D1081768

# Langenscheidt
# Universal German Dictionary

**German – English**
**English – German**

completely revised edition

edited by the
Langenscheidt editorial staff

**Langenscheidt**

Berlin · Munich · Vienna · Zurich
London · Madrid · New York · Warsaw

Project management:
Heike Pleisteiner

Lexicographical work:
Howard Atkinson, Martin Fellermayer, Stuart Fortey,
Heike Pleisteiner, Heike Richini, Robin Sawers, Karin Weindl

This dictionary uses the standardised German spelling system
valid as of 2006.

This dictionary has been created with the help of dictionary
databases owned by HarperCollins Publishers Ltd.

Neither the presence nor the absence of a designation
indicating that any entered word constitutes a trademark
should be regarded as affecting the legal status thereof.

# Contents

# How to use this dictionary

### Where do I find what I am looking for?

This dictionary contains over 36,000 references, which are listed **in alphabetical order**. The only exceptions to this strict rule are **phrasal verbs**, which are entered directly under the simple verb form. This means, to take an example, that **keep back**, **keep off**, **keep out**, **keep to** and **keep up** are all entered directly under **keep**. The entry for the word **keeper** follows the phrasal verbs, although strictly speaking it ought to come alphabetically between **keep back** and **keep off**.

The letters **ä**, **ö** and **ü** are treated on the same basis as **a, o** and **u**. Thus the entry for **träumen**, for example, comes between **Traum** and **traumhaft**.

For the **pronunciation** of German words, see the notes on pages 9–14.

### How do I find what I am looking for?

The structure of the individual entries is the same for both sections of the dictionary.

Each entry is structured using Arabic numerals (1, 2, 3 etc.). These can differentiate between different **parts of speech** (noun, adjective, adverb, verb, etc.):

> **search 1.** *n* Suche *f* (*for* nach);
> *do a ~ for* IT suchen nach; *in
> ~ of* auf der Suche nach **2.** *vi*
> suchen (*for* nach) **3.** *vt* durch-
> suchen

They can also differentiate between the different **meanings** of a word:

> **Druck 1.** *m* ⟨-(e)s, Drücke⟩
> PHYS pressure; *fig* (*strain*)
> stress; *jdn unter ~ setzen*
> put sb under pressure **2.** *m*
> ⟨-(e)s, -e⟩ TYPO printing;
> (*product, typeface*) print

**What can I find under each entry?**

Look at the following entry:

> **cash 1.** *n* Bargeld *nt*; *in ~* bar; *~*
> ***on delivery*** per Nachnahme
> **2.** *vt* (*check/cheque*) einlösen

This example will serve to illustrate the main elements, which are itemised and explained below:

| | |
|---|---|
| **cash** | the **word** itself **in bold print** |
| **1.** | Arabic numeral to differentiate between different parts of speech |
| *n* | part of speech (in this case, noun) in *italics* |
| Bargeld | German equivalent of the English word in standard script |
| *nt* | gender of the German equivalent (in this case, neuter) in *italics* |
| ; | semi-colon used to separate the translation from the typical usages which follow |
| *in ~* | the expression *in cash* in **bold italics** |
| ~ | the swung dash as part of the expression stands for the main word **cash** |
| bar | German equivalent of the English expression in standard script |
| *~ on delivery* | the expression *cash on delivery* in **bold italics** |
| per Nachnahme | German equivalent of the English expression in standard script |
| **2.** | Arabic numeral to differentiate between different parts of speech |
| *vt* | part of speech (in this case, transitive verb) in *italics* |

| (*check/ cheque*) | typical object of the equivalent German expression (in this case, 'cash a *check/cheque*') placed within brackets and *italicised* |
| einlösen | German equivalent of the English word in standard script |

### Are all the entries structured in this way?

Every entry more or less follows the simple structure outlined above. The clear differentiation between various forms and meanings will lead you to the correct translation. In addition, the *italicised* information in brackets can denote a subject or object of the given word, or else it can indicate the general context in which the word is used:

> **break down** *vi* (*car*) eine Panne haben; (*machine*) versagen; (*person*) zusammenbrechen; **break up 1.** *vi* aufbrechen; (*meeting, organisation*) sich auflösen; (*marriage*) in die Brüche gehen (...)

### What is the purpose of the information in *italics*?

Information in *italics*, with or without brackets, often provides a more precise indication of the different meanings of a word. This information might refer to synonyms (words with a similar meaning), possible subjects and objects, etc. and is included in order to indicate which translation should be used in any given context.

*Italics* are also used to provide grammatical information, as well as to clarify the meaning and use of a word for which there is no direct translation:

> **Mehlspeise** *f sweet dish made from flour, eggs and milk*
>
> **Einwohnermeldeamt** *nt registration office for residents*

Translations of verbs are often followed by the prepositions which they take in *italics*. Equivalents are then given in standard script and the cases they take in *italics*.

> **inform** *vt* informieren *(of, about* über + *acc)*; **keep sb ~ed** jdn auf dem Laufenden halten

For further information on the use of *italics*, you should refer to the **List of Abbreviations** on pages 15–16.

## What is the purpose of cross-references?

Cross-references are always indicated by the → symbol. They usually refer you to another word of similar meaning or to an alternative spelling of the given word. When you look up the cross-referenced word, you will then find the translation(s) and other relevant information:

> **Januar** *m* ⟨-(s), -e⟩ January; → **Juni**
>
> **Juni** *m* ⟨-(s), -s⟩ June; **im ~** in June; **am 4. ~ on** 4(th) June, on June 4(th) ; **Anfang/ Mitte/Ende ~** at the beginning/in the middle/at the end of June; **letzten/ nächsten ~** last/next June
>
> **homeopathic** *adj* (*US*) → **homoeopathic**
>
> **homoeopathic** *adj* homöopathisch

## What is the purpose of the context indicators?

These help you to differentiate between the various meanings of a word and the contexts in which they are used:

> **dressing** *n* GASTR Dressing *nt*, Soße *f*; MED Verband *m*

The most common of these indicators are written in SMALL CAPITAL LETTERS and can be found in the **List of Abbreviations** on pages 15–16. Less common indicators are not abbreviated and are given in *italics*.

> **knight** *n* Ritter *m*; (*in chess*)
> Pferd *nt*, Springer *m*

## How is the register of a word indicated?

This dictionary provides information on the following types of register: *fig* (figurative), *pej* (pejorative or derogatory), *fam* (familiar or informal) and *vulg* (vulgar). As far as possible, translations of words with such indicators have been chosen to reflect the same register. In other words, a vulgar German word or expression will be translated by a suitably vulgar English word or expression, and so on. These indicators can be found in the **List of Abbreviations** on pages 15–16.

## What type of grammatical information can I find in this dictionary?

A list of the **Irregular German Verbs** contained in this dictionary can be found in the appendix on pages 599–602. Irregular verb forms are given in italics immediately after the verb and are also listed as separate entries:

> **schwimmen** ⟨schwamm, ge-
> schwommen⟩ *vi* swim
>
> **schwamm** *imperf* → **schwim-
> men**
>
> **geschwommen** *pp* →
> **schwimmen**

Irregular **plural forms**, as well as the **genitive forms**, are given after the relevant nouns:

> **Haus** *nt* ⟨-es, Häuser⟩ house;
> **nach** ~**e** home; **zu** ~**e** at
> home

The **List of Abbreviations** on pages 15–16 contains all the indicators for grammatical information used in this dictionary.

**What can I find in the appendices?**

In addition to the **Irregular German Verbs** mentioned above (pp. 599–602), the appendices also include chapters on **Numbers** (pp. 603–605), **European currency** (p. 605), **Temperatures** (p. 606) and **Weights and measures** (pp. 607–608).

## Notes on the pronunciation of German words

The rules governing the pronunciation of German words tend to be more straightforward than their English equivalents – and there are fewer exceptions. This means that you can apply these rules consistently without any great fear of being incorrect.

In order to help you understand the basic rules, we have divided our guidelines into the following sections: **consonants, vowels, stress.**

We have concentrated on those German sounds which follow different rules from their English equivalents and on those which do not exist in English at all.

## Consonants

### Silent consonants

The only silent consonant in German is **h**, which is silent or not depending on its position in a word. It is pronounced at the beginning of a word (as in **Held** *hero*) or between two vowels (as in the name **Johannes**). It is silent when it comes between a vowel and a consonant (as in **Fehler** *mistake*) and when it comes at the end of a word (as in **froh** *happy*).

When **h** is used in combination with other consonants (such as in **sch** and **ch**), different rules apply (see under **combinations of consonants**).

## Single and double consonants

Most German single and double consonants are pronounced in the same way as their English equivalents.

The rules and examples below show **only** cases in which they are pronounced differently or (in the case of **ß**) do not exist in English at all.

| consonant | rule | example |
|---|---|---|
| b | often pronounced **p** (as in the English **p**oet) at the end of a word, | hal**b** |
| | sometimes at the end of a syllable | A**b**stieg |
| c | pronounced **ts** (as in the English bi**ts**) | **C**D |
| | pronounced **k** (as in the English **k**ite) in words of foreign derivation (most cases) | **C**annabis, **C**ola |
| d | often pronounced **t** (as in the English taxi) at the end of a word, | Lan**d** |
| | sometimes at the end of a syllable | un**d** so weiter |
| g | often pronounced **k** (as in the English **k**ite) at the end of a word, | Zu**g** |
| | sometimes at the end of a consonant; | Flu**g**zeug |
| | pronounced **ch** (as in the Scottish loch*) if the word ends in -ig | lusti**g** |
| h | see **silent consonants** (above) | |
| j | usually pronounced **y** (as in the English **y**oung) | **J**oghurt |
| q | pronounced **kv** in combination with the vowel **u** | **Q**uiz |
| r | rolled at the back of the mouth (similarly to the Scottish **r** sound) | **r**und |
| s | pronounced **z** (as in the English **z**ebra) when it comes between two vowels | le**s**en |

| ß | pronounced **s** (as in the English **s**ix) never occurs at the beginning of a word | Fu**ß**ball |
|---|---|---|
| t | pronounced **ts** (as in the English bi**ts**) when followed by the letters -ion | Intui**t**ion |
| v | mostly pronounced **f** (as in the English **f**ork) | **v**erstehen |
| | pronounced **v** (as in the English **v**ote) in words of Greek or Latin derivation | **V**eto |
| w | pronounced **v** (as in the English **v**ote) | **w**o, **W**under |
| z | pronounced **ts** (as in the English bi**ts**) | **Z**unge |
| * | This sound does not commonly exist in English. It can | |

best be described by comparing it to the sound made at the beginning of the word *human* in the phrase '**a hu**man being'.

**Double consonants within one syllable** always make the preceding vowel short (**Krabbe, paddeln, kommen, gewinnen, muss, fett**).

### Combinations of consonants

In German, certain combinations of consonants (if they are pronounced as part of the same syllable) produce a sound which is not found in English. The most difficult for English native speakers is the following sound:

**ch** This combination produces a guttural sound which can best be described by comparing it to the sound made at the beginning of the word *human* in the English phrase '**a h**uman being'. However, the sound can be pronounced in two slightly different basic ways, depending on the vowel sound which precedes it: in a word such as **lachen** (*to laugh*), it is produced at the back of the throat (as in Scottish lo**ch***), whereas in **ich** (*I*) it is produced at the front of the mouth and sounds a little more like the English **sh** (as in fi**sh**).

The following consonant combinations also produce sounds different from their English equivalents:

| chs | pronounced **ks** (as in the English kicks) | **Lachs**, **wachsen** |
| ng | always pronounced as in the English singer, never as in finger | Hu**ng**er |
| sch | always pronounced **sh** (as in the English shoe) | **Frosch**, **Schiff**, ver**sch**winden |
| sp | at the beginning of a word or syllable, pronounced **shp** (as in the English phrase ca**sh pr**ize) | **Sp**ort, ver**sp**ätet |
| st | at the beginning of a word or syllable, pronounced **sht** (as in the English phrase fi**sh t**ank) | **St**ein, ver**st**ehen |
| th | always pronounced **t** (as in the English taxi) | **Th**unfisch |
| tsch | pronounced **ch** (as in the English chicken) | Qua**tsch** |
| tz | pronounced **ts** (as in the English bits) | Ka**tz**e |

## Vowels

### Long and short vowel sounds

German vowel sounds can be long or short. Certain sounds (such as those produced by the letters **ä**, **ö** and **ü**) have no direct equivalent in English – in these cases we have given an approximation of the sound.

| letter (-s) | vowel sound produced | example |
| --- | --- | --- |
| a | short (close to the English fan) | H**a**mmer |
| a, ah, aa | long (close to the English marmalade) | V**a**ter, B**ah**n, **Aa**l |
| ä | short (close to the English set) | **ä**ndern |

| ä, äh | long (close to the English bear) | Käfig, ähnlich |
| e | short (as in the English wet) | endlich |
| e, ee, eh | long (close to the English gay, but with no concluding y sound) | edel, Fee, Fehler |
| i | short (as in the English igloo) | in, Kinn |
| i, ie | long (as in the English feel) | Kino, tief |
| o | short (as in the English hop) | kommen |
| o, oo, oh | long (close to the English fold) | los, Moos, Kohl |
| oh | long (close to the English more) | Ohr |
| ö | short (close to the English flirt, but shorter) | können |
| ö | long (close to the English flirt) | Löwe |
| u | short (as in the English full) | Mutter, unter |
| u, uh | long (as in the English pool) | tun, Kuh |
| ü | short* | dünn |
| ü, üh | long (close to the English tune, but with a raised tongue) | über, fühlen |

\* There is really no English equivalent to this sound. The word dünn, for example can best be produced by pronouncing the English word din with pursed lips.

## Diphthongs

A diphthong is in effect the combination of two vowel sounds. There are relatively few of these in German.

| ei, ai | as in the English my | fein, Haifisch |
| au | as in the English now | August |
| eu, äu | as in the English toy | neun, äußerst |

## Stress

Most German words are stressed on the first syllable. The only major exception to this rule concerns words beginning with prefixes such as **be-**, **ent-** and **ver-**, which are usually stressed on the subsequent syllable (**beantworten**, **Enttäuschung**, **vermuten**).

Additionally, some words of foreign (especially Latin) derivation are stressed on the final syllable (**Café**, **Elefant**, **Soldat**, **Station**).

# Abbreviations

| | | | |
|---|---|---|---|
| *a.* | also | | *(Imperfekt)* |
| *abbr* | abbreviation | *impers* | impersonal |
| *acc* | accusative | *in cpds* | in compounds |
| *acr* | acronym | *indef* | indefinite |
| *adj* | adjective | *interj* | interjection |
| *adv* | adverb | *inv* | invariable |
| AGR | agriculture | *irr* | irregular |
| ANAT | anatomy | IT | IT, computing |
| *art* | article | *jdm* | jemandem |
| ART | fine arts | *jdn* | jemanden |
| ASTR | astronomy, | *jds* | jemandes |
| | astrology | *jmd* | jemand |
| AUTO | automobiles, | LAW | law |
| | traffic | LING | linguistics |
| AVIAT | aviation | *m* | masculine |
| BIO | biology | MATH | mathematics |
| BOT | botany | MED | medicine |
| *Brit* | British | METEO | meteorology |
| CHEM | chemistry | MIL | military |
| COMM | commerce | MUS | music |
| *conj* | conjunction | *n* | noun |
| *contr* | contraction | NAUT | nautical |
| *dat* | dative | *nom* | nominative |
| ELEC | electricity | *npl* | plural noun |
| *esp* | especially | *nsing* | singular noun |
| *etw* | etwas | *nt* | neuter |
| *f* | feminine | *num* | numeral |
| *fam* | familiar, informal | *or* | or |
| *fig* | figurative | *pej* | pejorative |
| FILM | film, cinema | PHOT | photography |
| FIN | finance | PHYS | physics |
| GASTR | gastronomy, | *pl* | plural |
| | cooking | POL | politics |
| *gen* | genitive | *pp* | past participle |
| *hist* | historically | *pref* | prefix |
| HIST | history | *prep* | preposition |
| *imperf* | past tense | *pron* | pronoun |

| | | | |
|---|---|---|---|
| *pt* | past tense | THEAT | theater/theatre |
| ® | registered trade-mark | TV | television |
| | | TYPO | typography, printing |
| RADIO | radio | | |
| RAIL | railways | *US* | North American |
| REL | religion | *vaux* | auxiliary verb |
| *sb* | somebody | *vi* | intransitive verb |
| *Scot* | Scottish | *vr* | reflexive verb |
| *sg* | singular | *vt* | transitive verb |
| SPORT | sports | *vulg* | vulgar |
| *sth* | something | ZOOL | zoology |
| TECH | technology | ~ | swung dash |
| TEL | telecommunications | → | refer to |

# German – English

# A

**A** *abbr* → *Autobahn* ≈ M (*Brit*), ≈ I (*US*)

**à** *prep + acc* at … each; *4 Tickets à 8 Euro* 4 tickets at 8 euros each

**Aal** *m* ⟨-(e)s, -e⟩ eel

**ab 1.** *prep + dat* from; *von jetzt ~* from now on; *Berlin ~ 16:30 Uhr* departs Berlin 16.30; *~ Seite 17* from page 17; *~ 18* from the age of 18 **2.** *adv* off; *links ~* to the left; *~ und zu* (*or* **an**) now and then (*or* again); *der Knopf ist~* the button has come off

**abbauen** *vt* (*tent*) take down; (*in number, degree*) reduce

**abbeißen** *irr vt* bite off

**abbestellen** *vt* cancel

**abbiegen** *irr vi* turn off; (*road*) bend; *nach links / rechts ~* turn left / right

**Abbildung** *f* illustration

**abblasen** *irr vt fig* call off

**abblenden** *vt, vi* AUTO (*die Scheinwerfer*) *~* dip (*Brit*) (*or* dim (*US*)) one's headlights; **Abblendlicht** *nt* dipped (*Brit*) (*or* dimmed (*US*)) headlights *pl*

**abbrechen** *irr vt* break off; (*building*) pull down; (*end*) stop; (*computer program*) abort

**abbremsen** *vi* brake, slow down

**abbringen** *irr vt* *jdn von einer Idee ~* talk sb out of an idea; *jdn vom Thema ~* get sb away from the subject; *davon lasse ich mich nicht ~* nothing will make me change my mind about it

**abbuchen** *vt* to debit (*von* to)

**abdanken** *vi* resign

**abdrehen 1.** *vt* (*gas, water*) turn off; (*light*) switch off **2.** *vi* (*ship, plane*) change course

**Abend** *m* ⟨-s, -e⟩ evening; *am ~* in the evening; *zu ~ essen* have dinner; *heute / morgen / gestern ~* this / tomorrow / yesterday evening; *guten ~!* good evening; **Abendbrot** *nt* supper; **Abendessen** *nt* dinner; **Abendgarderobe** *f* evening dress (*or* gown); **Abendkasse** *f* box office; **Abendkleid** *nt* evening dress (*or* gown); **Abendmahl** *das ~* (Holy) Communion; **abends** *adv* in the evening; *montags ~* on

Monday evenings

**Abenteuer** nt ⟨-s, -⟩ adventure; **Abenteuerurlaub** m adventure holiday

**aber** conj but; (nevertheless) however; **oder ~** alternatively; **~ ja!** (but) of course; **das ist ~ nett von Ihnen** that's really nice of you

**abergläubisch** adj superstitious

**abfahren** irr vi leave (or depart) (nach for); (skier) ski down; **Abfahrt** f departure; (from motorway) exit; (in skiing) descent; (piste) run; **Abfahrtslauf** m (in skiing) downhill; **Abfahrtszeit** f departure time

**Abfall** m waste; (household) rubbish (Brit), garbage (US); **Abfalleimer** m rubbish bin (Brit), garbage can (US)

**abfällig** adj disparaging; **~ von jdm sprechen** make disparaging remarks about sb

**abfärben** vi (in the wash) run; fig rub off

**abfertigen** vt (parcel) prepare for dispatch; (at the border) clear; **Abfertigungsschalter** m (at airport) check-in desk

**abfinden** irr 1. vt pay off 2. vr **sich mit etw ~** come to terms with sth; **Abfindung** f (money) compensation; (for employee) redundancy payment

**abfliegen** irr vi (plane) take off; (passenger also) fly off; **Abflug** m departure; (becoming airborne) take-off; **Abflughalle** f departure lounge; **Abflugzeit** f departure time

**Abfluss** m drain; (of washbasin) plughole (Brit); **Abflussrohr** nt waste pipe; (outside) drainpipe

**abfragen** vt test; IT call up

**abführen 1.** vi MED have a laxative effect 2. vt (tax, charges) pay; **jdn ~ lassen** take sb into custody; **Abführmittel** nt laxative

**Abgabe** f handing in; (of ball) pass; (charge) tax; (of statement) making; **abgabenfrei** adj tax-free; **abgabenpflichtig** adj liable to tax

**Abgase** pl AUTO exhaust fumes pl; **Abgas(sonder)-untersuchung** f exhaust emission test

**abgeben** irr **1.** vt (luggage, key) leave (bei with); (homework etc) hand in; (heat) give off; (statement, judgment) make **2.** vr **sich mit jdm ~** associate with sb; **sich mit etw ~** bother with sth

**abgebildet** adj **wie oben ~** as shown above

**abgehen** irr vi (letters) go; (button etc) come off; (amount) be taken off; (road) branch off; **von der**

*Schule* ~ leave school; *sie geht mir ab* I really miss her; *was geht denn hier ab? fam* what's going on here?

**abgehetzt** *adj* exhausted, shattered

**abgelaufen** *adj* (*passport*) expired; (*time, period*) up; *die Milch ist* ~ the milk is past its sell-by date

**abgelegen** *adj* remote

**abgemacht** *interj* OK, it's a deal, that's settled, then

**abgeneigt** *adj einer Sache dat* ~ *sein* be averse to sth; *ich wäre nicht* ~, *das zu tun* I wouldn't mind doing that

**Abgeordnete(r)** *mf* Member of Parliament

**abgepackt** *adj* prepacked

**abgerissen** *adj der Knopf ist* ~ the button has come off

**abgesehen** *adj es auf jdn / etw* ~ *haben* be after sb/sth; ~ *von* apart from

**abgespannt** *adj* (*person*) exhausted, worn out

**abgestanden** *adj* stale; (*beer*) flat

**abgestorben** *adj* (*plant*) dead; (*fingers*) numb

**abgestumpft** *adj* (*person*) insensitive

**abgetragen** *adj* (*clothes*) worn

**abgewöhnen** *vt jdm etw* ~ cure sb of sth; *sich etw* ~ give sth up

**abhaken** *vt* tick off; *das* (*Thema*) *ist schon abgehakt* that's been dealt with

**abhalten** *irr vt* (*meeting*) hold; *jdn von etw* ~ keep sb away from sth; (*prevent*) keep sb from sth

**abhanden** *adj* ~ *kommen* get lost

**Abhang** *m* slope

**abhängen 1.** *vt* (*picture*) take down; (*trailer*) uncouple; (*pursuer*) shake off **2.** *irr vi von jdm / etw* ~ depend on sb/sth; *das hängt davon ab, ob* ... it depends (on) whether ...; *abhängig* dependent (*von* on)

**abhauen** *irr* **1.** *vt* (*branch, arm etc*) cut off **2.** *vi fam* clear off; *hau ab!* get lost!, beat it!

**abheben** *irr* **1.** *vt* (*money*) withdraw; (*receiver, playing card*) pick up **2.** *vi* (*plane*) take off; (*rocket*) lift off; (*in card game*) cut

**abholen** *vt* collect; (*at station etc*) meet; (*with car*) pick up; **Abholmarkt** *m* cash and carry

**abhorchen** *vt* MED listen to

**abhören** *vt* (*vocabulary*) test; (*phone call*) tap; (*tape etc*) listen to

**Abitur** *nt* ⟨-s, -e⟩ German school-leaving examination, ≈ A-levels (*Brit*), ≈ High School Diploma (*US*)

**abkaufen** *vt jdm etw* ~ buy

sth from sb; **das kauf ich dir nicht ab!** *fam* I don't believe you

**abklingen** *irr vi* (*pain*) ease; (*effect*) wear off

**abkommen** *irr vi* get away; **von der Straße ~** leave the road; **von einem Plan ~** give up a plan; **vom Thema ~** stray from the point

**Abkommen** *nt* ⟨-s, -⟩ agreement

**abkoppeln** *vt* (*trailer*) unhitch

**abkratzen** **1.** *vt* scrape off **2.** *vi fam* (*die*) kick the bucket, croak

**abkühlen** *vi, vr, vt* cool down

**abkürzen** *vt* (*word*) abbreviate; **den Weg ~** take a short cut; **Abkürzung** *f* (*of word*) abbreviation; (*path*) short cut

**abladen** *irr vt* unload

**Ablage** *f* (*for documents*) tray; (*for whole office*) filing system

**Ablauf** *m* drain; (*of events*) course; (*of deadline*) expiry; **ablaufen** *irr vi* (*liquid*) drain away; (*events*) happen; (*deadline, passport*) expire

**ablegen** **1.** *vt* put down; (*clothes*) take off; (*habit*) get out of; (*exam*) take, sit; (*documents*) file away **2.** *vt* (*ship*) cast off

**ablehnen** *vt* reject; (*invitation*) decline; (*be against*) disapprove of; (*applicant*)

turn down **2.** *vi* decline

**ablenken** *vt* distract; **jdn von der Arbeit ~** distract sb from their work; **vom Thema ~** change the subject; **Ablenkung** *f* distraction

**ablesen** *vt* (*text, speech*) read; **das Gas / den Strom ~** read the gas / electricity meter

**abliefern** *vt* deliver

**abmachen** *vt* take off; (*date, price etc*) agree; **Abmachung** *f* agreement

**abmelden** **1.** *vt* (*newspaper*) cancel; (*car*) take off the road **2.** *vr* give notice of one's departure; (*from hotel*) check out; (*member*) cancel one's membership

**abmessen** *irr vt* measure

**abnehmen** *irr vt* take off, remove; (*receiver*) pick up; (*driving licence*) take away; (*money*) get (*jdm* out of sb); (*purchase, fam: believe*) buy (*jdm* from sb) **2.** *vi* decrease; (*slim*) lose weight; TEL pick up the phone; **fünf Kilo ~** lose five kilos

**Abneigung** *f* dislike (*gegen* of); (*stronger*) aversion (*gegen* to)

**abnutzen** *vt, vr* wear out

**Abonnement** *nt* ⟨-s, -s⟩ subscription; **Abonnent(in)** *m(f)* subscriber; **abonnieren** *vt* subscribe to

**abraten** *irr vi* **jdm von etw ~** advise sb against sth

**abräumen** *vt* **den Tisch ~**

clear the table; *das Geschirr* ~ clear away the dishes; *(prize etc)* walk off with

**Abrechnung** f settlement; *(invoice)* bill

**abregen** vr fam calm (or cool) down; *reg dich ab!* take it easy

**Abreise** f departure; **abreisen** vi leave *(nach for)*; **Abreisetag** m day of departure

**abreißen** irr 1. vt *(house)* pull down; *(sheet of paper)* tear off; *den Kontakt nicht ~ lassen* stay in touch 2. vi *(button etc)* come off

**abrunden** vt *eine Zahl nach oben / unten ~* round a number up / down

**abrupt** adj abrupt

**ABS** nt abbr = *Antiblockiersystem* AUTO ABS

**Abs.** abbr → *Absender* from

**absagen** 1. vt cancel, call off; *(invitation)* turn down 2. vi decline; *ich muss leider ~* I'm afraid I can't come

**Absatz** m COMM sales pl; *(in text)* paragraph; *(of shoe)* heel

**abschaffen** vt abolish, do away with

**abschalten** vt, vi a. fig switch off

**abschätzen** vt estimate; *(situation)* assess

**abscheulich** adj disgusting

**abschicken** vt send off

**abschieben** irr vt *(asylum*

*seeker etc)* deport

**Abschied** m ⟨-(e)s, -e⟩ parting; ~ *nehmen* say good-bye *(von jdm to sb)*; **Abschiedsfeier** f farewell party

**Abschlagszahlung** f interim payment

**Abschleppdienst** m AUTO breakdown service; **abschleppen** vt tow; **Abschleppseil** nt towrope; **Abschleppwagen** m breakdown truck *(Brit)*, tow truck *(US)*

**abschließen** irr vt *(door)* lock; *(bring to an end)* conclude, finish; *(agreement, deal)* conclude; **Abschluss** m close, conclusion; *(of agreement, deal)* conclusion

**abschmecken** vt *(sample)* taste; *(with salt etc)* season

**abschminken** vr take one's make-up off 2. vt fam *sich dat etw ~* get sth out of one's mind

**abschnallen** vr undo one's seatbelt

**abschneiden** irr 1. vt cut off 2. vi *gut / schlecht ~* do well / badly

**Abschnitt** m *(of book, text)* section; *(of cheque, ticket)* stub

**abschrauben** vt unscrew

**abschrecken** vt deter, put off

**abschreiben** irr vt *(bei, von from, off)*; *(give up on)* write off; COMM deduct

**abschüssig** adj steep
**abschwächen** vt lessen; (statement, criticism) tone down
**abschwellen** irr vi (inflammation) go down; (noise) die down
**absehbar** adj foreseeable; **in ~er Zeit** in the foreseeable future; **absehen** irr **1.** vt (end, consequences) foresee **2.** vi **von etw ~** refrain from sth
**abseits 1.** adv out of the way; SPORT offside **2.** prep + gen away from; **Abseits** nt SPORT offside; **Abseitsfalle** f SPORT offside trap
**absenden** irr vt send off; (letter etc) post; **Absender(in)** m(f) ⟨-s, -⟩ sender
**absetzen 1.** vt (glass, spectacles etc) put down; (passenger) drop (off); COMM sell; FIN deduct; (cancel) drop **2.** vr (leave) clear off; (mud etc) be deposited
**Absicht** f intention; **mit ~** on purpose; **absichtlich** adj intentional, deliberate
**absolut** adj absolute
**abspecken** vi fam lose weight
**abspeichern** vt IT save
**absperren** vt block (or close) off; (door) lock; **Absperrung** f blocking (or closing) off; (obstacle) barricade
**abspielen 1.** vt (CD etc) play **2.** vr happen

**abspringen** irr vi jump down / off; (participant) drop out (von of)
**abspülen** vt rinse; (dishes) wash (up)
**Abstand** m distance; (time gap) interval; **~ halten** keep one's distance
**abstauben** vt, vi dust; fam (steal) pinch
**Abstecher** m ⟨-s, -⟩ detour
**absteigen** irr vi (from bicycle etc) get off, dismount; (at hotel) stay (in + dat at)
**abstellen** vt (bag, tray etc) put down; (car) park; (light, machine etc) turn (or switch) off; (bad practice etc) stop; **Abstellraum** m store room
**Abstieg** m ⟨-(e)s, -e⟩ (from mountain) descent; SPORT relegation
**abstimmen 1.** vi vote **2.** vt (aims, dates) fit in (auf + acc with); **Dinge aufeinander ~** coordinate things **3.** vr come to an agreement (or arrangement)
**abstoßend** adj repulsive
**abstrakt** adj abstract
**abstreiten** irr vt deny
**Abstrich** m MED smear; **~e machen** cut back (an + dat on); (expect less) lower one's sights
**Absturz** m fall; AVIAT, IT crash
**abstürzen** vi fall; AVIAT, IT crash
**absurd** adj absurd
**Abszess** m ⟨-es, -e⟩ abscess

**abtauen** *vt, vi* thaw; *(fridge)* defrost

**Abtei** *f* ⟨-, -en⟩ abbey

**Abteil** *nt* ⟨-(e)s, -e⟩ compartment

**Abteilung** *f (in firm, department store)* department; *(in hospital)* section

**abtreiben** *irr* **1.** *vt (child)* abort **2.** *vi* be driven off course; MED carry out an abortion; *(pregnant woman)* have an abortion; **Abtreibung** *f* abortion

**abtrocknen** *vt* dry

**abwarten 1.** *vt* wait for; *das bleibt abzuwarten* that remains to be seen **2.** *vi* wait

**abwärts** *adv* down

**Abwasch** *m* ⟨-(e)s⟩ washing-up; **abwaschen** *irr vt (dirt)* wash off; *(dishes)* wash (up)

**Abwasser** *nt* ⟨-s, Abwässer⟩ sewage

**abwechseln** *vr* alternate; *sich mit jdm ~* take turns with sb; **abwechselnd** *adv* alternately; **Abwechslung** *f* change; *zur ~* for a change

**abweisen** *irr vt* turn away; *(application)* turn down; **abweisend** *adj* unfriendly

**abwesend** *adj* absent; **Abwesenheit** *f* absence

**abwiegen** *irr vt* weigh (out)

**abwimmeln** *vt fam jdn ~* get rid of sb, give sb the elbow

**abwischen** *vt (face, table etc)* wipe; *(dirt)* wipe off

**abzählen** *vt* count; *(money)* count out

**Abzeichen** *nt* badge

**abzeichnen 1.** *vt* draw, copy; *(document)* initial **2.** *vr* stand out; *fig (be imminent)* loom

**abziehen** *irr* **1.** *vt* take off; *(bed)* strip; *(key)* take out; *(number, amount)* take away, subtract **2.** *vi* go away

**Abzug** *m (photo)* print; *(opening)* vent; *(of troops)* withdrawal; *(of amount)* deduction; *nach ~ der Kosten* charges deducted; **abzüglich** *prep + gen* minus; *~ 20% Rabatt* less 20% discount

**abzweigen 1.** *vi* branch off **2.** *vt* set aside; **Abzweigung** *f* junction

**Accessoires** *pl* accessories *pl*

**ach** *interj* oh; *~ so!* oh, I see; *~ was!* *(surprised)* really?; *(annoyed)* don't talk nonsense

**Achse** *f* ⟨-, -n⟩ axis; AUTO axle

**Achsel** *f* ⟨-, -n⟩ shoulder; armpit

**Achsenbruch** *m* AUTO broken axle

**acht** *num* eight; *heute in ~ Tagen* in a week('s time), a week from today

**Acht** *f* ⟨-⟩ *sich in ~ nehmen* be careful *(vor + dat* of), watch out *(vor + dat* for); *etw außer ~ lassen* disregard sth

**achte(r, s)** *adj* eighth; → *drit-*

# Achtel

**te**; **Achtel** nt ⟨-s, -⟩ (fraction) eighth; (liquid measure) eighth of a litre; (glass of wine) ≈ small glass

**achten 1.** vt respect **2.** vi pay attention (auf + acc to)

**Achterbahn** f big dipper, roller coaster

**achtgeben** vi take care (auf + acc of)

**achthundert** num eight hundred; **achtmal** adv eight times

**Achtung 1.** f attention; (esteem) respect **2.** interj look out

**achtzehn** num eighteen; **achtzehnte(r, s)** adj eighteenth; → **dritte**; **achtzig** num eighty; **in den ~er Jahren** in the eighties; **achtzigste(r, s)** adj eightieth

**Acker** m ⟨-s, Äcker⟩ field

**Action** f ⟨-, -s⟩ fam action; **Actionfilm** m action film

**Adapter** m ⟨-, -⟩ adapter

**addieren** vt add (up)

**Adel** m ⟨-s⟩ nobility; **adelig** adj noble

**Ader** f ⟨-, -n⟩ vein

**Adjektiv** nt adjective

**Adler** m ⟨-s, -⟩ eagle

**adoptieren** vt adopt; **Adoption** f adoption; **Adoptiveltern** pl adoptive parents pl; **Adoptivkind** nt adopted child

**Adrenalin** nt ⟨-s⟩ adrenalin

**Adressbuch** nt directory; (personal) address book; A-dresse f ⟨-, -n⟩ address; **adressieren** vt address (an + acc to)

**Advent** m ⟨-s, -⟩ Advent; **Adventskranz** m Advent wreath

**Adverb** nt adverb

**Aerobic** nt ⟨-s⟩ aerobics sg

**Affäre** f ⟨-, -n⟩ affair

**Affe** m ⟨-n, -n⟩ monkey

**Afghanistan** nt ⟨-s⟩ Afghanistan

**Afrika** nt ⟨-s⟩ Africa; **Afrikaner(in)** m(f) ⟨-s, -⟩ African; **afrikanisch** adj African

**After** m ⟨-s, -⟩ anus

**Aftershave** nt ⟨-(s), -s⟩ aftershave

**AG** f ⟨-, -s⟩ abbr → **Aktiengesellschaft** plc (Brit), corp. (US)

**Agent(in)** m(f) agent; **Agentur** f agency

**aggressiv** adj aggressive

**Ägypten** nt ⟨-s⟩ Egypt

**ah** interj ah, ooh

**äh** interj er, um; (disgusted) ugh

**aha** interj I see, aha

**ähneln 1.** vi + dat be like, resemble **2.** vr be alike (or similar)

**ahnen** vt suspect; **du ahnst es nicht!** would you believe it?

**ähnlich** adj similar (dat to); **jdm ~ sehen** look like sb; **Ähnlichkeit** f similarity

**Ahnung** f idea; (vague) suspicion; **keine ~!** no idea; **ah-**

**nungslos** *adj* unsuspecting

**Ahorn** *m* ⟨-s, -e⟩ maple

**Aids** *nt* ⟨-⟩ Aids; **aidskrank** *adj* suffering from Aids; **Aidstest** *m* Aids test

**Airbag** *m* ⟨-s, -s⟩ AUTO airbag; **Airbus** *m* airbus

**Akademie** *f* ⟨-, -n⟩ academy; **Akademiker(in)** *m(f)* ⟨-s, -⟩ (university) graduate

**akklimatisieren** *vr* acclimatize oneself

**Akkordeon** *nt* ⟨-s, -s⟩ accordion

**Akku** *m* ⟨-s, -s⟩ (storage) battery

**Akkusativ** *m* accusative (case)

**Akne** *f* ⟨-, -⟩ acne

**Akrobat(in)** *m(f)* ⟨-s, -en⟩ acrobat

**Akt** *m* ⟨-(e)s, -e⟩ act; ART nude

**Akte** *f* ⟨-, -n⟩ file; **etw zu den ~n legen** *a. fig* file sth away; **Aktenkoffer** *m* briefcase

**Aktie** *f* ⟨-, -n⟩ share; **Aktiengesellschaft** *f* public limited company (*Brit*), corporation (*US*)

**Aktion** *f* campaign; (*military, police*) operation

**Aktionär(in)** *m(f)* ⟨-s, -e⟩ shareholder

**aktiv** *adj* active; **aktivieren** *vt* activate

**aktualisieren** *vt* update; **aktuell** *adj* (*subject*) topical; (*modern*) up-to-date; (*problem*) current; **nicht mehr ~** no longer relevant

**Akupunktur** *f* acupuncture

**Akustik** *f* acoustics *sg*; **akustisch** *adj* acoustic

**akut** *adj* acute

**AKW** *nt* ⟨-s, -s⟩ *abbr* → **Atomkraftwerk** nuclear power station

**Akzent** *m* ⟨-(e)s, -e⟩ accent; (*emphasis*) stress; **mit starkem schottischen ~** with a strong Scottish accent

**akzeptieren** *vt* accept

**Alarm** *m* ⟨-(e)s, -e⟩ alarm; **Alarmanlage** *f* alarm system; **alarmieren** *vt* alarm; **die Polizei ~** call the police

**Albanien** *nt* ⟨-s⟩ Albania

**Albatros** *m* ⟨-ses, -se⟩ albatross

**albern** *adj* silly

**Albtraum** *m* nightmare

**Album** *nt* ⟨-s, Alben⟩ album

**Algen** *pl* algae *pl*, seaweed *sg*

**Algerien** *nt* ⟨-s⟩ Algeria

**Alibi** *nt* ⟨-s, -s⟩ alibi

**Alimente** *pl* maintenance *sg*

**Alkohol** *m* ⟨-s, -e⟩ alcohol; **alkoholfrei** *adj* non-alcoholic; **~es Getränk** soft drink; **Alkoholiker(in)** *m(f)* ⟨-s, -⟩ alcoholic; **alkoholisch** *adj* alcoholic; **Alkoholtest** *m* breathalyser® test (*Brit*), alcohol test (*US*)

**All** *nt* ⟨-s⟩ universe

**alle(r, s) 1.** *pron* all; **~ Passagiere** all passengers; **wir ~** all of us; **~ beide** both of us / you / them; **~ vier Jahre** every four years; **~ 100 Me-**

***ter*** every 100 metres; → **al-les 2.** *adv fam* finished

**Allee** *f* ⟨-, -n⟩ avenue

**allein** *adj, adv* alone; (*unaided*) on one's own, by oneself; *nicht ~* not only; **allein-erziehend** *adj* **~e Mutter** single mother; **Alleinerziehende(r)** *mf* single mother / father / parent; **alleinstehend** *adj* single, unmarried

**allerbeste(r, s)** *adj* very best

**allerdings** *adv* admittedly; (*definitely*) certainly, sure (*US*)

**allererste(r, s)** *adj* very first; *zu allererst* first of all

**Allergie** *f* allergy; **Allergiker(in)** *m(f)* ⟨-s, -⟩ allergy sufferer; **allergisch** *adj* allergic (*gegen* to)

**allerhand** *adj inv fam* all sorts of; *das ist doch ~!* (*reproaching*) that's the limit

**Allerheiligen** *nt* ⟨·⟩ All Saints' Day

**allerhöchste(r, s)** *adj* very highest; **allerhöchstens** *adv* at the very most; **allerlei** *adj inv* all sorts of; **allerletzte(r, s)** *adj* very last; **allerwenigste(r, s)** *adj* very least

**alles** *pron* everything; *~ Gute!* all the best!; *~ in allem* all in all; *~ alle*

**Alleskleber** *m* ⟨-s, -⟩ all-purpose glue

**allgemein** *adj* general; *im Allgemeinen* in general

**Allgemeinarzt** *m*, **Allge-**

**meinärztin** *f* GP (*Brit*), family practitioner (*US*)

**Alligator** *m* ⟨-s, -en⟩ alligator

**alljährlich** *adj* annual

**allmählich 1.** *adj* gradual **2.** *adv* gradually

**Allradantrieb** *m* all-wheel drive

**Alltag** *m* everyday life; **alltäglich** *adj* everyday; (*average*) ordinary; (*life, walk etc*) daily

**allzu** *adv* all too

**Allzweckreiniger** *m* ⟨-s, -⟩ multi-purpose cleaner

**Alpen** *pl* **die ~** the Alps *pl*

**Alphabet** *nt* ⟨-(e)s, -e⟩ alphabet; **alphabetisch** *adj* alphabetical

**Alptraum** *m* → **Albtraum**

**als** *conj* (*comparison*) than; (*time*) when; *das Zimmer ist größer ~ das andere* this room is bigger than the other; *das Essen war billiger ~ ich erwartet hatte* the meal was cheaper than I expected (it to be); *~ Kind* as a child; *nichts~* (*Ärger*) nothing but (trouble); *anders ~* different from; *erst ~* only when; *~ ob* as if

**also 1.** *conj* so, therefore **2.** *adv, interj* so; *~ gut* (*or schön*)! okay then

**alt** *adj* old; *wie ~ sind Sie?* how old are you?; *28 Jahre ~* 28 years old; *vier Jahre älter* four years older

**Altar** *m* ⟨-(e)s, Altäre⟩ altar

**Alter** *nt* ⟨-s, -⟩ age; (*last period of life*) old age; **im ~ von** at the age of; **er ist in meinem ~** he's my age

**alternativ** *adj* alternative; (*concerned for the environment*) ecologically minded; (*farming*) organic; **Alternative** *f* alternative

**Altersheim** *nt* old people's home

**Altglas** *nt* used glass; **Altglascontainer** *m* bottle bank; **altmodisch** *adj* old-fashioned; **Altpapier** *nt* waste paper; **Altstadt** *f* old town

**Alt-Taste** *f* Alt key

**Alufolie** *f* tin (*or* kitchen) foil

**Aluminium** *nt* ⟨-s⟩ aluminium (*Brit*), aluminum (*US*)

**Alzheimerkrankheit** *f* Alzheimer's (disease)

**am** *contr* = **an dem**; **~ 2. Januar** on January 2(nd); **~ Morgen** in the morning; **~ Strand** on the beach; **~ Bahnhof** at the station; **was gefällt Ihnen ~ besten?** what do you like best?; **~ besten bleiben wir hier** it would be best if we stayed here

**Amateur(in)** *m(f)* amateur

**ambulant** *adj* outpatient; **kann ich ~ behandelt werden?** can I have it done as an outpatient?; **Ambulanz** *f* ambulance; (*in hospital*) outpatients' department

**Ameise** *f* ⟨-, -n⟩ ant

**amen** *interj* amen

**Amerika** *nt* ⟨-s⟩ America; **Amerikaner(in)** *m(f)* ⟨-s, -⟩ American; **amerikanisch** *adj* American

**Ampel** *f* ⟨-, -n⟩ traffic lights *pl*

**Amphitheater** *nt* amphitheatre

**Amsel** *f* ⟨-, -n⟩ blackbird

**Amt** *nt* ⟨-(e)s, Ämter⟩ (*governmental agency*) office, department; (*position*) post; **amtlich** *adj* official; **Amtszeichen** *nt* TEL dialling tone (*Brit*), dial tone (*US*)

**amüsant** *adj* amusing; **amüsieren** **1.** *vt* amuse **2.** *vr* enjoy oneself, have a good time

**an** **1.** *prep* + *dat* **~ der Wand** on the wall; **~ der Themse** on the Thames; **alles ist ~ seinem Platz** everything is in its place; **~ einem kalten Tag** on a cold day; **~ Ostern** at Easter **2.** *prep* + *acc* **~ die Tür klopfen** knock at the door; **ans Meer fahren** go to the seaside; **die 40 Grad** nearly 40 degrees **3.** *adv* **von ... ~** from ... on; **das Licht / Radio ist ~** the light / radio is on

**anal** *adj* anal

**analog** *adj* analogous; IT analog

**Analyse** *f* ⟨-, -n⟩ analysis; **analysieren** *vt* analyse

**Ananas** *f* ⟨-, - *or* -se⟩ pineapple

## anbaggern

**anbaggern** vt fam chat up (Brit), come on to (US)

**Anbau** m AGR cultivation; (building) extension; **anbauen** vt AGR cultivate; (garage etc) build on

**anbehalten** irr vt keep on

**anbei** adv enclosed; **~ sende ich ...** please find enclosed ...

**anbeten** vt worship

**anbieten** irr 1. vt offer 2. vr volunteer

**anbinden** irr vt tie up

**Anblick** m sight

**anbraten** irr vt brown

**anbrechen** irr 1. vt start; (reserves, savings) break into; (bottle, packet) open 2. vi start; (day) break; (night) fall

**anbrennen** irr vt, vi burn; **das Fleisch schmeckt angebrannt** the meat tastes burnt

**anbringen** irr vt (along with one) bring; (fasten) fix, attach

**Andacht** f ⟨-, -en⟩ devotion; (church service) prayers pl

**andauern** vi continue, go on; **andauernd** adj continual

**Andenken** nt ⟨-s, -⟩ memory; (object) souvenir

**andere(r, s)** adj other; (not the same) different; (following) next; **am ~n Tag** the next day; **von etw/jdm ~m sprechen** talk about sth / sb else; **unter ~m** among other things; **andererseits** adv on the other hand

**ändern 1.** vt alter, change **2.** vr change

**andernfalls** adv otherwise

**anders** adv differently (als from); **jemand / irgendwo ~** someone / somewhere else; **sie ist ~ als ihre Schwester** she's not like her sister; **es geht nicht ~** there's no other way; **anders(he)rum** adv the other way round; **anderswo** adv somewhere else

**anderthalb** num one and a half

**Änderung** f change, alteration

**andeuten** vt indicate; (indirectly) hint at

**Andorra** nt ⟨-s⟩ Andorra

**Andrang** m **es herrschte großer ~** there was a huge crowd

**androhen** vt **jdm etw ~** threaten sb with sth

**aneinander** adv at/on / to one another (or each other); **~ denken** think of each other; **sich ~ gewöhnen** get used to each other; **aneinandergeraten** vi clash; **aneinanderlegen** vt put together

**anerkennen** irr vt (country, certificate etc) recognize; (efforts etc) appreciate; **Anerkennung** f recognition; (of efforts etc) appreciation

**anfahren** irr **1.** vt (pedestrian) run into; (place, port) stop (or call) at; (goods) deliver; **jdn** ~ fig (verbally) jump on sb **2.** vi start; (in car) drive off

**Anfall** m MED attack; **anfällig** adj delicate; (machine) temperamental; ~ **für** prone to

**Anfang** m ⟨-(e)s, Anfänge⟩ beginning, start; **zu|am** ~ to start with; ~ **Mai** at the beginning of May; **sie ist** ~ **20** she's in her early twenties; **anfangen** irr vt, vi begin; **damit kann ich nichts** ~ that's no use to me; **Anfänger(in)** m(f) ⟨-s, -⟩ beginner; **anfangs** adv at first; **Anfangsbuchstabe** m first (or initial) letter

**anfassen 1.** vt touch **2.** vi **kannst du mal mit** ~? can you give me a hand?

**Anflug** m AVIAT approach; (small amount) trace

**anfordern** vt demand; **Anforderung** f request (von for); (on sb or sth) demand

**Anfrage** f inquiry

**anfreunden** vr **sich mit jdm** ~ make (or become) friends with sb

**anfühlen** vr feel; **es fühlt sich gut an** it feels good

**Anführungszeichen** pl quotation marks pl

**Angabe** f TECH specification; fam (swanking) showing off; (in tennis) serve; ~**n** pl

(information) particulars pl; **die** ~**n waren falsch** the information was wrong; **angeben** irr **1.** vt (name, reason) give; (temperature, time etc) indicate; (course, pace) set **2.** vi fam boast; SPORT serve; **Angeber(in)** m(f) ⟨-s, -⟩ fam show-off; **angeblich** adj alleged

**angeboren** adj inborn

**Angebot** nt offer; COMM supply (an + dat of); ~ **und Nachfrage** supply and demand

**angebracht** adj appropriate

**angebunden** adj **kurz** ~ curt

**angeheitert** adj tipsy

**angehen** irr **1.** vt concern; **das geht dich nichts an** that's none of your business; **ein Problem** ~ tackle a problem; **was ihn angeht** as far as he's concerned, as for him **2.** vi (fire) catch; fam (start) begin; **angehend** adj prospective

**Angehörige(r)** mf relative

**Angeklagte(r)** mf accused, defendant

**Angel** f ⟨-, -n⟩ fishing rod; (of door) hinge

**Angelegenheit** f affair, matter

**Angelhaken** m fish hook; **angeln 1.** vt catch **2.** vi fish; **Angeln** nt ⟨-s⟩ angling, fishing; **Angelrute** f ⟨-, -n⟩ fishing rod

**angemessen** adj appropriate, suitable

**angenehm** adj pleasant; **~!** pleased to meet you

**angenommen 1.** adj assumed **2.** conj **~, es regnet, was machen wir dann?** suppose it rains, what do we do then?

**angesehen** adj respected

**angesichts** prep + gen in view of, considering

**Angestellte(r)** mf employee

**angetan** adj **von jdm / etw ~ sein** be impressed by (or taken with) sb/sth

**angewiesen** adj **auf jdn / etw ~ sein** be dependent on sb/sth

**angewöhnen** vt **sich etw ~** get used to doing sth; **Angewohnheit** f habit

**Angina** f ⟨-, Anginen⟩ tonsillitis; **Angina Pectoris** f ⟨-⟩ angina

**Angler(in)** m(f) ⟨-s, -⟩ angler

**Angora** nt ⟨-s⟩ angora

**angreifen** irr vt attack; (with hand) touch; (harm) damage; **Angriff** m attack; **etw in ~ nehmen** get started on sth

**Angst** f ⟨-, Ängste⟩ fear; **~ haben** be afraid (or scared) (vor + dat of or); **jdm ~ machen** scare sb; **ängstigen 1.** vt frighten **2.** vr worry (um, wegen + dat about); **ängstlich** adj nervous; (anxious) worried

**anhaben** irr vt (clothes) have on, wear; (light) have on

**anhalten** irr vi stop; (carry on) continue; **anhaltend** adj continuous; **Anhalter(in)** m(f) ⟨-s, -⟩ hitch-hiker; **per ~ fahren** hitch-hike

**anhand** prep + gen with; **~ von** by means of

**anhängen** vt hang up; RAIL (carriages) couple; (something extra) add (on); **jdm etw ~** fam (blame) pin sth on sb; **Anhänger** m ⟨-s, -⟩ AUTO trailer; (on suitcase) tag; (jewellery) pendant; **Anhänger(in)** m(f) ⟨-s, -⟩ supporter; **Anhängerkupplung** f towbar; **anhänglich** adj affectionate; pej clinging

**Anhieb** m **auf ~** straight away; **das kann ich nicht auf ~ sagen** I can't say offhand

**anhimmeln** vt worship, idolize

**anhören 1.** vt listen to **2.** vr sound; **das hört sich gut an** that sounds good

**Animateur(in)** m(f) host / hostess

**Anis** m ⟨-es, -e⟩ aniseed

**Anker** m ⟨-s, -⟩ anchor; **ankern** vt, vi anchor; **Ankerplatz** m anchorage

**anklicken** vt IT click on

**anklopfen** vi knock (an + acc on)

**ankommen** irr vi arrive; **bei jdm gut ~** go down well with sb; **es kommt darauf an** it depends (ob on whether); **darauf kommt es nicht an**

**annehmen**

that doesn't matter

**ankotzen** vt vulg **es kotzt mich an** it makes me sick

**ankreuzen** vt mark with a cross

**ankündigen** vt announce

**Ankunft** f ⟨-, Ankünfte⟩ arrival; **Ankunftszeit** f arrival time

**Anlage** f (tendency) disposition; (aptitude) talent; (park) gardens pl, grounds pl; (in letter etc) enclosure; (for CDs etc) stereo (system); TECH plant; FIN investment

**Anlass** m ⟨-es, Anlässe⟩ cause (zu for); (event) occasion; **aus diesem ~** for this reason; **anlassen** irr vt (engine) start; (light, garment) leave on; **Anlasser** m ⟨-s, -⟩ AUTO starter; **anlässlich** prep + gen on the occasion of

**Anlauf** m run-up; **anlaufen** irr vi begin; (film) open; (window) mist up; (metal) tarnish

**anlegen 1.** vt put (an + acc against / on); (jewellery) put on; (garden) lay out; (money) invest; (gun) aim (auf + acc at); **es auf etw** acc ~ be out for sth **2.** vi (ship) berth, dock **3.** vr **sich mit jdm ~** fam pick a quarrel with sb; **Anlegestelle** f moorings pl

**anlehnen 1.** vt lean (an + acc against); (door) leave ajar **2.**

vr lean (an + acc against)

**anleiern** vt etw ~ fam get sth going

**Anleitung** f instructions pl

**Anliegen** nt ⟨-s, -⟩ matter; (question) request

**Anlieger(in)** m(f) ⟨-s, -⟩ resident; **~ frei** residents only

**anlügen** irr vt lie to

**anmachen** vt (fasten) attach; (light, TV etc) switch on; (salad) dress; fam (excite) turn on; fam (talk to) chat up (Brit), come on to (US); fam (attack verbally) have a go at

**Anmeldeformular** nt application form; (for registering with the authorities) registration form; **anmelden 1.** vt (visit etc) announce **2.** vr (with doctor etc) make an appointment; (with the authorities, for course etc) register; **Anmeldeschluss** m deadline for applications, registration deadline; **Anmeldung** f registration; (request) application

**annähen** vt **einen Knopf (an den Mantel)** ~ sew a button on (one's coat)

**annähernd** adv roughly; **nicht** ~ nowhere near

**Annahme** f ⟨-, -n⟩ acceptance; (supposition) assumption; **annehmbar** adj acceptable; **annehmen** irr vt accept; (name) take; (child) adopt; (take as true) suppose, assume

**Annonce** f ⟨-, -n⟩ advertisement

**annullieren** vt cancel

**anöden** vt fam bore stiff (or silly)

**anonym** adj anonymous

**Anorak** m ⟨-s, -s⟩ anorak

**anpacken** vt (problem, task) tackle; **mit** ~ lend a hand

**anpassen** 1. vt fig adapt (dat to) 2. vr adapt (an + acc to)

**anpfeifen** irr vt **das Spiel** ~ start the game; **Anpfiff** m SPORT (starting) whistle; (start) kick-off; fam (reprimand) roasting

**anprobieren** vt try on

**Anrede** f form of address

**anreden** vt address

**anregen** vt stimulate; **Anregung** f stimulation; (idea) suggestion

**Anreise** f journey; **anreisen** vi arrive; **Anreisetag** m day of arrival

**Anreiz** m incentive

**anrichten** vt (food) prepare; (damage) cause

**Anruf** m call; **Anrufbeantworter** m ⟨-s, -⟩ answering machine, answerphone; **anrufen** irr vt TEL call, phone, ring (Brit)

**ans** contr = **an das**

**Ansage** f announcement; (on answerphone) recorded message; **ansagen** vt announce; **angesagt sein** be recommended; (fashiona-

ble) be the in thing

**anschaffen** vt buy

**anschauen** vt look at

**Anschein** m appearance; **dem** (or **allem**) ~ **nach** ~ it looks as if ...; **den** ~ **erwecken, hart zu arbeiten** give the impression of working hard; **anscheinend** 1. adj apparent 2. adv apparently

**anschieben** irr vt **könnten Sie mich mal** ~? AUTO could you give me a push?

**Anschlag** m notice; (on sb or sth) attack; **anschlagen** irr **1.** vt (poster) put up; (damage) chip **2.** vi (medicine etc) take effect; **mit etw an etw** acc ~ bang sth against sth

**anschließen** irr vt **1.** vt ELEC, TECH connect (an + acc to); (into socket) plug in **2.** vi, vr (**sich**) **an etw** acc ~ (building etc) adjoin sth; (happen after) follow sth **3.** vr join (jdm / einer Gruppe sb/a group); **anschließend 1.** adj adjacent; (happening afterwards) subsequent **2.** adv afterwards; ~ **an** + acc following; **Anschluss** m ELEC, RAIL following; (of water, gas etc) supply; **im** ~ **an** + acc following; **kein** ~ **unter dieser Nummer** TEL the number you have dialled has not been recognized; **Anschlussflug** m connecting flight

**anschnallen 1.** *vt* (*skis*) put on **2.** *vr* fasten one's seat belt

**Anschrift** *f* address

**anschwellen** *irr vi* swell (up)

**ansehen** *irr vt* look at; (*while sth happens*) watch; *jdn / etw als etw ~* look on sb/sth as sth; *das sieht man ihm an* he looks it

**an sein** *irr vi →* **an**

**ansetzen 1.** *vt* (*date*) fix; (*food*) prepare **2.** *vi* start, begin; *zu etw ~* prepare to do sth

**Ansicht** *f* view, opinion; (*act of seeing*) sight; *meiner ~ nach* in my opinion; *zur ~* on approval; **Ansichtskarte** *f* postcard

**ansonsten** *adv* otherwise

**anspielen** *vi auf etw acc ~* allude to sth; **Anspielung** *f* allusion (*auf + acc* to)

**ansprechen** *irr* **1.** *vt* speak to; (*interest*) appeal to **2.** *vi auf etw acc ~* (*patient*) respond to sth; **ansprechend** *adj* attractive; **Ansprechpartner(in)** *m(f)* contact

**anspringen** *irr vi* AUTO start

**Anspruch** *m* claim; (*entitlement*) right (*auf + acc* to); *etw in ~ nehmen* take advantage of sth; *~ auf etw haben* be entitled to sth; **anspruchslos** *adj* undemanding; (*life, accommodation etc*) modest; **anspruchsvoll** *adj* demanding

**Anstalt** *f* ⟨-, -en⟩ institution

**Anstand** *m* decency; **anständig** *adj* decent; *fig fam* proper; (*large*) considerable

**anstarren** *vt* stare at

**anstatt** *prep + gen* instead of

**anstecken 1.** *vt* pin on; MED infect; *jdn mit einer Erkältung ~* pass new's cold on to sb **2.** *vr* **ich habe mich bei ihm angesteckt** I caught it from him **3.** *vi fig* be infectious; **ansteckend** *adj* infectious; **Ansteckungsgefahr** *f* danger of infection

**anstehen** *irr vi* queue (*Brit*), stand in line (*US*); (*task etc*) be on the agenda

**anstelle** *prep + gen* instead of

**anstellen 1.** *vt* (*radio, heating etc*) turn on; (*worker*) employ; (*undertake*) do; *was hast du wieder angestellt?* what have you been up to now? **2.** *vr* queue (*Brit*), stand in line (*US*); *fam* **stell dich nicht so an!** stop making such a fuss

**Anstoß** *m* impetus; SPORT kick-off; **anstoßen** *irr* **1.** *vt* push; (*with foot*) kick **2.** *vi* knock, bump; (*chink glasses*) drink (a toast) (*auf + acc* to); **anstößig** *adj* offensive; (*clothes etc*) indecent

**anstrengen 1.** *vt* strain **2.** *vr* make an effort; **anstrengend** *adj* tiring

**Antarktis** *f* Antarctic

**Anteil** *m* share (*an + dat* in); *~*

***nehmen an*** + *dat* sympathize with; take an interest in

**Antenne** *f* ⟨-, -n⟩ aerial

**Antibabypille** *f die* ~ the pill; **Antibiotikum** *nt* ⟨-s, Antibiotika⟩ MED antibiotic

**antik** *adj* antique

**Antilope** *f* ⟨-, -n⟩ antelope

**Antiquariat** *nt* second-hand bookshop

**Antiquitäten** *pl* antiques *pl*; **Antiquitätenhändler(in)** *m(f)* antique dealer

**antörnen** *vt fam* turn on

**Antrag** *m* ⟨-(e)s, Anträge⟩ proposal; POL motion; (*document*) application form; *ei- nen ~ stellen auf* + *acc* make an application for

**antreffen** *irr vt* find

**antreiben** *irr vt* TECH drive; (*onto shore*) wash up; *jdn zur Arbeit* ~ make sb work

**antreten** *irr vt eine Reise* ~ set off on a journey

**Antrieb** *m* TECH drive; (*motivation*) impetus

**antun** *irr vt jdm etwas* ~ do sth to sb; *sich dat etwas* ~ (*commit suicide*) kill oneself

**Antwort** *f* ⟨-, -en⟩ answer, reply; *um* ~ *wird gebeten* RSVP (*répondez s'il vous plaît*); **antworten** *vi* answer, reply; *jdm* ~ answer sb; *auf etw* *acc* ~ answer sth

**anvertrauen** *vt jdm etw* ~ entrust sb with sth

**Anwalt** *m* ⟨-s, Anwälte⟩, An-

**wältin** *f* lawyer

**anweisen** *irr vt* instruct; (*flat, job etc*) allocate (*jdm etw* sth to sb); **Anweisung** *f* instruction; (*for making payment*) money order

**anwenden** *irr vt* use; (*law, rule*) apply; **Anwender(in)** *m(f)* ⟨-s, -⟩ user; **Anwendung** *f* use; IT application

**anwesend** *adj* present; **Anwesenheit** *f* presence

**anwidern** *vt* disgust

**Anwohner(in)** *m(f)* ⟨-s, -⟩ resident

**Anzahl** *f* number (*an* + *dat* of); **anzahlen** *vt* pay a deposit on; *100 Euro* ~ pay 100 euros as a deposit; **Anzahlung** *f* deposit

**Anzeichen** *nt* sign; MED symptom

**Anzeige** *f* ⟨-, -n⟩ (*in newspaper*) advertisement; (*electronic*) display; (*made to the police*) report; **anzeigen** *vt* (*temperature, time*) indicate, show; (*electronically*) display; (*make known*) announce; *jdn / einen Autodiebstahl bei der Polizei* ~ report sb/a stolen car to the police

**anziehen** *irr* **1.** *vt* attract; (*clothes*) put on; (*screw, rope*) tighten **2.** *vr* get dressed; **anziehend** *adj* attractive

**Anzug** *m* suit

**anzüglich** *adj* suggestive

**anzünden** *vt* light; (*house etc*)

set fire to

**anzweifeln** vt doubt

**Aperitif** m ⟨-s, -s (or -e)⟩ aperitif

**Apfel** m ⟨-s, Äpfel⟩ apple; **Apfelbaum** m apple tree; **Apfelkuchen** m apple cake; **Apfelmus** nt apple purée; **Apfelsaft** m apple juice; **Apfelsine** f orange; **Apfelwein** m cider

**Apostroph** m ⟨-s, -e⟩ apostrophe

**Apotheke** f ⟨-, -n⟩ chemist's (shop) (Brit), pharmacy (US); **apothekenpflichtig** adj only available at the chemist's (or pharmacy); **Apotheker(in)** m(f) ⟨-s, -⟩ chemist (Brit), pharmacist (US)

**Apparat** m ⟨-(e)s, -e⟩ (piece of) apparatus; TEL telephone; RADIO, TV set; **am ...!** TEL speaking; **am ~ bleiben** TEL hold the line

**Appartement** nt ⟨-s, -s⟩ studio flat (Brit) (or apartment (US))

**Appetit** m ⟨-(e)s, -e⟩ appetite; **guten ~!** bon appétit

**appetitlich** adj appetizing

**Applaus** m ⟨-es, -e⟩ applause

**Aprikose** f ⟨-, -n⟩ apricot

**April** m ⟨-(s), -e⟩ April; → **Juni** **~, ~!** April fool!; **Aprilscherz** m ⟨-es, -e⟩ April fool's joke

**apropos** adv by the way; **~ Urlaub ...** while we're on

the subject of holidays ...

**Aquajogging** nt aqua jogging; **Aquaplaning** nt ⟨-(s)⟩ aquaplaning

**Aquarell** nt ⟨-s, -e⟩ watercolour

**Aquarium** nt ⟨-s, Aquarien⟩ aquarium

**Äquator** m ⟨-s⟩ equator

**Araber(in)** m(f) ⟨-s, -⟩ Arab; **arabisch** adj Arab; (numeral, language) Arabic; (Sea, Desert) Arabian

**Arbeit** f ⟨-, -en⟩ work; (post) job; (product) piece of work; **arbeiten** vi work; **Arbeiter(in)** m(f) ⟨-s, -⟩ worker; (unskilled) labourer; **Arbeitgeber(in)** m(f) ⟨-s, -⟩ employer; **Arbeitnehmer(in)** m(f) ⟨-s, -⟩ employee; **Arbeitsagentur** f job agency (Brit), unemployment agency (US); **Arbeitsamt** nt job centre (Brit), employment office (US); **Arbeitserlaubnis** f work permit; **arbeitslos** adj unemployed; **Arbeitslose(r)** mf unemployed person; **die ~n** pl the unemployed pl; **Arbeitslosengeld** nt (income--related) unemployment benefit, job-seeker's allowance (Brit); **Arbeitslosenhilfe** f (non-income related) unemployment benefit; **Arbeitslosigkeit** f unemployment; **Arbeitsplatz** m job; (place) workplace; **Arbeits-**

**speicher** *m* IT main memory; **Arbeitszeit** *f* working hours *pl*; **Arbeitszimmer** *nt* study

**Archäologe** *m* ⟨-n, -n⟩, **Archäologin** *f* archaeologist

**Architekt(in)** *m(f)* ⟨-en, -en⟩ architect; **Architektur** *f* architecture

**Archiv** *nt* ⟨-s, -e⟩ archives *pl*

**arg 1.** *adj* bad; (*unpleasant, intense*) awful **2.** *adv* (*very*) terribly

**Argentinien** *nt* ⟨-s⟩ Argentina

**Ärger** *m* ⟨-s⟩ annoyance; (*stronger*) anger; (*difficulties*) trouble; **ärgerlich** *adj* angry; (*irritating*) annoying; **ärgern 1.** *vt* annoy **2.** *vr* get annoyed

**Argument** *nt* ⟨-s, -e⟩ argument

**Arktis** *f* ⟨-⟩ Arctic

**arm** *adj* poor

**Arm** *m* ⟨-(e)s, -e⟩ arm; (*of river*) branch

**Armaturenbrett** *nt* instrument panel; AUTO dashboard

**Armband** *nt* bracelet; **Armbanduhr** *f* (wrist)watch

**Armee** *f* ⟨-, -n⟩ army

**Ärmel** *m* ⟨-s, -⟩ sleeve; **Ärmelkanal** *m* (English) Channel

**Armut** *f* ⟨-⟩ poverty

**Aroma** *nt* ⟨-s, Aromen⟩ aroma

**arrogant** *adj* arrogant

**Arsch** *m* ⟨-es, Ärsche⟩ *vulg* arse (*Brit*), ass (*US*); **Arschloch** *nt* *vulg* (*person*) arse-

hole (*Brit*), asshole (*US*)

**Art** *f* ⟨-, -en⟩ (*manner*) way; (*type*) kind, sort; (*of animal*) species; **nach ~ des Hauses** à la maison; **auf diese ~ (und Weise)** in this way; **das ist nicht seine ~** that's not like him

**Arterie** *f* ⟨-, -n⟩ artery

**artig** *adj* good, well-behaved

**Artikel** *m* ⟨-s, -⟩ (*product*) article, item; (*in newspaper*) article

**Artischocke** *f* ⟨-, -n⟩ artichoke

**Artist(in)** *m(f)* ⟨-en, -en⟩ (*circus*) performer

**Arznei** *f* medicine; **Arzt** *m* ⟨-es, Ärzte⟩ doctor; **Arzthelfer(in)** *m(f)* doctor's assistant; **Ärztin** *f* (female) doctor; **ärztlich** *adj* medical; **sich ~ behandeln lassen** undergo medical treatment

**Asche** *f* ⟨-, -n⟩ ashes *pl*; (*from cigarette*) ash; **Aschenbecher** *m* ashtray; **Aschermittwoch** *m* Ash Wednesday

**Asiat(in)** *m(f)* ⟨-en, -en⟩ Asian; **asiatisch** *adj* Asian; **Asien** *nt* ⟨-s⟩ Asia

**Aspekt** *m* ⟨-(e)s, -e⟩ aspect

**Asphalt** *m* ⟨-(e)s, -e⟩ asphalt

**Aspirin®** *nt* ⟨-s, -e⟩ aspirin

**aß** *imperf* → **essen**

**Ass** *nt* ⟨-es, -e⟩ (*in card game, tennis*) ace

**Assistent(in)** *m(f)* assistant

**Ast** *m* ⟨-(e)s, Äste⟩ branch

**aufbauen**

**Asthma** nt ⟨-s⟩ asthma

**Astrologie** f astrology; **Astronaut(in)** m(f) ⟨-en, -en⟩ astronaut; **Astronomie** f astronomy

**ASU** f ⟨-, -s⟩ abbr = **Abgassonderuntersuchung** exhaust emission test

**Asyl** nt ⟨-s, -e⟩ asylum; (place) home; (for the homeless) shelter; **Asylant(in)** m(f), **Asylbewerber(in)** m(f) asylum seeker

**Atelier** nt ⟨-s, -s⟩ studio

**Atem** m ⟨-s⟩ breath; **atemberaubend** adj breathtaking; **Atembeschwerden** pl breathing difficulties pl; **atemlos** adj breathless; **Atempause** f breather

**Athen** nt Athens

**Äthiopien** nt ⟨-s⟩ Ethiopia

**Athlet(in)** m(f) ⟨-en, -en⟩ athlete

**Atlantik** m ⟨-s⟩ Atlantic (Ocean)

**Atlas** m ⟨- or Atlasses, Atlanten⟩ atlas

**atmen** vt, vi breathe; **Atmung** f breathing

**Atom** nt ⟨-s, -e⟩ atom; **Atombombe** f atom bomb; **Atomkraftwerk** nt nuclear power station; **Atommüll** m nuclear waste; **Atomwaffen** pl nuclear weapons pl

**Attentat** nt ⟨-(e)s, -e⟩ assassination (auf + acc of); (unsuccessful) assassination attempt

**Attest** nt ⟨-(e)s, -e⟩ certificate

**attraktiv** adj attractive

**Attrappe** f ⟨-, -n⟩ dummy

**ätzend** adj fam revolting; (bad) lousy

**au** interj ja! yeah

**Aubergine** f ⟨-, -n⟩ aubergine, eggplant (US)

**auch** conj also, too; even; (actually) really; **oder ~** or; **ich ~ so do I**; **ich ~ nicht** me neither; **wer / was ~ immer** whoever / whatever; **ich gehe jetzt - ich ~** I'm going now - so am I; **das weiß ich ~ nicht** I don't know either

**audiovisuell** adj audiovisual

**auf 1.** prep + acc or dat on; **~ der Reise / dem Tisch** on the way / the table; **~ der Post®/ der Party** at the post office / the party; **etw ~ den Tisch stellen** put sth on the table; **~ Deutsch** in German **2.** prep + acc (mountain, tree etc) up; (direction) to; (following) after; **~ eine Party gehen** go to a party; **bis ~ ihn** except for him; **~ einmal** suddenly; (simultaneously, in one go) at once **3.** adv (open) open; **~ sein** fam be open; (person) be up; **~ und ab** up and down; **~!** come on!; **~ dass** so that

**aufatmen** vi breathe a sigh of relief

**aufbauen** vt (erect) put up; (develop) build up; (form)

construct; (*establish*) found, base (*auf* + *acc* on); **sich eine Existenz ~** make a life for oneself

**aufbewahren** *vt* keep, store

**aufbleiben** *irr vi* (*door, shop etc*) stay open; (*person*) stay up

**aufblenden** *vi*, *vt* (*die Scheinwerfer*) ~ put one's headlights on full beam

**aufbrechen** *irr* **1.** *vt* break open **2.** *vi* burst open; (*go*) leave; (*on journey*) set off

**aufdrängen 1.** *vt jdm etw ~* force sth on sb **2.** *vr* intrude (*jdm* on sb); **aufdringlich** *adj* pushy

**aufeinander** *adv* on top of each other; ~ **achten** look after each other; ~ **vertrauen** trust each other; **aufeinanderfolgen** *vi* follow one another; **aufeinanderprallen** *vi* crash into one another

**Aufenthalt** *m* stay; (*of train*) stop; **Aufenthaltsgenehmigung** *f* residence permit; **Aufenthaltsraum** *m* lounge

**aufessen** *irr vt* eat up

**auffahren** *irr vi* (*car*) run (*or* crash) (*auf* + *acc* into); (*get closer*) drive up; **Auffahrt** *f* (*of building*) drive; (*onto motorway*) slip road (*Brit*), ramp (*US*); **Auffahrunfall** *m* rear-end collision; (*several vehicles*) pile-up

**auffallen** *irr vi* stand out; *jdm* ~ strike sb; *das fällt gar*

*nicht auf* nobody will notice; **auffallend** *adj* striking; **auffällig** *adj* conspicuous; (*clothes, colour*) striking

**auffangen** *irr vt* (*ball*) catch; (*in table, index*) list; (*blow*) cushion

**auffassen** *vt* understand; **Auffassung** *f* view; opinion; (*interpretation*) concept; (*comprehension*) grasp

**auffordern** *vt* (*order*) call upon; (*request*) ask

**auffrischen** *vt* (*knowledge*) brush up

**aufführen 1.** *vt* THEAT perform; (*in table, index*) list; (*example*) give **2.** *vr* behave; **Aufführung** *f* THEAT performance

**Aufgabe** *f* job, task; (*schoolwork*) exercise; homework

**Aufgang** *m* (*steps*) staircase

**aufgeben** *irr* **1.** *vt* (*job, smoking, plan etc*) give up; (*parcel*) post; (*luggage*) check in; (*order*) place; (*advertisement*) insert; (*puzzle, problem*) set **2.** *vi* give up

**aufgehen** *irr vi* (*sun, dough*) rise; (*door, flower*) open; (*become clear*) dawn (*jdm* on sb)

**aufgelegt** *adj* **gut / schlecht** ~ in a good / bad mood

**aufgeregt** *adj* excited

**aufgeschlossen** *adj* open (-minded)

**aufgeschmissen** *adj fam* in a fix

**aufgrund, auf Grund** *prep*

+ *gen* on the basis of; (*reason*) because of

**aufhaben** *irr* **1.** *vt* (*hat etc*) have on; **viel ~** have a lot of homework to do **2.** *vi* (*shop*) be open

**aufhalten** *irr* **1.** *vt* (*person*) detain; (*development*) stop; (*door, hand*) hold open; (*eyes*) keep open **2.** *vr* (*reside*) live; (*temporarily*) stay

**aufhängen** *irr vt* hang up

**aufheben** *irr vt* (*from ground etc*) pick up; (*not throw away*) keep

**aufholen 1.** *vt* (*time*) make up **2.** *vi* catch up

**aufhören** *vi* stop; **~, etw zu tun** stop doing sth

**aufklären** *vt* (*mystery etc*) clear up; **jdn ~** enlighten sb; (*about sex*) tell sb the facts of life

**Aufkleber** *m* ⟨-s, -⟩ sticker

**aufkommen** *irr vi* (*wind*) come up; (*doubt, feeling*) arise; (*fashion etc*) appear on the scene; **für den Schaden ~** pay for the damage

**Aufladegerät** *nt* charger; **aufladen** *irr vt* load; (*mobile phone etc*) charge; (*prepaid card etc*) top up

**Auflage** *f* edition; (*of newspaper*) circulation; (*imposed on sb*) condition

**auflassen** *vt* (*hat, glasses*) keep on; (*door*) leave open

**Auflauf** *m* crowd; (*dish*) bake

**auflegen 1.** *vt* (*CD, make-up*

*etc*) put on; (*receiver*) put down **2.** *vi* TEL hang up

**aufleuchten** *vi* light up

**auflösen 1.** *vt* (*in liquid*) dissolve **2.** *vr* (*in liquid*) dissolve; **der Stau hat sich aufgelöst** traffic is back to normal; **Auflösung** *f* (*of puzzle*) solution; (*of screen*) resolution

**aufmachen 1.** *vt* (*present, garment*) undo **2.** *vr* set out (*nach* for)

**aufmerksam** *adj* attentive; **jdn auf etw** *acc* **~ machen** draw sb's attention to sth; **Aufmerksamkeit** *f* attention; (*concentration*) attentiveness; (*present*) small token

**aufmuntern** *vt* encourage; (*make happier*) cheer up

**Aufnahme** *f* ⟨-, -n⟩ PHOT photo (-graph); (*in film*) shot; (*to club, hospital etc*) admission; (*start*) beginning; (*on tape etc*) recording; **Aufnahmeprüfung** *f* entrance exam; **aufnehmen** *irr vt* (*to hospital, club etc*) admit; (*music*) record; (*begin*) take up; (*in list*) include; (*understand*) take in; **mit jdm Kontakt ~** get in touch with sb

**aufpassen** *vi* pay attention; (*be careful*) take care; **auf jdn / etw ~** keep an eye on sb/sth

**Aufprall** *m* ⟨-s, -e⟩ impact; **aufprallen** *vi* **auf etw** *acc* **~**

hit sth, crash into sth

**Aufpreis** *m* extra charge

**aufpumpen** *vt* pump up

**Aufputschmittel** *nt* stimulant

**aufräumen** *vt*, *vi* clear away; *(room)* tidy up

**aufrecht** *adj* upright

**aufregen 1.** *vt* excite; *(irritate)* annoy **2.** *vr* get worked up; **aufregend** *adj* exciting; **Aufregung** *f* excitement

**aufreißen** *irr vt (parcel, bag etc)* tear open; *(door)* fling open; *(person)* fam pick up

**Aufruf** *m* AVIAT, IT call; *(public request)* appeal; **aufrufen** *irr vt (request)* call upon *(zu* for); *(names)* call out; AVIAT call; IT call up

**aufrunden** *vt (amount)* round up

**aufs** *contr* = **auf das**

**Aufsatz** *m* essay

**aufschieben** *irr vt* postpone; *(delay doing)* put off; *(door)* slide open

**Aufschlag** *m (on price)* extra charge; *(in tennis)* service; **aufschlagen** *irr* **1.** *vt (book, eyes)* open; *(knee etc)* cut open; *(tent)* pitch, put up; *(camp)* set up **2.** *vi (in tennis)* serve; *auf etw acc ~* hit sth

**aufschließen** *irr* **1.** *vt* unlock, open up **2.** *vi (people in a row)* close up

**aufschneiden** *irr* **1.** *vt* cut open; *(bread, meat etc)* slice **2.** *vi* boast, show off

**Aufschnitt** *m (slices pl of)* cold meat; *(cheese) (assorted)* sliced cheeses *pl*

**aufschreiben** *irr vt* write down

**Aufschrift** *f* inscription; *(piece of paper)* label

**Aufschub** *m* delay; *(until a later date)* postponement

**Aufsehen** *nt* ⟨-s⟩ stir; *großes ~ erregen* cause a sensation; **Aufseher(in)** *m(f)* ⟨-s, -⟩ guard; *(in firm)* supervisor; *(in museum)* attendant; *(in park)* keeper

**auf sein** *irr vi* → **auf**

**aufsetzen 1.** *vt* put on; *(document)* draw up **2.** *vi (plane)* touch down

**Aufsicht** *f* supervision; *(in exam)* invigilation; *die ~ haben* be in charge

**aufspannen** *vt (umbrella)* put up

**aufsperren** *vt (mouth)* open wide; *(door, flat)* unlock

**aufspringen** *irr vi* jump *(auf + acc* onto); *(stand up quickly)* jump up; *(door, suitcase)* spring open

**aufstehen** *irr vi* get up; *(door)* be open

**aufstellen** *vt* put up; *(in a row)* line up; *(candidate)* put up; *(list, schedule)* draw up; *(record)* set up

**Aufstieg** *m* ⟨-(e)s, -e⟩ *(up mountain)* ascent; *(progress)* rise; *(in career, sport)* promotion

**Aufstrich** m spread

**auftanken** vt, vi (car) tank up; (plane) refuel

**auftauchen** vi turn up; (from water etc) surface; (question, problem) come up

**auftauen 1.** vt (food) defrost **2.** vi thaw; fig (person) unbend

**Auftrag** m ⟨-(e)s, Aufträge⟩ COMM order; (allocated work) job; (orders) instructions pl; (mission) task; **im ~ von** on behalf of; **auftragen** irr vt (ointment etc) apply; (meal) serve

**auftreten** irr vi appear; (problem) come up; (act) behave; **Auftritt** m (of actor) entrance; fig (argument) scene

**aufwachen** vi wake up

**aufwachsen** irr vi grow up

**Aufwand** m ⟨-(e)s⟩ expenditure; (costs also) expense; (exertion) effort; **aufwändig** adj costly; **das ist zu ~** that's too much trouble

**aufwärmen** vt, vr warm up

**aufwärts** adv upwards; **mit etw geht es ~** things are looking up for sth

**aufwecken** vt wake up

**aufwendig** adj → **aufwändig**

**aufwischen** vt wipe up; (floor) wipe

**aufzählen** vt list

**aufzeichnen** vt sketch; (write) jot down; (on tape etc) record; **Aufzeichnung** f

f (written) note; (on tape etc) recording; (on film) record

**aufziehen** irr **1.** vt (drawer, curtains etc) pull open; (watch) wind (up); fam (make fun of) tease; (children) bring up; (animals) rear **2.** vi (storm) come up

**Aufzug** m lift (Brit), elevator (US); (clothes) get-up; THEAT act

**Auge** nt ⟨-s, -n⟩ eye; **jdm etw aufs ~ drücken** fam force sth on sb; **ins ~ gehen** fam go wrong; **unter vier ~n** in private; **etw im ~ behalten** keep sth in mind; **Augenarzt** m, **Augenärztin** f eye specialist, eye doctor (US); **Augenblick** m moment; **im ~** at the moment; **Augenbraue** f ⟨-, -n⟩ eyebrow; **Augenbrauenstift** m eyebrow pencil; **Augenfarbe** f eye colour; **seine ~** the colour of his eyes; **Augenlid** nt eyelid; **Augenoptiker(in)** m(f) ⟨-s, -⟩ optician; **Augentropfen** pl eyedrops pl; **Augenzeuge** m, **Augenzeugin** f eyewitness

**August** m ⟨-(e)s or -, -e⟩ August; → **Juni**

**Auktion** f auction

**aus 1.** prep + dat (from inside) out of; (source) from; (material) (made) of; **~ Berlin kommen** come from Berlin; **~ Versehen** by mistake; **~**

***Angst*** out of fear **2.** *adv* out; (*ended*) finished, over; *ein/*~ TECH on / off; ~ *sein fam* SPORT be out; (*finished*) be over; *auf etw acc* ~ *sein* be after sth; *von mir* ~ as far as I'm concerned; *von mir* ~*!* don't care! ; *zwischen uns ist es* ~ we're finished; **Aus** *nt* ⟨-⟩ SPORT touch; *fig* end

**ausatmen** *vi* breathe out

**ausbauen** *vt* (*house, road*) extend; (*engine etc*) remove

**ausbessern** *vt* repair; (*clothes*) mend

**ausbilden** *vt* educate; (*apprentice etc*) train; (*skills*) develop; **Ausbildung** *f* education; (*of apprentice etc*) training; (*of skills*) development

**Ausblick** *m* view; *fig* outlook

**ausbrechen** *irr vi* break out; *in Tränen* ~ burst into tears; *in Gelächter* ~ burst out laughing

**ausbreiten 1.** *vt* spread (out); (*arms*) stretch out **2.** *vr* spread

**Ausbruch** *m* (*of war, epidemic etc*) outbreak; (*of volcano*) eruption; (*of feelings*) outburst; (*from prison*) escape

**ausbuhen** *vt* boo

**Ausdauer** *f* perseverance; SPORT stamina

**ausdehnen** *vt* stretch; *fig* (*power*) extend

**ausdenken** *irr vt sich dat etw* ~ come up with sth

**Ausdruck 1.** *m* ⟨Ausdrücke pl⟩ expression **2.** *m* ⟨Ausdrücke pl⟩ (*from computer*) printout; **ausdrucken** *vt* IT print (out)

**ausdrücken 1.** *vt* (*facts, feelings etc*) express; (*cigarette*) put out; (*lemon etc*) squeeze **2.** *vr* express oneself; **ausdrücklich 1.** *adj* express **2.** *adv* expressly

**auseinander** *adv* apart; ~ *schreiben* write as separate words; **auseinandergehen** *irr vi* (*people*) separate; (*opinions*) differ; (*object*) fall apart; **auseinanderhalten** *irr vt* tell apart; **auseinandersetzen 1.** *vr* explain **2.** *vr* look (*mit* at); (*disagree*) argue (*mit* with); **Auseinandersetzung** *f* (*row*) argument; (*discussion*) debate

**Ausfahrt** *f* (*of train etc*) departure; (*from motorway, garage etc*) exit

**ausfallen** *irr vi* (*hair*) fall out; (*concert, class etc*) be cancelled; (*machine*) break down; (*electricity*) be cut off; (*well, badly etc*) turn out; *groß / klein* ~ (*clothes, shoes*) be too big / too small

**ausfindig machen** *vt* discover

**ausflippen** *vi fam* freak out

**Ausflug** *m* excursion, outing; **Ausflugsziel** *nt* destination

**Ausfluss** m MED discharge

**ausfragen** vt question

**Ausfuhr** f ‹-, -en› export

**ausführen** vt (order, task, plan) carry out; (person) take out; (comm) export; (theory etc) explain

**ausführlich 1.** adj detailed **2.** adv in detail

**ausfüllen** vt fill up; (questionnaire etc) fill in (or out)

**Ausgabe** f (money) expenditure; IT output; (of book) edition; (of magazine) issue

**Ausgang** m way out, exit; (at airport) gate; (conclusion) end; (outcome) result; „kein ~" 'no exit'

**ausgeben** irr **1.** vt (money) spend; (share out) distribute; **jdm etw ~** (treat sb) buy sb sth **2.** vr **sich für etw / jdn ~** pass oneself off as sth / sb

**ausgebucht** adj fully booked

**ausgefallen** adj unusual

**ausgehen** irr vi (in the evening etc) go out; (petrol, coffee etc) run out; (hair) fall out; (fire, light etc) go out; (well, badly etc) turn out; **davon ~, dass** assume that; **ihm ging das Geld aus** he ran out of money

**ausgelassen** adj exuberant

**ausgeleiert** adj worn out

**ausgenommen** conj, prep + gen or dat except

**ausgerechnet** adv **~ du** you of all people; **~ heute** today

of all days

**ausgeschildert** adj signposted

**ausgeschlafen** adj **bist du ~?** have you had enough sleep?

**ausgeschlossen** adj impossible, out of the question

**ausgesprochen 1.** adj out-and-out; (strong) marked **2.** adv extremely; **~ gut** really good

**ausgezeichnet** adj excellent

**ausgiebig** adj (use) thorough; (meal) substantial

**ausgießen** irr vt (drink) pour out; (jug, glass etc) empty

**ausgleichen** irr **1.** vt even out **2.** vi SPORT equalize

**Ausguss** m sink; (waste pipe) outlet

**aushalten** irr **1.** vt bear, stand; **nicht auszuhalten sein** be unbearable **2.** vi hold out

**aushändigen** vt **jdm etw ~** hand sth over to sb

**Aushang** m notice

**Aushilfe** f temporary help; (in office) temp

**auskennen** irr vr know a lot (bei, mit about); (in a place) know one's way around

**auskommen** irr vi **gut / schlecht mit jdm ~** get on well / badly with sb; **mit etw ~** get by with sth

**Auskunft** f ‹-, Auskünfte› information; (particulars) details pl; (counter) information desk; TEL (directory) enquiries *sg* (*Brit*), information (*US*)

**auslachen** *vt* laugh at

**ausladen** *irr vt* (*luggage etc*) unload; **jdn ~** (*guest*) tell sb not to come

**Auslage** *f* window display; **~n** *pl* (*costs*) expenses

**Ausland** *nt* foreign countries *pl*; **im / ins ~** abroad; **Ausländer(in)** *m(f)* ⟨-s, -⟩ foreigner; **ausländerfeindlich** *adj* hostile to foreigners, xenophobic; **ausländisch** *adj* foreign; **Auslandsgespräch** *nt* international call; **Auslandskrankenschein** *m* health insurance certificate for foreign countries, ≈ E111 (*Brit*); **Auslandsschutzbrief** *m* international (*motor*) insurance cover (*documents pl*)

**auslassen** *irr* **1.** *vt* leave out; (*word etc also*) omit; (*do without*) skip; (*anger*) vent (*an* + *dat* auf *acc*) **2.** *vr* **sich über etw** *acc* **~** speak one's mind about sth

**auslaufen** *irr vi* (*liquid*) run out; (*tank etc*) leak; (*ship*) leave port; (*contract*) expire

**auslegen** *vt* (*goods*) display; (*money*) lend; (*text etc*) interpret; (*machine, building*) design (*für, auf* + *acc* for sth)

**ausleihen** *irr vt* (*to sb*) lend; **sich** *dat* **etw ~** borrow sth

**ausloggen** *vi* IT log out (*or* off)

**auslösen** *vt* (*explosion, alarm*) set off; (*bring about*) cause; **Auslöser** *m* ⟨-s, -⟩ PHOT shutter release

**ausmachen** *vt* (*light, radio*) turn off; (*fire*) put out; (*date, price*) fix; (*arrange*) agree; (*proportion, amount etc*) represent; (*be significant*) matter; **macht es Ihnen etwas aus, wenn …?** would you mind if …?; **das macht mir nichts aus** I don't mind

**Ausmaß** *nt* extent

**Ausnahme** *f* ⟨-, -n⟩ exception; **ausnahmsweise** *adv* as an exception, just this once

**ausnutzen** *vt* (*time, opportunity, influence*) use; (*person, sb's good nature*) take advantage of

**auspacken** *vt* unpack

**ausprobieren** *vt* try (out)

**Auspuff** *m* ⟨-(e)s, -e⟩ TECH exhaust; **Auspuffrohr** *nt* exhaust (pipe); **Auspufftopf** *m* AUTO silencer (*Brit*), muffler (*US*)

**ausrauben** *vt* rob

**ausräumen** *vt* clear away; (*cupboard, room*) empty; (*misgivings*) put aside

**ausrechnen** *vt* calculate, work out

**Ausrede** *f* excuse

**ausreden 1.** *vi* finish speaking **2.** *vt* **jdm etw ~** talk sb out of sth

**ausreichend** *adj* sufficient,

satisfactory; *(mark in school)* ≈ D

**Ausreise** *f* departure; *bei der* ≈ on leaving the country; **Ausreiseerlaubnis** *f* exit visa; **ausreisen** *vi* leave the country

**ausreißen** *irr* **1.** *vt* tear out **2.** *vi* come off; *fam (abscond)* run away

**ausrenken** *vt* dislocate; *sich dat den Arm* ≈ dislocate one's arm

**ausrichten** *vt (message)* deliver; *(regards)* pass on; *ich konnte bei ihr nichts* ≈ I couldn't get anywhere with her; *jdm etw* ≈ tell sb sth

**ausrufen** *irr vt (over loud-speaker)* announce; *jdn lassen* page sb; **Ausrufezeichen** *nt* exclamation mark

**ausruhen** *vi, vr* rest

**Ausrüstung** *f* equipment

**ausrutschen** *vi* slip

**ausschalten** *vt* switch off; *fig* eliminate

**Ausschau** *f* ≈ *halten* look out *(nach* for)

**ausscheiden** *irr* **1.** *vt* MED give off, secrete **2.** *vi* leave *(aus etw* sth); SPORT be eliminated

**ausschlafen** *irr* **1.** *vi, vr* have a lie-in **2.** *vt* sleep off

**Ausschlag** *m* MED rash; *den* ≈ *geben fig* tip the balance; **ausschlagen** *irr* **1.** *vt (tooth)* knock out; *(invitation)* turn down **2.** *vi (horse)* kick out; **ausschlaggebend** *adj*

decisive

**ausschließen** *irr vt* lock out; *fig* exclude; **ausschließlich** **1.** *adv* exclusively **2.** *prep* + *gen* excluding

**Ausschnitt** *m (part)* section; *(of dress)* neckline; *(from newspaper)* cutting

**ausschütten** *vt (liquid)* pour out; *(container)* empty

**aussehen** *irr vi* look; *krank* ≈ look ill; *gut* ≈ *(person)* be good-looking; *(thing)* be looking good; *es sieht nach Regen aus* it looks like rain; *es sieht schlecht aus* things look bad

**aus sein** *irr vi* → *aus*

**außen** *adv* outside; *nach* ≈ outwards; *von* ≈ from (the) outside; **Außenbordmotor** *m* outboard motor; **Außenminister(in)** *m(f)* foreign minister, Foreign Secretary *(Brit)*; **Außenseite** *f* outside; **Außenseiter(in)** *m(f)* outsider; **Außenspiegel** *m* wing mirror *(Brit)*, side mirror *(US)*

**außer** **1.** *prep* + *dat* except (for); *nichts* ≈ nothing but; ≈ *Betrieb* out of order; *sich sein* be beside oneself *(vor* with); ≈ *Atem* out of breath **2.** *conj* except; *wenn* unless; ≈ *dass* except; **außerdem** *conj* besides

**äußere(r, s)** *adj* outer, external

**außergewöhnlich 1.** *adj* unusual **2.** *adv* exceptionally; **~ kalt** exceptionally cold; **außerhalb** *prep + gen* outside

**äußerlich** *adj* external

**äußern 1.** *vt* express; *(display)* show **2.** *vr* give one's opinion; *(be visible)* show itself

**außerordentlich** *adj* extraordinary; **außerplanmäßig** *adj* unscheduled

**äußerst** *adv* extremely; **äußerste(r, s)** *adj* utmost; *(in distance)* farthest; *(date)* last possible

**Äußerung** *f* remark

**aussetzen 1.** *vt* *(child, animal)* abandon; *(reward)* offer; **ich habe nichts daran auszusetzen** I have no objection to it **2.** *vi* stop; *(take a break)* drop out; *(in game)* miss a turn

**Aussicht** *f* view; *(chance)* prospect; **aussichtslos** *adj* hopeless; **Aussichtsplattform** *f* observation platform; **Aussichtsturm** *m* observation tower

**Aussiedler(in)** *m(f)* ‹-s, -› émigré *(person of German descent from Eastern Europe)*

**ausspannen 1.** *vi* relax **2.** *vt* **er hat ihm die Freundin ausgespannt** *fam* he's nicked his girlfriend

**aussperren 1.** *vt* lock out **2.** *vr* lock oneself out

**Aussprache** *f* *(of words)* pronunciation; *(talk)* (frank) discussion; **aussprechen** *irr* **1.** *vt* pronounce; *(thoughts etc)* express **2.** *vi* talk *(über + acc* about) **3.** *vi* finish speaking

**ausspülen** *vt* rinse (out)

**Ausstattung** *f* *(in hospital, office etc)* equipment; *(in flat etc)* furnishings *pl*; *(in car)* fittings *pl*

**ausstehen** *irr* **1.** *vt* endure; **ich kann ihn nicht ~** I can't stand him **2.** *vi* *(debt etc)* be outstanding

**aussteigen** *irr* *vi* get out *(aus* of); **aus dem Bus / Zug ~** get off the bus / train; **Aussteiger(in)** *m(f)* dropout

**ausstellen** *vt* display; *(at trade fair, in museum etc)* exhibit; *fam* *(radio, heating etc)* switch off; *(cheque etc)* make out; *(passport etc)* issue; **Ausstellung** *f* exhibition

**aussterben** *irr* *vi* die out

**ausstrahlen** *vt* radiate; *(programme)* broadcast; **Ausstrahlung** *f* RADIO, TV broadcast; *fig (of person)* charisma

**ausstrecken 1.** *vr* stretch out **2.** *vt* *(hand)* reach out *(nach* for)

**aussuchen** *vt* choose

**Austausch** *m* exchange; **austauschen** *vt* exchange *(gegen* for)

**austeilen** *vt* distribute; hand

out

**Auster** f ⟨-, -n⟩ oyster; **Austernpilz** m oyster mushroom

**austragen** irr vt (mail) deliver; (competition) hold

**Australien** nt ⟨-s⟩ Australia; **Australier(in)** m(f) ⟨-s, -⟩ Australian; **australisch** adj Australian

**austrinken** irr **1.** vt (glass) drain; (wine, coffee etc) drink up **2.** vi finish one's drink

**austrocknen** vi dry out; (river) dry up

**ausüben** vt (profession, sport) practise; (influence) exert

**Ausverkauf** m sale; **ausverkauft** adj (tickets, item) sold out

**Auswahl** f selection, choice (an + dat of); **auswählen** vt select, choose

**auswandern** vi emigrate

**auswärtig** adj not local; (relating to other countries) foreign; **auswärts** adv out of town; SPORT **~ spielen** play away; **Auswärtsspiel** nt away match

**auswechseln** vt replace; SPORT substitute

**Ausweg** m way out

**ausweichen** irr vi get out of the way; **jdm / einer Sache ~** move aside for sb/sth; fig avoid sb/sth

**Ausweis** m ⟨-es, -e⟩ (for individual) identity card, ID;

(for library etc) card; **ausweisen** irr **1.** vt expel **2.** vr prove one's identity; **Ausweiskontrolle** f ID check; **Ausweispapiere** pl identification documents pl

**auswendig** adv by heart

**auswuchten** vt AUTO (wheels) balance

**auszahlen 1.** vt (money) pay (out); (person) pay off **2.** vr be worth it

**auszeichnen 1.** vt (special person) honour; COMM price **2.** vr distinguish oneself

**ausziehen 1.** vt (clothes) take off **2.** vr undress **3.** vi (from flat) move out

**Auszubildende(r)** mf trainee

**authentisch** adj authentic, genuine

**Auto** nt ⟨-s, -s⟩ car; **~ fahren** drive; **Autoatlas** m road atlas; **Autobahn** f motorway (Brit), freeway (US); **Autobahnauffahrt** f motorway access road (Brit), on-ramp (US); **Autobahnausfahrt** f motorway exit (Brit), off-ramp (US); **Autobahngebühr** f toll; **Autobahnkreuz** nt motorway interchange; **Autobahnring** m motorway ring (Brit), beltway (US); **Autobombe** f car bomb; **Autofähre** f car ferry; **Autofahrer(in)** m(f) driver, motorist; **Autofahrt** f drive

**Autogramm** nt ⟨-s, -e⟩ autograph

**Automarke** f make of car
**Automat** m ⟨-en, -en⟩ vending machine
**Automatik** f ⟨-, -en⟩ AUTO automatic transmission; **Automatikschaltung** f automatic gear change (*Brit*) (*or* shift (*US*)); **Automatikwagen** m automatic
**automatisch 1.** *adj* automatic **2.** *adv* automatically
**Automechaniker(in)** m(f) car mechanic; **Autonummer** f registration (*Brit*) (*or* license (*US*)) number; **Autoradio** nt car radio; **Autoreifen** m car tyre; **Autoreisezug** m Motorail train® (*Brit*), auto train (*US*); Au-

torennen nt motor racing; (*single event*) motor race; **Autoschlüssel** m car key; **Autotelefon** nt car phone; **Autounfall** m car accident; **Autoverleih** m, **Autovermietung** f car hire (*Brit*) (*or* rental (*US*)); (*firm*) car hire (*Brit*) (*or* rental (*US*)) company; **Autowaschanlage** f car wash; **Autowerkstatt** f car repair shop, garage; **Autozubehör** nt car accessories pl
**Avocado** f ⟨-, -s⟩ avocado
**Axt** f ⟨-, Äxte⟩ axe
**Azubi** m ⟨-s, -s⟩ f ⟨-, -s⟩ acr → **Auszubildende**; trainee

# B

**B** abbr → **Bundesstraße**
**Baby** nt ⟨-s, -s⟩ baby; **Babybett** nt cot (*Brit*), crib (*US*); **Babyfläschchen** nt baby's bottle; **Babynahrung** f baby food; **Babysitter(in)** m(f) babysitter; **Babysitz** m child seat; **Babywickelraum** m baby-changing room
**Bach** m ⟨-(e)s, Bäche⟩ stream
**Backblech** nt baking tray (*Brit*), cookie sheet (*US*)
**Backbord** nt port (side)
**Backe** f ⟨-, -n⟩ cheek
**backen** ⟨backte, gebacken⟩ vt, vi bake

**Backenzahn** m molar
**Bäcker(in)** m(f) ⟨-s, -⟩ baker; **Bäckerei** f bakery; (*selling bread*) baker's shop
**Backofen** m oven; **Backpulver** nt baking powder
**Backspace-Taste** f IT backspace key
**Backstein** m brick
**Backwaren** pl bread, cakes and pastries pl
**Bad** nt ⟨-(e)s, Bäder⟩ bath; (*in sea etc*) swim; (*resort*) spa; *ein ~ nehmen* have (*or* take) a bath; **Badeanzug** m swimsuit, swimming costume (*Brit*); **Badehose** f swim-

ming trunks *pl*; **Badekappe** *f* swimming cap; **Bademantel** *m* bathrobe; **Bademeister(in)** *m(f)* pool attendant; **Bademütze** *f* swimming cap

**baden 1.** *vi* have a bath; (*in sea etc*) swim, bathe (*Brit*) **2.** *vt* bath (*Brit*), bathe (*US*)

**Baden-Württemberg** *nt* ⟨-s⟩ Baden-Württemberg

**Badeort** *m* spa; **Badesachen** *pl* swimming things *pl*; **Badeschaum** *m* bubble bath, bath foam; **Badetuch** *nt* bath towel; **Badewanne** *f* bath (tub); **Badezeug** *nt* swimming gear; **Badezimmer** *m* bathroom

**Badminton** *nt* badminton

**baff** *adj* ~ **sein** *fam* be flabbergasted (*or* gobsmacked)

**Bagger** *m* ⟨-s, -⟩ excavator; **Baggersee** *m* artificial lake in quarry etc, used for bathing

**Bahamas** *pl* **die** ~ the Bahamas *pl*

**Bahn** *f* ⟨-, -en⟩ railway (*Brit*), railroad (*US*); (*racetrack*) track; (*for single runner*) lane; ASTR orbit; *Deutsche ~* Germany's main railway operator; **bahnbrechend** *adj* groundbreaking; **Bahn-Card®** *f* ⟨-, -s⟩ rail card (*allowing 50% or 25% reduction on tickets*); **Bahnfahrt** *f* railway (*Brit*) *or* railroad (*US*) journey; **Bahnhof** *m* station; **am** (*or* **auf dem**) ~

at the station; **Bahnlinie** *f* railway (*Brit*) (*or* railroad (*US*)) line; **Bahnpolizei** *f* railway (*Brit*) (*or* railroad (*US*)) police; **Bahnsteig** *m* ⟨-(e)s, -e⟩ platform; **Bahnstrecke** *f* railway (*Brit*) (*or* railroad (*US*)) line; **Bahnübergang** *m* level crossing (*Brit*), grade crossing (*US*)

**Bakterien** *pl* bacteria *pl*, germs *pl*

**bald** *adv* soon; almost; *bis ~!* see you soon (*or* later); **baldig** *adj* quick, speedy

**Balkan** *m* ⟨-s⟩ *der* ~ the Balkans *pl*

**Balken** *m* ⟨-s, -⟩ beam

**Balkon** *m* ⟨-s, -s *or* -e⟩ balcony

**Ball** *m* ⟨-(e)s, Bälle⟩ ball; (*event*) dance, ball

**Ballett** *nt* ⟨-(e)s, -e⟩ ballet

**Ballon** *m* ⟨-s, -s⟩ balloon

**Ballspiel** *nt* ball game

**Ballungsgebiet** *nt* conurbation

**Baltikum** *nt* ⟨-s⟩ *das* ~ the Baltic States *pl*

**Bambus** *m* ⟨-ses, -se⟩ bamboo; **Bambussprossen** *pl* bamboo shoots *pl*

**banal** *adj* banal; (*question, remark*) trite

**Banane** *f* ⟨-, -n⟩ banana

**band** *imperf* → **binden**

**Band 1.** *m* ⟨-(e)s, Bände⟩ (*book*) volume **2.** *nt* ⟨-(e)s, Bänder⟩ (*of fabric*) ribbon, tape; (*in factory*) production line; (*for recording*) tape;

ANAT ligament; **etw auf ~ aufnehmen** tape sth 3. $f \langle$-, -s$\rangle$ (musicians) band

**Bandage** $f \langle$-, -n$\rangle$ bandage; **bandagieren** vt bandage

**Bande** $f \langle$-, -n$\rangle$ gang

**Bänderriss** m MED torn ligament

**Bandscheibe** $f$ ANAT disc; **Bandwurm** m tapeworm

**Bank 1.** $f \langle$-, Bänke$\rangle$ bench **2.** $f \langle$-, -en$\rangle$ FIN bank

**Bankautomat** m cash dispenser; **Bankkarte** $f$ bank card; **Bankkonto** nt bank account; **Bankleitzahl** $f$ bank sort code; **Banknote** $f$ banknote; **Bankverbindung** $f$ banking (or account) details pl

**bar** adj **~es Geld** cash; **etw (in) ~ bezahlen** pay sth (in) cash

**Bar** $f \langle$-, -s$\rangle$ bar

**Bär** m $\langle$-en, -en$\rangle$ bear

**barfuß** adj barefoot

**barg** imperf → **bergen**

**Bargeld** nt $\langle$-(e)s$\rangle$ cash; **bargeldlos** adj non-cash

**Barkeeper** m $\langle$-s, -$\rangle$, **Barmann** m barman, bartender (US)

**barock** adj baroque

**Barometer** m $\langle$-s, -$\rangle$ barometer

**barsch** adj brusque

**Barsch** m $\langle$-(e)s, -e$\rangle$ perch

**Barscheck** m open (or uncrossed) cheque

**Bart** m $\langle$-(e)s, Bärte$\rangle$ beard

**bärtig** adj bearded

**Barzahlung** $f$ cash payment

**Basar** m $\langle$-s, -e$\rangle$ bazaar

**Baseballmütze** $f$ baseball cap

**Basel** nt $\langle$-s$\rangle$ Basle

**Basilikum** nt $\langle$-s$\rangle$ basil

**Basis** $f \langle$-, Basen$\rangle$ basis

**Baskenland** nt Basque region

**Basketball** m basketball

**Bass** m $\langle$-es, Bässe$\rangle$ bass

**basta** interj **und damit ~!** and that's that

**basteln 1.** vt make **2.** vi make things, do handicrafts

**bat** imperf → **bitten**

**Batterie** $f$ battery; **batteriebetrieben** adj battery-powered

**Bau 1.** m $\langle$-(e)s$\rangle$ (constructing) building, construction; (organization) structure; (place) building site **2.** m $\langle$Baue pl$\rangle$ (of animal) burrow **3.** m $\langle$Bauten pl$\rangle$ (edifice) building; **Bauarbeiten** pl construction work sg; (on road) roadworks pl (Brit), roadwork (US); **Bauarbeiter(in)** m(f) construction worker

**Bauch** m $\langle$-(e)s, Bäuche$\rangle$ stomach; **Bauchnabel** m navel; **Bauchredner(in)** m(f) ventriloquist; **Bauchschmerzen** pl stomach-ache sg; **Bauchspeicheldrüse** $f$ pancreas; **Bauchtanz** m belly dance; (activity) belly dancing; **Bauchweh** nt ⟨-s⟩ stomach-ache

**bauen** vt, vi build; TECH construct

**Bauer** m ⟨-n or -s, -n⟩ farmer; (in chess) pawn; **Bäuerin** f farmer; farmer's wife; **Bauernhof** m farm

**baufällig** adj dilapidated; **Baujahr** adj year of construction; **der Wagen ist ~ 2002** the car is a 2002 model, the car was made in 2002

**Baum** m ⟨-(e)s, Bäume⟩ tree

**Baumarkt** m DIY centre

**Baumwolle** f cotton

**Bauplatz** m building site; **Baustein** m (for building) stone; (toy) brick; fig element; **elektronischer ~** chip; **Baustelle** f building site; (on road) roadworks pl (Brit), roadwork (US); **Bauteil** nt prefabricated part; **Bauunternehmer(in)** m(f) building contractor; **Bauwerk** nt building

**Bayern** nt ⟨-s⟩ Bavaria

**beabsichtigen** vt intend

**beachten** vt pay attention to; (rule etc) observe; **nicht ~** ignore; **beachtlich** adj considerable

**Beachvolleyball** nt beach volleyball

**Beamte(r)** m ⟨-n, -n⟩, **Beamtin** f official; (employed by the state) civil servant

**beanspruchen** vt claim; (time, space) take up; **jdn ~**

keep sb busy

**beanstanden** vt complain about; **Beanstandung** f complaint

**beantragen** vt apply for

**beantworten** vt answer

**bearbeiten** vt work; (material, data) process; CHEM treat; (case etc) deal with; (book etc) revise; fam (try to influence) work on; **Bearbeitungsgebühr** f handling (or service) charge

**beatmen** vt **jdn ~** give sb artificial respiration

**beaufsichtigen** vt supervise; (in exam) invigilate

**beauftragen** vt instruct; **jdn mit etw ~** give sb the job of doing sth

**Becher** m ⟨-s, -⟩ mug; (without handle) tumbler; (for yoghurt) pot; (made of cardboard) tub

**Becken** nt ⟨-s, -⟩ basin; (for washing) sink; (for swimming) pool; MUS cymbal; ANAT pelvis

**bedanken** vr say thank you; **sich bei jdm für etw ~** thank sb for sth

**Bedarf** m ⟨-(e)s⟩ need (an + dat for); COMM demand (an + dat for); **je nach ~** according to demand; **bei ~** if necessary; **Bedarfshaltestelle** f request stop, flag stop (US)

**bedauerlich** adj regrettable; **bedauern** vt regret; (person)

feel sorry for; **bedauerns-
wert** adj regrettable; (person) unfortunate

**bedeckt** adj covered; (sky)
overcast

**bedenken** irr vt consider; **Bedenken** nt ⟨-s, -⟩ (thought)
consideration; (reservation)
doubt; (moral doubt) scru-
ples pl; **bedenklich** adj dubious; (condition, situation)
serious

**bedeuten** vt mean; **jdm
nichts / viel ~** mean noth-
ing/a lot to sb; **bedeutend**
adj important; (large) considerable; **Bedeutung** f
meaning; importance

**bedienen 1.** vt serve; (machine) operate **2.** vr (when
eating) help oneself; **Bedienung** f service; (person)
waiter / waitress; shop assistant; (supplement) service
(charge); **Bedienungsanlei-
tung** f operating instructions pl; **Bedienungshand-
buch** nt instruction manual;
**Bedingung** f condition; **unter der ~, dass** on condition
that; **unter diesen ~en** under these circumstances

**bedrohen** vt threaten
**Bedürfnis** nt need
**beeilen** vr hurry
**beeindrucken** vt impress
**beeinflussen** vt influence
**beeinträchtigen** vt affect
**beenden** vt end; (complete)
finish

**beerdigen** vt bury; **Beerdigung** f burial; (ceremony)
funeral

**Beere** f ⟨-, -n⟩ berry; (for
wine) grape

**Beet** nt ⟨-(e)s, -e⟩ bed

**befahl** imperf → **befehlen**

**befahrbar** adj passable; NAUT
navigable; **befahren 1.** irr vt
(road) use; (mountain pass)
drive over; (river etc) navigate **2.** adj **stark / wenig ~**
busy / quiet

**Befehl** m ⟨-(e)s, -e⟩ order; IT
command; **befehlen** ⟨befahl,
befohlen⟩ **1.** vt order; **jdm ~,
etw zu tun** order sb to do
sth **2.** vi give orders

**befestigen** vt fix; (with string,
rope) attach; (with glue)
stick

**befeuchten** vt moisten

**befinden** irr vr be

**befohlen** pp → **befehlen**

**befolgen** vt (advice etc) follow

**befördern** vt transport; (at
work) promote; **Beförde-
rung** f transport; (at work)
promotion; **Beförderungs-
bedingungen** pl conditions
pl of carriage

**Befragung** f questioning;
(survey) opinion poll

**befreundet** adj friendly; **~
sein** be friends (mit jdm
with sb)

**befriedigen** vt satisfy; **befriedigend** adj satisfactory;
(mark for schoolwork) ≈

C; **Befriedigung** f satisfaction

**befristet** adj limited (auf + acc to)

**befruchten** vt fertilize; fig stimulate

**Befund** m ⟨-(e)s, -e⟩ findings pl; MED diagnosis

**befürchten** vt fear

**befürworten** vt support

**begabt** adj gifted, talented; **Begabung** f talent, gift

**begann** imperf → **beginnen**

**begegnen** vi (jdm sb), meet with (einer Sache dat sth)

**begehen** irr vt (offence) commit; (anniversary etc) celebrate

**begehrt** adj sought-after; (bachelor) eligible

**begeistern 1.** vt fill with enthusiasm; (stimulate) inspire **2.** vr **sich für etw ~** be / get enthusiastic about sth; **begeistert** adj enthusiastic

**Beginn** m ⟨-(e)s⟩ beginning; **zu ~** at the beginning; **beginnen** ⟨begann, begonnen⟩ vt, vi start, begin

**beglaubigen** vt certify; **Beglaubigung** f certification

**begleiten** vt accompany; **Begleiter(in)** m(f) companion; **Begleitung** f company; MUS accompaniment

**beglückwünschen** vt congratulate (zu on)

**begonnen** pp → **beginnen**

**begraben** irr vt bury; Begräbnis nt burial; (ceremony) funeral

**begreifen** irr vt understand

**Begrenzung** f boundary; fig restriction

**Begriff** m ⟨-(e)s, -e⟩ concept; (mental impression) idea; **im ~ sein, etw zu tun** be on the point of doing sth; **schwer von ~ sein** be slow on the uptake

**begründen** vt justify; **Begründung** f explanation; (vindication) justification

**begrüßen** vt greet; (guest) welcome; **Begrüßung** f greeting; (reception) welcome

**behaart** adj hairy

**behalten** irr vt keep; (keep in head) remember; **etw für sich ~** keep sth to oneself

**Behälter** m ⟨-s, -⟩ container

**behandeln** vt treat; **Behandlung** f treatment

**behaupten 1.** vt claim, maintain **2.** vr assert oneself; **Behauptung** f claim

**beheizen** vt heat

**behelfen** irr vr **sich mit / ohne etw ~** make do with / without sth

**beherbergen** vt accommodate

**beherrschen 1.** vt (situation, feelings) control; (instrument) master **2.** vr control oneself; **Beherrschung** f control (über + acc of); **die ~ verlieren** lose one's self-

control
**behilflich** adj helpful; **jdm ~ sein** help sb (bei with)
**behindern** vt hinder; (traffic, view) obstruct; **Behinderte(r)** mf disabled person; **behindertengerecht** adj suitable for disabled people
**Behörde** f (-, -n) authority; **die ~n** pl the authorities pl
**bei** prep + dat (place) near, by; (stay) at; (time) at, on; (in the course of) during; (circumstance) in; ~ **Friseur** at the hairdresser's; ~ **uns zuhause** at our place; in our country; ~ **Nacht** at night; ~ **Tag** by day; ~ **Nebel** in fog; ~ **Regen findet die Veranstaltung im Saal statt** if it rains the event will take place in the hall; **etw ~ sich haben** have sth on one; ~**m Fahren** while driving
**beibehalten** irr vt keep
**Beiboot** nt dinghy
**beibringen** irr vt **jdm etw ~** (tell) break sth to sb; (instruct) teach sb sth
**beide(s)** pron both; **meine ~n Brüder** my two brothers, both my brothers; **wir ~** both (or the two) of us; **keiner von ~n** neither of them; **alle ~** both (of them); ~**s ist sehr schön** both are very nice; **30 ~** (in tennis) 30 all
**beieinander** adv together
**Beifahrer(in)** m(f) passenger; **Beifahrerairbag** m pas-

senger airbag; **Beifahrersitz** m passenger seat
**Beifall** m (-(e)s) applause
**beige** adj inv beige
**Beigeschmack** m aftertaste
**Beil** nt (-(e)s, -e) axe
**Beilage** f GASTR side dish; vegetables pl; (of newspaper) supplement
**beiläufig 1.** adj casual **2.** adv casually
**Beileid** nt condolences pl; **(mein) herzliches ~** please accept my sincere condolences
**beiliegend** adj enclosed
**beim** contr = **bei dem**
**Bein** nt (-(e)s, -e) leg
**beinah(e)** adv almost, nearly
**beinhalten** vt contain
**Beipackzettel** m instruction leaflet
**beisammen** adv together; **Beisammensein** nt (-s) get-together
**beiseite** adv aside; **beiseitelegen** vt **etw ~** (save) put sth by
**Beispiel** nt (-(e)s, -e) example; **sich dat an jdm / etw ein ~ nehmen** take sb/sth as an example; **zum ~** for example
**beißen** (biss, gebissen) **1.** vt bite **2.** vi bite; (smoke, acid) sting **3.** vr (colours) clash
**Beitrag** m (-(e)s, Beiträge) contribution; (for membership) subscription; (for insurance) premium; **beitragen** irr vt, vi contribute (zu to)

**bekannt** *adj* well-known; (*recognizable*) familiar; **mit jdm ~ sein** know sb; **~ geben** announce; **jdn mit jdm ~ machen** introduce sb to sb; **Bekannte(r)** *mf* friend; (*less close*) acquaintance; **bekanntlich** *adv* as everyone knows; **Bekanntschaft** *f* acquaintance

**bekiffen** *vr fam* get stoned

**beklagen** *vr* complain

**Bekleidung** *f* clothing

**bekommen** *irr* **1.** *vt* get; (*letter, present etc*) receive; (*child*) have; (*train, cold*) catch, get; **wie viel ~ Sie dafür?** how much is that? **2.** *vi* **jdm ~** (*food*) agree with sb; **wir ~ schon** we're being served

**beladen** *irr vt* load

**Belag** *m* ⟨-(e)s, Beläge⟩ coating; (*on teeth*) plaque; (*on tongue*) fur

**belasten** *vt* load; (*body*) strain; (*environment*) pollute; *fig* (*with worries etc*) burden; COMM (*account*) debit; LAW incriminate

**belästigen** *vt* bother; (*stronger*) pester; (*sexually*) harass; **Belästigung** *f* annoyance; **sexuelle ~** sexual harassment

**belebt** *adj* (*street etc*) busy

**Beleg** *m* ⟨-(e)s, -e⟩ COMM receipt; (*written evidence*) proof; **belegen** *vt* (*bread*) spread; (*seat*) reserve; (*course*) register for; (*claim, expenditure etc*) prove

**belegt** *adj* TEL engaged (*Brit*), busy (*US*); (*hotel*) full; (*tongue*) coated; **~es Brötchen** sandwich; **der Platz ist ~** this seat is taken; **Belegtzeichen** *nt* TEL engaged tone (*Brit*), busy tone (*US*)

**beleidigen** *vt* insult; (*hurt feelings of*) offend; **Beleidigung** *f* insult; LAW slander; (*written*) libel

**beleuchten** *vt* light; (*light up*) illuminate; *fig* examine; **Beleuchtung** *f* lighting; (*lighting up*) illumination

**Belgien** *nt* ⟨-s⟩ Belgium; **Belgier(in)** *m(f)* ⟨-s, -⟩ Belgian; **belgisch** *adj* Belgian

**belichten** *vt* expose; **Belichtung** *f* exposure; **Belichtungsmesser** *m* ⟨-s, -⟩ light meter

**Belieben** *nt* (*ganz*) **nach ~** (just) as you wish

**beliebig 1.** *adj* **jedes ~e Muster** any pattern; **jeder ~e** anyone **2.** *adv* **~ lange** as long as you like; **~ viel** as many (*or much*) as you like

**beliebt** *adj* popular

**beliefern** *vt* supply

**bellen** *vi* bark

**Belohnung** *f* reward

**Belüftung** *f* ventilation

**belügen** *irr vt* lie to

**bemerkbar** *adj* noticeable; **sich ~ machen** (*person*) attract attention; (*thing*) become noticeable; **bemerken** vt notice; (say) remark; **bemerkenswert** adj remarkable; **Bemerkung** f remark

**bemitleiden** vt pity

**bemühen** vr try (hard), make an effort; **Bemühung** f effort

**bemuttern** vt mother

**benachbart** adj neighbouring

**benachrichtigen** vt inform; **Benachrichtigung** f notification

**benachteiligen** vt (put at a) disadvantage; (racially etc) discriminate against

**benehmen** irr vr behave; **Benehmen** nt ⟨-s⟩ behaviour

**beneiden** vt envy; **jdn um etw ~** envy sb sth

**Beneluxländer** pl Benelux countries pl

**benommen** adj dazed

**benötigen** vt need

**benutzen** vt use; **Benutzer(in)** m(f) ⟨-s, -⟩ user; **benutzerfreundlich** adj user-friendly; **Benutzerhandbuch** nt user's guide; **Benutzerkennung** f user ID; **Benutzeroberfläche** f IT user / system interface; **Benutzung** f use; **Benutzungsgebühr** f (hire) charge

**Benzin** nt ⟨-s, -e⟩ AUTO petrol (Brit), gas (US); **Benzinkanister** m petrol (Brit) or gas (US) can; **Benzinpumpe** f petrol (Brit) or gas

(US)) pump; **Benzintank** m petrol (Brit) (or gas (US)) tank; **Benzinuhr** f fuel gauge

**beobachten** vt observe; **Beobachtung** f observation

**bequem** adj comfortable; (excuse) convenient; (idle) lazy; **machen Sie es sich ~** make yourself at home; **Bequemlichkeit** f comfort; laziness

**beraten** irr **1.** vt advise; (plan etc) discuss **2.** vr consult; **Beratung** f advice; (at doctor's etc) consultation

**berauben** vt rob

**berechnen** vt calculate; COMM charge; **berechnend** adj (person) calculating

**berechtigen** vt entitle (zu to); fig justify; **berechtigt** adj justified; **zu etw ~ sein** be entitled to sth

**bereden** vt discuss

**Bereich** m ⟨-(e)s, -e⟩ area; (sphere) field

**bereisen** vt travel through

**bereit** adj ready; **zu etw ~ sein** be ready for sth; **sich ~ erklären, etw zu tun** agree to do sth

**bereiten** vt prepare; (grief) cause; (pleasure) give

**bereitlegen** vt lay out

**bereitmachen** vr get ready

**bereits** adv already

**Bereitschaft** f readiness; **~ haben** (doctor) be on call

**bereitstehen** vi be ready

**bereuen** *vt* regret

**Berg** *m* ⟨-(e)s, -e⟩ mountain; (*smaller*) hill; *in die ~e fahren* go to the mountains; **bergab** *adv* downhill; **bergauf** *adv* uphill; **Bergbahn** *f* mountain railway (*Brit*) (*or* railroad (*US*))

**bergen** ⟨barg, geborgen⟩ *vt* (*person*) rescue

**Bergführer(in)** *m(f)* mountain guide; **Berghütte** *f* mountain hut; **bergig** *adj* mountainous; **Bergschuh** *m* climbing boot; **Bergsteigen** *nt* ⟨-s⟩ mountaineering; **Bergsteiger(in)** *m(f)* ⟨-s, -⟩ mountaineer; **Bergtour** *f* mountain hike

**Bergung** *f* rescue; (*of body, vehicle*) recovery

**Bergwacht** *f* ⟨-, -en⟩ mountain rescue service; **Bergwerk** *nt* mine

**Bericht** *m* ⟨-(e)s, -e⟩ report; **berichten** *vt, vi* report

**berichtigen** *vt* correct

**Bermudadreieck** *nt* Bermuda triangle; **Bermudainseln** *pl* Bermuda *sg*; **Bermudashorts** *pl* Bermuda shorts *pl*

**Bernstein** *m* amber

**berüchtigt** *adj* notorious, infamous

**berücksichtigen** *vt* take into account; (*application, applicant*) consider

**Beruf** *m* ⟨-(e)s, -e⟩ occupation; (*requiring academic training*) profession; (*skilled,*

*self-employed*) trade; *was sind Sie von ~?* what do you do (for a living)?; **beruflich** *adj* professional

**Berufsausbildung** *f* vocational training; **Berufsschule** *f* vocational college; **berufstätig** *adj* employed; **Berufsverkehr** *m* commuter traffic

**beruhigen 1.** *vt* calm **2.** *vr* (*person, situation*) calm down; **beruhigend** *adj* reassuring; **Beruhigungsmittel** *nt* sedative

**berühmt** *adj* famous

**berühren 1.** *vt* touch; (*emotionally*) move; (*be important for*) affect; (*subject*) mention, touch on **2.** *vr* touch

**besaufen** *irr vr fam* get plastered

**beschädigen** *vt* damage

**beschäftigen 1.** *vt* occupy; (*worker*) employ **2.** *vr sich mit etw ~* occupy oneself with sth; (*problem etc*) deal with sth; **beschäftigt** *adj* busy, occupied; **Beschäftigung** *f* (*work*) employment; (*activity*) occupation; (*with problem etc*) preoccupation (*mit* with)

**Bescheid** *m* ⟨-(e)s, -e⟩ information; *~ wissen* be informed (*or* know) (*über* + *acc* about); *ich weiß ~* I know; *jdm ~ geben* (*or* *sagen*) let sb know

**bescheiden** adj modest

**bescheinigen** vt certify; (confirm) acknowledge; **Bescheinigung** f certificate; (for money) receipt

**bescheißen** irr vt vulg cheat (um out of)

**beschimpfen** vt swear at

**Beschiß** m ⟨-es⟩ **das ist ~** vulg that's a rip-off; **beschissen** adj vulg shitty

**beschlagnahmen** vt confiscate

**Beschleunigung** f acceleration; **Beschleunigungsspur** f acceleration lane

**beschließen** irr vt decide on; (conclude) end; **Beschluss** m decision

**beschränken 1.** vt limit, restrict (auf + acc to) **2.** vr restrict oneself (auf + acc to); **Beschränkung** f limitation, restriction

**beschreiben** irr vt describe; (paper) write on; **Beschreibung** f description

**beschuldigen** vt accuse (gen of); **Beschuldigung** f accusation

**beschummeln** vt, vi fam cheat (um out of)

**beschützen** vt protect (vor + dat from)

**Beschwerde** f ⟨-, -n⟩ complaint; **~n** pl (illness) trouble sg; **beschweren 1.** vt weight down; fig burden **2.** vr complain

**beschwipst** adj tipsy

**beseitigen** vt remove; (problem) get rid of; (rubbish) dispose of; **Beseitigung** f removal; (of rubbish) disposal

**Besen** m ⟨-s, -⟩ broom

**besetzen** vt (house, country) occupy; (seat) take; (post) fill; (role) cast; **besetzt** adj full; TEL engaged (Brit), busy (US); (seat) taken; (toilet) engaged; **Besetztzeichen** nt engaged tone (Brit), busy tone (US)

**besichtigen** vt (museum) visit; (sights) have a look at; (town) tour

**besiegen** vt defeat

**Besitz** m ⟨-es⟩ possession; (objects) property; **besitzen** irr vt own; (quality) have; **Besitzer(in)** m(f) ⟨-s, -⟩ owner

**besoffen** adj fam plastered

**besondere(r, s)** adj special; (specific, more than usual) particular; (strange) peculiar; **nichts ~s** nothing special; **Besonderheit** f special feature; (unusual characteristic) peculiarity; **besonders** adv especially, particularly; (individually) separately

**besorgen** vt (obtain) get (jdm for sb); (buy also) purchase; (task etc) deal with

**besprechen** irr vt discuss; **Besprechung** f discussion; (conference) meeting; **Besprechungsraum** m consultation room

**besser** *adj* better; **es geht ihm ~** he feels better; **~ gesagt** or rather; **~ werden** improve; **bessern 1.** *vt* improve **2.** *vr* improve; (*person*) mend one's ways; **Besserung** *f* improvement; **gute ~!** get well soon

**beständig** *adj* constant; (*weather*) settled

**Bestandteil** *m* component

**bestätigen** *vt* confirm; (*receipt, letter*) acknowledge; **Bestätigung** *f* confirmation; (*of letter*) acknowledgement

**beste(r, s)** **1.** *adj* best; **das ~ wäre, wir ...** it would be best if we ... **2.** *adv* **sie singt am ~n** she sings best; **so ist es am ~n** it's best that way; **am ~n gehst du gleich** you'd better go at once

**bestechen** *irr vt* bribe; **Bestechung** *f* bribery

**Besteck** *nt* ⟨-(e)s, -e⟩ cutlery

**bestehen** *irr* **1.** *vi* be, exist; (*continue*) last; **~ auf** + *dat* insist on; **~ aus** consist of **2.** *vt* (*test, exam*) pass; (*fight*) win

**bestehlen** *irr vt* rob

**bestellen** *vt* order; (*reserve*) book; (*regards, message*) pass on (*jdm* to sb); (*person*) send for; **Bestellnummer** *f* order number; **Bestellung** *f* COMM order; (*action*) ordering

**bestens** *adv* very well

**bestimmen** *vt* determine; (*rules*) lay down; (*day, place*) fix; (*person to a post*) appoint; (*intend*) mean (*für* for); **bestimmt 1.** *adj* definite; (*left unspecified*) certain; (*resolute*) firm **2.** *adv* definitely; (*know*) for sure; **Bestimmung** *f* (*rule*) regulation; (*intended use*) purpose

**Best.-Nr.** *abbr* → **Bestellnummer** order number

**bestrafen** *vt* punish

**bestrahlen** *vt* illuminate; MED treat with radiotherapy

**bestreiten** *irr vt* (*assertion etc*) deny

**Bestseller** *m* ⟨-s, -⟩ bestseller

**bestürzt** *adj* dismayed

**Besuch** *m* ⟨-(e)s, -e⟩ visit; (*person*) visitor; **~ haben** have visitors / a visitor; **besuchen** *vt* visit; (*school, cinema etc*) go to; **Besucher(in)** *m(f)* ⟨-s, -⟩ visitor; **Besuchszeit** *f* visiting hours *pl*

**betäuben** *vt* MED anaesthetize; **Betäubung** *f* anaesthetic; **örtliche ~** local anaesthetic; **Betäubungsmittel** *nt* anaesthetic

**Bete** *f* ⟨-, -n⟩ **Rote ~** beetroot

**beteiligen 1.** *vr* **sich an etw** *dat* **~** take part in sth, participate in sth **2.** *vt* **jdn an etw** *dat* **~** involve sb in sth; **Beteiligung** *f* participation; (*portion*) share; (*number of peo-*

*ple present*) attendance

**beten** *vi* pray

**Beton** *m* ⟨-s, -s⟩ concrete

**betonen** *vt* stress; (*give prominence to*) emphasize; **Betonung** *f* stress; *fig* emphasis

**Betr.** *abbr* = **Betreff** re

**Betracht** *m* in ~ **ziehen** take into consideration; **in ~ kommen** be a possibility; **nicht in ~ kommen** be out of the question; **betrachten** *vt* look at; ~ **als** regard as; **beträchtlich** *adj* considerable

**Betrag** *m* ⟨-(e)s, Beträge⟩ amount, sum; **betragen** *irr* **1.** *vt* amount (*or* come) to **2.** *vr* behave

**betreffen** *irr vt* concern; (*regulation etc*) affect; **was mich betrifft** as for me; **betreffend** *adj* relevant, in question

**betreten** *irr vt* enter; (*stage etc*) step onto; **„Betreten verboten‟** 'keep off / out'

**betreuen** *vt* look after; (*party of tourists, department*) be in charge of; **Betreuer(in)** *m(f)* ⟨-s, -⟩ (*of invalid, old person*) carer; (*of child*) child minder; (*of party of tourists*) groupleader

**Betrieb** *m* ⟨-(e)s, -e⟩ (*company*) firm; (*buildings etc*) plant; (*of machine, factory*) operation; (*in shops etc*) bustle; **außer ~ sein** be out of order; **in ~ sein** be in op-

eration; **betriebsbereit** *adj* operational; **Betriebsrat** *m* works council; **Betriebssystem** *nt* IT operating system

**betrinken** *irr vr* get drunk

**betroffen** *adj* (*upset*) shaken; **von etw ~ werden / sein** be affected by sth

**betrog** *imperf* → **betrügen**; **betrogen** *pp* → **betrügen**

**Betrug** *m* ⟨-(e)s⟩ deception; LAW fraud; **betrügen** ⟨betrog, betrogen⟩ *vt* deceive; LAW defraud; (*partner*) cheat on; **Betrüger(in)** *m(f)* ⟨-s, -⟩ cheat

**betrunken** *adj* drunk

**Bett** *nt* ⟨-(e)s, -en⟩ bed; **ins** (*or* **zu**) ~ **gehen** go to bed; **das ~ machen** make the bed; **Bettbezug** *m* duvet cover; **Bettdecke** *f* blanket

**betteln** *vi* beg

**Bettlaken** *nt* sheet

**Bettler(in)** *m(f)* ⟨-s, -⟩ beggar

**Bettsofa** *nt* sofa bed; **Betttuch** *nt* sheet; **Bettwäsche** *f* bed linen; **Bettzeug** *m* bedding

**beugen 1.** *vt* bend **2.** *vr* bend; (*yield*) submit (*dat* to)

**Beule** *f* ⟨-, -n⟩ bump; (*in car etc*) dent

**beunruhigen** *vt*, *vr* worry

**beurteilen** *vt* judge

**Beute** *f* ⟨-⟩ (*of thief*) booty, loot; (*of animal*) prey

**Beutel** *m* ⟨-s, -⟩ bag

**Bevölkerung** *f* population

**bevollmächtigt** *adj* authorized (*zu etw* to do sth)

**bevor** *conj* before; **bevorstehen** *irr vi* (*difficulties*) lie ahead; (*danger*) be imminent; **jdm ~** (*surprise etc*) be in store for sb; **bevorstehend** *adj* forthcoming; **bevorzugen** *vt* prefer

**bewachen** *vt* guard; **bewacht** *adj* **~er Parkplatz** supervised car park (*Brit*), guarded parking lot (*US*)

**bewegen** *vt, vr* move; **jdn dazu ~, etw zu tun** get sb to do sth; **es bewegt sich etwas** *fig* things are beginning to happen; **Bewegung** *f* movement; PHYS motion; (*inner*) emotion; (*bodily*) exercise; **Bewegungsmelder** *m* ⟨-s, -⟩ sensor (*which reacts to movement*)

**Beweis** *m* ⟨-es, -e⟩ proof; (*material, facts*) evidence; **beweisen** *irr vt* prove; (*demonstrate*) show

**bewerben** *irr vr* apply (*um* for); **Bewerbung** *f* application; **Bewerbungsunterlagen** *pl* application documents *pl*

**bewilligen** *vt* allow; (*money*) grant

**bewirken** *vt* cause, bring about

**bewohnen** *vt* live in; **Bewohner(in)** *m(f)* ⟨-s, -⟩ inhabitant; (*of house*) resident

**bewölkt** *adj* cloudy, overcast; **Bewölkung** *f* clouds *pl*

**bewundern** *vt* admire; **bewundernswert** *adj* admirable

**bewusst 1.** *adj* conscious; (*intentional*) deliberate; (*sich dat einer Sache gen ~ sein* be aware of sth **2.** *adv* consciously; (*intentionally*) deliberately; **bewusstlos** *adj* unconscious; **Bewusstlosigkeit** *f* unconsciousness; **Bewusstsein** *nt* ⟨-s⟩ consciousness; **bei ~** conscious

**bezahlen** *vt* pay; (*goods, service*) pay for; **sich bezahlt machen** be worth it

**Bezahlung** *f* payment

**bezeichnen** *vt* (*with sign etc*) mark; (*give name to*) call; (*categorize*) describe; **Bezeichnung** *f* name; (*expression*) term

**beziehen** *irr* **1.** *vt* (*bed*) change; (*house, position*) move into; (*get*) receive; (*newspaper*) take; **einen Standpunkt ~** *fig* take up a position **2.** *vr* refer (*auf + acc* to); **Beziehung** *f* (*between two things*) connection; (*between lovers*) relationship; **~en haben** (*influential*) have connections (*or contacts*); **in dieser ~** in this respect; **beziehungsweise** *adv* or; (*more precisely*) or rather

**Bezirk** *m* ⟨-(e)s, -e⟩ district

**Bezug** *m* ⟨-(e)s, Bezüge⟩ (*for cushion etc*) cover; (*for pil-*

*low)* pillowcase; **in ~ auf** *+ acc* with regard to; **bezüglich** *prep + gen* concerning

**bezweifeln** *vt* doubt

**BH** *m* ⟨-s, -s⟩ bra

**Bhf.** *abbr → Bahnhof* station

**Biathlon** *m* ⟨-s, -s⟩ biathlon

**Bibel** *f* ⟨-, -n⟩ Bible

**Biber** *m* ⟨-s, -⟩ beaver

**Bibliothek** *f* ⟨-, -en⟩ library

**biegen** ⟨bog, gebogen⟩ **1.** *vt, vr* bend **2.** *vi* turn *(in + acc* into); **Biegung** *f* bend

**Biene** *f* ⟨-, -n⟩ bee

**Bier** *nt* ⟨-(e)s, -e⟩ beer; **helles~** ≈ lager *(Brit)*, beer *(US)*; **dunkles ~** ≈ brown ale *(Brit)*, dark beer *(US)*; **zwei ~, bitte!** two beers, please; **Biergarten** *m* beer garden; **Bierzelt** *nt* beer tent

**bieten** ⟨bot, geboten⟩ **1.** *vt* offer; *(at auction)* bid; **sich** *dat* **etw ~ lassen** put up with sth **2.** *vr (opportunity)* present itself *(dat* to)

**Bikini** *m* ⟨-s, -s⟩ bikini

**Bild** *nt* ⟨-(e)s, -er⟩ picture; *(in one's mind)* image; PHOT photo

**bilden** **1.** *vt* form; *(intellectually)* educate; *(rule, basis etc)* constitute **2.** *vr (learn)* educate oneself

**Bilderbuch** *nt* picture book

**Bildhauer(in)** *m(f)* ⟨-s, -⟩ sculptor

**Bildschirm** *m* screen; **Bildschirmschoner** *m* ⟨-s, -⟩ screensaver; **Bildschirm-**

**text** *m* viewdata, videotext

**Bildung** *f* formation; *(knowledge, manners)* education; **Bildungsurlaub** *m* educational holiday; *(of employee)* study leave

**Billard** *nt* billiards *sg*

**billig** *adj* cheap; *(just)* fair

**Billigflieger** *m* budget airline; **Billigflug** *m* cheap flight

**Binde** *f* ⟨-, -n⟩ bandage; *(worn on arm)* band; *(for woman's period)* sanitary towel *(Brit)*, sanitary napkin *(US)*; **Bindehautentzündung** *f* conjunctivitis

**binden** ⟨band, gebunden⟩ *vt* tie; *(book)* bind; *(sauce)* thicken

**Bindestrich** *m* hyphen

**Bindfaden** *m* string

**Bindung** *f* bond, tie; *(on ski)* binding

**Bio-** *in cpds* bio-; **Biokost** *f* health food; **Biologie** *f* biology; **biologisch** *adj* biological; *(cultivation)* organic

**Birke** *f* ⟨-, -n⟩ birch

**Birne** *f* ⟨-, -n⟩ pear; ELEC *(light)* bulb

**bis 1.** *prep + acc (space)* to, as far as; *(time)* till, until; *(at the latest)* by; **Sie haben ~ Dienstag Zeit** you have until *(or* till*)* Tuesday; **~ Dienstag muss es fertig sein** it must be ready by Tuesday; **~ hierher** this far; **~ in die Nacht** into the night; **~ auf Weite-**

63 **bleifrei**

*res* until further notice; ~ *bald / gleich!* see you later / soon; ~ *auf etw acc* including sth; (*excluding*) except sth; ~ *zu* up to; *von ... ~ ...* from ... to ... **2.** *conj* (*numbers*) to; (*time*) until, till

**Bischof** *m* ⟨-s, Bischöfe⟩ bishop

**bisher** *adv* up to now, so far

**Biskuit** *nt* ⟨-(e)s, -s *or* -e⟩ sponge

**biss** *imperf* → **beißen**

**Biss** *m* ⟨-es, -e⟩ bite

**bisschen 1.** *adj ein* ~ a bit of; *ein* ~ *Salz / Liebe* a bit of salt / love; *ich habe kein* ~ *Hunger* I'm not a bit hungry **2.** *adv ein* ~ a bit; *kein* ~ not at all

**bissig** *adj* (*dog*) vicious; (*remark*) cutting

**Bit** *nt* ⟨-s, -s⟩ IT bit

**bitte** *interj* please; (*wie*) ~? (I beg your) pardon?; ~ (*schön*)! (*replying to thanks*) you're welcome, that's alright; *hier*, ~ here you are; **Bitte** *f* ⟨-, -n⟩ request; **bitten** ⟨bat, gebeten⟩ *vt, vi* ask (*um* for)

**bitter** *adj* bitter

**Blähungen** *pl* MED wind *sg*

**blamieren 1.** *vr* make a fool of oneself **2.** *vt jdn* ~ make sb look a fool

**Blankoscheck** *m* blank cheque

**Blase** *f* ⟨-, -n⟩ bubble; MED

blister; ANAT bladder

**blasen** ⟨blies, geblasen⟩ *vi* blow; *jdm einen* ~ *vulg* give sb a blow job

**Blasenentzündung** *f* cystitis

**blass** *adj* pale

**Blatt** *nt* ⟨-(e)s, Blätter⟩ leaf; (*of paper*) sheet; **blättern** *vi* IT scroll; *in etw dat* ~ leaf through sth; **Blätterteig** *m* puff pastry; **Blattsalat** *m* green salad; **Blattspinat** *m* spinach

**blau** *adj* blue; *fam* (*drunk*) plastered; GASTR boiled; ~*es Auge* black eye; ~*er Fleck* bruise; **Blaubeere** *f* bilberry, blueberry; **Blaulicht** *nt* flashing blue light; **blaumachen** *vi* skip work; (*pupil*) skip school; **Blauschimmelkäse** *m* blue cheese

**Blazer** *m* ⟨-s, -⟩ blazer

**Blech** *nt* ⟨-(e)s, -e⟩ sheet metal; (*for oven*) baking tray (*Brit*), cookie sheet (*US*); **Blechschaden** *m* AUTO damage to the bodywork

**Blei** *nt* ⟨-(e)s, -e⟩ lead

**bleiben** ⟨blieb, geblieben⟩ *vi* stay; *lass das* ~! stop it; *das bleibt unter uns* that's (just) between ourselves; *mir bleibt keine andere Wahl* I have no other choice

**bleich** *adj* pale; **bleichen** *vt* bleach

**bleifrei** *adj* (*petrol*) unleaded;

**bleihaltig** adj (petrol) leaded
**Bleistift** m pencil
**Blende** f ⟨-, -n⟩ PHOT aperture
**Blick** m ⟨-(e)s, -e⟩ look; (brief) glance; (from a place) view; **auf den ersten ~** at first sight; **einen ~ auf etw** acc **werfen** have a look at sth; **blicken** vi look; **sich ~ lassen** show up
**blieb** imperf → **bleiben**
**blies** imperf → **blasen**
**blind** adj blind; (glass etc) dull; **Blinddarm** m appendix; **Blinddarmentzündung** f appendicitis; **Blinde(r)** mf blind person / man / woman; **die ~n** pl the blind pl; **Blindenhund** m guide dog; **Blindenschrift** f braille
**blinken** vi (star, lights) twinkle; (brightly, briefly) flash; AUTO indicate; **Blinker** m ⟨-s, -⟩ AUTO indicator (Brit), turn signal (US)
**blinzeln** vi blink
**Blitz** m ⟨-es, -e⟩ (flash of) lightning; PHOT flash; **blitzen** vi PHOT use a/the flash; **es blitzte und donnerte** there was thunder and lightning; **Blitzlicht** nt flash
**Block** m ⟨-(e)s, Blöcke⟩ block; (of paper) pad; **Blockflöte** f recorder; **Blockhaus** nt log cabin; **blockieren 1.** vt block **2.** vi jam; (wheels) lock; **Blockschrift** f block letters pl
**blöd** adj stupid; **blödeln** vi

fam fool around
**Blog** nt ⟨-s, -s⟩ IT blog
**blond** adj blond; (woman) blonde
**bloß 1.** adj (without covering) bare; (nothing more than) mere **2.** adv only; **geh mir ~ aus dem Weg** just get out of my way
**blühen** vi bloom, fig flourish
**Blume** f ⟨-, -n⟩ flower; (of wine) bouquet; **Blumengeschäft** nt florist's (shop); **Blumenkohl** m cauliflower; **Blumenladen** m flower shop; **Blumenstrauß** m bunch of flowers; **Blumentopf** m flowerpot; **Blumenvase** f vase
**Bluse** f ⟨-, -n⟩ blouse
**Blut** nt ⟨-(e)s⟩ blood; **Blutbild** nt blood count; **Blutdruck** m blood pressure
**Blüte** f ⟨-, -n⟩ (part of plant) flower, bloom; (on tree) blossom; fig prime
**bluten** vi bleed
**Blütenstaub** m pollen
**Bluter** m ⟨-s, -⟩ MED haemophiliac; **Bluterguss** m haematoma; (on skin) bruise; **Blutgruppe** f blood group; **blutig** adj bloody; **Blutkonserve** f unit of stored blood; **Blutorange** f blood orange; **Blutprobe** f blood sample; **Blutspende** f blood donation; **Bluttransfusion** f blood transfusion; **Blutung** f bleeding; **Blutvergiftung**

f blood poisoning; **Blutwurst** f black pudding (Brit), blood sausage (US)

**BLZ** abbr → **Bankleitzahl**

**Bob** m ⟨-s, -s⟩ bob(sleigh)

**Bock** m ⟨-(e)s, Böcke⟩ (deer) buck; (sheep) ram; (stand) trestle; SPORT vaulting horse; **ich hab keinen ~ (drauf)** fam I don't feel like it

**Boden** m ⟨-s, Böden⟩ ground; (of room) floor; (of sea, barrel) bottom; (loft) attic; **Bodennebel** m ground mist; **Bodenpersonal** nt ground staff; **Bodenschätze** pl mineral resources pl

**Bodensee** m der ~ Lake Constance

**Body** m ⟨-s, -s⟩ body; **Bodybuilding** nt ⟨-s, -s⟩ bodybuilding

**bog** imperf → **biegen**

**Bogen** m ⟨-s, -⟩ curve; (in architecture) arch; (weapon, for violin etc) bow; (of paper) sheet

**Bohne** f ⟨-, -n⟩ bean; **grüne ~n** pl green (or French (Brit)) beans pl; **weiße ~n** pl haricot beans pl; **Bohnenkaffee** m real coffee; **Bohnensprosse** f bean sprout

**bohren** vt drill; **Bohrer** m ⟨-s, -⟩ drill

**Boiler** m ⟨-s, -⟩ water heater

**Boje** f ⟨-, -n⟩ buoy

**Bolivien** nt ⟨-s⟩ Bolivia

**Bombe** f ⟨-, -n⟩ bomb

**Bon** m ⟨-s, -s⟩ receipt; (exchangeable for goods etc) voucher, coupon

**Bonbon** m ⟨-s, -s⟩ sweet (Brit), candy (US)

**Bonus** m ⟨- or -ses, -se or Boni⟩ bonus; (in sport, school) bonus points pl; (in insurance) no-claims bonus

**Boot** nt ⟨-(e)s, -e⟩ boat; **Bootsverleih** m boat hire (Brit) (or rental (US))

**Bord** m ⟨-(e)s, -e⟩ (eines Schiffes) on board (a ship); **an ~ gehen** (ship) go on board; (plane) board; **von ~ gehen** disembark; **Bordcomputer** m dashboard computer

**Bordell** nt ⟨-s, -e⟩ brothel

**Bordkarte** f boarding card

**Bordstein** m kerb (Brit), curb (US)

**borgen** vt borrow; **jdm etw ~** lend sb sth; **sich** dat **etw ~** borrow sth

**Börse** f ⟨-, -n⟩ stock exchange; (for coins) purse

**bös** adj → **böse**; **bösartig** adj malicious; MED malignant

**Böschung** f slope; (along river) embankment

**böse** adj bad; (stronger) evil; (wound) nasty; (annoyed) angry; **bist du mir ~?** are you angry with me?

**boshaft** adj malicious

**Bosnien** nt ⟨-s⟩ Bosnia; **Bosnien-Herzegowina** nt ⟨-s⟩ Bosnia-Herzegovina

**böswillig** adj malicious

**bot** imperf → **bieten**

**botanisch** adj **~er Garten** botanical gardens pl

**Botschaft** f message; POL embassy; **Botschafter(in)** m(f) ambassador

**Botsuana** nt ⟨-s⟩ Botswana

**Bouillon** f ⟨-, -s⟩ stock

**Boutique** f ⟨-, -n⟩ boutique

**Bowle** f ⟨-, -n⟩ punch

**Box** f ⟨-, -en⟩ (container, for horse) box; (of stereo system) speaker; (in motor racing) pit

**boxen** vi box; **Boxer** m ⟨-s, -⟩ (dog, sportsman) boxer; **Boxershorts** pl boxer shorts pl; **Boxkampf** m boxing match

**Boykott** m ⟨-s, -e⟩ boycott

**brach** imperf → **brechen**

**brachte** imperf → **bringen**

**Brainstorming** nt ⟨-s⟩ brainstorming

**Branchenverzeichnis** nt yellow pages® pl

**Brand** m ⟨-(e)s, Brände⟩ fire

**Brandenburg** nt ⟨-s⟩ Brandenburg

**Brandsalbe** f ointment for burns

**Brandung** f surf

**Brandwunde** f burn

**brannte** imperf → **brennen**

**Brasilien** nt ⟨-s⟩ Brazil

**braten** ⟨briet, gebraten⟩ vt roast; grill; fry; **Braten** m ⟨-s, -⟩ roast; (uncooked) joint; **Bratensoße** f gravy; **Brathähnchen** nt roast

chicken; **Bratkartoffeln** pl fried potatoes pl; **Bratpfanne** f frying pan; **Bratspieß** m spit; **Bratwurst** f fried sausage; grilled sausage

**Brauch** m ⟨-s, Bräuche⟩ custom

**brauchen** vt need (für, zu for); (patience, care etc) require; (time) take; (make use of) use; **wie lange wird er ~?** how long will it take him?; **du brauchst es nur zu sagen** you only need to say; **das braucht (seine) Zeit** it takes time; **ihr braucht es nicht zu tun** you don't have (or need) to do it; **sie hätte nicht zu kommen ~** she needn't have come

**brauen** vt brew; **Brauerei** f brewery

**braun** adj brown; (from sun) tanned; **Bräune** f ⟨-, -n⟩ brownness; (from sun) tan; **Bräunungsstudio** nt tanning studio

**Brause** f ⟨-, -n⟩ (apparatus) shower; (drink) fizzy drink (Brit), soda (US)

**Braut** f ⟨-, Bräute⟩ bride; **Bräutigam** m ⟨-s, -e⟩ bridegroom

**brav** adj (child) good, well-behaved

**bravo** interj well done

**brechen** ⟨brach, gebrochen⟩ **1.** vt break; (vomit) bring up; **sich** dat **den Arm ~** break one's arm **2.** *vi* break; (*when unwell*) vomit, be sick; **Brechreiz** *m* nausea

**Brei** *m* ⟨-(e)s, -e⟩ mush, pulp; (*oats*) porridge; (*for children*) pap

**breit** *adj* wide; (*shoulders*) broad; **zwei Meter ~** two metres wide; **Breite** *f* ⟨-, -n⟩ breadth; (*in measurements*) width; GEO latitude; **der ~ nach** widthways; **Breitengrad** *m* (degree of) latitude

**Bremen** *nt* ⟨-s⟩ Bremen

**Bremsbelag** *m* brake lining; **Bremse** *f* ⟨-, -n⟩ brake; ZOOL horsefly; **bremsen 1.** *vi* brake **2.** *vt* (*car*) brake; *fig* slow down; **Bremsflüssigkeit** *f* brake fluid; **Bremslicht** *nt* brake light; **Bremspedal** *nt* brake pedal; **Bremsspur** *f* tyre marks *pl*; **Bremsweg** *m* braking distance

**brennen** ⟨brannte, gebrannt⟩ *vi* burn; (*house, forest*) be on fire; **es brennt!** fire!; **mir ~ die Augen** my eyes are smarting; **das Licht ~ lassen** leave the light on; **Brennholz** *nt* firewood; **Brennnessel** *f* stinging nettle; **Brennspiritus** *m* methylated spirits *pl*; **Brennstab** *m* fuel rod; **Brennstoff** *m* fuel

**Brett** *nt* ⟨-(e)s, -er⟩ board; (*longer*) plank; (*for books etc*) shelf; (*for game*) board;

---

**Schwarzes ~** notice board, bulletin board (*US*); **~er** *pl* skis *pl*; **Brettspiel** *nt* board game

**Brezel** *f* ⟨-, -n⟩ pretzel

**Brief** *m* ⟨-(e)s, -e⟩ letter; **Briefbombe** *f* letter bomb; **Brieffreund(in)** *m(f)* penfriend, pen pal; **Briefkasten** *m* letterbox (*Brit*), mailbox (*US*); **Briefmarke** *f* stamp; **Briefpapier** *nt* writing paper; **Brieftasche** *f* wallet; **Briefträger(in)** *m(f)* postman -woman; **Briefumschlag** *m* envelope; **Briefwaage** *f* letter scales *pl*

**brief** *imperf* → **braten**

**Brille** *f* ⟨-, -n⟩ glasses *pl*; (*protective*) goggles *pl*; **Brillenetui** *nt* glasses case

**bringen** ⟨brachte, gebracht⟩ *vt* bring; (*somewhere else*) take; (*go and come back with*) get, fetch; THEAT, FILM show; RADIO, TV broadcast; *Sie mir bitte noch ein Bier* could you bring me another beer, please?; *jdn nach Hause ~* take sb home; *jdn dazu ~, etw zu tun* make sb do sth; *jdn auf eine Idee ~* give sb an idea

**Brise** *f* ⟨-, -n⟩ breeze

**Brite** *m* ⟨-n, -n⟩, **Britin** *f* British person, Briton; *er ist ~* he is British; *die ~n* the British; **britisch** *adj* British

**Brocken** *m* ⟨-s, -⟩ bit; (*larger*) lump, chunk

**Brokkoli** m broccoli
**Brombeere** f blackberry
**Bronchitis** f ⟨-⟩ bronchitis
**Bronze** f ⟨-, -n⟩ bronze
**Brosche** f ⟨-, -n⟩ brooch
**Brot** nt ⟨-(e)s, -e⟩ bread; loaf;
**Brotaufstrich** m spread;
**Brötchen** nt roll; **Brotzeit** f
break; (food) snack; **~ machen** have a snack
**Browser** m ⟨-s, -⟩ IT browser
**Bruch** m ⟨-(e)s, Brüche⟩ (action) breaking; (crack etc;
with party, tradition etc)
break; MED rupture, hernia;
(of bone) fracture; MATH
fraction; **brüchig** adj brittle
**Brücke** f ⟨-, -n⟩ bridge
**Bruder** m ⟨-s, Brüder⟩ brother
**Brühe** f ⟨-, -n⟩ (clear) soup;
(basis for soup) stock; pej
(drink) muck; **Brühwürfel**
m stock cube
**brüllen** vi roar; (bull) bellow;
(in agony) scream (with
pain)
**brummen** 1. vi (bear, person)
growl; (mumble) mutter;
(insect) buzz; (engine, radio)
drone 2. vt growl
**brünett** adj brunette
**Brunnen** m ⟨-s, -⟩ fountain;
(deep) well; (natural) spring
**Brust** f ⟨-, Brüste⟩ breast; (of
man) chest; **Brustschwimmen** nt ⟨-s⟩ breaststroke;
**Brustwarze** f nipple
**brutal** adj brutal
**brutto** adv gross
**BSE** nt ⟨-⟩ abbr = **bovine**

*spongiforme Enzephalo-
pathie* BSE
**Bube** m ⟨-n, -n⟩ boy, lad;
(playing card) jack
**Buch** nt ⟨-(e)s, Bücher⟩ book
**Buche** f ⟨-, -n⟩ beech (tree)
**buchen** vt book; (amount)
enter
**Bücherei** f library
**Buchfink** m chaffinch
**Buchhalter(in)** m(f) ac-
countant
**Buchhandlung** f bookshop
**Büchse** f ⟨-, -n⟩ tin (Brit), can
**Buchstabe** m ⟨-ns, -n⟩ letter;
**buchstabieren** vt spell
**Bucht** f ⟨-, -en⟩ bay
**Buchung** f booking; COMM
entry
**Buckel** m ⟨-s, -⟩ hump
**bücken** vr bend down
**Buddhismus** m ⟨-⟩ Bud-
dhism
**Bude** f ⟨-, -en⟩ (at market)
stall; fam (flat) pad, place
**Büfett** nt ⟨-s, -s⟩ sideboard;
*kaltes ~* cold buffet
**Büffel** m ⟨-s, -⟩ buffalo
**Bügel** m ⟨-s, -⟩ (for clothes)
hanger; (on saddle) stirrup;
(of glasses) sidepiece; (of
ski-lift) T-bar; **Bügelbrett**
nt ironing board; **Bügeleisen** nt iron; **Bügelfalte** f
crease; **bügelfrei** adj non-
-iron; **bügeln** vt, vi iron
**buh** interj boo
**Bühne** f ⟨-, -n⟩ stage; **Büh-
nenbild** nt set
**Bulgare** m ⟨-n, -n⟩, **Bulgarin** f

Bulgarian; **Bulgarien** nt ⟨-s⟩ Bulgaria; **bulgarisch** adj Bulgarian; **Bulgarisch** nt Bulgarian

**Bulimie** f ⟨-⟩ bulimia

**Bulle** m ⟨-n, -n⟩ bull; fam (policeman) cop

**Bummel** m ⟨-s, -⟩ stroll; **bummeln** vi (stroll); (do things slowly) dawdle; (be idle) loaf around; **Bummelzug** m slow train

**bums** interj bang

**bumsen** vi vulg screw

**Bund 1.** m ⟨-(e)s, Bünde⟩ (of trousers, skirt) waistband; (between friends) bond; (organization) association; POL confederation; **der ~** fam (German military) the army **2.** nt ⟨-(e)s, -e⟩ bunch; (of straw etc) bundle

**Bundes-** in cpds Federal; (referring to Germany also) German; **Bundeskanzler(in)** m(f) Chancellor; **Bundesland** nt state, Land; **Bundesliga** f **erste / zweite ~** First / Second Division; **Bundespräsident(in)** m(f) President; **Bundesrat** m Upper House of the German Parliament); (in Switzerland) Council of Ministers; **Bundesregierung** f Federal Government; **Bundesrepublik** f Federal Republic; **~ Deutschland** Federal Republic of Germany; **Bundesstraße** f ≈ A road

(Brit), ≈ state highway (US); **Bundestag** m Lower House of the German Parliament); **Bundeswehr** f (German) armed forces pl

**Bündnis** nt alliance

**Bungalow** m ⟨-s, -s⟩ bungalow

**Bungeejumping** nt ⟨-s⟩ bungee jumping

**bunt 1.** adj colourful; (programme etc) varied; **~e Farben** bright colours **2.** adv (paint) in bright colours; **Buntstift** m crayon, coloured pencil

**Burg** f ⟨-, -en⟩ castle

**Bürger(in)** m(f) ⟨-s, -⟩ citizen; **bürgerlich** adj (rights, marriage etc) civil; (in social hierarchy) middle-class; pej bourgeois; **Bürgermeister(in)** m(f) mayor; **Bürgersteig** m ⟨-(e)s, -e⟩ pavement (Brit), sidewalk (US)

**Büro** nt ⟨-s, -s⟩ office; **Büroklammer** f paper clip

**Bürokratie** f bureaucracy

**Bursche** m ⟨-n, -n⟩ lad; (man) guy

**Bürste** f ⟨-, -n⟩ brush; **bürsten** vt brush

**Bus** m ⟨-ses, -se⟩ bus; (long--distance) coach (Brit), bus; **Busbahnhof** m bus station

**Busch** m ⟨-(e)s, Büsche⟩ bush; shrub

**Busen** m ⟨-s, -⟩ breasts pl, bosom

**Busfahrer(in)** m(f) bus driv-

er; **Bushaltestelle** f bus stop
**Businessclass** f ‹-› business
class
**Busreise** f coach tour (Brit),
bus tour
**Bußgeld** nt fine
**Büstenhalter** m ‹-s, -› bra
**Busverbindung** f bus con-
nection

**Butter** f ‹-› butter; **Butterbrot**
nt slice of bread and butter;
**Buttermilch** f buttermilk
**Button** m ‹-s, -s› badge (Brit),
button (US)
**b. w.** abbr = **bitte wenden** pto
**Byte** nt ‹-s, -s› byte
**bzw.** adv abbr → **beziehungsweise**

# C

**ca.** adv abbr → **circa** approx
**Cabrio** nt ‹-s, -s› convertible
**Café** nt ‹-s, -s› café
**Cafeteria** f ‹-, -s› cafeteria
**Call-Center** nt ‹-s, -s› call cen-
tre
**campen** vi camp; **Camping**
nt ‹-s› camping; **Camping-
bus** m camper; **Camping-
platz** m campsite, camping
ground (US)
**Cappuccino** m ‹-s, -› cappuc-
cino
**Carving** nt ‹-s› (in skiing)
carving; **Carvingski** m carv-
ing ski
**CD** f ‹-, -s› abbr → **Compact
Disc** CD; **CD-Brenner** m
‹-s, -› CD burner; **CD-Player** m
‹-s, -› CD player;
**CD-ROM** f ‹-, -s› abbr =
**Compact Disc Read Only
Memory** CD-ROM; **CD-
-ROM-Laufwerk** nt CD-
-ROM drive, **CD-Spieler** m
CD player
**Cello** nt ‹-s, -s or Celli› cello

**Celsius** nt celsius; **20 Grad ~**
20 degrees Celsius, 68 degrees Fahrenheit
**Cent** m ‹-, -s› (of dollar and
euro) cent
**Chamäleon** nt ‹-s, -s› chame-
leon
**Champagner** m ‹-s, -› champagne
**Champignon** m ‹-s, -s› mushroom
**Champions League** f ‹-, -s›
Champions League
**Chance** f ‹-, -n› chance; **die
~n stehen gut** the prospects
are good
**Chaos** nt ‹-› chaos; **Chaot(in)**
m(f) ‹-en, -en› fam disorganized person, scatterbrain;
**chaotisch** adj chaotic
**Charakter** m ‹-s, -e› character; **charakteristisch** adj
characteristic (für of)
**Charisma** nt ‹-s, Charismen or
Charismata› charisma
**charmant** adj charming
**Charterflug** m charter flight;

**chartern** *vt* charter

**Chat** *m* ⟨-s, -s⟩ IT chat; **chatten** *vi* IT chat

**checken** *vt* check; *fam (understand)* get

**Check-in** *m* ⟨-s, -s⟩ check-in; **Check-in-Schalter** *m* check-in desk

**Chef(in)** *m(f)* ⟨-s, -s⟩ boss; **Chefarzt** *m*, **Chefärztin** *f* senior consultant (*Brit*), medical director (*US*)

**Chemie** *f* ⟨-⟩ chemistry; **chemisch** *adj* chemical; **~e Reinigung** dry cleaning

**Chemotherapie** *f* ⟨-s⟩ chemotherapy

**Chicoree** *m* ⟨-s⟩ chicory

**Chiffre** *f* ⟨-, -n⟩ cipher; (*in newspaper*) box number

**Chile** *nt* ⟨-s⟩ Chile

**Chili** *m* ⟨-s, -s⟩ chilli

**China** *nt* ⟨-s⟩ China; **China-kohl** *m* Chinese leaves *pl* (*Brit*), bok choy (*US*); **Chinarestaurant** *nt* Chinese restaurant; **Chinese** *m* ⟨-n, -n⟩ Chinese; **Chinesin** *f* ⟨-, -nen⟩ Chinese (woman); **sie ist ~** she's Chinese; **chinesisch** *adj* Chinese; **Chinesisch** *nt* Chinese

**Chip** *m* ⟨-s, -s⟩ IT chip; **Chipkarte** *f* smart card

**Chips** *pl* (*snack*) crisps *pl* (*Brit*), chips *pl* (*US*)

**Chirurg(in)** *m(f)* ⟨-en, -en⟩ surgeon

**Chlor** *nt* ⟨-s⟩ chlorine

**Choke** *m* ⟨-s, -s⟩ choke

**Cholera** *f* ⟨-⟩ cholera

**Cholesterin** *nt* ⟨-s⟩ cholesterol

**Chor** *m* ⟨-(e), Chöre⟩ choir; THEAT chorus

**Choreografie** *f* choreography

**Christ(in)** *m(f)* ⟨-en, -en⟩ Christian; **Christbaum** *m* Christmas tree; **Christi Himmelfahrt** *f* the Ascension (of Christ); **Christkind** *nt* baby Jesus; (*bringing presents*) ≈ Father Christmas, Santa Claus; **christlich** *adj* Christian

**Chrom** *nt* ⟨-s⟩ chrome; CHEM chromium

**chronisch** *adj* chronic

**chronologisch 1.** *adj* chronological **2.** *adv* in chronological order

**Chrysantheme** *f* ⟨-, -n⟩ chrysanthemum

**circa** *adv* about, approximately

**City** *f* ⟨-⟩ city centre, downtown (*US*)

**Clementine** *f* ⟨-, -n⟩ clementine

**clever** *adj* clever, smart

**Clique** *f* ⟨-, -n⟩ group; *pej* clique; **David und seine ~** David and his lot *or* crowd

**Clown** *m* ⟨-s, -s⟩ clown

**Club** *m* ⟨-s, -s⟩ club; **Cluburlaub** *m* club holiday (*Brit*), club vacation (*US*)

**Cocktail** *m* ⟨-s, -s⟩ cocktail; **Cocktailtomate** *f* cherry tomato

**Cognac** *m* ⟨-s⟩ cognac

**Cola** *f* ⟨-, -s⟩ Coke®, cola

**Comic** *m* ⟨-s, -s⟩ comic strip; *(magazine)* comic

**Compact Disc** *f* ⟨-, -s⟩ compact disc

**Computer** *m* ⟨-s, -⟩ computer; **Computerfreak** *m* computer nerd; **computergesteuert** *adj* computer-controlled; **Computergrafik** *f* computer graphics *pl*; **computerlesbar** *adj* machine-readable; **Computerspiel** *nt* computer game; **Computertomografie** *f* computer tomography, scan; **Computervirus** *m* computer virus

**Container** *m* ⟨-s, -⟩ *(for transporting goods)* container; *(for refuse)* skip

**Control-Taste** *f* control key

**Cookie** *nt* ⟨-s, -s⟩ IT cookie

**cool** *adj fam* cool

**Cornflakes** *pl* cornflakes *pl*

**Couch** *f* ⟨-, -en⟩ couch; **Couchtisch** *m* coffee table

**Coupé** *nt* ⟨-s, -s⟩ coupé

**Coupon** *m* ⟨-s, -s⟩ coupon

**Cousin** *m* ⟨-s, -s⟩ cousin; **Cousine** *f* cousin

**Crack** *nt* ⟨-s⟩ *(drug)* crack

**Creme** *f* ⟨-, -s⟩ cream; GASTR mousse

**Creutzfeld-Jakob-Krankheit** *f* Creutzfeld-Jakob disease, CJD

**Croissant** *nt* ⟨-s, -s⟩ croissant

**Curry 1.** *m* ⟨-s⟩ curry powder **2.** *nt* ⟨-s⟩ *(dish)* curry; **Currywurst** *f* fried sausage with ketchup and curry powder

**Cursor** *m* ⟨-s, -⟩ IT cursor

**Cybercafé** *nt* cybercafé; **Cyberspace** *m* ⟨-⟩ cyberspace

# D

**da 1.** *adv* there; here; *(time)* then; **~ oben / drüben** up / over there; **~, wo** where; **~ sein** be there; **ist jemand ~?** is there anybody there?; **ich bin gleich wieder ~** I'll be right back; **ist noch Brot ~?** is there any bread left?; **es ist keine Milch mehr ~** we've run out of milk; **~, bitte!** there you are; **~ kann man nichts machen** there's nothing you can do **2.** *conj* as

**dabei** *adv* *(position)* close to it; *(simultaneously)* at the same time; *(but)* though; **sie hörte Radio und rauchte ~** she was listening to the radio and smoking (at the same time); **~ fällt mir ein ...** that reminds me ...; **~ kam es zu einem Unfall** this led to an accident; **... und ~ hat er gar keine Ahnung ...** even though he has no idea; **ich finde nichts**

~ I don't see anything wrong with it; *es bleibt ~* that's settled; *~ sein* be present; *(taking part)* be involved; *ich bin ~!* count me in; *er war gerade ~ zu gehen* he was just *(or* on the point of*)* leaving

**dabeibleiben** *irr vi* stick with it; *ich bleibe dabei* I'm not changing my mind

**dabeihaben** *irr vt* *er hat seine Schwester dabei* he's brought his sister along; *ich habe kein Geld dabei* I haven't got any money on me

**Dach** *nt* ⟨-(e)s, Dächer⟩ roof; **Dachboden** *m* attic; loft; **Dachgepäckträger** *m* roofrack; **Dachrinne** *f* gutter

**Dachs** *m* ⟨-es, -e⟩ badger

**dachte** *imperf* → **denken**

**Dackel** *m* ⟨-s, -⟩ dachshund

**dadurch 1.** *adv* *(space)* through it; *(means)* in that way; *(cause)* because of that, for that reason **2.** *conj* ~, *dass* because; ~, *dass er hart arbeitet* *(means)* by working hard

**dafür** *adv* for it; *(in place of it)* instead; *~ habe ich 50 Euro bezahlt* I paid 50 euros for it; *ich bin ~ zu bleiben* I'm for *(or* in favour of*)* staying; *~ ist er ja da* that's what he's there for; *er kann nichts ~* he can't help it

**dagegen** *adv* against it; *(dissimilarity)* in comparison; *(exchange)* for it; *ich habe*

*nichts ~* I don't mind

**daheim** *adv* at home

**daher 1.** *adv* from there; *(reason)* that's why **2.** *conj* that's why

**dahin** *adv* there; *(time)* then; *(past, used up)* gone; *bis ~* till then; *(place)* up to there; *bis ~ muss die Arbeit fertig sein* the work must be finished by then

**dahinter** *adv* behind it

**dahinterkommen** *vi* find out

**Dahlie** *f* dahlia

**Dalmatiner** *m* ⟨-s, -⟩ dalmatian

**damals** *adv* at that time, then

**Dame** *f* ⟨-, -n⟩ lady; *(card)* queen; *(game)* draughts *sg* *(Brit)*, checkers *sg* *(US)*; **Damenbinde** *f* sanitary towel *(Brit)*, sanitary napkin *(US)*; **Damenkleidung** *f* ladies' wear; **Damentoilette** *f* ladies' toilet *(or* restroom *(US))*

**damit 1.** *adv* with it; *(as a result)* by that; *was meint er ~?* what does he mean by that?; *genug ~!* that's enough **2.** *conj* so that

**Damm** *m* ⟨-(e)s, Dämme⟩ dyke; *(creating reservoir)* dam; *(in harbour)* mole; *(for railway, road)* embankment

**Dämmerung** *f* twilight; *(in morning)* dawn; *(in evening)* dusk

**Dampf** *m* ⟨-(e)s, Dämpfe⟩ steam; *(haze)* vapour;

**Dampfbad** nt Turkish bath; **Dampfbügeleisen** nt steam iron; **dampfen** vi steam

**dämpfen** vt GASTR steam; (sound) deaden; (enthusiasm) dampen

**Dampfer** m ⟨-s, -⟩ steamer

**Dampfkochtopf** m pressure cooker

**danach** adv after that; (time also) afterwards; (rules etc) accordingly; **mir ist nicht ~** I don't feel like it; **~ sieht es aus** that's what it looks like

**Däne** m ⟨-n, -n⟩ Dane

**daneben** adv beside it; (dissimilarity) in comparison

**Dänemark** nt ⟨-s⟩ Denmark; **Dänin** f Dane, Danish woman / girl; **dänisch** adj Danish; **Dänisch** nt Danish

**dank** prep + dat or gen thanks to; **Dank** m ⟨-(e)s⟩ thanks pl; **vielen ~!** thank you very much; **jdm ~ sagen** thank sb; **dankbar** adj grateful; (task) rewarding; **danke** interj thank you, thanks; **nein ~!** no, thank you; **~, gerne!** yes, please; **~, gleichfalls!** thanks, and the same to you; **danken** vi **jdm für etw ~** thank sb for sth; **nichts zu ~!** you're welcome

**dann** adv then; **bis ~!** see you (later); **~ eben nicht** okay, forget it, suit yourself

**daran** adv on it; (fix) to it; (bang) against it; **es liegt ~, dass ...** it's because ...

**darauf** adv on it; (direction) towards it; (time) afterwards; **es kommt ganz ~ an, ob ...** it all depends whether ...; **ich freue mich ~** I'm looking forward to it; **am Tag ~** the next day

**darauffolgend** adj (day, year) next, following

**daraus** adv from it; **was ist ~ geworden?** what became of it?

**darin** adv in it; **das Problem liegt ~, dass ...** the basic problem is that ...

**Darlehen** nt ⟨-s, -⟩ loan

**Darm** m ⟨-(e)s, Därme⟩ intestine; (of sausage) skin; **Darmgrippe** f gastroenteritis

**darstellen** vt represent; THEAT play; (give account of) describe; **Darsteller(in)** m(f) actor / actress; **Darstellung** f representation; (account) description

**darüber** adv above it, over it; (drive) over it; (amount) more; (time) meanwhile; (talk, argue, be pleased) about it

**darum** adv (reason) that's why; **es geht ~, dass ...** the point (or thing) is that ...

**darunter** adv under it; (group) among them; (amount) less; **was verstehen Sie ~?** what do you understand by that?

**darunterfallen** vi be included

**das 1.** art the; **er hat sich ~ Bein gebrochen** he's broken his leg; **vier Euro~ Kilo** four euros a kilo **2.** pron that (one), this (one); **~ Auto da** that car; **ich nehme ~ da** I'll take that one; **~ heißt** that is; **~ sind Amerikaner** they're American **3.** pron (thing) that, which; (person) who, that; **~ Auto, ~ er kaufte** the car (that (or which)) he bought; **~ Mädchen, ~ nebenan wohnt** the girl who (or that) lives next door

**da sein** irr vi **→ da**

**dass** conj that; **so ~** so that; **es sei denn, ~** unless; **ohne ~ er grüßte** without saying hello

**dasselbe** pron the same

**Datei** f fr file; **Dateimanager** m file manager

**Daten** pl data pl; **Datenbank** f database; **Datenmissbrauch** m misuse of data; **Datenschutz** m data protection; **Datenträger** m data carrier; **Datenverarbeitung** f data processing

**datieren** vt date

**Dativ** m dative (case)

**Dattel** f ⟨-, -n⟩ date

**Datum** nt ⟨-s, Daten⟩ date

**Dauer** f ⟨-, -n⟩ duration; (of film, visit etc) length; **auf die ~** in the long run; **für die ~ von zwei Jahren** for

(a period of) two years; **Dauerauftrag** m FIN standing order; **dauerhaft** adj lasting; (material) durable; **Dauerkarte** f season ticket; **dauern** vi last; (require time) take; **es hat sehr lange gedauert, bis er …** it took him a long time to …; **wie lange dauert es denn noch?** how much longer will it be?; **das dauert mir zu lange** I can't wait that long; **dauernd 1.** adj lasting; (continual) constant **2.** adv always, constantly; **er lachte ~** he kept laughing; **unterbrich mich nicht ~** stop interrupting me; **Dauerwelle** f perm (Brit), permanent (US)

**Daumen** m ⟨-s, -⟩ thumb

**Daunendecke** f eiderdown

**davon** adv of it; (distance) away; (separation) from it; (reason) because of it; **ich hätte gerne ein Kilo ~** I'd like one kilo of that; **~ habe ich gehört** I've heard of it; (event) I've heard about it; **das kommt ~, wenn …** that's what happens when …; **was habe ich ~?** what's the point?; **auf und ~** up and away; **davonlaufen** irr vi run away

**davor** adv in front of it; (time) before; **ich habe Angst ~** I'm afraid of it

**dazu** adv (in addition) on top of that, as well; (suitability) for it, for that purpose; **ich möchte Reis ~** I'd like rice with it; **und ~ noch** and in addition; **~ fähig sein, etw zu tun** be capable of doing sth; **wie kam es ~?** how did it happen?; **dazugehören** vi belong to it; **dazukommen** irr vi join sb; **kommt noch etwas dazu?** anything else?

**dazwischen** adv in between; (difference etc) between them; (in group) among them

**dazwischenkommen** irr vi **wenn nichts dazwischenkommt** if all goes well; **mir ist etwas dazwischengekommen** something has cropped up

**dealen** vi fam deal in drugs; **Dealer(in)** m(f) ⟨-s, -⟩ fam dealer, pusher

**Deck** nt ⟨-(e)s, -s or -e⟩ deck; **an ~ on** deck

**Decke** f ⟨-, -n⟩ cover; (for bed) blanket; (for table) tablecloth; (of room) ceiling

**Deckel** m ⟨-s, -⟩ lid

**decken 1.** vt cover; (table) lay, set **2.** vr (interests) coincide; (statements) correspond **3.** vi lay (or set) the table

**Decoder** m ⟨-s, -⟩ decoder

**defekt** adj faulty; **Defekt** m ⟨-(e)s, -e⟩ fault, defect

**definieren** vt define; **Definition** f ⟨-, -en⟩ definition

**deftig** adj (prices) steep; **ein**

**~es Essen** a good solid meal

**dehnbar** adj flexible, elastic; **dehnen** vt, vr stretch

**Deich** m ⟨-(e)s, -e⟩ dyke

**dein** pron (as adj) your; **deine(r, s)** pron (as noun) yours, of you; **deinetwegen** adv because of you; (to please you) for your sake

**deinstallieren** vt (program) uninstall

**Dekolleté** nt ⟨-s, -s⟩ low neckline

**Dekoration** f decoration; (in shop) window dressing; **dekorativ** adj decorative; **dekorieren** vt decorate; (shop window) dress

**Delfin** m ⟨-s, -e⟩ dolphin

**delikat** adj (food) delicious; (problem) delicate

**Delikatesse** f ⟨-, -n⟩ delicacy

**Delle** f ⟨-, -en⟩ fam dent

**Delphin** m ⟨-s, -e⟩ dolphin

**dem** dat sg = **der, = das; wie ~ auch sein mag** be that as it may

**demnächst** adv shortly, soon

**Demo** f ⟨-, -s⟩ fam demo

**Demokratie** f ⟨-, -n⟩ democracy; **demokratisch** adj democratic

**demolieren** vt demolish

**Demonstration** f demonstration; **demonstrieren** vt, vi demonstrate

**den 1.** art acc sg, dat pl = **der**, **sie hat sich ~ Arm gebrochen** she's broken her arm

**2.** *pron* him; (*thing*) that one; **~ hab ich schon ewig nicht mehr gesehen** I haven't seen him in ages **3.** *pron* (*person*) who, that, whom; (*thing*) which, that; **der Typ, auf ~ sie steht** the guy (who) she fancies; **der Berg, auf ~ wir geklettert sind** the mountain (that) we climbed

**denkbar 1.** *adj* **das ist ~** that's possible **2.** *adv* **~ einfach** extremely simple; **denken** ⟨dachte, gedacht⟩ **1.** *vt, vi* think ⟨*über + acc* about); **an jdn / etw ~** think of sb/sth; (*recall, take into consideration*) remember sb/sth; **woran denkst Du?** what are you thinking about?; **denk an den Kaffee!** don't forget the coffee **2.** *vr* imagine; **das kann ich mir ~** I can (well) imagine

**Denkmal** *nt* ⟨-s, Denkmäler⟩ monument; **Denkmalschutz** *m* monument preservation; **unter ~ stehen** be listed

**denn 1.** *conj* for, because **2.** *adv* then; (*after comparative*) than; **was ist ~?** what's wrong?; **ist das ~ so schwierig?** is it really that difficult?

**dennoch** *conj* still, nevertheless

**Deo** *nt* ⟨-s, -s⟩, **Deodorant** *nt* ⟨-s, -s⟩ deodorant; **Deoroller**

*m* roll-on deodorant; **Deospray** *m or nt* deodorant spray

**Deponie** *f* ⟨-, -n⟩ waste disposal site, tip

**Depressionen** *pl* **an ~ leiden** suffer from depression *sg*; **deprimieren** *vt* depress

**der 1.** *art* the; (*dative*) to the; (*genitive*) of the; **~ arme Marc** poor Marc; **~ Kundin habe es ~ Kundin geschickt** I sent it to the client; **Vater ~ Besitzerin** the owner's father **2.** *pron* that (one), this (one); **~ mit ~ Brille** the one (*or* him) with the glasses; **~ schreibt nicht mehr** (*pen etc*) that one doesn't write any more **3.** *pron* (*person*) who, that; (*thing*) which, that; **jeder, ~ ...** anyone who ...; **er war ~ erste, ~ es erfuhr** he was the first to know

**derart** *adv* so; (*before adj*) such; **derartig** *adj* **ein ~er Fehler** such a mistake, a mistake like that

**deren** *gen → die* **1.** *pron* (*person*) her; (*thing*) its; (*pl*) their **2.** *pron* (*person*) whose; (*thing*) of which

**dergleichen** *pron* **und ~ mehr** and the like, and so on; **nichts ~** no such thing

**derjenige** *pron* the one; **~, der** the one who (*or* that)

**dermaßen** *adv* so much; (*with adj*) so

**derselbe** *pron* the same (person / thing)

**deshalb** *adv* therefore; **~ frage ich ja** that's why I'm asking

**Design** *nt* ⟨-s, -s⟩ design; **Designer(in)** *m(f)* ⟨-s, -⟩ designer

**Desinfektionsmittel** *nt* disinfectant; **desinfizieren** *vt* disinfect

**dessen** *gen* → **der**, → **das 1.** *pron* (*thing*) his; (*thing*) its; **ich bin mir ~ bewusst** I'm aware of that **2.** *pron* (*person*) whose; (*thing*) of which

**Dessert** *nt* ⟨-s, -s⟩ dessert; **zum** (*or* **als**) **~** for dessert

**destilliert** *adj* distilled

**desto** *adv* **je eher, ~ besser** the sooner, the better

**deswegen** *conj* therefore

**Detail** *nt* ⟨-s, -s⟩ detail; **ins ~ gehen** go into detail

**Detektiv(in)** *m(f)* ⟨-s, -e⟩ detective

**deutlich** *adj* clear; (*difference*) distinct

**deutsch** *adj* German; **Deutsch** *nt* ⟨-(e)s, -⟩ German; **auf ~** in German; **ins ~e übersetzen** translate into German; **Deutsche(r)** *mf* German; **Deutschland** *nt* Germany

**Devise** *f* ⟨-, -n⟩ motto; **~n** *pl* FIN foreign currency *sg*; **Devisenkurs** *m* exchange rate

**Dezember** *m* ⟨-(s), -⟩ December; → **Juni**

**dezent** *adj* discreet

**d. h.** *abbr* = **das heißt** i.e.

**Dia** *nt* ⟨-s, -s⟩ slide

**Diabetes** *m* ⟨-, -⟩ MED diabetes; **Diabetiker(in)** *m(f)* ⟨-s, -⟩ diabetic

**Diagnose** *f* ⟨-, -n⟩ diagnosis

**diagonal** *adj* diagonal

**Dialekt** *m* ⟨-(e)s, -e⟩ dialect

**Dialog** *m* ⟨-(e)s, -e⟩ dialogue; IT dialog

**Dialyse** *f* ⟨-, -n⟩ MED dialysis

**Diamant** *m* ⟨-en, -en⟩ diamond

**Diaprojektor** *m* slide projector

**Diät** *f* ⟨-, -en⟩ diet; **eine ~ machen** be on a diet; (*start*) go on a diet

**dich** *pron acc* → **du**; you; **~ (selbst)** yourself; **pass auf ~ auf** look after yourself; **reg ~ nicht auf** don't get upset

**dicht 1.** *adj* dense; (*fog*) thick; (*weave*) close; (*shoes, boat etc*) watertight; (*traffic*) heavy **2.** *adv* **~ an / bei** close to; **~ bevölkert** densely populated

**Dichter(in)** *m(f)* ⟨-s, -⟩ poet; (*author*) writer

**Dichtung** *f* AUTO gasket; (*for tap etc*) washer; (*verse*) poetry

**Dichtungsring** *m* TECH washer

**dick** *adj* thick; (*person*) fat; **jdn ~ haben** be sick of sb; **Dickdarm** *m* colon; **Dick-**

**kopf** m stubborn (or pig-headed) person; **Dickmilch** f sour milk

**die 1.** art the; **~ arme Sarah** poor Sarah **2.** pron (sg) that (one), this (one); (pl) those (ones); **~ mit den langen Haaren** the one (or her) with the long hair; **ich nehme ~ da** I'll take that one / those **3.** pron (person) who, that; (thing) which, that; **sie war ~ erste, ~ es erfuhr** she was the first to know **4.** pl → **der**, → **die**, → **das**

**Dieb(in)** m(f) ⟨-(e)s, -e⟩ thief; **Diebstahl** m ⟨-(e)s, Diebstähle⟩ theft; **Diebstahlsicherung** f burglar alarm

**diejenige** pron the one; **~, die** the one who (or that); **~n** (pl) those pl, the ones

**Diele** f ⟨-, -n⟩ hall

**Dienst** m ⟨-(e)s, -e⟩ service; **außer ~** retired; **~ haben** be on duty

**Dienstag** m Tuesday; → **Mittwoch**; **dienstags** adv on Tuesdays; → **mittwochs**

**Dienstbereitschaft** f **~ haben** (doctor) be on call; **diensthabend** adj **der ~e Arzt** the doctor on duty; **Dienstleistung** f service; **dienstlich** adj official; **er ist ~ unterwegs** he's away on business; **Dienstreise** f business trip; **Dienststelle** f department; **Dienstwagen** m company car; **Dienstzeit**

f office hours pl; MIL period of service

**diesbezüglich** adj (formal) on this matter

**diese(r, s)** pron this (one); (pl) these; **~ Frau** this woman; **~r Mann** this man; **~s Mädchen** this girl; **~ Leute** these people; **ich nehme ~./~n/~s** I'll take this one; (there) I'll take that one; **ich nehme ~** pl I'll take these (ones); (there) I'll take those (ones)

**Diesel** m ⟨-s, -⟩ AUTO diesel

**dieselbe** pron the same; **es sind immer ~n** it's always the same people

**Dieselmotor** m diesel engine; **Dieselöl** nt diesel (oil)

**diesig** adj hazy, misty

**diesmal** adv this time

**Dietrich** m ⟨-s, -e⟩ skeleton key

**Differenz** f ⟨-, -en⟩ difference

**digital** adj digital; **Digital-** in cpds (display etc) digital; **Digitalfernsehen** nt digital television, digital TV; **Digitalkamera** f digital camera

**Diktat** nt ⟨-(e)s, -e⟩ dictation

**Diktatur** f dictatorship

**Dill** m ⟨-s⟩ dill

**DIN** abbr = **Deutsche Industrienorm** DIN; **~ A4** A4

**Ding** nt ⟨-(e)s, -e⟩ thing; **vor allen ~en** above all; **der Stand der ~e** the state of affairs; **das ist nicht mein ~** fam it's not my sort of thing (or cup of tea); **Dingsbums** nt ⟨-⟩ fam thingy, thingummybob

**Dinkel** m ⟨-s, -⟩ BOT spelt

**Dinosaurier** m ⟨-s, -⟩ dinosaur

**Diphtherie** f ⟨-, -n⟩ diphtheria

**Diplom** nt ⟨-(e)s, -e⟩ diploma

**Diplomat(in)** m(f) ⟨-en, -en⟩ diplomat

**dir** pron dat → **du**; (to) you; **hat er ~ geholfen?** did he help you?; **ich werde es ~ erklären** I'll explain it to you; **wasch ~ die Hände** go and wash your hands; **ein Freund von ~** a friend of yours

**direkt 1.** adj direct; (question) straight; (Verbindung) through service **2.** adv directly; (straightaway) immediately; **~ am Bahnhof** right next to the station; **Direktflug** m direct flight

**Direktor(in)** m(f) ⟨-s, -⟩ director; (of school) headmaster / -mistress (Brit), principal (US)

**Direktübertragung** f live broadcast

**Dirigent(in)** m(f) ⟨-en, -en⟩ conductor; **dirigieren** vt direct; MUS conduct

**Discman®** m ⟨-s, -s⟩ Discman®

**Diskette** f disk, diskette; **Diskettenlaufwerk** nt disk drive

**Diskjockey** m ⟨-s, -s⟩ disc jockey; **Disko** f ⟨-, -s⟩ fam

disco, club; **Diskothek** f ⟨-, -en⟩ discotheque, club

**diskret** adj discreet

**diskriminieren** vt discriminate against

**Diskussion** f discussion; **diskutieren** vt, vi discuss

**Display** nt ⟨-s, -s⟩ display

**disqualifizieren** vt disqualify

**Distanz** f distance

**Distel** f ⟨-, -n⟩ thistle

**Disziplin** f ⟨-, -en⟩ discipline

**divers** adj various

**dividieren** vt divide (durch by); **8 dividiert durch 2 ist 4** 8 divided by 2 is 4

**DJ** m ⟨-s, -s⟩ abbr → **Diskjockey** DJ

**doch 1.** adv **das ist nicht wahr! — ~!** that's not true — yes it is; **nicht ~!** oh no; **er kommt ~?** he will come, won't he?; **er hat es ~ gemacht** he did it after all; **setzen Sie sich ~** do sit down, please **2.** conj but

**Doktor(in)** m(f) doctor

**Dokument** nt document; **Dokumentarfilm** m documentary (film); **dokumentieren** vt document; **Dokumentvorlage** f IT document template

**Dolch** m ⟨-(e)s, -e⟩ dagger

**Dollar** m ⟨-s, -s⟩ dollar

**dolmetschen** vt, vi interpret; **Dolmetscher(in)** m(f) ⟨-s, -⟩ interpreter

**Dolomiten** pl Dolomites pl

**Dom** m ⟨-(e)s, -e⟩ cathedral

**Domäne** f ⟨-, -n⟩ domain, province; IT domain

**Dominikanische Republik** f Dominican Republic

**Domino** nt ⟨-s, -s⟩ dominoes sg

**Donau** f ⟨-⟩ Danube

**Döner** m ⟨-s, -⟩, **Döner Kebab** m ⟨-s, -s⟩ doner kebab

**Donner** m ⟨-s, -⟩ thunder; **donnern** vi **es donnert** it's thundering

**Donnerstag** m Thursday; → **Mittwoch**; **donnerstags** adv on Thursdays; → **mittwochs**

**doof** adj fam stupid

**dopen** vt dope; **Doping** nt ⟨-s⟩ doping; **Dopingkontrolle** f drugs test

**Doppel** nt ⟨-s, -⟩ duplicate; SPORT doubles sg; **Doppelbett** nt double bed; **Doppeldecker** m double-decker; **Doppelhaushälfte** f semi-detached house (Brit), duplex (US); **doppelklicken** vi double-click; **Doppelname** m double-barrelled name; **Doppelpunkt** m colon; **Doppelstecker** m two-way adaptor; **doppelt** adj double; **in ~er Ausführung** in duplicate; **Doppelzimmer** nt double room

**Dorf** nt ⟨-(e)s, Dörfer⟩ village

**Dorn** m ⟨-(e)s, -en⟩ BOT thorn

**Dörrobst** nt dried fruit

**Dorsch** m ⟨-(e)s, -e⟩ cod

**dort** adv there; **~ drüben** over

there; **dorther** adv from there

**Dose** f ⟨-, -n⟩ box; (for food) tin (Brit), can; (for beer) can

**dösen** vi doze

**Dosenbier** nt canned beer; **Dosenmilch** f canned milk, tinned milk (Brit); **Dosenöffner** m tin opener (Brit), can opener

**Dotter** m ⟨-s, -⟩ (egg) yolk

**downloaden** vt download

**Downsyndrom** nt ⟨-(e)s, -e⟩ MED Down's syndrome

**Dozent(in)** m(f) lecturer

**Dr.** abbr → **Doktor**

**Drache** m ⟨-n, -n⟩ dragon; **Drachen** m ⟨-s, -⟩ (toy) kite; SPORT hang-glider; **Drachenfliegen** nt ⟨-s⟩ hang-gliding; **Drachenflieger(in)** m(f) ⟨-s, -⟩ hang-glider

**Draht** m ⟨-(e)s, Drähte⟩ wire; **Drahtseilbahn** f cable railway

**Drama** nt ⟨-s, Dramen⟩ drama; **dramatisch** adj dramatic

**dran** adv fam contr → **daran**; **gut ~ sein** (rich) be well-off; (lucky) be fortunate; (healthy) be well; **schlecht ~ sein** be in a bad way; **wer ist ~?** whose turn is it?; **ich bin ~** it's my turn; **bleib ~!** TEL hang on

**drang** imperf → **dringen**

**Drang** m ⟨-(e)s, Dränge⟩ urge (nach for); (of circumstances etc) pressure

**drängeln** vt, vi push

**drängen 1.** vt push; (try to persuade) urge **2.** vi be urgent; (time) press; **auf etw** acc ~ press for sth

**drankommen** irr vi **wer kommt dran?** who's turn is it?, who's next?

**drauf** fam contr → **darauf**; **gut / schlecht ~ sein** to be in a good / bad mood

**Draufgänger(in)** m(f) ⟨-s, -⟩ daredevil

**draufkommen** irr vi remember; **ich komme nicht drauf** I can't think of it

**draufmachen** vi fam **einen ~** go on a binge

**draußen** adv outside

**Dreck** m ⟨-(e)s⟩ dirt, filth; **dreckig** adj dirty, filthy

**drehen 1.** vt vi turn; (cigarette) roll; (film) shoot **2.** vr turn; (revolve) rotate; **sich ~ um** (concern) be about

**Drehstrom** m three-phase current; **Drehtür** f revolving door; **Drehzahlmesser** m rev counter

**drei** num three; **~ viertel voll** three-quarters full; **es ist ~ viertel neun** it's a quarter to nine; **Drei** f ⟨-, -en⟩ three; (mark in school) ≈ C; **Dreieck** nt triangle; **dreieckig** adj triangular; **dreifach 1.** adj triple **2.** adv three times; **dreihundert** num three hundred; **Dreikönigstag** m Epiphany; **dreimal** adv three times; **Dreirad** nt tricy-

cle; **dreispurig** adj three-lane

**dreißig** num thirty; **dreißigste(r, s)** adj thirtieth; → **dritte**

**Dreiviertelstunde** f eine ~ three quarters of an hour

**dreizehn** num thirteen; **dreizehnte(r, s)** adj thirteenth; → **dritte**

**dressieren** vt train

**Dressing** nt ⟨-s, -s⟩ (salad) dressing

**Dressman** m ⟨-s, Dressmen⟩ (male) model

**Dressur** f ⟨-, -en⟩ training

**drin** fam contr → **darin**; in it; **mehr war nicht ~** that was the best I could do

**dringen** ⟨drang, gedrungen⟩ vi (water, light, cold) penetrate (durch through, in + acc into); **auf etw** acc ~ insist on sth; **dringend, dringlich** adj urgent

**drinnen** adv inside

**dritt** adv **wir sind zu ~** there are three of us; **dritte(r, s)** adj third; **die Dritte Welt** the Third World; **3. September** 3(rd) September; **am 3. September** on 3(rd) September, on September 3(rd); **München, den 3. September** Munich, September 3(rd); **Drittel** nt ⟨-s, -⟩ (fraction) third; **drittens** adv thirdly

**Droge** f ⟨-, -n⟩ drug; **drogenabhängig, drogensüchtig** adj addicted to drugs

**Dur**

**Drogerie** f chemist's (Brit), drugstore (US); **Drogeriemarkt** m discount chemist's (Brit) (or drugstore (US))

**drohen** vi threaten (jdm sb); **mit etw ~** threaten to do sth

**dröhnen** vi (engine) roar; (voice, music) boom; (room) resound

**Drohung** f threat

**Drossel** f ⟨-, -n⟩ thrush

**drüben** adv over there; on the other side

**drüber** fam contr → **darüber**

**Druck** 1. m ⟨-(e)s, Drücke⟩ PHYS pressure; (fig strain) stress; **jdn unter ~ setzen** put sb under pressure 2. m ⟨-(e)s, -e⟩ TYPO printing; (product, typeface) print; **Druckbuchstabe** m block letter; **in ~n schreiben** print; **drucken** vt, vi print

**drücken** 1. vt, vi (button, hand) press; (garment) pinch; (fig prices) keep down; **jdm etw in die Hand ~** press sth into sb's hand 2. vr **sich vor etw** dat ~ get out of sth; **drückend** adj oppressive

**Drucker** m ⟨-s, -⟩ IT printer; **Druckertreiber** m printer driver

**Druckknopf** m press stud (Brit), snap fastener (US); **Drucksache** f printed matter; **Druckschrift** f block letters pl

**drunten** adv down there

**drunter** fam contr → **darunter**

**Drüse** f ⟨-, -n⟩ gland

**Dschungel** m ⟨-s, -⟩ jungle

**du** pron you; **bist ~ es?** is it you?; **wir sind per ~** we're on first-name terms

**Dübel** m ⟨-s, -⟩ Rawlplug®

**ducken** vt, vr duck

**Dudelsack** m bagpipes pl

**Duett** nt ⟨-s, -e⟩ duet

**Duft** m ⟨-(e)s, Düfte⟩ scent; **duften** vi smell nice; **es duftet nach …** it smells of …

**dulden** vt tolerate

**dumm** adj stupid; **Dummkopf** m stupidity; (act) stupid thing; **Dummkopf** m idiot

**dumpf** adj (sound) muffled; (memory) vague; (pain) dull

**Düne** f ⟨-, -n⟩ dune

**Dünger** m ⟨-s, -⟩ fertilizer

**dunkel** adj dark; (voice) deep; (suspicion) vague; (mysterious) obscure; (suspicious) dubious; **im Dunkeln tappen** fig be in the dark; **dunkelblau** adj dark blue; **dunkelblond** adj light brown; **dunkelhaarig** adj dark-haired; **Dunkelheit** f darkness

**dünn** adj thin; (coffee) weak

**Dunst** m ⟨-es, Dünste⟩ haze; (light fog) mist; CHEM vapour

**dünsten** vt GASTR steam

**Duo** nt ⟨-⟩ MUS duo

**Dur** nt ⟨-⟩ MUS major (key); **in G~** in G major

**durch 1.** prep + acc through; (means) by; (time) during; **~ Amerika reisen** travel across the USA; **er verdient seinen Lebensunterhalt ~ den Verkauf von Autos** he makes his living by selling cars **2.** adv (meat) cooked through, well done; **das ganze Jahr ~** all through the year, the whole year long; **darf ich bitte ~?** can I get through, please?

**durchaus** adv absolutely; **~ nicht** not at all

**Durchblick** m view; **den ~ haben** fig know what's going on; **durchblicken** vi look through; fam understand (bei etw sth); **etw ~ lassen** fig hint at sth

**Durchblutung** f circulation

**durchbrennen** irr vi (fuse) blow; (wire) burn through; fam (abscond) run away

**durchdacht** adv **gut ~** well thought-out

**durchdrehen 1.** vt (meat) mince **2.** vi (wheels) spin; fam (under stress) crack up

**durcheinander** adv in a mess; fam (person) confused; **Durcheinander** nt ⟨-s⟩ (of people) confusion; (of things) mess; **durcheinanderbringen** irr vt mess up; (person) confuse; **durcheinanderreden** vi talk all at the same time; **durcheinandertrinken** irr vi mix one's drinks

**Durchfahrt** f way through; „**~ verboten!**" 'no thoroughfare'

**Durchfall** m MED diarrhoea

**durchfallen** irr vi fall through; (in exam) fail

**durchfragen** vr ask one's way

**durchführen** vt carry out

**Durchgang** m passage; SPORT round; (in election) ballot; **Durchgangsverkehr** m through traffic

**durchgebraten** adj well done

**durchgefroren** adj frozen to the bone

**durchgehen** irr vi go through (durch etw sth); (horse) break loose; (make off) run away; **durchgehend** adj (train) through; **~ geöffnet** open all day

**durchhalten** irr **1.** vi hold out **2.** vt (pace) keep up; **etw ~** (not give up) see sth through

**durchkommen** irr vi get through; (patient) pull through

**durchlassen** irr vt (person) let through; (water) let in

**durchlesen** irr vt read through

**durchleuchten** vt X-ray

**durchmachen** vt go through; (development) undergo; **die Nacht ~** make a night of it, have an all-nighter

**Durchmesser** m ⟨-s, -⟩ diameter

**Durchreise** f journey

through; **auf der ~** passing through; (goods) in transit; **Durchreisevisum** nt transit visa

**durchreißen** irr vt, vi tear (in two)

**durchs** contr = **durch das**

**Durchsage** f ⟨-, -n⟩ announcement

**durchschauen** vt (person, lie) see through

**durchschlagen** irr vr struggle through

**durchschneiden** irr vt cut (in two)

**Durchschnitt** m average; **im ~** on average; **durchschnittlich 1.** adj average **2.** adv on average

**durchsetzen 1.** vt get through **2.** vr (be successful) succeed; (assert oneself) get one's way

**durchsichtig** adj transparent, see-through

**durchstellen** vt TEL put through

**durchstreichen** irr vt cross out

**durchsuchen** vt search (nach for); **Durchsuchung** f search

**Durchwahl** f direct dialling; (number) extension

**durchziehen** irr vt (plan) carry through

**Durchzug** m draught

**dürfen** ⟨durfte, gedurft⟩ vi **etw tun ~** (permission) be allowed to do sth; **darf ich?** may I?; **das darfst du nicht (tun)!** you mustn't do that; **was darf es sein?** what can I do for you?; **er dürfte schon dort sein** he should be there by now

**dürr** adj (thin) skinny

**Durst** m ⟨-(e)s⟩ thirst; **~ haben** be thirsty; **durstig** adj thirsty

**Dusche** f ⟨-, -n⟩ shower; **duschen** vi, vr have a shower; **Duschgel** nt shower gel

**Düse** f ⟨-, -n⟩ nozzle; TECH jet; **Düsenflugzeug** nt jet (aircraft)

**düster** adj dark; (thoughts, future) gloomy

**Dutyfreeshop** m ⟨-s, -s⟩ duty-free shop

**duzen 1.** vt address as 'du' **2.** vr **sich ~** (mit jdm) address each other as 'du', be on first-name terms

**DVD** f ⟨-, -s⟩ abbr = **Digital Versatile Disk** DVD; **DVD-Player** m ⟨-s, -⟩ DVD player; **DVD-Rekorder** m ⟨-s, -⟩ DVD recorder

**dynamisch** adj dynamic

**Dynamo** m ⟨-s, -s⟩ dynamo

# E

**Ebbe** f ⟨-, -n⟩ low tide

**eben 1.** adj level; (even) smooth **2.** adv just; (confirming sth) exactly

**ebenfalls** adv also, as well; (reply) you too; **ebenso** adv just as; **~ gut** just as well; **~ viel** just as much

**EC** m ⟨-, -s⟩ abbr → **Eurocity-zug**

**Echo** nt ⟨-s, -s⟩ echo

**echt** adj (leather, gold) real, genuine; **ein ~er Verlust** a real loss

**EC-Karte** f ≈ debit card

**Ecke** f ⟨-, -n⟩ corner; MATH angle; **an der ~** at the corner; **gleich um die ~** just round the corner; **eckig** adj rectangular

**Economyclass** f ⟨-⟩ coach (class), economy class

**Ecstasy** f ⟨-⟩ (drug) ecstasy

**Efeu** m ⟨-s⟩ ivy

**Effekt** m ⟨-s, -e⟩ effect

**egal** adj **das ist ~** it doesn't matter; **das ist mir ~** I don't care, it's all the same to me; **~ wie teuer** no matter how expensive

**egoistisch** adj selfish

**ehe** conj before

**Ehe** f ⟨-, -n⟩ marriage; **Ehefrau** f wife

**ehemalig** adj former; **ehemals** adv formerly

**Ehemann** m husband; **Ehepaar** nt married couple

**eher** adv (time) sooner; (preference) rather; (passing judgment) more; **je ~, desto besser** the sooner the better

**Ehering** m wedding ring

**eheste(r, s) 1.** adj (earliest) first **2.** adv **am ~n** (probably) most likely

**Ehre** f ⟨-, -n⟩ honour; **ehren** vt honour; **Ehrenwort** nt word of honour; **~!** I promise

**ehrgeizig** adj ambitious

**ehrlich** adj honest

**Ei** nt ⟨-(e)s, -er⟩ egg

**Eiche** f ⟨-, -n⟩ oak (tree); **Eichel** f ⟨-, -n⟩ acorn

**Eichhörnchen** nt squirrel

**Eid** m ⟨-(e)s, -e⟩ oath

**Eidechse** f ⟨-, -n⟩ lizard

**Eierbecher** m eggcup; **Eierstock** m ovary; **Eieruhr** f egg timer

**Eifersucht** f jealousy; **eifersüchtig** adj jealous (auf + acc of)

**Eigelb** nt ⟨-(e)s, -⟩ egg yolk

**eigen** adj own; (typical) characteristic (jdm of sb); (strange) peculiar; **eigenartig** adj peculiar; **Eigenschaft** f quality; CHEM, PHYS property

**eigentlich 1.** adj actual, real **2.** adv actually, really; **was**

*denken Sie sich ~ dabei?* what on earth do you think you're doing?

**Eigentum** *nt* property; **Eigentümer(in)** *m(f)* owner; **Eigentumswohnung** *f* owner-occupied flat (Brit), condominium (US)

**eignen** *vr sich ~ für* be suited for; *er würde sich als Lehrer ~* he'd make a good teacher

**Eilbrief** *m* express letter, special-delivery letter; **Eile** *f* ‹-› hurry; **eilen** *vi* (letter, matter) be urgent; *es eilt nicht* there's no hurry; **eilig** *adj* hurried; (pressing) urgent; *es ~ haben* be in a hurry

**Eimer** *m* ‹-s, -› bucket

**ein** *adv* *nicht ~ noch aus wissen* not know what to do; *~ aus* (switch) on - off

**ein(e)** *art* a; an; *~ Mann* a man; *~ Apfel* an apple; *~e Stunde* an hour; *~ Haus* a house; *~ (gewisser) Herr Miller* a (certain) Mr Miller; *~es Tages* one day

**einander** *pron* one another, each other

**einarbeiten 1.** *vt* train **2.** *vr* get used to the work

**einatmen** *vt, vi* breathe in

**Einbahnstraße** *f* one-way street

**einbauen** *vt* build in; (engine etc) install, fit; **Einbauküche** *f* fitted kitchen

**einbiegen** *irr vi* turn (in + acc into)

**einbilden** *vt sich dat etw ~* imagine sth

**einbrechen** *irr vi* (into house) break in; (roof etc) fall in, collapse; **Einbrecher(in)** *m(f)* ‹-s, -› burglar

**einbringen** *irr* **1.** *vt* (harvest) bring in; (profit) yield; *jdm etw ~* bring (or earn) sb sth **2.** *vr sich in acc etw ~* make a contribution to sth

**Einbruch** *m* break-in, burglary; *bei ~ der Nacht* at nightfall

**Einbürgerung** *f* naturalization

**einchecken** *vt* check in

**eincremen** *vt, vr* put some cream on

**eindeutig 1.** *adj* clear, obvious **2.** *adv* clearly; *~ falsch* clearly wrong

**eindringen** *irr vi* force one's way in (in + acc -to); (into house) break in (in + acc -to); (gas, water) get in (in + acc -to)

**Eindruck** *m* impression; *großen ~ auf jdn machen* make a big impression on sb

**eine(r, s)** *pron* one; someone; *~r meiner Freunde* one of my friends; *~r nach dem andern* one after the other

**eineiig** *adj* (twins) identical

**eineinhalb** *num* one and a half

**einerseits** *adv* on the one hand

**einfach 1.** adj (not complicated) simple; (person) ordinary; (food) plain; (not multiple) single; **~e Fahrkarte** single ticket (Brit), one-way ticket (US) **2.** adv simply; (single time) once

**Einfahrt** f (in car) driving in; (of train) arrival; (place) entrance

**Einfall** m idea; **einfallen** irr vi (light etc) fall in; (roof, house) collapse; **ihm fiel ein, dass ...** it occurred to him that ...; **ich werde mir etwas ~ lassen** I'll think of something; **was fällt Ihnen ein!** what do you think you're doing?

**Einfamilienhaus** nt detached house

**einfarbig** adj all one colour; (fabric etc) self-coloured

**Einfluss** m influence

**einfrieren** irr vt, vi freeze

**einfügen** vt fit in; add; IT insert; **Einfügetaste** f IT insert key

**Einfuhr** f ⟨-, -en⟩ import; **Einfuhrbestimmungen** pl import regulations pl

**einführen** vt introduce; (goods) import; **Einführung** f introduction

**Eingabe** f (of data) input; **Eingabetaste** f IT return (or enter) key

**Eingang** m entrance; **Eingangshalle** f entrance hall, lobby (US)

**eingeben** irr vt (data etc) enter, key in

**eingebildet** adj imaginary; (conceited) arrogant

**Eingeborene(r)** mf native

**eingehen** irr vi (letter, money) come in, arrive; (animal, plant) die; (fabric) shrink; **auf etw ~** agree to sth; **auf jdn ~** respond to sb **2.** vt (contract) enter into; (bet) make; (risk) take

**eingelegt** adj (in vinegar) pickled

**eingeschaltet** adj (switched) on

**eingeschlossen** adj locked in; (in price) included

**eingewöhnen** vr settle in

**eingießen** irr vt pour

**eingreifen** irr vi intervene; **Eingriff** m intervention; (surgical) operation

**einhalten** irr vt (promise etc) keep

**einheimisch** adj (product, team) local; **Einheimische(r)** mf local

**Einheit** f unity; (measurement) unit; **einheitlich** adj uniform

**einholen** vt (car, person) catch up with; (lateness) make up for; (advice, permission) ask for

**Einhorn** nt unicorn

**einhundert** num one (or a) hundred

**einig** adj united; **sich** dat **~ sein** agree

**einige 1.** *pron pl* some; *(quite a few)* several **2.** *adj* some; *nach ~r Zeit* after some time; *~ hundert Euro* some hundred euros

**einigen** *vr* agree *(auf +* acc on)

**einigermaßen** *adv* fairly, quite; *(passably)* reasonably

**einiges** *pron* something; *(amount)* quite a bit; *(number)* a few things; *es gibt noch ~ zu tun* there's still a fair bit to do

**Einkauf** *m* purchase; *Einkäufe (machen)* (to do one's) shopping; **einkaufen 1.** *vt* buy **2.** *vi* go shopping; **Einkaufsbummel** *m* shopping trip; **Einkaufstasche** *f,* **Einkaufstüte** *f* shopping bag; **Einkaufswagen** *m* shopping trolley *(Brit)* (or cart *(US)*); **Einkaufszentrum** *nt* shopping centre *(Brit)* (or mall *(US)*)

**einklemmen** *vt* jam; *er hat sich zu den Finger eingeklemmt* he got his finger caught

**Einkommen** *nt* ⟨-s, -⟩ income

**einladen** *irr vt (person)* invite; *(things)* load up; *jdn zum Essen ~* take sb out for a meal; *ich lade dich ein (I'm paying)* it's my treat; **Einladung** *f* invitation

**Einlass** *m* ⟨-es, Einlässe⟩ admittance; *~ ab 18 Uhr* doors open at 6 pm; **einlassen** *irr*

*vr sich mit jdm / auf etw acc ~* get involved with sb/sth

**einleben** *vr* settle down

**einlegen** *vt (film etc)* put in; *(food before cooking)* marinate; *eine Pause ~* take a break

**einleiten** *vt* start; *(measures)* introduce; *(birth)* induce; *Einleitung* *f* introduction; *(of birth)* induction

**einleuchten** *vi jdm ~* be (or become) clear to sb; **einleuchtend** *adj* clear

**einloggen** *vi rr* log on (or in)

**einlösen** *vt (cheque)* cash; *(voucher)* redeem; *(promise)* keep

**einmal** *adv* once; *(at earlier time)* before; *(in the future)* some day; *(to begin with)* first; *~ im Jahr* once a year; *noch ~* once more, again; *ich war schon ~ hier* I've been here before; *warst du schon ~ in London?* have you ever been to London?; *nicht ~* not even; *auf ~* suddenly; *(simultaneously, in one go)* at once; **einmalig** *adj* unique; *(occurring only once)* single; *(excellent)* fantastic

**einmischen** *vr* interfere *(in* + acc with)

**Einnahme** *f* ⟨-, -n⟩ *(money)* takings *pl*; *(of medicine)* taking; **einnehmen** *irr vt (medicine)* take; *(money)* take in;

(*attitude, space*) take up; **jdn für sich ~** win sb over

**einordnen 1.** *vt* put in order; (*categorize*) classify; (*documents*) file **2.** *vr* AUTO get in lane; **sich rechts / links ~** get into the right / left lane

**einpacken** *vt* pack (up)

**einparken** *vi* park

**einplanen** *vt* allow for

**einprägen** *vt* **sich dat etw ~** remember (*or* memorize) sth

**einräumen** *vt* (*books, crockery*) put away; (*cupboard*) put things in

**einreden** *vt* **jdm / sich etw ~** talk sb / oneself into (believing) sth

**einreiben** *irr vt* **sich mit etw ~** rub sth into one's skin

**einreichen** *vt* hand in; (*application*) submit

Einreise *f* entry; Einreisebestimmungen *pl* entry regulations *pl*; Einreiseerlaubnis *f*, Einreisegenehmigung *f* entry permit; einreisen *vi* enter (*in ein Land* a country); Einreisevisum *nt* entry visa

**einrenken** *vt* (*arm, leg*) set

**einrichten 1.** *vt* (*house*) furnish; (*business etc*) establish, set up; (*fix*) arrange **2.** *vr* furnish one's home; (*get ready*) prepare oneself (*auf + acc* for); (*adjust*) adapt (*auf + acc* to); **Einrichtung** *f* (*in house*) furnishings *pl*;

(*organization*) institution; (*swimming pool etc*) facility

**eins** *num* one; **Eins** *f* ⟨-, -en⟩ one; (*mark in school*) ≈ A

**einsam** *adj* lonely

**einsammeln** *vt* collect

**Einsatz** *m* (*component*) insert; (*of machine, troops etc*) use; (*in gambling*) stake; (*of one's life*) risk; MUS entry

**einschalten** *vt* ELEC switch on

**einschätzen** *vt* estimate, assess

**einschenken** *vt* pour

**einschiffen** *vr* embark (*nach* for)

**einschlafen** *irr vi* fall asleep, drop off; **mir ist der Arm eingeschlafen** my arm's gone to sleep

**einschlagen** *irr* **1.** *vt* (*window*) smash; (*teeth, skull*) smash in; (*path, direction*) take **2.** *vi* hit (*in etw acc* sth, *auf jdn* sb); (*lightning*) strike; (*film, song etc*) be a success

**einschließen** *irr vt* (*person*) lock in; (*object*) lock away; (*encircle*) surround; *fig* include; **einschließlich 1.** *adv* inclusive **2.** *prep + gen* including; **von Montag bis ~ Freitag** from Monday up to and including Friday, Monday through Friday (*US*)

**einschränken 1.** *vt* limit, restrict; (*reduce*) cut down on

**2.** *vr* cut down (on expenditure)

**einschreiben** *irr vr* register; (*for school*) enrol; **Einschreiben** *nt* ‹-s, -› registered letter; **etw per ~ schicken** send sth by special delivery

**einschüchtern** *vt* intimidate

**einsehen** *irr vt* (*understand*) see; (*error*) recognize; (*files*) have a look at

**einseitig** *adj* one-sided

**einsenden** *irr vt* send in

**einsetzen 1.** *vt* put in; (*to a post*) appoint; (*money*) stake; (*machine, troops etc*) use **2.** *vi* (*rain etc*) set in; MUS begin, come in **3.** *vr* work hard; **sich für jdn / etw ~** support sb/sth

**Einsicht** *f* insight; **zu der ~ kommen, dass …** come to realize that …

**einsperren** *vt* lock up

**einspielen** *vt* (*money*) bring in

**einspringen** *irr vi* (*help out*) step in (*für* for)

**Einspruch** *m* objection (*gegen* to)

**einspurig** *adj* single-lane

**Einstand** *m* (*in tennis*) deuce

**einstecken** *vt* pocket; ELEC plug in; (*letter*) post, mail (*US*); (*keys, passport etc*) take; (*accept*) swallow

**einsteigen** *irr vi* (*into car*) get in; (*onto bus, train, plane*) get on; (*in business, project*

*etc*) get involved

**einstellen 1.** *vt* (*end*) stop; (*device etc*) adjust; (*camera*) focus; (*station, radio*) tune in; (*car, bicycle etc*) put; (*worker*) employ, take on **2.** *vr* **sich auf jdn / etw ~** adapt to sb / prepare oneself for sth; **Einstellung** *f* (*of device etc*) adjustment; (*of camera*) focusing; (*of worker*) taking on; (*opinion*) attitude

**einstürzen** *vi* collapse

**eintägig** *adj* one-day

**eintauschen** *vt* exchange (*gegen* for)

**eintausend** *num* one (*or* a) thousand

**einteilen** *vt* divide (up) (*in* + *acc* into); (*time*) organize

**eintönig** *adj* monotonous

**Eintopf** *m* stew

**eintragen** *irr* **1.** *vt* (*in list*) put down, enter **2.** *vr* put one's name down, register

**eintreffen** *irr vi* happen; (*person, train, letter etc*) arrive

**eintreten** *irr vi* enter (*in etw acc* sth); (*club, party*) join (*in etw acc* sth); (*event*) occur; **~ für** support; **Eintritt** *m* admission; **‚~ frei‘** 'admission free'; **Eintrittskarte** *f* (*entrance*) ticket; **Eintrittspreis** *m* admission charge

**einverstanden 1.** *interj* okay, all right **2.** *adj* **mit etwas ~ sein** agree to sth, accept sth

**Einwanderer** *m*, **Einwanderin** *f* immigrant; **einwan-**

**dern** vi immigrate
**einwandfrei** adj perfect, flawless
**Einwegflasche** f non-returnable bottle
**einweichen** vt soak
**einweihen** vt (building) inaugurate, open; **jdn in etw** acc **~** let sb in on sth; **Einweihungsparty** f housewarming party
**einwerfen** irr vt (ball, remark etc) throw in; (letter) post, mail (US); (money) put in, insert; (window) smash
**einwickeln** vt wrap up; fig **jdn ~** take sb in
**Einwohner(in)** m(f) ⟨-s, -⟩ inhabitant; **Einwohnermeldeamt** nt registration office for residents
**Einwurf** m (opening) slot; SPORT throw-in
**Einzahl** f singular
**einzahlen** vt pay in (auf ein Konto to an account)
**Einzel** nt ⟨-s, -⟩ (in tennis) singles sg; **Einzelbett** nt single bed; **Einzelfahrschein** m single ticket (Brit), one--way ticket (US); **Einzelgänger(in)** m(f) loner; **Einzelhandel** m retail trade; **Einzelkind** nt only child
**einzeln 1.** adj individual; (not together) separate; (solitary) single; **~e ...** several ..., some ...; **der / die Einzelne** the individual; **im Einzelnen** in detail **2.** adv sepa-

rately; (pack, list) individually; **~ angeben** specify; **~ eintreten** enter one by one
**Einzelzimmer** nt single room; **Einzelzimmerzuschlag** m single-room supplement
**einziehen** irr **1.** vt **den Kopf ~** duck **2.** vi (into house) move in
**einzig 1.** adj only; (solitary) single; (special) unique; **kein ~er Fehler** not a single mistake; **das Einzige** the only thing; **der / die Einzige** the only person **2.** adv only; **die ~ richtige Lösung** the only correct solution; **einzigartig** adj unique
**Eis** nt ⟨-es, -⟩ ice; (food) ice--cream; **Eisbahn** f ice (-skating) rink; **Eisbär** m polar bear; **Eisbecher** m (ice-cream) sundae; **Eisberg** m iceberg; **Eisbergsalat** m iceberg lettuce; **Eiscafé** nt, **Eisdiele** f ice-cream parlour
**Eisen** nt ⟨-s, -⟩ iron; **Eisenbahn** f railway (Brit), railroad (US); **eisern** adj iron
**eisgekühlt** adj chilled; **Eishockey** nt ice hockey; **Eiskaffee** m iced coffee; **eiskalt** adj ice-cold; (temperature) freezing; **Eiskunstlauf** m figure skating; **eislaufen** irr vi skate; **Eisschokolade** f iced chocolate; **Eisschrank** m fridge, ice-box (US); **Eistee** m iced

tea; **Eiswürfel** m ice cube;
**Eiszapfen** m icicle
**eitel** adj vain
**Eiter** m ⟨-s⟩ pus
**Eiweiß** nt ⟨-es, -e⟩ egg white;
CHEM, BIO protein
**ekelhaft, ek(e)lig** adj disgusting, revolting; **ekeln** vr be
disgusted (vor + dat at)
**EKG** nt ⟨-s, -s⟩ abbr = **Elektro-
kardiogramm** ECG
**Ekzem** nt ⟨-s, -e⟩ MED eczema
**elastisch** adj elastic
**Elch** m ⟨-(e)s, -e⟩ elk; (North
American) moose
**Elefant** m elephant
**elegant** adj elegant
**Elektriker(in)** m(f) ⟨-s, -⟩
electrician; **elektrisch** adj
electric; **Elektrizität** f electricity; **Elektroauto** nt electric car; **Elektrogerät** nt
electrical appliance; **Elekt-
rogeschäft** nt electrical
shop; **Elektroherd** m electric cooker; **Elektromotor**
m electric motor; **Elektro-
nik** f electronics sg; **elektronisch** adj electronic; **Elekt-
rorasierer** m ⟨-s, -⟩ electric
razor
**Element** nt ⟨-s, -e⟩ element
**elend** adj miserable; **Elend** nt
⟨-(e)s⟩ misery
**elf** num eleven; **Elf** f ⟨-, -en⟩
SPORT eleven
**Elfenbein** nt ivory
**Elfmeter** m SPORT penalty
(kick)
**elfte(r, s)** adj eleventh; →

---

*dritte*
**Ell(en)bogen** m elbow
**Elster** f ⟨-, -n⟩ magpie
**Eltern** pl parents pl
**EM** f abbr = **Europameister-
schaft** European Champi-
onship(s)
**E-Mail** f ⟨-, -s⟩ IT e-mail; **jdm
eine ~ schicken** e-mail sb,
send sb an e-mail; **jdm etwas per ~ schicken** e-mail
sth to sb; **E-Mail-Adresse** f
e-mail address; **e-mailen** vt
e-mail
**Emoticon** nt ⟨-s, -s⟩ emoticon
**emotional** adj emotional
**empfahl** imperf → **empfehlen**
**empfand** imperf → **empfinden**
**Empfang** m ⟨-(e)s, Empfänge⟩
(party; in hotel, office) reception; (of letter, goods) receipt; **in ~ nehmen** receive;
**empfangen** ⟨empfing, emp-
fangen⟩ vt receive; **Empfän-
ger(in)** 1. m(f) ⟨-s, -⟩ recipient; addressee 2. m TECH receiver; **Empfängnisverhü-
tung** f contraception; **Emp-
fangshalle** f reception area
**empfehlen** ⟨empfahl, empfoh-
len⟩ vt recommend; **Emp-
fehlung** f recommendation
**empfinden** ⟨empfand, empfun-
den⟩ vt feel; **empfindlich** adj
(person) sensitive; (spot)
sore; (easily offended)
touchy; (material) delicate
**empfing** imperf → **empfan-**

*gen*

empfohlen *pp* → **empfehlen**

empfunden *pp* → **empfinden**

empört *adj* indignant (*über* + *acc* at)

Ende *nt* ⟨-s, -n⟩ end; (*of film, novel*) ending; **am ~** at the end; (*when all is said and done*) in the end; **~ Mai** at the end of May; **~ der Achtzigerjahre** in the late eighties; **sie ist ~ zwanzig** she's in her late twenties; **zu ~** over, finished; **enden** *vi* end; **der Zug endet hier** this service (*or train*) terminates here; **endgültig** *adj* final; (*proof*) conclusive

Endivie *f* endive

endlich *adv* at last, finally; (*in the end*) eventually; **Endspiel** *nt* final; (*last round*) finals *pl*; **Endstation** *f* terminus; **Endung** *f* ending

Energie *f* energy; **~ sparend** energy-saving; **Energiebedarf** *m* energy requirement; **Energieverbrauch** *m* energy consumption

energisch *adj* (*firm*) forceful

eng **1.** *adj* narrow; (*clothes*) tight; *fig* (*friendship, relationship*) close; **das wird ~** *fam* (*deadline*) we're running out of time, it's getting tight **2.** *adv* **~ befreundet sein** be close friends

engagieren **1.** *vt* engage **2.** *vr* commit oneself, be committed (*für* to)

Engel *m* ⟨-s, -⟩ angel

England *nt* England; Engländer(in) *m(f)* ⟨-s, -⟩ Englishman / -woman; **die ~** *pl* the English; **englisch** *adj* English; GASTR rare; Englisch *nt* English; **ins ~e übersetzen** translate into English

Enkel *m* ⟨-s, -⟩ grandson; Enkelin *f* granddaughter

enorm *adj* enormous; *fig* tremendous

Entbindung *f* MED delivery

entdecken *vt* discover; Entdeckung *f* discovery

Ente *f* ⟨-, -n⟩ duck

entfernen **1.** *vt* remove; IT delete **2.** *vr* go away; **entfernt** *adj* distant; **15 km von X ~** 15 km away from X; **20 km voneinander ~** 20 km apart; Entfernung *f* distance; **aus der ~** from a distance

entführen *vt* kidnap; Entführer(in) *m(f)* kidnapper; Entführung *f* kidnapping

entgegen **1.** *prep* + *dat* contrary to **2.** *adv* towards; **dem Wind ~** against the wind; **entgegengesetzt** *adj* (*direction*) opposite; (*view*) opposing; **entgegenkommen** *irr vi* **jdm ~** come to meet sb; *fig* accommodate sb; **entgegenkommend** *adj* (*traffic*) oncoming; *fig* obliging

entgegnen *vt* reply (*auf* + *acc* to)

entgehen *irr vi jdm* ~ escape sb's notice; *sich dat etw* ~ *lassen* miss sth

entgleisen *irr vi* RAIL be derailed; *fig* (*person*) misbehave

Enthaarungscreme *f* hair remover

enthalten *irr* 1. *vt* contain; (*price*) include 2. *vr* abstain (*gen from*)

entkoffeiniert *adj* decaffeinated

entkommen *irr vi* escape

entkorken *vt* uncork

entlang *prep* + *acc or dat* ~ *dem Fluss, den Fluss* ~ along the river; entlanggehen *irr vi* walk along

entlassen *irr vt* (*patient*) discharge; (*worker*) dismiss

entlasten *vt jdn* ~ relieve sb of some of his / her work

entmutigen *vt* discourage

entnehmen *vt* take (*dat* from)

entrahmt *adj* (*milk*) skimmed

entschädigen *vt* compensate; Entschädigung *f* compensation

entscheiden *irr vi, vi, vr* decide; *sich für / gegen etw* ~ decide on / against sth; *wir haben uns entschieden, nicht zu gehen* we decided not to go; *das entscheidet sich morgen* that'll be decided tomorrow; entscheidend *adj* decisive; (*question, problem*) crucial; Ent-

scheidung *f* decision

entschließen *irr vr* decide (*zu, für* on), make up one's mind; Entschluss *m* decision

entschuldigen 1. *vt* excuse 2. *vr* apologize; *sich bei jdm für etw* ~ apologize to sb for sth 3. *vi* entschuldige!, ~ *Sie!* (*introducing question*) excuse me; (*apology*) (I'm) sorry, excuse me (*US*); Entschuldigung *f* apology; (*justification*) excuse; *jdn um* ~ *bitten* apologize to sb; ~*!* (*colliding with sb*) (I'm) sorry, excuse me (*US*); (*introducing question*) excuse me; (*could you repeat that?*) (I beg your) pardon?

entsetzlich *adj* dreadful, appalling

entsorgen *vt* dispose of

entspannen 1. *vt* (*body*) relax; POL (*situation*) ease 2. *vr* relax; *fam* chill out; Entspannung *f* relaxation

entsprechen *irr vi* + *dat* correspond to; (*requirements, wishes etc*) comply with; entsprechend 1. *adj* appropriate 2. *adv* accordingly 3. *prep* + *dat* according to, in accordance with

entstehen *vi* (*difficulties*) arise; (*town, building etc*) be built; (*work of art*) be created

enttäuschen *vt* disappoint;

**Enttäuschung** f disappointment

**entweder** conj ~ ... **oder** ... either ... or ...; ~ **oder!** take it or leave it

**entwerfen** irr vt (furniture, clothes) design; (plan, contract) draft

**entwerten** vt devalue; (ticket) cancel; **Entwerter** m ⟨-s, -⟩ ticket-cancelling machine

**entwickeln** vt, vr a. PHOT develop; (courage, energy) show, display; **Entwicklung** f development; PHOT developing; **Entwicklungshelfer(in)** m(f) ⟨-s, -⟩ development worker; **Entwicklungsland** nt developing country

**Entwurf** m outline; (of product) design; (of contract, novel etc) draft

**entzückend** adj delightful, charming

**Entzug** m withdrawal; (treatment) detox; **Entzugserscheinung** f withdrawal symptom

**entzünden** vr catch fire; MED become inflamed; **Entzündung** f MED inflammation

**Epidemie** f ⟨-, -n⟩ epidemic

**Epilepsie** f ⟨-, -n⟩ epilepsy

**epilieren** vt remove body hair, depilate; **Epiliergerät** nt Ladyshave®

**er** pron he; (thing) it; ~ **ist's** it's him; **wo ist mein Mantel? - ~ ist ...** where's my coat? - it's ...

**Erbe 1.** m ⟨-n, -n⟩ heir **2.** nt ⟨-s⟩ inheritance; fig heritage; **erben** vt inherit; **Erbin** f heiress; **erblich** adj hereditary

**erbrechen** irr vt, vr vomit; **Erbrechen** nt vomiting

**Erbschaft** f inheritance

**Erbse** f ⟨-, -n⟩ pea

**Erdapfel** m potato; **Erdbeben** nt earthquake; **Erdbeere** f strawberry; **Erde** f ⟨-, -n⟩ (planet) earth; (earth's surface) ground; **Erdgas** nt natural gas; **Erdgeschoss** nt ground floor (Brit), first floor (US); **Erdkunde** f geography; **Erdnuss** f peanut; **Erdöl** nt (mineral) oil; **Erdrutsch** m landslide; **Erdteil** m continent

**ereignen** vr happen, take place; **Ereignis** nt event

**erfahren 1.** irr vt learn, find out; (feeling) experience **2.** adj experienced; **Erfahrung** f experience

**erfinden** irr vt invent; **erfinderisch** adj inventive, creative; **Erfindung** f invention

**Erfolg** m ⟨-(e)s, -e⟩ success; (consequence) result; ~ **versprechend** promising; **viel ~!** good luck; **erfolglos** adj unsuccessful; **erfolgreich** adj successful

**erforderlich** adj necessary

**erforschen** vt explore; (problem etc) investigate

**erfreulich** adj pleasing, pleas-

ant; (news) good; **erfreulicherweise** adv fortunately
**erfrieren** irr vi freeze to death; (plants) be killed by frost

**Erfrischung** f refreshment
**erfüllen 1.** vt (room) fill; (request, wish etc) fulfil **2.** vr come true

**ergänzen 1.** vt (remark) add; (collection etc) complete **2.** vr complement one another; **Ergänzung** f completion; (thing added) supplement

**ergeben 1.** irr vt (amount) come to; (lead to) result in **2.** irr vr surrender; (arise) result (aus from) **3.** adj devoted; (unassuming) humble

**Ergebnis** nt result
**ergreifen** irr vt seize; (career) take up; (measure, opportunity) take; (fill with pity etc) move

**erhalten** irr vt receive; (building, custom etc) preserve; **gut ~ sein** be in good condition; **erhältlich** adj available

**erheblich** adj considerable
**erhitzen** vt heat (up)
**erhöhen 1.** vt raise; (on amount, degree) increase **2.** vr increase

**erholen** vr recover; (relax) have a rest; **erholsam** adj restful; **Erholung** f recovery; (on holiday etc) relaxation, rest

**erinnern 1.** vt remind (an + acc of) **2.** vr remember

(an etw acc sth); **Erinnerung** f memory; (object) souvenir; (letter etc) reminder

**erkälten** vr catch a cold; **erkältet** adj (**stark**) **~ sein** have a (bad) cold; **Erkältung** f cold

**erkennen** irr vt recognize; (discern, understand) see; **~, dass ...** realize that ...; **erkenntlich** adj **sich ~ zeigen** show one's appreciation

**Erker** m ⟨-s, -⟩ bay
**erklären** vt explain; (announce) declare; **Erklärung** f explanation; (announcement) declaration

**erkundigen** vr enquire (nach about)

**erlauben** vt allow, permit; **jdm ~, etw zu tun** allow (or permit) sb to do sth; **sich dat etw ~** permit oneself sth; **~ Sie(, dass ich rauche)?** do you mind (if I smoke)?; **was ~ Sie sich?** what do you think you're doing?; **Erlaubnis** f permission

**Erläuterung** f explanation; (on text) comment

**erleben** vt experience; (pleasant time etc) have; (bad experience etc) go through; (scene etc) witness; (be still alive for) live to see; **Erlebnis** nt experience

**erledigen** vt (matter, task) deal with; (fam (exhaust) wear out; fam (ruin) finish; **erledigt** adj finished; (sorted *out*) dealt with; *fam* (*exhausted*) whacked, knackered (*Brit*)

**erleichtert** *adj* relieved

**Erlös** *m* ‹-es, -e› proceeds *pl*

**ermahnen** *vt* (*against sth*) warn

**ermäßigt** *adj* reduced; **Ermäßigung** *f* reduction

**ermitteln 1.** *vt* find out; (*culprit*) trace **2.** *vi* LAW investigate

**ermöglichen** *vt* make possible (*dat* for)

**ermorden** *vt* murder

**ermüdend** *adj* tiring

**ermutigen** *vt* encourage

**ernähren** *vt* feed; (*family*) support **2.** *vr* support oneself; *sich ~ von* live on; **Ernährung** *f* food; **Ernährungsberater(in)** *m(f)* nutritional (*or* dietary) adviser

**erneuern** *vt* renew; (*to original condition*) restore; (*to good condition*) renovate; (*with new one*) replace

**ernst 1.** *adj* serious **2.** *adv* **jdn / etw ~ nehmen** take sb/sth seriously; **Ernst** *m* ‹-es› seriousness; *das ist mein ~* I'm quite serious; *im ~?* seriously?; **ernsthaft 1.** *adj* serious **2.** *adv* seriously

**Ernte** *f* ‹-, -n› harvest; **Erntedankfest** *nt* harvest festival (*Brit*), Thanksgiving (Day) (*US*); **ernten** *vt* harvest; (*praise etc*) earn

**erobern** *vt* conquer

**eröffnen** *vt* open; **Eröffnung** *f* opening

**erogen** *adj* erogenous

**erotisch** *adj* erotic

**erpressen** *vt* (*person*) blackmail; (*money etc*) extort; **Erpressung** *f* blackmail; (*of money*) extortion

**erraten** *irr vt* guess

**erregen** *vt* excite; (*sexually*) arouse; (*make angry*) annoy; (*cause*) arouse **2.** *vr* get worked up; **Erreger** *m* ‹-s, -› MED germ; virus

**erreichbar** *adj* ~ *sein* be within reach; (*person*) be available; *das Stadtzentrum ist zu Fuß / mit dem Wagen leicht ~* the city centre is within easy walking / driving distance; **erreichen** *vt* reach; (*train etc*) catch

**Ersatz** *m* ‹-es› replacement; (*temporary*) substitute; (*for loss etc*) compensation; **Ersatzreifen** *m* AUTO spare tyre; **Ersatzteil** *nt* spare (part)

**erscheinen** *irr vi* appear; (*give impression*) seem

**erschöpft** *adj* exhausted; **Erschöpfung** *f* exhaustion

**erschrecken 1.** *vt* frighten **2.** ‹erschrak, erschrocken› *vi* get a fright; **erschreckend** *adj* alarming; **erschrocken** *adj* frightened

**erschwinglich** *adj* affordable

**ersetzen** *vt* replace; (*expens-*

**es**) reimburse

**erst** *adv* first; (*initially*) at first; (*as recently as, merely*) only; (*no earlier than*) not until; **~ jetzt / gestern** only now / yesterday; **~ morgen** not until tomorrow; **es ist ~ 10 Uhr** it's only ten o'clock; **~ recht** all the more; **~ recht nicht** even less

**erstatten** *vt* (*costs*) refund; **Bericht ~** report (**über** + *acc* on) **Anzeige gegen jdn ~** report sb to the police

**erstaunlich** *adj* astonishing; **erstaunt** *adj* surprised

**erstbeste(r, s)** *adj* **das ~ Hotel** any old hotel; **der Erstbeste** just anyone

**erste(r, s)** *adj* first; → **dritte zum ~n Mal** for the first time; **er wurde Erster** he came first; **auf den ~n Blick** at first sight

**erstens** *adv* first(ly), in the first place

**ersticken** *vi* (*person*) suffocate; **in Arbeit ~** be snowed under with work

**erstklassig** *adj* first-class

**erstmals** *adv* for the first time

**erstrecken** *vr* extend, stretch (**auf** + *acc* to; **über** + *acc* over)

**ertappen** *vt* catch

**erteilen** *vt* (*advice, permission*) give

**Ertrag** *m* ⟨-(e)s, Erträge⟩ yield; (*profit*) proceeds *pl*; **ertra-**

**gen** *irr vt* (*pain*) bear, stand; (*tolerate*) put up with; **erträglich** *adj* bearable; (*fairly good*) tolerable

**ertrinken** *irr vi* drown

**erwachsen** *adj* grown-up; **~ werden** grow up; **Erwachsene(r)** *mf* adult, grown-up

**erwähnen** *vt* mention

**erwarten** *vt* expect; wait for; **ich kann den Sommer kaum ~** I can hardly wait for the summer

**erwerbstätig** *adj* employed

**erwidern** *vt* reply; (*greeting, visit*) return

**erwischen** *vt fam* catch (**bei etw** doing sth)

**erwünscht** *adj* desired; (*person*) welcome

**Erz** *nt* ⟨-es, -e⟩ ore

**erzählen** *vt* tell (**jdm etw** sb sth); **Erzählung** *f* story, tale

**erzeugen** *vt* produce; (*electricity*) generate; **Erzeugnis** *nt* product

**erziehen** *irr vt* bring up; (*intellectually*) educate; (*animal*) train; **Erzieher(in)** *m(f)* ⟨-s, -⟩ educator; (*in kindergarten*) nursery school teacher; **Erziehung** *f* upbringing; (*intellectual*) education

**es** *pron* it; (*baby, animal*) he / she; **ich bin ~** it's me; **~ ist kalt** it's cold; **~ gibt ...** there is .../there are ...; **ich hoffe ~** I hope so; **ich kann ~** I can do it

**Escape-Taste** f IT escape key

**Esel** m ⟨-s, -⟩ donkey

**Espresso** m ⟨-s, -⟩ espresso

**essbar** adj edible; **essen** ⟨aß, gegessen⟩ vt, vi eat; **zu Mittag / Abend** ~ have lunch / dinner; **was gibt's zu** ~? what's for lunch / dinner?; ~ **gehen** go out to eat; **Essen** nt ⟨-s, -⟩ meal; food

**Essig** m ⟨-s, -e⟩ vinegar

**Esslöffel** m dessert spoon; **Esszimmer** nt dining room

**Estland** nt Estonia

**Etage** f ⟨-, -n⟩ floor, storey; **in** (or **auf**) **der ersten** ~ on the first (Brit) (or second (US)) floor; **Etagenbett** nt bunk bed

**Etappe** f ⟨-, -n⟩ stage

**ethnisch** adj ethnic

**Etikett** nt ⟨-(e)s, -e⟩ label

**etliche** pron pl several, quite a few; **etliches** pron quite a lot

**etwa** adv (approximation) about; (possibility) perhaps; (example) for instance

**etwas 1.** pron something; (with negative, question) anything; (small amount) a little; ~ **Neues** something / anything new; ~ **zu essen** something to eat; ~ **Salz** some salt; **wenn ich noch** ~ **tun kann ...** if I can do anything else ... **2.** adv a bit, a little; ~ **mehr** a little more

**EU** f ⟨-⟩ abbr = **Europäische Union** EU

**euch** pron acc, dat → **ihr;** you, (to) you; ~ (**selbst**) yourselves; **wo kann ich** ~ **treffen?** where can I meet you?; **sie schickt es** ~ she'll send it to you; **ein Freund von** ~ a friend of yours; **setzt** ~ **bitte** please sit down; **habt ihr** ~ **amüsiert?** did you enjoy yourselves?

**euer** (as adj) your; ~ **David** (at end of letter) Yours, David; **euere(r, s)** pron → **eure**

**Eule** f ⟨-, -n⟩ owl

**eure(r, s)** pron (as noun) yours; **das ist** ~ that's yours; **euretwegen** adv because of you; (to please you) for your sake

**Euro** m ⟨-, -⟩ (currency) euro; **Eurocent** m eurocent; **Eurocity** m ⟨-(s), -s⟩, **Eurocityzug** m European Intercity train; **Europa** nt ⟨-s⟩ Europe; **Europäer(in)** m(f) ⟨-s, -⟩ European; **europäisch** adj European; **Europäische Union** European Union; **Europameister(in)** m(f) European champion; (team) European champions pl; **Europaparlament** nt European Parliament

**Euter** nt ⟨-s, -⟩ udder

**evangelisch** adj Protestant

**eventuell 1.** adj possible **2.** adv possibly, perhaps

**ewig** adj eternal; **er hat** ~ **gebraucht** it took him ages;

**Ewigkeit** f eternity

**Ex** mf ex; **Ex-** in cpds ex-, former; **Exfrau** f ex-wife; **Exfreund** m ex-boyfriend; **Exminister** m former minister

**exakt** adj precise

**Examen** nt ⟨-s, -⟩ exam

**Exemplar** nt ⟨-s, -e⟩ specimen; (book) copy

**Exil** nt ⟨-s, -e⟩ exile

**Existenz** f existence; (financial means) livelihood, living; **existieren** vi exist

**exklusiv** adj exclusive; **exklusive** adv, prep + gen excluding

**exotisch** adj exotic

**Experte** m ⟨-n, -n⟩, **Expertin** f expert

**explodieren** vi explode; **Explosion** f explosion

**Export** m ⟨-(e)s, -e⟩ export; **exportieren** vt export

**Express** m ⟨-es⟩, **Expresszug** m express (train)

**extra 1.** adj inv fam separate; (additional) extra **2.** adv separately; (for particular person or purpose) specially; (intentionally) on purpose; **Extra** nt ⟨-s, -s⟩ extra

**extrem 1.** adj extreme **2.** adv extremely; **~ kalt** extremely cold

**exzellent** adj excellent

**Eyeliner** m ⟨-s, -⟩ eyeliner

# F

**fabelhaft** adj fabulous, marvellous

**Fabrik** f factory

**Fach** nt ⟨-(e)s, Fächer⟩ compartment; (area of knowledge) subject; **Facharzt** m, **Fachärztin** f specialist; **Fachausdruck** m ⟨-s, Fachausdrücke⟩ technical term

**Fächer** m ⟨-s, -⟩ fan

**Fachfrau** f specialist, expert; **Fachmann** m ⟨-leute pl⟩ specialist, expert; **Fachwerkhaus** nt half-timbered house

**Fackel** f ⟨-, -n⟩ torch

**fad(e)** adj (food) bland; (boring) dull

**Faden** m ⟨-s, Fäden⟩ thread

**fähig** adj capable (zu, gen of); **Fähigkeit** f ability

**Fahndung** f search

**Fahne** f ⟨-, -n⟩ flag

**Fahrausweis** m ticket

**Fahrbahn** f road; (between lines) lane

**Fähre** f ⟨-, -n⟩ ferry

**fahren** ⟨fuhr, gefahren⟩ **1.** vt drive; (bicycle) ride; (convey) drive, take; **50 km/h ~** drive at (or do) 50 kph **2.** vi go; (in car) drive; (ship) sail; (depart) leave; **mit dem Auto / Zug ~** go by car / train; **rechts ~!** keep to the right; **Fahrer(in)** m(f) ⟨-s, -⟩ driver; **Fahrer-**

flucht f ~ **begehen** fail to stop after an accident; **Fahrersitz** m driver's seat

**Fahrgast** m passenger; **Fahrgeld** nt fare; **Fahrgemeinschaft** f car pool; **Fahrkarte** f ticket

**Fahrkartenautomat** m ticket machine; **Fahrkartenschalter** m ticket office

**fahrlässig** adj negligent

**Fahrlehrer(in)** m(f) driving instructor; **Fahrplan** m timetable; **Fahrpreis** m fare; **Fahrpreisermäßigung** f fare reduction

**Fahrrad** nt bicycle; **Fahrradschloss** nt bicycle lock; **Fahrradverleih** m cycle hire (Brit) (or rental (US)); **Fahrradweg** m cycle path

**Fahrschein** m ticket; **Fahrscheinautomat** m ticket machine; **Fahrscheinentwerter** m ticket-cancelling machine

**Fahrschule** f driving school; **Fahrschüler(in)** m(f) learner (driver) (Brit), student driver (US)

**Fahrstuhl** m lift (Brit), elevator (US)

**Fahrt** f ⟨-, -en⟩ journey; (short) trip; AUTO drive; **auf der ~ nach London** on the way to London; **nach drei Stunden** ~ after travelling for three hours; **gute ~!** have a good trip; **Fahrtkosten** pl travelling expenses pl

**fahrtüchtig** f (person) fit to drive; (vehicle) roadworthy

**Fahrtunterbrechung** f break in the journey, stop

**Fahrverbot** nt ~ **erhalten / haben** be banned from driving; **Fahrzeug** nt vehicle; **Fahrzeugbrief** m (vehicle) registration document; **Fahrzeughalter(in)** m(f) registered owner; **Fahrzeugpapiere** pl vehicle documents pl

**fair** adj fair

**Fakultät** f faculty

**Falke** m ⟨-n, -n⟩ falcon

**Fall** m ⟨-(e)s, Fälle⟩ (accident) fall; (instance, in law) case; **auf jeden ~, auf alle Fälle** in any case; (without fail) definitely; **auf keinen ~** on no account; **für den ~, dass** ... in case ...

**Falle** f ⟨-, -n⟩ trap

**fallen** ⟨fiel, gefallen⟩ vi fall; **etw ~ lassen** drop sth

**fällig** adj due

**falls** adv if; (allowing for eventuality) in case

**Fallschirm** m parachute; **Fallschirmspringen** nt parachuting, parachute jumping; **Fallschirmspringer(in)** m(f) parachutist

**falsch** adj wrong; (dishonest, not genuine) false; ~ **verbunden** sorry, wrong number; ~ **verbunden** sorry, wrong number; **fälschen** vt forge; **Falschgeld** nt counterfeit money; **Fälschung** f forgery, fake

**Faltblatt** nt leaflet

**Falte** f ⟨-, -n⟩ fold; (in skin) wrinkle; (in skirt) pleat; **falten** vt fold; **faltig** adj creased; (skin, face) wrinkled

**Familie** f family; **Familienangehörige(r)** mf family member; **Familienname** m surname; **Familienstand** m marital status

**Fan** m ⟨-s, -s⟩ fan

**fand** imperf → **finden**

**fangen** ⟨fing, gefangen⟩ **1.** vt catch **2.** vr (not fall) steady oneself; fig compose oneself

**Fantasie** f imagination

**fantastisch** adj fantastic

**Farbe** f ⟨-, -n⟩ colour; (substance) paint; (for fabric) dye; **färben** vt colour; (fabric, hair) dye; **Farbfilm** m colour film; **farbig** adj coloured; **Farbkopierer** m colour copier; **Farbstoff** m dye; (for food) colouring

**Farn** m ⟨-(e)s, -e⟩ fern

**Fasan** m ⟨-(e)s, -e(n)⟩ pheasant

**Fasching** m ⟨-s, -e⟩ carnival, Mardi Gras (US); **Faschingsdienstag** m ⟨-s, -e⟩ Shrove Tuesday, Mardi Gras (US)

**Faschismus** m fascism

**Faser** f ⟨-, -n⟩ fibre

**Fass** nt ⟨-, Fässer⟩ barrel; (for oil) drum

**fassen 1.** vt (take hold of) grasp; (be able to contain) hold; (decision) take; (comprehend) understand; **nicht zu ~!** unbelievable **2.** vr compose oneself; **Fassung** f (of jewel) mount; (of glasses) frame; (of lamp) socket; (of text) version; (self-control) composure; **jdn aus der ~ bringen** throw sb; **die ~ verlieren** lose one's cool

**fast** adv almost, nearly

**fasten** vi fast; **Fastenzeit** f **die ~** (Christian) Lent; (Muslim) Ramadan

**Fast Food** nt ⟨-s⟩ fast food

**Fastnacht** f carnival

**faul** adj (fruit, vegetables) rotten; (person) lazy; (excuse) lame; **faulen** vi rot

**faulenzen** vi do nothing, hang around; **Faulheit** f laziness

**faulig** adj rotten; (smell, taste) foul

**Faust** f ⟨-, Fäuste⟩ fist; **Fausthandschuh** m mitten

**Fax** nt ⟨-, -(e)⟩ fax; **faxen** vi, vt fax; **Faxgerät** nt fax machine; **Faxnummer** f fax number

**FCKW** nt ⟨-s, -s⟩ abbr = **Fluorchlorkohlenwasserstoff** CFC

**Februar** m ⟨-(s), -e⟩ February; → **Juni**

**Fechten** nt fencing

**Feder** f ⟨-, -n⟩ feather; (for writing) (pen-)nib; TECH spring; **Federball** m shuttle-

cock; (*game*) badminton;
**Federung** f suspension
**Fee** f ⟨-, -n⟩ fairy
**fegen** vi, vt sweep
**fehlen** vi (*from school etc*) to be
absent; *etw fehlt jdm* sb
lacks sth; *was fehlt ihm?*
what's wrong with him?;
*du fehlst mir* I miss you;
*es fehlt an ...* there's no...
**Fehler** m ⟨-s, -⟩ mistake, error;
(*defect, failing*) fault; **Fehlermeldung** f IT error message
**Fehlzündung** f AUTO misfire
**Feier** f ⟨-, -n⟩ celebration;
(*get-together*) party; **feierlich** adj solemn; **feiern** vt,
vi celebrate, have a party;
**Feiertag** m holiday; **gesetzlicher ~** public (or bank
(*Brit*) or legal (*US*)) holiday
**feig(e)** adj cowardly
**Feige** f ⟨-, -n⟩ fig
**Feigling** m coward
**Feile** f ⟨-, -n⟩ file
**fein** adj fine; (*gentleman,
manners*) refined
**Feind(in)** m(f) ⟨-(e)s, -e⟩ enemy; **feindlich** adj hostile
**Feinkost** f ⟨-⟩ delicacies pl;
**Feinkostladen** m delicates-
sen
**Feinstaub** m particulate mat-
ter
**Feinwaschmittel** nt washing
powder for delicate fabrics
**Feld** nt ⟨-(e)s, -er⟩ field; (*in
chess*) square; SPORT pitch;
**Feldweg** m path across the

fields
**Felge** f ⟨-, -n⟩ (wheel) rim
**Fell** nt ⟨-(e)s, -e⟩ fur; (*of sheep*)
fleece
**Fels** m ⟨-en, -en⟩, **Felsen** m ⟨-s,
-⟩ rock; (*rock face*) cliff; **fel-
sig** adj rocky
**feministisch** adj feminist
**Fenchel** m ⟨-s, -⟩ fennel
**Fenster** nt ⟨-s, -⟩ window;
**Fensterbrett** nt windowsill;
**Fensterladen** m shutter;
**Fensterplatz** m window-
seat; **Fensterscheibe** f windowpane
**Ferien** pl holidays pl (*Brit*),
vacation sg (*US*); **~ haben / machen** be/go on holiday (*Brit*) (or vacation
(*US*)); **Ferienhaus** nt holiday (*Brit*) (or vacation
(*US*)) home; **Ferienkurs** m
holiday (*Brit*) (or vacation
(*US*)) course; **Ferienlager**
nt holiday camp (*Brit*), vacation camp (*US*); (*for children in summer*) summer
camp; **Ferienort** m holiday
(*Brit*) (or vacation (*US*)) resort; **Ferienwohnung** f holiday flat (*Brit*), vacation
apartment (*US*)
**Ferkel** nt ⟨-s, -⟩ piglet
**fern** adj distant, far-off; **von ~**
from a distance; **Fernabfra-
ge** f remote-control access;
**Fernbedienung** f remote
control; **Ferne** f distance;
*aus der ~* from a distance
**ferner** adj, adv further; (*in ad-*

dition) besides
**Fernflug** m long-distance flight; **Ferngespräch** nt long-distance call; **ferngesteuert** adj remote-controlled; **Fernglas** nt binoculars pl; **Fernlicht** nt full beam (Brit), high beam (US)
**fernsehen** irr vi watch television; **Fernsehen** nt television; **im ~** on television; **Fernseher** m TV (set); **Fernsehkanal** m TV channel; **Fernsehprogramm** nt TV programme; (magazine) TV guide; **Fernsehserie** f TV series sg; **Fernsehturm** m TV tower
**Fernstraße** f major road; **Fernverkehr** m long-distance traffic
**Ferse** f ⟨-, -n⟩ heel
**fertig** adj ready; (completed) finished; **~ machen** (task etc) finish; **sich ~ machen** get ready; **mit etw ~ werden** be able to cope with sth; **auf die Plätze, ~, los!** on your marks, get set, go!; **Fertiggericht** nt ready meal; **fertigmachen** vt (criticize) give sb hell; (annoy) drive sb mad
**fest** adj firm; (food) solid; (salary) regular; (shoes) sturdy; (sleep) sound
**Fest** nt ⟨-(e)s, -e⟩ party; REL festival
**Festbetrag** m fixed amount
**festbinden** irr vt tie (an + dat

to); **festhalten** irr **1.** vt hold onto **2.** vr hold on (an + dat to)
**Festival** nt ⟨-s, -s⟩ festival
**Festland** nt mainland
**festlegen 1.** vt fix **2.** vr commit oneself
**festlich** adj festive
**festmachen** vt fasten; (date etc) fix; **festnehmen** irr vt arrest
**Festnetz** nt TEL fixed-line network; **Festplatte** f IT hard disk
**festsetzen** vt fix
**Festspiele** pl festival sg
**feststehen** irr vi be fixed
**feststellen** vt establish; (say) remark
**Festung** f fortress
**Festzelt** nt marquee
**Fete** f ⟨-, -n⟩ party
**fett** adj (person) fat; (food etc) greasy; (type) bold; **Fett** nt ⟨-(e)s, -e⟩ fat; TECH grease; **fettarm** adj low-fat; **fettig** adj fatty; (dirty) greasy
**feucht** adj damp; (air) humid; **Feuchtigkeit** f dampness; (of air) humidity; **Feuchtigkeitscreme** f moisturizing cream
**Feuer** nt ⟨-s, -⟩ fire; **haben Sie ~?** have you got a light?; **Feueralarm** m fire alarm; **feuerfest** adj fireproof; **Feuerlöscher** m ⟨-s, -⟩ fire extinguisher; **Feuermelder** m ⟨-s, -⟩ fire alarm; **Feuertreppe** f fire escape; **Feuerwehr** f ⟨-,

-en⟩ fire brigade; **Feuerwerk** nt fireworks pl; **Feuerzeug** nt (cigarette) lighter

**Fichte** f ⟨-, -n⟩ spruce

**ficken** vt, vi vulg fuck

**Fieber** nt ⟨-s, -⟩ temperature, fever; **~ haben** have a high temperature; **Fieberthermometer** nt thermometer

**fiel** imperf → **fallen**

**fies** adj fam nasty

**Figur** f ⟨-, -en⟩ figure; (in chess) piece

**Filet** nt ⟨-s, -s⟩ fillet

**Filiale** f ⟨-, -n⟩ COMM branch

**Film** m ⟨-(e)s, -e⟩ film, movie; **filmen** vt, vi film

**Filter** m ⟨-s, -⟩ filter; **Filterkaffee** m filter coffee; **filtern** vt filter; **Filterpapier** nt filter paper

**Filz** m ⟨-es, -e⟩ felt; **Filzschreiber** m, **Filzstift** m felt(-tip) pen, felt-tip

**Finale** nt ⟨-s, -⟩ SPORT final

**Finanzamt** nt tax office; **finanziell** adj financial; **finanzieren** vt finance

**finden** ⟨fand, gefunden⟩ vt find; (have opinion) think; **ich finde nichts dabei, wenn ...** I don't see what's wrong if ...; **ich finde es gut / schlecht** I like / don't like it

**fing** imperf → **fangen**

**Finger** m ⟨-s, -⟩ finger; **Fingerabdruck** m fingerprint; **Fingernagel** m fingernail

**Fink** m ⟨-en, -en⟩ finch

**Finne** m ⟨-n, -n⟩, **Finnin** f Finn, Finnish man / woman; **finnisch** adj Finnish; **Finnisch** nt Finnish; **Finnland** nt Finland

**finster** adj dark; (suspicious) dubious; (morose) grim; (thought) dark; **Finsternis** f darkness

**Firewall** f ⟨-, -s⟩ IT firewall

**Firma** f ⟨-, Firmen⟩ firm

**Fisch** m ⟨-(e)s, -e⟩ fish; **~e** pl ASTR Pisces sg; **fischen** vt, vi fish; **Fischer(in)** m(f) ⟨-s, -⟩ fisherman / -woman; **Fischerboot** nt fishing boat; **Fischgericht** nt fish dish; **Fischhändler(in)** m(f) fishmonger; **Fischstäbchen** nt fish finger (Brit) (or stick (US))

**Fisole** f ⟨-, -n⟩ French bean

**fit** adj fit; **Fitness** f ⟨-⟩ fitness; **Fitnesscenter** nt ⟨-s, -⟩ fitness centre; **Fitnesstrainer(in)** m(f) fitness trainer, personal trainer

**fix** adj quick; **~ und fertig** exhausted

**fixen** vi fam shoot up; **Fixer(in)** m(f) ⟨-s, -⟩ fam junkie

**FKK** f abbr = **Freikörperkultur** nudism; **FKK-Strand** m nudist beach

**flach** adj flat; (water, plate) shallow; **~er Absatz** low heel; **Flachbildschirm** m flat screen

**Fläche** f ⟨-, -n⟩ area; (of ob-

*ject*) surface

**Flagge** *f* ⟨-, -n⟩ flag

**flambiert** *adj* flambé(ed)

**Flamme** *f* ⟨-, -n⟩ flame

**Flasche** *f* ⟨-, -n⟩ bottle; *eine ~ sein fam* be useless; **Flaschenöffner** *m* bottle opener; **Flaschenpfand** *nt* deposit

**flatterhaft** *adj* fickle; **flattern** *vi* flutter

**flauschig** *adj* fluffy

**Flaute** *f* ⟨-, -n⟩ calm; COMM recession

**Flechte** *f* ⟨-, -n⟩ plait; MED scab; BOT lichen; **flechten** ⟨flocht, geflochten⟩ *vt* plait; (*wreath*) bind

**Fleck** *m* ⟨-(e)s, -e⟩, **Flecken** ⟨-s, -⟩ spot; (*dirt*) stain; **Fleckentferner** *m* ⟨-s, -⟩ stain remover; **fleckig** *adj* spotted; (*with dirt*) stained

**Fledermaus** *f* bat

**Fleisch** *nt* ⟨-(e)s⟩ flesh; (*food*) meat

**Fleischbrühe** *f* meat stock

**Fleischer(in)** *m(f)* ⟨-s, -⟩ butcher; **Fleischerei** *f* butcher's (shop)

**fleißig** *adj* diligent, hard-working

**flexibel** *adj* flexible

**flicken** *vt* mend; **Flickzeug** *nt* repair kit

**Flieder** *m* ⟨-s, -⟩ lilac

**Fliege** *f* ⟨-, -n⟩ fly; (*clothing*) bow tie

**fliegen** ⟨flog, geflogen⟩ *vt, vi* fly

**Fliese** *f* ⟨-, -n⟩ tile

**Fließband** *nt* conveyor belt; (*system*) production (*or* assembly) line; **fließen** ⟨floss, geflossen⟩ *vi* flow; **fließend** *adj* (*speech, German*) fluent; (*transition*) smooth; *~(es) Wasser* running water

**flippig** *adj fam* eccentric

**flirten** *vi* flirt

**Flitterwochen** *pl* honeymoon *sg*

**flocht** *imperf* → **flechten**

**Flocke** *f* ⟨-, -n⟩ flake

**flog** *imperf* → **fliegen**

**Floh** *m* ⟨-(e)s, Flöhe⟩ flea; **Flohmarkt** *m* flea market

**Flop** *m* ⟨-s, -s⟩ flop

**Floskel** *f* ⟨-, -n⟩ empty phrase

**floss** *imperf* → **fließen**

**Floß** *nt* ⟨-es, Flöße⟩ raft

**Flosse** *f* ⟨-, -n⟩ fin; (*of swimmer*) flipper

**Flöte** *f* ⟨-, -n⟩ flute; (*held vertically*) recorder

**Fluch** *m* ⟨-(e)s, Flüche⟩ curse; **fluchen** *vi* swear, curse

**Flucht** *f* ⟨-, -en⟩ flight; **flüchten** *vi* flee (*vor + dat* from); **flüchtig** *adj ich kenne ihn nur ~* I don't know him very well at all; **Flüchtling** *m* refugee

**Flug** *m* ⟨-(e)s, Flüge⟩ flight; **Flugbegleiter(in)** *m(f)* ⟨-s, -⟩ flight attendant; **Flugblatt** *nt* leaflet

**Flügel** *m* ⟨-s, -⟩ wing; MUS grand piano

**Fluggast** *m* passenger (*on a*

*plane*); **Fluggesellschaft** *f* airline; **Flughafen** *m* airport; **Fluglotse** *m* air-traffic controller; **Flugnummer** *f* flight number; **Flugplan** *m* flight schedule; **Flugplatz** *m* airport; (*small*) airfield; **Flugschein** *m* plane ticket; **Flugschreiber** *m* flight recorder, black box; **Flugsteig** *m* ⟨-s, -e⟩ gate; **Flugticket** *nt* plane ticket; **Flugverbindung** *f* flight connection; **Flugverkehr** *m* air traffic; **Flugzeit** *f* flying time; **Flugzeug** *nt* plane; **Flugzeugentführung** *f* hijacking

**Flunder** *f* ⟨-, -n⟩ flounder

**Fluor** *nt* ⟨-s⟩ fluorine

**Flur** *m* ⟨-(e)s, -e⟩ hall

**Fluss** *m* ⟨-es, Flüsse⟩ river; (*movement*) flow

**flüssig** *adj* liquid; **Flüssigkeit** *f* ⟨-, -en⟩ liquid; **Flüssigseife** *f* liquid soap

**flüstern** *vt, vi* whisper

**Flut** *f* ⟨-, -en⟩ flood; (*in sea*) high tide; **Flutlicht** *nt* floodlight

**Fohlen** *nt* ⟨-s, -⟩ foal

**Föhn** *m* ⟨-(e)s, -e⟩ hairdryer; (*wind*) foehn; **föhnen** *vt* dry; (*at hairdresser's*) blow-dry

**Folge** *f* ⟨-, -n⟩ (*one after another*) series *sg*; (*belonging together*) sequence; (*of novel*) instalment; (*of TV series*) episode; (*consequence*) result; **~n haben** have conse-

quences; **folgen** *vi* follow (*jdm* sb); (*do as told*) obey (*jdm* sb); **jdm ~ können** *fig* be able to follow sb; **folgend** *adj* following; **folgendermaßen** *adv* as follows; **folglich** *adv* consequently

**Folie** *f* foil; (*for projector*) transparency

**Fön®** *m* → **Föhn**

**Fondue** *nt* ⟨-s, -s⟩ fondue

**fönen** *vt* → **föhnen**

**fordern** *vt* demand

**fördern** *vt* promote; (*support*) help

**Forderung** *f* demand

**Forelle** *f* trout

**Form** *f* ⟨-, -en⟩ form; (*outer form*) shape; (*for casting*) mould; (*for baking*) baking tin (*Brit*) (*or* pan (*US*)); **in ~ sein** be in good form; **Formalität** *f* formality; **Format** *nt* format; **formatieren** *vt* (*disk*) format; (*text*) format; **formen** *vt* form, shape; **förmlich** *adj* formal; (*proper*) real; **formlos** *adj* informal; **Formular** *nt* ⟨-s, -e⟩ form; **formulieren** *vt* formulate

**forschen** *vi* search (*nach* for); (*academic*) do research; **Forscher(in)** *m(f)* researcher; **Forschung** *f* research

**Förster(in)** *m(f)* ⟨-s, -⟩ forester; (*for animals*) gamekeeper

**fort** *adv* away; (*missing*) gone; **fortbewegen 1.** *vt* move away **2.** *vr* move; **Fortbildung** *f* further education; (*vocational*) further training; **fortfahren** *irr vi* go away; (*carry on*) continue; **fortgehen** *irr vi* go away; **fortgeschritten** *adj* advanced; **Fortpflanzung** *f* reproduction

**Fortschritt** *m* progress; **~e machen** make progress; **fortschrittlich** *adj* progressive

**fortsetzen** *vt* continue; **Fortsetzung** *f* continuation; (*episode*) instalment; **~ folgt** to be continued

**Foto 1.** *nt* ⟨-s, -s⟩ photo **2.** *m* ⟨-s, -s⟩ camera; **Fotograf(in)** *m(f)* ⟨-en, -en⟩ photographer; **Fotografie** *f* photography; (*picture*) photograph; **fotografieren 1.** *vt* photograph **2.** *vi* take photographs; **Fotohandy** *nt* camera phone; **Fotokopie** *f* photocopy; **fotokopieren** *vt* photocopy

**Foul** *nt* ⟨-s, -s⟩ foul

**Foyer** *nt* ⟨-s, -s⟩ foyer

**Fr.** *f abbr* → **Frau** Mrs; (*unmarried, neutral*) Ms

**Fracht** *f* ⟨-, -en⟩ freight; NAUT cargo; **Frachter** *m* ⟨-s, -⟩ freighter

**Frack** *m* ⟨-(e)s, Fräcke⟩ tails *pl*

**Frage** *f* ⟨-, -n⟩ question; *das ist eine ~ der Zeit* that's a matter (*or* question) of time; **Fragebogen** *m* questionnaire; **fragen** *vt, vi* ask; **Fragezeichen** *nt* question mark; **fragwürdig** *adj* dubious

**Franken 1.** *m* ⟨-s, -⟩ Swiss franc **2.** *nt* ⟨-s⟩ (*region*) Franconia

**frankieren** *vt* stamp; (*with machine*) frank

**Frankreich** *nt* ⟨-s⟩ France; **Franzose** *m*, **Französin** *f* Frenchman / -woman; **die ~n** *pl* the French *pl*; **französisch** *adj* French; **Französisch** *nt* French

**fraß** *imperf* → **fressen**

**Frau** *f* ⟨-, -en⟩ woman; (*spouse*) wife; (*form of address*) Mrs; (*unmarried, neutral*) Ms; **Frauenarzt** *m*, **Frauenärztin** *f* gynaecologist

**Fräulein** *nt* young lady; (*old-fashioned form of address*) Miss

**Freak** *m* ⟨-s, -s⟩ *fam* freak

**frech** *adj* cheeky; **Frechheit** *f* cheek; *so eine ~!* what a cheek

**Freeclimbing** *nt* ⟨-s⟩ free climbing

**frei** *adj* free; (*road*) clear; (*worker*) freelance; *ein ~er Tag* a day off; *~e Arbeitsstelle* vacancy; *Zimmer ~* room(s) to let (*Brit*), room(s) for rent (*US*); *im Freien* in the open air

**Freibad** *nt* open-air (swimming) pool; **freiberuflich**

*adj* freelance; **freig(i)ebig**
*adj* generous; **Freiheit** *f* freedom; **Freikarte** *f* free ticket;
**freilassen** *irr vt* (set) free
**freilich** *adv* of course
**Freilichtbühne** *f* open-air
theatre; **freimachen** *vr* undress; **freinehmen** *irr vt*
**sich** *dat* **einen Tag** ~ take a
day off; **Freisprechanlage**
*f* hands-free phone; **Freistoß** *m* free kick
**Freitag** *m* Friday; → **Mittwoch**; **freitags** *adv* on Fri-
days; → **mittwochs**
**freiwillig** *adj* voluntary
**Freizeit** *f* spare (*or* free) time;
**Freizeithemd** *nt* sports
shirt; **Freizeitkleidung** *f* leisure wear; **Freizeitpark** *m*
leisure park
**fremd** *adj* (*unfamiliar*)
strange; (*of another country*)
foreign; (*not one's own*)
someone else's; (*from another
country*) foreign; **Fremde(r)**
*mf* stranger; (*from another
country*) foreigner; **Frem-
denführer(in)** *m(f)* (*tourist*)
guide; **Fremdenverkehr** *m*
tourism; **Fremdenverkehrsamt** *nt* tourist information
office; **Fremdsprache** *f* foreign language; **Fremdspra-
chenkenntnisse** *pl* knowledge *sg* of foreign lan-
guages; **Fremdwort** *nt* foreign word
**Frequenz** *f* RADIO frequency
**fressen** ⟨fraß, gefressen⟩ *vt, vi*
(*animal*) eat; (*person*) guz-
zle

**Freude** *f* ⟨-, -n⟩ joy, delight;
**freuen 1.** *vt* please; **es freut
mich, dass …** I'm pleased
that … **2.** *vr* be pleased
(*über +* acc *about*); **sich
auf etw** acc ~ look forward
to sth
**Freund** *m* ⟨-(e)s, -e⟩ friend; (*in
relationship*) boyfriend;
**Freundin** *f* friend; (*in relationship*) girlfriend; **freundlich** *adj* friendly; (*helpful
etc*) kind; **freundlicherwei-
se** *adv* kindly; **Freundschaft** *f* friendship
**Frieden** *m* ⟨-s, -⟩ peace; **Friedhof** *m* cemetery; **friedlich**
*adj* peaceful
**frieren** ⟨fror, gefroren⟩ *vt, vi*
freeze; **ich friere, es friert
mich** I'm freezing
**Frikadelle** *f* ⟨-, -n⟩ rissole
**Frisbee®** *nt*, **Frisbeeschei-
be®** *f* frisbee®
**frisch** *adj* fresh; (*full of life*)
lively; „~ **gestrichen**" 'wet
paint'; **sich ~ machen** fresh-
en up; **Frischhaltefolie** *f*
clingfilm® (*Brit*), plastic
wrap (*US*); **Frischkäse** *m*
cream cheese
**Friseur(in)** ⟨-s, -e⟩ *m(f)* hairdresser; **frisieren 1.** *vt jdn*
~ do sb's hair **2.** *vr* do one's
hair
**Frist** *f* ⟨-, -en⟩ period; (*last
date*) deadline; **innerhalb einer** ~ **von zehn Tagen** within
a ten-day period; **eine** ~ **ein-**

*halten* meet a deadline; *die ~ ist abgelaufen* the deadline has expired; **fristlos** *adj ~e Entlassung* dismissal without notice

**Frisur** *f* hairdo, hairstyle

**frittieren** *vt* deep-fry

**Frl.** *f abbr* → *Fräulein* Miss

**froh** *adj* happy; *~e Weihnachten!* Merry Christmas

**fröhlich** *adj* happy, cheerful

**fror** *imperf* → *frieren*

**Frosch** *m* ⟨-(e)s, Frösche⟩ frog

**Frost** *m* ⟨-(e)s, Fröste⟩ frost; *bei ~* in frosty weather; **Frostschutzmittel** *nt* anti-freeze

**Frottee** *nt* terry(cloth); **Frottier(hand)tuch** *nt* towel

**Frucht** *f* ⟨-, Früchte⟩ fruit; *(grain)* corn; **Fruchteis** *nt* fruit-flavoured ice-cream; **fruchtig** *adj* fruity; **Fruchtsaft** *m* fruit juice; **Fruchtsalat** *m* fruit salad

**früh** *adj, adv* early; *heute ~* this morning; *um fünf Uhr ~* at five (o'clock) in the morning; *~ genug* soon enough; *früher* **1.** *adj* earlier; *(ex-)* former **2.** *adv* formerly, in the past; **frühestens** *adv* at the earliest

**Frühjahr** *nt*, **Frühling** *m* spring; **Frühlingsrolle** *f* spring roll; **Frühlingszwiebel** *f* spring onion *(Brit)*, scallion *(US)*

**Frühstück** *nt* breakfast; **frühstücken** *vi* have breakfast;

**Frühstücksbüfett** *nt* breakfast buffet

**frühzeitig** *adj* early

**Frust** *m* ⟨-s⟩ *fam* frustration; **frustrieren** *vt* frustrate

**Fuchs** *m* ⟨-es, Füchse⟩ fox

**fühlen** *vt, vi, vr* feel

**fuhr** *imperf* → *fahren*

**führen** **1.** *vt* lead; *(business)* run; *(accounts)* keep **2.** *vi* lead, be in the lead **3.** *vr* behave; **Führerschein** *m* driving license *(Brit)*, driver's license *(US)*; **Führung** *f* leadership; *(of company)* management; MIL command; *(in museum, town)* guided tour; *in ~ liegen* be in the lead

**füllen** *vt, vr* fill; GASTR stuff **Füller** *m* ⟨-s, -⟩, **Füllfederhalter** *m* ⟨-s, -⟩ fountain pen

**Füllung** *f* filling

**Fund** *m* ⟨-(e)s, -e⟩ find; **Fundbüro** *nt* lost property office *(Brit)*, lost and found *(US)*; **Fundsachen** *pl* lost property *sg*

**fünf** *num* five; **Fünf** *f* ⟨-, -en⟩ five; *(mark in school)* ≈ E; **fünfhundert** *num* five hundred; **fünfmal** *adv* five times; **fünfte(r, s)** *adj* fifth; → *dritte*; **Fünftel** *nt* ⟨-s, -⟩ fifth; **fünfzehn** *num* fifteen; **fünfzehnte(r, s)** *adj* fifteenth; → *dritte*; **fünfzig** *num* fifty; **fünfzigste(r, s)** *adj* fiftieth

**Funk** *m* ⟨-s⟩ radio; *über ~* by

radio

**Funke** *m* ⟨-ns, -n⟩ spark; **funkeln** *vi* sparkle

**Funkgerät** *nt* radio set; **Funk-
taxi** *nt* radio taxi, radio cab

**Funktion** *f* function; **funktionieren** *vi* work, function

**für** *prep + acc* for; **was ~ (ein)
...?** what kind (*or* sort) of
...?; **Tag ~ Tag** day after day

**Furcht** *f* ⟨-⟩ fear; **furchtbar**
*adj* terrible; **fürchten 1.** *vt*
be afraid of, fear **2.** *vr* be
afraid (*vor* + *dat* of); **fürchterlich** *adj* awful

**füreinander** *adv* for each other

**fürs** *contr* = **für das**

**Fürst(in)** *m(f)* ⟨-en, -en⟩
prince / princess; **Fürsten-
tum** *nt* principality

**Furunkel** *nt* ⟨-s, -⟩ boil

**Furz** *m* ⟨-es, Fürze⟩ vulg fart; **furzen** *vi* vulg fart

**Fuß** *m* ⟨-es, Füße⟩ foot; (*of
glass, column etc*) base; (*of
furniture*) leg; **zu ~** on foot;

**zu ~ gehen** walk; **Fußball**
*m* football (*Brit*), soccer

**Fußballmannschaft** *f* football (*Brit*) (*or* soccer) team;
**Fußballplatz** *m* football
pitch (*Brit*), soccer field
(*US*); **Fußballspiel** *nt* football (*Brit*) (*or* soccer) match;
**Fußballspieler(in)** *m(f)*
footballer (*Brit*), soccer
player; **Fußboden** *m* floor;
**Fußgänger(in)** *m(f)* ⟨-s, -⟩
pedestrian; **Fußgänger-
überweg** *m* pedestrian
crossing (*Brit*), crosswalk
(*US*); **Fußgängerzone** *f* pedestrian precinct (*Brit*) (*or*
zone (*US*)); **Fußgelenk** *nt*
ankle; **Fußpilz** *m* athlete's
foot; **Fußtritt** *m* kick; **jdm einen ~ geben** give sb a kick,
kick sb; **Fußweg** *m* footpath

**Futter** *nt* ⟨-s, -⟩ feed; (*hay etc*)
fodder; (*material*) lining;
**füttern** *vt* feed; (*garment*)
line

**Fuzzi** *m* ⟨-s, -s⟩ fam guy

# G

**gab** *imperf* → **geben**

**Gabe** *f* ⟨-, -n⟩ gift

**Gabel** *f* ⟨-, -n⟩ fork; **Gabelung**
*f* fork

**gaffen** *vi* gape

**Gage** *f* ⟨-, -n⟩ fee

**gähnen** *vi* yawn

**Galerie** *f* gallery

**Galle** *f* ⟨-, -n⟩ gall; (*organ*) gall

bladder; **Gallenstein** *m* gallstone

**Galopp** *m* ⟨-s⟩ gallop; **galoppieren** *vi* gallop

**galt** *imperf* → **gelten**

**gammeln** *vi* loaf (*or* hang)
around

**Gang** *m* ⟨-(e)s, Gänge⟩ walk;
(*in plane*) aisle; (*of meal,*

events etc) course; (in building) corridor; (connecting way) passage; AUTO gear; **den zweiten ~ einlegen** change into second (gear); **etw in ~ bringen** get sth going; **Gangschaltung** f gears pl; **Gangway** f ⟨-, -s⟩ AVIAT steps pl; NAUT gangway

**Gans** f ⟨-, Gänse⟩ goose; **Gänseblümchen** nt daisy; **Gänsehaut** f goose pimples pl (Brit), goose bumps pl (US)

**ganz 1.** adj whole; (set etc) complete; **~ Europa** all of Europe; **sein ~es Geld** all his money; **den ~en Tag** all day; **die ~e Zeit** all the time **2.** adv quite; (totally) completely; **es hat mir ~ gut gefallen** I quite liked it; **~ schön viel** quite a lot; **ganztägig** adj all-day; (work, job) full-time

**gar 1.** adj done, cooked **2.** adv at all; **~ nicht / nichts / keiner** not / nothing / nobody at all; **~ nicht schlecht** not bad at all

**Garage** f ⟨-, -n⟩ garage

**Garantie** f guarantee; **garantieren** vt guarantee

**Garderobe** f ⟨-, -n⟩ (clothes) wardrobe; (in theatre, museum etc) cloakroom

**Gardine** f curtain

**Garn** nt ⟨-(e)s, -n⟩ thread

**Garnele** f ⟨-, -n⟩ shrimp

**garnieren** vt decorate; (food) garnish

**Garten** m ⟨-s, Gärten⟩ garden; **Gärtner(in)** m(f) ⟨-s, -⟩ gardener; **Gärtnerei** f market garden (Brit), truck farm (US)

**Garzeit** f cooking time

**Gas** nt ⟨-es, -e⟩ gas; **~ geben** AUTO accelerate; fig get a move on (inf); **Gasanzünder** m gas lighter; **Gasheizung** f gas heating; **Gasherd** m gas stove, gas cooker (Brit); **Gaskocher** m ⟨-s, -⟩ camping stove; **Gaspedal** nt accelerator, gas pedal (US)

**Gasse** f ⟨-, -n⟩ alley

**Gast** m ⟨-es, Gäste⟩ guest; **Gäste haben** have guests; **Gästebett** nt spare bed; **Gästebuch** nt visitors' book; **Gästehaus** nt guest house; **Gästezimmer** nt guest room; **gastfreundlich** adj hospitable; **Gastgeber(in)** m(f) ⟨-s, -⟩ host / hostess; **Gasthaus** nt, **Gasthof** m inn; **Gastland** nt host country

**Gastritis** f ⟨-⟩ gastritis

**Gastronomie** f catering trade

**Gastspiel** nt SPORT away game; **Gaststätte** f restaurant; pub (Brit), bar; **Gastwirt(in)** m(f) landlord / -lady

**Gaumen** m ⟨-s, -⟩ palate

**geb.** 1. adj abbr → **geboren** b. **2.** adj abbr = **geborene** née → **geboren**

**Gebäck** nt ⟨-(e)s, -e⟩ pastries

# gebacken                                                     114

*pl*, biscuits *pl* (*Brit*), cookies
*pl* (*US*)
**gebacken** *pp* → **backen**
**Gebärmutter** *f* womb
**Gebäude** *nt* ⟨-s, -⟩ building
**geben** ⟨gab, gegeben⟩ **1.** *vt*, *vi*
give (*jdm etw* sb sth, sth to
sb); (*cards*) deal; *lass dir eine Quittung ~* ask for a receipt **2.** *vt impers* **es gibt**
there is / are; (*in the future*)
there will be; *das gibt's
nicht* I don't believe it **3.**
*vr* (*person*) behave, act;
*das gibt sich wieder* it'll
sort itself out
**Gebet** *nt* ⟨-(e)s, -e⟩ prayer
**gebeten** *pp* → **bitten**
**Gebiet** *nt* ⟨-(e)s, -e⟩ area; (*British etc*) territory; *fig* field
**gebildet** *adj* educated; (*with
book learning*) well-read
**Gebirge** *nt* ⟨-s, -⟩ mountains
*pl*
**Gebiss** *nt* ⟨-es, -e⟩ teeth *pl*;
(*false*) dentures *pl*; **gebissen** *pp* → **beißen**; **Gebiss-
reiniger** *m* denture tablets
*pl*
**Gebläse** *nt* ⟨-s, -⟩ fan, blower
**geblasen** *pp* → **blasen**
**geblieben** *pp* → **bleiben**
**gebogen** *pp* → **biegen**
**geboren 1.** *pp* → **gebären 2.**
*adj* born; *Andrea Jordan,
~e Christian* Andrea Jor-
dan, née Christian
**geborgen 1.** *pp* → **bergen 2.**
*adj* secure, safe
**geboten** *pp* → **bieten**

**gebracht** *pp* → **bringen**
**gebrannt** *pp* → **brennen**
**gebraten** *pp* → **braten**
**gebrauchen** *vt* use; **Gebrauchsanweisung** *f* direc-
tions *pl* for use; **gebraucht**
*adj* used; *etw ~ kaufen* buy
sth secondhand; **Ge-
brauchtwagen** *m* second-
hand (*or* used) car
**gebrochen** *pp* → **brechen**
**Gebühr** *f* ⟨-, -en⟩ charge; (*for
using road*) toll; (*for doctor,
lawyer etc*) fee; **gebührenfrei** *adj* free of charge;
(*number*) freefone® (*Brit*),
toll-free (*US*); **gebühren-
pflichtig** *adj* subject to charges; *~e Straße* toll road
**gebunden** *pp* → **binden**
**Geburt** *f* ⟨-, -en⟩ birth; **gebür-
tig** *adj* **er ist ~er Schweizer**
he is Swiss by birth; **Ge-
burtsdatum** *nt* date of birth;
**Geburtsjahr** *nt* year of
birth; **Geburtsname** *m* birth
name; (*of woman*) maiden
name; **Geburtsort** *m* birthplace; **Geburtstag** *m* birthday; *herzlichen Glück-
wunsch zum ~!* Happy
Birthday; **Geburtsurkunde**
*f* birth certificate
**Gebüsch** *nt* ⟨-(e)s, -e⟩ bushes
*pl*
**gedacht** *pp* → **denken**
**Gedächtnis** *nt* memory; *im ~
behalten* remember
**Gedanke** *m* ⟨-ns, -n⟩ thought;
*sich dat über etw acc ~n*

*machen* think about sth; (*anxiously*) be worried about sth; **Gedankenstrich** *m* dash

**Gedeck** *nt* ⟨-(e)s, -e⟩ place setting; (*on menu*) set meal

**Gedenkstätte** *f* memorial

**Gedicht** *nt* ⟨-(e)s, -e⟩ poem

**Gedränge** *nt* ⟨-s⟩ crush, crowd

**gedrungen** *pp* → **dringen**

**Geduld** *f* ⟨-⟩ patience; **geduldig** *adj* patient

**gedurft** *pp* → **dürfen**

**geehrt** *adj* **Sehr ~er Herr Young** Dear Mr Young

**geeignet** *adj* suitable

**Gefahr** *f* ⟨-, -en⟩ danger; **auf eigene ~** at one's own risk; **gefährden** *vt* endanger

**gefahren** *pp* → **fahren**

**gefährlich** *adj* dangerous

**Gefälle** *nt* ⟨-s, -⟩ gradient, slope

**gefallen 1.** *pp* → **fallen 2.** *irr vi jdm ~* please sb; **er/es gefällt mir** I like him / it; **sich** *dat* **etw ~ lassen** put up with sth

**Gefallen** *nt*; **jdm einen ~ tun** do sb a favour

**gefangen** *pp* → **fangen**

**Gefängnis** *nt* prison

**Gefäß** *nt* ⟨-es, -e⟩ container, receptacle; ANAT, BOT vessel

**gefasst** *adj* composed, calm; **auf etw** *acc* **~ sein** be prepared (*or* ready) for sth

**geflochten** *pp* → **flechten**

**geflogen** *pp* → **fliegen**

**geflossen** *pp* → **fließen**

**Geflügel** *nt* ⟨-s⟩ poultry

**gefragt** *adj* in demand

**gefressen** *pp* → **fressen**

**Gefrierbeutel** *m* freezer bag; **Gefrierfach** *nt* freezer compartment; **Gefrierschrank** *m* (upright) freezer; **Gefriertruhe** *f* (chest) freezer

**gefroren** *pp* → **frieren**

**Gefühl** *nt* ⟨-(e)s, -e⟩ feeling

**gefunden** *pp* → **finden**

**gegangen** *pp* → **gehen**

**gegeben** *pp* → **geben**

**gegebenenfalls** *adv* if need be

**gegen** *prep* + *acc* against; (*exchange*) (in return) for; **~ 8 Uhr** about 8 o'clock; **Deutschland ~ England** Germany versus England; **etwas ~ Husten** something for coughs

**Gegend** *f* ⟨-, -en⟩ area; **hier in der ~** around here

**gegeneinander** *adv* against one another

**Gegenfahrbahn** *f* opposite lane; **Gegenmittel** *nt* remedy (*gegen* for); **Gegenrichtung** *f* opposite direction; **Gegensatz** *m* contrast; **im ~ zu** in contrast to; **gegensätzlich** *adj* conflicting; **gegenseitig** *adj* mutual; **sich ~ helfen** help each other

**Gegenstand** *m* object; (*topic*) subject

**Gegenteil** *nt* opposite; **im ~** on the contrary; **gegenteilig**

*adj* opposite, contrary

**gegenüber 1.** *prep* + *dat* opposite; *(with regard to person)* to(wards) **2.** *adv* opposite; **gegenüberstehen** *vt* face; *(problems)* be faced with; **gegenüberstellen** *vt* confront (*dat* with); *fig* compare (*dat* with)

**Gegenverkehr** *m* oncoming traffic; **Gegenwart** *f* ⟨-⟩ present (tense)

**gegessen** *pp* → **essen**

**geglichen** *pp* → **gleichen**

**geglitten** *pp* → **gleiten**

**Gegner(in)** *m(f)* ⟨-s, -⟩ opponent

**gegolten** *pp* → **gelten**

**gegossen** *pp* → **gießen**

**gegraben** *pp* → **graben**

**gegriffen** *pp* → **greifen**

**gehabt** *pp* → **haben**

**Gehalt 1.** *m* ⟨-(e)s, -e⟩ content **2.** *nt* ⟨-(e)s, Gehälter⟩ salary

**gehalten** *pp* → **halten**

**gehangen** *pp* → **hängen**

**gehässig** *adj* spiteful, nasty

**gehauen** *pp* → **hauen**

**gehbehindert** *adj* **sie ist ~** she can't walk properly

**geheim** *adj* secret; **etw ~ halten** keep sth secret; **Geheimnis** *nt* secret; *(puzzling)* mystery; **geheimnisvoll** *adj* mysterious; **Geheimnummer** *f*, **Geheimzahl** *f (of credit card)* PIN number

**geheißen** *pp* → **heißen**

**gehen** ⟨ging, gegangen⟩ **1.** *vt, vi* go; *(on foot)* walk; *(function)* work; **über die Straße ~** cross the street **2.** *vi impers* **wie geht es (dir)?** how are you *(or things)*?; **mir / ihm geht es gut** I'm/he's (doing) fine; **geht das?** is that possible?; **geht's noch?** can you still manage?; **es geht** not too bad, OK; **es geht um ...** it's about ...

**Gehirn** *nt* ⟨-(e)s, -e⟩ brain; **Gehirnerschütterung** *f* concussion

**gehoben** *pp* → **heben**

**geholfen** *pp* → **helfen**

**Gehör** *nt* ⟨-(e)s⟩ hearing

**gehorchen** *vi* obey (*jdm* sb)

**gehören 1.** *vi* belong (*jdm* to sb); **wem gehört das Buch?** whose book is this?; **gehört es dir?** is it yours? **2.** *vr impers* **das gehört sich nicht** it's not done

**Gehweg** *m* ⟨-s, -e⟩ pavement *(Brit)*, sidewalk *(US)*

**Geier** *m* ⟨-s, -⟩ vulture

**Geige** *f* ⟨-, -n⟩ violin

**geil** *adj* randy *(Brit)*, horny *(US)*; *fam (wonderful)* fantastic

**Geisel** *f* ⟨-, -n⟩ hostage

**Geist** *m* ⟨-(e)s, -er⟩ spirit; *(phantom)* ghost; *(intellect)* mind; **Geisterbahn** *f* ghost train, tunnel of horror *(US)*; **Geisterfahrer(in)** *m(f)* person driving the wrong way on the motorway

**geizig** *adj* stingy

**gekannt** pp → **kennen**

**geklungen** pp → **klingen**

**gekniffen** pp → **kneifen**

**gekommen** pp → **kommen**

**gekonnt 1.** pp → **können 2.** adj skilful

**gekrochen** pp → **kriechen**

**Gel** nt ⟨-s, -s⟩ gel

**Gelächter** nt ⟨-s, -⟩ laughter

**geladen 1.** pp → **laden 2.** adj loaded; ELEC live; fig furious

**gelähmt** adj paralysed

**Gelände** nt ⟨-s, -⟩ land, terrain; (of factory, for sport) grounds pl; (being built on) site

**Geländer** nt ⟨-s, -⟩ railing; (on stairs) banister

**Geländewagen** m off-road vehicle

**gelang** imperf → **gelingen**

**gelassen 1.** pp → **lassen 2.** adj calm, composed

**Gelatine** f gelatine

**gelaufen** pp → **laufen**

**gelaunt** adj **gut** / **schlecht** ~ in a good / bad mood

**gelb** adj yellow; (traffic light) amber, yellow (US); **gelblich** adj yellowish; **Gelbsucht** f jaundice

**Geld** nt ⟨-(e)s, -er⟩ money; **Geldautomat** m cash machine (or dispenser Brit), ATM (US); **Geldbeutel** m, **Geldbörse** f purse; **Geldschein** m (bank)note (Brit), bill (US); **Geldstrafe** f fine; **Geldstück** nt coin; **Geldwechsel** m exchange of money; **Geldwechselautomat** m, **Geldwechsler** m ⟨-s, -⟩ change machine

**Gelee** nt ⟨-s, -s⟩ jelly

**gelegen** pp → **liegen**

**Gelegenheit** f opportunity; (event) occasion

**gelegentlich 1.** adj occasional **2.** adv occasionally

**Gelenk** nt ⟨-(e)s, -e⟩ joint

**gelernt** adj skilled

**gelesen** pp → **lesen**

**geliehen** pp → **leihen**

**gelingen** ⟨gelang, gelungen⟩ vi succeed; **es ist mir gelungen, ihn zu erreichen** I managed to get hold of him

**gelitten** pp → **leiden**

**gelogen** pp → **lügen**

**gelten** ⟨galt, gegolten⟩ **1.** vt be worth; **jdm viel / wenig ~** mean a lot / not mean much to sb **2.** vi be valid; (in game etc) be allowed; **etw ~ lassen** accept sth

**gelungen** pp → **gelingen**

**gemahlen** pp → **mahlen**

**Gemälde** nt ⟨-s, -⟩ painting, picture

**gemäß 1.** prep + dat in accordance with **2.** adj appropriate (dat)

**gemein** adj mean, nasty

**Gemeinde** f ⟨-, -n⟩ district, community; (church district) parish; (people in church) congregation

**gemeinsam 1.** adj joint, common **2.** adv together, jointly; **das Haus gehört uns bei-**

**den ~** the house belongs to both of us

**Gemeinschaft** *f* community

**gemeint** *pp → meinen*; **das war nicht so ~** I didn't mean it like that

**gemessen** *pp → messen*

**gemieden** *pp → meiden*

**gemischt** *adj* mixed

**gemocht** *pp → mögen*

**Gemüse** *nt* ⟨-s, -⟩ vegetables *pl*; **Gemüsehändler(in)** *m(f)* greengrocer

**gemusst** *pp → müssen*

**gemustert** *adj* patterned

**gemütlich** *adj* comfortable, cosy; (*person*) good-natured, easy-going; **mach es dir ~** make yourself at home

**genannt** *pp → nennen*

**genau 1.** *adj* exact, precise **2.** *adv* exactly, precisely; **~ in der Mitte** right in the middle; **es mit etw ~ nehmen** be particular about sth; **~ genommen** strictly speaking; **ich weiß es ~** I know for certain (*or* for sure); **genauso** *adv* exactly the same (way); **~ gut / viel / viele Leute** just as well / much / many people (*wie* as)

**genehmigen** *vt* approve; **sich** *dat* **etw ~** indulge in sth; **Genehmigung** *f* approval

**Generalkonsulat** *nt* consulate general

**Generation** *f* generation

**Genf** *nt* ⟨-s⟩ Geneva; **~er See** Lake Geneva

**Genforschung** *f* genetic research

**genial** *adj* brilliant

**Genick** *nt* ⟨-(e)s, -e⟩ (back of the) neck

**Genie** *nt* ⟨-s, -s⟩ genius

**genieren** *vr* feel awkward; **ich geniere mich vor ihm** he makes me feel embarrassed

**genießen** ⟨genoss, genossen⟩ *vt* enjoy

**Genitiv** *m* genitive (case)

**genmanipuliert** *adj* genetically modified, GM

**genommen** *pp → nehmen*

**genoss** *imperf → genießen*

**genossen** *pp → genießen*

**Gentechnik** *f* genetic technology; **gentechnisch** *adv* **~ verändert** genetically modified, GM

**genug** *adv* enough

**genügen** *vi* be enough (*jdm* for sb); **danke, das genügt** thanks, that's enough (*or* that will do)

**Genuss** *m* ⟨-es, Genüsse⟩ pleasure; (*eating, drinking*) consumption

**geöffnet** *adj* (*shop etc*) open

**Geografie** *f* geography

**Geologie** *f* geology

**Georgien** *nt* ⟨-s⟩ Georgia

**Gepäck** *nt* ⟨-(e)s⟩ luggage (*Brit*), baggage; **Gepäckabfertigung** *f* luggage (*Brit*) (*or* baggage) check-in; **Gepäckannahme** *f* (*for*

*forwarding*) luggage (*Brit*) (*or* baggage) office; (*for safekeeping*) left-luggage office (*Brit*), baggage checkroom (*US*); **Gepäckaufbewahrung** *f* left-luggage office (*Brit*), baggage checkroom (*US*); **Gepäckausgabe** *f* luggage (*Brit*) (*or* baggage) office; (*at airport*) baggage reclaim; **Gepäckband** *nt* luggage (*Brit*) (*or* baggage) conveyor; **Gepäckkontrolle** *f* luggage (*Brit*) (*or* baggage) check; **Gepäckstück** *nt* item of luggage (*Brit*) (*or* baggage); **Gepäckträger** *m* porter; (*fixed to bicycle*) carrier; **Gepäckwagen** *m* luggage van (*Brit*), baggage car (*US*)
**gepfiffen** *pp* → **pfeifen**
**gepflegt** *adj* well-groomed; (*park*) well looked after
**gequollen** *pp* → **quellen**
**gerade 1.** *adj* straight; (*number*) even **2.** *adv* exactly; (*a short while ago*) just; **warum ~ ich?** why me (of all people)?; **~ weil** precisely because; **~ noch** only just; **~ neben** right next to; **geradeaus** *adv* straight ahead
**gerannt** *pp* → **rennen**
**Gerät** *nt* ⟨-(e)s, -e⟩ device, gadget; (*implement*) tool; (*radio, TV*) set; (*gear*) equipment
**geraten 1.** *pp* → **raten 2.** *irr vi* turn out; **gut / schlecht ~** turn out well / badly; **an**

*jdn* **~** come across sb; **in etw** *acc* **~** get into sth
**geräuchert** *adj* smoked
**geräumig** *adj* roomy
**Geräusch** *nt* ⟨-(e)s, -e⟩ sound; (*unpleasant*) noise
**gerecht** *adj* fair; (*punishment, reward*) just
**gereizt** *adj* irritable
**Gericht** *nt* ⟨-(e)s, -e⟩ LAW court; (*food*) dish
**gerieben** *pp* → **reiben**
**gering** *adj* small; (*minor*) slight; (*temperature, price etc*) low; (*time*) short; **geringfügig 1.** *adj* slight, minor **2.** *adv* slightly
**gerissen** *pp* → **reißen**
**geritten** *pp* → **reiten**
**gern(e)** *adv* willingly, gladly; **etw ~ tun** like doing sth; **~ geschehen** you're welcome; **gernhaben, gern mögen** *irr vt* like
**gerochen** *pp* → **riechen**
**Gerste** *f* ⟨-, -n⟩ barley; **Gerstenkorn** *nt* (*on eyelid*) stye
**Geruch** *m* ⟨-(e)s, Gerüche⟩ smell
**Gerücht** *nt* ⟨-(e)s, -e⟩ rumour
**gerufen** *pp* → **rufen**
**Gerümpel** *nt* ⟨-s⟩ junk
**gerungen** *pp* → **ringen**
**Gerüst** *nt* ⟨-(e)s, -e⟩ (*around building*) scaffolding; *fig* framework (*zu* of)
**gesalzen** *pp* → **salzen**
**gesamt** *adj* whole, entire; (*costs*) total; (*works*) complete; **Gesamtschule** *f* ≈

comprehensive school

**gesandt** pp → **senden**

**Gesäß** nt ⟨-es, -e⟩ bottom

**geschaffen** pp → **schaffen**

**Geschäft** nt ⟨-(e)s, -e⟩ business; shop; (transaction) deal; **geschäftlich 1.** adj commercial **2.** adv on business; **Geschäftsfrau** f businesswoman; **Geschäftsführer(in)** m(f) managing director; (of shop) manager; **Geschäftsleitung** f executive board; **Geschäftsmann** m businessman; **Geschäftsreise** f business trip; **Geschäftszeiten** pl business (or opening) hours pl

**geschehen** ⟨geschah, geschehen⟩ vi happen

**Geschenk** nt ⟨-(e)s, -e⟩ present, gift; **Geschenkgutschein** m gift voucher; **Geschenkpapier** nt giftwrap

**Geschichte** f ⟨-, -n⟩ story; (matter) affair; HIST history

**geschickt** adj skilful

**geschieden 1.** pp → **scheiden 2.** adj divorced

**geschienen** pp → **scheinen**

**Geschirr** nt ⟨-(e)s, -e⟩ crockery; (for cooking) pots and pans pl; (of horse) harness; ~ **spülen** do (or wash) the dishes, do the washing-up (Brit); **Geschirrspülmaschine** f dishwasher; **Geschirrspülmittel** nt washing-up liquid (Brit), dishwashing liquid (US); Ge-

**schirrtuch** nt tea towel (Brit), dish towel (US)

**geschissen** pp → **scheißen**

**geschlafen** pp → **schlafen**

**geschlagen** pp → **schlagen**

**Geschlecht** nt ⟨-(e)s, -er⟩ sex; LING gender; **Geschlechtskrankheit** f sexually transmitted disease, STD; **Geschlechtsverkehr** m sexual intercourse

**geschlichen** pp → **schleichen**

**geschliffen** pp → **schleifen**

**geschlossen** adj closed

**Geschmack** m ⟨-(e)s, Geschmäcke⟩ taste; **geschmacklos** adj tasteless; **Geschmack(s)sache** f das ist ~ that's a matter of taste; **geschmackvoll** adj tasteful

**geschmissen** pp → **schmeißen**

**geschmolzen** pp → **schmelzen**

**geschnitten** pp → **schneiden**

**geschoben** pp → **schieben**

**Geschoss** nt ⟨-es, -e⟩ (storey) floor

**geschossen** pp → **schießen**

**Geschrei** nt ⟨-s⟩ cries pl; fig fuss

**geschrieben** pp → **schreiben**

**geschrie(e)n** pp → **schreien**

**geschützt** adj protected

**Geschwätz** nt ⟨-es⟩ chatter; (about other people) gossip; **geschwätzig** adj talkative,

**getan**

gossipy

**geschweige** adv ~ **(denn)** let alone

**geschwiegen** pp → **schweigen**

**Geschwindigkeit** f speed; PHYS velocity; **Geschwindigkeitsbegrenzung** f speed limit

**Geschwister** pl brothers and sisters pl

**geschwollen** adj swollen; (speech) pompous

**geschwommen** pp → **schwimmen**

**geschworen** pp → **schwören**

**Geschwulst** f ⟨-, Geschwülste⟩ growth

**Geschwür** nt ⟨-(e)s, -e⟩ ulcer

**gesehen** pp → **sehen**

**gesellig** adj sociable; **Gesellschaft** f society; (people with sb) company

**gesessen** pp → **sitzen**

**Gesetz** nt ⟨-es, -e⟩ law; **gesetzlich** adj legal; **gesetzwidrig** adj illegal

**Gesicht** nt ⟨-(e)s, -er⟩ face; (look) expression; **mach doch nicht so ein ~!** stop pulling such a face; **Gesichtscreme** f face cream; **Gesichtswasser** nt toner

**gesoffen** pp → **saufen**

**gesogen** pp → **saugen**

**gespannt** adj tense; (keen) eager; **ich bin ~, ob ... I** wonder if ...; **auf etw ~/ jdn ~ sein** look forward to

sth / to seeing sb

**Gespenst** nt ⟨-(e)s, -er⟩ ghost

**gesperrt** adj closed

**gesponnen** pp → **spinnen**

**Gespräch** nt ⟨-(e)s, -e⟩ talk, conversation; discussion; (by phone) call

**gesprochen** pp → **sprechen**

**gesprungen** pp → **springen**

**Gestalt** f ⟨-, -en⟩ form, shape; (person) figure

**gestanden** pp → **stehen**, → **gestehen**

**Gestank** m ⟨-(e)s⟩ stench

**gestatten** vt permit, allow; ~ **Sie?** may I?

**Geste** f ⟨-, -n⟩ gesture

**gestehen** irr vt confess

**gestern** adv yesterday; ~ **Abend / Morgen** yesterday evening / morning

**gestiegen** pp → **steigen**

**gestochen** pp → **stechen**

**gestohlen** pp → **stehlen**

**gestorben** pp → **sterben**

**gestört** adj disturbed; (radio reception) poor

**gestoßen** pp → **stoßen**

**gestreift** adj striped

**gestrichen** pp → **streichen**

**gestritten** pp → **streiten**

**gestunken** pp → **stinken**

**gesund** adj healthy; **wieder ~ werden** get better; **Gesundheit** f health; ~**!** bless you!

**gesundheitsschädlich** adj unhealthy

**gesungen** pp → **singen**

**gesunken** pp → **sinken**

**getan** pp → **tun**

**getragen** pp → **tragen**

**Getränk** nt ⟨-(e)s, -e⟩ drink; **Getränkeautomat** m drinks machine; **Getränkekarte** f list of drinks

**Getreide** nt ⟨-s, -⟩ cereals pl, grain

**getrennt** adj separate; **~ leben** live apart; **~ zahlen** pay separately

**getreten** pp → **treten**

**Getriebe** nt ⟨-s, -⟩ AUTO gearbox

**getrieben** pp → **treiben**

**getroffen** pp → **treffen**

**getrunken** pp → **trinken**

**Getue** nt fuss

**geübt** adj experienced

**Gewähr** f ⟨-⟩ guarantee

**Gewalt** f ⟨-, -en⟩ power; (influence) control; (brute strength) force; (brutality) violence; **mit aller ~** with all one's might; **gewaltig** adj tremendous; (mistake) huge

**gewandt 1.** pp → **wenden 2.** adj (physically) nimble; (talented) skilful; (practised) experienced

**gewann** imperf → **gewinnen**

**gewaschen** pp → **waschen**

**Gewebe** nt ⟨-s, -⟩ fabric; BIO tissue

**Gewehr** nt ⟨-(e)s, -e⟩ rifle, gun

**Geweih** nt ⟨-(e)s, -e⟩ antlers pl

**gewellt** adj (hair) wavy

**gewendet** pp → **wenden**

**Gewerbe** nt ⟨-s, -⟩ trade; **Gewerbegebiet** nt industrial estate (Brit) (or park (US)); **gewerblich** adj commercial

**Gewerkschaft** f trade union

**gewesen** pp → **sein**

**Gewicht** nt ⟨-(e)s, -e⟩ weight; fig importance

**gewiesen** pp → **weisen**

**Gewinn** m ⟨-(e)s, -e⟩ profit; (from gambling) winnings pl; (gewann, gewonnen) **1.** vt win; (acquire) gain; (coal, oil) extract **2.** vi win; (profit) gain; **Gewinner(in)** m(f) ⟨-s, -⟩ winner

**gewiss 1.** adj certain **2.** adv certainly

**Gewissen** nt ⟨-s, -⟩ conscience; **ein gutes / schlechtes ~ haben** have a clear / bad conscience

**Gewitter** nt ⟨-s, -⟩ thunderstorm

**gewogen** pp → **wiegen**

**gewöhnen 1.** vt **jdn an etw** acc **~** accustom sb to sth **2.** vr **sich an jdn / etw ~** get used (or accustomed) to sb/sth; **Gewohnheit** f habit; (tradition) custom; **gewöhnlich** adj usual; (average) ordinary; pej common; **wie ~** as usual; **gewohnt** adj usual; **etw ~ sein** be used to sth

**Gewölbe** nt ⟨-s, -⟩ vault

**gewonnen** pp → **gewinnen**

**geworben** pp → **werben**

**geworden** pp → **werden**

**geworfen** pp → **werfen**

**Gewürz** nt ⟨-es, -e⟩ spice; Ge-

**würznelke** f clove; **gewürzt** adj seasoned

**gewusst** pp → **wissen**

**Gezeiten** pl tides pl

**gezogen** pp → **ziehen**

**gezwungen** pp → **zwingen**

**Gibraltar** nt ⟨-s⟩ Gibraltar

**Gicht** f ⟨-⟩ gout

**Giebel** m ⟨-s, -⟩ gable

**gierig** adj greedy

**gießen** ⟨goss, gegossen⟩ vt pour; ⟨flowers⟩ water; ⟨metal⟩ cast; **Gießkanne** f watering can

**Gift** nt ⟨-(e)s, -e⟩ poison; **giftig** adj poisonous

**Gigabyte** nt gigabyte

**Gin** m ⟨-s, -s⟩ gin

**ging** imperf → **gehen**; **Gin Tonic** m ⟨-(s), -s⟩ gin and tonic

**Gipfel** m ⟨-s, -⟩ summit, peak; POL summit; fig ⟨culmination⟩ height

**Gips** m ⟨-es, -e⟩ a. MED plaster; **Gipsverband** m plaster cast

**Giraffe** f ⟨-, -n⟩ giraffe

**Girokonto** nt current account ⟨Brit⟩, checking account ⟨US⟩

**Gitarre** f ⟨-, -n⟩ guitar

**Gitter** nt ⟨-s, -⟩ bars pl

**glänzen** vi a. fig shine; **glänzend** adj shining; fig brilliant

**Glas** nt ⟨-es, Gläser⟩ glass; ⟨for jam⟩ jar; **Glascontainer** m bottle bank; **Glaser(in)** m(f) glazier; **Glasscheibe** f pane (of glass); **Glassplitter** m splinter of glass

**Glasur** f glaze; GASTR icing

**glatt** adj smooth; ⟨floor, road etc⟩ slippery; ⟨lie⟩ downright; **Glatteis** nt (black) ice

**Glatze** f ⟨-, -n⟩ bald head

**glauben** vt, vi believe ⟨an + acc in⟩; ⟨have opinion⟩ think; **jdm ~** believe sb

**gleich 1.** adj equal; ⟨similar⟩ same, identical; **es ist mir ~** it's all the same to me **2.** adv equally; ⟨immediately⟩ straight away; ⟨soon⟩ in a minute; **~ groß / alt** the same size / age; **~ nach / an** right after / at; **Gleichberechtigung** f equal rights pl; **gleichen** ⟨glich, geglichen⟩ **1.** vi **jdm / einer Sache ~** be like sb/sth **2.** vr be alike; **gleichfalls** adv likewise; **danke ~!** thanks, and the same to you; **gleichgültig** adj indifferent; ⟨immaterial⟩ unimportant; **gleichmäßig** adj regular; ⟨distribution⟩ even, equal; **gleichzeitig 1.** adj simultaneous **2.** adv at the same time

**Gleis** nt ⟨-es, -e⟩ track, rails pl; ⟨area in station⟩ platform

**gleiten** ⟨glitt, geglitten⟩ vi glide; ⟨slip down⟩ slide; **Gleitschirmfliegen** nt ⟨-s⟩ paragliding

**Gletscher** m ⟨-s, -⟩ glacier

**glich** imperf → **gleichen**

**Glied** nt ⟨-(e)s, -er⟩ ⟨arm, leg⟩ limb; ⟨of chain⟩ link; ⟨male organ⟩ penis; **Gliedmaßen**

*pl* limbs *pl*

**glitschig** *adj* slippery

**glitt** *imperf* → **gleiten**

**glitzern** *vi* glitter; *(stars)* twinkle

**Glocke** *f* ⟨-, -n⟩ bell; **Glockenspiel** *nt* chimes *pl*

**Glotze** *f* ⟨-, -n⟩ *fam* (*TV*) box; **glotzen** *vi fam* stare

**Glück** *nt* ⟨-(e)s⟩ luck; *(pleasure)* happiness; **~ haben** be lucky; *viel ~!* good luck; *zum ~* fortunately; **glücklich** *adj* lucky; *(pleased)* happy; **glücklicherweise** *adv* fortunately; **Glückwunsch** *m* congratulations *pl*; *herzlichen ~ zur bestandenen Prüfung* congratulations on passing your exam; *herzlichen ~ zum Geburtstag!* Happy Birthday

**Glühbirne** *f* light bulb; **glühen** *vi* glow; **Glühwein** *m* mulled wine

**GmbH** *f* ⟨-, -s⟩ *abbr* = **Gesellschaft mit beschränkter Haftung** ≈ Ltd (*Brit*), ≈ Inc (*US*)

**Gokart** *m* ⟨-s⟩, -s⟩ go-kart

**Gold** *nt* ⟨-(e)s⟩ gold; **golden** *adj* gold; *fig* golden; **Goldfisch** *m* goldfish; **Goldmedaille** *f* gold medal; **Goldschmied(in)** *m(f)* goldsmith

**Golf 1.** *m* ⟨-(e)s, -e⟩ gulf; *der ~ von Biskaya* the Bay of Biscay **2.** *nt* ⟨-s⟩ golf; **Golfplatz** *m* golf course; **Golfschläger** *m* golf club

**Gondel** *f* ⟨-, -n⟩ gondola; *(of cable railway)* cable-car

**gönnen** *vt ich gönne es ihm* I'm really pleased for him; *sich dat etw ~* allow oneself sth

**goss** *imperf* → **gießen**

**gotisch** *adj* Gothic

**Gott** *m* ⟨-es, Götter⟩ God; *(deity)* god; **Gottesdienst** *m* service; **Göttin** *f* goddess

**Grab** *nt* ⟨-(e)s, Gräber⟩ grave

**graben** ⟨grub, gegraben⟩ *vt* dig; **Graben** *m* ⟨-s, Gräben⟩ ditch

**Grabstein** *m* gravestone

**Grad** *m* ⟨-(e)s, -e⟩ degree; *wir haben 30 ~ Celsius* it's 30 degrees Celsius, it's 86 degrees Fahrenheit; *bis zu einem gewissen ~* up to a certain extent

**Graf** *m* ⟨-en, -en⟩ count; *(in Britain)* earl

**Graffiti** *pl* graffiti *sg*

**Grafik** *f* ⟨-, -en⟩ graph; *(work of art)* graphic; *(illustration)* diagram; **Grafikkarte** *f* IT graphics card

**Gräfin** *f* ⟨-, -nen⟩ countess

**Gramm** *nt* ⟨-s⟩ gram(me)

**Grammatik** *f* grammar

**Grapefruit** *f* ⟨-, -s⟩ grapefruit

**Graphik** *f* → **Grafik**

**Gras** *nt* ⟨-es, Gräser⟩ grass

**grässlich** *adj* horrible

**Gräte** *f* ⟨-, -n⟩ (fish)bone

**gratis** *adj*, *adv* free (of charge)

**gratulieren** *vi jdm* (*zu etw*)

congratulate sb (on sth); (*ich*) *gratuliere!* congratulations!

**grau** *adj* grey, gray (*US*)

**grauhaarig** *adj* grey-haired

**grausam** *adj* cruel

**gravierend** *adj* (*error*) serious

**greifen** ⟨griff, gegriffen⟩ **1.** *vt* seize; *zu etw* ~ *fig* resort to sth **2.** *vi* (*rule etc*) have an effect (*bei* on)

**grell** *adj* harsh

**Grenze** *f* ⟨-, -n⟩ boundary; (*of country*) border; (*on sth*) limit; **grenzen** *vi* border (*an + acc* on); **Grenzkontrolle** *f* border control

**Grieche** *m* ⟨-n, -n⟩ Greek; **Griechenland** *nt* Greece; **Griechin** *f* Greek; **griechisch** *adj* Greek; **Griechisch** *nt* Greek

**Grieß** *m* ⟨-es, -e⟩ GASTR semolina

**griff** *imperf* → **greifen**

**Griff** *m* ⟨-(e)s, -e⟩ grip; (*of door etc*) handle; **griffbereit** *adj* handy

**Grill** *m* ⟨-s, -s⟩ grill; (*outdoors*) barbecue

**Grille** *f* ⟨-, -n⟩ cricket

**grillen** *vt* grill **2.** *vi* have a barbecue; **Grillfest** *nt*, **Grillfete** *f* barbecue; **Grillkohle** *f* charcoal

**grinsen** *vi* grin; (*mockingly*) sneer

**Grippe** *f* ⟨-, -n⟩ flu; **Grippeschutzimpfung** *f* flu vacci-

nation

**grob** *adj* coarse; (*error*, *breach*) gross; (*estimate*) rough

**Grönland** *nt* ⟨-s⟩ Greenland

**groß 1.** *adj* big, large; (*person*) tall; *fig* great; (*letter*) capital; (*adult*) grown-up; *im Großen und Ganzen* on the whole **2.** *adv* greatly; **großartig** *adj* wonderful

**Großbritannien** *nt* ⟨-s⟩ (Great) Britain

**Großbuchstabe** *m* capital letter

**Größe** *f* ⟨-, -n⟩ size; (*of person*) height; *fig* greatness; *welche ~ haben Sie?* what size do you take?

**Großeltern** *pl* grandparents *pl*; **Großhandel** *m* wholesale trade; **Großmarkt** *m* hypermarket; **Großmutter** *f* grandmother; **großschreiben** *irr* *vt* write with a capital letter; **Großstadt** *f* city; **Großvater** *m* grandfather; **großzügig** *adj* generous

**Grotte** *f* ⟨-, -n⟩ grotto

**grub** *imperf* → **graben**

**Grübchen** *nt* dimple

**Grube** *f* ⟨-, -n⟩ pit

**grüezi** *interj* (*Swiss*) hello

**grün** *adj* green; *~er Salat* lettuce; *~e Bohnen* French beans

**Grund** *m* ⟨-(e)s, Gründe⟩ reason; (*earth's surface*)

ground; (of sea, container) bottom; (belonging to sb) land, property; **aus gesundheitlichen Gründen** for health reasons; **aus diesem ~** for this reason

**gründen** vt found; **Gründer(in)** m(f) founder

**Grundgebühr** f basic charge

**gründlich** adj thorough

**grundsätzlich** adj fundamental, basic; **sie kommt zu spät** she's always late; **Grundschule** f primary school; **Grundstück** nt plot; (land) estate; (for building on) site

**Grüne(r)** m f POL Green; **die ~n** the Green Party

**Gruppe** f ⟨-, -n⟩ group; **Gruppenermäßigung** f group discount; **Gruppenreise** f group travel

**Gruß** m ⟨-es, Grüße⟩ greeting; **viele Grüße** best wishes; **Grüße an** + acc regards to; **mit freundlichen Grüßen** Yours sincerely (Brit), Sincerely yours (US); **grüßen** vt greet; **grüß deine Mutter von mir** give your mother my regards; **Julia lässt (euch) ~** Julia sends (you) her regards

**gucken** vi look

**Gulasch** nt ⟨-(e)s, -e⟩ goulash

**gültig** adj valid

**Gummi** m or nt ⟨-s, -s⟩ rubber; **Gummistiefel** m wellington (boot) (Brit), rubber boot

(US)

**günstig** adj favourable; (price) good

**gurgeln** vi gurgle; (with mouthwash) gargle

**Gurke** f ⟨-, -n⟩ cucumber; **saure ~** gherkin

**Gurt** m ⟨-(e)s, -e⟩ belt

**Gürtel** m ⟨-s, -⟩ belt; GEO zone; **Gürtelrose** f shingles sg

**gut 1.** adj good; (mark in school) ≈ B; **sehr ~** very good, excellent; (mark in school) ≈ A; **alles Gute!** all the best **2.** adv well; **~ gehen** (business etc) go well; **es geht ihm ~** he's doing fine; **~ aussehend** good-looking; **~ gelaunt** in a good mood; **~ gemeint** well meant; **schon ~!** it's all right; **mach's ~!** take care, bye

**Gutachten** nt ⟨-s, -⟩ report; **Gutachter(in)** m(f) ⟨-s, -⟩ expert

**gutartig** adj MED benign

**Güter** pl goods pl; **Güterzug** m goods train

**gutgläubig** adj trusting

**Guthaben** nt ⟨-s⟩ (credit) balance

**gutmütig** adj good-natured

**Gutschein** m voucher

**Gutschrift** f credit

**guttun** irr vi jdm~ do sb good

**Gymnasium** nt ≈ grammar school (Brit), ≈ high school (US)

**Gymnastik** f exercises pl,

keep-fit
**Gynäkologe** m, **Gynäkolo-**

**gin** f gynaecologist
**Gyros** nt ⟨-, -⟩ doner kebab

# H

**Haar** nt ⟨-(e)s, -e⟩ hair; **um ein ~** nearly; **sich** dat **die ~e schneiden lassen** have one's hair cut; **Haarbürste** f hairbrush; **Haarfestiger** m setting lotion; **Haargel** nt hair gel; **haarig** adj hairy; fig nasty; **Haarschnitt** m haircut; **Haarspange** f hair slide (Brit), barrette (US); **Haarspliss** m split ends pl; **Haarspray** nt hair spray; **Haartrockner** m ⟨-s, -⟩ hairdryer; **Haarwaschmittel** nt shampoo

**haben** ⟨hatte, gehabt⟩ vt, vaux have; **Hunger / Angst ~** be hungry / afraid; **Ferien ~** be on holiday (Brit) (or vacation (US)); **welches Datum ~ wir heute?** what's the date today?; **ich hätte gerne ...** I'd like ...; **hätten Sie etwas dagegen, wenn ich ...?** would you mind if ... I ...?; **was hast du denn?** what's the matter (with you)?

**Haben** nt COMM credit
**Habicht** m ⟨-s, -e⟩ hawk
**Hacke** f ⟨-, -n⟩ hoe; (of foot, shoe) heel; **hacken** vt chop; (hole) hack; (soil) hoe; **Hacker(in)** m(f) ⟨-s, -⟩ IT hacker; **Hackfleisch** nt mince(d

meat) (Brit), ground meat (US)
**Hafen** m ⟨-s, Häfen⟩ harbour; (larger) port; **Hafenstadt** f port
**Hafer** m ⟨-s, -⟩ oats pl; **Haferflocken** pl rolled oats pl
**Haft** f ⟨-⟩ custody; **haftbar** adj liable, responsible; **haften** vi stick; **~ für** be liable (or responsible) for; **Haftnotiz** f Post-it®; **Haftpflichtversicherung** f third party insurance; **Haftung** f liability
**Hagebutte** f ⟨-, -n⟩ rose hip
**Hagel** m ⟨-s⟩ hail; **hageln** vi impers hail
**Hahn** m ⟨-(e)s, Hähne⟩ cock; (for water) tap (Brit), faucet (US); **Hähnchen** nt cockerel; GASTR chicken
**Hai(fisch)** m ⟨-(e)s, -e⟩ shark
**Haken** m ⟨-s, -⟩ hook; (mark) tick
**halb** adj half; **~ eins** half past twelve; fam half twelve; **eine ~e Stunde** half an hour; **~ offen** half-open; **Halbfinale** nt semifinal; **halbieren** vt halve; **Halbinsel** f peninsula; **Halbjahr** nt half-year; **Halbmond** m ASTR half-moon; (symbol) crescent; **Halbpension** f half board;

**halbtags** adv (work) part-time; **halbwegs** adv (fairly) reasonably; **Halbzeit** f half; (interval) half-time

**half** imperf → **helfen**; **Hälfte** f ⟨-, -n⟩ half

**Halle** f ⟨-, -n⟩ hall; **Hallenbad** nt indoor (swimming) pool

**hallo** interj hello, hi

**Halogenlampe** f halogen lamp

**Hals** m ⟨-es, Hälse⟩ neck; (inside) throat; **Halsband** nt (for animal) collar; **Halsentzündung** f sore throat; **Halskette** f necklace; **Hals-Nasen-Ohren-Arzt** m, **Hals-Nasen-Ohren-Ärztin** f ear, nose and throat specialist; **Halsschmerzen** pl sore throat sg; **Halstuch** nt scarf

**halt 1.** interj stop **2.** adv **das ist ~ so** that's just the way it is; **Halt** m ⟨-(e)s, -e⟩ stop; (grip) hold; (inner strength) stability

**haltbar** adj durable; (food) non-perishable; **Haltbarkeitsdatum** nt best-before date

**halten** ⟨hielt, gehalten⟩ **1.** vt keep; (grip) hold; ~ **für** regard as; ~ **von** think of; **den Elfmeter ~** save the penalty; **eine Rede ~** give (or make) a speech **2.** vi hold; (stay fresh) keep; (come to standstill) stop; **zu jdm ~** stand by sb **3.** vr (stay fresh) keep

**Haltestelle** f stop; **Halteverbot** nt **hier ist ~** you can't stop here

**Haltung** f (of body) posture; fig attitude; (self-control) composure

**Hamburg** nt ⟨-s⟩ Hamburg; **Hamburger** m ⟨-s, -⟩ GASTR hamburger

**Hammelfleisch** nt mutton

**Hammer** m ⟨-s, Hämmer⟩ hammer; fig fam (mistake) howler

**Hämorr(ho)iden** pl haemorrhoids pl, piles pl

**Hamster** m ⟨-s, -⟩ hamster

**Hand** f ⟨-, Hände⟩ hand; **jdm die ~ geben** shake hands with sb; **zu Händen von** attention; **Handarbeit** f (school subject) handicraft; ~ **sein** be handmade; **Handball** m handball; **Handbremse** f handbrake; **Handbuch** nt handbook, manual; **Handcreme** f hand cream

**Handel** m ⟨-s⟩ trade; (deal) transaction; **handeln 1.** vi act; COMM trade; ~ **von** be about **2.** vr impers **es handelt sich um ...** it's about ...

**Handfeger** m ⟨-s, -⟩ brush; **Handfläche** f palm; **Handgelenk** nt wrist; **handgemacht** adj handmade; **Handgepäck** nt hand luggage (Brit) (or baggage)

**Händler(in)** m(f) ⟨-s, -⟩ dealer

**handlich** adj handy

**Handlung** f act, action; (of

*novel, film*) plot

**Handschellen** *pl* handcuffs *pl*; **Handschrift** *f* handwriting; **Handschuh** *m* glove; **Handschuhfach** *nt* glove compartment; **Handtasche** *f* handbag, purse (*US*)

**Handtuch** *nt* towel; **Handwerk** *nt* trade; **Handwerker** *m* ⟨-s, -⟩ workman

**Handy** *nt* ⟨-s, -s⟩ mobile (phone) (*Brit*), cell phone (*US*); **Handynummer** *f* mobile number (*Brit*), cell phone number (*US*)

**Hang** *m* ⟨-(e)s, Hänge⟩ slope; *fig* tendency

**Hängematte** *f* hammock

**hängen 1.** ⟨hing, gehangen⟩ *vi* hang; *an der Wand / an der Decke* ~ hang on the wall / from the ceiling; *an jdm* ~ *fig* be attached to sb; ~ *bleiben* get caught (*an + dat* on); *fig* get stuck (*an + acc* on) **2.** *vt* hang (*an + acc* on)

**Hantel** *f* ⟨-, -n⟩ dumbbell

**Hardware** *f* ⟨-, -s⟩ *IT* hardware

**Harfe** *f* ⟨-, -n⟩ harp

**harmlos** *adj* harmless

**harmonisch** *adj* harmonious

**Harn** *m* ⟨-(e)s, -e⟩ urine; **Harnblase** *f* bladder

**hart** *adj* hard; *fig* harsh; ~ *gekocht* (egg) hard-boiled; **hartnäckig** *adj* stubborn

**Haschisch** *nt* hashish

**Hase** *m* ⟨-n, -n⟩ hare

**Haselnuss** *f* hazelnut

**Hass** *m* ⟨-es⟩ hatred (*auf*

+ *acc, gegen* of), hate; **hassen** *vt* hate

**hässlich** *adj* ugly; (*mean*) nasty

**Hast** *f* ⟨-⟩ haste, hurry; **hastig** *adj* hasty

**hatte** *imperf* → **haben**

**Haube** *f* ⟨-, -n⟩ hood; (*hat*) cap; AUTO bonnet (*Brit*), hood (*US*)

**hauchdünn** *adj* (*layer, slice*) wafer-thin

**hauen** ⟨haute, gehauen⟩ *vt* hit

**Haufen** *m* ⟨-s, -⟩ pile; *ein* ~ *Geld* a lot of money

**häufig 1.** *adj* frequent **2.** *adv* frequently, often

**Haupt-** *in cpds* main; **Hauptbahnhof** *m* central (*or* main) station; **Haupteingang** *m* main entrance; **Hauptgericht** *nt* main course

**Häuptling** *m* chief

**Hauptquartier** *nt* headquarters *pl*; **Hauptrolle** *f* leading role; **Hauptsache** *f* main thing; **hauptsächlich** *adv* mainly, chiefly; **Hauptsaison** *f* high (*or* peak) season; **Hauptsatz** *m* main clause; **Hauptschule** *f* ≈ secondary school (*Brit*), ≈ junior high school (*US*); **Hauptstadt** *f* capital; **Hauptstraße** *f* main road; (*in town centre*) main street; **Hauptverkehrszeit** *f* rush hour

**Haus** *nt* ⟨-es, Häuser⟩ house; *nach* ~*e* home; *zu* ~*e* at home; *jdn nach* ~*e bringen*

take sb home; **Hausarbeit** f housework; **Hausaufgabe** f homework; **~n** pl homework sg; **Hausbesitzer(in)** m(f) ⟨-s, -⟩ house owner; (*renting out*) landlord / -lady; **Hausbesuch** m home visit; **Hausflur** m hall; **Hausfrau** f housewife; **hausgemacht** adj homemade; **Haushalt** m household; POL budget

**häuslich** adj domestic

**Hausmann** m house-husband; **Hausmannskost** f good plain cooking; **Hausmeister(in)** m(f) caretaker (*Brit*), janitor (*US*); **Hausnummer** f house number; **Hausschlüssel** m front-door key; **Hausschuh** m slipper; **Haustier** nt pet; **Haustür** f front door

**Haut** f ⟨-, Häute⟩ skin; **Hautarzt** m, **Hautärztin** f dermatologist; **Hautausschlag** m skin rash; **Hautcreme** f skin cream; **Hautfarbe** f skin colour

**Hawaii** nt ⟨-s⟩ Hawaii

**Hebamme** f ⟨-, -n⟩ midwife

**Hebel** m ⟨-s, -⟩ lever

**heben** ⟨hob, gehoben⟩ vt raise, lift

**Hebräisch** nt ⟨-⟩ Hebrew

**Hecht** m ⟨-(e)s, -e⟩ pike

**Heck** nt ⟨-(e)s, -e⟩ (*of boat*) stern; (*of car*) rear; **Heckantrieb** m rear-wheel drive

**Hecke** f ⟨-, -n⟩ hedge

**Heckklappe** f tailgate; **Heck-**

**scheibe** f rear window

**Hefe** f ⟨-, -n⟩ yeast

**Heft** nt ⟨-(e)s, -e⟩ notebook, exercise book; (*of magazine*) issue

**heftig** adj violent; (*criticism, argument*) fierce

**Heftklammer** f paper clip; **Heftpflaster** nt plaster (*Brit*), Band-Aid® (*US*)

**Heide** f ⟨-, -n⟩ heath, moor; **Heidekraut** nt heather

**Heidelbeere** f bilberry, blueberry

**heidnisch** adj (*custom*) pagan

**heikel** adj (*matter*) awkward; (*person*) fussy

**heil** adj (*thing*) in one piece, intact; **heilbar** adj curable

**Heilbutt** m ⟨-(e)s, -e⟩ halibut

**heilen 1.** vt cure **2.** vi heal

**heilig** adj holy; **Heiligabend** m Christmas Eve; **Heilige(r)** mf saint

**Heilpraktiker(in)** m(f) ⟨-s, -⟩ non-medical practitioner

**heim** adv home; **Heim** nt ⟨-(e), -e⟩ home

**Heimat** f ⟨-, -en⟩ home (town / country)

**heimfahren** irr vi drive home; **Heimfahrt** f journey home; **heimisch** adj (*population, customs*) local; (*animal, plant*) native; **heimkommen** irr vi come (or return) home

**heimlich** adj secret

**Heimreise** f journey home;

**Heimspiel** nt SPORT home game; **Heimweg** m way home; **Heimweh** nt ⟨-s⟩ homesickness; ~ **haben** be homesick

**Heirat** f ⟨-, -en⟩ marriage; **heiraten 1.** vi get married **2.** vt marry; **Heiratsantrag** m proposal; **er hat ihr einen ~ gemacht** he proposed to her

**heiser** adj hoarse

**heiß** adj hot; (discussion) heated; **mir ist ~** I'm hot

**heißen** ⟨hieß, geheißen⟩ **1.** vi be called; (have sense, consequence) mean; **ich heiße Tom** my name is Tom; **wie ~ Sie?** what's your name?; **wie heißt sie mit Nachmen?** what's her surname?; **wie heißt das auf Englisch?** what's that in English? **3.** vi impers **es heißt** (people say) it is said; **es heißt in dem Brief ...** it says in the letter ...; **das heißt** that is

**Heißluftherd** m fan-assisted oven

**heiter** adj cheerful; (weather) bright

**heizen** vt heat; **Heizkissen** m MED heated pad; **Heizkörper** m radiator; **Heizöl** nt fuel oil; **Heizung** f heating

**Hektar** nt ⟨-s, -⟩ hectare

**Hektik** f ⟨-, -en⟩ **nur keine ~!** take it easy; **hektisch** adj hectic

**Held** m ⟨-en, -en⟩ hero; **Heldin** f heroine

**helfen** ⟨half, geholfen⟩ **1.** vi help (jdm bei etw sb with sth); (thing) be of use **2.** vi impers **es hilft nichts, du musst ...** it's no use, you have to ...; **Helfer(in)** m(f) helper; (at work) assistant

**hell** adj bright; (colour) light; (complexion) fair; **hellblau** adj light blue; **hellblond** adj ash-blond; **hellgelb** adj pale yellow; **hellgrün** adj light green; **Hellseher(in)** m(f) clairvoyant

**Helm** m ⟨-(e)s, -e⟩ helmet; **Helmpflicht** f compulsory wearing of helmets

**Hemd** nt ⟨-(e)s, -en⟩ shirt

**hemmen** vt check; (hinder) hamper; **gehemmt sein** be inhibited; **Hemmung** f inhibition; (moral) scruple

**Henkel** m ⟨-s, -⟩ handle

**Henna** nt ⟨-s⟩ henna

**Henne** f ⟨-, -n⟩ hen

**Hepatitis** f ⟨-, Hepatitiden⟩ hepatitis

**her** adv here; **wo ist sie ~?** where is she from?; **das ist zehn Jahre ~** that was ten years ago

**herab** adv down; **herablassend** adj (remark) condescending; **herabsehen** irr vt **auf jdn ~** look down on sb; **herabsetzen** vt reduce; fig disparage

**heran** adv **näher ~!** come

closer; **herankommen** irr vi approach; **~ an** + acc be able to get at; fig be able to get hold of; **heranwachsen** irr vi grow up

**herauf** adv up; **heraufbeschwören** irr vt evoke; (crisis, dispute etc) cause; **heraufziehen** irr **1.** vt pull up **2.** vi approach; (storm) gather

**heraus** adv out; **herausbekommen** irr vt (secret) find out; (puzzle) solve; **herausbringen** irr vt bring out; **herausfinden** irr vt find out; **herausfordern** vt challenge; **Herausforderung** f challenge; **herausgeben** irr vt (book) edit; (issue) publish; **jdm zwei Euro ~** give sb two euros change; **herausholen** vt get out (aus of); **herauskommen** irr vi come out; **dabei kommt nichts heraus** nothing will come of it; **herausstellen** vr turn out (als to be); **herausziehen** irr vt pull out

**Herbst** m ⟨-(e)s, -e⟩ autumn, fall (US)

**Herd** m ⟨-(e)s, -e⟩ cooker, stove

**Herde** f ⟨-, -n⟩ herd; (of sheep) flock

**herein** adv in; **~!** come in; **hereinfallen** irr vi **wir sind auf einen Betrüger hereingefallen** we were taken in by a swindler; **hereinlegen** vt **jdn ~** fig take sb for a ride

**Herfahrt** f journey here; **auf der ~** on the way here

**Hergang** m course (of events); **schildern Sie mir den ~** tell me what happened

**Hering** m ⟨-s, -e⟩ herring

**herkommen** irr vi come; **wo kommt sie her?** where does she come from?

**Heroin** n ⟨-s⟩ heroin

**Herpes** m ⟨-⟩ MED herpes

**Herr** m ⟨-(e)n, -en⟩ (before name) Mr; (person) gentleman; (nobleman, God) Lord; **mein ~!** sir; **meine ~en!** gentlemen; **Sehr geehrte Damen und ~en** Dear Sir or Madam; **Herrentoilette** f men's toilet, gents

**herrichten** vt prepare

**herrlich** adj marvellous, splendid

**Herrschaft** f rule; power

**herrschen** vi rule; (exist) exist

**herstellen** vt make; (industrially) manufacture; **Hersteller(in)** m(f) manufacturer; **Herstellung** f production

**herüber** adv over

**herum** adv around; (in a circle) round; **um etw ~** around sth; **du hast den Pulli falsch ~ an** you're wearing your sweater inside out; **anders ~** the other way round; **herumfahren** irr vi drive around; **herumkommen** irr vi **sie ist viel in der Welt herumgekommen** she's been around the world; **um etw ~** (avoid) get out of sth; **herumkriegen** vt talk round; **herumtreiben** irr vr hang around

**herunter** adv down; **heruntergekommen** adj (building, area) run-down; (person) down-at-heel; **herunterhandeln** vt get down; **herunterholen** vt bring down; **herunterkommen** irr vi come down; **herunterladen** irr vt IT download

**hervor** adv out; **hervorbringen** irr vt produce; (word) utter; **hervorheben** irr vt emphasize, stress; **hervorragend** adj excellent; **hervorrufen** irr vt cause, give rise to

**Herz** nt ⟨-ens, -en⟩ heart; (card suit) hearts pl; **von ganzem ~en** wholeheartedly; **sich** dat **etw zu ~en nehmen** take sth to heart; **Herzanfall** m heart attack; **Herzbeschwerden** pl heart trouble sg; **herzhaft** adj (meal) substantial; **~ lachen** have a good laugh; **Herzinfarkt** m heart attack; **Herzklopfen** nt ⟨-s⟩ MED palpitations pl; **ich hatte ~** (vor Aufregung) my heart was pounding (with excitement); **herzkrank** adj **sie ist ~** she's got a heart condition; **herzlich** adj (reception, person) warm; **~en Glückwunsch**

congratulations

**Herzog(in)** m(f) ⟨-s, Herzöge⟩ duke / duchess

**Herzschlag** m heartbeat; (stopping) heart failure; **Herzschrittmacher** m pacemaker

**Hessen** nt ⟨-s⟩ Hessen

**heterosexuell** adj heterosexual

**Hetze** f ⟨-, -n⟩ rush; **hetzen** vt, vr rush

**Heu** nt ⟨-(e)s⟩ hay

**heuer** adv this year

**heulen** vi howl; (weep) cry

**Heuschnupfen** m hay fever

**Heuschrecke** f ⟨-, -n⟩ grasshopper; (larger) locust

**heute** adv today; **~ Abend / früh** this evening / morning; **~ Nacht** tonight; (just gone) last night; **~ in acht Tagen** a week (from) today; **sie hat bis ~ nicht bezahlt** she hasn't paid to this day; **heutig** adj **die ~e Zeitung / Generation** today's paper / generation; **heutzutage** adv nowadays

**Hexe** f ⟨-, -n⟩ witch; **Hexenschuss** m lumbago

**hielt** imperf → **halten**

**hier** adv here; **~ entlang** this way; **ich bin auch nicht von ~** I'm a stranger here myself; **hierbleiben** irr vi stay here; **hierher** adv here; **das gehört nicht ~** that doesn't belong here; **hierlassen** irr vt leave here;

**hiermit** 134

hiermit *adv* with this

hiesig *adj* local

heiß *imperf* → **heißen**

**Hi-Fi-Anlage** *f* hi-fi (system)

high *adj fam* high; Highlife *nt* ⟨-s⟩ high life; ~ **machen** live it up; Hightech *nt* ⟨-s⟩ high tech

Hilfe *f* ⟨-, -n⟩ help; (*financial, for those in need*) aid; ~! help!; Erste ~ **leisten** give first aid; um ~ **bitten** ask for help; hilflos *adj* helpless; hilfsbereit *adj* helpful; Hilfsmittel *nt* aid

Himbeere *f* raspberry

Himmel *m* ⟨-s, -⟩ sky; REL heaven; Himmelfahrt *f* Ascension; Himmelsrichtung *f* direction; himmlisch *adj* heavenly

hin *adv* there; ~ **und her** to and fro; ~ **und zurück** there and back; bis zur Mauer ~ up to the wall; das ist noch **lange** ~ (*in the future*) that's a long way off

hinab *adv* down; hinabgehen *irr vi* go down

hinauf *adv* up; hinaufgehen *irr vi, vt* go up; hinaufsteigen *irr vi* climb (up)

hinaus *adv* out; hinausgehen *irr vi* go out; ~ **über** + *acc* exceed; hinauslaufen *irr vi* run out; ~ **auf** + *acc* come to, amount to; hinausschieben *irr vt* put off, postpone; hinauswerfen *irr vt* throw out; (*employee*) fire,

sack (*Brit*); hinauszögern *vr* take longer than expected

hinbringen *irr vt* **ich bringe Sie hin** I'll take you there

hindern *vt* prevent; jdn daran ~, etw zu tun stop (or prevent) sb from doing sth; Hindernis *nt* obstacle

Hinduismus *m* Hinduism

hindurch *adv* through; das **ganze Jahr** ~ throughout the year, all year round; die **ganze Nacht** ~ all night (long)

hinein *adv* in; hineingehen *irr vi* go in; ~ **in** + *acc* go into, enter; hineinpassen *vi* fit in; ~ **in** + *acc* fit into

hinfahren *irr vi* **1.** go there **2.** *vt* take there; Hinfahrt *f* outward journey

hinfallen *irr vi* fall (down)

Hinflug *m* outward flight

hing *imperf* → **hängen**

hingehen *irr vi* go there; (*time*) pass; hinhalten *irr vt* hold out; (*keep waiting*) put off

hinken *vi* limp; der Vergleich **hinkt** the comparison doesn't work

hinlegen **1.** *vt* put down **2.** *vr* lie down; hinnehmen *irr vt fig* put up with, take; Hinreise *f* outward journey; hinsetzen *vr* sit down; hinsichtlich *prep* + *gen* with regard to; hinstellen **1.** *vt* put (down) **2.** *vr* stand

hinten *adv* at the back; (*in car*)

in the back; (*sth* / *sb else*) behind

**hinter** *prep* + *dat or acc* behind; (*beyond, in order of importance*) after; **~ jdm her sein** be after sb; **etw ~ sich** *acc* **bringen** get sth over (and done) with; **Hinterachse** *f* rear axle; **Hinterbein** *nt* hind leg; **Hinterbliebene(r)** *mf* dependant; **hintere(r, s)** *adj* rear, back; **hintereinander** *adv* (*in a row*) one behind the other; (*in continuous sequence*) one after the other; **drei Tage ~** three days running (*or* in a row); **Hintergedanke** *m* ulterior motive; **hintergehen** *irr vt* deceive; **Hintergrund** *m* background; **hinterher** *adv* afterwards; **los, ~!** come on, after him / her / them; **Hinterkopf** *m* back of the head; **hinterlassen** *vt* leave; **jdm eine Nachricht ~** leave a message for sb; **hinterlegen** *vt* leave (*bei* with)

**Hintern** *m* ⟨-, -⟩ *fam* backside, bum

**Hinterradantrieb** *m* AUTO rear-wheel drive; **Hinterteil** *nt* back (part); (*of person*) behind; **Hintertür** *f* back door

**hinüber** *adv* over; **~ sein** *fam* (*broken*) be ruined; (*food*) have gone bad; **hinübergehen** *irr vi* go over

**hinunter** *adv* down; hinun-

tergehen *irr vi*, *vt* go down; **hinunterschlucken** *vt a. fig* swallow

**Hinweg** *m* outward journey

**hinwegsetzen** *vr* **sich über etw** *acc* **~** ignore sth

**Hinweis** *m* ⟨-es, -e⟩ (*suggestion*) hint; (*for user etc*) instruction; **hinweisen** *irr vi* **jdn auf etw** *acc* **~** point sth out to sb

**hinzu** *adv* in addition; **hinzufügen** *vt* add

**Hirn** *nt* ⟨-(e)s, -e⟩ brain; (*intellect*) brains *pl*; **Hirnhautentzündung** *f* meningitis

**Hirsch** *m* ⟨-(e)s, -e⟩ deer; (*meat*) venison

**Hirse** *f* ⟨-, -n⟩ millet

**Hirte** *m* ⟨-n, -n⟩ shepherd

**historisch** *adj* historical

**Hit** *m* ⟨-s, -s⟩ MUS, IT hit; **Hitliste** *f*, **Hitparade** *f* charts *pl*

**Hitze** *f* ⟨-⟩ heat; **hitzebeständig** *adj* heat-resistant; **Hitzewelle** *f* heatwave; **hitzig** *adj* hot-tempered; (*debate*) heated; **Hitzschlag** *m* heatstroke

**HIV** *nt* ⟨-(s), -(s)⟩ *abbr* = **Human Immunodeficiency Virus** HIV; **HIV-negativ** *adj* HIV-negative; **HIV-positiv** *adj* HIV-positive

**H-Milch** *f* long-life milk

**hob** *imperf* → **heben**

**Hobby** *nt* ⟨-s, -s⟩ hobby

**Hobel** *m* ⟨-s, -⟩ plane

**hoch** *adj* high; (*tree, house*) tall; (*snow*) deep; **der Zaun**

**ist drei Meter ~** the fence is three metres high; **~ begabt** extremely gifted; **das ist mir zu ~** that's above my head; **~ soll sie leben!, sie lebe ~!** three cheers for her; **4 ~ 2 ist 16** 4 squared is 16; **4 ~ 5** 4 to the power of 5

**Hoch** nt ⟨-s, -s⟩ METEO high; **hochachtungsvoll** adv Yours faithfully; **Hochbetrieb** m **es herrscht ~** they / we are extremely busy; **Hochdeutsch** nt High German; **Hochgebirge** nt high mountains pl; **Hochhaus** nt high rise; **hochheben** irr vt lift (up); **Hochschule** f college; university; **Hochsommer** m midsummer; **Hochsprung** m high jump; **höchst** adv highly, extremely; **höchste(r, s)** adj highest; (very great) extreme; **höchstens** adv at the most; **Höchstgeschwindigkeit** f maximum speed **Hochstuhl** m high chair **höchstwahrscheinlich** adv very probably **Hochwasser** nt high water; floods pl **Hochzeit** f ⟨-, -en⟩ wedding; **Hochzeitsnacht** f wedding night; **Hochzeitsreise** f honeymoon; **Hochzeitstag** m wedding day; (yearly) wedding anniversary **hocken** vi, vr squat, crouch **Hocker** m ⟨-s, -⟩ stool

**Hockey** nt ⟨-s⟩ hockey **Hoden** m ⟨-s, -⟩ testicle **Hof** m ⟨-(e)s, Höfe⟩ yard; (surrounded by building) courtyard; (agricultural) farm; (royal) court **hoffen** vi hope (auf + acc for); **ich hoffe es** I hope so; **hoffentlich** adv hopefully; **~ nicht** I hope not; **Hoffnung** f hope; **hoffnungslos** adj hopeless **höflich** adj polite; **Höflichkeit** f politeness **hohe(r, s)** adj → **hoch** **Höhe** f ⟨-, -n⟩ height; (high land) hill; (of sum of money) amount; (flying height) altitude; **Höhenangst** f vertigo **Höhepunkt** m (of trip) high point; (of show etc) highlight; (sexual, of film) climax **höher** adj, adv higher **hohl** adj hollow **Höhle** f ⟨-, -n⟩ cave **holen** vt get, fetch; (collect) pick up; (breath) catch; **die Polizei ~** call the police; **jdn / etw ~ lassen** send for sb/sth **Holland** nt Holland; **Holländer(in)** m(f) ⟨-s, -⟩ Dutchman / -woman; **holländisch** adj Dutch **Hölle** f ⟨-, -n⟩ hell **Hologramm** nt hologram **holperig** adj bumpy **Holunder** m ⟨-s, -⟩ elder **Holz** nt ⟨-es, Hölzer⟩ wood; **Holzboden** m wooden floor; **hölzern** adj wooden; **holzig** adj (stem) woody; **Holzkohle** f charcoal

**Homebanking** nt ⟨-s⟩ home banking, online banking; **Homepage** f ⟨-, -s⟩ home page; **Hometrainer** m exercise machine

**Homoehe** f fam gay marriage **homöopathisch** adj homeopathic

**homosexuell** adj homosexual

**Honig** m ⟨-s, -e⟩ honey; **Honigmelone** f honeydew melon

**Honorar** nt ⟨-s, -e⟩ fee

**Hopfen** m ⟨-s, -⟩ BOT hop; (in brewing) hops pl

**hoppla** interj whoops, oops

**horchen** vi listen (auf + acc to); (at door) eavesdrop

**hören** vt, vi hear; (by chance) overhear; (attentively; radio, music) listen to; **ich habe schon viel von Ihnen gehört** I've heard a lot about you; **Hörer** m TEL receiver; **Hörer(in)** m(f) listener; **Hörgerät** nt hearing aid

**Horizont** m ⟨-(e)s, -e⟩ horizon; **das geht über meinen ~** that's beyond me

**Hormon** nt ⟨-s, -e⟩ hormone

**Hornhaut** f hard skin; (of eye) cornea

**Horoskop** nt ⟨-s, -e⟩ horoscope

**Hörsaal** m lecture hall; **Hörsturz** m acute hearing loss

**Hose** f ⟨-, -n⟩ trousers pl (Brit), pants pl (US); (undergarment) (under)pants pl; **eine ~** a pair of trousers / pants; **kurze ~** (pair of) shorts pl; **Hosenanzug** m trouser suit (Brit), pantsuit (US); **Hosenschlitz** m fly, flies (Brit); **Hosentasche** f trouser pocket (Brit), pant pocket (US); **Hosenträger** m braces pl (Brit), suspenders pl (US)

**Hospital** nt ⟨-s, Hospitäler⟩ hospital

**Hotdog** nt or m ⟨-s, -s⟩ hot dog

**Hotel** nt ⟨-s, -s⟩ hotel; **in welchem ~ seid ihr?** which hotel are you staying at?; **Hoteldirektor(in)** m(f) hotel manager; **Hotelkette** f hotel chain; **Hotelzimmer** nt hotel room

**Hotline** f ⟨-, -s⟩ hot line

**Hubraum** m cubic capacity

**hübsch** adj (girl, child, dress) pretty; (man, woman) good-looking, cute

**Hubschrauber** m ⟨-s, -⟩ helicopter

**Huf** m ⟨-(e)s, -e⟩ hoof; **Hufeisen** nt horseshoe

**Hüfte** f ⟨-, -n⟩ hip

**Hügel** m ⟨-s, -⟩ hill; **hügelig** adj hilly

**Huhn** nt ⟨-(e)s, Hühner⟩ hen; GASTR chicken; **Hühnchen** nt chicken; **Hühnerauge** nt corn; **Hühnerbrühe** f chicken broth

**Hülle** f ⟨-, -n⟩ cover; (for ID) case; (cellophane) wrapping

**Hummel** f ⟨-, -n⟩ bumblebee

**Hummer** m ⟨-s, -⟩ lobster; **Hummerkrabbe** f king prawn

**Humor** m ⟨-s⟩ humour; **~ haben** have a sense of humour; **humorvoll** adj humorous

**humpeln** vi hobble

**Hund** m ⟨-(e)s, -e⟩ dog; **Hundeleine** f dog lead (Brit), dog leash (US)

**hundert** num hundred; **hundertprozentig** adj, adv one hundred per cent; **hundertste(r, s)** adj hundredth

**Hündin** f bitch

**Hunger** m ⟨-s⟩ hunger; **~ haben / bekommen** be / get hungry; **hungern** vi go hungry; (seriously, constantly) starve

**Hupe** f ⟨-, -n⟩ horn; **hupen** vi sound one's horn

**Hüpfburg** f bouncy castle®;

**hüpfen** vi hop; jump

**Hürde** f ⟨-, -n⟩ hurdle

**Hure** f ⟨-, -n⟩ whore

**hurra** interj hooray

**husten** vi cough; **Husten** m ⟨-s⟩ cough; **Hustenbonbon** nt cough sweet; **Hustensaft** m cough mixture

**Hut** m ⟨-(e)s, Hüte⟩ hat

**hüten 1.** vt look after **2.** vr **sich ~, etw zu tun** take care not to do sth; **sich ~ vor** + dat beware of

**Hütte** f ⟨-, -n⟩ hut, cottage

**Hyäne** f ⟨-, -n⟩ hyena

**Hydrant** m hydrant

**hygienisch** adj hygienic

**Hyperlink** m ⟨-s, -s⟩ hyperlink

**Hypnose** f ⟨-, -n⟩ hypnosis; **Hypnotiseur(in)** m(f) hypnotist; **hypnotisieren** vt hypnotize

**Hypothek** f ⟨-, -en⟩ mortgage

**hysterisch** adj hysterical

# I

**IC** m ⟨-, -s⟩ abbr = **Intercity (-zug)** Intercity (train)

**ICE** m ⟨-, -s⟩ abbr = **Intercityexpress(zug)** German high-speed train

**ich** pron I; **~ bin's** it's me; **~ nicht** not me; **du und ~** you and me; **hier bin ~!** here I am; **~ Idiot!** stupid me

**Icon** nt ⟨-s, -s⟩ IT icon

**ideal** adj ideal; **Ideal** nt ⟨-s, -e⟩ ideal

**Idee** f ⟨-, -n⟩ idea

**identifizieren** vt, vr identify

**identisch** adj identical

**Idiot(in)** m(f) ⟨-en, -en⟩ idiot; **idiotisch** adj idiotic

**Idol** nt ⟨-s, -e⟩ idol

**Idylle** f idyll; **idyllisch** adj idyllic

**Igel** *m* ⟨-s, -⟩ hedgehog
**ignorieren** *vt* ignore

**ihm** *pron dat sg* → **er**, → **es**; (to) him; *(thing)* (to) it; **wie geht es ~?** how is he?; **ein Freund von ~** a friend of his

**ihn** *pron acc sg* → **er**; him; *(thing)*

**ihnen** *pron dat pl* → **sie**; (to) them; **wie geht es ~?** how are they?; **ein Freund von ~** a friend of theirs

**Ihnen** *pron dat sg and pl* → **Sie**; (to) you; **wie geht es ~?** how are you?; **ein Freund von ~** a friend of yours

**ihr 1.** *pron (2nd person pl)* you; **seid's** it's you **2.** *pron (dat sg)* → **sie**; (to) her; *(thing)* (to) it; **er schickte es ~** he sent it to her; **er hat ~ die Haare geschnitten** he cut her hair; **wie geht es ~?** how is she?; **ein Freund von ~** a friend of hers **3.** *pron (as adj)* her; *(thing)* its; *(pl)* their; **~ Vater** her father; **~ Auto** *(several owners)* their car

**Ihr** *pron* → **Sie**; *(as adj)* your; **~(e) XY** *(at end of letter)* Yours, XY

**ihre(r, s)** *pron (as noun, sg)* hers; *(pl)* theirs; **das ist ~r/ihr(e)s** that's hers; *(pl)* that's theirs

**Ihre(r, s)** *pron (as noun)* yours; **das ist ~r/Ihr(e)s** that's yours

**ihretwegen 1.** *adv (sg)* because of her; *(to please her)* for her sake **2.** *adv (pl)* because of them; *(to please them)* for their sake; **Ihretwegen** *adv* because of you; *(to please you)* for your sake

**Ikone** *f* ⟨-, -n⟩ icon

**illegal** *adj* illegal

**Illusion** *f* illusion; **sich** *dat* **~en machen** delude oneself; **illusorisch** *adj* illusory

**Illustration** *f* illustration

**Illustrierte** *f* ⟨-n, -n⟩ (glossy) magazine

**im** *contr* = **in dem**; **~ Bett** in bed; **~ Fernsehen** on TV; **~ Radio** on the radio; **~ Bus / Zug** on the bus / train; **~ Januar** in January; **~ Stehen** (while) standing up

**Imbiss** *m* ⟨-es, -e⟩ snack; **Imbissbude** *f* snack bar

**Imbussschlüssel** *m* hex key

**immer** *adv* always; **~ mehr** more and more; **~ wieder** again and again; **~ noch** still; **~ noch nicht** still not; **für ~** forever; **~ wenn ich ...** every time I ...; **~ schöner / trauriger** more and more beautiful / sadder and sadder; **was / wer / wo / wann (auch) ~** whatever / whoever / wherever / whenever; **immerhin** *adv* after all; **immerzu** *adv* all the time

**Immigrant(in)** *m(f)* immigrant

**Immobilien** pl property sg, real estate sg; **Immobilienmakler(in)** m(f) estate agent (Brit), realtor (US)

**immun** adj immune (gegen to); **Immunschwäche** f immunodeficiency; **Immunschwächekrankheit** f immune deficiency syndrome; **Immunsystem** nt immune system

**impfen** vt vaccinate; **Impfpass** m vaccination card; **Impfstoff** m vaccine; **Impfung** f vaccination

**imponieren** vi impress (jdm sb)

**Import** m ⟨-(e)s, -e⟩ import; **importieren** vt import

**impotent** adj impotent

**imstande** adj ~ **sein** be in a position; (capable) be able

**in 1.** prep + acc in(to); to; ~ **die Stadt** into town; ~ **die Schule gehen** go to school **2.** prep + dat in; (with time) in; (in the course of) during; (before the end of) within; ~ **der Stadt** in town; ~ **der Schule** at school; **noch** ~ **dieser Woche** by the end of this week; **heute** ~ **acht Tagen** a week (from) today; **Dienstag** ~ **einer Woche** a week on Tuesday **3.** adv ~ **sein** (fashionable) be in

**inbegriffen** adj included

**indem** conj **sie gewann,** ~ **sie mogelte** she won by cheating

**Inder(in)** m(f) ⟨-s, -⟩ Indian

**Indianer(in)** m(f) ⟨-s, -⟩ American Indian, Native American; **indianisch** adj American Indian, Native American

**Indien** nt ⟨-s⟩ India

**indirekt** adj indirect

**indisch** adj Indian

**individuell** adj individual

**Indonesien** nt ⟨-s⟩ Indonesia

**Industrie** f industry; **Industrie-** in cpds industrial

**ineinander** adv in(to) one another (or each other)

**Infarkt** m ⟨-(e)s, -e⟩ heart attack

**Infektion** f infection; **Infektionskrankheit** f infectious disease; **infizieren 1.** vt infect **2.** vr be infected

**Info** f ⟨-, -s⟩ fam info

**infolge** prep + gen as a result of, owing to; **infolgedessen** adv consequently

**Infomaterial** nt fam bumf, info

**Informatik** f computer science; **Informatiker(in)** m(f) ⟨-s, -⟩ computer scientist

**Information** f information; **Informationsschalter** m information desk; **informieren 1.** vt inform; **falsch** ~ misinform **2.** vr find out (über + acc about)

**infrage** adv **das kommt nicht** ~ that's out of the question; **etw** ~ **stellen** question sth

**Infrastruktur** *f* infrastructure
**Infusion** *f* infusion
**Ingenieur(in)** *m(f)* engineer
**Ingwer** *m* ⟨-s⟩ ginger
**Inhaber(in)** *m(f)* ⟨-s, -⟩ owner; *(of licence)* holder
**Inhalt** *m* ⟨-(e)s, -e⟩ contents *pl*; *(of book etc)* content; MATH volume; *(two-dimensional)* area; **Inhaltsangabe** *f* summary; **Inhaltsverzeichnis** *nt* table of contents
**Initiative** *f* initiative; *die ~ ergreifen* take the initiative
**Injektion** *f* injection
**inklusive** *adv*, *prep* inclusive *(gen* of)
**inkonsequent** *adj* inconsistent
**Inland** *nt* POL, COMM home; *im ~* at home; GEO inland; **Inlandsflug** *m* domestic flight; **Inlandsgespräch** *nt* national call
**Inliner(in)** *m(f)* ⟨-s, -⟩ insider
**Inliner** *pl*, **Inlineskates** *pl* SPORT in-line skates *pl*
**innen** *adv* inside; **Innenarchitekt(in)** *m(f)* interior designer; **Innenhof** *m* (inner) courtyard; **Innenminister(in)** *m(f)* minister of the interior, Home Secretary *(Brit)*; **Innenseite** *f* inside; **Innenspiegel** *m* rearview mirror; **Innenstadt** *f* town centre; city centre
**innere(r, s)** *adj* inner; *(in body, own country)* internal; **Innere(s)** *nt* inside; *(middle)* centre; *fig* heart

**innerhalb** *adv*, *prep* + *gen* within; *(with space)* inside
**innerlich** *adj* internal; *(calm etc)* inner
**innerste(r, s)** *adj* innermost
**Innovation** *f* innovation
**inoffiziell** *adj* unofficial; *(party etc)* informal
**ins** *contr* = *in das*
**Insasse** *m* ⟨-n, -n⟩, **Insassin** *f* AUTO passenger; *(of mental hospital, prison)* inmate
**insbesondere** *adv* particularly, in particular
**Inschrift** *f* inscription
**Insekt** *nt* ⟨-(e)s, -en⟩ insect, bug *(US)*; **Insektenschutzmittel** *nt* insect repellent; **Insektenstich** *m* insect bite
**Insel** *f* ⟨-, -n⟩ island
**Inserat** *nt* advertisement
**insgesamt** *adv* altogether, all in all
**Insider(in)** *m(f)* ⟨-s, -⟩ insider
**insofern 1.** *adv* in that respect; *(therefore)* (and) so **2.** *conj* if; *~ als* in so far as
**Installateur(in)** *m(f)* plumber; electrician; **installieren** *vt* IT install
**Instinkt** *m* ⟨-(e)s, -e⟩ instinct
**Institut** *nt* ⟨-(e)s, -e⟩ institute
**Institution** *f* institution
**Instrument** *nt* instrument
**Insulin** *nt* ⟨-s⟩ insulin
**Inszenierung** *f* production
**intakt** *adj* intact
**intellektuell** *adj* intellectual
**intelligent** *adj* intelligent; **Intelligenz** *f* intelligence

**intensiv** adj intensive; (feeling, pain) intense; **Intensivkurs** m crash course; **Intensivstation** f intensive care unit

**interaktiv** adj interactive

**interessant** adj interesting; **Interesse** nt ⟨-s, -n⟩ interest; ~ **haben an** + dat be interested in; **interessieren 1.** vt interest **2.** vr be interested (für in)

**Interface** nt ⟨-, -s⟩ IT interface

**Internat** nt boarding school

**international** adj international

**Internet** nt ⟨-s⟩ Internet, Net; **im** ~ on the Internet; **im** ~ **surfen** surf the Net; **Internetanschluss** m Internet connection; **Internetauktion** f Internet auction; **Internetcafé** nt Internet café, cybercafé; **Internetfirma** f dotcom company; **Internethandel** m e-commerce; **Internetseite** f web page; **Internetzugang** m Internet access

**interpretieren** vt interpret (als as)

**Interpunktion** f punctuation

**Interview** nt ⟨-s, -s⟩ interview; **interviewen** vt interview

**intim** adj intimate

**intolerant** adj intolerant

**investieren** vt invest

**inwiefern** adv in what way; (how far) to what extent; **inwieweit** adv to what extent

**inzwischen** adv meanwhile

**Irak** m ⟨-(s)⟩ **(der)** ~ Iraq

**Iran** m ⟨-(s)⟩ **(der)** ~ Iran

**Ire** m ⟨-n, -n⟩ Irishman

**irgend** adv ~ **so ein Idiot** some idiot; **wenn** ~ **möglich** if at all possible; **irgendein** pron, **irgendeine(r, s)** adj some; (with question, conditional clause; whichever) any; **irgendetwas** pron something; (with question, conditional clause) anything; **irgendjemand** pron somebody; (with question, conditional clause) anybody; **irgendwann** adv sometime; (whenever you like) any time; **irgendwie** adv somehow; **irgendwo** adv somewhere; (with question, conditional clause) anywhere

**Irin** f Irishwoman; **irisch** adj Irish; **Irland** nt Ireland

**ironisch** adj ironic

**irre** adj crazy, mad; (wonderful) terrific; **Irre(r)** mf lunatic; **irreführen** irr vt mislead; **irren** vi, vr be mistaken; **wenn ich mich nicht irre** if I'm not mistaken; **irrsinnig** adj mad, crazy; **Irrtum** m ⟨-s, -tümer⟩ mistake, error; **irrtümlich 1.** adj mistaken **2.** adv by mistake

**Ischias** m ⟨-⟩ sciatica

**Islam** m ⟨-s⟩ Islam; **islamisch** adj Islamic

**Island** nt Iceland; **Islän-**

**der(in)** *m(f)* ⟨-s, -⟩ Icelander; **isländisch** *adj* Icelandic; **Isländische** *nt* Icelandic

**Isolierband** *nt* insulating tape; **isolieren** *vt* isolate; ELEC insulate

**Isomatte f** thermomat, karrymat®

**Israel** *nt* Israel; **Israeli** *m*

⟨-(s), -(s)⟩ *f* ⟨-, -(s)⟩ Israeli; **israelisch** *adj* Israeli

**IT** *f* ⟨-⟩ *abbr* = **Informationstechnologie** IT

**Italien** *nt* ⟨-s⟩ Italy; **Italiener(in)** *m(f)* ⟨-s, -⟩ Italian; **italienisch** *adj* Italian; **Italienische** *nt* Italian

# J

**ja** *adv* yes; **aber ~!** yes, of course; **~, wissen Sie ...** well, you know ...; **ich glaube ~** I think so; **~?** (*on phone*) hello?; **sag's ihr ~ nicht!** don't you dare tell her; **das sag ich ~** that's what I'm trying to say

**Jacht** *f* ⟨-, -en⟩ yacht; **Jachthafen** *m* marina

**Jacke** *f* ⟨-, -n⟩ jacket; (*knitted*) cardigan

**Jackett** *nt* ⟨-s, -s *or* -e⟩ jacket

**Jagd** *f* ⟨-, -en⟩ hunt; (*activity*) hunting; **jagen 1.** *vi* hunt **2.** *vt* hunt; (*pursue*) chase; **Jäger(in)** *m(f)* hunter

**Jaguar** *m* ⟨-s, -e⟩ jaguar

**Jahr** *nt* ⟨-(e)s, -e⟩ year; **ein halbes ~** six months *pl*; **Anfang der neunziger ~e** in the early nineties; **mit sechzehn ~en** at (the age of) sixteen;

**Jahrestag** *m* anniversary; **Jahreszahl** *f* date, year; **Jahreszeit** *f* season; **Jahrgang** *m* (*of wine*) year, vintage; **der ~ 1989** (*people*) those born in 1989; **Jahrhundert** *nt* ⟨-s, -e⟩ century; **jährlich** *adj* yearly, annual; **Jahrmarkt** *m* fair; **Jahrtausend** *nt* millennium; **Jahrzehnt** *nt* decade

**jähzornig** *adj* hot-tempered

**Jakobsmuschel** *f* scallop

**Jalousie** *f* (*venetian*) blind

**Jamaika** *nt* ⟨-s⟩ Jamaica

**jämmerlich** *adj* pathetic

**jammern** *vi* moan

**Januar** *m* ⟨-(s), -e⟩ January; → **Juni**

**Japan** *nt* ⟨-s⟩ Japan; **Japaner(in)** *m(f)* ⟨-s, -⟩ Japanese; **japanisch** *adj* Japanese; **Japanische** *nt* Japanese

**jaulen** *vi* howl

**jawohl** *adv* yes (of course)

**Jazz** *m* ⟨-⟩ jazz

**je** *adv* ever; (*for every one*) each; **~ nach** depending on; **~ nachdem** it depends; **~ schneller desto besser** the faster the better

**Jeans** f ⟨-, -⟩ jeans pl
**jede(r, s) 1.** *indef num* every; (*considered singly*) each; (*whichever you like*) any; **~s Mal** every time, each time; **~n zweiten Tag** every other day; **bei ~m Wetter** in any weather **2.** *pron* everybody; (*every single one*) each; **~r von euch / uns** each of you / us; (*with question or negative*) anybody
**jedenfalls** *adv* in any case; **jederzeit** *adv* at any time; **jedesmal** *adv* every time
**jedoch** *adv* however
**jemals** *adv* ever
**jemand** *pron* somebody; (*with question or negative*) anybody
**Jemen** m ⟨-(s)⟩ Yemen
**jene(r, s)** *pron* that (one), those pl
**jenseits 1.** *adv* on the other side **2.** *prep + gen* on the other side of; *fig* beyond
**Jetlag** m ⟨-s⟩ jet lag
**jetzig** *adj* present
**jetzt** *adv* now; **erst ~** only now; **~ gleich** right now; **bis ~** so far, up to now; **von ~ an** from now on
**jeweils** *adv* **~ zwei zusammen** two at a time; **zu ~ 5 Euro** at 5 euros each
**Job** m ⟨-s, -s⟩ *fam* job; **jobben** vi *fam* work, have a job
**Jod** nt ⟨-(e)s⟩ iodine
**joggen** vi jog; **Jogging** nt ⟨-s⟩ jogging; **Jogginghose** f jogging pants pl

**Jog(h)urt** m or nt ⟨-s, -s⟩ yoghurt
**Johannisbeere** f **Schwarze ~** blackcurrant; **Rote ~** redcurrant
**Joint** m ⟨-s, -s⟩ *fam* joint
**jonglieren** vi juggle
**Jordanien** nt ⟨-s⟩ Jordan
**Journalist(in)** m(f) journalist
**Joystick** m ⟨-s, -s⟩ IT joystick
**jubeln** vi cheer
**Jubiläum** nt ⟨-s, Jubiläen⟩ jubilee; (*date*) anniversary
**jucken 1.** vi itch **2.** vt **es juckt mich am Arm** my arm is itching; **das juckt mich nicht** *fam* I couldn't care less; **Juckreiz** m itch
**Jude** m ⟨-n, -n⟩, **Jüdin** f Jew; **sie ist Jüdin** she's Jewish; **jüdisch** *adj* Jewish
**Judo** nt ⟨-(s)⟩ judo
**Jugend** f ⟨-⟩ youth; **Jugendgruppe** f youth group; **Jugendherberge** f ⟨-, -n⟩ youth hostel; **Jugendherbergsausweis** m youth hostel card; **jugendlich** *adj* youthful; **Jugendliche(r)** mf young person; **Jugendstil** m art nouveau; **Jugendzentrum** nt youth centre
**Jugoslawien** nt ⟨-s⟩ HIST Yugoslavia
**Juli** m ⟨-(s), -s⟩ July; → **Juni**
**jung** *adj* young
**Junge** m ⟨-n, -n⟩ boy
**Junge(s)** nt ⟨-n, -n⟩ young animal; **die ~n** pl the young pl
**Jungfrau** f virgin; ASTR Virgo

**Junggeselle** *m* ⟨-n, -n⟩ bachelor

**Juni** *m* ⟨-(s), -s⟩ June; **im ~** in June; **am 4. ~** on 4(th) June, on June 4(th) ; **Anfang / Mitte / Ende ~** at the beginning / in the middle / at the end of June; **letzten / nächsten ~** last / next June

**Jupiter** *m* ⟨-s⟩ Jupiter

**Jura** *no article* (*subject*) law; **~ studieren** study law; **Jurist(in)** *m(f)* lawyer; **juristisch** *adj* legal

**Justiz** *f* ⟨-⟩ justice; **Justizminister(in)** *m(f)* minister of justice

**Juwel** *nt* ⟨-s, -en⟩ jewel; **Juwelier(in)** *m(f)* ⟨-s, -e⟩ jeweller

# K

**Kabel** *nt* ⟨-s, -⟩ ELEC wire; (*thick*) cable; **Kabelfernsehen** *nt* cable television

**Kabeljau** *m* ⟨-s, -e *or* -s⟩ cod

**Kabine** *f* cabin; (*at swimming pool*) cubicle

**Kabrio** *nt* ⟨-s, -s⟩ convertible

**Kachel** *f* ⟨-, -n⟩ tile; **Kachelofen** *m* tiled stove

**Käfer** *m* ⟨-s, -⟩ beetle, bug (*US*)

**Kaff** *nt* ⟨-s, -s⟩ dump, hole

**Kaffee** *m* ⟨-s, -s⟩ coffee; **~ kochen** make some coffee; **Kaffeekanne** *f* coffeepot; **Kaffeelöffel** *m* coffee spoon; **Kaffeemaschine** *f* coffee maker (*or* machine); **Kaffeetasse** *f* coffee cup

**Käfig** *m* ⟨-s, -e⟩ cage

**kahl** *adj* (*person, head*) bald; (*tree, wall*) bare

**Kahn** *m* ⟨-(e)s, Kähne⟩ boat; (*for goods*) barge

**Kai** *m* ⟨-s, -e *or* -s⟩ quay

**Kaiser** *m* ⟨-s, -⟩ emperor; Kai-

serin *f* empress; **Kaiserschnitt** *m* MED caesarean (section)

**Kajak** *nt* ⟨-s, -s⟩ kayak; **Kajakfahren** *nt* kayaking

**Kajüte** *f* ⟨-, -n⟩ cabin

**Kakao** *m* ⟨-s, -s⟩ cocoa; (*drink*) (hot) chocolate

**Kakerlake** *f* ⟨-, -n⟩ cockroach

**Kaki** *f* ⟨-, -s⟩ kaki

**Kaktee** *f* ⟨-, -n⟩, **Kaktus** *m* ⟨-, -se⟩ cactus

**Kalb** *nt* ⟨-(e)s, Kälber⟩ calf; **Kalbfleisch** *nt* veal; **Kalbsbraten** *m* roast veal; **Kalbsschnitzel** *nt* veal cutlet; (*in breadcrumbs*) escalope of veal

**Kalender** *m* ⟨-s, -⟩ calendar; (*book*) diary

**Kalk** *m* ⟨-(e)s, -e⟩ lime; (*in bones*) calcium

**Kalorie** *f* calorie; **kalorienarm** *adj* low-calorie

**kalt** *adj* cold; **mir ist (es) ~** I'm cold; **kaltblütig** *adj* cold-

# Kälte

blooded; **Kälte** f ⟨-⟩ cold; fig coldness

**kam** imperf → **kommen**

**Kambodscha** nt ⟨-s⟩ Cambodia

**Kamel** nt ⟨-s, -e⟩ camel

**Kamera** f ⟨-, -s⟩ camera

**Kamerad(in)** m(f) ⟨-en, -en⟩ friend; (accompanying sb) companion

**Kamerafrau** f, **Kameramann** m camerawoman / -man

**Kamille** f ⟨-, -n⟩ camomile; **Kamillentee** m camomile tea

**Kamin** m ⟨-s, -e⟩ (outside) chimney; (inside) fireplace

**Kamm** m ⟨-(e)s, Kämme⟩ comb; (of mountain) ridge; (of cock) crest; **kämmen** vr sich ~, sich dat die Haare ~ comb one's hair

**Kampf** m ⟨-(e)s, Kämpfe⟩ fight; (in war) battle; (in sport etc) contest; fig struggle; **kämpfen** vi fight (für, um for); **Kampfsport** m martial art

**Kanada** m ⟨-s⟩ Canada; **Kanadier(in)** m(f) ⟨-s, -⟩ Canadian; **kanadisch** adj Canadian

**Kanal** m ⟨-s, Kanäle⟩ canal; (ditch, on TV) channel; **der ~** the (English) Channel; **Kanalinseln** pl Channel Islands pl; **Kanaltunnel** m Channel Tunnel

**Kanarienvogel** m canary

**Kandidat(in)** m(f) ⟨-en, -en⟩ candidate

**Kandis(zucker)** m ⟨-⟩ rock candy

**Känguru** nt ⟨-s, -s⟩ kangaroo

**Kaninchen** nt rabbit

**Kanister** m ⟨-s, -⟩ can

**Kännchen** nt ⟨-s⟩ pot; **ein ~ Kaffee / Tee** a pot of coffee / tea; **Kanne** f ⟨-, -n⟩ jug; (for coffee) pot; (for milk) churn; (for watering plants) can

**kannte** imperf → **kennen**

**Kante** f ⟨-, -n⟩ edge

**Kantine** f canteen

**Kanton** m ⟨-s, -e⟩ canton

**Kanu** nt ⟨-s, -s⟩ canoe

**Kanzler(in)** m(f) ⟨-s, -⟩ chancellor

**Kap** nt ⟨-s, -s⟩ cape

**Kapelle** f chapel; MUS band

**Kaper** f ⟨-, -n⟩ caper

**kapieren** vt, vi fam understand; **kapiert?** got it?

**Kapital** nt ⟨-s, -e or -ien⟩ capital

**Kapitän** m ⟨-s, -e⟩ captain

**Kapitel** nt ⟨-s, -⟩ chapter

**Kappe** f ⟨-, -n⟩ cap

**Kapsel** f ⟨-, -n⟩ capsule

**kaputt** adj fam broken; (person) exhausted; **kaputtgehen** irr vi break; (shoes) fall apart; **kaputtmachen** vt break; (person) wear out

**Kapuze** f ⟨-, -n⟩ hood

**Karaffe** f ⟨-, -n⟩ carafe; (with stopper) decanter

**Karamell** m ⟨-s⟩ caramel, toffee

**Karaoke** nt ⟨-(s)⟩ karaoke

**Karat** nt ⟨-s, -e⟩ carat

**Karate** nt ⟨-s⟩ karate

**Kardinal** m ⟨-s, Kardinäle⟩ cardinal

**Karfreitag** m Good Friday

**kariert** adj checked; (paper) squared

**Karies** f ⟨-⟩ (tooth) decay

**Karikatur** f caricature

**Karneval** m ⟨-s, -e or -s⟩ carnival

**Kärnten** nt ⟨-s⟩ Carinthia

**Karo** nt ⟨-s, -s⟩ square; (card suit) diamonds pl

**Karosserie** f AUTO body(-work)

**Karotte** f ⟨-, -n⟩ carrot

**Karpfen** m ⟨-s, -⟩ carp

**Karriere** f ⟨-, -n⟩ career

**Karte** f ⟨-, -n⟩ card; (of country etc) map; (in restaurant) menu; (for theatre, train etc) ticket; **mit ~ bezahlen** pay by credit card; **~n spielen** play cards; **die ~n mischen / geben** shuffle / deal the cards

**Kartei** f card index; **Karteikarte** f index card

**Kartenspiel** nt card game; **Kartentelefon** nt cardphone; **Kartenvorverkauf** m advance booking

**Kartoffel** f ⟨-, -n⟩ potato; **Kartoffelbrei** m mashed potatoes pl; **Kartoffelchips** pl crisps pl (Brit), chips pl (US); **Kartoffelsalat** m potato salad

**Karton** m ⟨-s, -s⟩ cardboard;

(container) (cardboard) box

**Karussell** nt ⟨-s, -s⟩ roundabout (Brit), merry-go-round

**Kaschmir** m ⟨-s, e⟩ cashmere

**Käse** m ⟨-s, -⟩ cheese; **Käsekuchen** m cheesecake; **Käseplatte** f cheeseboard

**Kasino** nt ⟨-s, -s⟩ casino

**Kasper(l)** m ⟨-s, -⟩ Punch; fig clown; **Kasperl(e)theater** nt Punch and Judy show

**Kasse** f ⟨-, -n⟩ (in shop) till, cash register; (in supermarket) checkout; (container) cashbox; (at theatre) box office; (at cinema) ticket office; (insurance scheme) health insurance; **Kassenbon** m ⟨-s, -s⟩, **Kassenzettel** m receipt

**Kassette** f (small) box; (tape) cassette; **Kassettenrekorder** m cassette recorder

**kassieren 1.** vt take **2.** vi **darf ich ~?** would you like to pay now?; **Kassierer(in)** m(f) cashier

**Kastanie** f chestnut

**Kasten** m ⟨-s, Kästen⟩ box; (for bottles) crate

**Kat** m abbr → **Katalysator**

**Katalog** m ⟨-(e)s, -e⟩ catalogue

**Katalysator** m AUTO catalytic converter

**Katar** nt ⟨-s⟩ Qatar

**Katarr(h)** m ⟨-s, -e⟩ catarrh

**Katastrophe** f ⟨-, -n⟩ catastrophe, disaster

**Kategorie** f ⟨-, -n⟩ category

**Kater** m ⟨-s, -⟩ tomcat; fam

hangover

**Kathedrale** f ⟨-, -n⟩ cathedral

**Katholik(in)** m(f) Catholic; **katholisch** adj Catholic

**Katze** f ⟨-, -n⟩ cat

**Kauderwelsch** nt ⟨-(s)⟩ gibberish

**kauen** vt, vi chew

**Kauf** m ⟨-(e)s, Käufe⟩ purchase; (action) buying; **ein guter ~** a bargain; **etw in ~ nehmen** put up with sth; **kaufen** vt buy; **Käufer(in)** m(f) buyer; **Kauffrau** f businesswoman; **Kaufhaus** nt department store; **Kaufmann** m businessman; (retailer) shopkeeper (Brit), storekeeper (US)

**Kaugummi** m chewing gum

**Kaulquappe** f ⟨-, -n⟩ tadpole

**kaum** adv hardly, scarcely

**Kaution** f ⟨-, -s⟩ deposit; LAW bail

**Kaviar** m caviar

**KB** nt⟨-,-⟩,**Kbyte** nt ⟨-, -⟩ abbr → **Kilobyte** KB

**Kebab** m ⟨-(s), -s⟩ kebab

**Kegel** m ⟨-s, -⟩ skittle; (in tenpin bowling) pin; MATH cone; **Kegelbahn** f bowling alley; **kegeln** vi play skittles; (in tenpin bowling) bowl

**Kehle** f ⟨-, -n⟩ throat; **Kehlkopf** m larynx

**kehren** vt (with brush) sweep

**Keilriemen** m AUTO fan belt

**kein** pron no, not ... any; **ich habe ~ Geld** I have no money, I don't have money; **keine(r, s)** pron no one, no-

body; (thing) not ... any, none; **~r von ihnen** none of them; (two people / things) neither of them; **ich will keins von beiden** I don't want either (of them); **keinesfalls** adv on no account, under no circumstances

**Keks** m ⟨-es, -e⟩ biscuit (Brit), cookie (US); **jdm auf den ~ gehen** fam get on sb's nerves

**Keller** m ⟨-s, -⟩ cellar; (storey) basement

**Kellner** m ⟨-s, -⟩ waiter; **Kellnerin** f waitress

**Kenia** nt ⟨-s⟩ Kenya

**kennen** ⟨kannte, gekannt⟩ vt know; **wir ~ uns seit 1990** we've known each other since 1990; **kennenlernen** vt get to know; **sich ~** get to know each other; (for the first time) meet

**Kenntnis** f knowledge; **seine ~se** his knowledge

**Kennwort** nt a. IT password; **Kennzeichen** nt mark, sign; AUTO number plate (Brit), license plate (US)

**Kerl** m ⟨-s, -e⟩ guy, bloke (Brit)

**Kern** m ⟨-(e)s, -e⟩ (of fruit) pip; (of peach, cherry etc) stone; (of nut) kernel; (of atom) nucleus; fig heart, core

**Kernenergie** f nuclear energy; **Kernkraft** f nuclear power; **Kernkraftwerk** nt nuclear power station

**Kerze** f ⟨-, -n⟩ candle; (*in engine*) plug

**Ket(s)chup** m or nt ⟨-(s), -s⟩ ketchup

**Kette** f ⟨-, -n⟩ chain; (*jewellery*) necklace

**keuchen** vi pant; **Keuchhusten** m whooping cough

**Keule** f ⟨-, -n⟩ club; GASTR leg; (*of chicken also*) drumstick

**Keyboard** nt ⟨-s, -s⟩ MUS keyboard

**Kfz** nt abbr → **Kraftfahrzeug**

**Kfz-Brief** m ≈ logbook

**Kfz-Steuer** f ≈ road tax (*Brit*), vehicle tax (*US*)

**Kichererbse** f chick pea

**kichern** vi giggle

**Kickboard**® nt ⟨-s, -s⟩ micro scooter

**Kicker** m ⟨-s, -⟩ table football (*Brit*), foosball (*US*)

**kidnappen** vt kidnap

**Kidney-Bohne** f kidney bean

**Kiefer 1.** m ⟨-s, -⟩ jaw **2.** f ⟨-, -n⟩ pine; **Kieferchirurg(in)** m(f) oral surgeon

**Kieme** f ⟨-, -n⟩ gill

**Kies** m ⟨-es, -e⟩ gravel; **Kiesel** m ⟨-s, -⟩, **Kieselstein** m pebble

**kiffen** vi fam smoke pot

**Kilo** nt ⟨-s, -(s)⟩ kilo; **Kilobyte** nt kilobyte; **Kilogramm** nt kilogram; **Kilometer** m kilometre; **Kilometerstand** m ≈ mileage; **Kilowatt** nt kilowatt

**Kind** nt ⟨-(e)s, -er⟩ child; *sie* **bekommt ein ~** she's having a baby; **Kinderarzt** m, **Kinderärztin** f paediatrician; **Kinderbetreuung** f childcare; **Kinderbett** nt cot (*Brit*), crib (*US*); **Kinderfahrkarte** f child's ticket; **Kindergarten** m nursery school, kindergarten; **Kindergärtner(in)** m(f) nursery-school teacher; **Kindergeld** nt child benefit; **Kinderkrankheit** f children's illness; **Kinderkrippe** f crèche (*Brit*), daycare center (*US*); **Kinderlähmung** f polio; **Kindermädchen** nt nanny (*Brit*), nurse(maid); **kindersicher** adj childproof; **Kindersicherung** f childproof safety catch; (*on bottle*) childproof cap; **Kindersitz** m child seat; **Kinderteller** m (*in restaurant*) children's portion; **Kinderwagen** m pram (*Brit*), baby carriage (*US*); **Kinderzimmer** nt children's (bed)room; **Kindheit** f childhood; **kindisch** adj childish; **kindlich** adj childlike

**Kinn** nt ⟨-(e)s, -e⟩ chin

**Kino** nt ⟨-s, -s⟩ cinema (*Brit*), movie theater (*US*); **ins ~ gehen** go to the cinema (*Brit*) (*or* to the movies (*US*))

**Kiosk** m ⟨-(e)s, -e⟩ kiosk

**Kippe** f fam cigarette end, fag end (*Brit*)

**Kirche** f ⟨-, -n⟩ church; **Kirchturm** m church tower; (pointed) steeple

**Kirmes** f ⟨-, -sen⟩ fair

**Kirsche** f ⟨-, -n⟩ cherry; **Kirschtomate** f cherry tomato

**Kissen** nt ⟨-s, -⟩ cushion; (on bed) pillow

**Kiste** f ⟨-, -n⟩ box; (trunk) chest

**KITA** f abbr = **Kindertagesstätte** day-care centre (Brit), daycare center (US)

**kitschig** adj kitschy, cheesy

**kitzelig** adj a. fig ticklish; **kitzeln** vt, vi tickle

**Kiwi** f ⟨-, -s⟩ kiwi (fruit)

**Klage** f ⟨-, -n⟩ complaint; LAW lawsuit; **klagen** vi complain (über + acc about, bei to); **kläglich** adj wretched

**Klammer** f ⟨-, -n⟩ (in text) bracket; (on documents) clip; (for washing) peg (Brit), clothespin (US); (on teeth) brace; **Klammeraffe** m fam at-sign, @; **klammern** vr cling (an + acc to)

**klang** imperf → **klingen**

**Klang** m ⟨-(e)s, Klänge⟩ sound

**Klappbett** nt folding bed

**klappen** vi impers (succeed) work; **es hat gut geklappt** it went well

**klappern** vi rattle; (pots and pans) clatter; **Klapperschlange** f rattlesnake

**Klappstuhl** m folding chair

**klar** adj clear; **sich** dat **im Kla-**

**ren sein** be clear (über + acc about); **alles ~?** everything okay?

**klären** 1. vt (liquid) purify; (problem, issue) clarify 2. vr clear itself up

**Klarinette** f ⟨-, -n⟩ clarinet

**klarkommen** irr vi **mit etw ~** cope with something; **kommst du klar?** are you managing all right?; **mit jdm ~** get along with sb; **klarmachen** vt **jdm etw ~** make sth clear to sb; **klarstellen** vt clarify

**Klärung** f (of problem, issue) clarification

**klasse** adj inv fam great, brilliant

**Klasse** f ⟨-, -n⟩ class; (year in school) form (Brit), grade (US); **erster ~ reisen** travel first class; **in welche ~ gehst du?** which form (Brit) (or grade (US)) are you in?; **Klassenarbeit** f test; **Klassenlehrer(in)** m(f) class teacher; **Klassenzimmer** nt classroom

**Klassik** f classical period; classical music

**Klatsch** m ⟨-(e)s, -e⟩ (talk) gossip; **klatschen** vi (hit) smack; (after concert etc) applaud, clap; (talk) gossip; **klatschnass** adj soaking (wet)

**Klaue** f ⟨-, -n⟩ claw; fam (handwriting) scrawl

**klauen** vt fam pinch

**Klavier** nt ⟨-s, -e⟩ piano

**Klebeband** nt adhesive tape; **kleben 1.** vt stick (an + acc to) **2.** vi (unpleasantly) be sticky; **klebrig** adj sticky; **Klebstoff** m glue; **Klebstreifen** m adhesive tape

**Klecks** m ⟨-es, -e⟩ blob; (of ink) blot

**Klee** m ⟨-s⟩ clover

**Kleid** nt ⟨-(e)s, -er⟩ dress; **~er** pl clothes pl; **Kleiderbügel** m coat hanger; **Kleiderschrank** m wardrobe (Brit), closet (US); **Kleidung** f clothing

**klein** adj small, little; (finger) little; **mein ~er Bruder** my little (or younger) brother; **als ich noch ~ war** when I was a little boy / girl; **etw ~ schneiden** chop sth up; **Kleinanzeige** f classified ad; **Kleinbuchstabe** m small letter; **Kleinbus** m minibus; **Kleingeld** nt change; **Kleinigkeit** f trifle; (meal) snack; **Kleinkind** nt toddler; **kleinschreiben** vt write with a small letter; **Kleinstadt** f small town

**Klempner(in)** m(f) plumber

**klettern** vi climb

**Klettverschluss** m Velcro® fastening

**klicken** vi a. IT click

**Klient(in)** m(f) ⟨-en, -en⟩ client

**Klima** nt ⟨-s, -s⟩ climate; **Klimaanlage** f air conditioning; **klimatisiert** adj air-conditioned

**Klinge** f ⟨-, -n⟩ blade

**Klingel** f ⟨-, -n⟩ bell; **klingeln** vi ring

**klingen** ⟨klang, geklungen⟩ vi sound

**Klinik** f clinic; (non-specialist) hospital

**Klinke** f ⟨-, -n⟩ handle

**Klippe** f ⟨-, -n⟩ cliff; (in sea) reef; fig hurdle

**Klischee** nt ⟨-s, -s⟩ fig cliché

**Klo** nt ⟨-s, -s⟩ fam loo (Brit), john (US); **Klobrille** f toilet seat; **Klopapier** nt toilet paper

**klopfen** vt, vi knock; (heart) thump

**Kloß** m ⟨-es, Klöße⟩ (in throat) lump; GASTR dumpling

**Kloster** nt ⟨-s, Klöster⟩ monastery; (for women) convent

**Klub** m ⟨-s, -s⟩ club

**klug** adj clever

**knabbern** vt, vi nibble

**Knäckebrot** nt crispbread

**knacken** vt, vi crack

**Knall** m ⟨-(e)s, -e⟩ bang; **knallen** vi bang

**knapp** adj (in short supply) scarce; (victory) narrow; **~ bei Kasse sein** be short of money; **~ zwei Stunden** just under two hours

**kneifen** ⟨kniff, gekniffen⟩ vt, vi pinch; (shirk) back out (vor + dat of)

**Kneipe** f ⟨-, -n⟩ fam pub (Brit), bar

**Knete** f ‹-› fam (money) dough; **kneten** vt knead; (shape) mould

**knicken** vt, vi break; (paper) fold

**Knie** nt ‹-s, -› knee; **in die ~ gehen** bend one's knees; **Kniebeuge** f knee bend; **Kniegelenk** nt knee joint; **Kniekehle** f back of the knee; **knien** vi kneel; **Kniescheibe** f kneecap; **Knieschoner** m ‹-s, -›, **Knieschützer** m ‹-s, -› knee pad

**kniff** imperf → **kneifen**

**knipsen 1.** vt, vi snap; PHOT snap **2.** vi PHOT take snaps

**knirschen** vi crunch; **mit den Zähnen ~** grind one's teeth

**knitterfrei** adj non-crease; **knittern** vi crease

**Knoblauch** m garlic; **Knoblauchbrot** nt garlic bread; **Knoblauchzehe** f clove of garlic

**Knöchel** m ‹-s, -› knuckle; (of foot) ankle

**Knochen** m ‹-s, -› bone; **Knochenbruch** m fracture; **Knochenmark** nt marrow

**Knödel** m ‹-s, -› dumpling

**Knopf** m ‹-(e)s, Knöpfe› button; **Knopfdruck** m **auf ~** at the touch of a button; **Knopfloch** nt buttonhole

**Knospe** f ‹-, -n› bud

**knoten** vt knot; **Knoten** m ‹-s, -› knot; MED lump

**Know-how** nt ‹-(s)› know-how, expertise

**knurren** vi (dog) growl; (stomach) rumble; (person) grumble

**knusprig** adj crisp; (biscuit) crunchy

**knutschen** vi fam smooch

**k. o.** adj inv SPORT knocked out; fig knackered

**Koalition** f coalition

**Koch** m ‹-(e)s, Köche› cook; **Kochbuch** nt cookery book, cookbook; **kochen** vt, vi cook; (water) boil; (coffee, tea) make; **Köchin** f cook; **Kochlöffel** m wooden spoon; **Kochnische** f kitchenette; **Kochplatte** f hotplate; **Kochrezept** nt recipe; **Kochtopf** m saucepan

**Kode** m ‹-s, -s› code

**Köder** m ‹-s, -› bait

**Koffein** nt ‹-s› caffeine; **koffeinfrei** adj decaffeinated

**Koffer** m ‹-s, -› (suit)case; **Kofferraum** m AUTO boot (Brit), trunk (US)

**Kognak** m ‹-s, -s› brandy

**Kohl** m ‹-(e)s, -e› cabbage

**Kohle** f ‹-, -n› coal; (made from wood) charcoal; fam (money) cash, dough; **Kohlehydrat** nt carbohydrate; **Kohlendioxid** nt carbon dioxide; **Kohlensäure** f (in drinks) fizz; **ohne ~** still, non-carbonated (US); **mit ~** sparkling, carbonated (US)

**Kohlrabi** m ‹-(s), -(s)› kohlrabi

**Koje** f ‹-, -n› cabin; (bed)

bunk

**Kokain** nt ⟨-s⟩ cocaine

**Kokosnuss** f coconut

**Kolben** m ⟨-s, -⟩ TECH piston

**Kolik** f ⟨-, -en⟩ colic

**Kollaps** m ⟨-es, -e⟩ collapse

**Kollege** m ⟨-n, -n⟩, **Kollegin** f colleague

**Köln** nt ⟨-s⟩ Cologne

**Kolonne** f ⟨-, -n⟩ convoy

**Kolumbien** nt ⟨-s⟩ Columbia

**Koma** nt ⟨-s, -s⟩ coma

**Kombi** m ⟨-(s), -s⟩ estate (car) (Brit), station wagon (US); **Kombination** f combination; (reasoning) deduction; **kombinieren 1.** vt combine **2.** vi reason; (suspect) guess

**Komfort** m ⟨-s⟩ conveniences pl; (of guest, room etc) comfort

**Komiker(in)** m(f) comedian, comic; **komisch** adj funny

**Komma** nt ⟨-s, -s⟩ comma

**kommen** ⟨kam, gekommen⟩ vi come; (come closer) approach; (occur) happen; (reach, begin) get; (become visible) appear; (to school, prison etc) go; **zu sich ~** come round (or to); **zu etw ~ (get)** acquire sth; (find time for) get round to sth; **wer kommt zuerst?** who's first?; **kommend** adj coming; **~e Woche** next week; **in den ~en Jahren** in the years to come

**Kommentar** m commentary; **kein ~** no comment

**Kommilitone** m ⟨-n, -n⟩, **Kommilitonin** f fellow student

**Kommissar(in)** m(f) inspector

**Kommode** f ⟨-, -n⟩ chest of drawers

**Kommunikation** f communication

**Kommunion** f REL communion

**Kommunismus** m communism

**Komödie** f comedy

**kompakt** adj compact

**Kompass** m ⟨-es, -e⟩ compass

**kompatibel** adj compatible

**kompetent** adj competent

**komplett** adj complete

**Kompliment** nt compliment; **jdm ein ~ machen** pay sb a compliment; **~!** congratulations

**kompliziert** adj complicated

**Komponist(in)** m(f) composer

**Kompost** m ⟨-(e)s, -e⟩ compost; **Komposthaufen** m compost heap

**Kompott** nt ⟨-(e)s, -e⟩ stewed fruit

**Kompresse** f ⟨-, -n⟩ compress

**Kompromiss** m ⟨-es, -e⟩ compromise

**Kondition** f condition; **sie hat eine gute ~** she's in good shape

**Konditorei** f cake shop; (serving coffee etc) café

**Kondom** nt ⟨-s, -e⟩ condom

**Konfektionsgröße** f size
**Konferenz** f conference
**Konfession** f religion; (within Christianity) denomination
**Konfetti** nt ⟨-(s)⟩ confetti
**Konfirmation** f REL confirmation
**Konflikt** m ⟨-(e)s, -e⟩ conflict
**konfrontieren** vt confront
**Kongo** m ⟨-s⟩ Congo
**Kongress** m ⟨-es, -e⟩ conference; **der ~** (US parliament) Congress
**König** m ⟨-(e)s, -e⟩ king; **Königin** f queen; **königlich** adj royal; **Königreich** nt kingdom
**Konkurrenz** f competition
**können** ⟨konnte, gekonnt⟩ vt, vi be able to, can; (poem, song) know; **~ Sie Deutsch?** can (or do) you speak German?; **ich kann nicht kommen** I can't come; **das kann sein** that's possible; **ich kann nichts dafür** it's not my fault
**konsequent** adj consistent
**konservativ** adj conservative
**Konserven** pl tinned food sg (Brit), canned food sg; **Konservendose** f tin (Brit), can
**konservieren** vt preserve; **Konservierungsmittel** nt preservative
**Konsonant** m consonant
**Konsul(in)** m(f) ⟨-s, -n⟩ consul; **Konsulat** nt consulate
**Kontakt** m ⟨-(e)s, -e⟩ contact;

**kontaktarm** adj **er ist ~** he lacks contact with other people; **kontaktfreudig** adj sociable; **Kontaktlinsen** pl contact lenses pl
**Kontinent** m continent
**Konto** nt ⟨-s, Konten⟩ account; **Kontoauszug** m (bank) statement; **Kontoinhaber(in)** m(f) account holder; **Kontonummer** f account number; **Kontostand** m balance
**Kontrabass** m double bass
**Kontrast** m ⟨-(e)s, -e⟩ contrast
**Kontrolle** f ⟨-, -n⟩ control; (checking) supervision; (at airport etc) passport control; **kontrollieren** vt control; (verify) check
**Konzentration** f concentration; **Konzentrationslager** nt HIST concentration camp; **konzentrieren** vt, vr concentrate
**Konzept** nt ⟨-(e)s, -e⟩ rough draft
**Konzern** m ⟨-(e)s, -e⟩ firm
**Konzert** nt ⟨-(e)s, -e⟩ concert; (piece of music) concerto; **Konzertsaal** m concert hall
**koordinieren** vt coordinate
**Kopf** m ⟨-(e)s, Köpfe⟩ head; **Kopfhörer** m headphones pl; **Kopfkissen** nt pillow; **Kopfsalat** m lettuce; **Kopfschmerzen** pl headache sg; **Kopfstütze** f headrest; **Kopftuch** nt headscarf
**Kopie** f copy; **kopieren** vt a. IT

copy; **Kopierer** m ⟨-s, -⟩, **Kopiergerät** nt copier

**Kopilot(in)** m(f) co-pilot

**Koralle** f ⟨-, -n⟩ coral

**Koran** m ⟨-s⟩ REL Koran

**Korb** m ⟨-(e)s, Körbe⟩ basket; **jdm einen ~ geben** fig turn sb down

**Kord** m ⟨-(e)s, -e⟩ corduroy

**Kordel** f ⟨-, -n⟩ cord

**Kork** m ⟨-(e)s, -e⟩ cork; **Korken** m ⟨-s, -⟩ cork; **Korkenzieher** m ⟨-s, -⟩ corkscrew

**Korn** nt ⟨-(e)s, Körner⟩ grain; **Kornblume** f cornflower

**Körper** m ⟨-s, -⟩ body; **Körperbau** m build; **Körpergeruch** m body odour; **körperlich** adj physical; **Körperverletzung** f physical injury

**korrekt** adj correct

**Korrespondent(in)** m(f) correspondent; **Korrespondenz** f correspondence

**korrigieren** vt correct

**Kosmetik** f cosmetics pl; **Kosmetikkoffer** m vanity case; **Kosmetiksalon** m beauty parlour

**Kost** f ⟨-⟩ food; (meals) board

**kostbar** adj precious; (dear) costly, expensive

**kosten 1.** vt cost **2.** vt, vi (sample) taste; **Kosten** pl costs pl, cost; (money spent) expenses pl; **auf ~ von** at the expense of; **kostenlos** adj free (of charge); **Kostenvoranschlag** m estimate

**köstlich** adj (food) delicious;

**sich ~ amüsieren** have a marvellous time

**Kostprobe** f taster; fig sample; **kostspielig** adj expensive

**Kostüm** nt ⟨-s, -e⟩ costume; (jacket and skirt) suit

**Kot** m ⟨-(e)s⟩ excrement

**Kotelett** nt ⟨-(e)s, -e or -s⟩ chop, cutlet

**Koteletten** pl sideboards pl (Brit), sideburns pl (US)

**Kotflügel** m AUTO wing

**kotzen** vi vulg puke, throw up

**Krabbe** f ⟨-, -n⟩ shrimp; (larger) prawn; (with pincers) crab

**krabbeln** vi crawl

**Krach** m ⟨-(e)s, -s or -e⟩ crash; (continuous) noise; fam (argument) row

**Kraft** f ⟨-, Kräfte⟩ strength; POL, PHYS force; (ability) power; **in ~ treten** come into effect; **Kraftausdruck** m swearword; **Kraftfahrzeug** nt motor vehicle; **Kraftfahrzeugbrief** m ≈ logbook; **Kraftfahrzeugschein** m vehicle registration document; **Kraftfahrzeugsteuer** f ≈ road tax (Brit), vehicle tax (US); **Kraftfahrzeugversicherung** f car insurance; **kräftig** adj strong; healthy; (colour) intense, strong; **Kraftstoff** m fuel; **Kraftwerk** nt power station

**Kragen** m ⟨-s, -⟩ collar

**Krähe** f ⟨-, -n⟩ crow

# Kralle

**Kralle** f ⟨-, -n⟩ claw; (on car) wheel clamp

**Kram** m ⟨-(e)s⟩ stuff

**Krampf** m ⟨-(e)s, Krämpfe⟩ cramp; (twitching) spasm; **Krampfader** f varicose vein

**Kran** m ⟨-(e)s, Kräne⟩ crane

**Kranich** m ⟨-s, -e⟩ ZOOL crane

**krank** adj ill, sick

**kränken** vt hurt

**Krankengymnastik** f physiotherapy; **Krankenhaus** nt hospital; **Krankenkasse** f health insurance; **Krankenpfleger** m ⟨-s, -⟩ (male) nurse; **Krankenschein** m health insurance certificate; **Krankenschwester** f nurse; **Krankenversicherung** f health insurance; **Krankenwagen** m ambulance; **Krankheit** f illness; (infectious) disease

**Kränkung** f insult

**Kranz** m ⟨-es, Kränze⟩ wreath

**krass** adj crass; fam (wonderful) wicked

**kratzen** vt, vi scratch; **Kratzer** m ⟨-s, -⟩ scratch

**kraulen 1.** vi (swim) do the crawl **2.** vt (stroke) pet

**Kraut** nt ⟨-(e)s, Kräuter⟩ cabbage; **Kräuter** pl herbs pl; **Kräuterbutter** f herb butter; **Kräutertee** m herbal tea; **Krautsalat** m coleslaw

**Krawatte** f tie

**kreativ** adj creative

**Krebs** m ⟨-es, -e⟩ ZOOL crab; MED cancer; ASTR Cancer

**Kredit** m ⟨-(e)s, -e⟩ credit; **auf ~ on** credit; **einen ~ aufnehmen** take out a loan; **Kreditkarte** f credit card

**Kreide** f ⟨-, -n⟩ chalk

**Kreis** m ⟨-es, -e⟩ circle; (administrative area) district

**Kreisel** m ⟨-s, -⟩ (toy) top; (on road) roundabout (Brit), traffic circle (US)

**Kreislauf** m MED circulation; fig (of nature etc) cycle; **Kreislaufstörungen** pl MED **ich habe ~** I've got problems with my circulation; **Kreisverkehr** m roundabout (Brit), traffic circle (US)

**Kren** m ⟨-s⟩ horseradish

**Kresse** f ⟨-, -n⟩ cress

**Kreuz** nt ⟨-es, -e⟩ cross; ANAT small of the back; (card suit) clubs pl; **mir tut das ~ weh** I've got backache; **Kreuzband** nt cruciate ligament; **Kreuzfahrt** f cruise; **Kreuzgang** m cloisters pl; **Kreuzotter** f ⟨-, -n⟩ adder; **Kreuzschlüssel** m AUTO wheel brace; **Kreuzschmerzen** pl backache sg; **Kreuzung** f crossroads sg, intersection; (animal, plant) cross; **Kreuzworträtsel** nt crossword (puzzle)

**kriechen** ⟨kroch, gekrochen⟩ vi crawl; (unobtrusively) creep; fig pej **(vor jdm) ~** crawl (to sb)

**Krieg** m ⟨-(e)s, -e⟩ war

**kriegen** vt fam get; (rascal)

*bus etc*) catch; **sie kriegt ein Kind** she's having a baby; **ich kriege noch Geld von dir** you still owe me some money

**Krimi** m ⟨-s, -s⟩ *fam* thriller; **Kriminalität** f criminality; **Kriminalpolizei** f detective force, ≈ CID (*Brit*), ≈ FBI (*US*); **Kriminalroman** m detective novel; **kriminell** *adj* criminal

**Krippe** f ⟨-, -n⟩ manger; (*Nativity scene*) crib (*Brit*), crèche (*US*); (*nursery*) crèche (*Brit*), daycare center (*US*)

**Krise** f ⟨-, -n⟩ crisis

**Kristall 1.** m ⟨-s, -e⟩ crystal **2.** nt ⟨-s⟩ (*glass*) crystal

**Kritik** f criticism; (*of film, book etc*) review; **Kritiker(in)** m(f) critic; **kritisch** *adj* critical

**kritzeln** *vt, vi* scribble, scrawl

**Kroate** m ⟨-n, -n⟩ Croat; **Kroatien** nt ⟨-s⟩ Croatia; **Kroatin** f Croat; **kroatisch** *adj* Croatian; **Kroatisch** nt Croatian

**kroch** *imperf* → **kriechen**

**Krokodil** nt ⟨-s, -e⟩ crocodile

**Krokus** m ⟨-, -*or*-se⟩ crocus

**Krone** f ⟨-, -n⟩ crown

**Kröte** f ⟨-, -n⟩ toad

**Krücke** f ⟨-, -n⟩ crutch

**Krug** m ⟨-(e)s, Krüge⟩ jug; (*for beer*) mug

**Krümel** m ⟨-s, -⟩ crumb

**krumm** *adj* crooked

**Kruste** f ⟨-, -n⟩ crust

**Kruzifix** nt ⟨-es, -e⟩ crucifix

**Kuba** nt ⟨-s⟩ Cuba

**Kübel** m ⟨-s, -⟩ tub; (*with handle*) bucket

**Kubikmeter** m cubic metre

**Küche** f ⟨-, -n⟩ kitchen; (*activity*) cooking

**Kuchen** m ⟨-s, -⟩ cake; **Kuchengabel** f cake fork

**Küchenmaschine** f food processor; **Küchenpapier** nt kitchen roll; **Küchenschrank** m (kitchen) cupboard

**Kuckuck** m ⟨-s, -e⟩ cuckoo

**Kugel** f ⟨-, -n⟩ ball; MATH sphere; MIL bullet; (*on Christmas tree*) bauble; **Kugellager** nt ball bearing; **Kugelschreiber** m (ball-point) pen, biro® (*Brit*); **Kugelstoßen** nt ⟨-s⟩ shot put

**Kuh** f ⟨-, Kühe⟩ cow

**kühl** *adj* cool; **Kühlbox** f cool box; **kühlen** *vt* cool; **Kühler** m ⟨-s, -⟩ AUTO radiator; **Kühlerhaube** f AUTO bonnet (*Brit*), hood (*US*); **Kühlschrank** m fridge, refrigerator; **Kühltasche** f cool bag; **Kühltruhe** f freezer

**Kuhstall** m cowshed

**Küken** nt ⟨-s, -⟩ chick

**Kuli** m ⟨-s, -s⟩ *fam* pen, biro® (*Brit*)

**Kulisse** f ⟨-, -n⟩ scenery

**Kult** m ⟨-(e)s, -e⟩ cult; **Kultfigur** f cult figure

**Kultur** f culture; (*way of life*) civilization; **Kulturbeutel** m toilet bag (Brit), washbag; **kulturell** adj cultural

**Kümmel** m ⟨-s, -⟩ caraway seeds pl

**Kummer** m ⟨-s⟩ grief, sorrow

**kümmern 1.** vr sich um jdn ~ look after sb; **sich um etw ~** see to sth **2.** vt concern; **das kümmert mich nicht** that doesn't worry me

**Kumpel** m ⟨-s, -⟩ fam mate, pal

**Kunde** m ⟨-n, -n⟩ customer; **Kundendienst** m after-sales (or customer) service; **Kunden(kredit)karte** f storecard, chargecard; **Kundennummer** f customer number

**kündigen 1.** vi hand in one's notice; (tenant) give notice that one is moving out; **jdm ~** give sb his / her notice; (landlord) give sb notice to quit **2.** vt cancel; (contract) terminate; **jdm die Stellung ~** give sb his / her notice; **Kündigung** f (from job) dismissal; (of contract) termination; (of subscription) cancellation; (period of notification) notice

**Kundin** f customer; **Kundschaft** f customers pl

**künftig** adj future

**Kunst** f ⟨-, Künste⟩ art; (ability) skill; **Kunstausstellung** f art exhibition; **Kunstgewerbe** nt arts and crafts pl; **Künstler(in)** m(f) ⟨-s, -⟩ art-

ist; **künstlerisch** adj artistic

**künstlich** adj artificial

**Kunststoff** m synthetic material; **Kunststück** nt trick; **Kunstwerk** nt work of art

**Kupfer** nt ⟨-s⟩ copper

**Kuppel** f ⟨-, -n⟩ dome

**kuppeln** vi AUTO operate the clutch; **Kupplung** f coupling; AUTO clutch

**Kur** f ⟨-, -en⟩ course of treatment; (at health resort) cure

**Kür** f ⟨-, -en⟩ SPORT free programme

**Kurbel** f ⟨-, -n⟩ winder

**Kürbis** m ⟨-ses, -se⟩ pumpkin

**Kurierdienst** m courier service

**Kurort** m health resort

**Kurs** m ⟨-es, -e⟩ course; FIN rate; (for foreign currency) exchange rate

**kursiv 1.** adj italic **2.** adv in italics

**Kursleiter(in)** m(f) course tutor; **Kursteilnehmer(in)** m(f) (course) participant

**Kurve** f ⟨-, -n⟩ curve; (in road) bend; **kurvenreich** adj (road) winding

**kurz** adj short; (with time also) brief; **~ vorher / darauf** shortly before / after; **kannst du ~ kommen?** could you come here for a minute?; **~ gesagt** in short; **kurzärmelig** adj short-sleeved; **kürzen** vt cut short; (in length) shorten; (salary) reduce; **kurzerhand** adv on

the spot; **kurzfristig** *adj*
short-term; ***das Konzert
wurde ~ abgesagt*** the concert was called off at short
notice; **Kurzgeschichte** *f*
short story; **kürzlich** *adv* recently; **Kurzparkzone** *f*
short-stay (*Brit*) (*or* short-
-term (*US*)) parking zone;
**Kurzschluss** *m* ELEC short
circuit; **kurzsichtig** *adj*
short-sighted; **Kurztrip** *m*
trip, break; **Kurzurlaub** *m*
short holiday (*Brit*), short
vacation (*US*)

**Kusine** *f* cousin
**Kuss** *m* ‹-es, Küsse› kiss; **küs-
sen** *vt, vr* kiss
**Küste** *f* ‹-, -n› coast; (*strip of
land*) shore; **Küstenwache** *f*
coastguard
**Kutsche** *f* ‹-, -n› carriage; (*en-
closed*) coach
**Kuvert** *nt* ‹-s, -s› envelope
**Kuvertüre** *f* ‹-, -n› coating
**Kuwait** *nt* ‹-s› Kuwait
**KZ** *nt* ‹-s, -s› *abbr* → **Konzen-
trationslager** HIST concen-
tration camp

# L

**Labor** *nt* ‹-s, -e *or* -s› lab
**Labyrinth** *nt* ‹-s, -e› maze
**lächeln** *vi* smile; **Lächeln** *nt*
‹-s› smile; **lachen** *vi* laugh;
**lächerlich** *adj* ridiculous
**Lachs** *m* ‹-es, -e› salmon
**Lack** *m* ‹-(e)s, -e› varnish;
(*coloured*) lacquer; (*for
car*) paint; **lackieren** *vt* varnish; (*car*) spray; **Lacksch-
aden** *m* scratch (on the paint-
work)
**Ladegerät** *nt* (battery) charger; **laden** ‹lud, geladen› *v a.*
IT load; (*guest*) invite; (*mobile phone etc*) charge
**Laden** *m* ‹-s, Läden› shop; (*on
window*) shutter; **Laden-
dieb(in)** *m(f)* shoplifter; **La-
dendiebstahl** *m* shoplifting
**Ladung** *f* load; NAUT, AVIAT

cargo
**lag** *imperf* → **liegen**
**Lage** *f* ‹-, -n› position, situation
**Lager** *nt* ‹-s, -› camp; COMM
warehouse; TECH bearing;
**Lagerfeuer** *nt* campfire; **lagern** *vt* store
**Lagune** *f* lagoon
**lahm** *adj* lame; (*dreary*) dull;
**lähmen** *vt* paralyse; **Läh-
mung** *f* paralysis
**Laib** *m* ‹-s, -e› loaf
**Laie** *m* ‹-n, -n› layman
**Laken** *nt* ‹-s, -› sheet
**Lakritze** *f* ‹-, -n› liquorice
**Lamm** *nt* ‹-(e)s, Lämmer› (*also
meat*) lamb
**Lampe** *f* ‹-, -n› lamp; (*in
lamp*) bulb; **Lampenfieber**
*nt* stage fright; **Lampen-**

**schirm** m lampshade

**Lampion** m ⟨-s, -s⟩ Chinese lantern

**Land** nt ⟨-(e)s, Länder⟩ land; (nation) country; (German federal division) state, Land; **auf dem ~(e)** in the country

**Landebahn** f runway; **landen** vt, vi land

**Länderspiel** nt international (match)

**Landesgrenze** f national border, frontier; **Landeswährung** f national currency; **landesweit** adj nationwide

**Landhaus** nt country house; **Landkarte** f map; **Landkreis** m administrative region, ≈ district

**ländlich** adj rural

**Landschaft** f countryside; (beautiful) scenery; ART landscape; **Landstraße** f country road, B road (Brit)

**Landung** f landing; **Landungsbrücke** f, **Landungssteg** m gangway

**Landwirt(in)** m(f) farmer; **Landwirtschaft** f agriculture, farming; **landwirtschaftlich** adj agricultural

**lang** adj long; (person) tall; **ein zwei Meter ~er Tisch** a table two metres long; **den ganzen Tag ~** all day long; **langärmelig** adj long-sleeved; **lange** adv (for) a long time; **ich musste ~ warten** I had to wait (for)

a long time; **ich bleibe nicht ~** I won't stay long; **es ist ~ her, dass wir uns gesehen haben** it's a long time since we saw each other; **Länge** f ⟨-, -n⟩ length; GEO longitude

**langen** vi fam be enough; fam (with hand) reach (nach for); **mir langt's** I've had enough

**Langeweile** f boredom

**langfristig 1.** adj long-term **2.** adv in the long term

**Langlauf** m cross-country skiing

**langsam 1.** adj slow **2.** adv slowly

**Langschläfer(in)** m(f) ⟨-s, -⟩ late riser

**längst** adv **das ist ~ fertig** that was finished a long time ago; **sie sollte ~ da sein** she should have been here long ago; **als sie kam, waren wir ~ weg** when she arrived we had long since left

**Langstreckenflug** m long-haul flight

**Languste** f ⟨-, -n⟩ crayfish, crawfish (US)

**langweilen** vt bore; **ich langweile mich** I'm bored; **langweilig** adj boring

**Laos** nt ⟨-⟩ Laos

**Lappen** m ⟨-s, -⟩ cloth, rag; (for dusting) duster

**läppisch** adj silly; (amount of money) ridiculous

**Laptop** m ⟨-s, -s⟩ laptop

**Lärche** f ⟨-, -n⟩ larch

**Lärm** *m* ⟨-(e)s⟩ noise

**las** *imperf* → **lesen**

**Lasche** *f* ⟨-, -n⟩ flap

**Laser** *m* ⟨-s, -⟩ laser; **Laserdrucker** *m* laser printer

**lassen** ⟨ließ, gelassen⟩ *vi, vt* (*allow*) let; (*in a place, a condition*) leave; (*cease*) stop; **etw machen** ~ have sth done; **sich** *dat* **die Haare schneiden** ~ have one's hair cut; **jdn etw machen** ~ make sb do sth; **lass das!** stop it!

**lässig** *adj* casual

**Last** *f* ⟨-, -en⟩ load; (*duty, obligation etc*) burden

**Laster** *m* ⟨-s, -⟩ vice; *fam* truck, lorry (*Brit*)

**lästern** *vi* **über jdn** / **etw** ~ make nasty remarks about sb/sth

**lästig** *adj* annoying; (*person*) tiresome

**Last-Minute-Angebot** *nt* last-minute offer; **Last-Minute-Flug** *m* last-minute flight; **Last-Minute-Ticket** *nt* last-minute ticket

**Lastwagen** *m* truck, lorry (*Brit*)

**Latein** *nt* ⟨-s⟩ Latin

**Laterne** *f* ⟨-, -n⟩ lantern; (*in street*) streetlight

**Latte** *f* ⟨-, -n⟩ slat; *SPORT* bar

**Latz** *m* ⟨-es, Lätze⟩ bib; **Lätzchen** *nt* bib; **Latzhose** *f* dungarees *pl*

**lau** *adj* (*wind, air*) mild

**Laub** *nt* ⟨-(e)s⟩ foliage; **Laubfrosch** *m* tree frog

**Lauch** *m* ⟨-(e)s, -e⟩ leeks *pl*; **eine Stange** ~ a leek; **Lauchzwiebel** *f* spring onions *pl* (*Brit*), scallions *pl* (*US*)

**Lauf** *m* ⟨-(e)s, Läufe⟩ run; (*contest*) race; (*development*) course; **Laufbahn** *f* career; **laufen** ⟨lief, gelaufen⟩ *vi, vt* walk; (*function*) work; **mir läuft die Nase** my nose is running; **was läuft im Kino?** what's on at the cinema?; **wie läuft's so?** how are things?; **laufend** *adj* running; (*month, expenses*) current; **auf dem Laufenden sein** / **halten** be / keep up-to-date; **Läufer** *m* ⟨-s, -⟩ (*carpet*) rug; (*in chess*) bishop; **Läufer(in)** *m(f)* SPORT runner; **Laufmasche** *f* ladder (*Brit*), run (*US*); **Laufwerk** *nt* IT drive

**Laune** *f* ⟨-, -n⟩ mood; **gute** / **schlechte** ~ **haben** be in a good / bad mood; **launisch** *adj* moody

**Laus** *f* ⟨-, Läuse⟩ louse

**lauschen** *vi* listen; (*secretly*) eavesdrop

**laut 1.** *adj* loud **2.** *adv* loudly; (*read*) aloud **3.** *prep* + *gen or dat* according to

**läuten** *vt, vi* ring

**lauter** *adv fam* nothing but

**Lautsprecher** *m* loudspeaker; **Lautstärke** *f* loudness; RADIO, TV volume

**lauwarm** *adj* lukewarm

**Lava** *f* ⟨-, Laven⟩ lava

**Lavendel** m ⟨-s, -⟩ lavender

**Lawine** f avalanche

**leasen** vt lease; **Leasing** nt ⟨-s⟩ leasing

**leben** vt, vi live; (not be dead) be alive; **wie lange ~ Sie schon hier?** how long have you been living here?; **von ... ~** (food etc) live on ...; (occupation, activity) make one's living from ...; **Leben** nt ⟨-s, -⟩ life; **lebend** adj living; **lebendig** adj alive; (full of live) lively; **lebensgefährlich** adj very dangerous; (injury) critical; **Lebensgefährte** m, **Lebensgefährtin** f partner; **Lebenshaltungskosten** pl cost sg of living; **lebenslänglich** adj for life; **~ bekommen** get life; **Lebenslauf** m curriculum vitae (Brit), CV (Brit), resumé (US); **Lebensmittel** pl food sg; **Lebensmittelgeschäft** nt grocer's (shop); **Lebensmittelvergiftung** f food poisoning; **lebensnotwendig** adj vital; **Lebensretter(in)** m(f) rescuer; **Lebensstandard** m standard of living; **Lebenszeichen** nt sign of life

**Leber** f ⟨-, -n⟩ liver; **Leberfleck** m mole; **Leberpastete** f liver pâté

**Lebewesen** nt living being

**lebhaft** adj lively; (memory, impression) vivid

**Lebkuchen** m gingerbread

**leblos** adj lifeless

**Leck** nt leak

**lecken 1.** vi (container, ship) leak **2.** vt, vi lick

**lecker** adj delicious, tasty

**Leder** nt ⟨-s, -⟩ leather

**ledig** adj single

**leer** adj empty; (page) blank; (battery) dead; **leeren** vt, vr empty; **Leerlauf** m (gear) neutral; **Leerung** f emptying; (from postbox) collection

**legal** adj legal, lawful

**legen 1.** vt put, place; (eggs) lay **2.** vr lie down; (storm, excitement) die down; (pain, feeling) wear off

**leger** adj casual

**Lehm** m ⟨-(e)s, -e⟩ loam; (for bricks etc) clay

**Lehne** f ⟨-, -n⟩ arm(rest); back (-rest); **lehnen** vt, vr lean

**Lehrbuch** nt textbook; **Lehre** f ⟨-, -n⟩ teaching; (vocational) apprenticeship; (moral) lesson; **lehren** vt teach; **Lehrer(in)** m(f) ⟨-s, -⟩ teacher; **Lehrgang** m course; **Lehrling** m apprentice; **lehrreich** adj instructive

**Leibwächter(in)** m(f) bodyguard

**Leiche** f ⟨-, -n⟩ corpse; **Leichenwagen** m hearse

**leicht 1.** adj light; (task etc) easy, simple; (illness) slight; **es sich dat ~ machen** take the easy way out **2.** adv easily; (a bit) slightly; **Leicht-**

**athletik** f athletics sg; **leichtfallen** irr vi be easy for sb; **leichtsinnig** adj careless; (stronger) reckless

**leid** adj jdn / etw ~ **sein** be tired of sb/sth; **Leid** nt ⟨-(e)s⟩ grief, sorrow; **leiden** ⟨litt, gelitten⟩ vi, vt suffer (an, unter + dat from); **ich kann ihn / es nicht ~** I can't stand him / it; **Leiden** nt ⟨-s, -⟩ suffering; (medical) illness

**Leidenschaft** f passion; **leidenschaftlich** adj passionate

**leider** adv unfortunately; **wir müssen jetzt ~ gehen** I'm afraid we have to go now; **~ ja / nein** I'm afraid so / not

**leidtun** irr vi **es tut mir / ihm leid** I'm/he's sorry; **er tut mir leid** I'm sorry for him

**leihen** ⟨lieh, geliehen⟩ vt jdm etw ~ lend sb sth; **sich dat etw von jdm ~** borrow sth from sb; **Leihwagen** m hire car (Brit), rental car (US)

**Leim** m ⟨-(e)s, -e⟩ glue

**Leine** f ⟨-, -n⟩ cord; (for washing) line; (for dog) lead (Brit), leash (US)

**Leinen** nt ⟨-s, -⟩ linen; **Leinwand** f ART canvas; FILM screen

**leise 1.** adj quiet; (music, steps etc) soft **2.** adv quietly

**Leiste** f ⟨-, -n⟩ ledge; (decorative) strip; ANAT groin

**leisten** vt (work) do; (accomplish) achieve; **jdm Gesellschaft ~** keep sb company; **sich dat etw ~** (as reward etc) treat oneself to sth; **ich kann es mir nicht ~** I can't afford it

**Leistenbruch** m hernia

**Leistung** f performance; (remarkable) achievement

**leiten** vt lead; (firm) run; (guide) direct; ELEC conduct

**Leiter** f ⟨-, -n⟩ ladder

**Leiter(in)** m(f) ⟨-s, -⟩ (of business) manager

**Leitplanke** f ⟨-, -n⟩ crash barrier

**Leitung** f (guidance) direction; TEL line; (of firm) management; (for water) pipe; (for electricity) cable; **eine lange ~ haben** be slow on the uptake; **Leitungswasser** nt tap water

**Lektion** f lesson

**Lektüre** f ⟨-, -n⟩ reading; (books etc) reading matter

**Lende** f ⟨-, -n⟩ (meat) loin; (of beef) sirloin

**lenken** vt steer; (gaze) direct (auf + acc towards); **jds Aufmerksamkeit auf etw** acc ~ draw sb's attention to sth; **Lenker** m handlebars pl; **Lenkrad** nt steering wheel; **Lenkradschloss** nt steering lock; **Lenkstange** f handlebars pl

**Leopard** m ⟨-en, -en⟩ leopard

**Lepra** f ⟨-⟩ leprosy

**Lerche** f ⟨-, -n⟩ lark

**lernen** vt, vi learn; (for exam) study, revise

**lesbisch** adj lesbian

**Lesebuch** nt reader; **lesen** ⟨las, gelesen⟩ vi, vt read; (fruit) pick; **Leser(in)** m(f) reader; **leserlich** adj legible; **Lesezeichen** nt bookmark

**Lettland** nt Latvia

**letzte(r, s)** adj last; (most recent) latest; (definitive) final; **zum ~n Mal** for the last time; **am ~n Montag** last Monday; **in ~r Zeit** lately, recently; **letztens** adv recently

**Leuchte** f ⟨-, -n⟩ lamp, light; **leuchten** vi shine; (fire, dial) glow; **Leuchter** m ⟨-s, -⟩ candlestick; **Leuchtreklame** f neon sign; **Leuchtturm** m lighthouse

**leugnen 1.** vt deny **2.** vi deny everything

**Leukämie** f leukaemia (Brit), leukemia (US)

**Leukoplast®** nt ⟨-(e)s, -e⟩ Elastoplast® (Brit), Band-Aid® (US)

**Leute** pl people pl

**Lexikon** nt ⟨-s, Lexika⟩ encyclopaedia (Brit), encyclopedia (US)

**Libanon** m ⟨-s⟩ **der ~** Lebanon

**Libelle** f dragonfly

**liberal** adj liberal

**Libyen** nt ⟨-s⟩ Libya

**Licht** nt ⟨-(e)s, -er⟩ light; **Lichtblick** m ray of hope; **licht-**

**empfindlich** adj sensitive to light; **Lichtempfindlichkeit** f PHOT speed; **Lichthupe** f **die ~ betätigen** flash one's lights; **Lichtjahr** nt light year; **Lichtmaschine** f dynamo; **Lichtschalter** m light switch; **Lichtschranke** f light barrier; **Lichtschutzfaktor** m sun protection factor, SPF

**Lichtung** f clearing

**Lid** nt ⟨-(e)s, -er⟩ eyelid; **Lidschatten** m eyeshadow

**lieb** adj (kind) nice; (loved) dear; (lovely) sweet; **das ist ~ von dir** that's nice of you; **Lieber Herr X** Dear Mr X; **Liebe** f ⟨-, -n⟩ love; **lieben** vt love; (sexually) make love to; **liebenswürdig** adj kind; **lieber** adv rather; **ich möchte ~ nicht** I'd rather not; **welches ist dir ~?** which one do you prefer?; → **gern**; → **lieb**; **Liebesbrief** m love letter; **Liebeskummer** m **~ haben** be lovesick; **Liebespaar** nt lovers pl; **liebevoll** adj loving; **Liebhaber(in)** m(f) ⟨-s, -⟩ lover; **lieblich** adj lovely; (wine) sweet; **Liebling** m darling; **Lieblings-** in cpds favourite; **liebste(r, s)** adj favourite; **liebsten** adv **am ~ esse ich ...** my favourite food is ...; **am ~ würde ich bleiben** I'd really like to stay

**Liechtenstein** nt ⟨-s⟩ Liechtenstein

**Lied** *nt* ⟨-(e)s, -er⟩ song; REL hymn

**lief** *imperf* → **laufen**

**liefern** *vt* deliver; (*provide*) supply; **Lieferung** *f* delivery

**Liege** *f* ⟨-, -n⟩ (*at doctor's*) couch; (*for overnight stay*) campbed; (*in garden*) lounger; **liegen** ⟨lag, gelegen⟩ *vi* lie; (*be situated*) be; **mir liegt nichts / viel daran** it doesn't matter to me/it matters a lot to me; **woran liegt es nur, dass ...?** why is it that ...?; **~ bleiben** (*person*) stay lying down; stay in bed; (*thing*) be left (behind); **~ lassen** (*forget*) leave behind; **Liegestuhl** *m* deck chair; **Liegestütz** *m* press-up (*Brit*), push-up (*US*); **Liegewagen** *m* RAIL couchette car

**lieh** *imperf* → **leihen**

**ließ** *imperf* → **lassen**

**Lift** *m* ⟨-(e)s, -e *or* -s⟩ lift, elevator (*US*)

**Liga** *f* ⟨-, Ligen⟩ league, division

**light** *adj* (*cola*) diet; (*food*) low-fat; low-calorie; (*cigarettes*) mild

**Likör** *m* ⟨-s, -e⟩ liqueur

**lila** *adj inv* purple

**Lilie** *f* lily

**Limette** *f* ⟨-, -n⟩ lime

**Limo** *f* ⟨-, -s⟩ *fam* fizzy drink (*Brit*), soda (*US*); **Limonade** *f* fizzy drink (*Brit*), soda

(*US*);    (*lemon-flavoured*) lemonade

**Limone** *f* ⟨-, -n⟩ lime

**Limousine** *f* ⟨-, -n⟩ saloon (car) (*Brit*), sedan (*US*); *fam* limo

**Linde** *f* ⟨-, -n⟩ lime tree

**lindern** *vt* relieve, soothe

**Lineal** *nt* ⟨-s, -e⟩ ruler

**Linie** *f* line; **Linienflug** *m* scheduled flight; **liniert** *adj* ruled, lined

**Link** *m* ⟨-s, -s⟩ IT link

**Linke** *f* ⟨-n, -n⟩ left-hand side; (*hand*) left hand; POL left (wing); **linke(r, s)** *adj* left; **auf der ~n Seite** on the left, on the left-hand side; **links** *adv* on the left; **~ abbiegen** turn left; **~ von** to the left of; **~ oben** at the top left; **Linkshänder(in)** *m(f)* ⟨-s, -⟩ left-hander; **linksherum** *adv* to the left, anticlockwise; **Linksverkehr** *m* driving on the left

**Linse** *f* ⟨-, -n⟩ lentil; (*optical*) lens

**Lipgloss** *nt* ⟨-, -⟩ lip gloss; **Lippe** *f* ⟨-, -n⟩ lip; **Lippenstift** *m* lipstick

**lispeln** *vi* lisp

**List** *f* ⟨-, -en⟩ (*ruse*) trick

**Liste** *f* ⟨-, -n⟩ list

**Litauen** *nt* ⟨-s⟩ Lithuania

**Liter** *m or nt* ⟨-s, -⟩ litre

**literarisch** *adj* literary; **Literatur** *f* literature

**Litschi** *f* ⟨-, -s⟩ lychee, litchi

**litt** imperf → **leiden**

**live** adv RADIO, TV live

**Lizenz** f licence

**Lkw** m ‹-(s), -(s)› abbr = **Lastkraftwagen** truck, lorry (Brit); **Lkw-Maut** f heavy goods vehicle toll

**Lob** nt ‹-(e)s› praise; **loben** vt praise

**Loch** nt ‹-(e)s, Löcher› hole; **lochen** vt (hair) curl; **Locher** m ‹-s, -› (hole) punch

**Locke** f ‹-, -n› curl; **locken** vt lure; (hair) curl; **Lockenstab** m curling tongs pl (Brit), curling irons pl (US); **Lockenwickler** m ‹-s, -› curler

**locker** adj (screw, tooth) loose; (posture) relaxed; (person) easy-going; **lockern** vt, vr loosen

**lockig** adj curly

**Löffel** m ‹-s, -› spoon; **einen ~ Mehl zugeben** add a spoonful of flour

**log** imperf → **lügen**

**Loge** f ‹-, -n› THEAT box

**logisch** adj logical

**Lohn** m ‹-(e)s, Löhne› reward; (for work) pay, wages pl; **lohnen** vr be worth it; **es lohnt sich nicht zu warten** it's no use waiting

**Lohnerhöhung** f pay rise (Brit), pay raise (US); **Lohnsteuer** f income tax

**Lokal** nt ‹-(e)s, -e› restaurant; pub (Brit), bar

**Lokomotive** f locomotive

**London** nt ‹-s› London

**Lorbeer** m ‹-s, -en› laurel; **Lorbeerblatt** nt GASTR bay leaf

**los** adj loose; **~!** go on!; **jdn / etw ~ sein** be rid of sb/sth; **was ist ~?** what's the matter?, what's up?; **dort ist nichts / viel ~** there's nothing/a lot going on there

**Los** nt ‹-es, -e› lot, fate; (in lottery etc) ticket

**löschen** vt (fire, light) put out, extinguish; (thirst) quench; (tape) erase; (data, line) delete

**lose** adj loose

**Lösegeld** nt ransom

**losen** vi draw lots

**lösen 1.** vt (knot, screw etc) loosen; (puzzle) solve; CHEM dissolve; (ticket for train etc) buy **2.** vr (wallpaper, paint etc) come off; (sugar etc) dissolve; (problem, difficulty) (re)solve itself

**losfahren** irr vi leave; **losgehen** irr vi set out; (begin) start; **loslassen** irr vt let go

**löslich** adj soluble

**Lösung** f (liquid, of puzzle, problem) solution

**loswerden** irr vt get rid of

**Lotterie** f lottery; **Lotto** nt ‹-s› National Lottery; **~ spielen** play the lottery

**Löwe** m ‹-n, -n› ZOOL lion; ASTR Leo; **Löwenzahn** m dandelion

**Luchs** m ‹-es, -e› lynx

**Lücke** f ⟨-, -n⟩ gap

**lud** imperf → **laden**

**Luft** f ⟨-, Lüfte⟩ air; (of person) breath; **Luftballon** m balloon; **luftdicht** adj airtight; **Luftdruck** m METEO atmospheric pressure; (in tyre) air pressure

**Luftfahrt** f aviation; **Luftfeuchtigkeit** f humidity; **Luftfilter** m air filter; **Luftfracht** f air freight; **Luftmatratze** f airbed; **Luftpirat** in m(f) hijacker; **Luftpost** f airmail; **Luftpumpe** f (bicycle) pump; **Luftröhre** f windpipe

**Lüftung** f ventilation

**Luftverschmutzung** f air pollution; **Luftwaffe** f air force; **Luftzug** m draught (Brit), (US)

**Lüge** f ⟨-, -n⟩ lie; **lügen** ⟨log, gelogen⟩ vi lie; **Lügner(in)** m(f) ⟨-s, -⟩ liar

**Luke** f ⟨-, -n⟩ hatch

**Lumpen** m ⟨-s, -⟩ rag

**Lunchpaket** nt packed lunch

**Lunge** f ⟨-, -n⟩ lungs pl; **Lungenentzündung** f pneumonia

**Lupe** f ⟨-, -n⟩ magnifying glass; **etw unter die ~ nehmen** fig have a close look at sth

**Lust** f ⟨-, Lüste⟩ joy, delight; (inclination) desire; **~ auf etw** acc **haben** feel like sth; **~ haben, etw zu tun** feel like doing sth

**lustig** adj amusing, funny; (jovial) cheerful

**lutschen 1.** vt suck **2.** vi **~ an** + dat suck; **Lutscher** m ⟨-s, -⟩ lollipop

**Luxemburg** nt ⟨-s⟩ Luxembourg

**luxuriös** adj luxurious

**Luxus** m ⟨-⟩ luxury

**Lymphdrüse** f lymph gland; **Lymphknoten** m lymph node

**Lyrik** f ⟨-⟩ poetry

# M

**machbar** adj feasible

**machen 1.** vt (produce, cause) make; (carry out, accomplish) do; (cost) be; **das Essen / einen Fehler ~** make dinner / a mistake; **ein Foto ~** take a photo; **was machst du?** what are you doing?; (as job) what do you do (for a living)?; **das kann man doch nicht ~!** you can't do that; **das Bett ~** make the bed; **was macht das?** how much is that?; **das macht zwanzig Euro** that's twenty euros; **einen Spaziergang ~** go for a walk; **Urlaub ~** go on holiday; **eine Pause ~** take a break; *einen Kurs* ~ take a course; *das macht nichts* it doesn't matter **2.** *vr sich an die Arbeit* ~ get down to work

**Macht** f ⟨-, Mächte⟩ power; **mächtig** adj powerful; fam enormous; **machtlos** adj powerless; *da ist man* ~ there's nothing you can do (about it)

**Mädchen** nt girl; **Mädchenname** m maiden name

**Made** f ⟨-, -n⟩ maggot

**Magazin** nt ⟨-s, -e⟩ magazine

**Magen** m ⟨-s, - or Mägen⟩ stomach; **Magenbeschwerden** pl stomach trouble sg; **Magen-Darm-Infektion** f gastroenteritis; **Magengeschwür** nt stomach ulcer; **Magenschmerzen** pl stomach-ache sg

**mager** adj (meat) lean; (person) thin; (cheese, yoghurt) low-fat; **Magermilch** f skimmed milk; **Magersucht** f anorexia; **magersüchtig** adj anorexic

**magisch** adj magical

**Magnet** m ⟨-s or -en, -en⟩ magnet

**mähen** vt, vi mow

**mahlen** ⟨mahlte, gemahlen⟩ vt grind

**Mahlzeit 1.** f meal; (for baby) feed **2.** interj enjoy your meal

**mahnen** vt urge; *jdn schriftlich* ~ send sb a reminder;

**Mahngebühr** f fine; **Mahnung** f warning; (written) reminder

**Mai** m ⟨-(s), -e⟩ May; → **Juni**; **Maifeiertag** m May Day; **Maiglöckchen** nt lily of the valley; **Maikäfer** m cockchafer

**Mail** f ⟨-, -s⟩ e-mail; *jdm eine* ~ *schicken* e-mail sb; **Mailbox** f IT mailbox; **mailen** vi, vt e-mail

**Mais** m ⟨-es, -e⟩ maize, corn (US); **Maiskolben** m corn cob; GASTR corn on the cob

**Majestät** f ⟨-, -en⟩ Majesty

**Majonäse** f ⟨-, -n⟩ mayonnaise

**Majoran** m ⟨-s, -e⟩ marjoram

**Make-up** nt ⟨-s, -s⟩ make-up

**Makler(in)** m(f) ⟨-s, -⟩ broker; (for houses etc) estate agent (Brit), realtor (US)

**Makrele** f ⟨-, -n⟩ mackerel

**Makrone** f ⟨-, -n⟩ macaroon

**mal** adv (in calculation) times, multiplied by; (in measurement) by; fam (in past) once; (in future) some day; *4 ~ 3 ist 12* 4 times 3 is (or equals) twelve; *da habe ich ~ gewohnt* I used to live there; *irgendwann ~ werde ich dort hinfahren* I'll go there one day

**Mal** nt ⟨-(e)s, -e⟩ time; (on skin) mark; *jedes* ~ every time; *ein paar* ~ a few times

**Malaria** f ⟨-⟩ malaria

**Malaysia** nt ⟨-s⟩ Malaysia

**Malbuch** nt colouring book

**Malediven** pl Maldives pl

**malen** vt, vi paint; **Maler(in)** m(f) ⟨-s, -⟩ painter; **Malerei** f painting; **malerisch** adj picturesque

**Mallorca** nt ⟨-s⟩ Majorca, Mallorca

**malnehmen** irr vt multiply (mit by)

**Malta** nt ⟨-s⟩ Malta

**Malz** nt ⟨-es⟩ malt; **Malzbier** nt malt beer

**Mama** f ⟨-, -s⟩ mum(my) (Brit), mom(my) (US)

**man** pron you; (formal) one; (unspecified person) someone, somebody; (unspecified persons) they, people pl; **wie schreibt ~ das?** how do you spell that?; ~ **sagt, dass ...** they (or people) say that ...

**managen** vt fam manage; **Manager(in)** m(f) ⟨-s, -⟩ manager

**manche(r, s)** pron some; (large number) many; ~ **Politiker** many politicians pl, many a politician; **manchmal** adv sometimes

**Mandant(in)** m(f) client

**Mandarine** f mandarin, tangerine

**Mandel** f ⟨-, -n⟩ almond; **~n** ANAT tonsils pl; **Mandelentzündung** f tonsillitis

**Manege** f ⟨-, -n⟩ ring

**Mangel** m ⟨-s, Mängel⟩ lack; (scarcity) shortage (an

+ dat of); (imperfection) defect, fault; (imperfection in goods) faulty; (mark in school) ≈ E

**Mango** f ⟨-, -s⟩ mango

**Manieren** pl manners pl

**Maniküre** f ⟨-, -n⟩ manicure

**manipulieren** vt manipulate

**Manko** nt ⟨-s, -s⟩ deficiency

**Mann** m ⟨-(e)s, Männer⟩ man; (spouse) husband; **Männchen** nt **es ist ein ~** (animal) it's a he; **männlich** adj masculine; BIO male

**Mannschaft** f SPORT, fig team; NAUT, AVIAT crew

**Mansarde** f ⟨-, -n⟩ attic

**Manschettenknopf** m cufflink

**Mantel** m ⟨-s, Mäntel⟩ coat

**Mappe** f ⟨-, -n⟩ briefcase; (cardboard, plastic) folder

**Maracuja** f ⟨-, -s⟩ passion fruit

**Marathon** m ⟨-s, -s⟩ marathon

**Märchen** nt fairy tale

**Marder** m ⟨-s, -⟩ marten

**Margarine** f margarine

**Marienkäfer** m ladybird (Brit), ladybug (US)

**Marihuana** nt ⟨-s⟩ marijuana

**Marille** f ⟨-, -n⟩ apricot

**Marine** f navy

**marinieren** vt marinate

**Marionette** f puppet

**Mark** nt ⟨-(e)s⟩ (in bone) marrow; (from fruit) pulp

**Marke** f ⟨-, -n⟩ (of food, cigarettes etc) brand; (of car, cooker etc) make; (for letter) stamp; (for meal) voucher,

**markieren** 170

ticket; *(made of metal etc)*
disc; *(of water level etc)*
mark

**markieren** *vt* mark; **Markierung** *f* marking; *(sign)* mark

**Markise** *f* ⟨-, -n⟩ awning

**Markt** *m* ⟨-(e)s, Märkte⟩ market; **auf den ~ bringen** launch; **Markthalle** *f* covered market; **Marktlücke** *f* gap in the market; **Marktplatz** *m* market place; **Marktwirtschaft** *f* market economy

**Marmelade** *f* jam; *(orange)* marmalade

**Marmor** *m* ⟨-s, -e⟩ marble; **Marmorkuchen** *m* marble cake

**Marokko** *nt* ⟨-s⟩ Morocco

**Marone** *f* ⟨-, -n⟩ chestnut

**Mars** *m* ⟨-⟩ Mars

**Marsch** *m* ⟨-(e)s, Märsche⟩ march

**Märtyrer(in)** *m(f)* ⟨-s, -⟩ martyr

**März** *m* ⟨-(es), -e⟩ March; → **Juni**

**Marzipan** *nt* ⟨-s, -e⟩ marzipan

**Maschine** *f* machine; *(of car)* engine; **Maschinenbau** *m* mechanical engineering

**Masern** *pl* MED measles *sg*

**Maske** *f* ⟨-, -n⟩ mask; **Maskenball** *m* fancy-dress ball

**Maskottchen** *nt* mascot

**maß** *imperf* → **messen**

**Maß** *nt* ⟨-es, -e⟩ measure; *(restraint)* moderation; *(scale)* degree, extent; **~e** *(of per-*

*son)* measurements; *(of room)* dimensions; **in gewissem / hohem ~e** to a certain / high degree

**Mass** *f* ⟨-, -(en)⟩ litre of beer

**Massage** *f* ⟨-, -n⟩ massage

**Masse** *f* ⟨-, -n⟩ mass; *(of people)* crowd; *(most)* majority; **massenhaft** *adv* masses (or loads) of; **Massenkarambolage** *f* pile-up; **Massenmedien** *pl* mass media *pl*

**Masseur(in)** *m(f)* masseur / masseuse

**maßgeschneidert** *adj* *(clothes)* made-to-measure

**massieren** *vt* massage

**mäßig** *adj* moderate

**massiv** *adj* solid; *fig* massive

**maßlos** *adj* extreme

**Maßnahme** *f* ⟨-, -n⟩ measure, step

**Maßstab** *m* rule, measure; *fig* standard; **im ~ von 1:5** on a scale of 1:5

**Mast** *m* ⟨-(e)s, -e(n)⟩ mast; *(ELEC)* pylon

**Material** *nt* ⟨-s, -ien⟩ material; *(for one's work)* materials *pl*; **materialistisch** *adj* materialistic

**Materie** *f* matter

**Mathematik** *f* mathematics *sg*; **Mathematiker(in)** *m(f)* mathematician

**Matinee** *f* ⟨-, -n⟩ ≈ matinee

**Matratze** *f* ⟨-, -n⟩ mattress

**Matrose** *m* ⟨-n, -n⟩ sailor

**Matsch** *m* ⟨-(e)s⟩ mud; *(snow)* slush; **matschig** *adj*

(*ground*) muddy; (*snow*) slushy; (*fruit*) mushy

**matt** *adj* weak; (*not shiny*) dull; PHOT matt; (*in chess*) mate

**Matte** *f* ⟨-, -n⟩ mat

**Matura** *f* ⟨-⟩ *Austrian school--leaving examination,* ≈ A-levels (*Brit*), ≈ High School Diploma (*US*)

**Mauer** *f* ⟨-, -n⟩ wall

**Maul** *nt* ⟨-(e)s, Mäuler⟩ mouth; *fam* gob; **halt's ~!** shut your face (*or* gob); **Maulesel** *m* mule; **Maulkorb** *m* muzzle; **Maulwurf** *m* mole

**Maurer(in)** *m(f)* ⟨-s, -⟩ bricklayer

**Mauritius** *nt* ⟨-⟩ Mauritius

**Maus** *f* ⟨-, Mäuse⟩ mouse; **Mausefalle** *f* mousetrap; **Mausklick** *m* ⟨-s, -s⟩ mouse click; **Mauspad** *nt* ⟨-s, -s⟩ mouse mat (*or* pad); **Maustaste** *f* mouse key (*or* button)

**Maut** *f* ⟨-, -en⟩ toll; **Mautgebühr** *f* toll; **mautpflichtig** *adj* **~e Straße** toll road, turnpike (*US*); **Mautstelle** *f* tollbooth, tollgate; **Mautstraße** *f* toll road, turnpike (*US*)

**maximal** *adv* **ihr habt ~ zwei Stunden Zeit** you've got two hours at (the) most; **~ will ich nicht ausgeben** a maximum of four people

**Mayonnaise** *f* → *Majonäse*

**Mazedonien** *nt* ⟨-s⟩ Macedonia

**MB** *nt* ⟨-, -⟩, **Mbyte** *nt* ⟨-, -⟩ *abbr* → *Megabyte* MB

**Mechanik** *f* mechanics *sg*; (*mechanism*) mechanics *pl*; **Mechaniker(in)** *m(f)* ⟨-s, -⟩ mechanic; **mechanisch** *adj* mechanical; **Mechanismus** *m* mechanism

**meckern** *vi* (*goat*) bleat; *fam* (*person*) moan

**Mecklenburg-Vorpommern** *nt* ⟨-s⟩ Mecklenburg-Western Pomerania

**Medaille** *f* ⟨-, -n⟩ medal

**Medien** *pl* media *pl*

**Medikament** *nt* medicine

**Meditation** *f* meditation; **meditieren** *vi* meditate

**medium** *adj* (*steak*) medium

**Medizin** *f* ⟨-, -en⟩ medicine (*gegen* for); **medizinisch** *adj* medical

**Meer** *nt* ⟨-(e)s, -e⟩ sea; **am ~** by the sea; **Meerenge** *f* straits *pl*; **Meeresfrüchte** *pl* seafood *sg*; **Meeresspiegel** *m* sea level; **Meerrettich** *m* horseradish; **Meerschweinchen** *nt* guinea pig

**Megabyte** *nt* megabyte

**Mehl** *nt* ⟨-(e)s, -e⟩ flour; **Mehlspeise** *f* sweet dish made from flour, eggs and milk

**mehr 1.** *pron* more; **~ will ich nicht ausgeben** I don't want to spend any more, that's as much as I want to spend; **was willst du ~?** what more do you want? **2.** *adv* **immer ~** (*Leute*) more

and more (people); **~ als
fünf Minuten** more than five
minutes; **es ist kein Brot ~
da** there's no bread left;
**nie ~** never again; **mehrdeu-
tig** adj ambiguous; **mehrere**
pron several; **mehreres**
pron several things; **mehrfach** adj multiple; **(done
again)** repeated; **Mehrfach-
stecker** m multiple plug;
**Mehrheit** f majority; **mehrmals** adv repeatedly; **mehrsprachig** adj multilingual;
**Mehrwertsteuer** f value
added tax, VAT; **Mehrzahl**
f majority; **(in grammar)**
plural

**meiden** ⟨mied, gemieden⟩ vt
avoid

**Meile** f ⟨-, -n⟩ mile

**mein** pron my; **meine(r, s)**
pron mine

**meinen** vt, vi think; say;
**(want to say, intend)** mean;
**das war nicht so gemeint**
I didn't mean it like that
**meinetwegen** adv because of
me; **(to please me)** for my
sake; **(for my part)** as far
as I'm concerned

**Meinung** f opinion; **meiner ~
nach** in my opinion; **Mei-
nungsumfrage** f opinion
poll; **Meinungsverschie-
denheit** f disagreement
**(über + acc** about)

**Meise** f ⟨-, -n⟩ tit; **eine ~ haben** fam be crazy

**Meißel** m ⟨-s, -⟩ chisel

**meist** adv mostly; **meiste(r,
s)** pron most; **die ~n (Leute)**
most people; **die ~ Zeit** most
of the time; **das ~ (davon)**
most of it; **die ~n von ihnen**
most of them; **meistens** adv
mostly; **(largely)** for the
most part

**Meister(in)** m(f) ⟨-s, -⟩ master; SPORT champion; **Meisterschaft** f championship;
**Meisterwerk** nt masterpiece

**melden 1.** vt report **2.** vr report **(bei** to); **(in class)** put
one's hand up; **(offer one's
services)** volunteer; **(on
phone, in response to advert
etc)** answer; **Meldung** f announcement; **(account)** report; IT message

**Melodie** f tune, melody

**Melone** f ⟨-, -n⟩ melon

**Memoiren** pl memoirs pl

**Menge** f ⟨-, -n⟩ quantity; **(of
people)** crowd; **eine ~ a** lot
**(gen** of)

**Meniskus** m ⟨-, Menisken⟩
meniscus

**Mensa** f ⟨-, Mensen⟩ canteen,
cafeteria **(US)**

**Mensch** m ⟨-en, -en⟩ human
being, man; **(individual)**
person; **kein ~** nobody; **~!**
wow!; **(annoyed)** bloody
hell!; **Menschenmenge** f
crowd; **Menschenrechte** pl
human rights pl; **Men-
schenverstand** m **gesunder ~** common sense;
**Menschheit** f humanity,

mankind; **menschlich** adj human; (kind) humane
**Menstruation** f menstruation
**Mentalität** f mentality, mindset
**Menthol** nt ⟨-s⟩ menthol
**Menü** nt ⟨-s, -s⟩ set meal; IT menu; **Menüleiste** f IT menu bar
**Merkblatt** nt leaflet; **merken** vt notice; **sich dat etw ~** remember sth; **Merkmal** nt feature
**Merkur** m ⟨-s⟩ Mercury
**merkwürdig** adj odd
**Messbecher** m measuring jug
**Messe** f ⟨-, -n⟩ fair; REL mass
**messen** ⟨maß, gemessen⟩ **1.** vt measure; (temperature, pulse) take **2.** vr compete
**Messer** nt ⟨-s, -⟩ knife
**Messing** nt ⟨-s⟩ brass
**Metall** nt ⟨-s, -e⟩ metal
**Meteorologe** m, **Meteorologin** f meteorologist
**Meter** m or nt ⟨-s, -⟩ metre; **Metermaß** nt tape measure
**Methode** f ⟨-, -n⟩ method
**Metzger(in)** m(f) ⟨-s, -⟩ butcher; **Metzgerei** f butcher's (shop)
**Mexiko** nt ⟨-s⟩ Mexico
**MEZ** f abbr = **mitteleuropäische Zeit** CET
**miau** interj miaow
**mich** pron acc → **ich**; me; ~ (**selbst**) myself; **stell dich hinter ~** stand behind me; **ich fühle ~ wohl** I feel fine

**mied** imperf → **meiden**
**Miene** f ⟨-, -n⟩ look, expression
**mies** adj fam lousy
**Miesmuschel** f mussel
**Mietauto** nt → **Mietwagen**
**Miete** f ⟨-, -n⟩ rent; **mieten** vt rent; (car) hire (Brit), rent (US); **Mieter(in)** m(f) ⟨-s, -⟩ tenant; **Mietshaus** nt block of flats (Brit), apartment house (US); **Mietvertrag** m rental agreement; **Mietwagen** m hire car (Brit), rental car (US); **sich dat einen ~ nehmen** hire (Brit) (or rent (US)) a car
**Migräne** f ⟨-, -n⟩ migraine
**Migrant(in)** m(f) ⟨-en, -en⟩ migrant (worker)
**Mikrofon** nt ⟨-s, -e⟩ microphone
**Mikrowelle** f ⟨-, -n⟩, **Mikrowellenherd** m microwave (oven)
**Milch** f ⟨-⟩ milk; **Milcheis** nt ice-cream (made with milk); **Milchkaffee** m milky coffee; **Milchpulver** nt powdered milk; **Milchreis** m rice pudding; **Milchshake** m milk shake; **Milchstraße** f Milky Way
**mild** adj mild; (judge) lenient; (friendly) kind
**Militär** nt ⟨-s⟩ military, army
**Milliarde** f ⟨-, -n⟩ billion; **Milligramm** nt milligram; **Milliliter** m millilitre; **Millimeter** m millimetre; **Million** f mil-

lion; **Millionär(in)** m(f) millionaire

**Milz** f ‹-, -en› spleen

**Minderheit** f minority

**minderjährig** adj underage

**minderwertig** adj inferior

**Mindest-** in cpds minimum; **mindeste(r, s)** adj least; **mindestens** adv at least

**Mine** f ‹-, -n› mine; (in pencil) lead; (in ballpoint pen) refill

**Mineralwasser** nt mineral water

**Minibar** f minibar; **Minigolf** nt miniature golf, crazy golf (Brit)

**minimal** adj minimal

**Minimum** nt ‹-s, Minima› minimum

**Minirock** m miniskirt

**Minister(in)** m(f) ‹-s, -› minister; **Ministerium** nt ministry; **Ministerpräsident(in)** m(f) Minister President (Prime Minister of a Bundesland)

**minus** adv minus; **Minus** nt ‹-, -› deficit; **im ~ sein** be in the red; (account) be overdrawn

**Minute** f ‹-, -n› minute

**Minze** f ‹-, -n› mint

**mir** pron dat → **ich**; (to) me; **kannst du ~ helfen?** can you help me?; **kannst du es ~ erklären?** can you explain it to me?; **ich habe ~ einen neuen Rechner gekauft** I bought (myself) a new computer; **ein Freund**

**von ~** a friend of mine

**mischen** vt mix; (cards) shuffle; **Mischung** f mixture (aus of)

**missachten** vt ignore; **Missbrauch** m abuse; (wrong use) misuse; **missbrauchen** vt misuse (zu for); (sexually) abuse; **Misserfolg** m failure; **Missgeschick** nt mishap; **misshandeln** v ill-treat

**Mission** f mission

**misslingen** ‹misslang, misslungen› vi fail; **misstrauen** vi + dat distrust; **Misstrauen** nt ‹-s› mistrust, suspicion (gegenüber of); **misstrauisch** adj distrustful; (suspecting sth) suspicious; **Missverständnis** nt misunderstanding; **missverstehen** irr vt misunderstand

**Mist** m ‹-(e)s› fam rubbish; (from cows) dung; (as fertilizer) manure

**Mistel** f ‹-, -n› mistletoe

**mit 1.** prep + dat with; (by means of) by; **~ der Bahn** by train; **~ der Kreditkarte bezahlen** pay by credit card; **~ 10 Jahren** at the age of 10; **wie wär's ~ ...?** how about ...? **2.** adv along, too; **wollen Sie ~?** do you want to come along?

**Mitarbeiter(in)** m(f) employee

**mitbekommen** irr vt fam catch; (learn about) hear; (understand) get

**mitbenutzen** *vt* share

**Mitbewohner(in)** *m(f)* flat-mate (*Brit*), roommate (*US*)

**mitbringen** *irr vt* bring along; **Mitbringsel** *nt* ⟨-s, -⟩ small present

**miteinander** *adv* with one another; (*jointly*) together

**miterleben** *vt* see (with one's own eyes)

**Mitesser** *m* ⟨-s, -⟩ blackhead

**Mitfahrgelegenheit** *f* ≈ lift, ride (*US*); **Mitfahrzentrale** *f* agency for arranging lifts

**mitgeben** *irr vt* **jdm etw ~** give sb sth (to take along)

**Mitgefühl** *nt* sympathy

**mitgehen** *irr vi* go / come along

**mitgenommen** *adj* worn out, exhausted

**Mitglied** *nt* member

**mithilfe** *prep* + *gen or* **~ von** with the help of

**mitkommen** *irr vi* come along; (*understand*) follow

**Mitleid** *nt* pity; **~ haben mit** feel sorry for

**mitmachen 1.** *vt* take part in **2.** *vt* take part

**mitnehmen** *irr vt* take along; (*tire*) wear out, exhaust

**mitschreiben 1.** *vi* take notes **2.** *vt* take down

**Mitschüler(in)** *m(f)* schoolmate

**mitspielen** *vi* (*in team*) play; (*in game*) join in; **in einem Film / Stück ~** act in a film / play

**Mittag** *m* midday; **gestern ~** at midday yesterday, yesterday lunchtime; **zu ~ essen** have lunch; **Mittagessen** *nt* lunch; **mittags** *adv* at lunchtime, at midday; **Mittagspause** *f* lunch break

**Mitte** *f* ⟨-, -n⟩ middle; **~ Juni** in the middle of June; **sie ist ~ zwanzig** she's in her mid-twenties

**mitteilen** *vt* **jdm etw ~** inform sb of sth; **Mitteilung** *f* notification

**Mittel** *nt* ⟨-s -⟩ means *sg*; (*practical measure, way*) method; MED remedy (*gegen* for)

**Mittelalter** *nt* Middle Ages *pl*; **mittelalterlich** *adj* medieval; **Mittelamerika** *nt* Central America; **Mitteleuropa** *nt* Central Europe; **Mittelfeld** *nt* midfield; **Mittelfinger** *m* middle finger; **mittelmäßig** *adj* mediocre; **Mittelmeer** *nt* Mediterranean (Sea); **Mittelohrentzündung** *f* inflammation of the middle ear; **Mittelpunkt** *m* centre; **im ~ stehen** be the centre of attention

**mittels** *prep* + *gen* by means of

**Mittelstürmer(in)** *m(f)* striker, centre-forward

**mitten** *adv* in the middle; **~ auf der Straße / in der Nacht** in the middle of the street / night

**Mitternacht** f midnight
**mittlere(r, s)** adj middle; (ordinary) average
**mittlerweile** adv meanwhile
**Mittwoch** m ⟨-s, -e⟩ Wednesday; (am) ~ on Wednesday; (am) ~ Morgen / Nachmittag / Abend (on) Wednesday morning / afternoon / evening; diesen / letzten / nächsten ~ this / last / next Wednesday; jeden ~ every Wednesday; ~ in einer Woche a week on Wednesday, Wednesday week; mittwochs (am) ~ on Wednesdays; ~ abends on Wednesday evenings
**mixen** vt mix; **Mixer** m ⟨-s, -⟩ (kitchen appliance) blender
**mobben** vt harass (or bully) (at work)
**Möbel** nt ⟨-s, -⟩ piece of furniture; die ~ pl the furniture sg; **Möbelwagen** m removal van
**mobil** adj mobile; **Mobiltelefon** nt mobile phone
**möblieren** vt furnish
**mochte** imperf → **mögen**
**Mode** f ⟨-, -n⟩ fashion
**Model** nt ⟨-s, -s⟩ model
**Modell** nt ⟨-s, -e⟩ model
**Modem** m ⟨-s, -s⟩ IT modem
**Mode(n)schau** f fashion show
**Moderator(in)** m(f) presenter
**modern** adj modern; (stylish) fashionable; **modisch** adj

fashionable
**Modus** m ⟨-, Modi⟩ IT mode; fig way
**Mofa** nt ⟨-s, -s⟩ moped
**mogeln** vi cheat
**mögen** ⟨mochte, gemocht⟩ vt, vi like; ich möchte ... I would like ...; ich möchte lieber bleiben I'd rather stay; möchtest du lieber Tee oder Kaffee? would you prefer tea or coffee?
**möglich** adj possible; so bald wie ~ as soon as possible; **möglicherweise** adv possibly; **Möglichkeit** f possibility; **möglichst** adv as ... as possible
**Mohn** m ⟨-(e)s, -e⟩ poppy; (for cake etc) poppy seed
**Möhre** f ⟨-, -n⟩, **Mohrrübe** f carrot
**Mokka** m ⟨-s, -s⟩ mocha
**Moldawien** nt ⟨-s⟩ Moldova
**Molkerei** f ⟨-, -en⟩ dairy
**Moll** nt ⟨-⟩ minor (key); a-~ A minor
**mollig** adj cosy; (person) plump
**Moment** m ⟨-(e)s, -e⟩ moment; im ~ at the moment; einen ~ bitte! just a minute; momentan **1.** adj momentary **2.** adv at the moment
**Monaco** nt ⟨-s⟩ Monaco
**Monarchie** f monarchy
**Monat** m ⟨-(e)s, -e⟩ month; sie ist im dritten ~ she's three months pregnant; **monatlich** adj, adv monthly; ~

**muffig**

*100 Euro zahlen* pay 100 euros a month (*or* every month); **Monatskarte** *f* monthly season ticket

**Mönch** *m* ⟨-s, -e⟩ monk

**Mond** *m* ⟨-(e)s, -e⟩ moon; **Mondfinsternis** *f* lunar eclipse

**Mongolei** *f* ⟨-⟩ **die ~** Mongolia

**Monitor** *m* IT monitor

**monoton** *adj* monotonous

**Monsun** *m* ⟨-s, -e⟩ monsoon

**Montag** *m* Monday; → **Mittwoch**; **montags** *adv* on Mondays; → **mittwochs**

**Montenegro** *nt* ⟨-s⟩ Montenegro

**Monteur(in)** *m(f)* ⟨-s, -e⟩ fitter; **montieren** *vt* assemble, set up

**Monument** *nt* monument

**Moor** *nt* ⟨-(e)s, -e⟩ moor

**Moos** *nt* ⟨-es, -e⟩ moss

**Moped** *nt* ⟨-s, -s⟩ moped

**Moral** *f* ⟨-⟩ morals *pl*; **moralisch** *adj* moral

**Mord** *m* ⟨-(e)s, -e⟩ murder; **Mörder(in)** *m(f)* ⟨-s, -⟩ murderer / murderess

**morgen** *adv* tomorrow; **~ früh** tomorrow morning

**Morgen** *m* ⟨-s, -⟩ morning; **am ~** in the morning; **Morgenmantel** *m* dressing gown; **Morgenmuffel** *m* **er ist ein ~** he's not a morning person; **morgens** *adv* in the morning; **um 3 Uhr ~** at 3 (o'clock) in the morning,

at 3 am

**Morphium** *nt* ⟨-s⟩ morphine

**morsch** *adj* rotten

**Mosaik** *nt* ⟨-s, -e(n)⟩ mosaic

**Mosambik** *nt* ⟨-s⟩ Mozambique

**Moschee** *f* ⟨-, -n⟩ mosque

**Moskau** *nt* ⟨-s⟩ Moscow

**Moskito** *m* ⟨-s, -s⟩ mosquito; **Moskitonetz** *nt* mosquito net

**Moslem** *m* ⟨-s, -s⟩, **Moslime** *f* ⟨-, -n⟩ Muslim

**Most** *m* ⟨-(e)s, -e⟩ (unfermented) fruit juice; (*fermented, from apples*) cider

**Motel** *nt* ⟨-s, -s⟩ motel

**motivieren** *vt* motivate

**Motor** *m* engine; ELEC motor; **Motorboot** *nt* motorboat; **Motorenöl** *nt* engine oil; **Motorhaube** *f* bonnet (*Brit*), hood (*US*); **Motorrad** *nt* motorbike, motorcycle; **Motorradfahrer(in)** *m(f)* motorcyclist; **Motorroller** *m* (motor) scooter; **Motorschaden** *m* engine trouble

**Motte** *f* ⟨-, -n⟩ moth

**Motto** *nt* ⟨-s, -s⟩ motto

**Mountainbike** *nt* ⟨-s, -s⟩ mountain bike

**Möwe** *f* ⟨-, -n⟩ (sea)gull

**MP3-Player** *m* ⟨-s, -⟩ MP3 player

**Mücke** *f* ⟨-, -n⟩ midge; (*in the tropics*) mosquito; **Mückenstich** *m* mosquito bite

**müde** *adj* tired

**muffig** *adj* (*smell*) musty;

(*face, person*) grumpy

**Mühe** f ⟨-, -n⟩ trouble, pains *pl*; **sich** *dat* **große ~ geben** go to a lot of trouble

**Mühle** f ⟨-, -n⟩ mill; (*for coffee*) grinder

**Müll** m ⟨-(e)s⟩ rubbish (*Brit*), garbage (*US*); **Müllabfuhr** f rubbish (*Brit*) (*or* garbage (*US*)) disposal

**Mullbinde** f gauze bandage

**Müllcontainer** m waste container; **Mülleimer** m rubbish bin (*Brit*), garbage can (*US*); **Mülltonne** f dustbin (*Brit*), garbage can (*US*); **Müllwagen** m dustcart (*Brit*), garbage truck (*US*)

**multikulturell** *adj* multicultural

**Multimedia-** *in cpds* multimedia

**Multiple-Choice-Verfahren** *nt* multiple choice

**multiple Sklerose** f ⟨-n, -n⟩ multiple sclerosis

**Multiplexkino** *nt* multiplex (cinema)

**multiplizieren** *vt* multiply (*mit* by)

**Mumie** f mummy

**Mumps** m ⟨-⟩ mumps *sg*

**München** *nt* ⟨-s⟩ Munich

**Mund** m ⟨-(e)s, Münder⟩ mouth; **halt den ~!** shut up; **Mundart** f dialect; **Munddusche** f dental water jet

**münden** *vi* flow (*in* + *acc* into)

**Mundgeruch** m bad breath; **Mundharmonika** f ⟨-, -s⟩ mouth organ

**mündlich** *adj* oral

**Mundschutz** m mask; **Mundwasser** *nt* mouthwash

**Munition** f ammunition

**Münster** *nt* ⟨-s, -⟩ minster, cathedral

**munter** *adj* lively

**Münzautomat** m vending machine; **Münze** f ⟨-, -n⟩ coin; **Münzeinwurf** m slot; **Münzrückgabe** f coin return; **Münztelefon** *nt* pay phone; **Münzwechsler** m change machine

**murmeln** *vt, vi* murmur, mutter

**Murmeltier** *nt* marmot

**mürrisch** *adj* sullen, grumpy

**Muschel** f ⟨-, -n⟩ mussel; (*empty*) shell

**Museum** *nt* ⟨-s, Museen⟩ museum

**Musical** *nt* ⟨-s, -s⟩ musical

**Musik** f music; **musikalisch** *adj* musical; **Musiker(in)** m(f) ⟨-s, -⟩ musician; **Musikinstrument** *nt* musical instrument; **musizieren** *vi* play music

**Muskat** m ⟨-(e)s⟩ nutmeg

**Muskel** m ⟨-s, -n⟩ muscle; **Muskelkater** m **~ haben** be stiff; **Muskelriss** m torn muscle; **Muskelzerrung** f pulled muscle; **muskulös** *adj* muscular

**Müsli** *nt* ⟨-s, -⟩ muesli

**Muslim(in)** *m(f)* ⟨-s, -s⟩ Muslim

**Muss** *nt* ⟨-⟩ must

**müssen** ⟨musste, gemusst⟩ *vi* must, have to; **er hat gehen ~** he (has) had to go; **sie müsste schon längst hier sein** she should have arrived a long time ago; **du musst es nicht tun** you don't have to do it, you needn't do it; **ich muss mal** I need to / got to the loo *(Brit)*, I have to go to the bathroom *(US)*

**mutwillig** *adj* deliberate

**Mütze** *f* ⟨-, -n⟩ cap

**Muster** *nt* ⟨-s, -⟩ pattern, design; *(small quantity)* sample

**Mut** *m* ⟨-(e)s⟩ courage; **jdm ~ machen** encourage sb; **mutig** *adj* brave, courageous

**Mutter 1.** *f* ⟨-, Mütter⟩ mother **2.** *f* ⟨-, -n⟩ *(for bolt)* nut; **Muttersprache** *f* mother tongue; **Muttertag** *m* Mother's Day; **Mutti** *f* mum(my) *(Brit)*, mom(my) *(US)*

**Myanmar** *nt* ⟨-s⟩ Myanmar

# N

**na** *interj* **~ also!, ~ bitte!** see?, what did I tell you?; **~ ja** well; **~ und?** so what?

**Nabel** *m* ⟨-s, -⟩ navel

**nach** *prep + dat after*; *(direction)* to; *(consistent with)* according to; **~ zwei Stunden** after two hours, two hours later; **es ist fünf ~ sechs** it's five past *(Brit)* (or after *(US)*) six; **der Zug ~ London** the train for (or to) London; **~ rechts / links** to the right / left; **~ Hause** home; **~ oben / hinten / unten** up / back / down; **~ und ~** gradually

**nachahmen** *vt* imitate

**Nachbar(in)** *m(f)* ⟨-n, -n⟩ neighbour; **Nachbarschaft** *f* neighbourhood

**nachdem** *conj after*; *(because)* since; **je ~ (ob / wie)** depending on (whether / how)

**nachdenken** *irr vi* think *(über + acc* about); **nachdenklich** *adj* thoughtful

**nacheinander** *adv* one after another (or the other)

**Nachfolger(in)** *m(f)* ⟨-s, -⟩ successor

**nachforschen** *vt* investigate

**nachgeben** *irr vi* give in *(jdm* to sb)

**nachgehen** *irr vi* follow *(jdm* sb); *(investigate)* inquire *(einer Sache dat* into sth); **die Uhr geht (zehn Minuten) nach** this watch is (ten minutes) slow

**nachher** *adv* afterwards; **bis ~!** see you later

**Nachhilfe** *f* extra tuition

**nachholen** vt catch up with; (what one has missed) make up for

**nachkommen** irr vi follow; **einer Verpflichtung** dat ~ fulfil an obligation

**nachlassen** irr **1.** vt (sum of money) take off **2.** vi decrease, ease off; (get worse) deteriorate; **nachlässig** adj negligent, careless

**nachlaufen** irr vi run after, chase (jdm sb)

**nachmachen** vt imitate, copy (jdm etw sth from sb); (fake) counterfeit

**Nachmittag** m afternoon; **heute** ~ this afternoon; **am** ~ in the afternoon; **nachmittags** adv in the afternoon; **um 3 Uhr** ~ at 3 (o'clock) in the afternoon, at 3 pm

**Nachnahme** f ⟨-, -n⟩ cash on delivery; **per** ~ COD

**Nachname** m surname

**nachprüfen** vt check

**nachrechnen** vt check

**Nachricht** f ⟨-, -en⟩ (piece of) news sg; (notification) message; **Nachrichten** pl news sg

**Nachsaison** f off-season

**nachschauen 1.** vi jdm ~ gaze after sb **2.** vt check

**nachschicken** vt forward

**nachschlagen** irr vt look up

**nachsehen** irr vt check

**Nachspeise** f dessert

**nächste(r, s)** adj next; (in space) nearest

**Nacht** f ⟨-, Nächte⟩ night; **in der** ~ during the night; (when dark) at night; **Nachtclub** m nightclub; **Nachtdienst** m night duty; ~ **haben** (chemist's) be open all night

**Nachteil** m disadvantage

**Nachtflug** m night flight; **Nachthemd** nt nightdress; (for men) nightshirt

**Nachtigall** f ⟨-, -en⟩ nightingale

**Nachtisch** m dessert, sweet (Brit), pudding (Brit)

**Nachtleben** nt nightlife

**nachträglich** adv ~ **alles Gute zum Geburtstag!** Happy belated birthday

**nachts** adv at night; **um 11 Uhr** ~ at 11 (o'clock) at night, at 11 pm; **um 2 Uhr** ~ at 2 (o'clock) in the morning, at 2 am; **Nachtschicht** f night shift; **Nachttisch** m bedside table; **Nachtzug** m night train

**Nachweis** m ⟨-es, -e⟩ proof

**Nachwirkung** f after-effect

**nachzahlen 1.** vi pay extra **2.** vt **20 Euro** ~ pay 20 euros extra

**nachzählen** vt check

**Nacken** m ⟨-s, -⟩ (nape of the) neck

**nackt** adj naked; (facts) plain, bare; **Nacktbadestrand** m nudist beach

**Nadel** f ⟨-, -n⟩ needle; (with head) pin

**Nagel** m ⟨-s, Nägel⟩ nail; **Nagelbürste** f nail brush; **Nagelfeile** f nail-file; **Nagellack** m nail varnish (or polish); **Nagellackentferner** m ⟨-s, -⟩ nail-varnish (or nail-polish) remover; **Nagelschere** f nail scissors pl

**nah(e) 1.** adj, adv near(by); (in time) near; (relative, friend) close **2.** prep + dat near (to), close to; **Nähe** f ⟨-⟩ vicinity; **in der ~** nearby; **in der ~ von** near to; **nahegehen** irr vi jdm ~ upset sb; **naheliegen** irr vi be obvious

**nähen** vt, vi sew

**nähere(r, s)** adj (explanation, investigation) more detailed; **die ~ Umgebung** the immediate area; **Nähere(s)** nt details pl; **nähern** vr approach

**nahezu** adv virtually, almost

**nahm** imperf → **nehmen**

**Nähmaschine** f sewing machine

**nahrhaft** adj nourishing, nutritious; **Nahrung** f food; **Nahrungsmittel** nt food

**Naht** f ⟨-, Nähte⟩ seam; MED stitches pl, suture; TECH join

**Nahverkehr** m local traffic

**Nähzeug** nt sewing kit

**naiv** adj naive

**Name** m ⟨-ns, -n⟩ name

**nämlich** adv that is to say, namely; (because) since

**nannte** imperf → **nennen**

**Napf** m ⟨-(e)s, Näpfe⟩ bowl, dish

**Narbe** f ⟨-, -n⟩ scar

**Narkose** f ⟨-, -n⟩ anaesthetic

**Narzisse** f ⟨-, -n⟩ narcissus

**naschen** vt, vi nibble

**Nase** f ⟨-, -n⟩ nose; **Nasenbluten** nt ⟨-s⟩ nosebleed; **~ haben** have a nosebleed; **Nasenloch** nt nostril; **Nasentropfen** pl nose drops pl

**Nashorn** nt rhinoceros

**nass** adj wet; **Nässe** f ⟨-⟩ wetness; **nässen** vi (wound) weep

**Nation** f ⟨-, -en⟩ nation; **national** adj national; **Nationalfeiertag** m national holiday; **Nationalhymne** f ⟨-, -n⟩ national anthem; **Nationalität** f nationality; **Nationalmannschaft** f national team; **Nationalpark** m National Park; **Nationalspieler(in)** m(f) international (player)

**NATO** f ⟨-⟩ abbr = **North Atlantic Treaty Organization** NATO, Nato

**Natur** f nature; **Naturkost** f health food; **natürlich 1.** adj natural **2.** adv naturally; (certainly, obviously) of course; **Naturpark** m nature reserve; **Naturschutz** m conservation; **Naturschutzgebiet** nt nature reserve; **Naturwissenschaft** f (natural) science; **Naturwissenschaftler(in)** m(f) scientist

**Navigationssystem** nt AUTO navigation system

**n. Chr.** *abbr* = *nach Christus* AD

**Nebel** *m* ⟨-s, -⟩ fog, mist; **nebelig** *adj* foggy, misty; **Nebelscheinwerfer** *m* foglamp; **Nebelschlussleuchte** *f* AUTO rear foglight

**neben** *prep* + *acc or dat* next to; *(in addition to)* apart from, besides; **nebenan** *adv* next door; **nebenbei** *adv* at the same time; *(as an extra)* additionally; *(by the way)* incidentally; **nebeneinander** *adv* side by side; **Nebenfach** *nt* subsidiary subject

**nebenher** *adv* *(in addition)* besides; *(simultaneously)* at the same time; *(at the side)* alongside

**Nebenkosten** *pl* extra charges *pl*, extras *pl*; **nebensächlich** *adj* minor; **Nebensaison** *f* low season; **Nebenstraße** *f* side street; **Nebenwirkung** *f* side effect

**neblig** *adj* foggy, misty

**necken** *vt* tease

**Neffe** *m* ⟨-n, -n⟩ nephew

**negativ** *adj* negative; **Negativ** *nt* PHOT negative

**nehmen** ⟨nahm, genommen⟩ *vt* take; **den Bus / Zug ~** take the bus / train; **jdn / etw ernst ~** take sb/sth seriously

**neidisch** *adj* envious

**neigen** *vi* **zu etw ~** tend towards sth; **Neigung** *f* slope; *(tendency)* inclination; *(in-*

*terest)* liking

**nein** *adv* no

**Nektarine** *f* nectarine

**Nelke** *f* ⟨-, -n⟩ carnation; *(spice)* clove

**nennen** ⟨nannte, genannt⟩ *vt* name; *(by a name)* call

**Nepal** *nt* ⟨-s⟩ Nepal

**Neptun** *m* ⟨-s⟩ Neptune

**Nerv** *m* ⟨-s, -en⟩ nerve; **jdm auf die ~en gehen** get on sb's nerves; **nerven** *vt* **jdn ~** *fam* get on sb's nerves; **Nervenzusammenbruch** *m* nervous breakdown; **nervös** *adj* nervous

**Nest** *nt* ⟨-(e)s, -er⟩ nest; *pej* *(place)* dump

**nett** *adj* nice; *(friendly)* kind; **sei so ~ und ...** do me a favour and ...

**netto** *adv* net

**Netz** *nt* ⟨-es, -e⟩ net; *(system)* network; *(electricity supply)* mains, power *(US)*; **Netzanschluss** *m* mains connection; **Netzwerk** *nt* IT network

**neu** *adj* new; *(languages, history)* modern; **die ~esten Nachrichten** the latest news; **Neubau** *m* new building; **neuerdings** *adv* recently; **Neuerung** *f* innovation; *(change)* reform

**Neugier** *f* curiosity; **neugierig** *adj* curious *(auf* + *acc* about); **ich bin ~, ob ...** I wonder whether *(or* if) ...

**Neuheit** *f* novelty; **Neuigkeit** *f* news *sg*; **Neujahr** *nt* New

Year; *prosit ~!* Happy New Year; **neulich** *adv* recently, the other day

**neun** *num* nine; **neunhundert** *num* nine hundred; **neunmal** *adv* nine times; **neunte(r, s)** *adj* ninth; → *dritte*; **Neuntel** *nt* ⟨-s, -⟩ (*fraction*) ninth; **neunzehn** *num* nineteen; **neunzehnte(r, s)** *adj* nineteenth; → *dritte*; **neunzig** *num* ninety; *in den ~er Jahren* in the nineties; **Neunzigerjahre** *pl* nineties *pl*; **neunzigste(r, s)** *adj* ninetieth

**neureich** *adj* nouveau riche

**Neurologe** *m*, **Neurologin** *f* neurologist; **Neurose** *f* ⟨-, -n⟩ neurosis; **neurotisch** *adj* neurotic

**Neuseeland** *nt* New Zealand

**Neustart** *m* IT restart, reboot

**neutral** *adj* neutral

**neuwertig** *adj* nearly new

**Nicaragua** *nt* ⟨-s⟩ Nicaragua

**nicht 1.** *adv* not; *er kommt ~* he doesn't come; (*on this occasion*) he isn't coming; *sie wohnt ~ mehr hier* she doesn't live here any more; *gar ~* not at all; *ich kenne ihn auch ~* I don't know him either; *noch ~* not yet; *~ berühren!* do not touch **2.** *pref* non-

**Nichte** *f* ⟨-, -n⟩ niece

**Nichtraucher(in)** *m(f)* non--smoker; **Nichtraucherzone** *f* non-smoking area

**nichts** *pron* nothing; *ich habe ~ gesagt* I didn't say anything; *macht ~* never mind

**Nichtschwimmer(in)** *m(f)* non-swimmer

**nichtssagend** *adj* meaningless

**nicken** *vi* nod

**Nickerchen** *nt* nap

**nie** *adv* never; *~ wieder* (*or mehr*) never again; *fast ~* hardly ever

**nieder 1.** *adj* low; (*in status*) inferior **2.** *adv* down; **niedergeschlagen** *adj* depressed; **Niederlage** *f* defeat

**Niederlande** *pl* Netherlands *pl*; **Niederländer(in)** *m(f)* Dutchman / Dutchwoman; **niederländisch** *adj* Dutch; **Niederländisch** *nt* Dutch

**Niederlassung** *f* branch

**Niederösterreich** *nt* Lower Austria; **Niedersachsen** *nt* Lower Saxony

**Niederschlag** *m* METEO precipitation; rainfall

**niedlich** *adj* sweet, cute

**niedrig** *adj* low

**niemals** *adv* never

**niemand** *pron* nobody, no one; *ich habe ~en gesehen* I haven't seen anyone; *~ von ihnen* none of them

**Niere** *f* ⟨-, -n⟩ kidney; **Nierensteine** *pl* kidney stones *pl*

**nieseln** *vi impers* drizzle; **Nieselregen** *m* drizzle

**niesen** *vi* sneeze

**Niete** *f* ⟨-, -n⟩ (*losing ticket*)

blank; *pej* (*person*) failure;
TECH rivet

**Nigeria** *nt* ⟨-s⟩ Nigeria

**Nikotin** *nt* ⟨-s⟩ nicotine

**Nilpferd** *nt* hippopotamus

**nippen** *vi* sip; *an etw dat* ~ sip
sth

**nirgends** *adv* nowhere

**Nische** *f* ⟨-, -n⟩ niche

**Niveau** *nt* ⟨-s, -s⟩ level; *sie hat*
~ she's got class

**nobel** *adj* generous; *fam*
classy, posh

**Nobelpreis** *m* Nobel Prize

**noch 1.** *adv* still; (*in addition*)
else; *wer kommt* ~? who
else is coming?; ~ *nie* never;
~ *nicht* not yet; *immer* ~
still; ~ *einmal* (once) again;
~ *am selben Tag* that (very)
same day; ~ *besser / mehr /
jetzt* even better / more /
now; *wie heißt sie* ~? what's
her name again?; ~ *ein Bier,
bitte* another beer, please **2.**
*conj* nor; **nochmal(s)** *adv*
again, once more

**Nominativ** *m* nominative
(case)

**Nonne** *f* ⟨-, -n⟩ nun

**Nonstop-Flug** *m* nonstop
flight

**Nord** north; **Nordamerika** *nt*
North America; **Nord-
deutschland** *nt* Northern
Germany; **Norden** *m* ⟨-s⟩
north; **Nordeuropa** *nt*
Northern Europe

**Nordic Walking** *nt* SPORT
Nordic Walking

**Nordirland** *nt* Northern Ireland; **nordisch** *adj* Nordic;
**Nordkorea** *nt* ⟨-s⟩ North Korea; **nördlich** *adj* northern;
(*course, direction*) norther-
ly; **Nordost(en)** *m* northeast; **Nordpol** *m* North Pole;
**Nordrhein-Westfalen** *nt* ⟨-s⟩
North Rhine-Westphalia;
**Nordsee** *f* North Sea; **nord-
wärts** *adv* north, northwards; **Nordwest(en)** *m*
northwest; **Nordwind** *m*
north wind

**nörgeln** *vi* grumble

**Norm** *f* ⟨-, -en⟩ norm; (*technical, industrial*) standard

**normal** *adj* normal; **normalerweise** *adv* normally

**Norwegen** *nt* ⟨-s⟩ Norway;
**Norweger(in)** *m*(*f*) Norwegian; **norwegisch** *adj* Norwegian; **Norwegisch** *nt*
Norwegian

**Not** *f* ⟨-, Nöte⟩ need; poverty;
(*distress*) hardship; (*emergency situation*) trouble;
**zur** ~ if necessary; (*with time
to spare*) just about

**Notar(in)** *m*(*f*) public notary

**Notarzt** *m*, **Notärztin** *f* emergency doctor; **Notarztwa-
gen** *m* emergency ambu-
lance; **Notaufnahme** *f*
A&E, casualty (*Brit*), emergency room (*US*); **Notausgang** *m* emergency exit;
**Notbremse** *f* emergency
brake; **Notdienst** *m* emergency service, after-hours

service; **notdürftig** *adj*
scanty; *(rough and ready)*
makeshift
**Note** *f* ⟨-, -n⟩ *(in school)* mark,
grade *(US)*; MUS note
**Notebook** *nt* ⟨-(s), -s⟩ IT notebook
**Notfall** *m* emergency; **not-**
**falls** *adv* if necessary
**notieren** *vt* note down
**nötig** *adj* necessary; **etw ~ ha-**
**ben** need sth
**Notiz** *f* ⟨-, -en⟩ note; **Notiz-**
**block** *m* notepad; **Notiz-**
**buch** *nt* notebook
**notlanden** *vi* make a forced
*(or* emergency*)* landing;
**Notlandung** *f* emergency
landing; **Notruf** *m* emergency call; **Notrufnummer** *f*
emergency number; **Notruf-**
**säule** *f* emergency telephone
**notwendig** *adj* necessary
**Nougat** *m or nt* ⟨-s, -s⟩ nougat
**November** *m* ⟨-(s), -⟩ November; → **Juni**
**Nr.** *abbr* → **Nummer** No., no.
**Nu** *m* **im ~** in no time
**nüchtern** *adj* sober; *(stom-*
*ach)* empty
**Nudel** *f* ⟨-, -n⟩ noodle; **~n** *pl*
*(Italian)* pasta *sg*

**null** *num* zero; TEL O *(Brit)*,
zero *(US)*; **~ Fehler** no mis-
takes; **~ Uhr** midnight; **Null** *f*
⟨-, -en⟩ nought, zero; *pej*
*(person)* dead loss; **Nulltarif**
*m* **zum ~** free of charge
**Nummer** *f* ⟨-, -n⟩ number;
**nummerieren** *vt* number;
**Nummernschild** *nt* AUTO
number plate *(Brit)*, license
plate *(US)*
**nun 1.** *adv* now; **von ~ an**
from now on **2.** *interj* well;
**~ gut!** all right, then; **es ist**
**~ mal so** that's the way it is
**nur** *adv* only; **nicht ~ ..., son-**
**dern auch ...** not only ...,
but also ...
**Nürnberg** *nt* ⟨-s⟩ Nuremberg
**Nuss** *f* ⟨-, Nüsse⟩ nut; **Nuss-**
**knacker** *m* ⟨-s, -⟩ nutcracker
**Nutte** *f* ⟨-, -n⟩ *fam* tart
**nutz, nütze** *adj* **zu nichts ~**
**sein** be useless; **nutzen,**
**nützen 1.** *vt* use *(zu etw*
for sth*)*; **was nützt es?** what
use is it? **2.** *vi* be of use; **das**
**nützt nicht viel** that doesn't
help much; **Nutzen** *m* ⟨-s, -⟩
usefulness; *(financial)* profit; **nützlich** *adj* useful
**Nylon** *nt* ⟨-s⟩ nylon

# O

**o** *interj* oh

**Oase** *f* ‹-, -n› oasis

**ob** *conj* if, whether; **so als ~** as if; **und ..!** you bet

**obdachlos** *adj* homeless

**oben** *adv* at the top; (*in pile, on cupboard etc*) on (the) top; (*in house*) upstairs; (*in text*) above; **da ~** up there; **von ~ bis unten** from top to bottom; **siehe ~** see above

**Ober** *m* ‹-s, -› waiter

**obere(r, s)** *adj* upper, top

**Oberfläche** *f* surface; **oberflächlich** *adj* superficial

**Obergeschoss** *nt* upper floor

**oberhalb** *adv, prep* + *gen* above

**Oberkörper** *m* upper body; **Oberlippe** *f* upper lip; **Oberösterreich** *nt* Upper Austria; **Oberschenkel** *m* thigh

**oberste(r, s)** *adj* very top, topmost

**Oberteil** *nt* top; **Oberweite** *f* bust / chest measurement

**Objekt** *nt* ‹-(e)s, -e› object

**objektiv** *adj* objective

**Objektiv** *nt* lens

**obligatorisch** *adj* compulsory, obligatory

**Oboe** *f* ‹-, -n› oboe

**Observatorium** *nt* observatory

**Obst** *nt* ‹-(e)s› fruit; **Obstkuchen** *m* fruit tart; **Obstsalat** *m* fruit salad

**obwohl** *conj* although

**Ochse** *m* ‹-n, -n› ox

**ocker** *adj* ochre

**öd(e)** *adj* waste; *fig* dull

**oder** *conj* or; **~ aber** or else; **er kommt doch, ~?** he's coming, isn't he?

**Ofen** *m* ‹-s, Öfen› oven; (*for heating*) heater; (*using coal etc*) stove; (*kitchen appliance*) cooker, stove; **Ofenkartoffel** *f* baked (*or* jacket) potato

**offen 1.** *adj* open; (*honest*) frank; (*job*) vacant **2.** *adv* frankly; **~ gesagt** to be honest

**offenbar** *adj* obvious; **offensichtlich** *adj* evident, obvious

**öffentlich** *adj* public; **Öffentlichkeit** *f* public

**offiziell** *adj* official

**offline** *adv* IT offline

**öffnen** *vt, vr* open; **Öffner** *m* ‹-s, -› opener; **Öffnung** *f* opening; **Öffnungszeiten** *pl* opening times *pl*

**oft** *adv* often; **schon ~** many times; **öfter** *adv* more often (*or* frequently); **öfters** *adv* often, frequently

**ohne** *conj, prep* + *acc* without; **~ Weiteres** without a second thought; (*without delay*) immediately; **~ mich** count me out

**Ohnmacht** f ⟨-machten pl⟩ unconsciousness; **in ~ fallen** faint; **ohnmächtig** *adj* unconscious; **sie ist ~** she has fainted

**Ohr** nt ⟨-(e)s, -en⟩ ear; (*faculty*) hearing

**Öhr** nt ⟨-(e)s, -e⟩ eye

**Ohrenarzt** m, **Ohrenärztin** f ear specialist; **Ohrenschmerzen** pl earache; **Ohrentropfen** pl ear drops pl; **Ohrfeige** f slap (in the face); **Ohrläppchen** nt earlobe; **Ohrringe** pl earrings pl

**oje** *interj* oh dear

**okay** *interj* OK, okay

**Ökoladen** m health food store; **ökologisch** *adj* ecological; **~e Landwirtschaft** organic farming

**ökonomisch** *adj* economic; (*money-saving*) economical

**Ökosystem** nt ecosystem

**Oktober** m ⟨-(s), -⟩ October; → **Juni**

**Öl** nt ⟨-(e)s, -e⟩ oil; **Ölbaum** m olive tree; **ölen** vt oil; TECH lubricate; **Ölfarbe** f oil paint; **Ölfilter** m oil filter; **Ölgemälde** nt oil painting; **Ölheizung** f oil-fired central heating; **ölig** *adj* oily

**oliv** *adj inv* olive-green; **Olive** f ⟨-, -n⟩ olive; **Olivenöl** nt olive oil

**Ölsardine** f sardine in oil; **Ölteppich** m oil slick; **Ölwechsel** m oil change

**Olympiade** f Olympic Games pl; **olympisch** *adj* Olympic

**Oma** f, **Omi** f ⟨-, -s⟩ grandma, gran(ny)

**Omelett** nt ⟨-(e)s, -s⟩, **Omelette** f omelette

**Omnibus** m bus

**onanieren** vi masturbate

**Onkel** m ⟨-s, -⟩ uncle

**online** *adv* IT online

**OP** m ⟨-s, -s⟩ *abbr* = **Operationssaal** operating theatre (*Brit*) (or room (*US*))

**Opa** m, **Opi** m ⟨-s, -s⟩ grandpa, grandad

**Open-Air-Konzert** nt open-air concert

**Oper** f ⟨-, -n⟩ opera; (*building*) opera house

**Operation** f operation

**Operette** f operetta

**operieren 1.** vi operate **2.** vt operate on

**Opernhaus** nt opera house, opera; **Opernsänger(in)** m(f) opera singer

**Opfer** nt ⟨-s, -⟩ sacrifice; (*person*) victim; **ein ~ bringen** make a sacrifice

**Opium** nt ⟨-s⟩ opium

**Opposition** f opposition

**Optiker(in)** m(f) ⟨-s, -⟩ optician

**optimal** *adj* optimal, optimum

**optimistisch** *adj* optimistic

**oral** *adj* oral; **Oralverkehr** m

oral sex

**orange** adj inv orange; **Orange** f ⟨-, -n⟩ orange; **Orangenmarmelade** f marmalade; **Orangensaft** m orange juice

**Orchester** nt ⟨-s, -⟩ orchestra

**Orchidee** f ⟨-, -n⟩ orchid

**Orden** m ⟨-s, -⟩ REL order; MIL decoration

**ordentlich 1.** adj respectable; (orderly) tidy, neat **2.** adv properly

**ordinär** adj common, vulgar; (joke) dirty

**ordnen** vt sort out; **Ordner** m ⟨-s, -⟩ steward; (for documents) file; **Ordnung** f order; (orderliness) tidiness; (**geht**) **in ~!** (that's) all right

**Oregano** m ⟨-s⟩ oregano

**Organ** nt ⟨-s, -e⟩ organ; voice

**Organisation** f organization; **organisieren 1.** vt organize; fam (obtain) get hold of **2.** vr organize

**Organismus** m organism

**Orgasmus** m orgasm

**Orgel** f ⟨-, -n⟩ organ

**Orgie** f orgy

**orientalisch** adj oriental

**orientieren** vr get one's bearings; **Orientierung** f orientation; **Orientierungssinn** m sense of direction

**original** adj original; (real) genuine; **Original** nt ⟨-s, -e⟩ original

**originell** adj original; (humorous) witty

**Orkan** m ⟨-(e)s, -e⟩ hurricane

**Ort** m ⟨-(e)s, -e⟩ place; (small town) village

**Orthopäde** m ⟨-n, -n⟩, **Orthopädin** f orthopaedist

**örtlich** adj local; **Ortschaft** f village, small town; **Ortsgespräch** nt local call; **Ortstarif** m local rate; **Ortszeit** f local time

**Ost** m; **Ostdeutschland** nt Eastern Germany; HIST East Germany; **Osten** m ⟨-s⟩ east

**Osterei** nt Easter egg; **Osterglocke** f daffodil; **Osterhase** m Easter bunny; **Ostermontag** m Easter Monday; **Ostern** nt ⟨-, -⟩ Easter; **an** (or **zu**) **~** at Easter; **frohe ~** Happy Easter

**Österreich** nt ⟨-s⟩ Austria; **Österreicher(in)** m(f) ⟨-s, -⟩ Austrian; **österreichisch** adj Austrian

**Ostersonntag** m Easter Sunday

**Osteuropa** nt Eastern Europe; **Ostküste** f east coast; **östlich** adj eastern; (course, direction) easterly; **Ostsee** f **die ~** the Baltic (Sea); **Ostwind** m east(erly) wind

**Otter** m ⟨-s, -⟩ otter

**out** adj fam out; **outen** vt out; **oval** adj oval; **Oval** nt oval

**Overheadprojektor** m overhead projector

**Ozean** m ⟨-s, -e⟩ ocean; **der Stille ~** the Pacific (Ocean)

**Ozon** nt ⟨-s⟩ ozone; **Ozon-**

**loch** nt hole in the ozone layer; **Ozonschicht** f ozone

layer; **Ozonwerte** pl ozone levels pl

## P

**paar** adj inv **ein ~** a few; **ein ~ Mal** a few times; **ein ~ Äpfel** some apples

**Paar** nt ⟨-(e)s, -e⟩ pair; (married) couple

**pachten** vt lease

**Päckchen** nt package; (of cigarettes) packet; (sent by post) small parcel; **packen** vt pack; (get hold of) grasp, seize; fam (succeed with) manage; fig (film, story etc) grip; **Packpapier** nt brown paper; **Packung** f packet, pack (US); **Packungsbeilage** f package insert

**Pädagoge** m ⟨-n, -n⟩, **Pädagogin** f teacher; **pädagogisch** adj educational

**Paddel** nt ⟨-s, -⟩ paddle; **Paddelboot** nt canoe; **paddeln** vi paddle

**Paket** nt ⟨-(e)s, -e⟩ packet; (sent by post) parcel; IT package; **Paketbombe** f parcel bomb

**Pakistan** nt ⟨-s⟩ Pakistan

**Palast** m ⟨-es, Paläste⟩ palace

**Palästina** nt ⟨-s⟩ Palestine; **Palästinenser(in)** m(f) ⟨-s, -⟩ Palestinian

**Palatschinken** pl filled pancakes pl

**Palette** f (of painter) palette; (for moving goods) pallet; (variety) range

**Palme** f ⟨-, -n⟩ palm (tree); **Palmsonntag** m Palm Sunday

**Pampelmuse** f ⟨-, -n⟩ grapefruit

**pampig** adj fam cheeky; (food etc) gooey

**Panda(bär)** m ⟨-s, -s⟩ panda

**Pandemie** f ⟨-, -n⟩ pandemic

**panieren** vt GASTR coat with breadcrumbs; **paniert** adj breaded

**Panik** f panic

**Panne** f ⟨-, -n⟩ AUTO breakdown; (mishap) slip; **Pannendienst** m, **Pannenhilfe** f breakdown (or rescue) service

**Pant(h)er** m ⟨-s, -⟩ panther

**Pantomime** f ⟨-, -n⟩ mime

**Panzer** m ⟨-s, -⟩ MIL (vehicle) tank

**Papa** m ⟨-s, -s⟩ dad(dy), pa (US)

**Papagei** m ⟨-s, -en⟩ parrot

**Papaya** f ⟨-, -s⟩ papaya

**Papier** nt ⟨-s, -e⟩ paper; **~e** pl (ID) papers pl; (official texts) papers pl, documents pl; **Papierkorb** m wastepaper basket; IT recycle bin;

Papiertaschentuch nt (paper) tissue; Papiertonne f paper bank

Pappbecher m paper cup; Pappe f ⟨-, -n⟩ cardboard; Pappkarton m cardboard box; Pappteller m paper plate

Paprika m ⟨-s, -s⟩ (spice) paprika; (vegetable) pepper

Papst m ⟨-(e)s, Päpste⟩ pope

Paradeiser m ⟨-s, -⟩ tomato

Paradies nt ⟨-es, -e⟩ paradise

Paragliding nt ⟨-s⟩ paragliding

Paragraph m ⟨-en, -en⟩ paragraph; LAW section

parallel adj parallel

Paranuss f Brazil nut

Parasit m ⟨-en, -en⟩ parasite

parat adj ready; etw ~ haben have sth ready

Pärchen nt couple

Parfüm nt ⟨-s, -s or -e⟩ perfume

Park m ⟨-s, -s⟩ park; Parkbank f park bench

Parkdeck nt parking level; parken vt, vi park

Parkett nt ⟨-s, -e⟩ parquet flooring; THEAT stalls pl (Brit), parquet (US)

Parkhaus nt multi-storey car park (Brit), parking garage (US)

parkinsonsche Krankheit f Parkinson's disease

Parkkralle f AUTO wheel clamp; Parklicht nt parking light; Parklücke f parking

space; Parkplatz m parking space; (for many cars) car park (Brit), parking lot (US); Parkscheibe f parking disc; Parkscheinautomat m pay point; (issuing ticket) ticket machine; Parkuhr f parking meter; Parkverbot nt no-parking zone; hier ist ~ you can't park here

Parlament nt parliament

Parmesan m ⟨-s⟩ Parmesan (cheese)

Partei f party

Parterre nt ⟨-s, -s⟩ ground floor (Brit), first floor (US)

Partitur f MUS score

Partizip nt ⟨-s, -ien⟩ participle

Partner(in) m(f) ⟨-s, -⟩ partner; Partnerschaft f partnership; eingetragene ~ civil partnership; Partnerstadt f twin town

Party f ⟨-, -s⟩ party; Partymuffel m ⟨-s, -⟩ party pooper; Partyservice m catering service

Pass m ⟨-es, Pässe⟩ pass; (ID) passport

passabel adj reasonable

Passagier m ⟨-s, -e⟩ passenger

Passamt nt passport office; Passbild nt passport photo

passen vi (size) fit; (colour, style) go (zu with); (not answer) pass; passt (es) dir morgen? does tomorrow suit you?; das passt mir gut that suits me fine; pas-

**send** adj suitable; (in colour, style) matching; (appropriate) fitting; (time) convenient

**passieren** vi happen

**passiv** adj passive

**Passkontrolle** f passport control

**Passwort** nt password

**Paste** f ⟨-, -n⟩ paste

**Pastete** f ⟨-, -n⟩ pie; (small) vol-au-vent; (for spreading) pâté

**Pastor** m/(f) ⟨-⟩ minister, vicar

**Pate** m ⟨-n, -n⟩ godfather; **Patenkind** nt godchild

**Patient(in)** m(f) patient

**Patin** f godmother

**Patrone** f ⟨-, -n⟩ cartridge

**patschnass** adj soaking wet

**pauschal** adj (cost) inclusive; (judgment) sweeping; **Pauschale** f ⟨-, -n⟩, **Pauschalgebühr** f flat rate (charge); **Pauschalpreis** m flat rate; (for hotel, trip) all-inclusive price; **Pauschalreise** f package tour

**Pause** f ⟨-, -n⟩ break; THEAT interval; (in cinema) intermission; (when speaking) pause

**Pavian** m ⟨-s, -e⟩ baboon

**Pavillon** m ⟨-s, -s⟩ pavilion

**Pay-TV** nt ⟨-s⟩ pay-per-view television, pay TV

**Pazifik** m ⟨-s⟩ Pacific (Ocean)

**PC** m ⟨-s, -s⟩ abbr = **Personal Computer** PC

**Pech** nt ⟨-s, -e⟩ fig bad luck; **~ haben** be unlucky; **~ gehabt!** tough (luck)

**Pedal** nt ⟨-s, -e⟩ pedal

**Pediküre** f ⟨-, -en⟩ pedicure

**Peeling** nt ⟨-s, -s⟩ (facial / body) scrub

**peinlich** adj embarrassing, awkward; (conscientious) painstaking; **es war mir sehr ~** I was totally embarrassed

**Peitsche** f ⟨-, -n⟩ whip

**Pelikan** m ⟨-s, -e⟩ pelican

**Pellkartoffeln** pl potatoes pl boiled in their skins

**Pelz** m ⟨-es, -e⟩ fur; **pelzig** adj (tongue) furred

**pendeln** vi (train, bus) shuttle; (person) commute; **Pendelverkehr** m shuttle traffic; (for commuters) commuter traffic; **Pendler(in)** m(f) ⟨-s, -⟩ commuter

**Penis** m ⟨-, -se⟩ penis

**Pension** f (money) pension; (period) retirement; (building) guesthouse, B&B; **pensioniert** adj retired

**Peperoni** f ⟨-, -⟩ chilli

**per** prep + acc by, per; (each) per; (not later than) by

**perfekt** adj perfect

**Periode** f ⟨-, -n⟩ period

**Perle** f ⟨-, -n⟩ a. fig pearl

**perplex** adj dumbfounded

**Person** f ⟨-, -en⟩ person; **ein Tisch für drei ~en** a table for three; **Personal** nt ⟨-s⟩ staff, personnel; **Personal-**

**ausweis** m identity card; **Personalien** pl particulars pl; **Personenschaden** m injury to persons; **persönlich** 1. adj personal; (on letter) private 2. adv personally; (oneself) in person; **Persönlichkeit** f personality

**Peru** nt ⟨-s⟩ Peru

**Perücke** f ⟨-, -n⟩ wig

**pervers** adj perverted

**pessimistisch** adj pessimistic

**Pest** f ⟨-⟩ plague

**Petersilie** f parsley

**Petroleum** nt ⟨-s⟩ paraffin (Brit), kerosene (US)

**Pfad** m ⟨-(e)s, -e⟩ path; **Pfadfinder** m ⟨-s, -⟩ boy scout; **Pfadfinderin** f girl guide

**Pfahl** m ⟨-(e)s, Pfähle⟩ post, stake

**Pfand** nt ⟨-(e)s, Pfänder⟩ security; (on bottle) deposit; (in game) forfeit; **Pfandflasche** f returnable bottle

**Pfanne** f ⟨-, -n⟩ (frying) pan

**Pfannkuchen** m pancake

**Pfarrei** f parish; **Pfarrer(in)** m(f) ⟨-s, -⟩ priest

**Pfau** m ⟨-(e)s, -en⟩ peacock

**Pfeffer** m ⟨-s, -⟩ pepper; **Pfefferkuchen** m gingerbread; **Pfefferminze** f ⟨-e⟩ peppermint; **Pfefferminztee** m peppermint tea; **Pfeffermühle** f pepper mill; **Pfefferstreuer** m ⟨-s, -⟩ pepper pot

**Pfeife** f ⟨-, -n⟩ whistle; (for to-

bacco, of organ) pipe; **pfeifen** ⟨pfiff, gepfiffen⟩ vt, vi whistle

**Pfeil** m ⟨-(e)s, -e⟩ arrow

**Pferd** nt ⟨-(e)s, -e⟩ horse; **Pferdeschwanz** m ponytail; **Pferdestall** m stable

**pfiff** imperf → **pfeifen**

**Pfifferling** m chanterelle

**Pfingsten** nt ⟨-, -⟩ Whitsun, Pentecost (US); **Pfingstmontag** m Whit Monday; **Pfingstsonntag** m Whit Sunday, Pentecost (US)

**Pfirsich** m ⟨-s, -e⟩ peach

**Pflanze** f ⟨-, -n⟩ plant; **pflanzen** vt plant; **Pflanzenfett** nt vegetable fat

**Pflaster** nt ⟨-s, -⟩ (for wound) plaster, Band Aid® (US); (on road) road surface, pavement (US)

**Pflaume** f ⟨-, -n⟩ plum

**Pflege** f ⟨-, -n⟩ care; (of patient) nursing; (of car, machine) maintenance; **pflegebedürftig** adj in need of care; **pflegeleicht** adj easy-care; fig easy to handle; **pflegen** vt look after; (patient) nurse; (relations) foster; (fingernails, face) take care of; (data) maintain; **Pflegepersonal** nt nursing staff; **Pflegeversicherung** f long-term care insurance

**Pflicht** f ⟨-, -en⟩ duty; SPORT compulsory section; **pflichtbewusst** adj conscientious; **Pflichtfach** nt compulsory subject

**pflücken** vt pick

**Pforte** f ⟨-, -n⟩ gate; **Pfört-ner(in)** m(f) ⟨-s, -⟩ porter

**Pfosten** m ⟨-s, -⟩ post

**Pfote** f ⟨-, -n⟩ paw

**pfui** interj ugh

**Pfund** nt ⟨-(e)s, -e⟩ pound

**pfuschen** vi fam be sloppy

**Pfütze** f ⟨-, -n⟩ puddle

**Phantasie** f → **Fantasie**; **phantastisch** adj → **fantastisch**

**Phase** f ⟨-, -n⟩ phase

**Philippinen** pl Philippines pl

**Philosophie** f philosophy

**pH-neutral** adj pH-balanced

**Photo** nt → **Foto**

**Physalis** f ⟨-, Physalen⟩ physalis

**Physik** f physics sg

**physisch** adj physical

**Pianist(in)** m(f) ⟨-en, -en⟩ pianist

**Pickel** m ⟨-s, -⟩ pimple; (tool) pickaxe

**Picknick** nt ⟨-s, -e or -s⟩ picnic; **ein ~ machen** have a picnic

**piepsen** vi chirp

**piercen** vt **sich die Nase ~ lassen** have one's nose pierced; **Piercing** nt ⟨-s⟩ (body) piercing

**pieseln** vi fam pee

**Pik** nt ⟨-, -⟩ (card suit) spades pl

**pikant** adj spicy

**Pilates** nt SPORT Pilates

**Pilger(in)** m(f) pilgrim; Pil-

gerfahrt f pilgrimage

**Pille** f ⟨-, -n⟩ pill; **sie nimmt die ~** she's on the pill

**Pilot(in)** m(f) ⟨-en, -en⟩ pilot

**Pilz** m ⟨-es, -e⟩ mushroom; (poisonous) toadstool; MED fungus

**PIN** f ⟨-, -s⟩ PIN (number)

**pingelig** adj fam fussy

**Pinguin** m ⟨-s, -e⟩ penguin

**Pinie** f ⟨-, -n⟩ pine; **Pinienkern** m pine nut

**pink** adj shocking pink

**pinkeln** vi fam pee

**Pinsel** m ⟨-s, -⟩ (paint)brush

**Pinzette** f tweezers pl

**Pistazie** f pistachio

**Piste** f ⟨-, -n⟩ piste; AVIAT runway

**Pistole** f ⟨-, -n⟩ pistol

**Pixel** nt ⟨-s⟩ IT pixel

**Pizza** f ⟨-, -s⟩ pizza; **Pizzaservice** m pizza delivery service; **Pizzeria** f ⟨-, Pizzerien⟩ pizzeria

**Pkw** m ⟨-(s), -(s)⟩ abbr = **Personenkraftwagen** car

**Plakat** nt poster

**Plan** m ⟨-(e)s, Pläne⟩ plan; (of town) map; **planen** vt plan

**Planet** m ⟨-en, -en⟩ planet; **Planetarium** nt planetarium

**planmäßig** adj scheduled

**Plan(t)schbecken** nt paddling pool; **plan(t)schen** vi splash around

**Planung** f planning

**Plastik 1.** f sculpture **2.** nt ⟨-s⟩ plastic; **Plastikfolie** f plastic film; **Plastiktüte** f plastic bag

**Platin** nt ⟨-s⟩ platinum

**platsch** interj splash

**platt** adj flat; fam (surprised) flabbergasted; fig (remarks etc) flat, boring

**Platte** f ⟨-, -n⟩ PHOT, TECH, GASTR plate; (stone slab) flag; (LP) record; **Plattenspieler** m record player

**Plattform** f platform; **Plattfuß** m flat foot; (on vehicle) flat (tyre)

**Platz** m ⟨-es, Plätze⟩ place; (in train, theatre etc) seat; (vacant area) space, room; (in town) square; (for sports) playing field; **nehmen Sie ~** please sit down, take a seat; **ist dieser ~ frei?** is this seat taken?

**Plätzchen** nt spot; (sweet food) biscuit

**platzen** vi burst; (bomb) explode

**Platzkarte** f seat reservation; **Platzreservierung** f seat reservation; **Platzverweis** m **er erhielt einen ~** he was sent off; **Platzwunde** f laceration, cut

**plaudern** vi chat, talk

**pleite** adj fam broke; **Pleite** f ⟨-, -n⟩ bankruptcy; fam (party, play etc) flop

**Plombe** f ⟨-, -n⟩ lead seal; (in tooth) filling; **plombieren** vt (tooth) fill

**plötzlich 1.** adj sudden **2.** adv suddenly, all at once

**plumps** interj thud; (in liquid) plop

**Plural** m ⟨-s, -e⟩ plural

**plus** adv plus; **fünf ~ sieben ist zwölf** five plus seven is (or are) twelve; **zehn Grad ~** ten degrees above zero; **Plus** nt ⟨-, -⟩ plus; FIN profit; (benefit) advantage

**Plüsch** m ⟨-(e)s, -e⟩ plush

**Pluto** m ⟨-⟩ Pluto

**Po** m ⟨-s, -s⟩ fam bottom, bum

**Pocken** pl smallpox sg

**poetisch** adj poetic

**Pointe** f ⟨-, -n⟩ punch line

**Pokal** m ⟨-s, -e⟩ goblet; SPORT cup

**pökeln** vt pickle

**Pol** m ⟨-s, -e⟩ pole

**Pole** m ⟨-n, -n⟩ Pole; **Polen** nt ⟨-s⟩ Poland

**Police** f ⟨-, -n⟩ (insurance) policy

**polieren** vt polish

**Polin** f Pole, Polish woman

**Politik** f politics sg; (course of action) policy; **Politiker(in)** m(f) politician; **politisch** adj political

**Politur** f polish

**Polizei** f police pl; **Polizeibeamte(r)** m, **Polizeibeamtin** f police officer; **Polizeirevier** nt, **Polizeiwache** f police station; **Polizist(in)** m(f) policeman / -woman

**Pollen** m ⟨-s, -⟩ pollen; **Pollenflug** m ⟨-s⟩ pollen count

**polnisch** adj Polish; **Polnisch** nt Polish

**Polo** *nt* ⟨-s⟩ polo; **Polohemd** *nt* polo shirt

**Polterabend** *m party prior to a wedding, at which old crockery is smashed to bring good luck*

**Polyester** *m* ⟨-s, -⟩ polyester

**Polypen** *pl* MED adenoids *pl*

**Pommes frites** *pl* chips *pl* (*Brit*), French fries *pl* (*US*)

**Pony 1.** *m* ⟨-s⟩ (*hairstyle*) fringe (*Brit*), bangs *pl* (*US*) **2.** *nt* ⟨-s⟩ (*horse*) pony

**Popcorn** *nt* ⟨-s⟩ popcorn

**Popmusik** *f* pop (music)

**populär** *adj* popular

**Pore** *f* ⟨-, -n⟩ pore

**Pornografie** *f* pornography

**Porree** *m* ⟨-s, -s⟩ leeks *pl*; *eine Stange* ~ a leek

**Portemonnaie, Portmonee** *nt* ⟨-s, -s⟩ purse

**Portion** *f* portion, helping

**Porto** *nt* ⟨-s, -s⟩ postage

**Portrait, Porträt** *nt* ⟨-s, -s⟩ portrait

**Portugal** *nt* ⟨-s⟩ Portugal; **Portugiese** *m* ⟨-n, -n⟩ Portuguese; **Portugiesin** *f* ⟨-, -nen⟩ Portuguese; **portugiesisch** *adj* Portuguese; **Portugiesisch** *nt* Portuguese

**Portwein** *m* ⟨-s, -e⟩ port

**Porzellan** *nt* ⟨-s, -e⟩ china

**Posaune** *f* ⟨-, -n⟩ trombone

**Position** *f* position

**positiv** *adj* positive

**Post®** *f* ⟨-, -en⟩ post office; (*letters*) post (*Brit*), mail; **Postamt** *nt* post office;

**Postanweisung** *f* postal order (*Brit*), money order (*US*); **Postbank** *f German post office bank*; **Postbote** *m*, **-botin** *f* postman / -woman

**Posten** *m* ⟨-s, -⟩ post, position

**Poster** *nt* ⟨-s, -⟩ poster

**Postfach** *nt* post-office box, PO box; **Postkarte** *f* postcard; **Postleitzahl** *f* postcode (*Brit*), zip code (*US*)

**Poststempel** *m* postmark

**Potenz** *f* MATH power; (*of man*) potency

**PR** *f* ⟨-, -s⟩ *abbr* = **Public Relations** PR

**prächtig** *adj* splendid

**prahlen** *vi* boast, brag

**Praktikant(in)** *m(f)* trainee; **Praktikum** *nt* ⟨-s, Praktika⟩ work experience; **praktisch** *adj* practical; *~er Arzt* general practitioner

**Praline** *f* chocolate

**Prämie** *f* (*for insurance*) premium; (*as recompense*) reward; (*from employer*) bonus

**Präservativ** *nt* condom

**Präsident(in)** *m(f)* president

**Praxis** *f* ⟨-, Praxen⟩ practice; (*treatment room*) surgery; (*of lawyer*) office; **Praxisgebühr** *f surgery surcharge*

**präzise** *adj* precise, exact

**predigen** *vt, vi* preach; **Predigt** *f* ⟨-, -en⟩ sermon

**Preis** *m* ⟨-es, -e⟩ price; (*for winner*) prize; **Preisaus-**

**schreiben** *nt* competition
**Preiselbeere** *f* cranberry
**preisgünstig** *adj* inexpensive; **Preisliste** *f* price list; **Preisschild** *nt* price tag; **Preisträger(in)** *m(f)* prizewinner; **preiswert** *adj* inexpensive

**Prellung** *f* bruise

**Premiere** *f* ⟨-, -n⟩ premiere, first night

**Premierminister(in)** *m(f)* prime minister, premier

**Prepaidhandy** *nt* prepaid mobile (*Brit*), prepaid cell phone (*US*); **Prepaidkarte** *f* prepaid card

**Presse** *f* ⟨-, -n⟩ press

**pressen** *vt* press

**prickeln** *vi* tingle

**Priester(in)** *m(f)* ⟨-s, -⟩ priest / (woman) priest

**Primel** *f* ⟨-, -n⟩ primrose

**primitiv** *adj* primitive

**Prinz** *m* ⟨-en, -en⟩ prince; **Prinzessin** *f* princess

**Prinzip** *nt* ⟨-s, -ien⟩ principle; *im ~* basically; *aus ~* on principle

**privat** *adj* private; **Privatfernsehen** *nt* commercial television; **Privatgrundstück** *nt* private property; **privatisieren** *vt* privatize

**pro** *prep* + *acc* per; *5 Euro ~ Stück / Person* 5 euros each / per person; **Pro** *nt* ⟨-s⟩ pro

**Probe** *f* ⟨-, -n⟩ test; (*small quantity*) sample; THEAT re-

hearsal; **Probefahrt** *f* test drive; *eine ~ machen* go for a test drive; **Probezeit** *f* trial period; **probieren** *vt, vi* try; (*wine, food*) taste, sample

**Problem** *nt* ⟨-s, -e⟩ problem

**Produkt** *nt* ⟨-(e)s, -e⟩ product; **Produktion** *f* production; (*amount produced*) output; **produzieren** *vt* produce

**Professor(in)** *m(f)* ⟨-s, -en⟩ professor

**Profi** *m* ⟨-s, -s⟩ pro

**Profil** *nt* ⟨-s, -e⟩ profile; (*of tyre, sole of shoe*) tread

**Profit** *m* ⟨-(e)s, -e⟩ profit; **profitieren** *vi* profit (*von* from)

**Prognose** *f* ⟨-, -n⟩ prediction; (*of weather*) forecast

**Programm** *nt* ⟨-s, -e⟩ programme; IT program; TV channel; **Programmheft** *nt* programme; **programmieren** *vt* program; **Programmierer(in)** *m(f)* ⟨-s, -⟩ programmer

**Projekt** *nt* ⟨-(e)s, -e⟩ project

**Projektor** *m* projector

**Promenade** *f* ⟨-, -n⟩ promenade

**Promille** *nt* ⟨-(s), -⟩ (blood) alcohol level; *0,8 ~* 0,08 per cent; **Promillegrenze** *f* legal alcohol limit

**prominent** *adj* prominent; **Prominenz** *f* VIPs *pl*, prominent figures *pl*; *fam* (*celebrities*) the glitterati *pl*

**Propeller** *m* ⟨-s, -⟩ propeller

**prosit** *interj* cheers

**Prospekt** *m* ⟨-(e)s, -e⟩ leaflet, brochure

**prost** *interj* cheers

**Prostituierte(r)** *mf* prostitute

**Protest** *m* ⟨-(e)s, -e⟩ protest

**Protestant(in)** *m(f)* Protestant; **protestantisch** *adj* Protestant

**protestieren** *vi* protest (*gegen* against)

**Prothese** *f* ⟨-, -n⟩ artificial arm / leg; (*false teeth*) dentures *pl*

**Protokoll** *nt* ⟨-s, -e⟩ (*of meeting*) minutes *pl*; IT protocol; (*given to police*) statement

**protzen** *vi* show off; **protzig** *adj* flashy

**Proviant** *m* ⟨-s, -e⟩ provisions *pl*

**Provider** *m* ⟨-s, -⟩ IT (*service*) provider

**Provinz** *f* ⟨-, -en⟩ province

**Provision** *f* COMM commission

**provisorisch** *adj* provisional; **Provisorium** *nt* ⟨-s, Provisorien⟩ stopgap; (*tooth*) provisional filling

**provozieren** *vt* provoke

**Prozent** *nt* ⟨-(e)s, -e⟩ per cent

**Prozess** *m* ⟨-es, -e⟩ process; LAW trial; (*lawsuit*) (court) case; **prozessieren** *vi* go to law (*mit* against)

**Prozession** *f* procession

**Prozessor** *m* ⟨-s, -en⟩ IT processor

**prüde** *adj* prudish

**prüfen** *vt* test; (*verify*) check; *f* exam; (*verification*) check; *eine ~ machen* take an exam

**Prügelei** *f* fight; **prügeln 1.** *vt* beat **2.** *vr* fight

**PS 1.** *abbr* = **Pferdestärke** hp **2.** *abbr* = **Postskript(um)** PS

**pseudo-** *pref* pseudo; **Pseudonym** *nt* ⟨-s, -e⟩ pseudonym

**pst** *interj* ssh

**Psychiater(in)** *m(f)* ⟨-s, -⟩ psychiatrist; **psychisch** *adj* psychological; (*illness*) mental; **Psychoanalyse** *f* psychoanalysis; **Psychologe** *m* ⟨-n, -n⟩, **Psychologin** *f* psychologist; **Psychologie** *f* psychology; **psychosomatisch** *adj* psychosomatic; **Psychoterror** *m* psychological intimidation; **Psychotherapie** *f* psychotherapy

**Pubertät** *f* puberty

**Publikum** *nt* ⟨-s⟩ audience; SPORT crowd

**Pudding** *m* ⟨-s, -e *or* -s⟩ blancmange

**Pudel** *m* ⟨-s, -⟩ poodle

**Puder** *m* ⟨-s, -⟩ powder; **Puderzucker** *m* icing sugar

**Puerto Rico** *nt* ⟨-s⟩ Puerto Rico

**Pulli** *m* ⟨-s, -s⟩, **Pullover** *m* ⟨-s, -⟩ sweater, pullover, jumper (*Brit*)

**Puls** *m* ⟨-es, -e⟩ pulse

**Pulver** *nt* ⟨-s, -⟩ powder; **Pulverkaffee** *m* instant coffee; **Pulverschnee** *m* powder snow

**Pumpe** f ⟨-, -n⟩ pump; **pumpen** vt pump; fam (to sb) lend; fam (from sb) borrow

**Pumps** pl court shoes pl (Brit), pumps pl (US)

**Punk** m ⟨-s, -s⟩ (music, person) punk

**Punkt** m ⟨-(e)s, -e⟩ point; (in pattern) dot; (punctuation mark) full stop (Brit), period (US); ~ **zwei Uhr** at two o'clock sharp

**pünktlich** adj punctual, on time; **Pünktlichkeit** f punctuality

**Punsch** m ⟨-(e)s, -e⟩ punch

**Pupille** f ⟨-, -n⟩ pupil

**Puppe** f ⟨-, -n⟩ doll

**pur** adj pure; (absolute) sheer;

(whisky) neat

**Püree** nt ⟨-s, -s⟩ puree; mashed potatoes pl

**Puste** f ⟨-⟩ fam puff; **außer ~ sein** be puffed; **pusten** vi blow; (pant) puff

**Pute** f ⟨-, -n⟩ turkey

**Putz** m ⟨-es⟩ (on wall) plaster

**putzen** vt clean; **sich dat die Nase ~** blow one's nose; **sich dat die Zähne ~** brush one's teeth; **Putzfrau** f cleaner; **Putzlappen** m cloth; **Putzmittel** nt cleaning agent, cleaner

**Puzzle** nt ⟨-s, -s⟩ jigsaw (puzzle)

**Pyjama** m ⟨-s, -s⟩ pyjamas pl

**Pyramide** f ⟨-, -n⟩ pyramid

**Python** m ⟨-s, -s⟩ python

# Q

**Quadrat** nt square; **quadratisch** adj square; **Quadratmeter** m square metre

**quaken** vi (frog) croak; (duck) quack

**Qual** f ⟨-, -en⟩ pain, agony; (mental) anguish; **quälen 1.** vt torment **2.** vr struggle; (mentally) torment oneself; **Quälerei** f torture, torment

**qualifizieren** vt, vr qualify; (classify) label

**Qualität** f quality

**Qualle** f ⟨-, -n⟩ jellyfish

**Qualm** m ⟨-(e)s⟩ thick smoke; **qualmen** vt, vi smoke

**Quantität** f quantity

**Quarantäne** f ⟨-, -n⟩ quarantine

**Quark** m ⟨-s⟩ quark; fam (nonsense) rubbish

**Quartett** nt ⟨-s, -e⟩ quartet; (card game) happy families sg

**Quartier** nt ⟨-s, -e⟩ accommodation

**quasi** adv more or less

**Quatsch** m ⟨-es⟩ fam rubbish; **quatschen** vi fam chat

**Quecksilber** nt mercury

**Quelle** f ⟨-, -n⟩ spring; (of river) source

**quer** *adv* crossways, diagonally; at right angles; **Querflöte** *f* flute; **Querschnitt** *m* cross section; **querschnittsgelähmt** *adj* paraplegic; **Querstraße** *f* side street

**quetschen** *vt* squash, crush; MED bruise; **Quetschung** *f* bruise

**Queue** *m* ⟨-s, -s⟩ (billiard) cue

**quietschen** *vi* squeal; (*door, bed*) squeak; (*brakes*) screech

**quitt** *adj* quits, even

**Quitte** *f* ⟨-, -n⟩ quince

**Quittung** *f* receipt

**Quiz** *nt* ⟨-, -⟩ quiz

**Quote** *f* ⟨-, -n⟩ rate; COMM quota

# R

**Rabatt** *m* ⟨-(e)s, -e⟩ discount

**Rabbi** *m* ⟨-(s), -(s)⟩ rabbi; **Rabbiner** *m* ⟨-s, -⟩ rabbi

**Rabe** *m* ⟨-n, -n⟩ raven

**Rache** *f* ⟨-⟩ revenge, vengeance

**Rachen** *m* ⟨-s, -⟩ throat

**rächen 1.** *vt* avenge **2.** *vr* take (one's) revenge (*an* + *dat* on)

**Rad** *nt* ⟨-(e)s, Räder⟩ wheel; (*vehicle*) bike; **~ fahren** cycle; **mit dem ~ fahren** go by bike

**Radar** *m or nt* ⟨-s⟩ radar; **Radarfalle** *f* speed trap; **Radarkontrolle** *f* radar speed check

**radeln** *vi fam* cycle; **Radfahrer(in)** *m(f)* cyclist; **Radfahrweg** *m* cycle track (*or* path)

**Radicchio** *m* ⟨-s⟩ radicchio

**radieren** *vt* rub out, erase; **Radiergummi** *m* rubber (*Brit*), eraser; **Radierung** *f* ART etching

**Radieschen** *nt* radish

**radikal** *adj* radical

**Radio** *nt* ⟨-s, -s⟩ radio; **im ~** on the radio

**radioaktiv** *adj* radioactive

**Radiologe** *m* ⟨-n, -n⟩, **Radiologin** *f* radiologist

**Radiowecker** *m* radio alarm (clock)

**Radkappe** *f* AUTO hub cap

**Radler(in)** *m(f)* ⟨-s, -⟩ cyclist

**Radler** *nt* ⟨-s, -⟩ ≈ shandy

**Radlerhose** *f* cycling shorts *pl*; **Radrennen** *nt* cycle racing; (*single event*) cycle race; **Radtour** *f* cycling tour; **Radweg** *m* cycle track (*or* path)

**raffiniert** *adj* crafty, cunning; (*sugar*) refined

**Rafting** *nt* ⟨-s⟩ white water rafting

**Ragout** *nt* ⟨-s, -s⟩ ragout

**Rahm** *m* ⟨-s⟩ cream

**rahmen** *vt* frame; **Rahmen** *m* ⟨-s, -⟩ frame

**Rakete** *f* ⟨-, -n⟩ rocket

**rammen** vt ram

**Rampe** f ⟨-, -n⟩ ramp

**ramponieren** vt fam damage, batter

**Ramsch** m ⟨-(e)s, -e⟩ junk

**ran** fam contr → **heran**

**Rand** m ⟨-(e)s, Ränder⟩ edge; (of spectacles, cup etc) rim; (on paper) margin; (of dirt, under eyes) ring; fig verge, brink

**randalieren** vi (go on the) rampage

**rang** imperf → **ringen**

**Rang** m ⟨-(e)s, Ränge⟩ rank; (in competition) place; THEAT circle

**rannte** imperf → **rennen**

**ranzig** adj rancid

**Rap** m ⟨-(s), -s⟩ MUS rap; **rappen** vi MUS rap; **Rapper(in)** m(f) ⟨-s, -⟩ MUS rapper

**rar** adj rare, scarce

**rasant** adj quick, rapid

**rasch** adj quick

**rascheln** vi rustle

**rasen** vi (rush) race; (behave wildly) rave; (jdm sb) **gegen einen Baum ~** crash into a tree

**Rasen** m ⟨-s, -⟩ lawn

**rasend** adj furious

**Rasenmäher** m ⟨-s, -⟩ lawn-mower

**Rasierapparat** m razor; (electric) shaver; **Rasiercreme** f shaving cream; **rasieren** vt, vr shave; **Rasierer** m shaver; **Rasiergel** nt shaving gel; **Rasierklinge** f razor blade; **Rasiermesser** nt

(cutthroat) razor; **Rasierpinsel** m shaving brush; **Rasierschaum** m shaving foam; **Rasierzeug** nt shaving tackle, shaving equipment

**Rasse** f ⟨-, -n⟩ race; (animals) breed

**Rassismus** m racism; **Rassist(in)** m(f) racist; **rassistisch** adj racist

**Rast** f ⟨-, -en⟩ rest, break; **~ machen** have a rest (or break); **Raststätte** f AUTO service area; (café) motorway (Brit) (or highway (US)) restaurant

**Rasur** f shave

**Rat** m ⟨-(e)s, Ratschläge⟩ (piece of) advice; **um ~ fragen** ask for advice

**Rate** f ⟨-, -n⟩ instalment; **etw auf ~n kaufen** buy sth in instalments (Brit), buy sth on the instalment plan (US)

**raten** ⟨riet, geraten⟩ vt, vi guess; (recommend) advise (jdm sb)

**Rathaus** nt town hall

**Ration** f ration

**ratlos** adj at a loss, helpless; **ratsam** adj advisable

**Rätsel** nt ⟨-s, -⟩ puzzle; (word puzzle) riddle; **das ist mir ein ~** it's a mystery to me; **rätselhaft** adj mysterious

**Ratte** f ⟨-, -n⟩ rat

**rau** adj rough, coarse; (weather) harsh

**Raub** m ⟨-(e)s⟩ robbery; (sto-

*len things*) steal; **rau-
ben** vt steal; **jdm etw ~** rob
sb of sth; **Räuber(in)** m(f)
⟨-s, -⟩ robber; **Raubkopie** f
pirate copy; **Raubmord** m
robbery with murder; **Raub-
tier** nt predator; **Raubüberfall** m mugging; **Raubvogel**
m bird of prey

**Rauch** m ⟨-(e)s⟩ smoke; (*from
exhaust*) fumes pl; **rauchen**
vt, vi smoke; **Raucher(in)**
m(f) ⟨-s, -⟩ smoker

**Räucherlachs** m smoked
salmon; **räuchern** vt smoke

**rauchig** adj smoky; **Rauchmelder** m smoke detector;
**Rauchverbot** nt smoking
ban; **hier ist ~** there's no
smoking here

**rauf** fam contr → **herauf**

**rauh** adj → **rau**; **Rauhreif** m
→ **Raureif**

**Raum** m ⟨-(e)s, Räume⟩ space;
(*part of building, space for a
purpose*) room; (*district*) area

**räumen** vt clear; (*house, seat*)
vacate; (*take away*) shift,
move; (*into cupboard etc*)
put away

**Raumfähre** f space shuttle;
**Raumfahrt** f space travel;
**Raumschiff** nt spacecraft,
spaceship; **Raumsonde** f
space probe; **Raumstation**
f space station

**Raupe** f ⟨-, -n⟩ caterpillar

**Raureif** m hoarfrost

**raus** fam contr → **heraus**; →

**hinaus**; **~!** (get) out!

**Rausch** m ⟨-(e)s, Räusche⟩ intoxication; **einen ~ haben** /
**kriegen** be / get drunk;
**Rauschgift** nt drug;
**Rauschgiftsüchtige(r)** mf
drug addict

**rausfliegen** irr vi fam be
kicked out

**raushalten** irr vr fam **halt du
dich da raus!** you (just)
keep out of it

**räuspern** vr clear one's
throat

**rausschmeißen** irr vt fam
throw out

**Razzia** f ⟨-, Razzien⟩ raid

**reagieren** vi react (*auf* + *acc*
to); **Reaktion** f reaction

**real** adj real; **realisieren** vt
(*danger, problem*) realize;
(*plan, idea*) implement; **realistisch** adj realistic; **Realität** f ⟨-, -en⟩ reality; **Reali-
ty-TV** nt ⟨-s⟩ reality TV

**Realschule** f ≈ secondary
school, junior high (school)
(*US*)

**rebellieren** vi rebel

**Rebhuhn** nt partridge

**rechnen 1.** vt, vi calculate; **~
mit** expect; (*rely on*) count
on **2.** vr pay off, turn out
to be profitable; **Rechner**
m ⟨-s, -⟩ calculator; (*larger*)
computer; **Rechnung** f cal-
culation(s); COMM bill (*Brit*),
check (*US*); **die ~, bitte!** can
I have the bill, please?; **das
geht auf meine ~** this is on

me

**recht 1.** *adj* right; **mir soll's ~ sein** it's alright by me; **mir ist es ~** I don't mind; **~ haben** be right; **jdm ~ geben** agree with sb **2.** *adv* really, quite; *(correctly)* right(ly); **ich weiß nicht ~** I don't really know; **es geschieht ihm ~** it serves him right

**Recht** *nt* ⟨-(e)s, -e⟩ right; LAW law

**Rechte** *f* ⟨-n, -n⟩ right-hand side; *(hand)* right hand; POL right (wing); **rechte(r, s)** *adj* right; **auf der ~ Seite** on the right, on the right-hand side

**Rechteck** *nt* ⟨-s, -e⟩ rectangle; **rechteckig** *adj* rectangular

**rechtfertigen 1.** *vt* justify **2.** *vr* justify oneself

**rechtlich** *adj* legal; **rechtmäßig** *adj* legal, lawful

**rechts** *adv* on the right; **~ abbiegen** turn right; **~ von** to the right of; **~ oben** at the top right

**Rechtsanwalt** *m*, **-anwältin** *f* lawyer

**Rechtschreibung** *f* spelling

**Rechtshänder(in)** *m(f)* ⟨-s, -⟩ right-hander; **rechtsherum** *adv* to the right, clockwise; **rechtsradikal** *adj* POL extreme right-wing

**Rechtsschutzversicherung** *f* legal costs insurance

**Rechtsverkehr** *m* driving on the right

**rechtswidrig** *adj* illegal

**rechtwinklig** *adj* right-angled; **rechtzeitig 1.** *adj* timely **2.** *adv* in time

**recyceln** *vt* recycle; **Recycling** *nt* ⟨-s⟩ recycling

**Redakteur(in)** *m(f)* editor; **Redaktion** *f* editing; *(people)* editorial staff; *(place)* editorial office(s)

**Rede** *f* ⟨-, -n⟩ speech; *(conversation)* talk; **eine ~ halten** make a speech; **reden 1.** *vi* talk, speak **2.** *vt* talk; *(nonsense etc)* talk; **Redewendung** *f* idiom; **Redner(in)** *m(f)* speaker

**reduzieren** *vt* reduce

**Referat** *nt* ⟨-s, -e⟩ paper; **ein ~ halten** give a paper *(über + acc* on)

**reflektieren** *vt* reflect

**Reform** *f* ⟨-, -en⟩ reform; **Reformhaus** *nt* health food shop; **reformieren** *vt* reform

**Regal** *nt* ⟨-s, -e⟩ shelf; *(piece of furniture)* shelves *pl*

**Regel** *f* ⟨-, -n⟩ rule; MED period; **regelmäßig** *adj* regular; **regeln** *vt* regulate, control; *(matter)* settle; **Regelung** *f* regulation

**Regen** *m* ⟨-s, -⟩ rain; **Regenbogen** *m* rainbow; **Regenmantel** *m* raincoat; **Regenschauer** *m* shower; **Regenschirm** *m* umbrella; **Regenwald** *m* rainforest; **Regenwurm** *m* earthworm

**Regie** *f* direction

**regieren** vt, vi govern, rule; **Regierung** f government; (of monarch) reign

**Region** f region; **regional** adj regional

**Regisseur(in)** m(f) director

**regnen** vi impers rain; **regnerisch** adj rainy

**regulär** adj regular; **regulieren** vt regulate, adjust

**Reh** nt ⟨-(e)s, -e⟩ deer; (meat) venison

**Reibe** f ⟨-, -n⟩, **Reibeisen** nt grater; **reiben** ⟨rieb, gerieben⟩ vt rub; GASTR grate; **reibungslos** adj smooth

**reich** adj rich

**Reich** nt ⟨-(e)s, -e⟩ empire; (of king) kingdom

**reichen 1.** vi reach; (money, food etc) be enough, be sufficient (jdm for sb) **2.** vt hold out; (give) pass, hand; (serve) offer

**reichhaltig** adj ample, rich; **reichlich** adj (tip) generous; (meal) ample; **~ Zeit** plenty of time; **Reichtum** m ⟨-s, -tümer⟩ wealth

**reif** adj ripe; (person, judgment) mature

**Reif 1.** m ⟨-(e)s⟩ hoarfrost **2.** m ⟨-(e)s, -e⟩ ring, hoop

**reifen** vi mature; (fruit) ripen

**Reifen** m ⟨-s, -⟩ ring, hoop; (of car) tyre; **Reifendruck** m tyre pressure; **Reifenpanne** f puncture; **Reifenwechsel** m tyre change

**Reihe** f ⟨-, -n⟩ row; (of days

etc) fam (number) series sg; **der ~ nach** one after the other; **er ist an der ~** it's his turn; **Reihenfolge** f order, sequence; **Reihenhaus** nt terraced house (Brit), row house (US)

**Reiher** m ⟨-s, -⟩ heron

**rein 1.** fam contr → **herein;** → **hinein 2.** adj pure; (shirt, air) clean

**Reinfall** m fam letdown; **reinfallen** irr vi fam **auf etw** acc **~** fall for sth

**reinigen** vt clean; **Reinigung** f cleaning; (shop) cleaner's; **Reinigungsmittel** nt cleaning agent, cleaner

**reinlegen** vt **jdn ~** take sb for a ride

**Reis** m ⟨-es, -e⟩ rice

**Reise** f ⟨-, -n⟩ journey; (on ship) voyage; **Reiseapotheke** f first-aid kit; **Reisebüro** nt travel agent's; **Reisebus** m coach; **Reiseführer(in)** m(f) courier; (book) guide (-book); **Reisegepäck** nt luggage (Brit), baggage; **Reisegesellschaft** f tour operator; **Reisegruppe** f tourist party; (travelling by coach) coach party; **Reiseleiter(in)** m(f) courier; **reisen** vi travel; **~ nach** go to; **Reisende(r)** mf traveller; **Reisepass** m passport; **Reisescheck** m traveller's cheque; **Reisetasche** f holdall (Brit), carryall (US); **Rei-**

**severanstalter** *m* tour operator; **Reiseverkehr** *m* holiday traffic; **Reiseversicherung** *f* travel insurance; **Reiseziel** *nt* destination

**Reiskocher** *m* ⟨-s, -⟩ rice steamer

**reißen** ⟨riss, gerissen⟩ *vt, vi* tear; (*move*) pull, drag

**Reißnagel** *m* drawing pin (*Brit*), thumbtack (*US*); **Reißverschluss** *m* zip (*Brit*), zipper (*US*); **Reißzwecke** *f* drawing pin (*Brit*), thumbtack (*US*)

**reiten** ⟨ritt, geritten⟩ *vt, vi* ride; **Reiter(in)** *m(f)* rider

**Reiz** *m* ⟨-es, -e⟩ stimulus; (*delightfulness*) charm; (*appeal*) attraction; **reizen** *vt* stimulate; (*make angry*) annoy; (*interest*) appeal to, attract; **reizend** *adj* charming; **Reizung** *f* irritation

**Reklamation** *f* complaint

**Reklame** *f* ⟨-, -n⟩ advertising; (*on TV*) commercial

**reklamieren** *vi* complain (*wegen* about)

**Rekord** *m* ⟨-(e)s, -e⟩ record

**relativ 1.** *adj* relative **2.** *adv* relatively

**relaxen** *vi* relax, chill out

**Religion** *f* religion; **religiös** *adj* religious

**Remoulade** *f* ⟨-, -n⟩ tartar sauce

**Renaissance** *f* renaissance, revival; HIST Renaissance

**rennen** ⟨rannte, gerannt⟩ *vt, vi* run; **Rennen** *nt* ⟨-s, -⟩ running; (*competition*) race; **Rennrad** *nt* racing bike

**renommiert** *adj* famous, noted (*wegen, für* for)

**renovieren** *vt* renovate; **Renovierung** *f* renovation

**rentabel** *adj* profitable

**Rente** *f* ⟨-, -n⟩ pension; **Rentenversicherung** *f* pension scheme

**Rentier** *nt* reindeer

**rentieren** *vr* pay, be profitable

**Rentner(in)** *m(f)* ⟨-s, -⟩ pensioner, senior citizen

**Reparatur** *f* repair; **Reparaturwerkstatt** *f* repair shop; AUTO garage; **reparieren** *vt* repair

**Reportage** *f* report; **Reporter(in)** *m(f)* ⟨-s, -⟩ reporter

**Republik** *f* republic

**Reservat** *nt* ⟨-s, -e⟩ nature reserve; **Reserve** *f* ⟨-, -n⟩ reserve; **Reservekanister** *m* spare can; **Reserverad** *nt* AUTO spare wheel; **reservieren** *vt* reserve; **Reservierung** *f* reservation

**resignieren** *vi* give up; **resigniert** *adj* resigned

**Respekt** *m* ⟨-(e)s⟩ respect; **respektieren** *vt* respect

**Rest** *m* ⟨-(e)s, -e⟩ rest, remainder; (*left over*) remains *pl*

**Restaurant** *nt* ⟨-s, -s⟩ restaurant

**restaurieren** *vt* restore

**restlich** *adj* remaining

**Resultat** *nt* result

**retten** *vt* save, rescue

**Rettich** *m* ⟨-s, -e⟩ radish (*large white or red variety*)

**Rettung** *f* rescue; (*assistance*) help; (*medical team*) ambulance service; **Rettungsboot** *nt* lifeboat; **Rettungshubschrauber** *m* rescue helicopter; **Rettungsring** *m* lifebelt, life preserver (*US*); **Rettungswagen** *m* ambulance

**Reue** *f* ⟨-⟩ remorse; regret

**revanchieren** *vr* (*for help etc*) return the favour

**Revolution** *f* revolution

**Rezept** *nt* ⟨-(e)s, -e⟩ GASTR recipe; MED prescription; **rezeptfrei** *adj* over-the-counter, non-prescription

**Rezeption** *f* (*at hotel*) reception

**rezeptpflichtig** *adj* available only on prescription

**Rhabarber** *m* ⟨-s⟩ rhubarb

**Rhein** *m* ⟨-(e)s⟩ Rhine; **Rheinland-Pfalz** *nt* ⟨-⟩ Rhineland-Palatinate

**Rheuma** *nt* ⟨-s⟩ rheumatism

**Rhythmus** *m* rhythm

**richten** 1. *vt* direct (*auf + acc* to); (*weapon, camera*) point (*auf + acc* at); (*letter, inquiry*) address (*an + acc* to) 2. *vr* **sich ~ nach** (*rule etc*) keep to; (*fashion, example*) follow; (*vary according to*) depend on

**Richter(in)** *m(f)* ⟨-s, -⟩ judge

**Richtgeschwindigkeit** *f* recommended speed

**richtig** 1. *adj* right, correct; (*genuine*) proper 2. *adv fam* (*very*) really; **richtigstellen** *vt* **etw ~** correct sth

**Richtlinie** *f* guideline

**Richtung** *f* direction; (*trend*) tendency

**rieb** *imperf* → **reiben**

**riechen** ⟨roch, gerochen⟩ *vt, vi* smell; ***nach etw ~*** smell of sth

**rief** *imperf* → **rufen**

**Riegel** *m* ⟨-s, -⟩ bolt; GASTR (*of chocolate*) bar

**Riese** *m* ⟨-n, -n⟩ giant; **Riesengarnele** *f* king prawn; **riesengroß** *adj* gigantic, huge; **Riesenrad** *nt* big wheel; **riesig** *adj* enormous, huge

**riet** *imperf* → **raten**

**Riff** *nt* ⟨-(e)s, -e⟩ reef

**Rind** *nt* ⟨-(e)s, -er⟩ cow; (*male*) bull; GASTR beef; ***~er*** *pl* cattle *pl*

**Rinde** *f* ⟨-, -n⟩ (*of tree*) bark; (*of cheese*) rind; (*of bread*) crust

**Rinderbraten** *m* roast beef

**Rindfleisch** *nt* beef

**Ring** *m* ⟨-(e)s, -e⟩ ring; (*round town*) ring road; **Ringfinger** *m* ring finger; **ringsherum** *adv* round about

**Rippe** *f* ⟨-, -n⟩ rib

**Risiko** *nt* ⟨-s, -s or Risiken⟩ risk; ***auf eigenes ~*** at one's own risk; **riskant** *adj* risky;

**riskieren** vt risk

**riss** imperf → **reißen**

**Riss** m ⟨-es, -e⟩ tear; (in wall, cup etc) crack; **rissig** adj cracked; (skin) chapped

**ritt** imperf → **reiten**

**Ritter** m ⟨-s, -⟩ knight

**Rivale** m ⟨-n, -n⟩, **Rivalin** f rival

**Robbe** f ⟨-, -n⟩ seal

**Roboter** m ⟨-s, -⟩ robot

**robust** adj robust

**roch** imperf → **riechen**

**Rock** m ⟨-(e)s, Röcke⟩ skirt

**Rockmusik** f rock (music)

**Rodelbahn** f toboggan run; **rodeln** vi toboggan

**Roggen** m ⟨-s, -⟩ rye; **Roggenbrot** nt rye bread

**roh** adj raw; (person) coarse, crude; **Rohkost** f raw vegetables and fruit pl

**Rohr** nt ⟨-(e)s, -e⟩ pipe; **Röhre** f ⟨-, -n⟩ tube; (in cooker) oven; **Rohrzucker** m cane sugar

**Rohstoff** m raw material

**Rokoko** nt ⟨-s⟩ rococo

**Rolle** f ⟨-, -n⟩ roll; THEAT role

**rollen** vt, vi roll

**Roller** m ⟨-s, -⟩ scooter

**Rollerskates** pl roller skates pl

**Rollkragenpullover** m polo-neck (Brit) (or turtleneck (US)) sweater; **Rollladen** m, **Rollo** m ⟨-s, -s⟩ (roller) shutters pl; **Rollschuh** m roller skate; **Rollstuhl** m wheelchair; **rollstuhlge-**

**recht** adj suitable for wheelchairs; **Rolltreppe** f escalator

**Roman** m ⟨-s, -e⟩ novel

**Romantik** f romance; **romantisch** adj romantic

**römisch-katholisch** adj Roman Catholic

**röntgen** vt X-ray; **Röntgenaufnahme** f, **Röntgenbild** nt X-ray; **Röntgenstrahlen** pl X-rays pl

**rosa** adj inv pink

**Rose** f ⟨-, -n⟩ rose

**Rosenkohl** m (Brussels) sprouts pl

**Rosé(wein)** m rosé (wine)

**rosig** adj rosy

**Rosine** f raisin

**Rosmarin** m ⟨-s⟩ rosemary

**Rost** m ⟨-(e)s, -e⟩ rust; (for roasting) grill, gridiron; **Rostbratwurst** f grilled sausage; **rosten** vi rust; **rösten** vt roast, grill; (bread) toast; **rostfrei** adj rustproof; (steel) stainless; **rostig** adj rusty

**rot** adj red; **~ werden** blush; **Rote Karte** red card; **Rote Bete** beetroot; **bei Rot über die Ampel fahren** jump the lights; **das Rote Kreuz** the Red Cross

**Röteln** pl German measles sg

**rothaarig** adj red-haired

**rotieren** vi rotate

**Rotkehlchen** nt robin; **Rotkohl** m, **Rotkraut** nt red cabbage; **Rotlichtviertel** nt red-light district; **Rotwein** m red wine

**Rouge** nt ⟨-s, -s⟩ rouge

**Route** f ⟨-, -n⟩ route

**Routine** f experience; (drudgery) routine

**Rubbellos** nt scratchcard; **rubbeln** vt rub

**Rübe** f ⟨-, -n⟩ turnip; **Gelbe ~** carrot; **Rote ~** beetroot

**rüber** fam contr → **herüber**; → **hinüber**

**rückbestätigen** vt (flight etc) reconfirm

**rücken** vt, vi move; **könntest du ein bisschen ~?** could you move over a bit?

**Rücken** m ⟨-s, -⟩ back; **Rückenlehne** f back(rest); **Rückenmark** nt spinal cord; **Rückenschmerzen** pl backache sg; **Rückenschwimmen** nt ⟨-s⟩ backstroke; **Rückenwind** m tailwind

**Rückerstattung** f refund; **Rückfahrkarte** f return ticket (Brit), round-trip ticket (US); **Rückfahrt** f return journey; **Rückfall** m relapse; **Rückflug** m return flight; **Rückgabe** f return; **rückgängig** adj **etw ~ machen** cancel sth; **Rückgrat** nt ⟨-(e)s, -e⟩ spine, backbone; **Rückkehr** f ⟨-, -en⟩ return; **Rücklicht** nt rear light; **Rückreise** f return journey; **auf der ~** on the way back

**Rucksack** m rucksack, backpack; **Rucksacktourist(in)** m(f) backpacker

**Rückschritt** m step back; **Rückseite** f back; **siehe ~** see overleaf

**Rücksicht** f consideration; **~ nehmen auf** + acc show consideration for; **rücksichtslos** adj inconsiderate; (driving) reckless; **rücksichtsvoll** adj considerate

**Rücksitz** m back seat; **Rückspiegel** m AUTO rear-view mirror; **Rückvergütung** f refund; **rückwärts** adv backwards, back; **Rückwärtsgang** m AUTO reverse (gear); **Rückweg** m return journey, way back; **Rückzahlung** f repayment

**Ruder** nt ⟨-s, -⟩ oar; (at back of boat) rudder; **Ruderboot** nt rowing boat (Brit), rowboat (US); **rudern** vt, vi row

**Ruf** m ⟨-(e)s, -e⟩ call, cry; (of artist, company etc) reputation; **rufen** ⟨rief, gerufen⟩ vt, vi call; (shout) cry; **Rufnummer** f telephone number

**Ruhe** f ⟨-⟩ rest; (untroubled state) peace, quiet; (stillness) calm; (no talking) silence; **lass mich in ~!** leave me alone; **ruhen** vi rest; **Ruhestand** m retirement; **im ~ sein** be retired; **Ruhetag** m closing day; **montags ~ haben** be closed on Mondays

**ruhig** adj quiet; (motionless) still; (hand) steady; (com-

*posed, peaceful)* calm

**Ruhm** *m* ‹-(e)s› fame, glory

**Rührei** *nt* scrambled egg(s); **rühren 1.** *vt* move; *(with spoon etc)* stir **2.** *vr* move; *(speak)* say something; **rührend** *adj* touching, moving

**Ruine** *f* ‹-, -n› ruin; **ruinieren** *vt* ruin

**rülpsen** *vi* burp, belch

**rum** *fam contr → herum*

**Rum** *m* ‹-s, -s› rum

**Rumänien** *nt* ‹-s› Romania

**Rummel** *m* ‹-s› hustle and bustle; *(event)* fair; *(in the media)* hype; **Rummelplatz** *m* fairground

**rumoren** *vi* **es rumort in meinem Bauch / Kopf** my stomach is rumbling / my head is spinning

**Rumpf** *m* ‹-(e)s, Rümpfe› ANAT trunk; AVIAT fuselage; NAUT hull

**Rumpsteak** *nt* rump steak

**rund 1.** *adj* round **2.** *adv (approximately)* around; **~ um etw** (a)round sth; **Runde** *f* ‹-, -n› round; *(in race)* lap; **Rundfahrt** *f* tour *(durch*

of *)*; **Rundfunk** *m (organization)* broadcasting service; **im ~** on the radio; **Rundgang** *m* tour *(durch* of *)*; *(of guard etc)* round; **Rundreise** *f* tour *(durch* of *)*

**runter** *fam contr → herunter*, **→ hinunter**; **runterscrollen** *vt* IT scroll down

**runzelig** *adj* wrinkled; **runzeln** *vt* **die Stirn ~** frown

**ruppig** *adj* gruff

**Ruß** *m* ‹-es› soot

**Russe** *m* ‹-n, -n› Russian

**Rüssel** *m* ‹-s, -› *(of elephant)* trunk; *(of pig)* snout

**Russin** *f* Russian; **russisch** *adj* Russian; **Russisch** *nt* Russian; **Russland** *nt* Russia

**Rüstung** *f (of knight)* armour; *(weapons etc)* armaments *pl*

**Rutsch** *m* ‹-(e)s, -e› **guten ~ (ins neue Jahr)!** Happy New Year; **Rutschbahn** *f*, **Rutsche** *f* slide; **rutschen** *vi* slide; *(accidentally)* slip; **rutschig** *adj* slippery

**rütteln** *vt, vi* shake

# S

**s.** *abbr* = **siehe** see; **S.** *abbr →* **Seite** p.

**Saal** *m* ‹-(e)s, Säle› hall; *(for meetings)* room

**Saarland** *nt* Saarland

**sabotieren** *vt* sabotage

**Sache** *f* ‹-, -n› thing; *(situation, event)* affair, business; *(issue)* matter; **bei der ~ bleiben** keep to the point; **sachkundig** *adj* competent; **Sachlage** *f* situation; **sach-**

**lich** *adj* objective; (*unemotional*) matter-of-fact; (*error, account*) factual; **sächlich** LING neuter; **Sachschaden** *m* material damage

**Sachsen** *nt* ⟨-s⟩ Saxony; **Sachsen-Anhalt** *nt* ⟨-s⟩ Saxony-Anhalt

**sacht(e)** *adv* softly, gently

**Sachverständige(r)** *mf* expert

**Sack** *m* ⟨-(e)s, Säcke⟩ sack; *pej* bastard, bugger; **Sackgasse** *f* dead end, cul-de-sac

**Safe** *m* ⟨-s, -s⟩ safe

**Safer Sex** *m* safe sex

**Safran** *m* ⟨-s⟩ saffron

**Saft** *m* ⟨-(e)s, Säfte⟩ juice; **saftig** *adj* juicy

**Sage** *f* ⟨-, -n⟩ legend

**Säge** *f* ⟨-, -n⟩ saw

**sagen** *vt, vi* say (*jdm* to sb), tell (*jdm* sb); **wie sagt man ... auf Englisch?** what's ... in English?

**sägen** *vt, vi* saw

**sah** *imperf* → **sehen**

**Sahne** *f* ⟨-⟩ cream

**Saison** *f* ⟨-, -s⟩ season; **außerhalb der ~** out of season

**Saite** *f* ⟨-, -n⟩ string

**Sakko** *nt* ⟨-s, -s⟩ jacket

**Salami** *f* ⟨-, -s⟩ salami

**Salat** *m* ⟨-(e)s, -e⟩ salad; (*vegetable*) lettuce; **Salatbar** *f* salad bar; **Salatschüssel** *f* salad bowl; **Salatsoße** *f* salad dressing

**Salbe** *f* ⟨-, -n⟩ ointment

**Salbei** *m* ⟨-s⟩ sage

**Salmonellenvergiftung** *f* salmonella (poisoning)

**Salsamusik** *f* salsa (music)

**Salto** *m* ⟨-s, -s⟩ somersault

**Salz** *nt* ⟨-es, -e⟩ salt; **salzarm** *adj* low-salt; **salzen** ⟨salzte, gesalzen⟩ *vt* salt; **salzig** *adj* salty; **Salzkartoffeln** *pl* boiled potatoes *pl*; **Salzstange** *f* pretzel stick; **Salzstreuer** *m* salt cellar (*Brit*) (*or* shaker (*US*)); **Salzwasser** *nt* salt water

**Samba** *m* ⟨-, -s⟩ samba

**Samen** *m* ⟨-, -⟩ seed; (*of male*) sperm

**sammeln** *vt* collect; **Sammlung** *f* collection

**Samstag** *m* Saturday; → **Mittwoch**; **samstags** *adv* on Saturdays; → **mittwochs**

**samt** *prep* + *dat* (along) with, together with

**Samt** *m* ⟨-(e)s, -e⟩ velvet

**sämtliche(r, s)** *adj* all (the)

**Sanatorium** *nt* ⟨-s, Sanatorien⟩ sanatorium (*Brit*), sanitarium (*US*)

**Sand** *m* ⟨-(e)s, -e⟩ sand

**Sandale** *f* ⟨-, -n⟩ sandal

**sandig** *adj* sandy; **Sandkasten** *m* sandpit (*Brit*), sandbox (*US*); **Sandstrand** *m* sandy beach

**sandte** *imperf* → **senden**

**sanft** *adj* soft, gentle

**sang** *imperf* → **singen**

**Sänger(in)** *m(f)* ⟨-s, -⟩ singer

**Sangria** *f* ⟨-, -s⟩ sangria

**sanieren** vt redevelop; (building) renovate; (business) restore to profitability

**sanitär** adj sanitary; **~e Anlagen** pl sanitation

**Sanitäter(in)** m(f) ⟨-s, -⟩ ambulance man / woman, paramedic

**sank** imperf → **sinken**

**Sardelle** f anchovy

**Sarg** m ⟨-(e)s, Särge⟩ coffin

**saß** imperf → **sitzen**

**Satellit** m ⟨-en, -en⟩ satellite; **Satellitenfernsehen** nt satellite TV; **Satellitenschüssel** f fam satellite dish

**satt** adj full; (colour) rich, deep; (after meal) be full; **~ machen** be filling; **jdn / etw ~ sein** be fed up with sb/sth

**Sattel** m ⟨-s, Sättel⟩ saddle

**satthaben** irr vt **jdn / etw ~** be fed up with sb/sth

**Saturn** m ⟨-s⟩ Saturn

**Satz** m ⟨-es, Sätze⟩ LING sentence; MUS movement; (in tennis) set; (of coffee) grounds pl; (leap) jump; COMM rate

**Sau** f ⟨-, Säue⟩ sow; pej dirty bugger

**sauber** adj clean; (ironic) fine; **~ machen** clean; **Sauberkeit** f cleanness; (hygiene) cleanliness; **säubern** vt clean

**saublöd** adj fam really stupid, dumb

**Sauce** f ⟨-, -n⟩ sauce; (with meat) gravy

**Saudi-Arabien** nt ⟨-s⟩ Saudi Arabia

**sauer** adj sour; CHEM acid; fam (annoyed) cross; **saurer Regen** acid rain; **Sauerkirsche** f sour cherry; **Sauerkraut** nt sauerkraut; **säuerlich** adj slightly sour; **Sauerrahm** m sour cream; **Sauerstoff** m oxygen

**saufen** ⟨soff, gesoffen⟩ **1.** vt drink; fam (person) knock back **2.** vi drink; fam (person) booze

**saugen** ⟨sog or saugte, gesogen or gesaugt⟩ vt, vi suck; (with cleaner) vacuum, hoover (Brit); **Säugetier** nt mammal; **Säugling** m infant, baby

**Säule** f ⟨-, -n⟩ column, pillar

**Saum** m ⟨-s, Säume⟩ hem; (join) seam

**Sauna** f ⟨-, -s⟩ sauna

**Säure** f ⟨-, -n⟩ acid

**Saustall** m pigsty; **Sauwetter** nt **was für ein ~** fam what lousy weather

**Saxophon** nt ⟨-s, -e⟩ saxophone

**S-Bahn** f suburban railway; **S-Bahn-Haltestelle** f, **S-Bahnhof** m suburban (train) station

**scannen** vt scan; **Scanner** m ⟨-s, -⟩ scanner

**schäbig** adj shabby

**Schach** nt ⟨-s, -s⟩ chess; (position) check; **Schachbrett** nt chessboard; **Schachfigur** f chess piece; **schachmatt** adj checkmate

**Schacht** m ⟨-(e)s, Schächte⟩ shaft

**Schachtel** f ⟨-, -n⟩ box

**schade** interj what a pity

**Schädel** m ⟨-s, -⟩ skull; **Schädelbruch** m fractured skull

**schaden** vi damage, harm (jdm sb); **das schadet nichts** it won't do any harm; **Schaden** m ⟨-s, Schäden⟩ damage; (to body) injury; (bad thing) disadvantage; **einen ~ verursachen** cause damage; **Schadenersatz** m compensation, damages pl; **schadhaft** adj faulty; damaged; **schädigen** vt damage; (person) do harm to, harm; **schädlich** adj harmful (für to); **Schadstoff** m harmful substance; **schadstoffarm** adj low-emission

**Schaf** nt ⟨-(e)s, -e⟩ sheep; **Schäfer** m ⟨-s, -⟩ shepherd; **Schäferhund** m Alsatian (Brit), German shepherd; **Schäferin** f shepherdess

**schaffen 1.** ⟨schuf, geschaffen⟩ vt create; (room) make **2.** vt manage, do; (complete) finish; (exam) pass; **jdm zu ~ machen** cause sb trouble

**Schaffner(in)** m(f) ⟨-s, -⟩ (in bus) conductor / conductress; RAIL guard

**Schafskäse** m sheep's (milk) cheese

**schal** adj (drink) flat

**Schal** m ⟨-s, -e or -s⟩ scarf

**Schale** f ⟨-, -n⟩ skin; (removed) peel; (of nut, mussel, egg) shell; (container) bowl, dish

**schälen 1.** vt peel; (tomato, almonds) skin; (peas, eggs, nuts) shell; (grain) husk **2.** vr peel

**Schall** m ⟨-(e)s, -e⟩ sound; **Schalldämpfer** m ⟨-s, -⟩ AUTO silencer (Brit), muffler (US); **Schallplatte** f record

**Schalotte** f ⟨-, -n⟩ shallot

**schalten 1.** vt switch **2.** vi AUTO change gear; **Schalter** m ⟨-s, -⟩ (at post office, bank) counter; (electrical) switch; **Schalterhalle** f main hall; **Schalthebel** m gear lever (Brit) (or shift (US)); **Schaltjahr** nt leap year; **Schaltknüppel** m gear lever (Brit) (or shift (US)); **Schaltung** f gear change (Brit), gearshift (US)

**Scham** f ⟨-⟩ shame; modesty; **schämen** vr be ashamed

**Schande** f ⟨-⟩ disgrace

**Schanze** f ⟨-, -n⟩ ski jump

**Schar** f ⟨-, -en⟩ (of birds) flock; (of people) crowd; **in ~en** in droves

**scharf** adj (knife; criticism) sharp; (spicy) hot; **auf etw** acc **~ sein** fam be keen on sth

**Schärfe** f ⟨-, -n⟩ sharpness; (severity) rigour; PHOT focus

**Scharlach** m ⟨-s⟩ MED scarlet
fever

**Scharnier** nt ⟨-s, -e⟩ hinge

**Schaschlik** m or nt ⟨-s, -s⟩
(shish) kebab

**Schatten** m ⟨-s, -⟩ shadow; **30
Grad im ~** 30 degrees in the
shade; **schattig** adj shady

**Schatz** m ⟨-es, Schätze⟩ treasure; (*person*) love

**schätzen** vt estimate; (*object*)
value; (*appreciate*) value, esteem; (*think*) reckon;
**Schätzung** f estimate; (*action*) estimation; (*of object*)
valuation; **schätzungswei-
se** adv roughly, approximately

**schauen** vi look; **ich schau
mal, ob ...** I'll go and have
a look whether ...; **schau,
dass ...** see (to it) that ...

**Schauer** m ⟨-s, -⟩ (*rain*) shower; (*shiver*) shudder

**Schaufel** f ⟨-, -n⟩ shovel; **~
und Besen** dustpan and
brush; **schaufeln** vt shovel

**Schaufenster** nt shop window

**Schaukel** f ⟨-, -n⟩ swing;
**schaukeln** vi rock; (*on a
swing*) swing

**Schaum** m ⟨-(e)s, Schäume⟩
foam; (*from soap*) lather;
(*on beer*) froth; **Schaumbad**
nt bubble bath; **schäumen**
vi foam; **Schaumfestiger**
m ⟨-s, -⟩ styling mousse;
**Schaumgummi** m foam
(rubber); **Schaumwein** m

sparkling wine

**Schauplatz** m scene

**Schauspiel** nt spectacle;
THEAT play; **Schauspie-
ler(in)** m(f) actor / actress

**Scheck** m ⟨-s, -s⟩ cheque;
**Scheckheft** nt chequebook;
**Scheckkarte** f cheque card

**Scheibe** f ⟨-, -n⟩ disc; (*of
bread, cheese etc*) slice; (*of
glass*) pane; **Scheibenwischer** m ⟨-s, -⟩ AUTO windscreen (*Brit*) or windshield
(*US*)) wiper

**Scheich** m ⟨-s, -s⟩ sheik(h)

**Scheide** f ⟨-, -n⟩ ANAT vagina

**scheiden** ⟨schied, geschieden⟩
vt separate; **sich ~ lassen**
get a divorce; **sie hat sich
von ihm ~ lassen** she divorced him; **Scheidung** f divorce

**Schein** m ⟨-(e)s, -e⟩ light; (*external impression*) appearance; (*money*) (bank)note;
**scheinbar** adj apparent;
**scheinen** ⟨schien, geschie-
nen⟩ vi (*sun*) shine; (*appear*)
seem; **Scheinwerfer** m ⟨-s,-⟩
floodlight; THEAT spotlight;
AUTO headlight

**Scheiß-** in cpds vulg damned,
bloody (*Brit*); **Scheiße** f ⟨-⟩
vulg shit, crap; **scheißegal**
adj vulg **das ist mir ~** I don't
give a damn (*or toss*); **scheißen** ⟨schiss, geschissen⟩ vi
vulg shit

**Scheitel** m ⟨-s, -⟩ parting
(*Brit*), part (*US*)

**scheitern** *vi* fail (*an* + *dat* because of)

**Schellfisch** *m* haddock

**Schema** *nt* ⟨-s, -s *or* Schemata⟩ scheme, plan; (*drawing*) diagram

**Schenkel** *m* ⟨-s, -⟩ thigh

**schenken** *vt* give; *er hat es mir geschenkt* he gave it to me (as a present); *sich dat etw ~* *fam* skip sth

**Scherbe** *f* ⟨-, -n⟩ broken piece, fragment

**Schere** *f* ⟨-, -n⟩ scissors *pl*; (*large*) shears *pl*; *eine ~* a pair of scissors / shears

**Scherz** *m* ⟨-es, -e⟩ joke

**scheu** *adj* shy

**scheuen 1.** *vr sich ~ vor* + *dat* be afraid of, shrink from **2.** *vt* shun **3.** *vi* (*horse*) shy

**scheuern** *vt* scrub; *jdm eine ~* fam slap sb in the face

**Scheune** *f* ⟨-, -n⟩ barn

**scheußlich** *adj* dreadful

**Schi** *m* ⟨-s, -er⟩ → **Ski**

**Schicht** *f* ⟨-, -en⟩ layer; (*in society*) class; (*in factory etc*) shift

**schick** *adj* stylish, chic

**schicken** **1.** *vt* send **2.** *vr* hurry up

**Schickimicki** *m* ⟨-(s), -s⟩ fam trendy

**Schicksal** *nt* ⟨-s, -e⟩ fate

**Schiebedach** *nt* AUTO sunroof; **schieben** ⟨schob, geschoben⟩ *vt, vi* push; *die Schuld auf jdn ~* put the blame on sb; **Schiebetür** *f*

sliding door

**schied** *imperf* → **scheiden**

**Schiedsrichter(in)** *m(f)* referee, umpire

**schief 1.** *adj* crooked **2.** *adv* crooked(ly); **schiefgehen** *irr vi* fam go wrong

**schielen** *vi* squint

**schien** *imperf* → **scheinen**

**Schienbein** *nt* shin

**Schiene** *f* ⟨-, -n⟩ rail; MED splint

**schießen** ⟨schoss, geschossen⟩ **1.** *vt* shoot; (*ball*) kick; (*goal*) score; (*photo*) take **2.** *vi* shoot (*auf* + *acc* at)

**Schiff** *nt* ⟨-(e)s, -e⟩ ship; (*in church*) nave; **Schifffahrt** *f* shipping; **Schiffsreise** *f* voyage

**schikanieren** *vt* harass; (*at school*) bully

**Schild 1.** *m* ⟨-(e)s, -e⟩ (*of warrior*) shield **2.** *nt* ⟨-(e)s, -er⟩ sign; *was steht auf dem ~?* what does the sign say?

**Schilddrüse** *f* thyroid gland

**schildern** *vt* describe

**Schildkröte** *f* tortoise; (*living in water*) turtle

**Schimmel** *m* ⟨-s, -⟩ mould; (*animal*) white horse; **schimmeln** *vi* go mouldy

**schimpfen** **1.** *vt* tell off **2.** *vi* complain; *mit jdm ~* tell sb off; **Schimpfwort** *nt* swearword

**Schinken** *m* ⟨-s, -⟩ ham

**Schirm** *m* ⟨-(e)s, -e⟩ umbrella; (*for sun*) parasol, sunshade

**schiss** *imperf* → *scheißen*

**Schlacht** f ⟨-, -en⟩ battle; **schlachten** vt slaughter; **Schlachter(in)** m(f) ⟨-s, -⟩ butcher

**Schlaf** m ⟨-(e)s⟩ sleep; **Schlafanzug** m pyjamas pl; **Schlafcouch** f bed settee

**Schläfe** f ⟨-, -n⟩ temple

**schlafen** ⟨schlief, geschlafen⟩ vi sleep; *schlaf gut!* sleep well; *hast du gut geschlafen?* did you sleep all right?; *er schläft noch* he's still asleep; ~ *gehen* go to bed

**schlaff** adj slack; (*weak*) limp; (*tired*) exhausted

**Schlafgelegenheit** f place to sleep; **Schlaflosigkeit** f sleeplessness; **schläfrig** adj sleepy; **Schlafsack** m sleeping bag; **Schlaftablette** f sleeping pill; **Schlafwagen** m sleeping car, sleeper; **Schlafzimmer** nt bedroom

**Schlag** m ⟨-(e)s, Schläge⟩ blow; ELEC shock; **Schlagader** f artery; **Schlaganfall** m MED stroke; **schlagartig** adj sudden

**schlagen** ⟨schlug, geschlagen⟩ 1. vt hit; (*hit repeatedly, defeat*) beat; (*cream*) whip 2. vi (*heart*) beat; (*clock*) strike; *mit dem Kopf gegen etw* ~ bang one's head against sth 3. vr fight

**Schläger** m ⟨-s, -⟩ SPORT bat; racket; (*golf*) club; hockey stick; (*person*) brawler;

**Schlägerei** f fight, brawl

**schlagfertig** adj quick-witted; **Schlagloch** nt pothole; **Schlagsahne** f whipping cream; (*beaten*) whipped cream; **Schlagzeile** f headline; **Schlagzeug** nt drums pl; (*in orchestra*) percussion

**Schlamm** m ⟨-(e)s, -e⟩ mud

**schlampig** adj fam sloppy

**schlang** *imperf* → *schlingen*

**Schlange** f ⟨-, -n⟩ snake; (*of people*) queue (*Brit*), line (*US*); ~ *stehen* queue (*Brit*), stand in line (*US*)

**schlank** adj slim

**schlapp** adj limp

**Schlappe** f ⟨-, -n⟩ fam setback

**Schlauch** m ⟨-(e)s, Schläuche⟩ hose; (*in tyre*) inner tube; **Schlauchboot** nt rubber dinghy

**schlecht** 1. adj bad; *mir ist* ~ I feel sick; *die Milch ist* ~ the milk has gone off 2. adv badly; *es geht ihm* ~ he's having a hard time; (*health-wise*) he's not feeling well; (*financially*) he's pretty hard up; **schlechtmachen** vt jdn ~ run sb down

**schleichen** ⟨schlich, geschlichen⟩ vi creep

**Schleier** m ⟨-s, -⟩ veil

**Schleife** f ⟨-, -n⟩ IT, AVIAT, ELEC loop; (*ribbon*) bow

**Schleim** m ⟨-(e)s, -e⟩ slime; MED mucus; **Schleimer** m

⟨-s, -⟩ *fam* creep; **Schleimhaut** *f* mucous membrane
**schlendern** *vi* stroll
**schlenkern** *vt* drag; (*car, ship*) tow; (*carry*) lug; **Schlepplift** *m* ski tow
**Schleswig-Holstein** *nt* ⟨-s⟩ Schleswig-Holstein
**Schleuder** *f* ⟨-, -n⟩ catapult; (*for washing*) spin-dryer; **schleudern 1.** *vt* hurl; (*washing*) spin-dry **2.** *vi* AUTO skid; **Schleudersitz** *m* ejector seat
**schlich** *imperf* → **schleichen**
**schlicht** *adj* simple, plain
**schlichten** *vt* (*dispute*) settle
**schlief** *imperf* → **schlafen**
**schließen** ⟨schloss, geschlossen⟩ *vt, vi, vr* close, shut; (*bring to an end*) close; (*friendship, alliance, marriage*) enter into; (*deduce*) infer (*aus* from); **Schließfach** *nt* locker
**schließlich** *adv* finally; (*when all is said and done*) after all
**schliff** *imperf* → **schleifen**
**schlimm** *adj* bad; **schlimmer** *adj* worse; **schlimmste(r, s)** *adj* worst; **schlimmstenfalls** *adv* at (the) worst
**Schlips** *m* ⟨-es, -e⟩ tie
**Schlitten** *m* ⟨-s, -⟩ sledge, toboggan; (*with horses*) sleigh; **Schlittenfahren** *nt* ⟨-s⟩ tobogganing
**Schlittschuh** *m* ice skate; ~ **laufen** ice-skate

**Schlitz** *m* ⟨-es, -e⟩ slit; (*for coin*) slot; (*on trousers*) flies *pl*
**schloss** *imperf* → **schließen**
**Schloss** *nt* ⟨-es, Schlösser⟩ lock; (*building*) castle
**Schlosser(in)** *m(f)* mechanic
**Schlucht** *f* ⟨-, -en⟩ gorge, ravine
**schluchzen** *vi* sob
**Schluckauf** *m* ⟨-s⟩ hiccups *pl*; **schlucken** *vt, vi* swallow
**schlug** *imperf* → **schlagen**
**schlürfen** *vt, vi* slurp
**Schluss** *m* ⟨-es, Schlüsse⟩ end; (*deduction*) conclusion; **am ~** at the end; **mit jdm ~ machen** finish (*or* split up) with sb
**Schlüssel** *m* ⟨-s, -⟩ *a. fig* key; **Schlüsselbein** *nt* collarbone; **Schlüsselbund** *m* bunch of keys; **Schlüsselloch** *nt* keyhole
**Schlussfolgerung** *f* conclusion; **Schlusslicht** *nt* taillight; *fig* tail-ender; **Schlussverkauf** *m* clearance sale
**schmal** *adj* narrow; (*person, book etc*) slim
**Schmalz** *nt* ⟨-es, -e⟩ dripping, lard
**schmatzen** *vi* eat noisily
**schmecken** *vt, vi* taste (*nach* of); **es schmeckt ihm** he likes it; **lass es dir ~!** bon appétit
**Schmeichelei** *f* flattery; **schmeichelhaft** *adj* flatter-

ing; **schmeicheln** *vi* jdm ~ flatter sb

**schmeißen** ⟨schmiss, geschmissen⟩ *vt fam* chuck, throw

**schmelzen** ⟨schmolz, geschmolzen⟩ *vt, vi* melt

**Schmerz** *m* ⟨-es, -en⟩ pain; *(sorrow)* grief; **~en haben** be in pain; **~en im Rücken haben** have a pain in one's back; **schmerzen** *vt, vi* hurt; **Schmerzensgeld** *nt* compensation; **schmerzhaft**, **schmerzlich** *adj* painful; **Schmerzmittel** *nt* painkiller; **schmerzstillend** *adj* painkilling; **Schmerztablette** *f* painkiller

**Schmetterling** *m* butterfly

**schmieden** *vt* forge; *(plans)* make

**schmieren** 1. *vt* smear; *(machine, bicycle etc)* lubricate, grease; *(person)* bribe 2. *vt, vi* *(write)* scrawl; **Schmiergeld** *nt fam* bribe; **schmierig** *adj* greasy

**Schminke** *f* ⟨-, -n⟩ make-up; **schminken** *vr* put one's make-up on

**schmiss** *imperf* → **schmeißen**

**schmollen** *vi* sulk

**schmolz** *imperf* → **schmelzen**

**Schmuck** *m* ⟨-(e)s, -e⟩ jewellery *(Brit)*, jewelry *(US)*; *(ornament)* decoration; **schmücken** *vt* decorate

**schmuggeln** *vt, vi* smuggle

**schmunzeln** *vi* smile

**schmusen** *vi* (kiss and) cuddle

**Schmutz** *m* ⟨-es⟩ dirt, filth; **schmutzig** *adj* dirty

**Schnabel** *m* ⟨-s, Schnäbel⟩ beak, bill; *(for pouring)* spout

**Schnake** *f* ⟨-, -n⟩ mosquito

**Schnäppchen** *nt fam* bargain; **schnappen** 1. *vt* catch 2. *vi* **nach Luft ~** gasp for breath; *(mouth)* trap; **PHOT** snap(shot); **Schnappschuss** *m*

**Schnaps** *m* ⟨-es, Schnäpse⟩ schnapps

**schnarchen** *vi* snore

**schnaufen** *vi* puff, pant

**Schnauzbart** *m* moustache; **Schnauze** *f* ⟨-, -n⟩ snout, muzzle; *(for pouring)* spout; *fam (mouth)* trap; **die ~ voll haben** have had enough

**schnäuzen** *vr* blow one's nose

**Schnecke** *f* ⟨-, -n⟩ snail; **Schneckenhaus** *nt* snail's shell

**Schnee** *m* ⟨-s⟩ snow; **Schneeball** *m* snowball; **Schneebrille** *f* snow goggles *pl*; **Schneeflocke** *f* snowflake; **Schneeglöckchen** *nt* snowdrop; **Schneegrenze** *f* snowline; **Schneekanone** *f* snow thrower; **Schneekette** *f* AUTO snow chain; **Schneemann** *m* snowman; **Schneepflug** *m* snowplough;

**schön**

**Schneeregen** m sleet; **Schneesturm** m snowstorm, blizzard; **Schneetreiben** nt light blizzards pl; **Schneewehe** f snowdrift

**Schneide** f ⟨-, -n⟩ edge; (part of knife) blade; **schneiden** ⟨schnitt, geschnitten⟩ **1.** vt cut; **sich dat die Haare ~ lassen** have one's hair cut **2.** vr cut oneself; **Schneider(in)** m(f) ⟨-s, -⟩ tailor; dressmaker; **Schneidezahn** m incisor

**schneien** vi impers snow

**schnell 1.** adj quick, fast **2.** adv quickly, fast; **mach ~!** hurry up; **Schnelldienst** m express service; **Schnellhefter** m loose-leaf binder; **Schnellimbiss** m snack bar; **Schnellstraße** f expressway

**schneuzen** vr → **schnäuzen**

**schnitt** imperf → **schneiden**

**Schnitt** m ⟨-(e)s, -e⟩ cut; (where lines cross) intersection; (diagram) (cross) section; (of quantities) average; **Schnitte** f ⟨-, -n⟩ slice; (with filling) sandwich; **Schnittkäse** m cheese slices pl; **Schnittlauch** m chives pl; **Schnittstelle** f IT, fig interface; **Schnittwunde** f cut, gash

**Schnitzel** nt ⟨-s, -⟩ (of paper) scrap; GASTR escalope

**schnitzen** vt carve

**Schnorchel** m ⟨-s, -⟩ snorkel

**schnorcheln** vi go snorkelling, snorkel

**schnüffeln** vi sniff

**Schnuller** m ⟨-s, -⟩ dummy (Brit), pacifier (US)

**Schnulze** f ⟨-, -n⟩ (film, novel) weepie

**Schnupfen** m ⟨-s, -⟩ cold

**schnuppern** vi sniff

**Schnur** f ⟨-, Schnüre⟩ string, cord; ELEC lead; **schnurlos** adj cordless

**Schnurrbart** m moustache

**schnurren** vi purr

**Schnürsenkel** m ⟨-s, -⟩ shoelace

**schob** imperf → **schieben**

**Schock** m ⟨-(e)s, -e⟩ shock; **unter ~ stehen** be in a state of shock; **schockieren** vt shock

**Schokolade** f chocolate; **Schokoriegel** m chocolate bar

**Scholle** f ⟨-, -n⟩ plaice; (on sea) ice floe

**schon** adv already; **ist er ~ da?** is he here yet?; **warst du ~ einmal da?** have you ever been there?; **ich war ~ einmal da** I've been there before; **~ damals** even then; **~ 1999** as early (or as long ago) as 1999

**schön** adj beautiful; (kind) nice; (woman) beautiful; pretty; (man) beautiful, handsome; (weather) fine; **~e Grüße** best wishes; **~es Wochenende** have a nice

weekend
**schonen 1.** vt look after **2.** vr take it easy
**Schönheit** f beauty
**Schonkost** f light diet
**Schöpfung** f creation
**Schoppen** m ⟨-s, -⟩ glass (of wine)
**Schorf** m ⟨-(e)s, -e⟩ scab
**Schorle** f ⟨-, -n⟩ spritzer
**Schornstein** m chimney; **Schornsteinfeger(in)** m(f) ⟨-s, -⟩ chimney sweep
**schoss** imperf → **schießen**
**Schoß** m ⟨-es, Schöße⟩ lap
**Schotte** m ⟨-n, -n⟩ Scot, Scotsman; **Schottin** f Scot, Scotswoman; **schottisch** adj Scottish, Scots; **Schottland** nt Scotland
**schräg** adj slanting; (roof) sloping; (line) diagonal; fam (unconventional) wacky
**Schrank** m ⟨-(e)s, Schränke⟩ cupboard; (for clothes) wardrobe (Brit), closet (US)
**Schranke** f ⟨-, -n⟩ barrier
**Schrankwand** f wall unit
**Schraube** f ⟨-, -n⟩ screw; **schrauben** vt screw; **Schraubenschlüssel** m spanner; **Schraubenzieher** m ⟨-s, -⟩ screwdriver; **Schraubverschluss** m screw top, screw cap
**Schreck** m ⟨-(e)s, -e⟩, **Schrecken** m ⟨-s, -⟩ terror; (momentary) fright; **jdm einen ~ einjagen** give sb a fright;

**schreckhaft** adj jumpy;
**schrecklich** adj terrible, dreadful
**Schrei** m ⟨-(e)s, -e⟩ scream; (call) shout
**Schreibblock** m writing pad; **schreiben** ⟨schrieb, geschrieben⟩ vt, vi write; spell; **wie schreibt man …?** how do you spell …?; **Schreiben** nt ⟨-s, -⟩ writing; (sent to sb) letter; **Schreibfehler** m spelling mistake; **schreibgeschützt** adj write-protected; **Schreibtisch** m desk; **Schreibwaren** pl stationery sg; **Schreibwarenladen** m stationer's
**schreien** ⟨schrie, geschrie(e)n⟩ vt, vi scream; (call) shout
**Schreiner(in)** m(f) joiner; **Schreinerei** f joiner's workshop
**schrie** imperf → **schreien**
**schrieb** imperf → **schreiben**
**Schrift** f ⟨-, -en⟩ (by hand) handwriting; (printing style) typeface; (type) font; **schriftlich 1.** adj written **2.** adv in writing; **würden Sie uns das bitte ~ geben?** could we have that in writing, please?; **Schriftsteller(in)** m(f) ⟨-s, -⟩ writer
**Schritt** m ⟨-(e)s, -e⟩ step; **~ für ~** step by step; **Schrittgeschwindigkeit** f walking speed; **Schrittmacher** m MED pacemaker
**Schrott** m ⟨-(e)s, -e⟩ scrap

**schützen**

metal; *fig* rubbish

**schrubben** *vi*, *vt* scrub; **Schrubber** *m* ⟨-s, -⟩ scrubbing brush

**schrumpfen** *vi* shrink

**Schubkarren** *m* ⟨-s, -⟩ wheelbarrow; **Schublade** *f* drawer

**schubsen** *vt* shove, push

**schüchtern** *adj* shy

**schuf** *imperf* → **schaffen**

**Schuh** *m* ⟨-(e)s, -e⟩ shoe; **Schuhcreme** *f* shoe polish; **Schuhgeschäft** *nt* shoe shop; **Schuhgröße** *f* shoe size; **Schuhlöffel** *m* shoehorn;

**Schulabschluss** *m* school-leaving qualification

**schuld** *adj* **wer ist ~ daran?** whose fault is it?; **er ist ~** it's his fault; **he's to blame; Schuld** *f* ⟨-⟩ guilt; (*blame*) fault; **~ haben** be to blame (*an* + *dat* for); **er hat ~** it's his fault; **schulden** *vt* owe (*jdm etw* sb sth); **Schulden** *pl* debts *pl*; **~ haben** be in debt; **~ machen** run up debts; **seine ~ bezahlen** pay off one's debts; **schuldig** *adj* guilty (*an* + *dat* of); (*proper*) due; **jdm etw ~ sein** owe sb sth

**Schule** *f* ⟨-, -n⟩ school; **in der ~** at school; **in die ~ gehen** go to school; **Schüler(in)** *m(f)* ⟨-s, -⟩ pupil; (*older*) student; **Schüleraustausch** *m* school exchange; **Schulfach** *nt* subject; **Schulferien** *pl*

school holidays *pl* (*Brit*) (*or* vacation (*US*)); **schulfrei** *adj* **morgen ist ~** there's no school tomorrow; **Schulfreund(in)** *m(f)* schoolmate; **Schuljahr** *nt* school year; **Schulkenntnisse** *pl* **~ in Französisch** school(-level) French; **Schulklasse** *f* class; **Schulleiter(in)** *m(f)* headmaster / headmistress (*Brit*), principal (*US*)

**Schulter** *f* ⟨-, -n⟩ shoulder

**Schulung** *f* training; (*event*) training course

**Schuppe** *f* ⟨-, -n⟩ (*of fish*) scale; **Schuppen** *pl* dandruff *sg*

**Schürfwunde** *f* graze

**Schürze** *f* ⟨-, -n⟩ apron

**Schuss** *m* ⟨-es, Schüsse⟩ shot; **mit einem ~ Wodka** with a dash of vodka

**Schüssel** *f* ⟨-, -n⟩ bowl

**Schuster(in)** *m(f)* ⟨-s, -⟩ shoemaker

**Schutt** *m* ⟨-(e)s⟩ rubble

**Schüttelfrost** *m* shivering fit; **schütteln** *vt*, *vr* shake

**schütten 1.** *vt* pour; (*sugar, gravel etc*) tip **2.** *vi impers* pour (down)

**Schutz** *m* ⟨-es⟩ protection (*gegen, vor* against, from); (*place*) shelter; **jdn in ~ nehmen** stand up for sb; **Schutzblech** *nt* mudguard

**Schütze** *m* ⟨-n, -n⟩ (*in football*) scorer; *ASTR* Sagittarius

**schützen** *vt* **jdn gegen / vor**

*etw* ~ protect sb against / from sth; **Schutzimpfung** *f* inoculation, vaccination

**schwach** *adj* weak; **~e Augen** poor eyesight *sg*; **Schwäche** *f* ⟨-, -n⟩ weakness; **Schwachstelle** *f* weak point

**Schwager** *m* ⟨-s, Schwäger⟩ brother-in-law; **Schwägerin** *f* sister-in-law

**Schwalbe** *f* ⟨-, -n⟩ swallow; (*in football*) dive

**schwamm** *imperf* → **schwimmen**

**Schwamm** *m* ⟨-(e)s, Schwämme⟩ sponge

**Schwan** *m* ⟨-(e)s, Schwäne⟩ swan

**schwanger** *adj* pregnant; **im vierten Monat ~ sein** be four months pregnant; **Schwangerschaft** *f* pregnancy; **Schwangerschaftsabbruch** *m* abortion; **Schwangerschaftstest** *m* pregnancy test

**schwanken** *vi* sway; (*prices, figures*) fluctuate; (*be uncertain*) hesitate; (*drunkard etc*) stagger

**Schwanz** *m* ⟨-es, Schwänze⟩ tail; *vulg* (*penis*) cock

**Schwarm** *m* ⟨-(e)s, Schwärme⟩ swarm; *fam* (*pop star etc*) heartthrob; **schwärmen** *vi* swarm; **~ für** be mad about

**schwarz** *adj* black; **mir wurde ~ vor Augen** everything went black; **Schwarzarbeit** *f* illicit work; **Schwarzbrot**

*nt* black bread; **schwarzfahren** *irr vi* travel without a ticket; **Schwarzfahrer(in)** *m(f)* fare-dodger; **Schwarzmarkt** *m* black market; **schwarzsehen** *irr vi fam* be pessimistic (*für* about); **Schwarzwald** *m* Black Forest; **schwarzweiß** *adj* black and white

**schwatzen** *vi* chatter; **Schwätzer(in)** *m(f)* ⟨-s, -⟩ chatterbox; (*long-winded*) gasbag; (*about other people*) gossip

**schweben** *vi* float; (*upwards*) soar

**Schwede** *m* ⟨-n, -n⟩ Swede; **Schweden** *nt* ⟨-s⟩ Sweden; **Schwedin** *f* Swede; **schwedisch** *adj* Swedish; **Schwedisch** *nt* Swedish

**Schwefel** *m* ⟨-s⟩ sulphur

**schweigen** ⟨schwieg, geschwiegen⟩ *vi* be silent; stop talking; **Schweigen** *nt* ⟨-s⟩ silence

**Schwein** *nt* ⟨-(e)s, -e⟩ pig; *fam* luck; *fam* (*vile person*) swine; **Schweinebraten** *m* roast pork; **Schweinefleisch** *nt* pork; **Schweinerei** *f* mess; (*act*) dirty trick

**Schweiß** *m* ⟨-es⟩ sweat

**schweißen** *vt, vi* weld

**Schweiz** *f* ⟨-⟩ **die** ~ Switzerland; **Schweizer(in)** *m(f)* ⟨-s, -⟩ Swiss; **Schweizerdeutsch** *nt* Swiss German; **schweizerisch** *adj* Swiss

**Schwelle** f ⟨-, -n⟩ doorstep; a. fig threshold

**schwellen** ⟨schwoll, geschwollen⟩ vi swell (up); **Schwellung** f swelling

**schwer 1.** adj heavy; (task, life, question) difficult, hard; (illness, mistake) serious, bad **2.** adv (very) really; (injured etc) seriously, badly; **Schwerbehinderte(r)** mf severely disabled person; **schwerfallen** irr vi jdm ~ be difficult for sb; **schwerhörig** adj hard of hearing

**Schwert** nt ⟨-(e)s, -er⟩ sword

**Schwester** f ⟨-, -n⟩ sister; MED nurse

**schwieg** imperf → **schweigen**

**Schwiegereltern** pl parents-in-law pl; **Schwiegermutter** f mother-in-law; **Schwiegersohn** m son-in-law; **Schwiegertochter** f daughter-in-law; **Schwiegervater** m father-in-law

**schwierig** adj difficult, hard; **Schwierigkeit** f difficulty; **in ~en kommen** get into trouble; **jdm ~en machen** make things difficult for sb

**Schwimmbad** nt swimming pool; **Schwimmbecken** nt swimming pool; **schwimmen** ⟨schwamm, geschwommen⟩ vi swim; (drift, not sink) float; fig be all at sea; **Schwimmer(in)** m(f) swimmer; **Schwimmflosse**

f flipper; **Schwimmflügel** m water wing; **Schwimmreifen** m rubber ring; **Schwimmweste** f life jacket

**Schwindel** m ⟨-s⟩ dizziness; (fit) dizzy spell; (deception) swindle; **schwindelfrei** adj **nicht ~ sein** suffer from vertigo; **~ sein** have a head for heights; **schwindlig** adj dizzy; **mir ist ~** I feel dizzy

**Schwips** m **einen ~ haben** be tipsy

**schwitzen** vi sweat

**schwoll** imperf → **schwellen**

**schwor** imperf → **schwören**

**schwören** ⟨schwor, geschworen⟩ vt, vi swear; **einen Eid ~** take an oath

**schwul** adj gay

**schwül** adj close

**Schwung** m ⟨-(e)s, Schwünge⟩ swing; (force when moving) momentum; fig energy; fam (quantity) batch; **in ~ kommen** get going

**Schwur** m ⟨-s, Schwüre⟩ oath

**scrollen** vi IT scroll

**sechs** num six; **Sechs** f ⟨-, -en⟩ six; (mark in school) ≈ F; **sechshundert** num six hundred; **sechsmal** adv six times; **sechste(r, s)** adj sixth; → **dritte**; **Sechstel** nt ⟨-s, -⟩ (fraction) sixth; **sechzehn** num sixteen; **sechzehnte(r, s)** adj sixteenth; → **dritte**; **sechzig** num sixty; **in den ~er Jahren** in the sixties; **sechzigste(r, s)** adj sixtieth

**Secondhandladen** *m* secondhand shop

**See 1.** *f* ⟨-, -n⟩ sea; *an der* ~ by the sea **2.** *m* ⟨-s, -n⟩ lake; *am* ~ by the lake; **Seehund** *m* seal; **Seeigel** *m* sea urchin; **seekrank** *adj* seasick

**Seele** *f* ⟨-, -n⟩ soul

**Seeleute** *pl* seamen *pl*, sailors *pl*

**seelisch** *adj* mental, psychological

**Seelöwe** *m* sea lion; **Seemann** *m* sailor, seaman; **Seemeile** *f* nautical mile; **Seemöwe** *f* seagull; **Seepferdchen** *nt* sea horse; **Seerose** *f* water lily; **Seestern** *m* starfish; **Seezunge** *f* sole

**Segel** *nt* ⟨-s, -⟩ sail; **Segelboot** *nt* yacht; **Segelfliegen** *nt* ⟨-s⟩ gliding; **Segelflugzeug** *nt* glider; **segeln** *vt, vi* sail; **Segelschiff** *nt* sailing ship

**sehbehindert** *adj* partially sighted

**sehen** ⟨sah, gesehen⟩ *vt, vi* see; *(in specific direction)* look; *gut / schlecht* ~ have good / bad eyesight; *kann ich das mal* ~? can I have a look at it?; *wir* ~ *uns morgen!* see you tomorrow; **Sehenswürdigkeiten** *pl* sights *pl*

**Sehne** *f* ⟨-, -n⟩ tendon; *(on bow)* string

**sehnen** *vr* long *(nach* for)

**Sehnenzerrung** *f* MED pulled tendon

**Sehnsucht** *f* longing; **sehnsüchtig** *adj* longing

**sehr** *adv* very; *(with verbs)* a lot, very much; *zu* ~ too much

**seicht** *adj* shallow

**Seide** *f* ⟨-, -n⟩ silk

**Seife** *f* ⟨-, -n⟩ soap; **Seifenoper** *f* soap (opera); **Seifenschale** *f* soap dish

**Seil** *nt* ⟨-(e)s, -e⟩ rope; *(metal)* cable; **Seilbahn** *f* cable railway

**sein** ⟨war, gewesen⟩ *vi, vaux* be; *lass das* ~! leave that!; *(sth annoying)* stop that!; *das kann* ~ that's possible

**sein** *pron* his; her; its; *das ist* ~*e Tasche* that's his bag; *jeder hat* ~*e Sorgen* everyone has their problems; **seine(r, s)** *pron* his; hers; *das ist* ~*r/*~*/*~*s* that's his / hers; **seinetwegen** *adv* because of him; *(to please him)* for his sake

**seit** *conj* since; *(period)* for; *er ist* ~ *Montag hier* he's been here since Monday; *er ist* ~ *einer Woche hier* he's been here for a week; ~ *Langem* for a long time; **seitdem** *adv, conj* since

**Seite** *f* ⟨-, -n⟩ side; *(in book)* page; *zur* ~ *gehen* step aside; **Seitensprung** *m* affair; **Seitenstechen** *nt* ⟨-s⟩ ~ *haben / bekommen*

have / get a stitch; **Seitenstraße** f side street; **Seitenstreifen** m hard shoulder (*Brit*), shoulder (*US*); **Seitenwind** m crosswind

**seither** adv since (then)

**seitlich** adj side

**Sekretär(in)** m(f) ⟨-s, -e⟩ secretary; **Sekretariat** nt ⟨-(e)s, -e⟩ secretary's office

**Sekt** m ⟨-(e)s, -e⟩ sparkling wine

**Sekte** f ⟨-, -n⟩ sect

**Sekunde** f ⟨-, -n⟩ second; **Sekundenkleber** m ⟨-s, -⟩ superglue

**selbst 1.** pron **ich ~** I … myself; **du / Sie ~** you … yourself; **er ~** he … himself; **sie ~** she … herself; they … themselves; **wir haben es ~ gemacht** we did it ourselves; **mach es ~** do it yourself; **von ~** by itself; **das versteht sich ja von ~** that goes without saying **2.** adv even; **~ mir gefiel's** even I liked it

**selbständig** adj → **selbstständig**

**Selbstauslöser** m ⟨-s, -⟩ PHOT self-timer; **Selbstbedienung** f self-service; **Selbstbefriedigung** f masturbation; **Selbstbeherrschung** f self-control; **Selbstbeteiligung** f (*on insurance*) excess; **selbstbewusst** adj (self-)confident; **selbstgemacht** adj self-made; **selbstklebend** adj self-adhesive; **Selbstlaut** m vowel; **Selbstmord** m suicide; **Selbstmordattentat** nt suicide bombing; **Selbstmordattentäter(in)** m(f) suicide bomber; **selbstsicher** adj self-assured; **selbstständig** adj independent; (*working*) self-employed; **selbstverständlich 1.** adj obvious; **ich halte das für ~** I take that for granted **2.** adv naturally; **Selbstvertrauen** nt self-confidence

**selten 1.** adj rare **2.** adv seldom, rarely

**seltsam** adj strange; **~ schmecken / riechen** taste / smell strange

**Semester** nt ⟨-s, -⟩ semester; **Semesterferien** pl vacation sg

**Seminar** nt ⟨-s, -e⟩ seminar

**Semmel** f ⟨-, -n⟩ roll; **Semmelbrösel** pl breadcrumbs pl

**Senat** m ⟨-(e)s, -e⟩ senate

**senden 1.** ⟨sandte, gesandt⟩ vt send **2.** vt, vi RADIO, TV broadcast; **Sender** m ⟨-s, -⟩ (*TV*) channel; (*radio*) station; (*apparatus*) transmitter; **Sendung** f RADIO, TV broadcasting; (*single broadcast*) programme

**Senf** m ⟨-(e)s, -e⟩ mustard

**Senior(in)** m(f) senior citizen; **Seniorenpass** m senior citizen's travel pass

**senken 1.** vt lower **2.** vr sink

**senkrecht** adj vertical

**Sensation** f ⟨-, -en⟩ sensation

**sensibel** adj sensitive

**sentimental** adj sentimental

**separat** adj separate

**September** m ⟨-(s), -⟩ September; → **Juni**

**Serbien** nt ⟨-s⟩ Serbia

**Serie** f series sg

**seriös** adj serious; (firm, people) respectable

**Serpentine** f hairpin (bend)

**Serum** nt ⟨-s, Seren⟩ serum

**Server** m ⟨-s, -⟩ IT server

**Service 1.** nt ⟨-(s), -⟩ (crockery) service **2.** m ⟨-, -s⟩ service

**servieren** vt, vi serve

**Serviette** f napkin, serviette

**Servolenkung** f AUTO power steering

**Sesam** m ⟨-s, -s⟩ sesame seeds pl

**Sessel** m ⟨-s, -⟩ armchair; **Sessellift** m chairlift

**Set** m or nt ⟨-s, -s⟩ set; (under plate etc) tablemat

**setzen 1.** vt put; (sail) set **2.** vr settle; (person) sit down; **~ Sie sich doch** please sit down

**Seuche** f ⟨-, -n⟩ epidemic

**seufzen** vt, vi sigh

**Sex** m ⟨-(es)⟩ sex; **sexistisch** adj sexist; **Sexualität** f sexuality; **sexuell** adj sexual

**Seychellen** pl Seychelles pl

**sfr** abbr = **Schweizer Fran-**

**ken** Swiss franc(s)

**Shampoo** nt ⟨-s, -s⟩ shampoo

**Shorts** pl shorts pl

**Shuttlebus** m shuttle bus

**sich** pron himself; herself; itself; (plural) themselves; (after 'Sie') yourself; yourselves; (indefinite, after 'man') oneself; **er hat ~ verletzt** he hurt himself; **sie kennen ~** they know each other; **sie hat ~ sehr gefreut** she was very pleased; **er hat ~ das Bein gebrochen** he's broken his leg

**sicher** adj safe (vor + dat from); (sure) certain (gen of); (method, source) reliable; (self-assured) confident; **aber ~!** of course, sure; **Sicherheit** f safety; (protective measures) FIN security; (sureness) certainty; (self-assurance) confidence; **mit ~** definitely; **Sicherheitsabstand** m safe distance; **Sicherheitsgurt** m seat belt; **sicherheitshalber** adv just to be on the safe side; **Sicherheitsnadel** f safety pin; **Sicherheitsvorkehrung** f safety precaution; **sicherlich** adv certainly; (in all likelihood) probably

**sichern** vt secure (gegen against); (guard) IT protect; (data) back up; **Sicherung** f securing; (on machine etc) safety device; (on gun) safety catch; ELEC fuse; IT back-up; **die ~ ist durchgebrannt** the fuse has blown

**Sicht** f ⟨-⟩ sight; (*scene*) view; **sichtbar** *adj* visible; **sichtlich** *adj* evident, obvious; **Sichtverhältnisse** *pl* visibility *sg*; **Sichtweite** f **in / außer ~** within / out of sight

**sie** *pron* she; (*plural*) they; (*accusative*) her; them; (*thing*) it; **da ist ~ ja** there she is; **da sind ~ ja** there they are; **ich kenne~** I know her; I know them

**Sie** *pron* you

**Sieb** *nt* ⟨-(e)s, -e⟩ sieve; (*for tea*) strainer

**sieben** *num* seven; **siebenhundert** *num* seven hundred; **siebenmal** *adv* seven times; **siebte(r, s)** *adj* seventh; → **dritte**; **Siebtel** *nt* ⟨-s, -⟩ (*fraction*) seventh; **siebzehn** *num* seventeen; **siebzehnte(r, s)** *adj* seventeenth; → **dritte**; **siebzig** *num* seventy; **in den ~er Jahren** in the seventies; **siebzigste(r, s)** *adj* seventieth

**Siedlung** f ⟨-, -en⟩ housing estate (*Brit*) (or development (*US*))

**Sieg** m ⟨-(e)s, -e⟩ victory; **siegen** *vi* win; **Sieger(in)** *m(f)* ⟨-s, -⟩ winner; **Siegerehrung** f presentation ceremony

**siezen** *vt* address as 'Sie'

**Signal** *nt* ⟨-s, -e⟩ signal

**Silbe** f ⟨-, -n⟩ syllable

**Silber** *nt* ⟨-s⟩ silver; **Silberhochzeit** f silver wedding; **Silbermedaille** f silver medal

**Silikon** *nt* ⟨-s, -e⟩ silicone

**Silvester** *nt* ⟨-s, -⟩, **Silvesterabend** m New Year's Eve, Hogmanay (*Scot*)

**Simbabwe** *nt* ⟨-s⟩ Zimbabwe

**simpel** *adj* simple

**simsen** *vt, vi* fam text

**simultan** *adj* simultaneous

**Sinfonie** f ⟨-, -n⟩ symphony; **Sinfonieorchester** *nt* symphony orchestra

**Singapur** *nt* ⟨-s⟩ Singapore

**singen** ⟨sang, gesungen⟩ *vt, vi* sing; **richtig / falsch ~** sing in tune / out of tune

**Single 1.** f ⟨-, -s⟩ (*CD*) single **2.** m ⟨-s, -s⟩ (*person*) single

**Singular** m singular

**sinken** ⟨sank, gesunken⟩ *vi* sink; (*prices etc*) fall, go down

**Sinn** m ⟨-(e)s, -e⟩ (*of word, speech etc*) sense, meaning; **~ machen** make sense; **das hat keinen ~** it's no use; **sinnlich** *adj* sensuous; (*erotic*) sensual; (*perception*) sensory; **sinnlos** *adj* stupid; (*behaviour*) senseless; (*futile*) pointless; (*talk etc*) meaningless; **sinnvoll** *adj* meaningful; (*reasonable*) sensible

**Sirup** m ⟨-s, -e⟩ syrup

**Sitte** f ⟨-, -n⟩ custom

**Situation** f situation

**Sitz** m ⟨-es, -e⟩ seat; **sitzen** ⟨saß, gesessen⟩ vi sit; *(remark, blow)* strike home; *(what one has learnt)* have sunk in; *der Rock sitzt gut* the skirt is a good fit; **Sitzgelegenheit** f place to sit down; **Sitzplatz** m seat; **Sitzung** f meeting

**Sizilien** nt ⟨-s⟩ Sicily

**Skandal** m ⟨-s, -e⟩ scandal

**Skandinavien** nt ⟨-s⟩ Scandinavia

**Skateboard** nt ⟨-s, -s⟩ skateboard

**Skelett** nt ⟨-s, -e⟩ skeleton

**skeptisch** adj sceptical

**Ski** m ⟨-s, -er⟩ ski; **~ laufen** (or **fahren**) ski; **Skianzug** m ski suit; **Skibrille** f ski goggles pl; **Skifahren** nt ⟨-s⟩ skiing; **Skigebiet** nt ⟨-s, -e⟩ skiing area; **Skihose** f skiing trousers pl; **Skikurs** m skiing course; **Skiläufer(in)** m(f) skier; **Skilehrer(in)** m(f) ski instructor; **Skilift** m ski-lift

**Skinhead** m ⟨-s, -s⟩ skinhead

**Skischuh** m ski boot; **Skispringen** nt ⟨-s, -n⟩ ski jumping; **Skistiefel** m ⟨-s, -⟩ ski boot; **Skistock** m ski pole; **Skiurlaub** m skiing holiday *(Brit)* or vacation *(US)*

**Skizze** f ⟨-, -n⟩ sketch

**Skonto** m or nt ⟨-s, -s⟩ discount

**Skorpion** m ⟨-s, -e⟩ zool scorpion; astr Scorpio

**Skulptur** f ⟨-, -en⟩ sculpture

**S-Kurve** f double bend

**Slalom** m ⟨-s, -s⟩ slalom

**Slip** m ⟨-s, -s⟩ (pair of) briefs pl; **Slipeinlage** f panty liner

**Slowakei** f ⟨-⟩ Slovakia; **slowakisch** adj Slovakian; **Slowakisch** nt Slovakian

**Slowenien** nt ⟨-s⟩ Slovenia; **slowenisch** adj Slovenian; **Slowenisch** nt Slovenian

**Smiley** m ⟨-s, -s⟩ smiley

**Smog** m ⟨-s⟩ smog; **Smogalarm** m smog alert

**Smoking** m ⟨-s, -s⟩ dinner jacket *(Brit)*, tuxedo *(US)*

**SMS 1.** nt abbr = **Short Message Service 2.** f text message; **ich schicke dir eine ~** I'll text you, I'll send you a text (message)

**Snowboard** nt ⟨-s, -s⟩ snowboard; **Snowboardfahren** nt ⟨-s⟩ snowboarding; **Snowboardfahrer(in)** m(f) snowboarder

**so 1.** adv so; *(in this way)* like this; *(approximately)* about; **fünf Euro oder ~** five euros or so; **~ ein** such a; **~ ... wie** ... as ... as ...; **und ~ weiter** and so on; **~ viel** as much *(wie* as); **~ weit sein** be ready; **~ weit wie** (or **als**) **möglich** as far as possible **2.** conj so; *(before adjective)* as

**sobald** conj as soon as

**Socke** f ⟨-, -n⟩ sock

**Sodbrennen** nt ⟨-s⟩ heartburn

**Sofa** *nt* ⟨-s, -s⟩ sofa

**sofern** *conj* if, provided (that)

**soff** *imperf* → **saufen**

**sofort** *adv* immediately, at once

**Softeis** *nt* soft ice-cream

**Software** *f* ⟨-, -s⟩ software

**sog** *imperf* → **saugen**

**sogar** *adv* even; **kalt, ~ sehr kalt** cold, in fact very cold

**sogenannt** *adj* so-called

**Sohle** *f* ⟨-, -n⟩ sole

**Sohn** *m* ⟨-(e)s, Söhne⟩ son

**Soja** *f* ⟨-, Sojen⟩ soya; **Sojasprossen** *pl* bean sprouts *pl*

**solang(e)** *conj* as long as

**Solarium** *nt* solarium

**Solarzelle** *f* solar cell

**solche(r, s)** *pron* such; **eine ~ Frau, solch eine Frau** such a woman, a woman like that; **~ Sachen** things like that, such things; **ich habe ~ Kopfschmerzen** I've got such a headache; **ich habe ~n Hunger** I'm so hungry

**Soldat(in)** *m(f)* ⟨-en, -en⟩ soldier

**solid(e)** *adj* solid; (*life, person*) respectable

**solidarisch** *adj* showing solidarity

**Soll** *nt* ⟨-(s), -(s)⟩ FIN debit; (*amount of work*) quota, target

**sollen** *vi* be supposed to; (*obligation*) shall, ought to; **soll ich?** shall I?; **du solltest besser nach Hause gehen** you'd better go home; **sie soll sehr reich sein** she's said to be very rich; **was soll das?** what's all that about?

**Solo** *nt* ⟨-s, -⟩ solo

**Sommer** *m* ⟨-s, -⟩ summer; **Sommerfahrplan** *m* summer timetable; **Sommerferien** *pl* summer holidays *pl* (*Brit*) (*or* vacation *sg* (*US*)); **sommerlich** *adj* summery; (*clothes*) summer; **Sommerreifen** *m* normal tyre; **Sommersprossen** *pl* freckles *pl*; **Sommerzeit** *f* summertime; (*by the clock*) daylight saving time

**Sonderangebot** *nt* special offer; **sonderbar** *adj* strange, odd; **Sondermüll** *m* hazardous waste

**sondern** *conj* but; **nicht nur ..., ~ auch** not only ..., but also

**Sonderpreis** *m* special price; **Sonderschule** *f* special school; **Sonderzeichen** *nt* IT special character

**Song** *m* ⟨-s, -s⟩ song

**Sonnabend** *m* Saturday; → **Mittwoch**; **sonnabends** *adv* on Saturdays; → **mittwochs**

**Sonne** *f* ⟨-, -n⟩ sun; **sonnen** *vr* sunbathe; **Sonnenaufgang** *m* sunrise; **Sonnenblume** *f* sunflower; **Sonnenbrand** *m* sunburn; **Sonnenbrille** *f* sunglasses *pl*, shades *pl*; **Sonnencreme** *f* sun cream;

**Sonnendach** nt (of car) sunroof; **Sonnendeck** nt sun deck; **Sonnenmilch** f suntan lotion; **Sonnenöl** nt suntan oil; **Sonnenschein** m sunshine; **Sonnenschirm** m parasol, sunshade; **Sonnenstich** m sunstroke; **Sonnenstudio** nt solarium; **Sonnenuhr** f sundial; **Sonnenuntergang** m sunset; **sonnig** adj sunny

**Sonntag** m Sunday; → **Mittwoch**; **sonntags** adv on Sundays; → **mittwochs**

**sonst** adv else; (if not) otherwise, (or) else; (at other times) normally, usually; ~ **noch etwas?** anything else?; ~ **nichts** nothing else

**sooft** conj whenever

**Sopran** m ⟨-s, -e⟩ soprano

**Sorge** f ⟨-, -n⟩ worry; (looking after) care; **sich** dat **um jdn** ~**n machen** be worried about sb; **sorgen 1.** vi **für jdn** ~ look after sb; **für etw** ~ take care of sth, see to sth **2.** vr worry (um about); **sorgfältig** adj careful

**sortieren** vt sort (out)

**sosehr** conj however much

**Soße** f ⟨-, -n⟩ sauce; (with meat) gravy

**Soundkarte** f IT sound card

**Souvenir** nt ⟨-s, -s⟩ souvenir

**soviel** conj as far as

**soweit** conj as far as

**sowie** conj as well as; (with time) as soon as

**sowohl** conj ~ … **als** (or **wie**) **auch** both … and

**sozial** adj social; **Sozialhilfe** f income support (Brit), welfare (aid) (US); **Sozialismus** m socialism; **Sozialversicherung** f social security; **Sozialwohnung** f council flat (Brit), state-subsidized apartment (US)

**Soziologie** f sociology

**sozusagen** adv so to speak

**Spachtel** m ⟨-s, -⟩ spatula

**Spag(h)etti** pl spaghetti sg

**Spalte** f ⟨-, -n⟩ crack; (in glacier) crevasse; (in text) column

**spalten** vt, vr split

**Spange** f ⟨-, -n⟩ clasp; (for hair) hair slide (Brit), barrette (US)

**Spanien** nt ⟨-s⟩ Spain; **Spanier(in)** m(f) ⟨-s, -⟩ Spaniard; **spanisch** adj Spanish; **Spanisch** nt Spanish

**spann** imperf → **spinnen**

**spannen 1.** vt (make taut) tighten **2.** vi be tight

**spannend** adj exciting, gripping; **Spannung** f tension; ELEC voltage; fig suspense

**Sparbuch** nt savings book; (account) savings account; **sparen** vt, vi save

**Spargel** m ⟨-s, -⟩ asparagus; **Spargelsuppe** f asparagus soup

**Sparkasse** f savings bank; **Sparkonto** f savings account

**spärlich** adj meagre; (cloth-

ing) scanty
**sparsam** *adj* economical;
**Sparschwein** *nt* piggy bank
**Spaß** *m* ⟨-es, Späße⟩ joke;
(*pleasure*) fun; *es macht
mir ~* I enjoy it, it's (great)
fun; *viel ~!* have fun
**spät** *adj, adv* late; *zu ~ kommen* be late
**Spaten** *m* ⟨-s, -⟩ spade
**später** *adj, adv* later; **spätestens** *adv* at the latest; **Spät-
vorstellung** *f* late-night performance
**Spatz** *m* ⟨-en, -en⟩ sparrow
**spazieren** *vi* stroll, walk; *~
gehen* go for a walk; **Spaziergang** *m* walk
**Specht** *m* ⟨-(e)s, -e⟩ woodpecker
**Speck** *m* ⟨-(e)s, -e⟩ bacon fat;
(*streaky*) bacon
**Spedition** *f* removal firm
**Speiche** *f* ⟨-, -n⟩ spoke
**Speichel** *m* ⟨-s⟩ saliva
**Speicher** *m* ⟨-s, -⟩ (*in building*) attic; IT memory; **speichern** *vt* IT store; (*send to
disk etc*) save
**Speise** *f* ⟨-, -n⟩ food; (*prepared*) dish; **Speisekarte** *f*
menu; **Speiseröhre** *f* gullet,
oesophagus; **Speisesaal** *m*
dining hall; **Speisewagen**
*m* dining car
**Spende** *f* ⟨-, -n⟩ donation;
**spenden** *vt* donate, give
**spendieren** *vt jdm etw ~*
treat sb to sth
**Sperre** *f* ⟨-, -n⟩ barrier; (*on sb*

or *sth*) ban; **sperren** *vt*
block; SPORT suspend; (*ex-
ports etc*) ban; **Sperrstunde**
*f* closing time; **Sperrung** *f*
closing
**Spesen** *pl* expenses *pl*
**spezialisieren** *vr* specialize
(*auf + acc* in); **Spezialist(in)**
*m(f)* specialist; **Spezialität** *f*
speciality (*Brit*), specialty
(*US*); **speziell 1.** *adj* special
**2.** *adv* especially
**Spiegel** *m* ⟨-s, -⟩ mirror;
**Spiegelei** *nt* fried egg (sun-
ny-side up (*US*)); **spiegel-
glatt** *adj* very slippery;
**Spiegelreflexkamera** *f* reflex camera
**Spiel** *nt* ⟨-(e)s, -e⟩ game; (*activity*) play(ing); (*of playing
cards*) pack, deck; **Spielautomat** *m* gaming machine;
(*with cash payout*) slot machine; **spielen** *vt, vi* play;
(*for money*) gamble; THEAT
perform, act; *Klavier ~* play
the piano; **spielend** *adv* easily; **Spieler(in)** *m(f)* ⟨-s, -⟩
player; (*for money*) gam-
bler; **Spielfeld** *nt* (*for football, hockey*) field; (*for basketball*) court; **Spielfilm** *m*
feature film; **Spielkasino**
*nt* casino; **Spielplatz** *m* playground; **Spielraum** *m* room
to manoeuvre; **Spielregel** *f*
rule; *sich an die ~n halten*
stick to the rules; **Spielsa-
chen** *pl* toys *pl*; **Spielzeug**
*nt* toys *pl*; (*single item*) toy

**Spieß** m ⟨-es, -e⟩ spear; (for roasting) spit; **Spießer(in)** m(f) ⟨-s, -⟩ square, stuffy type; **spießig** adj square, uncool

**Spikes** pl SPORT spikes pl; AUTO studs pl

**Spinat** m ⟨-(e)s, -e⟩ spinach

**Spinne** f ⟨-, -n⟩ spider; **spinnen** ⟨spann, gesponnen⟩ vt, vi spin; fam talk rubbish; be crazy; **du spinnst!** you must be mad; **Spinnwebe** f ⟨-, -n⟩ cobweb

**Spion(in)** m(f) ⟨-s, -e⟩ spy; **spionieren** vi spy; fig snoop around

**Spirale** f ⟨-, -n⟩ spiral; MED coil

**Spirituosen** pl spirits pl, liquor sg (US)

**Spiritus** m ⟨-, -se⟩ spirit

**spitz** adj (nose, chin) pointed; (pencil, knife) sharp; (angle) acute; **Spitze** f ⟨-, -n⟩ point; (of finger, nose) tip; (of remark) taunt, dig; (in race etc) lead; (fabric) lace; **Spitzer** m ⟨-s, -⟩ pencil sharpener; **Spitzname** m nickname

**Spliss** m ⟨-⟩ split ends pl

**sponsern** vt sponsor; **Sponsor(in)** m(f) ⟨-s, -en⟩ sponsor

**spontan** adj spontaneous

**Sport** m ⟨-(e)s, -e⟩ sport; **~ treiben** do sport; **Sportanlage** f sports grounds pl; **Sportart** f sport; **Sportbekleidung** f sportswear; **Sportgeschäft** nt sports shop; **Sporthalle** f

gymnasium, gym; **Sportlehrer(in)** m(f) ⟨-s, -⟩ sports instructor, PE teacher; **Sportler(in)** m(f) ⟨-s, -⟩ sportsman / -woman; **sportlich** adj sporting; (person) sporty; **Sportplatz** m playing field; **Sportverein** m sports club; **Sportwagen** m sports car

**sprach** imperf → **sprechen**

**Sprache** f ⟨-, -n⟩ language; (faculty) speech; **Sprachenschule** f language school; **Sprachkurs** m language course; **Sprachunterricht** m language teaching

**sprang** imperf → **springen**

**Spray** m or nt ⟨-s, -s⟩ spray

**Sprechanlage** f intercom; **sprechen** ⟨sprach, gesprochen⟩ vt, vi speak (jdn, mit jdm to sb); (converse) talk (mit to, über, von about); **~ Sie Deutsch?** do you speak German?; **kann ich bitte mit David ~?** (on phone) can I speak to David, please?; **Sprecher(in)** m(f) speaker; (on TV, radio) announcer; **Sprechstunde** f consultation; (of doctor) surgery hours pl; (of solicitor etc) office hours pl; **Sprechzimmer** nt consulting room

**Sprichwort** nt proverb

**Springbrunnen** m fountain

**springen** ⟨sprang, gesprungen⟩ vi jump; (glass) crack; (headfirst) dive

**Sprit** m ⟨-(e)s, -e⟩ fam petrol (Brit), gas (US)

**Spritze** f ⟨-, -n⟩ syringe; (jab) injection; (on hose) nozzle; **spritzen 1.** vt spray; MED inject **2.** vi splash; MED give injections

**Spruch** m ⟨-(e)s, Sprüche⟩ saying

**Sprudel** m ⟨-s, -⟩ sparkling mineral water; (sweet) fizzy drink (Brit), soda (US); **sprudeln** vi bubble

**Sprühdose** f aerosol (can); **sprühen** vt, vi spray; fig sparkle; **Sprühregen** m drizzle

**Sprung** m ⟨-(e)s, Sprünge⟩ jump; (in glass etc) crack; **Sprungbrett** nt springboard; **Sprungschanze** f ski jump; **Sprungturm** m diving platforms pl

**Spucke** f ⟨-⟩ spit; **spucken** vt, vi spit

**spuken** vi (ghost) walk; **hier spukt es** this place is haunted

**Spülbecken** nt sink

**Spule** f ⟨-, -n⟩ spool; ELEC coil

**Spüle** f ⟨-, -n⟩ sink; **spülen** vt, vi rinse; (after meal) wash up; (toilet) flush; **Spülmaschine** f dishwasher; **Spülmittel** nt washing-up liquid (Brit), dishwashing liquid (US); **Spültuch** nt dishcloth; **Spülung** f (of toilet) flush

**Spur** f ⟨-, -en⟩ trace; (of feet, wheels) track; (followed by police etc) trail; (on road) lane; **die~wechseln** change lanes pl

**spüren** vt feel; (observe) notice; **Spürhund** m sniffer dog

**Squash** nt ⟨-⟩ squash; **Squashschläger** m squash racket

**Sri Lanka** nt ⟨-s⟩ Sri Lanka

**Staat** m ⟨-(e)s, -en⟩ state; **staatlich** adj state(-); (industry, museum etc) state-run; **Staatsangehörigkeit** f nationality; **Staatsanwalt** m, **-anwältin** f prosecuting counsel (Brit), district attorney (US); **Staatsbürger(in)** m(f) citizen; **Staatsbürgerschaft** f nationality

**Stab** m ⟨-(e)s, Stäbe⟩ rod; (in cage, window) bar; **Stäbchen** nt chopstick; **Stabhochsprung** m pole vault

**stabil** adj stable; (furniture) sturdy

**stach** imperf → **stechen**

**Stachel** m ⟨-s, -n⟩ spike; (of animal) spine; (of insect) sting; **Stachelbeere** f gooseberry; **Stacheldraht** m barbed wire; **stachelig** adj prickly

**Stadion** nt ⟨-s, Stadien⟩ stadium

**Stadt** f ⟨-, Städte⟩ town; (large) city; (in der ~ in town; **Stadtautobahn** f urban motorway (Brit) (or expressway (US)); **Stadtführer** m (booklet) city guide; **Stadtführung** f city sightseeing tour; **Stadthalle** f municipal hall; **städtisch** adj municipal; **Stadtmauer** f city wall(s); **Stadtmitte** f town / city centre, downtown (US); **Stadtplan** m (street) map; **Stadtrand** m outskirts pl; **Stadtrundfahrt** f city tour

**stahl** imperf → **stehlen**

**Stahl** m ⟨-(e)s, Stähle⟩ steel

**Stall** m ⟨-(e)s, Ställe⟩ stable; (for rabbit) hutch; (for pigs) pigsty; (for poultry) henhouse

**Stamm** m ⟨-(e)s, Stämme⟩ (of tree) trunk; (people) tribe; **stammen** vi ~ **aus** come from; **Stammgast** m regular (guest); **Stammkunde** m, **Stammkundin** f regular (customer); **Stammtisch** m table reserved for regulars

**stand** imperf → **stehen**

**Stand** m ⟨-(e)s, Stände⟩ (of water, petrol) level; (posture) standing position; (situation) state; (in game) score; (at fair etc) stall

**Stand-by-Betrieb** m standby; **Stand-by-Ticket** nt stand-by ticket

**Ständer** m ⟨-s, -⟩ stand; fam (erection) hard-on

**Standesamt** nt registry office

**ständig** adj permanent; (uninterrupted) constant, continual

**Standlicht** nt sidelights pl

(Brit), parking lights pl (US); **Standort** m position; **Standpunkt** m standpoint; **Standspur** f AUTO hard shoulder (Brit), shoulder (US)

**Stange** f ⟨-, -n⟩ stick; (long, round) pole; (metal) bar; (of cigarettes) carton

**stank** imperf → **stinken**

**Stapel** m ⟨-s, -⟩ pile

**Star 1.** m ⟨-(e)s, -e⟩ (bird) starling; MED cataract **2.** m ⟨-s, -s⟩ (in film etc) star

**starb** imperf → **sterben**

**stark** adj strong; (intense, big) heavy; (in measurements) thick; **Stärke** f ⟨-, -n⟩ strength; (dimension) thickness; (in washing, food) starch; **stärken** vt strengthen; (washing) starch; **Stärkung** f strengthening; (food) refreshment

**starr** adj stiff; (unyielding) rigid; (look) staring; **starren** vi stare

**Start** m ⟨-(e)s, -e⟩ start; AVIAT takeoff; **Startbahn** f runway; **starten** vt, vi start; AVIAT take off; **Startmenü** nt IT start menu

**Station** f stop; (on railway) station; (in hospital) ward; **stationär** adj stationary; **~e Behandlung** in-patient treatment; **jdn ~ behandeln** treat sb as an in-patient

**Statistik** f statistics pl

**Stativ** nt tripod

**statt** conj, prep + gen or dat instead of; ~ **zu arbeiten** instead of working

**stattfinden** irr vi take place

**Statue** f ⟨-, -n⟩ statue

**Statusleiste** f, **Statuszeile** f IT status bar

**Stau** m ⟨-(e)s, -e⟩ (traffic) jam; **im ~ stehen** be stuck in a traffic jam

**Staub** m ⟨-(e)s⟩ dust; ~ **wischen** dust; **staubig** adj dusty; **staubsaugen** vt, vi vacuum, hoover (Brit); **Staubsauger** m vacuum cleaner, hoover® (Brit); **Staubtuch** nt duster

**Staudamm** m dam

**staunen** vi be astonished (über + acc at)

**Stausee** m reservoir; **Stauung** f (of water) damming-up; (of blood, traffic) congestion

**Stauwarnung** f traffic report

**Steak** nt ⟨-s, -s⟩ steak

**stechen** ⟨stach, gestochen⟩ vt, vi (with needle etc) prick; (with knife) stab; (with finger) poke; (bee) sting; (mosquito) bite; (sun) burn; (in card game) trump; **Stechen** nt ⟨-s, -⟩ sharp pain, stabbing pain; **Stechmücke** f mosquito

**Steckdose** f socket; **stecken** **1.** vt put; (pin) stick; (in sewing) pin **2.** vi (not move) be stuck; (pin) be (sticking); **der Schlüssel steckt** the key is in the door; **Stecker** m ⟨-s, -⟩ plug

**Steg** m ⟨-s, -e⟩ bridge

**stehen** ⟨stand, gestanden⟩ **1.** vi stand (zu by); (with location, circumstance) be; (watch, machine, traffic) have stopped; **was steht im Brief?** what does it say in the letter?; **jdm (gut) ~** suit sb; ~ **bleiben** (clock) stop; ~ **lassen** leave **2.** vi impers **wie steht's?** SPORT what's the score?

**stehlen** ⟨stahl, gestohlen⟩ vt steal

**Stehplatz** m (in concert etc) standing ticket

**Steiermark** f ⟨-⟩ Styria

**steif** adj stiff

**steigen** ⟨stieg, gestiegen⟩ vi (prices, temperature) rise; (person) climb

**steigern** vt, vr increase

**Steigung** f incline, gradient

**steil** adj steep; **Steilhang** m steep slope; **Steilküste** f steep coast

**Stein** m ⟨-(e)s, -e⟩ stone; **Steinbock** m ZOOL ibex; ASTR Capricorn; **steinig** adj stony; **Steinschlag** m falling rocks pl

**Stelle** f ⟨-, -n⟩ place, spot; (work) place, job; (department) office; **ich an deiner ~** if I were you; **stellen 1.** vt put; (clock etc) set (auf + acc to); (make available) provide **2.** vr (to the police)

give oneself up; *sich schlafend ~* pretend to be asleep; **Stellenangebot** *nt* job offer, vacancy; **stellenweise** *adv* in places; **Stellplatz** *m* parking space; **Stellung** *f* position; *zu etw ~ nehmen* comment on sth; **Stellvertreter(in)** *m(f)* representative; (*as official post*) deputy

**Stempel** *m* ⟨-s, -⟩ stamp; **stempeln** *vt* stamp; (*postage stamp*) cancel

**sterben** ⟨starb, gestorben⟩ *vi* die

**Stereoanlage** *f* stereo (system)

**steril** *adj* sterile; **sterilisieren** *vt* sterilize

**Stern** *m* ⟨-(e)s, -e⟩ star; **Sternbild** *nt* constellation; (*in astrology*) star sign, sign of the zodiac; **Sternfrucht** *f* star fruit; **Sternschnuppe** *f* ⟨-, -n⟩ shooting star; **Sternwarte** *f* ⟨-e, -n⟩ observatory; **Sternzeichen** *nt* star sign, sign of the zodiac; *welches ~ bist du?* what's your star sign?

**stets** *adv* always

**Steuer 1.** *nt* ⟨-s, -⟩ AUTO steering wheel **2.** *f* ⟨-, -n⟩ tax; **Steuerberater(in)** *m(f)* tax adviser; **Steuerbord** *nt* starboard; **Steuererklärung** *f* tax declaration; **steuerfrei** *adj* tax-free; (*goods*) duty-free; **Steuerknüppel** *m* control column; AVIAT, IT joy-

stick; **steuern** *vt, vi* steer; (*plane*) pilot; (*development, volume*) IT control; **steuerpflichtig** *adj* taxable; **Steuerung** *f* AUTO steering; (*instruments*) controls *pl*; AVIAT piloting; *fig* control

**Stich** *m* ⟨-(e)s, -e⟩ (*of insect*) sting; (*of mosquito*) bite; (*with knife*) stab; (*in sewing*) stitch; (*of colour*) tinge; (*in card game*) trick; ART engraving

**sticken** *vt, vi* embroider

**Sticker** *m* ⟨-s, -⟩ sticker

**Stickerei** *f* embroidery

**stickig** *adj* stuffy, close

**Stiefbruder** *m* stepbrother

**Stiefel** *m* ⟨-s, -⟩ boot

**Stiefmutter** *f* stepmother

**Stiefmütterchen** *nt* pansy

**Stiefschwester** *f* stepsister; **Stiefsohn** *m* stepson; **Stieftochter** *f* stepdaughter; **Stiefvater** *m* stepfather

**stieg** *imperf →* **steigen**

**Stiege** *f* ⟨-, -n⟩ steps *pl*

**Stiel** *m* ⟨-(e)s, -e⟩ handle; BOT stalk; *ein Eis am ~* an ice lolly (*Brit*), a Popsicle® (*US*)

**Stier** *m* ⟨-(e)s, -e⟩ ZOOL bull; ASTR Taurus; **Stierkampf** *m* bullfight

**stieß** *imperf →* **stoßen**

**Stift** *m* ⟨-(e)s, -e⟩ (*wooden*) peg; (*nail*) tack; (*for writing, drawing*) pen; crayon; pencil

**Stil** *m* ⟨-s, -e⟩ style

**still** *adj* quiet; (*motionless*) still

**stillen** *vt* breast-feed
**stillhalten** *irr vi* keep still; **stillstehen** *irr vi* stand still
**Stimme** *f* ⟨-, -n⟩ voice; (*in election*) vote
**stimmen** *vi* be right; **that's right; *hier stimmt was nicht*** there's something wrong here; **stimmt so!** keep the change
**Stimmung** *f* mood; (*in group etc*) atmosphere
**stinken** ⟨stank, gestunken⟩ *vi* stink (*nach* of)
**Stipendium** *nt* scholarship; (*as means of support*) grant
**Stirn** *f* ⟨-, -en⟩ forehead; **Stirnhöhle** *f* sinus
**Stock** 1. *m* ⟨-(e)s, Stöcke⟩ stick; BOT stock 2. *m* ⟨Stockwerke *pl*⟩ floor, storey; **im ersten ~** on the first floor (*Brit*), on the second floor (*US*); **Stockbett** *nt* bunk bed; **Stöckelschuhe** *pl* high-heels; **Stockwerk** *nt* floor
**Stoff** *m* ⟨-(e)s, -e⟩ (*fabric*) material; (*substance*) matter; (*of book etc*) subject (matter); *fam* (*drugs*) stuff
**stöhnen** *vi* groan (*vor* with)
**stolpern** *vi* stumble, trip
**stolz** *adj* proud
**stopp** *interj* hold it; (*introducing new thought*) hang on a minute; **stoppen** *vt, vi* stop; (*with watch*) time; **Stoppschild** *nt* stop sign; **Stoppuhr** *f* stopwatch
**Stöpsel** *m* ⟨-s, -⟩ plug; (*for*

*bottle*) stopper
**Storch** *m* ⟨-(e)s, Störche⟩ stork
**stören** *vt* disturb; (*hinder*) interfere with; **darf ich dich kurz ~?** can I trouble you for a minute?; **stört es dich, wenn...?** do you mind if ...?
**stornieren** *vt* cancel
**Störung** *f* disturbance; (*on phone line*) fault
**Stoß** *m* ⟨-es, Stöße⟩ push; (*with fist, elbow*) blow; (*with foot*) kick; (*of books, washing*) pile; **Stoßdämpfer** *m* ⟨-s, -⟩ shock absorber
**stoßen** ⟨stieß, gestoßen⟩ 1. *vt* shove, push; (*with a blow*) knock; (*with foot*) kick; (*head etc*) bump 2. *vr* bang oneself
**Stoßstange** *f* AUTO bumper
**stottern** *vt, vi* stutter
**Strafe** *f* ⟨-, -n⟩ punishment; SPORT penalty; (*in prison*) sentence; (*money*) fine; **strafen** *vt* punish; **Straftat** *f* (*criminal*) offence; **Strafzettel** *m* ticket
**Strahl** *m* ⟨-s, -en⟩ ray, beam; (*of water*) jet; **strahlen** *vi* radiate; *fig* beam
**Strähne** *f* ⟨-, -n⟩ strand; (*white, coloured*) streak
**Strand** *m* ⟨-(e)s, Strände⟩ beach; **am ~** on the beach; **Strandcafé** *nt* beach café
**strapazieren** *vt* be hard on; (*person, nerves*) be a strain on
**Straße** *f* ⟨-, -n⟩ road; (*in town*)

street; **Straßenarbeiten** pl roadworks pl (Brit), road repairs pl (US); **Straßenbahn** f tram (Brit), streetcar (US); **Straßencafé** nt pavement café (Brit), sidewalk café (US); **Straßenfest** nt street party; **Straßenglätte** f slippery roads pl; **Straßenrand** m **am ~** at the roadside; **Straßenschild** nt street sign; **Straßensperre** f roadblock; **Straßenverhältnisse** pl road conditions pl

**Strategie** f ⟨-, -n⟩ strategy

**Strauch** m ⟨-(e)s, Sträucher⟩ bush, shrub

**Strauß 1.** m ⟨-es, Sträuße⟩ bunch; (as gift) bouquet **2.** m ⟨Sträuße (0)⟩ ostrich

**Strecke** f ⟨-, -n⟩ route; distance; RAIL line

**strecken** vt, vr stretch

**streckenweise** adv in parts; (occasionally) at times

**Streich** m ⟨-(e)s, -e⟩ trick, prank

**streicheln** vt stroke

**streichen** ⟨strich, gestrichen⟩ vt paint; (word etc) delete; (flight, race etc) cancel

**Streichholz** nt match; **Streichholzschachtel** f matchbox; **Streichkäse** m cheese spread

**Streifen** m ⟨-s, -⟩ stripe; (piece) strip; (movie) film

**Streifenwagen** m patrol car

**Streik** m ⟨-(e)s, -s⟩ strike; **streiken** vi be on strike

**Streit** m ⟨-(e)s, -e⟩ argument (um, wegen about, over); **streiten** ⟨stritt, gestritten⟩ vi, vr argue (um, wegen about, over)

**streng** adj (look, appearance) severe; (teacher, measure) strict; (smell etc) sharp

**Stress** m ⟨-es⟩ stress; **stressen** vt stress (out); **stressig** adj fam stressful

**Stretching** nt ⟨-s⟩ SPORT stretching exercises pl

**streuen** vt scatter

**strich** imperf → **streichen**

**Strich** m ⟨-(e)s, -e⟩ line; **Stricher** m fam rent boy (Brit), boy prostitute; **Stricherin** f fam hooker; **Strichkode** m ⟨-s, -s⟩ bar code; **Strichpunkt** m semicolon

**Strick** m ⟨-(e)s, -e⟩ rope

**stricken** vt, vi knit; **Strickjacke** f cardigan; **Stricknadel** f knitting needle

**String** m ⟨-s, -s⟩ G-string; **Stringtanga** m G-string

**Stripper(in)** m(f) stripper; **Striptease** m ⟨-⟩ striptease

**stritt** imperf → **streiten**

**Stroh** nt ⟨-(e)s⟩ straw; **Strohdach** nt thatched roof; **Strohhalm** m (drinking) straw

**Strom** m ⟨-(e)s, Ströme⟩ river; fig stream; ELEC current; **Stromanschluss** m connection; **Stromausfall** m power failure

**strömen** vi stream, pour;

**Strömung** f current

**Stromzähler** m electricity meter

**Strophe** f ⟨-, -n⟩ verse

**Strudel** m ⟨-s, -⟩ (in river) whirlpool; (dessert) strudel

**Struktur** f structure; (of material) texture

**Strumpf** m ⟨-(e)s, Strümpfe⟩ stocking; sock; **Strumpfhose** f (pair of) tights pl (Brit), pantyhose (US)

**Stück** nt ⟨-(e)s, -e⟩ piece; (some) bit; (of sugar) lump; THEAT play

**Student(in)** m(f) student; **Studentenausweis** m student card; **Studentenwohnheim** nt hall of residence (Brit), dormitory (US); **Studienabschluss** m qualification (at the end of a course of higher education); **Studienfahrt** f study trip; **Studienplatz** m university / college place; **studieren** vt, vi study; **Studium** nt studies pl; **während seines ~s** while he is / was studying

**Stufe** f ⟨-, -n⟩ step; (in development) stage

**Stuhl** m ⟨-(e)s, Stühle⟩ chair

**stumm** adj silent; MED dumb

**stumpf** adj blunt; (apathetic, not shiny) dull; **stumpfsinnig** adj dull

**Stunde** f ⟨-, -n⟩ hour; (in school etc) lesson; **eine halbe ~** half an hour; **Stundenkilometer** m **80 ~** 80 kilo-

metres an hour; **stundenlang** adv for hours; **Stundenplan** m timetable; **stündlich** adj hourly

**Stuntman** m ⟨-s, Stuntmen⟩ stuntman; **Stuntwoman** f ⟨-, Stuntwomen⟩ stuntwoman

**stur** adj stubborn; (stronger) pigheaded

**Sturm** m ⟨-(e)s, Stürme⟩ storm; **stürmen** vi (wind) blow hard; (rush) storm; **Stürmer(in)** m(f) striker, forward; **Sturmflut** f storm tide; **stürmisch** adj stormy; fig tempestuous; (time) turbulent; (lover) passionate; (applause, welcome) tumultuous; **Sturmwarnung** f gale warning

**Sturz** m ⟨-es, Stürze⟩ fall; POL overthrow; **stürzen 1.** vt hurl; POL overthrow; (container) overturn **2.** vi fall; (rush) dash; **Sturzhelm** m crash helmet

**Stute** f ⟨-, -n⟩ mare

**Stütze** f ⟨-, -n⟩ support; (person who helps) help; fam (for unemployed person) dole (Brit), welfare (US)

**stutzig** adj perplexed, puzzled; (distrustful) suspicious

**Styropor®** nt ⟨-s⟩ polystyrene (Brit), styrofoam (US)

**subjektiv** adj subjective

**Substanz** f ⟨-, -en⟩ substance

**subtrahieren** vt subtract

**Subvention** f subsidy; **sub-**

ventionieren *vt* subsidize

**Suche** *f* search (*nach* for); **auf der ~ nach etw sein** be looking for sth; **suchen 1.** *vt* look for; IT search **2.** *vi* look, search (*nach* for); **Suchmaschine** *f* IT search engine

**Sucht** *f* ⟨-, Süchte⟩ mania; MED addiction; **süchtig** *adj* addicted; **Süchtige(r)** *mf* addict

**Süd** south; **Südafrika** *nt* South Africa; **Südamerika** *nt* South America; **Süddeutschland** *nt* Southern Germany; **Süden** *m* ⟨-s⟩ south; **im ~ Deutschlands** in the south of Germany; **Südeuropa** *nt* Southern Europe; **Südkorea** *nt* ⟨-s⟩ South Korea; **südlich** *adj* southern; (*course, direction*) southerly; **Südost(en)** *m* southeast; **Südpol** *m* South Pole; **Südstaaten** *pl* (*in USA*) the Southern States *pl*, the South *sg*; **südwärts** *adv* south, southwards; **Südwest(en)** *m* southwest; **Südwind** *m* south wind

**Sülze** *f* ⟨-, -n⟩ jellied meat

**Summe** *f* ⟨-, -n⟩ sum; (*altogether*) total

**summen** *vi, vt* hum; (*insect*) buzz

**Sumpf** *m* ⟨-(e)s, Sümpfe⟩ marsh; (*in the tropics*) swamp; **sumpfig** *adj* marshy

**Sünde** *f* ⟨-, -n⟩ sin

**super** *adj fam* super, great;

**Super** *nt* ⟨-s⟩ four star (petrol) (*Brit*), premium (*US*); **Supermarkt** *m* supermarket

**Suppe** *f* ⟨-, -n⟩ soup; **Suppengrün** *nt* bunch of herbs and vegetables for flavouring soup; **Suppenwürfel** *m* stock cube

**Surfbrett** *nt* surfboard; **surfen** *vi* surf; **im Internet ~** surf the Internet; **Surfer(in)** *m(f)* ⟨-s, -⟩ surfer

**Surrealismus** *m* surrealism

**Sushi** *nt* ⟨-s, -s⟩ sushi

**süß** *adj* sweet; **süßen** *vt* sweeten; **Süßigkeit** *f* sweet (*Brit*), candy (*US*); **Süßkartoffel** *f* sweet potato (*Brit*), yam (*US*); **süßsauer** *adj* sweet-and-sour; **Süßspeise** *f* dessert; **Süßstoff** *m* sweetener; **Süßwasser** *nt* fresh water

**Sweatshirt** *nt* ⟨-s, -s⟩ sweatshirt

**Swimmingpool** *m* ⟨-s, -s⟩ (swimming) pool

**Sylvester** *nt* → *Silvester*

**Symbol** *nt* ⟨-s, -e⟩ symbol; **Symbolleiste** *f* IT toolbar

**Symmetrie** *f* ⟨-, -n⟩ symmetry; **symmetrisch** *adj* symmetrical

**sympathisch** *adj* nice; **jdn ~ finden** like sb

**Symphonie** *f* ⟨-, -n⟩ symphony

**Symptom** *nt* ⟨-s, -e⟩ symptom (*für* of)

**Synagoge** *f* ⟨-, -n⟩ synagogue

**Tannenzapfen**

**synchronisiert** *adj* (*film*) dubbed; **Synchronstimme** *f* dubbing voice

**Synthetik** *f* ⟨-, -en⟩ synthetic (fibre); **synthetisch** *adj* synthetic

**Syrien** *nt* ⟨-s⟩ Syria

**System** *nt* ⟨-s, -e⟩ system; **systematisch** *adj* systematic; **Systemsteuerung** *f* IT control panel

**Szene** *f* ⟨-, -n⟩ scene

# T

**Tabak** *m* ⟨-s, -e⟩ tobacco; **Tabakladen** *m* tobacconist's

**Tabelle** *f* table

**Tablett** *nt* ⟨-s, -s⟩ tray

**Tablette** *f* tablet, pill

**Tabulator** *m* tabulator, tab

**Tacho(meter)** *m* ⟨-s, -⟩ AUTO speedometer

**Tafel** *f* ⟨-, -n⟩ *a.* MATH table; (*for notices*) board; (*in classroom*) blackboard; (*commemorative*) plaque; **eine ~ Schokolade** a bar of chocolate

**Tag** *m* ⟨-(e)s, -e⟩ day; daylight; **guten ~!** good morning / afternoon; **am ~** during the day; **sie hat ihre ~e** she's got her period; **eines ~es** one day; **Tagebuch** *nt* diary; **tagelang** *adj* for days (on end); **Tagesanbruch** *m* daybreak; **Tagesausflug** *m* day trip; **Tagescreme** *f* day cream; **Tagesgericht** *nt* dish of the day; **Tageskarte** *f* day ticket; **die ~** (*at restaurant*) today's menu; **Tageslicht** *nt* daylight; **Tagesordnung** *f* agenda; **Tagestour** *f* day

trip; **Tageszeitung** *f* daily newspaper; **täglich** *adj*, *adv* daily; **tags(über)** *adv* during the day; **Tagung** *f* conference

**Tai Chi** *nt* ⟨-⟩ tai chi

**Taille** *f* ⟨-, -n⟩ waist

**Taiwan** *nt* ⟨-s⟩ Taiwan

**Takt** *m* ⟨-(e)s, -e⟩ tact; MUS time

**Taktik** *f* ⟨-, -en⟩ tactics *pl*

**Tal** *nt* ⟨-(e)s, Täler⟩ valley

**Talent** *nt* ⟨-(e)s, -e⟩ talent; **talentiert** *adj* talented

**Talkmaster(in)** *m(f)* ⟨-s, -⟩ talk-show host; **Talkshow** *f* ⟨-, -s⟩ talkshow

**Tampon** *m* ⟨-s, -s⟩ tampon

**Tandem** *nt* ⟨-s, -s⟩ tandem

**Tang** *m* ⟨-s, -e⟩ seaweed

**Tanga** *m* ⟨-s, -s⟩ thong

**Tank** *m* ⟨-s, -s⟩ tank; **Tankanzeige** *f* fuel gauge; **Tankdeckel** *m* fuel cap; **tanken** *vi* get some petrol (*Brit*) (*or* gas (*US*)); AVIAT refuel; **Tanker** *m* ⟨-s, -⟩ (oil) tanker; **Tankstelle** *f* petrol station (*Brit*), gas station (*US*)

**Tanne** *f* ⟨-, -n⟩ fir; **Tannenzapfen** *m* fir cone

**Tansania** nt ⟨-s⟩ Tanzania

**Tante** f ⟨-, -n⟩ aunt; **Tante-Emma-Laden** m corner shop (Brit), grocery store (US)

**Tanz** m ⟨-es, Tänze⟩ dance; **tanzen** vi, vt dance; **Tänzer(in)** m(f) dancer; **Tanzfläche** f dance floor; **Tanzkurs** m dancing course; **Tanzlehrer(in)** m(f) dancing instructor; **Tanzstunde** f dancing lesson

**Tapete** f ⟨-, -n⟩ wallpaper; **tapezieren** vt, vi wallpaper

**Tarif** m ⟨-s, -e⟩ tariff, (scale of) fares / charges pl

**Tasche** f ⟨-, -n⟩ bag; (in trousers etc) pocket; (handbag) bag (Brit), purse (US); **Taschen-** in cpds pocket; **Taschenbuch** nt paperback; **Taschendieb(in)** m(f) pickpocket; **Taschengeld** nt pocket money; **Taschenlampe** f torch (Brit), flashlight (US); **Taschenmesser** nt penknife; **Taschenrechner** m pocket calculator; **Taschentuch** nt handkerchief

**Tasse** f ⟨-, -n⟩ cup; **eine ~ Kaffee** a cup of coffee

**Tastatur** f keyboard; **Taste** f ⟨-, -n⟩ button; (of piano, computer) key; **Tastenkombination** f IT shortcut

**tat** imperf → **tun**

**Tat** f ⟨-, -en⟩ action

**Tatar** nt ⟨-s, -s⟩ raw minced beef

**Täter(in)** m(f) ⟨-s, -⟩ culprit

**Tätigkeit** f activity; (job) occupation

**tätowieren** vt tattoo; **Tätowierung** f tattoo (an + dat on)

**Tatsache** f fact; **tatsächlich 1.** adj actual **2.** adv really

**Tau** **1.** nt ⟨-(e)s, -e⟩ rope **2.** m ⟨-(e)s⟩ dew

**taub** adj deaf

**Taube** f ⟨-, -n⟩ pigeon, dove

**taubstumm** adj deaf-and-dumb; **Taubstumme(r)** mf deaf-mute

**tauchen 1.** vt dip **2.** vi dive; NAUT submerge; **Tauchen** nt ⟨-s⟩ diving; **Taucher(in)** m(f) ⟨-s, -⟩ diver; **Taucheranzug** m diving (or wet) suit; **Taucherbrille** f diving goggles pl; **Tauchermaske** f diving mask; **Tauchkurs** m diving course

**tauen** vi impers thaw

**Taufe** f ⟨-, -n⟩ baptism; **taufen** vt baptize; (name) christen

**taugen** vi be suitable (für for); **nichts ~** be no good

**Tausch** m ⟨-(e)s, -e⟩ exchange; **tauschen** vt exchange, swap

**täuschen 1.** vt deceive **2.** vi be deceptive **3.** vr be wrong; **täuschend** adj deceptive; **Täuschung** f deception; (optical) illusion

**tausend** num a thousand; **vier~** four thousand; **~ Dank!** thanks a lot; **tausendmal** adv a thousand times; **tausendste(r, s)** adj thousandth; **Tausendstel** nt ⟨-s, -⟩ (fraction) thousandth

**Taxi** nt taxi; **Taxifahrer(in)** m(f) taxi driver; **Taxistand** m taxi rank (Brit), taxi stand (US)

**Team** nt ⟨-s, -s⟩ team; **Teamarbeit** f team work; **teamfähig** adj able to work in a team

**Technik** f technology; (applied) engineering; (method, skill) technique; **Techniker(in)** m(f) ⟨-s, -⟩ engineer; SPORT, MUS technician; **technisch** adj technical

**Techno** m ⟨-s⟩ MUS techno

**Teddybär** m teddy bear

**Tee** m ⟨-s, -s⟩ tea; **Teebeutel** m teabag; **Teekanne** f teapot; **Teelöffel** m teaspoon

**Teer** m ⟨-(e)s, -e⟩ tar

**Teesieb** nt tea strainer; **Teetasse** f teacup

**Teich** m ⟨-(e)s, -e⟩ pond

**Teig** m ⟨-(e)s, -e⟩ dough; **Teigwaren** pl pasta sg

**Teil 1.** m ⟨-(e)s, -e⟩ part; (due to sb) share; **zum ~** partly **2.** nt ⟨-(e)s, -e⟩ part; (part of whole) component; **teilen** vt, vr divide; (with sb) share (mit with); **20 durch 4 ~** divide 20 by 4

**Teilnahme** f ⟨-, -n⟩ participation (an + dat in); **teilnehmen** irr vi take part (an + dat in); **Teilnehmer(in)** m(f) ⟨-s, -⟩ participant

**teils** adv partly; **teilweise** adv partially, in part; **Teilzeit** f **~**

**arbeiten** work part-time

**Teint** m ⟨-s, -s⟩ complexion

**Telefon** nt ⟨-s, -e⟩ telephone; **Telefonanruf** m, **Telefonat** nt (tele)phone call; **Telefonanschluss** m telephone connection; **Telefonauskunft** f directory enquiries pl (Brit), directory assistance (US); **Telefonbuch** nt telephone directory; **Telefongebühren** pl telephone charges pl; **Telefongespräch** nt telephone conversation; **telefonieren** vi **ich telefoniere gerade (mit …)** I'm on the phone (to …); **telefonisch** adj telephone; (notification) by telephone; **Telefonkarte** f phonecard; **Telefonnummer** f (tele)phone number; **Telefonrechnung** f phone bill; **Telefonverbindung** f telephone connection; **Telefonzelle** f phone box (Brit), phone booth

**Telegramm** nt telegram; **Teleobjektiv** nt telephoto lens; **Teleshopping** nt ⟨-s⟩ teleshopping; **Teleskop** nt ⟨-s, -e⟩ telescope

**Teller** m ⟨-s, -⟩ plate

**Tempel** m ⟨-s, -⟩ temple

**Temperament** nt temperament; liveliness; **temperamentvoll** adj lively

**Temperatur** f temperature; **bei ~en von 30 Grad** at temperatures of 30 degrees

**Tempo** nt ⟨-s, -s⟩ speed; **Tempolimit** nt ⟨-s, -s⟩ speed limit

**Tempotaschentuch®** nt (paper) tissue, ≈ Kleenex®

**Tendenz** f tendency; intention

**Tennis** nt ⟨-⟩ tennis; **Tennisball** m tennis ball; **Tennisplatz** m tennis court; **Tennisschläger** m tennis racket; **Tennisspieler(in)** m(f) tennis player

**Tenor** m ⟨-s, Tenöre⟩ tenor

**Teppich** m ⟨-s, -e⟩ carpet; **Teppichboden** m (wall-to-wall) carpet

**Termin** m ⟨-s, -e⟩ date; (for finishing sth) deadline; (with doctor etc) appointment

**Terminal** nt ⟨-s, -s⟩ IT, AVIAT terminal

**Terminkalender** m diary; **Terminplaner** m personal organizer, Filofax®; (pocket computer) personal digital assistant, PDA

**Terrasse** f ⟨-, -n⟩ terrace; (adjoining house) patio

**Terror** m ⟨-s⟩ terror; **Terroranschlag** m terrorist attack; **terrorisieren** vt terrorize; **Terrorismus** m terrorism; **Terrorist(in)** m(f) terrorist

**Tesafilm®** m ≈ sellotape® (Brit), ≈ Scotch tape® (US)

**Test** m ⟨-s, -s⟩ test

**Testament** nt will; **das Alte / Neue ~** the Old / New Testament

**testen** vt test; **Testergebnis** nt test results pl

**Tetanus** m ⟨-⟩ tetanus; **Tetanusimpfung** f (anti-)tetanus injection

**teuer** adj expensive, dear (Brit)

**Teufel** m ⟨-s, -⟩ devil; **Teufelskreis** m vicious circle

**Text** m ⟨-(e)s, -e⟩ text; (of song) words pl, lyrics pl; **Textmarker** m ⟨-s, -⟩ highlighter; **Textverarbeitung** f word processing

**Thailand** nt Thailand

**Theater** nt ⟨-s, -⟩ theatre; fam fuss; **ins ~ gehen** go to the theatre; **Theaterkasse** f box office; **Theaterstück** nt (stage) play

**Theke** f ⟨-, -n⟩ bar; (in shop) counter

**Thema** nt ⟨-s, Themen⟩ subject, topic; **kein ~!** no problem

**Themse** f ⟨-⟩ Thames

**Theologie** f theology

**theoretisch** adj theoretical; **~ stimmt das** that's right in theory; **Theorie** f theory

**Therapeut(in)** m(f) therapist; **Therapie** f therapy; **eine ~ machen** undergo therapy

**Thermalbad** nt thermal bath; (resort) thermal spa; **Thermometer** nt ⟨-s, -⟩ thermometer; **Thermoskanne** f Thermos® (flask); **Thermostat** m ⟨-(e)s, -e⟩ thermostat

**These** f ⟨-, -n⟩ theory

**Thron** m ⟨-(e)s, -e⟩ throne

**Thunfisch** *m* tuna

**Thüringen** *nt* ⟨-s⟩ Thuringia

**Thymian** *m* ⟨-s, -e⟩ thyme

**Tick** *m* ⟨-(e)s, -s⟩ tic; *(idiosyncrasy)* quirk; *(mania)* craze; **ticken** *vi* tick; **er tickt nicht ganz richtig** he's off his rocker

**Ticket** *nt* ⟨-s, -s⟩ (plane) ticket

**tief** *adj* deep; *(neckline, note, sun)* low; *2 Meter ~* 2 metres deep; **Tief** *nt* ⟨-s, -s⟩ METEO low; *(mood)* depression; **Tiefdruck** *m* METEO low pressure; **Tiefe** *f* ⟨-, -n⟩ depth; **Tiefgarage** *f* underground car park *(Brit)* (or garage *(US)*); **tiefgekühlt** *adj* frozen; **Tiefkühlfach** *nt* freezer compartment; **Tiefkühlkost** *f* frozen food; **Tiefkühltruhe** *f* freezer; **Tiefpunkt** *m* low

**Tier** *nt* ⟨-(e)s, -e⟩ animal; **Tierarzt** *m*, **Tierärztin** *f* vet; **Tiergarten** *m* zoo; **Tierhandlung** *f* pet shop; **Tierheim** *nt* animal shelter; **tierisch 1.** *adj* animal **2.** *adv fam* really; *~ ernst* deadly serious; **ich hatte ~ Angst** I was dead scared; **Tierkreiszeichen** *nt* sign of the zodiac; **Tierpark** *m* zoo; **Tierquälerei** *f* cruelty to animals; **Tierschützer(in)** *m(f)* ⟨-s, -⟩ animal rights campaigner; **Tierversuch** *m* animal experiment

**Tiger** *m* ⟨-s, -⟩ tiger

**timen** *vt* time; **Timing** *nt* ⟨-s⟩ timing

**Tinte** *f* ⟨-, -n⟩ ink; **Tintenfisch** *m* cuttlefish; *(small)* squid; *(with eight arms)* octopus; **Tintenfischringe** *pl* calamari *pl*

**Tipp** *m* ⟨-s, -s⟩ tip; **tippen** *vt, vi* tap; *fam* type; *fam* guess

**Tirol** *nt* ⟨-s⟩ Tyrol

**Tisch** *m* ⟨-(e)s, -e⟩ table; **Tischdecke** *f* tablecloth; **Tischtennis** *nt* table tennis; **Tischtennisschläger** *m* table-tennis bat

**Titel** *m* ⟨-s, -⟩ title; **Titelbild** *nt* cover picture

**Toast** *m* ⟨-(e)s, -s⟩ toast; **toasten** *vt* toast; **Toaster** *m* ⟨-s, -⟩ toaster

**Tochter** *f* ⟨-, Töchter⟩ daughter

**Tod** *m* ⟨-(e)s, -e⟩ death; **Todesopfer** *nt* casualty; **Todesstrafe** *f* death penalty; **todkrank** *adj* terminally ill; *(not life-threatening)* seriously ill; **tödlich** *adj* deadly, fatal; *er ist ~ verunglückt* he was killed in an accident; **todmüde** *adj fam* dead tired; **todsicher** *adj fam* dead certain

**Tofu** *m* ⟨-(s)⟩ tofu, bean curd

**Toilette** *f* toilet, restroom *(US)*; **Toilettenpapier** *nt* toilet paper

**toi, toi, toi** *interj* good luck

**tolerant** *adj* tolerant *(gegen* of)

**toll** *adj* mad; *(activity)* wild; *fam (wonderful)* great; **Toll-**

wut f rabies sg

**Tomate** f ⟨-, -n⟩ tomato; **Tomatenmark** nt tomato purée (Brit) (or paste (US)); **Tomatensaft** m tomato juice

**Tombola** f ⟨-, -s⟩ raffle, tombola (Brit)

**Ton 1.** m ⟨-(e)s, -e⟩ clay **2.** m ⟨Töne pl⟩ sound; MUS note; (in voice) tone; (hue, nuance) shade

**tönen 1.** vi sound **2.** vt shade; (hair) tint

**Toner** m ⟨-s, -⟩ toner; **Tonerkassette** f toner cartridge

**Tonne** f ⟨-, -n⟩ barrel; (weight) tonne, metric ton

**Tontechniker(in)** m(f) sound engineer

**Tönung** f hue; (for hair) rinse

**Top** nt ⟨-s, -s⟩ top

**Topf** m ⟨-(e)s, Töpfe⟩ pot

**Töpfer(in)** m(f) ⟨-s, -⟩ potter; **Töpferei** f pottery; (item) piece of pottery

**Tor** nt ⟨-(e)s, -e⟩ gate; SPORT goal; **ein ~ schießen** score a goal; **Torhüter(in)** m(f) goalkeeper

**torkeln** vi stagger

**Tornado** m ⟨-s, -s⟩ tornado

**Torschütze** m, **Torschützin** f (goal)scorer

**Torte** f ⟨-, -n⟩ cake; (fruit tart) flan; (with layers of cream) gateau

**Torwart(in)** m(f) ⟨-s, -e⟩ goalkeeper

**tot** adj dead; **~er Winkel** blind spot

**total** adj total, complete; **Totalschaden** m complete write-off

**Tote(r)** mf dead man / woman; (body) corpse; **töten** vt, vi kill; **Totenkopf** m skull

**totlachen** vr kill oneself laughing

**Toto** m or nt ⟨-s, -s⟩ pools pl

**totschlagen** irr vt beat to death; **die Zeit ~** kill time

**Touchscreen** m ⟨-s, -s⟩ touch screen

**Tour** f ⟨-, -en⟩ trip; (circular) tour

**Tourismus** m tourism; **Tourist(in)** m(f) tourist; **touristisch** adj tourist; pej touristy

**Tournee** f ⟨-, -n⟩ tour

**traben** vi trot

**Tracht** f ⟨-, -en⟩ traditional costume

**Tradition** f tradition; **traditionell** adj traditional

**traf** imperf → **treffen**

**Trafik** f ⟨-, -en⟩ tobacconist's

**tragbar** adj portable

**träge** adj sluggish, slow

**tragen** ⟨trug, getragen⟩ vt carry; (clothes, glasses, hair) wear; (name, fruit) bear; **Träger** m ⟨-s, -⟩ (on dress etc) strap; **Tragflügelboot** nt hydrofoil

**tragisch** adj tragic; **Tragödie** f tragedy

**Trainer(in)** m(f) ⟨-s, -⟩ trainer, coach; **trainieren** vt, vi train; (person also) coach; (exercise) practise; **Training** nt

⟨-s, -s⟩ training; **Trainings-anzug** m tracksuit

**Traktor** m tractor

**Trambahn** f tram (Brit), streetcar (US)

**trampen** vi hitchhike; **Tramper(in)** m(f) hitchhiker

**Träne** f ⟨-, -n⟩ tear; **tränen** vi water; **Tränengas** nt teargas

**trank** imperf → **trinken**

**Transfusion** f transfusion

**Transitverkehr** m transit traffic; **Transitvisum** nt transit visa

**Transplantation** f transplant; (of skin) graft

**Transport** m ⟨-(e)s, -e⟩ transport; **transportieren** vt transport

**Transvestit** m ⟨-en, -en⟩ transvestite

**trat** imperf → **treten**

**Traube** f ⟨-, -n⟩ grape; bunch of grapes; **Traubensaft** m grape juice; **Traubenzucker** m glucose

**trauen** 1. vi jdm / einer Sache ~ trust sb/sth 2. vr dare 3. vt marry; **sich ~ lassen** get married

**Trauer** f ⟨-⟩ sorrow; (for deceased person) mourning

**Traum** m ⟨-(e)s, Träume⟩ dream; **träumen** vt, vi dream (von of, about); **traumhaft** adj dreamlike; fig wonderful

**traurig** adj sad (über + acc about)

**Trauschein** m marriage certificate; **Trauung** f wedding ceremony; **Trauzeuge** m, **Trauzeugin** f witness (at wedding ceremony); ≈ best man / maid of honour

**Travellerscheck** m traveller's cheque

**treffen** ⟨traf, getroffen⟩ 1. vr meet 2. vt, vi hit; (remark) hurt; (friend etc) meet; (decision) make; (measures) take; **Treffen** nt ⟨-s, -⟩ meeting; **Treffer** m ⟨-s, -⟩ goal; **Treffpunkt** m meeting place

**treiben** ⟨trieb, getrieben⟩ 1. vt drive; (sport) do 2. vi (on water) drift; (plant) sprout; (tea, coffee) be diuretic; **Treiber** m ⟨-s, -⟩ IT driver; **Treibhaus** nt greenhouse; **Treibstoff** m fuel

**trennen** 1. vt separate; (split into parts) divide 2. vr separate; **sich von jdm ~** leave sb; **sich von etw ~** part with sth; **Trennung** f separation

**Treppe** f ⟨-, -n⟩ stairs pl; (outside) steps pl

**Tresen** m ⟨-s, -⟩ bar; (in shop) counter

**Tresor** m ⟨-s, -e⟩ safe

**Tretboot** nt pedal boat; **treten** ⟨trat, getreten⟩ 1. vi step 2. vt kick

**treu** adj (to partner) faithful; (customer, fan) loyal; **Treue** f ⟨-⟩ (in marriage) faithfulness; (of customer, fan) loyalty

**Triathlon** m ⟨-s, -s⟩ triathlon

**Tribüne** f ⟨-, -n⟩ stand; (for speaker) platform

**Trick** m ⟨-s, -e or -s⟩ trick; **Trickfilm** m cartoon

**trieb** imperf → **treiben**

**Trieb** m ⟨-(e)s, -e⟩ urge; (instinct) drive; (on tree etc) shoot; **Triebwerk** nt engine

**Trikot** nt ⟨-s, -s⟩ shirt, jersey

**trinkbar** adj drinkable; **trinken** ⟨trank, getrunken⟩ vt, vi drink; **einen ~ gehen** go out for a drink; **Trinkgeld** nt tip; **Trinkhalm** m (drinking) straw; **Trinkwasser** nt drinking water

**Trio** nt ⟨-s, -s⟩ trio

**Tritt** m ⟨-(e)s, -e⟩ step; kick

**Triumph** m ⟨-(e)s, -e⟩ triumph; **triumphieren** vi triumph (über + acc over)

**trivial** adj trivial

**trocken** adj dry; **Trockenheit** f dryness; **trockenlegen** vt (baby) change; **trocknen** vt, vi dry; **Trockner** m ⟨-s, -⟩ dryer

**Trödel** m ⟨-s⟩ fam junk; **Trödelmarkt** m flea market

**trödeln** vi fam dawdle

**Trommel** f ⟨-, -n⟩ drum; **Trommelfell** nt eardrum; **trommeln** vt, vi drum

**Trompete** f ⟨-, -n⟩ trumpet

**Tropen** pl tropics pl

**Tropf** m ⟨-(e)s, -e⟩ MED drip; **am ~ hängen** be on a drip; **tröpfeln** vi drip; **es tröpfelt** it's drizzling; **tropfen** vt, vi drip; **Tropfen** m ⟨-s, -⟩ drop;

**tropfenweise** adv drop by drop; **tropfnass** adj dripping wet; **Tropfsteinhöhle** f stalactite cave

**tropisch** adj tropical

**Trost** m ⟨-es⟩ consolation, comfort; **trösten** vt console, comfort; **trostlos** adj bleak; (conditions) wretched; **Trostpreis** m consolation prize

**trotz** prep + gen or dat in spite of; **Trotz** m ⟨-es⟩ defiance; **trotzdem 1.** adv nevertheless **2.** conj although; **trotzig** adj defiant

**trüb** adj dull; (liquid, glass) cloudy; fig gloomy

**Trüffel** f ⟨-, -n⟩ truffle

**trug** imperf → **tragen**

**trügerisch** adj deceptive

**Truhe** f ⟨-, -n⟩ chest

**Trumpf** m ⟨-(e)s, Trümpfe⟩ trump

**Trunkenheit** f intoxication; **~ am Steuer** drink driving (Brit), drunk driving (US)

**Truthahn** m turkey

**Tscheche** m ⟨-n, -n⟩, **Tschechin** f Czech; **Tschechien** nt ⟨-s⟩ Czech Republic; **tschechisch** adj Czech; **Tschechisch** nt Czech

**Tschetschenien** nt ⟨-s⟩ Chechnya

**tschüs(s)** interj bye

**T-Shirt** nt ⟨-s, -s⟩ T-shirt

**Tube** f ⟨-, -n⟩ tube

**Tuberkulose** f ⟨-, -n⟩ tuberculosis, TB

**Tuch** nt ⟨-(e)s, Tücher⟩ cloth; (for neck) scarf; (for head) headscarf

**Tüchtig** adj competent; (hard-working) efficient

**Tugend** f ⟨-, -en⟩ virtue; **tugendhaft** adj virtuous

**Tulpe** f ⟨-, -n⟩ tulip

**Tumor** m ⟨-s, -en⟩ tumour

**tun** ⟨tat, getan⟩ **1.** vt do; (sth somewhere) put; **was tust du da?** what are you doing?; **das tut man nicht** you shouldn't do that; **jdm etw ~** (harm) do sth to sb **2.** vi act; **so ~, als ob** act as if **3.** vr impers **es tut sich etwas / viel** something/a lot is happening

**Tuner** m ⟨-s, -⟩ tuner

**Tunesien** nt ⟨-s⟩ Tunisia

**Tunfisch** m tuna

**Tunnel** m ⟨-s, -s or -⟩ tunnel

**Tunte** f ⟨-, -n⟩ pej fam fairy

**tupfen** vt, vi dab; (with colour) dot; **Tupfen** m ⟨-s, -⟩ dot

**Tür** f ⟨-, -en⟩ door; **vor / an der ~** at the door; **an die ~ gehen** answer the door

**Türke** m ⟨-n, -n⟩ Turk; **Türkei** f ⟨-⟩ **die ~** Turkey; **Türkin** f Turk

**Türkis** m ⟨-es, -e⟩ turquoise

**türkisch** adj Turkish; **Türkisch** nt Turkish

**Turm** m ⟨-(e)s, Türme⟩ tower; (pointed church tower) steeple; (in chess) rook, castle

**turnen** vi do gymnastics; **Turnen** nt ⟨-s⟩ gymnastics sg, physical education, PE; **Turner(in)** m(f) gymnast; **Turnhalle** f gym(nasium); **Turnhose** f gym shorts pl

**Turnier** nt ⟨-s, -e⟩ tournament

**Turnschuh** m gym shoe, sneaker (US)

**Türschild** nt doorplate; **Türschloss** nt lock

**tuscheln** vt, vi whisper

**Tussi** f ⟨-, -s⟩ pej fam chick

**Tüte** f ⟨-, -n⟩ bag

**TÜV** m ⟨-s, -s⟩ acr = **Technischer Überwachungsverein**; ≈ MOT (Brit), vehicle inspection (US)

**Tweed** m ⟨-s, -s⟩ tweed

**Typ** m ⟨-s, -en⟩ type; (car) model; (man) guy, bloke

**Typhus** m ⟨-⟩ typhoid

**typisch** adj typical (für of); **ein ~er Fehler** a common mistake; **~ Marcus!** that's just like Marcus; **~ amerikanisch!** that's so American

# U

**u. a.** *abbr* = **und andere(s)** and others; = **unter anderem, unter anderen** among other things

**u. A. w. g.** *abbr* = **um Antwort wird gebeten** RSVP

**U-Bahn** *f* underground (*Brit*), subway (*US*)

**übel** *adj* bad; (*morally*) wicked; **mir ist ~** I feel sick; **diese Bemerkung hat er mir ~ genommen** he took offence at my remark; **Übelkeit** *f* nausea

**üben** *vt, vi* practise

**über** *prep + dat or acc* (*throw, jump*) over; (*with position also*) above; (*from one side to the other*) across; (*farther up from*) above; (*route*) via; (*concerning*) about; (*quantity*) over, more than; **~ das Wochenende** over the weekend

**überall** *adv* everywhere

**überbacken** *adj* (*mit Käse*) **~** au gratin; **überbelichten** *vt* PHOT overexpose; **überbieten** *irr vt* outbid; (*be better than*) surpass; (*record*) break

**Überbleibsel** *nt* ⟨-s, -⟩ remnant

**Überblick** *m* overview; *fig* survey; (*understanding*) grasp (*über + acc of*)

**überbuchen** *vt* overbook; **Überbuchung** *f* overbooking

**übereinander** *adv* on top of each other; (*talk etc*) about each other

**übereinstimmen** *vi* agree (*mit* with)

**überfahren** *irr vt* AUTO run over; **Überfahrt** *f* crossing

**Überfall** *m* robbery; MIL raid; (*on sb*) assault; **überfallen** *irr vt* attack; (*bank*) raid

**überfällig** *adj* overdue

**überfliegen** *irr vt* fly over; (*book*) skim through

**überflüssig** *adj* superfluous

**überfordern** *vt* demand too much of; (*strength etc*) overtax; **da bin ich überfordert** you've got me there

**Überführung** *f* flyover (*Brit*), overpass (*US*)

**überfüllt** *adj* overcrowded

**Übergabe** *f* handover

**Übergang** *m* crossing; (*change, passing*) transition; **Übergangslösung** *f* temporary solution, stopgap

**übergeben** *irr vt* **1.** *vt* hand over **2.** *vr* be sick, vomit

**Übergepäck** *nt* excess baggage

**Übergewicht** *nt* excess weight; (**10 Kilo**) **~ haben** be (10 kilos) overweight

**überglücklich** *adj* overjoyed; *fam* over the moon

**überhaupt** *adv* at all; in general

**überheblich** *adj* arrogant

**überholen** *vt* overtake; TECH overhaul; **Überholspur** *f* overtaking (*Brit*) *or* passing (*US*) lane; **überholt** *adj* outdated

**überhören** *vt* miss, not catch; (*deliberately*) ignore; **überladen** *irr vt* overload **2.** *adj fig* cluttered; **überlassen** *irr vt jdm etw ~* leave sth to sb; **überlaufen** *irr vi* (*liquid*) overflow

**überleben** *vt, vi* survive; **Überlebende(r)** *mf* survivor

**überlegen 1.** *vt* consider; **sich** *dat* **etw ~** think about sth; **er hat es sich** *dat* **anders überlegt** he's changed his mind **2.** *adj* superior (*dat* to); **Überlegung** *f* consideration

**übermäßig** *adj* excessive

**übermorgen** *adv* the day after tomorrow

**übernächste(r, s)** *adj ~* **Woche** the week after next

**übernachten** *vi* spend the night (*bei jdm* at sb's place); **Übernachtung** *f* overnight stay; **~ mit Frühstück** bed and breakfast

**übernehmen** *irr vt* **1.** take on; (*post, business*) take over **2.** *vr* take on too much

**überprüfen** *vt* check; **Über-**

**prüfung** *f* check; (*action*) checking

**überqueren** *vt* cross

**überraschen** *vt* surprise; **Überraschung** *f* surprise

**überreden** *vt* persuade; **er hat mich überredet** he talked me into it

**überreichen** *vt* hand over

**überschätzen** *vt* overestimate; **überschlagen** *irr* **1.** *vt* estimate **2.** *vr* somersault; (*car*) overturn; (*voice*) crack; **überschneiden** *irr vr* (*lines etc*) intersect; (*dates*) clash

**Überschrift** *f* heading

**Überschwemmung** *f* flood

**übersehen** *irr vt* look (out) over; (*ignore*) overlook

**übersetzen** *vt* translate (*aus* from, *in* + *acc* into); **Übersetzer(in)** *m(f)* ⟨-s, -⟩ translator; **Übersetzung** *f* translation

**Übersicht** *f* overall view; (*résumé*) survey; **übersichtlich** *adj* clear

**überstehen** *irr vt* get over

**Überstunden** *pl* overtime *sg*

**überstürzt** *adj* hasty

**übertragbar** *adj* transferable; MED infectious; **übertragen** *irr* **1.** *vt* transfer (*auf* + *acc* to); RADIO broadcast; (*disease*) transmit **2.** *vr* spread (*auf* + *acc* to) **3.** *adj* figurative; **Übertragung** *f* RADIO broadcast; (*of data*) transmission

**übertreffen** *irr vt* surpass

**übertreiben** *irr vt, vi* exaggerate, overdo; **Übertreibung** *f* exaggeration; **übertrieben** *adj* exaggerated, overdone

**überwachen** *vt* supervise; (*suspect*) keep under surveillance

**überwand** *imperf* → **überwinden**

**überweisen** *irr vt* transfer; (*patient*) refer (*an + acc* to); **Überweisung** *f* transfer; (*of patient*) referral

**überwiegend** *adv* mainly

**überwinden** ⟨überwand, überwunden⟩ **1.** *vt* overcome **2.** *vr* make an effort, force oneself; **überwunden** *pp* → **überwinden**

**überzeugen** *vt* convince; **Überzeugung** *f* conviction

**überziehen** *irr vt* cover; (*jacket etc*) put on; (*account*) overdraw; **die Betten frisch ~** change the sheets

**üblich** *adj* usual

**übrig** *adj* remaining; **ist noch Saft ~?** is there any juice left?; **~ bleiben** be left (over); **die Übrigen** *pl* the rest *pl*; **im Übrigen** besides; **übrigens** *adv* besides; (*incidentally*) by the way; **übrighaben** *irr vi* **für jdn etwas ~** *fam* have a soft spot for sb

**Übung** *f* practice; (*set of movements, task etc*) exercise

**Ufer** *nt* ⟨-s, -⟩ (*of river*) bank; (*of sea, lake*) shore; **am ~** on the bank / shore

**Uhr** *f* ⟨-, -en⟩ clock; watch; **wie viel ~ ist es?** what time is it?; **1 ~** 1 o'clock; **20 ~** 8 o'clock, 8 pm; **Uhrzeit** *f* time (of day)

**Ukraine** *f* ⟨-⟩ **die ~** the Ukraine

**UKW** *abbr* → **Ultrakurzwelle** VHF

**Ulme** *f* ⟨-, -n⟩ elm

**Ultrakurzwelle** *f* very high frequency; **Ultraschallaufnahme** *f* MED scan

**um 1.** *prep + acc* (*space*) (a)round; (*time*) at; **~ etw kämpfen** fight for sth **2.** *conj* (in order) to; **zu klug, ~ zu ...** too clever to ... **3.** *adv* (*approximately*) about; **die Ferien sind ~** the holidays are over; **die Zeit ist ~** time's up; → **umso**

**umarmen** *vt* embrace

**Umbau** *m* rebuilding; (*into sth*) conversion (*zu* into); **umbauen** *vt* rebuild; (*into sth*) convert (*zu* into)

**umblättern** *vi, vt* turn over

**umbringen** *irr vt* kill

**umbuchen** *vi* change one's reservation / flight

**umdrehen** *vt, vr* turn (round); (*retrace steps*) turn back; **Umdrehung** *f* turn; PHYS, AUTO revolution

**umfahren** *irr vt* knock down

**umfallen** *irr vi* fall over

**Umfang** *m* extent; (*of book*) size; (*of voice, instrument*) range; MATH circumference;

**umfangreich** *adj* extensive

**Umfrage** *f* survey

**Umgang** *m* company; (*with sb*) dealings *pl*; **umgänglich** *adj* sociable; **Umgangssprache** *f* colloquial language, slang

**Umgebung** *f* surroundings *pl*; (*social*) environment; (*friends, colleagues etc*) people around one

**umgehen 1.** *irr vi* go round; **~ (können) mit** (know how to) handle **2.** *irr vt* avoid; (*problems*) get round; **Umgehungsstraße** *f* bypass

**umgekehrt 1.** *adj* reverse; (*contrary*) opposite **2.** *adv* the other way round; **und ~** and vice versa

**umhören** *vr* ask around; **umkehren 1.** *vi* turn back **2.** *vt* reverse; **umkippen 1.** *vt* tip over **2.** *vi* overturn; (*fig* change one's mind; *fam* (*faint*) pass out

**Umkleidekabine** *f* changing cubicle (*Brit*), dressing room (*US*); **Umkleideraum** *m* changing room

**umleiten** *vt* divert; **Umleitung** *f* diversion

**umrechnen** *vt* convert (*in + acc* into); **Umrechnung** *f* conversion; **Umrechnungskurs** *m* rate of exchange

**Umriss** *m* outline

**umrühren** *vi, vt* stir

**ums** *contr* = **um das**

**Umsatz** *m* turnover

**umschalten** *vi* turn over

**Umschlag** *m* cover; (*of book*) jacket; MED compress; (*of letter*) envelope

**Umschulung** *f* retraining

**umsehen** *irr vr* look around; (*search*) look out (*nach* for)

**umso** *adv* all the; **~ mehr** all the more; **~ besser** so much the better

**umsonst** *adv* in vain; (*free*) for nothing

**Umstand** *m* circumstance; **Umstände** *pl* fine fuss; **in anderen Umständen sein** be pregnant; **jdm Umstände machen** cause sb a lot of trouble; **unter diesen / keinen Umständen** under these / no circumstances; **unter Umständen** possibly; **umständlich** *adj* (*method*) complicated; (*way of expressing oneself*) long-winded; (*person*) ponderous

**umsteigen** *irr vi* change (trains / buses)

**umstellen 1.** *vt* (*move*) change round **2.** *vr* adapt (*auf + acc* to); **Umstellung** *f* change; (*adapting*) adjustment

**Umtausch** *m* exchange; **umtauschen** *vt* exchange; (*currency*) change

**Umweg** *m* detour

**Umwelt** *f* environment; **Umweltbelastung** *f* ecological damage; **Umweltschutz** *m* environmental protection;

**Umweltschützer(in)** *m(f)*
⟨-s, -⟩ environmentalist; **Umweltverschmutzung** *f* pollution; **umweltverträglich** *adj* environment-friendly

**umwerfen** *irr vt* knock over; *fig (change)* upset; *fig fam* flabbergast

**umziehen** *irr* **1.** *vt, vr* change **2.** *vi* move (house); **Umzug** *m* procession; *(to new house)* move

**unabhängig** *adj* independent; **Unabhängigkeitstag** *m* Independence Day, Fourth of July (*US*)

**unabsichtlich** *adv* unintentionally

**unangenehm** *adj* unpleasant; **Unannehmlichkeit** *f* inconvenience; **~en** *pl* trouble *sg*

**unanständig** *adj* indecent; **unappetitlich** *adj (food)* unappetizing; *(repulsive)* off-putting; **unbeabsichtigt** *adj* unintentional; **unbedeutend** *adj* insignificant, unimportant; *(error)* slight

**unbedingt 1.** *adj* unconditional **2.** *adv* absolutely

**unbefriedigend** *adj* unsatisfactory; **unbegrenzt** *adj* unlimited; **unbekannt** *adj* unknown; **unbeliebt** *adj* unpopular; **unbemerkt** *adj* unnoticed; **unbequem** *adj (chair, person)* uncomfortable; **unbeständig** *adj (weather)* unsettled; *(situa-*

*tion)* unstable; *(person)* unreliable; **unbestimmt** *adj* indefinite; **unbewusst** *adj* unconscious; **unbezahlt** *adj* unpaid; **unbrauchbar** *adj* useless

**und** *conj* and; **~ so weiter** and so on; **na ~?** so what?

**undankbar** *adj (person)* ungrateful; *(task)* thankless; **undenkbar** *adj* inconceivable; **undeutlich** *adj* indistinct; **undicht** *adj* leaky; **uneben** *adj* uneven; **unecht** *adj (jewellery etc)* fake; **unehelich** *adj (child)* illegitimate; **unendlich** *adj* endless; MATH infinite; **unentbehrlich** *adj* indispensable; **unentgeltlich** *adj* free (of charge)

**unentschieden** *adj* undecided; **~ enden** SPORT end in a draw

**unerfreulich** *adj* unpleasant; **unerlässlich** *adj* indispensable; **unerträglich** *adj* unbearable; **unerwartet** *adj* unexpected; **unfähig** *adj* incompetent; **~ sein, etw zu tun** be incapable of doing sth; **unfair** *adj* unfair

**Unfall** *m* accident; **Unfallstation** *f* casualty ward; **Unfallstelle** *f* scene of the accident; **Unfallversicherung** *f* accident insurance

**unfreundlich** *adj* unfriendly

**Ungarn** *nt* ⟨-s⟩ Hungary

**Ungeduld** *f* impatience; **un-**

**geduldig** *adj* impatient
**ungeeignet** *adj* unsuitable
**ungefähr 1.** *adj* approximate
**2.** *adv* approximately; **~ 10
Kilometer** about 10 kilometres; **wann~?** about what
time?; **wo~?** whereabouts?
**ungefährlich** *adj* harmless;
(*involving no danger*) safe
**ungeheuer 1.** *adj* huge **2.** *adv
fam* enormously; **Ungeheu-
er** *nt* ⟨-s, -⟩ monster
**ungehorsam** *adj* disobedient
(*gegenüber* to); **ungemüt-
lich** *adj* unpleasant; (*person*) disagreeable; **ungenießbar** *adj* inedible; un-
drinkable; **ungenügend**
*adj* unsatisfactory; (*mark
in school*) ≈ F; **ungepflegt**
*adj* (*garden*) untended; (*appearance*) unkempt; (*hands*)
neglected; **ungerade** *adj*
odd
**ungerecht** *adj* unjust; **unge-
rechtfertigt** *adj* unjustified;
**Ungerechtigkeit** *f* injustice,
unfairness
**ungern** *adv* reluctantly; **ungeschickt** *adj* clumsy; **un-
geschminkt** *adj* without
make-up; **ungesund** *adj* unhealthy; **ungewiss** *adj* uncertain; **ungewöhnlich** *adj*
unusual
**Ungeziefer** *nt* ⟨-s⟩ vermin *pl*
**ungezwungen** *adj* relaxed
**unglaublich** *adj* incredible
**Unglück** *nt* ⟨-(e)s, -e⟩ misfortune; (*in game, career etc*)

bad luck; (*train or plane
crash*) disaster; **das bringt
~** that's unlucky; **unglücklich** *adj* unhappy; (*unsuccessful*) unlucky; (*unfavour-
able*) unfortunate; **unglück-
licherweise** *adv* unfortunately
**ungültig** *adj* invalid
**ungünstig** *adj* inconvenient
**unheilbar** *adj* incurable; **~
krank sein** be terminally ill
**unheimlich 1.** *adj* eerie **2.** *adv
fam* incredibly
**unhöflich** *adj* impolite
**uni** *adj* plain
**Uni** *f* ⟨-, -s⟩ uni
**Uniform** *f* ⟨-, -en⟩ uniform
**Universität** *f* university
**Unkenntnis** *f* ignorance
**unklar** *adj* unclear
**Unkosten** *pl* expenses *pl*
**Unkraut** *nt* weeds *pl*
**unlogisch** *adj* illogical
**unmissverständlich** *adj* un-
ambiguous
**unmittelbar** *adj* immediate; **~
darauf** immediately afterwards
**unmöbliert** *adj* unfurnished
**unmöglich** *adj* impossible
**unnötig** *adj* unnecessary
**UNO** *f* ⟨-⟩ *acr* = **United Nations Organization**; UN
**unordentlich** *adj* untidy; **Unordnung** *f* disorder
**unpassend** *adj* inappropriate; (*time*) inconvenient; **un-
persönlich** *adj* impersonal;
**unpraktisch** *adj* impractical

**Unrecht** *nt* wrong; **zu ~** wrongly; **im ~ sein** be wrong; **unrecht** *adj* wrong; **~ haben** be wrong

**unregelmäßig** *adj* irregular; **unreif** *adj* unripe; **unruhig** *adj* restless; **~ schlafen** have a bad night

**uns** *pron acc, dat → wir;* us, (to) us; **~ (selbst)** *(reflexive)* ourselves; **sehen Sie ~?** can you see us?; **er schickte es ~** he sent it to us; **lasst ~ in Ruhe** leave us alone; **ein Freund von ~** a friend of ours; **wir haben ~ hingesetzt** we sat down; **wir haben ~ amüsiert** we enjoyed ourselves; **wir mögen ~** we like each other

**unscharf** *adj* PHOT blurred, out of focus

**unschlüssig** *adj* undecided

**unschuldig** *adj* innocent

**unser** *pron* our; **unsere(r, s)** *pron* ours; **unseretwegen** *adv* because of us; *(to please us)* for our sake

**unseriös** *adj* dubious; **unsicher** *adj* uncertain; *(lacking confidence)* insecure

**Unsinn** *m* nonsense

**unsterblich** *adj* immortal; **~ verliebt** madly in love

**unsympathisch** *adj* unpleasant; **er ist mir ~** I don't like him

**unten** *adv* below; *(in house)* downstairs; *(at lower end)* at the bottom; **nach ~** down;

**unter** *prep + acc or dat* under, below; *(people)* among; *(time)* during

**Unterarm** *m* forearm

**Unterbewusstsein** *nt* subconscious

**unterbrechen** *irr vt* interrupt; **Unterbrechung** *f* interruption; **ohne ~** nonstop

**unterdrücken** *vt* suppress; *(people)* oppress

**untere(r, s)** *adj* lower

**untereinander** *adv (in space)* one below the other; *(reciprocally)* each other; among themselves / yourselves / ourselves

**Unterführung** *f* underpass

**untergehen** *irr vi* go down; *(sun also)* set; *(nation)* perish; *(world)* come to an end; *(by noise)* be drowned out

**Untergeschoss** *nt* basement; **Untergewicht** *nt* **(10 Kilo) ~ haben** be (10 kilos) underweight; **Untergrund** *m* foundation; POL underground; **Untergrundbahn** *f* underground (Brit), subway (US)

**unterhalb** *adv, prep + gen* below; **~ von** below

**Unterhalt** *m* maintenance; **unterhalten** *irr* **1.** *vt* maintain; *(audience, guest)* entertain **2.** *vr* talk; *(have a good time)* enjoy oneself; **Unterhaltung** *f* entertainment; talk, conversation

**Unterhemd** *nt* vest (Brit), undershirt (US); **Unterhose** *f* underpants *pl*; (*for women*) briefs *pl*

**unterirdisch** *adj* underground

**Unterkiefer** *m* lower jaw

**Unterkunft** *f* ⟨-, -künfte⟩ accommodation

**Unterlage** *f* document; (*for resting on when writing*) pad

**unterlassen** *irr vt* **es ~, etw zu tun** fail to do sth; (*hold back*) refrain from doing sth

**unterlegen** *adj* inferior (*dat* to); (*beaten*) defeated

**Unterleib** *m* abdomen

**Unterlippe** *f* lower lip

**Untermiete** *f* **zur ~ wohnen** be a subtenant; **Untermieter(in)** *m(f)* subtenant

**unternehmen** *irr vt* (*trip*) go on; (*attempt*) make; **etwas ~** do something (*gegen* about); **Unternehmen** *nt* ⟨-s, -⟩ undertaking; (*attempt*) COMM company; **Unternehmensberater(in)** *m(f)* ⟨-s, -⟩ management consultant; **Unternehmer(in)** *m(f)* ⟨-s, -⟩ entrepreneur

**Unterricht** *m* ⟨-(e)s, -e⟩ lessons *pl*; **unterrichten** *vt* teach

**unterschätzen** *vt* underestimate

**unterscheiden** *irr* **1.** *vt* distinguish (*von* from, *zwischen + dat* between) **2.** *vr* differ (*von* from)

**Unterschenkel** *m* lower leg

**Unterschied** *m* ⟨-(e)s, -e⟩ difference; **im ~ zu dir** unlike you; **unterschiedlich** *adj* different

**unterschreiben** *irr vt* sign; **Unterschrift** *f* signature

**Untersetzer** *m* ⟨-s, -⟩ tablemat; (*for glass*) coaster

**unterste(r, s)** *adj* lowest, bottom

**unterstellen** *vr* take shelter

**unterstreichen** *irr vt a. fig* underline

**unterstützen** *vt* support; **Unterstützung** *f* support

**untersuchen** *vt* MED examine; (*police*) investigate; **Untersuchung** *f* examination; (*by police*) investigation

**Untertasse** *f* saucer; **Unterteil** *nt* lower part, bottom; **Untertitel** *m* subtitle

**untervermieten** *vt* sublet

**Unterwäsche** *f* underwear

**unterwegs** *adv* on the way

**unterzeichnen** *vt* sign

**untreu** *adj* unfaithful; **unüberlegt 1.** *adj* ill-considered **2.** *adv* without thinking; **unüblich** *adj* unusual; **unverantwortlich** *adj* irresponsible

**unverbindlich 1.** *adj* not binding; (*reply*) noncommittal **2.** *adv* COMM without obligation

**unverbleit** *adj* unleaded; **unverheiratet** *adj* unmarried, single; **unvermeidlich** *adj* unavoidable; **unvernünftig**

*adj* silly; **unverschämt** *adj* impudent; **unverständlich** *adj* incomprehensible; **unverträglich** *adj* (*food*) indigestible; **unverzüglich** *adj* immediate; **unvollständig** *adj* incomplete; **unvorsichtig** *adj* careless

**unwahrscheinlich 1.** *adj* improbable, unlikely **2.** *adv fam* incredibly

**Unwetter** *nt* thunderstorm

**unwichtig** *adj* unimportant

**unwiderstehlich** *adj* irresistible

**unwillkürlich 1.** *adj* involuntary **2.** *adv* instinctively

**unwohl** *adj* unwell, ill

**unzählig** *adj* innumerable, countless

**unzerbrechlich** *adj* unbreakable; **unzertrennlich** *adj* inseparable; **unzufrieden** *adj* dissatisfied; **unzugänglich** *adj* inaccessible; **unzumutbar** *adj* unacceptable; **unzutreffend** *adj* inapplicable; (*wrong*) incorrect; **unzuverlässig** *adj* unreliable

**Update** *nt* ⟨-s, -s⟩ IT update

**üppig** *adj* (*meal*) lavish; (*vegetation*) lush

**uralt** *adj* ancient, very old

**Uran** *nt* ⟨-s⟩ uranium

**Uranus** *m* ⟨-⟩ Uranus

**Uraufführung** *f* premiere

**Urenkel** *m* great-grandson; **Urenkelin** *f* great-granddaughter; **Urgroßeltern** *pl*

great-grandparents *pl*; **Urgroßmutter** *f* great-grandmother; **Urgroßvater** *m* great-grandfather

**Urheber(in)** *m(f)* ⟨-s, -⟩ originator; (*writer*) author

**Urin** *m* ⟨-s, -e⟩ urine; **Urinprobe** *f* urine specimen

**Urkunde** *f* ⟨-, -n⟩ document

**Urlaub** *m* ⟨-(e)s, -e⟩ holiday (*Brit*), vacation (*US*); **im ~** on holiday (*Brit*), on vacation (*US*); **in ~ fahren** go on holiday (*Brit*) (*or* vacation (*US*)); **Urlauber(in)** *m(f)* ⟨-s, -⟩ holiday-maker (*Brit*), vacationer (*US*); **Urlaubsort** *m* holiday resort; **urlaubsreif** *adj* ready for a holiday (*Brit*) (*or* vacation (*US*)); **Urlaubszeit** *f* holiday season (*Brit*), vacation period (*US*)

**Urologe** *m*, **Urologin** *f* urologist

**Ursache** *f* cause (*für* of); **keine ~!** not at all; (*in reply to apology*) that's all right

**Ursprung** *m* origin; **ursprünglich 1.** *adj* original **2.** *adv* originally

**Urteil** *nt* ⟨-s, -e⟩ opinion; LAW verdict; (*penalty*) sentence; **urteilen** *vi* judge

**Uruguay** *nt* ⟨-⟩ Uruguay

**Urwald** *m* jungle

**USA** *nt* USA *sg*

**User(in)** *m(f)* ⟨-s, -⟩ IT user

**usw.** *abbr* = **und so weiter** etc

# V

**vage** *adj* vague

**Vagina** *f* ‹-, Vaginen› vagina

**Valentinstag** *m* St Valentine's Day

**Vandalismus** *m* vandalism

**Vanille** *f* ‹-› vanilla

**variieren** *vt, vi* vary

**Vase** *f* ‹-, -n› vase

**Vater** *m* ‹-s, -s› father; **väterlich** *adj* paternal; **Vaterschaft** *f* fatherhood; LAW paternity; **Vatertag** *m* Father's Day; **Vaterunser** *nt* **das ~ (beten)** (to say) the Lord's Prayer

**V-Ausschnitt** *m* V-neck

**v. Chr.** *abbr* = **vor Christus** BC

**Veganer(in)** *m(f)* ‹-s, -/-› vegan; **Vegetarier(in)** *m(f)* ‹-s, -› vegetarian; **vegetarisch** *adj* vegetarian

**Veilchen** *nt* violet

**Velo** *nt* ‹-s, -s› (*Swiss*) bicycle

**Vene** *f* ‹-, -n› vein

**Venedig** *nt* ‹-s› Venice

**Venezuela** *nt* ‹-s› Venezuela

**Ventil** *nt* ‹-s, -e› valve

**Ventilator** *m* ventilator

**Venus** *f* ‹-› Venus

**Venusmuschel** *f* clam

**verabreden 1.** *vt* arrange **2.** *vr* arrange to meet (*mit jdm* sb); **ich bin schon verabredet** I'm already meeting someone; **Verabredung** *f* arrangement; (*meeting*) appointment; (*with friend*) date

**verabschieden 1.** *vt* say goodbye to; (*law*) pass **2.** *vr* say goodbye

**verachten** *vt* despise; **verächtlich** *adj* contemptuous; (*deserving contempt*) contemptible; **Verachtung** *f* contempt

**verallgemeinern** *vt* generalize

**Veranda** *f* ‹-, Veranden› veranda, porch (*US*)

**veränderlich** *adj* changeable; **verändern** *vt, vr* change; **Veränderung** *f* change

**veranlassen** *vt* cause

**veranstalten** *vt* organize; **Veranstalter(in)** *m(f)* ‹-s, -› organizer; **Veranstaltung** *f* event; **Veranstaltungsort** *m* venue

**verantworten 1.** *vt* take responsibility for **2.** *vr* **sich für etw~** answer for sth; **verantwortlich** *adj* responsible (*für* for); **Verantwortung** *f* responsibility (*für* for)

**verärgern** *vt* annoy

**verarschen** *vt fam* take the piss out of (*Brit*), make a sucker out of (*US*)

**Verb** *nt* ‹-s, -en› verb

**Verband** *m* MED bandage; (*or-*

*ganization)* association; **Verband(s)kasten** *m* first--aid box; **Verband(s)zeug** *nt* dressing material

**verbergen** *irr vt, vr* hide (*vor* + *dat* from)

**verbessern 1.** *vt* improve; (*error, person speaking)* correct **2.** *vr* improve; (*when speaking)* correct oneself; **Verbesserung** *f* improvement; (*of error)* correction

**verbiegen** *irr vt, vr* bend

**verbieten** *irr vt* forbid; *jdm ~, etw zu tun* forbid sb to do sth

**verbinden** *irr* **1.** *vt* connect; (*do or have at the same time)* combine; MED bandage; **können Sie mich mit ... ?** TEL can you put me through to ...?; **ich verbinde** TEL I'm putting you through **2.** *vr* CHEM combine; **Verbindung** *f* connection

**verbleit** *adj* leaded

**Verbot** *nt* ⟨-(e)s, -e⟩ ban (*für, von* on); **verboten** *adj* forbidden; **es ist ~** it's not allowed; **es ist ~, hier zu parken** you're not allowed to park here; **Rauchen ~** no smoking

**verbrannt** *adj* burnt

**Verbrauch** *m* ⟨-(e)s⟩ consumption; **verbrauchen** *vt* use up; **Verbraucher(in)** *m(f)* ⟨-s, -⟩ consumer

**Verbrechen** *nt* ⟨-s, -⟩ crime; **Verbrecher(in)** *m(f)* ⟨-s, -⟩

criminal

**verbreiten** *vt, vr* spread

**verbrennen** *irr vt* burn; **Verbrennung** *f* burning; (*in engine)* combustion

**verbringen** *irr vt* spend

**verbunden** *adj* **falsch ~** sorry, wrong number

**Verdacht** *m* ⟨-(e)s⟩ suspicion; **verdächtig** *adj* suspicious; **verdächtigen** *vt* suspect

**verdammt** *interj fam* damn

**verdanken** *vt* **jdm etw ~** owe sth to sb

**verdarb** *imperf* → **verderben**

**verdauen** *vt a. fig* digest; **Verdauung** *f* digestion

**Verdeck** *nt* ⟨-(e)s, -e⟩ top

**verderben** ⟨verdarb, verdorben⟩ **1.** *vt* spoil; (*damage)* ruin; (*morally)* corrupt; **ich habe mir den Magen verdorben** I've got an upset stomach **2.** *vi* (*food)* go off

**verdienen** *vt* earn; (*morally)* deserve; **Verdienst 1.** *m* ⟨-(e)s, -e⟩ earnings *pl* **2.** *nt* ⟨-(e)s, -e⟩ merit; (*contribution)* service (*um* to)

**verdoppeln** *vt* double

**verdorben 1.** *pp* → **verderben 2.** *adj* spoilt; (*damaged)* ruined; (*morally)* corrupt

**verdrehen** *vt* twist; (*eyes)* roll; *jdm den Kopf ~ fig* turn sb's head

**verdünnen** *vt* dilute

**verdunsten** *vi* evaporate

**verdursten** *vi* die of thirst

**verehren** *vt* admire; REL worship; **Verehrer(in)** *m(f)* ⟨-s, -⟩ admirer

**Verein** *m* ⟨-(e)s, -e⟩ association; (*for sport, hobby*) club; **vereinbaren** *vt* arrange; **Vereinbarung** *f* agreement, arrangement

**vereinigen** *vt* unite; **Vereinigtes Königreich** *nt* United Kingdom; **Vereinigte Staaten (von Amerika)** *pl* United States *sg* (of America); **Vereinigung** *f* union; (*organization*) association; **Vereinte Nationen** *pl* United Nations *pl*

**vereisen 1.** *vi* (*road*) freeze over; (*window*) ice up **2.** *vt* MED freeze

**verfahren irr 1.** *vi* proceed **2.** *vr* get lost; **Verfahren** *nt* ⟨-s, -⟩ procedure; TECH method; LAW proceedings *pl*

**verfallen** *irr vi* decline; (*ticket etc*) expire; **~ in** + *acc* lapse into; **Verfallsdatum** *nt* expiry (*Brit*) (*or* expiration (*US*)) date; (*of food*) best-before date

**verfärben** *vr* change colour; (*washing*) discolour

**Verfasser(in)** *m(f)* ⟨-s, -⟩ author, writer; **Verfassung** *f* condition; POL constitution

**verfaulen** *vi* rot

**verfehlen** *vt* miss

**Verfilmung** *f* film (*or* screen) version

**verfluchen** *vt* curse

**verfolgen** *vt* pursue; POL persecute

**verfügbar** *adj* available; **verfügen** *vi* **über etw** *acc* **~** have sth at one's disposal; **Verfügung** *f* order; **jdm zur ~ stehen** be at sb's disposal

**verführen** *vt* tempt; (*sexually*) seduce; **verführerisch** *adj* seductive

**vergangen** *adj* past; **~e Woche** last week; **Vergangenheit** *f* past

**Vergaser** *m* ⟨-s, -⟩ AUTO carburettor

**vergaß** *imperf* → **vergessen**

**vergeben** *irr vt* forgive (*jdm etw* sb for sth); **vergebens** *adv* in vain; **vergeblich 1.** *adv* in vain **2.** *adj* vain, futile

**vergehen irr 1.** *vi* pass **2.** *vr* **sich an jdm ~** indecently assault sb; **Vergehen** *nt* ⟨-s, -⟩ offence

**vergessen** ⟨vergaß, vergessen⟩ *vt* forget; **vergesslich** *adj* forgetful

**vergeuden** *vt* squander, waste

**vergewaltigen** *vt* rape; **Vergewaltigung** *f* rape

**vergewissern** *vr* make sure

**vergiften** *vt* poison; **Vergiftung** *f* poisoning

**Vergissmeinnicht** *nt* ⟨-(e)s, -e⟩ forget-me-not

**Vergleich** *m* ⟨-(e)s, -e⟩ comparison; LAW settlement; **im ~ zu** compared to (*or* with); **vergleichen** *irr vt* compare (*mit* to, with)

**Vergnügen** nt ⟨-s, -⟩ pleasure; *viel ~!* enjoy yourself; **vergnügt** adj cheerful; **Vergnügungspark** m amusement park

**vergriffen** adj (book) out of print; (product) out of stock

**vergrößern** vt enlarge; (in quantity) increase; (with lens) magnify; **Vergrößerung** f enlargement; (in quantity) increase; (with lens) magnification; **Vergrößerungsglas** nt magnifying glass

**verhaften** vt arrest

**verhalten** irr vr behave; **Verhalten** nt ⟨-s⟩ behaviour

**Verhältnis** nt relationship (zu with); MATH ratio; *~se* pl circumstances pl, conditions pl; *im ~ von 1 zu 2* in a ratio of 1 to 2; **verhältnismäßig 1.** adj relative **2.** adv relatively

**verhandeln** vi negotiate (über etw acc sth); **Verhandlung** f negotiation

**verheimlichen** vt keep secret (jdm from sb)

**verheiratet** adj married

**verhindern** vt prevent; *sie ist verhindert* she can't make it

**Verhör** nt ⟨-(e)s, -e⟩ interrogation; (in court) examination; **verhören 1.** vt interrogate; (in court) examine **2.** vr mishear

**verhungern** vi starve to death

**verhüten** vt prevent; **Verhütung** f prevention; (with pill, condom etc) contraception; **Verhütungsmittel** nt contraceptive

**verirren** vr get lost

**Verkauf** m sale; **verkaufen** vt sell; *zu ~* for sale; **Verkäufer(in)** m(f) seller; (professional) salesperson; (in shop) shop assistant (Brit), salesperson (US); **verkäuflich** adj for sale

**Verkehr** m ⟨-s, -e⟩ traffic; (sexual) intercourse; (general use) circulation; **verkehren** vi (bus etc) run; *~ mit* associate (or mix) with; **Verkehrsampel** f traffic lights pl; **Verkehrsamt** nt tourist information office; **Verkehrsfunk** m travel news sg; **Verkehrsinsel** f traffic island; **Verkehrsmeldung** f traffic report; **Verkehrsmittel** nt means sg of transport; *öffentliche ~* pl public transport sg; **Verkehrsschild** nt traffic sign; **Verkehrsunfall** m road accident; **Verkehrszeichen** nt traffic sign

**verkehrt** adj wrong; the wrong way round, inside out; *du machst es ~* you're doing it wrong

**verklagen** vt take to court

**verkleiden 1.** vt, vr dress up (als as) **2.** vr dress up (als as); (to avoid being recognized) disguise oneself; **Verkleidung** f fancy dress

**verkleinern** *vt* reduce; (*room, area etc*) make smaller; **verkommen 1.** *irr vi* deteriorate; (*person*) go downhill **2.** *adj* (*house etc*) dilapidated; (*morally*) depraved; **verkraften** *vt* cope with

**verkratzt** *adj* scratched

**verkühlen** *vr* catch a chill

**verkürzen** *vt* shorten

**Verlag** *m* ⟨-(e)s, -e⟩ publishing company

**verlangen 1.** *vt* demand; want; (*price*) ask; (*expect*) ask (*von* of); (*person*) ask for; (*passport etc*) ask to see; **~ Sie Herrn X** ask for Mr X **2.** *vi* **~ nach** ask for

**verlängern** *vt* extend; (*passport, permit*) renew; **Verlängerung** *f* extension; SPORT extra time; (*of passport, permit*) renewal; **Verlängerungsschnur** *f* extension cable; **Verlängerungswoche** *f* extra week

**verlassen 1.** *irr vt* leave **2.** *irr vr* rely (*auf* + *acc* on) **3.** *adj* desolate; (*person*) abandoned; **verlässlich** *adj* reliable

**Verlauf** *m* course; **verlaufen** *irr* **1.** *vi* (*path, border*) run (*entlang* along); (*in time*) pass; (*colours*) run **2.** *vr* get lost; (*crowd*) disperse

**verlegen 1.** *vt* move; (*lose*) mislay; (*book*) publish **2.** *adj* embarrassed; **Verlegenheit** *f* embarrassment; (*situ-*

*ation*) difficulty

**Verleih** *m* ⟨-(e)s, -e⟩ hire company (*Brit*), rental company (*US*); **verleihen** *irr vt* lend; (*commercially*) hire (out) (*Brit*), rent (out) (*US*); (*prize, medal*) award

**verleiten** *vt* **jdn dazu ~, etw zu tun** induce sb to do sth

**verlernen** *vt* forget

**verletzen** *vt* injure; *fig* hurt; **Verletzte(r)** *mf* injured person; **Verletzung** *f* injury; (*of law etc*) violation

**verlieben** *vr* fall in love (*in jdn* with sb); **verliebt** *adj* in love

**verlieren** ⟨verlor, verloren⟩ *vt, vi* lose

**verloben** *vr* get engaged (*mit* to); **Verlobte(r)** *mf* fiancé / fiancée; **Verlobung** *f* engagement

**verlor** *imperf* → **verlieren**

**verloren** *pp* → **verlieren**

**verlosen** *vt* raffle; **Verlosung** *f* raffle

**Verlust** *m* ⟨-(e)s, -e⟩ loss

**vermehren** *vt, vr* multiply; (*amount*) increase

**vermeiden** *irr vt* avoid

**vermeintlich** *adj* supposed

**vermieten** *vt* rent (out), let (out) (*Brit*); (*car*) hire (out) (*Brit*), rent (out) (*US*); **Vermieter(in)** *m(f)* landlord / landlady

**vermischen** *vt, vr* mix

**vermissen** *vt* miss; **vermisst** *adj* missing; **jdn als ~ mel-**

**den** report sb missing

**Vermögen** nt ⟨-s, -⟩ fortune

**vermuten** vt suppose; (sth bad) suspect; **vermutlich 1.** adj probable **2.** adv probably; **Vermutung** f supposition; (of sth bad) suspicion

**vernachlässigen** vt neglect

**vernichten** vt destroy; **vernichtend** adj fig crushing; (look) withering; (criticism) scathing

**Vernunft** f ⟨-, no pl⟩ reason; **vernünftig** adj sensible; (price) reasonable

**veröffentlichen** vt publish

**verordnen** vt MED prescribe; **Verordnung** f order; MED prescription

**verpachten** vt lease (out) (an + acc to)

**verpacken** vt pack; (in paper) wrap up

**Verpackung** f packaging

**verpassen** vt miss

**verpflegen** vt feed; **Verpflegung** f feeding; food; (in hotel) board

**verpflichten 1.** vt oblige; (employ) engage **2.** vr commit oneself (etw zu tun to doing sth)

**verprügeln** vt beat up

**verraten** irr **1.** vt betray; (secret) divulge; **aber nicht ~!** but don't tell anyone **2.** vr give oneself away

**verrechnen 1.** vt ~ **mit** set off against **2.** vr miscalculate; **Verrechnungsscheck** m

crossed cheque (Brit), check for deposit only (US)

**verregnet** adj rainy

**verreisen** vi go away (nach to); **sie ist (geschäftlich) verreist** she's away (on business); **verrenken** vt contort; MED dislocate; **sich dat den Knöchel ~** sprain (or twist) one's ankle; **verringern** vt reduce

**verrostet** adj rusty

**verrückt** adj mad, crazy; **es macht mich ~** it's driving me mad

**versagen** vi fail; **Versagen** nt ⟨-s⟩ failure; **Versager(in)** m(f) ⟨-s, -⟩ failure

**versalzen** irr vt put too much salt in/on

**versammeln** vt, vr assemble, gather; **Versammlung** f meeting

**Versand** m ⟨-(e)s⟩ dispatch; (in company) dispatch department; **Versandhaus** nt mail-order company

**versäumen** vt miss; (not do) neglect; **~, etw zu tun** fail to do sth

**verschätzen** vr miscalculate

**verschenken** vt give away; (chance) waste

**verschicken** vt send off

**verschieben** irr vt postpone, put off; (push) move

**verschieden** adj different; (several) various; **sie sind ~ groß** they are of different sizes; **Verschiedene** pl vari-

ous people / things pl; **Ver-
schiedenes** various things
pl

**verschimmelt** adj mouldy

**verschlafen** irr **1.** vt sleep
through; fig miss **2.** vi, vr
oversleep

**verschlechtern** vr deteriorate, get worse; **Verschlech-
terung** f deterioration

**verschließbar** adj lockable;
**verschließen** irr vt close;
(with key) lock

**verschlimmern 1.** vt make
worse **2.** vr get worse

**verschlossen** adj locked; fig
reserved

**verschlucken 1.** vt swallow **2.**
vr choke (an + dat on)

**Verschluss** m lock; (on dress)
fastener; PHOT shutter;
(bung) stopper

**verschmutzen** vt get dirty;
(environment) pollute

**verschnaufen** vi **ich muss
mal** ~ I need to get my
breath back

**verschneit** adj snow-covered

**verschnupft** adj **~ sein** have
a cold; fam be peeved

**verschonen** vt spare (jdn mit
etw sb sth)

**verschreiben** irr vt MED prescribe; **verschreibungs-
pflichtig** adj available only
on prescription

**verschwand** imperf → **verschwinden**

**verschweigen** irr vt keep secret; **jdm etw** ~ keep sth

from sb

**verschwenden** vt waste; **Verschwendung** f waste

**verschwiegen** adj discreet;
(place) secluded

**verschwinden** ⟨verschwand,
verschwunden⟩ vi disappear,
vanish; **verschwinde!** get
lost!; **verschwunden** pp →
**verschwinden**

**Versehen** nt ⟨-s, -⟩ **aus** ~ by
mistake; **versehentlich** adv
by mistake

**versenden** irr vt send off

**versetzen 1.** vt transfer; (jewellery etc) pawn; fam (on a
date) stand up **2.** vr **sich in
jdn** (or **jds Lage**) ~ put oneself in sb's place

**verseuchen** vt contaminate

**versichern** vt insure; (confirm) assure; **versichert
sein** be insured; **Versicher-
tenkarte** f health-insurance
card; **Versicherung** f insurance; **Versicherungskarte**
f **grüne** ~ green card (Brit),
insurance document for
driving abroad; **Versicherungspolice** f insurance
policy

**versilbert** adj silver-plated

**versinken** irr vi sink

**versöhnen 1.** vt reconcile **2.**
vr become reconciled

**versorgen 1.** vt provide, supply (mit with); (family) look
after **2.** vr look after oneself;
**Versorgung** f provision;
(care) maintenance; (mon-

*ey*) benefit
**verspäten** *vr* be late; **verspätet** *adj* late; **Verspätung** *f* delay; (*eine Stunde*) ~ **haben** be (an hour) late
**versprechen** *irr* **1.** *vt* promise **2.** *vr* **ich habe mich versprochen** I didn't mean to say that
**Verstand** *m* mind; (common) sense; **den** ~ **verlieren** lose one's mind; **verständigen 1.** *vt* inform **2.** *vr* communicate; (*agree*) come to an understanding; **Verständigung** *f* communication; **verständlich** *adj* understandable; **Verständnis** *nt* understanding (*für* of); (*compassion*) sympathy; **verständnisvoll** *adj* understanding
**verstauchen** *vt* sprain; **verstaucht** *pp* = **verstauchen** sprained
**Versteck** *nt* ⟨-(e)s, -e⟩ hiding place; ~ **spielen** play hide-and-seek; **verstecken** *vt, vr* hide (*vor* + *dat* from)
**verstehen** *irr* **1.** *vt* understand; **falsch** ~ misunderstand **2.** *vr* get on (*mit* with)
**verstellbar** *adj* adjustable; **verstellen 1.** *vt* move; (*clock*) adjust; (*obstruct*) block; (*voice, handwriting*) disguise **2.** *vr* pretend, put on an act
**verstopfen** *vt* block up; **MED** constipate; **Verstopfung** *f* obstruction; **MED** constipa-

tion
**Verstoß** *m* infringement, violation (*gegen* of)
**Versuch** *m* ⟨-(e)s, -e⟩ attempt; (*scientific*) experiment; **versuchen** *vt* try
**vertauschen** *vt* exchange; (*by mistake*) mix up
**verteidigen** *vt* defend
**verteilen** *vt* distribute
**Vertrag** *m* ⟨-(e)s, Verträge⟩ contract; **POL** treaty
**vertragen 1.** *vt* stand, bear **2.** *vr* get along (with each other); (*be reconciled*) make it up
**vertrauen** *vi* **jdm** / **einer Sache** ~ trust sb/sth; **Vertrauen** *nt* ⟨-s⟩ trust (*in* + *acc* in, *zu* in); **ich habe kein** ~ **zu ihm** I don't trust him; **ich hab's ihm im** ~ **gesagt** I told him in confidence; **vertraulich** *adj* confidential; **vertraut** *adj* **sich mit etw** ~ **machen** familiarize oneself with sth
**vertreten** *irr* *vt* represent; (*opinion*) hold; **Vertreter(in)** *m(f)* ⟨-s, -⟩ representative
**Vertrieb** *m* ⟨-(e)s, -e⟩ sales department
**verunglücken** *vi* have an accident; **tödlich** ~ be killed in an accident
**verursachen** *vt* cause
**verurteilen** *vt* condemn
**verwählen** *vr* dial the wrong number
**verwalten** *vt* manage; (*offi-*

*cials*) administer; **Verwalter(in)** *m(f)* ⟨-s, -⟩ manager; **Verwaltung** *f* management; (*by officials*) administration

**verwandt** *adj* related (*mit* to); **Verwandte(r)** *mf* relative, relation; **Verwandtschaft** *f* relationship; (*people*) relations *pl*

**verwarnen** *vt* warn; SPORT caution

**verwechseln** *vt* confuse (*mit* with); (*for sb or sth else*) mistake (*mit* for)

**verweigern** *vt* refuse

**verwenden** *vt* use; **Verwendung** *f* use

**verwirklichen** *vt* realize; **sich selbst ~** fulfil oneself

**verwirren** *vt* confuse; **Verwirrung** *f* confusion

**verwöhnen** *vt* spoil

**verwunderlich** *adj* surprising; **Verwunderung** *f* astonishment

**verwüsten** *vt* devastate

**verzählen** *vr* miscount

**verzehren** *vt* consume

**Verzeichnis** *nt* list; (*of books, products*) catalogue; (*in book*) index; IT directory

**verzeihen** ⟨verzieh, verziehen⟩ *vt*, *vi* forgive (*jdm etw* sb for sth); **~ Sie bitte, ...** excuse me, ...; **→ Sie die Störung** sorry to disturb you; **Verzeihung** *f* ↗! sorry; **, ...** excuse me, ...; (*jdn*) **um ~ bitten** apologize (to sb)

**verzichten** *vi* **auf etw** *acc* ~ do

without sth; (*abandon*) give sth up

**verzieh** *imperf* → **verzeihen**

**verziehen** *pp* → **verzeihen**

**verziehen** *irr* **1.** *vt* (*child*) spoil; **das Gesicht ~** pull a face **2.** *vr* go out of shape; (*go away*) disappear

**verzieren** *vt* decorate

**verzögern 1.** *vt* delay **2.** *vr* be delayed; **Verzögerung** *f* delay

**verzweifeln** *vi* despair (*an* + *dat* of); **verzweifelt** *adj* desperate; **Verzweiflung** *f* despair

**Vetter** *m* ⟨-s, -n⟩ cousin

**vgl.** *abbr* → **vergleiche** cf

**Viagra®** *nt* ⟨-s⟩ Viagra®

**Vibrator** *m* ⟨-s, -en⟩ vibrator; **vibrieren** *vi* vibrate

**Video** *nt* ⟨-s, -s⟩ video; **auf ~ aufnehmen** video; **Videoclip** *m* ⟨-s, -s⟩ video clip; **Videofilm** *m* video; **Videogerät** *nt* video (recorder); **Videokamera** *f* video camera; **Videokassette** *f* video (cassette); **Videorekorder** *m* video recorder; **Videospiel** *nt* video game; **Videothek** *f* ⟨-, -en⟩ video library

**Vieh** *nt* ⟨-(e)s⟩ cattle

**viel 1.** *pron* a lot (of), lots of; **~ Arbeit** a lot of work, lots of work; **~e Leute** a lot of people, lots of people, many people; **zu ~** too much; **zu ~e** too many; **sehr ~** a great deal of; **sehr ~e** a great many; *ziemlich ~/~e* quite a lot of; *nicht ~* not much, not a lot of; *nicht ~e* not many, not a lot of; *sie sagt nicht ~* she doesn't say a lot; *gibt es ~?* is there much?, is there a lot?; *gibt es ~e?* are there many?, are there a lot? **2.** *adv* a lot; *er geht ~ ins Kino* he goes a lot to the cinema; *sehr ~* a great deal; *ziemlich ~* quite a lot; *~ besser* much better; *~ teurer* much more expensive; *~ zu ~* far too much

**vielleicht** *adv* perhaps; *~ ist sie krank* perhaps she's ill, she might be ill; *weißt du ~, wo er ist?* do you know where he is (by any chance)?

**vielmal(s)** *adv* many times; *danke vielmals* many thanks; **vielmehr** *adv* rather; **vielseitig** *adj* very varied; (*person, device*) versatile

**vier** *num* four; *auf allen ~en* on all fours; *unter ~ Augen* in private, privately; **Vier** *f* ⟨-, -en⟩ four; (*mark in school*) ≈ D; **Vierbettzimmer** *nt* four-bed room; **Viereck** *nt* ⟨-(e)s, -e⟩ four-sided figure; square; **viereckig** *adj* four-sided; square; **vierfach** *adj* die *~e Menge* four times the amount; **vierhundert** *num* four hundred; **viermal** *adv* four times; **vierspurig** *adj* four-lane

**viert** *adv* *wir sind zu ~* there

are four of us; **vierte(r, s)** *adj* fourth; → *dritte*

**Viertel** *nt* ⟨-s, -⟩ (*of town*) quarter, district; (*fraction*) quarter; (*of wine etc*) quarter-litre; *~ vor / nach drei* a quarter to / past three; *viertel drei* a quarter past two; *drei viertel drei* a quarter to three; **Viertelfinale** *nt* quarter-final; **vierteljährlich** *adj* quarterly; **Viertelstunde** *f* quarter of an hour

**vierzehn** *num* fourteen; *in ~ Tagen* in two weeks, in a fortnight (*Brit*); **vierzehntägig** *adj* two-week, fortnightly (*Brit*); **vierzehnte(r, s)** *adj* fourteenth; → *dritte*; **vierzig** *num* forty; **vierzigste(r, s)** *adj* fortieth

**Vietnam** *nt* ⟨-s⟩ Vietnam

**Vignette** *f* ⟨-, Villen⟩ (*Brit*) (*or freeway US*)) permit

**Villa** *f* ⟨-, Villen⟩ villa

**violett** *adj* purple

**Violine** *f* violin

**Virus** *m or nt* ⟨-, Viren⟩ virus

**Visitenkarte** *f* card

**Visum** *nt* ⟨-s, Visa *or* Visen⟩ visa

**Vitamin** *nt* ⟨-s, -e⟩ vitamin

**Vitrine** *f* ⟨-, -n⟩ (*glass*) cabinet; (*in museum etc*) display case

**Vogel** *m* ⟨-s, Vögel⟩ bird; **Vogelgrippe** *f* bird flu, avian flu; **vögeln** *vi, vt* vulg screw

**Voicemail** *f* ⟨-, -s⟩ voice mail

**Vokal** *m* ⟨-s, -e⟩ vowel

**Volk** *nt* ⟨-(e)s, Völker⟩ people

*pl*; (*community*) nation; **Volksfest** *nt* festival; (*with rides etc*) funfair; **Volkshochschule** *f* adult education centre; **Volkslied** *nt* folksong; **Volksmusik** *f* folk music; **volkstümlich** *adj* popular; traditional; (*art*) folk

**voll** *adj* full (*von* of); **Vollbremsung** *f* **eine ~ machen** slam on the brakes; **vollends** *adv* completely

**Volleyball** *m* volleyball

**Vollgas** *nt* **mit ~** at full throttle; **~ geben** step on it

**völlig 1.** *adj* complete **2.** *adv* completely

**volljährig** *adj* of age; **Vollkaskoversicherung** *f* fully comprehensive insurance; **vollklimatisiert** *adj* fully air-conditioned; **vollkommen 1.** *adj* perfect; **~er Unsinn** complete rubbish **2.** *adv* completely

**Vollkornbrot** *nt* wholemeal (*Brit*) (*or* whole wheat (*US*)) bread

**vollmachen** *vt* fill (up)

**Vollmacht** *f* ⟨-, -en⟩ authority; (*document*) power of attorney

**Vollmilch** *f* full-fat milk (*Brit*), whole milk (*US*); **Vollmilchschokolade** *f* milk chocolate; **Vollmond** *m* full moon; **Vollnarkose** *f* general anaesthetic; **Vollpension** *f* full board

**vollständig** *adj* complete

**volltanken** *vi* fill up

**Vollwertkost** *f* wholefood; **vollzählig** *adj* complete

**Volt** *nt* ⟨-, -⟩ volt

**Volumen** *nt* ⟨-s, -⟩ volume

**vom** *contr* = **von dem**; (*with space, time, cause*) from; **ich kenne sie nur ~ Sehen** I only know her by sight

**von** *prep* + *dat* (*with space, time*) from; (*replacing genitive, consisting of*) of; (*passive*) by; **ein Freund ~ mir** a friend of mine; **~ mir aus** *fam* if you like; **~ wegen!** no way; **voneinander** *adv* from each other

**vor** *prep* + *dat or acc* before; (*in space*) in front of; **fünf ~ drei** five to three; **~ 2 Tagen** 2 days ago; **~ Wut / Liebe** with rage / love; **~ allem** above all

**vorangehen** *irr vi* go ahead; **einer Sache** *dat* ~ precede sth; **vorankommen** *irr vi* make progress

**voraus** *adv* ahead; **im Voraus** in advance; **jdm ~ sein** be ahead of sb; **vorausfahren** *irr vi* drive on ahead; **vorausgesetzt** *conj* provided (that); **Voraussage** *f* prediction; (*for weather*) forecast; **voraussagen** *vt* predict; **voraussehen** *irr vt* foresee; **voraussetzen** *vt* assume; **Voraussetzung** *f* requirement, prerequisite; **voraus-**

**sichtlich 1.** adj expected **2.** adv probably; **vorauszahlen** vt pay in advance

**vorbei** adv past, over, finished; **vorbeibringen** irr vt drop by (or in); **vorbeifahren** irr vi drive past; **vorbeigehen** irr vi pass by, go past; (elapse, end) pass; **vorbeikommen** irr vi drop by; **vorbeilassen** vt **kannst du die Leute ~?** would you let these people pass?; **lässt du mich bitte mal vorbei?** can I get past, please?

**vorbereiten 1.** vt prepare **2.** vr get ready (auf + acc, für for); **Vorbereitung** f preparation

**vorbestellen** vt book in advance; (meal) order in advance; **Vorbestellung** f booking, reservation

**vorbeugen** vi prevent (dat sth); **vorbeugend** adj preventive; **Vorbeugung** f prevention

**Vorbild** nt (role) model; **vorbildlich** adj model, ideal

**Vorderachse** f front axle; **vordere(r, s)** adj front; **Vordergrund** m foreground; **Vorderradantrieb** m AUTO front-wheel drive; **Vorderseite** f front; **Vordersitz** m front seat; **Vorderteil** m or nt (part)

**voreilig** adj hasty, rash; **~e Schlüsse ziehen** jump to conclusions; **voreingenom-**

**men** adj biased

**vorenthalten** irr vt **jdm etw ~** withhold sth from sb

**vorerst** adv for the moment

**vorfahren** irr vi drive on ahead; **vor das Haus ~** drive up to the house; **fahren Sie bis zur Ampel vor** drive as far as the traffic lights

**Vorfahrt** f AUTO right of way; **~ achten** give way (Brit), yield (US); **Vorfahrtsschild** nt give way (Brit) (or yield (US)) sign; **Vorfahrtsstraße** f major road

**Vorfall** m incident

**vorführen** vt demonstrate; (film) show; THEAT perform

**Vorgänger(in)** m(f) predecessor

**vorgehen** irr vi go on ahead; (to the front) go forward; (take action) act, proceed; (clock, watch) be fast; (be more important) take precedence; (happen) go on; **Vorgehen** nt ⟨-s⟩ procedure

**Vorgesetzte(r)** mf superior

**vorgestern** adv the day before yesterday

**vorhaben** irr vt plan; **hast du schon was vor?** have you got anything on?; **ich habe vor, nach Rom zu fahren** I'm planning to go to Rome

**vorhalten** irr vt **jdm etw ~** accuse sb

**Vorhand** f forehand

**vorhanden** adj existing; available

**Vorhang** *m* curtain

**Vorhaut** *f* foreskin

**vorher** *adv* before; **zwei Tage** ~ two days before; ~ **essen wir** we'll eat first; **Vorhersage** *f* forecast; **vorhersehen** *irr vt* foresee

**vorhin** *adv* just now, a moment ago

**vorkommen** *irr vi* come forward; (*take place*) happen; (*appear*) seem (to be); **sich** *dat* **dumm** ~ feel stupid

**Vorlage** *f* model

**vorlassen** *irr vt* **jdn** ~ let sb go first

**vorläufig** *adj* temporary

**vorlesen** *irr vt* read out

**vorletzte(r, s)** *adj* last but one; **am** ~n **Samstag** (on) the Saturday before last

**Vorliebe** *f* preference

**vormachen** *kannst du es mir* ~? can you show me how to do it?; **jdm etwas** ~ *fig* fool sb

**Vormittag** *m* morning; **am** ~ in the morning; **heute** ~ this morning; **vormittags** *adv* in the morning; **um 9 Uhr** ~ at 9 (o'clock) in the morning, at 9 am

**vorn(e)** *adv* in front; **von** ~ **anfangen** start at the beginning; **nach** ~ to the front; **weiter** ~ further up; **von** ~ **bis hinten** from beginning to end

**Vorname** *m* first name; **wie heißt du mit** ~n? what's your first name?

**vornehm** *adj* distinguished; (*behaviour*) refined; (*clothes, hotel etc*) elegant

**vornehmen** *irr vt* **sich** *dat* **etw** ~ start on sth; **sich** *dat* ~, **etw zu tun** decide to do sth

**vornherein** *adv* **von** ~ from the start

**Vorort** *m* suburb

**vorrangig** *adj* priority

**Vorrat** *m* stock, supply; **vorrätig** *adj* in stock

**Vorrecht** *nt* privilege; **Vorruhestand** *m* early retirement; **Vorsaison** *f* early season

**Vorsatz** *m* intention; **LAW** intent; **vorsätzlich** *adj* intentional; **LAW** premeditated

**Vorschau** *f* preview; (*for film*) trailer

**Vorschlag** *m* suggestion, proposal; **vorschlagen** *irr vt* suggest, propose; **ich schlage vor, dass wir gehen** I suggest we go

**vorschreiben** *irr vt* stipulate; **jdm etw** ~ dictate sth to sb

**Vorschrift** *f* regulation, rule; instruction; **vorschriftsmäßig** *adj* correct

**Vorsicht** *f* care; ~! look out; (*on sign*) caution; ~ **Stufe!** mind the step; **vorsichtig** *adj* careful; **vorsichtshalber** *adv* just in case

**Vorsorge** *f* precaution; (*stopping*) prevention; **Vorsorgeuntersuchung** *f* checkup;

**vorsorglich** *adv* as a precaution

**Vorspeise** *f* starter

**vorstellen** *vt* (*person*) introduce, put forward; (*in front of sth else*) put in front; **sich dat etw ~** imagine sth; **Vorstellung** *f* (*to sb*) introduction; THEAT performance; (*concept*) idea; **Vorstellungsgespräch** *nt* interview

**vortäuschen** *vt* feign

**Vorteil** *m* advantage (*gegenüber* over); **die Vor- und Nachteile** the pros and cons; **vorteilhaft** *adj* advantageous

**Vortrag** *m* ⟨-(e)s, Vorträge⟩ talk (*über* + *acc* on); (*academic*) lecture; **einen ~ halten** give a talk

**vorüber** *adv* over; **vorübergehen** *irr vi* pass; **vorübergehend 1.** *adj* temporary **2.** *adv* temporarily, for the time being

**Vorurteil** *nt* prejudice

**Vorverkauf** *m* advance booking

**vorverlegen** *vt* bring forward

**Vorwahl** *f* TEL dialling code (*Brit*), area code (*US*)

**Vorwand** *m* ⟨-(e)s, Vorwände⟩ pretext, excuse; **unter dem ~, dass** with the excuse that

**vorwärts** *adv* forward; **vorwärtsgehen** *irr vi* fig progress

**vorweg** *adv* in advance; **vorwegnehmen** *irr vt* anticipate

**vorwerfen** *irr vt* **jdm etw ~** accuse sb of sth

**vorwiegend** *adv* mainly

**Vorwort** *nt* preface

**Vorwurf** *m* reproach; **sich dat Vorwürfe machen** reproach oneself; **jdm Vorwürfe machen** accuse sb; **vorwurfsvoll** *adj* reproachful

**vorzeigen** *vt* show

**vorzeitig** *adj* premature, early

**vorziehen** *irr vt* prefer

**vorzüglich** *adj* excellent

**vulgär** *adj* vulgar

**Vulkan** *m* ⟨-s, -e⟩ volcano; **Vulkanausbruch** *m* volcanic eruption

# W

**Waage** *f* ⟨-, -n⟩ scales *pl*; ASTR Libra; **waagerecht** *adj* horizontal

**wach** *adj* awake; **~ werden** wake up; **Wache** *f* ⟨-, -n⟩ guard

**Wachs** *nt* ⟨-es, -e⟩ wax

**wachsen** ⟨wuchs, gewachsen⟩ *vi* grow

**wachsen** *vt* (*skis*) wax

**Wachstum** *nt* growth

**Wächter(in)** *m(f)* ⟨-s, -⟩

**wandeln**

**guard;** *(of car park)* attendant

**wackelig** *adj* wobbly; *fig* shaky; **Wackelkontakt** *m* loose connection; **wackeln** *vi (chair)* be wobbly; *(tooth, screw)* be loose; *mit dem Kopf ~* waggle one's head

**Wade** *f* ⟨-, -n⟩ ANAT calf

**Waffe** *f* ⟨-, -n⟩ weapon

**Waffel** *f* ⟨-, -n⟩ waffle; *(biscuit, for ice cream)* wafer

**wagen** *v* risk; *es ~, etw zu tun* dare to do sth

**Wagen** *m* ⟨-s, -⟩ AUTO car; RAIL carriage; **Wagenheber** *m* ⟨-s, -⟩ jack; **Wagentyp** *m* model, make

**Wahl** *f* ⟨-, -en⟩ choice; POL election

**wählen 1.** *vt* choose; TEL dial; POL vote for; *(as president, to board etc)* elect **2.** *vi* choose; TEL dial; POL vote; **Wähler(in)** *m(f)* ⟨-s, -⟩ voter; **wählerisch** *adj* choosy

**Wahlkampf** *m* election campaign; **wahllos** *adv* at random; **Wahlwiederholung** *f* redial

**Wahnsinn** *m* madness; *~!* amazing!; **wahnsinnig 1.** *adj* insane, mad **2.** *adv fam* incredibly

**wahr** *adj* true; *das darf doch nicht ~ sein!* I don't believe it; *nicht ~?* that's right, isn't it?

**während 1.** *prep + gen* during **2.** *conj* while; **währenddes-**

**-sen** *adv* meanwhile, in the meantime

**Wahrheit** *f* truth

**wahrnehmbar** *adj* noticeable, perceptible; **wahrnehmen** *irr vt* perceive

**Wahrsager(in)** *m(f)* ⟨-s, -⟩ fortune-teller

**wahrscheinlich 1.** *adj* probable, likely **2.** *adv* probably; *ich komme ~ zu spät* I'll probably be late; **Wahrscheinlichkeit** *f* probability

**Währung** *f* currency

**Wahrzeichen** *nt* symbol

**Waise** *f* ⟨-, -n⟩ orphan

**Wal** *m* ⟨-(e)s, -e⟩ whale

**Wald** *m* ⟨-(e)s, Wälder⟩ wood; *(extensive)* forest; **Waldbrand** *m* forest fire; **Waldsterben** *nt* ⟨-s⟩ forest dieback

**Wales** *nt* ⟨-⟩ Wales; **Waliser(in)** *m(f)* ⟨-s, -⟩ Welshman / Welshwoman; **walisisch** *adj* Welsh; **Walisisch** *nt* Welsh

**Walkman**® *m* ⟨-s, -s⟩ walkman®, personal stereo

**Wallfahrt** *f* pilgrimage; **Wallfahrtsort** *m* place of pilgrimage

**Walnuss** *f* walnut

**Walross** *nt* ⟨-es, -e⟩ walrus

**wälzen 1.** *vt* roll; *(books)* pore over; *(problems)* deliberate on **2.** *vr* wallow; *(in pain)* roll about; *(in bed)* toss and turn

**Walzer** *m* ⟨-s, -⟩ waltz

**Wand** *f* ⟨-, Wände⟩ wall

**Wandel** *m* ⟨-s⟩ change; **wan-**

deln *vt, vr* change
**Wanderer** *m* ⟨-s, -⟩, **Wanderin**
*f* hiker; **Wanderkarte** *f* hiking map; **wandern** *vi* hike;
(*gaze*) wander; (*thoughts*)
stray; **Wanderschuh** *m*
walking shoe; **Wanderstiefel** *m* hiking boot; **Wanderung** *f* hike; *eine ~ machen*
go on a hike; **Wanderweg** *m*
walking (*or* hiking) trail;
**Wandschrank** *m* built-in
cupboard (*Brit*), closet (*US*)
**wandte** *imperf* → **wenden**
**Wange** *f* ⟨-, -n⟩ cheek
**wann** *adv* when; *seit ~ ist sie
da?* how long has she been
here?; *bis ~ bleibt ihr?*
how long are you staying?
**Wanne** *f* ⟨-, -n⟩ (bath) tub
**Wappen** *nt* ⟨-s, -⟩ coat of arms
**war** *imperf* → **sein**
**warb** *imperf* → **werben**
**Ware** *f* ⟨-, -n⟩ product; *~n*
goods *pl*; **Warenhaus** *nt* department store; **Warenprobe** *f* sample; **Warenzeichen**
*nt* trademark
**warf** *imperf* → **werfen**
**warm** *adj* warm; (*meal*) hot; *~
laufen* warm up; *mir ist es
zu ~* I'm too warm; **Wärme**
*f* ⟨-, -n⟩ warmth; **wärmen** 1.
*vt* warm; (*food*) warm (*or*
heat) up 2. *vi* (*clothes, sun*)
be warm 3. *vr* warm up;
(*by holding each other*) keep
each other warm; **Wärmflasche** *f* hot-water bottle
**Warnblinkanlage** *f* AUTO

warning flasher; **Warndreieck** *nt* AUTO warning triangle; **warnen** *vt* warn (*vor*
+ *dat* about, of); **Warnung**
*f* warning
**Warteliste** *f* waiting list; **warten** 1. *vi* wait (*auf* + *acc* for);
*warte mal!* wait (*or* hang on)
a minute 2. *vt* TECH service
**Wärter(in)** *m(f)* attendant
**Wartesaal** *m*, **Wartezimmer**
*nt* waiting room
**Wartung** *f* service; (*action*)
servicing
**warum** *adv* why
**Warze** *f* ⟨-, -n⟩ wart
**was** 1. *pron* what; *~ kostet
das?* what does it cost?,
how much is it?; *~ für ein
Auto ist das?* what kind of
car is that?; *~ für eine Farbe / Größe?* what colour /
size?; *fam ~?* what?; *~ ist /
gibt's?* what is it?, what's
up? 2. *pron Du weißt, ~
ich meine* you know what
I mean; *~ (auch) immer*
whatever 3. *fam* something;
*soll ich dir ~ mitbringen?*
do you want me to bring
you anything?
**Waschanlage** *f* AUTO car
wash; **waschbar** *adj* washable; **Waschbecken** *nt* washbasin
**Wäsche** *f* ⟨-, -n⟩ washing;
(*dirty*) laundry; *in der ~* in
the wash; **Wäscheklammer**
*f* clothes peg (*Brit*) (*or* pin
(*US*)); **Wäscheleine**

**wechseln**

clothesline

**waschen** 〈wusch, gewaschen〉 **1.** vt, vi wash; **Waschen und Legen** shampoo and set **2.** vr (have a) wash; **sich** dat **die Haare ~** wash one's hair

**Wäscherei** f laundry; **Wäscheständer** m clothes horse; **Wäschetrockner** m tumble-drier

**Waschgelegenheit** f washing facilities pl; **Waschlappen** m flannel (Brit), washcloth (US); fam (person) wet blanket; **Waschmaschine** f washing machine; **Waschmittel** nt, **Waschpulver** nt washing powder; **Waschraum** m washroom; **Waschsalon** m 〈-s, -s〉 launderette (Brit), laundromat (US); **Waschstraße** f car wash

**Wasser** nt 〈-s, -〉 water; **fließendes ~** running water; **Wasserball** m SPORT water polo; **wasserdicht** adj watertight; (fabric, watch) waterproof; **Wasserfall** m waterfall; **Wasserfarbe** f watercolour; **wasserfest** adj watertight, waterproof; **Wasserhahn** m tap (Brit), faucet (US); **wässerig** adj watery; **Wasserkessel** m 〈-s, -〉 kettle; **Wasserkocher** m 〈-s, -〉 electric kettle; **Wasserleitung** f water pipe; **wasserlöslich** adj water-soluble; **Wassermann** m ASTR Aquarius; **Wassermelone** f water melon; **Wasserrutschbahn** f water chute; **Wasserschaden** m water damage; **wasserscheu** adj scared of water; **Wasserski** nt water-skiing; **Wassersport** m water sports pl; **wasserundurchlässig** adj watertight, waterproof; **Wasserverbrauch** m water consumption; **Wasserversorgung** f water supply; **Wasserwerk** nt waterworks pl

**waten** vi wade

**Watt¹** nt 〈-(e)s, -en〉 GEO mud flats pl **2.** nt 〈-s, -〉 ELEC watt

**Watte** f 〈-, -n〉 cotton wool; **Wattestäbchen** nt cotton bud, Q-tip® (US)

**WC** nt 〈-s, -s〉 toilet, restroom (US); **WC-Reiniger** m toilet cleaner

**Web** nt 〈-s〉 IT Web; **Webseite** f IT web page

**Wechsel** m 〈-s, -〉 change; SPORT substitution; **Wechselgeld** nt change; **wechselhaft** adj (weather) changeable; **Wechseljahre** pl menopause sg; **Wechselkurs** m exchange rate; **wechseln 1.** vt change; (looks) exchange; **Geld ~** change some money; (into smaller coins or notes) get some change; **Euro in Pfund ~** change euros into pounds **2.** vi change; **kannst**

***du ~?*** can you change this?;
**Wechselstrom** *m* alternating current, AC; **Wechselstube** *f* bureau de change

**Weckdienst** *m* wake-up call service; **wecken** *vt* wake (up); **Wecker** *m* ⟨-s, -⟩ alarm clock; **Weckruf** *m* wake-up call

**wedeln** *vi* SKI wedel; ***der Hund wedelte mit dem Schwanz*** the dog wagged its tail

**weder** *conj* **~ ... noch ...** neither ... nor ...

**weg** *adv* away; *(leaving, removed)* off; ***er war schon ~*** he had already left *(or* gone*)*; ***Hände ~!*** hands off; ***weit ~*** a long way away *(or* off*)*

**Weg** *m* ⟨-(e)s, -e⟩ way; *(for walking)* path; *(way travelled)* route; ***jdn nach dem ~ fragen*** ask sb the way; ***auf dem ~ sein*** be on the way

**wegbleiben** *irr vi* stay away; **wegbringen** *irr vt* take away

**wegen** *prep* + *gen or dat* because of

**wegfahren** *irr vi* drive away; *(depart)* leave; *(car)* go away; **Wegfahrsperre** *f* AUTO *(engine)* immobilizer; **weggehen** *irr vi* go away; **wegkommen** *irr vi* get away; ***fig gut / schlecht ~*** come off well / badly; **weglassen** *irr vt* leave out; **weglaufen** *irr vi* run away; weg-

**legen** *vt* put aside; **wegmüssen** *irr vi* **ich muss weg** I've got to go; **wegnehmen** *irr vt* take away; **wegräumen** *vt* clear away; **wegrennen** *irr vi* run away; **wegschicken** *vt* send away; **wegschmeißen** *irr vt* throw away; **wegsehen** *irr vi* look away; **wegtun** *irr vt* put away

**Wegweiser** *m* ⟨-s, -⟩ signpost
**wegwerfen** *irr vt* throw away; **wegwischen** *vt* wipe off; **wegziehen** *irr vi* move (away)

**weh** *adj* sore; → **wehtun**
**wehen** *vt, vi* blow; *(flag)* flutter

**Wehen** *pl* labour pains *pl*
**Wehrdienst** *m* military service

**wehren** *vr* defend oneself
**wehtun** *irr vi* hurt; ***jdm / sich ~*** hurt sb / oneself

**Weibchen** *nt* **es ist ein ~** *(animal)* it's a she; **weiblich** *adj* feminine; BIO female

**weich** *adj* soft; **~ gekocht** *(egg)* soft-boiled

**Weichspüler** *m* ⟨-s, -⟩ *(fabric)* softener

**Weide** *f* ⟨-, -n⟩ *(tree)* willow; *(field)* meadow

**weigern** *vr* refuse; **Weigerung** *f* refusal

**Weiher** *m* ⟨-s, -⟩ pond
**Weihnachten** *nt* ⟨-, -⟩ Christmas; **Weihnachtsabend** *m* Christmas Eve; **Weih-**

**nachtsbaum** m Christmas tree; **Weihnachtsfeier** f Christmas party; **Weihnachtsferien** pl Christmas holidays pl (Brit), Christmas vacation sg (US); **Weihnachtsgeld** nt Christmas bonus; **Weihnachtsgeschenk** nt Christmas present; **Weihnachtskarte** f Christmas card; **Weihnachtslied** nt Christmas carol; **Weihnachtsmann** m Father Christmas, Santa (Claus); **Weihnachtstag** m **erster** ~ Christmas Day; **zweiter** ~ Boxing Day; **Weihnachtszeit** f Christmas season

**weil** conj because

**Weile** f ⟨-⟩ while, short time; **es kann noch eine ~ dauern** it could take some time

**Wein** m ⟨-(e)s, -e⟩ wine; (plant) vine; **Weinbrand** m brandy

**weinen** vt, vi cry

**Weinglas** nt wine glass; **Weinkarte** f wine list; **Weinkeller** m wine cellar; **Weinprobe** f wine tasting; **Weintraube** f grape

**weise** adj wise

**Weise** f ⟨-, -n⟩ manner, way; **auf diese (Art und) ~** this way

**weisen** ⟨wies, gewiesen⟩ vt show

**Weisheit** f wisdom; **Weisheitszahn** m wisdom tooth

**weiß** adj white; **Weißbier** nt ≈

wheat beer; **Weißbrot** nt white bread; **Weißkohl** m, **Weißkraut** nt (white) cabbage; **Weißwein** m white wine

**weit 1.** adj wide; (concept) broad; (journey, throw) long; (dress) loose; **wie ~ ist es ...?** how far is it ...?; **so ~ sein** be ready **2.** adv far; **~ verbreitet** widespread; **~ gereist** widely travelled; **~ offen** wide open; **das geht zu ~** that's going too far, that's pushing it

**weiter 1.** adj (more distant) farther (away); (additional) further; **~e Informationen** further information sg **2.** adv further; **~!** go on; (to people walking) keep moving; **~ nichts / niemand** nothing / nobody else; **und so ~** and so on; **Weiterbildung** f further training (or education); **weiterempfehlen** irr vt recommend; **weitererzählen** vt **nicht ~!** I don't tell anyone; **weiterfahren** irr vi go on (nach to, bis as far as); **weitergeben** irr vt pass on; **weitergehen** irr vi go on; **weiterhelfen** irr vi **jdm ~** help sb

**weiterhin** adv **etw ~ tun** go on doing sth

**weitermachen** vt, vi continue; **weiterreisen** vi continue one's journey

**weitgehend 1.** *adj* considerable **2.** *adv* largely; **weitsichtig** *adj* long-sighted; *fig* far-sighted; **Weitsprung** *m* long jump; **Weitwinkelobjektiv** *nt* PHOT wide-angle lens

**Weizen** *m* ‹-s, -› wheat; **Weizenbier** *nt* ≈ wheat beer

**welche(r, s) 1.** *pron* what; (*when choosing*) which (one); ~ *Geschmacksrichtung willst du?* which flavour do you want?; ~*r ist es?* which (one) is it? **2.** *pron* (*relative, person*) who; (*relative, thing*) which, that; *zeig mir,* ~*r es war* show me which one of them it was **3.** *pron fam* some; *hast du Kleingeld? - ja, ich hab'* ~*s* have you got any change? - yes, I've got some

**welk** *adj* withered; **welken** *vi* wither

**Welle** *f* ‹-, -n› wave; **Wellengang** *m* waves *pl*; *starker* ~ heavy seas *pl*; **Wellenlänge** *f* wavelength; **Wellenreiten** *nt* surfing; **Wellensittich** *m* ‹-s, -e› budgerigar, budgie

**Wellness** *f* health and beauty (*Brit*), wellness (*US*)

**Welpe** *m* ‹-n, -n› puppy

**Welt** *f* ‹-, -en› world; *auf der* ~ in the world; *auf die* ~ *kommen* be born; **Weltall** *nt* universe; **weltbekannt** *adj*, **weltberühmt** *adj* world-famous; **Weltkrieg** *m* world war; **Weltmacht** *f* world power; **Weltmeister(in)** *m(f)* world champion; **Weltmeisterschaft** *f* world championship; (*in football*) World Cup; **Weltraum** *m* space; **Weltreise** *f* trip round the world; **Weltrekord** *m* world record; **Weltstadt** *f* metropolis; **weltweit** *adj* worldwide, global

**wem** *pron dat* → **wer**; who; to, (*to*) whom; ~ *hast du's gegeben?* who did you give it to?; ~ *gehört es?* who does it belong to?; *auch immer es gehört* whoever it belongs to

**wen** *pron acc* → **wer**; who, whom; ~ *hast du besucht?* who did you visit?; ~ *möchten Sie sprechen?* who would you like to speak to?

**Wende** *f* ‹-, -n› turning point; (*transformation*) change; *die* ~ HIST the fall of the Berlin Wall; **Wendekreis** *m* AUTO turning circle

**wenden** ‹wendete *or* wandte, gewendet *or* gewandt› *vt, vi, vr* turn (round); (*by 180°*) make a U-turn; *sich an jdn* ~ turn to sb; *bitte* ~*!* please turn over, PTO

**wenig 1.** *pron* little; ~(*e*) *pl* few; (*nur*) *ein (klein)* ~ (just) a little (bit); *ein* ~ *Zucker* a little bit of sugar, a little sugar; *wir haben* ~ *Zeit* we haven't got much time; *zu* ~ too little; *pl* too few; *nur*

~ *wissen* only a few know 2. *adv* *er spricht* ~ he doesn't talk much; ~ *bekannt* little known; *wenigstens* *adv* at least

**wenn** *conj* if; (*with time*) when; *wennschon* *adv* *na* ~ so what?

**wer** 1. *pron* who; ~ *war das?* who was that?; ~ *von euch?* which (one) of you? 2. *pron* anybody who, anyone who; ~ *das glaubt, ist dumm* anyone who believes that is stupid; ~ *auch immer* whoever 3. *pron* somebody, someone; anybody, anyone; *ist da* ~*?* is (there) anybody there?

**Werbefernsehen** *nt* TV commercials *pl*; **werben** ⟨warb, geworben⟩ 1. *vt* win; (*member*) recruit 2. *vi* advertise; **Werbespot** *m* ⟨-s, -s⟩ commercial; **Werbung** *f* advertising

**werden** ⟨wurde, geworden⟩ 1. *vi* get, become; *alt / müde / reich* ~ get old / tired / rich; *was willst du* ~*?* what do you want to be? 2. *vaux* (*future*) will; (*definitely*) be going to; (*passive*) be; *er wird uns (schon) fahren* he'll drive us; *ich werde kommen* I'll come; *er wird uns abholen* he's going to pick us up; *wir* ~ *dafür bezahlt* we're paid for it; *er wird gerade diskutiert*

he's being discussed

**werfen** ⟨warf, geworfen⟩ *vt* throw

**Werft** *f* ⟨-, -en⟩ shipyard, dockyard

**Werk** *nt* ⟨-(e)s, -e⟩ (*of art, literature etc*) work; (*industrial*) factory; (*mechanism*) works *pl*; **Werkstatt** *f* ⟨-, -stätten⟩ workshop; AUTO garage; **Werktag** *m* working day; **werktags** *adv* on weekdays, during the week; **Werkzeug** *nt* tool; **Werkzeugkasten** *m* toolbox

**wert** *adj* worth; *es ist etwa 50 Euro* ~ it's worth about 50 euros; *das ist nichts* ~ it's worthless; **Wert** *m* ⟨-(e)s, -e⟩ worth; FIN value; ~ *legen auf* + *acc* attach importance to; *es hat doch keinen* ~ (*sense*) it's pointless; **Wertangabe** *f* declaration of value; **Wertbrief** *m* insured letter; **Wertgegenstand** *m* valuable object; **wertlos** *adj* worthless; **Wertmarke** *f* token; **Wertpapiere** *pl* securities *pl*; **Wertsachen** *pl* valuables *pl*; **Wertstoff** *m* recyclable waste; **wertvoll** *adj* valuable

**Wesen** *nt* ⟨-s, -⟩ being; (*character*) nature

**wesentlich** 1. *adj* significant; (*substantial*) considerable 2. *adv* considerably

**weshalb** *adv* why

**Wespe** *f* ⟨-, -n⟩ wasp; Wes-

penstich *m* wasp sting
**wessen** *pron gen* → **wer**;
whose
**West** west; **Westdeutschland**
*nt* Western Germany; HIST
West Germany
**Weste** *f* ⟨-, -n⟩ waistcoat
(*Brit*), vest (*US*); (*woollen*)
cardigan
**Westen** *m* ⟨-s⟩ west; **im ~**
**Englands** in the west of
England; **Westeuropa** *nt*
Western Europe; **Westküste**
*f* west coast; **westlich**
*adj* western; (*course, direction*) westerly; **Westwind** *m*
west(erly) wind
**weswegen** *adv* why
**Wettbewerb** *m* competition;
**Wettbüro** *nt* betting office;
**Wette** *f* ⟨-, -n⟩ bet; **eine ~ abschließen** make a bet; **die ~**
**gilt!** you're on; **wetten** v*t*, *vi*
bet (*auf + acc* on); **ich habe**
**mit ihm gewettet, dass ...** I
bet him that ...; **ich wette**
**mit dir um 50 Euro** I'll bet
you 50 euros; **~, dass?** wanna bet?
**Wetter** *nt* ⟨-s, -⟩ weather; **Wetterbericht** *m*, **Wettervorhersage** *f* weather forecast
**Wettkampf** *m* contest; **Wettlauf** *m*, **Wettrennen** *nt* race
**WG** *f* ⟨-, -⟩ *abbr* → **Wohngemeinschaft**
**Whirlpool®** *m* ⟨-s, -s⟩ jacuzzi®
**Whisky** *m* ⟨-s, -s⟩ (*Scottish*)
whisky; (*Irish, American*)
whiskey

**wichtig** *adj* important
**wickeln** *vt* (*string*) wind (*um*
round); (*paper, scarf, blanket*) wrap (*um* round); **ein**
**Baby ~** change a baby's nappy (*Brit*) (*or* diaper (*US*));
**Wickelraum** *m* baby-changing room; **Wickeltisch** *m*
baby-changing table
**Widder** *m* ⟨-s, -⟩ ZOOL ram;
ASTR Aries *sg*
**wider** *prep + acc* against
**widerlich** *adj* disgusting
**widerrufen** *irr vt* withdraw;
(*contract, order*) cancel
**widersprechen** *irr vi* contradict (*jdm* sb); **Widerspruch**
*m* contradiction
**Widerstand** *m* resistance; **widerstandsfähig** *adj* resistant (*gegen* to)
**widerwärtig** *adj* disgusting
**widerwillig** *adj* unwilling, reluctant
**widmen 1.** *vt* dedicate **2.** *vr*
**sich** *jdm* / *etw* **~** devote
oneself to sb/sth; **Widmung**
*f* dedication
**wie 1.** *adv* how; **~ viel** how
much; **~ viele Menschen?**
how many people?; **~**
**geht's?** how are you?; **~**
**das?** how come?; **~ bitte?**
pardon, sorry? (*Brit*) **2.**
(*so*) **schön ~ ...** as beautiful
as ...; **~ du weißt** as you
know; **~ ich das hörte** when
I heard that; **ich sah ~ er**
**rauskam** I saw him coming
out

**wieder** adv again; ~ **ein(e)** ...
another ...; ~ **erkennen** recognize; **etw** ~ **gutmachen**
make up for sth; ~ **verwerten** recycle

**wiederbekommen** irr vt get
back

**wiederholen** vt repeat; **Wiederholung** f repetition

**Wiederhören** nt TEL **auf** ~
goodbye

**wiederkommen** irr vi come
back

**wiedersehen** irr vt see again;
(person) meet again; **Wiedersehen** nt ⟨-s, -e⟩ reunion;
**auf** ~! goodbye

**Wiedervereinigung** f reunification

**Wiege** f ⟨-, -n⟩ cradle; **wiegen**
⟨wog, gewogen⟩ vt, vi weigh

**Wien** nt ⟨-s⟩ Vienna

**wies** imperf → **weisen**

**Wiese** f ⟨-, -n⟩ meadow

**Wiesel** nt ⟨-s, -⟩ weasel

**wieso** adv why

**wievielmal** adv how often;
**wieviel(r, s)** adj **zum** ~ **in**
**Mal?** how many times?;
**den Wievielten haben wir**
**heute?** what's the date today?; **am Wievielten hast**
**du Geburtstag?** which day
is your birthday?

**wieweit** conj to what extent

**wild** adj wild

**Wild** nt ⟨-(e)s⟩ game

**wildfremd** adj fam **ein** ~**er**
**Mensch** a complete (or total) stranger; **Wildleder** nt

suede; **Wildpark** m game
park; **Wildschwein** nt (wild)
boar; **Wildwasserfahren** nt
⟨-s⟩ whitewater canoeing
(or rafting)

**Wille** m ⟨-ns, -ns⟩ will

**willen** prep + gen **um** ... ~
for the sake of ...; **um Himmels** ~! for heaven's sake;
(shocked) goodness me

**willkommen** adj welcome

**Wimper** f ⟨-, -n⟩ eyelash;
**Wimperntusche** f mascara

**Wind** m ⟨-(e)s, -e⟩ wind

**Windel** f ⟨-, -n⟩ nappy (Brit),
diaper (US)

**windgeschützt** adj sheltered
from the wind; **windig** adj
windy; fig dubious; **Windjacke** f windcheater; **Windmühle** f windmill; **Windpocken** pl chickenpox sg;
**Windschutzscheibe** f AUTO
windscreen (Brit), windshield (US); **Windstärke** f
wind force; **Windsurfen** nt
⟨-s⟩ windsurfing; **Windsurfer(in)** m(f) windsurfer

**Winkel** m ⟨-s, -⟩ MATH angle;
(in room) corner

**winken** vt, vi wave

**Winter** m ⟨-s, -⟩ winter; **Winterausrüstung** f winter
equipment; **Winterfahrplan**
m winter timetable; **winterlich** adj wintry; **Wintermantel** m winter coat; **Winterreifen** m winter tyre; **Winterschlussverkauf** m winter
sales pl; **Wintersport** m win-

ter sports *pl*

**Winterzeit** *f* (*by the clock*) winter time (*Brit*), standard time (*US*)

**winzig** *adj* tiny

**wir** *pron* we; ~ *alle* all of us; ~ *drei* the three of us; ~ *sind's* it's us; ~ *nicht* not us

**Wirbel** *m* ⟨-s, -⟩ whirl; (*activity*) hurly-burly; (*about sb or sth*) fuss; ANAT vertebra; **Wirbelsäule** *f* spine

**wirken** *vi* be effective; (*be successful*) work; (*appear to be*) seem

**wirklich** *adj* real; **Wirklichkeit** *f* reality

**wirksam** *adj* effective; **Wirkung** *f* effect

**wirr** *adj* confused; **Wirrwarr** *m* ⟨-s⟩ confusion

**Wirsing** *m* ⟨-s⟩ savoy cabbage

**Wirt** *m* ⟨-(e)s, -e⟩ landlord; **Wirtin** *f* landlady

**Wirtschaft** *f* economy; (*place*) pub; **wirtschaftlich** *adj* economic; (*not wasteful*) economical

**Wirtshaus** *nt* pub

**wischen** *vt, vi* wipe; **Wischer** *m* ⟨-s, -⟩ wiper

**wissen** ⟨wusste, gewusst⟩ *vt* know; *weißt du schon, ...?* did you know ...?; *woher weißt du das?* how do you know?; *das musst du selbst* ~ that's up to you; **Wissen** *nt* ⟨-s⟩ knowledge

**Wissenschaft** *f* science; **Wissenschaftler(in)** *m(f)* ⟨-s, -⟩

scientist; (*in the arts*) academic; **wissenschaftlich** *adj* scientific; (*in the arts*) academic

**Witwe** *f* ⟨-, -n⟩ widow; **Witwer** *m* ⟨-s, -⟩ widower

**Witz** *m* ⟨-(e)s, -e⟩ joke; *mach keine ~e!* you're kidding!; *das soll wohl ein ~ sein* you've got to be joking; **witzig** *adj* funny

**wo 1.** *adv* where; *überall,* ~ *ich hingehe* wherever I go **2.** *conj* jetzt, ~ *du da bist* now that you're here; ~ *ich dich gerade spreche* while I'm talking to you; **woanders** *adv* somewhere else

**wobei** *adv* ~ *mir einfällt ...* which reminds me ...

**Woche** *f* ⟨-, -n⟩ week; *während* (*or unter*) *der* ~ during the week; *einmal die* ~ once a week; **Wochenende** *nt* weekend; *am* ~ *at* (*Brit*) (*or on* (*US*)) the weekend; *wir fahren übers* ~ *weg* we're going away for the weekend; **Wochenendhaus** *nt* weekend cottage; **Wochenendtrip** *m* weekend trip; **Wochenendurlaub** *m* weekend break; **Wochenkarte** *f* weekly (season) ticket; **wochenlang** *adv* for weeks (on end); **Wochenmarkt** *m* weekly market; **Wochentag** *m* weekday; **wöchentlich** *adj, adv* weekly

**woraus**

**Wodka** m ⟨-s, -s⟩ vodka

**wodurch** adv ~ **unterscheiden sie sich?** what's the difference between them?; ~ **hast du es gemerkt?** how did you notice?; **wofür** adv (relative) for which; (question) what … for; ~ **brauchst du das?** what do you need that for?

**wog** imperf → **wiegen**

**woher** adv where … from; **wohin** adv where … to

**wohl** adv well; at ease, comfortable; probably; certainly; **Wohl** nt ⟨-(e)s⟩ **zum ~!** cheers; **wohlbehalten** adv safe and sound; **Wohlstand** m prosperity, affluence

**Wohnblock** m block of flats (Brit), apartment house (US); **wohnen** vi live; **Wohngemeinschaft** f shared flat (Brit) (or apartment (US)); **ich wohne in einer ~** I share a flat (or an apartment); **wohnhaft** adj resident; **Wohnküche** f kitchen-cum-living-room; **Wohnmobil** nt ⟨-s, -e⟩ camper, RV (US); **Wohnort** m place of residence; **Wohnsitz** m place of residence; **Wohnung** f flat (Brit), apartment (US); **Wohnungstür** f front door; **Wohnwagen** m caravan; **Wohnzimmer** nt living room

**Wolf** m ⟨-(e)s, Wölfe⟩ wolf

**Wolke** f ⟨-, -n⟩ cloud; **Wolkenkratzer** m skyscraper; **wolkenlos** adj cloudless; **wolkig** adj cloudy

**Wolldecke** f (woollen) blanket; **Wolle** f ⟨-, -n⟩ wool

**wollen 1.** vaux want; **sie wollte ihn nicht sehen** she didn't want to see him; ~ **wir gehen?** shall we go?; ~ **Sie bitte …** will (or would) you please … **2.** vt want; **ich will lieber bleiben** I'd prefer to stay; **er will, dass ich aufhöre** he wants me to stop; **ich wollte, ich wäre / hätte …** I wish I were / had … **3.** vi want to; **ich will nicht** I don't want to; **was du willst** whatever you like; **ich will nach Hause** I want to go home; **wo willst du hin?** where do you want to go?; (to person heading somewhere) where are you going?

**Wolljacke** f cardigan

**womit** adv what … with; ~ **habe ich das verdient?** what have I done to deserve that?

**womöglich** adv possibly

**woran** adv ~ **denkst du?** what are you thinking of?; ~ **ist er gestorben?** what did he die of?; ~ **sieht man das?** how can you tell?

**worauf** adv ~ **wartest du?** what are you waiting for?

**woraus** adv ~ **ist das gemacht?** what is it made of?

# Wort

**Wort 1.** *nt* ⟨-(e)s, Wörter⟩ word **2.** *nt* ⟨-(e)s, -e⟩ word; *mit anderen ~en* in other words; *jdn beim ~ nehmen* take sb at his / her word; **Wörterbuch** *nt* dictionary; **wörtlich** *adj* literal

**worüber** *adv* **~ redet sie?** what is she talking about?

**worum** *adv* **~ geht's?** what is it about?

**worunter** *adv* **~ leidet er?** what is he suffering from?

**wovon** *adv* (*relative*) from which; **~ redest du?** what are you talking about? **wozu** *adv* (*relative*) to / for which; (*question*) what ... for / to; (*for what reason*) why; **~?** what for?; **~ brauchst du das?** what do you need it for?; **~ soll das gut sein?** what's that for?

**Wrack** *nt* ⟨-(e)s, -s⟩ wreck

**wuchs** *imperf* → **wachsen**

**wühlen** *vi* rummage; (*animal*) root; (*mole*) burrow

**wund** *adj* sore; **Wunde** *f* ⟨-, -n⟩ wound

**Wunder** *nt* ⟨-s, -⟩ miracle; *es ist kein ~* it's no wonder; **wunderbar** *adj* wonderful, marvellous; **Wunderkerze** *f* sparkler; **wundern 1.** *vr* be surprised (*über + acc* at) **2.** *vt* surprise; **wunderschön** *adj* beautiful; **wundervoll** *adj* wonderful

**Wundsalbe** *f* antiseptic oint-

ment; **Wundstarrkrampf** *m* tetanus

**Wunsch** *m* ⟨-(e)s, Wünsche⟩ wish (*nach* for); **wünschen** *vt* wish; *sich dat etw ~* want sth; *ich wünsche dir alles Gute* I wish you all the best; **wünschenswert** *adj* desirable

**wurde** *imperf* → **werden**

**Wurf** *m* ⟨-s, Würfe⟩ throw; ZOOL litter

**Würfel** *m* ⟨-s, -⟩ dice; MATH cube; **würfeln 1.** *vi* throw (the dice); (*as game*) play dice **2.** *vt* (*number*) throw; GASTR dice; **Würfelzucker** *m* lump sugar

**Wurm** *m* ⟨-(e)s, Würmer⟩ worm

**Wurst** *f* ⟨-, Würste⟩ sausage; *das ist mir ~ fam* I couldn't care less

**Würstchen** *nt* frankfurter

**Würze** *f* ⟨-, -n⟩ seasoning, spice

**Wurzel** *f* ⟨-, -n⟩ root; **Wurzelbehandlung** *f* root canal treatment

**würzen** *vt* season, spice; **würzig** *adj* spicy

**wusch** *imperf* → **waschen**

**wusste** *imperf* → **wissen**

**wüst** *adj* (*untidy*) chaotic; (*party, life, person*) wild; (*place*) desolate; *fam* (*intense*) terrible

**Wüste** *f* ⟨-, -n⟩ desert

**Wut** *f* ⟨-⟩ rage, fury; *ich habe eine ~ auf ihn* I'm really mad at him; **wütend** adj furious

**WWW** nt ⟨-⟩ abbr = **World Wide Web** WWW

# X, Y

**X-Beine** pl knock-knees pl; **x-beinig** adj knock-kneed
**x-beliebig** adj **ein ~es Buch** any book (you like)
**x-mal** adv umpteen times

**Xylophon** nt ⟨-s, -e⟩ xylophone
**Yoga** m or nt ⟨-(s)⟩ yoga
**Yuppie** m ⟨-s, -s⟩ f ⟨-, -s⟩ yuppie

# Z

**zackig** adj (line etc) jagged; fam (speed) brisk
**zaghaft** adj timid
**zäh** adj tough
**Zahl** f ⟨-, -en⟩ number; **zahlbar** adj payable; **zahlen** vt, vi pay; ~ **bitte!** could I have the bill (Brit) (or check (US)) please?; **bar ~** pay cash; **zählen** vt, vi count (auf + acc on); ~ **zu** be one of; **Zahlenschloss** nt combination lock; **Zähler** m ⟨-s, -⟩ counter; (for electricity, water) meter; **zahlreich** adj numerous; **Zahlung** f payment
**zahm** adj tame; **zähmen** vt tame
**Zahn** m ⟨-(e)s, Zähne⟩ tooth; **Zahnarzt** m, **Zahnärztin** f dentist; **Zahnbürste** f toothbrush; **Zahncreme** f toothpaste; **Zahnersatz** m dentures pl; **Zahnfleisch** nt

gums pl; **Zahnfleischbluten** nt bleeding gums pl; **Zahnfüllung** f filling; **Zahnklammer** f brace; **Zahnpasta** f, **Zahnpaste** f toothpaste; **Zahnschmerzen** pl toothache sg; **Zahnseide** f dental floss; **Zahnspange** f brace; **Zahnstocher** m ⟨-s, -⟩ toothpick
**Zange** f ⟨-, -n⟩ pliers pl; (for sugar) tongs pl; ZOOL pincers pl
**zanken** vi, vr quarrel
**Zäpfchen** nt ANAT uvula; MED suppository
**zapfen** vt (beer) pull; **Zapfsäule** f petrol (Brit) (or gas (US)) pump
**zappen** vi zap, channel-hop
**zart** adj (meat etc) tender; (fine, weakly) delicate; **zartbitter** adj (chocolate)

plain, dark

**zärtlich** adj tender, affectionate; **Zärtlichkeit** f tenderness; **~en** pl hugs and kisses pl

**Zauber** m ⟨-s, -⟩ magic; (*magic power*) spell; **Zauberei** f magic; **Zauberer** m ⟨-s, -⟩ magician; (*entertainer*) conjuror; **Zauberformel** f (*magic*) spell; **zauberhaft** adj enchanting; **Zauberin** f sorceress; **Zauberkünstler(in)** m(f) magician, conjuror; **Zaubermittel** nt magic cure; **zaubern** vi do magic; (*entertainer*) do conjuring tricks; **Zauberspruch** m (*magic*) spell

**Zaun** m ⟨-(e)s, Zäune⟩ fence

**z. B.** abbr = **zum Beispiel** e.g., eg

**Zebra** nt ⟨-s, -s⟩ zebra; **Zebrastreifen** m zebra crossing (*Brit*), crosswalk (*US*)

**Zecke** f ⟨-, -n⟩ tick

**Zehe** f ⟨-, -n⟩ toe; (*of garlic*) clove; **Zehennagel** m toenail; **Zehenspitze** f tip of the toes

**zehn** num ten; **Zehnerkarte** f ticket valid for ten trips; **Zehnkampf** m decathlon; **Zehnkämpfer(in)** m(f) decathlete; **zehnmal** adv ten times; **zehntausend** num ten thousand; **zehnte(r, s)** adj tenth; → **dritte**; **Zehntel** nt ⟨-s, -⟩ tenth

**Zeichen** nt ⟨-s, -⟩ sign; (*letter,* numeral) character; **Zeichenblock** m sketch pad; **Zeichensetzung** f punctuation; **Zeichensprache** f sign language; **Zeichentrickfilm** m cartoon

**zeichnen** vt, vi draw; **Zeichnung** f drawing

**Zeigefinger** m index finger; **zeigen 1.** vt show; *sie zeigte uns die Stadt* she showed us around the town; *zeig mal!* let me see **2.** vi point (*auf* + *acc* to, at) **3.** vr show oneself; *es wird sich ~* time will tell; **Zeiger** m ⟨-s, -⟩ pointer; (*of clock, watch*) hand

**Zeile** f ⟨-, -n⟩ line

**Zeit** f ⟨-, -en⟩ time; *ich habe keine ~* I haven't got time; *lass dir ~* take your time; *von ~ zu ~* from time to time; **Zeitansage** f TEL speaking clock (*Brit*), correct time (*US*); **Zeitarbeit** f temporary work; **zeitgenössisch** adj contemporary, modern; **zeitgleich 1.** adj simultaneous **2.** adv at exactly the same time; **zeitig** adj early; **Zeitkarte** f season ticket; **zeitlich** adj (*order*) chronological; *es passt ~ nicht* it isn't a convenient time; **Zeitlupe** f slow motion; **Zeitplan** m schedule; **Zeitpunkt** m point in time; **Zeitraum** m period (of time)

**Zeitschrift** f magazine; (*academic, scientific*) periodical

**Zeitung** f newspaper; **es steht in der ~** it's in the paper(s); **Zeitungsartikel** m newspaper article; **Zeitungskiosk** m, **Zeitungsstand** m newsstand

**Zeitunterschied** m time difference; **Zeitverschiebung** f time lag; **Zeitvertreib** m ⟨-(e)s, -e⟩ **zum ~** to pass the time; **Zeitzone** f time zone

**Zelle** f ⟨-, -n⟩ cell

**Zellophan**® nt ⟨-s⟩ cellophane

**Zelt** nt ⟨-(e)s, -e⟩ tent; **zelten** vi camp, go camping; **Zeltplatz** m campsite, camping site

**Zement** m ⟨-(e)s, -e⟩ cement

**Zentimeter** m or nt centimetre

**Zentner** m ⟨-s, -⟩ (metric) hundredweight; (in Germany) fifty kilos; (in Austria and Switzerland) one hundred kilos

**zentral** adj central; **Zentrale** f ⟨-, -n⟩ central office; TEL exchange; **Zentralheizung** f central heating; **Zentralverriegelung** f AUTO central locking; **Zentrum** nt ⟨-s, Zentren⟩ centre

**zerbrechen** irr vt, vi break; **zerbrechlich** adj fragile

**Zeremonie** f ⟨-, -n⟩ ceremony

**zerkleinern** vt cut up; (roughly) chop (up); **zerkratzen** vt scratch; **zerlegen** vt take to pieces; (meat) carve; (machine, engine) dismantle;

**zerquetschen** vt squash; **zerreißen** irr **1.** vt tear to pieces **2.** vi tear

**zerren 1.** vt drag; **sich** dat **einen Muskel ~** pull a muscle **2.** vi tug (an + dat at); **Zerrung** f MED pulled muscle

**zerschlagen** irr **1.** vt smash **2.** vr come to nothing

**zerschneiden** irr vt cut up

**zerstören** vt destroy; **Zerstörung** f destruction

**zerstreuen 1.** vt scatter; (crowd) disperse; (doubts, fears) dispel **2.** vr (crowd) disperse; **zerstreut** adj scattered; (person) absent-minded; (temporarily) distracted

**zerteilen** vt split up

**Zertifikat** nt ⟨-(e)s, -e⟩ certificate

**Zettel** m ⟨-s, -⟩ piece of paper; (message, reminder) note

**Zeug** nt ⟨-(e)s, -e⟩ stuff; (equipment) gear; **dummes ~** nonsense

**Zeuge** m ⟨-n, -n⟩, **Zeugin** f witness

**Zeugnis** nt certificate; (from school) report; (from former employer) reference

**zickig** adj fam touchy, bitchy

**Zickzack** m ⟨-(e)s, -e⟩ **im ~ fahren** zigzag (across the road)

**Ziege** f ⟨-, -n⟩ goat

**Ziegel** m ⟨-s, -⟩ brick; (on roof) tile

**Ziegenkäse** m goat's cheese

**ziehen** ⟨zog, gezogen⟩ **1.** vt draw; (tug, drag) pull; (piece in game) move; (breed) rear **2.** vi pull; (go) move; (smoke, cloud etc) drift; **den Tee ~ lassen** let the tea stand **3.** vi impers **es zieht** there's a draught **4.** vr (meeting, speech) drag on

**Ziel** nt ⟨-(e)s, -e⟩ (of journey) destination; SPORT finish; (intention) goal, aim; **zielen** vi aim (auf + acc at); **Zielgruppe** f target group; **ziellos** adj aimless; **Zielscheibe** f target

**ziemlich 1.** adj considerable; **ein ~es Durcheinander** quite a mess; **mit ~er Sicherheit** with some certainty **2.** adv rather, quite; **~ viel** quite a lot

**zierlich** adj dainty; (woman) petite

**Ziffer** f ⟨-, -n⟩ figure; **arabische / römische ~n** pl Arabic / Roman numerals pl; **Zifferblatt** nt dial, face

**zig** adj umpteen

**Zigarette** f cigarette; **Zigarettenautomat** m cigarette machine; **Zigarettenschachtel** f cigarette packet; **Zigarettenstummel** m cigarette end; **Zigarillo** ⟨-s, -s⟩ m or nt cigarillo; **Zigarre** f ⟨-, -n⟩ cigar

**Zimmer** nt ⟨-s, -⟩ room; **haben Sie ein ~ für zwei Personen?** do you have a room for two?; **Zimmerlautstärke**

f reasonable volume; **Zimmermädchen** nt chambermaid; **Zimmermann** m carpenter; **Zimmerpflanze** f house plant; **Zimmerschlüssel** m room key; **Zimmerservice** m room service; **Zimmervermittlung** f accommodation agency

**Zimt** m ⟨-(e)s, -e⟩ cinnamon

**Zink** nt ⟨-(e)s⟩ zinc

**Zinn** nt ⟨-(e)s⟩ tin; (alloy) pewter

**Zinsen** pl interest sg

**Zipfel** m ⟨-s, -⟩ corner; (pointed) tip; (of shirt) tail; (of sausage) end

**Zirkel** m ⟨-s, -⟩ MATH (pair of) compasses pl

**Zirkus** m ⟨-, -se⟩ circus

**zischen** vi hiss

**Zitat** nt ⟨-(e)s, -e⟩ quotation (aus from); **zitieren** vt quote

**Zitronat** nt candied lemon peel; **Zitrone** f ⟨-, -n⟩ lemon; **Zitronenlimonade** f lemonade; **Zitronensaft** m lemon juice

**zittern** vi tremble (vor + dat with)

**zivil** adj civilian; (price) reasonable; **Zivil** nt ⟨-s⟩ plain clothes pl; MIL civilian clothes pl; **Zivildienst** m community service (for conscientious objectors)

**zocken** vi fam gamble

**Zoff** m ⟨-s⟩ fam trouble

**zog** imperf → **ziehen**

**zögerlich** adj hesitant; **zö-**

**gern** *vi* hesitate

**Zoll** *m* ⟨-(e)s, Zölle⟩ customs *pl*; (*tax*) duty; **Zollabfertigung** *f* customs clearance; **Zollamt** *nt* customs office; **Zollbeamte(r)** *m*, **Zollbeamtin** *f* customs official; **Zollerklärung** *f* customs declaration; **zollfrei** *adj* duty-free; **Zollgebühren** *pl* customs duties *pl*; **Zollkontrolle** *f* customs check; **Zöllner(in)** *m(f)* customs officer; **zollpflichtig** *adj* liable to duty

**Zone** *f* ⟨-, -n⟩ zone

**Zoo** *m* ⟨-s, -s⟩ zoo

**Zoom** *nt* ⟨-s, -s⟩ zoom (shot); zoom (lens)

**Zopf** *m* ⟨-(e)s, Zöpfe⟩ plait (*Brit*), braid (*US*)

**Zorn** *m* ⟨-(e)s⟩ anger; **zornig** *adj* angry (*über etw acc* about sth, *auf jdn* with sb)

**zu 1.** *conj* (*with infinitive*) to **2.** *prep* + *dat* (*direction, action*) to; (*place, time, price*) at; (*purpose*) for; **~r Post® gehen** go to the post office; **~ Hause** at home; **~ Weihnachten** at Christmas; **fünf Bücher ~ 20 Euro** five books at 20 euros each; **~m Fenster herein** through the window; **~ meiner Zeit** in my time **3.** *adv* too; **~ viel** too much; **~ wenig** not enough **4.** *adj fam* shut; **Tür ~!** shut the door

**zuallererst** *adv* first of all; **zu-**

**allerletzt** *adv* last of all

**Zubehör** *nt* ⟨-(e)s, -e⟩ accessories *pl*

**zubereiten** *vt* prepare; **Zubereitung** *f* preparation

**zubinden** *irr vt* do (*or* tie) up

**Zucchini** *pl* courgettes *pl* (*Brit*), zucchini *pl* (*US*)

**züchten** *vt* (*animals*) breed; (*plants*) grow

**zucken** *vi* jerk; (*convulsively*) twitch; **mit den Schultern ~** shrug (one's shoulders)

**Zucker** *m* ⟨-s, -⟩ sugar; MED diabetes *sg*; **Zuckerdose** *f* sugar bowl; **zuckerkrank** *adj* diabetic; **Zuckerrohr** *nt* sugar cane; **Zuckerwatte** *f* candy-floss (*Brit*), cotton candy (*US*)

**zudecken** *vt* cover up

**zudrehen** *vt* turn off

**zueinander** *adv* to one another; (*as part of verb*) together; **zueinanderhalten** *irr vi* stick together

**zuerst** *adv* first; (*at the start*) at first; **~ einmal** first of all

**Zufahrt** *f* access; (*of house*) drive(way); **Zufahrtsstraße** *f* access road; (*onto motorway*) slip road (*Brit*), ramp (*US*)

**Zufall** *m* chance; (*event*) coincidence; **durch ~** by accident; **so ein ~!** what a coincidence; **zufällig 1.** *adj* chance **2.** *adv* by chance; **weißt du ~, ob ...?** do you happen to know whether

...?

**zufrieden** *adj* content(ed); (*with sth*) satisfied; **lass sie ~** leave her alone (*or* in peace); **zufriedengeben** *irr vr* **sich mit etw ~** settle for sth; **Zufriedenheit** *f* contentment; (*with sth*) satisfaction; **zufriedenstellen** *vt* **sie ist schwer zufriedenzustellen** she is hard to please

**zufügen** *vt* add (*dat* to); **jdm Schaden / Schmerzen ~** cause sb harm / pain

**Zug** *m* ‹-(e)s, Züge› RAIL train; (*air*) draught; (*tug*) pull; (*in chess*) move; (*of character*) trait; (*on cigarette*) puff, drag; (*swallow*) gulp

**Zugabe** *f* extra; (*at concert etc*) encore

**Zugabteil** *nt* train compartment

**Zugang** *m* access; „**kein ~!**" ‘no entry'

**Zugauskunft** *f* train information office / desk; **Zugbegleiter(in)** *m(f)* guard (*Brit*), conductor (*US*)

**zugeben** *irr vt* admit; **zugegeben** *adv* admittedly

**zugehen** *irr* **1.** *vi* (*door, cupboard etc*) shut; **auf jdn / etw ~** walk towards sb/sth; **dem Ende ~** be coming to a close **2.** *vi impers* happen; **es ging lustig zu** we / they had a lot of fun

**Zügel** *m* ‹-s, -› rein

**Zugführer(in)** *m(f)* guard

(*Brit*), conductor (*US*)

**zugig** *adj* draughty

**zügig** *adj* speedy

**Zugluft** *f* draught

**Zugpersonal** *nt* train staff

**zugreifen** *irr vi* fig seize the opportunity; (*when eating*) help oneself; **~ auf** + *acc* IT access

**Zugrestaurant** *nt* dining car, diner (*US*)

**Zugriffsberechtigung** *f* IT access right

**zugrunde** *adv* **~ gehen** perish; **~ gehen an** + *dat* die of

**Zugschaffner(in)** *m(f)* ticket inspector; **Zugunglück** *nt* train crash

**zugunsten** *prep* + *gen* or *dat* in favour of

**Zugverbindung** *f* train connection

**zuhaben** *irr vi* be closed

**zuhalten** *irr vt* **sich** *dat* **die Nase ~** hold one's nose; **sich** *dat* **die Ohren ~** hold one's hands over one's ears; **die Tür ~** hold the door shut

**Zuhause** *nt* ‹-s› home

**zuhören** *vi* listen (*dat* to); **Zuhörer(in)** *m(f)* listener

**zukleben** *vt* seal

**zukommen** *irr vi* come up (*auf* + *acc* to); **jdm etw ~ lassen** give / send sb sth; **etw auf sich** *acc* **~ lassen** take sth as it comes

**Zukunft** *f* ‹-, Zukünfte› future; **zukünftig 1.** *adj* future **2.** *adv* in future

**zulassen** *irr vt (let in)* admit; *(allow)* permit; *(car)* license; *fam (not open)* keep shut; **zulässig** *adj* permissible, permitted

**zuletzt** *adv* finally, at last

**zuliebe** *adv* **jdm ~** for sb's sake

**zum** *contr = zu dem*; **~ dritten Mal** for the third time; **~ Trinken** for drinking

**zumachen** **1.** *vt* shut; *(clothes)* do up **2.** *vi* shut

**zumindest** *adv* at least

**zumuten** **1.** *vt* **jdm etw ~** expect sth of sb **2.** *vr* **sich** *dat* **zu viel ~** overdo things

**zunächst** *adv* first of all; **~ einmal** to start with

**Zunahme** *f* ⟨-, -n⟩ increase

**Zuname** *m* surname, last name

**zünden** *vt, vi* AUTO ignite; fire; **Zündkabel** *f* AUTO ignition cable; **Zündkerze** *f* AUTO spark plug; **Zündschloss** *nt* ignition lock; **Zündschlüssel** *m* ignition key; **Zündung** *f* ignition

**zunehmen** *irr* **1.** *vi* increase; *(person)* put on weight **2.** *vt* **5 Kilo ~** put on 5 kilos

**Zunge** *f* ⟨-, -n⟩ tongue

**Zungenkuss** *m* French kiss

**zunichtemachen** *vt* ruin

**zunutze** *adv* **sich** *dat* **etw ~ machen** make use of sth

**zuparken** *vt* block

**zur** *contr = zu der*

**zurechtfinden** *irr vr* find

one's way around; **zurechtkommen** *irr vi* cope *(mit etw* with sth); **zurechtmachen** **1.** *vt* prepare **2.** *vr* get ready

**Zürich** *nt* ⟨-s⟩ Zurich

**zurück** *adv* back

**zurückbekommen** *irr vt* get back; **zurückblicken** *vi* look back *(auf + acc* at); **zurückbringen** *irr vt* bring back; *(somewhere else)* take back; **zurückerstatten** *vt* refund; **zurückfahren** *irr vi* go back; **zurückgeben** *irr vt* give back; **zurückgehen** *irr vi* go back; *(in time)* date back *(auf + acc* to)

**zurückhalten** *irr* **1.** *vt* hold back; *(hinder)* prevent **2.** *vr* hold back; **zurückhaltend** *adj* reserved

**zurückholen** *vt* fetch back; **zurückkommen** *irr vi* come back; **auf etw** *acc* **~** return *(or* get back) to sth; **zurücklassen** *irr vt* leave behind; **zurücklegen** *vt* put back; *(money)* put by; *(keep in reserve)* keep back; *(distance)* cover; **zurücknehmen** *irr vt* take back; **zurückrufen** *irr vt* call back; **zurückschicken** *vt* send back; **zurückstellen** *vt* put back; **zurücktreten** *irr vi* step back; *(from office)* retire; **zurückverlangen** *vt* **etw ~** ask for sth back; **zurückzahlen** *vt* pay back

**zurzeit** *adv* at present

**Zusage** f promise; (of invitation) acceptance; **zusagen 1.** vt promise **2.** vi accept; **jdm ~** (please) appeal to sb
**zusammen** adv together
**Zusammenarbeit** f collaboration; **zusammenarbeiten** vi work together
**zusammenbrechen** irr vi collapse; (mentally) break down; **Zusammenbruch** m collapse; (mental) breakdown
**zusammenfassen** vt summarize; (bring together) unite; **Zusammenfassung** f summary
**zusammengehören** vi belong together; **zusammenhalten** irr vi stick together
**Zusammenhang** m connection; **im / aus dem ~** in / out of context; **zusammenhängen** irr vi be connected; **zusammenhängend** adj coherent; **zusammenhang(s)los** adj incoherent
**zusammenklappen** vi, vt fold up; **zusammenlegen 1.** vt fold up **2.** vi club together; **zusammennehmen** irr **1.** vt summon up; **alles zusammengenommen** all in all **2.** vr pull oneself together; fam get a grip, get one's act together; **zusammenpassen** vi go together; (people) be suited; **zusammenrechnen** vt add up
**Zusammensein** nt ⟨-s⟩ get-together
**zusammensetzen 1.** vt put together **2.** vr **sich ~ aus** be composed of; **Zusammensetzung** f composition
**Zusammenstoß** m crash, collision; **zusammenstoßen** irr vi crash (mit into)
**zusammenzählen** vt add up
**zusammenziehen** irr vi (into flat etc) move in together
**Zusatz** m addition; IT add-on; **zusätzlich 1.** adj additional **2.** adv in addition
**zuschauen** vi watch; **Zuschauer(in)** m(f) ⟨-s, -⟩ spectator; **die ~** pl THEAT the audience sg; **Zuschauertribüne** f stand
**zuschicken** vt send
**Zuschlag** m extra charge; (on ticket) supplement
**zuschlagpflichtig** adj subject to an extra charge; RAIL subject to a supplement
**zuschließen** irr vt lock up
**zusehen** irr vi watch (jdm sb); **~, dass** make sure that
**zusichern** vt jdm etw ~ assure sb of sth
**Zustand** m state, condition
**zustande** adv **~ bringen** bring about; **~ kommen** come about
**zuständig** adj (authority) relevant; **~ für** responsible for
**Zustellung** f delivery
**zustimmen** vi agree (einer Sache dat to sth, jdm with sb); **Zustimmung** f approval

**zustoßen** *irr vi fig* happen (*jdm* to sb)

**Zutaten** *pl* ingredients *pl*

**zutrauen** *vt jdm etw* ~ think sb is capable of sth; *das hätte ich ihm nie zugetraut* I'd never have thought he was capable of it; *ich würde es ihr* ~ (*sth negative*) I wouldn't put it past her; **Zutrauen** *nt* ⟨-s⟩ confidence (*zu* in); **zutraulich** *adj* trusting; (*animal*) friendly

**zutreffen** *irr vi* be correct; ~ *auf* + *acc* apply to; *Zutreffendes bitte streichen* please delete as applicable

**Zutritt** *m* entry; (*permission to enter*) access; *„~ verboten!"* 'no entry'

**zuverlässig** *adj* reliable; **Zuverlässigkeit** *f* reliability

**Zuversicht** *f* confidence; **zuversichtlich** *adj* confident

**zuvor** *adv* before; (*before anything else*) first; **zuvorkommen** *irr vi jdm* ~ beat sb to it

**Zuwachs** *m* ⟨-es, Zuwächse⟩ increase, growth; *fam* (*baby*) addition to the family

**zuwider** *adv es ist mir* ~ I hate (*or* detest) it

**zuzüglich** *prep + gen* plus

**zwang** *imperf* → **zwingen**

**Zwang** *m* ⟨-(e)s, Zwänge⟩ (*inner urge*) compulsion; (*against will*) force; **zwängen** *vt, vr* squeeze (*in + acc* into); **zwanglos** *adj* informal

**zwanzig** *num* twenty; **zwanzigste(r, s)** *adj* twentieth; → *dritte*

**zwar** *adv und* ~ ...., to be precise; *das ist* ~ *schön, aber* ... it is nice, but ...

**Zweck** *m* ⟨-(e)s, -e⟩ purpose; **zwecklos** *adj* pointless

**zwei** *num* two; **Zwei** *f* ⟨-, -en⟩ two; (*mark in school*) ≈ B; **Zweibettzimmer** *nt* twin room; **zweideutig** *adj* ambiguous; (*indecent*) suggestive; **zweifach** *adj, adv* double

**Zweifel** *m* ⟨-s, -⟩ doubt; **zweifellos** *adv* undoubtedly; **zweifeln** *vi* doubt (*an etw dat* sth); **Zweifelsfall** *m im* ~ in case of doubt

**Zweig** *m* ⟨-(e)s, -e⟩ branch; **Zweigstelle** *f* branch

**zweihundert** *num* two hundred; **zweimal** *adv* twice; **zweisprachig** *adj* bilingual; **zweispurig** *adj* AUTO two-lane; *zwei adv wir sind zu* ~ there are two of us; **zweite(r, s)** *adj* second; → *dritte*; **zweitens** *adv* secondly; (*when listing*) second; **zweitgrößte(r, s)** *adj* second largest; **Zweitschlüssel** *m* spare key

**Zwerg(in)** *m(f)* ⟨-(e)s, -e⟩ dwarf

**Zwetschge** *f* ⟨-, -n⟩ plum

**zwicken** *vt* pinch

**Zwieback** *m* ⟨-(e)s, -e⟩ rusk

**Zwiebel** *f* ⟨-, -n⟩ onion; (*of*

*flower)* bulb; **Zwiebelsuppe** *f* onion soup

**Zwilling** *m* ⟨-s, -e⟩ twin; **~e** *pl* ASTR Gemini *sg*

**zwingen** ⟨zwang, gezwungen⟩ *vt* force

**zwinkern** *vi* blink; *(deliberately)* wink

**zwischen** *prep + acc or dat* between; **Zwischenablage** *f* IT clipboard; **zwischendurch** *adv* in between; **Zwischenlandung** *f* stopover;

**Zwischenraum** *m* space; **Zwischenstopp** *m* ⟨-s, -s⟩ stopover; **Zwischenzeit** *f* **in der ~** in the meantime

**zwitschern** *vt, vi* twitter, chirp

**zwölf** *num* twelve; **zwölfte(r, s)** *adj* twelfth; → *dritte*

**Zylinder** *m* ⟨-s, -⟩ cylinder; top hat

**zynisch** *adj* cynical

**Zypern** *nt* ⟨-s⟩ Cyprus

# English – German

## A

**a, an** *art* ein / eine / ein; **~ man** ein Mann; **~ woman** eine Frau; **~n apple** ein Apfel; **he's ~ student** er ist Student; **three times ~ week** dreimal pro Woche / in der Woche

**AA** *abbr* = **Automobile Association** britischer Automobilklub, ≈ ADAC *m*

**aback** *adv* **taken ~** erstaunt

**abandon** *vt* (*desert*) verlassen; (*give up*) aufgeben

**abbey** *n* Abtei *f*

**abbreviation** *n* Abkürzung *f*

**abdication** *n* Abdankung *f*

**abdomen** *n* Unterleib *m*

**ability** *n* Fähigkeit *f*; **able** *adj* fähig; **be ~ to do sth** etw tun können

**aboard** *adv, prep* an Bord + *gen*

**abolish** *vt* abschaffen

**aborigine** *n* Ureinwohner(in) *m(f)* (Australiens)

**abortion** *n* Abtreibung *f*

**about 1.** *adv* (*around*) herum, umher; (*approximately*) ungefähr; (*with time*) gegen; **be ~ to** im Begriff sein zu; **there are a lot of people ~** es sind eine Menge Leute

da **2.** *prep* (*concerning*) über + *acc*; **there is nothing you can do ~ it** da kann man nichts machen

**above 1.** *adv* oben; **children aged 8 and ~** Kinder ab 8 Jahren; **on the floor ~** ein Stockwerk höher **2.** *prep* über; **~ 40 degrees** über 40 Grad; **~ all** vor allem **3.** *adj* obig

**abroad** *adv* im Ausland; **go ~** ins Ausland gehen

**absent** *adj* abwesend; **be ~** fehlen; **absent-minded** *adj* zerstreut

**absolute** *adj* absolut; (*rubbish*) vollkommen, total; **absolutely** *adv* absolut; (*true, stupid*) vollkommen; **~!** genau!; **you're ~ right** du hast / Sie haben völlig recht

**absorb** *vt* absorbieren; *fig* (*information*) in sich aufnehmen; **absorbed** *adj* **~ in sth** in etw vertieft; **absorbent** *adj* absorbierend; **~ cotton** (*US*) Watte *f*; **absorbing** *adj fig* faszinierend, fesselnd

**abstract** *adj* abstrakt

**abundance** *n* Reichtum *m* (*of* an + *dat*)

**abuse 1.** n (*rude language*) Beschimpfungen pl; (*mistreatment*) Missbrauch m **2.** vt (*misuse*) missbrauchen; **abusive** adj beleidigend

**AC 1.** abbr → **alternating current** Wechselstrom m **2.** abbr → **air conditioning** Klimaanlage f

**a/c** abbr → **account** Kto.

**academic 1.** n Wissenschaftler(in) m(f) **2.** adj wissenschaftlich

**accelerate** vi (*car etc*) beschleunigen; (*driver*) Gas geben; **acceleration** n Beschleunigung f; **accelerator** n Gas(pedal) nt

**accent** n Akzent m

**accept** vt (*agree to*) akzeptieren; (*responsibility*) übernehmen; **acceptable** adj annehmbar

**access** n Zugang m; IT Zugriff m; **accessible** adj (leicht) zugänglich / erreichbar; **accessory** n Zubehörteil m; **access road** n Zufahrtsstraße f

**accident** n Unfall m; **by ~** zufällig; **accidental** adj unbeabsichtigt; (*meeting*) zufällig; (*death*) durch Unfall; **accident-prone** adj vom Pech verfolgt

**acclimatize** vt **~ oneself** sich gewöhnen (*to* an + *acc*)

**accommodate** vt unterbringen; **accommodation, s** n Unterkunft f

**accompany** vt begleiten

**accomplish** vt erreichen

**accord** n **of one's own ~** freiwillig; **according to** prep nach, laut + dat

**account** n (*in bank etc*) Konto nt; (*narrative*) Bericht m; **on ~ of** wegen; **on no ~** auf keinen Fall; **take into ~** berücksichtigen, in Betracht ziehen; (*explain*) erklären; (*expenditure*) Rechenschaft ablegen für; **account number** n Kontonummer f

**accurate** adj genau

**accusation** n Anklage f, Beschuldigung f; **accuse** vt beschuldigen; LAW anklagen (*of* wegen gen); **accused** n LAW Angeklagte(r) mf

**accustom** vt gewöhnen (*to* an + *acc*); **accustomed** adj gewohnt; **get ~ to sth** sich an etw acc gewöhnen

**ace 1.** n Ass nt **2.** adj Star-

**ache 1.** n Schmerz m **2.** vi wehtun

**achieve** vt erreichen; **achievement** n Leistung f

**acid 1.** n Säure f **2.** adj sauer

**acknowledge** vt (*recognize*) anerkennen; (*admit*) zugeben; (*receipt of letter etc*) bestätigen; **acknowledgement** n Anerkennung f; (*of letter*) Empfangsbestätigung f

**acne** n Akne f

**acorn** n Eichel f

**acoustic** *adj* akustisch;
**acoustics** *npl* Akustik *f*
**acquaintance** *n* (*person*) Bekannte(r) *mf*
**acquire** *vt* erwerben, sich aneignen; **acquisition** *n* (*of skills etc*) Erwerb *m*; (*object*) Anschaffung *f*
**across 1.** *prep* über + *acc*; **he lives ~ the street** er wohnt auf der anderen Seite der Straße **2.** *adv* hinüber, herüber; **100m ~** 100m breit
**act 1.** *n* (*deed*) Tat *f*; LAW Gesetz *nt*; THEAT Akt *m*; **be in the ~ of doing sth** gerade dabei sein, etw zu tun **2.** *vi* (*take action*) handeln; (*behave*) sich verhalten; THEAT spielen; **~ as** (*person*) fungieren als; (*thing*) dienen als **3.** *vt* (*a part*) spielen
**action** *n* (*of play, novel etc*) Handlung *f*; (*in film etc*) Action *f*; MIL Kampf *m*; **take ~** etwas unternehmen; **put a plan into ~** einen Plan in die Tat umsetzen; **action replay** *n* SPORT, TV Wiederholung *f*
**activate** *vt* aktivieren; **active** *adj* aktiv; (*child*) lebhaft; **activity** *n* Aktivität *f*; (*occupation*) Beschäftigung *f*; (*organized event*) Veranstaltung *f*
**actor** *n* Schauspieler(in) *m(f)*;
**actress** *n* Schauspielerin *f*
**actual** *adj* wirklich; **actually** *adv* eigentlich; (*said in sur-*

*prise*) tatsächlich
**acupuncture** *n* Akupunktur *f*
**acute** *adj* (*pain*) akut; MATH (*angle*) spitz
**ad** *abbr* → **advertisement**
**AD** *abbr* = **Anno Domini** nach Christi, n. Chr.
**adapt 1.** *vi* sich anpassen (*to* + *dat*) **2.** *vt* anpassen (*to* + *dat*); (*rewrite*) bearbeiten (*for* für); **adaptation** *n* (*of book etc*) Bearbeitung *f*; **adapter** *n* ELEC Zwischenstecker *m*, Adapter *m*
**add** *vt* (*ingredient*) hinzufügen; (*numbers*) addieren; **add up 1.** *vi* (*make sense*) stimmen **2.** *vt* (*numbers*) addieren
**addicted** *adj* **~ to alcohol / drugs** alkohol- / drogensüchtig
**addition** *n* Zusatz *m*; (*to bill*) Aufschlag *m*; MATH Addition *f*; **in ~** außerdem, zusätzlich (*to* zu); **additional** *adj* zusätzlich, weiter; **additive** *n* Zusatz *m*; **add-on** *n* Zusatzgerät *nt*
**address 1.** *n* Adresse *f* **2.** *vt* (*letter*) adressieren; (*person*) anreden
**adequate** *adj* (*appropriate*) angemessen; (*sufficient*) ausreichend
**adhesive** *n* Klebstoff *m*; **adhesive tape** *n* Klebstreifen *m*
**adjacent** *adj* benachbart
**adjoining** *adj* benachbart,

Neben-

**adjust 1.** vt einstellen; (put right also) richtig stellen; (speed, flow) regulieren; (in position) verstellen **2.** vi sich anpassen (to + dat); **adjustable** adj verstellbar

**admin** n fam Verwaltung f; **administration** n Verwaltung f; POL Regierung f

**admirable** adj bewundernswert; **admiration** n Bewunderung f; **admire** vt bewundern

**admission** n (entrance) Zutritt m; (to university etc) Zulassung f; (fee) Eintritt m; **admission charge, admission fee** n Eintrittspreis m; **admit** vt (let in) hereinlassen (to in + acc); (to university etc) zulassen; (confess) zugeben, gestehen; **be ~ted to hospital** ins Krankenhaus eingeliefert werden

**adolescent** n Jugendliche(r) mf

**adopt** vt (child) adoptieren; (idea) übernehmen; **adoption** n (of child) Adoption f; (of idea) Übernahme f

**adorable** adj entzückend; **adore** vt anbeten; (person) über alles lieben, vergöttern

**adult 1.** adj (person) erwachsen; (film etc) für Erwachsene **2.** n Erwachsene(r) mf

**adultery** n Ehebruch m

**advance 1.** n (money) Vorschuss m; (progress) Fortschritt m; **in ~** im Voraus; **book in ~** vorbestellen **2.** vi (move forward) vorrücken **3.** vt (money) vorschießen; **advance booking** n Reservierung f; THEAT Vorverkauf m; **advanced** adj (modern) fortschrittlich; (course, study) für Fortgeschrittene; **advance payment** n Vorauszahlung f

**advantage** n Vorteil m; **take ~** (exploit) ausnutzen; (profit from) Nutzen ziehen aus; **it's to your ~** es ist in deinem / Ihrem Interesse

**adventure** n Abenteuer nt; **adventure holiday** n Abenteuerurlaub m; **adventure playground** n Abenteuerspielplatz m

**adverse** adj (conditions etc) ungünstig; (effect, comment etc) negativ

**advert** n Anzeige f; **advertise 1.** vt werben für; (in newspaper) inserieren; (job) ausschreiben **2.** vi Reklame machen; **advertisement** n Werbung f; (announcement) Anzeige f; **advertising** n Werbung f

**advice** n Rat(schlag) m; **take my ~** hör auf mich; **advisable** adj ratsam; **advise** vt raten (sb jdm); **~ sb to do sth / not to do sth** jdm zuraten / abraten, etw zu tun

**aerial 1.** n Antenne f **2.** adj Luft-

**aerobics** *nsing* Aerobic *nt*

**aeroplane** *n* Flugzeug *nt*

**afaik** *abbr* **= as far as I know** (*SMS etc*) ≈ soweit ich weiß

**affair** *n* (*matter, business*) Sache *f*, Angelegenheit *f*; (*scandal*) Affäre *f*; (*love affair*) Verhältnis *nt*

**affect** *vt* (*influence*) (ein)wirken auf + *acc*; (*health, organ*) angreifen; (*move deeply*) berühren; (*concern*) betreffen;

**affection** *n* Zuneigung *f*; **affectionate** *adj* liebevoll

**affluent** *adj* wohlhabend

**afford** *vt* sich leisten; **I can't ~ it** ich kann es mir nicht leisten; **affordable** *adj* erschwinglich

**Afghanistan** *n* Afghanistan *nt*

**aforementioned** *adj* oben genannt

**afraid** *adj* **be ~** Angst haben (*of* +*gen* + *dat*); **be ~ that ...** fürchten, dass ...; **I'm ~ I don't know** das weiß ich leider nicht

**Africa** *n* Afrika *nt*; **African 1.** *adj* afrikanisch **2.** *n* Afrikaner(in) *m(f)*; **African American, Afro-American** *n* Afroamerikaner(in) *m(f)*

**after 1.** *prep* nach; **ten ~ five** (*US*) zehn nach fünf; **be ~ sb / sth** (*following, seeking*) hinter jdm / etw her sein; **~ all** schließlich **2.** *conj* nachdem **3.** *adv* **soon ~** bald danach; **aftercare** *n* Nachbe-

handlung *f*

**afternoon** *n* Nachmittag *m*; **in the ~** nachmittags

**afters** *npl* Nachtisch *m*; **after-sales service** *n* Kundendienst *m*; **after-shave** (lotion) *n* Rasierwasser *nt*; **afterwards** *adv* nachher; (*after that*) danach

**again** *adv* wieder; (*one more time*) noch einmal; **~ and ~** immer wieder; **the same ~ please** das Gleiche noch mal bitte

**against** *prep* gegen; **~ my will** wider Willen; **~ the law** unrechtmäßig, illegal

**age 1.** *n* Alter *nt*; (*period of history*) Zeitalter *nt*; **at the ~ of four** im Alter von vier (Jahren); **what ~ is she?, what is her ~?** wie alt ist sie?; **under ~** minderjährig **2.** *vi* altern, alt werden; **aged 1.** *adj* **~ thirty** dreißig Jahre alt; **a son ~ twenty** ein zwanzigjähriger Sohn **2.** *adj* (*elderly*) betagt; **age group** *n* Altersgruppe *f*; **age limit** *n* Altersgrenze *f*

**agency** *n* Agentur *f*

**agenda** *n* Tagesordnung *f*

**agent** *n* COMM Vertreter(in) *m(f)*; (*for writer, actor etc*) Agent(in) *m(f)*

**aggression** *n* Aggression *f*; **aggressive** *adj* aggressiv

**AGM** *abbr* **= Annual General Meeting** JHV *f*

**ago** *adv* **two days ~** heute vor

zwei Tagen; **not long ~** (erst) vor Kurzem

**agonize** *vi* sich den Kopf zerbrechen (*over* über + *acc*); **agonizing** *adj* qualvoll; **agony** *n* Qual *f*

**agree 1.** *vt* (*date, price etc*) vereinbaren; **~ to do sth** sich bereit erklären, etw zu tun; **~ that ...** sich *dat* einig sein, dass ...; (*decide*) beschließen, dass ...; (*admit*) zugeben, dass ... **2.** *vi* (*have same opinion, correspond*) übereinstimmen (*with* mit); (*consent*) zustimmen; (*come to an agreement*) sich einigen (*about, on* auf + *acc*); (*food*) **not ~ with sb** jdm nicht bekommen; **agreement** *n* (*agreeing*) Übereinstimmung *f*; (*contract*) Abkommen *nt*, Vereinbarung *f*

**agricultural** *adj* landwirtschaftlich, Landwirtschafts-; **agriculture** *n* Landwirtschaft *f*

**ahead** *adv* **be ~** führen, vorne liegen; **~ of** vor + *dat*; **be 3 metres ~** 3 Meter Vorsprung haben

**aid 1.** *n* Hilfe *f*; **in ~ of** zugunsten + *gen*; **with the ~ of** mithilfe + *gen* **2.** *vt* helfen + *dat*; (*support*) unterstützen

**Aids** *n acr* = **acquired immune deficiency syndrome**; Aids *nt*

**aim 1.** *vt* (*gun, camera*) richten (*at* auf + *acc*) **2.** *vi* **~ at** (*with*

*gun etc*) zielen auf + *acc*; *fig* abzielen auf + *acc*; **~ to do sth** beabsichtigen, etw zu tun **3.** *n* Ziel *nt*

**air 1.** *n* Luft *f*; **in the open ~** im Freien **2.** *vt* lüften; **airbag** *n* AUTO Airbag *m*; **air-conditioned** *adj* mit Klimaanlage; **air conditioning** *n* Klimaanlage *f*; **aircraft** *n* Flugzeug *nt*; **airfield** *n* Flugplatz *m*; **air force** *n* Luftwaffe *f*; **airline** *n* Fluggesellschaft *f*; **airmail** *n* Luftpost *f*; **by ~** mit Luftpost; **airplane** *n* (*US*) Flugzeug *nt*; **air pollution** *n* Luftverschmutzung *f*; **airport** *n* Flughafen *m*; **airsick** *adj* luftkrank; **airtight** *adj* luftdicht; **air-traffic controller** *n* Fluglotse *m*, Fluglotsin *f*

**aisle** *n* Gang *m*; (*in church*) Seitenschiff *nt*; **~ seat** Sitz *m* am Gang

**ajar** *adj* (*door*) angelehnt

**alarm 1.** *n* (*warning*) Alarm *m*; (*bell etc*) Alarmanlage *f* **2.** *vt* beunruhigen; **alarm clock** *n* Wecker *m*; **alarmed** *adj* (*protected*) alarmgesichert; **alarming** *adj* beunruhigend

**Albania** *n* Albanien *nt*; **Albanian 1.** *adj* albanisch **2.** *n* (*person*) Albaner(in) *m(f)*; (*language*) Albanisch *nt*

**album** *n* Album *nt*

**alcohol** *n* Alkohol *m*; **alcohol-free** *adj* alkoholfrei; **alcoholic 1.** *adj* (*drink*) alkoholisch **2.** n Alkoholiker(in) m(f)

**ale** n Ale nt (helles englisches Bier)

**alert 1.** adj wachsam **2.** n Alarm m **3.** vt warnen (to vor + dat)

**algebra** n Algebra f

**Algeria** n Algerien nt

**alibi** n Alibi nt

**alien** n (foreigner) Ausländer(in) m(f); (from space) Außerirdische(r) m/f

**alike** adj, adv gleich; (similar) ähnlich

**alive** adj lebendig; **keep sth ~** etw am Leben erhalten; **he's still ~** er lebt noch

**all 1.** adj (plural, every one of) alle; (singular, the whole of) ganz; **~ the children** alle Kinder; **~ the time** die ganze Zeit; **~ his life** sein ganzes Leben; **why me of ~ people?** warum ausgerechnet ich? **2.** pron (everything) alles; (everybody) alle; **~ of** ganz; **~ of them came** sie kamen alle **3.** n alles **4.** adv (completely) ganz; **it's ~ over** es ist ganz aus; **~ along** von Anfang an; **~ at once** auf einmal

**allegation** n Behauptung f; **alleged** adj angeblich

**allergic** adj allergisch (to gegen); **allergy** n Allergie f

**alleviate** vt (pain) lindern

**alley** n (enge) Gasse; (passage) Durchgang m; (bowl-

ing) Bahn f

**alliance** n Bündnis nt

**alligator** n Alligator m

**all-night** adj (café, cinema) die ganze Nacht geöffnet

**allocate** vt zuweisen, zuteilen (to dat)

**allotment** n (plot) Schrebergarten m

**allow** vt (permit) erlauben (sb jdm); (grant) bewilligen; (time) einplanen; **allow for** vt berücksichtigen; (cost etc) einkalkulieren; **allowance** n (from state) Beihilfe f; (from parent) Unterhaltsgeld nt

**all right 1.** adj okay, in Ordnung; **I'm ~** mir geht's gut **2.** adv (satisfactorily) ganz gut **3.** interj okay

**allusion** n Anspielung f (to auf + acc)

**ally** n Verbündete(r) mf; HIST Alliierte(r) m/f

**almond** n Mandel f

**almost** adv fast

**alone** adj, adv allein

**along 1.** prep entlang + acc; **~ the river** den Fluss entlang; (position) am Fluss entlang **2.** adv (onward) weiter; **~ with** zusammen mit; **all ~** die ganze Zeit, von Anfang an; **alongside 1.** prep neben + dat **2.** adv (walk) nebenher

**aloud** adv laut

**alphabet** n Alphabet nt

**Alps** npl **the ~** die Alpen

**already** adv schon, bereits

**Alsace** *n* Elsass *nt*; **Alsatian 1.** *adj* elsässisch **2.** *n* Elsässer(in) *m(f)*; *(Brit, dog)* Schäferhund *m*

**also** *adv* auch

**altar** *n* Altar *m*

**alter** *vt* ändern; **alteration** *n* Änderung *f*; *~s (to building)* Umbau *m*

**alternate 1.** *adj* abwechselnd **2.** *vi* abwechseln *(with* mit); **alternating current** *n* Wechselstrom *m*; **alternative 1.** *adj* Alternativ- **2.** *n* Alternative *f*

**although** *conj* obwohl

**altitude** *n* Höhe *f*

**altogether** *adv (in total)* insgesamt; *(entirely)* ganz und gar

**aluminium, aluminum** *(US)* *n* Aluminium *nt*

**always** *adv* immer

**am** *present* → **be**; bin

**am, a.m.** *abbr* = **ante meridiem** vormittags, vorm.

**amateur 1.** *n* Amateur(in) *m(f)* **2.** *adj* Amateur-; *(theatre, choir)* Laien-

**amazed** *adj* erstaunt *(at* über + *acc)*; **amazing** *adj* erstaunlich

**Amazon** *n* ~ *(river)* Amazonas *m*

**ambassador** *n* Botschafter *m*

**ambiguity** *n* Zweideutigkeit *f*; **ambiguous** *adj* zweideutig

**ambition** *n* Ambition *f*; *(ambitious nature)* Ehrgeiz *m*;

**ambitious** *adj* ehrgeizig

**ambulance** *n* Krankenwagen *m*

**America** *n* Amerika *nt*; **American 1.** *adj* amerikanisch **2.** *n* Amerikaner(in) *m(f)*; **native** ~ Indianer(in) *m(f)*

**amiable** *adj* liebenswürdig

**amicable** *adj* freundlich; *(relations)* freundschaftlich

**amnesia** *n* Gedächtnisverlust *m*

**among(st)** *prep* unter + *dat*

**amount 1.** *n (quantity)* Menge *f*; *(of money)* Betrag *m*; **a large / small** ~ **of** ... ziemlich viel / wenig ... **2.** *vi* ~ **to** *(total)* sich belaufen auf + *acc*

**amp, ampere** *n* Ampere *nt*

**amplifier** *n* Verstärker *m*

**Amtrak®** *n* amerikanische Eisenbahngesellschaft

**amuse** *vt* amüsieren; *(entertain)* unterhalten; **amused** *adj* **I'm not** ~ das finde ich gar nicht lustig; **amusement** *n (enjoyment)* Vergnügen *nt*; *(recreation)* Unterhaltung *f*; **amusement park** *n* Vergnügungspark *m*; **amusing** *adj* amüsant

**an** *art* ein(e)

**anaemic** *adj* blutarm

**anaesthetic** *n* Narkose *f*; *(substance)* Narkosemittel *nt*

**analyse, analyze** *vt* analysieren; **analysis** *n* Analyse *f*

**anatomy** *n* Anatomie *f*;

*(structure)* Körperbau *m*

**ancestor** *n* Vorfahr *m*

**anchor 1.** *n* Anker *m* **2.** *vt* verankern

**anchovy** *n* Sardelle *f*

**ancient** *adj* alt; *fam (person, clothes etc)* uralt

**and** *conj* und

**Andorra** *n* Andorra *nt*

**anemic** *adj (US)* → **anaemic**

**anesthetic** *n (US)* → **anaesthetic**

**angel** *n* Engel *m*

**anger 1.** *n* Zorn *m* **2.** *vt* ärgern

**angina, angina pectoris** *n* Angina Pectoris *f*

**angle** *n* Winkel *m*; *fig* Standpunkt *m*

**angling** *n* Angeln *nt*

**angry** *adj* verärgert; *(stronger)* zornig; *be* **~** *with sb* auf jdn böse sein

**angular** *adj* eckig; *(face)* kantig

**animal** *n* Tier *nt*; *animal rights npl* Tierrechte *pl*

**animated** *adj* lebhaft; **~** *film* Zeichentrickfilm *m*

**aniseed** *n* Anis *m*

**ankle** *n* (Fuß)knöchel *m*

**annex** *n* Anbau *m*

**anniversary** *n* Jahrestag *m*

**announce** *vt* bekannt geben; RADIO, TV ansagen; **announcement** *n* Bekanntgabe *f*; *(official)* Bekanntmachung *f*; RADIO, TV Ansage *f*; **announcer** *n* RADIO, TV Ansager(in) *m(f)*

**annoy** *vt* ärgern; **annoyance**

*n* Ärger *m*; **annoyed** *adj* ärgerlich; *be* **~** *with sb (about sth)* sich über jdn (über etw) ärgern; **annoying** *adj* ärgerlich; *(person)* lästig, nervig

**annual 1.** *adj* jährlich **2.** *n* Jahrbuch *nt*

**anonymous** *adj* anonym

**anorak** *n* Anorak *m*; *(Brit) fam pej* Freak *m*

**anorexia** *n* Magersucht *f*; **anorexic** *adj* magersüchtig

**another** *adj, pron (different)* ein(e) andere(r, s); *(additional)* noch eine(r, s); *let me put it* **~** *way* lass es mich anders sagen

**answer 1.** *n* Antwort *f* (*to* auf + *acc*) **2.** *vi* antworten; *(on phone)* sich melden **3.** *vt (person)* antworten + *dat*; *(letter, question)* beantworten; *(telephone)* gehen an + *acc*, abnehmen; *(door)* öffnen; **answering machine, answerphone** *n* Anrufbeantworter *m*

**ant** *n* Ameise *f*

**Antarctic** *n* Antarktis *f*; **Antarctic Circle** *n* südlicher Polarkreis

**antelope** *n* Antilope *f*

**antenna** *n* ZOOL Fühler *m*; RADIO Antenne *f*

**anti-** *pref* Anti-, anti-; **antibiotic** *n* Antibiotikum *nt*

**anticipate** *vt (expect: trouble, question)* erwarten, rechnen mit; **anticipation** *n* Erwartung *f*

**anticlimax** n Enttäuschung f; **anticlockwise** adv entgegen dem Uhrzeigersinn; **antifreeze** n Frostschutzmittel nt

**antiquarian** adj ~ **bookshop** Antiquariat nt

**antique 1.** n Antiquität f **2.** adj antik; **antique shop** n Antiquitätengeschäft nt

**antiseptic 1.** n Antiseptikum nt **2.** adj antiseptisch

**antlers** npl Geweih nt

**anxiety** n Sorge f (about um); **anxious** adj besorgt (about um); (apprehensive) ängstlich

**any 1.** adj (in question: untranslated) **do you have ~ money?** hast du / haben Sie Geld?; (with negative) **I don't have ~ money** ich habe kein Geld; (whichever one likes) **take ~ card** nimm / nehmen Sie irgendeine Karte **2.** pron (in question) **do you want ~?** (singular) willst du / wollen Sie etwas (davon)?; (plural) willst du / wollen Sie welche?; (with negative) **I don't have ~** ich habe keine / keinen / keins; (whichever one likes) **you can take ~ of them** du kannst / Sie können jede(n, s) beliebige(n) nehmen **3.** adv (in question) **are there ~ more strawberries?** gibt es noch Erdbeeren?; **can't you work ~ faster?** kannst

du / können Sie nicht schneller arbeiten?; (with negative) **not ~ longer** nicht mehr; **this isn't ~ better** das ist auch nicht besser; **anybody** pron (whoever one likes) irgendjemand; (everyone) jeder; (in question) jemand; **anyhow** adv **I don't want to talk about it, not now ~** ich möchte nicht darüber sprechen, jedenfalls nicht jetzt; **they asked me not to go, but I went ~** sie baten mich, nicht hinzugehen, aber ich bin trotzdem hingegangen; **anyone** pron (whoever one likes) irgendjemand; (everyone) jeder; (in question) jemand; **isn't there ~ you can ask?** gibt es denn niemanden, den du fragen kannst / den Sie fragen können?; **anyplace** adv (US) irgendwo; (direction) irgendwohin; (everywhere) überall; **anything** pron (whatever one likes, in question) (irgend)etwas; (everything) alles; ~ **else?** sonst noch etwas?; ~ **but that** alles, nur das nicht; **she didn't tell me** ~ sie hat mir nichts gesagt; **anytime** adv jederzeit; **anyway** adv **I didn't want to go there ~** ich wollte da sowieso nicht hingehen; **thanks ~** trotzdem danke; **~, as I was saying, ...** jedenfalls, wie ich schon sagte, ...;

**anywhere** *adv* irgendwo; (*direction*) irgendwohin; (*everywhere*) überall

**apart** *adv* auseinander; **~ from** außer; **live~** getrennt leben

**apartment** *n* Wohnung *f*; **apartment block** *n* Wohnblock *m*

**ape** *n* (Menschen)affe *m*

**aperitif** *n* Aperitif *m*

**aperture** *n* Öffnung *f*; PHOT Blende *f*

**apologize** *vi* sich entschuldigen; **apology** *n* Entschuldigung *f*

**apostrophe** *n* Apostroph *m*

**appalled** *adj* entsetzt (*at* über + *acc*); **appalling** *adj* entsetzlich

**apparatus** *n* Apparat *m*; (*piece of apparatus*) Gerät *nt*

**apparent** *adj* (*obvious*) offensichtlich (*to* für); (*seeming*) scheinbar; **apparently** *adv* anscheinend

**appeal 1.** *vi* (dringend) bitten (*for* um, *to* + *acc*); LAW Berufung einlegen; **~ to sb** (*be attractive*) jdm zusagen **2.** *n* Aufruf *m* (*to an* + *acc*); LAW Berufung *f*; (*attraction*) Reiz *m*; **appealing** *adj* ansprechend, attraktiv

**appear** *vi* erscheinen; THEAT auftreten; (*seem*) scheinen; **appearance** *n* Erscheinen *nt*; THEAT Auftritt *m*; (*look*) Aussehen *nt*

**appendicitis** *n* Blinddarmentzündung *f*; **appendix** *n*

Blinddarm *m*; (*to book*) Anhang *m*

**appetite** *n* Appetit *m*; *fig* (*desire*) Verlangen *nt*; **appetizing** *adj* appetitlich

**applause** *n* Beifall *m*, Applaus *m*

**apple** *n* Apfel *m*; **apple juice** *n* Apfelsaft *m*; **apple pie** *n* gedeckter Apfelkuchen *m*; **apple puree, apple sauce** *n* Apfelmus *nt*; **apple tart** *n* Apfelkuchen *m*; **apple tree** *n* Apfelbaum *m*

**appliance** *n* Gerät *nt*; **applicable** *adj* anwendbar; (*on forms*) zutreffend; **applicant** *n* Bewerber(in) *m(f)*; **application** *n* (*request*) Antrag *m* (*for auf* + *acc*); (*for job*) Bewerbung *f* (*for* um); **application form** *n* Anmeldeformular *nt*; **apply 1.** *vi* (*be relevant*) zutreffen (*to auf* + *acc*); (*for job etc*) sich bewerben (*for* um) **2.** *vt* (*cream, paint etc*) auftragen; (*put into practice*) anwenden; (*brakes*) betätigen

**appoint** *vt* (*to post*) ernennen; **appointment** *n* Verabredung *f*; (*at doctor, hairdresser etc, in business*) Termin *m*; **by ~** nach Vereinbarung

**appreciate 1.** *vt* (*value*) zu schätzen wissen; (*understand*) einsehen **2.** *vi* (*increase in value*) im Wert steigen; **appreciation** *n* (*esteem*) Anerkennung *f*, Würdigung *f*

**apprehensive** *adj* ängstlich

**approach 1.** *vi* sich nähern **2.** *vt (place)* sich nähern + *dat;* *(person)* herantreten an + *acc*

**appropriate** *adj* passend; *(to occasion)* angemessen; *(remark)* treffend; **appropriately** *adv* passend; *(expressed)* treffend

**approval** *n (show of satisfaction)* Anerkennung *f; (permission)* Zustimmung *f (of* zu); **approve 1.** *vt* billigen **2.** *vi ~ of sth / sb* etw billigen / von jdm etwas halten; **I don't ~** ich missbillige das

**approx** → **approximately;** ca.; **approximate** *adj* ungefähr; **approximately** *adv* ungefähr, circa

**apricot** *n* Aprikose *f*

**April** *n* April *m;* → **September**

**apron** *n* Schürze *f*

**aptitude** *n* Begabung *f*

**aquaplaning** *n* AUTO Aquaplaning *n*

**aquarium** *n* Aquarium *n*

**Aquarius** *n* ASTR Wassermann *m*

**Arab** *n* Araber(in) *m(f);* **Arabian** *adj* arabisch; **Arabic 1.** *n (language)* Arabisch *nt* **2.** *adj* arabisch

**arbitrary** *adj* willkürlich

**arcade** *n* Arkade *f; (shopping arcade)* Einkaufspassage *f*

**arch** *n* Bogen *m*

**archaeologist, archeologist** *(US) n* Archäologe *m,* Archäologin *f;* **archaeology, archeology** *(US) n* Archäologie *f*

**archaic** *adj* veraltet

**archbishop** *n* Erzbischof *m*

**architect** *n* Architekt(in) *m(f);* **architecture** *n* Architektur *f*

**archive(s)** *n(pl)* Archiv *nt*

**archway** *n* Torbogen *m*

**Arctic** *n* Arktis *f;* **Arctic Circle** *n* nördlicher Polarkreis

**are** *present* → **be**

**area** *n (region, district)* Gebiet *nt,* Gegend *f; (amount of space)* Fläche *f; (part of building etc)* Bereich *m,* Zone *f; fig (field)* Bereich *m;* **the London ~** der Londoner Raum; **area code** *n (US)* Vorwahl *f*

**aren't** *contr* → **are not**

**Argentina** *n* Argentinien *nt*

**argue** *vi* streiten *(about, over* über + *acc); ~ that ...* behaupten, dass ...; *~* **for / against ...** sprechen für / gegen ...; **argument** *n (reasons)* Argument *nt; (quarrel)* Streit *m;* **have an ~** sich streiten

**Aries** *nsing* ASTR Widder *m*

**arise** *vi* sich ergeben, entstehen; *(problem, question, wind)* aufkommen

**aristocracy** *n (class)* Adel *m;* **aristocrat** *n* Adlige(r) *mf;* **aristocratic** *adj* aristokratisch, adlig

**arm 1.** n Arm m; (sleeve) Ärmel m; (of armchair) Armlehne f **2.** vt bewaffnen; **armchair** n Lehnstuhl m

**armed** adj bewaffnet

**armpit** n Achselhöhle f

**arms** npl Waffen pl

**army** n Armee f

**A road** n (Brit) ≈ Bundesstraße f

**aroma** n Duft m, Aroma nt; **aromatherapy** n Aromatherapie f

**arose** pt → **arise**

**around 1.** adv herum, umher; (present) hier (irgendwo); (approximately) ungefähr; (with time) gegen; **he's somewhere** er ist hier irgendwo in der Nähe **2.** prep (surrounding) um ... (herum); (about in) in ... herum

**arr.** abbr → **arrival, arrives** Ank.

**arrange** vt (put in order) (an)ordnen; (artistically) arrangieren; (agree to: meeting etc) vereinbaren, festsetzen; (organize) planen; **~ that ...** es so einrichten, dass ...; **we ~d to meet at eight o'clock** wir haben uns für acht Uhr verabredet; **arrangement** n (layout) Anordnung f; (agreement) Vereinbarung f, Plan m; **make ~s** Vorbereitungen treffen

**arrest 1.** vt (person) verhaften **2.** n Verhaftung f

**arrival** n Ankunft f; **new ~** (person) Neuankömmling m; Familienzuwachs m; **arrivals** n (airport) Ankunftshalle f; **arrive** vi ankommen (at bei, in einer); **~ at a solution** eine Lösung finden

**arrogant** adj arrogant

**arrow** n Pfeil m

**arse** n vulg Arsch m

**art** n Kunst f, **the ~s** pl Geisteswissenschaften pl

**artery** n Schlagader f, Arterie f

**art gallery** n Kunstgalerie f, Kunstmuseum nt

**arthritis** n Arthritis f

**artichoke** n Artischocke f

**article** n Artikel m; (object) Gegenstand m

**artificial** adj künstlich, Kunst-

**artist** n Künstler(in) m(f); **artistic** adj künstlerisch

**as 1.** adv (like) wie; (in role of) als; **such ~** (for example) ... wie etwa ...; **~ ... ~** so ... wie; **~ soon ~ he comes** sobald er kommt; **twice ~ much** zweimal so viel; **~ for ...** was ... betrifft; **~ of ...** (time) ab ... + dat **2.** conj (since) da,`weil; (while) als, während; **~ if, ~ though** als ob; **leave it ~ it is** lass es so (wie es ist); **~ it were** sozusagen

**asap** acr = **as soon as possible**; möglichst bald

**ash** n (dust) Asche f; (tree) Esche f

**ashamed** adj beschämt; **be ~**

**(of sb / sth)** sich (für jdn / etw) schämen

**ashore** adv an Land

**ashtray** n Aschenbecher m

**Asia** n Asien nt; **Asian 1.** adj asiatisch **2.** n Asiat(in) m(f)

**aside** adv beiseite, zur Seite; **~ from** (esp, US) außer

**ask** vt, vi fragen; (question) stellen; (request) bitten um; **~ the way** jdn nach dem Weg fragen; **~ sb to do sth** jdn darum bitten, etw zu tun; **ask for** vt bitten um

**asleep** adj, adv **be~** schlafen; **fall ~** einschlafen

**asparagus** n Spargel m

**aspirin** n Aspirin® nt

**ass** n a. fig Esel m; (US) vulg Arsch m

**assassinate** vt ermorden; **assassination** n Ermordung f

**assault 1.** n Angriff m; LAW Körperverletzung f **2.** vt überfallen, herfallen über + acc

**assemble 1.** vt (parts) zusammensetzen **2.** vi sich versammeln; **assembly** n (of people) Versammlung f; **assembly hall** n Aula f; **assertion** n Behauptung f

**assess** vt einschätzen; **assessment** n Einschätzung f

**asset** n Vermögenswert m; fig Vorteil m; **~s** pl Vermögen nt

**assign** vt zuweisen; **assignment** n Aufgabe f; (mission) Auftrag m

**assist** vt helfen + dat; **assist-**

**ance** n Hilfe f; **assistant** n Assistent(in) m(f), Mitarbeiter(in) m(f); (in shop) Verkäufer(in) m(f); **assistant referee** n SPORT Schiedsrichterassistent(in) m(f)

**associate** vt verbinden (with mit); **association** n (organization) Verband m, Vereinigung f; **in ~ with** ... in Zusammenarbeit mit ...

**assorted** adj gemischt; **assortment** n Auswahl f (of an + dat); (of sweets) Mischung f

**assume** vt annehmen (that ... dass ...); (role, responsibility) übernehmen; **assumption** n Annahme f

**assurance** n Versicherung f; (confidence) Zuversicht f; **assure** vt (say confidently) versichern + dat; **be ~d of sth** einer Sache sicher sein

**asterisk** n Sternchen nt

**asthma** n Asthma nt

**astonished** adj erstaunt (at über); **astonishing** adj erstaunlich; **astonishment** n Erstaunen nt

**astound** vt sehr erstaunen; **astounding** adj erstaunlich

**astray** adv **go~** (letter etc) verloren gehen; (person) vom Weg abkommen

**astrology** n Astrologie f

**astronaut** n Astronaut(in) m(f)

**astronomy** n Astronomie f

**asylum** n (home) Anstalt f;

(*political asylum*) Asyl *nt*; **asylum seeker** *n* Asylbewerber(in) *m(f)*

**at** *prep* (*place*) ~ **the door** an der Tür; ~ **home** zu Hause; ~ **John's** bei John; ~ **school** in der Schule; ~ **the theatre** / **cinema** im Theater / Kino; ~ **lunch** / **work** beim Essen / bei der Arbeit; (*direction*) **point** ~ **sb** auf jdn zeigen; **he looked** ~ **me** er sah mich an; (*time*) ~ **2 o'clock** um 2 Uhr; ~ **Easter** / **Christmas** zu Ostern / Weihnachten; **the moment** im Moment; ~ (**the age of**) **16** im Alter von 16 Jahren, mit 16; (*price*) ~ **£5 each** zu je 5 Pfund; (*speed*) ~ **20 mph** mit 20 Meilen pro Stunde

**ate** *pret* → **eat**

**athlete** *n* Athlet(in) *m(f)*; (*track and field*) Leichtathlet(in) *m(f)*; ~**'s foot** Fußpilz *m*; **athletic** *adj* sportlich; (*build*) athletisch; **athletics** *npl* Leichtathletik *f*

**Atlantic** *n* **the** ~ (*Ocean*) der Atlantik

**atlas** *n* Atlas *m*

**ATM** *abbr* = **automated teller machine** Geldautomat *m*

**atmosphere** *n* Atmosphäre *f*, Stimmung *f*

**atom** *n* Atom *nt*; **atom(ic) bomb** *n* Atombombe *f*; **atomic** *adj* Atom-; ~ **energy** Atomenergie *f*; ~ **power** Atomkraft *f*

**A to Z®** *n* Stadtplan *m* (in Buchform)

**atrocious** *adj* grauenhaft; **atrocity** *n* Grausamkeit *f*; (*deed*) Gräueltat *f*

**attach** *vt* befestigen, anheften (*to* an + *dat*); **be** ~**ed to sb** / **sth** an jdm / etw hängen; **attachment** *n* (*affection*) Zuneigung *f*; IT Attachment *nt*, Anhang *m*

**attack 1.** *vt, vi* angreifen **2.** *n* Angriff + *acc* (*on* auf *m*); MED Anfall *m*

**attempt 1.** *n* Versuch *m* **2.** *vt* versuchen

**attend 1.** *vt* (*go to*) teilnehmen an + *dat*; (*lectures, school*) besuchen **2.** *vi* (*be present*) anwesend sein; **attend to** *vt* sich kümmern um; (*customer*) bedienen; **attendance** *n* (*presence*) Anwesenheit *f*; **attendant** *n* (*in car park etc*) Wächter(in) *m(f)*; (*in museum*) Aufseher(in) *m(f)*

**attention** *n* Aufmerksamkeit *f*; (*your*) ~ **please!** Achtung!; **pay** ~ **to sth** etw beachten; **pay** ~ **to sb** jdm aufmerksam zuhören

**attic** *n* Dachboden *m*; (*lived in*) Mansarde *f*

**attitude** *n* (*mental*) Einstellung *f* (*to, towards* zu); (*more general, physical*) Haltung *f*

**attorney** *n* (*US, lawyer*) Rechtsanwalt *m*, Rechtsanwältin *f*

**attract** *vt* anziehen; (*attention*)

erregen; *be* ~*ed to* or *by sb* sich zu jdm hingezogen fühlen; **attraction** *n* Anziehungskraft *f*; (*thing*) Attraktion *f*; **attractive** *adj* attraktiv; (*thing, idea*) reizvoll

**aubergine** *n* Aubergine *f*

**auction 1.** *n* Versteigerung *f*, Auktion *f* **2.** *vt* versteigern

**audience** *n* Publikum *nt*; RADIO Zuhörer *pl*; TV Zuschauer *pl*

**audio** *adj* Ton-

**audition 1.** *n* Probe *f* **2.** *vi* THEAT vorspielen, vorsingen

**auditorium** *n* Zuschauerraum *m*

**August** *n* August *m*; → **September**

**aunt** *n* Tante *f*

**au pair** *n* Aupairmädchen *nt*, Aupairjunge *m*

**Australia** *n* Australien *nt*; **Australian 1.** *adj* australisch **2.** *n* Australier(in) *m(f)*

**Austria** *n* Österreich *nt*; **Austrian 1.** *adj* österreichisch **2.** *n* Österreicher(in) *m(f)*

**authentic** *adj* echt; (*signature*) authentisch; **authenticity** *n* Echtheit *f*

**author** *n* Autor(in) *m(f)*; (*of report etc*) Verfasser(in) *m(f)*

**authority** *n* (*power, expert*) Autorität *f*; *the authorities* *pl* die Behörden *pl*; **authorize** *vt* (*permit*) genehmigen

**auto** *n* (*US*) Auto *nt*

**autograph** *n* Autogramm *nt*

**automatic 1.** *adj* automatisch;

~ *gear change* (*Brit*) / ~ *gear shift* (*US*) Automatikschaltung *f* **2.** *n* (*car*) Automatikwagen *m*

**automobile** *n* (*US*) Auto (-mobil) *nt*; **autotrain** *n* (*US*) Autoreisezug *m*

**autumn** *n* (*Brit*) Herbst *m*

**auxiliary 1.** *adj* Hilfs- **2.** *n* Hilfskraft *f*

**availability** *n* (*of product*) Lieferbarkeit *f*; (*of resources*) Verfügbarkeit *f*; **available** *adj* erhältlich; (*existing*) vorhanden; (*product*) lieferbar; (*person*) erreichbar; *be* / *make* ~ *to sb* jdm zur Verfügung stehen / stellen

**avalanche** *n* Lawine *f*

**Ave** *abbr* → **avenue**

**avenue** *n* Allee *f*

**average 1.** *n* Durchschnitt *m*; *on* ~ im Durchschnitt **2.** *adj* durchschnittlich

**aviation** *n* Luftfahrt *f*

**avocado** *n* Avocado *f*

**avoid** *vt* vermeiden; ~ *sb* aus dem Weg gehen; **avoidable** *adj* vermeidbar

**awake 1.** *vi* aufwachen **2.** *adj* wach

**award 1.** *n* (*prize*) Preis *m*; (*for bravery etc*) Auszeichnung *f* **2.** *vt* zuerkennen (*to sb* jdm); (*present*) verleihen (*to sb* jdm)

**aware** *adj* bewusst; *be* ~ *of sth* sich *dat* einer Sache *gen* bewusst sein; *I was not* ~ *that* ... es war mir nicht klar, dass

...

**away** *adv* weg; **look ~** wegsehen; **he's ~** er ist nicht da; (*on a trip*) er ist verreist; (*from school, work*) er fehlt; SPORT **they are** (*playing*) **~** sie spielen auswärts; (*with distance*) **three miles ~** drei Meilen (von hier) entfernt

**awful** *adj* schrecklich, furcht-

bar; **awfully** *adv* furchtbar

**awkward** *adj* (*clumsy*) ungeschickt; (*embarrassing*) peinlich; (*difficult*) schwierig

**awning** *n* Markise *f*

**awoke** *pt* → **awake**

**awoken** *pp* → **awake**

**ax** (*US*), **axe** *n* Axt *f*

**axle** *n* TECH Achse *f*

# B

**B & B** *abbr* → **bed and breakfast**

**BA** *abbr* = **Bachelor of Arts**

**babe** *n fam* Baby *nt*; (*affectionate*) Schatz *m*, Kleine(r) *mf*

**baby** *n* Baby *nt*; (*of animal*) Junge(s) *nt*; *fam* (*affectionate*) Schatz *m*, Kleine(r) *mf*; **have a ~** ein Kind bekommen; **baby carriage** *n* (*US*) Kinderwagen *m*; **baby food** *n* Babynahrung *f*; **baby shower** *n* (*US*) Party für die werdende Mutter; **baby-sit** *irr vi* babysitten; **baby-sitter** *n* Babysitter(in) *m*(*f*)

**bachelor** *n* Junggeselle *m*; **Bachelor of Arts** / **Science** *erster akademischer Grad*, ≈ Magister / Diplom; **bachelorette** *n* Junggesellin *f*; **bachelorette party** *n* (*US*) Junggesellinnenabschied; **bachelor party** *n* (*US*) Junggesellenabschied

**back 1.** *n* (*of person, animal*) Rücken *m*; (*of house, coin etc*) Rückseite *f*; (*of chair*) Rückenlehne *f*; (*of car*) Rücksitz *m*; (*of train*) Ende *nt*; SPORT (*defender*) Verteidiger(in) *m*(*f*); **at the ~ of ...**, **in ~ of** (*inside*) hinten in ...; (*outside*) hinter ... *m*; **~ to front** verkehrt herum **2.** *vt* (*support*) unterstützen; (*car*) rückwärtsfahren **3.** *vi* (*go backwards*) rückwärtsgehen or rückwärtsfahren **4.** *adj* Hinter-; **~ wheel** Hinterrad *nt* **5.** *adv* zurück; **they're ~** sie sind wieder da; **back down** *vi* nachgeben; **back up 1.** *vi* (*car etc*) zurücksetzen **2.** *vt* (*support*) unterstützen; IT sichern; (*car*) zurückfahren

**backache** *n* Rückenschmerzen *pl*; **backbone** *n* Rückgrat *nt*; **backdoor** *n* Hintertür *f*; **backfire** *vi* (*plan*) fehlschlagen; AUTO fehlzünden; **background** n Hintergrund m; **backhand** n SPORT Rückhand f; **backlog** n (of work) Rückstand m; **backpack** n (US) Rucksack m; **backpacker** n Rucksacktourist(in) m(f); **backpacking** n Rucksacktourismus m; **back seat** n Rücksitz m; **backside** n fam Po m; **back street** n Seitensträßchen nt; **backstroke** n Rückenschwimmen nt; **back-up** n (support) Unterstützung f; **~ (copy)** IT Sicherungskopie f; **backward** adj (region) rückständig; **~ movement** Rückwärtsbewegung f; **backwards** adv rückwärts; **backyard** n Hinterhof m

**bacon** n Frühstücksspeck m

**bacteria** npl Bakterien pl

**bad** adj schlecht, schlimm; (smell) übel; **I have a ~ back** mir tut der Rücken weh; **I'm ~ at maths / sport** ich bin schlecht in Mathe / Sport; **go ~** schlecht werden, verderben

**badge** n Abzeichen nt

**badger** n Dachs m

**badly** adv schlecht; **~ wounded** schwer verwundet; **need sth ~** etw dringend brauchen; **bad-tempered** adj schlecht gelaunt

**bag** n (small) Tüte f; (larger) Beutel m; (handbag) Tasche f

**baggage** n Gepäck nt; **baggage (re)claim** n Gepäckrückgabe f

**baggy** adj (zu) weit; (trousers, suit) ausgebeult

**bagpipes** npl Dudelsack m

**Bahamas** npl **the ~** die Bahamas pl

**bail** n (money) Kaution f

**bait** n Köder m

**bake** vt, vi backen; **baked beans** npl weiße Bohnen in Tomatensoße; **baked potato** n in der Schale gebackene Kartoffel, Ofenkartoffel f; **baker** n Bäcker(in) m(f); **bakery** n Bäckerei f; **baking powder** n Backpulver nt

**balance 1.** n (equilibrium) Gleichgewicht nt **2.** vt (make up for) ausgleichen; **balance sheet** n Bilanz f

**balcony** n Balkon m

**bald** adj kahl; **be~** eine Glatze haben

**Balkans** npl **the ~** der Balkan, die Balkanländer pl

**ball** n Ball m; **have a ~** fam sich prima amüsieren

**ballet** n Ballett nt; **ballet dancer** n Balletttänzer(in) m(f)

**balloon** n (Luft)ballon m

**ballot** n (geheime) Abstimmung

**ballpoint (pen)** n Kugelschreiber m

**ballroom** n Tanzsaal m

**Baltic** adj **~ Sea** Ostsee f; **the ~ States** die baltischen Staa-

**barrel organ**

ten; **Baltics** *n* **the** ~ das Baltikum *nt*

**bamboo** *n* Bambus *m*; **bamboo shoots** *npl* Bambussprossen *pl*

**ban** 1. *n* Verbot *nt* 2. *vt* verbieten

**banana** *n* Banane *f*; **he's** ~ s er ist völlig durchgeknallt; **banana split** *n* Bananensplit *nt*

**band** *n* (*group*) Gruppe *f*; (*of criminals*) Bande *f*; (*pop, rock etc*) Band *f*; (*strip*) Band *nt*

**bandage** 1. *n* Verband *m*; (*elastic*) Bandage *f* 2. *vt* verbinden

**bang** 1. *n* (*noise*) Knall *m*; (*blow*) Schlag *m* 2. *vt, vi* knallen; (*door*) zuschlagen, zuknallen; **banger** *n* (*Brit fam*) (*firework*) Knallkörper *m*; (*sausage*) Würstchen *nt*; (*old car*) Klapperkiste *f*

**bangs** *npl* (*US, von Frisur*) Pony *m*

**banish** *vt* verbannen

**banister(s)** *n* (Treppen)geländer *nt*

**bank** *n* FIN Bank *f*; (*of river etc*) Ufer *nt*; **bank account** *n* Bankkonto *nt*; **bank balance** *n* Kontostand *m*; **bank card** *n* Bankkarte *f*; **bank code** *n* Bankleitzahl *f*; **bank holiday** *n* gesetzlicher Feiertag

**bankrupt** *vt* ruinieren; **go** ~ Pleite gehen

**bank statement** *n* Kontoaus-

zug *m*

**baptism** *n* Taufe *f*; **baptize** *vt* taufen

**bar** 1. *n* (*for drinks*) Bar *f*; (*less smart*) Lokal *nt*; (*rod*) Stange *f*; (*of chocolate etc*) Riegel *m*, Tafel *f*; (*of soap*) Stück *nt*; (*counter*) Theke *f* 2. *prep* außer; ~ **none** ohne Ausnahme

**barbecue** *n* (*device*) Grill *m*; (*party*) Barbecue *nt*, Grillfete *f*; **have a** ~ grillen

**bar code** *n* Strichcode *m*

**bare** *adj* nackt; ~ **patch** kahle Stelle; **barefoot** *adj, adv* barfuß; **bareheaded** *adj, adv* ohne Kopfbedeckung; **barely** *adv* kaum; (*with age*) knapp

**bargain** 1. *n* (*cheap offer*) günstiges Angebot, Schnäppchen *nt*; (*transaction*) Geschäft *nt*; **what a** ~ das ist aber günstig! 2. *vi* (ver)handeln

**barge** *n* (*for freight*) Lastkahn *m*; (*unpowered*) Schleppkahn *m*

**bark** 1. *n* (*of tree*) Rinde *f*; (*of dog*) Bellen *nt* 2. *vi* (*dog*) bellen

**barley** *n* Gerste *f*

**barmaid** *n* Barkeeperin *f*; **barman** *n* Barkeeper *m*

**barn** *n* Scheune *f*

**barometer** *n* Barometer *nt*

**baroque** *adj* barock, Barock-

**barracks** *npl* Kaserne *f*

**barrel** *n* Fass *nt*; **barrel organ** *n* Drehorgel *f*

**barrier** n (*obstruction*) Absperrung f; (*across road etc*) Schranke f

**bartender** n (US) Barkeeper (in) m(f)

**base** n Basis f; (*of lamp, pillar etc*) Fuß m; MIL Stützpunkt m **2.** vt gründen (*on* auf + *acc*); **be ~d on sth** auf etw dat basieren

**baseball** n Baseball m; **baseball cap** n Baseballmütze f

**basement** n Kellergeschoss nt

**bash** fam **1.** n Schlag m, Party f **2.** vt hauen

**basic** adj einfach; (*fundamental*) Grund-; (*importance, difference*) grundlegend; (*in principle*) grundsätzlich; **basically** adv im Grunde; **basics** npl **the ~** das Wesentliche

**basil** n Basilikum nt

**basin** n (*for washing, valley*) (Wasch)becken nt

**basis** n Basis f; **on the ~ of** aufgrund + gen; **on a monthly ~** monatlich

**basket** n Korb m; **basketball** n Basketball m

**Basque 1.** n (*person*) Baske m, Baskin f; (*language*) Baskisch nt **2.** adj baskisch

**bass** **1.** n MUS Bass m; ZOOL Barsch m **2.** adj MUS Bass-

**bastard** n vulg (*awful person*) Arschloch nt

**bat** n ZOOL Fledermaus f; SPORT (*cricket, baseball*)

Schlagholz nt; (*table tennis*) Schläger m

**bath 1.** n Bad nt; (*tub*) Badewanne f; **have a ~** baden **2.** vt (*child etc*) baden

**bathe** vt, vi (*wound etc*) baden; **bath foam** n Badeschaum m; **bathing cap** n Badekappe f; **bathing costume**, **bathing suit** (US) n Badeanzug m

**bathmat** n Badevorleger m; **bathrobe** n Bademantel m; **bathroom** n Bad(ezimmer) nt; **bath towel** n Badetuch nt; **bathtub** n Badewanne f

**baton** n MUS Taktstock m; (*police*) Schlagstock m

**batter 1.** n Teig m **2.** vt heftig schlagen; **battered** adj übel zugerichtet; (*hat, car*) verbeult; (*wife, baby*) misshandelt

**battery** n ELEC Batterie f; **battery charger** n Ladegerät m

**battle** n Schlacht f; fig Kampf m (*for* um ); **battlefield** n Schlachtfeld nt

**Bavaria** n Bayern nt

**bay** n (*of sea*) Bucht f; (*on house*) Erker m; (*tree*) Lorbeerbaum m; **bay leaf** n Lorbeerblatt nt; **bay window** n Erkerfenster nt

**BBC** abbr = **British Broadcasting Corporation** BBC f

**BC** abbr = **before Christ** vor Christi Geburt, v. Chr.

**be 1.** vi sein; (*become*) werden; (*be situated*) liegen,

**beech**

sein; *she's French* sie ist Französin; *he wants to ~ a doctor* er will Arzt werden; *I'm too hot* mir ist zu warm; *she's not well* (*health*) ihr geht's nicht gut; *the book is 5 dollars* (*cost*) das Buch kostet 5 Dollar; *how much is that altogether?* was macht das zusammen?; *how long have you been here?* wie lange bist du / sind Sie schon da?; *have you ever been to Rome?* warst du / waren Sie schon einmal in Rom?; *there is / are* es gibt, es ist / sind; *there are two left* es sind noch zwei übrig 2. *vaux* (*passive*) werden; *he was run over* er wurde überfahren, er wurde überfahren; (*continuous tenses*) *I was walking on the beach* ich ging am Strand spazieren; *they're coming tomorrow* sie kommen morgen; (*infinitive: intention, obligation*) *the car is to ~ sold* das Auto soll verkauft werden; *you are not to mention it* du darfst / Sie dürfen es nicht erwähnen

**beach** *n* Strand *m*; **beachwear** *n* Strandkleidung *f*
**bead** *n* (*of glass, wood etc*) Perle *f*; (*drop*) Tropfen *m*
**beak** *n* Schnabel *m*
**beam 1.** (*of wood etc*) Balken *m*; (*of light*) Strahl *m* **2.** *vi*

(*smile etc*) strahlen
**bean** *n* Bohne *f*; **bean curd** *n* Tofu *m*
**bear 1.** *vt* (*carry*) tragen; (*tolerate*) ertragen **2.** *n* Bär *m*; **bearable** *adj* erträglich
**beard** *n* Bart *m*
**beat 1.** *vt* schlagen; (*as punishment*) prügeln; *~ sb at tennis* jdn im Tennis schlagen **2.** *n* (*of heart, drum etc*) Schlag *m*; MUS Takt *m*; **beat up** *vt* zusammenschlagen; **beaten** *pp* → **beat**; *off the ~ track* abgelegen
**beautiful** *adj* schön; (*splendid*) herrlich; **beauty** *n* Schönheit *f*; **beauty spot** *n* (*place*) lohnendes Ausflugsziel
**beaver** *n* Biber *m*
**became** *pt* → **become**
**because** *n* adv, conj weil **2.** *prep ~ of* wegen + *gen or dat*
**become** *vt* werden; *what's ~ of him?* was ist aus ihm geworden?
**bed** *n* Bett *nt*; (*in garden*) Beet *nt*; **bed and breakfast** *n* Übernachtung *f* mit Frühstück; Pension *f*; **bedding** *n* Bettzeug *nt*; **bed linen** *n* Bettwäsche *f*; **bedroom** *n* Schlafzimmer *nt*; **bed-sit(ter)** *n* fam möblierte Einzimmerwohnung; **bedspread** *n* Tagesdecke *f*; **bedtime** *n* Schlafenszeit *f*
**bee** *n* Biene *f*
**beech** *n* Buche *f*

**beef** n Rindfleisch nt; **beefburger** n Hamburger m; **beef tomato** n Fleischtomate f

**beehive** n Bienenstock m

**been** pp → **be**

**beer** n Bier nt

**beetle** n Käfer m

**beetroot** n Rote Bete

**before 1.** prep vor; **the year ~ last** vorletztes Jahr; **the day ~ yesterday** vorgestern **2.** conj bevor **3.** adv (of year) vorher; **have you been there ~?** waren Sie schon einmal dort?; **beforehand** adv vorher

**beg 1.** vt **~ sb to do sth** jdn inständig bitten, etw zu tun **2.** vi (beggar) betteln (for um)

**began** pt → **begin**

**beggar** n Bettler(in) m(f)

**begin** vt, vi anfangen, beginnen; **beginner** n Anfänger(in) m(f); **beginning** n Anfang m; **begun** pp → **begin**

**behalf** n **on ~ of, in ~ of** (US) im Namen / Auftrag von; **on my ~** für sich

**behave** vi sich benehmen; **behavior** (US), **behaviour** n Benehmen nt

**behind 1.** prep hinter **2.** adv hinten; **be~ with one's work** mit seiner Arbeit im Rückstand sein **3.** n fam Hinterteil nt

**beige** adj beige

**being** n (existence) Dasein nt; (person) Wesen nt

**Belarus** n Weißrussland nt

**belch 1.** n Rülpser m **2.** vi rülpsen

**Belgian 1.** adj belgisch **2.** n Belgier(in) m(f); **Belgium** n Belgien nt

**belief** n Glaube m (in an + acc); (conviction) Überzeugung f; **it's my ~ that ...** ich bin der Überzeugung, dass ...; **believe** vt glauben; **believe in** vi glauben an + acc

**bell** n (church) Glocke f; (bicycle, door) Klingel f; **bellboy** n (esp, US) Page m

**bellows** npl (for fire) Blasebalg m

**belly** n Bauch m; **bellyache 1.** n Bauchweh nt; **belly button** n fam Bauchnabel m; **bellyflop** n fam Bauchklatscher m

**belong** vi gehören (to sb jdm); (to club) angehören + dat; **belongings** npl Habe f

**below 1.** prep unter **2.** adv unten

**belt 1.** n (round waist) Gürtel m; (safety belt) Gurt m; **below the~** unter die Gürtellinie **2.** vi fam (go fast) rasen, düsen; **beltway** n (US) Umgehungsstraße f

**bench** n Bank f

**bend 1.** n Biegung f; (in road) Kurve f **2.** vt (curve) biegen; (head, arm) beugen **3.** vi sich biegen; (person) sich beugen; **bend down** *vi* sich bücken

**beneath 1.** *prep* unter **2.** *adv* darunter

**beneficial** *adj* gut, nützlich (*to* für); **benefit 1.** *n* (*advantage*) Vorteil *m*; (*profit*) Nutzen *m*; **for your / his ~** deinetwegen / seinetwegen **2.** *vt* guttun (+ *dat* **3.** *vi* Nutzen ziehen (*from* aus)

**bent 1.** *pt, pp* → **bend 2.** *adj* krumm; *fam* korrupt

**Bermuda 1.** *n* the **~s** *pl* die Bermudas *pl* **2.** *adj* **~ shorts** *pl* Bermudashorts *pl*

**berry** *n* Beere *f*

**beside** *prep* neben; **~ the sea / lake** am Meer / See; **besides 1.** *prep* außer **2.** *adv* außerdem

**best 1.** *adj* beste(r, s); **my ~ friend** mein bester *or* engster Freund; **the ~ thing (to do) would be to …** das Beste wäre zu …; (*on food packaging*) **~ before …** mindestens haltbar bis … **2.** *n* the / die / das Beste; **all the ~** alles Gute; **make the ~ of it** das Beste daraus machen **3.** *adv* am besten; **I like this ~** das mag ich am liebsten; **~-before date** *n* Mindesthaltbarkeitsdatum *nt*; **best man** *n* Trauzeuge *m*

**bet 1.** *vt, vi* wetten (*on* auf + *acc*); **you ~** *fam* und ob!; **I**

**~ he'll be late** er kommt mit Sicherheit zu spät **2.** *n* Wette *f*

**betray** *vt* verraten

**better** *adj, adv* besser; **get ~** (*healthwise*) sich erholen, wieder gesund werden; (*improve*) sich verbessern; **I'm much ~ today** es geht mir heute viel besser; **you'd go** du solltest / Sie sollten lieber gehen; **a change for the ~** eine Wendung zum Guten

**between 1.** *prep* zwischen; (*among*) unter; **~ you and me, …** unter uns gesagt, … **2.** *adv* (*in*) **~** dazwischen

**beverage** *n* (*formal*) Getränk *nt*

**beware** *vt* of *sth* sich vor etw + *dat* hüten; **'~ of the dog'** "Vorsicht, bissiger Hund!"

**beyond 1.** *prep* (*place*) jenseits + *gen*; (*time*) über … hinaus; (*out of reach*) außerhalb + *gen*; **it's ~ me** da habe ich keine Ahnung, da bin ich überfragt **2.** *adv* darüber hinaus

**bias** *n* (*prejudice*) Vorurteil *nt*, Voreingenommenheit *f*; **biased** *adj* voreingenommen

**bib** *n* Latz *m*

**Bible** *n* Bibel *f*

**bicycle** *n* Fahrrad *nt*

**bid 1.** *vt* (*offer*) bieten **2.** *n* (*attempt*) Versuch *m*; (*offer*) Gebot *nt*

**big** *adj* groß; **it's no ~ deal** *fam*

es ist nichts Besonderes; **big dipper** *n* (*Brit*) Achterbahn *f*; **big-headed** *adj* eingebildet

**bike** *n fam* Rad *nt*

**bikini** *n* Bikini *m*

**bilberry** *n* Heidelbeere *f*

**bilingual** *adj* zweisprachig

**bill** *n* (*account*) Rechnung *f*; (*US, banknote*) Banknote *f*; POL Gesetzentwurf *m*; ZOOL Schnabel *m*; **billfold** *n* (*US*) Brieftasche *f*

**billiards** *nsing* Billard *nt*

**billion** *n* Milliarde *f*

**bin** *n* Behälter *m*; (*rubbish bin*) (Müll)eimer *m*; (*for paper*) Papierkorb *m*

**bind** *vt* binden; (*bind together*) zusammenbinden; (*wound*) verbinden; **binding** (*ski*) Bindung *f*; (*book*) Einband *m*

**binge** *n fam* (*drinking*) Sauferei *f*; **go on a ~** auf Sauftour gehen

**bingo** *n* Bingo *nt*

**binoculars** *npl* Fernglas *nt*

**biological** *adj* biologisch; **biology** *n* Biologie *f*

**birch** *n* Birke *f*

**bird** *n* Vogel *m*; (*Brit*) *fam* (*girl, girlfriend*) Tussi *f*; **bird flu** *n* Vogelgrippe *f*; **bird watcher** *n* Vogelbeobachter(in) *m(f)*

**birth** *n* Geburt *f*; **birth certificate** *n* Geburtsurkunde *f*; **birthday** *n* Geburtstag *m*; **happy ~** herzlichen Glückwunsch zum Geburtstag; **birthday card** *n* Geburtstagskarte *f*; **birthday party** *n* Geburtstagsfeier *f*; **birthplace** *n* Geburtsort *m*

**biscuit** *n* (*Brit*) Keks *m*

**bisexual** *adj* bisexuell

**bishop** *n* Bischof *m*; (*in chess*) Läufer *m*

**bit 1.** *pt* → **bite 2.** *n* (*piece*) Stück(chen) *nt*; IT Bit *nt*; **a ~ (of ...)** (*small amount*) ein bisschen ...; **a ~ tired** etwas müde; **~ by ~** allmählich; (*time*) **for a ~** ein Weilchen; **quite a ~** (*a lot*) ganz schön viel

**bitch** *n* (*dog*) Hündin *f*, *pej* (*woman*) Miststück *nt*, Schlampe *f*; **son of a ~** (*US*) *vulg* Hurensohn *m*, Scheißkerl *m*; **bitchy** *adj* gemein, zickig

**bite 1.** *vt*, *vi* beißen **2.** *n* Biss *m*; (*mouthful*) Bissen *m*; (*insect*) Stich *m*; **have a ~** eine Kleinigkeit essen; **bitten** *pp* → **bite**

**bitter 1.** *adj* bitter; (*memory etc*) schmerzlich **2.** *n* (*Brit, beer*) halbdunkles Bier; **bitter lemon** *n* Bitter Lemon *nt*

**black** *adj* schwarz; **blackberry** *n* Brombeere *f*; **blackbird** *n* Amsel *f*; **blackboard** *n* (Wand)tafel *f*; **black box** *n* AVIAT Flugschreiber *m*; **blackcurrant** *n* Schwarze Johannisbeere *f*; **black eye** *n* blaues Auge; **Black Forest**

**blood orange**

*n* Schwarzwald *m*; **black-mail 1.** *n* Erpressung *f* **2.** *vt* erpressen; **black market** *n* Schwarzmarkt *m*; **blackout** *n* MED Ohnmacht *f*; *have a* ~ ohnmächtig werden; **black pudding** *n* ≈ Blutwurst *f*; **Black Sea** *n the* ~ das Schwarze Meer; **blacksmith** *n* Schmied(in) *m(f)*; **black tie** *n* Abendanzug *m*, Smoking *m*; *is it* ~*?* ist / besteht da Smokingzwang?

**bladder** *n* Blase *f*

**blade** *n* (*of knife*) Klinge *f*; (*of propeller*) Blatt *nt*; (*of grass*) Halm *m*

**blame 1.** *n* Schuld *f* **2.** *vt* ~ *sth on sb* jdm die Schuld an etw *dat* geben; *he is to* ~ er ist daran schuld

**bland** *adj* (*taste*) fade; (*comment*) nichtssagend

**blank** *adj* (*page, space*) leer, unbeschrieben; (*look*) ausdruckslos; ~ *cheque* Blankoscheck *m*

**blanket** *n* (Woll)decke *f*

**blast 1.** *n* (*of wind*) Windstoß *m*; (*of explosion*) Druckwelle *f* **2.** *vt* (*blow up*) sprengen

**blatant** *adj* (*undisguised*) offen; (*obvious*) offensichtlich

**blaze 1.** *vi* lodern; (*sun*) brennen **2.** *n* (*building*) Brand *m*; (*other fire*) Feuer *nt*

**bleach 1.** *n* Bleichmittel *nt* **2.** *vt* bleichen

**bleary** *adj* (*eyes*) trübe, verschlafen

**bleed** *vi* bluten

**bleeper** *n fam* Piepser *m*

**blend 1.** *n* Mischung *f* **2.** *vt* mischen **3.** *vi* sich mischen; **blender** *n* Mixer *m*

**bless** *vt* segnen; ~ *you!* Gesundheit!; **blessing** *n* Segen *m*

**blew** *pt* → **blow**

**blind 1.** *adj* blind; (*corner*) unübersichtlich; *turn a* ~ *eye to sth* bei etw ein Auge zudrücken **2.** *n* (*for window*) Rollo *nt* **3.** *vt* blenden; **blind alley** *n* Sackgasse *f*; **blind spot** *n* AUTO toter Winkel; *fig* schwacher Punkt

**blink** *vi* blinzeln; (*light*) blinken

**bliss** *n* (Glück)seligkeit *f*

**blister** *n* Blase *f*

**blizzard** *n* Schneesturm *m*

**block 1.** *n* (*wood, stone, ice*) Block *m*, Klotz *m*; (*of buildings*) Häuserblock *m*; ~ *of flats* (*Brit*) Wohnblock *m* **2.** *vt* (*road*) blockieren; (*nose, pipe*) verstopfen; **blockage** *n* Verstopfung *f*; **blockbuster** *n* Knüller *m*; **block letters** *npl* Blockschrift *f*

**blog** *n* IT Blog *nt*

**bloke** *n* (*Brit*) *fam* Kerl *m*, Typ *m*

**blond(e) 1.** *adj* blond **2.** *n* (*person*) Blondine *f*, blonder Typ

**blood** *n* Blut *nt*; **blood count** *n* Blutbild *nt*; **blood donor** *n* Blutspender(in) *m(f)*; **blood group** *n* Blutgruppe *f*; **blood orange**

**orange** n Blutorange f; **blood poisoning** n Blutvergiftung f; **blood pressure** n Blutdruck m; **blood sample** n Blutprobe f; **bloodsports** npl Sportarten, bei denen Tiere getötet werden; **bloody** adj (Brit) fam verdammt, Scheiß-; (literal sense) blutig

**bloom 1.** n Blüte f **2.** vi blühen

**blossom 1.** n Blüte f **2.** vi blühen

**blouse** n Bluse f; **big girl's ~** fam Schwächling m, femininer Typ

**blow 1.** n Schlag m **2.** vi, vt (wind) wehen, blasen; (person: trumpet etc) blasen; **~ one's nose** sich dat die Nase putzen; **blow out** vt (candle etc) ausblasen; **blow up 1.** vi explodieren **2.** vt sprengen; (balloon, tyre) aufblasen; PHOT (enlarge) vergrößern; **blow-dry** vt föhnen; **blowjob** n fam **give sb a ~** jdm einen blasen; **blown** pp → **blow**

**BLT** n abbr = **bacon, lettuce and tomato sandwich** mit Frühstücksspeck, Kopfsalat und Tomaten belegtes Sandwich

**blue** adj blau; fam (unhappy) trübsinnig, niedergeschlagen; (film) pornografisch; (joke) anzüglich; (language) derb; **bluebell** n Glockenblume f; **blueberry** n Blaubeere f; **blue cheese** n Blau-

schimmelkäse m; **blues** npl the ~ MUS der Blues; **have the ~** fam niedergeschlagen sein

**blunder** n Schnitzer m

**blunt** adj (knife) stumpf; fig unverblümt; **bluntly** adv geradeheraus

**blurred** adj verschwommen, unklar

**blush** vi erröten

**board 1.** n (of wood) Brett nt; (committee) Ausschuss m; (of firm) Vorstand m; **~ and lodging** Unterkunft und Verpflegung; **on ~** an Bord **2.** vt (train, bus) einsteigen in + acc; (ship) an Bord + gen gehen; **boarder** n Pensionsgast m, Internatsschüler(in) m(f); **board game** n Brettspiel nt; **boarding card, boarding pass** n Bordkarte f, Einsteigekarte f; **boarding school** n Internat nt; **board meeting** n Vorstandssitzung f; **boardroom** n Sitzungssaal m (des Vorstands)

**boast 1.** vi prahlen (about mit) **2.** n Prahlerei f

**boat** n Boot nt; (ship) Schiff nt; **boatman** n (hirer) Bootsverleiher m; **boat race** n Regatta f

**bob(sleigh)** n Bob m

**bodily 1.** adj körperlich **2.** adv (forcibly) gewaltsam; **body** n Körper m; (dead) Leiche f; (of car) Karosserie f; **bod-**

**bored**

**ybuilding** n Bodybuilding nt; **bodyguard** n Leibwächter m; (group) Leibwache f; **body jewellery** n Intimschmuck m; **body odour** n Körpergeruch m; **body piercing** n Piercing nt; **bodywork** n Karosserie f

**boil 1.** vt, vi kochen **2.** n MED Geschwür nt; **boiler** n Boiler m; **boiling** adj (water etc) kochend (heiß); **I was ~ (hot)** mir war fürchterlich heiß; (with rage) ich kochte vor Wut; **boiling point** n Siedepunkt m

**bold** adj kühn, mutig; (colours) kräftig; (type) fett

**Bolivia** n Bolivien f

**bomb 1.** n Bombe f **2.** vt bombardieren

**bond** (link) Bindung f

**bone** n Knochen m; (of fish) Gräte f

**boner** n (US) fam Schnitzer m; (vulg: erection) Ständer m

**bonfire** n Feuer nt (im Freien)

**bonnet** n (Brit) AUTO Haube f; (for baby) Häubchen nt

**bonny** adj (esp Scot) hübsch

**bonus** n Bonus m, Prämie f

**boo 1.** vt auspfeifen **2.** vi buhen **3.** n Buhruf m

**book 1.** n Buch nt; (of tickets, stamps) Heft nt **2.** vt (table etc) bestellen; (hotel, flight etc) buchen; **fully ~ed (up)** ausgebucht; (performance) ausverkauft; **book in** vt eintragen; **be booked in at a**

**hotel** ein Zimmer in einem Hotel bestellt haben; **bookcase** n Bücherregal nt; **booking** n Buchung f; **booking office** n RAIL Fahrkartenschalter m; THEAT Vorverkaufsstelle f; **booklet** n Broschüre f; **bookmark** n a. IT Lesezeichen nt; **bookshelf** n Bücherbord nt; **bookshelves** Bücherregal nt; **bookshop, bookstore** n (esp US) Buchhandlung f

**boom 1.** n (of business) Boom m; (noise) Dröhnen nt **2.** vi (business) boomen; fam florieren

**boomerang** n Bumerang m

**boost 1.** n Auftrieb m **2.** vt (production, sales) ankurbeln; (power, profits etc) steigern; **booster (injection)** n Wiederholungsimpfung f

**boot 1.** n Stiefel m; (Brit) AUTO Kofferraum m **2.** vt IT laden, booten

**booth** n (at fair etc) Bude f; (at trade fair etc) Stand m

**booze 1.** n fam Alkohol m **2.** vi fam saufen

**border** n Grenze f; (edge) Rand m; **north / south of the Border** (Brit) in Schottland / England; **borderline** n Grenze f

**bore 1.** pt → **bear 2.** vt (hole etc) bohren; (person) langweilen **3.** n (person) Langweiler(in) m f(s); (thing) langweilige Sache; **bored** adj be

~ sich langweilen; **boredom** n Langeweile f; **boring** adj langweilig

**born** adj he was ~ **in London** er ist in London geboren

**borne** pp → **bear**

**borough** n Stadtbezirk m

**borrow** vt borgen

**Bosnia-Herzegovina** n Bosnien-Herzegowina nt; **Bosnian 1.** adj bosnisch **2.** n Bosnier(in) m(f)

**boss** n Chef(in) m(f), Boss m

**botanical** adj botanisch; ~ **garden(s)** botanischer Garten

**both 1.** adj beide; ~ **the books** beide Bücher **2.** pron (people) beide; (things) beides; ~ **(of) the boys** die beiden Jungs; **I like ... ~ of them** ich mag sie (alle) beide **3.** adv ~ **X and Y** sowohl X als auch Y

**bother 1.** vt ärgern, belästigen; **it doesn't ~ me** das stört mich nicht; **he can't be ~ed with details** er sich nicht ab; **I'm not ~ed** das ist mir egal **2.** vi sich kümmern (about um); **don't ~** (das ist) nicht nötig, lass es! **3.** n (trouble) Mühe f; (annoyance) Ärger m

**bottle 1.** n Flasche f **2.** vt (in Flaschen) abfüllen; **bottle bank** n Altglascontainer m; **bottled** adj in Flaschen; ~ **beer** Flaschenbier nt; **bottleneck** n fig Engpass m;

**bottle opener** n Flaschenöffner m

**bottom 1.** n (of container) Boden m; (underside) Unterseite f; fam (of person) Po m; **at the ~ of the sea / table / page** auf dem Meeresgrund / am Tabellenende / unten auf der Seite **2.** adj unterste(r, s); **be ~ of the class / league** Klassenletzte(r)/Tabellenletzte(r) sein; ~ **gear** AUTO erster Gang

**bought** pt, pp → **buy**

**bounce** vi (ball) springen, aufprallen; ~ **up and down** (person) herumhüpfen; **bouncy** adj (ball) gut springend; (person) munter; **bouncy castle**® n Hüpfburg f

**bound 1.** pt, pp → **bind 2.** adj (tied up) gebunden; (obliged) verpflichtet; **be ~ to do sth** (sure to) etw bestimmt tun (werden); (have to) etw tun müssen; **it's ~ to happen** es muss so kommen; **be ~ for ...** auf dem Weg nach ... sein; **boundary** n Grenze f

**bouquet** n (flowers) Strauß m; (of wine) Blume f

**bow 1.** n (ribbon) Schleife f; (instrument, weapon) Bogen m **2.** vi sich verbeugen **3.** n (with head) Verbeugung f; (of ship) Bug m

**bowels** npl Darm m

**bowl 1.** n (basin) Schüssel f; (shallow) Schale f; (for animal) Napf m **2.** vt, vi (in cricket) werfen

**bowling** n Kegeln nt; **bowling alley** n Kegelbahn f; **bowling green** n Rasen m zum Bowling-Spiel; **bowls** nsing (game) Bowling-Spiel n

**bow tie** n Fliege f

**box** n Schachtel f; (cardboard) Karton m; (bigger) Kasten m; (space on form) Kästchen nt; THEAT Loge f

**boxer** n Boxer(in) m(f); **boxers**, **boxer shorts** npl Boxershorts pl; **boxing** n SPORT Boxen nt; **Boxing Day** n zweiter Weihnachtsfeiertag; **boxing gloves** npl Boxhandschuhe m; **box office** n (cinema, theatre) Kasse f

**boy** n Junge m

**boycott 1.** n Boykott m **2.** vt boykottieren

**boyfriend** n (fester) Freund m; **boy scout** n Pfadfinder m

**bra** n BH m

**brace** n (on teeth) Spange f

**bracelet** n Armband nt

**braces** npl (Brit) Hosenträger pl

**bracket 1.** n (in text) Klammer f; TECH Träger m **2.** vt einklammern

**brag** vi angeben

**brain** n ANAT Gehirn nt; (mind) Verstand m; ~s pl (intelligence) Grips m; **brainy**

adj schlau, clever

**brake 1.** n Bremse f **2.** vi bremsen; **brake fluid** n Bremsflüssigkeit f; **brake light** n Bremslicht nt; **brake pedal** n Bremspedal nt

**branch** n (of tree) Ast m; (of family, subject) Zweig m; (of firm) Filiale f, Zweigstelle f; **branch off** vi (road) abzweigen

**brand** n COMM Marke f

**brand-new** adj (funkel)nagelneu

**brandy** n Weinbrand m

**brass** n Messing nt; (Brit) fam (money) Knete f; **brass band** n Blaskapelle f

**brave** adj tapfer, mutig

**brawn** n (strength) Muskelkraft f; GASTR Sülze f; **brawny** adj muskulös

**Brazil** n Brasilien nt; **Brazilian 1.** adj brasilianisch **2.** n Brasilianer(in) m(f); **brazil nut** n Paranuss f

**bread** n Brot nt; **breadbin** n (Brit), **breadbox** (US) n Brotkasten m; **breadcrumbs** npl Brotkrumen pl; GASTR Paniermehl nt; **breaded** adj paniert; **breadknife** n Brotmesser nt

**breadth** n Breite f

**break 1.** n (fracture) Bruch m; (rest) Pause f; (short holiday) Kurzurlaub m; **give me a** ~ hör / hören Sie auf damit! **2.** vt (fracture) brechen; (in pieces) zerbrechen; (toy, de-

*vice)* kaputt machen; *(promise)* nicht halten; *(silence)* brechen; *(law)* verletzen; *(news)* mitteilen *(to sb* jdm); *I broke my leg* ich habe mir das Bein gebrochen; *he broke it to her gently* er hat es ihr schonend beigebracht **3.** *vi (come apart)* (auseinander)brechen; *(in pieces)* zerbrechen; *(toy, device)* kaputtgehen; *(day, dawn)* anbrechen; *(news)* bekannt werden; **break down** *vi (car)* eine Panne haben; *(machine)* versagen; *(person)* zusammenbrechen; **break in** *vi (burglar)* einbrechen; **break into** *vt* einbrechen in + *acc;* **break off** *vi, vt* abbrechen; **break out** *vi* ausbrechen; **~ in a rash** einen Ausschlag bekommen; **break up 1.** *vi* aufbrechen; *(meeting, organisation)* sich auflösen; *(marriage)* in die Brüche gehen; *(couple)* sich trennen; **school breaks up on Friday** am Freitag beginnen die Ferien **2.** *vt* aufbrechen; *(marriage)* zerstören; *(meeting)* auflösen; **breakable** *adj* zerbrechlich; **breakdown** *n (of car)* Panne *f;* *(of machine)* Störung *f;* *(of person, relations, system)* Zusammenbruch *m;* **breakdown service** *n* Pannendienst *m;* **breakdown truck** *n* Abschleppwagen *m*

**breakfast** *n* Frühstück *nt;* **have ~** frühstücken

**break-in** *n* Einbruch *m;* **breakup** *n (of meeting, organisation)* Auflösung *f; (of marriage)* Zerrüttung *f*

**breast** *n* Brust *f;* **breastfeed** *vt* stillen; **breaststroke** *n* Brustschwimmen *nt*

**breath** *n* Atem *m;* **out of ~** außer Atem; **breathalyse, breathalyze** *vt* (ins Röhrchen) blasen lassen; **breathalyser, breathalyzer** *n* Promillemesser *m;* **breathe** *vt, vi* atmen; **breathe in** *vt, vi* einatmen; **breathe out** *vt, vi* ausatmen; **breathless** *adj* atemlos; **breathtaking** *adj* atemberaubend

**bred** *pt, pp* → **breed**

**breed 1.** *n (race)* Rasse *f* **2.** *vi* sich vermehren **3.** *vt* züchten; **breeder** *n* Züchter(in) *m(f);* *fam* Hetero *m;* **breeding** *n (of animals)* Züchtung *f*

**breeze** *n* Brise *f*

**brevity** *n* Kürze *f*

**brew** *vt (beer)* brauen; *(tea)* kochen; **brewery** *n* Brauerei *f*

**bribe 1.** *n* Bestechungsgeld *nt* **2.** *vt* bestechen; **bribery** *n* Bestechung *f*

**brick** *n* Backstein *m;* **bricklayer** *n* Maurer(in) *m(f)*

**bride** *n* Braut *f;* **bridegroom** *n* Bräutigam *m;* **bridesmaid** *n* Brautjungfer *f*

**bridge** n Brücke f, Bridge nt

**brief 1.** adj kurz **2.** vt instruieren (on über + acc)

**briefcase** n Aktentasche f

**briefs** npl Slip m

**bright** adj hell; (colour) leuchtend; (cheerful) heiter; (intelligent) intelligent; (idea) glänzend; **brighten up 1.** vt aufhellen; (person) aufheitern **2.** vi sich aufheitern; (person) fröhlicher werden

**brilliant** adj (sunshine, colour) strahlend; (person) brillant; (idea) glänzend; (Brit) fam **it was ~** es war fantastisch

**brim** n Rand m

**bring** vt bringen; (with one) mitbringen; **bring about** vt herbeiführen, bewirken; **bring back** vt zurückbringen; (memories) wecken; **bring down** vt (reduce) senken; (government etc) zu Fall bringen; **bring in** vt hereinbringen; (introduce) einführen; **bring out** vt herausbringen; **bring up** vt (child) aufziehen; (question) zur Sprache bringen

**bristle** n Borste f

**Brit** n fam Brite m, Britin f; **Britain** n Großbritannien nt; **British 1.** adj britisch; **the ~ Isles** pl die Britischen Inseln pl **2.** n **the ~** pl die Briten pl

**brittle** adj spröde

**broad** adj breit; (accent) stark; **in ~ daylight** am helllichten Tag

**B road** n (Brit) ≈ Landstraße f

**broadcast** n Sendung f **2.** irr vt/i, vi senden; (event) übertragen

**broaden** vt ~ **the mind** den Horizont erweitern; **broad-minded** adj tolerant

**broccoli** n Brokkoli pl

**brochure** n Prospekt m, Broschüre f

**broke 1.** pt → **break 2.** adj (Brit) fam pleite; **broken** pp → **break**; **broken-hearted** adj untröstlich

**broker** n Makler(in) m(f)

**bronchitis** n Bronchitis f

**brooch** n Brosche f

**broom** n Besen m

**Bros** abbr = **brothers** Gebr.

**broth** n Fleischbrühe f

**brothel** n Bordell m

**brother** n Bruder m; **~s** pl comm Gebrüder pl; **brother-in-law** n Schwager m

**brought** pt, pp → **bring**

**brow** n (eyebrow) (Augen)braue f; (forehead) Stirn f

**brown** adj braun; **brown bread** n Mischbrot nt; (wholemeal) Vollkornbrot nt; **brownie** n gastr Brownie m; (Brit) junge Pfadfinderin; **brown paper** n Packpapier nt; **brown rice** n Naturreis m; **brown sugar** n brauner Zucker

**browse** vi (in book) blättern;

*(in shop)* herumschauen;
**browser** *n* IT Browser *m*

**bruise 1.** *n* blauer Fleck **2.** *vt ~*
**one's arm** sich *dat* einen
blauen Fleck (am Arm) ho-
len

**brush 1.** *n* Bürste *f*; *(for
sweeping)* Handbesen *m*;
*(for painting)* Pinsel *m* **2.** *vt*
bürsten; *(sweep)* fegen; *~*
**one's teeth** sich *dat* die
Zähne putzen; **brush up** *vt*
*(French etc)* auffrischen

**Brussels sprouts** *npl* Rosenkohl *m*, Kohlsprossen *pl*

**brutality** *n* Brutalität *f*

**BSc** *abbr* = *Bachelor of Science* erster akademischer
Grad in technisch-naturwis-
senschaftlichen Fächern, ≈
Diplom

**BSE** *abbr* = *bovine spongi-
form encephalopathy* BSE

**bubble** *n* Blase *f*; **bubble bath**
*n* Schaumbad *nt*, Bade-
schaum *m*; **bubbly 1.** *adj*
sprudelnd; *(person)* temperamentvoll **2.** *n fam* Scham-
pus *m*

**buck** *n (animal)* Bock *m*; *(US)*
*fam* Dollar *m*

**bucket** *n* Eimer *m*

**buckle 1.** *n* Schnalle *f* **2.** *vi*
TECH sich verbiegen **3.** *vt* zu-
schnallen

**bud** *n* Knospe *f*

**Buddhism** *n* Buddhismus *m*;
**Buddhist 1.** *adj* buddhistisch
**2.** *n* Buddhist(in) *m(f)*

**buddy** *n fam* Kumpel *m*

**budget 1.** *n* Budget *nt* **2.** *adj*
preisgünstig; **budget airline**
*n* Billigflieger *m*

**budgie** *n fam* Wellensittich *m*

**buffalo** *n* Büffel *m*

**buffet** *n (food)* (kaltes) Büfett
*nt*

**bug 1.** *n* IT Bug *m*, Programm-
fehler *m*; *(listening device)*
Wanze *f*; *(US, insect)* Insekt
*nt*; *fam (illness)* Infektion *f*
**2.** *vt fam* nerven

**bugger 1.** *n vulg* Scheißkerl *m*
**2.** *interj vulg* Scheiße *f*; **bugger off** *vi (Brit) vulg* abhau-
en, Leine ziehen

**buggy®** *n (for baby)* Buggy®
*m*; *(US, pram)* Kinderwagen
*m*

**build** *vt* bauen; **build up** *vt*
aufbauen; **building** *n* Gebäude *nt*; **building site** *n*
Baustelle *f*

**built** *pt, pp →* **build**; **built-in**
*adj (cupboard)* Einbau-, ein-
gebaut

**bulb** *n* BOT (Blumen)zwiebel *f*;
ELEC Glühbirne *f*

**Bulgaria** *n* Bulgarien *nt*; **Bulgarian 1.** *adj* bulgarisch **2.** *n*
*(person)* Bulgare *m*, Bulgarin *f*; *(language)* Bulgarisch
*nt*

**bulimia** *n* Bulimie *f*

**bulk** *n (size)* Größe *f*; *(greater
part)* Großteil *m (of + gen)*;
**in ~** en gros; **bulky** *adj
(goods)* sperrig; *(person)*
stämmig

**bull** n Stier m; **bulldog** n Bulldogge f; **bulldoze** vt planieren; **bulldozer** n Planierraupe f

**bullet** n Kugel f

**bulletin** n Bulletin nt; (announcement) Bekanntmachung f; MED Krankenbericht m; **bulletin board** n (US) IT schwarzes Brett

**bullshit** n fam Scheiß m

**bully** n Tyrann m

**bum** n fam (Brit, backside) Po m; (US, vagrant) Penner m

**bumblebee** n Hummel f

**bumf** n fam Infomaterial nt, Papierkram m

**bump 1.** n fam (swelling) Beule f; (road) Unebenheit f; (blow) Stoß m **2.** vt stoßen; ~ **one's head** sich dat den Kopf anschlagen (on an + dat); **bump into** vt stoßen gegen; fam (meet) (zufällig) begegnen (+ dat); **bumper 1.** n AUTO Stoßstange f **2.** adj (edition etc) Riesen-; (crop etc) Rekord-; **bumpy** adj holp(e)rig

**bun** n süßes Brötchen

**bunch** n (of flowers) Strauß m; (pear of people) Haufen m; ~ **of keys** Schlüsselbund m

**bundle** n Bündel nt

**bungee jumping** n Bungeejumping nt

**bunk** n Koje f; **bunk bed(s)** n(pl) Etagenbett nt

**bunker** n Bunker m

**bunny** n Häschen nt

**buoy** n Boje f; **buoyant** adj (floating) schwimmend

**burden** n Last f

**bureau** n Büro nt; (government department) Amt nt; **bureaucracy** n Bürokratie f; **bureau de change** n Wechselstube f

**burger** n Hamburger m

**burglar** n Einbrecher(in) m(f); **burglar alarm** n Alarmanlage f; **burglarize** vt (US) einbrechen in + acc; **burglary** n Einbruch m; **burgle** vt einbrechen in + acc

**burial** n Beerdigung f

**burn 1.** vt verbrennen; (food, slightly) anbrennen; ~ **one's hand** sich dat die Hand verbrennen **2.** vi brennen **3.** n (injury) Brandwunde f; (on material) verbrannte Stelle

**burp 1.** vi rülpsen **2.** vt (baby) aufstoßen lassen

**bursary** n Stipendium nt

**burst 1.** vt platzen lassen **2.** vi platzen; ~ **into tears** in Tränen ausbrechen

**bury** vt begraben; (in grave) beerdigen; (hide) vergraben

**bus** n Bus m; **bus driver** n Busfahrer(in) m(f)

**bush** n Busch m

**business** n Geschäft nt; (enterprise) Unternehmen nt; (concern, affair) Sache f;

*I'm here on* ~ ich bin geschäftlich hier; *it's none of your* ~ das geht dich / Sie nichts an; **business card** n Visitenkarte f; **business class** n AVIAT Businessclass f; **business hours** npl Geschäftsstunden pl; **businessman** n Geschäftsmann m; **business studies** npl Betriebswirtschaftslehre f; **businesswoman** n Geschäftsfrau f

**bus service** n Busverbindung f; **bus shelter** n Wartehäuschen nt; **bus station** n Busbahnhof m; **bus stop** n Bushaltestelle f

**bust 1.** n Büste f **2.** adj (broken) kaputt; *go* ~ Pleite gehen

**busy** adj beschäftigt; (street, place) belebt; (esp US, telephone) besetzt; ~ *signal* (US) Besetztzeichen nt

**but 1.** conj aber; (only) nur; *not this* ~ *that* nicht dies, sondern das **2.** prep (except) außer; *any colour* ~ *blue* jede Farbe, nur nicht blau; *nothing* ~ ... nichts als ...; *the last / next house* ~ *one* das vorletzte / übernächste Haus

**butcher** n Metzger(in) m(f)

**butt** n fam Hintern m

**butter 1.** n Butter f; **buttercup** n Butterblume f; **butterfly** n Schmetterling m

**buttocks** npl Gesäß nt

**button 1.** n Knopf m **2.** vt zuknöpfen; **buttonhole** n Knopfloch n

**buy 1.** n Kauf m **2.** vt kaufen (*from* von); **buyer** n Käufer(in) m(f)

**buzz 1.** n Summen nt; *give sb a* ~ fam jdn anrufen **2.** vi summen; **buzzer** n Summer m

**by 1.** prep (cause, author) von; (means) mit; (beside, near) bei, an; (via) durch; (before) bis; (according to) nach; *go* ~ *train / bus / car* mit dem Zug / Bus / Auto fahren; *send* ~ *post* mit der Post® schicken; *a house* ~ *the river* ein Haus am or beim Fluss; ~ *her side* neben ihr, an ihrer Seite; *leave* ~ *the back door* durch die Hintertür rausgehen; ~ *day / night* tags / nachts; *they'll be here* ~ *five* bis fünf Uhr müssten sie hier sein; *judge* ~ *appearances* nach dem Äußeren urteilen; *rise* ~ *10 %* um 10 % steigen; *it missed me* ~ *inches* es hat mich um Zentimeter verfehlt; *divided / multiplied* ~ *7* dividiert durch / multipliziert mit 7; ~ *oneself* allein **2.** adv (past) vorbei; *rush* ~ vorbeirasen

**bye-bye** interj fam Wiedersehen, tschüss

**by-election** n Nachwahl f; **bypass** n Umgehungsstraße f;

MED Bypass *m*; **byroad** *n* Nebenstraße *f*; **bystander** *n*

Zuschauer(in) *m(f)*

**byte** *n* Byte *nt*

# C

**C** *abbr* = *Celsius* C

**c** *abbr* → *circa* ca.

**cab** *n* Taxi *nt*

**cabbage** *n* Kohl *m*

**cabin** *n* NAUT Kajüte *f*; AVIAT Passagierraum *m*; (*wooden house*) Hütte *f*; **cabin crew** *n* Flugbegleitpersonal *nt*

**cabinet** *n* Schrank *m*; (*for display*) Vitrine *f*; POL Kabinett *nt*

**cable** *n* ELEC Kabel *nt*; **cable-car** *n* Seilbahn *f*; **cable television**, **cablevision** (*US*) *n* Kabelfernsehen *nt*

**cactus** *n* Kaktus *m*

**CAD** *abbr* = *computer-aided design* CAD *nt*

**Caesarean** *adj* ~ (*section*) Kaiserschnitt *m*

**café** *n* Café *nt*; **cafeteria** *n* Cafeteria *f*; **cafetiere** *n* Kaffeebereiter *m*

**caffein(e)** *n* Koffein *nt*

**cage** *n* Käfig *m*

**Cairo** *n* Kairo *nt*

**cake** *n* Kuchen *m*; **cake shop** *n* Konditorei *f*

**calculate** *vt* berechnen; (*estimate*) kalkulieren; **calculating** *adj* berechnend; **calculation** *n* Berechnung *f*; (*estimate*) Kalkulation *f*; **calculator** *n* Taschenrechner *m*

**calendar** *n* Kalender *m*

**calf** *n* Kalb *nt*; ANAT Wade *f*

**California** *n* Kalifornien *nt*

**call 1.** *vt* rufen; (*name, describe as*) nennen; TEL anrufen; IT, AVIAT aufrufen; **what's this ~ed?** wie heißt das? **2.** *vi* (*shout*) rufen (*for help* um Hilfe); (*visit*) vorbeikommen; **~ at the doctor's** beim Arzt vorbeigehen; (*of train*) **~ at ... in ...** halten **3.** *n* (*shout*) Ruf *m*; TEL Anruf *m*; IT, AVIAT Aufruf *m*; **make a ~** telefonieren; **give sb a ~** jdn anrufen; **be on ~** Bereitschaftsdienst haben; **call back** *vt*, *vi* zurückrufen; **call for** *vt* (*come to pick up*) abholen; (*demand, require*) verlangen; **call off** *vt* absagen

**call centre** *n* Callcenter *nt*; **caller** *n* Besucher(in) *m(f)*; TEL Anrufer(in) *m(f)*

**calm 1.** *n* Stille *f*; (*also of person*) Ruhe *f*; (*of sea*) Flaute *f* **2.** *vt* beruhigen **3.** *adj* ruhig; **calm down** *vi* sich beruhigen

**calorie** *n* Kalorie *f*

**calves** *pl* → *calf*

**Cambodia** *n* Kambodscha *nt*

**camcorder** *n* Camcorder *m*

**came** *pt* → *come*

**camel** n Kamel nt

**camera** n Fotoapparat m, Kamera f; **camera phone** n Fotohandy nt

**camomile** n Kamille f

**camouflage** n Tarnung f

**camp 1.** n Lager nt; (camping place) Zeltplatz m **2.** vi zelten, campen **3.** adj fam theatralisch, tuntig

**campaign 1.** n Kampagne f; POL Wahlkampf m **2.** vi sich einsetzen   (for / against für / gegen)

**campbed** n Campingliege f; **camper** n (person) Camper(in) m(f); (van) Wohnmobil nt; **camping** n Zelten nt, Camping nt; **campsite** n Zeltplatz m, Campingplatz m

**campus** n (of university) Universitätsgelände nt, Campus m

**can 1.** vaux (be able) können; (permission) dürfen; I **~not** or **~'t see** I go now? darf ich jetzt gehen? **2.** n (for food, beer) Dose f; (for water, milk) Kanne f

**Canada** n Kanada nt; **Canadian 1.** adj kanadisch **2.** n Kanadier(in) m(f)

**canal** n Kanal m

**canary** n Kanarienvogel m

**cancel** vt (plans) aufgeben; (meeting, event) absagen; COMM (order etc) stornieren; IT löschen; AVIAT streichen;

**be ~led** (event, train, bus) ausfallen; **cancellation** n Absage f; COMM Stornierung f; AVIAT gestrichener Flug

**cancer** n MED Krebs m; **Cancer** n ASTR Krebs m

**candid** adj (person, conversation) offen

**candidate** n (for post) Bewerber(in) m(f); POL Kandidat(in) m(f)

**candle** n Kerze f; **candlelight** n Kerzenlicht nt; **candlestick** n Kerzenhalter m

**candy** n (US) Bonbon nt; (quantity) Süßigkeiten pl; **candy-floss** n (Brit) Zuckerwatte f

**canned** adj Dosen-

**cannot** negative → **can**

**canoe** n Kanu nt; **canoeing** n Kanufahren nt

**can opener** n Dosenöffner m

**canopy** n Baldachin m; (awning) Markise f; (over entrance) Vordach nt

**can't** contr → **cannot**

**canteen** n (in factory) Kantine f; (in university) Mensa f

**canvas** n (for sails, shoes) Segeltuch nt; (for tent) Zeltstoff m; (for painting) Leinwand f

**canvass** vi um Stimmen werben (for für)

**canyon** n Felsenschlucht f; **canyoning** n Canyoning nt

**cap** n Mütze f; (lid) Verschluss m, Deckel m

**capability** n Fähigkeit f; **ca-**

**pable** adj fähig; **be ~ of sth** zu etw fähig (or imstande) sein

**capacity** n (of building, container) Fassungsvermögen nt; (ability) Fähigkeit f; (function) **in his ~ as ...** in seiner Eigenschaft als ...

**cape** n (garment) Cape nt, Umhang m; (piece of land) Kap nt

**caper** n (for cooking) Kaper f

**capital** n FIN Kapital nt; (letter) Großbuchstabe m; (city) Hauptstadt f; **capitalism** n Kapitalismus m; **capital punishment** n die Todesstrafe

**Capricorn** n ASTR Steinbock m

**capsule** n Kapsel f

**captain** n Kapitän m; (army) Hauptmann m

**captive** n Gefangene(r) mf; **capture 1.** vt (person) fassen, gefangen nehmen; (town etc) einnehmen; IT (data) erfassen **2.** n Gefangennahme f; IT Erfassung f

**car** n Auto nt; (US) RAIL Wagen m

**caravan** n Wohnwagen m; **caravan site** n Campingplatz m für Wohnwagen

**caraway** (seed) n Kümmel m

**carbohydrate** n Kohle(n)-hydrat nt

**car bomb** n Autobombe f

**carbon** n Kohlenstoff m

**carburettor, carburetor** (US)

n Vergaser m

**card** n Karte f; (material) Pappe f; **cardboard** n Pappe f; **~ (box)** Karton m; (smaller) Pappschachtel f; **card game** n Kartenspiel nt

**cardigan** n Strickjacke f

**cardphone** n Kartentelefon nt

**care 1.** n (worry) Sorge f; (carefulness) Sorgfalt f; (looking after things, people) Pflege f; **with ~** sorgfältig; (cautiously) vorsichtig; **take ~** (watch out) vorsichtig sein; (in address) **~ of** bei; **take~ of** sorgen für, sich kümmern um **2.** vi **I don't ~** es ist mir egal; **~ about sth** Wert auf etw acc legen; **he ~s about her** sie liegt ihm am Herzen; **care for** vt (look after) sorgen für, sich kümmern um; (like) mögen

**career** n Karriere f, Laufbahn f; **careers adviser** n Berufsberater(in) m(f)

**carefree** adj sorgenfrei; **careful, carefully** adj, adv sorgfältig; (cautious, cautiously) vorsichtig; **careless, carelessly** adj, adv nachlässig; (driving etc) leichtsinnig; (remark) unvorsichtig; **carer** n Betreuer(in) m(f), Pfleger(in) m(f); **caretaker** n Hausmeister(in) m(f); **careworker** n Pfleger(in) m(f)

**car-ferry** n Autofähre f

**cargo** n Ladung f

**car hire, car hire company** n
Autovermietung f

**Caribbean 1.** n Karibik f **2.** adj
karibisch

**caring** adj mitfühlend; (parent, partner) liebevoll; (looking after sb) fürsorglich

**car insurance** n Kraftfahrzeugversicherung f

**carnation** n Nelke f

**carnival** n Volksfest nt; (before Lent) Karneval m

**carol** n Weihnachtslied nt

**carp** n (fish) Karpfen m

**car park** n (Brit) Parkplatz m;
(multi-storey car park) Parkhaus nt

**carpenter** n Zimmermann m

**carpet** n Teppich m

**car phone** n Autotelefon nt;
**carpool 1.** n Fahrgemeinschaft f; (vehicles) Fuhrpark
m **2.** vi eine Fahrgemeinschaft bilden; **car rental** n
Autovermietung f

**carriage** n (Brit) RAIL (coach)
Wagen m; (compartment)
Abteil nt; (horse-drawn)
Kutsche f; (transport) Beför-
derung f; **carriageway** n
(Brit, on road) Fahrbahn f

**carrier** n COMM Spediteur(in)
m(f); **carrier bag** n Trageta-
sche f

**carrot** n Karotte f

**carry** vt tragen; (in vehicle) befördern; (have on one) bei
sich haben; **carry on 1.** vi
(continue) weitermachen **2.**
vt (continue) fortführen; ~

**on working** weiter arbeiten;
**carry out** vt (orders, plan)
ausführen, durchführen

**carrycot** n Babytragetasche f

**carsick** adj he gets ~ ihm wird
beim Autofahren übel

**cart** n Wagen m, Karren m;
(US, shopping trolley) Einkaufswagen m

**carton** n (Papp)karton m; (of
cigarettes) Stange f

**cartoon** n Cartoon m or nt;
(one drawing) Karikatur f;
(film) (Zeichen)trickfilm m

**cartridge** n (for film) Kassette
f; (for gun, pen, printer)
Patrone f; (for copier) Kar-
tusche f

**carve** vt, vi (wood) schnitzen;
(stone) meißeln; (meat)
schneiden, tranchieren;
**carving** n (in wood) Schnit-
zerei f; (in stone) Skulptur f,
Carving

**car wash** n Autowaschanlage
f

**case** n (crate) Kiste f; (box)
Schachtel f; (for spectacles)
Etui nt; (matter) LAW Fall
m; in ~ falls; **in that** ~ in
dem Fall; **in** ~ **of fire** bei
Brand; **it's a** ~ **of ...** es handelt sich hier um ...

**cash 1.** n Bargeld nt; **in** ~ bar;
~ **on delivery** per Nachnah-
me **2.** vt (check / cheque) einlösen; **cash desk** n Kasse f;
**cash dispenser** n Geldautomat m; **cashier** n Kassie-
rer(in) m(f); **cash machine** n

*n* (*Brit*) Geldautomat *m*

**cashmere** *n* Kaschmirwolle *f*

**cash payment** *n* Barzahlung *f*; **cashpoint** *n* (*Brit*) Geldautomat *m*

**casing** *n* Gehäuse *n*

**casino** *n* Kasino *n*

**cask** *n* Fass *nt*

**casserole** *n* Kasserole *f*; (*food*) Schmortopf *m*

**cassette** *n* Kassette *f*; **cassette recorder** *n* Kassettenrecorder *m*

**cast 1.** *vt* (*throw*) werfen; THEAT, FILM besetzen; (*roles*) verteilen **2.** *n* THEAT, FILM Besetzung *f*; MED Gipsverband *m*

**caster** *n* ~ **sugar** Streuzucker *m*

**castle** *n* Burg *f*

**casual** *adj* (*arrangement, remark*) beiläufig; (*attitude, manner*) (nach)lässig, zwanglos; (*dress*) leger; (*work, earnings*) Gelegenheits-; (*look, glance*) flüchtig; ~ **wear** Freizeitkleidung *f*; ~ **sex** Gelegenheitssex *m*; **casually** *adv* (*remark, say*) beiläufig; (*meet*) zwanglos; (*dressed*) leger

**casualty** *n* Verletzte(r) *mf*; (*dead*) Tote(r) *mf*; (*department in hospital*) Notaufnahme *f*

**cat** *n* Katze *f*; (*male*) Kater *m*

**catalog** (*US*), **catalogue** *n* Katalog *m*

**cataract** *n* Wasserfall *m*; MED

grauer Star

**catarrh** *n* Katarr(h) *m*

**catastrophe** *n* Katastrophe *f*

**catch 1.** *n* (*in fish etc*) Fang *m* **2.** *vt* fangen; (*thief*) fassen; (*train, bus etc*) nehmen; (*not miss*) erreichen; ~ **a cold** sich erkälten; ~ **fire** Feuer fangen; **I didn't ~ that** das habe ich nicht verstanden; **catch up** *vt, vi* ~ **with sb** jdn einholen; ~ **on sth** etw nachholen; **catching** *adj* ansteckend

**category** *n* Kategorie *f*

**cater** *vi* die Speisen und Getränke liefern (*for* für); **cater for** *vt* (*have facilities for*) eingestellt sein auf + *acc*; **catering** *n* Versorgung *f* mit Speisen und Getränken, Gastronomie *f*; **catering service** *n* Partyservice *m*

**caterpillar** *n* Raupe *f*

**cathedral** *n* Kathedrale *f*, Dom *m*

**Catholic 1.** *adj* katholisch **2.** *n* Katholik(in) *m(f)*

**cat nap** *n* (*Brit*) kurzer Schlaf; **cat's eyes** *npl* Katzenaugen *pl*, Reflektoren *pl*

**catsup** (*US*) Ketchup *nt* or *m*

**cattle** *npl* Vieh *nt*

**caught** *pt, pp* → **catch**

**cauliflower** *n* Blumenkohl *m*; **cauliflower cheese** *n* Blumenkohl *m* in Käsesoße

**cause 1.** *n* (*origin*) Ursache *f* (*of* für); (*reason*) Grund *m*

*(for zu); (purpose)* Sache *f*;
**for a good ~** für wohltätige
Zwecke; **no ~ for alarm /
complaint** kein Grund zur
Aufregung / Klage **2.** *vt* verursachen
**causeway** *n* Damm *m*
**caution 1.** *n* Vorsicht *f*; LAW,
SPORT Verwarnung *f* **2.** *vt*
(ver)warnen; **cautious** *adj*
vorsichtig
**cave** *n* Höhle *f*
**cavity** *n* Hohlraum *m*; (*in
tooth*) Loch *nt*
**cayenne (pepper)** *n* Cayennepfeffer *m*
**CCTV** *abbr* → **closed circuit
television** Videoüberwachungsanlage *f*
**CD** *abbr* → **compact disc** CD
*f*; **CD player** *n* CD-Spieler
*m*; **CD-ROM** *abbr* = **Compact Disc Read Only Memory** CD-ROM *f*
**cease 1.** *vi* aufhören **2.** *vt* beenden; **~ doing sth** aufhören, etw zu tun; **cease fire**
*n* Waffenstillstand *m*
**ceiling** *n* Decke *f*
**celebrate** *vt*, *vi* feiern; **celebrated** *adj* gefeiert; **celebration** *n* Feier *f*; **celebrity** *n*
Berühmtheit *f*, Star *m*
**celeriac** *n* (Knollen)sellerie
*m* or *f*; **celery** *n* (Stangen)sellerie *m* or *f*
**cell** *n* Zelle *f*; (*US*) → **cellphone**
**cellar** *n* Keller *m*
**cello** *n* Cello *nt*

**cellphone, cellular phone** *n*
Mobiltelefon *nt*, Handy *nt*
**Celt** *n* Kelte *m*, Keltin *f*; **Celtic
1.** *adj* keltisch **2.** *n* (*language*)
Keltisch *nt*
**cement** *n* Zement *m*
**cemetery** *n* Friedhof *m*
**cent** *n* (*of dollar, euro etc*)
Cent *m*
**center** *n* (*US*) → **centre**
**centiliter** (*US*), **centilitre** *n*
Zentiliter *m*; **centimeter**
(*US*), **centimetre** *n* Zentimeter *m*
**central** *adj* zentral; **Central
America** *n* Mittelamerika
*nt*; **Central Europe** *n* Mitteleuropa *nt*; **central heating** *n*
Zentralheizung *f*; **centralize**
*vt* zentralisieren; **central
locking** *n* AUTO Zentralverriegelung *f*; **central reservation** *n* (*Brit*) Mittelstreifen
*m*; **central station** *n* Hauptbahnhof *m*
**centre 1.** *n* Mitte *f*; (*building,
of city*) Zentrum *nt* **2.** *vt* zentrieren; **centre forward** *n*
SPORT Mittelstürmer *m*
**century** *n* Jahrhundert *nt*
**ceramic** *adj* keramisch
**cereal** *n* (*any grain*) Getreide
*nt*; (*breakfast cereal*) Frühstücksflocken *pl*
**ceremony** *n* Feier *f*, Zeremonie *f*
**certain** *adj* sicher (*of* + *gen*);
(*particular*) bestimmt; **for ~**
mit Sicherheit; **certainly**
*adv* sicher; (*without doubt*)

bestimmt; **~!** aber sicher!; **~ not** ganz bestimmt nicht!

**certificate** *n* Bescheinigung *f*; (*in school, of qualification*) Zeugnis *nt*; **certify** *vt, vi* bescheinigen

**cervical smear** *n* Abstrich *m*

**CFC** *abbr* = *chlorofluorocarbon* FCKW *nt*

**chain 1.** *n* Kette *f* **2.** *vt ~ (up)* anketten

**chair** *n* Stuhl *m*; (*university*) Lehrstuhl *m*; (*armchair*) Sessel *m*; (*chairperson*) Vorsitzende(r) *mf*; **chairlift** *n* Sessellift *m*; **chairman** *n* Vorsitzende(r) *m*; (*of firm*) Präsident *m*; **chairperson** *n* Vorsitzende(r) *m*; (*of firm*) Präsident(in) *m(f)*; **chairwoman** *n* Vorsitzende *f*; (*of firm*) Präsidentin *f*

**chalet** *n* (*in mountains*) Berghütte *f*; (*holiday dwelling*) Ferienhäuschen *nt*

**chalk** *n* Kreide *f*

**challenge 1.** *n* Herausforderung *f* **2.** *vt* (*person*) herausfordern; (*statement*) bestreiten

**chambermaid** *n* Zimmermädchen *nt*

**champagne** *n* Champagner *m*

**champion** *n* SPORT Meister(in) *m(f)*; **championship** *n* Meisterschaft *f*

**chance** *n* (*fate*) Zufall *m*; (*possibility*) Möglichkeit *f*; (*opportunity*) Gelegenheit

*f*; (*risk*) Risiko *nt*; *by~* zufällig; *he doesn't stand a ~ (of winning)* er hat keinerlei Chance(, zu gewinnen)

**chancellor** *n* Kanzler(in) *m(f)*

**chandelier** *n* Kronleuchter *m*

**change 1.** *vt* verändern; (*alter*) ändern; (*money, wheel, nappy*) wechseln; (*exchange*) (um)tauschen; **~ one's clothes** sich umziehen; **~ trains** umsteigen; **~ gear** AUTO schalten **2.** *vi* sich ändern; (*esp outwardly*) sich verändern; (*get changed*) sich umziehen **3.** *n* Veränderung *f*; (*alteration*) Änderung *f*; (*money*) Wechselgeld *nt*; (*coins*) Kleingeld *nt*; *for a ~* zur Abwechslung; *can you give me ~ for £10?* können Sie mir auf 10 Pfund herausgeben?; **change down** *vi* (*Brit*) AUTO herunterschalten; **change over** *vi* sich umstellen (*to auf + acc*); **change up** *vi* (*Brit*) AUTO hochschalten

**changeable** *adj* (*weather*) veränderlich, wechselhaft; **change machine** *n* Geldwechsler *m*; **changing room** *n* Umkleideraum *m*

**channel** *n* Kanal *m*; RADIO, TV Kanal *m*, Sender *m*; *the (English) Channel* der Ärmelkanal; *the Channel Islands* die Kanalinseln; **channel-hopping** *n* Zappen *nt*

**chaos** *n* Chaos *nt*; **chaotic** *adj* chaotisch

**chap** *n* (*Brit*) *fam* Bursche *m*, Kerl *m*

**chapel** *n* Kapelle *f*

**chapped** *adj* (*lips*) aufgesprungen

**chapter** *n* Kapitel *nt*

**character** *n* Charakter *m*, Wesen *nt*; (*in a play, novel etc*) Figur *f*; TYPO Zeichen *nt*; **he's a real~** er ist ein echtes Original; **characteristic** *n* typisches Merkmal

**charcoal** *n* Holzkohle *f*

**charge 1.** *n* (*cost*) Gebühr *f*; LAW Anklage *f*; **free of~** gratis, kostenlos; **be in ~ of** verantwortlich sein für **2.** *vt* (*money*) verlangen; LAW anklagen; (*battery*) laden

**charity** *n* (*institution*) wohltätige Organisation *f*; **a collection for~** eine Sammlung für wohltätige Zwecke; **charity shop** *n* Geschäft einer 'charity', in dem freiwillige Helfer gebrauchte Kleidung, Bücher etc verkaufen

**charm 1.** *n* Charme *m* **2.** *vt* bezaubern; **charming** *adj* reizend, charmant

**chart 1.** *n* Diagramm *nt*; (*map*) Karte *f*; **the~s** *pl* die Charts, die Hitliste

**charter 1.** *n* Urkunde *f* **2.** *vt* NAUT, AVIAT chartern; **charter flight** *n* Charterflug *m*

**chase 1.** *vt* jagen, verfolgen **2.**

*n* Verfolgungsjagd *f*; (*hunt*) Jagd *f*

**chassis** *n* AUTO Fahrgestell *nt*

**chat 1.** *vi* plaudern; IT chatten **2.** *n* Plauderei *f*; **chat up** *vt* anmachen, anbaggern; **chatroom** *n* IT Chatroom *m*; **chat show** *n* Talkshow *f*

**chauffeur** *n* Chauffeur(in) *m(f)*, Fahrer(in) *m(f)*

**cheap** *adj* billig; (*of poor quality*) minderwertig

**cheat** *n, vi* betrügen; (*in school, game*) mogeln

**Chechnya** *n* Tschetschenien *nt*

**check 1.** *vt* (*examine*) überprüfen (*for* + *acc*); TECH (*adjustment etc*) kontrollieren; (*US, tick*) abhaken; AVIAT (*luggage*) einchecken; (*US, coat*) abgeben **2.** *n* (*examination, restraint*) Kontrolle *f*; (*US, restaurant bill*) Rechnung *f*; (*pattern*) Karo (-muster) *nt*; (*US*) → **cheque**; **check in** *vt, vi* AVIAT einchecken; (*into hotel*) sich anmelden; **check out** *vi* sich anmelden; **check up** *vi* nachprüfen; **~ on sb** Nachforschungen über jdn anstellen

**checkers** *nsing* (*US*) Damespiel *nt*

**check-in** *n* (*airport*) Check-in *m*; (*hotel*) Anmeldung *f*; **check-in desk** *n* Abfertigungsschalter *m*; **checking account** *n* (*US*) Scheckkonto nt; **check list** n Kontrollliste f; **checkout** n (*supermarket*) Kasse f; **checkout time** n (*hotel*) Abreise(zeit) f; **checkpoint** n Kontrollpunkt m; **checkroom** n (*US*) Gepäckaufbewahrung f; **checkup** n MED (ärztliche) Untersuchung

**cheddar** n Cheddarkäse m
**cheek** n Backe f, Wange f; (*insolence*) Frechheit f; **what a** ~ so eine Frechheit!; **cheekbone** n Backenknochen m; **cheeky** adj frech

**cheer 1.** n Beifallsruf m; ~**s** (*when drinking*) prost!; (*Brit fam*) (*thanks*) danke; (*Brit, goodbye*) tschüs **2.** vt zujubeln + dat **3.** vi jubeln; **cheer up 1.** vt aufmuntern **2.** vi fröhlicher werden; **cheerful** adj fröhlich

**cheese** n Käse m; **cheeseboard** n Käsebrett nt; (*as course*) (gemischte) Käseplatte; **cheesecake** n Käsekuchen m

**chef** n Koch m; (*in charge of kitchen*) Küchenchef(in) m(f)

**chemical 1.** adj chemisch **2.** n Chemikalie f; **chemist** n (*pharmacist*) Apotheker(in) m(f); (*industrial chemist*) Chemiker(in) m(f); ~**'s** (*shop*) Apotheke f; **chemistry** n Chemie f

**cheque** n (*Brit*) Scheck m; **cheque account** n (*Brit*) Gi-

rokonto nt; **cheque book** n (*Brit*) Scheckheft nt; **cheque card** n (*Brit*) Scheckkarte f

**chequered** adj kariert
**cherish** vt (*look after*) liebevoll sorgen für; (*hope*) hegen; (*memory*) bewahren

**cherry** n Kirsche f; **cherry tomato** n Kirschtomate f

**chess** n Schach nt; **chessboard** n Schachbrett nt

**chest** n Brust f; (*box*) Kiste f; ~ **of drawers** Kommode f

**chestnut** n Kastanie f
**chew** vt, vi kauen; **chewing gum** n Kaugummi m

**chick** n Küken nt; **chicken** n Huhn nt; (*food: roast*) Hähnchen nt; (*coward*) Feigling m; **chicken breast** n Hühnerbrust f; **chicken Kiev** n paniertes Hähnchen, mit Knoblauchbutter gefüllt; **chickenpox** n Windpocken pl; **chickpea** n Kichererbse f

**chicory** n Chicorée f
**chief 1.** n (*of department etc*) Leiter(in) m(f); (*boss*) Chef(in) m(f); (*of tribe*) Häuptling m **2.** adj Haupt-; **chiefly** adv hauptsächlich

**child** n Kind nt; **child allowance**, **child benefit** (*Brit*) n Kindergeld nt; **childhood** n Kindheit f; **childish** adj kindisch; **child lock** n Kindersicherung f; **childproof** adj kindersicher; **children** pl → **child**; **child seat** n Kindersitz m

Chile n Chile nt

chill 1. n Kühle f; MED Erkältung f 2. vt (wine) kühlen; chill out vi fam chillen, relaxen; chilled adj gekühlt

chilli n Pepperoni pl; (spice) Chili m; (dish) con carne m Chili con carne m

chilly adj kühl, frostig

chimney n Schornstein m; chimneysweep n Schornsteinfeger(in) m(f)

chimpanzee n Schimpanse m

chin n Kinn nt

china n Porzellan nt

China n China nt; Chinese 1. adj chinesisch 2. n (person) Chinese m, Chinesin f; (language) Chinesisch nt; Chinese leaves npl Chinakohl m

chip 1. n (of wood etc) Splitter m; (damage) angeschlagene Stelle; IT Chip m; ~s (Brit, potatoes) Pommes (frites) pl; (US, crisps) Kartoffelchips pl 2. vt anschlagen, beschädigen; chippie fam, chip shop n Frittenbude f

chiropodist n Fußpfleger(in) m(f)

chirp vi zwitschern

chisel n Meißel m

chives npl Schnittlauch m

chlorine n Chlor nt

chocaholic, chocoholic n Schokoladenfreak m; choc-ice n Eis nt mit Schokoladenüberzug; chocolate n

Schokolade f; (chocolate-coated sweet) Praline f; a bar of ~ eine Tafel Schokolade; a box of ~s eine Schachtel Pralinen; chocolate cake n Schokoladenkuchen m

choice 1. n Wahl f; (selection) Auswahl f 2. adj auserlesen; (product) Qualitäts-

choir n Chor m

choke 1. vi sich verschlucken; SPORT die Nerven verlieren 2. vt erdrosseln 3. n AUTO Choke m

cholera n Cholera f

cholesterol n Cholesterin nt

choose vt wählen; (pick out) sich aussuchen; there are three to ~ from es stehen drei zur Auswahl

chop 1. vt (zer)hacken; (meat etc) klein schneiden 2. n (meat) Kotelett nt; get the ~ gefeuert werden; chopsticks npl Essstäbchen pl

chorus n Chor m; (in song) Refrain m

chose, chosen pt, pp → choose

chowder n (US) dicke Suppe mit Meeresfrüchten

christen vt taufen; christening n Taufe f; Christian 1. adj christlich 2. n Christ(in) m(f); Christian name n (Brit) Vorname m

Christmas n Weihnachten pl; Christmas bonus n Weihnachtsgeld nt; Christmas card n Weihnachtskarte f

**Christmas carol** n Weihnachtslied nt; **Christmas Day** n der erste Weihnachtstag; **Christmas Eve** n Heiligabend m; **Christmas pudding** n Plumpudding m; **Christmas tree** n Weihnachtsbaum m

**chronic** adj MED chronisch

**chubby** adj (child) pummelig; (adult) rundlich

**chuck** vt fam schmeißen; **chuck in** vt fam (job) hinschmeißen; **chuck out** vt fam rausschmeißen; **chuck up** vi fam kotzen

**chunk** n Klumpen m; (of bread) Brocken m; (of meat) Batzen m; **chunky** adj (person) stämmig

**Chunnel** n fam Kanaltunnel m

**church** n Kirche f; **churchyard** n Kirchhof m

**chute** n Rutsche f

**chutney** n Chutney m

**CIA** abbr = **Central Intelligence Agency** (US) CIA f

**CID** abbr = **Criminal Investigation Department** (Brit) ≈ Kripo f

**cider** n ≈ Apfelmost m

**cigar** n Zigarre f; **cigarette** n Zigarette f

**cinema** n Kino nt

**cinnamon** n Zimt m

**circle 1.** n Kreis m **2.** vi kreisen; **circuit** n Rundfahrt f; (on foot) Rundgang m; (for racing) Rennstrecke f; ELEC

Stromkreis m; **circular 1.** adj (kreis)rund, kreisförmig f **2.** n Rundschreiben nt; **circulation** n (of blood) Kreislauf m; (of newspaper) Auflage f

**circumstances** npl (facts) Umstände pl; (financial condition) Verhältnisse pl; **in / under the ~** unter den Umständen; **under no ~** auf keinen Fall

**circus** n Zirkus m

**cissy** n fam Weichling m

**cistern** n Zisterne f; (of WC) Spülkasten m

**citizen** n Bürger(in) m(f); (of nation) Staatsangehörige(r) mf; **citizenship** n Staatsangehörigkeit f

**city** n Stadt f; (large) Großstadt f; **the ~** (London's financial centre) die (Londoner) City; **city centre** n Innenstadt f, Zentrum nt

**civil** adj (of town) Bürger-; (of state) staatsbürgerlich; (not military) zivil; **civil ceremony** n standesamtliche Hochzeit; **civil engineering** n Hoch- und Tiefbau m, Bauingenieurwesen nt; **civilian** n Zivilist(in) m(f); **civilization** n Zivilisation f, Kultur f; **civilized** adj zivilisiert, kultiviert; **civil partnership** n eingetragene Partnerschaft; **civil rights** npl Bürgerrechte pl; **civil servant** n (Staats)beamte(r) m,

(Staats)beamtin f; **civil service** n Staatsdienst m; **civil war** n Bürgerkrieg m

**CJD** abbr = **Creutzfeld-Jakob disease** Creutzfeld-Jakob-Krankheit f

**cl** abbr = **centilitre(s)** cl

**claim 1.** vt beanspruchen; (apply for) beantragen; (demand) fordern; (assert) behaupten (that dass) **2.** n (demand) Forderung f (for für); (right) Anspruch m (to auf + acc); **~ for damages** Schadensersatzforderung f; **make** or **put in a ~** (insurance) Ansprüche geltend machen; **claimant** n Antragsteller(in) m(f)

**clam** n Venusmuschel f; **clam chowder** n (US) dicke Muschelsuppe (mit Sellerie, Zwiebeln etc)

**clap** vi (Beifall) klatschen

**claret** n roter Bordeaux(wein)

**clarify** vt klären

**clash 1.** vi (physically) zusammenstoßen (with mit); (argue) sich auseinandersetzen (with mit); fig (colours) sich beißen **2.** n Zusammenstoß m; (argument) Auseinandersetzung f

**class 1.** n Klasse f **2.** vt einordnen, einstufen

**classic 1.** adj (mistake, example etc) klassisch **2.** n Klassiker m; **classical** adj (music, ballet etc) klassisch

**classification** n Klassifizie-

rung f; **classify** vt klassifizieren; **classified advertisement** Kleinanzeige f

**classroom** n Klassenzimmer nt

**classy** adj fam nobel, exklusiv

**clause** n LING Satz m; LAW Klausel f

**claw** n Kralle f

**clay** n Lehm m; (for pottery) Ton m

**clean 1.** adj sauber; **~ driving licence** Führerschein ohne Strafpunkte **2.** vt sauber machen; (carpet etc) reinigen; (window, shoes, vegetables) putzen; (wound) säubern; **clean up 1.** vt sauber machen **2.** vi aufräumen; **cleaner** n (person) Putzmann m, Putzfrau f; (substance) Putzmittel nt; **~'s** (firm) Reinigung f

**cleanse** vt reinigen; (wound) säubern; **cleanser** n Reinigungsmittel nt

**clear 1.** adj klar; (distinct) deutlich; (conscience) rein; (free, road etc) frei; **be ~ about sth** sich über etw im Klaren sein **2.** adv **stand ~** zurücktreten **3.** vt (road, room etc) räumen; (table) abräumen; LAW (find innocent) freisprechen (of von) **4.** vi (fog, mist) sich verziehen; (weather) aufklaren; **clear away** vt wegräumen; (dishes) abräumen; **clear off** vi fam abhauen; **clear**

**up 1.** vi (tidy up) aufräumen; (weather) sich aufklären **2.** vt (room) aufräumen; (litter) wegräumen; (matter) klären

**clearance sale** n Räumungsverkauf m; **clearing** n Lichtung f; **clearly** adv klar; (speak, remember) deutlich; (obviously) eindeutig; **clearway** n (Brit) Straße f mit Halteverbot m

**clench** vt (fist) ballen; (teeth) zusammenbeißen

**clergyman** n Geistliche(r) m; **clergywoman** n Geistliche f

**clerk** (US) n (in office) Büroangestellte(r) mf; (US, salesperson) Verkäufer(in) m(f)

**clever** adj schlau, klug

**cliché** n Klischee nt

**click 1.** n Klicken nt; IT Mausklick m **2.** vi klicken; ~ **on sth** IT etw anklicken; **it** ~**ed** fam ich hab's / er hat's etc geschnallt; **they** ~**ed** sie haben sich gleich verstanden; **click on** vt IT anklicken

**client** n Kunde m, Kundin f; LAW Mandant(in) m(f)

**cliff** n Klippe f

**climate** n Klima nt

**climax** n Höhepunkt m

**climb 1.** vi (person) klettern; (aircraft, sun) steigen; (road) ansteigen **2.** vt (mountain) besteigen; (tree etc) klettern auf + acc **3.** n Aufstieg m; **climbing** n Klettern nt, Bergsteigen nt; **climbing frame** n Klettergerüst nt

**cling** vi sich klammern (to an + acc); **cling film®** n Frischhaltefolie f

**clinic** n Klinik f

**clip 1.** n Klammer f **2.** vt (fix) anklemmen (to an + acc); (fingernails) schneiden; **clippers** npl (for nails) Schere f; (for nails) Zwicker m

**cloak** n Umhang m; **cloakroom** n (for coats) Garderobe f

**clock** n Uhr f; AUTO fam Tacho m; **round the** ~ rund um die Uhr; **clockwise** adv im Uhrzeigersinn

**cloister** n Kreuzgang m

**clone 1.** n Klon m **2.** vt klonen

**close 1.** adj nahe (to + dat); (friend, contact) eng; (resemblance) groß; ~ **to the beach** in der Nähe des Strandes; ~ **win** knapper Sieg; **on** ~**r examination** bei näherer or genauerer Untersuchung **2.** adv dicht; **he lives** ~ **by** er wohnt ganz in der Nähe **3.** vt schließen; (road) sperren; (discussion, matter) abschließen **4.** vi schließen **5.** n Ende nt; **close down 1.** vi schließen; (factory) stillgelegt werden **2.** vt (shop) schließen; (factory) stilllegen; **closed** adj (road) gesperrt; (shop etc) geschlossen; **closed circuit television** n Videoüberwachungsanlage f; **closely** adv (related) eng, nah; (packed, fol-

*low)* dicht; *(attentively)* genau

**closet** *n (esp US)* Schrank *m*

**close-up** *n* Nahaufnahme *f*

**closing** *adj* ~ **date** letzter Termin; *(for competition)* Einsendeschluss *m*; ~ **time** *n (of shop)* Ladenschluss *m*; *(Brit, of pub)* Polizeistunde *f*

**closure** *n* Schließung *f*; Abschluss *m*; **look for** ~ mit etw abschließen wollen

**clot 1.** *(blood)* ~ Blutgerinnsel *nt*; *fam (idiot)* Trottel *m* **2.** *vi (blood)* gerinnen

**cloth** *n (material)* Tuch *nt*; *(for cleaning)* Lappen *m*

**clothe** *vt* kleiden; **clothes** *npl* Kleider *pl*, Kleidung *f*; **clothes peg**, **clothespin** *(US)* *n* Wäscheklammer *f*; **clothing** *n* Kleidung *f*

**clotted** *adj* ~ **cream** dicke Sahne (aus erhitzter Milch)

**cloud** *n* Wolke *f*; **cloudy** *adj (sky)* bewölkt; *(liquid)* trüb

**clove** *n* Gewürznelke *f*; ~ **of garlic** Knoblauchzehe *f*

**clover** *n* Klee *m*; **cloverleaf** *n* Kleeblatt *n*

**clown** *n* Clown *m*

**club** *adj* ~ **cream** Knüppel *m*; *(society)* Klub *m*, Verein *m*; *(nightclub)* Disko *f*; *(golf club)* Golfschläger *m*; ~**s**, Kreuz *nt*; **clubbing** *n* **go** ~ in die Disko gehen; **club class** *n* AVIAT Businessclass *f*

**clue** *n* Anhaltspunkt *m*, Hinweis *m*; **he hasn't a** ~ er hat keine Ahnung

**clumsy** *adj* unbeholfen, ungeschickt

**clung** *pt, pp* → **cling**

**clutch** *n* AUTO Kupplung *f*

**cm** *abbr* = **centimetre(s)** cm

**c/o** *abbr* → **care of** bei

**Co** *abbr* → **company**

**coach 1.** *n (Brit, bus)* Reisebus *m*; RAIL (Personen)wagen *m*; SPORT (Trainer(in) *m(f)* **2.** *vt* Nachhilfeunterricht geben + *dat*; SPORT trainieren; **coach (class)** *n* AVIAT Economyclass *f*; **coach driver** *n* Busfahrer(in) *m(f)*; **coach party** *n* Reisegruppe *f (im Bus)*; **coach station** *n* Busbahnhof *m*; **coach trip** *n* Busfahrt *f*; *(tour)* Busreise *f*

**coal** *n* Kohle *f*

**coalition** *n* POL Koalition *f*

**coast** *n* Küste *f*; **coastguard** *n* Küstenwache *f*; **coastline** *n* Küste *f*

**coat** *n* Mantel *m*; *(jacket)* Jacke *f*; *(on animals)* Fell *nt*, Pelz *m*; *(of paint)* Schicht *f*; ~ **of arms** Wappen *nt*; **coathanger** *n* Kleiderbügel *m*; **coating** *n* Überzug *m*; *(layer)* Schicht *f*

**cobble(stone)s** *npl* Kopfsteinpflaster *nt*; *(surface)* Kopfsteinpflaster *nt*

**cobweb** *n* Spinnennetz *nt*

**cocaine** *n* Kokain *nt*

**cock** *n* Hahn *m*; *vulg (penis)* Schwanz *m*

cockle n Herzmuschel f

cockpit n (in plane, racing car) Cockpit nt; cockroach n Kakerlake f; cocktail n Cocktail m; cock-up n (Brit) fam make a ~ of sth bei etw Mist bauen; cock up vt (Brit) fam vermasseln, versauen; cocky adj großspurig, von sich selbst überzeugt

cocoa n Kakao m

coconut n Kokosnuss f

COD abbr = cash on delivery per Nachnahme

code n Kode m

coffee n Kaffee m; coffee bar n Café nt; coffee break n Kaffeepause f; coffee maker n Kaffeemaschine f; coffee pot n Kaffeekanne f; coffee shop n Café nt; coffee table n Couchtisch m

coffin n Sarg m

coil n Rolle f; ELEC Spule f; MED Spirale f

coin n Münze f

coincide vi (happen together) zusammenfallen (with mit); coincidence n Zufall m

coke n Koks m; Coke® Cola f

cola n Cola f

cold 1. adj kalt; I'm ~ mir ist kalt, ich friere 2. n Kälte f; (illness) Erkältung f, Schnupfen m; catch a ~ sich erkälten; cold box n Kühlbox f; cold sore n Herpes f

coleslaw n Krautsalat m

collaborate vi zusammenar-

beiten (with mit); collaboration n Zusammenarbeit f; (of one party) Mitarbeit f

collapse 1. vi zusammenbrechen; (building etc) einstürzen 2. n Zusammenbruch m; (of building) Einsturz m

collar n Kragen m; (for dog, cat) Halsband nt; collarbone n Schlüsselbein nt

colleague n Kollege m, Kollegin f

collect 1. vt sammeln; (fetch) abholen 2. vi sich sammeln; collect call n (US) R-Gespräch nt; collected adj (works) gesammelt; (person) gefasst; collection n Sammlung f, REL Kollekte f; (from postbox) Leerung f; collector n Sammler(in) m(f)

college n (residential) College nt; (specialist) Fachhochschule f; (vocational) Berufsschule f; (US, university) Universität f; go to ~ (US) studieren

collide vi zusammenstoßen; collision n Zusammenstoß m

colloquial adj umgangssprachlich

Cologne n Köln nt

colon n (punctuation mark) Doppelpunkt m

colonial adj kolonial; colony n Kolonie f

color n (US), colour 1. n Farbe f; (of skin) Hautfarbe f 2.

*vt* anmalen; *(bias)* färben; **colour-blind** *adj* farbenblind; **coloured** *adj* farbig; *(biased)* gefärbt; **colour film** *n* Farbfilm *m*; **colourful** *adj* lit, fig bunt; *(life, past)* bewegt; **colouring** *n* (*in food etc*) Farbstoff *m*; *(complexion)* Gesichtsfarbe *f*; **colourless** *adj* farblos; **colour photo(graph)** *n* Farbfoto *nt*; **colour television** *n* Farbfernsehen *nt*

**column** *n* Säule *f*; *(of print)* Spalte *f*

**comb 1.** *n* Kamm *m* **2.** *vt* kämmen; **~ one's hair** sich kämmen

**combination** *n* Kombination *f*; *(mixture)* Mischung *f* *(of* aus*)*; **combine** *vt* verbinden *(with* mit*)*; *(two things)* kombinieren

**come** *vi* kommen; *(arrive)* ankommen; *(on list, in order)* stehen; *(with adjective: become)* werden; **~ and see us** besuchen Sie uns mal; **coming** ich komm ja schon!; **~ first / second** erster / zweiter werden; **~ true** wahr werden; **~ loose** sich lockern; **the years to ~** die kommenden Jahre; **there's one more to ~** es kommt noch eins / noch einer; **how ~ ...?** *fam* wie kommt es, dass ...?; **~ to think of it** *fam* wo es mir gerade einfällt; **come across** *vt (find)*

stoßen auf + *acc*; **come back** *vi* zurückkommen; **I'll ~ to that** ich komme darauf zurück; **come down** *vi* herunterkommen; *(rain, snow, price)* fallen; **come from** *vt (result)* kommen von; **where do you ~?** wo kommst du / kommen Sie her?; **I~ London** ich komme aus London; **come in** *vi* hereinkommen; *(arrive)* ankommen; **come off** *vi (button, handle etc)* abgehen; *(succeed)* gelingen; **~ well / badly** gut / schlecht wegkommen; **come on** *vi (progress)* vorankommen; **~!** komm!; *(hurry)* beeil dich!; *(encouraging)* los!; **come out** *vi* herauskommen; *(photo)* was werden; *(homosexual)* sich outen; **come round** *vi (visit)* vorbeikommen; *(regain consciousness)* wieder zu sich kommen; **come to 1.** *vi (regain consciousness)* wieder zu sich kommen **2.** *vt (sum)* sich belaufen auf + *acc*; **when it comes to ~** wenn es um ... geht; **come up** *vi* hochkommen; *(sun, moon)* aufgehen; **~ (for discussion)** zur Sprache kommen; **come up to** *vt (approach)* zukommen auf + *acc*; *(water)* reichen bis zu; *(expectations)* entsprechen + *dat*; **come up with** *vt (idea)* haben; *(solution, answer)* kommen auf

+ *acc*; ~ *a suggestion* einen Vorschlag machen

**comedian** *n* Komiker(in) *m(f)*; **comedy** *n* Komödie *f*, Comedy *f*

**comfort 1.** *n* Komfort *m*; (*consolation*) Trost *m* **2.** *vt* trösten; **comfortable** *adj* bequem; (*income*) ausreichend; (*temperature, life*) angenehm; **comforting** *adj* tröstlich

**comic 1.** *n* (*magazine*) Comic (-heft) *nt*; (*comedian*) Komiker(in) *m(f)* **2.** *adj* komisch

**coming** *adj* kommend; (*event*) bevorstehend

**comma** *n* Komma *nt*

**command 1.** *n* Befehl *m*; (*control*) Führung *f*; MIL Kommando *nt* **2.** *vt* befehlen + *dat*

**commemorate** *vt* gedenken + *gen*; **commemoration** *n* **in ~ of** in Gedenken an + *acc*

**comment 1.** *n* (*remark*) Bemerkung *f*; (*note*) Anmerkung *f*; (*official*) Kommentar *m* (*on* zu); **no ~** kein Kommentar **2.** *vi* sich äußern (*on* zu); **commentary** *n* Kommentar *m* (*on* zu); TV, SPORT Livereportage *f*; **commentator** *n* Kommentator(in) *m(f)*; TV, SPORT Reporter(in) *m(f)*

**commerce** *n* Handel *m*; **commercial 1.** *adj* kommerziell; (*training*) kaufmännisch; ~ **break** Werbepause **2.** *n* TV

Werbespot *m*

**commission 1.** *n* Auftrag *m*; (*fee*) Provision *f*; (*reporting body*) Kommission *f* **2.** *vt* beauftragen

**commit 1.** *vt* (*crime*) begehen **2.** *vr* ~ **oneself** (*undertake*) sich verpflichten (*to* zu); **commitment** *n* Verpflichtung *f*; POL Engagement *nt*

**committee** *n* Ausschuss *m*, Komitee *nt*

**common 1.** *adj* (*experience*) allgemein, alltäglich; (*shared*) gemeinsam; (*widespread, frequent*) häufig; *pej* gewöhnlich, ordinär; **have sth in ~** etw gemein haben **2.** *n* (*Brit, land*) Gemeindewiese *f*; **commonly** *adv* häufig, allgemein; **commonplace** *adj* alltäglich; *pej* banal; **commonroom** *n* Gemeinschaftsraum *m*; **Commons** *n* (*Brit*) POL **the (House of)** ~ das Unterhaus; **common sense** *n* gesunder Menschenverstand

**communal** *adj* gemeinsam; (*of a community*) Gemeinschafts-, Gemeinde-

**communicate** *vi* kommunizieren (*with* mit); **communication** *n* Kommunikation *f*, Verständigung *f*; **communicative** *adj* gesprächig

**communion** *n* (*Holy*) **Communion** Heiliges Abendmahl; (*Catholic*) Kommunion *f*

**communism** n Kommunismus m; **communist 1.** adj kommunistisch **2.** n Kommunist(in) m(f)

**community** n Gemeinschaft f; **community centre** n Gemeindezentrum nt; **community service** n LAW Sozialdienst m

**commutation ticket** n (US) Zeitkarte f; **commute** vi pendeln; **commuter** n Pendler(in) m(f)

**compact 1.** adj kompakt **2.** n (for make-up) Puderdose f; (US, car) ≈ Mittelklassewagen m; **compact camera** n Kompaktkamera f; **compact disc** n Compact Disc f, CD f

**companion** n Begleiter(in) m(f)

**company** n Gesellschaft f; COMM Firma f; **keep sb ~** jdm Gesellschaft leisten; **company car** n Firmenauto nt

**comparable** adj vergleichbar (with, to mit); **comparatively** adv verhältnismäßig; **compare** vt vergleichen (with, to mit); **~d with or to** im Vergleich zu; **beyond ~** unvergleichlich; **comparison** n Vergleich m; **in ~ with** im Vergleich mit (or zu)

**compartment** n RAIL Abteil nt; (in desk etc) Fach nt

**compass** n Kompass m; **~es** pl Zirkel m

**compassion** n Mitgefühl nt

**compatible** adj vereinbar (with mit); IT kompatibel; **we're not ~** wir passen nicht zueinander

**compensate 1.** vt (person) entschädigen (for für) **2.** vi **~ for sth** Ersatz für etw leisten; (make up for) etw ausgleichen; **compensation** n Entschädigung f; (money) Schadenersatz m; LAW Abfindung f

**compete** vi konkurrieren (for um); SPORT kämpfen (for um); (take part) teilnehmen (in an + dat)

**competence** n Fähigkeit f; LAW Zuständigkeit f; **competent** adj fähig; LAW zuständig

**competition** n (contest) Wettbewerb m; COMM Konkurrenz f (for um); **competitive** adj (firm, price, product) konkurrenzfähig; **competitor** n COMM Konkurrent(in) m(f); SPORT Teilnehmer(in) m(f)

**complain** vi klagen; (formally) sich beschweren (about über + acc); **complaint** n Klage f, Beanstandung f; (formal) Beschwerde f; MED Leiden nt

**complement** vt ergänzen

**complete 1.** adj vollständig; (finished) fertig; (failure, disaster) total; (happiness) vollkommen; **are we ~?** sind

wir vollzählig? **2.** vt vervoll-
ständigen; (form) ausfüllen;
**completely** adv völlig; **not ~
... nicht ganz ...**
**complex 1.** adj (task, theory
etc) kompliziert **2.** n Kom-
plex m
**complexion** n Gesichtsfarbe
f, Teint m
**complicated** adj kompliziert;
**complication** n Komplikati-
on f
**compliment** n Kompliment
nt; **complimentary** adj lo-
bend; (free of charge) Gra-
tis~; **~ ticket** Freikarte f
**component** n Bestandteil m
**compose** vt (music) kompo-
nieren; **~ oneself** sich zusammennehmen; **com-
posed** adj gefasst; **be ~ of**
bestehen aus; **composition**
n (of a group) Zusammen-
setzung f; MUS Komposition f
**comprehend** vt verstehen;
**comprehension** n Ver-
ständnis nt
**comprehensive** adj umfas-
send; **~ school** Gesamtschule f
**comprise** vt umfassen, bestehen aus
**compromise 1.** n Kompromiss m **2.** vi einen Kompromiss schließen
**compulsory** adj obligatorisch
**computer** n Computer m;
**computer-aided** adj compu-
tergestützt; **computer-con-**

**trolled** adj rechnergesteu-
ert; **computer game** n Computerspiel nt; **computer-lit-
erate** adj **be ~** mit dem Computer umgehen können;
**computer scientist** n Infor-
matiker(in) m(f); **comput-
ing** n (subject) Informatik f
**con** fam **1.** n Schwindel m **2.** vt
betrügen (out of um)
**conceal** vt verbergen (from
vor + dat)
**conceive** vt (imagine) sich
vorstellen; (child) empfangen
**concentrate** vi sich konzentrieren (on auf + acc); **concentration** n Konzentration
f
**concept** n Begriff m
**concern 1.** n (affair) Angelegenheit f; (worry) Sorge f;
**it's not my ~** das geht mich
nichts an; **there's no cause
for ~** kein Grund zur Beun-
ruhigung **2.** vt (affect) angehen; (have connection with)
betreffen; (be about) handeln von; **those ~ed** die Be-
troffenen; **as far as I'm ~ed**
was mich betrifft; **con-
cerned** adj (anxious) besorgt; **concerning** prep bezüglich, hinsichtlich + gen
**concert** n Konzert nt; **~ hall**
Konzertsaal m
**concession** n Zugeständnis
nt; (reduction) Ermäßigung f
**conclude** vt (end) beenden,
(ab)schließen; (infer) folgern

*(from* aus); **~ that** ... zu dem Schluss kommen, dass ...; **conclusion** *n* Schluss *m*, Schlussfolgerung *f*

**concrete 1.** *n* Beton *m* **2.** *adj* konkret

**concussion** *n* Gehirnerschütterung *f*

**condition** *n* (*state*) Zustand *m*; (*requirement*) Bedingung *f*; **on ~ that** ... unter der Bedingung, dass ...; **~s** *pl* (*circumstances, weather*) Verhältnisse *pl*

**conditioner** *n* Weichspüler *m*; (*for hair*) Pflegespülung *f*

**condo** *n* → **condominium**

**condolences** *npl* Beileid *nt*

**condom** *n* Kondom *nt*

**condominium** *n* (*US, apartment*) Eigentumswohnung *f*

**conduct 1.** *n* (*behaviour*) Verhalten *nt* **2.** *vt* führen, leiten; (*orchestra*) dirigieren

**conductor** *n* MUS Dirigent(in) *m(f)*; (*Brit*) Schaffner(in) *m(f)*; (*US*) Zugführer(in) *m(f)*

**cone** *n* Kegel *m*; (*for ice cream*) Waffeltüte *f*; (*fir cone*) (Tannen)zapfen *m*

**conference** *n* Konferenz *f*

**confess** *vt, vi* **~ that** ... gestehen, dass ...; **confession** *n* Geständnis *nt*; REL Beichte *f*

**confidence** *n* Vertrauen *nt* (*in* zu); (*assurance*) Selbstvertrauen *nt*; **confident** *adj* (*sure*) zuversichtlich (*that* ... dass ...), überzeugt (*of*

von); (*self-assured*) selbstsicher; **confidential** *adj* vertraulich

**confine** *vt* beschränken (*to* auf + *acc*)

**confirm** *vt* bestätigen; **confirmation** *n* Bestätigung *f*; REL Konfirmation *f*; **confirmed** *adj* überzeugt; (*bachelor*) eingefleischt

**confuse** *vt* verwirren; (*sth with sth*) verwechseln (*with* mit); (*several things*) durcheinanderbringen; **confused** *adj* (*person*) konfus, verwirrt; (*account*) verworren; **confusing** *adj* verwirrend; **confusion** *n* Verwirrung *f*; (*of two things*) Verwechslung *f*; (*muddle*) Chaos *nt*

**congestion** *n* Stau *m*

**congratulate** *vt* gratulieren (*on* zu); **congratulations** *npl* Glückwünsche *pl*; **~!** gratuliere!, herzlichen Glückwunsch!

**congregation** *n* REL Gemeinde *f*

**congress** *n* Kongress *m*; (*US*) **Congress** der Kongress; **congressman**, **congresswoman** *n* (*US*) Mitglied *nt* des Repräsentantenhauses

**conjunction** *n* LING Konjunktion *f*; **in ~ with** in Verbindung mit

**connect 1.** *vt* verbinden (*with, to* mit); ELEC, TECH (*appliance etc*) anschließen (*to* an + *acc*) **2.** *vi* (*train, plane*) Anschluss haben (*with* an + *acc*); **~ing flight** Anschlussflug *m*; **~ing train** Anschlusszug *m*; **connection** *n* Verbindung *f*; (*link*) Zusammenhang *m*; (*for train, plane, electrical appliance*) Anschluss *m* (*with, to* an + *acc*); (*business etc*) Beziehung *f*; **in ~ with** in Zusammenhang mit; **bad ~** TEL schlechte Verbindung; ELEC Wackelkontakt *m*; **connector** *n* IT (*computer*) Stecker *m*

**conscience** *n* Gewissen *nt*; **conscientious** *adj* gewissenhaft

**conscious** *adj* (*act*) bewusst; MED bei Bewusstsein

**consecutive** *adj* aufeinanderfolgend

**consent** 1. *n* Zustimmung *f* 2. *vi* zustimmen (*to dat*)

**consequence** *n* Folge *f*, Konsequenz *f*; **consequently** *adv* folglich, deshalb

**conservation** *n* Erhaltung *f*; (*nature conservation*) Naturschutz *m*; **conservation area** *n* Naturschutzgebiet *nt*

**conservative**, (POL) **Conservative** *adj* konservativ

**conservatory** *n* (*greenhouse*) Gewächshaus *nt*; (*room*) Wintergarten *m*

**consider** *vt* (*reflect on*) nachdenken über, sich überlegen; (*take into account*) in Betracht ziehen; (*regard*) hal-

ten für; **he is ~ed** (**to be**) ... er gilt als ...; **considerable** *adj* beträchtlich; **considerate** *adj* aufmerksam, rücksichtsvoll; **consideration** *n* (*thoughtfulness*) Rücksicht *f*; (*thought*) Überlegung *f*; **take sth into ~** etw in Betracht ziehen; **considering** 1. *prep* in Anbetracht + *gen* 2. *conj* da

**consist** *vi* **~ of** ... bestehen aus

**consistent** *adj* (*behaviour, process etc*) konsequent; (*statements*) übereinstimmend; (*argument*) folgerichtig; (*performance, results*) beständig

**consolation** *n* Trost *m*; **console** *vt* trösten

**consonant** *n* Konsonant *m*

**conspicuous** *adj* auffällig, auffallend

**conspiracy** *n* Komplott *nt*

**constable** *n* (*Brit*) Polizist(in) *m(f)*

**Constance** *n* Konstanz *nt*; **Lake ~** der Bodensee

**constant** *adj* (*continual*) ständig, dauernd; (*unchanging: temperature etc*) gleichbleibend; **constantly** *adv* dauernd

**consternation** *n* (*dismay*) Bestürzung *f*

**constituency** *n* Wahlkreis *m*

**constitution** *n* Verfassung *f*; (*of person*) Konstitution *f*

**construct** *vt* bauen; **con-**

**struction** n (process, result)
Bau m; (method) Bauweise
f; **under~** im Bau befindlich;
**construction site** n Baustelle f

**consulate** n Konsulat nt

**consult** vt um Rat fragen;
(doctor) konsultieren;
(book) nachschlagen in
+ dat; **consultant** n MED
Facharzt m, Fachärztin f;
**consultation** n Beratung f;
MED Konsultation f; **~ room**
Besprechungsraum m,
Sprechzimmer nt

**consume** vt verbrauchen;
(food) konsumieren; **consumer** n Verbraucher(in)
m(f)

**contact 1.** n (touch) Berührung f; (communication)
Kontakt m; (person) Kontaktperson f; **be / keep in ~
(with sb)** (mit jdm) in Kontakt sein / bleiben **2.** vt sich
in Verbindung setzen mit;
**contact lenses** npl Kontaktlinsen pl

**contagious** adj ansteckend

**contain** vt enthalten; **container** n Behälter m; (for
transport) Container m

**contaminate** vt verunreinigen; (chemically) verseuchen; **~d by radiation** strahlenverseucht, verstrahlt;
**contamination** n Verunreinigung f; (by radiation) Verseuchung f

**contemporary** adj zeitgenös-

sisch

**contempt** n Verachtung f;
**contemptuous** adj verächtlich

**content** adj zufrieden

**content(s)** n(pl) Inhalt m

**contest 1.** n (Wett)kampf m
(for um); (competition)
Wettbewerb m **2.** vt kämpfen
um + acc; (dispute) bestreiten; **contestant** n Teilnehmer(in) m(f)

**context** n Zusammenhang m;
**out of ~** aus dem Zusammenhang gerissen

**continent** n Kontinent m,
Festland nt; **the Continent**
(Brit) das europäische Festland, der Kontinent; **continental** adj kontinental; **~
breakfast** kleines Frühstück
mit Brötchen und Marmelade, Kaffee oder Tee

**continual** adj (endless) ununterbrochen; (constant) dauernd, ständig; **continually**
adv dauernd; (again and
again) immer wieder; **continuation** n Fortsetzung f;
**continue 1.** vi weitermachen
(with mit); (esp talking) fortfahren (with mit); (travelling) weiterfahren; (state,
conditions) fortdauern, anhalten **2.** vt fortsetzen; **to
be ~d** Fortsetzung folgt;
**continuous** adj (endless) ununterbrochen; (constant)
ständig

**contraceptive** n Verhütungsmittel *nt*

**contract** *n* Vertrag *m*

**contradict** *vt* widersprechen + *dat*; **contradiction** *n* Widerspruch *m*

**contrary 1.** *n* Gegenteil *nt*; **on the** ~ im Gegenteil **2.** *adj* ~ **to** entgegen + *dat*

**contrast 1.** *n* Kontrast *m*, Gegensatz *m*; **in** ~ **to** im Gegensatz zu **2.** *vt* entgegensetzen

**contribute** *vt*, *vi* beitragen (*to* zu); (*money*) spenden (*to* für); **contribution** *n* Beitrag *m*

**control 1.** *vt* (*master*) beherrschen; (*temper etc*) im Griff haben; (*esp*) TECH steuern; ~ **oneself** sich beherrschen **2.** *n* Kontrolle *f*; (*mastery*) Beherrschung *f*; (*esp*) TECH Steuerung *f*; ~**s** *pl* (*knobs, switches etc*) Bedienungselemente *pl*; (*collectively*) Steuerung *f*; **be out of** ~ außer Kontrolle sein; **control knob** *n* Bedienungsknopf *m*; **control panel** *n* Schalttafel *f*

**controversial** *adj* umstritten

**convalesce** *vi* gesund werden; **convalescence** *n* Genesung *f*

**convenience** *n* (*quality, thing*) Annehmlichkeit *f*; **at your** ~ wann es Ihnen passt; **with all modern** ~**s** mit allem Komfort; **convenience food** *n* Fertiggericht *nt*; **convenient** *adj* günstig, passend

**convent** *n* Kloster *nt*

**convention** *n* (*custom*) Konvention *f*; (*meeting*) Konferenz *f*; **conventional** *adj* herkömmlich, konventionell

**conversation** *n* Gespräch *nt*, Unterhaltung *f*

**conversion** *n* Umwandlung *f* (*into* in + *acc*); (*of building*) Umbau *m* (*into* zu); (*calculation*) Umrechnung *f*; **conversion table** *n* Umrechnungstabelle *f*; **convert** *vt* umwandeln; (*person*) bekehren; IT konvertieren; ~ **into Euros** in Euro umrechnen; **convertible** *n* AUTO Kabrio *nt*

**convey** *vt* (*carry*) befördern; (*feelings*) vermitteln; **conveyor belt** *n* Förderband *nt*, Fließband *nt*

**convict 1.** *vt* verurteilen (*of* wegen) **2.** *n* Strafgefangene(r) *mf*; **conviction** *n* LAW Verurteilung *f*; (*strong belief*) Überzeugung *f*

**convince** *vt* überzeugen (*of* von); **convincing** *adj* überzeugend

**cook 1.** *vt*, *vi* kochen **2.** *n* Koch *m*, Köchin *f*; **cookbook** *n* Kochbuch *nt*; **cooker** *n* Herd *m*; **cookie** *n* (*US*) Keks *m*; **cooking** *n* Kochen *nt*; (*style of cooking*) Küche *f*

**cool 1.** *adj* kühl, gelassen; *fam* (*brilliant*) cool, stark **2.** *vt*, *vi* (ab)kühlen; ~ **it** reg dich ab! **3.** *n* **keep / lose one's** ~ *fam* ruhig bleiben / durchdrehen; **cool down** vi abkühlen; (*calm down*) sich beruhigen

**cooperate** vi zusammenarbeiten, kooperieren; **cooperation** n Zusammenarbeit f, Kooperation f; **cooperative 1.** adj hilfsbereit **2.** n Genossenschaft f

**cop** n fam (*policeman*) Bulle m

**cope** vi zurechtkommen, fertig werden (*with* mit)

**Copenhagen** n Kopenhagen nt

**copier** n Kopierer m

**copper** n Kupfer nt; (*Brit fam*) (*policeman*) Bulle m; fam (*coin*) Kupfermünze f; ~s Kleingeld nt

**copy 1.** n Kopie f; (*of book*) Exemplar nt **2.** vt kopieren; (*imitate*) nachahmen; **copyright** n Urheberrecht nt

**coral** n Koralle f

**cord** n Schnur f; (*material*) Kordsamt m; **cordless** adj (*phone*) schnurlos

**core** n Kern m; (*of apple, pear*) Kerngehäuse nt; **core business** n Kerngeschäft nt

**cork** n (*material*) Kork m; (*stopper*) Korken m; **corkscrew** n Korkenzieher m

**corn** n Getreide nt, Korn nt; (*US, maize*) Mais m; (*on foot*) Hühnerauge nt; ~ **on the cob** (gekochter) Maiskolben; **corned beef** n Cornedbeef nt

**corner 1.** n Ecke f; (*on road*)

Kurve f; sport Eckstoß m **2.** vt in die Enge treiben; **corner shop** n Laden m an der Ecke

**cornflakes** npl Cornflakes pl

**Cornish** adj kornisch; ~ **pasty** mit Fleisch und Kartoffeln gefüllte Pastete; **Cornwall** n Cornwall nt

**corporation** n (*US*) comm Aktiengesellschaft f

**corpse** n Leiche f

**correct 1.** adj (*accurate*) richtig; (*proper*) korrekt **2.** vt korrigieren, verbessern; **correction** n (*esp written*) Korrektur f

**correspond** vi entsprechen (*to dat*); (*two things*) übereinstimmen; **corresponding** adj entsprechend

**corridor** n (*in building*) Flur m; (*in train*) Gang m

**corrupt** adj korrupt

**cosmetic** adj kosmetisch; **cosmetics** npl Kosmetika pl; **cosmetic surgery** n Schönheitschirurgie f

**cosmopolitan** adj international; (*attitude*) weltoffen

**cost 1.** vt kosten **2.** n Kosten pl; **at all** ~**s, at any** ~ um jeden Preis; ~ **of living** Lebenshaltungskosten pl; **costly** adj kostspielig

**costume** n THEAT Kostüm nt

**cosy** adj gemütlich

**cot** n (*Brit*) Kinderbett nt; (*US*) Campingliege f

**cottage** n kleines Haus;

*(country cottage)* Landhäuschen *nt*; **cottage cheese** *n* Hüttenkäse *m*; **cottage pie** *n* Hackfleisch mit Kartoffelbrei überbacken

**cotton** *n* Baumwolle *f*; **cotton candy** *n* *(US)* Zuckerwatte *f*; **cotton wool** *n* *(Brit)* Watte *f*

**couch** *n* Couch *f*; *(sofa)* Sofa *nt*; **couchette** *n* Liegewagen (-platz) *m*

**cough 1.** *vi* husten **2.** *n* Husten *m*; **cough mixture** *n* Hustensaft *m*; **cough sweet** *n* Hustenbonbon *nt*

**could** *pt* → **can**; konnte *conditional* könnte; **~ you come earlier?** könntest du / könnten Sie früher kommen?; **couldn't** *contr* = **could not**

**council** *n* POL Rat *m*; *(local council)* Gemeinderat *m*; *(town council)* Stadtrat *m*; **council estate** *n* Siedlung *f* des sozialen Wohnungsbaus; **council house** *n* Sozialwohnung *f*; **council tax** *n* Gemeindesteuer *f*

**count 1.** *vt, vi* zählen; *(include)* mitrechnen **2.** *n* Zählung *f*; *(noble)* Graf *m*; **count on** *vt (rely on)* sich verlassen auf + *acc*; *(expect)* rechnen mit

**counter** *n (in shop)* Ladentisch *m*; *(in café)* Theke *f*; *(in bank, post office)* Schalter *m*; **counter attack 1.** *n* Gegenangriff *m* **2.** *vi* zurück-

schlagen; **counter-clockwise** *adv* *(US)* entgegen dem Uhrzeigersinn

**counterpart** *n* Gegenstück *nt* *(of zu)*

**countess** *n* Gräfin *f*

**countless** *adj* zahllos, unzählig

**country** *n* Land *nt*; **in the ~** auf dem Land(e); **in this ~** hierzulande; **country cousin** *n fam* Landei *nt*; **country dancing** *n* Volkstanz *m*; **countryman** *n (compatriot)* Landsmann *m*; **country music** *n* Countrymusic *f*; **country road** *n* Landstraße *f*; **countryside** *n* Landschaft *f*; *(rural area)* Land *nt*

**county** *n (Brit)* Grafschaft *f*; *(US)* Verwaltungsbezirk *m*; **county town** *n (Brit)* ≈ Kreisstadt *f*

**couple** *n* Paar *nt*; **a ~ of** ein paar

**coupon** *n (voucher)* Gutschein *m*

**courage** *n* Mut *m*

**courgette** *n (Brit)* Zucchini *f*

**courier** *n (for tourists)* Reiseleiter(in) *m(f)*; *(messenger)* Kurier *m*

**course** *n (of study)* Kurs *m*; *(for race)* Strecke *f*; NAUT, AVIAT Kurs *m*; *(at university)* Studiengang *m*; *(in meal)* Gang *m*; **of** ~ natürlich; **in the ~ of** während

**court** *n* SPORT Platz *m*; LAW Gericht *nt*

**courtesy** n Höflichkeit f; ~ **bus / coach** (gebührenfreier) Zubringerbus

**courthouse** n (US) Gerichtsgebäude nt; **court order** n Gerichtsbeschluss m; **courtroom** n Gerichtssaal m; **courtyard** n Hof m

**cousin** n (male) Cousin m; (female) Cousine f

**cover** 1. vt bedecken (in, with mit); (distance) zurücklegen; (loan, costs) decken 2. n (for bed etc) Decke f; (of cushion) Bezug m; (lid) Deckel m; (of book) Umschlag m; (insurance) ~ Versicherungsschutz m; **cover up** vt zudecken; (error etc) vertuschen; **coverage** n Berichterstattung f (of über + acc); **cover charge** n Kosten pl für ein Gedeck; **covering letter** n Begleitbrief m; **cover story** n (newspaper) Titelgeschichte f

**cow** n Kuh f

**coward** n Feigling m; **cowardly** adj feig(e)

**cowboy** n Cowboy m

**cozy** adj (US) gemütlich

**CPU** abbr = **central processing unit** Zentraleinheit f

**crab** n Krabbe f

**crabby** adj mürrisch, reizbar

**crack** 1. n Riss m; (in pottery, glass) Sprung m; (drug) Crack nt; **have a ~ at sth** etw ausprobieren 2. vi (pottery, glass) einen Sprung be-

kommen; (wood, ice etc) einen Riss bekommen; **get ~ing** fam loslegen 3. vt (bone) anbrechen; (nut, code) knacken

**cracker** n (biscuit) Kräcker m; (Christmas cracker) Knallbonbon nt; **crackers** adj fam verrückt, bekloppt

**crackle** vi knistern; (telephone, radio) knacken; **crackling** n GASTR Kruste f (des Schweinebratens)

**cradle** n Wiege f

**craft** n Handwerk nt; (art) Kunsthandwerk nt; **craftsman** n Handwerker m

**cram** 1. vt stopfen (into in + acc); **be ~med with ...** mit ... vollgestopft sein 2. vi (revise for exam) pauken (for für)

**cramp** n Krampf m

**cranberry** n Preiselbeere f

**crane** n (machine) Kran m; (bird) Kranich m

**crap** 1. n vulg Scheiße f; (rubbish) Mist m 2. adj beschissen, Scheiß-

**crash** 1. n einen Unfall haben; (two vehicles) zusammenstoßen; (plane, computer) abstürzen; (economy) zusammenbrechen; ~ **into sth** gegen etw knallen 2. vt einen Unfall haben mit 3. n (car) Unfall m; (train) Unglück nt; (collision) Zusammenstoß m; AVIAT, IT Absturz m; (noise) Krachen nt; **crash**

barrier n Leitplanke f; **crash course** n Intensivkurs m; **crash helmet** n Sturzhelm m

crate n Kiste f; (of beer) Kasten m

crater n Krater m

craving n starkes Verlangen, Bedürfnis nt

crawl 1. vi kriechen; (baby) krabbeln 2. n (swimming) Kraul nt; **crawler lane** n Kriechspur f

crayfish n Languste f

crayon n Buntstift m

crazy adj verrückt (about nach)

cream 1. n (from milk) Sahne f, Rahm m; (polish, cosmetic) Creme f 2. adj cremefarben; **cream cake** n (small) Sahnetörtchen nt; (big) Sahnetorte f; **cream cheese** n Frischkäse m; **creamer** n Kaffeeweißer m; **creamy** adj sahnig

crease 1. n Falte f 2. vt falten; (untidy) zerknittern

create vt schaffen; (cause) verursachen; **creative** adj (person) kreativ; **creature** n Geschöpf nt

crèche n Kinderkrippe f

credibility n Glaubwürdigkeit f; **credible** adj (person) glaubwürdig

credit n FIN (amount allowed) Kredit m; (amount possessed) Guthaben nt; (recognition) Anerkennung f; **~s** (of film) Abspann m; **credit card** n Kreditkarte f

creep vi kriechen; **creeps** n **he gives me the ~** er ist mir nicht ganz geheuer; **creepy** adj (frightening) gruselig, unheimlich

crept pt, pp → **creep**

cress n Kresse f

crest n Kamm m; (coat of arms) Wappen nt

crew n Besatzung f, Mannschaft f

crib n (US) Kinderbett nt

cricket n (insect) Grille f; (game) Cricket nt

crime n Verbrechen nt; **criminal 1.** n Verbrecher(in) m(f) **2.** adj kriminell, strafbar

crisis n Krise f

crisp adj knusprig; **crispbread** n Knäckebrot nt; **crisps** npl (Brit) Chips pl

criterion n Kriterium nt; **critic** n Kritiker(in) m(f); **critical** adj kritisch; **critically** adv kritisch; **~ ill / injured** schwer krank / verletzt; **criticism** n Kritik f; **criticize** vt kritisieren

Croat n Kroate m, Kroatin f; **Croatia** n Kroatien nt; **Croatian** adj kroatisch

crockery n Geschirr nt

crocodile n Krokodil nt

crocus n Krokus m

crop (harvest) Ernte f; **crops** npl Getreide nt

croquette n Krokette f

cross 1. n Kreuz nt; **mark sth with a ~** etw ankreuzen 2. vt

(road, river etc) überqueren;
(legs) übereinanderschlagen; **it ~ed my mind** es fiel mir ein; **~ one's fingers** die Daumen drücken **3.** adj ärgerlich, böse; **cross out** vt durchstreichen

**crossbar** n (of bicycle) Stange f; SPORT Querlatte f; **cross-country** adj **~ running** Geländelauf m; **~ skiing** Langlauf m; **cross-eyed** adj **be ~** schielen; **crossing** n (in crossroads) (Straßen)kreuzung f; (for pedestrians) Fußgängerüberweg m; (on ship) Überfahrt f; **crossroads** nsing or pl Straßenkreuzung f; **cross section** n Querschnitt m; **crosswalk** n (US) Fußgängerüberweg m; **crossword (puzzle)** n Kreuzworträtsel nt

**crouch** vi hocken
**crouton** n Croûton m
**crow** n Krähe f
**crowd 1.** n Menge f **2.** vi sich drängen (into in +acc; round um); **crowded** adj überfüllt
**crown 1.** n Krone f **2.** vt krönen
**crucial** adj entscheidend
**crude 1.** adj primitiv; (humour, behaviour) derb, ordinär **2.** n **~ (oil)** Rohöl nt
**cruel** adj grausam (to zu, gegen); (unfeeling) gefühllos; **cruelty** n Grausamkeit f; **~ to animals** Tierquälerei f
**cruise 1.** n Kreuzfahrt f **2.** vi

(ship) kreuzen; (car) mit Reisegeschwindigkeit fahren; **cruise liner** n Kreuzfahrtschiff nt; **cruise missile** n Marschflugkörper m
**crumb** n Krume f
**crumble 1.** vt, vi zerbröckeln **2.** n mit Streuseln überbackenes Kompott
**crumpet** n weiches Hefegebäck zum Toasten (attractive woman) fam Schnecke f
**crumple** vt zerknittern
**crunchy** adj (Brit) knusprig
**crusade** n Kreuzzug m
**crush 1.** vt zerdrücken; (finger etc) quetschen; (spices, stone) zerstoßen **2.** n **have a ~ on sb** in jdn verknallt sein; **crushing** adj (defeat, remark) vernichtend
**crust** n Kruste f; **crusty** adj knusprig
**crutch** n Krücke f
**cry 1.** vi (call) rufen; (scream) schreien; (weep) weinen **2.** n (call) Ruf m; (louder) Schrei m
**crypt** n Krypta f
**cu** abbr = **see you** (SMS, E-Mail) ≈ bis bald
**Cuba** n Kuba nt
**cube** n Würfel m
**cubic** adj Kubik
**cubicle** n Kabine f
**cuckoo** n Kuckuck m
**cucumber** n Salatgurke f
**cuddle 1.** vt in den Arm nehmen; (amorously) schmusen mit **2.** n Liebkosung f, Umar-

mung f; **have a ~** schmusen; **cuddly** adj verschmust; **cuddly toy** n Plüschtier nt

**cuff** n Manschette f; (US, trouser cuff) Aufschlag m; **cufflink** n Manschettenknopf m

**cuisine** n Kochkunst f, Küche f

**cul-de-sac** n (Brit) Sackgasse f;

**culprit** n Schuldige(r) mf, Übeltäter(in) m(f)

**cult** n Kult m

**cultivate** vt AGR (land) bebauen; (crop) anbauen; **cultivated** adj (person) kultiviert, gebildet

**cultural** adj kulturell, Kultur-; **culture** n Kultur f; **cultured** adj gebildet, kultiviert; **culture vulture** fam (Brit) n Kulturfanatiker(in) m(f)

**cumbersome** adj (object) unhandlich

**cumin** n Kreuzkümmel m

**cunning** adj schlau; (person a.) gerissen

**cup** n Tasse f; (prize) Pokal m; **it's not his ~ of tea** das ist nicht sein Fall; **cupboard** n Schrank m; **cup final** n Pokalendspiel nt

**curable** adj heilbar

**curb** n (US) → **kerb**

**curd** n ~ **cheese**, **~s** ≈ Quark m

**cure 1.** n Heilmittel nt (for gegen); (process) Heilung f **2.** vt heilen; GASTR (salt) pö-

keln; (smoke) räuchern

**curious** adj neugierig; (strange) seltsam

**curl 1.** n Locke f **2.** vi sich kräuseln; **curly** adj lockig

**currant** n (dried) Korinthe f; (red, black) Johannisbeere f

**currency** n Währung f; **foreign ~** Devisen pl

**current 1.** n (in water) Strömung f; (electric current) Strom m **2.** adj (issue, affairs) aktuell, gegenwärtig; (expression) gängig; **current account** n Girokonto nt; **currently** adv zur Zeit

**curriculum** n Lehrplan m; **curriculum vitae** n (Brit) Lebenslauf m

**curry** n Currygericht nt; **curry powder** n Curry(pulver) nt

**curse 1.** vi (swear) fluchen (at auf + acc) **2.** n Fluch m

**cursor** n IT Cursor m

**curtain** n Vorhang m; **it was ~s for Benny** für Benny war alles vorbei

**curve** n Kurve f; **curved** adj gebogen

**cushion** n Kissen nt

**custard** n dicke Vanillesoße, die warm oder kalt zu vielen englischen Nachspeisen gegessen wird

**custom** n Brauch m; (habit) Gewohnheit f; **customary** adj üblich; **custom-built** adj nach Kundenangaben gefertigt; **customer** n Kunde m, Kundin f; **customer**

**loyalty card** n Kundenkarte f; **customer service** n Kundendienst m

**customs** npl (organization, location) Zoll m; **pass through** ~ durch den Zoll gehen; **customs officer** n Zollbeamte(r) m, Zollbeamtin f

**cut 1.** vt schneiden; (cake) anschneiden; (wages, benefits) kürzen; (prices) heruntersetzen; **I ~ my finger** ich habe mir in den Finger geschnitten **2.** n Schnitt m; (wound) Schnittwunde f; (reduction) Kürzung f (in gen); **price / tax ~** Preissenkung / Steuersenkung f; **cut back** vt (workforce etc) reduzieren; **cut down** vt (tree) fällen; **~ on sth** etwas einschränken; **cut in** vi AUTO scharf einscheren; **cut off** vt abschneiden; (gas, electricity) abdrehen, abstellen; TEL **I was ~** ich wurde unterbrochen

**cute** adj putzig, niedlich; (US, shrewd) clever

**cutlery** n Besteck nt

**cutlet** n (pork) Kotelett nt; (veal) Schnitzel nt

**cut-price** adj verbilligt

**cutting 1.** n (from paper) Ausschnitt m; (of plant) Ableger m **2.** adj (comment) verletzend

**CV** abbr → **curriculum vitae**

**cwt** abbr → **hundredweight** ≈ Zentner, Ztr.

**cybercafé** n Internetcafé nt; **cyberspace** n Cyberspace m

**cycle 1.** n Fahrrad nt **2.** vi Rad fahren; **cycle lane, cycle path** n Radweg m; **cycling** n Radfahren nt; **cyclist** n Radfahrer(in) m(f)

**cylinder** n Zylinder m

**cynical** adj zynisch

**cypress** n Zypresse f

**Cypriot 1.** adj zypriotisch **2.** n Zypriote m, Zypriotin f; **Cyprus** n Zypern nt

**czar** n Zar m; **czarina** n Zarin f

**Czech 1.** adj tschechisch **2.** n (person) Tscheche m, Tschechin f; (language) Tschechisch nt; **Czech Republic** n Tschechische Republik, Tschechien nt

# D

**dab** vt (wound, nose etc) betupfen (with mit)

**dad(dy)** n Papa m, Vati m; **daddy-longlegs** nsing (Brit) Schnake f; (US) Weberknecht m

**daffodil** n Osterglocke f

**daft** adj fam blöd, doof

**daily 1.** adj, adv täglich **2.** n (paper) Tageszeitung f

**dairy** n (on farm) Molkerei f;
   **dairy products** npl Milch-
   produkte pl
**daisy** n Gänseblümchen nt
**dam 1.** n Staudamm **m 2.** vt
   stauen
**damage 1.** n Schaden m; **~s** pl
   LAW Schadenersatz **m 2.** vt
   beschädigen; (reputation,
   health) schädigen, schaden
   + dat
**damn 1.** adj fam verdammt **2.**
   vt (condemn) verurteilen; **~**
   (it)! verflucht! **3.** n **he**
   **doesn't give a ~** es ist ihm
   völlig egal
**damp 1.** adj feucht **2.** n Feuchtigkeit f; **dampen** vt befeuchten
**dance 1.** n Tanz m; (event)
   Tanzveranstaltung f **2.** vi tanzen; **dance floor** n Tanzfläche f; **dancer** n Tänzer(in)
   m(f); **dancing** n Tanzen nt
**dandelion** n Löwenzahn m
**dandruff** n Schuppen pl
**Dane** n Däne m, Dänin f
**danger** n Gefahr f; **be in ~** in
   Gefahr sein; **dangerous** adj
   gefährlich
**Danish 1.** adj dänisch **2.** n
   (language) Dänisch nt; **the**
   **~** pl die Dänen; **Danish pas-**
   **try** n Plundergebäck nt
**Danube** n Donau f
**dare** vi **~** (**to**) **do sth** es wagen,
   etw zu tun; **I didn't ~ ask** ich
   traute mich nicht, zu fragen;
   **how ~ you** was fällt dir ein!;
**daring** adj (person) mutig;

(film, clothes etc) gewagt
**dark 1.** adj dunkel; (gloomy)
   düster, trübe; (sinister) finster; **~ chocolate** Bitterscho-
   kolade f; **~ green / blue**
   dunkelgrün / dunkelblau **2.**
   n Dunkelheit f; **dark glass-**
   **es** npl Sonnenbrille f; **dark-**
   **ness** n Dunkelheit nt
**darling** n Schatz m; (also favourite) Liebling m
**darts** nsing (game) Darts nt
**dash 1.** vi stürzen, rennen **2.** vt
   **~ hopes** Hoffnungen zerstören **3.** n (in text) Gedankenstrich m; (of liquid) Schuss
   m; **dashboard** n Armaturenbrett nt
**data** npl Daten pl; **data bank**,
   **data base** n Datenbank f;
   **data capture** n Datenerfas-
   sung f; **data processing** n
   Datenverarbeitung f; **data**
   **protection** n Datenschutz m
**date 1.** n Datum nt; (for meeting, delivery etc) Termin m;
   (with person) Verabredung
   f; (with girlfriend / boyfriend etc) Date nt; (fruit)
   Dattel f; **what's the ~ (to-**
   **day)?** der Wievielte ist heute?; **out of ~** adj veraltet; **up**
   **to ~** adj (news) aktuell; (fashion) zeitgemäß **2.** vt (letter
   etc) datieren; (person) gehen
   mit; **dated** adj altmodisch;
   **date of birth** n Geburtsda-
   tum nt; **dating agency** n
   Partnervermittlung f
**daughter** n Tochter f; **daugh-**

**dawn**

ter-in-law *n* Schwiegertochter *f*

**dawn 1.** *n* Morgendämmerung *f* **2.** *vi* dämmern; *it ~ed on me* mir ging ein Licht auf

**day** *n* Tag *m*; *one ~* eines Tages; *by~* bei Tage; *~ after~,~ by.~* Tag für Tag; *the ~ after / before* am Tag danach / zuvor; *the ~ before yesterday* vorgestern; *the ~ after tomorrow* übermorgen; *the ~s* heutzutage; *in those ~s* damals; *let's call it a ~* Schluss für heute!; **day-care center** *n* (*US*), **day-care centre** *f* (*Brit*) Kita *f* (*Kindertagesstätte*); **daydream 1.** *n* Tagtraum *m* **2.** *vi* (mit offenen Augen) träumen; **daylight** *n* Tageslicht *nt*; **day nursery** *n* Kita *f* (*Kindergesstätte*); **day return** *n* (*Brit*) RAIL Tagesrückfahrkarte *f*; **daytrip** *n* Tagesausflug *m*

**dazzle** *vt* blenden

**dead 1.** *adj* tot; (*limb*) abgestorben **2.** *adv* genau; *fam* total, völlig; *~ tired* *adj* todmüde; *~ slow* (*sign*) Schritt fahren; **dead end** *n* Sackgasse *f*; **deadline** *n* Termin *m*; (*period*) Frist *f*; *~ for applications* Anmeldeschluss *m*; **deadly 1.** *adj* tödlich **2.** *adv ~ dull* todlangweilig

**deaf** *adj* taub; **deafen** *vt* taub machen; **deafening** *adj* ohrenbetäubend

**deal 1.** *vt, vi* (*cards*) geben, austeilen **2.** *n* (*business deal*) Geschäft *nt*; (*agreement*) Abmachung *f*; *it's a ~* abgemacht!; *a good / great ~* of ziemlich / sehr viel; **deal in** *vt* handeln mit; **deal with** *vt* (*matter*) sich beschäftigen mit; (*book, film*) behandeln; (*successfully: person, problem*) fertig werden mit; (*matter*) erledigen; **dealer** *n* COMM Händler(in) *m(f)*; (*drugs*) Dealer(in) *m(f)*

**dealt** *pt, pp* → **deal**

**dear 1.** *adj* lieb, teuer; *Dear Sir or Madam* Sehr geehrte Damen und Herren; *Dear David* Lieber David **2.** *n* Schatz *m*; (*as address*) mein Schatz, Liebling; **dearly** *adv* (*love*) (heiß und) innig; (*pay*) teuer

**death** *n* Tod *m*; (*of project, hopes*) Ende *nt*; (*in accident*) Todesfall *m*, Todesopfer *nt*; **death certificate** *n* Totenschein *m*; **death penalty** *n* Todesstrafe *f*; **death toll** *n* Zahl *f* der Todesopfer

**debatable** *adj* fraglich; (*question*) strittig; **debate 1.** *n* Debatte *f* **2.** *vt* debattieren

**debit 1.** *n* Soll *nt* **2.** *vt* (*account*) belasten; **debit card** *n* Geldkarte *f*

**debris** *n* Trümmer *pl*

**debt** *n* Schuld *f*; *be in ~* verschuldet sein

**decade** *n* Jahrzehnt *nt*

**decaff** *n fam* koffeinfreier Kaffee; **decaffeinated** *adj* koffeinfrei

**decanter** *n* Dekanter *m*, Karaffe *f*

**decay 1.** *n* Verfall *m*; (*rotting*) Verwesung *f*; (*of tooth*) Karies *f* **2.** *vi* verfallen; (*rot*) verwesen; (*wood*) vermodern; (*teeth*) faulen; (*leaves*) verrotten

**deceased** *n* **the** ~ der / die Verstorbene

**deceive** *vt* täuschen

**December** *n* Dezember *m*; → **September**

**decent** *adj* anständig

**decide 1.** *vt* (*question*) entscheiden; (*body of people*) beschließen; **I can't** ~ **what to do** ich kann mich nicht entscheiden, was ich tun soll **2.** *vi* sich entscheiden; ~ **on sth** (*in favour of sth*) sich für etw entscheiden; sich zu etw entschließen; **decided** *adj* entschieden; (*clear*) deutlich; **decidedly** *adv* entschieden

**decimal** *adj* Dezimal-; **decimal system** *n* Dezimalsystem *nt*

**decipher** *vt* entziffern

**decision** *n* Entscheidung *f* (*on* über + *acc*); (*of committee, jury etc*) Beschluss *m*; **make a** ~ eine Entscheidung treffen; **decisive** *adj* entscheidend; (*person*) entscheidungsfreudig

**deck** *n* NAUT Deck *nt*; (*of cards*) Blatt *nt*; **deckchair** *n* Liegestuhl *m*

**declaration** *n* Erklärung *f*; **declare** *vt* erklären; (*state*) behaupten (*that* dass); (*at customs*) **have you anything to** ~**?** haben Sie etwas zu verzollen?

**decline 1.** *n* Rückgang *m* **2.** *vt* (*invitation, offer*) ablehnen **3.** *vi* (*become less*) sinken, abnehmen; (*health*) sich verschlechtern

**decode** *vt* entschlüsseln

**decorate** *vt* (aus)schmücken; (*wallpaper*) tapezieren; (*paint*) anstreichen; **decoration** *n* Schmuck *m*; (*process*) Schmücken *nt*; (*wallpapering*) Tapezieren *nt*; (*painting*) Anstreichen *nt*; **Christmas** ~**s** Weihnachtsschmuck *m*; **decorator** *n* Maler(in) *m(f)*

**decrease 1.** *n* Abnahme *f* **2.** *vi* abnehmen

**dedicate** *vt* widmen (*to sb* jdm); **dedicated** *adj* (*person*) engagiert; **dedication** *n* (*in book*) Widmung *f*; (*commitment*) Hingabe *f*, Engagement *nt*

**deduce** *vt* folgern, schließen (*from* aus, *that* dass)

**deduct** *vt* abziehen (*from* von); **deduction** *n* (*of money*) Abzug *m*; (*conclusion*) (Schluss)folgerung *f*

**deed** *n* Tat *f*

**deep** *adj* tief; **deepen** *vt* ver-

tiefen; **deep-freeze** n Tiefkühltruhe f; (upright) Gefrierschrank m; **deep-fry** vt
frittieren

**deer** n Reh nt; (with stag)
Hirsch m

**defeat 1.** n Niederlage f; **admit ~** sich geschlagen geben
**2.** vt besiegen

**defect** n Defekt m, Fehler m;
**defective** adj fehlerhaft

**defence** n Verteidigung f; **defend** vt verteidigen; **defendant** n LAW Angeklagte(r) mf;
**defender** n SPORT Verteidi-
ger(in) m(f); **defensive** adj
defensiv

**deficiency** n Mangel m; **deficit** n Defizit m

**define** vt (word) definieren;
(duties, powers) bestimmen;
**definite** adj (clear) klar, eindeutig; (certain) sicher; **it's ~**
es steht fest; **definitely** adv
bestimmt; **definition** n Definition f; PHOT Schärfe f

**defrost** vt (fridge) abtauen;
(food) auftauen

**degree** n Grad m; (at university) akademischer Grad; **to
a certain ~** einigermaßen; **I
have a ~ in chemistry** ≈
ich habe einen Abschluss
in Chemie

**dehydrated** adj (food) getrocknet, Trocken-; (person)
ausgetrocknet

**de-ice** vt enteisen

**delay 1.** vt (postpone) verschieben, aufschieben; **be**

**~ed** (event) sich verzögern;
**the train / flight was ~ed**
der Zug / die Maschine hatte
Verspätung **2.** vi warten; (hesitate) zögern **3.** n Verzögerung f; (of train etc) Verspätung f; **without ~** unverzüglich; **delayed** adj (train etc)
verspätet

**delegation** n Abordnung f;
(foreign) Delegation f

**delete** vt (aus)streichen; IT löschen; **deletion** n Streichung
f; IT Löschung f

**deli** n fam Feinkostgeschäft nt

**deliberate** adj (intentional)
absichtlich; **deliberately**
adv mit Absicht, extra

**delicate** adj (fine) fein; (fragile) zart; a. MED empfindlich;
(situation) heikel

**delicatessen** nsing Feinkostgeschäft nt

**delicious** adj köstlich, lecker

**delight** n Freude f; **delighted**
adj sehr erfreut (with über
+ acc); **delightful** adj entzückend; (weather, meal etc)
herrlich

**deliver** vt (goods) liefern (to
sb jdm); (letter, parcel) zu-
stellen; (speech) halten; (baby) entbinden; **delivery** n
(of letter, parcel)
Zustellung f; (of baby) Entbindung f; **delivery van** n
Lieferwagen m

**delude** vt täuschen; **don't ~
yourself** mach dir nichts
vor; **delusion** n Irrglaube m

**de luxe** adj Luxus-

**demand 1.** vt verlangen (from von); (time, patience etc) erfordern **2.** n (request) Forderung f, Verlangen nt (for nach); COMM (for goods) Nachfrage f; **on ~** auf Wunsch; **very much in ~** sehr gefragt; **demanding** adj anspruchsvoll

**demerara** n ~ **(sugar)** brauner Zucker

**demister** n Defroster m

**demo** n fam Demo f

**democracy** n Demokratie f; **democrat, Democrat** (US) POL Demokrat(in) m(f); **democratic** adj demokratisch; **the Democratic Party** (US) POL die Demokratische Partei

**demolish** vt abreißen; fig zerstören

**demonstrate** vt, vi demonstrieren, beweisen; **demonstration** n Demonstration f

**denial** n Leugnung f; (official denial) Dementi nt

**denim** n Jeansstoff m; **denim jacket** n Jeansjacke f; **denims** npl Bluejeans pl

**Denmark** n Dänemark nt

**denomination** n REL Konfession f; COMM Nennwert m

**dense** adj dicht; fam (stupid) schwer von Begriff; **density** n Dichte f

**dent 1.** n Beule f, Delle f **2.** vt einbeulen

**dental** adj Zahn-; **~ care** Zahnpflege f; **~ floss** Zahnseide f; **dentist** n Zahnarzt m, Zahnärztin f; **dentures** npl Zahnprothese f; (full) Gebiss nt

**deny** vt leugnen, bestreiten; (refuse) ablehnen

**deodorant** n Deo(dorant) nt

**depart** vi abreisen; (bus, train) abfahren (for nach, from von); (plane) abfliegen (for nach, from von)

**department** n Abteilung f; (at university) Institut nt; POL (ministry) Ministerium nt; **department store** n Kaufhaus nt

**departure** n (of person) Weggang m; (on journey) Abreise f (for nach); (of train etc) Abfahrt f (for nach); (of plane) Abflug m (for nach); **departure lounge** n AVIAT Abflughalle f; **departure time** n Abfahrtzeit f; AVIAT Abflugzeit f

**depend** vi **it~s** es kommt darauf an (whether, if ob); **depend on** vt (thing) abhängen von; (person: rely on) sich verlassen auf + acc; (person, area etc) angewiesen sein auf + acc; **it depends on the weather** es kommt auf das Wetter an; **dependable** adj zuverlässig; **dependent** adj abhängig (on von)

**deport** vt ausweisen, abschieben; **deportation** n Abschiebung f

**deposit 1.** n (*down payment*) Anzahlung f; (*security*) Kaution f; (*for bottle*) Pfand nt; (*to bank account*) Einzahlung f; (*in river etc*) Ablagerung f **2.** vt (*put down*) abstellen, absetzen; (*to bank account*) einzahlen; (*sth valuable*) deponieren; **deposit account** n Sparkonto nt

**depot** n Depot nt

**depress** vt (*in mood*) deprimieren; **depressed** adj (*person*) niedergeschlagen, deprimiert; **~ area** Notstandsgebiet nt; **depressing** adj deprimierend; **depression** n (*mood*) Depression f; METEO Tief nt

**deprive** vt **~ sb of sth** jdn einer Sache berauben; **deprived** adj (*child*) (sozial) benachteiligt

**dept** abbr → **department** Abt.

**depth** n Tiefe f

**deputy 1.** adj stellvertretend, Vize- **2.** n Stellvertreter(in) m(f); (*US*) POL Abgeordnete(r) mf

**derail** vt entgleisen lassen; **be ~ed** entgleisen

**dermatitis** n Hautentzündung f

**derogatory** adj abfällig

**descend** vt, vi hinabsteigen, hinuntergehen; (*person*) or **be ~ed from** abstammen von; **descendant** n Nachkomme m; **descent** n (*coming down*) Abstieg m; (*origin*) Abstammung f

**describe** vt beschreiben; **description** n Beschreibung f

**desert 1.** n Wüste f **2.** vt verlassen; (*abandon*) im Stich lassen; **deserted** adj verlassen; (*empty*) menschenleer

**deserve** vt verdienen

**design 1.** n (*plan*) Entwurf m; (*of vehicle, machine*) Konstruktion f; (*of object*) Design nt; (*planning*) Gestaltung f **2.** vt entwerfen; (*machine etc*) konstruieren; **~ed for sb / sth** (*intended*) für jdn / etw konzipiert; **designer** n Designer(in) m(f); TECH Konstrukteur(in) m(f); **designer drug** n Designerdroge f

**desirable** adj wünschenswert; (*person*) begehrenswert; **desire 1.** n Wunsch m (*for* nach); (*esp sexual*) Begierde f (*for* nach) **2.** vt wünschen; (*ask for*) verlangen; **if ~d** auf Wunsch

**desk** n Schreibtisch m; (*reception desk*) Empfang m; (*at airport etc*) Schalter m; **desktop publishing** n Desktoppublishing nt

**despair 1.** n Verzweiflung f (*at* über + acc) **2.** vi verzweifeln (*of* an + dat)

**despatch** n → **dispatch**

**desperate** adj verzweifelt; (*situation*) hoffnungslos; **be ~ for sth** etw dringend brauchen, unbedingt wollen;

**desperation** *n* Verzweiflung *f*

**despicable** *adj* verachtenswert; **despise** *vt* verachten

**despite** *prep* trotz + *gen*

**dessert** *n* Nachtisch *m*; **dessert spoon** *n* Dessertlöffel *m*

**destination** *n* (*of person*) (Reise)ziel *nt*; (*of goods*) Bestimmungsort *m*

**destiny** *n* Schicksal *nt*

**destroy** *vt* zerstören; (*completely*) vernichten; **destruction** *n* Zerstörung *f*; (*complete*) Vernichtung *f*; **destructive** *adj* zerstörerisch, destruktiv

**detach** *vt* abnehmen; (*from form etc*) abtrennen; (*free*) lösen (*from* von); **detachable** *adj* abnehmbar; (*from form etc*) abtrennbar; **detached** *adj* (*attitude*) distanziert, objektiv; **~ house** Einzelhaus *nt*

**detail** (*US*) *n* Einzelheit *f*, Detail *nt*; (*further*) **~s from** ...: Näheres erfahren Sie bei ...; *go into* ~ ins Detail gehen; *in* ~ ausführlich; **detailed** *adj* detailliert, ausführlich

**detain** *vt* aufhalten; (*police*) in Haft nehmen

**detect** *vt* entdecken; (*notice*) wahrnehmen; **detection** *n* Detektiv(in) *m(f)*; **detective** *n* Detektiv(in) *m(f)*; **detective story** *n* Krimi *m*

**detergent** *n* Reinigungsmit-

tel *nt*; (*soap powder*) Waschmittel *nt*

**deteriorate** *vi* sich verschlechtern

**determination** *n* Entschlossenheit *f*; **determine** *vt* bestimmen; **determined** *adj* (*fest*) entschlossen

**detest** *vt* verabscheuen; **detestable** *adj* abscheulich

**detour** *n* Umweg *m*; (*of traffic*) Umleitung *f*

**deuce** *n* (*tennis*) Einstand *m*

**devastate** *vt* verwüsten; **devastating** *adj* verheerend

**develop 1.** *vt* entwickeln; (*illness*) bekommen **2.** *vi* sich entwickeln; **developing country** *n* Entwicklungsland *nt*; **development** *n* Entwicklung *f*; (*of land*) Erschließung *f*

**device** *n* Vorrichtung *f*, Gerät *nt*

**devil** *n* Teufel *m*

**devoted** *adj* liebend; (*servant etc*) treu ergeben; **devotion** *n* Hingabe *f*

**devour** *vt* verschlingen

**dew** *n* Tau *m*

**diabetes** *n* Diabetes *m*, Zuckerkrankheit *f*; **diabetic 1.** *adj* zuckerkrank, für Diabetiker **2.** *n* Diabetiker(in) *m(f)*

**diagnosis** *n* Diagnose *f*

**diagonal** *adj* diagonal

**diagram** *n* Diagramm *nt*

**dial 1.** *n* Skala *f*; (*of clock*) Zifferblatt *nt* **2.** *vt* TEL wählen; **dial code** *n* (*US*) Vorwahl *f*

**dialect** n Dialekt m

**dialling code** n (Brit) Vorwahl f; **dialling tone** n (Brit) Amtszeichen nt

**dialogue, dialog** (US) n Dialog m

**dial tone** n (US) Amtszeichen nt

**dialysis** n MED Dialyse f

**diameter** n Durchmesser m

**diamond** n Diamant m, Karo nt

**diaper** n (US) Windel f

**diarrhoea** n Durchfall m

**diary** n (Taschen)kalender m; (account) Tagebuch nt

**dice** npl Würfel pl

**dictation** n Diktat nt

**dictator** n Diktator(in) m(f); **dictatorship** n Diktatur f

**dictionary** n Wörterbuch nt

**did** pt → **do**

**didn't** contr = **did not**

**die** vi sterben (of an + dat); (plant, animal) eingehen; (engine) absterben; **be dying to do sth** darauf brennen, etw zu tun; **I'm dying for a drink** ich brauche unbedingt was zu trinken; **die away** vi schwächer werden; (wind) sich legen; **die down** vi nachlassen; **die out** vi aussterben

**diesel** n (fuel, car) Diesel m

**diet** n **1.** Kost f; (special food) Diät f **2.** vi eine Diät machen

**differ** vi (be different) sich unterscheiden; (disagree) anderer Meinung sein; **difference** n Unterschied m; **it**

**makes no ~ (to me)** es ist (mir) egal; **it makes a big ~** es macht viel aus; **different** adj verschieden; (with pl) verschieden; **be quite ~** ganz anders sein (from als); (two people, things) völlig verschieden sein; **differentiate** vt, vi unterscheiden; **differently** adv anders (from als); (from one another) unterschiedlich

**difficult** adj schwierig; **I find it ~** es fällt mir schwer; **difficulty** n Schwierigkeit f

**dig** vt, vi (hole) graben; **dig in** vi fam (to food) reinhauen; **~! greif(t) zu!; dig up** vt ausgraben

**digest** vt verdauen; **digestion** n Verdauung f; **digestive** adj **~ biscuit** (Brit) Vollkornkeks m

**digit** n Ziffer f; **digital** adj digital; **digital camera** n Digitalkamera f; **digital television** n, **digital TV** n Digitalfernsehen nt

**dignified** adj würdevoll; **dignity** n Würde f

**dilapidated** adj baufällig

**dill** n Dill m

**dilute** vt verdünnen

**dim 1.** adj (light) schwach; (outline) undeutlich; (stupid) schwer von Begriff **2.** vt verdunkeln; (US) AUTO abblenden; **~ med headlights** (US) Abblendlicht nt

**dime** n (US) Zehncentstück

*nt*

**dimension** *n* Dimension *f*; **~s** *pl* Maße *pl*

**diminish 1.** *vt* verringern **2.** *vi* sich verringern

**dimple** *n* Grübchen *nt*

**dine** *vi* speisen; **dine out** *vi* außer Haus essen; **diner** *n* Gast *m*; RAIL Speisewagen *m*; (*US*) Speiselokal *nt*

**dinghy** *n* Ding(h)i *nt*; (*inflatable*) Schlauchboot *nt*

**dining car** *n* Speisewagen *m*; **dining room** *n* Esszimmer *nt*; (*in hotel*) Speiseraum *m*

**dinner** *n* Abendessen *nt*; (*lunch*) Mittagessen *nt*; (*public*) Diner *nt*; **be at ~** beim Essen sein; **have ~** zu Abend / Mittag essen; **dinner jacket** *n* Smoking *m*; **dinnertime** *n* Essenszeit *f*

**dinosaur** *n* Dinosaurier *m*

**dip 1.** *vt* tauchen (*in* in + *acc*); **~** (*one's headlights*) (*Brit*) AUTO abblenden; **~ped headlights** Abblendlicht *nt* **2.** *n* (*in ground*) Bodensenke *f*; (*sauce*) Dip *m*

**diploma** *n* Diplom *nt*

**diplomatic** *adj* diplomatisch

**dipstick** *n* Ölmessstab *m*

**direct 1.** *adj* direkt; (*cause, consequence*) unmittelbar; **~ debit** (*mandate*) Einzugsermächtigung *f*; **~ train** durchgehender Zug **2.** *vt* (*aim, send*) richten (*at, to* an + *acc*); (*film*) die Regie führen bei; (*traffic*) regeln;

**direct current** *n* ELEC Gleichstrom *m*

**direction** *n* (*course*) Richtung *f*; FILM Regie *f*; **in the ~ of ...** in Richtung ...; **~s** *pl* (*to a place*) Wegbeschreibung *f*

**directly** *adv* direkt; (*at once*) sofort

**director** *n* Direktor(in) *m(f)*, Leiter(in) *m(f)*; (*of film*) Regisseur(in) *m(f)*

**directory** *n* Adressbuch *nt*, Telefonbuch *nt*; **~ enquiries** *or* (*US*) **assistance** TEL Auskunft *f*

**dirt** *n* Schmutz *m*, Dreck *m*; **dirt cheap** *adj* spottbillig; **dirty** *adj* schmutzig

**disability** *n* Behinderung *f*; **disabled 1.** *adj* behindert, Behinderten- **2.** *npl* **the ~** die Behinderten

**disadvantage** *n* Nachteil *m*; **at a ~** benachteiligt; **disadvantageous** *adj* unvorteilhaft, ungünstig

**disagree** *vi* anderer Meinung sein; (*two people*) sich nicht einig sein; (*two reports etc*) nicht übereinstimmen; **disagreeable** *adj* unangenehm; (*person*) unsympathisch; **disagreement** *n* Meinungsverschiedenheit *f*

**disappear** *vi* verschwinden

**disappoint** *vt* enttäuschen; **disappointing** *adj* enttäuschend; **disappointment** *n* Enttäuschung *f*

**disapprove** *vi* missbilligen

(*of acc*)

**disarm 1.** *vt* entwaffnen **2.** *vi* POL abrüsten; **disarmament** *n* Abrüstung *f*; **disarming** *adj* (*smile*, *look*) gewinnend

**disaster** *n* Katastrophe *f*; **disastrous** *adj* katastrophal

**disbelief** *n* Ungläubigkeit *f*

**disc** *n* Scheibe *f*, CD *f*; → **disk** ANAT Bandscheibe *f*

**discharge 1.** *n* MED Ausfluss *m* **2.** *vt* (*person*) entlassen; (*emit*) ausstoßen; MED ausscheiden

**discipline** *n* Disziplin *f*

**disc jockey** *n* Diskjockey *m*

**disclose** *vt* bekannt geben; (*secret*) enthüllen

**disco** *n* Disko *f*, Diskomusik *f*

**discomfort** *n* (*slight pain*) leichte Schmerzen *pl*; (*unease*) Unbehagen *nt*

**disconnect** *vt* (*electricity*, *gas*, *phone*) abstellen; (*unplug*) **the TV** (*from the mains*) den Stecker des Fernsehers herausziehen; TEL **I've been ~ed** das Gespräch ist unterbrochen worden

**discontinue** *vt* einstellen; (*product*) auslaufen lassen

**discount** *n* Rabatt *m*

**discover** *vt* entdecken; **discovery** *n* Entdeckung *f*

**discredit 1.** *vt* in Verruf bringen **2.** *n* Misskredit *m*

**discreet** *adj* diskret

**discrepancy** *n* Unstimmigkeit *f*, Diskrepanz *f*

**discriminate** *vi* unterschei-

den; **~ against sb** jdn diskriminieren; **discrimination** *n* (*different treatment*) Diskriminierung *f*

**discus** *n* Diskus *m*

**discuss** *vt* diskutieren, besprechen; **discussion** *n* Diskussion *f*

**disease** *n* Krankheit *f*

**disembark** *vi* von Bord gehen

**disgrace 1.** *n* Schande *f* **2.** *vt* Schande machen + *dat*; (*family etc*) Schande bringen über + *acc*; (*less strong*) blamieren; **disgraceful** *adj* skandalös

**disguise 1.** *vt* verkleiden; (*voice*) verstellen **2.** *n* Verkleidung *f*

**disgust 1.** *n* Abscheu *m*; (*physical*) Ekel *m* **2.** *vt* anekeln, anwidern; **disgusting** *adj* widerlich; (*physically*) ekelhaft

**dish** *n* Schüssel *f*; (*food*) Gericht *nt*; **~es** *pl* (*crockery*) Geschirr *nt*; **do / wash the ~es** abwaschen; **dishcloth** *n* (*for washing*) Spültuch *nt*; (*for drying*) Geschirrtuch *nt*

**dishearten** *vt* entmutigen; **don't be ~ed** lass den Kopf nicht hängen!

**dishonest** *adj* unehrlich

**dish towel** *n* (*US*) Geschirrtuch *nt*; **dish washer** *n* Geschirrspülmaschine *f*

**dishy** *adj* (*Brit*) *fam* gut aussehend

**disillusioned** adj desillusioniert

**disinfect** vt desinfizieren; **disinfectant** n Desinfektionsmittel nt

**disk** n IT (floppy) Diskette f; **disk drive** n Diskettenlaufwerk nt; **diskette** n Diskette f

**dislike 1.** n Abneigung f **2.** vt nicht mögen; **~ doing sth** etw ungern tun

**dislocate** vt MED verrenken, ausrenken

**dismal** adj trostlos

**dismantle** vt auseinandernehmen; (machine) demontieren

**dismay** n Bestürzung f; **dismayed** adj bestürzt

**dismiss** vt (employee) entlassen; **dismissal** n Entlassung f

**disobedience** n Ungehorsam m; **disobedient** adj ungehorsam; **disobey** vt nicht gehorchen + dat

**disorder** n (mess) Unordnung f; (riot) Aufruhr m; MED Störung f, Leiden nt

**disorganized** adj chaotisch

**disparaging** adj geringschätzig

**dispatch** vt abschicken, abfertigen

**dispensable** adj entbehrlich; **dispense** vt verteilen; **dispense with** vt verzichten auf + acc; **dispenser** n Automat m

**disperse** vi sich zerstreuen

**display 1.** n (exhibition) Ausstellung f, Show f; (of goods) Auslage f; TECH Anzeige f, Display nt **2.** vt zeigen; (goods) ausstellen

**disposable** adj (container, razor etc) Wegwerf-; **~ nappy** Wegwerfwindel f; **disposal** n Loswerden nt; (of waste) Beseitigung f; **be at sb's ~** jdm zur Verfügung stehen; **have at one's ~** verfügen über; **dispose of** vt loswerden; (waste etc) beseitigen

**dispute 1.** n Streit m; (industrial) Auseinandersetzung f **2.** vt bestreiten

**disqualification** n Disqualifikation f; **disqualify** vt disqualifizieren

**disregard** vt nicht beachten

**disreputable** adj verrufen

**disrespect** n Respektlosigkeit f

**disrupt** vt stören; (interrupt) unterbrechen; **disruption** n Störung f; (interruption) Unterbrechung f

**dissatisfied** adj unzufrieden

**dissent** n Widerspruch m

**dissolve 1.** vt auflösen **2.** vi sich auflösen

**dissuade** vt (davon abbringen) **~ sb from doing sth** jdn davon abbringen, etw zu tun

**distance** n Entfernung f; **in the / from a ~** in / aus der Ferne; **distant** adj (a. in time) fern; (relative etc) entfernt; (person) distanziert

**distaste** n Abneigung f (for gegen)

**distil** vt destillieren; **distillery** n Brennerei f

**distinct** adj verschieden; (clear) klar, deutlich; **distinction** n (difference) Unterschied m; (in exam etc) Auszeichnung f; **distinctive** adj unverkennbar; **distinctly** adv deutlich

**distinguish** vt unterscheiden (sth from sth etw von etw)

**distort** vt verzerren; (truth) verdrehen

**distract** vt ablenken; **distraction** n Ablenkung f (diversion) Zerstreuung f

**distress** 1. n (need, danger) Not f; (suffering) Leiden nt; (mental) Qual f; (worry) Kummer m 2. vt mitnehmen, erschüttern; **distressed area** n Notstandsgebiet nt

**distribute** vt verteilen; COMM (goods) vertreiben; **distribution** n Verteilung f, COMM (of goods) Vertrieb m; **distributor** n AUTO Verteiler m; COMM Händler(in) m(f)

**district** n Gegend f; (administrative) Bezirk m; **district attorney** n (US) Staatsanwalt m, Staatsanwältin f

**distrust** 1. vt misstrauen + dat 2. n Misstrauen nt

**disturb** vt stören; (worry) beunruhigen; **disturbance** n

Störung f; **disturbing** adj beunruhigend

**ditch** 1. n Graben m 2. vt fam (person) den Laufpass geben + dat; (plan etc) verwerfen

**ditto** n dito, ebenfalls

**dive** 1. n (into water) Kopfsprung m; AVIAT Sturzflug m; fam zwielichtiges Lokal 2. vi (under water) tauchen; **diver** n Taucher(in) m(f)

**diverse** adj verschieden; **diversion** n (of traffic) Umleitung f; (distraction) Ablenkung f; **divert** vt ablenken; (traffic) umleiten

**divide** 1. vt teilen; (in several parts, between people) aufteilen 2. vi sich teilen; **dividend** n Dividende f

**divine** adj göttlich

**diving** n (Sport)tauchen nt; (jumping in) Springen nt; SPORT (from board) Kunstspringen nt; **diving board** n Sprungbrett nt; **diving goggles** npl Taucherbrille f; **diving mask** n Tauchmaske f

**division** n Teilung f; MATH Division f; (department) Abteilung f; SPORT Liga f

**divorce** 1. n Scheidung f 2. vt sich scheiden lassen von; **divorced** adj geschieden; **get~** sich scheiden lassen; **divorcee** n Geschiedene(r) mf

**DIY** abbr → **do-it-yourself**; **DIY centre** n Baumarkt m

**dizzy** adj schwindlig

**DJ** 1. abbr → **disc jockey**

**Diskjockey** *m*, **DJ** *m* **2.** *abbr* → **dinner jacket** Smoking *m*

**do 1.** *vaux* (*in negatives*) **I don't know** ich weiß es nicht; **he didn't come** er ist nicht gekommen; (*in questions*) **does she swim?** schwimmt sie?; (*for emphasis*) **he does like talking** er redet sehr gern; (*replacing verb*) **they drink more than we do** sie trinken mehr als wir; **please don't!** bitte tun Sie / tu das nicht!; (*in question tags*) **you know him, don't you?** du kennst / Sie kennen ihn doch, oder? **2.** *vt* tun, machen; (*clean: room etc*) sauber machen; (*study*) studieren; AUTO (*speed*) fahren; (*distance*) zurücklegen; **he has nothing to ~** sie hat nichts zu tun; **~ the dishes** abwaschen; **you can't ~ Cambridge in a day** Cambridge kann man nicht an einem Tag besichtigen **3.** *vi* (*get on*) vorankommen; (*be enough*) reichen; **~ well / badly** gut / schlecht vorankommen; (*in exam etc*) gut / schlecht abschneiden; **how are you doing?** wie geht's denn so?; **that (much) should ~** das dürfte reichen **4.** *n* (*party*) Party *f*; **do away with** *vt* abschaffen; **do up** *vt* (*fasten*) zumachen; (*parcel*) verschnüren; (*renovate*) wiederherrichten; **do with** *vt*

(*need*) brauchen; **I could ~ a drink** ich könnte einen Drink gebrauchen; **do without** *vt* auskommen ohne; **I can ~ your comments** auf deine / Ihre Kommentare kann ich verzichten

**dock** *n* Dock *nt*; LAW Anklagebank *f*; **dockyard** *n* Werft *f*

**doctor** *n* Arzt *m*, Ärztin *f*; (*in title, also academic*) Doktor *m*

**document** *n* Dokument *nt*; **documentary** *n* Dokumentarfilm *m*; **documentation** *n* Dokumentation *f*

**docusoap** *n* Reality-Serie *f*, Dokusoap *f*

**dodgy** *adj* nicht ganz in Ordnung; (*dishonest, unreliable*) zwielichtig; **he has a ~ stomach** er hat sich den Magen verdorben

**dog** *n* Hund *m*; **doggie bag** *n* Tüte oder Box, in die Essensreste aus dem Restaurant mit nach Hause genommen werden können

**do-it-yourself 1.** *n* Heimwerken *nt*, Do-it-yourself *nt* **2.** *adj* Heimwerker-; **do-it-yourselfer** *n* Bastler(in) *m(f)*, Heimwerker(in) *m(f)*

**doll** *n* Puppe *f*

**dollar** *n* Dollar *m*

**dolphin** *n* Delphin *m*

**domain** *n* Domäne *f*; IT Domain *f*

**dome** *n* Kuppel *f*

**domestic** adj häuslich; (within country) Innen-, Binnen-; **domesticated** adj (person) häuslich; (animal) zahm; **domestic flight** n Inlandsflug m

**domicile** n (ständiger) Wohnsitz

**dominant** adj dominierend, vorherrschend

**dominoes** npl Domino(spiel) nt

**donate** vt spenden; **donation** n Spende f

**done 1.** pp → **do 2.** adj (cooked) gar; **well ~** durchgebraten

**doner (kebab)** n Döner (Kebab) m

**donkey** n Esel m

**donor** n Spender(in) m(f)

**don't** contr = **do not**

**door** n Tür f; **doorbell** n Türklingel f; **door handle** n Türklinke f; **doorknob** n Türknauf m; **doormat** n Fußabtreter m; **doorstep** n Türstufe f; **right on our ~** direkt vor unserer Haustür

**dope** sport n (for athlete) Aufputschmittel nt **2.** vt dopen

**dormitory** n Schlafsaal m; (US) Studentenwohnheim nt

**dosage** n Dosierung f; **dose 1.** n Dosis f **2.** vt dosieren

**dot** n Punkt m; **on the ~** auf die Minute genau

**double 1.** adj, adv doppelt; **~**

**the quantity** die zweifache Menge, doppelt so viel **2.** vt verdoppeln **3.** n (person) Doppelgänger(in) m(f); FILM Double nt; **double bass** n Kontrabass m; **double bed** n Doppelbett nt; **double-click** vt IT doppelklicken; **double cream** n Sahne mit hohem Fettgehalt; **doubledecker** n Doppeldecker m; **double glazing** n Doppelverglasung f; **double-park** vi in zweiter Reihe parken; **double room** n Doppelzimmer nt; **doubles** npl sport (also match) Doppel nt

**doubt 1.** n Zweifel m; **no ~** ohne Zweifel, zweifellos, wahrscheinlich; **have one's ~s** Bedenken haben **2.** vt bezweifeln; (statement, word) anzweifeln; **I ~ it** das bezweifle ich; **doubtful** adj zweifelhaft, zweifelnd; **it is ~ whether ...** es ist fraglich, ob ...; **doubtless** adv ohne Zweifel, sicherlich

**dough** n Teig m; **doughnut** n Donut m (rundes Hefegebäck)

**dove** n Taube f

**down 1.** n Daunen pl; (fluff) Flaum m **2.** adv unten; (motion) nach unten; (towards speaker) herunter; (away from speaker) hinunter; **~ here / there** hier / dort unten; (downstairs) **they came ~ for breakfast** sie kamen

**draw up**

zum Frühstück herunter **3.** *prep* (*towards speaker*) herunter; (*away from speaker*) hinunter; **drive ~ the hill / road** den Berg / die Straße hinunter fahren; (*along*) **walk ~ the street** die Straße entlang gehen; **he's ~ the pub** *fam* er ist in der Kneipe **4.** *vt fam* (*drink*) runterkippen **5.** *adj* niedergeschlagen, deprimiert

**downcast** *adj* niedergeschlagen; **downfall** *n* Sturz *m*; **down-hearted** *adj* entmutigt; **downhill** *adj* bergab

**download** *vt* downloaden, herunterladen; **down payment** *n* Anzahlung *f*; **downs** *npl* Hügelland *nt*; **downsize 1.** *vt* (*business*) verkleinern **2.** *vi* sich verkleinern

**Down's syndrome** *n* MED Downsyndrom *nt*

**downstairs** *adv* unten; (*motion*) nach unten; **downstream** *adv* flussabwärts; **downtown 1.** *adv* (*be, work etc*) in der Innenstadt; (*go*) in die Innenstadt **2.** *adj* (*US*) in der Innenstadt; **~ Chicago** die Innenstadt von Chicago; **down under** *adv fam* (*in / to Australia*) in / nach Australien; (*in / to New Zealand*) in / nach Neuseeland; **downwards** *adv*, *adj* nach unten; (*movement, trend*) Abwärts-

**doze 1.** *vi* dösen **2.** *n* Nicker-

chen *nt*

**dozen** *n* Dutzend *nt*

**DP** *abbr* → **data processing** DV *f*

**draft** *n* (*outline*) Entwurf *m*; (*US*) MIL Einberufung *f*

**drag 1.** *vt* schleppen **2.** *n fam* **be a ~** (*boring*) stinklangweilig sein; (*laborious*) ein ziemlicher Schlauch sein; **drag on** *vi* sich in die Länge ziehen

**dragon** *n* Drache *m*; **dragonfly** *n* Libelle *f*

**drain 1.** *n* Abfluss *m* **2.** *vt* (*water, oil*) ablassen; (*vegetables etc*) abgießen; (*land*) entwässern, trockenlegen **3.** *vi* (*of water*) abfließen; **drainpipe** *n* Abflussrohr *nt*

**drama** *n* Drama *nt*; **dramatic** *adj* dramatisch

**drank** *pt* → **drink**

**drapes** *npl* (*US*) Vorhänge *pl*

**drastic** *adj* drastisch

**draught** *n* (Luft)zug *m*; **there's a ~** es zieht; **on ~** (*beer*) vom Fass; **draughts** *nsing* Damespiel *nt*; **draughty** *adj* zugig

**draw 1.** *vt* (*pull*) ziehen; (*crowd*) anlocken, anziehen; (*picture*) zeichnen **2.** *vi* SPORT unentschieden spielen **3.** *n* SPORT Unentschieden *nt*; (*attraction*) Attraktion *f*; (*for lottery*) Ziehung *f*; **draw out** *vt* herausziehen; (*money*) abheben; **draw up 1.** *vt* (*formulate*) entwerfen; (*list*) erstellen **2.** *vi* (*car*) anhalten; **drawback** *n* Nachteil *m*

**drawer** *n* Schublade *f*

**drawing** *n* Zeichnung *f*; **drawing pin** *n* Reißzwecke *f*

**drawn** *pp* → **draw**

**dread 1.** *n* Furcht *f* (*of* vor + *dat*) **2.** *vt* sich fürchten vor + *dat*; **dreadful** *adj* furchtbar; **dreadlocks** *npl* Rastalocken *pl*

**dream 1.** *vt, vi* träumen (*about* von) **2.** *n* Traum *m*; **dreamt** *pt, pp* → **dream**

**dreary** *adj* (*weather, place*) trostlos; (*book etc*) langweilig

**drench** *vt* durchnässen

**dress 1.** *n* Kleidung *f*; (*garment*) Kleid *nt* **2.** *vt* anziehen; MED (*wound*) verbinden; **get ~ed** sich anziehen; **dress up** *vi* sich fein machen; (*in costume*) sich verkleiden (*as* als); **dress circle** *n* THEAT erster Rang; **dresser** *n* Anrichte *f*; (*US, dressing table*) (Frisier)kommode *f*; **dressing** *n* GASTR Dressing *nt*, Soße *f*; MED Verband *m*; **dressing gown** *n* Bademantel *m*; **dressing room** *n* THEAT Künstlergarderobe *f*; **dressing table** *n* Frisierkommode *f*; **dress rehearsal** *n* THEAT Generalprobe *f*

**drew** *pt* → **draw**

**dried** *adj* getrocknet; (*milk, flowers*) Trocken-; **~ fruit** Dörrobst *nt*; **drier** *n* → **dryer**

**drift 1.** *vi* treiben **2.** *n* (*of snow*) Verwehung *f*; *fig* Tendenz *f*; **if you get my ~** wenn du mich richtig verstehst / Sie mich richtig verstehen

**drill 1.** *n* Bohrer *m* **2.** *vt, vi* bohren

**drink 1.** *vt, vi* trinken **2.** *n* Getränk *nt*; (*alcoholic*) Drink *m*; **drink-driving** *n* (*Brit*) Trunkenheit *f* am Steuer; **drinking water** *n* Trinkwasser *nt*

**drip 1.** *n* Tropfen *m* **2.** *vi* tropfen; **dripping 1.** *n* Bratenfett *nt* **2.** *adj* **~ (wet)** tropfnass

**drive 1.** *vt* (*car, person in car*) fahren; (*force: person, animal*) treiben; TECH antreiben; **~ sb mad** jdn verrückt machen **2.** *vi* fahren **3.** *n* Fahrt *f*; (*entrance*) Einfahrt *f*, Auffahrt *f*; IT Laufwerk *nt*; **drive away, drive off 1.** *vt* vertreiben; **drive-in** *adj* Drive-in-; **~ cinema** (*US*) Autokino *nt*; **driven** *pp* → **drive**

**driver** *n* Fahrer(in) *m(f)*; IT Treiber *m*; **~'s license** (*US*) Führerschein *m*; **~'s seat** Fahrersitz *m*; **driving** *n* (Auto)fahren *nt*; **driving lesson** *n* Fahrstunde *f*; **driving licence** *n* (*Brit*) Führerschein *m*; **driving school** *n* Fahrschule *f*; **driving seat** *n* (*Brit*) Fahrersitz *m*; **driving test** *n* Fahrprüfung *f*

**drizzle 1.** *n* Nieselregen *m* **2.**

**dummy**

*vi* nieseln

**drop 1.** *n* (*of liquid*) Tropfen *m*; (*fall in price etc*) Rückgang *m* **2.** *vt a. fig* (*give up*) fallen lassen **3.** *vi* (*fall*) herunterfallen; (*figures, temperature*) sinken, zurückgehen; **drop by, drop in** *vi* vorbeikommen; **drop off** *vi* (*to sleep*) einnicken; **drop out** *vi* (*withdraw*) aussteigen; (*university*) das Studium abbrechen; **dropout** *n* Aussteiger(in) *m(f)*

**drove** *pt* → **drive**

**drown 1.** *vi* ertrinken **2.** *vt* ertränken

**drowsy** *adj* schläfrig

**drug 1.** *n* MED Medikament *nt*, Arznei *f*; (*addictive*) Droge *f*; (*narcotic*) Rauschgift *nt*; **be on ~s** drogensüchtig sein **2.** *vt* (*mit Medikamenten*) betäuben; **drug addict** *n* Rauschgiftsüchtige(r) *m(f)*; **drug dealer** *n* Drogenhändler(in) *m(f)*; **druggist** *n* (*US*) Drogist(in) *m(f)*; **drugstore** *n* (*US*) Drogerie *f*

**drum** *n* Trommel *f*; **~s** *pl* Schlagzeug *nt*

**drunk 1.** *pp* → **drink 2.** *adj* betrunken; **get~** sich betrinken **3.** *n* Betrunkene(r) *m/f*; (*alcoholic*) Trinker(in) *m(f)*; **drunk-driving** *n* (*US*) Trunkenheit *f* am Steuer; **drunken** *adj* betrunken, besoffen

**dry 1.** *adj* trocken **2.** *vt* trocknen; (*dishes, oneself, one's*

*hands etc*) abtrocknen **3.** *vi* trocknen, trocken werden; **dry out** *vi* trocknen; **dry-clean** *vt* chemisch reinigen; **dry-cleaning** *n* chemische Reinigung; **dryer** *n* Trockner *m*; (*for hair*) Föhn *m*; (*over head*) Trockenhaube *f*

**DTP** *abbr* → **desktop publishing** DTP *nt*

**dual** *adj* doppelt; **~ carriageway** (*Brit*) zweispurige Schnellstraße *f*; **~ nationality** doppelte Staatsangehörigkeit

**dubbed** *adj* (*film*) synchronisiert

**dubious** *adj* zweifelhaft

**duchess** *n* Herzogin *f*

**duck** *n* Ente *f*

**dude** *n* (*US*) *fam* Typ *m*; **a cool ~** ein cooler Typ

**due 1.** *adj* (*time*) fällig; (*fitting*) angemessen; **in ~ course** zu gegebener Zeit; **~ to** infolge + *gen*, wegen + *gen* **2.** *adv* **~ south / north etc** direkt nach Norden / Süden etc

**dug** *pt, pp* → **dig**

**duke** *n* Herzog *m*

**dull** *adj* (*colour, light, weather*) trübe; (*boring*) langweilig

**duly** *adv* ordnungsgemäß; (*as expected*) wie erwartet

**dumb** *adj* stumm; *fam* (*stupid*) doof, blöde

**dumb-bell** *n* Hantel *f*

**dummy 1.** *n* (*sham*) Attrappe

f; (in shop) Schaufenster-
puppe f; (Brit, teat) Schnuller m; fam (person) Dumm-
kopf m **2.** adj unecht,
Schein-; ~ **run** Testlauf m

**dump 1.** n Abfallhaufen m;
fam (place) Kaff nt **2.** vt lit,
fig abladen; fam **he ~ed
her** er hat mir ihr Schluss gemacht

**dumpling** n Kloß m, Knödel
m

**dune** n Düne f

**dung** n Dung m; (manure)
Mist m

**dungeon** n Kerker m

**duplex** n zweistöckige Wohnung; (US) Doppelhaus-
hälfte f

**duplicate 1.** n Duplikat nt **2.**
vt (make copies of) kopie-
ren; (repeat) wiederholen

**durable** adj haltbar; **duration**
n Dauer f

**during** prep (time) während
+ gen

**dusk** n Abenddämmerung f

**dust 1.** n Staub m **2.** vt abstauben; **dustbin** n (Brit) Mülleimer m; **dustcart** n (Brit)

Müllwagen m; **duster** n
Staubtuch nt; **dustman** n
(Brit) Müllmann m; **dustpan** n Kehrschaufel f; **dusty**
adj staubig

**Dutch 1.** adj holländisch **2.** n
(language) Holländisch nt;
speak / talk **Dutch** ~ fam
Quatsch reden; **the** ~ pl die
Holländer; **Dutchman** n
Holländer m; **Dutchwoman**
n Holländerin f

**duty 1.** n Pflicht f; (task) Aufgabe f; (tax) Zoll m; **on / off** ~
im Dienst / nicht im Dienst;
**be on** ~ Dienst haben; **duty-free** adj zollfrei; ~ **shop**
Dutyfreeshop m

**duvet** n Federbett nt

**DVD** n abbr = **digital versatile
disk** DVD f; **DVD player** n
DVD-Player m; **DVD re-
corder** n DVD-Rekorder m

**dwelling** n Wohnung f

**dye 1.** n Farbstoff m **2.** vt färben

**dynamo** n Dynamo m

**dyslexia** n Legasthenie f;
**dyslexic** adj legasthenisch;
**be** ~ Legastheniker(in) sein

# E

**E** abbr → **ecstasy** (drug) Ecstasy nt

**E111 form** n ≈ Auslandskrankenschein m

**each 1.** adj jeder / jede / jedes
**2.** pron jeder / jede / jedes;

**I'll have one of** ~ ich nehme
von jedem eins; **they** ~ **have
a car** jeder von ihnen hat ein
Auto; ~ **other** einander, sich;
**for / against** ~ **other** füreinander / gegeneinander **3.**

*adv* je; **they cost 10 dollars ~** sie kosten 10 Dollar das Stück

**eager** *adj* eifrig; **be ~ to do sth** darauf brennen, etw zu tun

**eagle** *n* Adler *m*

**ear** *n* Ohr *nt*; **earache** *n* Ohrenschmerzen *pl*; **eardrum** *n* Trommelfell *nt*

**earl** *n* Graf *m*

**early** *adj* früh; **be 10 minutes ~** 10 Minuten zu früh kommen; **at the earliest** frühestens; **in ~ June / 2008** Anfang Juni / 2008; **~ retirement** vorzeitiger Ruhestand; **~ warning system** Frühwarnsystem *nt*

**earn** *vt* verdienen; **earnings** *npl* Verdienst *m*, Einkommen *nt*

**earplug** *n* Ohrenstöpsel *m*, Ohropax® *nt*; **earring** *n* Ohrring *m*

**earth** 1. *n* Erde *f*; **what on ~ ...?** was in aller Welt ...? 2. *vt* erden; **earthquake** *n* Erdbeben *nt*

**ease** 1. *vt* (*pain*) lindern 2. *n* (*easiness*) Leichtigkeit *f*; **feel at ~** sich wohlfühlen; **feel ill at ~** sich nicht wohlfühlen; **easily** *adv* leicht; **he is ~ the best** er ist mit Abstand der Beste

**east** 1. *n* Osten *m*; **to the ~ of** östlich von 2. *adv* (*go, face*) nach Osten 3. *adj* Ost-; **~ wind** Ostwind *m*; **eastbound** *adj* (in) Richtung Os-

ten

**Easter** *n* Ostern *nt*; **at ~** zu Ostern; **Easter egg** *n* Osterei *nt*

**eastern** *adj* Ost-, östlich; **Eastern Europe** Osteuropa *nt*

**Easter Sunday** *n* Ostersonntag *m*

**East Germany** *n* Ostdeutschland *nt*; **eastwards** *adv* nach Osten

**easy** *adj* leicht; (*task, solution*) einfach; (*life*) bequem; (*manner*) ungezwungen; **easy-going** *adj* gelassen

**eat** *vt* essen; (*animal*) fressen; **eat out** *vi* zum Essen ausgehen; **eat up** *vt* aufessen

**eaten** *pp* → **eat**

**eavesdrop** *vi* (heimlich) lauschen; **~ on sb** jdn belauschen

**eccentric** *adj* exzentrisch

**echo** 1. *n* Echo *nt* 2. *vi* widerhallen

**ecological** *adj* ökologisch; **~ disaster** Umweltkatastrophe *f*; **ecology** *n* Ökologie *f*

**economic** *adj* wirtschaftlich, Wirtschafts-; **economical** *adj* wirtschaftlich; (*person*) sparsam; **economics** *nsing or pl* Wirtschaftswissenschaft *f*; **economist** *n* Wirtschaftswissenschaftler(in) *m(f)*; **economize** *vi* sparen (**on** an + *dat*); **economy** *n* (*of state*) Wirtschaft *f*; (*thrift*) Sparsamkeit *f*; **economy class** *n* AVIAT Economyclass *f*

**ecstasy** *n* Ekstase *f*; *(drug)* Ecstasy *f*

**eczema** *n* Ekzem *nt*

**edge** *n* Rand *m*; *(of knife)* Schneide *f*; **on ~** nervös; **edgy** *adj* nervös

**edible** *adj* essbar

**Edinburgh** *n* Edinburg *nt*

**edit** *vt (series, newspaper etc)* herausgeben; *(text)* redigieren; *(film)* schneiden; IT editieren; **edition** *n* Ausgabe *f*; **editor** *n* Redakteur(in) *m(f)*; *(of series etc)* Herausgeber(in) *m(f)*

**educate** *vt (child)* erziehen; *(at school, university)* ausbilden; *(public)* aufklären; **educated** *adj* gebildet; **education** *n* Erziehung *f*; *(studies, training)* Ausbildung *f*; *(subject of study)* Pädagogik *f*; *(system)* Schulwesen *nt*; *(knowledge)* Bildung *f*; **educational** *adj* pädagogisch; **~ television** Schulfernsehen *nt*

**eel** *n* Aal *m*

**eerie** *adj* unheimlich

**effect** *n* Wirkung *f (on* auf + *acc)*; **come into ~** in Kraft treten; **effective** *adj* wirksam, effektiv

**efficiency** *n* Leistungsfähigkeit *f*; *(of method)* Wirksamkeit *f*; **efficient** *adj* TECH leistungsfähig; *(method)* wirksam, effizient

**effort** *n* Anstrengung *f*; *(attempt)* Versuch *m*; **make an**

**~ sich anstrengen; effortless** *adj* mühelos

**e.g.** *abbr = exempli gratia (for example)* z. B.

**egg** *n* Ei *nt*; **eggcup** *n* Eierbecher *m*; **eggplant** *n (US)* Aubergine *f*; **eggshell** *n* Eierschale *f*

**ego** *n* Ich *nt*; *(self-esteem)* Selbstbewusstsein *nt*

**Egypt** *n* Ägypten *nt*; **Egyptian 1.** *adj* ägyptisch **2.** *n* Ägypter(in) *m(f)*

**eiderdown** *n* Daunendecke *f*

**eight 1.** *num* acht; **at the age of ~** im Alter von acht Jahren; **it's ~** *(o'clock)* es ist acht Uhr **2.** *n (a. bus etc)* Acht *f*; *(boat)* Achter *m*; **eighteen 1.** *num* achtzehn **2.** *n* Achtzehn *f*; **~ eight; eighteenth** *adj* achtzehnte(r, s); **~ eighth; eighth 1.** *adj* achte(r, s); **the ~ of June** der achte Juni **2.** *n (fraction)* Achtel *nt*; **an ~ of a litre** ein Achtelliter; **eightieth** *adj* achtzigste(r, s); **~ eighth; eighty 1.** *num* achtzig **2.** *n* Achtzig *f*; **~ eight**

**Eire** *n* die Republik Irland

**either 1.** *conj* **~ ... or** entweder ... oder **2.** *pron* **~ of the two** eine(r, s) von beiden **3.** *adj* **on ~ side** auf beiden Seiten **4.** *adv* **I won't go ~** ich gehe auch nicht

**elaborate 1.** *adj (complex)* kompliziert; *(plan)* ausgeklügelt; *(decoration)* kunstvoll **2.** *vi* **could you ~ on that?** könntest du / könnten Sie mehr darüber sagen?

**elastic** *adj* elastisch; **~ band** Gummiband *nt*

**elbow** *n* Ellbogen *m*; **give sb the ~** *fam* jdm den Laufpass geben

**elder 1.** *adj* (*of two*) älter **2.** *n* Ältere(r) *mf*; вот Holunder *m*; **elderly 1.** *adj* ältere(r, s) **2. n the ~** die älteren Leute; **eldest** *adj* älteste(r, s)

**elect** *vt* wählen; **he was ~ed chairman** er wurde zum Vorsitzenden gewählt; **election** *n* Wahl *f*; **election campaign** *n* Wahlkampf *m*

**electric** *adj* elektrisch; (*car, motor, razor etc*) Elektro-; **~ blanket** Heizdecke *f*; **~ cooker** Elektroherd *m*; **~ current** elektrischer Strom; **~ shock** Stromschlag *m*; **electrical** *adj* elektrisch; **~ goods / appliances** Elektrogeräte; **electrician** *n* Elektriker(in) *m(f)*; **electricity** *n* Elektrizität *f*; **electronic** *adj* elektronisch

**elegant** *adj* elegant

**element** *n* Element *nt*; **an ~ of truth** ein Körnchen Wahrheit; **elementary** *adj* einfach; (*basic*) grundlegend; **~ stage** Anfangsstadium *nt*; **~ school** (*US*) Grundschule *f*; **maths / French** Grundkenntnisse in Mathematik / Französisch

**elephant** *n* Elefant *m*

**elevator** *n* (*US*) Fahrstuhl *m*

**eleven 1.** *num* elf **2.** *n* (*team, bus etc*) Elf *f* → *eighth*; **eleventh 1.** *adj* elfte(r, s) **2.** *n* (*fraction*) Elftel *nt* → *eighth*

**eligible** *adj* infrage kommend; (*for grant etc*) berechtigt; **~ bachelor** begehrter Junggeselle

**eliminate** *vt* ausschließen (*from* aus), ausschalten; (*problem etc*) beseitigen

**elm** *n* Ulme *f*

**elope** *vi* durchbrennen (*with sb* mit jdm)

**eloquent** *adj* redegewandt

**else** *adv* **anybody / anything ~** (*in addition*) sonst (noch) jemand / etwas; (*other*) ein anderer / etwas anderes; **somebody ~** jemand anders; **everyone ~** alle anderen; **or ~** sonst; **elsewhere** *adv* anderswo, woanders; (*direction*) woandershin

**ELT** *abbr* = **English Language Teaching**

**e-mail, E-mail 1.** *vi, vt* mailen (*sth to sb* jdm etw) **2.** *n* (*message*) E-Mail *f*; **e-mail address** *n* E-Mail-Adresse *f*

**embankment** *n* Böschung *f*; (*for railway*) Bahndamm *m*

**embargo** *n* Embargo *nt*

**embark** *vi* an Bord gehen

**embarrass** *vt* in Verlegenheit bringen; **embarrassed** *adj* verlegen; **embarrassing** *adj* peinlich embassy n Botschaft f

embrace 1. vt umarmen 2. n Umarmung f

embroider vt besticken; embroidery n Stickerei f

embryo n Embryo m

emerge vi auftauchen; it ~d that ... es stellte sich heraus, dass ...

emergency 1. n Notfall m 2. adj Not-; ~ exit Notausgang m; ~ landing Notlandung f; ~ room (US) Notaufnahme f; ~ service Notdienst m; ~ stop Vollbremsung f

emigrate vi auswandern

emotion n Emotion f, Gefühl nt; emotional adj (person) emotional; (experience, moment, scene) ergreifend

emperor n Kaiser m

emphasis n Betonung f; emphasize vt betonen; emphatic, emphatically adj, adv nachdrücklich

empire n Reich nt

employ vt beschäftigen; (hire) anstellen; (use) anwenden; employee n Angestellte/r mf; employer n Arbeitgeber(in) m(f); employment n Beschäftigung f; (position) Stellung f

empress n Kaiserin f

empty 1. adj leer 2. vt (contents) leeren; (container) ausleeren

enable vt ~ sb to do sth es jdm ermöglichen, etw zu tun

enamel n Email nt; (of teeth) Zahnschmelz m

enchanting adj bezaubernd

enclose vt einschließen; (in letter) beilegen (in, with dat); enclosure n (for animals) Gehege nt; (in letter) Anlage f

encore n Zugabe f

encounter 1. n Begegnung f 2. vt (person) begegnen + dat; (difficulties) stoßen auf + acc

encourage vt ermutigen; encouragement n Ermutigung f

encyclopaedia n Lexikon nt, Enzyklopädie f

end 1. n Ende nt; (of film, play etc) Schluss m; (purpose) Zweck m; at the ~ of May Ende Mai; in the ~ schließlich; come to an ~ zu Ende gehen 2. vt beenden 3. vi enden; end up vi enden

endanger vt gefährden; ~ed species vom Aussterben bedrohte Art

ending n (of book) Ausgang m; (last part) Schluss m; (of word) Endung f; endless adj endlos; (possibilities) unendlich

endurance n Ausdauer f; endure vt ertragen

enemy 1. n Feind(in) m(f) 2. adj feindlich

energetic adj energiegeladen; (active) aktiv; energy n Energie f

enforce vt durchsetzen; (obe-

*dience*) erzwingen

**engage** *vt* (*employ*) einstellen; (*singer, performer*) engagieren; **engaged** *adj* verlobt; (*toilet, telephone line*) besetzt; **get** ~ sich verloben (*to* mit); **engaged tone** *n* (*Brit*) TEL Belegzeichen *nt*; **engagement** *n* (*marry*) Verlobung *f*

**engine** *n* AUTO Motor *m*; RAIL Lokomotive *f*; ~ **failure** AUTO Motorschaden *m*; ~ **trouble** AUTO Defekt *m* am Motor; **engineer** *n* Ingenieur(in) *m(f)*; (*US*) RAIL Lokomotivführer(in) *m(f)*; **engineering** *n* Technik *f*; (*mechanical engineering*) Maschinenbau *m*; (*subject*) Ingenieurwesen *nt*; **engine immobilizer** *n* AUTO Wegfahrsperre *f*

**England** *n* England *nt*; **English 1.** *adj* englisch; **he's** ~ er ist Engländer; **the** ~ **Channel** *der* Ärmelkanal **2.** *n* (*language*) Englisch *nt*; **in** ~ auf Englisch; **translate into** ~ ins Englische übersetzen; (*people*) **the** ~ *pl* die Engländer; **Englishman** *n* Engländer *m*; **Englishwoman** *n* Engländerin *f*

**engrave** *vt* eingravieren; **engraving** *n* Stich *m*

**engrossed** *adj* vertieft (*in sth* in etw *acc*)

**enjoy** *vt* genießen; **I** ~ **reading** ich lese gern; **he** ~**s teasing her** es macht ihm Spaß, sie

aufzuziehen; **did you** ~ **the film?** hat dir der Film gefallen?; **enjoyable** *adj* angenehm; (*entertaining*) unterhaltsam; **enjoyment** *n* Vergnügen *nt*; (*stronger*) Freude *f* (*of* an + *dat*)

**enlarge** *vt* vergrößern; (*expand*) erweitern; **enlargement** *n* Vergrößerung *f*

**enormous, enormously** *adj, adv* riesig, ungeheuer

**enough 1.** *adj* genug; **that's** ~ das reicht!; (*stop it*) Schluss damit!; **I've had** ~ das hat mir gereicht; (*eat*) ich bin satt **2.** *adv* genug, genügend

**enquire** *vi* sich erkundigen (*about* nach); **enquiry** *n* (*question*) Anfrage *f*; (*for information*) Erkundigung *f* (*about* über + *acc*); (*investigation*) Untersuchung *f*; '**Enquiries**' „Auskunft"

**enrol** *vi* sich einschreiben; (*for course, school*) sich anmelden; **enrolment** *n* Einschreibung *f*, Anmeldung *f*

**en suite** *adj*, **room with** ~ (**bathroom**) Zimmer *nt* mit eigenem Bad

**ensure** *vt* sicherstellen

**enter 1.** *vt* eintreten in + *acc*, betreten; (*drive into*) einfahren in + *acc*; (*country*) einreisen in + *acc*; (*in list*) eintragen; IT eingeben; (*race, contest*) teilnehmen an + *dat* **2.** *vi* (*towards speaker*) hereinkommen; (*away from speak-*

*er)* hineingehen

**enterprise** *n* COMM Unternehmen *nt*

**entertain** *vt (guest)* bewirten; *(amuse)* unterhalten; **entertaining** *adj* unterhaltsam; **entertainment** *n (amusement)* Unterhaltung *f*

**enthusiasm** *n* Begeisterung *f*; **enthusiastic** *adj* begeistert *(about* von)

**entire, entirely** *adj, adv* ganz

**entitle** *vt (qualify)* berechtigen *(to* zu); *(name)* betiteln

**entrance** *n* Eingang *m*; *(for vehicles)* Einfahrt *f*; *(entering)* Eintritt *m*; THEAT Auftritt *m*; **entrance exam** *n* Aufnahmeprüfung *f*; **entrance fee** *n* Eintrittsgeld *nt*

**entrust** *vt ~* **sb with sth** jdm etw anvertrauen

**entry** *n (way in)* Eingang *m*; *(entering)* Eintritt *m*; *(in vehicle)* Einfahrt *f*; *(into country)* Einreise *f*; *(admission)* Zutritt *m*; *(in diary, accounts)* Eintrag *m*; **'no ~'** „Eintritt verboten"; *(for vehicles)* „Einfahrt verboten"; **entry phone** *n* Türsprechanlage *f*

**envelope** *n (Brief )umschlag *m*

**enviable** *adj* beneidenswert; **envious** *adj* neidisch

**environment** *n* Umgebung *f*; *(ecology)* Umwelt *f*; **environmental** *adj* Umwelt-; **environmentalist** *n* Umwelt-

schützer(in) *m(f)*

**envy 1.** *n* Neid *m (of* auf *+ acc)* **2.** *vt* beneiden *(sb* sth jdn um etw)

**epidemic** *n* Epidemie *f*

**epilepsy** *n* Epilepsie *f*; **epileptic** *adj* epileptisch

**episode** *n* Episode *f*; TV Folge *f*

**epoch** *n* Zeitalter *nt*, Epoche *f*

**equal 1.** *adj* gleich *(to + dat)* **2.** *n* Gleichgestellte(r) *mf* **3.** *vt* gleichen; *(match)* gleichkommen *+ dat*; **two times two ~s four** zwei mal zwei ist gleich vier; **equality** *n* Gleichheit *f*; *(equal rights)* Gleichberechtigung *f*; **equalize** *vi* SPORT ausgleichen; **equalizer** *n* SPORT Ausgleichstreffer *m*; **equally** *adv* gleich; *(on the other hand)* andererseits; **equation** *n* MATH Gleichung *f*

**equator** *n* Äquator *m*

**equilibrium** *n* Gleichgewicht *nt*

**equip** *vt* ausrüsten; *(kitchen)* ausstatten; **equipment** *n* Ausrüstung *f*; *(for kitchen)* Ausstattung *f*; **electrical ~** Elektrogeräte *pl*

**equivalent 1.** *adj* gleichwertig *(to* dat); *(corresponding)* entsprechend *(to* dat) **2.** *n* Äquivalent *nt*; *(amount)* gleiche Menge; *(in money)* Gegenwert *m*

**era** *n* Ära *f*, Zeitalter *nt*

**erase** *vt* ausradieren; *(tape, disk)* löschen; **eraser** *n* Radiergummi *m*

**erect 1.** *adj* aufrecht **2.** *vt (building, monument)* errichten; *(tent)* aufstellen; **erection** *n* Errichtung *f*; ANAT Erektion *f*

**erotic** *adj* erotisch

**err** *vi* sich irren

**erratic** *adj (behaviour)* unberechenbar; *(bus link etc)* unregelmäßig; *(performance)* unbeständig

**error** *n* Fehler *m*; **error message** *n* IT Fehlermeldung *f*

**erupt** *vi* ausbrechen

**escalator** *n* Rolltreppe *f*

**escalope** *n* Schnitzel *nt*

**escape 1.** *n* Flucht *f*; *(from prison etc)* Ausbruch *m*; **there's no ~** es gibt keinen Ausweg; **have a narrow ~** gerade noch davonkommen **2.** *vt (pursuers)* entkommen + *dat*; *(punishment etc)* entgehen + *dat* **3.** *vi (from pursuers)* entkommen *(from dat)*; *(from prison etc)* ausbrechen *(from dat)*; *(leak: gas)* ausströmen; *(water)* auslaufen

**escort 1.** *n (companion)* Begleiter(in) *m(f)*; *(guard)* Eskorte *f* **2.** *vt (lady)* begleiten

**especially** *adv* besonders

**espionage** *n* Spionage *f*

**essay** *n* Aufsatz *m*; *(literary)* Essay *m*

**essential 1.** *adj (necessary)* unentbehrlich, unverzichtbar; *(basic)* wesentlich **2.** *n* **the ~s** *pl* das Wesentliche; **essentially** *adv* im Wesentlichen

**establish** *vt (set up)* gründen; *(introduce)* einführen; *(relations)* aufnehmen; *(prove)* nachweisen; **~ that ...** feststellen, dass ...; **establishment** *n* Institution *f*; *(business)* Unternehmen *nt*

**estate** *n* Gut *nt*; *(housing ~)* Siedlung *f*; *(country house)* Landsitz *m*; **estate agent** *n (Brit)* Grundstücksmakler(in) *m(f)*, Immobilienmakler(in) *m(f)*; **estate car** *n (Brit)* Kombiwagen *m*

**estimate 1.** *n* Schätzung *f*; COMM *(of price)* Kostenvoranschlag *m* **2.** *vt* schätzen

**Estonia** *n* Estland *nt*; **Estonian 1** *adj* estnisch **2** *n (person)* Este *m*, Estin *f*; *(language)* Estnisch *nt*

**estuary** *n* Mündung *f*

**etching** *n* Radierung *f*

**eternal, eternally** *adj, adv* ewig; **eternity** *n* Ewigkeit *f*

**ethical** *adj* ethisch; **ethics** *npl* Ethik *f*

**Ethiopia** *n* Äthiopien *nt*

**ethnic** *adj* ethnisch; *(clothes etc)* landesüblich; **~ minority** ethnische Minderheit

**EU** *abbr* = **European Union** EU *f*

**euro** *n* FIN Euro *m*; **Europe** *n*

Europa *nt*; **European 1.** *adj*
europäisch; **~ Parliament**
Europäisches Parlament; **~
Union** Europäische Union
**2.** *n* Europäer(in) *m(f)*; **Eu-
rosceptic** *n* Euroskepti-
ker(in) *m(f)*; **Eurotunnel** *n*
Eurotunnel *m*

**evacuate** *vt* (*place*) räumen;
(*people*) evakuieren

**evaluate** *vt* auswerten

**evaporate** *vi* verdampfen; *fig*
verschwinden; **~d milk** Kon-
densmilch *f*

**even 1.** *adj* (*flat*) eben; (*regular*) gleichmäßig; (*equal*)
gleich; (*number*) gerade;
**the score is ~** es steht unentschieden **2.** *adv* sogar; **~ you**
selbst (*or* sogar) du / Sie; **~ if**
selbst wenn, wenn auch; **~
though** obwohl; **not ~** nicht
einmal; **~ better** noch besser; **even out** *vi* (*prices*) sich
einpendeln

**evening** *n* Abend *m*; **in the ~**
abends, am Abend; **this ~**
heute Abend; **evening
class** *n* Abendkurs *m*; **evening dress** *f* (*generally*)
Abendkleidung *f*; (*wom-
an's*) Abendkleid *nt*

**evenly** *adv* gleichmäßig

**event** *n* Ereignis *nt*; (*organized*) Veranstaltung *f*; SPORT
(*discipline*) Disziplin *f*; **in
the ~ of** im Falle + gen

**eventual** *adj* (*final*) letztend-
lich; **eventually** *adv* (*at last*)
am Ende; (*given time*)

schließlich

**ever** *adv* (*at any time*) je(mals);
**don't ~ do that again** tu /
tun Sie das ja nie wieder;
**he's the best.~** er ist der Beste, den es je gegeben hat;
**have you ~ been to the
States?** bist du / sind Sie
schon einmal in den Staaten
gewesen?; **for ~** (für) immer;
**for ~ and ~** auf immer und
ewig; **~ so ...** *fam* äußerst
...;; **~ so drunk** ganz schön
betrunken

**every** *adj* jeder / jede / jedes;
**~ day** jeden Tag; **~ other
day** jeden zweiten Tag; **~ five
days** alle fünf Tage; **I have ~
reason to believe that ...** ich
habe allen Grund anzuneh-
men, dass ...; **everybody**
*pron* jeder, alle *pl*; **everyday**
*adj* (*commonplace*) alltäglich; (*clothes, language etc*)
Alltags-; **everyone** *pron* jeder, alle *pl*; **everything** *pron*
alles; **everywhere** *adv* überall; (*with direction*) überall-
hin

**evidence** *n* Beweise *pl*; (*single piece*) Beweis *m*; (*testi-
mony*) Aussage *f*; **evident,
evidently** *adj*, *adv* offensichtlich

**evil 1.** *adj* böse **2.** *n* Böse(s) *nt*

**evolution** *n* Entwicklung *f*;
(*of life*) Evolution *f*; **evolve**
*vi* sich entwickeln

**ex-** *pref* Ex-, ehemalig; **~boy-
friend** Exfreund; **~wife** frü-

here Frau, Exfrau f; **ex** n fam Verflossene(r) mf, Ex mf

**exact** adj genau; **exactly** adv genau; **not ~ fast** nicht gerade schnell

**exaggerate** vt, vi übertreiben; **exaggerated** adj übertrieben; **exaggeration** n Übertreibung f

**exam** n Prüfung f; **examination** n MED (etc) Untersuchung f, Prüfung f; (at university) Examen nt; (at customs etc) Kontrolle f; **examine** vt untersuchen (for auf + acc); (check) kontrollieren, prüfen; **examiner** n Prüfer(in) m(f)

**example** n Beispiel nt (of für + acc); **for ~** zum Beispiel

**excavation** n Ausgrabung f

**exceed** vt überschreiten, übertreffen; **exceedingly** adv äußerst

**excel 1.** vt übertreffen **2.** vi sich auszeichnen (in in + dat, at bei); **excellent, excellently** adj, adv ausgezeichnet

**except 1.** prep ~ außer + dat; ~ **for** abgesehen von **2.** vt ausnehmen; **exception** n Ausnahme f; **exceptional, exceptionally** adj, adv außergewöhnlich

**excess** n Übermaß nt (of an + dat); **excess baggage** n Übergepäck nt; **excessive, excessively** adj, adv übermäßig; **excess weight** n

Übergewicht nt

**exchange 1.** n Austausch m (for gegen); (of bought items) Umtausch m (for gegen); FIN Wechsel m; TEL Vermittlung f, Zentrale f **2.** vt austauschen; (goods) tauschen; (bought items) umtauschen (for gegen); (money, blows) wechseln; **exchange rate** n Wechselkurs m

**excited** adj aufgeregt; **exciting** adj aufregend; (book, film) spannend

**exclamation** n Ausruf m; **exclamation mark, exclamation point** (US) n Ausrufezeichen nt

**exclude** vt ausschließen; **exclusion** n Ausschluss m; **exclusive** adj (select) exklusiv; (sole) ausschließlich; **exclusively** adv ausschließlich

**excruciating** adj fürchterlich, entsetzlich

**excursion** n Ausflug m

**excuse 1.** vt entschuldigen; ~ **me** Entschuldigung! **2.** n Entschuldigung f, Ausrede f

**ex-directory** adj **be ~** (Brit) TEL nicht im Telefonbuch stehen

**execution** n (killing) Hinrichtung f; **executive** n leitender Angestellter, leitende Angestellte

**exemplary** adj beispielhaft

**exercise** n (in school, sports) Übung f; (movement) Bewegung f; **get more ~** mehr

Sport treiben

**exert** vt (influence) ausüben

**exhaust** n (fumes) Abgase pl; AUTO ~ **(pipe)** Auspuff m; **exhausted** adj erschöpft; **exhausting** adj anstrengend

**exhibit** n (in exhibition) Ausstellungsstück nt; **exhibition** n Ausstellung f; **exhibitionist** n Selbstdarsteller(in) m(f)

**exhilarating** adj belebend, erregend

**exile 1.** n Exil nt; (person) Verbannte(r) mf **2.** vt verbannen

**exist** vi existieren; (live) leben (on von); **existence** n Existenz f; **come into ~** entstehen; **existing** adj bestehend

**exit** n Ausgang m; (for vehicles) Ausfahrt f

**exotic** adj exotisch

**expand 1.** vt ausdehnen, erweitern **2.** vi sich ausdehnen; **expansion** n Expansion f, Erweiterung f

**expect 1.** vt erwarten; (suppose) annehmen; **he ~s me to do it** er erwartet, dass ich es mache; **I ~ it'll rain** es wird wohl regnen; **I ~ so** ich denke schon **2.** vi **she's ~ing** sie erwartet ein Kind

**expenditure** n Ausgaben pl

**expense** n Kosten pl; (single cost) Ausgabe f; (business) ~**s** pl Spesen pl; **at sb's ~** auf jds Kosten; **expensive** adj teuer

**experience 1.** n Erfahrung f;

(particular incident) Erlebnis nt; **by / from ~** aus Erfahrung **2.** vt erfahren, erleben; (hardship) durchmachen; **experienced** adj erfahren

**experiment 1.** n Versuch m, Experiment nt **2.** vi experimentieren

**expert 1.** n Experte m, Expertin f; (professional) Fachmann m, Fachfrau f; LAW Sachverständige(r) mf **2.** adj fachmännisch, Fach-; **expertise** n Sachkenntnis f

**expire** vi (end) ablaufen; **expiry date** n Verfallsdatum nt

**explain** vt erklären (sth to sb jdm etw); **explanation** n Erklärung f

**explicit** adj ausdrücklich, eindeutig

**explode** vi explodieren

**exploit** vt ausbeuten

**explore** vt erforschen

**explosion** n Explosion f; **explosive 1.** adj explosiv **2.** n Sprengstoff m

**export 1.** vt, vi exportieren **2.** n Export m **3.** adj (trade) Export-

**expose** vt (to danger etc) aussetzen (to dat); (uncover) freilegen; (imposter) entlarven; **exposed** adj (position) ungeschützt; **exposure** n MED Unterkühlung f; PHOT (time) Belichtung(szeit) f; **24 ~s** 24 Aufnahmen

**express 1.** adj (speedy) Express-, Schnell-; **~ delivery**

Eilzustellung f **2.** n RAIL Schnellzug m **3.** vt ausdrücken **4.** vr ~ **oneself** sich ausdrücken; **expression** n (phrase) Ausdruck m; (look) Gesichtsausdruck m; **expressway** n (US) Schnellstraße f

**extend** vt (arms) ausstrecken; (lengthen) verlängern; (building) vergrößern, ausbauen; (business, limits) erweitern; **extension** n (lengthening) Verlängerung f; (of building) Anbau m; TEL Anschluss m; **extensive** adj (knowledge) umfangreich; (use) häufig; **extent** n (length) Länge f; (size) Ausdehnung f; (scope) Umfang m, Ausmaß nt; **to a certain / large** ~ in gewissem / hohem Maße

**exterior** n Äußere(s) nt
**external** adj äußere(r, s), Außen-; **externally** adv äußerlich
**extinct** adj (species) ausgestorben
**extinguish** vt löschen; **extinguisher** n Löschgerät nt
**extra 1.** adj zusätzlich; ~ **charge** Zuschlag m; ~ **time** SPORT Verlängerung f **2.** adv besonders; ~ **large** (clothing)

übergroß **3.** npl ~**s** zusätzliche Kosten pl; (food) Beilagen pl; (accessories) Zubehör nt; (for car etc) Extras pl
**extract 1.** vt herausziehen (from aus); (tooth) ziehen **2.** n (from book etc) Auszug m

**extraordinary** adj außerordentlich; (unusual) ungewöhnlich; (amazing) erstaunlich
**extreme 1.** adj äußerste(r, s); (drastic) extrem **2.** n Extrem nt; **extremely** adv äußerst, höchst; **extreme sports** npl Extremsportarten pl; **extremist 1.** adj extremistisch **2.** n Extremist m
**extrovert** adj extrovertiert
**exultation** n Jubel m
**eye 1.** n Auge nt; **keep an** ~ **on sb / sth** auf jdn / etw aufpassen **2.** vt mustern; **eyebrow** n Augenbraue f; **eyelash** n Wimper f; **eyelid** n Augenlid nt; **eyeliner** n Eyeliner m; **eyeopener** n **that was an** ~ das hat mir die Augen geöffnet; **eyeshadow** n Lidschatten m; **eyesight** n Sehkraft f; **eyesore** n Schandfleck m; **eye witness** n Augenzeuge m, Augenzeugin f

# F

**fabric** n Stoff m

**fabulous** adj sagenhaft

**façade** n Fassade f

**face 1.** n Gesicht nt; (of clock) Zifferblatt nt; (of mountain) Wand f; **in the ~ of** trotz + gen; **be ~ to ~** (people) einander gegenüberstehen **2.** vt, vi (person) gegenüberstehen + dat; (at table) gegenübersitzen + dat; **~ north** (room) nach Norden gehen; **~ (up to) the facts** den Tatsachen ins Auge sehen; **be ~d with sth** mit etw konfrontiert sein

**facet** n fig Aspekt m

**face value** n Nennwert m

**facial 1.** adj Gesichts- **2.** n fam (kosmetische) Gesichtsbehandlung

**facilitate** vt erleichtern

**facility** n (building etc to be used) Einrichtung f, Möglichkeit f

**fact** n Tatsache f; **as a matter of ~, in ~** eigentlich, tatsächlich

**factor** n Faktor m

**factory** n Fabrik f; **factory outlet** n Fabrikverkauf m

**factual** adj sachlich

**faculty** n Fähigkeit f; (at university) Fakultät f; (US, teaching staff) Lehrkörper m

**fade** vi verblassen

**fag** n (Brit) fam (cigarette) Kippe f; (US) fam pej Schwule(r) m

**Fahrenheit** n Fahrenheit

**fail 1.** vt (exam) nicht bestehen **2.** vi versagen; (plan, marriage) scheitern; (student) durchfallen; (eyesight) nachlassen; **words ~ me** ich bin sprachlos; **failure** n (person) Versager(in) m(f); (act) Versagen nt; (of engine etc) Ausfall m; (of plan, marriage) Scheitern nt

**faint 1.** adj schwach; (sound) leise; fam **I haven't the ~est** (idea) ich habe keinen blassen Schimmer **2.** vi ohnmächtig werden (with vor + dat); **faintness** n MED Schwächegefühl nt

**fair 1.** adj (hair) (dunkel)blond; (skin) hell; (just) gerecht, fair; (reasonable) ganz ordentlich; (in school) befriedigend; (weather) schön; (wind) günstig; **a ~ number / amount of** ziemlich viele / viel **2.** adv play **~** fair spielen; fig fair sein; **~ enough** in Ordnung! **3.** n (funfair) Jahrmarkt m; COMM Messe f; **fair-haired** adj (dunkel)blond; **fairly** adv (honestly) fair; (rather) ziemlich

**fairy** n Fee f; **fairy tale** n Märchen nt

**faith** n (trust) Vertrauen nt (in sb zu jdm); REL Glaube m; **faithful, faithfully** adj, adv treu; **Yours ~ly** Hochachtungsvoll

**fake 1.** n (thing) Fälschung f **2.** adj vorgetäuscht **3.** vt fälschen

**fall 1.** vi fallen; (from a height, badly) stürzen; **~ ill** krank werden; **~ asleep** einschlafen; **~ in love** sich verlieben **2.** n Fall m; (accident) Sturz m; (decrease) Sinken nt (in + gen); (US, autumn) Herbst m; **fall apart** vi auseinanderfallen; **fall behind** vi zurückbleiben; (with work, rent) in Rückstand geraten; **fall down** vi (person) hinfallen; **fall off** vi herunterfallen; (decrease) zurückgehen; **fall out** vi herausfallen; (quarrel) sich streiten; **fall over** vi hinfallen; **fall through** vi (plan etc) ins Wasser fallen

**fallen** pp → **fall**

**false** adj falsch; (artificial) künstlich; **false alarm** n blinder Alarm; **false start** n in SPORT Fehlstart m; **false teeth** npl (künstliches) Gebiss

**fame** n Ruhm m

**familiar** adj vertraut, bekannt; **be ~ with** vertraut sein mit, gut kennen; **familiarity** n Vertrautheit f

**family** n Familie f; (including relations) Verwandtschaft f; **family man** n Familienvater m; **family name** n Familienname m, Nachname m; **family practitioner** n (US) Allgemeinarzt m, Allgemeinärztin f

**famine** n Hungersnot f

**famous** adj berühmt

**fan** n (hand-held) Fächer m; ELEC Ventilator m; (admirer) Fan m

**fanatic** n Fanatiker(in) m(f)

**fancy 1.** adj (elaborate) kunstvoll; (unusual) ausgefallen **2.** vt (like) gernhaben; **he fancies her** er steht auf sie; **~ that** stell dir vor!, so was!; **fancy dress** n Kostüm nt, Verkleidung f

**fan heater** n Heizlüfter m

**fantasise** vi träumen (about von); **fantastic** adj fantastisch; **that's ~** fam das ist ja toll!; **fantasy** n Fantasie f

**far 1.** adj weit; **the ~ end of the room** das andere Ende des Zimmers; **the Far East** der Ferne Osten **2.** adv weit; **~ better** viel besser; **by ~ the best** bei weitem der / die / das Beste; **as ~ as ...** bis zum or zur ...; (with place name) bis nach ...; **as ~ as I'm concerned** was mich betrifft, von mir aus; **so ~** soweit, bisher; **faraway** adj weit entfernt; (look) verträumt

**fare** n Fahrpreis m

**farm** n Bauernhof m, Farm f; **farmer** n Bauer m, Bäuerin f, Landwirt(in) m(f); **farmhouse** n Bauernhaus nt; **farming** n Landwirtschaft f; **farmland** n Ackerland nt; **farmyard** n Hof m

**far-reaching** adj weit reichend; **far-sighted** adj weitsichtig

**fart 1.** n fam Furz m; **old~** fam (person) alter Sack **2.** vi fam furzen

**farther** adj, adv comparative → **far**; **farthest** adj, adv superlative → **far**, → **furthest**

**fascinating** adj faszinierend; **fascination** n Faszination f

**fashion** n (clothes) Mode f; (manner) Art (und Weise) f; **be in ~** (in) Mode sein; **out of ~** unmodisch; **fashionable**, **fashionably** adj, adv (clothes, person) modisch

**fast 1.** adj schnell **be ~** (clock) vorgehen **2.** adv schnell; (firmly) fest; **be ~ asleep** fest schlafen **3.** n Fasten nt **4.** vi fasten

**fasten** vt (attach) befestigen (to an + dat); (do up) zumachen; **~ your seatbelts** bitte anschnallen; **fastener**, **fastening** n Verschluss m

**fast food** n Fast Food nt; **fast forward** n (for tape) Schnellvorlauf m; **fast lane** n Über-

holspur f

**fat 1.** adj dick; (meat) fett **2.** n Fett nt

**fatal** adj tödlich

**fat-free** adj (food) fettfrei

**father 1.** n Vater m; (priest) Pfarrer m **2.** vt (child) zeugen; **Father Christmas** n der Weihnachtsmann; **father-in-law** n Schwiegervater m

**fatigue** n Ermüdung f

**fattening** adj **be ~** dick machen; **fatty** adj (food) fettig

**faucet** n (US) Wasserhahn m

**fault** n Fehler m; TECH Defekt m; ELEC Störung f; (blame) Schuld f; **it's your ~** du bist daran schuld; **faulty** adj fehlerhaft; TECH defekt

**favor** (US), **favour** n **1.** (approval) Gunst f; (kindness) Gefallen m; **in ~ of** für; **I'm in ~ (of going)** ich bin dafür(, dass wir gehen); **do sb a ~** jdm einen Gefallen tun **2.** vt (prefer) vorziehen; **favourite** n Liebling m, Favorit(in) m(f) **3.** adj Lieblings-

**fax 1.** vt faxen **2.** n Fax nt; **fax number** n Faxnummer f

**FBI** abbr = **Federal Bureau of Investigation** FBI nt

**fear 1.** n Angst f (of vor + dat) **2.** vt befürchten; **fearful** adj (timid) ängstlich, furchtsam; (terrible) fürchterlich

**feasible** adj machbar

**feast** n Festessen nt

**feather** n Feder f

**feature 1.** n (facial) (Gesichts)zug m; (characteristic) Merkmal nt; (of car etc) Ausstattungsmerkmal nt; (in the press) Feature nt **2.** vt bringen, (als Besonderheit) zeigen; **feature film** n Spielfilm m

**February** n Februar m; → **September**

**fed** pt, pp → **feed**

**federal** adj Bundes-; **the Federal Republic of Germany** die Bundesrepublik Deutschland

**fed-up** adj **be ~ with** etw satthaben; **I'm ~** ich habe die Nase voll

**fee** n Gebühr f; (of doctor, lawyer) Honorar nt

**feeble** adj schwach

**feed 1.** vt (baby, animal) füttern; (support) ernähren **2.** n (for baby) Mahlzeit f; (for animals) Futter nt; IT (paper feed) Zufuhr f; **feed in** vt (information) eingeben; **feedback** n (information) Feed-back nt

**feel 1.** vt (sense) fühlen; (pain) empfinden; (think) meinen **2.** vi (person) sich fühlen; **I ~ cold** mir ist kalt; **do you ~ like a walk?** hast du Lust, spazieren zu gehen?; **feeling** n Gefühl nt

**feet** pl → **foot**

**fell 1.** pt → **fall 2.** vt (tree) fällen

**fellow** n Kerl m, Typ m; **~ citizen** Mitbürger(in) m(f)

**felt 1.** pt, pp → **feel 2.** n Filz m; **felt tip, felt-tip pen** n Filzstift m

**female 1.** n (of animals) Weibchen nt **2.** adj weiblich; **~ doctor** Ärztin f; **feminine** adj weiblich

**fence** n Zaun m

**fencing** n SPORT Fechten nt

**fender** n (US) AUTO Kotflügel m

**fennel** n Fenchel m

**fern** n Farn m

**ferocious** adj wild

**ferry 1.** n Fähre f **2.** vt übersetzen

**festival** n REL Fest nt; ART, MUS Festspiele pl; (pop music) Festival nt; **festive** adj festlich; **festivities** n Feierlichkeiten pl

**fetch** vt holen; (collect) abholen; (in sale, money) einbringen; **fetching** adj reizend

**fetish** n Fetisch m

**fetus** n (US) Fötus m

**fever** n Fieber nt; **feverish** adj MED fieberig; **fig** fieberhaft

**few** adj, pron ζ wenige pl; **a ~** pl ein paar; **fewer** adj weniger; **fewest** adj wenigste(r, s)

**fiancé** n Verlobte(r) m; **fiancée** n Verlobte f

**fiber** (US), **fibre** n Faser f; (material) Faserstoff m

**fiction** n (novels) Prosaliteratur f; **fictional, fictitious** adj erfunden

**fiddle 1.** n Geige f; (trick) Betrug m **2.** vt (accounts, results) frisieren; **fiddle with** vt herumfummeln an + dat

**fidelity** n Treue f

**fidget** vi zappeln; **fidgety** adj zappelig

**field** n Feld nt; (grass-covered) Wiese f; fig (of work) (Arbeits)gebiet nt

**fierce** adj heftig; (animal, appearance) wild; (criticism, competition) scharf

**fifteen 1.** num fünfzehn **2.** n Fünfzehn f; → **eight**; **fifteenth** adj fünfzehnte(r, s); → **eighth**; **fifth 1.** adj fünfte(r, s) **2.** n (fraction) Fünftel nt; → **eighth**; **fiftieth** adj fünfzigste(r, s); → **eighth**; **fifty 1.** num fünfzig **2.** n Fünfzig f; → **eight**

**fig** n Feige f

**fight 1.** vi kämpfen (with, against gegen, for, over um) **2.** vt (person) kämpfen mit; fig (disease, fire etc) bekämpfen **3.** n Kampf m; (brawl) Schlägerei f; (argument) Streit m; **fight back** vi zurückschlagen; **fight off** vt abwehren

**figurative** adj übertragen

**figure 1.** n (person) Gestalt f; (of person) Figur f; (number) Zahl f, Ziffer f; (amount) Betrag m; **a four-figure sum** eine vierstellige Summe **2.** vt (US, think) glauben **3.** vi (appear) erscheinen; **figure out**

vt (work out) herausbekommen; **I can't figure him out** ich werde aus ihm nicht schlau; **figure skating** n Eiskunstlauf m

**file 1.** n (tool) Feile f; (dossier) Akte f; IT Datei f; (folder) Aktenordner m; **on ~** in den Akten **2.** vt (metal, nails) feilen; (papers) ablegen (under unter)

**fill** vt füllen; (tooth) plombieren; (post) besetzen; **fill in** vt (hole) auffüllen; (form) ausfüllen; (tell) informieren (on über); **fill out** vt (form) ausfüllen; **fill up** vi AUTO volltanken

**fillet** n Filet nt

**filling** n GASTR Füllung f; (for tooth) Plombe f; **filling station** n Tankstelle f

**film 1.** n Film m **2.** vt (scene) filmen; **film star** n Filmstar m; **film studio** n Filmstudio nt

**filter 1.** n Filter m; (traffic lane) Abbiegespur f **2.** vt filtern

**filth** n Dreck m; **filthy** adj dreckig

**fin** n Flosse f

**final 1.** adj letzte(r, s); (stage, round) End-; (decision, version) endgültig; **~ score** Schlussstand m **2.** n SPORT Endspiel nt; (competition) Finale nt; **~s** pl, Abschlussexamen nt; **finalize** vt die endgültige Form geben

+ *dat*; **finally** *adv* (*lastly*) zuletzt; (*eventually*) schließlich, endlich

**finance 1.** *n* Finanzwesen *nt*; **~s** *pl* Finanzen *pl* **2.** *vt* finanzieren; **financial** *adj* finanziell; (*adviser, crisis, policy etc*) Finanz-

**find** *vt* finden; **he was found dead** er wurde tot aufgefunden; **I~ myself in difficulties** ich befinde mich in Schwierigkeiten; **she ~s it difficult / easy** es fällt ihr schwer / leicht; **find out** *vt* herausfinden; **findings** *npl* LAW Ermittlungsergebnis *nt*; MED Befund *m*

**fine 1.** *adj* (*thin*) dünn, fein; (*good*) gut; (*splendid*) herrlich; (*weather*) schön; **I'm ~** es geht mir gut; **that's ~** das ist OK **2.** *adv* (*well*) gut **3.** *n* LAW Geldstrafe *f* **4.** *vt* LAW mit einer Geldstrafe belegen; **fine arts** *npl* **the ~** die schönen Künste *pl*

**finger 1.** *n* Finger *m* **2.** *vt* herumfingern an + *dat*; **fingernail** *n* Fingernagel *m*; **fingerprint** *n* Fingerabdruck *m*; **fingertip** *n* Fingerspitze *f*

**finicky** *adj* (*person*) pingelig; (*work*) knifflig

**finish 1.** *n* Ende *nt*; SPORT Finish *nt*; (*line*) Ziel *nt*; (*of product*) Verarbeitung *f* **2.** *vt* beenden; (*book etc*) zu Ende lesen; (*food*) aufessen; (*drink*) austrinken **3.** *vi* zu

Ende gehen; (*song, story*) enden; (*person*) fertig sein; (*stop*) aufhören; **have you ~ed?** bist du fertig?; **~ first / second** SPORT als erster / zweiter durchs Ziel gehen; **finishing line** *n* Ziellinie *f*

**Finland** *n* Finnland *nt*; **Finn** *n* Finne *m*, Finnin *f*; **Finnish 1.** *adj* finnisch **2.** *n* (*language*) Finnisch *nt*

**fir** *n* Tanne *f*

**fire 1.** *n* Feuer *nt*; (*house etc*) Brand *m*; **set ~ to sth** etw in Brand stecken; **be on ~** brennen **2.** *vt* (*bullets, rockets*) abfeuern; *fam* (*dismiss*) feuern **3.** *vi* AUTO (*engine*) zünden; **~ at sb** auf jdn schießen; **fire alarm** *n* Feuermelder *m*; **fire brigade** *n* Feuerwehr *f*; **fire engine** *n* Feuerwehrauto *nt*; **fire escape** *n* Feuerleiter *f*; **fire extinguisher** *n* Feuerlöscher *m*; **firefighter** *n* Feuerwehrmann *m*, Feuerwehrfrau *f*; **fireman** *n* Feuerwehrmann *m*; **fireplace** *n* (offener) Kamin; **fireproof** *adj* feuerfest; **fire station** *n* Feuerwache *f*; **fireworks** *npl* Feuerwerk *nt*

**firm 1.** *adj* fest; (*person*) **be ~** entschlossen auftreten **2.** *n* Firma *f*

**first 1.** *adj* erste(r, s) **2.** *adv* (*at first*) zuerst; (*firstly*) erstens; (*arrive, finish*) als erste(r); (*happen*) zum ersten Mal; **~**

**of all** zuallererst **3.** n (person)
Erste(r) mf; AUTO (gear) erster Gang; **at ~** zuerst; anfangs; **first aid** n erste Hilfe;
**first-class 1.** adj erstklassig
(compartment, ticket) erster
Klasse; **~ mail** (Brit) bevorzugt beförderte Post **2.** adv
(travel) erster Klasse; **first floor** n (Brit) erster Stock;
(US) Erdgeschoss nt; **first lady** n (US) Frau f des Präsidenten; **firstly** adv erstens;
**first name** n Vorname m; **first night** n THEAT Premiere
f; **first-rate** adj erstklassig

**fir tree** n Tannenbaum m

**fish 1.** n Fisch m **2.** vi fischen;
(with rod) angeln; **go ~ing** fischen / angeln gehen

**fishbone** n Gräte f; **fish farm**
n Fischzucht f; **fish finger** n
(Brit) Fischstäbchen nt; **fishing** n Fischen nt; (with
rod) Angeln nt; **fishing boat**
n Fischerboot nt; **fishing line** n Angelschnur f; **fishing rod** n Angelrute f; **fishmonger** n Fischhändler(in)
m(f); **fish stick** n (US)
Fischstäbchen nt; **fish tank**
n Aquarium nt

**fishy** adj fam (suspicious) faul

**fist** n Faust f

**fit 1.** adj MED gesund; SPORT in
Form, fit; **keep ~** sich in
Form halten **2.** vt passen
+ dat; (attach) anbringen
(to an + dat); (install) einbauen (in in + acc) **3.** vi pas-

sen; (in space, gap) hineinpassen **4.** n (of clothes) Sitz
m; MED Anfall m; **it's a good
~** es passt gut; **fit in 1.** vt (accommodate) unterbringen;
(find time for) einschieben
**2.** vi (in space) hineinpassen;
(plans, ideas) passen; **he
doesn't ~ (here)** er passt
nicht hierher; **~ with sb's
plans** vereinbaren lassen; **fitness**
n MED Gesundheit f; SPORT
Fitness f; **fitness trainer** n
SPORT Fitnesstrainer(in)
m(f); **fitted carpet** n Teppichboden m; **fitted kitchen**
n Einbauküche f; **fitting 1.**
adj passend **2.** n (of dress)
Anprobe f; **~s** pl Ausstattung f

**five 1.** num fünf **2.** n Fünf f; →
**eight**; (money) n (Brit) fam
Fünfpfundschein m

**fix** vt befestigen (to an + dat);
(settle) festsetzen; (place,
time) ausmachen; (repair)
reparieren; **fixer** n (drug addict) Fixer(in) m(f); **fixture**
n **~s (and fittings)** pl Ausstattung f

**fizzy** adj sprudelnd; **~ drink**
Limo f

**flabbergasted** adj fam platt
**flabby** adj (fat) wabbelig
**flag** n Fahne f
**flake 1.** n Flocke f **2.** vi **~ (off)**
abblättern
**flamboyant** adj extravagant
**flame** n Flamme f; (person) **an**

**float**

*old* ~ eine alte Liebe

**flan** n (*fruit flan*) Obstkuchen m

**flannel 1.** n Flanell m; (*Brit, face flannel*) Waschlappen m **2.** vi herumlabern

**flap 1.** n Klappe f; *fam* **be in a** ~ **rotieren 2.** vt (*wings*) schlagen mit **3.** vi flattern

**flared** *adj* (*trousers*) mit Schlag; **flares** npl Schlaghose f

**flash 1.** n Blitz m; (*news flash*) Kurzmeldung f; PHOT Blitzlicht nt; **in a** ~ im Nu **2.** vt ~ **one's (head)lights** die Lichthupe betätigen **3.** vi aufblinken; (*brightly*) aufblitzen; **flashback** n Rückblende f; **flashlight** n PHOT Blitzlicht nt; (*US, torch*) Taschenlampe f; **flashy** *adj* grell, schrill; *pej* protzig

**flat 1.** *adj* flach; (*surface*) eben; (*drink*) abgestanden; (*tyre*) platt; (*battery*) leer; (*refusal*) glatt **2.** n (*Brit, rooms*) Wohnung f; AUTO Reifenpanne f; **flat screen** n TFT-Flachbildschirm m; **flatten** vt platt machen, einebnen

**flatter** vt schmeicheln + *dat*; **flattering** *adj* schmeichelhaft

**flatware** n (*US*) Besteck nt

**flavor** (*US*), **flavour 1.** n Geschmack m **2.** vt Geschmack geben + *dat*; (*with spices*) würzen; **flavouring** n Aroma nt

**flaw** n Fehler m; **flawless** *adj* fehlerlos; (*complexion*) makellos

**flea** n Floh m

**fled** pt, pp → **flee**

**flee** vi fliehen

**fleece** n (*of sheep*) Vlies nt; (*soft material*) Fleece m; (*jacket*) Fleecejacke f

**fleet** n Flotte f

**flesh** n Fleisch nt

**flew** pt → **fly**

**flex** n (*Brit*) ELEC Schnur f

**flexibility** n Biegsamkeit f; *fig* Flexibilität f; **flexible** *adj* biegsam; (*plans, person*) flexibel; **flexitime** n gleitende Arbeitszeit, Gleitzeit f

**flicker** vi flackern; TV flimmern

**flies** pl → **fly 2**

**flight** n Flug m; (*escape*) Flucht f; ~ **of stairs** Treppe f; **flight attendant** n Flugbegleiter(in) m(f); **flight recorder** n Flugschreiber m

**flimsy** *adj* schlecht gebaut, nicht stabil; (*thin*) hauchdünn; (*excuse*) fadenscheinig

**fling 1.** vt schleudern **2.** n **have a** ~ eine (kurze) Affäre haben

**flip** vt schnippen; ~ **a coin** eine Münze werfen; **flip through** vt (*book*) durchblättern; **flipchart** n Flipchart f

**flipper** n Flosse f

**flirt** vi flirten

**float** vi schwimmen; (*in air*)

schweben

**flock** n (of sheep) Herde f; (of birds) Schwarm m; (of people) Schar f

**flood 1.** n Hochwasser nt, Überschwemmung f; fig Flut f **2.** vt überschwemmen; **floodlight** n Flutlicht nt; **floodlit** adj (building) angestrahlt

**floor** n Fußboden m; (storey) Stock m; **ground ~** (Brit), **first ~** (US) Erdgeschoss nt; **first ~** (Brit), **second ~** (US) erster Stock

**flop 1.** n fam (failure) Reinfall m, Flop m **2.** vi misslingen, floppen

**floppy disk** n Diskette f

**Florence** n Florenz nt

**florist's (shop)** n Blumengeschäft nt

**flounder** n (fish) Flunder f

**flour** n Mehl nt

**flourish 1.** vi gedeihen; (business) gut laufen; (boom) florieren **2.** vt (wave about) schwenken; **flourishing** adj blühend

**flow 1.** n Fluss m; **go with the ~** mit dem Strom schwimmen **2.** vi fließen

**flower 1.** n Blume f **2.** vi blühen; **flower bed** n Blumenbeet nt; **flowerpot** n Blumentopf m

**flown** pp → **fly**

**flu** n fam Grippe f

**fluent** adj (Italian etc) fließend; **be ~ in German** fließend Deutsch sprechen

**fluid 1.** n Flüssigkeit f **2.** adj flüssig

**flung** pt, pp → **fling**

**flush 1.** n (lavatory) Wasserspülung f; (blush) Röte f **2.** vi (lavatory) spülen

**flute** n Flöte f

**fly 1.** vt, vi fliegen; **how time flies** wie die Zeit vergeht! **2.** n (insect) Fliege f; **~ /flies** pl (on trousers) Hosenschlitz m; **fly-drive** n Urlaub m mit Flug und Mietwagen; **flyover** n (Brit) Straßenüberführung f, Eisenbahnüberführung f; **flysheet** n Überzelt nt

**foal** n Fohlen nt

**foam 1.** n Schaum m **2.** vi schäumen

**focus 1.** n Brennpunkt m; **in / out of ~** (photo) scharf / unscharf **2.** vt (camera) scharf stellen **3.** vi sich konzentrieren (on auf + acc)

**foetus** n Fötus m

**fog** n Nebel m; **foggy** adj neblig; **fog light** n AUTO (at rear) Nebelschlussleuchte f

**foil** n Folie f

**fold 1.** vt falten **2.** vi fam (business) eingehen **3.** n Falte f; **fold up 1.** vt (map etc) zusammenfalten; (chair etc) zusammenklappen **2.** vi (business) fam eingehen; **folder** n (portfolio) Aktenmappe f; (pamphlet) Broschüre f; IT Ordner m; **folding** adj zusammenklappbar; (bicycle, chair) Klapp-

**folk 1.** n Leute pl; MUS Folk m; **my ~s** pl fam meine Leute **2.** adj Volks-

**follow 1.** vt folgen + dat; (pursue) verfolgen; (understand) folgen können + dat; (career, news etc) verfolgen; **as ~s** wie folgt **2.** vi folgen; (result) sich ergeben (from aus); **follow up** vt (request, rumour) nachgehen + dat, weiter verfolgen; **follower** n Anhänger(in) m(f); **following 1.** adj folgend; **the ~ day** am (darauf) folgenden Tag **2.** prep nach

**fond** adj **be ~ of** gernhaben; **fondly** adv (with love) liebevoll; **fondness** n Vorliebe f, (for people) Zuneigung f

**fondue** n Fondue nt

**font** n Taufbecken nt; TYPO Schrift(art) f

**food** n Essen nt, Lebensmittel pl; (for animals) Futter nt; **food poisoning** n Lebensmittelvergiftung f; **food processor** n Küchenmaschine f; **foodstuff** n Lebensmittel nt

**fool 1.** n Idiot m, Narr m; **make a ~ of oneself** sich blamieren **2.** vt (deceive) hereinlegen **3.** vi **~ around** herumalbern; (waste time) herumtrödeln; **foolish** adj dumm; **foolproof** adj idiotensicher

**foot 1.** n Fuß m; (measure) Fuß m (30,48 cm); **on ~** zu Fuß **2.** vt (bill) bezahlen; **foot-and-mouth disease** n Maul- und Klauenseuche f; **football** n Fußball m; (US) Football m; **footballer** n Fußballspieler(in) m(f); **footbridge** n Fußgängerbrücke f; **footing** n (hold) Halt m; **footnote** n Fußnote f; **footpath** n Fußweg m; **footprint** n Fußabdruck m; **footwear** n Schuhwerk nt

**for 1.** prep für; **I'm all ~ it** ich bin ganz dafür; (purpose) **what ~?** wozu?; (pleasure) **what's ~ lunch?** was gibt es zum Mittagessen?; (destination) **the train ~ London** der Zug nach London; (because of) **~ this reason** aus diesem Grund; **famous** bekannt für, berühmt wegen; (with time) **we talked ~ two hours** wir redeten zwei Stunden lang; (up to now) **we've been talking ~ two hours** wir reden seit zwei Stunden; (with distance) **~ miles (and miles)** meilenweit; **bends ~ 2 miles** kurvenreich auf 2 Meilen; **as ~ ...** was ... betrifft **2.** conj denn

**forbade** pt → **forbid**

**forbid** vt verbieten

**force 1.** n Kraft f, Gewalt f; **come into ~** in Kraft treten; **the Forces** pl die Streitkräfte **2.** vt zwingen; **forced** adj (*smile*) gezwungen

**forceps** *npl* Zange *f*

**forearm** *n* Unterarm *m*

**forecast 1.** *vt* voraussagen; (*weather*) vorhersagen **2.** *n* Vorhersage *f*

**forefinger** *n* Zeigefinger *m*

**foreground** *n* Vordergrund *m*

**forehand** *n* SPORT Vorhand *f*

**forehead** *n* Stirn *f*

**foreign** *adj* ausländisch; **foreigner** *n* Ausländer(in) *m(f)*; **foreign exchange** *n* Devisen *pl*; **foreign language** *n* Fremdsprache *f*; **foreign minister** *n* Außenminister(in) *m(f)*; **Foreign Office** *n* (*Brit*) Außenministerium *nt*; **Foreign Secretary** *n* (*Brit*) Außenminister(in) *m(f)*

**foremost** *adj* erste(r, s); (*leading*) führend

**forerunner** *n* Vorläufer(in) *m(f)*

**foresee** *irr vt* vorhersehen; **foreseeable** *adj* absehbar

**forest** *n* Wald *m*; **forestry** *n* Forstwirtschaft *f*

**forever** *adv* für immer

**forgave** *pt* → **forgive**

**forge 1.** *n* Schmiede *f* **2.** *vt* schmieden; (*fake*) fälschen; **forgery** *n* Fälschung *f*

**forget** *vt, vi* vergessen; **~ about sth** etw vergessen; **forgetful** *adj* vergesslich; **forget-me-not** *n* Vergissmeinnicht *nt*

**forgive** *irr vt* verzeihen; **~ sb**

**for sth** jdm etw verzeihen

**forgot** *pt* → **forget**

**forgotten** *pp* → **forget**

**fork 1.** *n* Gabel *f*; (*in road*) Gabelung *f* **2.** *vi* (*road*) sich gabeln

**form 1.** *n* (*shape*) Form *f*, Klasse *f*; (*document*) Formular *nt*; (*person*) **be in (good) ~** in Form sein **2.** *vt* bilden

**formal** *adj* förmlich, formell; **formality** *n* Formalität *f*

**format 1.** *n* Format *nt* **2.** *vt* formatieren

**former** *adj* frühere(r, s); (*opposite of latter*) erstere(r, s); **formerly** *adv* früher

**formula** *n* Formel *f*

**forth** *adv* **and so ~** und so weiter; **forthcoming** *adj* kommend, bevorstehend

**fortieth** *adj* vierzigste(r, s); → **eighth**

**fortnight** *n* vierzehn Tage *pl*

**fortress** *n* Festung *f*

**fortunate** *adj* glücklich; **I was ~** ich hatte Glück; **fortunately** *adv* zum Glück; **fortune** *n* (*money*) Vermögen *nt*; **good ~** Glück *nt*; **fortune-teller** *n* Wahrsager(in) *m(f)*

**forty** **1.** *num* vierzig **2.** *n* Vierzig *f*; → **eighty**

**forward 1.** *adv* vorwärts **2.** *n* SPORT Stürmer(in) *m(f)* **3.** *vt* (*send on*) nachsenden; IT weiterleiten; **forwards** *adv* vorwärts

**foster child** *n* Pflegekind *nt*; **foster parents** *npl* Pflegetern pl

**fought** pt, pp → **fight**

**foul 1.** adj (weather) schlecht; (smell) übel **2.** n SPORT Foul nt

**found 1.** pt, pp → **find 2.** vt (establish) gründen; **foundations** npl Fundament nt

**fountain** n Springbrunnen m; **fountain pen** n Füller m

**four 1.** num Vier f; → **eight; fourteen 1.** num vierzehn **2.** n Vierzehn f; → **eight; fourteenth** adj vierzehnte(r, s); → **eighth; fourth** adj vierte(r, s); → **eighth**

**four-wheel drive** n Allradantrieb m; (car) Geländewagen m

**fowl** n Geflügel nt

**fox** n Fuchs m

**fraction** n MATH Bruch m; (part) Bruchteil m; **fracture 1.** n MED Bruch m **2.** vt brechen

**fragile** adj zerbrechlich

**fragment** n Bruchstück nt

**fragrance** n Duft m; **fragrant** adj duftend

**frail** adj gebrechlich

**frame 1.** n Rahmen m; (of spectacles) Gestell nt; ~ **of mind** Verfassung f **2.** vt einrahmen; **framework** n Rahmen m, Struktur f

**France** n Frankreich nt

**frank** adj offen

**frankfurter** n (Frankfurter) Würstchen nt

**frankly** adv offen gesagt; **quite** ~ ganz ehrlich

**frantic** adj (activity) hektisch; (effort) verzweifelt; ~ **with worry** außer sich vor Sorge

**fraud** n (trickery) Betrug m; (person) Schwindler(in) m(f)

**freak 1.** n Anomalie f; (animal, person) Missgeburt f; fam (fan) Fan m, Freak m **2.** adj (conditions) außergewöhnlich, seltsam; **freak out** vi fam ausflippen

**freckle** n Sommersprosse f

**free 1.** adj, adv frei; (without payment) gratis, kostenlos; **for** ~ umsonst **2.** vt befreien; **freebie** n fam Werbegeschenk nt; **freedom** n Freiheit f; **freephone** adj a ~-**number** eine gebührenfreie Nummer; **free kick** n SPORT Freistoß m

**freelance 1.** adj freiberuflich tätig; (artist) freischaffend **2.** n Freiberufler(in) m(f)

**free-range** adj (hen) frei laufend; ~ **eggs** pl Freilandeier pl

**freeway** n (US) (gebührenfreie) Autobahn

**freeze 1.** vi (feel cold) frieren; (of lake etc) zufrieren; (water etc) gefrieren **2.** vt einfrieren; **freezer 2** n Tiefkühltruhe f; (in fridge) Gefrierfach nt; **freezing** adj eiskalt; **I'm** ~ mir ist eiskalt; **freezing point** n Gefrierpunkt m

# freight                                                        398

**freight** n (*goods*) Fracht f;
(*money charged*) Frachtge-
bühr f; **freight car** n (*US*)
Güterwagen m; **freight train**
n (*US*) Güterzug m

**French 1.** *adj* französisch **2.** n
(*language*) Französisch nt;
*the ~ pl* die Franzosen;
**French bean** n grüne Bohne; **French bread** n Ba-
guette f; **French dressing**
n Vinaigrette f; **French fries**
(*US*) npl Pommes frites pl;
**French kiss** n Zungenkuss
m; **French toast** n (*US*) in
Ei und Milch getunktes ge-
bratenes Brot; **French win-
dow(s)** n(pl) Balkontür f,
Terrassentür f; **Frenchwom-
an** n Französin f

**frequency** n Häufigkeit f;
PHYS Frequenz f; **frequent**
*adj* häufig; **frequently** *adv*
häufig

**fresco** n Fresko nt

**fresh** *adj* frisch; (*new*) neu;
**freshen** *vi ~* (**up**) (*person*)
sich frisch machen; **fresher**,
**freshman** n Erstsemester
nt; **freshwater fish** n Süß-
wasserfisch m

**Fri** *abbr* → **Friday** Fr

**friction** n Reibung f

**Friday** n Freitag m; → **Tuesday**

**fridge** n Kühlschrank m

**fried** *adj* gebraten; **~ potatoes**
Bratkartoffeln pl; **~ egg**
Spiegelei nt; **~ rice** gebrate-
ner Reis

**friend** n Freund(in) m(f); (*less
close*) Bekannte(r) mf;
**make ~s with sb** sich mit
jdm anfreunden; **we're
good ~s** wir sind gut befreundet; **friendly 1.** *adj*
freundlich **2.** n SPORT
Freundschaftsspiel nt;
**friendship** n Freundschaft f

**fright** n Schrecken m; **frighten**
*vt* erschrecken; **be ~ed**
Angst haben; **frightening**
*adj* beängstigend

**frill** n Rüsche f; **~s** fam
Schnickschnack

**fringe** n (*edge*) Rand m; (*on
shawl etc*) Fransen pl; (*hair*)
Pony m

**frizzy** *adj* kraus

**frog** n Frosch m

**from** prep von; (*place, out of*)
aus; (*with date, time*) ab;
**travel ~ A to B** von A nach
B fahren; **the train ~ Bath**
der Zug aus Bath; **where
does she come ~?** woher
kommt sie?; **it's ten miles
~ here** es ist zehn Meilen
von hier (entfernt); **~ May
5th(onwards)** ab dem 5. Mai

**front 1.** n Vorderseite f; (*of
house*) Fassade f; (*in war,
of weather*) Front f; (*at seaside*) Promenade f; **in ~, at
the ~** vorne; **in ~ of** vor; **up
~** (*in advance*) vorher, im Voraus **2.** *adj* vordere(r, s), Vor-
der-; (*first*) vorderste(r, s);
**~ door** Haustür f; **~ page** Ti-

telseite f; ~ **seat** Vordersitz m; ~ **wheel** Vorderrad nt

**frontier** n Grenze f

**front-wheel drive** n AUTO Frontantrieb m

**frost** n Frost m; (white frost) Reif m; **frosting** n (US) Zuckerguss m; **frosty** adj frostig

**froth** n Schaum m

**frown** vi die Stirn runzeln

**froze** pt → **freeze**

**frozen 1.** pp → **freeze 2.** adj (food) tiefgekühlt, Tiefkühl-

**fruit** n (as collective, a. type) Obst nt; (single fruit) Frucht f; **fruit machine** n Spielautomat m; **fruit salad** n Obstsalat m

**frustrated** adj frustriert; **frustration** n Frustration f, Frust m

**fry** vt braten; **frying pan** n Bratpfanne f

**fuchsia** n Fuchsie f

**fuck** vt vulg ficken; ~ **off** verpiss dich!; **fucking** adj vulg Scheiß-

**fudge** n ≈ weiche Karamellsüßigkeit

**fuel** n Kraftstoff m; (for heating) Brennstoff m; **fuel consumption** n Kraftstoffverbrauch m; **fuel gauge** n Benzinuhr f

**fugitive** n Flüchtling m

**fulfil** vt erfüllen

**full** adj voll; (person: satisfied) satt; (member, employment) Voll(zeit)-; (complete) voll-

ständig; ~ **of** ... voller ...  gen; **full beam** n AUTO Fernlicht nt; **full moon** n Vollmond m; **full stop** n Punkt m; **full-time** adj ~ **job** Ganztagsarbeit f; **fully** adv völlig; (recover) voll und ganz; (discuss) ausführlich

**fumble** vi herumfummeln (with, at an + dat)

**fumes** npl Dämpfe pl; (of car) Abgase pl

**function 1.** n Funktion f; (event) Feier f; (reception) Empfang m **2.** vi funktionieren

**fund** n Fonds m; ~**s** pl Geldmittel pl

**fundamental** adj grundlegend; **fundamentally** adv im Grunde

**funding** n finanzielle Unterstützung

**funeral** n Beerdigung f

**funfair** n Jahrmarkt m

**fungus** n Pilz m

**funnel** n Trichter m; (of steamer) Schornstein m

**funny** adj (amusing) komisch, lustig; (strange) seltsam

**fur** n Pelz m; (of animal) Fell nt

**furious** adj wütend (with sb auf jdn)

**furnished** adj möbliert; **furniture** n Möbel pl; **piece of ~**

Möbelstück *nt*

**further** *comparative* → **far 1.** *adj* weitere(r, s); **~ education** Weiterbildung *f;* **until ~ notice** bis auf weiteres **2.** *adv* weiter; **furthest** *superlative* → **far 1.** *adj* am weitesten entfernt **2.** *adv* am weitesten

**fury** *n* Wut *f*

**fuse 1.** *n* ELEC Sicherung *f* **2.** *vi* ELEC durchbrennen; **fuse**

**box** *n* Sicherungskasten *m*

**fuss** *n* Theater *nt;* **make a ~** (ein) Theater machen; **fussy** *adj* (*difficult*) schwierig, kompliziert; (*attentive to detail*) pingelig

**future 1.** *adj* künftig **2.** *n* Zukunft *f*

**fuze** (*US*) → **fuse**

**fuzzy** *adj* (*indistinct*) verschwommen; (*hair*) kraus

# G

**gable** *n* Giebel *m*

**gadget** *n* Vorrichtung *f*, Gerät *nt*

**Gaelic 1.** *adj* gälisch **2.** *n* (*language*) Gälisch *nt*

**gain 1.** *vt* (*obtain, win*) gewinnen; (*advantage, respect*) sich verschaffen; (*wealth*) erwerben; (*weight*) zunehmen **2.** *vi* (*improve*) gewinnen (*in* an + *dat*); (*clock*) vorgehen **3.** *n* Gewinn *m* (*in* an + *dat*)

**gale** *n* Sturm *m*

**gall bladder** *n* Gallenblase *f*

**gallery** *n* Galerie *f*, Museum *nt*

**gallon** *n* Gallone *f;* (*Brit*) 4,546 l (*US*) 3,79 l

**gallop 1.** *n* Galopp *m* **2.** *vi* galoppieren

**gallstone** *n* Gallenstein *m*

**Gambia** *n* Gambia *nt*

**gamble 1.** *vi* um Geld spielen, wetten **2.** *n* **it's a ~** es ist ris-

kant; **gambling** *n* Glücksspiel *nt*

**game** *n* Spiel *nt;* (*animals*) Wild *nt;* **~s** (*in school*) Sport *m*

**gammon** *n* geräucherter Schinken

**gang** *n* (*of criminals, youths*) Bande *f*, Gang *f*, Clique *f*

**gangster** *n* Gangster *m*

**gangway** *n* (*Brit, aisle*) Gang *m*, Gangway *f*

**gap** *n* (*hole*) Lücke *f;* (*in time*) Pause *f;* (*in age*) Unterschied *m*

**gape** *vi* (mit offenem Mund) starren

**gap year** *n* Jahr zwischen Schulabschluss und Studium, das oft zu Auslandsaufenthalten genutzt wird

**garage** *n* Garage *f;* (*for repair*) (Auto)werkstatt *f*

**garbage** *n* (*US*) Müll *m; fam* (*nonsense*) Quatsch *m;* gar-

**general**

**bage can** n (US) Mülleimer m; (outside) Mülltonne f; **garbage truck** n (US) Müllwagen m

**garden** n Garten m; (public) ~s Park m; **garden centre** n Gartencenter nt; **gardener** n Gärtner(in) m(f); **gardening** n Gartenarbeit f

**gargle** vi gurgeln

**gargoyle** n Wasserspeier m

**garlic** n Knoblauch m; **garlic bread** n Knoblauchbrot nt; **garlic butter** n Knoblauchbutter f

**gas** n Gas nt; (US, petrol) Benzin nt; **step on the ~** Gas geben; **gas cooker** n Gasherd m; **gas cylinder** n Gasflasche f; **gas fire** n Gasofen m

**gasket** n Dichtung f

**gas lighter** n (for cigarettes) Gasfeuerzeug nt; **gas mask** n Gasmaske f; **gas meter** n Gaszähler m

**gasoline** n (US) Benzin nt

**gasp** vi keuchen; (in surprise) nach Luft schnappen

**gas pedal** n (US) Gaspedal nt; **gas pump** n (US) Zapfsäule f; **gas station** n (US) Tankstelle f; **gas tank** n (US) Benzintank m

**gastric** adj Magen-; **~ flu** Magen-Darm-Grippe f; **~ ulcer** Magengeschwür nt

**gasworks** n Gaswerk nt

**gate** n Tor nt; (barrier) Schranke f, AVIAT Gate nt,

Flugsteig m

**gateau** n Torte f

**gateway** n Tor nt

**gather 1.** vt (collect) sammeln; **~ speed** beschleunigen **2.** vi (assemble) sich versammeln; (understand) schließen (from aus); **gathering** n Versammlung f

**gauge** n Meßgerät nt

**gauze** n Gaze f; (for bandages) Mull m

**gave** pt → **give**

**gay** adj (homosexual) schwul; **~ marriage** Homoehe f fam

**gaze 1.** n Blick m **2.** vi starren

**GCSE** abbr = **general certificate of secondary education** Abschlussprüfung f der Sekundarstufe, ≈ mittlere Reife

**gear** n AUTO Gang m; (equipment) Ausrüstung f; (clothes) Klamotten pl; **change ~** schalten; **gearbox** n Getriebe nt; **gear change**, **gear lever**, **gear stick** (US) n Schalthebel m; **gear shift** (US) n Gangschaltung f; **gear lever**, **gear stick** (US) n Schalthebel m

**geese** pl → **goose**

**gel 1.** n Gel nt **2.** vi gelieren; **they really ~led** sie verstanden sich auf Anhieb

**gem** n Edelstein m; fig Juwel nt

**Gemini** nsing ASTR Zwillinge pl

**gender** n Geschlecht nt

**gene** n Gen nt

**general** adj allgemein; ~

*knowledge* Allgemeinbildung f; **~ election** Parlamentswahlen pl; **generalize** vi verallgemeinern; **generally** adv im Allgemeinen

**generation** n Generation f; **generation gap** n Generationsunterschied m

**generosity** n Großzügigkeit f; **generous** adj großzügig; (portion) reichlich

**genetic** adj genetisch; **~ research** Genforschung; **~ technology** Gentechnik; **genetically modified** adj gentechnisch verändert, genmanipuliert; → **GM**

**Geneva** n Genf nt; **Lake ~** der Genfer See

**genitals** npl Geschlechtsteile pl

**genius** n Genie nt

**gentle** adj sanft; (touch) zart; **gentleman** n Herr m; (polite man) Gentleman m

**gents** n '**~**' (lavatory) „Herren"; **the ~** pl die Herrentoilette

**genuine** adj echt

**geographical** adj geografisch; **geography** n Geografie f; (at school) Erdkunde f

**geometry** n Geometrie f

**geranium** n Geranie f

**gerbil** n ZOOL Wüstenrennmaus f

**germ** n Keim m; MED Bazillus m

**German 1.** adj deutsch; **she's ~** sie ist Deutsche; **~ shep-**

**herd** Deutscher Schäferhund **2.** n (person) Deutsche(r) mf; (language) Deutsch nt; **in ~** auf Deutsch; **German measles** n sg Röteln pl; **Germany** n Deutschland nt

**gesture** n Geste f

**get 1.** vt (receive) bekommen, kriegen; **~ a cold / flu** sich erkälten / eine Grippe bekommen; (buy) kaufen; (obtain) sich besorgen; (to keep) sich anschaffen; **~ sb sth** jdm etw besorgen; **~ a life!** fam (annoyed) mach dich mal locker!, red dich bloß ab!; (fetch) jdm etw holen; **where did you ~ that (from)?** woher hast du / haben Sie das?; **~ a taxi** ein Taxi nehmen; (persuade) **~ sb to do sth** jdn dazu bringen, etw zu tun; (manage) **~ sth to work** etw zum Laufen bringen; **~ sth done** (oneself) etw machen; (by sb else) etw machen lassen; (things) **this isn't ~ting us anywhere** so kommen wir nicht weiter; (understand) **don't ~ me wrong** versteh / verstehen Sie mich nicht falsch! **2.** vi (become) werden; **~ old** alt werden; **it's ~ting dark** es wird dunkel; **~ dressed / washed** sich anziehen / waschen; **I'll ~ ready** ich mache mich fertig; **~ lost** sich verirren; (arrive) **we got to Dover**

*at 5* wir kamen um 5 in Dover an; ~ *somewhere* / *nowhere* fig (in career) es zu etwas / nichts bringen; (with task, discussion) weiterkommen / nicht weiterkommen; **get across 1.** vi ~ *sth* über etw acc kommen **2.** vt *get sth across* (communicate) etw klarmachen; **get along** vi (manage) zurechtkommen; (people) gut auskommen (with mit); **get at** vt (reach) herankommen an + acc; *what are you getting at?* worauf willst du / wollen Sie hinaus?, was meinst du / meinen Sie damit?; **get away** vi (leave) wegkommen; (escape) entkommen (from dat); *he got away with it* er kam ungeschoren davon; **get back 1.** vi zurückkommen; TEL ~ *to s.o.* jdn zurückrufen **2.** vt *get sth back* etw zurückbekommen; **get by** vi (manage) auskommen (on mit); **get down 1.** vi heruntersteigen; ~ *to business* zur Sache kommen **2.** vt *get sth down* (write) etw aufschreiben; *it gets me down* fam es macht mich fertig; **get in** vi (arrive home) heimkommen; (into car etc) einsteigen; **get into** vt (car, bus etc) einsteigen in + acc; (rage, panic etc) geraten in + acc; ~ *trouble* in Schwierigkeiten kommen; **get off**

**1.** vi (train etc) aussteigen (aus); (horse) absteigen (von); fam (be enthusiastic) ~ *on sth* auf etw abfahren **2.** vt (nail, sticker) los- / abbekommen; (clothes) ausziehen; **get on 1.** vi (train etc) einsteigen (in + acc); (horse) aufsteigen (auf + acc); (progress) vorankommen; (be friends) auskommen (with mit); *be getting on* alt werden **2.** vt etw vorantreiben, mit etw loslegen; **get out 1.** vi herauskommen; (of vehicle) aussteigen (of aus); ~! raus! **2.** vt (take out) herausholen; (stain, nail) herausbekommen; **get over** vt (recover from) hinwegkommen über + acc; (illness) sich erholen von; (loss) sich abfinden mit; **get through** vi durchkommen; **get up** vi aufstehen; **get-together** n Treffen nt

**Ghana** n Ghana nt
**gherkin** n Gewürzgurke f
**ghetto** n Ghetto nt
**ghost** n Gespenst nt; (of sb) Geist m
**giant 1.** n Riese m **2.** adj riesig
**giblets** npl Geflügelinnereien pl
**Gibraltar** n Gibraltar nt
**giddy** adj schwindlig
**gift** n Geschenk nt; (talent) Begabung f; **gifted** adj begabt; **giftwrap** vt als Geschenk verpacken

**gigantic** *adj* riesig

**giggle 1.** *vi* kichern **2.** *n* Gekicher *nt*

**gill** *n* (*of fish*) Kieme *f*

**gimmick** *n* (*for sales, publicity*) Gag *m*

**gin** *n* Gin *m*

**ginger 1.** *n* Ingwer *m* **2.** *adj* (*colour*) kupferrot; (*cat*) rötlichgelb; **ginger ale** *n* Gingerale *nt*; **ginger beer** *n* Ingwerlimonade *f*; **gingerbread** *n* Lebkuchen *m* (*mit Ingwergeschmack*); **ginger (-haired)** *adj* rotblond; **gingerly** *adv* (*move*) vorsichtig

**giraffe** *n* Giraffe *f*

**girl** *n* Mädchen *nt*; **girlfriend** *n* (*feste*) Freundin *f*; **girl guide** *n* (*Brit*), **girl scout** (*US*) Pfadfinderin *f*

**gist** *n* **get the ~** (*of it*) das Wesentliche verstehen

**give 1.** *vt* geben; (*as present*) schenken (*to sb* jdm); (*state*: *name etc*) angeben; (*speech*) halten; (*blood*) spenden; **~ sb sth** jdm etw geben / schenken (*to sb* jdm); **2.** *vi* (*yield*) nachgeben; **give away** *vt* (*give free*) verschenken; (*secret*) verraten; **give back** *vt* zurückgeben; **give in** *vi* aufgeben; **give up** *vt, vi* aufgeben; **give way** *vi* (*collapse, yield*) nachgeben; (*traffic*) die Vorfahrt beachten

**given 1.** *pp* → **give 2.** *adj* (*fixed*) festgesetzt; (*certain*) bestimmt; **~ name** (*US*) Vorname *m* **3.** *conj* **~ that** ... angesichts der Tatsache, dass ...

**glacier** *n* Gletscher *m*

**glad** *adj* froh (*about* über); **I was ~ (to hear) that** ... es hat mich gefreut, dass ...; **gladly** *adv* gerne

**glance 1.** *n* Blick *m* **2.** *vi* einen Blick werfen (*at* auf + *acc*)

**gland** *n* Drüse *f*; **glandular fever** *n* Drüsenfieber *nt*

**glare 1.** *n* grelles Licht; (*stare*) stechender Blick **2.** *vi* (*angrily*) **~ at sb** jdn böse anstarren

**glass** *n* Glas *nt*; **~es** *pl* Brille *f*

**glen** *n* (*Scot*) (enges) Bergtal *nt*

**glide** *vi* gleiten; (*hover*) schweben; **glider** *n* Segelflugzeug *nt*; **gliding** *n* Segelfliegen *nt*

**glimpse** *n* flüchtiger Blick

**glitter** *vi* glitzern; (*eyes*) funkeln

**glitzy** *adj fam* glanzvoll, Schickimicki-

**global** *adj* global, Welt-; **~ warming** die Erwärmung der Erdatmosphäre; **globe** *n* (*sphere*) Kugel *f*; (*world*) Erdball *m*; (*map*) Globus *m*

**gloomily, gloomy** *adv, adj* düster

**glorious** *adj* (*victory, past*) ruhmreich; (*weather, day etc*) herrlich; **glory** *n* Herrlichkeit *f*

**gloss** *n* (*shine*) Glanz *m*

**glossary** *n* Glossar *nt*

**glossy 1.** *adj* (*surface*) glänzend **2.** *n* (*magazine*) Hochglanzmagazin *nt*

**glove** *n* Handschuh *m*; **glove compartment** *n* Handschuhfach *nt*

**glow** *vi* glühen

**glucose** *n* Traubenzucker *m*

**glue 1.** *n* Klebstoff *m* **2.** *vt* kleben

**glutton** *n* Vielfraß *m*; **a ~ for punishment** *fam* Masochist *m*

**GM** *abbr* → **genetically modified** Gen-; **~ foods** gentechnisch veränderte Lebensmittel

**GMT** *abbr* → **Greenwich Mean Time** WEZ *f*

**go 1.** *vi* gehen; (*in vehicle, travel*) fahren; (*plane*) fliegen; (*road*) führen (*to* nach); (*depart: train, bus*) (ab)fahren; (*person*) (fort)gehen; (*disappear*) verschwinden; (*time*) vergehen; (*function*) gehen, funktionieren; (*machine, engine*) laufen; (*fit, suit*) passen (*with* zu); (*fail*) nachlassen; **I have to ~ to the doctor / to London** ich muss zum Arzt / nach London; **~ shopping** einkaufen gehen; **~ for a walk / swim** spazieren / schwimmen gehen; **has he gone yet?** ist er schon weg?; **the wine ~es in the cupboard** der Wein kommt in den Schrank; **get sth ~ing** etw in Gang setzen; **keep ~ing** weitermachen; (*machine etc*) weiterlaufen; **how's the job ~ing?** was macht der Job?; **~ deaf / mad / grey** taub / verrückt / grau werden **2. vaux be ~ing to do sth** etw tun werden; **I was ~ing to do it** ich wollte es tun **3.** *n* (*attempt*) Versuch *m*; **can I have another ~?** darf ich noch mal (probieren)?; **it's my ~** ich bin dran; (*drink*) in einem Zug; **go after** *vt* nachlaufen + *dat*; (*in vehicle*) hinterherfahren + *dat*; **go ahead** *vi* (*in front*) vorausgehen; (*start*) anfangen; **go away** *vi* weggehen; (*on holiday, business*) verreisen; **go back** *vi* (*return*) zurückgehen; **go by 1.** *vi* vorbeigehen; (*vehicle*) vorbeifahren; (*years, time*) vergehen **2.** *vt* (*judge by*) gehen nach; **go down** *vi* (*sun, ship*) untergehen; (*flood, temperature*) zurückgehen; (*price*) sinken; **~ well / badly** gut / schlecht ankommen; **go in** *vi* hineingehen; **go into** *vt* (*enter*) hineingehen in + *acc*; (*crash*) fahren gegen, hineinfahren in + *acc*; **~ teaching / politics / the army** Lehrer werden / in die Politik gehen / zum Militär gehen; **go off 1.** *vi* (*depart*) weggehen; (*in vehicle*) wegfahren; (*lights*) ausgehen;

(*milk etc*) sauer werden; (*gun, bomb, alarm*) losgehen **2.** *vt* (*dislike*) nicht mehr mögen; **go on** *vi* (*continue*) weitergehen; (*lights*) angehen; **~ with** *or* **doing sth** etw weitermachen; **go out** *vi* (*leave house*) hinausgehen; (*fire, light, person socially*) ausgehen; **~ for a meal** essen gehen; **go up** *vi* (*temperature, price*) steigen; (*lift*) hochfahren; **go without** *vi* verzichten auf + *acc*; (*food, sleep*) auskommen ohne

**go-ahead 1.** *adj* (*progressive*) fortschrittlich **2.** *n* grünes Licht

**goal** *n* (*aim*) Ziel *nt*; SPORT Tor *nt*; **goalie, goalkeeper** *n* Torwart *m*; **goalpost** *n* Torpfosten *m*

**goat** *n* Ziege *f*

**gob 1.** *n* (*Brit*) *fam* Maul *nt*; **shut your ~** halt's Maul! **2.** *vi* spucken; **gobsmacked** *fam* (*surprised*) platt

**god** *n* Gott *m*; **thank God** Gott sei Dank; **godchild** *n* Patenkind *nt*; **goddaughter** *n* Patentochter *f*; **goddess** *n* Göttin *f*; **godfather** *n* Pate *m*; **godmother** *n* Patin *f*; **godson** *n* Patensohn *m*

**goggles** *npl* Schutzbrille *f*; (*for skiing*) Skibrille *f*; (*for diving*) Taucherbrille *f*

**going** *adj* (*rate*) üblich; **goings-on** *npl* Vorgänge *pl*

**go-kart** *n* Gokart *m*

**gold** *n* Gold *nt*; **golden** *adj* golden; **goldfish** *n* Goldfisch *m*; **gold-plated** *adj* vergoldet

**golf** *n* Golf *nt*; **golf ball** *n* Golfball *m*; **golf club** *n* Golfschläger *m*; (*association*) Golfklub *m*; **golf course** *n* Golfplatz *m*

**gone 1.** *pp* → **go**; **he's ~** er ist weg **2.** *prep* **just ~ three** kurz nach drei

**good 1.** *n* (*benefit*) Wohl *nt*; (*morally good things*) Gute(s) *nt*; **it's for your own ~** es ist zu deinem / Ihrem Besten *or* Vorteil; **it's no ~** (*doing sth*) es hat keinen Sinn *or* Zweck; (*thing*) es taugt nichts; **for ~** für immer **2.** *adj* gut; (*suitable*) passend; (*thorough*) gründlich; (*well-behaved*) brav; (*kind*) nett, lieb; **be ~ at sport / maths** gut in Sport / Mathe sein; **be no ~ at sport / maths** schlecht in Sport / Mathe sein; **too ~ to be true** zu schön, um wahr zu sein; **this is just not ~ enough** so geht das nicht; **a ~ three hours** gute drei Stunden; **~ morning / evening** guten Morgen / Abend; **~ night** gute Nacht; **have a ~ time** sich gut amüsieren

**goodbye** *interj* auf Wiedersehen

**Good Friday** *n* Karfreitag *m*

**good-looking** *adj* gut aussehend

**goods** npl Waren pl, Güter pl;
**goods train** n (Brit) Güterzug m

**goose** n Gans f; **gooseberry**
n Stachelbeere f; **goose
bumps** n, **goose pimples**
npl Gänsehaut f

**gorge** n Schlucht f

**gorgeous** adj wunderschön;
**he's ~** er sieht toll aus

**gorilla** n Gorilla m

**gossip 1.** n (talk) Klatsch m;
(person) Klatschtante f **2.**
vi klatschen, tratschen

**got** pt, pp → **get**

**gotten** (US) pp → **get**

**govern** vt regieren; (province
etc) verwalten; **government**
n Regierung f; governor n
Gouverneur(in) m(f); **govt**
abbr → **government** Regierung f

**gown** n Abendkleid nt; (academic) Robe f

**GP** abbr = **General Practitioner** Allgemeinarzt m,
Allgemeinärztin f

**GPS** n abbr = **global positioning system** GPS nt

**grab** vt packen; (person)
schnappen

**graceful** adj anmutig

**grade** n Niveau nt; (of goods)
Güteklasse f; (mark) Note f;
(US, year) Klasse f; **make
the ~** es schaffen; **grade
crossing** n (US) Bahnübergang m; **grade school** n
(US) Grundschule f

**gradient** n (upward) Steigung
f; (downward) Gefälle nt

**gradual, gradually** adj, adv
allmählich

**graduate 1.** n Uniabsolvent(in) m(f) **2.** vi einen akademischen Grad erwerben

**grain** n (cereals) Getreide nt;
(of corn, sand) Korn nt

**gram** n Gramm nt

**grammar** n Grammatik f;
**grammar school** n (Brit) ≈
Gymnasium nt

**gran** n fam Oma f

**grand 1.** adj pej hochnäsig;
(posh) vornehm **2.** n fam
1000 Pfund bzw. 1000 Dollar

**grand(d)ad** n fam Opa m;
**granddaughter** n Enkelin
f; **grandfather** n Großvater
m; **grandma** n fam Oma f;
**grandmother** n Großmutter
f; **grandpa** n fam Opa m;
**grandparents** npl Großeltern pl; **grandson** n Enkel m

**grandstand** n SPORT Tribüne f

**granny** n fam Oma f

**grant 1.** n gewähren (sb sth
jdm etw); **take sb/sth for
~ed** jdn/etw als selbstverständlich hinnehmen **2.** n
Subvention f, finanzielle
Unterstützung f; (for university) Stipendium nt

**grape** n Weintraube f; **grapefruit** n Grapefruit f; **grape
juice** n Traubensaft m

**graph** n Diagramm nt; **graphic** adj grafisch; (description)
anschaulich

**grasp** vt ergreifen; (under-stand) begreifen

**grass** n Gras nt; (lawn) Rasen m; (**grasshopper** n Heu-schrecke f

**grate 1.** n Feuerrost m **2.** vi kratzen **3.** vt (cheese) reiben

**grateful, gratefully** adj, adv dankbar

**grater** n Reibe f

**gratifying** adj erfreulich

**gratitude** n Dankbarkeit f

**grave 1.** n Grab nt **2.** adj ernst; (mistake) schwer

**gravel** n Kies m

**graveyard** n Friedhof m

**gravity** n Schwerkraft f; (seriousness) Ernst m

**gravy** n Bratensoße f

**gray** adj (US) grau

**graze 1.** vi (of animals) grasen **2.** vt (touch) streifen; MED abschürfen **3.** n MED Abschürfung f

**grease 1.** n (fat) Fett nt; (lubricant) Schmiere f **2.** vt einfetten; TECH schmieren; **greasy** adj fettig; (hands, tools) schmierig; fam (person) schleimig

**great** adj groß; fam (good) großartig, super; **a ~ deal of** viel; **Great Britain** n Großbritannien nt; **great-grandfather** n Urgroßvater m; **great-grandmother** n Urgroßmutter f; **greatly** adv sehr; **~ disappointed** zutiefst enttäuscht

**Greece** n Griechenland nt

**greed** n Gier f (for nach); (for food) Gefräßigkeit f; **greedy** adj gierig; (for food) gefräßig

**Greek 1.** adj griechisch **2.** n (person) Grieche m, Griechin f; (language) Griechisch nt; **it's all ~ to me** ich verstehe nur Bahnhof

**green 1.** adj grün; **~ with envy** grün / gelb vor Neid **2.** n (colour, for golf) Grün nt; (village green) Dorfwiese f; **~s** (vegetables) grünes Gemüse; **the Greens, the Green Party** POL die Grünen; **green card** n (US, work permit) Arbeitserlaubnis f; (Brit, for car) grüne Versicherungskarte; **greengage** n Reneklode f; **greengrocer** n Obst- und Gemüsehändler(in) m(f); **greenhouse** n Gewächshaus nt; **~ effect** Treibhauseffekt m; **Greenland** n Grönland nt; **green pepper** n grüner Paprika; **green salad** n grüner Salat

**greet** vt grüßen; **greeting** n Gruß m

**grew** pt → **grow**

**grey** adj grau; **grey-haired** adj grauhaarig; **greyhound** n Windhund m

**grid** n Gitter nt; **gridlock** n Verkehrsinfarkt m; **gridlocked** adj (roads) völlig verstopft; (talks) festgefahren

**grief** n Kummer m; (over loss) Trauer f

**grievance** n Beschwerde f

**grieve** vi trauern (for um)

**grill 1.** n (on cooker) Grill m **2.** vt grillen

**grim** adj (face, humour) grimmig; (situation, prospects) trostlos

**grin 1.** n Grinsen nt **2.** vi grinsen

**grind** vt mahlen; (sharpen) schleifen; (US, meat) durchdrehen

**grip** n Griff m; **get a~** nimm dich zusammen!; **get to ~s with sth** etw in den Griff bekommen **2.** vt packen

**groan** vi stöhnen (with vor + dat)

**grocer** n Lebensmittelhändler(in) m(f); **groceries** npl Lebensmittel pl

**groin** n ANAT Leiste f; **groin strain** n MED Leistenbruch m

**groom 1.** n Bräutigam m **2.** vt **well ~ed** gepflegt

**grope 1.** vi tasten **2.** vt (sexually harrass) befummeln

**gross** adj (coarse) derb; (extreme: negligence, error) grob; (disgusting) ekelhaft; COMM brutto; **~ salary** Bruttogehalt nt

**grotty** adj fam mies, vergammelt

**ground 1.** pt, pp → **grind 2.** n Boden m, Erde f; SPORT Platz m; **~s** pl (around house) (Garten)anlagen pl; (reasons) Gründe pl; (of coffee) Satz m; **on (the) ~s of** auf-

grund von; **ground floor** n (Brit) Erdgeschoss nt; **ground meat** n (US) Hackfleisch nt

**group** n Gruppe f

**grouse** n (bird) Schottisches Moorhuhn; (complaint) Nörgelei f

**grow 1.** vi wachsen; (increase) zunehmen (in an); (become) werden; **~ old** alt werden; **~ into ...** sich entwickeln zu ... **2.** vt (crop, plant) ziehen; (commercially) anbauen; **I'm ~ing a beard** ich lasse mir einen Bart wachsen; **grow up** vi aufwachsen; (mature) erwachsen werden; **growing** adj wachsend; **a ~ number of people** immer mehr Leute

**growl** vi knurren

**grown** pp → **grow**

**grown-up 1.** adj erwachsen **2.** n Erwachsene(r) m/f; **growth** n Wachstum nt; (increase) Zunahme f; MED Wucherung f

**grubby** adj schmuddelig

**grudge 1.** n Abneigung f (against gegen) **2.** vt **~ sb sth** jdm etw nicht gönnen

**gruelling** adj aufreibend; (pace) mörderisch

**gruesome** adj grausig

**grumble** vi murren (about über + acc)

**grumpy** adj fam mürrisch, grantig

**grunt** vi grunzen

**G-string** n String m, Stringtanga m

**guarantee 1.** n Garantie f (of
für) **2.** vt garantieren

**guard 1.** n (sentry) Wache f;
(in prison) Wärter(in) m(f);
(Brit) RAIL Schaffner(in)
m(f) **2.** vt bewachen

**guardian** n Vormund m; ~ **angel** Schutzengel m

**guess 1.** n Vermutung f; (estimate) Schätzung f; **have a** ~
rate mal! **2.** vt, vi raten; (estimate) schätzen; **I** ~ **you're
right** du hast wohl recht; **I**
~ **so** ich glaube schon

**guest** n Gast m; **be my** ~ nur
zu!; **guest-house** n Pension
f; **guest room** n Gästezimmer nt

**guidance** n (direction) Leitung f; (advice) Rat m;
(counselling) Beratung f;
**for your** ~ zu Ihrer Orientierung; **guide 1.** n (person)
Führer(in) m(f); (tour) Rei-
seleiter(in) m(f); (book)
Führer m **2.** vt führen;
**guidebook** n Reiseführer
m; **guide dog** n Blindenhund m; **guided tour** n Führung f (of durch); **guidelines**
npl Richtlinien pl

**guilt** n Schuld f; **guilty** adj
schuldig (of gen); (look)
schuldbewusst; **have a** ~
**conscience** ein schlechtes
Gewissen haben

**guinea pig** n Meerschweinchen nt; (person) Versuchs-
kaninchen nt

**guitar** n Gitarre f

**gulf** n Golf m; **Gulf States** npl
Golfstaaten pl

**gull** n Möwe f

**gullible** adj leichtgläubig

**gulp 1.** n (kräftiger) Schluck
**2.** vi schlucken

**gum** n (around teeth, usu pl)
Zahnfleisch nt; (chewing
gum) Kaugummi m

**gun** n Schusswaffe f; (rifle)
Gewehr nt; (pistol) Pistole
f; **gunfire** n Schüsse pl; **gun-
powder** n Schießpulver nt

**gush** vi (heraus)strömen
(from aus)

**gut** n Darm m; ~**s** pl (intes-
tines) Eingeweide; (courage)
Mumm m

**gutter** n (for roof) Dachrinne
f; (in street) Rinnstein m,
Gosse f

**guy** n (man) Typ m, Kerl m; ~**s**
pl (US) Leute pl

**gym** n Turnhalle f; (for working out) Fitnesscenter nt;
**gymnasium** n Turnhalle f;
**gymnastics** nsing Turnen
nt; **gym-toned** adj durchtrai-
niert

**gynaecologist** n Frauenarzt
m, Frauenärztin f, Gynäkologe m, Gynäkologin f; **gyn-
aecology** n Gynäkologie f

# H

**habit** *n* Gewohnheit *f*; **habitual** *adj* gewohnt; *(drinker, liar)* gewohnheitsmäßig

**hack** *vt* hacken; **hacker** *n* ɪᴛ Hacker(in) *m(f)*

**had** *pt, pp* → **have**

**haddock** *n* Schellfisch *m*

**hadn't** *contr* of **had not**

**haemophiliac, hemophiliac** *(US)* *n* Bluter(in) *m(f)*;

**haemorrhage, hemorrhage** *(US)* **1.** *n* Blutung *f* **2.** *vi* bluten; **haemorrhoids, hemorrhoids** *(US)* *npl* Hämorrhoiden *pl*

**haggis** *n* (Scot) mit gehackten Schafsinnereien und Haferschrot gefüllter Schafsmagen

**hail 1.** *n* Hagel *m* **2.** *vi* hageln **3.** *vt* ~ **sb as sth** jdn als etw feiern; **hailstone** *n* Hagelkorn *nt*; **hailstorm** *n* Hagelschauer *m*

**hair** *n* Haar *nt*, Haare *pl*; **get one's ~ cut** sich *dat* die Haare schneiden lassen; **hairbrush** *n* Haarbürste *f*; **hair conditioner** *n* Haarspülung *f*; **haircut** *n* Haarschnitt *m*; **hairdo** *n* Frisur *f*; **hairdresser** *n* Friseur *m*, Friseurin *f*; **hairdryer** *n* Haartrockner *m*; *(hand-held)* Fön® *m*; *(over head)* Trockenhaube *f*; **hair gel** *n* Haargel *nt*; **hair remover** *n* Enthaarungsmittel *nt*; **hair spray** *n* Haarspray *nt*; **hair style** *n* Frisur *f*; **hairy** *adj* haarig, behaart; *fam (dangerous)* brenzlig

**hake** *n* Seehecht *m*

**half 1.** *n* Hälfte *f*; sᴘᴏʀᴛ *(of game)* Halbzeit *f*; **cut in ~** halbieren **2.** *adj* halb; **three and a ~ pounds** dreieinhalb Pfund; **~ an hour, a ~ hour** eine halbe Stunde; **one and a ~** eineinhalb, anderthalb **3.** *adv* halb, zur Hälfte; **~ asleep** fast eingeschlafen; **~ as big (as)** halb so groß (wie); **half board** *n* Halbpension *f*; **half fare** *n* halber Fahrpreis; **half-hearted** *adj* halbherzig; **half-hour** *n* halbe Stunde; **half moon** *n* Halbmond *m*; **half pint** *n* ≈ Viertelliter *m* or *nt*; **half price** *n* (at) ~ zum halben Preis; **half-term** *n* (at school) Ferien *pl* in der Mitte des Trimesters; **half-time** *n* Halbzeit *f*; **halfway** *adv* auf halbem Wege; **halfwit** *n* *fam* Trottel *m*

**halibut** *n* Heilbutt *m*

**hall** *n* (building) Halle *f*; *(for audience)* Saal *m*; *(entrance hall)* Flur *m*; *(large)* Diele *f*; **~ of residence** (Brit) Studentenwohnheim *nt*

**hallo** *interj* hallo

**halt 1.** n Pause f, Halt m; **come to a ~** zum Stillstand kommen **2.** vt, vi anhalten

**halve** vt halbieren

**ham** n Schinken m

**hamburger** n GASTR Hamburger m

**hammer 1.** n Hammer m **2.** vt, vi hämmern

**hammock** n Hängematte f

**hamper 1.** n behindern **2.** n (as gift) Geschenkkorb m; (for picnic) Picknickkorb m

**hamster** n Hamster m

**hand** n Hand f; (of clock, instrument) Zeiger m; (in card game) Blatt nt; **~s off!** Finger weg!; **on the one ~ ..., on the other ~...** einerseits ..., andererseits ...; **give sb a ~** jdm helfen (with bei); **it's in his ~s** er hat es in der Hand; **be in good ~s** gut aufgehoben sein; **get out of ~** außer Kontrolle geraten **2.** vt (pass) reichen (to sb jdm); **hand down** vt (tradition) überliefern; (heirloom) vererben; **hand in** vt einreichen; (at school, university etc) abgeben; **hand out** vt verteilen; **hand over** vt übergeben

**handbag** n Handtasche f; **handbook** n Handbuch nt; **handbrake** n (Brit) Handbremse f; **handcuffs** npl Handschellen pl; **handheld PC** n Handheld m

**handicap 1.** n Behinderung f,

Handikap nt **2.** vt benachteiligen; **handicapped** adj behindert; **the ~** die Behinderten

**handicraft** n Kunsthandwerk nt

**handkerchief** n Taschentuch nt

**handle 1.** n Griff m; (of door) Klinke f; (of cup etc) Henkel m; (for winding) Kurbel f **2.** vt (touch) anfassen; (deal with: matter) sich befassen mit; (people, machine etc) umgehen mit; (situation, problem) fertig werden mit; **handlebars** npl Lenkstange f

**hand luggage** n Handgepäck nt; **handmade** adj handgefertigt; **be ~** Handarbeit sein; **handout** n (sheet) Handout nt, Thesenpapier nt; **handset** n Hörer m; **please replace the ~** bitte legen Sie auf; **hands-free phone** n Freisprechanlage f; **handshake** n Händedruck m

**handsome** adj (man) gut aussehend

**hands-on** adj praxisorientiert; **~ experience** praktische Erfahrung

**handwriting** n Handschrift f

**handy** adj (useful) praktisch

**hang 1.** vt (auf)hängen; (execute: hanged, hanged) hängen **2.** vi hängen **3.** n **he's got the ~ of it** er hat den

Dreh raus; **hang about** vi sich herumtreiben, rumhängen; **hang on** vi sich festhalten (*to an + dat*); *fam* (*wait*) warten; **~ to sth** etw behalten; **hang up 1.** vi TEL auflegen **2.** vt aufhängen

**hanger** n Kleiderbügel m

**hang glider** n (*Flug*)drachen m; (*person*) Drachenflieger(in) m(f); **hang-gliding** n Drachenfliegen nt

**hangover** n (*bad head*) Kater m; (*relic*) Überbleibsel nt

**hankie** n fam Taschentuch nt

**happen** vi geschehen; (*sth strange, unpleasant*) passieren; **if anything should ~ to me** wenn mir etwas passieren sollte; **it won't ~ again** es wird nicht wieder vorkommen; **I ~ed to be passing** ich kam zufällig vorbei; **happening** n Ereignis nt

**happily** adv fröhlich, glücklich; (*luckily*) glücklicherweise; **happiness** n Glück nt; **happy** adj glücklich; (*satisfied*) **~ with sth** mit etw zufrieden; (*willing*) **be ~ to do sth** etw gerne tun; **Happy Christmas** fröhliche Weihnachten!; **Happy New Year** ein glückliches Neues Jahr!; **Happy Birthday** herzlichen Glückwunsch zum Geburtstag!; **happy hour** n Happy Hour f

**harass** vt (*ständig*) belästigen; **harassment** n Belästi-

gung f; (*at work*) Mobbing nt; **sexual ~** sexuelle Belästigung

**harbor** (*US*), **harbour** n Hafen m

**hard 1.** adj hart; (*difficult*) schwer, schwierig; (*harsh*) hart(herzig); **don't be ~ on him** sei nicht zu streng zu ihm; **it's ~ to believe** es ist kaum zu glauben **2.** adv (*work*) schwer; (*run*) schnell; (*rain, snow*) stark; **try ~/~er** sich dat große/mehr Mühe geben; **hardback** n gebundene Ausgabe; **hard-boiled** adj (*egg*) hart gekocht; **hard copy** n IT Ausdruck m; **hard disk** n IT Festplatte f; **harden 1.** vt härten **2.** vi hart werden; **hardly** adv kaum; **~ ever** fast nie; **hardship** n Not f; **hard shoulder** n (*Brit*) Standspur f; **hardware** n IT Hardware f, Haushalts- und Eisenwaren pl; **hard-working** adj fleißig, tüchtig

**hare** n Hase m

**harm 1.** n Schaden m; (*bodily*) Verletzung f; **it wouldn't do any ~** es würde nicht schaden **2.** vt schaden + dat; (*person*) verletzen; **harmful** adj schädlich; **harmless** adj harmlos

**harp** n Harfe f

**harsh** adj (*climate, voice*) rau; (*light, sound*) grell; (*severe*) hart, streng

**harvest 1.** *n* Ernte *f*; *(time)*
Erntezeit *f* **2.** *vt* ernten

**has** *3rd person sg present →*
**have**

**hash** *n* GASTR Haschee *nt*; *fam*
*(hashish)* Haschisch *nt*;
**make a ~ of sth** etw vermasseln; **hash browns** *npl (US)*
≈ Kartoffelpuffer / Rösti mit
Zwiebeln *pl*

**hasn't** *abbr of* **has not**

**hassle 1.** *n* Ärger *m*; *(fuss)*
Theater *nt*; **no ~** kein Problem **2.** *vt* bedrängen

**haste** *n* Eile *f*; **hastily, hasty**
*adv, adj* hastig; *(rash)* vorschnell

**hat** *n* Hut *m*

**hatch** *n* NAUT Luke *f*; *(in
house)* Durchreiche *f*;
**hatchback** *n (car)* Wagen
*m* mit Hecktür

**hate 1.** *vt* hassen; **I ~ doing
this** ich mache das sehr ungern **2.** *n* Hass *m (of* auf
*+ acc)*

**haul 1.** *vt* ziehen, schleppen **2.**
*n (booty)* Beute *f*; **haulage** *n*
Transport *m*; *(trade)* Spedition *f*

**haunted** *adj* **a ~ house** ein
Haus, in dem es spukt

**have 1.** *vt* hassen; *(possess)* ~
**you got** or **do you ~ a light?**
hast du / haben Sie Feuer?;
*(receive)* **I've just had a letter from ...** ich habe soeben
einen Brief von ... erhalten;
**~ a baby** ein Kind bekommen; *(have to eat / drink)*

**what are you having?** was
möchtest du / möchten Sie
(essen / trinken)?; **I had too
much wine** ich habe zu viel
Wein getrunken; **~ lunch /
dinner** zu Mittag / Abend
essen; **~ a party** eine
Party geben; *(take)* **~ a
bath / shower** ein Bad nehmen / duschen; *(causative)* **~
sth done** etw machen lassen; **they had a good time**
sie haben sich gut amüsiert;
*(phrases with 'it')* **I won't ~ it**
das lasse ich mir nicht bieten!; **we've had it** *fam* wir
sind geliefert **2.** *vaux (forming perfect tenses)* haben /
sein; **he has seen it** er hat
es gesehen; **she has come**
sie ist gekommen; *(expressing compulsion)* **~ (got) to
do sth** etw tun müssen;
**you don't ~ to go** du
musst / Sie müssen nicht gehen; *(in tag questions)*
**you've been there, ~n't
you?** du bist / Sie sind schon
mal dort gewesen, nicht
wahr?; **have on** *vt (be wearing)* anhaben; *(have arranged)* vorhaben; *(Brit)*
**you're having me on** du verarschst / Sie verarschen mich
doch

**Hawaii** *n* Hawaii *nt*

**hawk** *n* Habicht *m*

**hay** *n* Heu *nt*; **hay fever** *n*
Heuschnupfen *m*

**hazard** *n* Gefahr *f*; *(risk)* Risiko nt; **hazardous** adj gefährlich; ~ **waste** Sondermüll m; **hazard warning lights** npl Warnblinkanlage f

**haze** n Dunst m

**hazelnut** n Haselnuss f

**hazy** adj (misty) dunstig; (vague) verschwommen

**he** pron er

**head 1.** n Kopf m; (leader) Leiter(in) m(f); (at school) Schulleiter(in) m(f); ~ **of state** Staatsoberhaupt nt; (tossing coin) ~**s or tails?** Kopf oder Zahl? **2.** adj (leading) Ober-; ~ **boy** Schulsprecher m; ~ **girl** Schulsprecherin f **3.** vt anführen; (organization) leiten; **head for** vt zusteuern auf + acc; **he's heading for trouble** er wird Ärger bekommen

**headache** n Kopfschmerzen pl, Kopfweh nt; **header** n (soccer) Kopfball m; (dive) Kopfsprung m; **headfirst** adj kopfüber; **headhunt** vt COMM abwerben; **heading** n Überschrift f; **headlamp, headlight** n Scheinwerfer m; **headline** n Schlagzeile f; **headmaster** n Schulleiter m; **headmistress** n Schulleiterin f; **headphones** npl Kopfhörer m; **headquarters** npl (of firm) Zentrale f; **headrest** n Kopfstütze f; **headscarf** n Kopftuch nt; **head teacher**

n Schulleiter(in) m(f)

**heal** vt, vi heilen

**health** n Gesundheit f; **good / bad for one's** ~ gesund / ungesund ~ **and beauty** Wellness f; **health centre** n Ärztezentrum nt; **health club** n Fitnesscenter nt; **health food** n Reformkost f; ~ **store,** ~ **shop** Bioladen m; **health insurance** n Krankenversicherung f; **health service** n Gesundheitswesen nt; **healthy** adj gesund

**heap 1.** n Haufen m; ~**s of** fam jede Menge **2.** vt, vi häufen

**hear** vt, vi hören; ~ **about sth** von etw erfahren; **I've** ~**d of it / him** ich habe schon davon / von ihm gehört; **hearing** n Gehör nt; LAW Verhandlung f; **hearing aid** n Hörgerät nt; **hearsay** n from ~ vom Hörensagen

**heart** n Herz nt; **lose / take** ~ den Mut verlieren / Mut fassen; **learn by** ~ auswendig lernen; (cards) ~**s** Herz nt; **queen of** ~**s** Herzdame f; **heart attack** n Herzanfall m; **heartbeat** n Herzschlag m; **heartbreaking** adj herzzerreißend; **heartbroken** adj todunglücklich, untröstlich; **heartburn** n Sodbrennen nt; **heart failure** n Herzversagen nt; **heartfelt** adj tief empfunden; **heart-throb** n fam Schwarm m; **heart-to-**

**heart** n offene Aussprache; **hearty** adj (meal, appetite) herzhaft; (welcome) herzlich
**heat 1.** n Hitze f; (pleasant) Wärme f; (temperature) Temperatur f; SPORT Vorlauf m **2.** vt (house, room) heizen; **heat up 1.** vi warm werden **2.** vt aufwärmen; **heated** adj beheizt; fig hitzig; **heater** n Heizofen m; AUTO Heizung f
**heath** n (Brit) Heide f; **heather** n Heidekraut nt
**heating** n Heizung f
**heaven** n Himmel m; **heavenly** adj himmlisch
**heavily** adv (rain, drink etc) stark; **heavy** adj schwer; (rain, traffic, smoker etc) stark
**Hebrew 1.** adj hebräisch **2.** n (language) Hebräisch nt
**hectic** adj hektisch
**he'd** contr of **he had; he would**
**hedge** n Hecke f
**hedgehog** n Igel m
**heel** n ANAT Ferse f; (of shoe) Absatz m
**hefty** adj schwer; (person) stämmig; (fine, amount) saftig
**height** n Höhe f; (of person) Größe f
**heir** n Erbe m; **heiress** n Erbin f
**held** pt, pp → **hold**
**helicopter** n Hubschrauber m; **heliport** n Hubschrauberlandeplatz m

**hell 1.** n Hölle f; **go to ~** scher dich zum Teufel; **that's a ~ of a lot of money** das ist verdammt viel Geld **2.** interj verdammt
**he'll** contr of **he will; he shall**
**hello** interj hallo
**helmet** n Helm m
**help 1.** n Hilfe f **2.** vt, vi helfen + dat (with bei); **~ sb (to) do sth** jdm helfen, etw zu tun; **can I ~?** kann ich (Ihnen) behilflich sein?; **I couldn't ~ laughing** ich musste einfach lachen; **I can't ~ it** ich kann nichts dafür; **~ yourself** bedienen Sie sich; **helpful** adj (person) hilfsbereit; (useful) nützlich; **helping** n Portion f; **helpless** adj hilflos
**hem** n Saum m
**hemophiliac** n (US) Bluter m; **hemorrhage** n (US) Blutung f; **hemorrhoids** npl (US) Hämorrhoiden pl
**hen** n Henne f
**hence** adv (reason) daher
**hen night** n (Brit) Junggesellinnenabschied
**hepatitis** n Hepatitis f
**her 1.** adj ihr; **she's hurt ~ leg** sie hat sich dat das Bein verletzt **2.** pron (direct object) sie; (indirect object) ihr; **do you know ~?** kennst du sie?; **can you help ~?** kannst du ihr helfen?; **it's ~** sie ist's
**herb** n Kraut nt
**herd** n Herde f
**here** adv hier; (to this place)

hierher; *come* ~ komm her; *I won't be* ~ *for lunch* ich bin zum Mittagessen nicht da

**hereditary** *adj* erblich; **hereditary disease** *n* Erbkrankheit *f*; **heritage** *n* Erbe *nt*

**hernia** *n* Leistenbruch *m*, Eingeweidebruch *m*

**hero** *n* Held *m*

**heroin** *n* Heroin *nt*

**heroine** *n* Heldin *f*

**herring** *n* Hering *m*

**hers** *pron* ihre(r, s); *this is* ~ das gehört ihr; *a friend of* ~ ein Freund von ihr

**herself** *pron* (*reflexive*) sich; *she's bought* ~ *a flat* sie hat sich eine Wohnung gekauft; (*emphatic*) *she did it* ~ sie hat es selbst gemacht; (*all*) *by* ~ allein

**he's** *contr of* **he is; he has**

**hesitate** *vi* zögern; *don't* ~ *to ask* fragen Sie ruhig; **hesitation** *n* Zögern *nt*; *without* ~ ohne zu zögern

**heterosexual** *adj* heterosexuell

**hi** *interj* hi, hallo

**hiccup** *n* Schluckauf *m*

**hid** *pt* → **hide**

**hidden** *pp* → **hide**

**hide 1.** *vt* verstecken (*from* vor + *dat*), (*feelings, truth*) verbergen; (*cover*) verdecken **2.** *vi* sich verstecken (*from* vor + *dat*)

**hideous** *adj* scheußlich

**hiding** *n* (*beating*) Tracht *f*

Prügel; (*concealment*) *be in* ~ sich versteckt halten; **hiding place** *n* Versteck *nt*

**hi-fi** *n* Hi-Fi *nt*; (*system*) Hi-Fi-Anlage *f*

**high 1.** *adj* hoch; (*wind*) stark; (*on drugs*) high **2.** *adv* hoch **3.** *n* METEO Hoch *nt*; **highchair** *n* Hochstuhl *m*; **higher** *adj* höher; **higher education** *n* Hochschulbildung *f*; **high heels** *npl* Stöckelschuhe *pl*; **high jump** *n* Hochsprung *m*; **Highlands** *npl* (schottisches) Hochland *nt*; **highlight 1.** *n* (*in hair*) Strähnchen *nt*; *fig* Höhepunkt *m* **2.** *vt* (*with pen*) hervorheben; **highlighter** *n* Textmarker *m*; **highly** *adj* hoch, sehr; ~ *paid* hoch bezahlt; *I think* ~ *of him* ich habe eine hohe Meinung von ihm; **high school** *n* (*US*) Highschool *f*, ≈ Gymnasium *nt*; **high-speed** *adj* Schnell-; ~ *train* Hochgeschwindigkeitszug *m*; **high street** *n* Hauptstraße *f*; **high tech 1.** *adj* Hightech- **2.** *n* Hightech *nt*; **high tide** *n* Flut *f*; **highway** *n* (*US*) ≈ Autobahn *f*; (*Brit*) Landstraße *f*

**hijack** *vt* entführen, hijacken; **hijacker** *n* Entführer(in) *m(f)*, Hijacker *m*

**hike 1.** *vi* wandern **2.** *n* Wanderung *f*; **hiker** *n* Wanderer *m*, Wanderin *f*; **hiking** *n* Wandern *nt*

**hilarious** *adj* zum Schreien

komisch

**hill** n Hügel m; (*higher*) Berg m; **hilly** adj hügelig

**him** pron (*direct object*) ihn; (*indirect object*) ihm; **do you know ~?** kennst du ihn?; **can you help ~?** kannst du ihm helfen?; **it's ~** er ist's; **~ too** er auch

**himself** pron (*reflexive*) sich; **he's bought ~ a flat** er hat sich eine Wohnung gekauft; (*emphatic*) **he did it ~** er hat es selbst gemacht; (**all**) **by ~** allein

**hinder** vt behindern; **hindrance** n Behinderung f

**Hindu 1.** adj hinduistisch **2.** n Hindu m; **Hinduism** n Hinduismus m

**hinge** n Scharnier nt; (*on door*) Angel f

**hint 1.** n Wink m, Andeutung f **2.** vi andeuten (*at acc*)

**hip** n Hüfte f

**hippopotamus** n Nilpferd nt

**his 1.** adj sein; **he's hurt ~ leg** er hat sich das Bein verletzt **2.** pron seine(r, s); **it's ~** es gehört ihm; **a friend of ~** ein Freund von ihm

**historic** adj (*significant*) historisch; **historical** adj (*mon-*

*ument etc*) historisch; (*studies etc*) geschichtlich; **history** n Geschichte f

**hit 1.** n (*blow*) Schlag m; (*on target*) Treffer m; (*successful film, CD etc*) Erfolg m; Hit m **2.** vt schlagen; (*bullet, stone etc*) treffen; **the car ~ the tree** das Auto fuhr gegen einen Baum; **~ one's head on sth** sich den Kopf an etw dat stoßen; **hit (up)on** vt stoßen auf + acc; **hit-and-run** adj **~ accident** Unfall m mit Fahrerflucht

**hitch-hike** vi trampen; **hitch-hiker** n Tramper(in) m(f); **hitchhiking** n Trampen nt

**HIV** abbr = **human immunodeficiency virus** HIV nt; **~ positive / negative** HIV-positiv / negativ

**hive** n Bienenstock m

**HM** abbr = **His / Her Majesty**

**HMS** abbr = **His / Her Majesty's Ship**

**hoarse** adj heiser

**hoax** n Streich m, Jux m; (*false alarm*) blinder Alarm

**hob** n (*of cooker*) Kochfeld nt

**hobble** vi humpeln

**hobby** n Hobby nt

**hobo** n (*US*) Penner(in) m(f)

**hockey** n Hockey nt; (*US*) Eishockey nt

**hold 1.** vt halten; (*contain*) enthalten; (*be able to contain*) fassen; (*post, office*) innehaben; (*value*) behalten; (*meeting*) abhalten; (*person* *as prisoner*) gefangen halten; ~ **one's breath** den Atem anhalten; ~ **hands** Händchen halten; ~ **the line** TEL bleiben Sie am Apparat **2.** *vi* halten; (*weather*) sich halten **3.** *n* (*grasp*) Halt *m*; (*of ship, aircraft*) Laderaum *m*; **hold back** *vt* zurückhalten; (*keep secret*) verheimlichen; **hold on** *vi* sich festhalten; TEL dranbleiben; ~ **to sth** *vt* etw festhalten; **hold out** *vt* ausstrecken; (*offer*) hinhalten; (*offer*) bieten **2.** *vi* durchhalten; **hold up** *vt* hochhalten; (*support*) stützen; (*delay*) aufhalten; **holdall** *n* Reisetasche *f*; **holder** *n* (*person*) Inhaber(in) *m(f)*; **holdup** *n* (*in traffic*) Stau *m*; (*robbery*) Überfall *m*

**hole** *n* Loch *nt*; (*of fox, rabbit*) Bau *m*; ~ **in the wall** (*cash dispenser*) Geldautomat *m*

**holiday** *n* (*day off*) freier Tag; (*public holiday*) Feiertag *m*; (*vacation*) Urlaub *m*; (*at school*) Ferien *pl*; **on** ~ im Urlaub; **go on** ~ Urlaub machen; **holiday camp** *n* Ferienlager *nt*; **holiday home** *n* Ferienhaus *nt*; (*flat*) Ferienwohnung *f*; **holidaymaker** *n* Urlauber(in) *m(f)*; **holiday resort** *n* Ferienort *m*

**Holland** *n* Holland *nt*

**hollow 1.** *adj* hohl; (*words*) leer **2.** *n* Vertiefung *f*

**holly** *n* Stechpalme *f*

**holy** *adj* heilig; **Holy Week** *n* Karwoche *f*

**home 1.** *n* Zuhause *nt*; (*area, country*) Heimat *f*; (*institution*) Heim *nt*; **at** ~ zu Hause; **make oneself at** ~ es sich dir bequem machen; **away from** ~ verreist **2.** *adv* **go** ~ nach Hause gehen / fahren; **home address** *n* Heimatadresse *f*; **home country** *n* Heimatland *nt*; **home game** *n* SPORT Heimspiel *nt*; **homeless** *adj* obdachlos; **homely** *adj* häuslich; (*US, ugly*) unscheinbar; **home-made** *adj* selbst gemacht; **Home Office** *n* (*Brit*) Innenministerium *nt*

**homeopathic** *adj* (*US*) → **homoeopathic**

**home page** *n* IT Homepage *f*; **Home Secretary** *n* (*Brit*) Innenminister(in) *m(f)*; **homesick** *adj* **be** ~ Heimweh haben; **homework** *n* Hausaufgaben *pl*

**homicide** *n* (*US*) Totschlag *m*

**homoeopathic** *adj* homöopathisch

**homosexual** *adj* homosexuell

**Honduras** *n* Honduras *nt*

**honest** *adj* ehrlich; **honesty** *n* Ehrlichkeit *f*

**honey** *n* Honig *m*; **honeydew melon** *n* Honigmelone *f*; **honeymoon** *n* Flitterwochen *pl*

**Hong Kong** *n* Hongkong *nt*

**honor** (US) → **honour**; honorary adj (member, title etc) Ehren-, ehrenamtlich; **honour 1.** vt ehren; (cheque) einlösen; (contract) einhalten **2.** n Ehre f; **in ~ of** zu Ehren von; **honourable** adj ehrenhaft; **honours degree** n akademischer Grad mit Prüfung im Spezialfach

**hood** n Kapuze f; AUTO Verdeck nt; (US) AUTO Kühlerhaube f

**hoof** n Huf m

**hook** n Haken m; **hooked** adj (keen) besessen (on von); (drugs) abhängig (on von)

**hooligan** n Hooligan m

**hoot** vi AUTO hupen

**Hoover**® **1.** n Staubsauger m; **hoover** n, vt staubsaugen

**hop 1.** vi hüpfen **2.** n BOT Hopfen m

**hope 1.** vi, vt hoffen (for auf + acc); **I ~ so/~ not** hoffentlich / hoffentlich nicht; **I ~ (that) we'll meet** ich hoffe, dass wir uns sehen werden **2.** n Hoffnung f; **there's no ~** es ist aussichtslos; **hopeful** adj hoffnungsvoll; **hopefully** adv (full of hope) hoffnungsvoll; (I hope so) hoffentlich; **hopeless** adj hoffnungslos; (incompetent) miserabel

**horizon** n Horizont m; **horizontal** adj horizontal

**hormone** n Hormon nt

**horn** n Horn nt; AUTO Hupe f

**hornet** n Hornisse f

**horny** adj fam geil

**horoscope** n Horoskop nt

**horrible, horribly** adj, adv schrecklich; **horrid, horridly** adj, adv abscheulich; **horrify** vt entsetzen; **horror** n Entsetzen nt; (things) Schrecken pl

**hors d'oeuvre** n Vorspeise f

**horse** n Pferd nt; **horse chestnut** n Rosskastanie f; **horsepower** n Pferdestärke f, PS nt; **horse racing** n Pferderennen nt; **horseradish** n Meerrettich m; **horse riding** n Reiten nt; **horseshoe** n Hufeisen nt

**hose, hosepipe** n Schlauch m

**hospitable** adj gastfreundlich

**hospital** n Krankenhaus nt

**hospitality** n Gastfreundschaft f

**host 1.** n Gastgeber m; TV (of show) Moderator(in) m(f); Talkmaster(in) m(f) **2.** vt (party) geben; TV (TV show) moderieren

**hostage** n Geisel f

**hostel** n Wohnheim nt; (youth hostel) Jugendherberge f

**hostess** n (of a party) Gastgeberin f

**hostile** adj feindlich; **hostility** n Feindseligkeit f

**hot** adj heiß; (drink, food, water) warm; (spiced) scharf; **I'm (feeling) ~** mir ist heiß; **hot dog** n Hotdog nt

**hotel** n Hotel nt; **hotel room** n

Hotelzimmer *nt*

**hothouse** *n* Treibhaus *nt*;
**hotline** *n* Hotline *f*; **hotplate**
*n* Kochplatte *f*; **hotpot** *n*
Fleischeintopf mit Kartoffeleinlage; **hot-water bottle** *n*
Wärmflasche *f*

**hour** *n* Stunde *f*; **wait for ~s**
stundenlang warten; **~s** *pl*
(*of shops etc*) Geschäftszeiten *pl*; **hourly** *adj* stündlich

**house 1.** *n* Haus *nt*; **at my ~**
bei mir (zu Hause); **to my ~**
zu mir (nach Hause); **on
the~** auf Kosten des Hauses;
**the House of Commons /
Lords** das britische Unterhaus / Oberhaus; **the Houses of Parliament** das britische Parlamentsgebäude **2.**
*vt* unterbringen; **houseboat**
*n* Hausboot *nt*; **household** *n*
Haushalt *m*; **~ appliance**
Haushaltsgerät *nt*; **househusband** *n* Hausmann *m*;
**housekeeping** *n* Haushaltung *f*; (*money*) Haushaltsgeld *nt*; **house-trained** *adj*
stubenrein; **house-warming (party)** *n* Einzugsparty
*f*; **housewife** *n* Hausfrau *f*;
**house wine** *n* Hauswein
*m*; **housework** *n* Hausarbeit
*f*

**housing** *n* (*houses*) Wohnungen *pl*; (*house building*)
Wohnungsbau *m*; **housing
benefit** *n* Wohngeld *nt*;
**housing development**,
**housing estate** (*Brit*) *n*

Wohnsiedlung *f*

**hover** *vi* schweben; **hovercraft** *n* Luftkissenboot *nt*

**how** *adv* wie; **~ many** wie viele; **~ much** wie viel; **~ are
you?** wie geht es Ihnen?; **~
are things?** wie geht's?; **~'s
work?** was macht die Arbeit?; **~ about ...?** wie wäre
es mit ...?; **however 1.** *conj*
(*but*) jedoch, aber **2.** *adv*
(*no matter how*) wie ... auch;
**~ much it costs** wie viel es
auch kostet

**howl** *vi* heulen; **howler** *n fam*
grober Schnitzer

**HQ** *abbr* → **headquarters**

**hubcap** *n* Radkappe *f*

**hug 1.** *vt* umarmen *2. n* Umarmung *f*

**huge** *adj* riesig

**hum** *vi*, *vt* summen

**human 1.** *adj* menschlich; **~
rights** Menschenrechte *pl*
**2.** *n* ~ (**being**) Mensch *m*; **humanitarian** *adj* humanitär;
**humanity** *n* Menschheit *f*;
(*kindliness*) Menschlichkeit
*f*; **humanities** Geisteswissenschaften *pl*

**humble** *adj* demütig; (*modest*) bescheiden

**humid** *adj* feucht; **humidity** *n*
(Luft)feuchtigkeit *f*

**humiliate** *vt* demütigen; **humiliation** *n* Erniedrigung *f*,
Demütigung *f*

**humor** (*US*) → **humour**; **humorous** *adj* humorvoll; (*story*) lustig, witzig; **humour** *n*

Humor *m*; **sense of** ~ Sinn *m* für Humor

**hump** *n* Buckel *m*

**hundred** *num* **one** ~, **a** ~ (ein)hundert; **a** ~ **and one** hundert(und)eins; **two** ~ zweihundert; **hundredth 1.** *adj* hundertste(r, s) **2.** *n* (*fraction*) Hundertstel *nt*; **hundredweight** *n* Zentner *m* (*50,8 kg*)

**hung** *pt, pp* → **hang**

**Hungarian 1.** *adj* ungarisch **2.** *n* (*person*) Ungar(in) *m(f)*; (*language*) Ungarisch *nt*; **Hungary** *n* Ungarn *nt*

**hunger** *n* Hunger *m*; **hungry** *adj* hungrig; **be** ~ Hunger haben

**hunk** *n* *fam* gut gebauter Mann; **hunky** *adj* *fam* (*man*) gut gebaut

**hunt 1.** *n* Jagd *f*; (*search*) Suche *f* (*for* nach) **2.** *vt, vi* jagen; (*search*) suchen (*for* nach); **hunting** *n* Jagen *nt*, Jagd *f*

**hurdle** *n a. fig* Hürde *f*; **the 400m** ~**s** der 400m-Hürdenlauf

**hurl** *vt* schleudern

**hurricane** *n* Orkan *m*

**hurried** *adj* eilig; **hurry 1.** *n* Eile *f*; **be in a** ~ es eilig haben; **there's no** ~ es eilt nicht **2.** *vi* sich beeilen; ~ (**up**) mach schnell! **3.** *vt* antreiben

**hurt 1.** *n* wehtun + *dat*;

(*wound: person, feelings*) verletzen; **I've** ~ **my arm** ich habe mir am Arm wehgetan **2.** *vi* wehtun; **my arm** ~**s** mir tut der Arm weh

**husband** *n* Ehemann *m*

**husky 1.** *adj* rau **2.** *n* Schlittenhund *m*

**hut** *n* Hütte *f*

**hyacinth** *n* Hyazinthe *f*

**hybrid** *n* Kreuzung *f*

**hydroelectric** *adj* ~ **power station** Wasserkraftwerk *nt*

**hydrofoil** *n* Tragflächenboot *nt*

**hydrogen** *n* Wasserstoff *m*

**hygiene** *n* Hygiene *f*; **hygienic** *adj* hygienisch

**hymn** *n* Kirchenlied *nt*

**hypermarket** *n* Großmarkt *m*; **hypersensitive** *adj* überempfindlich

**hyphen** *n* Bindestrich *m*

**hypnosis** *n* Hypnose *f*; **hypnotize** *vt* hypnotisieren

**hypochondriac** *n* eingebildete(r) Kranke(r)

**hypocrisy** *n* Heuchelei *f*; **hypocrite** *n* Heuchler(in) *m(f)*

**hypodermic** *adj, n* ~ (**needle**) Spritze *f*

**hypothetical** *adj* hypothetisch

**hysteria** *n* Hysterie *f*; **hysterical** *adj* hysterisch; (*amusing*) zum Totlachen

# I

**I** *pron* ich

**ice 1.** *n* Eis *nt* **2.** *vt* (*cake*) glasieren; **iceberg** *n* Eisberg *m*; **icebox** *n* (*US*) Kühlschrank *m*; **icecold** *adj* eiskalt; **ice cream** *n* Eis *nt*; **ice cube** *n* Eiswürfel *m*; **iced** *adj* eisgekühlt; (*coffee, tea*) Eis-; (*cake*) glasiert; **ice hockey** *n* Eishockey *nt*

**Iceland** *n* Island *nt*; **Icelander** *n* Isländer(in) *m(f)*; **Icelandic 1.** *adj* isländisch **2.** *n* (*language*) Isländisch *nt*

**ice lolly** *n* (*Brit*) Eis *nt* am Stiel; **ice rink** *n* Kunsteisbahn *f*; **ice skating** *n* Schlittschuhlaufen *nt*

**icing** *n* (*on cake*) Zuckerguss *m*

**icon** *n* Ikone *f*; **IT** Icon *nt*, Programmsymbol *nt*

**icy** *adj* (*slippery*) vereist; (*cold*) eisig

**I'd** *contr = I would; I had*

**ID** *abbr = identification* Ausweis *m*

**idea** *n* Idee *f*; (*I've*) **no ~** (ich habe) keine Ahnung; *that's my ~ of ...* so stelle ich mir ... vor

**ideal 1.** *n* Ideal *nt* **2.** *adj* ideal; **ideally** *adv* ideal; (*before statement*) idealerweise

**identical** *adj* identisch; **~ twins** eineiige Zwillinge

**identify** *vt* identifizieren; **identity** *n* Identität *f*; **identity card** *n* Personalausweis *m*

**idiom** *n* Redewendung *f*; **idiomatic** *adj* idiomatisch

**idiot** *n* Idiot(in) *m(f)*

**idle** *adj* (*doing nothing*) untätig; (*lazy*) faul; (*promise, threat*) leer

**idol** *n* Idol *nt*; **idolize** *vt* vergöttern

**idyllic** *adj* idyllisch

**i.e.** *abbr = id est* d. h.

**if** *conj* wenn, falls; (*whether*) ob; **~ so** wenn ja; **~ I were you** wenn ich du / Sie wäre; *I don't know ~ he's coming* ich weiß nicht, ob er kommt

**ignition** *n* Zündung *f*; **ignition key** *n* AUTO Zündschlüssel *m*

**ignorance** *n* Unwissenheit *f*; **ignorant** *adj* unwissend; **ignore** *vt* ignorieren, nicht beachten

**I'll** *contr = I will; I shall*

**ill** *adj* krank; **~ at ease** unbehaglich

**illegal** *adj* illegal

**illegitimate** *adj* unzulässig; (*child*) unehelich

**illiterate** *adj* **be ~** Analphabet(in) sein

**illness** *n* Krankheit *f*

**illuminate** *vt* beleuchten; **illuminating** *adj* (*remark*) aufschlussreich

**illusion** n Illusion f; **be under the ~ that** ... sich einbilden, dass ...

**illustrate** vt illustrieren; **illustration** n Abbildung f, Bild nt

**I'm** contr = **I am**

**image** n Bild nt; (public image) Image nt; **imagination** n Fantasie f; (mistaken) Einbildung f; **imaginative** adj fantasievoll; **imagine** vt sich vorstellen; (wrongly) sich einbilden; **~!** stell dir vor!

**imitate** vt nachahmen, nachmachen; **imitation 1.** n Nachahmung f **2.** adj imitiert, Kunst-

**immaculate** adj tadellos; (spotless) makellos

**immature** adj unreif

**immediate** adj unmittelbar; (instant) sofortig; (reply) umgehend; **immediately** adv sofort

**immense, immensely** adj, adv riesig, enorm

**immersion heater** n Boiler m

**immigrant** n Einwanderer m, Einwanderin f; **immigration** n Einwanderung f; (facility) Einwanderungskontrolle f

**immobilize** vt lähmen; **immobilizer** n AUTO Wegfahrsperre f

**immoral** adj unmoralisch

**immortal** adj unsterblich

**immune** adj MED immun (from, to gegen); **immune**

**system** n Immunsystem nt

**impact** n Aufprall m; (effect) Auswirkung f (on auf + acc)

**impatience** n Ungeduld f; **impatient, impatiently** adj, adv ungeduldig

**impede** vt behindern

**imperfect** adj unvollkommen; (goods) fehlerhaft

**imperial** adj kaiserlich, Reichs-; **imperialism** n Imperialismus m

**impertinence** n Unverschämtheit f, Zumutung f; **impertinent** adj unverschämt

**implant** n MED Implantat nt

**implausible** adj unglaubwürdig

**implement 1.** n Werkzeug nt, Gerät nt **2.** vt durchführen

**implication** n Folge f, Auswirkung f; (logical) Schlussfolgerung f; **implicit** adj implizit, unausgesprochen; **imply** vt (indicate) andeuten; (mean) bedeuten; **are you ~ing that** ... wollen Sie damit sagen, dass ...

**impolite** adj unhöflich

**import 1.** vt einführen, importieren **2.** n Einfuhr f, Import m

**importance** n Bedeutung f; **of no ~** unwichtig; **important** adj wichtig (to sb für jdn); (significant) bedeutend; (influential) einflussreich

**import duty** n Einfuhrzoll m;

**import licence** n Einfuhrgenehmigung f

**impose** vt (conditions) auferlegen (on dat); (penalty, sanctions) verhängen (on gegen); **imposing** adj eindrucksvoll, imposant

**impossible** adj unmöglich

**impotence** n Machtlosigkeit f; (sexual) Impotenz f; **impotent** adj machtlos; (sexually) impotent

**impractical** adj unpraktisch; (plan) undurchführbar

**impress** vt beeindrucken; **impression** n Eindruck m; **impressive** adj eindrucksvoll

**imprison** vt inhaftieren; **imprisonment** n Inhaftierung f

**improper** adj (indecent) unanständig; (use) unsachgemäß

**improve 1.** vt verbessern **2.** vi sich verbessern, besser werden; (patient) Fortschritte machen; **improvement** n Verbesserung f (in + gen; on gegenüber); (in appearance) Verschönerung f

**improvise** vt, vi improvisieren

**impulse** n Impuls m; **impulsive** adj impulsiv

**in 1.** prep in + dat; (expressing motion) in + acc; (in the case of) bei; **put it ~ the drawer** tu es in die Schublade; **~ the army** beim Militär; **~ itself** an sich; (time) **~ the morning / afternoon / evening** am Morgen / Nachmittag /

Abend; **at three ~ the afternoon** um drei Uhr nachmittags; **~ 2007** (im Jahre) 2007; **~ July** im Juli; **~ a week** in einer Woche; **~ writing** schriftlich; **~ German** auf Deutsch; **one ~ ten** einer von zehn, jeder zehnte; **~ all** insgesamt **2.** adv (go) hinein; (come) herein; **be ~** zu Hause sein; (in fashion) in sein, modisch sein; (arrived) angekommen sein; **sb is ~ for sth** jdm steht etw bevor; (sth unpleasant) jmd kann sich auf etw acc gefasst machen; **be ~ on sth** an etw dat beteiligt sein

**inability** n Unfähigkeit f

**inaccessible** adj a. fig unzugänglich

**inaccurate** adj ungenau

**inadequate** adj unzulänglich

**inappropriate** adj unpassend; (clothing) ungeeignet; (remark) unangebracht

**incapable** adj unfähig (of zu); **be ~ of doing sth** nicht imstande sein, etw zu tun

**incense** n Weihrauch m

**incentive** n Anreiz m

**incessant, incessantly** adj, adv unaufhörlich

**incest** n Inzest m

**inch** n Zoll m (2,54 cm)

**incident** n Vorfall m; (disturbance) Zwischenfall m; **incidentally** adv nebenbei bemerkt, übrigens

**inclination** n Neigung f; **inclined** adj **be ~ to do sth** dazu neigen, etw zu tun

**include** vt einschließen; (on list, in group) aufnehmen; **including** prep einschließlich (+ gen); **not ~ service** Bedienung nicht inbegriffen; **inclusive** adj einschließlich (of + gen); (price) Pauschal-

**incoherent** adj zusammenhanglos

**income** n Einkommen nt; (from business) Einkünfte pl; **income tax** n Einkommensteuer f; (on wages, salary) Lohnsteuer f; **incoming** adj ankommend; (mail) eingehend

**incompatible** adj unvereinbar; (people) unverträglich; IT nicht kompatibel

**incompetent** adj unfähig

**incomplete** adj unvollständig

**incomprehensible** adj unverständlich

**inconceivable** adj unvorstellbar

**inconsiderate** adj rücksichtslos

**inconsistency** n Inkonsequenz f; (contradictory) Widersprüchlichkeit f; **inconsistent** adj inkonsequent; (contradictory) widersprüchlich; (work) unbeständig

**inconvenience** n Unannehmlichkeit f; (trouble) Umstände pl; **inconvenient** adj ungünstig, unbequem;

(time) **it's ~ for me** es kommt mir ungelegen; **if it's not too ~ for you** wenn es dir / Ihnen passt

**incorporate** vt aufnehmen (into in + acc); (include) enthalten

**incorrect** adj falsch; (improper) inkorrekt

**increase 1.** n Zunahme f (in an + dat); (in amount, speed) Erhöhung f (in + gen) **2.** vt (price, taxes, salary, speed etc) erhöhen; (wealth) vermehren; (number) vergrößern **3.** vi zunehmen (in an + dat); (prices) steigen; (in size) größer werden; (in number) sich vermehren; **increasingly** adv zunehmend

**incredible, incredibly** adj, adv unglaublich; (very good) fantastisch

**incredulous** adj ungläubig, skeptisch

**incriminate** vt belasten

**incubator** n Brutkasten m

**incurable** adj unheilbar

**indecent** adj unanständig

**indecisive** adj (person) unentschlossen; (result) nicht entscheidend

**indeed** adv tatsächlich; (as answer) allerdings; **very hot ~** wirklich sehr heiß

**indefinite** adj unbestimmt; **indefinitely** adv endlos; (postpone) auf unbestimmte Zeit

**independence** n Unabhängigkeit *f*; **independent** *adj* unabhängig (*of* von); (*person*) selbstständig

**indescribable** *adj* unbeschreiblich

**index** *n* Index *m*, Verzeichnis *nt*; **index finger** *n* Zeigefinger *m*

**India** *n* Indien *nt*; **Indian 1.** *adj* indisch; (*Native American*) indianisch **2.** *n* Inder(in) *m(f)*; (*Native American*) Indianer(in) *m(f)*; **Indian Ocean** *n* Indischer Ozean; **Indian summer** *n* Spätsommer *m*, Altweibersommer *m*

**indicate 1.** *vt* (*show*) zeigen; (*instrument*) anzeigen; (*suggest*) hinweisen auf + *acc* **2.** *vi* AUTO blinken; **indication** *n* (*sign*) Anzeichen *nt* (*of* für); **indicator** *n* AUTO Blinker *m*

**indifferent** *adj* (*not caring*) gleichgültig (*to, towards* gegenüber); (*mediocre*) mittelmäßig

**indigestible** *adj* unverdaulich; **indigestion** *n* Verdauungsstörung *f*

**indignity** *n* Demütigung *f*

**indirect, indirectly** *adj, adv* indirekt

**indiscreet** *adj* indiskret

**indispensable** *adj* unentbehrlich

**indisposed** *adj* unwohl

**indisputable** *adj* unbestreitbar; (*evidence*) unanfechtbar

**individual 1.** *n* Einzelne(r) *mf*

**2.** *adj* einzeln; (*distinctive*) eigen, individuell; **~ case** Einzelfall *m*; **individually** *adv* (*separately*) einzeln

**Indonesia** *n* Indonesien *nt*

**indoor** *adj* (*shoes*) Haus-; (*plant, games*) Zimmer-; SPORT (*soccer, championship, record etc*) Hallen-; **indoors** *adv* drinnen, im Haus

**indulge** *vi* **~ in sth** sich *dat* etw gönnen; **indulgence** *n* Nachsicht *f*; (*enjoyment*) (übermäßiger) Genuss; (*luxury*) Luxus *m*; **indulgent** *adj* nachsichtig (*with* gegenüber)

**industrial** *adj* Industrie-, industriell; **~ estate** Industriegebiet *nt*; **industry** *n* Industrie *f*

**inedible** *adj* nicht essbar, ungenießbar

**ineffective** *adj* unwirksam, wirkungslos; **inefficient** *adj* unwirksam; (*use, machine*) unwirtschaftlich; (*method etc*) unrationell

**inequality** *n* Ungleichheit *f*

**inevitable** *adj* unvermeidlich; **inevitably** *adv* zwangsläufig

**inexcusable** *adj* unverzeihlich

**inexpensive** *adj* preisgünstig

**inexperience** *n* Unerfahrenheit *f*; **inexperienced** *adj* unerfahren

**inexplicable** *adj* unerklärlich

**infallible** *adj* unfehlbar

**infamous** *adj* (*person*) berüchtigt (for wegen); (deed) niederträchtig

**infancy** n frühe Kindheit; **infant** n Säugling m; (small child) Kleinkind nt; **infant school** n Vorschule f

**infatuated** adj vernarrt or verknallt (with in + acc)

**infect** vt (person) anstecken; (wound) infizieren; **infection** n Infektion f; **infectious** adj ansteckend

**inferior** adj (in quality) minderwertig; (in rank) untergeordnet; **inferiority** n Minderwertigkeit f

**infertile** adj unfruchtbar

**inflame** vt MED entzünden; **inflammation** n MED Entzündung f

**inflatable** adj aufblasbar; **inflate** vt aufpumpen; (by blowing) aufblasen; (prices) hochtreiben

**inflation** n Inflation f

**inflexible** adj unflexibel

**in-flight** adj (catering, magazine) Bord-

**influence 1.** n Einfluss m (on auf + acc) **2.** vt beeinflussen; **influential** adj einflussreich

**influenza** n Grippe f

**inform** vt informieren (of, about über + acc); **keep sb ~ed** jdn auf dem Laufenden halten

**informal** adj zwanglos, ungezwungen

**information** n Auskunft f, Informationen pl; **for your ~** zu

deiner / Ihrer Information; **further ~** weitere Informationen, Weiteres; **information desk** n Auskunftsschalter m; **information technology** n Informationstechnik f, Informationstechnologie f; **informative** adj aufschlussreich

**infra-red** adj infrarot

**infrastructure** n Infrastruktur f

**infuriate** vt wütend machen; **infuriating** adj äußerst ärgerlich

**infusion** n (herbal tea) Aufguss m; MED Infusion f

**ingenious** adj (person) erfinderisch; (device) raffiniert; (idea) genial

**ingredient** n GASTR Zutat f

**inhabit** vt bewohnen; **inhabitant** n Einwohner(in) m(f)

**inhale** vt einatmen; (cigarettes) MED inhalieren; **inhaler** n Inhalationsgerät nt

**inherit** vt erben; **inheritance** n Erbe nt

**in-house** adj intern

**inhuman** adj unmenschlich

**initial 1.** adj anfänglich; **~ stage** Anfangsstadium nt **2.** vt mit Initialen unterschreiben; **initially** adv anfangs; **initials** npl Initialen pl

**initiative** n Initiative f

**inject** vt (drug etc) einspritzen; **~ sb with sth** jdm etw (ein)spritzen; **injection** n Spritze f, Injektion f

**injure** vt verletzen; **~ one's leg** sich dat das Bein verletzen; **injury** n Verletzung f

**injustice** n Ungerechtigkeit f

**ink** n Tinte f; **ink-jet printer** n Tintenstrahldrucker m

**inland 1.** adj Binnen- **2.** adv landeinwärts; **inland revenue** n (Brit) Finanzamt nt

**in-laws** npl fam Schwiegereltern pl

**inline skates** npl Inlineskates pl, Inliner pl

**inmate** n Insasse m

**inn** n Gasthaus nt

**inner** adj innere(r, s); **~ city** Innenstadt f

**innocence** n Unschuld f; **innocent** adj unschuldig

**innovation** n Neuerung f

**innumerable** adj unzählig

**inoculate** vt impfen (against gegen); **inoculation** n Impfung f

**in-patient** n stationärer Patient, stationäre Patientin

**input** n (contribution) Beitrag m; IT Eingabe f

**inquire** → **enquire**; **inquiry** → **enquiry**

**insane** adj wahnsinnig; MED geisteskrank; **insanity** n Wahnsinn m

**insatiable** adj unersättlich

**inscription** n (on stone etc) Inschrift f

**insect** n Insekt nt

**insecure** adj (person) unsicher; (shelves) instabil

**insensitive** adj unempfind-

lich (to gegen); (unfeeling) gefühllos

**inseparable** adj unzertrennlich

**insert 1.** vt einfügen; (coin) einwerfen; (key etc) hineinstecken **2.** n (in magazine) Beilage f; **insertion** n (in text) Einfügen nt

**inside 1. n the ~** das Innere; (surface) die Innenseite; **from the ~** von innen **2.** adj innere(r, s), Innen-; **~ lane** AUTO Innenspur f; SPORT Innenbahn f **3.** adv (place) innen; (direction) hinein; **go ~** hineingehen **4.** prep (place) in + dat; (into) in + acc ... hinein; (time, within) innerhalb + gen; **inside out** adv verkehrt herum; (know) in und auswendig; **insider** n Eingeweihte(r) mf, Insider(in) m(f)

**insight** n Einblick m (into in + acc)

**insincere** adj unaufrichtig, falsch

**insinuation** n Andeutung f

**insist** vi darauf bestehen; **~ on sth** auf etw dat bestehen; **insistent** adj hartnäckig

**insomnia** n Schlaflosigkeit f

**inspect** vt prüfen, kontrollieren; **inspection** n Prüfung f; (check) Kontrolle f; **inspector** n (police) Inspektor(in) m(f); (senior) Kommissar(in) m(f); (on bus etc) Kontrolleur(in) m(f)

**inspiration** n Inspiration f; **inspire** vt (respect) einflößen (in dat); (person) inspirieren

**install** vt (software) installieren

**installment, instalment** n Rate f; (of story) Folge f; **pay in ~s** auf Raten zahlen; **installment plan** n (US) Ratenkauf m

**instance** n (of discrimination) Fall m; (example) Beispiel m (of für + acc); **for ~** zum Beispiel

**instant 1.** n Augenblick m **2.** adj sofortig; **instant coffee** n löslicher Kaffee m; **instantly** adv sofort

**instead** adv stattdessen; **instead of** prep (an)statt + gen

**instinct** n Instinkt m; **instinctive, instinctively** adj, adv instinktiv

**institute** n Institut nt; **institution** n (organisation) Institution f, Einrichtung f; (home) Anstalt f

**instruct** vt anweisen; **instruction** n (teaching) Unterricht m; (command) Anweisung f; **~s for use** Gebrauchsanweisung f; **instructor** n Lehrer(in) m(f); (US) Dozent(in) m(f)

**instrument** n Instrument nt; **instrument panel** n Armaturenbrett nt

**insufficient** adj ungenügend

**insulate** vt ELEC isolieren; insulating tape n Isolierband nt; **insulation** n Isolierung f

**insulin** n Insulin nt

**insult 1.** n Beleidigung f **2.** vt beleidigen; **insulting** adj beleidigend

**insurance** n Versicherung f; **~ company** Versicherungsgesellschaft f; **~ policy** Versicherungspolice f; **insure** vt versichern (against gegen)

**intake** n Aufnahme f

**integrate** vt integrieren (into in + acc)

**integrity** n Integrität f, Ehrlichkeit f

**intellect** n Intellekt m; **intellectual** adj intellektuell; (interests etc) geistig

**intelligence** n (understanding) Intelligenz f; **intelligent** adj intelligent

**intend** vt beabsichtigen; **~ to do sth** vorhaben, etw zu tun

**intense** adj intensiv; (pressure) enorm; (competition) heftig; **intensity** n Intensität f; **intensive** adj intensiv; **intensive care unit** n Intensivstation f

**intention** n Absicht f; **intentional, intentionally** adj, adv absichtlich

**interact** vi aufeinander einwirken; **interaction** n Interaktion f, Wechselwirkung f; **interactive** adj interaktiv

**interchange** n (of motorways) Autobahnkreuz nt; **interchangeable** adj austauschbar

**intercity** n Intercityzug m, IC m

**intercom** n (Gegen)sprechanlage f

**intercourse** n (sexual) Geschlechtsverkehr m

**interest 1.** n Interesse nt; FIN (on money) Zinsen pl; comm (share) Anteil m; **be of ~** von Interesse sein (to für) **2.** vt interessieren; **interested** adj interessiert (in an + dat); **be ~ in** sich interessieren für; **are you ~ in coming?** hast du Lust, mitzukommen?; **interesting** adj interessant; **interest rate** n Zinssatz m

**interface** n IT Schnittstelle f

**interfere** vi (meddle) sich einmischen (with, in in + acc); **interference** n Einmischung f; TV, RADIO Störung f

**interior 1.** adj Innen- **2.** n Innere(s) nt; (of car) Innenraum m; (of house) Innenausstattung f

**intermediate** adj Zwischen-

**intermission** n Pause f

**intern** n Assistent(in) m(f)

**internal** adj innere(r, s); (flight) Inlands-; **~ revenue** (US) Finanzamt nt; **internally** adv innen; (in body) innerlich

**international 1.** adj international; **~ match** Länderspiel nt; **~ flight** Auslandsflug m **2.** n sport (player) National-

spieler(in) m(f)

**Internet** n IT Internet nt; **Internet access** n Internetzugang m; **Internet auction** n Internetauktion f; **Internet banking** n Onlinebanking nt; **Internet café** n Internetcafé nt; **Internet connection** n Internetanschluss m; **Internet provider** n Internetprovider m

**interpret** vi, vt (translate) dolmetschen; (explain) interpretieren; **interpretation** n Interpretation f; **interpreter** n Dolmetscher(in) m(f)

**interrogate** vt verhören; **interrogation** n Verhör nt

**interrupt** vt unterbrechen; **interruption** n Unterbrechung f

**intersection** n (of roads) Kreuzung f

**interstate** n (US) zwischenstaatlich; **~ highway** ≈ Bundesautobahn f

**interval** n (space, time) Abstand m; (theatre etc) Pause f

**intervene** vi eingreifen (in in); **intervention** n Eingreifen nt; POL Intervention f

**interview 1.** n Interview nt; (for job) Vorstellungsgespräch nt **2.** vt interviewen; (job applicant) ein Vorstellungsgespräch führen mit; **interviewer** n Interviewer(in) m(f)

**intestine** n Darm m; **~s** pl Eingeweide pl

# intimate

**intimate** adj (friends) vertraut, eng; (atmosphere) gemütlich; (sexually) intim

**intimidate** vt einschüchtern; **intimidation** n Einschüchterung f

**into** prep in + acc; (crash) gegen; **translate ~ French** ins Französische übersetzen; **be ~ sth** fam auf etw acc stehen

**intolerable** adj unerträglich

**intolerant** adj intolerant

**intoxicated** adj betrunken; fig berauscht

**intricate** adj kompliziert

**intrigue** vt faszinieren; **intriguing** adj faszinierend, fesselnd

**introduce** vt (person) vorstellen (to sb jdm); (sth new) einführen (to in + acc); **introduction** n Einführung f (to in + acc); (to book) Einleitung f (to zu); (to person) Vorstellung f

**introvert** n Introvertierte(r) mf

**intuition** n Intuition f

**invade** vt einfallen in + acc

**invalid 1.** n Kranke(r) mf; (disabled) Invalide m **2.** adj (not valid) ungültig

**invaluable** adj äußerst wertvoll, unschätzbar

**invariably** adv ständig; (every time) jedes Mal, ohne Ausnahme

**invasion** n Invasion f (of in + acc)

**invent** vt erfinden; **invention** n Erfindung f; **inventor** n Erfinder(in) m(f)

**inverted commas** npl Anführungszeichen pl

**invest** vt, vi investieren (in in + acc)

**investigate** vt untersuchen; **investigation** n Untersuchung f (into + gen)

**investment** n Investition f; **it's a good ~** es ist eine gute Anlage

**invigorating** adj erfrischend, belebend; (tonic) stärkend

**invisible** adj unsichtbar

**invitation** n Einladung f; **invite** vt einladen

**invoice** n (bill) Rechnung f

**involuntary** adj unbeabsichtigt

**involve** vt verwickeln (in sth in etw acc); (entail) zur Folge haben; **be ~d in sth** (participate in) an etw dat beteiligt sein; **I'm not ~d** (affected) ich bin nicht betroffen

**inward** adj innere(r, s); **inwardly** adv innerlich; **inwards** adv nach innen

**iodine** n Jod nt

**IOU** abbr = **I owe you** Schuldschein m

**IQ** abbr = **intelligence quotient** IQ m

**Iran** n der Iran

**Iraq** n der Irak

**Ireland** n Irland nt

**iris** n (flower) Schwertlilie f; (of eye) Iris f

**Irish 1.** adj irisch; **~ coffee** Irish Coffee m; **~ Sea** die Irische See **2.** n (language) Irisch nt; **the ~** pl die Iren pl; **Irishman** n Ire m; **Irishwoman** n Irin f

**iron 1.** n Eisen nt; (for ironing) Bügeleisen nt **2.** adj eisern **3.** vt bügeln

**ironic(al)** adj ironisch

**ironing board** n Bügelbrett nt

**irony** n Ironie f

**irrational** adj irrational

**irregular** adj unregelmäßig

**irrelevant** adj belanglos, irrelevant

**irreplaceable** adj unersetzlich

**irresistible** adj unwiderstehlich

**irresponsible** adj verantwortungslos

**irretrievable** adv unwiederbringlich; (loss) unersetzlich

**irritable** adj reizbar; **irritate** vt (annoy) ärgern; (deliberately) reizen; **irritation** n (anger) Ärger m; MED Reizung f

**is** 3rd person sg present → **be**; ist

**Islam** n Islam m; **Islamic** adj islamisch

**island** n Insel f; **Isle** n (in names) **the ~ of Man** die Insel Man; **the British ~s** die Britischen Inseln

**isn't** contr = **is not**

**isolate** vt isolieren; **isolated** adj (remote) abgelegen; **isolation** n Isolierung f

**Israel** n Israel nt; **Israeli 1.** adj israelisch **2.** n Israeli m or f

**issue 1.** n (matter) Frage f; (problem) Problem nt; (subject) Thema nt; (of newspaper etc) Ausgabe f; **that's not the~** darum geht es nicht **2.** vt ausgeben; (document) ausstellen; (orders) erteilen; (book) herausgeben

**it** pron (as subject) er / sie / es; (as direct object) ihn / sie / es; (as indirect object) ihm / ihr / ihm; **the worst thing about ~** das Schlimmste daran; **who is ~?** ~**'s me/~'s him** wer ist da? ich bin's/er ist's; **~'s your turn** du bist dran; **that's ~** ja genau!; ~**'s raining** es regnet; ~**'s Charlie here,** hier spricht Charlie

**IT** abbr → **information technology** IT f

**Italian 1.** adj italienisch **2.** n Italiener(in) m(f); (language) Italienisch nt

**italic 1.** adj kursiv **2.** npl **in ~s** kursiv

**Italy** n Italien nt

**itch 1.** n Juckreiz m; **I have an ~** mich juckt es **2.** vi jucken; **he is ~ing to …** es juckt ihn, zu …; **itchy** adj juckend

**it'd** contr = **it would; it had**

**item** n (article) Gegenstand m; (in catalogue) Artikel m; (on list, in accounts) Posten m; (on agenda) Punkt m; (in news) Bericht m; TV (radio)

Meldung f

**itinerary** n Reiseroute f

**it'll** contr = **it will; it shall**

**its** pron sein; (feminine form) ihr

**it's** contr = **it is; it has**

**itself** pron (reflexive) sich; (emphatic) **the house ~** das

Haus selbst or an sich; **by ~** allein; **the door closes (by) ~** die Tür schließt sich von selbst

**I've** contr = **I have**

**ivory** n Elfenbein nt

**ivy** n Efeu m

# J

**jab 1.** vt (needle, knife) stechen (into in + acc) **2.** n fam Spritze f

**jack** n AUTO Wagenheber m, Bube m; **jack in** vt fam aufgeben, hinschmeißen; **jack up** vt (car etc) aufbocken

**jacket** n Jacke f; (of man's suit) Jackett nt; (of book) Schutzumschlag m; **jacket potato** n (in der Schale) gebackene Kartoffel

**jack-knife 1.** n Klappmesser nt **2.** vi (truck) sich quer stellen

**jacuzzi®** n (bath) Whirlpool® m

**jail 1.** n Gefängnis nt **2.** vt einsperren

**jam 1.** n Konfitüre f, Marmelade f; (traffic jam) Stau m **2.** vt (street) verstopfen; **be ~med** (stuck) klemmen; **~ on the brakes** eine Vollbremsung machen

**Jamaica** n Jamaika nt

**jam-packed** adj proppenvoll

**janitor** n (US) Hausmeister(in) m(f)

**January** n Januar m

**Japan** n Japan nt; **Japanese 1.** adj japanisch **2.** n (person) Japaner(in) m(f); (language) Japanisch nt

**jar** n Glas nt

**jaundice** n Gelbsucht f

**javelin** n Speer m; SPORT Speerwerfen nt

**jaw** n Kiefer m

**jazz** n Jazz m

**jealous** adj eifersüchtig (of auf + acc); **don't make me ~** mach mich nicht neidisch; **jealousy** n Eifersucht f

**jeans** npl Jeans pl

**jelly** n Gelee nt; (dessert) Götterspeise f; (US, jam) Marmelade f; **jelly baby** n (sweet) Gummibärchen nt; **jellyfish** n Qualle f

**jeopardize** vt gefährden

**jerk 1.** n Ruck m; fam (idiot) Trottel m **2.** vt ruckartig bewegen **3.** vi (rope) rucken; (muscles) zucken

**Jerusalem** n Jerusalem nt

**jet** n (of water etc) Strahl m; (nozzle) Düse f; (aircraft) Düsenflugzeug nt; **jet foil** n Tragflächenboot nt; **jetlag** n Jetlag m (Müdigkeit nach langem Flug)

**Jew** n Jude m, Jüdin f

**jewel** n Edelstein m; (esp fig) Juwel nt; **jeweller, jeweler** (US) n Juwelier(in) m(f); **jewellery, jewelery** (US) n Schmuck m

**Jewish** adj jüdisch; **she's ~** sie ist Jüdin

**jigsaw** (puzzle) n Puzzle nt

**jilt** vt den Laufpass geben + dat

**jitters** npl fam **have the ~** Bammel haben; **jittery** adj fam ganz nervös

**job** n (piece of work) Arbeit f; (task) Aufgabe f; (occupation) Stellung f, Job m; **what's your ~?** was machen Sie beruflich?; **jobcentre** n Arbeitsvermittlungsstelle f, Arbeitsamt nt; **job-hunting** n **go ~** auf Arbeitssuche gehen; **jobless** adj arbeitslos; **job seeker** n Arbeitssuchende(r) m/f; **jobseeker's allowance** n Arbeitslosengeld nt; **job-sharing** n Arbeitsplatzteilung f

**jockey** n Jockey m

**jog** 1. vt (person) anstoßen 2. vi (run) joggen; **jogging** n Jogging nt; **go ~** joggen gehen

**john** n (US) fam Klo nt

**join** 1. vt (put together) verbinden (to mit); (club etc) beitreten + dat; **~ sb** sich jdm anschließen; (sit with) sich zu jdm setzen 2. vi (unite) sich vereinigen; (rivers) zusammenfließen; **join in** vi, vt mitmachen (sth bei etw)

**joint** 1. n (of bones) Gelenk nt; (in pipe etc) Verbindungsstelle f; (of meat) Braten m; (of marijuana) Joint m 2. adj gemeinsam; **joint account** n Gemeinschaftskonto nt; **jointly** adv gemeinsam

**joke** 1. n (jest) Witz m; (prank) Streich m; **for a ~** zum Spaß; **it's no ~** das ist nicht zum Lachen 2. vi Witze machen; **you must be joking** das ist ja wohl nicht dein Ernst!

**jolly** adj lustig, vergnügt

**Jordan** n (country) Jordanien nt; (river) Jordan m

**jot down** vt etw notieren; **jotter** n Notizbuch nt

**journal** n (diary) Tagebuch nt; (magazine) Zeitschrift f; **journalism** n Journalismus m; **journalist** n Journalist(in) m(f)

**journey** n Reise f; (esp on stage, by car, train) Fahrt f

**joy** n Freude f (at über + acc); **joystick** n Joystick m, AVIAT Steuerknüppel m

**judge** 1. n Richter(in) m(f); SPORT Punktrichter(in) m(f) 2. vt beurteilen (by nach) 3. vi urteilen (by nach);

**judg(e)ment** *n* LAW Urteil *nt*; (*opinion*) Ansicht *f*; **an error of ~** Fehleinschätzung *f*

**judo** *n* Judo *nt*

**jug** *n* Krug *m*

**juggle** *vi* jonglieren (*with* mit)

**juice** *n* Saft *m*; **juicy** *adj* saftig

**July** *n* Juli *m*; → **September**

**jumble** *n* Durcheinander *nt* **2.** *vt ~ (up)* durcheinanderwerfen; (*facts*) durcheinanderbringen; **jumble sale** *n* Flohmarkt *m*, (*for charity*) Wohltätigkeitsbasar *m*

**jump 1.** *vi* springen; (*nervously*) zusammenzucken; **~ to conclusions** voreilige Schlüsse ziehen **2.** *vt* (*omit*) überspringen; **~ the lights** bei Rot über die Kreuzung fahren; **~ the queue** sich vordrängen **3.** *n* Sprung *m*; (*for horses*) Hindernis *nt*; **jumper** *n* Pullover *m*; (*US, dress*) Trägerkleid *nt*; (*person, horse*) Springer(in) *m(f)*; **jumper cable** *n* (*US*), **jump lead** *n* (*Brit*) Starthilfekabel *nt*

**junction** *n* (*of roads*) Kreuzung *f*; RAIL Knotenpunkt *m*

**June** *n* Juni *m*; → **September**

**jungle** *n* Dschungel *m*

**junior 1.** *adj* (*younger*) jünger; (*lower position*) untergeordnet (*to sb* jdm) **2.** *n* **she's two years my ~** sie ist zwei Jahre jünger als ich; **junior high (school)** *n* (*US*) ≈ Mittel-

schule *f*; **junior school** *n* (*Brit*) Grundschule *f*

**junk** *n* (*trash*) Plunder *m*; **junk food** *n* Nahrungsmittel *pl* mit geringem Nährwert, Junkfood *nt*; **junkie** *n fam* Junkie *m*, Fixer(in) *m(f)*; *fig* (*fan*) Freak *m*; **junk mail** *n* Reklame *f*; IT Junkmail *f*; **junk shop** *n* Trödelladen *m*

**jury** *n* Geschworene *pl*; (*in competition*) Jury *f*

**just 1.** *adj* gerecht **2.** *adv* (*recently*) gerade; (*exactly*) genau; **~ as expected** wie erwartet; **~ as nice** genauso nett; (*barely*) **~ in time** gerade noch rechtzeitig; (*immediately*) **~ before / after ...** gleich vor / nach ...; (*small distance*) **~ round the corner** gleich um die Ecke; (*a little*) **~ over an hour** etwas mehr als eine Stunde; (*only*) **~ the two of us** nur wir beide; **~ a moment** Moment mal; (*absolutely, simply*) **it was ~ fantastic** es war einfach klasse; **~ about** so etwa; (*more or less*) mehr oder weniger; **~ about ready** fast fertig

**justice** *n* Gerechtigkeit *f*; **justifiable** *adj* berechtigt; **justifiably** *adv* zu Recht; **justify** *vt* rechtfertigen

**juvenile 1.** *adj* Jugend-, jugendlich **2.** *n* Jugendliche(r) *mf*

# K

**k** *abbr* → **thousand**; **15k** 15 000

**K** *abbr* → **kilobyte** KB

**kangaroo** *n* Känguru *nt*

**karaoke** *n* Karaoke *nt*

**karate** *n* Karate *nt*

**kart** *n* Gokart *m*

**kayak** *n* Kajak *m or nt*; **kayaking** *n* Kajakfahren *nt*

**Kazakhstan** *n* Kasachstan *nt*

**kebab** *n* (*shish kebab*) Schaschlik *nt or m*; (*doner kebab*) Kebab *m*

**keel** *n* NAUT Kiel *m*; **keel over** *vi* (*boat*) kentern; (*person*) umkippen

**keen** *adj* begeistert (*on* von); (*hardworking*) eifrig; (*mind, wind*) scharf; (*interest, feeling etc*) stark; **be ~ on sb** von jdm angetan sein; **she's ~ on riding** sie reitet gern; **be ~ to do sth** darauf erpicht sein, etw zu tun

**keep 1.** *vt* (*retain*) behalten; (*secret*) für sich behalten; (*observe*) einhalten; (*promise*) halten; (*run: shop, diary, accounts*) führen; (*animals*) halten; (*store*) aufbewahren; (*support, family etc*) unterhalten, versorgen; **~ sb waiting** jdn warten lassen; **~ sb from doing sth** jdn davon abhalten, etw zu tun; **~ sth clean / secret** etw sauber / geheim halten; **'~ clear'** „(bitte) frei halten"; **~ this to yourself** behalt das für dich / behalten Sie das für sich **2.** *vi* (*food*) sich halten; (*remain, with adj*) bleiben; **~ quiet** sei / seien Sie ruhig!; **~ left** links fahren; **~ doing sth** (*repeatedly*) etw immer wieder tun; **~ at it** mach weiter so!; **it ~s happening** es passiert immer wieder; **keep back 1.** *vi* zurückbleiben **2.** *vt* zurückhalten; (*information*) verschweigen (*from sb* jdm); **keep off** *vt* (*person, animal*) fernhalten; **~ the grass** „Betreten des Rasens verboten"; **keep on 1.** *vi* weitermachen; (*walking*) weitergehen; (*in car*) weiterfahren; **~ doing sth** (*persistently*) etw immer wieder tun **2.** *vt* (*coat etc*) anbehalten; **keep out 1.** *vt* nicht hereinlassen **2.** *vi* draußen bleiben; **~** (*on sign*) Eintritt verboten; **keep to** *vt* (*road, path*) bleiben bei *auf + dat*; (*plan etc*) sich halten an + *acc*; **~ the point** bei der Sache bleiben; **keep up 1.** *vi* Schritt halten (*with* mit) **2.** *vt* (*maintain*) aufrechterhalten; (*speed*) halten; **~ appearances** den Schein wahren; **keep it up!**

*fam* weiter so!

**keeper** n (museum etc) Aufseher(in) m(f); (goalkeeper) Torwart m; (zoo keeper) Tierpfleger(in) m(f); **keep-fit** n Fitnesstraining nt; **~ exercises** Gymnastik f

**kennel** n Hundehütte f; **kennels** n Hundepension f

**Kenya** n Kenia nt

**kept** pt, pp →**keep**

**kerb** n Randstein m

**kerosene** n (US) Petroleum nt

**ketchup** n Ketchup nt or m

**kettle** n Kessel m

**key 1.** n Schlüssel m; (of piano, computer) Taste f; MUS Tonart f; (for map etc) Zeichenerklärung f **2.** vt **~ (in)** IT eingeben **3.** adj entscheidend; **keyboard** n (of piano, computer) Tastatur f; **keyhole** n Schlüsselloch m; **keypad** n IT Nummernblock m; **keyring** n Schlüsselring m

**kick 1.** n Tritt m; SPORT Stoß m **2.** vt, vi treten; **kick out** n fam rausschmeißen (of aus); **kick-off** n SPORT Anstoß m

**kid 1.** n (child) Kind nt **2.** vt (tease) auf den Arm nehmen **3.** vi Witze machen; **you're ~ding** das ist doch nicht dein Ernst!; **no ~ding** aber echt!

**kidnap** vt entführen; **kidnapper** n Entführer(in) m(f); **kidnapping** n Entführung f

**kidney** n Niere f; **kidney machine** n künstliche Niere

**kill** vt töten; (esp intentionally) umbringen; (weeds) vernichten; **killer** n Mörder(in) m(f)

**kilo** n Kilo nt; **kilobyte** n Kilobyte nt; **kilogramme** n Kilogramm nt; **kilometer** (US), **kilometre** n Kilometer m; **~s per hour** Stundenkilometer pl; **kilowatt** n Kilowatt nt

**kilt** n Schottenrock m

**kind 1.** adj nett, freundlich (to zu) **2.** n Art f; (of coffee, cheese etc) Sorte f; **what ~ of ... ?** was für ein(e) ...?; **this ~ of ...** so ein(e) ...; **~ of** (+ adj) fam irgendwie

**kindergarten** n Kindergarten m

**kindly 1.** adj nett, freundlich **2.** adv liebenswürdigerweise

**king** n König m; **kingdom** n Königreich nt; **king-size** adj im Großformat; (bed) extra groß

**kipper** n Räucherhering m

**kiss 1.** n Kuss m; **~ of life** Mund-zu-Mund-Beatmung f **2.** vt küssen

**kit** n (equipment) Ausrüstung f; fam Sachen pl; (sports kit) Sportsachen pl; (for building sth) Bausatz m

**kitchen** n Küche f; **kitchen foil** n Alufolie f; **kitchen scales** n Küchenwaage f; **kitchenware** n Küchengeschirr nt

**kite** n Drachen m

**kitten** n Kätzchen nt

**kiwi** n (fruit) Kiwi f
**km** abbr = **kilometre(s)** km
**knack** n Dreh m, Trick m; **get / have got the ~** den Dreh herauskriegen / heraushaben; **knackered** adj (Brit) fam fix und fertig, kaputt
**knee** n Knie nt; **kneecap** n Kniescheibe f; **knee-jerk** adj (reaction) reflexartig; **kneel** vi knien; (action, kneel down) sich hinknien
**knelt** pt, pp → **kneel**
**knew** pt → **know**
**knickers** npl (Brit fam) Schlüpfer m
**knife** n Messer nt
**knight** n Ritter m; (in chess) Pferd nt, Springer m
**knit** vt, vi stricken; **knitting** n (piece of work) Strickarbeit f; (activity) Stricken nt; **knitwear** n Strickwaren pl
**knob** n (on door) Knauf m; (on radio etc) Knopf m
**knock 1.** vt (with hammer etc) schlagen; (accidentally) stoßen; **~ one's head** sich dat den Kopf anschlagen **2.** vi klopfen (on, at an + acc) **3.** n (blow) Schlag m; (on door) Klopfen nt; **there was a ~ (at the door)** es hat geklopft; **knock down** vt (object) umstoßen; (person) niederschlagen; (with car) anfahren; (building) abreißen;

**knock out** vt (stun) bewusstlos schlagen; (boxer) k.o. schlagen
**knot** n Knoten m
**know** vt, vi wissen; (be acquainted with: people, places) kennen; (recognize) erkennen; (language) können; **I'll let you ~** ich sage dir / Ihnen Bescheid; **I ~ some French** ich kann etwas Französisch; **get to ~ sb** jdn kennenlernen; **be ~ as** bekannt sein als; **know of** vt kennen; **not that I ~** nicht dass ich wüsste; **know-all** n fam Klugscheißer m; **know-how** n Kenntnis f, Knowhow nt; **knowing** adj wissend; (look, smile) vielsagend; **knowledge** n Wissen nt; (of a subject) Kenntnisse pl; **to (the best of) my ~** meines Wissens
**known** pp → **know**
**knuckle** n (Finger)knöchel m; GASTR Hachse f; **knuckle down** vi sich an die Arbeit machen
**Koran** n Koran m
**Korea** n Korea nt
**Kosovo** n der Kosovo m
**kph** abbr = **kilometres per hour** km/h
**Kremlin** n the ~ der Kreml
**Kurd** n Kurde m, Kurdin f; **Kurdish** adj kurdisch
**Kuwait** n Kuwait nt

# L

**L** abbr (Brit) AUTO → **learner**

**LA** abbr = **Los Angeles**

**lab** n fam Labor nt

**label 1.** n Etikett nt; (tied) Anhänger m; (adhesive) Aufkleber m; (record label) Label nt **2.** vt etikettieren; pej abstempeln

**labor** (US), **labour 1.** n Arbeit f; MED Wehen pl; **be in ~** Wehen haben **2.** adj POL Labour-; **Labour Party** Labour Party f

**laboratory** n Labor nt

**laborious** adj mühsam; **labor union** n (US) Gewerkschaft f; **labourer** n Arbeiter(in) m(f)

**lace 1.** n (fabric) Spitze f; (of shoe) Schnürsenkel m **2.** vt (~ up) zuschnüren

**lack 1.** vt, vi **be ~ing** fehlen; **we ~ the time** uns fehlt die Zeit **2.** n Mangel m (of an + dat)

**lacquer** n Lack m; (Brit, hair lacquer) Haarspray m

**lad** n Junge m

**ladder** n (in fabric) Leiter f; (in tight) Laufmasche f

**laddish** adj (Brit) machohaft

**laden** adj beladen (with mit)

**ladies, ladies' room** n Damentoilette f

**lad mag** n Männerzeitschrift f

**lady** n Dame f; (as title) Lady f;

**ladybird, ladybug** (US) n Marienkäfer m; **Lady-shave®** n Epiliergerät nt

**lag 1.** vi (~ **behind**) zurückliegen **2.** vt (pipes) isolieren

**lager** n helles Bier; **~ lout** betrunkener Rowdy

**laid** pt, pp → **lay**; **laid-back** adj fam cool, gelassen

**lain** pp → **lie**

**lake** n See m

**lamb** n Lamm nt; (meat) Lammfleisch nt; **lamb chop** n Lammkotelett nt

**lame** adj lahm; (excuse) faul; (argument) schwach

**lament 1.** n Klage f **2.** vt beklagen

**laminated** adj beschichtet

**lamp** n Lampe f; (in street) Laterne f; (in car) Licht nt, Scheinwerfer m

**land 1.** n Land nt **2.** vi (from ship) an Land gehen; AVIAT landen; **landing** n Landung f; (on stairs) Treppenabsatz m; **landing stage** n Landesteg m; **landing strip** n Landebahn f

**landlady** n Hauswirtin f, Vermieterin f; **landlord** n (of house) Hauswirt m, Vermieter m; (of pub) Gastwirt m; **landowner** n Grundbesitzer(in) m(f); **landscape** n Landschaft f; (format) Querformat *nt*; **landslide** *n* Erdrutsch *m*

**lane** *n* (*in country*) enge Landstraße, Weg *m*; (*in town*) Gasse *f*; (*of motorway*) Spur *f*; sport Bahn *f*; **get in ~** (*in car*) sich einordnen

**language** *n* Sprache *f*

**lantern** *n* Laterne *f*

**lap** *n* **1.** Schoß *m*; (*in race*) Runde *f* **2.** *vt* (*in race*) überholen

**lapse** *n* **1.** (*mistake*) Irrtum *m*; (*moral*) Fehltritt *m* **2.** *vi* ablaufen

**laptop** *n* Laptop *m*

**large** *adj* groß; **by and ~** im Großen und Ganzen; **largely** *adv* zum größten Teil; **large-scale** *adj* groß angelegt, Groß-

**lark** *n* (*bird*) Lerche *f*

**larynx** *n* Kehlkopf *m*

**laser** *n* Laser *m*; **laser printer** *n* Laserdrucker *m*

**lash** *vt* peitschen; **lash out** *vi* (*with fists*) um sich schlagen; (*spend money*) sich in Unkosten stürzen (*on* mit)

**lass** *n* Mädchen *nt*

**last 1.** *adj* letzte(r, s); **the ~ but one** der / die / das vorletzte; **~ night** gestern Abend; **but not least** nicht zuletzt **2.** *adv* zuletzt; (*last time*) das letzte Mal; **at ~** endlich **3.** *n* (*person*) Letzte(r) *mf*; (*thing*) Letzte(s) *nt*; **he was the ~ to leave** er ging als Letzter **4.** *vi* (*continue*) dauern; (*re-main in good condition*) durchhalten; (*remain good*) sich halten; (*money*) ausreichen; **lasting** *adj* dauerhaft; (*impression*) nachhaltig; **lastly** *adv* schließlich; **last-minute** *adj* in letzter Minute; **last name** *n* Nachname *m*

**late 1.** *adj* spät; (*after proper time*) zu spät; (*train etc*) verspätet; (*dead*) verstorben; **be ~** zu spät kommen; (*train etc*) Verspätung haben **2.** *adv* spät; (*after proper time*) zu spät; **late availibility flight** *n* Last-Minute-Flug *m*; **lately** *adv* in letzter Zeit; **late opening** *n* verlängerte Öffnungszeiten *pl*; **later** *adj*, *adv* später; **see you ~** bis später; **latest 1.** *adj* späteste(r, s) (*most recent*) neueste(r, s) **2.** *n* **the ~** (*news*) das Neueste; **at the ~** spätestens

**Latin 1.** *n* Latein *nt* **2.** *adj* lateinisch; **Latin America** *n* Lateinamerika *nt*; **Latin-American 1.** *adj* lateinamerikanisch **2.** *n* Lateinamerikaner(in) *m(f)*

**latter** *adj* (*second of two*) letztere(r, s); (*last: part, years*) letzte(r, s), später

**Latvia** *n* Lettland *nt*; **Latvian 1** *adj* lettisch **2** *n* (*person*) Lette *m*, Lettin *f*; (*language*) Lettisch *nt*

**laugh 1.** *n* Lachen *nt*; **for a ~** aus Spaß **2.** *vi* lachen (*at*, *about* über + *acc*); **~ at sb** sich über jdn lustig machen; **it's no ~ing matter** es ist nicht zum Lachen; **laughter** *n* Gelächter *nt*

**launch 1.** *n (launching, of ship)* Stapellauf *m*; *(of rocket)* Abschuss *m*; *(of product)* Markteinführung *f*; *(event)* Eröffnungsfeier *f* **2.** *vt (ship)* vom Stapel lassen; *(rocket)* abschießen; *(product)* einführen; *(project)* in Gang setzen

**laundrette** *n (Brit)*, **laundromat** *n (US)* Waschsalon *m*; **laundry** *n (place)* Wäscherei *f*; *(clothes)* Wäsche *f*

**lavatory** *n* Toilette *f*

**lavender** *n* Lavendel *m*

**lavish** *adj* verschwenderisch; *(furnishings etc)* üppig; *(gift)* großzügig

**law** *n* Gesetz *nt*; *(system)* Recht *nt*; *(for study)* Jura; *(of sport)* Regel *f*; **against the ~** gesetzwidrig; **law-abiding** *adj* gesetzestreu; **law court** *n* Gerichtshof *m*; **lawful** *adj* rechtmäßig

**lawn** *n* Rasen *m*; **lawnmower** *n* Rasenmäher *m*

**lawsuit** *n* Prozess *m*; **lawyer** *n* Rechtsanwalt *m*, Rechtsanwältin *f*

**laxative** *n* Abführmittel *nt*

**lay 1.** *pt →* **lie 2.** *vt* **1.** *vt* legen; *(table)* decken; *vulg* poppen, bumsen; *(egg)* legen **3.** *adj* Laien-; **lay down** *vt* hinle-

gen; **lay on** *vt (provide)* anbieten; *(organize)* veranstalten, bereitstellen; **layabout** *n* Faulenzer(in) *m(f)*

**layer** *n* Schicht *f*

**layman** *n* Laie *m*

**layout** *n* Gestaltung *f*; *(of book etc)* Lay-out *nt*

**laze** *vi* faulenzen; **laziness** *n* Faulheit *f*; **lazy** *adj* faul; *(day, idea)* faul

**lb** *abbr →* **pound** Pfd.

**lead 1.** *n* Blei *nt* **2.** *vt, vi* führen; *(group etc)* leiten; **~ the way** vorangehen **3.** *n (race)* Führung *f*; *(distance, time ahead)* Vorsprung *m* (*over* vor + *dat*); THEAT Hauptrolle *f*; *(dog's)* Leine *f*; ELEC *(flex)* Leitung *f*; **lead astray** *vt* irreführen; **lead away** *vt* wegführen; **lead back** *vi* zurückführen; **lead to** *vt (street)* hinführen nach; *(result in)* führen zu; **lead up to** *vt (drive)* führen zu

**leaded** *adj (petrol)* verbleit

**leader** *n* Führer(in) *m(f)*; *(of party)* Vorsitzende(r) *mf*; *(of project, expedition)* Leiter(in) *m(f)*; SPORT *(in race)* der / die Erste; *(in league)* Tabellenführer *m*; **leadership** *n* Führung *f*

**lead-free** *adj (petrol)* bleifrei

**leading** *adj* führend, wichtig

**leaf** *n* Blatt *nt*; **leaflet** *n* Prospekt *m*; *(pamphlet)* Flugblatt *nt*; *(with instructions)* Merkblatt *nt*

**league** n Bund m; SPORT Liga f
**leak 1.** n (gap) undichte Stelle; (escape) Leck nt **2.** vi (pipe etc) undicht sein; (liquid etc) auslaufen; **leaky** adj undicht
**lean 1.** adj (meat) mager **2.** vi (not vertical) sich neigen; (rest) ~ **against sth** sich an etw acc lehnen; (support oneself) ~ **on sth** sich auf etw acc stützen **3.** vt lehnen (on, against an + acc); **lean back** vi sich zurücklehnen; **lean towards** vt tendieren zu
**leant** pt, pp → **lean**
**leap 1.** n Sprung m **2.** vi springen; **leap year** n Schaltjahr nt
**learn** vt, vi lernen; (find out) erfahren; ~ (**how**) **to swim** schwimmen lernen; **learned** adj gelehrt; **learner** n Anfänger(in) m(f); (Brit, driver) Fahrschüler(in) m(f)
**learnt** pt, pp → **learn**
**lease 1.** n (of land, premises etc) Pacht f; (contract) Pachtvertrag m; (of house, car etc) Miete f; (contract) Mietvertrag m **2.** vt pachten; (house, car etc) mieten; **lease out** vt vermieten; **leasing** n Leasing nt
**least 1.** adj wenigste(r, s); (slightest) geringste(r, s) **2.** adv am wenigsten; ~ **expensive** billigste(r, s) **3.** n **the** ~ das Mindeste; **not in the** ~ nicht im geringsten; **at** ~ we-

nigstens; (with number) mindestens
**leather 1.** n Leder nt **2.** adj ledern, Leder-
**leave 1.** n (time off) Urlaub m; **on** ~ auf Urlaub; **take one's** ~ Abschied nehmen (of von) **2.** vt (place, person) verlassen; (leave behind: message, scar etc) hinterlassen; (after death) hinterlassen (to sb jdm); (entrust) überlassen (to sb jdm); **be left** (remain) übrig bleiben; ~ **me alone** lass mich in Ruhe!; **don't** ~ **it to the last minute** warte nicht bis zur letzten Minute **3.** vi (weg)gehen, (weg)fahren; (on journey) abreisen; (bus, train) abfahren (for nach); **leave behind** vt zurücklassen; (scar etc) hinterlassen; **leave out** vt auslassen; (person) ausschließen (of von)
**leaves** pl → **leaf**
**leaving do** n Abschiedsfeier f
**Lebanon** n **the** ~ der Libanon
**lecture** n Vortrag m; (at university) Vorlesung f; **give a** ~ einen Vortrag halten; (in the Vorlesung) eine Vorlesung halten; **lecturer** n Dozent(in) m(f); **lecture theatre** n Hörsaal m
**led** pt, pp → **lead**
**LED** abbr = **light-emitting diode** Leuchtdiode f
**leek** n Lauch m
**left 1.** pt, pp → **leave 2.** adj linke(r, s) **3.** adv (position)

links; (*movement*) nach links
4. *n* (*side*) linke Seite; **the
Left** POL die Linke; **on/to
the ~** links (*of* von); left-
-hand *adj* linke(r, s); **~ bend**
Linkskurve *f*; **~ drive** Links-
steuerung *f*; **left-handed** *adj*
linkshändig; **left-hand side**
*n* linke Seite

**left-luggage locker** *n* Ge-
päckschließfach *nt*; **left-luggage office** *n* Gepäckaufbewahrung *f*

**leftovers** *npl* Reste *pl*

**left wing** *n* linker Flügel; **left-
-wing** *adj* POL linksgerichtet

**leg** *n* Bein *nt*; (*of meat*) Keule *f*

**legacy** *n* Erbe *nt*, Erbschaft *f*

**legal** *adj* Rechts-, rechtlich;
(*allowed*) legal; (*limit, age*)
gesetzlich; **~ aid** Rechtshilfe
*f*; **legalize** *vt* legalisieren; **le-
gally** *adv* legal

**legible, legibly** *adj, adv* leserlich

**legislation** *n* Gesetze *pl*

**legitimate** *adj* rechtmäßig, le-
gitim

**legroom** *n* Beinfreiheit *f*

**leisure** *n* (*at*) (*time*) Freizeit *f* 2.
*adj* Freizeit-; **~ centre** Frei-
zeitzentrum *nt*; **leisurely**
*adj* gemächlich

**lemon** *n* Zitrone *f*; **lemonade**
*n* Limonade *f*; **lemon curd** *n*
Brotaufstrich *aus Zitronen,
Butter, Eiern und Zucker*;
**lemon juice** *n* Zitronensaft
*m*; **lemon sole** *n* Seezunge *f*

**lend** *vt* leihen; **~ sb sth** jdm

etw leihen

**length** *n* Länge *f*; **4 metres in
~** 4 Meter lang; **what~ is it?**
wie lange ist es?; **lengthy** *adj*
sehr lange; (*dragging*) lang-
wierig

**lenient** *adj* nachsichtig

**lens** *n* Linse *f*; PHOT Objektiv
*nt*

**lent** *pt, pp* → **lend**

**Lent** *n* Fastenzeit *f*

**lentil** *n* BOT Linse *f*

**Leo** *n* ASTR Löwe *m*

**leopard** *n* Leopard *m*

**lept** *pt, pp* → **leap**

**lesbian 1.** *adj* lesbisch **2.** *n*
Lesbe *f*

**less** *adj, adv n* weniger; **~ and
~** immer weniger; (*less often*)
immer seltener; **lessen 1.** *vi*
abnehmen, nachlassen **2.** *vt*
verringern; (*pain*) lindern;
**lesser** *adj* geringer;
(*amount*) kleiner

**lesson** *n* (*at school*) Stunde *f*;
(*unit of study*) Lektion *f*; *fig*
Lehre *f*; REL Lesung *f*; **~s
start at 9** der Unterricht be-
ginnt um 9

**let** *vt* lassen; (*lease*) vermieten; **~ sb have sth** jdm etw
geben; **~'s go** gehen wir; **~
go (of sth)** (etw) loslassen;
**let down** *vt* herunterlassen;
(*fail to help*) im Stich lassen;
(*disappoint*) enttäuschen; **let
in** *vt* hereinlassen; **let out** *vt*
hinauslassen; (*secret*) verraten; (*scream etc*) ausstoßen

**lethal** *adj* tödlich

**let's** abbr = **let us**

**letter** n (of alphabet) Buchstabe m; (message) Brief m; (official letter) Schreiben nt; **letterbox** n Briefkasten m

**lettuce** n Kopfsalat m

**leukaemia, leukemia** (US) n Leukämie f

**level 1.** adj (horizontal) waagerecht; (ground) eben; (two things, two runners) auf selber Höhe; **~ on points** punktgleich **2.** adv (run etc) auf gleicher Höhe, gleich auf; **draw ~** (in race) gleichziehen (with mit); (in game) ausgleichen **3.** n (altitude) Höhe f; (standard) Niveau nt; **be on a ~ with** auf gleicher Höhe sein mit **4.** vt (ground) einebnen; **level crossing** n (Brit) (schienengleicher) Bahnübergang m; **level-headed** adj vernünftig

**lever** n (a. fig Hebel m; fig Druckmittel nt; **lever up** vt hochstemmen

**liability** n Haftung f; (burden) Belastung f; (obligation) Verpflichtung f; **liable** adj **be ~ for sth** (responsible) für etw haften

**liar** n Lügner(in) m(f)

**liberal** adj (generous) großzügig; (broad-minded) liberal; **Liberal Democrat 1.** n (Brit) POL Liberaldemokrat(in) m(f) **2.** adj liberaldemokratisch

**liberate** vt befreien; libera-

tion n Befreiung f

**liberty** n Freiheit f

**Libra** n ASTR Waage f

**library** n Bibliothek f; (lending library) Bücherei f

**Libya** n Libyen nt

**lice** pl → **louse**

**licence** n (permit) Genehmigung f; COMM Lizenz f; (driving licence) Führerschein m; **License 1.** n (US) → **licence 2.** vt genehmigen; **licensed** adj (restaurant etc) mit Schankerlaubnis; **license plate** n (US) AUTO Nummernschild nt; **licensing hours** npl Ausschankzeiten pl

**lick 1.** vt lecken **2.** n Lecken nt

**licorice** n Lakritze f

**lid** n Deckel m; (eyelid) Lid nt

**lie 1.** n Lüge f; **~ detector** Lügendetektor m **2.** vi lügen; **~ to sb** jdn belügen **3.** vi (rest, be situated) liegen; (lie down) sich legen; (snow) liegen bleiben; **be lying third** an dritter Stelle liegen; **lie about** vi herumliegen; **lie down** vi sich hinlegen

**lie in** n **have a ~** ausschlafen

**life** n Leben nt; **get ~** lebenslänglich bekommen; **life assurance** n Lebensversicherung f; **lifebelt** n Rettungsring m; **lifeboat** n Rettungsboot nt; **lifeguard** n Bademeister(in) m(f), Rettungsschwimmer(in) m(f); **life insurance** n Lebensversiche-

rung f; **life jacket** n
Schwimmweste f; **lifeless**
adj (dead) leblos; **lifelong**
adj lebenslang; **life preserver** n (US) Rettungsring m;
**life-saving** adj lebensret-
tend; **life-size(d)** adj in Le-
bensgröße; **life span** n Le-
bensspanne f; **life style** n Le-
bensstil m; **lifetime** n Le-
benszeit f

**lift 1.** vt (hoch)heben; (ban)
aufheben **2.** n (Brit, elevator)
Aufzug m, Lift m; **give sb a
~** jdn im Auto mitnehmen;
**lift up** vt hochheben

**ligament** n Band nt

**light 1.** vt beleuchten; (fire,
cigarette) anzünden **2.** n
Licht nt; (lamp) Lampe f;
**~s** pl AUTO Beleuchtung f;
(traffic lights) Ampel f; **in
the ~ of** angesichts + gen **3.**
adj (bright) hell; (not heavy,
easy) leicht; (punishment)
milde; (taxes) niedrig; **~
blue / green** hellblau / hellgrün; **light up 1.** vt (illuminate) beleuchten; (cigarette)
anzünden **2.** vi (a. eyes) aufleuchten

**light bulb** n Glühbirne f

**lighten 1.** vi hell werden **2.** vt
(give light to) erhellen;
(make less heavy) leichter
machen; fig erleichtern

**lighter** n (cigarette lighter)
Feuerzeug nt

**light-hearted** adj unbe-
schwert; **lighthouse** n

Leuchtturm m; **lighting** n
Beleuchtung f; **lightly** adv
leicht; **light meter** n PHOT
Belichtungsmesser m

**lightning** n Blitz m

**like 1.** vt mögen, gernhaben;
**he ~s swimming** er
schwimmt gern; **would you
~ ...?** hättest du / hätten Sie
gern ...?; **I'd ~ to go home**
ich möchte nach Hause (gehen); **I don't ~ the film** der
Film gefällt mir nicht **2.** prep
wie; **what's it/he ~?** wie ist
es/er?; **he looks ~ you** er
sieht dir / Ihnen ähnlich; **~
that / this** so; **likeable** adj
sympathisch

**likelihood** n Wahrscheinlichkeit f; **likely** adj wahrscheinlich; **the bus is ~ to be late**
der Bus wird wahrscheinlich
Verspätung haben

**like-minded** adj gleich ge-
sinnt

**likewise** adv ebenfalls; **do ~**
das Gleiche tun

**liking** n (for person) Zuneigung f; (for type, things) Vorliebe f (for für)

**lilac 1.** n Flieder m **2.** adj flie-
derfarben

**lily** n Lilie f; **~ of the valley**
Maiglöckchen nt

**limb** n Glied nt

**limbo** n in **~** (plans) auf Eis ge-
legt

**lime** n (tree) Linde f; (fruit) Limone f; (substance) Kalk m;
**lime juice** n Limonensaft m;

**limelight** *n fig* Rampenlicht *nt*; **limestone** *n* Kalkstein *m*
**limit 1.** *n* Grenze *f*; *(for pollution etc)* Grenzwert *m*; *be over the ~ (speed)* das Tempolimit überschreiten; *(alcohol consumption)* fahruntüchtig sein; *that's the ~* jetzt reicht's!, das ist die Höhe! **2.** *vt* beschränken *(to* auf *+ acc)*; *(freedom, spending)* einschränken; **limitation** *n* Beschränkung *f*; *(of freedom, spending)* Einschränkung *f*; **limited** *adj* begrenzt; *~ liability company* Gesellschaft *f* mit beschränkter Haftung, GmbH *f*; *public ~ company* Aktiengesellschaft *f*
**limp 1.** *vi* hinken **2.** *adj* schlaff
**line 1.** *n* Linie *f*; *(written)* Zeile *f*; *(on face)* Falte *f*; *(row)* Reihe *f*; *(US, queue)* Schlange *f*; RAIL Bahnlinie *f*; TEL Leitung *f*; *(range of items)* Kollektion *f*; *hold the ~* bleiben Sie am Apparat; *stand in ~* Schlange stehen; *something along those ~s* etwas in diesem Sinne; *drop me a ~* schreib mir ein paar Zeilen; *~s* THEAT Text *m* **2.** *vt (clothes)* füttern; *(streets)* säumen; **lined** *adj (paper)* liniert; *(face)* faltig; **line up** *vi* sich aufstellen; *(US, form queue)* sich anstellen
**linen** *n* Leinen *nt*; *(sheets etc)* Wäsche *f*

**liner** *n* Überseedampfer *m*, Passagierschiff *nt*
**lingerie** *n* Damenunterwäsche *f*
**lining** *n (of clothes)* Futter *nt*; *(brake lining)* Bremsbelag *m*
**link 1.** *n (connection)* Verbindung *f*; *(of chain)* Glied *nt*; *(relationship)* Beziehung *f (with* zu*)*; *(between events)* Zusammenhang *m*; *(Internet)* Link *m* **2.** *vt* verbinden
**lion** *n* Löwe *m*
**lip** *n* Lippe *f*; **lipstick** *n* Lippenstift *m*
**liqueur** *n* Likör *m*
**liquid 1.** *n* Flüssigkeit *f* **2.** *adj* flüssig
**liquor** *n* Spirituosen *pl*
**liquorice** *n* Lakritze *f*
**Lisbon** *n* Lissabon *nt*
**lisp** *vt*, *vi* lispeln
**list 1.** *n* Liste *f* **2.** *vt* auflisten, aufzählen; *~ed building* unter Denkmalschutz stehendes Gebäude
**listen** *vi* zuhören; **listen to** *vt (person)* zuhören + *dat*; *(radio)* hören; *(advice)* hören auf; **listener** *n* Zuhörer(in) *m(f)*; *(to radio)* Hörer(in) *m(f)*
**lit** *pt, pp → light*
**liter** *n (US)* Liter *m*
**literacy** *n* Fähigkeit *f* zu lesen und zu schreiben; **literal** *adj (translation, meaning)* wörtlich; *(actual)* buchstäblich; **literally** *adv (translate, take sth)* wörtlich; **literary** *adj* li-

terarisch; (critic, journal etc) Literatur-; **literature** n Literatur f; (brochures etc) Informationsmaterial nt

**Lithuania** n Litauen nt; **Lithuanian 1** adj litauisch **2** n (person) Litauer(in) m(f); (language) Litauisch nt

**litre** n Liter m

**litter 1.** n Abfälle pl; (of animals) Wurf m **2.** vt **be ~ed with** übersät sein mit; **litter bin** n Abfalleimer m

**little 1.** adj klein; (in quantity) wenig; **a ~ while ago** vor kurzer Zeit **2.** adv, n wenig; **a ~** ein bisschen, ein wenig; **as ~ as possible** so wenig wie möglich; **for as ~ as £5** schon für 5 Pfund; **I see very ~ of them** ich sehe sie selten; **~ by ~** nach und nach; **little finger** n kleiner Finger

**live 1.** adj lebendig; ELEC geladen, unter Strom; TV (radio, event) live; **~ broadcast** Direktübertragung f **2.** vi leben; (not die) überleben; (dwell) wohnen; **you ~ and learn** man lernt nie aus **3.** vt (life) führen; **live on 1.** vi weiterleben **2.** vt **~ sth** von etw leben; (feed) sich von etw ernähren; **earn enough to ~** genug verdienen, um davon zu leben; **live together** vi zusammenleben; **live up to** vt (reputation) gerecht werden + dat; (expectations) entsprechen + dat; **live with**

vt (parents etc) wohnen bei; (partner) zusammenleben mit; (difficulty) **you'll just have to ~ it** da musst dich / Sie müssen sich eben damit abfinden

**liveliness** n Lebhaftigkeit f; **lively** adj lebhaft

**liver** n Leber f

**lives** pl → **life**

**livestock** n Vieh nt

**living 1.** n Lebensunterhalt m; **what do you do for a ~?** was machen Sie beruflich? **2.** adj lebend; **living room** n Wohnzimmer nt

**lizard** ZOOL n Eidechse f

**llama** ZOOL n Lama nt

**load 1.** n Last f; (cargo) Ladung f; TECH fig Belastung f; **~s of** fam massenhaft; **it was a ~ of rubbish** fam es war grottenschlecht **2.** vt (vehicle) beladen; IT laden; (film) einlegen

**loaf** n **a ~ of bread** ein (Laib) Brot (m)nt

**loan 1.** n (item leant) Leihgabe f; FIN Darlehen nt; **on ~** geliehen **2.** vt leihen (to sb jdm)

**loathe** vt verabscheuen

**loaves** pl → **loaf**

**lobby** n Vorhalle f; POL Lobby f

**lobster** n Hummer m

**local 1.** adj (traffic, time etc) Orts-; (radio, news, paper) Lokal-; (government, authority) Kommunal-; (anaesthetic) örtlich; **~ call** TEL

Ortsgespräch nt; ~ **elections** Kommunalwahlen pl; ~ **time** Ortszeit f; ~ **train** Nahverkehrszug m; **the** ~ **shops** die Geschäfte am Ort **2.** n (pub) Stammlokal nt; **the** ~**s** pl die Ortsansässigen pl; **locally** adv örtlich, am Ort

**locate** vt (find) ausfindig machen; (establish) errichten; **be** ~**d** sich befinden (in, at in + dat); **location** n (position) Lage f; FILM Drehort m

**loch** n (Scot) See m

**lock 1.** n Schloss nt; NAUT Schleuse f; (of hair) Locke f **2.** vt (door etc) abschließen **3.** vi (door etc) sich abschließen lassen; (wheels) blockieren; **lock in** vt einschließen, einsperren; **lock out** vt aussperren; **lock up** vt (house) abschließen; (person) einsperren

**locker** n Schließfach nt; **locker room** n (US) Umkleideraum m

**locksmith** n Schlosser(in) m(f)

**locust** n Heuschrecke f

**lodge 1.** n (small house) Pförtnerhaus nt; (porter's lodge) Pförtnerloge f **2.** vi in Untermiete wohnen (with bei); **lodger** n Untermieter(in) m(f); **lodging** n Unterkunft f

**loft** n Dachboden m

**log** n Klotz m; NAUT Log nt; **keep a ~ of sth** über etw

Buch führen; **log in** vi IT sich einloggen; **log off** vi IT sich ausloggen; **log on** vi IT sich einloggen; **log out** vi IT sich ausloggen

**logic** n Logik f; **logical** adj logisch

**logo** n Logo nt

**loin** n Lende f

**loiter** vi sich herumtreiben

**lollipop** n Lutscher m; ~ **man / lady** (Brit) Schülerlotse m, Schülerlotsin f

**lolly** n Lutscher m; fam (money) Knete f

**London** n London nt

**loneliness** n Einsamkeit f; **lonely, lonesome** (esp US) adj einsam

**long 1.** adj lang; (distance) weit; **it's a ~ way** es ist weit (to nach); **for a ~ time** lange; **how ~ is the film?** wie lange dauert der Film?; **in the ~ run** auf die Dauer **2.** adv lange; **not for ~** nicht lange; ~ **ago** vor langer Zeit; **before ~** bald; **all day ~** den ganzen Tag; **no ~er** nicht mehr; **as ~ as** solange **3.** vi sich sehnen (for nach); (be waiting) sehnsüchtig warten (for auf); **long-distance call** n Ferngespräch nt; **long drink** n Longdrink m; **long-haul flight** n Langstreckenflug m; **longing** n Sehnsucht f (for nach); **longingly** adv sehnsüchtig; **longitude** n Länge f; **long jump** n Weitsprung *m*; **long-life milk** *n* H-Milch *f*; **long-range** *adj* Langstrecken-, Fern-; **~ missile** Langstreckenrakete *f*; **long-sighted** *adj* weitsichtig; **long-standing** *adj* alt, langjährig; **long-term** *adj* (*car park, effect etc*) Langzeit-; **~ unemployment** Langzeitarbeitslosigkeit *f*

**loo** *n* (*Brit*) *fam* Klo *nt*

**look 1.** *n* Blick *m*; (*appearance*) ~(**s**) *pl* Aussehen *nt*; **I'll have a ~** ich schau mal nach; **have a ~ at sth** sich *dat* etw ansehen; **can I have a ~?** darf ich mal sehen? **2.** *vi* schauen, gucken; (*search*) nachsehen; (*appear*) aussehen; (**I'm**) **just ~ing** ich schaue nur; **it ~s like rain** es sieht nach Regen aus **3.** *vt* **~ what you've done** sieh dir mal an, was du da angestellt hast; (*appear*) **he ~s his age** man sieht ihm sein Alter an; **~ one's best** sehr vorteilhaft aussehen; **look after** *vt* (*care for*) sorgen für; (*keep an eye on*) aufpassen auf + *acc*; **look at** *vt* ansehen, anschauen; **look back** *vi* sich umsehen; *fig* zurückblicken; **look down on** *vt fig* herabsehen auf + *acc*; **look for** *vt* suchen; **look forward to** *vt* sich freuen auf + *acc*; **look into** *vt* (*investigate*) untersuchen; **look out**

*vi* hinaussehen (*of the window* zum Fenster); (*watch out*) Ausschau halten (*for* nach); **~!** Vorsicht!; **look up to** *vt* aufsehen zu

**loop** *n* Schleife *f*

**loose** *adj* locker (*knot, button*) lose; **loosen** *vt* lockern; (*knot*) lösen

**loot** *n* Beute *f*

**lop-sided** *adj* schief

**lord** *n* (*ruler*) Herr *m*; (*Brit, title*) Lord *m*; **the Lord** (*God*) Gott der Herr; (**the House of**) **Lords** (*Brit*) das Oberhaus

**lorry** *n* (*Brit*) Lastwagen *m*

**lose 1.** *vt* verlieren; **~ weight** abnehmen; **~ one's life** umkommen **2.** *vi* verlieren; (*clock, watch*) nachgehen; **loss** *n* Verlust *m*; **lost 1.** *pt, pp → lose*; **we're ~** wir haben uns verlaufen **2.** *adj* verloren; **lost-and-found** (*US*), **lost property** (**office**) *n* Fundbüro *nt*

**lot** *n* (*batch*) *fam* Menge *f*, Haufen *m*; **a ~** viel(e); **a ~ of money** viel Geld; **~s of people** viele Leute; **the** (**whole**) **~** alles; (*people*) alle; (**parking**) **~** (*US*) Parkplatz *m*

**lotion** *n* Lotion *f*

**lottery** *n* Lotterie *f*

**loud** *adj* laut; (*colour*) schrei-

end; **loudspeaker** n Lautsprecher m; (of stereo) Box f
**lounge 1.** n Wohnzimmer nt; (in hotel) Aufenthaltsraum m; (at airport) Warteraum m **2.** vi sich herumlümmeln
**louse** n Laus f; **lousy** adj fam lausig
**lout** n Rüpel m
**lovable** adj liebenswert
**love 1.** n Liebe f (of zu); (person, address) Liebling m, Schatz m; SPORT null; **be in ~** verliebt sein (with sb in jdn); **fall in ~** sich verlieben (with sb in jdn); **make ~** (sexually) sich lieben; **make ~ to** (or **with**) sb mit jdm schlafen; **give her my ~** grüße sie von mir; **~, Tom** liebe Grüße, Tom **2.** vt (person) lieben; (activity) sehr gerne mögen; **~ to do** sth etw für sein Leben gerne tun; **I'd ~ a cup of tea** ich hätte liebend gern eine Tasse Tee; **love affair** n (Liebes)verhältnis nt; **love letter** n Liebesbrief m; **love life** n Liebesleben nt; **lovely** adj schön, wunderschön; (charming) reizend; **we had a ~ time** es war sehr schön; **lover** n Liebhaber(in) m(f); **loving** adj liebevoll
**low 1.** adj niedrig; (level, note, neckline) tief; (quality, standard) schlecht; (not loud) leise; (depressed) niedergeschlagen; **we're ~ on petrol** wir haben kaum noch

Benzin **2.** n METEO Tief nt;
**low-calorie** adj kalorienarm; **low-emission** adj schadstoffarm; **lower 1.** adj niedriger; (storey, class etc) untere(r, s) **2.** vt herunterlassen; (eyes, price) senken; (pressure) verringern; **low-fat** adj fettarm; **low tide** n Ebbe f
**loyal** adj treu; **loyalty** n Treue f
**lozenge** n Pastille f
**Ltd** abbr = **limited** ≈ GmbH f
**luck** n Glück nt; **bad ~** Pech nt; **luckily** adv glücklicherweise, zum Glück; **lucky** adj (number, day etc) Glücks-; **be ~** Glück haben
**ludicrous** adj grotesk
**luggage** n Gepäck nt; **luggage compartment** n Gepäckraum m; **luggage rack** n Gepäcknetz nt
**lukewarm** adj lauwarm
**lullaby** n Schlaflied nt
**lumbago** n Hexenschuss m
**luminous** adj leuchtend
**lump** n Klumpen m; MED Schwellung f; (in breast) Knoten m; (of sugar) Stück nt; **lump sum** n Pauschalsumme f
**lunacy** n Wahnsinn m; **lunatic 1.** adj wahnsinnig **2.** n Wahnsinnige(r) mf
**lunch, luncheon** n Mittagessen nt; **have ~** zu Mittag essen; **lunch break, lunch hour** n Mittagspause f;

**lunchtime** n Mittagszeit f

**lung** n Lunge f

**lurch** n; **leave sb in the ~** jdn im Stich lassen

**lurk** vi lauern

**lust** n (sinnliche) Begierde (for nach)

**Luxembourg** n Luxemburg

nt

**luxurious** adj luxuriös, Luxus-; luxury n (a. luxuries pl) Luxus m; **~ goods** Luxusgüter pl

**lynx** n Luchs m

**lyrics** npl (words for song) Liedtext m

# M

**m** abbr = **metre(s)** m

**M** abbr → **motorway** A; (size) → **medium** M

**ma** n fam Mutti f

**mac** n (Brit) fam Regenmantel m

**macaroon** n Makrone f

**Macedonia** n Mazedonien nt

**machine** n Maschine f; **machine gun** n Maschinengewehr nt; **machinery** n Maschinen pl; fig Apparat m

**mackerel** n Makrele f

**macro** n IT Makro nt

**mad** adj wahnsinnig, verrückt; (dog) tollwütig; (angry) wütend, sauer (at auf + acc); fam **~ about** (fond of) verrückt nach; **work like ~** wie verrückt arbeiten; **are you ~?** spinnst du / spinnen Sie?

**madam** n gnädige Frau

**mad cow disease** n Rinderwahnsinn m; **maddening** adj zum Verrücktwerden

**made** pt, pp → **make**

**made-to-measure** adj nach

Maß; **~ suit** Maßanzug m

**madly** adv wie verrückt; (with adj) wahnsinnig; **madman** n Verrückte(r) m; **madness** n Wahnsinn m; **madwoman** n Verrückte f

**magazine** n Zeitschrift f

**maggot** n Made f

**magic 1.** n Magie f; (activity) Zauberei f; fig (effect) Zauber m; **as if by ~** wie durch Zauberei **2.** adj Zauber-; (powers) magisch; **magician** n Zauberer m, Zaub(r)erin f

**magnet** n Magnet m; **magnetic** adj magnetisch

**magnificent, magnificently** adj, adv herrlich, großartig

**magnify** vt vergrößern; **magnifying glass** n Vergrößerungsglas nt, Lupe f

**magpie** n Elster f

**maid** n Dienstmädchen nt; **maiden name** n Mädchenname m; **maiden voyage** n Jungfernfahrt f

**mail 1.** n Post f; (e-mail) Mail f **2.** vt (post) aufgeben; (send) mit der Post® schicken (*to an + acc*); **mailbox** *n* (*US*) Briefkasten *m*; **IT** Mailbox *f*; **mailing list** *n* Adressenliste *f*; **mailman** *n* (*US*) Briefträger *m*; **mail order** *n* Bestellung *f* per Post; **mail order firm** *n* Versandhaus *nt*

**main 1.** *adj* Haupt-; **~ course** Hauptgericht *nt*; **the ~ thing** die Hauptsache **2.** *n* (*pipe*) Hauptleitung *f*; **mainframe** *n* Großrechner *m*; **mainland** *n* Festland *nt*; **mainly** *adv* hauptsächlich; **main road** *n* Hauptverkehrsstraße *f*; **main street** *n* (*US*) Hauptstraße *f*

**maintain** *vt* (*keep up*) aufrechterhalten; (*machine, roads*) instand halten; (*service*) warten; **maintenance** *n* Instandhaltung *f*; **TECH** Wartung *f*

**maize** *n* Mais *m*

**majestic** *adj* majestätisch; **majesty** *n* Majestät *f*; **Your / His / Her Majesty** Eure / Seine / Ihre Majestät

**major 1.** *adj* (*bigger*) größer; (*important*) bedeutend; **~ part** Großteil *m*; (*role*) wichtige Rolle; **~ road** Hauptverkehrsstraße *f*; **MUS A ~** A-Dur *nt* **2.** *vi* (*US*) **~ in sth** etw als Hauptfach studieren

**Majorca** *n* Mallorca *nt*

**majority** *n* Mehrheit *f*; **be in the ~** in der Mehrzahl sein

**make 1.** *n* Marke *f* **2.** *vt* machen; (*manufacture*) herstellen; (*clothes*) anfertigen; (*dress*) nähen; (*soup*) zubereiten; (*bread, cake*) backen; (*tea, coffee*) kochen; (*speech*) halten; (*earn*) verdienen; (*decision*) treffen; *it's made of gold* es ist aus Gold; **~ sb do sth** jdn dazu bringen, etw zu tun; (*force*) jdn zwingen, etw zu tun; *she made us wait* sie ließ uns warten; *what ~s you think that?* wie kommen Sie darauf?; *he never really made it* er hat es nie zu etwas gebracht; *she didn't ~ it through the night* sie hat die Nacht nicht überlebt; (*calculate*) *I ~ it £5/a quarter to six* nach meiner Rechnung kommt es auf 5 Pfund / nach meiner Uhr ist es dreiviertel sechs; *he's just made for this job* er ist für diese Arbeit wie geschaffen; **make for** *vt* zusteuern auf + *acc*; **make of** *vt* (*think of*) halten von; *I couldn't make anything of it* ich wurde daraus nicht schlau; **make off** *vi* sich davonmachen (*with* mit); **make out** *vt* (*cheque*) ausstellen; (*list*) aufstellen; (*understand*) verstehen; (*discern*) ausmachen; **~ (that) ...** es so hinstellen, als ob ...; **make up 1.** *vt* (*team etc*) bilden; (*face* schminken; (*invent: story etc*) erfinden; **~ one's mind** sich entscheiden; **make (it) up with sb** sich mit jdm aussöhnen **2.** *vi* sich versöhnen; **make up for** *vt* ausgleichen; (*time*) aufholen

**make-believe** *adj* Fantasie-; **makeover** *n* gründliche Veränderung, Verschönerung *f*; **maker** *n* COMM Hersteller(in) *m(f)*; **makeshift** *adj* behelfsmäßig; **make-up** *n* Make-up *nt*, Schminke *f*; **making** *n* Herstellung *f*

**malaria** *n* Malaria *f*

**Malaysia** *n* Malaysia *nt*

**male 1.** *n* Mann *m*; (*animal*) Männchen *nt* **2.** *adj* männlich; **~ chauvinist** Chauvi *m*, Macho *m*; **~ nurse** Krankenpfleger *m*

**malfunction 1.** *vi* nicht richtig funktionieren **2.** *n* Defekt *m*

**malice** *n* Bosheit *f*; **malicious** *adj* boshaft; (*damage*) mutwillig

**malignant** *adj* bösartig

**mall** *n* (*US*) Einkaufszentrum *nt*

**malnutrition** *n* Unterernährung *f*

**malt** *n* Malz *nt*

**Malta** *n* Malta *nt*; **Maltese 1.** *adj* maltesisch **2.** *n* (*person*) Malteser(in) *m(f)*; (*language*) Maltesisch *nt*

**maltreat** *vt* schlecht behandeln; (*violently*) misshandeln

**mammal** *n* Säugetier *nt*

**mammoth** *adj* Mammut-, Riesen-

**man 1.** *n* (*male*) Mann *m*; (*human race*) der Mensch, die Menschen *pl*; (*in chess*) Figur *f* **2.** *vt* besetzen

**manage 1.** *vi* zurechtkommen; **can you ~?** schaffst du es?; **~ without sth** ohne etw auskommen, auf etw verzichten können **2.** *vt* (*control*) leiten; (*musician, sportsman*) managen; (*cope with*) fertig werden mit; (*task, portion, climb etc*) schaffen; **~ to do sth** es schaffen, etw zu tun; **manageable** *adj* (*object*) handlich; (*task*) zu bewältigen; **management** *n* Leitung *f*; (*directors*) Direktion *f*; (*subject*) Management *nt*, Betriebswirtschaft *f*; **management consultant** *n* Unternehmensberater(in) *m(f)*; **manager** *n* Geschäftsführer(in) *m(f)*; (*departmental manager*) Abteilungsleiter(in) *m(f)*; (*of branch, bank*) Filialleiter(in) *m(f)*; (*of musician, sportsman*) Manager(in) *m(f)*; **managing director** *n* Geschäftsführer(in) *m(f)*

**mane** *n* Mähne *f*

**maneuver** (*US*) → **manoeuvre**

**mango** *n* Mango *f*

**man-hour** *n* Arbeitsstunde *f*

**married**

**manhunt** n Fahndung f
**mania** n Manie f; **maniac** n Wahnsinnige(r) mf; (fan) Fanatiker(in) m(f)
**manicure** n Maniküre f
**manipulate** vt manipulieren
**mankind** n Menschheit f
**manly** adj männlich
**man-made** adj (product) künstlich
**manner** n Art f; **in this ~** auf diese Art und Weise; **~s** pl Manieren pl
**manoeuvre 1.** n Manöver nt **2.** vt, vi manövrieren
**manor** n **~** (house) Herrenhaus nt
**manpower** n Arbeitskräfte pl
**mansion** n Villa f; (of old family) Herrenhaus nt
**manslaughter** n Totschlag m
**manual 1.** adj manuell, Hand- **2.** n Handbuch nt
**manufacture 1.** vt herstellen **2.** n Herstellung f; **manufacturer** n Hersteller m
**manure** n Dung m; (esp artificial) Dünger m
**many** adj, pron viele; **~ times** oft; **not ~ people** nicht viele Leute; **too ~ problems** zu viele Probleme
**map** n Landkarte f; (of town) Stadtplan m
**maple** n Ahorn m
**marathon** n Marathon m
**marble** n Marmor m; (for playing) Murmel f
**march 1.** vi marschieren **2.** n Marsch m; (protest) Demonstration f
**March** n März m; → **September**
**mare** n Stute f
**margarine** n Margarine f
**margin** n Rand m; (extra amount) Spielraum m; COMM Gewinnspanne f; **marginal** adj (difference etc) geringfügig
**marijuana** n Marihuana nt
**marinated** adj mariniert
**marine** adj Meeres-
**marital** adj ehelich; **~ status** Familienstand m
**maritime** adj See-
**marjoram** n Majoran m
**mark 1.** n (spot) Fleck m; (at school) Note f; (sign) Zeichen nt **2.** vt (indicate) markieren; (schoolwork) benoten, korrigieren, Flecken machen auf + acc; **marker** n (in book) Lesezeichen nt; (pen) Marker m
**market 1.** n Markt m **2.** vt COMM (new product) auf den Markt bringen; (goods) vertreiben; **marketing** n Marketing nt; **market leader** n Marktführer m; **market place** n Marktplatz m; **market research** n Marktforschung f
**marmalade** n Orangenmarmelade f
**maroon** adj rötlich braun
**marquee** n großes Zelt
**marriage** n Ehe f; (wedding) Heirat f (to mit); **married**

*adj (person)* verheiratet

**marrow** *n (bone marrow)* Knochenmark *nt; (vegetable)* Kürbis *m*

**marry 1.** *vt* heiraten; *(join)* trauen **2.** *vi* ~ / **get married** heiraten

**marsh** *n* Marsch *f*, Sumpf *m*

**marshal** *n (at rally etc)* Ordner *m; (US, police)* Bezirkspolizeichef *m*

**martial arts** *npl* Kampfsportarten *pl*

**martyr** *n* Märtyrer(in) *m(f)*

**marvel 1.** *n* Wunder *nt* **2.** *vi* staunen *(at* über + *acc)*; **marvellous, marvelous** (*US*) *adj* wunderbar

**mascara** *n* Wimperntusche *f*

**mascot** *n* Maskottchen *nt*

**masculine** *adj* männlich

**mashed** *adj* ~ **potatoes** *pl* Kartoffelbrei *m*, Kartoffelpüree *nt*

**mask 1.** *n* Maske *f* **2.** *vt (feelings)* verbergen

**masochist** *n* Masochist(in) *m(f)*

**mason** *n (stonemason)* Steinmetz(in) *m(f);* **masonry** *n* Mauerwerk *nt*

**mass 1.** *n* Masse *f; (of people)* Menge *f;* REL Messe *f;* **~es of** massenhaft

**massacre** *n* Blutbad *nt*

**massage 1.** *n* Massage *f* **2.** *vt* massieren

**massive** *adj (powerful)* gewaltig; *(very large)* riesig

**mass media** *npl* Massenme-

dien *pl;* **mass production** *n* Massenproduktion *f*

**master 1.** *n* Herr *m; (of dog)* Besitzer *m*, Herrchen *nt; (artist)* Meister *m* **2.** *vt* meistern; *(language etc)* beherrschen; *(masterly adj* meisterhaft; **masterpiece** *n* Meisterwerk *nt*

**masturbate** *vi* masturbieren

**mat** *n* Matte *f; (for table)* Untersetzer *m*

**match 1.** *n* Streichholz *nt;* SPORT Wettkampf *m; (ball games)* Spiel *nt; (tennis)* Match *nt* **2.** *vt (be like, suit)* passen zu; *(equal)* gleichkommen + *dat* **3.** *vi* zusammenpassen; **matchbox** *n* Streichholzschachtel *f;* **matching** *adj (one item)* passend; *(two items)* zusammenpassend

**mate 1.** *n (companion)* Kumpel *m; (of animal)* Weibchen *nt*/Männchen *nt* **2.** *vi* sich paaren

**material** *n* Material *nt; (for book etc, cloth)* Stoff *m;* **materialistic** *adj* materialistisch; **materialize** *vi* zustande kommen; *(hope)* wahr werden

**maternal** *adj* mütterlich; **maternity** *adj* ~ **dress** Umstandskleid *nt;* ~ **leave** Elternzeit *f* (der Mutter); ~ **ward** Entbindungsstation *f*

**math** *n (US) fam* Mathe *f;* **mathematical** *adj* mathematisch; **mathematics** *nsing* Mathematik *f*; **maths** *nsing* (*Brit*) *fam* Mathe *f*

**matter 1.** *n* (*substance*) Materie *f*; (*affair*) Sache *f*; **a personal** ~ eine persönliche Angelegenheit; **a** ~ **of taste** eine Frage des Geschmacks; **no** ~ **how / what** egal wie / was; **what's the** ~**?** was ist los?; **as a** ~ **of fact** eigentlich; **a** ~ **of time** eine Frage der Zeit **2.** *vi* darauf ankommen, wichtig sein; **it doesn't** ~ es macht nichts; **matter-of-fact** *adj* sachlich, nüchtern

**mattress** *n* Matratze *f*

**mature 1.** *adj* reif **2.** *vi* reif werden; **maturity** *n* Reife *f*

**maximum 1.** *adj* Höchst-, höchste(r, s); ~ **speed** Höchstgeschwindigkeit *f* **2.** *n* Maximum *nt*

**may** *vaux* (*be possible*) können; (*have permission*) dürfen; **it** ~ **rain** es könnte regnen; ~ **I smoke?** darf ich rauchen?; **we** ~ **as well go** wir können ruhig gehen

**May** *n* Mai *m*; → **September**

**maybe** *adv* vielleicht

**mayo** (*US*) *fam*, **mayonnaise** *n* Mayo *f*, Mayonnaise *f*, Majonäse *f*

**mayor** *n* Bürgermeister *m*

**maze** *n* Irrgarten *m*; *fig* Wirrwarr *nt*

**MB** *abbr* → **megabyte** MB *nt*

**me** *pron* (*direct object*) mich; (*indirect object*) mir; **it's** ~

ich bin's

**meadow** *n* Wiese *f*

**meal** *n* Essen *nt*, Mahlzeit *f*; **go out for a** ~ essen gehen; **meal pack** *n* (*US*) tiefgekühltes Fertiggericht; **meal time** *n* Essenszeit *f*

**mean 1.** *vt* (*signify*) bedeuten; (*have in mind*) meinen; (*intend*) vorhaben; **I** ~ **it** ich meine das ernst; **what do you** ~ (*by that*)**?** was willst du damit sagen?; ~ **to do sth** etw tun wollen; **it was** ~**t for you** es war für dich bestimmt (*or* gedacht); **it was** ~**t to be a joke** es sollte ein Witz sein **2.** *vi* **he's well** er meint es gut **3.** *adj* (*stingy*) geizig; (*spiteful*) gemein (*to* zu); **meaning** *n* Bedeutung *f*; (*of life, poem*) Sinn *m*; **meaningful** *adj* sinnvoll; **meaningless** *adj* (*text*) ohne Sinn

**means** *n* Mittel *nt*; (*funds*) Mittel *pl*; **by** ~ **of** durch, mittels; **by all** ~ selbstverständlich; **by no** ~ keineswegs; ~ **of transport** Beförderungsmittel

**meant** *pt*, *pp* → **mean**

**meantime** *adv* **in the** ~ inzwischen; **meanwhile** *adv* inzwischen

**measles** *nsing* Masern *pl*; **German** ~ Röteln *pl*

**measure 1.** *vt*, *vi* messen **2.** *n* (*unit, device for measuring*) Maß *nt*; (*step*) Maßnahme *f*; **take** ~**s** Maßnahmen er-

# measurement 458

greifen; **measurement** n (*amount measured*) Maß nt

**meat** n Fleisch nt; **meatball** n Fleischbällchen m

**mechanic** n Mechaniker(in) m(f); **mechanical** adj mechanisch; **mechanics** nsing Mechanik f; **mechanism** n Mechanismus m

**medal** n Medaille f; (*decoration*) Orden m; **medalist** (*US*), **medallist** n Medaillengewinner(in) m(f)

**media** npl Medien pl

**median strip** n (*US*) Mittelstreifen m

**mediate** vi vermitteln

**medical 1.** adj medizinisch; (*treatment etc*) ärztlich; ~ **student** Medizinstudent(in) m(f) **2.** n Untersuchung f; **Medicare** n (*US*) Krankenkasse f für ältere Leute; **medication** n Medikamente pl; **be on** ~ Medikamente nehmen; **medicinal** adj Heil-; ~ **herbs** Heilkräuter pl; **medicine** n Arznei f; (*science*) Medizin f

**medieval** adj mittelalterlich

**mediocre** adj mittelmäßig

**meditate** vi meditieren; fig nachdenken (*on* über + acc)

**Mediterranean** n (*sea*) Mittelmeer nt; (*region*) Mittelmeerraum m

**medium 1.** adj (*quality, size*) mittlere(r, s); (*steak*) halbdurch; ~ (*dry*) (*wine*) halbtrocken; ~ **sized** mittelgroß;

~ **wave** Mittelwelle f **2.** n Medium nt; (*means*) Mittel nt

**meet 1.** vt treffen; (*by arrangement*) sich treffen mit; (*difficulties*) stoßen auf + acc; (*get to know*) kennenlernen; (*requirement, demand*) gerecht werden + dat; (*deadline*) einhalten; **pleased to ~ you** sehr angenehm!; ~ **sb at the station** jdn von Bahnhof abholen **2.** vi sich treffen; (*become acquainted*) sich kennenlernen; **we've met** (*before*) wir kennen uns schon; **meet up** vr sich treffen (*with* mit); **meet with** vt (*group*) zusammenkommen mit; (*difficulties, resistance etc*) stoßen auf + acc; **meeting** n Treffen nt; (*business meeting*) Besprechung f; (*of committee*) Sitzung f; (*assembly*) Versammlung f; **meeting place**, **meeting point** n Treffpunkt m

**megabyte** n Megabyte nt

**melody** n Melodie f

**melon** n Melone f

**melt** vt, vi schmelzen

**member** n Mitglied nt; (*of tribe, species*) Angehörige(r) mf; **Member of Parliament** Parlamentsabgeordnete(r) mf; **membership** n Mitgliedschaft f; **membership card** n Mitgliedskarte f

**memo** n Mitteilung f, Memo nt; **memo pad** n Notizblock m

**memorable** *adj* unvergesslich; **memorial** *n* Denkmal *nt* (*to* für); **memorize** *vt* sich einprägen, auswendig lernen; **memory** *n* Gedächtnis *nt*; IT (*of computer*) Speicher *m*; (*sth recalled*) Erinnerung *f*; **in ~ of** zur Erinnerung an + *acc*

**men** *pl* → **man**

**menace** *n* Bedrohung *f*; (*danger*) Gefahr *f*

**mend 1.** *vt* reparieren; (*clothes*) flicken **2.** *n* **be on the ~** auf dem Wege der Besserung sein

**meningitis** *n* Hirnhautentzündung *f*

**menopause** *n* Wechseljahre *pl*

**mental** *adj* geistig; **mentality** *n* Mentalität *f*; **mentally** *adv* geistig; **~ handicapped** geistig behindert; **~ ill** geisteskrank

**mention 1.** *n* Erwähnung *f* **2.** *vt* erwähnen (*to sb* jdm gegenüber); **don't ~ it** bitte sehr, gern geschehen

**menu** *n* Speisekarte *f*; IT Menü *nt*

**merchandise** *n* Handelsware *f*; **merchant** *adj* Handels-

**merciful** *adj* gnädig; **mercifully** *adv* glücklicherweise

**mercury** *n* Quecksilber *nt*

**mercy** *n* Gnade *f*

**mere** *adj* bloß; **merely** *adv* bloß, lediglich

**merge** *vi* verschmelzen; AUTO sich einfädeln; COMM fusionieren; **merger** *n* COMM Fusion *f*

**meringue** *n* Baiser *nt*

**merit** *n* Verdienst *nt*; (*advantage*) Vorzug *m*

**merry** *adj* fröhlich; *fam* (*tipsy*) angeheitert; **Merry Christmas** Fröhliche Weihnachten!; **merry-go-round** *n* Karussell *nt*

**mess** *n* Unordnung *f*; (*muddle*) Durcheinander *nt*; (*dirty*) Schweinerei *f*; (*trouble*) Schwierigkeiten *pl*; **in a ~** (*muddled*) durcheinander; (*untidy*) unordentlich; *fig* (*person*) in der Klemme; **make a ~ of sth** etw verpfuschen; **mess about** *vi* (*tinker with*) herummurksen (*with* an + *dat*); (*play the fool*) herumalbern; (*do nothing in particular*) herumgammeln; **mess up** *vt* verpfuschen; (*make untidy*) in Unordnung bringen; (*dirty*) schmutzig machen

**message** *n* Mitteilung *f*, Nachricht *f*; **can I give him a ~?** kann ich ihm etwas ausrichten?; **please leave a ~** (*on answerphones*) bitte hinterlassen Sie eine Nachricht; **I get the ~** ich hab's verstanden

**messenger** *n* Bote *m*

**messy** *adj* (*untidy*) unordentlich; (*situation etc*) verfahren

**met** *pt, pp* → **meet**

**metal** 460

**metal** *n* Metall *nt*; **metallic** *adj* metallisch

**meteorology** *n* Meteorologie *f*

**meter** *n* Zähler *m*; *(parking meter)* Parkuhr *f*; *(US)* → **metre**

**method** *n* Methode *f*

**meticulous** *adj* (peinlich) genau

**metre** *n* Meter *m or nt*; **metric** *adj* metrisch; ~ **system** Dezimalsystem *nt*

**Mexico** *n* Mexiko *nt*

**mice** *pl* → **mouse**

**mickey** *n* **take the** ~ *(out of sb)* *fam* (jdn) auf den Arm nehmen

**microchip** *n* IT Mikrochip *m*; **microphone** *n* Mikrofon *nt*; **microscope** *n* Mikroskop *nt*; **microwave (oven)** *n* Mikrowelle(nherd) *f(m)*

**mid** *adj* **in** ~ **January** Mitte Januar; **he's in his** ~ **forties** er ist Mitte vierzig

**midday** *n* Mittag *m*; **at** ~ mittags

**middle 1.** *n* Mitte *f*; **in the** ~ **of** mitten in + *dat*; **be in the** ~ **of doing sth** gerade dabei sein, etw zu tun **2.** *adj* mittlere(r, s), Mittel-; **middle-aged** *adj* mittleren Alters; **Middle Ages** *npl* **the** ~ das Mittelalter; **middle-class** *adj* mittelständisch; *(bourgeois)* bürgerlich; **middle classes** *npl* **the** ~ der Mittelstand; **Middle East** *n* **the** ~ der Nahe

Osten; **middle name** *n* zweiter Vorname

**Midlands** *npl* **the** ~ Mittelengland *nt*

**midnight** *n* Mitternacht *f*

**midst** *n* **in the** ~ **of** mitten in + *dat*

**midsummer** *n* Hochsommer *m*; **Midsummer's Day** Sommersonnenwende *f*

**midway** *adv* auf halbem Wege; ~ **through the film** nach der Hälfte des Films; **midweek** *adj*, *adv* in der Mitte der Woche

**midwife** *n* Hebamme *f*

**midwinter** *n* tiefster Winter

**might 1.** *pt* → **may**; *(possibility)* könnte; *(permission)* dürfte; *(would)* würde; **they** ~ **still come** sie könnten noch kommen; **I thought she** ~ **change her mind** ich dachte schon, sie würde sich anders entscheiden **2.** *n* Macht *f*, Kraft *f*

**mighty** *adj* gewaltig; *(powerful)* mächtig

**migraine** *n* Migräne *f*

**migrant** *n* *(bird)* Zugvogel *m*; ~ **worker** Gastarbeiter(in) *m(f)*; **migrate** *vi* abwandern; *(birds)* nach Süden ziehen

**mike** *n* *fam* Mikro *nt*

**Milan** *n* Mailand *nt*

**mild** *adj* mild; *(person)* sanft; **mildly** *adv* **put it** ~ gelinde gesagt; **mildness** *n* Milde *f*

**mile** *n* Meile *f* (= *1,609 km*); **for** ~**s (and** ~**s)** ≈ kilometer-

weit; **~s per hour** Meilen pro
Stunde; **~s better than** hundertmal besser als; **mileage**
*n* Meilen *pl*, Meilenzahl *f*;
**mileometer** *n* ≈ Kilometerzähler *m*; **milestone** *n a.*
*fig* Meilenstein *m*

**militant** *adj* militant; **military**
*adj* Militär-, militärisch

**milk** *n* Milch *f* **2.** *vt* melken;
**milk chocolate** *n* Vollmilchschokolade *f*; **milkman** *n*
Milchmann *m*; **milk shake**
*n* Milkshake *m*, Milchmixgetränk *nt*

**mill** *n* Mühle *f*; (*factory*) Fabrik *f*

**millennium** *n* Jahrtausend *nt*

**milligramme** *n* Milligramm
*nt*; **millilitre** (*US*), **millilitre**
*n* Milliliter *m*; **millimeter** *n*
(*US*), **millimetre** *n* Millimeter *m*

**million** *n* Million *f*; **five ~** fünf
Millionen; **~s of people** Millionen von Menschen; **millionaire** *n* Millionär(in) *m(f)*

**mime 1.** *n* Pantomime *f* **2.** *vt*, *vi*
mimen; **mimic 1.** *n* Imitator(in) *m(f)* **2.** *vt*, *vi* nachahmen; **mimicry** *n* Nachahmung *f*

**mince 1.** *vt* (zer)hacken **2.** *n*
(*meat*) Hackfleisch *nt*;
**mincemeat** *n* süße Gebäckfüllung aus Rosinen, Äpfeln,
Zucker, Gewürzen und Talg;
**mince pie** *n* mit 'mincemeat'
gefülltes süßes Weihnachtsgebäck

**mind 1.** *n* (*intellect*) Verstand
*m*; (*also person*) Geist *m*;
**out of sight, out of ~** aus
den Augen, aus dem Sinn;
**he is out of his ~** er ist nicht
bei Verstand; **keep sth in ~**
etw im Auge behalten; **I
have a lot on my ~** mich beschäftigt so vieles im Moment; **change one's ~** es sich
*dat* anders überlegen **2.** *vt*
(*look after*) aufpassen auf
+ *acc*; (*object to*) etwas haben gegen; **~ you, ...** allerdings ...; **I wouldn't ~ ...**
ich hätte nichts gegen ...; **~
the step** „Vorsicht Stufe!"
**3.** *vi* etwas dagegen haben;
**do you ~ if I ...** macht es Ihnen etwas aus, wenn ich ...; **I
don't ~** es ist mir egal, meinetwegen; **never ~** macht es
nichts

**mine 1.** *pron* meine(r, s); **this
is ~** das gehört mir; **a friend
of ~** ein Freund von mir **2.** *n*
(*coalmine*) Bergwerk *nt*; MIL
Mine *f*

**miner** *n* Bergarbeiter(in) *m(f)*

**mineral** *n* Mineral *nt*; **mineral
water** *n* Mineralwasser *nt*

**mingle** *vi* sich mischen (*with*
unter + *acc*)

**minibar** *n* Minibar *f*; **minibus**
*n* Kleinbus *m*; **minicab** *n*
Kleintaxi *nt*

**minimal** *adj* minimal; **minimize** *vt* auf ein Minimum reduzieren; **minimum 1.** *n* Minimum *nt* **2.** *adj* Mindest-

**mining** n Bergbau m
**miniskirt** n Minirock m
**minister** n POL Minister(in)
m(f); REL Pastor(in) m(f),
Pfarrer(in) m(f); **ministry** n
POL Ministerium nt
**minor 1.** adj kleiner; (insignificant) unbedeutend; (operation, offence) harmlos; ~
**road** Nebenstraße f; MUS **A**
~ a-Moll nt **2.** n (Brit, under
18) Minderjährige(r) mf;
**minority** n Minderheit f
**mint** n Minze f; (sweet)
Pfefferminz(bonbon) nt;
**mint sauce** n Minzsoße f
**minus** prep minus; (without)
ohne
**minute 1.** adj winzig; **in ~ detail** genauestens **2.** n Minute
f; **just a ~** Moment mal!; **any**
~ jeden Augenblick; **~s** pl (of
meeting) Protokoll nt
**miracle** n Wunder nt; **miraculous** adj unglaublich
**mirage** n Fata Morgana f,
Luftspiegelung f
**mirror** n Spiegel m
**misbehave** vi sich schlecht
benehmen
**miscalculation** n Fehlkalkulation f; (misjudgement)
Fehleinschätzung f
**miscarriage** n MED Fehlgeburt f
**miscellaneous** adj verschieden
**mischief** n Unfug m; **mischievous** adj (person)
durchtrieben; (glance) ver-

schmitzt
**misconception** n falsche
Vorstellung
**misconduct** n Vergehen nt
**miser** n Geizhals m
**miserable** adj (person) todunglücklich; (conditions,
life) elend; (pay, weather)
miserabel
**miserly** adj geizig
**misery** n Elend nt; (suffering)
Qualen pl
**misfit** n Außenseiter(in) m(f)
**misfortune** n Pech nt
**misguided** adj irrig; (optimism) unangebracht
**misinform** vt falsch informieren
**misinterpret** vt falsch auslegen
**misjudge** vt falsch beurteilen
**mislay** irr vt verlegen
**mislead** irr vt irreführen;
**misleading** adj irreführend
**misprint** n Druckfehler m
**mispronounce** vt falsch aussprechen
**miss 1.** vt (fail to hit, catch)
verfehlen; (not notice, hear)
nicht mitbekommen; (be too
late for) verpassen; (chance)
versäumen; (regret the absence of) vermissen; **I ~
you** du fehlst mir **2.** vi nicht
treffen; (shooting) danebenschießen; (ball, shot etc) danebengehen; **miss out 1.** vt
auslassen **2.** vi ~ **on sth** etw
verpassen
**Miss** n (unmarried woman)

Fräulein *nt*

**missile** *n* Geschoss *nt*; (*rocket*) Rakete *f*

**missing** *adj* (*person*) vermisst; (*thing*) fehlend; **be/go ~** vermisst werden, fehlen

**mission** *n* POL, MIL, REL Auftrag *m*, Mission *f*; **missionary** *n* Missionar(in) *m(f)*

**mist** *n* (feiner) Nebel *m*; (*haze*) Dunst *m*; **mist over**, **mist up** *vi* sich beschlagen

**mistake 1.** *n* Fehler *m*; **by ~** aus Versehen **2.** *irr vt* (*misunderstand*) falsch verstehen; (*mix up*) verwechseln (*for* mit); **mistaken** *adj* (*idea*, *identity*) falsch; **be ~** sich irren, falschliegen

**mistletoe** *n* Mistel *f*

**mistreat** *vt* schlecht behandeln

**mistress** *n* (*lover*) Geliebte *f*

**mistrust 1.** *n* Misstrauen *nt* (*of* gegen) **2.** *vt* misstrauen + *dat*

**misty** *adj* neblig; (*hazy*) dunstig

**misunderstand** *irr vt*, *vi* falsch verstehen; **misunderstanding** *n* Missverständnis *nt*; (*disagreement*) Differenz *f*

**mitten** *n* Fausthandschuh *m*

**mix 1.** *n* (*mixture*) Mischung *f* **2.** *vt* mischen; (*blend*) vermischen (*with* mit); (*drinks*, *music*) mixen; **~ business with pleasure** das Angenehme mit dem Nützlichen verbinden **3.** *vi* (*liquids*) sich

vermischen lassen; **mix up** *vt* (*mix*) zusammenmischen; (*confuse*) verwechseln (*with* mit); **mixed** *adj* gemischt; **a ~ bunch** eine bunt gemischte Truppe; **~ grill** Mixed Grill *m*; **~ vegetables** Mischgemüse *nt*; **mixer** *n* (*for food*) Mixer *m*; **mixture** *n* Mischung *f*; MED Saft *m*; **mix-up** *n* Durcheinander *nt*; Missverständnis *nt*

**ml** *abbr* = **millilitre(s)** ml

**mm** *abbr* = **millimetre(s)** mm

**moan 1.** *n* Stöhnen *nt*; (*complaint*) Gejammer *nt* **2.** *vi* stöhnen; (*complain*) jammern, meckern (*about* über + *acc*)

**mobile 1.** *adj* beweglich; (*on wheels*) fahrbar **2.** *n* (*phone*) Handy *nt*; **mobile phone** *n* Mobiltelefon *nt*, Handy *nt*

**mobility** *n* Beweglichkeit *f*

**mock 1.** *vt* verspotten **2.** *adj* Schein-; **mockery** *n* Spott *m*

**mod cons** *abbr* = **modern conveniences** (moderner) Komfort

**mode** *n* Art *f*; IT Modus *m*

**model 1.** *n* Modell *nt*; (*example*) Vorbild *nt*; (*fashion*) Model *m* **2.** *adj* (*miniature*) Modell-; (*perfect*) Muster- **3.** *vt* (*make*) formen **4.** *vi* **she ~s for Versace** sie arbeitet als Model bei Versace

**modem** *n* Modem *nt*

**moderate 1.** *adj* mäßig; (*views*, *politics*) gemäßigt;

(*income, success*) mittelmäßig **2.** *n* POL Gemäßigte(r)
*mf* **3.** *vt* mäßigen

**modern** *adj* modern; ~ *history* neuere Geschichte; ~
*Greek* Neugriechisch *nt*;

**modernize** *vt* modernisieren

**modest** *adj* bescheiden;

**modesty** *n* Bescheidenheit *f*

**modification** *n* Abänderung
*f*; **modify** *vt* abändern

**moist** *adj* feucht; **moisten** *vt*
befeuchten; **moisture** *n*
Feuchtigkeit *f*; **moisturizer**
*n* Feuchtigkeitscreme *f*

**molar** *n* Backenzahn *m*

**mold** (US) → **mould**

**mole** *n* (*spot*) Leberfleck *m*;
(*animal*) Maulwurf *m*

**molecule** *n* Molekül *nt*

**molest** *vt* belästigen

**molt** (US) → **moult**

**molten** *adj* geschmolzen

**mom** *n* (US) Mutti *f*

**moment** *n* Moment *m*, Augenblick *m*; *just a* ~ Moment
mal!; *at* (*or* **for**) *the* ~ im Augenblick; *in a* ~ gleich

**momentous** *adj* bedeutsam

**Monaco** *n* Monaco *nt*

**monarchy** *n* Monarchie *f*

**monastery** *n* (*for monks*)
Kloster *nt*

**Monday** *n* Montag *m*; →
**Tuesday**

**monetary** *adj* (*reform, policy,
union*) Währungs-; ~ *unit*
Geldeinheit *f*

**money** *n* Geld *nt*

**monitor 1.** *n* (*screen*) Monitor

*m* **2.** *vt* (*progress etc*) überwachen

**monk** *n* Mönch *m*

**monkey** *n* Affe *m*; ~ *business* Unfug *m*

**monsoon** *n* Monsun *m*

**monster 1.** *n* (*animal, thing*)
Monstrum *nt* **2.** *adj* Riesen-;
**monstrosity** *n* Monstrosität
*f*; (*thing*) Ungetüm *nt*

**Montenegro** *n* Montenegro
*nt*

**month** *n* Monat *m*; **monthly 1.**
*adj* monatlich; (*ticket, salary*) Monats- **2.** *adv* monatlich
**3.** *n* (*magazine*) Monats-
(zeit)schrift *f*

**monty** *n* *go the full* ~ *fam*
(*strip*) alle Hüllen fallen lassen; (*go the whole hog*) aufs
Ganze gehen

**monument** *n* Denkmal *nt* (*to*
für); **monumental** *adj*
(*huge*) gewaltig

**mood** *n* (*of person*) Laune *f*;
(*a. general*) Stimmung *f*; *be
in a good / bad* ~ gute /
schlechte Laune haben,
gut / schlecht drauf sein; *be
in the* ~ *for sth* für etw aufgelegt sein; **moody** *adj* launisch

**moon** *n* Mond *m*; *be over the
~ fam* überglücklich sein;
**moonlight 1.** *n* Mondlicht
*nt* **2.** *vi* schwarzarbeiten;
**moonlit** *adj* (*night, landscape*) mondhell

**moor 1.** *n* Moor *nt* **2.** *vt, vi* festmachen; **moorings** *npl* Lie-

**mostly**

geplatz *m*;  **moorland** *n*
Moorland *nt*, Heideland *nt*
**moose** *n* Elch *m*
**mop** *n* Mopp *m*; **mop up** *vt*
aufwischen
**moped** *n* (*Brit*) Moped *nt*
**moral 1.** *adj* moralisch; (*values*) sittlich **2.** *n* Moral *f*; **~s**
*pl* Moral *f*; **morale** *n* Stimmung *f*, Moral *f*; **morality** *n*
Moral *f*, Ethik *f*
**more** *adj, pron adv* mehr; (*additional*) noch; **three** **~** noch
drei; **some ~ tea?** noch etwas Tee?; **are there any ~?**
gibt es noch welche?; **I don't
go there any ~** ich gehe nicht
mehr hin; (*forming comparative*) **~ important** wichtiger;
**~ slowly** langsamer; **~ and ~**
immer mehr; **~ and ~ beautiful** immer schöner; **~ or
less** mehr oder weniger;
**moreish** *adj* (*food*) **these
crisps are really ~** ich kann
mit diesen Chips einfach
nicht aufhören; **moreover**
*adv* außerdem
**morgue** *n* Leichenschauhaus
*nt*
**morning 1.** *n* Morgen *m*; **in
the ~** am Morgen, morgens;
(*tomorrow*) morgen früh;
**this ~** heute morgen **2.** *adj*
Morgen-; (*early*) Früh-;
(*walk etc*) morgendlich;
**morning after pill** *n* die Pille
danach; **morning sickness**
*n* Schwangerschaftsübelkeit
*f*

**Morocco** *n* Marokko *nt*
**moron** *n* Idiot(in) *m(f)*
**morphine** *n* Morphium *nt*
**morsel** *n* Bissen *m*
**mortal 1.** *adj* sterblich;
(*wound*) tödlich **2.** *n* Sterbliche(r) *mf*; **mortality** *n* (*death
rate*) Sterblichkeitsziffer *f*
**mortgage 1.** *n* Hypothek *f* **2.**
*vt* mit einer Hypothek belasten
**mosaic** *n* Mosaik *nt*
**Moscow** *n* Moskau *nt*
**Moslem** *adj, n* → **Muslim**
**mosque** *n* Moschee *f*
**mosquito** *n* (Stech)mücke *f*;
(*tropical*) Moskito *m*; **~ net**
Moskitonetz *nt*
**moss** *n* Moos *nt*
**most 1.** *adj* meiste *pl*, die
meisten; **in ~ cases** in den
meisten Fällen **2.** *adv* (*with
verbs*) am meisten; (*with
adj*) ...ste; (*with adv*) am
...sten; (*very*) äußerst,
höchst; **he ate (the)** **~** er
hat am meisten gegessen;
**the ~ beautiful / interesting** der / die / das schönste / interessanteste; **~ interesting** hochinteressant! **3.**
*n* das meiste, der größte Teil;
(*people*) die meisten; **~ of
the money / players** das
meiste Geld / die meisten
Spieler; **for the ~ part** zum
größten Teil; **five at the ~**
höchstens fünf; **make the ~
of sth** etw voll ausnützen;
**mostly** *adv* (*most of the*

**MOT**                 466

*time*) meistens; (*mainly*) hauptsächlich; (*for the most part*) größtenteils

**MOT** *abbr* = **Ministry of Transport**; ~ (**test**) ≈ TÜV *m*

**motel** *n* Motel *nt*

**moth** *n* Nachtfalter *m*; (*wool-eating*) Motte *f*; **mothball** *n* Mottenkugel *f*

**mother 1.** *n* Mutter *f* **2.** *vt* bemuttern; **mother-in-law** *n* Schwiegermutter *f*; **mother-to-be** *n* werdende Mutter

**motion** *n* Bewegung *f*; (*in meeting*) Antrag *m*

**motivate** *vt* motivieren

**motor 1.** *n* Motor *m*; *fam* (*car*) Auto *nt* **2.** *adj* Motor-; **Motorail train**® *n* (*Brit*) Autoreisezug *m*; **motorbike** *n* Motorrad *nt*; **motorboat** *n* Motorboot *nt*; **motorcycle** *n* Motorrad *nt*; **motorist** *n* Autofahrer(in) *m(f)*; **motor oil** *n* Motorenöl *nt*; **motor racing** *n* Autorennsport *m*; **motor scooter** *n* Motorroller *m*; **motor vehicle** *n* Kraftfahrzeug *nt*; **motorway** *n* (*Brit*) Autobahn *f*

**mould 1.** *n* Form *f*; (*mildew*) Schimmel *m* **2.** *vt* formen; **mouldy** *adj* schimmelig

**mount 1.** *vt* (*horse*) steigen auf + *acc*; (*exhibition etc*) organisieren; (*painting*) mit einem Passepartout versehen **2.** *vi ~* (**up**) (an)steigen **3.** *n* Passepartout *nt*

**mountain** *n* Berg *m*; **moun-**

**taineer** *n* Bergsteiger(in) *m(f)*; **mountaineering** *n* Bergsteigen *nt*; **mountainside** *n* Berghang *m*

**mourn 1.** *vt* betrauern **2.** *vi* trauern (*for* um); **mourning** *n* Trauer *f*; **be in ~** trauern (*for* um)

**mouse** *n* *a.* IT Maus *f*; **mouse mat, mouse pad** (*US*) *n* Mauspad *nt*; **mouse trap** *n* Mausefalle *f*

**mousse** *n* GASTR Creme *f*; (*styling mousse*) Schaumfestiger *m*

**moustache** *n* Schnurrbart *m*

**mouth** *n* Mund *m*; (*of animal*) Maul *nt*; (*of cave*) Eingang *m*; (*of bottle etc*) Öffnung *f*; (*of river*) Mündung *f*; **keep one's ~ shut** *fam* den Mund halten; **mouthful** *n* (*of drink*) Schluck *m*; (*of food*) Bissen *m*; **mouth organ** *n* Mundharmonika *f*; **mouthwash** *n* Mundwasser *nt*; **mouthwatering** *adj* appetitlich, lecker

**move 1.** *n* (*movement*) Bewegung *f*; (*in game*) Zug *m*; (*step*) Schritt *m*; (*moving house*) Umzug *m*; **make a ~** (*in game*) ziehen; (*leave*) sich auf den Weg machen; **get a ~ on (with sth)** sich (mit etw) beeilen **2.** *vt* bewegen; (*object*) rücken; (*car*) wegfahren; (*transport: goods*) befördern; (*people*) transportieren; (*in job*) versetzen;

(emotionally) bewegen, rühren; **I can't ~ it** (stuck, too heavy) ich bringe es nicht von der Stelle; **~ (house)** umziehen **3.** vi sich bewegen; (change place) gehen; (vehicle, ship) fahren; (move house, town etc) umziehen; (in game) ziehen; **move about** vi sich bewegen; (travel) unterwegs sein; **move away** vi weggehen; (move town) wegziehen; **move in** vi (to house) einziehen; **move on** vi weitergehen; (vehicle) weiterfahren; **move out** vi ausziehen; **move up** vi (in queue etc) aufrücken; **movement** n Bewegung f

**movie** n Film m; **the ~s** (the cinema) das Kino; **movie theater** n (US) Kino nt

**moving** adj (emotionally) ergreifend, berührend

**mow** vt mähen; **mower** n (lawnmower) Rasenmäher m

**mown** pp → **mow**

**Mozambique** n Mosambik nt

**MP** abbr = **Member of Parliament** Parlamentsabgeordnete(r) mf

**MP3 player** n MP3-Player m

**mph** abbr = **miles per hour** Meilen pro Stunde

**Mr** n (written form of address) Herr

**Mrs** n (written form of address) Frau

**Ms** n (written form of address for any woman, married or unmarried) Frau

**Mt** abbr = **Mount** Berg m

**much 1.** adj viel; **we haven't got ~ time** wir haben nicht viel Zeit **2.** adv viel; (with verb) sehr; **I like it very ~** es gefällt mir sehr gut; **I don't like it ~** ich mag es nicht besonders; **thank you very ~** danke sehr; **~ as I like him** so sehr ich ihn mag; **we don't see them ~** wir sehen sie nicht sehr oft; **~ the same** fast gleich **3.** n viel; **as ~ as you want** so viel du willst / Sie wollen; **he's not ~ of a cook** er ist kein großer Koch

**muck** n fam Dreck m; **muck about** vi fam herumalbern; **muck up** vt fam dreckig machen; (spoil) vermasseln; **mucky** adj dreckig

**mucus** n Schleim m

**mud** n Schlamm m

**muddle 1.** n Durcheinander nt; **be in a ~** ganz durcheinander sein **2.** vt ~ (**up**) durcheinanderbringen; **muddled** adj konfus

**muddy** adj schlammig; (shoes) schmutzig; **mudguard** n Schutzblech nt

**muesli** n Müsli m

**muffin** n Muffin m; (Brit) weiches, flaches Milchbrötchen aus Hefeteig, das meist getoastet und mit Butter geges-

*sen wird*

**muffle** vt (*sound*) dämpfen; **muffler** n (US) Schalldämpfer m

**mug 1.** n (*cup*) Becher m; fam (*fool*) Trottel m **2.** vt (*attack and rob*) überfallen; **mugging** n Raubüberfall m

**mule** n Maulesel m

**mulled** adj **~ wine** Glühwein m

**multicolored** (US), **multicoloured** adj bunt; **multicultural** adj multikulturell; **multi-grade** ~ **oil** Mehrbereichsöl nt; **multilingual** adj mehrsprachig

**multiple 1.** n Vielfache(s) nt **2.** adj mehrfach; (*several*) mehrere; **multiple-choice** (*method*) n Multiple-Choice-Verfahren nt

**multiplex** adj, n ~ (*cinema*) Multiplexkino nt

**multiply 1.** vt multiplizieren (*by* mit) **2.** vi sich vermehren

**multi-purpose** adj Mehrzweck-; **multistorey** (*car park*) n Parkhaus nt

**mum** n fam (*mother*) Mutti f, Mami f

**mumble** vt, vi murmeln

**mummy** n (*dead body*) Mumie f; fam (*mother*) Mutti f, Mami f

**mumps** nsing Mumps m

**munch** vt, vi mampfen

**Munich** n München nt

**municipal** adj städtisch

**murder 1.** n Mord m; **the traf-fic was ~** der Verkehr war die Hölle **2.** vt ermorden; **murderer** n Mörder(in) m(f)

**murky** adj düster; (*water*) trüb

**murmur** vt, vi murmeln

**muscle** n Muskel m; **muscular** adj (*strong*) muskulös; (*cramp, pain etc*) Muskel-

**museum** n Museum nt

**mushroom** n (essbarer) Pilz; (*button mushroom*) Champignon m

**mushy** adj breiig

**music** n Musik f; **musical 1.** adj (*sound*) melodisch; (*person*) musikalisch; ~ **instrument** Musikinstrument nt **2.** n (*show*) Musical nt; **musically** adv musikalisch; **musician** n Musiker(in) m(f)

**Muslim 1.** adj moslemisch **2.** n Moslem m, Muslime f

**mussel** n Miesmuschel f

**must 1.** vaux (*need to*) müssen; (*in negation*) dürfen; **I ~n't forget that** ich darf das nicht vergessen; (*certainty*) **he ~ be there by now** er ist inzwischen bestimmt schon da; (*assumption*) **I ~ have lost it** ich habe es wohl verloren; **~ you?** muss das sein? **2.** n Muss nt

**mustache** n (US) Schnurrbart m

**mustard** n Senf m

**mustn't** contr = **must not**

**mute** adj stumm

**mutter** vt, vi murmeln

**mutton** n Hammelfleisch nt

**mutual** adj gegenseitig; **by ~ consent** in gegenseitigem Einvernehmen

**my** adj mein; **I've hurt ~ leg** ich habe mir das Bein verletzt

**Myanmar** n Myanmar nt

**myself** pron (reflexive) mich acc, mir dat; **I've hurt ~** ich habe mich verletzt; **I've bought ~ a flat** ich habe mir eine Wohnung gekauft;

(emphatic) **I did it ~** ich habe es selbst gemacht; **(all) by ~** allein

**mysterious** adj geheimnisvoll, mysteriös; (inexplicable) rätselhaft; **mystery** n Geheimnis nt; (puzzle) Rätsel nt

**myth** n Mythos m; fig (untrue story) Märchen nt; **mythology** n Mythologie f

# N

**naan bread** n (warm serviertes) indisches Fladenbrot

**nag** vt, vi herumnörgeln (sb an jdm); **nagging** n Nörgelei f

**nail 1.** n Nagel m **2.** vt nageln (to an); **nail down** vt festnageln; **nailbrush** n Nagelbürste f; **nail clippers** npl Nagelknipser m; **nailfile** n Nagelfeile f; **nail polish** n Nagellack m; **nail polish remover** n Nagellackentferner m; **nail scissors** npl Nagelschere f; **nail varnish** n Nagellack m

**naive** adj naiv

**naked** adj nackt

**name 1.** n Name m; **his ~ is ...** er heißt ...; **what's your ~?** wie heißen Sie?; (reputation) **have a good / bad ~** einen guten / schlechten Ruf haben **2.** vt nennen (after nach); (sth new) benennen; (nomi-

nate) ernennen (as als / zu); **a boy ~d ...** ein Junge namens ...; **namely** adv nämlich; **name plate** n Namensschild nt

**nanny** n Kindermädchen nt

**nap** n **have / take a ~** ein Nickerchen machen

**napkin** n (at table) Serviette f

**Naples** n Neapel nt

**nappy** n (Brit) Windel f

**narrow 1.** adj eng, schmal; (victory, majority) knapp; **have a ~ escape** mit knapper Not davonkommen **2.** vi sich verengen; **narrow down** vt einschränken (to sth auf etw acc); **narrow-minded** adj engstirnig

**nasty** adj ekelhaft; (person) fies; (remark) gehässig; (accident, wound etc) schlimm

**nation** n Nation f; **national 1.** adj national; **~ anthem** Nationalhymne f; **National Health Service** (Brit) staatlicher Gesundheitsdienst; ~ **insurance** (Brit) Sozialversicherung f; ~ **park** Nationalpark m **2.** n Staatsbürger(in) m(f); **nationality** n Staatsangehörigkeit f, Nationalität f; **nationwide** adj, adv landesweit

**native 1.** adj einheimisch; (inborn) angeboren, natürlich; **Native American** Indianer(in) m(f); ~ **country** Heimatland nt; **a ~ German** ein gebürtiger Deutscher, eine gebürtige Deutsche; ~ **language** Muttersprache f; ~ **speaker** Muttersprachler(in) m(f) **2.** n Einheimische(r) mf; (in colonial context) Eingeborene(r) mf

**nativity play** n Krippenspiel nt

**NATO** acr = **North Atlantic Treaty Organization**; Nato f

**natural** adj natürlich; (law, science, forces etc) Natur-; (inborn) angeboren; ~ **resources** Bodenschätze pl; **naturally** adv natürlich; (by nature) von Natur aus

**nature** n Natur f; (type) Art f; **by ~** von Natur aus; **nature reserve** n Naturschutzgebiet nt

**naughty** adj (child) ungezogen; (cheeky) frech

**nausea** n Übelkeit f

**nautical** adj nautisch; ~ **mile** Seemeile f

**nave** n Hauptschiff nt

**navel** n Nabel m

**navigate** vi navigieren; (in car) lotsen, dirigieren; **navigation** n Navigation f; (in car) Lotsen nt

**navy** n Marine f

**near 1.** adj nahe; **in the ~ future** in nächster Zukunft; **that was a ~ miss** (or thing) das war knapp; (with price) **... or ~est offer** Verhandlungsbasis ... **2.** adv in der Nähe; **come ~er** näher kommen; (event) näher rücken **3.** prep ~ **(to)** (space) nahe an + dat; (vicinity) in der Nähe + gen; ~ **the station** in der Nähe des Bahnhofs, in Bahnhofsnähe; **nearby 1.** adj nahe gelegen **2.** adv in der Nähe; **nearly** adv fast; **near-sighted** adj kurzsichtig

**neat** adj ordentlich; (work, writing) sauber; (undiluted) pur

**necessarily** adv notwendigerweise; **not ~** nicht unbedingt; **necessary** adj notwendig, nötig; **it's ~ to ...** man muss ...; **it's not ~ for him to come** er braucht nicht mitzukommen; **necessity** n Notwendigkeit f; **the bare necessities** das absolut Notwendigste

**neck** n Hals m; (size) Halsweite f; **necklace** n Halskette f; **necktie** n (US) Krawatte f

**nectarine** n Nektarine f

**née** adj geborene

**need 1.** n (requirement) Bedürfnis nt (for für); (necessity) Notwendigkeit f; (poverty) Not f; **be in ~ of sth** etw brauchen; **if ~(s) be** wenn nötig **2.** vt brauchen; **I ~ to speak to you** ich muss mit dir reden; **you ~n't go** du brauchst nicht (zu) gehen, du musst nicht gehen

**needle** n Nadel f

**needless, needlessly** adj, adv unnötig; **~ to say** selbstverständlich

**negative 1.** n LING Verneinung f; PHOT Negativ nt **2.** adj negativ; (answer) verneinend

**neglect 1.** n Vernachlässigung f **2.** vt vernachlässigen; **negligence** n Nachlässigkeit f; **negligent** adj nachlässig

**negotiate** vi verhandeln; **negotiation** n Verhandlung f

**neigh** vi (horse) wiehern

**neighbor** (US), **neighbour** n Nachbar(in) m(f); **neighbo(u)rhood** n Nachbarschaft f

**neighbo(u)ring** adj benachbart

**neither 1.** adj, pron keine(r, s) von beiden; **~ of you / us** keiner von euch / uns beiden **2.** adv **~ ... nor ...** weder ... noch ... **3.** conj **I'm not going -~ am I** ich gehe nicht - ich auch nicht

**nephew** n Neffe m

**nerd** n fam Schwachkopf m; **he's a real computer ~** er ist ein totaler Computerfreak

**nerve** n Nerv m; **he gets on my ~s** er geht mir auf die Nerven; (courage) **keep / lose one's ~** die Nerven behalten / verlieren; (cheek) **have the ~ to do sth** die Frechheit besitzen, etw zu tun; **nerve-racking** adj nervenaufreibend; **nervous** adj (apprehensive) ängstlich; (on edge) nervös; **nervous breakdown** n Nervenzusammenbruch m

**nest 1.** n Nest nt **2.** vi nisten

**net 1.** n Netz nt; **the Net** (Internet) das Internet; **on the ~** im Netz **2.** adj (price, weight) Netto-; **~ profit** Reingewinn m

**Netherlands** npl **the ~** die Niederlande pl

**network** n Netz nt; TV, RADIO Sendenetz nt; IT Netzwerk nt; **networking** n Networking nt (das Knüpfen und Pflegen von Kontakten, die dem beruflichen Fortkommen dienen)

**neurosis** n Neurose f; **neurotic** adj neurotisch

**neuter** adj BIO geschlechtslos; LING sächlich

**neutral 1.** adj neutral **2.** n (gear in car) Leerlauf m

**never** adv nie(mals); **~ before** noch nie; **~ mind** macht nichts!; **never-ending** *adj* endlos; **nevertheless** *adv* trotzdem

**new** *adj* neu; **this is all ~ to me** das ist für mich noch ungewohnt

**New England** *n* Neuengland *nt*

**Newfoundland** *n* Neufundland *nt*

**newly** *adv* neu; **~ made** (*cake*) frisch gebacken; **newly-weds** *npl* Frischvermählte *pl*; **new moon** *n* Neumond *nt*

**news** *nsing* (*item of news*) Nachricht *f*; RADIO, TV Nachrichten *pl*; **good ~** eine erfreuliche Nachricht; **what's the ~?** was gibt's Neues?; **have you heard the ~?** hast du das Neueste gehört?; **newsagent, news dealer** (*US*) *n* Zeitungshändler(in) *m(f)*; **news bulletin** *n* Nachrichtensendung *f*; **news flash** *n* Kurzmeldung *f*; **newsgroup** *n* IT Diskussionsforum *nt*, Newsgroup *f*; **newsletter** *n* Mitteilungsblatt *nt*; **newspaper** *n* Zeitung *f*

**New Year** *n* das neue Jahr; **Happy ~** (ein) frohes Neues Jahr!; (*toast*) Prosit Neujahr!; **~'s Day** Neujahr *nt*, Neujahrstag *m*; **~'s Eve** Silvesterabend *m*; **~'s resolution** guter Vorsatz fürs neue Jahr

**New York** *n* New York *nt*

**New Zealand 1.** *n* Neuseeland *nt* **2.** *adj* neuseeländisch; **New Zealander** *n* Neuseeländer(in) *m(f)*

**next 1.** *adj* nächste(r, s); **the week after ~** übernächste Woche; **~ time I see him** wenn ich ihn das nächste Mal sehe; **you're ~** du bist / Sie sind jetzt dran **2.** *adv* als Nächstes; (*then*) dann, darauf; **~ to** neben + *dat*; **~ to last** vorletzte(r, s); **~ to impossible** nahezu unmöglich; **the ~ best thing** das Zweitbeste; **~ door** nebenan

**NHS** *abbr* = **National Health Service**

**Niagara Falls** *npl* Niagarafälle *pl*

**nibble** *vt* knabbern an + *dat*; **nibbles** *npl* Knabberzeug *nt*

**Nicaragua** *n* Nicaragua *nt*

**nice** *adj* nett, sympathisch; (*taste, food, drink*) gut; (*weather*) schön; **have a ~ day** (*US*) schönen Tag noch!; **nicely** *adv* nett; (*well*) gut; **that'll do ~** das genügt vollauf

**nick** *vt fam* (*steal*) klauen

**nickel** *n* CHEM Nickel *nt*; (*US, coin*) Nickel *m*

**nickname** *n* Spitzname *m*

**nicotine** *n* Nikotin *nt*; **nicotine patch** *n* Nikotinpflaster *nt*

**niece** *n* Nichte *f*

**Nigeria** *n* Nigeria *nt*

**night** n Nacht f; (before bed) Abend m; **good ~** gute Nacht!; **at** (or **by**) **~** nachts; **have an early ~** früh schlafen gehen; **nightcap** n Schlummertrunk m; **nightclub** n Nachtklub m; **nightdress** n Nachthemd nt; **nightie** n fam Nachthemd nt

**nightingale** n Nachtigall f

**night life** n Nachtleben nt; **nightly** adv (every evening) jeden Abend; (every night) jede Nacht; **nightmare** n Albtraum m; **nighttime** n Nacht f; **at ~** nachts

**nil** n SPORT null

**Nile** n Nil m

**nine 1.** num neun; **~ times out of ten** so gut wie immer **2.** n (a. bus etc) Neun f; → **eight**; **nineteen 1.** num neunzehn **2.** n (a. bus etc) Neunzehn f; → **eight**; **nineteenth** adj neunzehnte(r, s); → **eighth**; **ninetieth** adj neunzigste(r, s); → **eighth**; **ninety 1.** num neunzig **2.** n Neunzig f; → **eight**; **ninth 1.** adj neunte(r, s) **2.** n (fraction) Neuntel nt; → **eighth**

**nipple** n Brustwarze f

**nitrogen** n Stickstoff m

**no 1.** adv nein; (after comparative) nicht; **I can wait ~ longer** ich kann nicht länger warten; **I have ~ more money** ich habe kein Geld mehr **2.** adj kein; **in ~ time** im Nu; **~ way** fam keinesfalls; **it's ~**

**use** (or **good**) es hat keinen Zweck; **~ smoking** Rauchen verboten **3.** n Nein nt

**nobody 1.** pron niemand; (emphatic) keiner; **~ knows** keiner weiß es; **~ else** sonst niemand, kein anderer **2.** n Niemand m

**no-claims bonus** n Schadenfreiheitsrabatt m

**nod** vi, vt nicken; **nod off** vi einnicken

**noise** n (loud) Lärm m; (sound) Geräusch nt; **noisy** adj laut; (crowd) lärmend

**nominate** vt (in election) aufstellen; (appoint) ernennen

**non-** pref Nicht-; (with adj) nicht-, un-; **non-alcoholic** adj alkoholfrei

**none** pron keine(r, s); **~ of them** keiner von ihnen; **~ of it is any use** nichts davon ist brauchbar; **there are ~ left** es sind keine mehr da; (with comparative) **be ~ the wiser** auch nicht schlauer sein

**nonetheless** adv nichtsdestoweniger

**non-fiction** n Sachbücher pl; **non-resident** n **'open to ~s'** „auch für Nichthotelgäste"; **non-returnable** adj **~ bottle** Einwegflasche f

**nonsense** n Unsinn m

**non-smoker** n Nichtraucher(in) m(f); **non-smoking** adj Nichtraucher-; **nonstop 1.** adj (train) durchgehend;

(*flight*) Nonstop- **2.** *adv* (*talk*) ununterbrochen; (*fly*) ohne Zwischenlandung

**noodles** *npl* Nudeln *pl*

**noon** *n* Mittag *m*; **at ~** um 12 Uhr mittags

**no one** *pron* niemand; (*emphatic*) keiner; **~ else** sonst niemand, kein anderer

**nor** *conj* **neither ... ~ ...** weder ... noch ...; **I don't smoke, ~ does he** ich rauche nicht, er auch nicht

**normal** *adj* normal; **get back to ~** sich wieder normalisieren; **normally** *adv* (*usually*) normalerweise

**north 1.** *n* Norden *m*; **to the ~ of** nördlich von **2.** *adv* (*go, face*) nach Norden **3.** *adj* Nord-; **North America** *n* Nordamerika *nt*; **northbound** *adj* (in) Richtung Norden; **northeast 1.** *n* Nordosten *m*; **to the ~ of** nordöstlich von **2.** *adv* (*go, face*) nach Nordosten **3.** *adj* Nordost-; **northern** *adj* nördlich; **~ France** Nordfrankreich *nt*; **Northern Ireland** *n* Nordirland *nt*; **North Pole** *n* Nordpol *m*; **North Sea** *n* Nordsee *f*; **northwards** *adv* nach Norden; **northwest 1.** *n* Nordwesten *m*; **to the ~ of** nordwestlich von **2.** *adv* (*go, face*) nach Nordwesten **3.** *adj* Nordwest-

**Norway** *n* Norwegen *nt*; **Nor-**

**wegian 1.** *adj* norwegisch **2.** *n* (*person*) Norweger(in) *m(f)*; (*language*) Norwegisch *nt*

**nose** *n* Nase *f*; **nosebleed** *n* Nasenbluten *nt*; **nose-dive** *n* Sturzflug *m*

**nosey** → **nosy**

**nostril** *n* Nasenloch *nt*

**nosy** *adj* neugierig

**not** *adv* nicht; **~ one of them** kein einziger von ihnen; **I told him ~ to (do it)** ich sagte ihm, er solle es nicht tun; **~ at all** überhaupt nicht, keineswegs; (*don't mention it*) gern geschehen; **~ yet** noch nicht

**notable** *adj* bemerkenswert; **note 1.** *n* (*written*) Notiz *f*; (*short letter*) paar Zeilen *pl*; (*comment in book etc*) Anmerkung *f*; (*banknote*) Schein *m*; MUS (*sign*) Note *f*; (*sound*) Ton *m*; **make a ~ of sth** sich etw notieren; **~s** (*of lecture etc*) Aufzeichnungen *pl*; **take ~s** sich der Notizen machen (*of über + acc*) **2.** *vt* (*notice*) bemerken (*that* dass); (*write down*) notieren; **notebook** *n* Notizbuch *nt*; IT Notebook *nt*; **notepad** *n* Notizblock *m*; **notepaper** *n* Briefpapier *nt*

**nothing** *n* nichts; **~ but ...** lauter ...; **for ~** umsonst; **he thinks ~ of it** er macht sich nichts daraus

**notice 1.** *n* (*announcement*) Bekanntmachung *f*; (*on no-*

*tice board)* Anschlag *m*; *(attention)* Beachtung *f*; *(advance warning)* Ankündigung *f*; *(to leave job, flat etc)* Kündigung *f*; **at short ~** kurzfristig; **until further ~** bis auf weiteres; **give sb ~** jdm kündigen; **hand in one's ~** kündigen; **take (no) ~ of** *(sth)* etw (nicht) beachten **2.** *vt* bemerken; **noticeable** *adj* erkennbar; *(visible)* sichtbar; **be ~ auf**fallen; **notice board** *n* Anschlagtafel *f*

**notification** *n* Benachrichtigung *f* *(of* von*)*; **notify** *vt* benachrichtigen *(of* von*)*

**notorious** *adj* berüchtigt

**nought** *n* Null *f*

**noun** *n* Substantiv *nt*

**novel 1.** *n* Roman *m* **2.** *adj* neuartig; **novelty** *n* Neuheit *f*

**November** *n* November *m*; → **September**

**novice** *n* Neuling *m*

**now** *adv (at the moment)* jetzt; *(introductory phrase)* also; **right ~** jetzt gleich; **just ~** gerade; **by ~** inzwischen; **from ~ on** ab jetzt; **~ and again** *(or then)* ab und zu; **nowadays** *adv* heutzutage

**nowhere** *adv* nirgends; **we're getting ~** wir kommen nicht weiter; **~ near** noch lange nicht

**nozzle** *n* Düse *f*

**nuclear** *adj (energy etc)*

Kern-; **~ power station** Kernkraftwerk *nt*

**nude 1.** *adj* nackt **2.** *n (person)* Nackte(r) *mf*; *(painting etc)* Akt *m*; **nudist** *n* Nudist(in) *m(f)*, FKK-Anhänger(in) *m(f)*; **nudist beach** *n* FKK-Strand *m*

**nuisance** *n* Ärgernis *nt*; *(person)* Plage *f*; **what a ~** wie ärgerlich!

**numb 1.** *adj* taub, gefühllos **2.** *vt* betäuben

**number 1.** *n* Nummer *f*; MATH Zahl *f*; *(quantity)* (An)zahl *f*; **in small / large ~s** in kleinen / großen Mengen; **a ~ of times** mehrmals **2.** *vt (give a number to)* nummerieren; *(count)* zählen *(among* zu*)*; **his days are ~ed** seine Tage sind gezählt; **number plate** *n (Brit)* AUTO Nummernschild *nt*

**numeral** *n* Ziffer *f*; **numerical** *adj* numerisch; *(superiority)* zahlenmäßig; **numerous** *adj* zahlreich

**nun** *n* Nonne *f*

**Nuremberg** *n* Nürnberg *nt*

**nurse 1.** *n* Krankenschwester *f*; *(male nurse)* Krankenpfleger *m* **2.** *vt (patient)* pflegen; *(baby)* stillen; **nursery** *n* Kinderzimmer *nt*; *(for plants)* Gärtnerei *f*; *(tree)* Baumschule *f*; **nursery rhyme** *n* Kinderreim *m*; **nursery school** *n* Kindergarten *m*; **~ teacher** Kindergärtner(in) *m(f)*, Erzieher(in) *m(f)*; **nursing** *n (profession)* Krankenpflege *f*; **~ home** Privatklinik *f*

**nut** *n* Nuss *f*; TECH *(for bolt)* Mutter *f*; **nutcase** *n fam* Spinner(in) *m(f)*; **nutcracker** *n*, **nutcrackers** *npl* Nussknacker *m*

**nutmeg** *n* Muskat *m*, Muskatnuss *f*

**nutrition** *n* Ernährung *f*; **nutritious** *adj* nahrhaft

**nuts** *fam* **1.** *adj* verrückt; **be ~ about sth** nach etw verrückt sein **2.** *npl (testicles)* Eier *pl*

**nutshell** *n* Nussschale *f*; **in a ~** kurz gesagt

**nutter** *n fam* Spinner(in) *m(f)*; **nutty** *adj fam* verrückt

**nylon** ® **1.** *n* Nylon® *nt* **2.** *adj* Nylon-

# O

**O** *n* TEL Null *f*

**oak 1.** *n* Eiche *f* **2.** *adj* Eichen-

**OAP** *abbr* = **old-age pensioner** Rentner(in) *m(f)*

**oar** *n* Ruder *nt*

**oasis** *n* Oase *f*

**oath** *n (statement)* Eid *m*

**oats** *npl* Hafer *m*; GASTR Haferflocken *pl*

**obedience** *n* Gehorsam *m*; **obedient** *adj* gehorsam; **obey** *vt, vi* gehorchen + *dat*

**object 1.** *n* Gegenstand *m*; *(abstract)* Objekt *nt*; *(purpose)* Ziel *nt* **2.** *vi* dagegen sein; *(raise objection)* Einwände erheben *(to* gegen); *(morally)* Anstoß nehmen *(to* an + *dat)*; **do you ~ to my smoking?** haben Sie etwas dagegen, wenn ich rauche?; **objection** *n* Einwand *m*

**objective 1.** *n* Ziel *nt* **2.** *adj* objektiv; **objectivity** *n* Objek-

tivität *f*

**obligation** *n (duty)* Pflicht *f*; *(commitment)* Verpflichtung *f*; **no ~** unverbindlich; **obligatory** *adj* obligatorisch; **oblige** *vt* **~ sb to do sth** jdn zwingen, etw zu tun; **he felt ~d to accept the offer** er fühlte sich verpflichtet, das Angebot anzunehmen

**oboe** *n* Oboe *f*

**obscene** *adj* obszön

**observation** *n (watching)* Beobachtung *f*; *(remark)* Bemerkung *f*; **observe** *vt (notice)* bemerken; *(watch)* beobachten; *(customs)* einhalten

**obsessed** *adj* besessen *(with an idea etc* von einem Gedanken etc)*; **obsession** *n* Manie *f*

**obsolete** *adj* veraltet

**obstacle** *n* Hindernis *nt (to*

für)

**obstinate** *adj* hartnäckig

**obstruct** *vt* versperren; *(pipe)* verstopfen; *(hinder)* behindern, aufhalten; **obstruction** *n* Blockierung *f*; *(of pipe)* Verstopfung *f*; *(obstacle)* Hindernis *nt*

**obtain** *vt* erhalten; **obtainable** *adj* erhältlich

**obvious** *adj* offensichtlich; *it was ~ to me that ...* es war mir klar, dass ...; **obviously** *adj* offensichtlich

**occasion** *n* Gelegenheit *f*; *(special event)* (großes) Ereignis; *on the ~ of* anlässlich + *gen*; *special ~* besonderer Anlass; **occasional**, **occasionally** *adj, adv* gelegentlich

**occupant** *n (of house)* Bewohner(in) *m(f)*; *(of vehicle)* Insasse *m*, Insassin *f*; **occupation** *n* Beruf *m*; *(pastime)* Beschäftigung *f*; *(of country etc)* Besetzung *f*; **occupied** *adj (country, seat, toilet)* besetzt; *(person)* beschäftigt; *keep sb / oneself* ~ jdn / sich beschäftigen; **occupy** *vt (country)* besetzen; *(time)* beanspruchen; *(mind, person)* beschäftigen

**occur** *vi* vorkommen; *~ to sb* jdm einfallen

**ocean** *n* Ozean *m*; *(US, sea)* das Meer *nt*

**o'clock** *adv 5 ~* 5 Uhr; *at 10 ~* um 10 Uhr

**octagon** *n* Achteck *nt*

**October** *n* Oktober *m*; → *September*

**octopus** *n* Tintenfisch *m*

**odd** *adj (strange)* sonderbar; *(not even)* ungerade; *(one missing)* einzeln; *be the ~ one out* nicht dazugehören; **odds** *npl* Chancen *pl*; *against all ~* entgegen allen Erwartungen

**odometer** *n (US)* AUTO Meilenzähler *m*

**odor** *(US)*, **odour** *n* Geruch *m*

**of** *prep* von; *(material, origin)* aus; *the name ~ the hotel* der Name des Hotels; *the works ~ Shakespeare* Shakespeares Werke; *a friend ~ mine* ein Freund von mir; *the fourth ~ June* der vierte Juni; *(quantity)* a *glass ~ water* ein Glas Wasser; *a litre ~ wine* ein Liter Wein; *a girl ~ ten* ein zehnjähriges Mädchen; *(US, in time)* *it's five ~ three* es ist fünf vor drei; *(cause)* *die ~ cancer* an Krebs sterben

**off 1.** *adv (away)* weg, fort; *(free)* frei; *(switch)* ausgeschaltet; *(milk)* sauer; *a mile ~* eine Meile entfernt; *I'll be ~ now* ich gehe jetzt; *have the day / Monday ~* heute / Montag freihaben; *the lights are ~* die Lichter sind aus; *the concert is ~* das Konzert fällt aus; *I got 10 % ~* ich habe 10 % Nachlass bekommen **2.**

*prep* (*away from*) von; **jump** / **fall** ~ **the roof** vom Dach springen / fallen; **get** ~ **the bus** aus dem Bus aussteigen; **he's** ~ **work** / **school** er hat frei / schulfrei; **take £20** ~ **the price** den Preis um 20 Pfund herabsetzen

**offence** *n* (*crime*) Straftat *f*; (*minor*) Vergehen *nt*; (*to feelings*) Kränkung *f*; **cause** / **take** ~ Anstoß erregen / nehmen; **offend** *vt* kränken; (*eye, ear*) beleidigen; **offender** *n* Straffällige(r) *mf*; **offense** (*US*) → **offence**; **offensive 1.** *adj* anstößig; (*insulting*) beleidigend; (*smell*) übel, abstoßend **2.** *n* MIL Offensive *f*

**offer 1.** *n* Angebot *nt*; ~ COMM *n* Angebot **2.** *vt* anbieten (*to sb* jdm); (*money, a chance etc*) bieten

**offhand 1.** *adj* lässig **2.** *adv* (*say*) auf Anhieb

**office** *n* Büro *nt*; (*position*) Amt *nt*; **doctor's** ~ (*US*) Arztpraxis *f*; **office block** *n* Bürogebäude *nt*; **office hours** *npl* Dienstzeit *f*; (*notice*) Geschäftszeiten *pl*; **officer** *n* MIL Offizier(in) *m(f)*; (*official*) Polizeibeamte(r) *m*, Polizeibeamtin *f*; **office worker** *n* Büroangestellte(r) *mf*; **official 1.** *adj* offiziell; (*report etc*) amtlich; ~ **language** Amtssprache *f* **2.** *n*

Beamte(r) *m*, Beamtin *f*, Repräsentant(in) *m(f)*

**off-licence** *n* (*Brit*) Wein- und Spirituosenhandlung *f*; **off-line** *adj* IT offline; **off-peak** *adj* außerhalb der Stoßzeiten; (*rate, ticket*) verbilligt; **off-putting** *adj*, abstoßend; **off-season** *adj* außerhalb der Saison

**offshore** *adj* küstennah, Küsten-; (*oil rig*) im Meer; **offside** *n* AUTO Fahrerseite *f*; SPORT Abseits *nt*

**often** *adv*; **every so** ~ von Zeit zu Zeit

**oil 1.** *n* Öl *nt* **2.** *vt* ölen; **oil level** *n* Ölstand *m*; **oil painting** *n* Ölgemälde *nt*; **oil-rig** *n* (Öl-)bohrinsel *f*; **oil slick** *n* Ölteppich *m*; **oil tanker** *n* Öltanker *m*; (*truck*) Tankwagen *m*; **oily** *adj* ölig; (*skin, hair*) fettig

**ointment** *n* Salbe *f*

**OK, okay** *adj fam* okay, in Ordnung; **that's** ~ **by** (*or* **with**) **me** das ist mir recht

**old** *adj* alt; **old age** *n* Alter *nt*; ~ **pensioner** *n* Rentner(in) *m(f)*; **old-fashioned** *adj* altmodisch; **old people's home** *n* Altersheim *nt*

**olive** *n* Olive *f*; **olive oil** *n* Olivenöl *nt*

**Olympic** *adj* olympisch; **the** ~ **Games, the** ~ **s** *pl* die Olympischen Spiele *pl*, die Olympiade

**omelette** *n* Omelett *nt*

**omit** *vt* auslassen

**on 1.** *prep (position)* auf + *dat*; *(with motion)* auf + *acc*; *(vertical surface, day)* an + *acc*; *(with motion)* an + *acc*; *it's ~ the table* es ist auf dem Tisch; *hang it ~ the wall* häng es an die Wand; *I haven't got it ~ me* ich habe es nicht bei mir; *~ TV* im Fernsehen; *~ the left* links; *~ the right* rechts; *~ the train / bus* im Zug / Bus; *~ the twelfth* am zwölften; *~ Sunday* am Sonntag; *~ Sundays* sonntags **2.** *adj, adv (light etc)* TV, ELEC an; *what's ~ at the cinema?* was läuft im Kino?; *I've nothing ~ (nothing arranged)* ich habe nichts vor; *(no clothes)* ich habe nichts an; *leave the light ~* das Licht brennen lassen

**once 1.** *adv (one time, in the past)* einmal; *at ~* sofort; *(at the same time)* gleichzeitig; *~ more* noch einmal; *for ~* ausnahmsweise einmal; *~ in a while* ab und zu mal **2.** *conj* wenn ~ einmal; *~ you've got used to it* sobald Sie sich daran gewöhnt haben

**oncoming** *adj* entgegenkommend; *~ traffic* Gegenverkehr *m*

**one 1.** *num* eins **2.** *adj* ein, eine, ein; *(only)* einzige(r, s); *~ day* eines Tages; *the ~ and only ...* der / die unver-

gleichliche ... **3.** *pron* eine(r, s); *(people, you)* man; *the ~ who / that ...* der(jenige), der / die(jenige), die / das(jenige), das ...; *this ~, that ~* dieser / diese / dieses; *the blue ~* der / die / das Blaue; *which ~?* welcher / welche / welches?; *~ another* einander; **one-off 1.** *adj* einmalig **2.** *n a ~* etwas Einmaliges; **one-parent family** *n* Einelternfamilie *f*; **one-piece** *adj* einteilig; **oneself** *pron (reflexive)* sich; **one-way** *adj ~ street* Einbahnstraße *f*; *~ ticket (US)* einfache Fahrkarte

**onion** *n* Zwiebel *f*

**on-line** *adj* IT online; *~ banking* Homebanking *nt*

**only 1.** *adv* nur; *(with time)* erst; *~ yesterday* erst gestern; *he's ~ four* er ist erst vier; *~ just arrived* gerade erst angekommen **2.** *adj* einzige(r, s); *~ child* Einzelkind *nt*

**o.n.o.** *abbr = or nearest offer* VHB *f (Verhandlungsbasis)*

**onside** *adv* SPORT nicht im Abseits

**onto** *prep* auf + *acc*; *(vertical surface)* an + *acc*

**onwards** *adv* voran, vorwärts; *from today ~* von heute an, ab heute

**open 1.** *adj* offen; *in the ~ air* im Freien; *~ to the public* für die Öffentlichkeit zugänglich; *the shop is ~ all day* das Geschäft hat den ganzen Tag offen **2.** *vt* öffnen, aufmachen; (*meeting, account, new building*) eröffnen; (*road*) dem Verkehr übergeben **3.** *vi* (*door, window etc*) aufgehen, sich öffnen; (*shop, bank*) öffnen, aufmachen; (*begin*) anfangen (*with* mit); **open day** *n* Tag *m* der offenen Tür; **opening** *n* Öffnung *f*; (*beginning*) Anfang *m*; (*official, of exhibition etc*) Eröffnung *f*; **~ hours** (*or times*) Öffnungszeiten *pl*; **openly** *adv* offen; **open-minded** *adj* aufgeschlossen; **open-plan** *adj* **~ office** Großraumbüro *nt*

**opera** *n* Oper *f*; **opera glasses** *npl* Opernglas *nt*; **opera house** *n* Oper *f*, Opernhaus *nt*

**operate 1.** *vt* (*machine*) bedienen; (*brakes, lights*) betätigen **2.** *vi* (*machine*) laufen; (*bus etc*) verkehren (*between* zwischen); **~ (on sb)** MED (jdn) operieren; **operating theatre** *n* Operationssaal *m*; **operation** *n* (*of machine*) Bedienung *f*; MED Operation *f*(*on an + dat*); (*undertaking*) Unternehmen *nt*; **in ~** (*machine*) in Betrieb; **have an ~** operiert werden (*for* wegen)

**opinion** *n* Meinung *f*(*on* zu); *in my ~* meiner Meinung

nach

**opponent** *n* Gegner(in) *m(f)*

**opportunity** *n* Gelegenheit *f*

**oppose** *vt* sich widersetzen + *dat*; (*idea*) ablehnen; **opposed 1. ~ to sth** gegen etw sein; *as ~ to* im Gegensatz zu; **opposing** (*team*) gegnerisch; (*points of view*) entgegengesetzt

**opposite 1.** *adj* (*house*) gegenüberliegend; (*direction*) entgegengesetzt; *the ~ sex* das andere Geschlecht **2.** *adv* gegenüber + *dat*; **~ me** mir gegenüber **4.** *n* Gegenteil *nt*

**opposition** *n* Widerstand *m* (*to* gegen); POL Opposition *f*

**oppress** *vt* unterdrücken

**opt** *vi* **~ for sth** sich für etw entscheiden

**optician** *n* Optiker(in) *m(f)*

**optimist** *n* Optimist(in) *m(f)*; **optimistic** *adj* optimistisch

**option** *n* Möglichkeit *f*; COMM Option *f*; *have no ~* keine Wahl haben; **optional** *adj* freiwillig; **~ extras** AUTO Extras *pl*

**or** *conj* oder; (*otherwise*) sonst; *hurry up, ~ (else) we'll be late* beeil dich, sonst kommen wir zu spät

**oral 1.** *adj* mündlich; **~ sex** Oralverkehr *m* **2.** *n* (*exam*) Mündliche(s) *nt*; **oral surgeon** *n* Kieferchirurg(in) *m(f)*

**orange 1.** *n* Orange *f* **2.** *adj*

orangefarben; **orange juice**
*n* Orangensaft *m*

**orbit 1.** *n* Umlaufbahn *f* **2.** *vt*
umkreisen

**orchard** *n* Obstgarten *m*

**orchestra** *n* Orchester *nt*;
(*US*) THEAT Parkett *nt*

**orchid** *n* Orchidee *f*

**ordeal** *n* Tortur *f*; (*emotional*)
Qual *f*

**order 1.** *n* (*sequence*) Reihenfolge *f*; (*good arrangement*)
Ordnung *f*; (*command*) Befehl *m*; LAW Anordnung *f*;
(*condition*) Zustand *m*, Bestellung *f*; **out of ~** (*not func-
tioning*) außer Betrieb; (*unsuitable*) nicht angebracht;
**in ~** (*items*) richtig geordnet;
(*all right*) in Ordnung; **in ~ to
do sth** um etw zu tun **2.** *vt*
(*arrange*) ordnen; (*command*) befehlen; **~ sb to do
sth** jdm befehlen, etw zu
tun; (*food, product*) bestellen; **order form** Bestell-
schein *m*

**ordinary** *adj* gewöhnlich, normal

**ore** *n* Erz *nt*

**organ** *n* MUS Orgel *f*; ANAT Organ *nt*

**organic** *adj* organisch; (*farming, vegetables*) Bio-, Öko-; **~
farmer** Biobauer *m*, Bio-
bäuerin *f*; **~ food** Biokost *f*

**organization** *n* Organisation
*f*; (*arrangement*) Ordnung *f*;
**organize** *vt* organisieren; **organizer** *n* (elektronisches)

Notizbuch

**orgasm** *n* Orgasmus *m*

**oriental** *adj* orientalisch

**orientation** *n* Orientierung *f*

**origin** *n* Ursprung *m*; (*of person*) Herkunft *f*; **original 1.**
*adj* (*first*) ursprünglich;
(*painting*) original; (*idea*)
originell **2.** *n* Original *nt*;
**originally** *adv* ursprünglich

**Orkneys** *npl*, **Orkney Islands**
*npl* Orkneyinseln *pl*

**ornamental** *adj* dekorativ

**orphan** *n* Waise *f*, Waisenkind
*nt*; **orphanage** *n* Waisen-
haus *nt*

**orthodox** *adj* orthodox

**orthopaedic**, **orthopedic**
(*US*) *adj* orthopädisch

**ostrich** *n* ZOOL Strauß *m*

**other** *adj, pron* andere(r, s);
**any ~ questions?** sonst
noch Fragen?; **the ~ day** neulich; **every ~ day** jeden zweiten Tag; **someone /
something or ~** irgendjemand / irgendetwas; **otherwise** *adv* sonst; (*differently*)
anders

**OTT** *adj abbr* = **over the top**
übertrieben

**otter** *n* Otter *m*

**ought** *vaux* (*obligation*)
sollte; (*probability*) dürfte;
(*stronger*) müsste; **you ~ to
do that** du solltest / Sie sollten das tun; **that ~ to do** das
müsste (*or* dürfte) reichen

**ounce** *n* Unze *f* (*28,35 g*)

**our** *adj* unser; **ours** *pron* unsere(r, s); **this is ~** das gehört uns; **a friend of ~** ein Freund von uns; **ourselves** pron (reflexive) uns; **we enjoyed ~** wir haben uns amüsiert; **we've got the house to ~** wir haben das Haus für uns; (emphatic) **we did it ~** wir haben es selbst gemacht; (all) **by ~** allein

**out 1.** adv hinaus / heraus; (not indoors) draußen; (not at home) nicht zu Hause; (not alight) aus; (unconscious) bewusstlos; (published) herausgekommen; (results) bekannt gegeben; **have you been ~ yet?** warst du / waren Sie schon draußen?; **I was ~ when they called** ich war nicht da, als sie vorbeikamen; **be ~ and about** unterwegs sein; **the fire is ~** das Feuer ist ausgegangen **2.** vt fam outen

**outback** n (in Australia) **the ~** das Hinterland

**outboard** adj **~ motor** Außenbordmotor m

**outbreak** n Ausbruch m

**outcome** n Ergebnis nt

**outcry** n (public protest) Protestwelle f (against gegen)

**outdo** irr vt übertreffen

**outdoor** adj Außen-; SPORT im Freien; **~ swimming pool** Freibad nt; **outdoors** adv draußen, im Freien

**outer** adj äußere(r, s); **outer space** n Weltraum m

**outfit** n Ausrüstung f; (clothes) Kleidung f

**outgoing** adj kontaktfreudig

**outgrow** irr vt (clothes) herauswachsen aus

**outing** n Ausflug m

**outlet** n Auslass m; Abfluss m; (US) Steckdose f; (shop) Verkaufsstelle f

**outline** n Umriss m; (summary) Abriss m

**outlive** vt überleben

**outlook** n Aussicht(en) f(pl); (attitude) Einstellung f (on zu)

**outnumber** vt zahlenmäßig überlegen sein + dat; **~ed** zahlenmäßig unterlegen

**out of** prep (motion, motive, origin) aus; (position, away from) außerhalb + gen; **~ danger / sight / breath** außer Gefahr / Sicht / Atem; **made ~ wood** aus Holz gemacht; **we are ~ bread** wir haben kein Brot mehr; **out-of-date** adj veraltet; **out-of-the-way** adj abgelegen

**outpatient** n ambulanter Patient, ambulante Patientin

**output** n Produktion f; (of engine) Leistung f; IT Ausgabe f

**outrage** n (great anger) Empörung f (at über); (wicked deed) Schandtat f; (crime) Verbrechen nt; (indecency) Skandal m; **outrageous** adj unerhört; (clothes, behaviour etc) unmöglich, schrill

**outright 1.** adv (killed) sofort

**2.** adj total; (denial) völlig; (winner) unbestritten

**outside 1.** n Außenseite f; **on the ~** außen **2.** adj äußere(r, s), Außen-; (chance) sehr gering **3.** adv außen; **go ~** nach draußen gehen **4.** prep außerhalb + gen; **outsider** n Außenseiter(in) m(f)

**outskirts** npl (of town) Stadtrand m

**outstanding** adj hervorragend; (debts etc) ausstehend

**outward** adj äußere(r, s); **~ journey** Hinfahrt f; **outwardly** adv nach außen hin; **outwards** adv nach außen

**oval** adj oval

**ovary** n Eierstock m

**ovation** n Ovation f, Applaus m

**oven** n Backofen m; **oven-proof** adj feuerfest

**over 1.** prep (position) über + dat; (motion) über + acc; **they spent a long time ~ it** sie haben lange dazu gebraucht; **from all ~ England** aus ganz England; **~ £20** mehr als 20 Pfund; **~ the phone / radio** am Telefon / im Radio; **talk ~ a glass of wine** sich bei einem Glas Wein unterhalten; **~ the summer** während des Sommers **2.** adv (across) hinüber / herüber; (finished) vorbei; (match, play etc) zu Ende; (left) übrig; **~ there /**

**in America** da drüben / drüben in Amerika; **~ to you** du bist / Sie sind dran; **it's (all) ~ between us** es ist aus zwischen uns; **~ and ~ again** immer wieder; **start (all) ~ again** noch einmal von vorn anfangen; **children of 8 and ~** Kinder ab 8 Jahren

**over-** pref über

**overall 1.** n (Brit) Kittel m **2.** adj (situation) allgemein; (length) Gesamt-; **~ majority** absolute Mehrheit **3.** adv insgesamt; **overalls** npl Overall m

**overboard** adv über Bord

**overbooked** adj überbucht

**overcharge** vt zu viel verlangen von

**overcome** irr vt überwinden; **~ by sleep / emotion** von Schlaf / Rührung übermannt

**overcooked** adj zu lange gekocht; (meat) zu lange gebraten

**overcrowded** adj überfüllt

**overdo** irr vt übertreiben; **overdone** adj übertrieben; (food) zu lange gekocht; (meat) zu lange gebraten

**overdose** n Überdosis f

**overdraft** n Kontoüberziehung f; **overdrawn** adj überzogen

**overdue** adj überfällig

**overestimate** vt überschätzen

**overexpose** vt PHOT überbelichten

**overflow** vi überlaufen

**overhead 1.** adj AVIAT ~ **locker** Gepäckfach nt; ~ **projector** Overheadprojektor m **2.** adv oben; **overhead** n, (Brit) **overheads** n COMM allgemeine Geschäftskosten pl

**overhear** irr vt zufällig mit anhören

**overheat** vi (engine) heiß laufen

**overjoyed** adj überglücklich (at über)

**overland 1.** adj Überland- **2.** adv (travel) über Land

**overlap** vi (dates etc) sich überschneiden; (objects) sich teilweise decken

**overload** vt überladen

**overlook** vt (view from above) überblicken; (not notice) übersehen; (pardon) hinwegsehen über + acc

**overnight 1.** adj (journey, train) Nacht-; ~ **bag** Reisetasche f; ~ **stay** Übernachtung f **2.** adv über Nacht

**overpass** n Überführung f

**overpay** vt überbezahlen

**overrule** vt verwerfen; (decision) aufheben

**overseas 1.** adj Übersee-; ausländisch; fam Auslands- **2.** adv (go) nach Übersee; (live, work) in Übersee

**oversee** irr vt beaufsichtigen

**overshadow** vt überschatten

**oversimplify** vt zu sehr vereinfachen

**oversleep** irr vi verschlafen

**overtake** irr vt, vi überholen

**overtime** n Überstunden pl

**overturn** vt, vi umkippen

**overweight** adj **be** ~ Übergewicht haben

**overwhelm** vt überwältigen; **overwhelming** adj überwältigend

**overwork 1.** n Überarbeitung f **2.** vi sich überarbeiten; **overworked** adj überarbeitet

**owe** vt schulden; ~ **sth to sb** (money) jdm etw schulden; (favour etc) jdm etw verdanken; **how much do I** ~ **you?** was bin ich dir / Ihnen schuldig?; **owing to** prep wegen + gen

**owl** n Eule f

**own 1.** vt besitzen **2.** adj eigen; **on one's** ~ allein; **he has a flat of his** ~ er hat eine eigene Wohung; **owner** n Besitzer(in) m(f); (of business) Inhaber(in) m(f); **ownership** n Besitz m; **under new** ~ unter neuer Leitung

**ox** n Ochse m; **oxtail** n Ochsenschwanz m; ~ **soup** Ochsenschwanzsuppe f

**oxygen** n Sauerstoff m

**oyster** n Auster f

**oz** abbr = **ounces** Unzen pl

**Oz** n fam Australien nt

**ozone** n Ozon nt; ~ **layer** Ozonschicht f

# P

**p 1.** abbr → **page** S. **2.** n abbr → **penny**; → **pence**

**p&p** abbr = **postage and packing**

**p.a.** abbr = **per annum**

**pace** n (speed) Tempo nt; (step) Schritt m; **pacemaker** n MED Schrittmacher m

**Pacific** n the ∼ (Ocean) der Pazifik

**pacifier** n (US, for baby) Schnuller m

**pack 1.** n (of cards) Spiel nt; (esp US, of cigarettes) Schachtel f; (gang) Bande f; (US, backpack) Rucksack m **2.** vt (case) packen; (clothes) einpacken **3.** vi (for holiday) packen; **pack in** vt (Brit) fam (job) hinschmeißen; **package** n Paket nt; **package deal** n Pauschalangebot nt; **package holiday**, **package tour** n Pauschalreise f; **packaging** n (material) Verpackung f; **packed lunch** n (Brit) Lunchpaket nt; **packet** n Päckchen nt; (of cigarettes) Schachtel f

**pad** n (of paper) Schreibblock m; (padding) Polster nt; **padded envelope** n wattierter Umschlag; **padding** n (material) Polsterung f

**paddle 1.** n (for boat) Paddel

**nt 2.** vi (in boat) paddeln; **paddling pool** n (Brit) Planschbecken nt

**padlock** n Vorhängeschloss nt

**page** n (of book etc) Seite f

**pager** n Piepser m

**paid 1.** pt, pp → **pay 2.** adj bezahlt

**pain** n Schmerz m; **be in** ∼ Schmerzen haben; **she's a (real)** ∼ sie nervt; **painful** adj (physically) schmerzhaft; **painkiller** n schmerzstillendes Mittel

**painstaking** adj sorgfältig

**paint 1.** n Farbe f **2.** vt anstreichen; (picture) malen; **paintbrush** n Pinsel m; **painter** n Maler(in) m(f); **painting** n (picture) Bild nt, Gemälde nt

**pair** n Paar nt; **a** ∼ **of shoes** ein Paar Schuhe; **a** ∼ **of scissors** eine Schere; **a** ∼ **of trousers** eine Hose

**pajamas** npl (US) Schlafanzug m

**Pakistan** n Pakistan nt

**pal** n fam Kumpel m

**palace** n Palast m

**pale** adj (face) blass, bleich; (colour) hell

**palm** (of hand) Handfläche f; ∼ **(tree)** Palme f; **palmtop** (computer) n Palmtop (-computer) m

**pamper** vt verhätscheln

**pan** n (*saucepan*) Topf m; (*frying pan*) Pfanne f; **pancake** n Pfannkuchen m; **Pancake Day** n (*Brit*) Fastnachtsdienstag m

**panda** n Panda m

**pandemic** n Pandemie f

**panel** n (*of wood*) Tafel f; (*in discussion*) Diskussionsteilnehmer pl; (*in jury*) Jurymitglieder pl

**panic 1.** n Panik f **2.** vi in Panik geraten; **panicky** adj panisch

**pansy** n (*flower*) Stiefmütterchen nt

**panties** npl (Damen)slip m

**pantomime** n (*Brit*) um die Weihnachtszeit aufgeführte Märchenkomödie

**pants** npl Unterhose f; (*esp US, trousers*) Hose f

**pantyhose** npl (*US*) Strumpfhose f; **panty-liner** n Slipeinlage f

**paper 1.** n Papier nt; (*newspaper*) Zeitung f; (*exam*) Klausur f; (*for reading at conference*) Referat nt; **~s** pl (*identity papers*) Papiere pl; **~ bag** Papiertüte f; **~ cup** Pappbecher m **2.** vt (*wall*) tapezieren; **paperback** n Taschenbuch nt; **paper clip** n Büroklammer f; **paper feed** n (*of printer*) Papiereinzug m; **paperwork** n Schreibarbeit f

**paracetamol** n (*tablet*) Paracetamoltablette f

**parachute 1.** n Fallschirm m **2.** vi abspringen

**parade 1.** n (*procession*) Umzug m; MIL Parade f **2.** vi vorbeimarschieren

**paradise** n Paradies nt

**paragliding** n Gleitschirmfliegen nt

**paragraph** n Absatz m

**parallel 1.** adj parallel **2.** n MATH fig Parallele f

**paralyze** vt lähmen; fig lahmlegen

**paranoid** adj paranoid

**paraphrase** vt umschreiben; (*sth spoken*) anders ausdrücken

**parasailing** n Parasailing nt

**parasol** n Sonnenschirm m

**parcel** n Paket nt

**pardon** n LAW Begnadigung f; **~ me/I beg your ~** verzeih / verzeihen Sie bitte; (*objection*) aber ich bitte dich / Sie; **I beg your ~?/~ me?** wie bitte?

**parent** n Elternteil m; **~s** pl Eltern pl; **~s-in-law** pl Schwiegereltern pl; **parental** adj elterlich, Eltern-

**parish** n Gemeinde f

**park 1.** n Park m **2.** vt, vi parken; **parking** n Parken nt; **'no ~'** „Parken verboten"; **parking brake** n (*US*) Handbremse f; **parking disc** n Parkscheibe f; **parking fine** n Geldbuße f für falsches Parken; **parking lights** npl (*US*) Standlicht nt; **parking**

**lot** n (US) Parkplatz m; **parking meter** n Parkuhr f; **parking place**, **parking space** n Parkplatz m; **parking ticket** n Strafzettel m

**parliament** n Parlament nt

**parsley** n Petersilie f

**parrot** n Papagei m

**parsnip** n Pastinake f (längliches, weißes Wurzelgemüse)

**part 1.** n Teil m; (of machine) Teil nt; THEAT Rolle f; (US, in hair) Scheitel m; **take ~** teilnehmen (in an + dat); **for the most ~** zum größten Teil **2.** adj Teil- **3.** vt (separate) trennen; (hair) scheiteln **4.** vi (people) sich trennen

**partial** adj (incomplete) teilweise, Teil-

**participant** n Teilnehmer(in) m(f); **participate** vi teilnehmen (in an + dat)

**particular 1.** adj (specific) bestimmt; (exact) genau; (fussy) eigen; **in ~** insbesondere **2.** n **~s** pl (details) Einzelheiten pl; (about person) Personalien pl; **particularly** adv besonders

**parting** n (farewell) Abschied m; (Brit, in hair) Scheitel m; **partly** adv teilweise

**partner** n Partner(in) m(f); **partnership** n Partnerschaft f

**partridge** n Rebhuhn nt

**part-time 1.** adj Teilzeit- **2.** adv **work ~** Teilzeit arbeiten

**party 1.** n (celebration) Party f; POL, LAW Partei f; (group) Gruppe f **2.** vi feiern

**pass 1.** vt (on foot) vorbeigehen an + dat; (in car etc) vorbeifahren an + dat; (time) verbringen; (exam) bestehen; (law) verabschieden; **~ sth to sb**, **~ sb sth** jdm etw reichen; **~ the ball to sb** jdm den Ball zuspielen **2.** vi (on foot) vorbeigehen; (in car etc) vorbeifahren; (years) vergehen; (in exam) bestehen **3.** n (document) Ausweis m; SPORT Pass m; **pass away** vi (die) verscheiden; **pass by 1.** vi (on foot) vorbeigehen; (in car etc) vorbeifahren **2.** vt (on foot) vorbeigehen an + dat; (in car etc) vorbeifahren an + dat; **pass on** vt weitergeben (to an + acc); (disease) übertragen (to auf + acc); **pass out** vi (faint) ohnmächtig werden; **pass round** vt herumreichen

**passage** n (corridor) Gang m; (in book, music) Passage f; **passageway** n Durchgang m

**passenger** n Passagier(in) m(f); (on bus) Fahrgast m; (on train) Reisende(r) m/f; (in car) Mitfahrer(in) m(f)

**passer-by** n Passant(in) m(f)

**passion** n Leidenschaft f; **passionate** adj leidenschaftlich; **passion fruit** n

Passionsfrucht f
**passive 1.** adj passiv; ~ **smoking** Passivrauchen nt **2.** n ~ **(voice)** LING Passiv nt
**passport** n (Reise)pass m; **passport control** n Passkontrolle f
**password** n IT Passwort nt
**past 1.** n Vergangenheit f **2.** adv (by) vorbei; **it's five ~** es ist fünf nach **3.** adj (years) vergangen; (president etc) ehemalig; **in the ~ two months** in den letzten zwei Monaten **4.** prep (telling time) nach; **half ~ 10** halb 11; **go ~ sth** an etw dat vorbeigehen / -fahren
**pasta** n Nudeln pl
**paste 1.** vt (stick) kleben; **~** einfügen **2.** n (glue) Kleister m
**pastime** n Zeitvertreib m
**pastry** n Teig m; (cake) Stückchen nt
**pasty** n (Brit) Pastete f
**patch 1.** n (area) Fleck m; (for mending) Flicken m **2.** vt flicken
**pâté** n Pastete f
**paternal** adj väterlich; **~ grandmother** Großmutter f väterlicherseits; **paternity leave** n Elternzeit f (des Vaters)
**path** n a. IT Pfad m; a. fig Weg m
**pathetic** adj (bad) kläglich, erbärmlich; **it's ~** es ist zum Heulen

**patience** n Geduld f; (Brit, ) Patience f; **patient 1.** adj geduldig **2.** n Patient(in) m(f)
**patio** n Terrasse f
**patriotic** adj patriotisch
**patrol car** n Streifenwagen m; **patrolman** n (US) Streifenpolizist m
**patron** n (sponsor) Förderer m, Förderin f; (in shop) Kunde m, Kundin f
**patronize** vt (treat condescendingly) von oben herab behandeln; **patronizing** adj (attitude) herablassend
**pattern** n Muster nt
**pause 1.** n Pause f **2.** vi (speaker) innehalten
**pavement** n (Brit) Bürgersteig m; (US) Pflaster m
**pay 1.** vt bezahlen; **he paid (me) £20 for it** er hat (mir) 20 Pfund dafür gezahlt; **~ attention** Acht geben (to auf + acc); **~ sb a visit** jdn besuchen **2.** vi zahlen; (be profitable) sich bezahlt machen; **~ for sth** etw bezahlen **3.** n Bezahlung f, Lohn m; **pay back** vt (money) zurückzahlen; **pay in** vt (into account) einzahlen; **payable** adj zahlbar; (due) fällig; **payday** n Zahltag m; **payee** n Zahlungsempfänger(in) m(f); **payment** n Bezahlung f; (money) Zahlung f; **pay phone** n Münzfernsprecher m
**PC 1.** abbr = **personal computer** PC m **2.** abbr = **politi-**

**pepper**

*cally correct* politisch korrekt

**PDA** *abbr* = *personal digital assistant* PDA *m*

**PE** *abbr* = *physical education* Sport *m*

**pea** *n* Erbse *f*

**peace** *n* Frieden *m*; **peaceful** *adj* friedlich

**peach** *n* Pfirsich *m*

**peacock** *n* Pfau *m*

**peak** *n* (*of mountain*) Gipfel *m*; *fig* Höhepunkt *m*; **peak period** *n* Stoßzeit *f*; (*season*) Hochsaison *f*

**peanut** *n* Erdnuss *f*; **peanut butter** *n* Erdnussbutter *f*

**pear** *n* Birne *f*

**pearl** *n* Perle *f*

**pebble** *n* Kiesel *m*

**pecan** *n* Pekannuss *f*

**peck** *vt, vi* picken; **peckish** *adj* (*Brit*) *fam* ein bisschen hungrig

**peculiar** *adj* (*odd*) seltsam; ~ **to** charakteristisch für; **peculiarity** *n* (*singular quality*) Besonderheit *f*; (*strangeness*) Eigenartigkeit *f*

**pedal** *n* Pedal *nt*

**pedestrian** *n* Fußgänger(in) *m(f)*; **pedestrian crossing** *n* Fußgängerüberweg *m*

**pee** *vi fam* pinkeln

**peel** 1. *n* Schale *f* 2. *vt* schälen 3. *vi* (*paint etc*) abblättern; (*skin etc*) sich schälen

**peer** 1. *n* Gleichaltrige(r) *mf* 2. *vi* starren

**peg** *n* (*for coat etc*) Haken *m*;

(*for tent*) Hering *m*; (*clothes*) ~ (Wäsche)klammer *f*

**pelvis** *n* Becken *nt*

**pen** *n* (*ball-point*) Kuli *m*, Kugelschreiber *m*; (*fountain pen*) Füller *m*

**penalize** *vt* (*punish*) bestrafen; **penalty** *n* (*punishment*) Strafe *f*; (*in soccer*) Elfmeter *m*

**pence** *pl* → **penny**

**pencil** *n* Bleistift *m*; **pencil sharpener** *n* (Bleistift)spitzer *m*

**penetrate** *vt* durchdringen; (*enter into*) eindringen in + *acc*

**penfriend** *n* Brieffreund(in) *m(f)*

**penguin** *n* Pinguin *m*

**penicillin** *n* Penizillin *nt*

**peninsula** *n* Halbinsel *f*

**penis** *n* Penis *m*

**penknife** *n* Taschenmesser *nt*

**penny** *n* (*Brit*) Penny *m*; (*US*) Centstück *nt*

**pension** *n* Rente *f*; (*for civil servants, executives etc*) Pension *f*; **pensioner** *n* Rentner(in) *m(f)*; **pension plan**, **pension scheme** *n* Rentenversicherung *f*

**penultimate** *adj* vorletzte(r, s)

**people** *npl* (*persons*) Leute *pl*; (*von Staat*) Volk *nt*; (*inhabitants*) Bevölkerung *f*; **people carrier** *n* Minivan *m*

**pepper** *n* Pfeffer *m*; (*vegeta-*

*ble)* Paprika *m;* **peppermint** *n (sweet)* Pfefferminz *nt*

**per** *prep* pro; **~ annum** pro Jahr; **~ cent** Prozent *nt*

**percentage** *n* Prozentsatz *m*

**percolator** *n* Kaffeemaschine *f*

**percussion** *n* MUS Schlagzeug *nt*

**perfect 1.** *adj* perfekt; *(utter)* völlig **2.** *vt* vervollkommnen; **perfectly** *adv* perfekt; *(utterly)* völlig

**perform 1.** *vt (task)* ausführen; *(play)* aufführen; MED *(operation)* durchführen **2.** *vi* THEAT auftreten; **performance** *n (show)* Vorstellung *f;* *(efficiency)* Leistung *f*

**perfume** *n* Duft *m;* *(substance)* Parfüm *nt*

**perhaps** *adv* vielleicht

**period** *n (length of time)* Zeit *f;* *(in history)* Zeitalter *nt,* Stunde *f;* MED Periode *f;* *(US, full stop)* Punkt *m;* **for a ~ of three years** für einen Zeitraum von drei Jahren; **periodical** *n* Zeitschrift *f*

**peripheral** *n* IT Peripheriegerät *nt*

**perjury** *n* Meineid *m*

**perm** *n* Dauerwelle *f*

**permanent, permanently** *adj, adv* ständig

**permission** *n* Erlaubnis *f;* **permit 1.** *n* Genehmigung *f* **2.** *vt* erlauben, zulassen; **~ sb to do sth** jdm erlauben,

etw zu tun

**persecute** *vt* verfolgen

**perseverance** *n* Ausdauer *f*

**persist** *vi (in belief etc)* bleiben *(in* bei); *(rain, smell)* andauern; **persistent** *adj* beharrlich

**person** *n* Mensch *m;* *(in official context)* Person *f;* **in ~** persönlich; **personal** *adj* persönlich; *(private)* privat; **personality** *n* Persönlichkeit *f;* **personal organizer** *n* Organizer *m;* **personal stereo** *n* Walkman® *m;* **personnel** *n* Personal *nt*

**perspective** *n* Perspektive *f*

**persuade** *vt* überreden; *(convince)* überzeugen; **persuasive** *adj* überzeugend

**perverse** *adj* eigensinnig; abwegig; **pervert 1.** *n* Perverse(r) *mf* **2.** *vt (morally)* verderben; **perverted** *adj* pervers

**pessimist** *n* Pessimist(in) *m(f);* **pessimistic** *adj* pessimistisch

**pest** *n (insect)* Schädling *m;* *fig (person)* Nervensäge *f;* *(thing)* Plage *f;* **pester** *vt* plagen; **pesticide** *n* Schädlingsbekämpfungsmittel *nt*

**pet** *n (animal)* Haustier *nt;* *(person)* Liebling *m*

**petition** *n* Petition *f*

**petrol** *n (Brit)* Benzin *nt;* **petrol pump** *n (at garage)* Zapfsäule *f;* **petrol station** *n* Tankstelle *f;* **petrol tank** *n*

**pig**

Benzintank *m*

**pharmacy** *n* (*shop*) Apotheke *f*; (*science*) Pharmazie *f*

**phase** *n* Phase *f*

**PhD** *abbr* = **Doctor of Philosophy** Dr. phil.; (*dissertation*) Doktorarbeit *f*; **do one's ~** promovieren

**pheasant** *n* Fasan *m*

**phenomenon** *n* Phänomen *nt*

**Philippines** *npl* Philippinen *pl*

**philosophical** *adj* philosophisch; *fig* gelassen; **philosophy** *n* Philosophie *f*

**phone 1.** *n* Telefon *nt* **2.** *vt*, *vi* anrufen; **phone bill** *n* Telefonrechnung *f*; **phone book** *n* Telefonbuch *nt*; **phone booth**, **phone box** (*Brit*) *n* Telefonzelle *f*; **phonecall** *n* Telefonanruf *m*; **phonecard** *n* Telefonkarte *f*; **phone number** *n* Telefonnummer *f*

**photo** *n* Foto *nt*; **photo booth** *n* Fotoautomat *m*; **photocopier** *n* Kopiergerät *nt*; **photocopy 1.** *n* Fotokopie *f* **2.** *vt* fotokopieren; **photograph 1.** *n* Fotografie *f*, Aufnahme *f* **2.** *vt* fotografieren; **photographer** *n* Fotograf(in) *m(f)*; **photography** *n* Fotografie *f*

**phrase** *n* (*expression*) Redewendung *f*, Ausdruck *m*; **phrase book** *n* Sprachführer *m*

**physical 1.** *adj* (*bodily*) körperlich, physisch **2.** *n* ärztli-

che Untersuchung; **physically** *adv* (*bodily*) körperlich, physisch; **~ handicapped** körperbehindert

**physics** *nsing* Physik *f*

**physiotherapy** *n* Physiotherapie *f*

**physique** *n* Körperbau *m*

**piano** *n* Klavier *nt*

**pick** *vt* (*flowers*, *fruit*) pflücken; (*choose*) auswählen; (*team*) aufstellen; **pick out** *vt* auswählen; **pick up** *vt* (*lift up*) aufheben; (*collect*) abholen; (*learn*) lernen

**pickle 1.** *n* (*food*) (Mixed) Pickles *pl* **2.** *vt* einlegen

**pickpocket** *n* Taschendieb(in) *m(f)*

**picnic** *n* Picknick *nt*

**picture 1.** *n* Bild *nt*; **go to the ~s** (*Brit*) ins Kino gehen **2.** *vt* (*visualize*) sich vorstellen; **picture book** *n* Bilderbuch *nt*; **picturesque** *adj* malerisch

**pie** *n* (*meat*) Pastete *f*; (*fruit*) Kuchen *m*

**piece** *n* Stück *nt*; (*part*) Teil *nt*; (*in chess*) Figur *f*; (*in draughts*) Stein *m*; **a ~ of cake** ein Stück Kuchen; **fall to ~s** auseinanderfallen

**pier** *n* Pier *m*

**pierce** *vt* durchstechen, durchbohren; (*cold*, *sound*) durchdringen; **pierced** *adj* (*part of body*) gepierct; **piercing** *adj* durchdringend

**pig** *n* Schwein *nt*

**pigeon** n Taube f

**piggy** adj fam verfressen; **pig-headed** adj dickköpfig; **piglet** n Ferkel nt; **pigsty** n Schweinestall m; **pigtail** n Zopf m

**pile** n (heap) Haufen m; (one on top of another) Stapel m; **pile up** vi (accumulate) sich anhäufen

**pile-up** n AUTO Massenkarambolage f

**pill** n Tablette f; **the ~** die (Antibaby)pille; **be on the ~** die Pille nehmen

**pillar** n Pfeiler m

**pillow** n (Kopf)kissen nt; **pillowcase** n (Kopf)kissenbezug m

**pilot** n AVIAT Pilot(in) m(f)

**pimple** n Pickel m

**pin 1.** n (for fixing) Nadel f; (in sewing) Stecknadel f; TECH Stift m; **I've got ~s and needles in my leg** mein Bein ist mir eingeschlafen **2.** vt (fix with pin) heften (to an + acc)

**PIN** acr = **personal identification number**; **~ (number)** PIN f, Geheimzahl f

**pinch 1.** n (of salt) Prise f **2.** vt zwicken; fam (steal) klauen **3.** vi (shoe) drücken

**pine** n Kiefer f

**pineapple** n Ananas f

**pink** adj rosa

**pint** n Pint nt (Brit: 0,57 l, US: 0,473l); (Brit, glass of beer) Bier nt

**pious** adj fromm

**pip** n (of fruit) Kern m

**pipe** n (for smoking) Pfeife f; (for water, gas) Rohrleitung f

**pirate** n Pirat(in) m(f); **pirated copy** n Raubkopie f

**Pisces** n ASTR Fische pl; **she's a ~** sie ist Fisch

**piss 1.** vi vulg pissen **2.** n vulg Pisse f; **take the ~ out of sb** jdn verarschen; **piss off** vi vulg sich verpissen; **pissed** adj (Brit, fam: drunk) sturzbesoffen; (US, fam: annoyed) stocksauer

**pistachio** n Pistazie f

**piste** n, Piste f

**pistol** n Pistole f

**pit** n (hole) Grube f; (coalmine) Zeche f; **the ~s** (motor racing) die Box; **be the ~s** fam grottenschlecht sein

**pitch 1.** n SPORT Spielfeld nt; MUS (of instrument) Tonlage f; (of voice) Stimmlage f **2.** vt (tent) aufschlagen; (throw) werfen; **pitch-black** adj pechschwarz

**pitcher** n (US, jug) Krug m

**pitiful** adj (contemptible) jämmerlich

**pitta bread** n Pittabrot nt

**pity 1.** n Mitleid nt; **what a ~** wie schade; **it's a ~** es ist schade **2.** vt Mitleid haben mit

**pizza** n Pizza f

**place 1.** n (spot, in text) Stelle f; (town etc) Ort; (house) Haus nt; (position, seat, on course) Platz m; **~ of birth**

Geburtsort *m*; **at my ~** bei mir; **in third ~** auf den dritten Platz; **out of ~** nicht an der richtigen Stelle; (*remark*) unangebracht; **in ~ of** anstelle von; **in the first ~** (*firstly*) erstens; (*immediately*) gleich; (*in any case*) überhaupt **2.** *vt* (*put*) stellen, setzen; (*lay flat*) legen; (*advertisement*) setzen (*in* in + *acc*); COMM (*order*) aufgeben; **place mat** *n* Set *nt*

**plague** *n* Pest *f*

**plaice** *n* Scholle *f*

**plain 1.** *adj* (*clear*) klar, deutlich; (*simple*) einfach; (*not beautiful*) unattraktiv; (*yoghurt*) Natur-; (*Brit, chocolate*) (Zart)bitter- **2.** *n* Ebene *f*; **plainly** *adv* (*frankly*) offen; (*simply*) einfach; (*obviously*) eindeutig

**plait 1.** *n* Zopf *m* **2.** *vt* flechten

**plan 1.** *n* Plan *m*; (*for essay etc*) Konzept *nt* **2.** *vt* planen; **~ to do sth, ~ on doing sth** vorhaben, etw zu tun **3.** *vi* planen

**plane** *n* (*aircraft*) Flugzeug *nt*; (*tool*) Hobel *m*

**planet** *n* Planet *m*

**plank** *n* Brett *nt*

**plant 1.** *n* Pflanze *f*; (*factory*) Werk *nt* **2.** *vt* (*tree etc*) pflanzen; **plantation** *n* Plantage *f*

**plaque** *n* Gedenktafel *f*; (*on teeth*) Zahnbelag *m*

**plaster** *n* (*Brit*) MED (*sticking plaster*) Pflaster *nt*; (*on wall*)

Verputz *m*; **to have one's arm in ~** den Arm in Gips haben

**plastered** *adj fam* besoffen; **get** (**absolutely**) **~** sich besaufen

**plastic 1.** *n* Kunststoff *m*; **pay with ~** mit Kreditkarte bezahlen **2.** *adj* Plastik-; **plastic bag** *n* Plastiktüte *f*; **plastic surgery** *n* plastische Chirurgie *f*

**plate** *n* (*for food*) Teller *m*; (*flat sheet*) Platte *f*; (*plaque*) Schild *nt*

**platform** *n* RAIL Bahnsteig *m*

**platinum** *n* Platin *nt*

**play 1.** *n* Spiel *nt*; THEAT (Theater)stück *nt* **2.** *vt* spielen; (*another player or team*) spielen gegen; **~ the piano** Klavier spielen **3.** *vi* spielen; **play at** *vt* **what are you playing at?** was soll das?; **play back** *vt* abspielen; **play down** *vt* herunterspielen

**playacting** *n* Schauspielerei *f*; **playback** *n* Wiedergabe *f*; **player** *n* Spieler(in) *m(f)*; **playful** *adj* (*person*) verspielt; (*remark*) scherzhaft; **playground** *n* Spielplatz *m*; (*in school*) Schulhof *m*; **playgroup** *n* Spielgruppe *f*; **playing card** *n* Spielkarte *f*; **playing field** *n* Sportplatz *m*; **playmate** *n* Spielkamerad(in) *m(f)*; **playwright** *n* Dramatiker(in) *m(f)*

**plc** *abbr* = **public limited**

*company* AG f

**plea** n Bitte f (*for* um)

**plead** vi dringend bitten (*with sb* jdn); LAW **~ guilty** sich schuldig bekennen

**pleasant, pleasantly** adj, adv angenehm

**please 1.** adv bitte; **more tea? - yes,** nicht Tee? - ja, bitte **2.** vt (*be agreeable to*) gefallen + dat; **~ yourself** wie du willst / Sie wollen; **pleased** adj zufrieden; (*glad*) erfreut; **~ to meet you** freut mich, angenehm; **pleasing** adj erfreulich; **pleasure** n Vergnügen nt, Freude f; **it's a ~** gern geschehen

**pledge 1.** n (*promise*) Versprechen nt **2.** vt (*promise*) versprechen

**plenty 1.** n **~ of** eine Menge, viel(e); **be ~** genug sein, reichen; **I've got ~** ich habe mehr als genug **2.** adv (US) fam ganz schön

**plimsoll** n (*Brit*) Turnschuh m

**plonk 1.** n (*Brit*) fam (*wine*) billiger Wein **2.** vt **~ sth (down)** etw hinknallen

**plot 1.** n (*of story*) Handlung f; (*conspiracy*) Komplott nt; (*of land*) Stück nt Land, Grundstück nt **2.** vi ein Komplott schmieden

**plough, plow** (US) **1.** n Pflug m **2.** vt, vi AGR pflügen; **ploughman's lunch** n (*Brit*) in einer Kneipe serviertes Gericht aus Käse, Brot,

*Mixed Pickles etc*

**pluck** vt (*eyebrows, guitar*) zupfen; (*chicken*) rupfen; **pluck up** vt **~ (one's) courage** Mut aufbringen

**plug 1.** n (*for sink, bath*) Stöpsel m; ELEC Stecker m; AUTO (Zünd)kerze f; fam (*publicity*) Schleichwerbung f **2.** vt fam (*advertise*) Reklame machen für; **plug in** vt anschließen

**plum 1.** n Pflaume f **2.** adj fam (*job etc*) Super-

**plumber** n Klempner(in) m(f)

**plump** adj rundlich

**plunge 1.** vt (*knife*) stoßen; (*into water*) tauchen **2.** vi stürzen; (*into water*) tauchen

**plural** n Plural m

**plus 1.** prep plus; (*as well as*) und **2.** adj Plus-; **20 ~** mehr als 20 **3.** n fig Plus nt

**plywood** n Sperrholz nt

**pm** abbr = *post meridiem*: **at 3 ~** um 3 Uhr nachmittags; **at 8 ~** um 8 Uhr abends

**pneumonia** n Lungenentzündung f

**poached** adj (*egg*) pochiert, verloren

**PO Box** abbr → *post office box* Postfach nt

**pocket 1.** n Tasche f **2.** vt (*put in pocket*) einstecken; **pocketbook** n (US, *wallet*) Brieftasche f; **pocket calculator** n Taschenrechner m; **pocket money** n Taschengeld nt

**poem** n Gedicht nt; **poet** n

**ponytail**

Dichter(in) *m(f)*; **poetic** *adj*
poetisch; **poetry** *n* (*art*)
Dichtung *f*; (*poems*) Gedichte *pl*

**point 1.** *n* Punkt *m*; (*spot*) Stelle *f*; (*sharp tip*) Spitze *f*; (*moment*) Zeitpunkt *m*; (*purpose*) Zweck *m*; (*idea*) Argument *nt*; (*decimal*) Dezimalstelle *f*; **~s** *pl* RAIL Weiche *f*; **~ of view** drei Komma zwei; **at some ~** irgendwann (mal); **get to the ~** zur Sache kommen; **there's no ~** es hat keinen Sinn; **I was on the ~ of leaving** ich wollte gerade gehen **2.** *vt* (*gun etc*) richten (*at* auf + *acc*); **~ one's finger at** mit dem Finger zeigen auf + *acc* **3.** *vi* (*with finger etc*) zeigen (*at, to* auf + *acc*); **point out** *vt* (*indicate*) aufzeigen; (*mention*) hinweisen auf + *acc*; **~ed** *adj* spitz; (*question*) gezielt; **pointer** *n* (*on dial*) Zeiger *m*; (*tip*) Hinweis *m*; **pointless** *adj* sinnlos

**poison 1.** *n* Gift *nt* **2.** *vt* vergiften; **poisonous** *adj* giftig

**poke** *vt* (*with stick, finger*) stoßen, stupsen, (*put*) stecken

**Poland** *n* Polen *nt*

**polar** *adj* Polar-, polar; **~ bear** Eisbär *m*

**pole** *n* Stange *f*; Pol *m*

**Pole** *n* Pole *m*, Polin *f*

**pole vault** *n* Stabhochsprung

*m*

**police** *n* Polizei *f*; **police car** *n* Polizeiwagen *m*; **policeman** *n* Polizist *m*; **police station** *n* (Polizei)wache *f*; **policewoman** *n* Polizistin *f*

**policy** *n* (*plan*) Politik *f*; (*principle*) Grundsatz *m*; (*insurance policy*) (Versicherungs)police *f*

**polio** *n* Kinderlähmung *f*

**polish 1.** *n* (*for furniture*) Politur *f*; (*for floor*) Wachs *nt*; (*for shoes*) Creme *f*; (*shine*) Glanz *m*; fig Schliff *m* **2.** *vt* polieren; (*shoes*) putzen; fig den letzten Schliff geben + *dat*

**Polish 1.** *adj* polnisch **2.** *n* Polnisch *nt*

**polite** *adj* höflich; **politeness** *n* Höflichkeit *f*

**political, politically** *adj, adv* politisch; **~ly correct** politisch korrekt; **politician** *n* Politiker(in) *m(f)*; **politics** *nsing or pl* Politik *f*

**poll** *n* (*election*) Wahl *f*; (*opinion poll*) Umfrage *f*

**pollen** *n* Pollen *m*, Blütenstaub *m*; **pollen count** *n* Pollenflug *m*

**polling station** *n* Wahllokal *nt*

**pollute** *vt* verschmutzen; **pollution** *n* Verschmutzung *f*

**pompous** *adj* aufgeblasen; (*language*) geschwollen

**pond** *n* Teich *m*

**pony** *n* Pony *nt*; **ponytail** *n*

Pferdeschwanz *m*

**pool 1.** *n* (*swimming pool*)
Schwimmbad *nt*; (*private*)
Schwimmingpool *m*; (*game*)
Poolbillard *nt* **2.** *vt* (*money
etc*) zusammenlegen

**poor 1.** *adj* arm; (*not good*)
schlecht **2.** *npl* **the ~** die Ar-
men *pl*; **poorly 1.** *adv* (*badly*)
schlecht **2.** *adj* (*Brit*) krank

**pop 1.** *n* (*music*) Pop *m*;
(*noise*) Knall *m* **2.** *vt* (*put*)
stecken; (*balloon*) platzen
lassen **3.** *vi* (*balloon*) platzen; (*cork*) knallen; **~ in**
(*person*) vorbeischauen;
**popcorn** *n* Popcorn *nt*

**Pope** *n* Papst *m*

**poppy** *n* Mohn *m*

**Popsicle®** *n* (*US*) Eis *nt* am
Stiel

**popular** *adj* (*well-liked*) beliebt (*with* bei); (*widespread*) weit verbreitet

**population** *n* Bevölkerung *f*;
(*of town*) Einwohner *pl*

**porcelain** *n* Porzellan *nt*

**porch** *n* Vorbau *m*; (*US, ve-
randah*) Veranda *f*

**porcupine** *n* Stachelschwein
*nt*

**pork** *n* Schweinefleisch *nt*;
**pork chop** *n* Schweinekote-
lett *nt*; **pork pie** *n* Schweine-
fleischpastete *f*

**porn** *n* Porno *m*; **porno-
graphic** *adj* pornografisch;
**pornography** *n* Pornografie
*f*

**porridge** *n* Haferbrei *m*

**port** *n* (*harbour*) Hafen *m*;
NAUT (*left side*) Backbord
*nt*; (*wine*) Portwein *m*; IT Anschluss *m*

**portable** *adj* tragbar; (*radio*)
Koffer-

**portal** *n* IT Portal *nt*

**porter** *n* Pförtner(in) *m(f)*;
(*for luggage*) Gepäckträger
*m*

**porthole** *n* Bullauge *nt*

**portion** *n* Teil *m*; (*of food*)
Portion *f*

**portrait** *n* Porträt *nt*

**Portugal** *n* Portugal *nt*; **Portuguese 1.** *adj* portugiesisch
**2.** *n* Portugiese *m*, Portugiesin *f*; (*language*) Portugiesisch *nt*

**pose 1.** *n* Haltung *f* **2.** *vi* posie-
ren **3.** *vt* (*threat, problem*)
darstellen

**posh** *adj fam* piekfein

**position 1.** *n* Stellung *f*;
(*place*) Position *f*, Lage *f*;
(*job*) Stelle *f*; (*opinion*)
Standpunkt *m*; **be in a ~ to
do sth** in der Lage sein,
etw zu tun **2.** *vt* aufstellen;
IT (*cursor*) positionieren

**positive** *adj* positiv; (*con-
vinced*) sicher

**possess** *vt* besitzen; **possession** *n* **~(s** *pl*) Besitz *m*

**possibility** *n* Möglichkeit *f*;
**possible** *adj* möglich; **if ~**
wenn möglich; **as big /
soon as ~** so groß / bald
wie möglich; **possibly** *adv*
(*perhaps*) vielleicht; **I've**

**done all I ~ can** ich habe mein Möglichstes getan

**post 1.** n (mail) Post f; (pole) Pfosten m; (job) Stelle f **2.** vt (letters) aufgeben; **keep sb ~ed** jdn auf dem Laufenden halten; **postage** n Porto nt; **postal** adj Post-; **postbox** n Briefkasten m; **postcard** n Postkarte f; **postcode** n (Brit) Postleitzahl f

**poster** n Plakat nt, Poster nt

**postgraduate** n jmd, der seine Studien nach dem ersten akademischen Grad weiterführt

**postman** n Briefträger m; **postmark** n Poststempel m

**postmortem** n Autopsie f

**post office** n Post® f

**postpone** vt verschieben (till auf + acc)

**posture** n Haltung f

**pot 1.** n Topf m; (teapot, coffee pot) Kanne f **2.** vt (plant) eintopfen

**potato** n Kartoffel f

**potential 1.** adj potenziell **2.** n Potenzial nt; **potentially** adv potenziell

**pottery** n (objects) Töpferwaren pl

**potty 1.** adj (Brit) fam verrückt **2.** n Töpfchen nt

**poultry** n Geflügel nt

**pound** n (money) Pfund nt; (weight) Pfund nt (0,454 kg); **a ~ of cherries** ein Pfund Kirschen; **ten-~ note** Zehnpfundschein m

**pour** vt (liquid) gießen; (rice, sugar etc) schütten; **~ sb sth** (drink) jdm etw eingießen; **pouring** adj (rain) strömend

**poverty** n Armut f

**powder** n Pulver nt; (cosmetic) Puder m; **powder room** n Damentoilette f

**power 1.** n Macht f; (ability) Fähigkeit f; (strength) Stärke f; ELEC Strom m; **be in ~** an der Macht sein **2.** vt betreiben, antreiben; **power-assisted steering** n Servolenkung f; **power cut** n Stromausfall m; **powerful** adj (politician etc) mächtig; (engine, government) stark; (argument) durchschlagend; **powerless** adj machtlos; **power station** n Kraftwerk nt

**PR 1.** abbr = **public relations** **2.** abbr = **proportional representation**

**practical, practically** adj, adv praktisch; **practice 1.** n (training) Übung f; (custom) Gewohnheit f; (doctor's, lawyer's) Praxis f; **in ~** (in reality) in der Praxis; **out of ~** außer Übung; **put sth into ~** etw in die Praxis umsetzen **2.** vt, vi (US) = **practise**; **practise 1.** vt (instrument, movement) üben; (profession) ausüben **2.** vi üben; (doctor, lawyer) praktizieren

**Prague** n Prag nt

**praise 1.** n Lob nt **2.** vt loben

**pram** n (Brit) Kinderwagen m

**prawn** n Garnele f, Krabbe f; **prawn crackers** npl Krabbenchips pl

**pray** vi beten; **prayer** n Gebet nt

**pre-** pref vor-, prä-

**preach** vi predigen

**precaution** n Vorsichtsmaßnahme f

**precede** vt vorausgehen + dat; **preceding** adj vorhergehend

**precinct** n (Brit, pedestrian precinct) Fußgängerzone f; (Brit, shopping precinct) Einkaufsviertel nt; (US, district) Bezirk m

**precious** adj kostbar; ~ **stone** Edelstein m

**précis** n Zusammenfassung f

**precise, precisely** adj, adv genau

**precondition** n Vorbedingung f

**predecessor** n Vorgänger(in) m(f)

**predict** vt voraussagen; **predictable** adj vorhersehbar; (person) berechenbar

**predominant** adj vorherrschend; **predominantly** adv überwiegend

**preface** n Vorwort nt

**prefer** vt vorziehen (to dat), lieber mögen (to als); ~ **to do sth** etw lieber tun; **preferably** adv vorzugsweise, am liebsten; **preference** n (liking) Vorliebe f; **preferential** adj **get** ~ **treatment** be-

vorzugt behandelt werden

**prefix** n (US) TEL Vorwahl f

**pregnancy** n Schwangerschaft f; **pregnant** adj schwanger; **two months** ~ im zweiten Monat schwanger

**prejudice** n Vorurteil nt; **prejudiced** adj (person) voreingenommen

**preliminary** adj (measures) vorbereitend; (results) vorläufig; (remarks) einleitend

**premature** adj vorzeitig; (hasty) voreilig

**première** n Premiere f

**premises** npl (offices) Räumlichkeiten pl; (of factory, school) Gelände nt

**premium-rate** adj TEL zum Höchsttarif

**preoccupied** adj **be** ~ **with sth** mit etw sehr beschäftigt sein

**prepaid** adj vorausbezahlt; (envelope) frankiert

**preparation** n Vorbereitung f; **prepare** 1. vt vorbereiten (for auf + acc); (food) zubereiten; **be** ~ **d to do sth** bereit sein, etw zu tun 2. vi sich vorbereiten (for auf + acc)

**prerequisite** n Voraussetzung f

**prescribe** vt vorschreiben; MED verschreiben; **prescription** n Rezept nt

**presence** n Gegenwart f; **present 1.** adj (in attendance) anwesend (at bei); (current) gegenwärtig; **~ tense** Gegenwart *f*; Präsens *nt* **2.** *n* Gegenwart *f*; (*gift*) Geschenk *nt*; **at ~** zurzeit **3.** *vt* TV, RADIO präsentieren; (*problem*) darstellen; (*report etc*) vorlegen; **present-day** *adj* heutig; **presently** *adv* bald; (*at present*) zurzeit

**preservative** *n* Konservierungsmittel *nt*; **preserve** *vt* erhalten; (*food*) einmachen, konservieren

**president** *n* Präsident(in) *m*(*f*); **presidential** *adj* Präsidenten-; (*election*) Präsidentschafts-

**press 1.** *n* (*newspapers, machine*) Presse *f* **2.** *vt* (*push*) drücken; **~ a button** auf einen Knopf drücken **3.** *vi* (*push*) drücken; **pressing** *adj* dringend; **press-stud** *n* Druckknopf *m*; **press-up** *n* (*Brit*) Liegestütz *m*; **be under ~** unter Druck stehen; **put ~ on sb** jdn unter Druck setzen; **pressure cooker** *n* Schnellkochtopf *m*; **pressurize** *vt* (*person*) unter Druck setzen

**presumably** *adv* vermutlich; **presume** *vt, vi* annehmen; **presumptuous** *adj* anmaßend

**presuppose** *vt* voraussetzen

**pretend 1.** *vt* **~ that** so tun als ob; **~ to do sth** vorgeben, etw zu tun **2.** *vi* **she's ~ing** sie tut

nur so

**pretentious** *adj* anmaßend; (*person*) wichtigtuerisch

**pretty 1.** *adj* hübsch **2.** *adv* ziemlich

**prevent** *vt* verhindern; **~ sb from doing sth** jdn daran hindern, etw zu tun

**preview** *n* FILM Voraufführung *f*; (*trailer*) Vorschau *f*

**previous, previously** *adj, adv* früher

**prey** *n* Beute *f*

**price 1.** *n* Preis *m* **2.** *vt* **it's ~d at £10** es ist mit 10 Pfund ausgezeichnet; **priceless** *adj* unbezahlbar; **price list** *n* Preisliste *f*; **price tag** *n* Preisschild *nt*

**prick 1.** *n* Stich *m*; *vulg* (*penis*) Schwanz *m*; *vulg* (*person*) Arsch *m* **2.** *vt* stechen in + *acc*; **~ one's finger** sich *dat* in den Finger stechen; **prickly** *adj* stachelig

**pride 1.** *n* Stolz *m*; (*arrogance*) Hochmut *m* **2.** *vt* **~ oneself on sth** auf etw *acc* stolz sein

**priest** *n* Priester *m*

**primarily** *adv* vorwiegend; **primary** *adj* Haupt-; **~ school** Grundschule *f*

**prime 1.** *adj* (*excellent*) erstklassig **2.** *n* **in one's ~** in den besten Jahren; **prime minister** *n* Premierminister(in) *m*(*f*); **prime time** *n* TV Hauptsendezeit *f*

**primitive** *adj* primitiv

**prince** *n* Prinz *m*; (*ruler*) Fürst

*m*; **princess** *n* Prinzessin *f*; Fürstin *f*

**principal 1.** *adj* Haupt-, wichtigste(r, s) **2.** *n*, Rektor(in) *m(f)*

**principle** *n* Prinzip *nt*; **in ~** im Prinzip; **on ~** aus Prinzip

**print 1.** *n* (*picture*) Druck *m*; PHOT Abzug *m*; (*made by feet, fingers*) Abdruck *m*; **out of ~** vergriffen **2.** *vt* drucken; (*photo*) abziehen; **print out** *vt* IT ausdrucken; **printed matter** *n* Drucksache *f*; **printer** *n* Drucker *m*; **printout** *n* IT Ausdruck *m*

**prior** *adj* früher; **a ~ engagement** eine vorher getroffene Verabredung

**priority** *n* (*thing having precedence*) Priorität *f*

**prison** *n* Gefängnis *nt*; **prisoner** *n* Gefangene(r) *mf*

**privacy** *n* Privatleben *nt*; **private 1.** *adj* (*confidential*) vertraulich **2.** *n* einfacher Soldat; **in ~** privat; **privately** *adv* (*confidentially*) vertraulich; **privatize** *vt* privatisieren

**privilege** *n* Privileg *nt*; **privileged** *adj* privilegiert

**prize** *n* Preis *m*; **prize money** *n* Preisgeld *nt*; **prizewinner** *n* Gewinner(in) *m(f)*; **prizewinning** *adj* preisgekrönt

**pro** *n* (*professional*) Profi *m*; **the ~s and cons** *pl* das Für und Wider

**pro-** *pref* pro-

**probability** *n* Wahrscheinlichkeit *f*; **probable, probably** *adj, adv* wahrscheinlich

**probation** *n* Probezeit *f*; LAW Bewährung *f*

**probe 1.** *n* (*investigation*) Untersuchung *f* **2.** *vt* untersuchen

**problem** *n* Problem *nt*; **no ~** kein Problem!

**procedure** *n* Verfahren *nt*

**proceed 1.** *vi* (*continue*) fortfahren; (*set about sth*) vorgehen **2.** *vt* **~ to do sth** anfangen, etw zu tun; **proceedings** *npl* LAW Verfahren *nt*; **proceeds** *npl* Erlös *m*

**process 1.** *n* Prozess *m*, Vorgang *m*; (*method*) Verfahren *nt* **2.** *vt* (*application etc*) bearbeiten; (*food, data*) verarbeiten; (*film*) entwickeln

**procession** *n* Umzug *m*

**processor** *n* IT Prozessor *m*; GASTR Küchenmaschine *f*

**produce 1.** *n* AGR Produkte *pl*, Erzeugnisse *pl* **2.** *vt* (*manufacture*) herstellen, produzieren; (*on farm*) erzeugen; (*film, play, record*) produzieren; (*cause*) hervorrufen; **producer** *n* (*manufacturer*) Hersteller(in) *m(f)*; (*of film, play, record*) Produzent(in) *m(f)*; **product** *n* Produkt *nt*, Erzeugnis *nt*; **production** *n* Produktion *f*; THEAT Inszenierung *f*; **productive** *adj* produktiv; (*land*) ertragreich

**prof** *n fam* Prof *m*

**profession** *n* Beruf *m*; **professional 1.** *n* Profi *m* **2.** *adj* beruflich; (*expert*) fachlich; (*sportsman, actor etc*) Berufs-

**professor** *n* Professor(in) *m(f)*; (*US, lecturer*) Dozent(in) *m(f)*

**proficient** *adj* kompetent (*in* in + *dat*)

**profile** *n* Profil *nt*; **keep a low** ~ sich rarmachen

**profit 1.** *n* Gewinn *m* **2.** *vi* profitieren (*by, from* von); **profitable** *adj* rentabel

**profound** *adj* tief; (*idea, thinker*) tiefgründig; (*knowledge*) profund

**program 1.** *n* IT Programm *nt*; (*US*) → **programme 2.** *vt* IT programmieren; (*US*) → **programme**

**programme 1.** *n* Programm *nt*; TV, RADIO Sendung *f* **2.** *vt* programmieren; **programmer** *n* Programmierer(in) *m(f)*; **programming** *n* IT Programmieren *nt*; ~ **language** Programmiersprache *f*

**progress 1.** *n* Fortschritt *m*; **make** ~ Fortschritte machen **2.** *vi* (*work, illness etc*) fortschreiten; (*improve*) Fortschritte machen; **progressive** *adj* (*person, policy*) fortschrittlich; **progressively** *adv* zunehmend

**prohibit** *vt* verbieten

**project** *n* Projekt *nt*

**prolong** *vt* verlängern

**prom** *n* (*at seaside*) Promenade *f*; (*Brit, concert*) Konzert *nt* (*bei dem ein Großteil des Publikums im Parkett Stehplätze hat*); (*US, dance*) Ball für die Schüler und Studenten von Highschools oder Colleges

**prominent** *adj* (*politician, actor etc*) prominent; (*easily seen*) auffallend

**promiscuous** *adj* promisk

**promise 1.** *n* Versprechen *nt* **2.** *vt* versprechen; ~ **sb sth** jdm etw versprechen; ~ **to do sth** versprechen, etw zu tun **3.** *vi* versprechen; **promising** *adj* vielversprechend

**promote** *vt* (*in rank*) befördern; (*help on*) fördern; COMM werben für; **promotion** *n* (*in rank*) Beförderung *f*; COMM Werbung *f* (*of* für)

**prompt 1.** *adj* prompt; (*punctual*) pünktlich **2.** *adv* **at two o'clock** ~ Punkt zwei Uhr **3.** *vt* THEAT (*actor*) soufflieren + *dat*

**prone** *adj* **be** ~ **to sth** zu etw neigen

**pronounce** *vt* (*word*) aussprechen; **pronunciation** *n* Aussprache *f*

**proof** *n* Beweis *m*; (*of alcohol*) Alkoholgehalt *m*

**prop 1.** *n* Stütze *f*; THEAT Requisit *nt* **2.** *vt* ~ **sth against sth** etw gegen etw lehnen;

**prop up** vt stützen; fig unterstützen

**proper** adj richtig; (morally correct) anständig

**property** n (possession) Eigentum nt; (characteristic) Eigenschaft f

**proportion** n Verhältnis nt; (share) Teil m; **~s** pl (size) Proportionen pl; **in ~ to** im Verhältnis zu; **proportional** adj proportional; **~ representation** Verhältniswahlrecht nt

**proposal** n Vorschlag m; **~ (of marriage)** (Heirats)antrag m; **propose 1.** vt vorschlagen **2.** vi (offer marriage) einen Heiratsantrag machen (to sb jdm)

**proprietor** n Besitzer(in) m(f); (of pub, hotel) Inhaber(in) m(f)

**prose** n Prosa f

**prosecute** vt verfolgen (for wegen)

**prospect** n Aussicht f

**prosperity** n Wohlstand m; **prosperous** adj wohlhabend; (business) gut gehend

**prostitute** n Prostituierte(r) mf

**protect** vt schützen (from, against vor + dat, gegen); **protection** n Schutz m (from, against vor + dat, gegen); **protective** adj beschützend; (clothing etc) Schutz-

**protein** n Protein nt, Eiweiß nt

**protest 1.** n Protest m; (demonstration) Protestkundgebung f **2.** vi protestieren (against gegen); (demonstrate) demonstrieren

**Protestant 1.** adj protestantisch **2.** n Protestant(in) m(f)

**proud, proudly** adj, adv stolz (of auf + acc)

**prove** vt beweisen; (turn out to be) sich erweisen als

**proverb** n Sprichwort nt

**provide** vt zur Verfügung stellen; (drinks, music etc) sorgen für; (person) versorgen (with mit); **provide for** vt (family etc) sorgen für; **provided** conj vt (that) vorausgesetzt, dass; **provider** n IT Provider m

**provision** n (condition) Bestimmung f; **~s** pl (food) Proviant m

**provoke** vt provozieren; (cause) hervorrufen

**proximity** n Nähe f

**prudent** adj klug; (person) umsichtig

**prudish** adj prüde

**prune 1.** n Backpflaume f **2.** vt (tree etc) zurechtstutzen

**PS** abbr = **postscript** PS nt

**pseudo** adj pseudo-, Pseudo-; **pseudonym** n Pseudonym nt

**psychiatric** adj psychiatrisch; (illness) psychisch; **psychiatrist** n Psychiater(in) m(f); **psychiatry** n Psychiatrie f; **psychic** adj übersinnlich;

*I'm not ~* ich kann keine Gedanken lesen; **psychoanalysis** n Psychoanalyse f; **psychoanalyst** n Psychoanalytiker(in) m(f); **psychological** adj psychologisch; **psychology** n Psychologie f; **psychopath** n Psychopath(in) m(f)

**pto** abbr = *please turn over* b. w.

**pub** n (Brit) Kneipe f
**puberty** n Pubertät f
**public 1.** n *the (general)* ~ die (breite) Öffentlichkeit; *in ~* in der Öffentlichkeit **2.** adj öffentlich; (relating to the state) Staats- f; ~ *convenience* (Brit) öffentliche Toilette; ~ *holiday* gesetzlicher Feiertag; ~ *opinion* die öffentliche Meinung; ~ *relations* pl Öffentlichkeitsarbeit f, Public Relations pl; ~ *school* (Brit) Privatschule f; **publication** n Veröffentlichung f; **publicity** n Publicity f; (advertisements) Werbung f; **publish** vt veröffentlichen; **publisher** n Verleger(in) m(f); (company) Verlag m; **publishing** n Verlagswesen nt

**pudding** n (course) Nachtisch m
**puddle** n Pfütze f
**puff** vi (pant) schnaufen
**puffin** n Papageientaucher m
**puff paste** (US), **puff pastry** n Blätterteig m

**pull 1.** n Ziehen nt; *give sth a ~* an etw dat ziehen **2.** vt (cart, tooth) ziehen; (rope, handle) ziehen an + dat; (fam (date) abschleppen; ~ *a muscle* sich dat einen Muskel zerren; ~ *sb's leg* jdn auf den Arm nehmen **3.** vi ziehen; **pull apart** vt (separate) auseinanderziehen; **pull down** vt (blind) herunterziehen; (house) abreißen; **pull in** vi hineinfahren; (stop) anhalten; **pull off** vt (deal etc) zuwege bringen; (clothes) ausziehen; **pull on** vt (clothes) anziehen; **pull out 1.** vi (car from lane) ausscheren; (train) abfahren; (withdraw) aussteigen (of aus) **2.** vt herausziehen; (tooth) ziehen; (troops) abziehen; **pull up 1.** vt (raise) hochziehen; (chair) heranziehen **2.** vi anhalten

**pullover** n Pullover m
**pulp** n Brei m; (of fruit) Fruchtfleisch nt
**pulpit** n Kanzel f
**pulse** n Puls m
**pump** n Pumpe f; (in petrol station) Zapfsäule f; **pump up** vt (tyre etc) aufpumpen
**pumpkin** n Kürbis m
**pun** n Wortspiel nt
**punch 1.** n (blow) (Faust)schlag m; (tool) Locher m; (hot drink) Punsch m; (cold drink) Bowle f **2.** vt (strike) schlagen; (ticket, paper) lo-

chen

**punctual, punctually** adj, adv pünktlich

**punctuation** n Interpunktion f; **punctuation mark** n Satzzeichen nt

**puncture** n (flat tyre) Reifenpanne f

**punish** vt bestrafen; **punishment** n Strafe f; (action) Bestrafung f

**pupil** n, Schüler(in) m(f)

**puppet** n Marionette f

**puppy** n junger Hund

**purchase 1.** n Kauf m **2.** vt kaufen

**pure** adj rein; (clean) sauber; (utter) pur; **purely** adv rein; **purify** vt reinigen; **purity** n Reinheit f

**purple** adj violett

**purpose** n Zweck m; (of person) Absicht f; **on ~** absichtlich

**purr** vi (cat) schnurren

**purse** n Geldbeutel m; (US, handbag) Handtasche f

**pursue** vt (person, car) verfolgen; (hobby, studies) nachgehen + dat

**pus** n Eiter m

**push 1.** n Stoß m **2.** vt (person) stoßen; (car, chair etc) schieben; (button) drücken; (drugs) dealen **3.** vi (in crowd) drängeln; **push in** vi (in queue) sich vordrängeln; **push off** vi fam (leave) abhauen; **push on** vi (with job) weitermachen; **push**

up vt (prices) hochtreiben; **pushchair** n (Brit) Sport-(kinder)wagen m; **pusher** n (of drugs) Dealer(in) m(f); **push-up** n (US) Liegestütz m; **pushy** adj fam aufdringlich, penetrant

**put** vt tun; (upright) stellen; (flat) legen; (express) ausdrücken; (write) schreiben; **he ~ his hand in his pocket** er steckte die Hand in die Tasche; **he ~ his hand on her shoulder** er legte ihr die Hand auf die Schulter; **~ money into one's account** Geld auf sein Konto einzahlen; **put aside** vt (money) zurücklegen; **put away** vt (tidy away) wegräumen; **put back** vt zurücklegen; (clock) zurückstellen; **put down** vt (in writing) aufschreiben; (Brit, animal) einschläfern; (rebellion) niederschlagen; **put the phone down** (den Hörer) auflegen; **put one's name down for sth** sich für etw eintragen; **put forward** vt (idea) vorbringen; (name) vorschlagen; (clock) vorstellen; **put off** vt (switch off) ausschalten; (postpone) verschieben; **put sb off doing sth** jdn davon abbringen, etw zu tun; **put on** vt (switch on) anmachen; (clothes) anziehen; (hat, glasses) aufsetzen; (make-up, CD) auflegen; **put the kettle on** Wasser aufsetzen; *put weight on* zunehmen; **put out** *vt* (*hand, foot*) ausstrecken; (*light, cigarette*) ausmachen; **put up** *vt* (*hand*) hochheben; (*picture*) aufhängen; (*tent*) aufstellen; (*building*) errichten; (*price*) erhöhen; (*person*) unterbringen; **~** sich abfinden mit; *I won't **~** with it* das lasse ich mir nicht gefallen

**putt** *vt*, *vi* SPORT putten
**puzzle 1.** *n* Rätsel *nt*; (*toy*) Geduldsspiel *nt*; (*jigsaw*) ~ Puzzle *nt* **2.** *vt* vor ein Rätsel stellen; *it ~s me* es ist mir ein Rätsel; **puzzling** *adj* rätselhaft
**pyjamas** *npl* Schlafanzug *m*
**pylon** *n* Mast *m*
**pyramid** *n* Pyramide *f*

# Q

**quack** *vi* quaken
**quaint** *adj* (*idea, tradition*) kurios; (*picturesque*) malerisch
**qualification** *n* (*for job*) Qualifikation *f*; (*from school, university*) Abschluss *m*; **qualified** *adj* (*for job*) qualifiziert; **qualify 1.** *vt* (*limit*) einschränken; *be qualified to do sth* berechtigt sein, etw zu tun **2.** *vi* (*finish training*) seine Ausbildung abschließen; (*contest etc*) sich qualifizieren
**quality** *n* Qualität *f*; (*characteristic*) Eigenschaft *f*
**quantity** *n* Menge *f*, Quantität *f*
**quarantine** *n* Quarantäne *f*
**quarrel 1.** *n* Streit *m* **2.** *vi* sich streiten
**quarter 1.** *n* Viertel *nt*; (*of year*) Vierteljahr *nt*; (*US, coin*) Vierteldollar *m*; *a ~ of an hour* eine Viertelstun-

de **2.** *vt* vierteln
**quarter final** *n* Viertelfinale *nt*
**quartet** *n* Quartett *nt*
**quay** *n* Kai *m*
**queen** *n* Königin *f*; (*in cards, chess*) Dame *f*
**queer 1.** *adj* (*strange*) seltsam, sonderbar; *pej* (*homosexual*) schwul **2.** *n pej* Schwule(r) *m*
**quench** *vt* (*thirst*) löschen
**query 1.** *n* Frage *f* **2.** *vt* infrage stellen; (*bill*) reklamieren
**question 1.** *n* Frage *f*; *that's out of the ~* das kommt nicht infrage **2.** *vt* (*person*) befragen; (*suspect*) verhören; (*express doubt about*) bezweifeln; **questionable** *adj* zweifelhaft; (*improper*) fragwürdig; **question mark** *n* Fragezeichen *nt*; **questionnaire** *n* Fragebogen *m*
**queue 1.** *n* (*Brit*) Schlange *f*;

**jump the ~** sich vordrängeln
**2.** vi ~ **(up)** Schlange stehen
**quibble** vi kleinlich sein;
(argue) streiten
**quiche** n Quiche f
**quick** adj schnell; (short)
kurz; **be ~** mach schnell!;
**quickly** adv schnell
**quid** n (Brit) fam Pfund nt
**quiet 1.** adj (not noisy) leise;
(peaceful, calm) still, ruhig;
**be ~** sei still!; **keep ~ about**
**sth** über etw acc nichts sagen
**2.** n Stille f, Ruhe f; **quietly**
adv leise; (calmly) ruhig
**quilt** n (Stepp)decke f
**quit 1.** vt (leave) verlassen;
(job) aufgeben **2.** vi (stop)
aufhören, etw zu tun **2.** vi
aufhören; (resign) kündigen

**quite** adv (fairly) ziemlich;
(completely) ganz, völlig; **I**
**don't ~ understand** ich verstehe das nicht ganz; **~ a few**
ziemlich viele; **~ so** richtig!;
**quits** adj **be ~ with sb** mit jdm
quitt sein
**quiver** vi zittern
**quiz** n (competition) Quiz nt
**quota** n Anteil m; COMM, POL
Quote f
**quotation** n Zitat nt; (price)
Kostenvoranschlag m; **quo-**
**tation marks** npl Anführungszeichen pl; **quote 1.** vt
(text, author) zitieren;
(price) nennen **2.** n Zitat
nt; (price) Kostenvoran-
schlag m; **in ~s** in Anführungszeichen

# R

**rabbi** n Rabbiner m
**rabbit** n Kaninchen nt
**rabies** nsing Tollwut f
**raccoon** n Waschbär m
**race 1.** n (competition) Rennen nt; (people) Rasse f **2.**
vt um die Wette laufen/
fahren **3.** vi (rush) rennen;
**racecourse** n Rennbahn f;
**racetrack** n Rennbahn f
**racial** adj Rassen-; **~ discrim-**
**ination** Rassendiskriminie-
rung f
**racing** n (horse) ~ Pferderennen nt; (motor) ~ Autoren-
nen nt; **racing car** n Renn-

wagen m
**racism** n Rassismus m; **racist**
**1.** n Rassist(in) m(f) **2.** adj
rassistisch
**rack 1.** n Ständer m, Gestell nt
**2.** vt ~ **one's brains** sich dat
den Kopf zerbrechen
**racket** n SPORT Schläger m;
(noise) Krach m
**radar** n Radar nt or m
**radiation** n (radioactive)
Strahlung f
**radiator** n Heizkörper m;
AUTO Kühler m
**radical** adj radikal
**radio** n Rundfunk m, Radio n

**rape**

**radioactivity** n Radioaktivität f

**radio alarm** n Radiowecker m; **radio station** n Rundfunkstation f

**radiotherapy** n Strahlenbehandlung f

**radish** n Radieschen nt

**radius** n Radius m; **within a five-mile ~** im Umkreis von fünf Meilen (of um)

**raffle** n Tombola f; **raffle ticket** n Los nt

**raft** n Floß nt

**rag** n Lumpen m; (for cleaning) Lappen m

**rage 1.** n Wut f; **be all the~** der letzte Schrei sein **2.** vi toben; (disease) wüten

**raid 1.** n Überfall m (on auf + acc); (by police) Razzia f (on gegen) **2.** vt (bank etc) überfallen; (by police) eine Razzia machen in + dat

**rail** n (on stairs, balcony etc) Geländer nt; (of ship) Reling f; RAIL Schiene f; **railcard** n (Brit) ≈ Bahncard® f; **railing** n Geländer nt; **~s** pl (fence) Zaun m; **railroad** n (US) Eisenbahn f; **railroad station** n (US) Bahnhof m; **railway** n (Brit) Eisenbahn f; **railway station** n Bahnhof m

**rain 1.** n Regen m **2.** vi regnen; **it's ~ing** es regnet; **rainbow** n Regenbogen m; **raincoat** n Regenmantel m; **rainforest** n Regenwald m; **rainy** adj regnerisch

**raise 1.** n (US, of wages / salary) Gehalts- / Lohnerhöhung f **2.** vt (lift) hochheben; (increase) erhöhen; (family) großziehen; (livestock) züchten; (money) aufbringen; (objection) erheben; **~ one's voice** (in anger) laut werden

**raisin** n Rosine f

**rally** n POL Kundgebung f; AUTO Rallye f

**RAM** acr = **random access memory**; RAM m

**ramble 1.** n Wanderung f **2.** vi (walk) wandern; (talk) schwafeln

**ramp** n Rampe f

**ran** pt → **run**

**ranch** n Ranch f

**rancid** adj ranzig

**random 1.** adj willkürlich **2.** n **at ~** (choose) willkürlich; (fire) ziellos

**rang** pt → **ring**

**range 1.** n (selection) Auswahl f (of an + dat); COMM Sortiment nt (of an + dat); (of missile, telescope) Reichweite f; (of mountains) Kette f; **in this price ~** in dieser Preisklasse **2.** vi **~ from ... to ...** (temperature, sizes, prices) liegen zwischen ... und ...

**rank 1.** n Rang m; (social position) Stand m **2.** vt einstufen

**ransom** n Lösegeld nt

**rap** n MUS Rap m

**rape 1.** n Vergewaltigung f **2.**

*vt* vergewaltigen

**rapid, rapidly** *adj, adv* schnell

**rapist** *n* Vergewaltiger *m*

**rare** *adj* selten, rar; (*especially good*) vortrefflich; (*steak*) blutig; **rarely** *adv* selten; **rarity** *n* Seltenheit *f*

**rash 1.** *adj* unbesonnen **2.** *n* MED (Haut)ausschlag *m*

**rasher** *n* ~ (*of bacon*) (Speck)scheibe *f*

**raspberry** *n* Himbeere *f*

**rat** *n* Ratte *f*

**rate 1.** *n* (*proportion, frequency*) Rate *f*; (*speed*) Tempo *nt*; ~ *of exchange* (Wechsel)kurs *m*; ~ *of interest* Zinssatz *m*; *at any* ~ auf jeden Fall **2.** *vt* (*evaluate*) einschätzen (*as* als)

**rather** *adv* (*in preference*) lieber; (*fairly*) ziemlich; *I'd* ~ *stay here* ich würde lieber hierbleiben; *I'd* ~ *not* lieber nicht; *or* ~ (*more accurately*) vielmehr

**ratio** *n* Verhältnis *nt*

**rational** *adj* rational; **rationalize** *vt* rationalisieren

**rattle 1.** *n* (*toy*) Rassel *f* **2.** *vt* (*keys, coins*) klimpern mit; (*person*) durcheinanderbringen **3.** *vi* (*window*) klappern; (*bottles*) klirren; **rattle off** *vt* herunterrasseln; **rattlesnake** *n* Klapperschlange *f*

**rave 1.** *vi* (*talk wildly*) fantasieren; (*rage*) toben; (*enthuse*) schwärmen (*about* von) **2.** *n* (*Brit, event*) Raveparty *f*

**raven** *n* Rabe *m*

**raving** *adv* ~ *mad* total verrückt

**ravishing** *adj* hinreißend

**raw** *adj* (*food*) roh; (*skin*) wund; (*climate*) rau

**ray** *n* (*of light*) Strahl *m*; ~ *of hope* Hoffnungsschimmer *m*

**razor** *n* Rasierapparat *m*; **razor blade** *n* Rasierklinge *f*

**Rd** *n abbr* → *road* Str.

**re** *prep* betreffs + *gen*

**reach 1.** *n* *within / out of* (*sb's*) ~ in / außer (jds) Reichweite; *within easy* ~ *of the shops* nicht weit von den Geschäften **2.** *vt* (*arrive at, contact*) erreichen; (*come down / up as far as*) reichen bis zu; (*contact*) *can you* ~ *it?* kommst du / kommen Sie dran?; **reach for** *vt* greifen nach; **reach out** *vi* die Hand ausstrecken; ~ *for* greifen nach

**react** *vi* reagieren (*to* auf + *acc*); **reaction** *n* Reaktion *f* (*to* auf + *acc*); **reactor** *n* Reaktor *m*

**read 1.** *vt* lesen; (*meter*) ablesen; ~ *sth to sb* jdm etw vorlesen **2.** *vi* lesen; ~ *to sb* jdm vorlesen; *it* ~*s well* es liest sich gut; *it* ~*s as follows* es lautet folgendermaßen; **read out** *vt* vorlesen; **read through** *vt* durchlesen; **read**

**up on** vt nachlesen über + acc; **readable** adj (book) lesenswert; (handwriting) lesbar; **reader** n Leser(in) m(f); **readership** n Leserschaft f

**readily** adv (willingly) bereitwillig; **~ available** leicht erhältlich

**reading** n (action) Lesen nt; (from meter) Zählerstand m; **reading glasses** npl Lesebrille f; **reading lamp** n Leselampe f; **reading matter** n Lektüre f

**readjust 1.** vt (mechanism etc) neu einstellen **2.** vi sich wieder anpassen (to an + acc)

**ready** adj fertig, bereit; **be ~ to do sth** (willing) bereit sein, etw zu tun; **are you ~ to go?** bist du so weit?; **get sth ~** etw fertig machen; **ready cash** n Bargeld nt; **ready-made** adj (product) Fertig-; (clothes) Konfektions-; **~ meal** Fertiggericht nt

**real 1.** adj wirklich; (actual) eigentlich; (genuine) echt; (idiot etc) richtig; **for ~** echt; **this time it's for ~** diesmal ist es ernst; **get ~** sei realistisch! **2.** adv fam (esp US) echt

**real estate** n Immobilien pl

**realistic, realistically** adj, adv realistisch; **reality** n Wirklichkeit f; **in ~** in Wirklichkeit; **realization** n (aware-ness) Erkenntnis f; **realize** vt (understand) begreifen; (plan, idea) realisieren; **I ~d (that)** ... mir wurde klar, dass ...

**really** adv wirklich

**real time** n IT **in ~** in Echtzeit

**realtor** n (US) Grundstücksmakler(in) m(f)

**reappear** vi wieder erscheinen

**rear 1.** adj hintere(r, s), Hinter- **2.** n (of building, vehicle) hinterer Teil; **at the ~ of** hinter + dat; (inside) hinten in + dat; **rear light** n AUTO Rücklicht nt

**rearm** vi wieder aufrüsten

**rearrange** vt (furniture, system) umstellen; (meeting) verlegen (for auf + acc)

**rear-view mirror** n Rückspiegel m; **rear window** n AUTO Heckscheibe f

**reason 1.** n (cause) Grund m (for für); (ability to think) Verstand m; (common sense) Vernunft f; **for some ~** aus irgendeinem Grund **2.** vi **with sb** mit jdm vernünftig reden; **reasonable** adj (person, price) vernünftig; (offer) akzeptabel; (chance) reell; (food, weather) ganz gut; **reasonably** adv vernünftig; (fairly) ziemlich

**reassure** vt beruhigen; **she ~d me that** ... sie versicherte mir, dass ...

**rebel 1.** n Rebell(in) m(f) **2.** vi

rebellieren; **rebellion** n Aufstand m

**reboot** vt, vi IT rebooten

**rebuild** irr vt wieder aufbauen

**recall** vt (remember) sich erinnern an + acc; (call back) zurückrufen

**recap** vt, vi rekapitulieren

**receipt** n (document) Quittung f; (receiving) Empfang m; ~s pl (money) Einnahmen pl

**receive** vt (news etc) erhalten, bekommen; (visitor) empfangen; **receiver** n TEL Hörer m; RADIO Empfänger m

**recent** adj (event) vor Kurzem stattgefunden; (photo) neueste(r,s); (invention) neu; **in ~ years** in den letzten Jahren; **recently** adv vor Kurzem; (in the last few days or weeks) in letzter Zeit

**reception** n Empfang m; **receptionist** n (in hotel) Empfangschef m, Empfangsdame f; (woman in firm) Empfangsdame f; MED Sprechstundenhilfe f

**recess** n (in wall) Nische f; (US, in school) Pause f

**recession** n Rezession f

**recharge** vt (battery) aufladen; **rechargeable** adj wiederaufladbar

**recipe** n Rezept nt (for für)

**recipient** n Empfänger(in) m(f)

**reciprocal** adj gegenseitig

**recite** vt vortragen

**reckless** adj leichtsinnig; (driving) gefährlich

**reckon 1.** vt (calculate) schätzen; (think) glauben **2.** vi **~ with / on** rechnen mit

**reclaim** vt (baggage) abholen; (expenses, tax) zurückverlangen

**recline** vi (person) sich zurücklehnen; **reclining seat** n Liegesitz m

**recognition** n (acknowledgement) Anerkennung f; **in ~ of** in Anerkennung + gen; **recognize** vt erkennen; (approve officially) anerkennen

**recommend** vt empfehlen; **recommendation** n Empfehlung f

**reconfirm** vt (flight etc) rückbestätigen

**reconsider** vt noch einmal überdenken

**reconstruct** vt wieder aufbauen; (crime) rekonstruieren

**record 1.** n MUS (Schall)platte f; (best performance) Rekord m; **keep a ~ of** Buch führen über + acc **2.** adj (time etc) Rekord- **3.** vt (write down) aufzeichnen; (on tape etc) aufnehmen; **~ed message** Ansage f; **recorded delivery** n (Brit) **by ~** per Einschreiben

**recorder** n MUS Blockflöte f; (cassette) ~ (Kassetten)rekorder m; **recording** n (on tape etc) Aufnahme f

**refined**

**recover 1.** *vt (money, item)* zurückbekommen; *(appetite, strength)* wiedergewinnen **2.** *vi* sich erholen

**recreation** *n* Erholung *f*; **recreational** *adj* Freizeit-; ~ **vehicle** (US) Wohnmobil *nt*

**recruit 1.** *n* MIL Rekrut(in) *m(f)*; *(in firm, organization)* neues Mitglied **2.** *vt* MIL rekrutieren; *(members)* anwerben; *(staff)* einstellen; **recruitment agency** *n* Personalagentur *f*

**rectangle** *n* Rechteck *nt*; **rectangular** *adj* rechteckig

**recuperate** *vi* sich erholen

**recyclable** *adj* recycelbar, wiederverwertbar; **recycle** *vt* recyceln, wiederverwerten; ~ **d paper** Recyclingpapier *nt*; **recycling** *n* Recycling *nt*, Wiederverwertung *f*

**red 1.** *adj* rot **2.** *n* **in the** ~ in den roten Zahlen; **red cabbage** *n* Rotkohl *m*; **redcurrant** *n* (rote) Johannisbeere

**redeem** *vt* COMM einlösen

**red-handed** *adj* **catch sb** ~ jdn auf frischer Tat ertappen

**redhead** *n* Rothaarige(r) *mf*

**redial** *vt, vi* nochmals wählen

**redirect** *vt* *(traffic)* umleiten; *(forward)* nachsenden

**red light** *n* *(traffic signal)* rotes Licht; **go through the** ~ bei Rot über die Ampel fahren

**red meat** *n* Rind-, Lamm-, Rehfleisch

**redo** *irr vt* nochmals machen

**reduce** *vt* reduzieren (*to* auf + *acc*, *by* um); **reduction** *n* Reduzierung *f*; *(in price)* Ermäßigung *f*

**redundant** *adj* überflüssig; **be made** ~ entlassen werden

**red wine** *n* Rotwein *m*

**reef** *n* Riff *nt*

**reel** *n* Spule *f*; *(on fishing rod)* Rolle *f*; **reel off** *vt* herunterrasseln

**ref** *n* *fam (referee)* Schiri *m*

**refectory** *n* *(at college)* Mensa *f*

**refer 1.** *vt* ~ **sb to sb / sth** jdn an jdn / etw verweisen; ~ **sth to sb** *(query, problem)* etw an jdn weiterleiten **2.** *vi* ~ **to** *(mention, allude to)* sich beziehen auf + *acc*; *(book)* nachschlagen in + *dat*

**referee** *n* Schiedsrichter(in) *m(f)*; *(in boxing)* Ringrichter *m*; *(Brit, for job)* Referenz *f*

**reference** *n* *(allusion)* Anspielung *f* *(to* auf + *acc)*; *(for job)* Referenz *f*; *(in book)* Verweis *m*; ~ *(number* in document) Aktenzeichen *nt*; **with** ~ **to** mit Bezug auf + *acc*; **reference book** *n* Nachschlagewerk *nt*

**referendum** *n* Referendum *nt*

**refill 1.** *vt* nachfüllen **2.** *n* *(for ballpoint pen)* Ersatzmine *f*

**refine** *vt* *(purify)* raffinieren; *(improve)* verfeinern; **refined** *adj* *(genteel)* fein

**reflect 1.** vt reflektieren; fig widerspiegeln **2.** vi nachdenken (on über + acc); **reflection** n (image) Spiegelbild nt; (thought) Überlegung f; **on** ~ nach reiflicher Überlegung

**reflex** n Reflex m

**reform 1.** n Reform f **2.** vt reformieren; (person) bessern

**refrain** n ~ **from doing sth** es unterlassen, etw zu tun

**refresh** vt erfrischen; **refreshing** adj erfrischend; **refreshments** npl Erfrischungen pl

**refrigerator** n Kühlschrank m

**refuel** vt, vi auftanken

**refugee** n Flüchtling m

**refund 1.** n (of money) Rückerstattung f; **get a ~ (on sth)** sein Geld (für etw) zurückbekommen **2.** vt zurückerstatten

**refusal** n (to do sth) Weigerung f; **refuse 1.** n Müll m, Abfall m **2.** vt ablehnen; ~ **sb sth** jdm etw verweigern; ~ **to do sth** sich weigern, etw zu tun **3.** vi sich weigern

**regain** vt wiedergewinnen, wiedererlangen

**regard 1.** n **with ~ to** in Bezug auf + acc; **in this ~** in dieser Hinsicht; ~**s** (at end of letter) mit freundlichen Grüßen; **give my ~s to ...** viele Grüße an ... + acc **2.** vt ~ **sb / sth as sth** jdn / etw als etw betrachten; **as ~s ...** was ... betrifft; **regarding** prep bezüglich

+ gen; **regardless 1.** adj ~ **of** ohne Rücksicht auf + acc **2.** adv trotzdem; **carry on** ~ einfach weitermachen

**regime** n POL Regime nt

**region** n (of country) Region f, Gebiet nt; **regional** adj regional

**register 1.** n Register nt, Namensliste f **2.** vt (with an authority) registrieren lassen; (birth, death, vehicle) anmelden **3.** vi (at hotel, for course) sich anmelden; (at university) sich einschreiben; **registered** adj eingetragen; (letter) eingeschrieben; **by ~ post** per Einschreiben; **registration** n (for course) Anmeldung f; (at university) Einschreibung f; AUTO (number) (polizeiliches) Kennzeichen; **registration form** n Anmeldeformular nt; **registration number** n AUTO (polizeiliches) Kennzeichen; **registry office** n Standesamt nt

**regret 1.** n Bedauern nt **2.** vt bedauern; **regrettable** adj bedauerlich

**regular 1.** adj regelmäßig; (size) normal **2.** n (client) Stammkunde m, Stammkundin f; (in bar) Stammgast m; (petrol) Normalbenzin nt; **regularly** adv regelmäßig

**regulate** vt regulieren; (using rules) regeln; **regulation** n (rule) Vorschrift f

**rehabilitation** n Rehabilition f

**rehearsal** n Probe f; **rehearse** vt, vi proben

**reign 1.** n Herrschaft f **2.** vi herrschen (over über + acc)

**reimburse** vt (person) entschädigen; (expenses) zurückerstatten

**reindeer** n Rentier nt

**reinforce** vt verstärken

**reinstate** vt (employee) wieder einstellen

**reject 1.** n COMM Ausschussartikel m **2.** vt ablehnen; **rejection** n Ablehnung f

**relapse** n Rückfall m

**relate 1.** vt (story) erzählen; (connect) in Verbindung bringen (to mit) **2.** vi ~ **to** (refer) sich beziehen auf + acc; **related** adj verwandt (to mit); **relation** n (relative) Verwandte(r) mf; (connection) Beziehung f; **relationship** n (connection) Beziehung f; (between people) Verhältnis n

**relative 1.** n Verwandte(r) mf **2.** adj relativ; **relatively** adv relativ, verhältnismäßig

**relax 1.** vi sich entspannen; ~! reg dich nicht auf! **2.** vt (grip, conditions) lockern; **relaxation** n (rest) Entspannung f; **relaxed** adj entspannt

**release 1.** n (from prison) Entlassung f; **new / recent** ~ (film, CD) Neuerscheinung f **2.** vt (animal, hostage) freilassen; (prisoner) entlas-

sen; (handbrake) lösen; (news) veröffentlichen; (film, CD) herausbringen

**relent** vi nachgeben; **relentless, relentlessly** adj, adv (merciless) erbarmungslos; (neverending) unaufhörlich

**relevance** n Relevanz f (to für); **relevant** adj relevant (to für)

**reliable, reliably** adj, adv zuverlässig; **reliant** adj ~ **on** abhängig von

**relic** n (from past) Relikt nt

**relief** n (from anxiety, pain) Erleichterung f; (assistance) Hilfe f; **relieve** vt (pain) lindern; (boredom) überwinden; (take over from) ablösen; **I'm~d** ich bin erleichtert

**religion** n Religion f; **religious** adj religiös

**relish 1.** n (for food) würzige Soße f **2.** vt (enjoy) genießen; **I don't ~ the thought of it** der Gedanke behagt mir gar nicht

**reluctant** adj widerwillig; **be ~ to do sth** etw nur ungern tun; **reluctantly** adv widerwillig

**rely on** vt sich verlassen auf + acc; (depend on) abhängig sein von

**remain** vi bleiben; (be left over) übrig bleiben; **remainder** n a. MATH Rest m; **remaining** adj übrig; **remains** npl Überreste pl

**remark 1.** n Bemerkung f **2.** vt

~ *that* bemerken, dass; remarkable, remarkably *adj,
adv* bemerkenswert
remedy *n* Mittel *nt (for* gegen)
remember **1.** *vt* sich erinnern
an + *acc;* ~ *to do sth* daran
denken, etw zu tun; *I must
~ that* das muss ich mir merken **2.** *vi* sich erinnern
remind *vt ~ sb of* / *about sb* /
*sth* jdn an jdn / etw erinnern;
~ *sb to do sth* jdn daran erinnern, etw zu tun; *that ~s
me* dabei fällt mir ein ...; reminder *n (to pay)* Mahnung *f*
remnant *n* Rest *m*
remote **1.** *adj (place)* abgelegen; *(slight)* gering **2.** *n* TV
Fernbedienung *f;* remote
control *n* Fernsteuerung *f;
(device)* Fernbedienung *f*
removal *n* Entfernung *f;
(Brit, move from house)* Umzug *m;* removal firm *n (Brit)*
Spedition *f;* remove *vt* entfernen; *(lid)* abnehmen;
*(doubt, suspicion)* zerstreu-
en
rename *vt* umbenennen
renew *vt* erneuern *(licence,
passport, library book)* verlängern lassen
renovate *vt* renovieren
renowned *adj* berühmt *(for*
für)
rent **1.** *n* Miete *f; for~ (US)* zu
vermieten **2.** *vt (as hirer, tenant)* mieten; *(as owner)* vermieten; *~ed car* Mietwagen

*m;* rent out *vt* vermieten;
rental **1.** *n* Miete *f; (for car,
TV etc)* Leihgebühr *f* **2.** *adj*
Miet-
reorganize *vt* umorganisie-
ren
rep *n* COMM Vertreter(in) *m(f)*
repair **1.** *n* Reparatur *f* **2.** *vt* reparieren; *(damage)* wieder-
gutmachen
repay *irr vt (money)* zurückzahlen; *~ sb for sth* fig sich
bei jdm für etw revanchieren
repeat **1.** *n* RADIO, TV Wiederholung *f* **2.** *vt* wiederholen;
repetition *n* Wiederholung *f*
replace *vt* ersetzen *(with*
durch); *(put back)* zurückstellen, zurücklegen; re-
placement *n (thing, person)*
Ersatz *m; (temporarily in
job)* Vertretung *f*
replay **1.** *n (action) ~* Wiederholung *f* **2.** *n (game)* wiederholen
replica *n* Kopie *f*
reply **1.** *n* Antwort *f* **2.** *vi* antworten; *~ to sb / sth* jdm /
auf etw *acc* antworten **3.** *vt
~ that* antworten, dass
report **1.** *n* Bericht *m,* Zeugnis
*nt* **2.** *vt (tell)* berichten; *(give
information against)* mel-
den; *(to police)* anzeigen **3.**
*vi (present oneself)* sich melden; *~ sick* sich krankmel-
den; report card *n (US, in
school)* Zeugnis *nt;* reporter
*n* Reporter(in) *m(f)*
represent *vt* darstellen;

(speak for) vertreten; **representation** n (picture etc) Darstellung f; **representative 1.** n (person) Vertreter(in) m(f); (US) POL Abgeordnete(r) mf **2.** adj repräsentativ (of für)

**reproduce 1.** vt (copy) reproduzieren **2.** vi BIO sich fortpflanzen; **reproduction** n (copy) Reproduktion f; BIO Fortpflanzung f

**reptile** n Reptil nt

**republic** n Republik f; **republican 1.** adj republikanisch **2.** n Republikaner(in) m(f)

**repulsive** adj abstoßend

**reputation** n Ruf m

**request 1.** n Bitte f (for um); **on ~** auf Wunsch **2.** vt bitten um

**require** vt (need) brauchen; (desire) verlangen; **required** adj erforderlich; **requirement** n (condition) Anforderung f; (need) Bedingung f

**rerun** n Wiederholung f

**rescue 1.** n Rettung f; **come to sb's ~** jdm zu Hilfe kommen **2.** vt retten

**research 1.** n Forschung f **2.** vi forschen (into über + acc) **3.** vt erforschen; **researcher** n Forscher(in) m(f)

**resemblance** n Ähnlichkeit f (to mit); **resemble** vt ähneln + dat

**resent** vt übel nehmen

**reservation** n (booking) Reservierung f; (doubt) Vorbehalt m; **I have a ~** (in hotel, restaurant) ich habe reserviert; **reserve 1.** n (store) Vorrat m (of an + dat); (manner) Zurückhaltung f; SPORT Reservespieler(in) m(f); (game reserve) Naturschutzgebiet nt **2.** vt (book in advance) reservieren; **reserved** adj reserviert

**residence** n Wohnsitz m; (living) Aufenthalt m; **~ permit** Aufenthaltsgenehmigung f; **~ hall** Studentenwohnheim nt; **resident** n (in house) Bewohner(in) m(f); (in town, area) Einwohner(in) m(f)

**resign 1.** vt (post) zurücktreten von; (job) kündigen **2.** vi (from post) zurücktreten; (from job) kündigen; **resignation** n (from post) Rücktritt m; (from job) Kündigung f

**resist** vt widerstehen + dat; **resistance** n Widerstand m (to gegen)

**resit** (Brit) **1.** irr vt wiederholen **2.** n Wiederholungsprüfung f

**resolution** n (intention) Vorsatz m; (decision) Beschluss m

**resolve** vt (problem) lösen

**resort 1.** n (holiday resort) Urlaubsort m; **as a last ~** als letzter Ausweg **2.** vi **~ to** greifen zu; (violence) anwenden

**resources** npl (money) (Geld)mittel pl; (mineral re-

*sources)* Bodenschätze *pl*

**respect 1.** *n* Respekt *m (for vor + dat);* (consideration) Rücksicht *f (for auf + acc);* **with ~ to** in Bezug auf *+ acc;* **in this ~** in dieser Hinsicht; **with all due ~** bei allem Respekt **2.** *vt* respektieren; **respectable** *adj (person, family)* angesehen; *(district)* anständig; *(achievement, result)* beachtlich; **respected** *adj* angesehen

**respective** *adj* jeweilig; **respectively** *adv* **5 % and 10 %** ~ 5 % beziehungsweise 10 %

**respond** *vi* antworten *(to auf + acc);* (react) reagieren *(to auf + acc);* (to treatment) ansprechen *(to auf + acc);* **response** *n* Antwort *f;* (reaction) Reaktion *f;* **in ~ to** als Antwort auf *+ acc*

**responsibility** *n* Verantwortung *f;* **that's her ~** dafür ist sie verantwortlich; **responsible** *adj* verantwortlich *(for für);* (trustworthy) verantwortungsbewusst; *(job)* verantwortungsvoll

**rest 1.** *n* (relaxation) Ruhe *f;* (break) Pause *f;* (remainder) Rest *m;* **have** (or **take**) **a ~** sich ausruhen; (break) Pause machen **2.** *vi* (relax) sich ausruhen; (lean) lehnen *(on, against* an + *dat,* gegen)

**restaurant** *n* Restaurant *nt;* **restaurant car** *n (Brit)* Spei-

sewagen *m*

**restful** *adj* (holiday etc) erholsam, ruhig; **restless** *adj* unruhig

**restore** *vt* (painting, building) restaurieren; (order) wiederherstellen; (give back) zurückgeben

**restrain** *vt* (person, feelings) zurückhalten; **~ oneself** sich beherrschen

**restrict** *vt* beschränken *(to auf + acc);* **restricted** *adj* beschränkt; **restriction** *n* Einschränkung *f (on + gen)*

**rest room** *n (US)* Toilette *f*

**result 1.** *n* Ergebnis *nt;* (consequence) Folge *f;* **as a ~ of** infolge *+ gen* **2.** *vi* **~ in** führen zu; **~ from** sich ergeben aus

**resume** *vt* (work, negotiations) wieder aufnehmen; (journey) fortsetzen

**résumé** *n* Zusammenfassung *f;* (US, curriculum vitae) Lebenslauf *m*

**resuscitate** *vt* wiederbeleben

**retail** *adv* im Einzelhandel; **retailer** *n* Einzelhändler(in) *m(f)*

**retain** *vt* behalten; (heat) halten

**rethink** *irr vt* noch einmal überdenken

**retire** *vi* (from work) in den Ruhestand treten; (withdraw) sich zurückziehen; **retired** *adj* (person) pensioniert; **retirement** *n* (time of life) Ruhestand *m;* **retire-**

**ment age** *n* Rentenalter *nt*

**retrain** *vi* sich umschulen lassen

**retreat 1.** *n* Rückzug *m* (*from* aus); (*refuge*) Zufluchtsort *m* **2.** *vi* sich zurückziehen

**retrieve** *vt* (*recover*) wiederbekommen; (*rescue*) retten; (*data*) abrufen

**retrospect** *n* **in ~** rückblickend

**return 1.** *n* (*going back*) Rückkehr *f*; (*giving back*) Rückgabe *f*; (*profit*) Gewinn *m*; (*Brit, returr ticket*) Rückfahrkarte *f*; (*plane ticket*) Rückflugticket *nt*, Return *m*; **in ~** als Gegenleistung (*for* für); *many happy ~s* (*of the day*) herzlichen Glückwunsch zum Geburtstag! **2.** *vi* (*person*) zurückkehren; (*doubts, symptoms*) wieder auftreten **3.** *vt* (*give back*) zurückgeben; *I ~ed his call* ich habe ihn zurückgerufen; **return** *adj* (*bottle*) Pfand-; **return flight** *n* (*Brit*) Rückflug *m*; (*both ways*) Hin- und Rückflug *m*; **return key** *n* IT Eingabetaste *f*; **return ticket** *n* (*Brit*) Rückfahrkarte *f*; (*for plane*) Rückflugticket *nt*

**reunification** *n* Wiedervereinigung *f*; **reunion** *n* (*party*) Treffen *nt*; **reunite** *vt* wieder vereinigen

**reveal** *vt* (*make known*) enthüllen; (*secret*) verraten; **re-**

**vealing** *adj* aufschlussreich; (*dress*) freizügig

**revenge** *n* Rache *f*; (*in game*) Revanche *f*; **take~ on sb** (*for sth*) sich an jdm (für etw) rächen

**revenue** *n* Einnahmen *pl*

**reverse 1.** *n* (*back*) Rückseite *f*; (*opposite*) Gegenteil *nt*; AUTO **~** (*gear*) Rückwärtsgang *m* **2.** *adj* **in ~** order in umgekehrter Reihenfolge **3.** *vt* (*order*) umkehren; (*decision*) umstoßen; (*car*) zurücksetzen **4.** *vi* rückwärtsfahren

**review 1.** *n* (*of book, film etc*) Rezension *f*; Kritik *f*; *be under ~* überprüft werden **2.** *vt* (*book, film etc*) rezensieren; (*re-examine*) überprüfen

**revise 1.** *vt* revidieren; (*text*) überarbeiten; (*Brit, in school*) wiederholen **2.** *vi* (*Brit*) (für eine Prüfung) lernen; **revision** *n* (*of text*) Überarbeitung *f*; (*Brit*) Wiederholung *f*

**revitalize** *vt* neu beleben

**revive** *vt* (*person*) wiederbeleben; (*tradition, interest*) wieder aufleben lassen

**revolt** *n* Aufstand *m*; **revolting** *adj* widerlich

**revolution** *n* POL *fig* Revolution *f*; **revolutionary 1.** *adj* revolutionär **2.** *n* Revolutionär(in) *m(f)*

**revolve** *vi* sich drehen (*around* um); **revolver** *n* Re-

volver *m*; **revolving door** *n*
Drehtür *f*

**reward 1.** *n* Belohnung *f* **2.** *vt*
belohnen; **rewarding** *adj*
lohnend

**rewind** *irr vt* (*tape*) zurück-
spulen

**rheumatism** *n* Rheuma *nt*

**rhinoceros** *n* Nashorn *nt*

**Rhodes** *n* Rhodos *nt*

**rhubarb** *n* Rhabarber *m*

**rhyme 1.** *n* Reim *m* **2.** *vi* sich
reimen (*with* auf + *acc*)

**rhythm** *n* Rhythmus *m*

**rib** *n* Rippe *f*

**ribbon** *n* Band *nt*

**rice** *n* Reis *m*; **rice pudding** *n*
Milchreis *m*

**rich 1.** *adj* reich; (*food*) schwer
**2.** *npl* **the ~** die Reichen *pl*

**rickety** *adj* wackelig

**rid** *vt* **get ~ of sb / sth** jdn /
etw loswerden

**ridden** *pp* → **ride**

**riddle** *n* Rätsel *nt*

**ride 1.** *vt* (*horse*) reiten; (*bicycle*) fahren **2.** *vi* (*on horse*)
reiten; (*on bike*) fahren **3.** *n*
(*in vehicle, on bike*) Fahrt *f*;
(*on horse*) (Aus)ritt *m*; **go
for a ~** (*in car, on bike*) spazieren fahren; (*on horse*) reiten gehen; **take sb for a ~**
*fam* jdn verarschen; **rider** *n*
(*on horse*) Reiter(in) *m(f)*

**ridiculous** *adj* lächerlich;
**don't be ~** red keinen Unsinn!

**riding 1.** *n* Reiten *nt* **2.** *adj*
Reit-

**rifle** *n* Gewehr *nt*

**right 1.** *adj* (*correct, just*) richtig; (*opposite of left*) rech-
te(r, s); (*clothes, job etc*) passend; **be ~** (*person*) recht haben; (*clock*) richtig gehen;
**that's ~** das stimmt! **2.** *n*
Recht *nt* (*to* auf + *acc*); (*side*)
rechte Seite; **the Right** POL
die Rechte; **take a ~** AUTO
rechts abbiegen; **on the ~**
rechts (*of* von); **to the ~** nach
rechts, rechts (*of* von) **3.** *adv*
(*towards the right*) nach
rechts; (*directly*) direkt; (*exactly*) genau; **turn ~** AUTO
rechts abbiegen; **~ away** sofort; **~ now** im Moment; (*immediately*) sofort; **right angle** *n* rechter Winkel; **right-
-hand drive 1.** *n* Rechtssteue-
rung *f* **2.** *adj* rechtsgesteuert;
**right-handed** *adj* **he is ~** er
ist Rechtshänder; **right-
-hand side** *n* rechte Seite;
**on the ~** auf der rechten Seite; **rightly** *adv* zu Recht;
**right of way** *n* **have ~** AUTO
Vorfahrt haben; **right wing**
*n* POL, SPORT rechter Flügel;
**right-wing** *adj* Rechts-; **~ extremist** Rechtsradikale(r)
*mf*

**rigid** *adj* (*stiff*) starr; (*strict*)
streng

**rim** *n* (*of cup etc*) Rand *m*; (*of
wheel*) Felge *f*

**rind** *n* (*of cheese*) Rinde *f*; (*of
bacon*) Schwarte *f*; (*of fruit*)
Schale *f*

**rock**

**ring 1.** vt, vi (bell) läuten; TEL anrufen **2.** n (on finger, in boxing) Ring m; (circle) Kreis m; (at circus) Manege f; **give sb a ~** TEL jdn anrufen; **ring back** vt, vi zurückrufen; **ring up** vt, vi anrufen
**ring road** n (Brit) Umgehungsstraße f
**ringtone** n Klingelton m
**rink** n (ice rink) Eisbahn f; (for roller-skating) Rollschuhbahn f
**rinse** vt spülen
**riot** n Aufruhr m
**rip 1.** n Riss m **2.** vt zerreißen; **~ sth open** etw aufreißen **3.** vi reißen; **rip off** vt fam (person) übers Ohr hauen; **rip up** vt zerreißen
**ripe** adj (fruit) reif; **ripen** vi reifen
**rip-off** n that's a ~ fam (too expensive) das ist Wucher
**rise 1.** vi (from sitting, lying) aufstehen; (sun) aufgehen; (prices, temperature) steigen; (ground) ansteigen **2.** n (increase) Anstieg m (in + gen); (pay rise) Gehaltserhöhung f; (to power, fame) Aufstieg m (to zu); (slope) Steigung f; **risen** pp → **rise**
**risk 1.** n Risiko nt **2.** vt riskieren; **risky** adj riskant
**ritual** n Ritual nt
**rival** n Rivale m, Rivalin f (for um); COMM Konkurrent(in) m(f); **rivalry** n Rivalität f; COMM, SPORT Konkurrenz f

**river** n Fluss m; **the River Thames** (Brit), **the Thames River** (US) die Themse; **riverside** n Flussufer nt **2.** adj am Flussufer
**road** n Straße f; fig Weg m; **on the ~** (travelling) unterwegs; **roadblock** n Straßensperre f; **roadmap** n Straßenkarte f; **road rage** n aggressives Verhalten im Straßenverkehr; **roadside** n at (or by) the ~ am Straßenrand; **roadsign** n Verkehrsschild nt; **road tax** n Kraftfahrzeugsteuer f; **roadworks** npl Bauarbeiten pl; **roadworthy** adj fahrtüchtig
**roar 1.** n (of person, lion) Brüllen nt; (von Verkehr) Donnern nt **2.** vi (person, lion) brüllen (with vor + dat)
**roast 1.** n Braten m **2.** adj ~ **beef** Rinderbraten m; ~ **chicken** Brathähnchen nt; ~ **pork** Schweinebraten m; ~ **potatoes** pl im Backofen gebratene Kartoffeln **3.** vt (meat) braten
**rob** vt bestehlen; (bank, shop) ausrauben; **robbery** n Raub m
**robe** n (US, dressing gown) Morgenrock m; (of judge, priest etc) Robe f, Talar m
**robin** n Rotkehlchen nt
**robot** n Roboter m
**rock 1.** n (substance) Stein m; (boulder) Felsbrocken m; MUS Rock m; **on the ~s**

(drink) mit Eis; (marriage) gescheitert 2. vt, vi (swing) schaukeln; (dance) rocken; **rock climbing** n Klettern nt

**rocket** n Rakete f; (in salad) Rucola m

**rocking chair** n Schaukelstuhl m

**rocky** adj (landscape) felsig; (path) steinig

**rod** n (bar) Stange f; (fishing rod) Rute f

**rode** pt → **ride**

**rogue** n Schurke m

**role** n Rolle f; **role model** n Vorbild nt

**roll** 1. n (of film, paper etc) Rolle f; (bread roll) Brötchen nt 2. vt (move by rolling) rollen; (cigarette) drehen 3. vi (move by rolling) rollen; **roll out** vt (pastry) ausrollen; **roll over** vi (person) sich umdrehen; **roll up** 1. vi (fam) (arrive) antanzen 2. vt (carpet) aufrollen; **roll one's sleeves up** die Ärmel hochkrempeln

**roller** n (hair roller) (Locken)wickler m; **roller coaster** n Achterbahn f; **roller skates** npl Rollschuhe pl; **roller-skating** n Rollschuhlaufen nt; **rolling pin** n Nudelholz nt; **roll-on** (deodorant) n Deoroller m

**ROM** acr = **read only memory**; ROM m

**Roman** 1. adj römisch 2. n Römer(in) m(f); **Roman Cath-**

olic 1. adj römisch-katholisch 2. n Katholik(in) m(f)

**romance** n Romantik f; (love affair) Romanze f

**Romania** n Rumänien nt; **Romanian** 1. adj rumänisch 2. n Rumäne m, Rumänin f; (language) Rumänisch nt

**romantic** adj romantisch

**roof** n Dach nt; **roof rack** n Dachgepäckträger m

**rook** n (in chess) Turm m

**room** n Zimmer nt, Raum m; (large, for gatherings etc) Saal m; (space) Platz m; fig Spielraum m; **make ~ for** Platz machen für; **roommate** n Zimmergenosse m, Zimmergenossin f; **room service** n Zimmerservice m

**root** n Wurzel f; **root out** vt ausrotten; **root vegetable** n Wurzelgemüse nt

**rope** n Seil nt; **know the ~s** sich auskennen

**rose** 1. pt → **rise** 2. n Rose f

**rosé** n Rosé(wein) m

**rot** vi verfaulen

**rotate** 1. vt (turn) rotieren lassen 2. vi rotieren; **rotation** n (turning) Rotation f; **in ~** abwechselnd

**rotten** adj (decayed) faul; (mean) gemein; (unpleasant) scheußlich; (ill) elend

**rough** 1. adj (not smooth) rau; (path) uneben; (coarse, violent) grob; (crossing) stürmisch; (without comforts) hart; (unfinished, makeshift) grob; *(approximate)* ungefähr; **~ draft** Rohentwurf m; *I have a ~ idea* ich habe eine ungefähre Vorstellung **2.** *adv* **sleep ~** im Freien schlafen **3.** *vt* **~ it** primitiv leben; **roughly** *adv* grob; *(approximately)* ungefähr

**round 1.** *adj* rund **2.** *adv* **all ~** *(on all sides)* rundherum; *I'll be ~ at 8* ich werde um acht Uhr da sein; *the other way ~* umgekehrt **3.** *prep* *(surrounding)* um *(... herum)*; **~ (about)** *(approximately)* ungefähr; **~ the corner** um die Ecke; *go ~ the world* um die Welt reisen; *she lives ~ here* sie wohnt hier in der Gegend **4.** *n* Runde f; *(of bread, toast)* Scheibe f; *it's my ~ (of drinks)* die Runde geht auf mich **5.** *vt* *(corner)* biegen um; **round off** *vt* abrunden; **round up** *vt (number, price)* aufrunden

**roundabout 1.** *n (Brit)* AUTO Kreisverkehr m; *(Brit, merry-go-round)* Karussell nt **2.** *adj* umständlich; **round-the-clock** *adj* rund um die Uhr; **round trip** *n* Rundreise f; **round-trip ticket** *n (US)* Rückfahrkarte f; *(for plane)* Rückflugticket nt

**route** *n* Route f; *(bus, plane etc service)* Linie f; *fig* Weg m

**routine 1.** *n* Routine f **2.** *adj* Routine-

**row 1.** *n (line)* Reihe f; *three*

*times in a ~* dreimal hintereinander **2.** *vt, vi (boat)* rudern **3.** *n (noise)* Krach m; *(dispute)* Streit m

**rowboat** *n (US)* Ruderboot nt

**row house** *n (US)* Reihenhaus nt

**rowing** *n* Rudern nt; **rowing boat** *n (Brit)* Ruderboot nt; **rowing machine** *n* Rudergerät nt

**royal** *adj* königlich; **royalty** *n (family)* Mitglieder pl der königlichen Familie; **royalties** pl *(from book, music)* Tantiemen pl

**RSPCA** *abbr* = **Royal Society for the Prevention of Cruelty to Animals** britischer Tierschutzverein

**RSVP** *abbr* = **répondez s'il vous plaît** u. A. w. g.

**rub** *vt* reiben; *fig* in vt massieren; **rub out** *vt (with eraser)* ausradieren

**rubber** *n* Gummi m; *(Brit, eraser)* Radiergummi m; *(US) fam (contraceptive)* Gummi m; **rubber stamp** *n* Stempel m

**rubbish** *n* Abfall m; *(non-sense)* Quatsch m; *(poor-quality thing)* Mist m; *don't talk ~* red keinen Unsinn!; **rubbish bin** *n* Mülleimer m; **rubbish dump** *n* Müllabladeplatz m

**rubble** *n* Schutt m

**ruby** *n (stone)* Rubin m

**rucksack** *n* Rucksack m

**rude** adj (impolite) unhöflich; (indecent) unanständig

**rug** n Teppich m; (next to bed) Bettvorleger m; (for knees) Wolldecke f

**rugby** n Rugby nt

**rugged** adj (coastline) zerklüftet; (features) markant

**ruin 1.** n Ruine f; (financial, social) Ruin m **2.** vt ruinieren

**rule 1.** n (governing) Herrschaft f; **as a ~** in der Regel **2.** vt, vi (govern) regieren; (decide) entscheiden;

**ruler** n Lineal nt; (person) Herrscher(in) m(f)

**rum** n Rum m

**rumble** vi (stomach) knurren; (train, truck) rumpeln

**rummage** vi ~ (**around**) herumstöbern

**rumor** (US), **rumour** n Gerücht nt

**run 1.** vt (race, distance) laufen; (machine, engine, computer program, water) laufen lassen; (manage) leiten, führen; (car) unterhalten; **I ran her home** ich habe sie nach Hause gefahren **2.** vi (move quickly) rennen; (bus, train) fahren; (path etc) verlaufen; (machine, engine, computer program) laufen; (flow) fließen; (colours, make-up) verlaufen; ~ **for President** für die Präsidentschaft kandidieren; **be ~ning low** knapp werden; **my nose is ~ning** mir läuft

die Nase; **it ~s in the family** es liegt in der Familie **3.** n (on foot) Lauf m; (in car) Spazierfahrt f; (series) Reihe f; (sudden demand) Ansturm m (on auf + acc); (in tights) Laufmasche f; (in cricket, baseball) Lauf m; **go for a ~** laufen gehen; (in car) eine Spazierfahrt machen; **in the long ~** auf die Dauer; **on the ~** auf der Flucht (from vor + dat); **run about** vi herumlaufen; **run away** vi weglaufen; **run down** vt (with car) umfahren; (criticize) heruntermachen; **be ~** (tired) abgespannt sein; **run into** vt (meet) zufällig treffen; (problem) stoßen auf + acc; **run off** vi weglaufen; **run out** vi (person) hinausrennen; (lease, time) ablaufen; (money, supplies) ausgehen; **he ran out of money** ihm ging das Geld aus; **run over** vt (with car) überfahren; **run up** vt (debt, bill) machen

**rung** pp → **ring**

**runner** n (athlete) Läufer(in) m(f); **do a ~** fam wegrennen; **runner bean** n (Brit) Stangenbohne f

**running 1.** n SPORT Laufen nt; (management) Leitung f, Führung f **2.** adj (water) fließend; ~ **costs** Betriebskosten pl; (for car) Unterhaltskosten pl; **3 days ~** 3 Tage hintereinander

**runny** adj (food) flüssig; (nose) laufend

**runway** n Start- und Landebahn f

**rural** adj ländlich

**rush 1.** n Eile f; (for tickets etc) Ansturm m (for auf + acc); **be in a ~** es eilig haben; **there's no ~** es ist nicht 2. vt (do too quickly) hastig machen; (meal) hastig essen; **~ sb to hospital** jdn auf dem schnellsten Weg ins Krankenhaus bringen; **don't ~**

**me** dräng mich nicht 3. vi (hurry) eilen; **rush hour** n Hauptverkehrszeit f

**rusk** n Zwieback m

**Russia** n Russland nt; **Russian 1.** adj russisch **2.** n Russe m, Russin f; (language) Russisch nt

**rust 1.** n Rost m 2. vi rosten; **rustproof** adj rostfrei; **rusty** adj rostig

**ruthless** adj rücksichtslos; (treatment, criticism) schonungslos

**rye** n Roggen m

# S

**sabotage** vt sabotieren

**sachet** n Päckchen nt

**sack 1.** n (bag) Sack m; **get the ~** fam rausgeschmissen werden **2.** vt fam rausschmeißen

**sacred** adj heilig

**sacrifice 1.** n Opfer nt **2.** vt opfern

**sad** adj traurig

**saddle** n Sattel m

**sadistic** adj sadistisch

**sadly** adv (unfortunately) leider

**safe 1.** adj (free from danger) sicher; (out of danger) in Sicherheit; (careful) vorsichtig; **have a ~ journey** gute Fahrt! **2.** n Safe m; **safeguard 1.** n Schutz m **2.** vt

schützen (against vor + dat); **safely** adv sicher; (arrive) wohlbehalten; (drive) vorsichtig; **safety** n Sicherheit f; **safety belt** n Sicherheitsgurt m; **safety pin** n Sicherheitsnadel f

**Sagittarius** n ASTR Schütze m

**Sahara** n **the ~** (Desert) die (Wüste) Sahara

**said** pt, pp → **say**

**sail 1.** n Segel m; **set ~** losfahren (for nach) **2.** vi (in yacht) segeln; (on ship) mit dem Schiff fahren; (ship) auslaufen (for nach) **3.** vt (yacht) segeln mit; (ship) steuern; **sailboat** n (US) Segelboot nt; **sailing** n **go ~** segeln gehen; **sailing boat** n (Brit) Segelboot nt; **sailor** n Seemann m; (in navy) Matrose m

**saint** n Heilige(r) mf

**sake** n for the ~ of um + gen ... willen; **for your** ~ deinetwegen, dir zuliebe

**salad** n Salat m; **salad cream** n (Brit) majonäseartige Salatsoße; **salad dressing** n Salatsoße f

**salary** n Gehalt nt

**sale** n Verkauf m; (at reduced prices) Ausverkauf m; **for** ~ zu verkaufen; **sales clerk** n (US) Verkäufer(in) m(f); **salesman** n Verkäufer m; (rep) Vertreter m; **sales rep** n Vertreter(in) m(f); **saleswoman** n Verkäuferin f; (rep) Vertreterin f

**salmon** n Lachs m

**saloon** n (ship's lounge) Salon m; (US, bar) Kneipe f

**salt 1.** n Salz nt **2.** vt (flavour) salzen; (roads) mit Salz streuen; **salt cellar**, **salt shaker** (US) n Salzstreuer m; **salty** adj salzig

**same 1.** adj the ~ (similar) der / die / das gleiche, die gleichen pl; (identical) der- / die- / dasselbe, dieselben pl; **they live in the ~ house** sie wohnen im selben Haus **2.** pron the ~ (similar) der / die / das Gleiche, die Gleichen pl; (identical) der- / die- / dasselbe, dieselben pl; **all the** ~ trotzdem; **the ~ to you** gleichfalls; **it's**

**all the** ~ **to me** es ist mir egal **3.** adv the ~ gleich

**sample 1.** n Probe f; (of fabric) Muster nt **2.** vt probieren

**sanctions** npl POL Sanktionen pl

**sanctuary** n (refuge) Zuflucht f; (for animals) Schutzgebiet nt

**sand** n Sand m

**sandal** n Sandale f

**sandwich** n Sandwich nt

**sandy** adj (full of sand) sandig; ~ **beach** Sandstrand m

**sane** adj geistig gesund, normal; (sensible) vernünftig

**sang** pt → **sing**

**sanitary** adj hygienisch; **sanitary napkin** (US), **sanitary towel** n Damenbinde f

**sank** pt → **sink**

**Santa (Claus)** n der Weihnachtsmann

**sarcastic** adj sarkastisch

**sardine** n Sardine f

**sari** n Sari m (von indischen Frauen getragenes Gewand)

**sat** pt, pp → **sit**

**Sat** abbr → **Saturday** Sa.

**satellite** n Satellit m; **satellite dish** n Satellitenschüssel f

**satin** n Satin m

**satisfaction** n (contentment) Zufriedenheit f; **is that to your** ~? bist du / sind Sie damit zufrieden?; **satisfactory** adj zufriedenstellend; **satisfied** adj zufrieden (with mit); **satisfy** vt zufriedenstellen; (conditions) erfüllen; (need, demand) befriedigen; **satis-fying** adj befriedigend

**Saturday** n Samstag m, Sonnabend m; → **Tuesday**

**sauce** n Soße f; **saucepan** n Kochtopf m; **saucer** n Untertasse f

**Saudi Arabia** n Saudi-Arabien nt

**sauna** n Sauna f

**sausage** n Wurst f; **sausage roll** n mit Wurst gefülltes Blätterteigröllchen

**savage** adj (person, attack) brutal; (animal) wild

**save 1.** vt (rescue) retten (from vor + dat); (money, time, electricity etc) sparen; (strength) schonen; IT speichern; ~ **sb's life** jdm das Leben retten **2.** vi sparen **3.** n (in soccer) Parade f; **save up** vi sparen (for auf + acc); **saving** n (of money) Sparen nt; ~**s** pl Ersparnisse pl; ~**s account** Sparkonto nt

**savory** (US), **savoury** adj (not sweet) pikant

**saw 1.** vt, vi sägen **2.** n (tool) Säge f **3.** pt → **see**; **sawdust** n Sägemehl nt

**saxophone** n Saxophon nt

**say 1.** vt sagen (to sb jdm); (prayer) sprechen; **what does the letter ~?** was steht im Brief?; **the rules... that...** in den Regeln heißt es, dass ...; **he's said to be rich** er soll reich sein **2.** n **have a ~ in sth** bei etw ein Mitspra-

cherecht haben **3.** adv zum Beispiel; **saying** n Sprichwort nt

**scab** n (on cut) Schorf m

**scaffolding** n (Bau)gerüst nt

**scale 1.** n (of map etc) Maßstab m; (on thermometer etc) Skala f; (of pay) Tarifsystem nt; MUS Tonleiter f; (of fish, snake) Schuppe f; **to ~** maßstabsgerecht; **on a large / small ~** in großem / kleinem Umfang; **scales** npl (for weighing) Waage f

**scalp** n Kopfhaut f

**scan 1.** vt (examine) genau prüfen; (read quickly) überfliegen; IT scannen **2.** n MED Ultraschall m; **scan in** vt IT einscannen

**scandal** n Skandal m

**Scandinavia** n Skandinavien nt; **Scandinavian 1.** adj skandinavisch **2.** n Skandinavier(in) m(f)

**scanner** n Scanner m

**scapegoat** n Sündenbock m

**scar** n Narbe f

**scarce** adj selten; (in short supply) knapp; **scarcely** adv kaum

**scare 1.** n (general alarm) Panik f **2.** vt erschrecken; **be ~d** Angst haben (of vor + dat)

**scarf** n Schal m; (on head) Kopftuch nt

**scarlet** adj scharlachrot; **scarlet fever** n Scharlach m

**scary** adj (film, story) gruselig

**scatter** vt verstreuen; (seed,

*gravel*) streuen; (*disperse*) auseinandertreiben

**scene** n (*location*) Ort m; (*division of play*) THEAT Szene f; (*view*) Anblick m; **make a ~** eine Szene machen; **scenery** n (*landscape*) Landschaft f; THEAT Kulissen pl; **scenic** adj (*landscape*) malerisch; **~ route** landschaftlich schöne Strecke

**scent** n (*perfume*) Parfüm nt; (*smell*) Duft m

**sceptical** adj (*Brit*) skeptisch

**schedule** 1. n (*plan*) Programm nt; (*of work*) Zeitplan m; (*list*) Liste f; (*US, of trains, buses, air traffic*) Fahr-, Flugplan m; **on ~** planmäßig; **be behind ~ with sth** mit etw in Verzug sein 2. vt **the meeting is ~d for next Monday** die Besprechung ist für nächsten Montag angesetzt; **scheduled** adj (*departure, arrival*) planmäßig; **~ flight** Linienflug m

**scheme** 1. n (*plan*) Plan m; (*project*) Projekt nt; (*dishonest*) Intrige f 2. vi intrigieren

**scholar** n Gelehrte(r) mf; **scholarship** n (*grant*) Stipendium nt

**school** n Schule f; (*university department*) Fachbereich m; (*US, university*) Universität f; **school bag** n Schultasche f; **schoolbook** n Schulbuch nt; **schoolboy** n Schüler m;

**schoolgirl** n Schülerin f; **schoolteacher** n Lehrer(in) m(f); **schoolwork** n Schularbeiten pl

**sciatica** n Ischias m

**science** n Wissenschaft f; (*natural science*) Naturwissenschaft f; **science fiction** n Sciencefiction f; **scientific** adj wissenschaftlich; **scientist** n Wissenschaftler(in) m(f); (*natural sciences*) Naturwissenschaftler(in) m(f)

**scissors** npl Schere f

**scone** n kleines süßes Hefebrötchen mit oder ohne Rosinen, das mit Butter oder Dickrahm und Marmelade gegessen wird

**scoop** 1. n (*exclusive story*) Exklusivbericht m; **a ~ of ice-cream** eine Kugel Eis 2. vt (*up*) schaufeln

**scooter** n (*Motor*)roller m; (*toy*) (Tret)roller m

**scope** n Umfang m; (*opportunity*) Möglichkeit f

**score** 1. n SPORT Spielstand m; (*final result*) Spielergebnis nt; (*in quiz etc*) Punktestand m; MUS Partitur f; **keep (the) ~** zählen 2. vt (*goal*) schießen; (*points*) punkten 3. vi (*keep score*) mitzählen; **scoreboard** n Anzeigetafel f

**scorn** n Verachtung f; **scornful** adj verächtlich

**Scorpio** n ASTR Skorpion m

**scorpion** n Skorpion m

**Scot** n Schotte m, Schottin f

**Scotch** n (whisky) schottischer Whisky, Scotch m
**Scotch tape®** n (US) Tesafilm® m
**Scotland** n Schottland nt; **Scotsman** n Schotte m; **Scotswoman** n Schottin f; **Scottish** adj schottisch
**scout** n (boy scout) Pfadfinder m
**scrambled eggs** npl Rührei nt
**scrap 1.** n (bit) Stückchen nt, Fetzen m; (metal) Schrott m **2.** vt (car) verschrotten; (plan) verwerfen
**scrape 1.** n (scratch) Kratzer m **2.** vt (car) schrammen; (wall) streifen; ~ **one's knee** sich das Knie schürfen; **scrape through** vi (exam) mit knapper Not bestehen
**scrap heap** n Schrotthaufen m; **scrap metal** n Schrott m; **scrap paper** n Schmierpapier f
**scratch 1.** n (mark) Kratzer m; **start from** ~ von vorne anfangen **2.** vt kratzen; (car) zerkratzen; ~ **one's arm** sich am Arm kratzen
**scream 1.** n Schrei m **2.** vi schreien (with vor + dat); ~ **at sb** jdn anschreien
**screen 1.** n TV, IT Bildschirm m; FILM Leinwand f **2.** vt (film) zeigen; (applicants, luggage) überprüfen; **screenplay** n Drehbuch nt; **screensaver** n IT Bild-

schirmschoner m
**screw 1.** n Schraube f **2.** vt vulg (have sex with) ficken; ~ **sth to sth** etw an etw acc schrauben; ~ **off / on** (lid) ab- / aufschrauben; **screw up** vt (paper) zusammenknüllen; (make a mess of) vermasseln; **screwdriver** n Schraubenzieher m
**scribble** vt, vi kritzeln
**script** n (of play) Text m; (of film) Drehbuch nt; (style of writing) Schrift f
**scroll** vi IT scrollen; **scroll down** vi IT runterscrollen; **scroll up** vi IT raufscrollen; **scroll bar** n IT Scrollbar f
**scrub** vt schrubben
**scruffy** adj vergammelt
**scuba-diving** n Sporttauchen nt
**sculptor** n Bildhauer(in) m(f); **sculpture** n ART Bildhauerei f; (statue) Skulptur f
**sea** n Meer nt, See f; **seafood** n Meeresfrüchte pl; **sea front** n Strandpromenade f; **seagull** n Möwe f
**seal 1.** n (animal) Robbe f; (stamp, impression) Siegel nt; TECH Verschluss m; (ring etc) Dichtung f **2.** vt versiegeln; (envelope) zukleben
**seam** n Naht f
**search 1.** n Suche f (for nach); **do a** ~ **for** IT suchen nach; **in** ~ **of** auf der Suche nach **2.** vi suchen (for nach) **3.** vt durchsuchen; **search en-**

gine n IT Suchmaschine f
**seashell** n Muschel f; **seashore** n Strand m; **seasick** adj seekrank; **seaside** n **at the ~** am Meer; **seaside resort** n Seebad nt
**season** 1. n Jahreszeit f, Saison f; **high / low ~** Hoch- / Nebensaison f 2. vt (flavour) würzen
**seasoning** n Gewürz nt
**season ticket** n RAIL Zeitkarte f; THEAT Abonnement nt; SPORT Dauerkarte f
**seat** 1. n (place) Platz m; (chair) Sitz m; **take a ~** setzen Sie sich 2. vt **the hall ~s 300** der Saal hat 300 Sitzplätze; **please be ~ed** bitte setzen Sie sich; **remain ~ed** sitzen bleiben; **seat belt** n Sicherheitsgurt m
**sea view** n Seeblick m; **seaweed** n Seetang m
**secluded** adj abgelegen
**second** 1. adj zweite(r, s); **the ~ of June** der zweite Juni 2. adv (in second position) an zweiter Stelle; (secondly) zweitens; **he came ~** er ist Zweiter geworden 3. n (of time) Sekunde f; (moment) Augenblick m; **~ (gear)** der zweite Gang; (second helping) zweite Portion; **just a ~** (einen) Augenblick!; **secondary** adj (less important) zweitrangig; **~ education** höhere Schulbildung f; **~ school** weiterführende

Schule; **second-class** 1. adj (ticket) zweiter Klasse; **~ stamp** Briefmarke für nicht bevorzugt beförderte Sendungen 2. adv (travel) zweiter Klasse; **second-hand** adj, adv gebraucht en; (information) aus zweiter Hand; **secondly** adv zweitens; **second-rate** adj pej zweitklassig
**secret** 1. n Geheimnis nt 2. adj geheim; (admirer) heimlich
**secretary** n Sekretär(in) m(f); (minister) Minister(in) m(f); **Secretary of State** n (US) Außenminister(in) m(f); **secretary's office** n Sekretariat nt
**secretive** adj geheimnistuerisch; **secretly** adv heimlich
**sect** n Sekte f
**section** n (part) Teil m; (of document) Abschnitt m; (department) Abteilung f
**secure** 1. adj (safe) sicher (from vor + dat); (firmly fixed) fest 2. vt (make firm) befestigen; (window, door) fest verschließen; **securely** adv (safely) sicher; **security** n Sicherheit f
**sedative** n Beruhigungsmittel nt
**seduce** vt verführen; **seductive** adj verführerisch
**see** 1. vt sehen; (understand) verstehen; (check) nachsehen; (accompany) bringen; (visit) besuchen; (talk to)

sprechen; ~ *the doctor* zum
Arzt gehen; ~ *sb home* jdn
nach Hause begleiten; ~
*you* tschüs!; ~ *you on Friday*
bis Freitag! **2.** *vi* sehen;
(*understand*) verstehen;
(*check*) nachsehen; (*you*)
siehst du / sehen Sie! *we'll
~ mal* sehen; **see about** *vt*
(*attend to*) sich kümmern
um; **see off** *vt* (*say goodbye
to*) verabschieden; **see out**
*vt* (*show out*) zur Tür bringen; **see through** *vt* **see
sth through** etw zu Ende
bringen; ~ *sb / sth* jdn /
etw durchschauen; **see to** *vt*
sich kümmern um; ~ *it that
... it that ...* sieh zu / sehen Sie zu, dass

**seed** *n* (*of plant*) Samen *m*; (*in
fruit*) Kern *m*; **seedless** *adj*
kernlos; **seedy** *adj* zwielichtig

**seek** *vi* suchen; (*fame*) stre-
ben nach; ~ *sb's advice*
jdn um Rat fragen

**seem** *vi* scheinen; *he ~s (to
be) honest* er scheint ehrlich
zu sein

**seen** *pp* → **see**

**seesaw** *n* Wippe *f*

**see-through** *adj* durchsichtig

**segment** *n* Teil *m*

**seize** *vt* packen; (*confiscate*)
beschlagnahmen; (*opportu-
nity, power*) ergreifen

**seldom** *adv* selten

**select 1.** *adj* (*exclusive*) exklusiv **2.** *vt* auswählen; **selec-**

tion *n* Auswahl *f* (*of* an + *dat*)
**self** *n* Selbst *nt*, Ich *nt*; *he's his
old ~ again* er ist wieder
ganz der Alte; **self-adhesive** *adj* selbstklebend;
**self-assured** *adj* selbstsicher;
**self-catering** *adj* für Selbst-
versorger; **self-centred** *adj*
egozentrisch; **self-confidence** *n* Selbstbewusstsein
*nt*; **self-confident** *adj* selbstbewusst; **self-conscious** *adj*
befangen, verklemmt; **self-
-contained** *adj* (*flat*) separat;
**self-control** *n* Selbstbeherrschung *f*; **self-defence** *n*
Selbstverteidigung *f*; **self-
-employed** *adj* selbstständig

**selfish**, **selfishly** *adj*, *adv*
egoistisch, selbstsüchtig

**self-pity** *n* Selbstmitleid *nt*;
**self-respect** *n* Selbstach-
tung *f*; **self-service 1.** *n*
Selbstbedienung *f* **2.** *adj*
Selbstbedienungs-

**sell 1.** *vt* verkaufen; ~ *sb sth,
~ sth to sb* jdm etw verkaufen;
*do you ~ postcards?* haben
Sie Postkarten? **2.** *vi* (*product*) sich verkaufen; **sell
out** *vt* **be sold out** ausverkauft sein; **sell-by date** *n*
Haltbarkeitsdatum *nt*

**Sellotape®** *n* (*Brit*) Tesafilm®
*m*

**semi** *n* (*Brit, house*) Doppelhaushälfte *f*; **semicircle** *n*
Halbkreis *m*; **semicolon** *n*
Semikolon *nt*; **semide-
tached** (**house**) *n* (*Brit*)

Doppelhaushälfte f; **semifinal** n Halbfinale nt

**seminar** n Seminar nt

**senate** n Senat m; **senator** n Senator(in) m(f)

**send** vt schicken; **~ sb sth, ~ sth to sb** jdm etw schicken; **~ her my best wishes** grüße sie von mir; **send away 1.** vt wegschicken **2.** vi **~ for** anfordern; **send back** vt zurückschicken; **send for** vt (person) holen lassen; (by post) anfordern; **send off** vt (by post) abschicken

**sender** n Absender(in) m(f)

**senior 1.** adj (older) älter; (high-ranking) höher; (pupils) älter; **he's ~ to me** er ist mir übergeordnet **2.** n **he's eight years my ~** er ist acht Jahre älter als ich; **senior citizen** n Senior(in) m(f)

**sensation** n Gefühl nt; (excitement, person, thing) Sensation f; **sensational** adj sensationell

**sense 1.** n (faculty, meaning) Sinn m; (feeling) Gefühl n; (understanding) Verstand m; **~ of smell / taste** Geruchs- / Geschmackssinn m; **have a ~ of humour** Humor haben; **make ~** (sentence etc) einen Sinn ergeben; (be sensible) Sinn machen; **in a ~** gewissermaßen **2.** vt spüren; **senseless** adj (stupid) sinnlos

**sensible, sensibly** adj, adv vernünftig

**sensitive** adj empfindlich (to gegen); (easily hurt) sensibel; (subject) heikel

**sent** pt, pp **→ send**

**sentence 1.** n LING Satz m; LAW Strafe f **2.** vt verurteilen (to zu)

**sentiment** n (sentimentality) Sentimentalität f; (opinion) Ansicht f; **sentimental** adj sentimental

**separate 1.** adj getrennt, separat; (individual) einzeln **2.** vt trennen (from von); **they are ~d** (couple) sie leben getrennt **3.** vi sich trennen; **separately** adv getrennt; (singly) einzeln

**September** n September m; **in ~** im September; **on the 2nd of ~** am 2. September; **at the beginning / in the middle / at the end of ~** Anfang / Mitte / Ende September; **last / next ~** letzten / nächsten September

**septic** adj vereitert

**sequel** n (to film, book) Fortsetzung f (to von)

**sequence** n (order) Reihenfolge f

**Serbia** n Serbien nt

**sergeant** n Polizeimeister(in) m(f); MIL Feldwebel(in) m(f)

**serial 1.** n TV Serie f; (in newspaper etc) Fortsetzungsroman m **2.** adj IT seriell; **~**

***number*** Seriennummer *f*
**series** *n sing* Reihe *f*; TV, RADIO
Serie *f*
**serious** *adj* ernst; *(injury, illness, mistake)* schwer; *(discussion)* ernsthaft; *are you
~?* ist das dein Ernst?; **seriously** *adv* ernsthaft; *(hurt)*
schwer; *~?* im Ernst?; *take
sb ~* jdn ernst nehmen
**sermon** *n* REL Predigt *f*
**servant** *n* Diener(in) *m(f)*;
**serve 1.** *vt (customer)* bedienen; *(food)* servieren; *(one's
country etc)* dienen + *dat*;
*(sentence)* verbüßen; *I'm being ~d* ich werde schon be-
dient; *it ~s him right* es geschieht ihm recht **2.** *vi* dienen *(as* als*)*, aufschlagen **3.**
*n*, Aufschlag *m*
**server** *n* IT Server *m*
**service 1.** *n (in shop, hotel)*
Bedienung *f*; *(activity, amen-
ity)* Dienstleistung *f*; *(set of
dishes)* Service *nt*; AUTO Ins-
pektion *f*; TECH Wartung *f*;
REL Gottesdienst *m*, Aufschlag *m*; *train / bus*
Zug- / Busverbindung *f*; *~
not included* „Bedienung
nicht inbegriffen" **2.** *vt* AUTO,
TECH warten; **service area** *n
(on motorway)* Raststätte *f*
*(mit* Tankstelle*)*; **service
charge** *n* Bedienung *f*; **service provider** *n* IT Provider
*m*; **service station** *n* Tankstelle *f*
**session** *n (of court, assembly)*

Sitzung *f*
**set 1.** *vt (place)* stellen; *(lay
flat)* legen; *(arrange)* anord-
nen; *(table)* decken; *(trap, record)* aufstellen; *(time,
price)* festsetzen; *(watch,
alarm)* stellen *(for* auf
+ *acc)*; *~ sb a task* jdm eine
Aufgabe stellen; *~ free* freilassen; *~ a good example*
ein gutes Beispiel geben;
*the novel is ~ in London*
der Roman spielt in London
**2.** *vi (sun)* untergehen; *(be-
come hard)* fest werden; *(bone)* zusammenwachsen
**3.** *n (collection of things)*
Satz *m*; *(of cutlery, furniture)*
Garnitur *f*; *(group of people)*
Kreis *m*; RADIO, TV Apparat
*m*, Satz *m*; THEAT Bühnen-
bild *nt*; FILM (Film)kulisse *f*
**4.** *adj (agreed, prescribed)*
festgelegt; *(ready)* bereit; *~
meal* Menü *nt*; **set aside** *vt
(money)* beiseitelegen;
*(time)* einplanen; **set off 1.**
*vi* aufbrechen *(for* nach*)* **2.**
*vt (alarm)* auslösen; *(en-
hance)* hervorheben; **set
out 1.** *vi* aufbrechen *(for*
nach*)* **2.** *vt (chairs, chesspiec-
es etc)* aufstellen; *(state)* dar-
legen; *~ to do sth (intend)*
beabsichtigen, etw zu tun;
**set up 1.** *vt (firm, organization)* gründen; *(stall, tent,
camera)* aufbauen; *(meeting)* vereinbaren **2.** *vi ~ as
a doctor* sich als Arzt nieder-

lassen

**setback** n Rückschlag m

**settee** n Sofa nt, Couch f

**setting** n (of novel, film) Schauplatz m; (surroundings) Umgebung f

**settle** 1. vt (bill, debt) begleichen; (dispute) beilegen; (question) klären; (stomach) beruhigen 2. vi ~ (**down**) (feel at home) sich einleben; (calm down) sich beruhigen; **settle in** vi (in place) sich einleben; (in job) sich eingewöhnen; **settlement** n (of bill, debt) Begleichung f; (colony) Siedlung f; **reach a ~** sich einigen

**setup** n (organization) Organisation f; (situation) Situation f

**seven** 1. num sieben 2. n Sieben f; → **eight**; **seventeen** 1. num siebzehn 2. n Siebzehn f; → **eight**; **seventeenth** adj siebzehnte(r, s); → **eighth**; **seventh** 1. adj siebte(r, s) 2. n (fraction) Siebtel nt; → **eighth**; **seventieth** adj siebzigste(r, s); → **eighth**; **seventy** 1. num siebzig; **~one** einundsiebzig 2. n Siebzig f; **be in one's seventies** in den Siebzigern sein; → **eight**

**several** adj, pron mehrere

**severe** adj (strict) streng; (serious) schwer; (pain) stark; (winter) hart; **severely** adv (harshly) hart; (seriously) schwer

**sew** vt, vi nähen

**sewage** n Abwasser nt; **sewer** n Abwasserkanal m

**sewing** n Nähen nt; **sewing machine** n Nähmaschine f

**sewn** → **sew**

**sex** n Sex m; (gender) Geschlecht nt; **have ~** Sex haben (with mit); **sexism** n Sexismus m; **sexist** 1. adj sexistisch 2. n Sexist(in) m(f); **sex life** n Sex(ual)leben nt

**sexual** adj sexuell; **~ discrimination / harassment** sexuelle Diskriminierung / Belästigung; **~ intercourse** m; Geschlechtsverkehr m; **sexuality** n Sexualität f

**sexy** adj sexy; geil

**Seychelles** npl Seychellen pl

**shack** n Hütte f

**shade** 1. n (shadow) Schatten m; (for lamp) (Lampen)schirm m; (colour) Farbton m; **~s** (US, sunglasses) Sonnenbrille f 2. vt (from sun) abschirmen; (in drawing) schattieren

**shadow** n Schatten m

**shady** adj schattig; fig zwielichtig

**shake** 1. vt (shock) erschüttern; **~ hands with sb** jdm die Hand geben; **~ one's head** den Kopf schütteln 2. vi (tremble) zittern; (building, ground) schwanken; **shake off** vt abschütteln; **shaken** pp → **shake**; **shaky** adj (trembling) zittrig; (*table, chair, position*) wackelig

**shall** *vaux* werden; (*in questions*) sollen; **I ~ do my best** ich werde mein Bestes tun; **~ I come too?** soll ich mitkommen?; **where ~ we go?** wo gehen wir hin?

**shallow** *adj* seicht; (*person*) oberflächlich

**shame** *n* (*feeling*) Scham *f*; (*disgrace*) Schande *f*; **what a ~!** wie schade!; **~ on you** schäm dich / schämen Sie sich!; **it's a ~ that ...** schade, dass ...

**shampoo** 1. *n* Shampoo *nt*; **have a ~ and set** sich die Haare waschen und legen lassen 2. *vt* (*hair*) waschen; (*carpet*) schamponieren

**shandy** *n* Radler *m*, Alsterwasser *nt*

**shan't** *contr* = **shall not**

**shape** 1. *n* Form *f*; (*unidentified figure*) Gestalt *f*; **in the ~ of** in Form + *gen*; **be in good ~** (*healthwise*) in guter Verfassung sein; **take ~** (*plan, idea*) annehmen 2. *vt* (*clay, person*) formen; **-shaped** *suf* -förmig

**share** 1. *n* Anteil + *dat* (*in, of* an *m*); FIN Aktie *f* 2. *vt, vi* teilen; **shareholder** *n* Aktionär(in) *m(f)*

**shark** *n* Haifisch *m*

**sharp** 1. *adj* scharf; (*pin*) spitz; (*person*) scharfsinnig; (*pain*) heftig; (*increase, fall*) abrupt; **C/F ~** MUS Cis / Dis *nt* 2. *adv* **at 2 o'clock ~** Punkt 2 Uhr; **sharpen** *vt* (*knife*) schärfen; (*pencil*) spitzen; **sharpener** *n* (*pencil sharpener*) Spitzer *m*

**shatter** 1. *vt* zerschmettern; *fig* zerstören 2. *vi* zerspringen; **shattered** *adj* (*exhausted*) kaputt

**shave** 1. *vt* rasieren 2. *vi* sich rasieren 3. *n* Rasur *f*; **that was a close ~** *fig* das war knapp; **shave off** *vt* **shave one's beard off** sich den Bart abrasieren; **shaven** 1. *pp* → **shave** 2. *adj* (*head*) kahl geschoren; **shaver** *n* ELEC Rasierapparat *m*; **shaving brush** *n* Rasierpinsel *m*; **shaving foam** *n* Rasierschaum *m*; **shaving tackle** *n* Rasierzeug *nt*

**shawl** *n* Tuch *nt*

**she** *pron* sie

**shed** 1. *n* Schuppen *m* 2. *vt* (*tears, blood*) vergießen; (*hair, leaves*) verlieren

**she'd** *contr* = **she had; she would**

**sheep** *n* Schaf *nt*; **sheepdog** *n* Schäferhund *m*; **sheepskin** *n* Schaffell *nt*

**sheer** *adj* (*madness*) rein; (*steep*) steil; **by ~ chance** rein zufällig

**sheet** *n* (*on bed*) Betttuch *nt*; (*of paper*) Blatt *nt*; (*of metal*) Platte *f*; (*of glass*) Scheibe *f*

**shelf** *n* Bücherbord *nt*, Regal

*nt;* **shelves** *pl (item of furniture)* Regal *nt*

**she'll** *contr* = **she will; she shall**

**shell 1.** *n (of egg, nut)* Schale *f;* *(seashell)* Muschel *f* **2.** *vt (peas, nuts)* schälen; **shellfish** *n (as food)* Meeresfrüchte *pl*

**shelter 1.** *n (protection)* Schutz *m;* *(accommodation)* Unterkunft *f;* *(bus shelter)* Wartehäuschen *nt* **2.** *vt* schützen *(from* vor + *dat)* **3.** *vi* sich unterstellen; **sheltered** *adj (spot)* geschützt; *(life)* behütet

**shelve** *vt fig* aufschieben; **shelves** *pl →* **shelf**

**shepherd** *n* Schäfer *m;* **shepherd's pie** *n* Hackfleischauflauf mit Decke aus Kartoffelpüree

**sherry** *n* Sherry *m*

**she's** *contr* = **she is; she has**

**shield 1.** *n* Schild *m;* *fig* Schutz *m* **2.** *vt* schützen *(from* vor + *dat)*

**shift 1.** *n (change)* Veränderung *f;* *(period at work, workers)* Schicht *f;* *(on keyboard)* Umschalttaste *f* **2.** *vt (furniture etc)* verrücken **3.** *vi (move)* sich bewegen; *(move up)* rutschen; **shift key** *n* Umschalttaste *f*

**shin** *n* Schienbein *nt*

**shine 1.** *vi (be shiny)* glänzen; *(sun)* scheinen; *(lamp)*

leuchten **2.** *vt (polish)* polieren **3.** *n* Glanz *m*

**shingles** *nsing* MED Gürtelrose *f*

**shiny** *adj* glänzend

**ship 1.** *n* Schiff *nt* **2.** *vt (send)* versenden; *(by ship)* verschiffen; **shipment** *n (goods)* Sendung *f;* *(sent by ship)* Ladung *f;* **shipwreck** *n* Schiffbruch *m;* **shipyard** *n* Werft *f*

**shirt** *n* Hemd *nt*

**shit** *n vulg* Scheiße *f;* **~!** Scheiße!; **shitty** *adj fam* beschissen

**shiver** *vi* zittern *(with* vor + *dat)*

**shock 1.** *n (mental, emotional)* Schock *m;* **be in ~** unter Schock stehen; **get a ~** ELEC einen Schlag bekommen **2.** *vt* schockieren; **shock absorber** *n* Stoßdämpfer *m;* **shocked** *adj* schockiert *(by* über + *acc)*; **shocking** *adj* schockierend

**shoe** *n* Schuh *m;* **shoelace** *n* Schnürsenkel *m;* **shoe polish** *n* Schuhcreme *f*

**shone** *pt, pp →* **shine**

**shook** *pt →* **shake**

**shoot 1.** *vt (wound)* anschießen; *(kill)* erschießen; FILM drehen; *fam (heroin)* drücken **2.** *vi (with gun, move quickly)* schießen; **~ at sb** auf jdn schießen **3.** *n (of plant)* Trieb *m;* **shooting** *n (exchange of gunfire)* Schie-

**show**

ßerei f; (killing) Erschie-
ßung f

**shop 1.** n Geschäft nt, Laden
m **2.** vi einkaufen; **shopper**
n Käufer(in) m(f); **shop
assistant** n Verkäufer(in)
m(f); **shopkeeper** n Ge-
schäftsinhaber(in) m(f);
**shoplifting** n (activity) Einkaufen nt; (goods)
Einkäufe pl; **do the ~** einkaufen; **go ~** einkaufen gehen; **shopping bag** n Einkaufstasche f; **shopping
cart** n (US) Einkaufswagen
m; **shopping centre** (US),
**shopping centre** n Einkaufszentrum nt; **shopping
list** n Einkaufszettel m;
**shopping trolley** n (Brit)
Einkaufswagen m; **shop
window** n Schaufenster nt
**shore** n Ufer nt; **~ on** an Land
**short** adj kurz; (person) klein;
**be ~ of money** knapp bei
Kasse sein; **be ~ of time** wenig Zeit haben; **~ of breath**
kurzatmig; **cut ~** (holiday)
abbrechen; **we are two ~**
wir haben zwei zu wenig;
**it's ~ for ...** das ist die Kurz-
form von ...; **shortage** n
Knappheit f (of an + dat);
**shortbread** n Buttergebäck
nt; **short circuit** n Kurzschluss m; **shortcoming** n
Unzulänglichkeit f; (of person) Fehler m; **shortcut** n
(quicker route) Abkürzung
f; IT Shortcut m; **shorten** vt

kürzen; (in time) verkürzen;
**shortlist** n **be on the ~** in der
engeren Wahl sein; **short-
lived** adj kurzlebig; **shortly**
adv bald; **shorts** npl Shorts
pl; **short-sighted** adj kurzsichtig; **short-sleeved** adj
kurzärmelig; **short-stay
car park** n Kurzzeitpark-
platz m; **short story** n Kurzgeschichte f; **short-term** adj
kurzfristig

**shot 1.** pt, pp → **shoot 2.** n
(from gun, in soccer) Schuss
m; PHOT, FILM Aufnahme f;
(injection) Spritze f; (of alcohol) Schuss m

**should 1.** pt → **shall 2.** vaux **I ~
go now** ich sollte jetzt ge-
hen; **you ~n't have said** that
das hättest du / hätten Sie
nicht sagen sollen; **that ~ be
enough** das müsste reichen
**shoulder** n Schulter f
**shouldn't** contr = **should not**
**should've** contr = **should
have**
**shout 1.** n Schrei m; (call) Ruf
m **2.** vt rufen; (order) brüllen
**3.** vi schreien; **~ at** anschrei-
en
**shove 1.** vt (person) schubsen;
(car, table etc) schieben **2.** vi
(in crowd) drängeln
**shovel 1.** n Schaufel f **2.** vt
schaufeln
**show 1.** vt zeigen; **~ sb sth,
sth to sb** jdm etw zeigen; **~
sb in** jdn hereinführen; **~
sb out** jdn zur Tür bringen

**2.** n FILM, THEAT Vorstellung f; TV Show f; (exhibition) Ausstellung f; **show off** vi pej angeben; **show round** vt herumführen; **show sb round the house / the town** jdm das Haus / die Stadt zeigen; **show up** vi (arrive) auftauchen

**shower 1.** n Dusche f; (rain) Schauer m; **have** or **take a ~** duschen **2.** vi (wash) sich duschen

**showing** n FILM Vorstellung f

**shown** pp → **show**

**showroom** n Ausstellungsraum m

**shrank** pt → **shrink**

**shred 1.** n (of paper, fabric) Fetzen m **2.** vt (in shredder) (im Reißwolf) zerkleinern; **shredder** n (for paper) Reißwolf m

**shrimp** n Garnele f

**shrink** vi schrumpfen; (clothes) eingehen

**shrivel** vi (**up**) schrumpfen; (skin) runzlig werden

**Shrove Tuesday** n Fastnachtsdienstag m

**shrub** n Busch m, Strauch m

**shrug** vt, vi (**one's shoulders**) die Achseln zucken

**shrunk** pp → **shrink**

**shudder** vi schaudern; (ground, building) beben

**shuffle** vt, vi mischen

**shut 1.** vt zumachen, schließen; **~ your face!** fam halt den Mund! **2.** vi schließen

**3.** adj geschlossen; **we're ~** wir haben geschlossen; **shut down 1.** vt schließen; (computer) ausschalten **2.** vi schließen; (computer) sich ausschalten; What is **shut in** vt einschließen; **shut out** vt (lock out) aussperren; **shut oneself out** sich aussperren; **shut up 1.** vt (lock up) abschließen; (silence) zum Schweigen bringen **2.** vi (keep quiet) den Mund halten; **~!** halt den Mund!; **shutter** n (on window) (Fenster)laden m; **shutter release** n Auslöser m

**shuttle bus** n Shuttlebus m

**shuttlecock** n Federball m

**shuttle service** n Pendelverkehr m

**shy** adj schüchtern; (animal) scheu

**Sicily** n Sizilien nt

**sick** adj krank; (joke) makaber; **be ~** (Brit, vomit) sich übergeben; **be off ~** wegen Krankheit fehlen; **I feel ~** mir ist schlecht; **be ~ of sb / sth** jdn / etw satthaben; **it makes me ~** fig es ekelt mich an; **sickbag** n Spucktüte f; **sick leave** n **be on ~** krankgeschrieben sein; **sickness** n Krankheit f; (Brit, nausea) Übelkeit f

**side** n Seite f; (of road) Rand m; (of mountain) Hang m; SPORT Mannschaft f; **by my ~** neben mir; **~ by ~**

beneinander 2. *adj* (*door, entrance*) Seiten-; **sideboard** *n* Anrichte *f*; **sideburns** *npl* Koteletten *pl*; **side dish** *n* Beilage *f*; **side effect** *n* Nebenwirkung *f*; **side order** *n* Beilage *f*; **side road** *n* Nebenstraße *f*; **sidewalk** *n* (US) Bürgersteig *m*; **sideways** *adv* seitwärts

**sieve** *n* Sieb *nt*

**sift** *vt* (*flour etc*) sieben

**sigh** *vi* seufzen

**sight** *n* (*power of seeing*) Sehvermögen *nt*; (*view, thing seen*) Anblick *m*; **~s** *pl* (*of city etc*) Sehenswürdigkeiten *pl*; **have bad ~** schlecht sehen; **lose ~ of** aus den Augen verlieren; **out of ~** außer Sicht; **sightseeing** *n* **go ~** Sehenswürdigkeiten besichtigen; **~ tour** Rundfahrt *f*

**sign** *n* (*notice, road sign*) Schild *nt* 2. *vt* unterschreiben 3. *vi* unterschreiben; **~ for sth** den Empfang einer Sache *gen* bestätigen; **~ in / out** sich ein- / austragen; **sign up** *vi* (*for course*) sich einschreiben; MIL sich verpflichten

**signal** 1. *n* Signal *nt* 2. *vi* (*car driver*) blinken

**signature** *n* Unterschrift *f*

**significant** *adj* (*important*) bedeutend, wichtig; (*meaning sth*) bedeutsam

**sign language** *n* Zeichen-

sprache *f*; **signpost** *n* Wegweiser *m*

**silence** 1. *n* Stille *f*; (*of person*) Schweigen *nt*; **~!** Ruhe! 2. *vt* zum Schweigen bringen; **silent** *adj* still; (*taciturn*) schweigsam; **she remained ~** sie schwieg

**silk** 1. *n* Seide *f* 2. *adj* Seiden-

**silly** *adj* dumm, albern; **don't do anything ~** mach keine Dummheiten; **the ~ season** das Sommerloch

**silver** 1. *n* Silber *nt*; (*coins*) Silbermünzen *pl* 2. *adj* Silber-; **silver wedding** *n* silberne Hochzeit

**similar** *adj* ähnlich (*to dat*); **similarity** *n* Ähnlichkeit *f* (*to mit*); **similarly** *adv* (*equally*) ebenso

**simple** *adj* einfach; (*unsophisticated*) einfach; **simplify** *vt* vereinfachen; **simply** *adv* einfach; (*merely*) bloß; (*dress*) schlicht

**simulate** *vt* simulieren

**simultaneous, simultaneously** *adj, adv* gleichzeitig

**sin** 1. *n* Sünde *f* 2. *vi* sündigen

**since** 1. *adv* seitdem; (*in the meantime*) seitdem 2. *prep* seit + *dat*; **ever ~ 1995** schon seit 1995 3. *conj* (*time*) seit, seitdem; (*because*) da, weil; **ever ~ I've known her** seit ich sie kenne; **it's ages ~ I've seen him** ich habe ihn seit Langem nicht mehr gesehen

**sincere** *adj* aufrichtig; **sincerely** *adv* aufrichtig; **Yours** ~ mit freundlichen Grüßen

**sing** *vt, vi* singen

**Singapore** *n* Singapur *nt*

**singer** *n* Sänger(in) *m(f)*

**single 1.** *adj* (*one only*) einzig; (*not double*) einfach; (*bed, room*) Einzel-; (*unmarried*) ledig; (*Brit, ticket*) einfach **2.** *n* (*Brit, ticket*) einfache Fahrkarte; MUS Single *f*; **single out** *vt* (*choose*) auswählen; **single-handed, single-handedly** *adv* im Alleingang; **single parent** *n* Alleinerziehende(r) *mf*

**singular** *n* Singular *m*

**sinister** *adj* unheimlich

**sink 1.** *vt* (*ship*) versenken **2.** *vi* sinken **3.** *n* Spülbecken *nt*; (*in bathroom*) Waschbecken *nt*

**sip** *vt* nippen an + *dat*

**sir** *n* yes, ~ ja(, mein Herr); *can I help you,* **~?** kann ich Ihnen helfen?; *Sir James* (*title*) Sir James

**sister** *n* Schwester *f*; (*Brit, nurse*) Oberschwester *f*; **sister-in-law** *n* Schwägerin *f*

**sit** *vi* (*be sitting*) sitzen; (*sit down*) sich setzen; (*committee, court*) tagen **2.** *vt* (*Brit, exam*) machen; **sit down** *vi* sich hinsetzen; **sit up** *vi* (*from lying position*) sich aufsetzen

**site** *n* Platz *m*; (*building site*) Baustelle *f*; (*website*) Site *f*

**sitting** *n* (*meeting, for portrait*) Sitzung *f*; **sitting room** *n* Wohnzimmer *nt*

**situated** *adj* **be** ~ liegen

**situation** *n* (*circumstances*) Situation *f*, Lage *f*; (*job*) Stelle *f*; **'~s vacant / wanted'** (*Brit*) „Stellenangebote / Stellengesuche"

**six 1.** *num* sechs **2.** *n* Sechs *f*; → *eight*; **sixpack** *n* (*of beer etc*) Sechserpack *nt*; **sixteen 1.** *num* sechzehn **2.** *n* Sechzehn *f*; → *eight*; **sixteenth** *adj* sechzehnte(r, s); → *eighth*; **sixth 1.** *adj* sechste(r, s); **~ form** (*Brit*) ≈ Oberstufe *f* **2.** *n* (*fraction*) Sechstel *nt*; → *eighth*; **sixtieth** *adj* sechzigste(r, s); → *eighth*; **sixty 1.** *num* sechzig; **~one** einundsechzig **2.** *n* Sechzig *f*; **be in one's sixties** in den Sechzigern sein; → *eight*

**size** *n* Größe *f*; **what ~ are you?** welche Größe hast du / haben Sie?; *a ~ too big* eine Nummer zu groß

**sizzle** *vi* brutzeln

**skate 1.** *n* Schlittschuh *m*; (*roller skate*) Rollschuh *m* **2.** *vi* Schlittschuh laufen; (*roller-skate*) Rollschuh laufen; **skateboard** *n* Skateboard *nt*; **skating** *n* Eislauf *m*; (*roller-skating*) Rollschuhlauf *m*; **skating rink** *n* Eisbahn *f*; (*for roller-skating*) Rollschuhbahn *f*

**skeleton** n Skelett nt
**skeptical** n (US) → **sceptical**
**sketch 1.** n Skizze f; THEAT Sketch m **2.** vt skizzieren
**ski 1.** n Ski m **2.** vi Ski laufen; **ski boot** n Skistiefel m
**skid** vi AUTO schleudern
**skier** n Skiläufer(in) m(f); **skiing** n Skilaufen nt; **go ~** Ski laufen gehen; **~ holiday** Skiurlaub m; **skiing instructor** n Skilehrer(in) m(f)
**skilful, skilfully** adj, adv geschickt
**ski-lift** n Skilift m
**skill** n Geschick nt; (acquired technique) Fertigkeit f; **skilled** adj geschickt (at, in in + dat); (worker) Fach-; (work) fachmännisch
**skim** vt **~ (off)** (fat etc) abschöpfen; **~ (through)** (read) überfliegen; **skimmed milk** n Magermilch f
**skin** n Haut f; (fur) Fell nt; (peel) Schale f; **skinny** adj dünn
**skip 1.** vi hüpfen; (with rope) seilspringen **2.** vt (miss out) überspringen; (meal) ausfallen lassen; (school, lesson) schwänzen
**ski pants** npl Skihose f; **ski pass** n Skipass m; **ski pole** n Skistock m; **ski resort** n Skiort m
**skirt** n Rock m
**ski run** n (Ski)abfahrt f; **ski stick** n Skistock m; **ski tow** n Schlepplift m

**skittle** n Kegel m; **~s** (game) Kegeln nt
**skive** vi **~ (off)** (from school) schwänzen; (from work) blaumachen
**skull** n Schädel m
**sky** n Himmel m; **skydiving** n Fallschirmspringen nt; **skylight** n Dachfenster nt; **skyscraper** n Wolkenkratzer m
**slam 1.** vt (door) zuschlagen; **slam on** vt **slam the brakes on** voll auf die Bremse treten
**slander 1.** n Verleumdung f **2.** vt verleumden
**slang** n Slang m
**slap 1.** n Klaps m; (across face) Ohrfeige f **2.** vt **~ sb's face** jdn ohrfeigen
**slash 1.** n (punctuation mark) Schrägstrich m **2.** vt (face, tyre) aufschlitzen; (prices) stark herabsetzen
**slate** n (rock) Schiefer m; (roof slate) Schieferplatte f
**slaughter** vt (animals) schlachten; (people) abschlachten
**Slav 1.** adj slawisch **2.** n Slawe m, Slawin f
**slave 1.** n Sklave m, Sklavin f; **slave away** vi schuften; **slave-driver** n fam Sklaventreiber(in) m(f); **slavery** n Sklaverei f
**sleaze** n (corruption) Korruption f; **sleazy** adj (bar, district) zwielichtig
**sledge** n Schlitten m
**sleep 1.** vi schlafen **2.** n Schlaf

*m*; **put to ~** (*animal*) einschläfern; **sleep in** *vi* (*lie in*) ausschlafen; **sleeper** *n* RAIL (*train*) Schlafwagenzug *m*; (*carriage*) Schlafwagen *m*; **sleeping bag** *n* Schlafsack *m*; **sleeping car** *n* Schlafwagen *m*; **sleeping pill** *n* Schlaftablette *f*; **sleepless** *adj* schlaflos; **sleepy** *adj* schläfrig; (*place*) verschlafen

**sleet** *n* Schneeregen *m*

**sleeve** *n* Ärmel *m*; **sleeveless** *adj* ärmellos

**sleigh** *n* (Pferde)schlitten *m*

**slender** *adj* schlank; *fig* gering

**slept** *pt, pp* → **sleep**

**slice 1.** *n* Scheibe *f*; (*of cake, tart, pizza*) Stück *nt* **2.** *vt* ~ (**up**) in Scheiben schneiden

**slid** *pt, pp* → **slide**

**slide 1.** *vt* gleiten lassen; (*push*) schieben **2.** *vi* gleiten; (*slip*) rutschen **3.** *n* PHOT Dia *nt*; (*in playground*) Rutschbahn *f*; (*Brit, for hair*) Spange *f*

**slight** *adj* leicht; (*problem, difference*) klein; **not in the ~est** nicht im Geringsten; **slightly** *adv* etwas; (*injured*) leicht

**slim 1.** *adj* (*person*) schlank; (*book*) dünn; (*chance, hope*) gering **2.** *vi* abnehmen

**slime** *n* Schleim *m*; **slimy** *adj* schleimig

**sling 1.** *vt* werfen **2.** *n* (*for*

*arm*) Schlinge *f*

**slip 1.** *n* (*mistake*) Flüchtigkeitsfehler *m*; **~ of paper** Zettel *m*; **~ in** (*put*) stecken; **~ on / off** (*garment*) an- / ausziehen; **it ~ped my mind** ich habe es vergessen **3.** *vi* (*lose balance*) (aus)rutschen; **slipper** *n* Hausschuh *m*; **slippery** *adj* (*path, road*) glatt; (*soap, fish*) glitschig; **slip-road** *n* (*Brit, onto motorway*) Auffahrt *f*; (*off motorway*) Ausfahrt *f*

**slit 1.** *vt* aufschlitzen **2.** *n* Schlitz *m*

**slope 1.** *n* Neigung *f*; (*side of hill*) Hang *m* **2.** *vi* (*be sloping*) schräg sein; **sloping** *adj* (*floor, roof*) schräg

**sloppy** *adj* (*careless*) schlampig

**slot** *n* (*opening*) Schlitz *m*; IT Steckplatz *m*; **we have a ~ free at 2** (*free time*) um 2 ist noch ein Termin frei; **slot machine** *n* Automat *m*; (*for gambling*) Spielautomat *m*

**Slovak 1.** *adj* slowakisch **2.** *n* (*person*) Slowake *m*, Slowakin *f*; (*language*) Slowakisch *nt*; **Slovakia** *n* Slowakei *f*

**Slovene, Slovenian 1.** *adj* slowenisch **2.** *n* (*person*) Slowene *m*, Slowenin *f*; (*language*) Slowenisch *nt*; **Slovenia** *n* Slowenien *nt*

**slow** *adj* langsam; (*business*) flau; **be ~** (*clock*) nachgehen; (*stupid*) begriffstutzig sein; **slow down** vi langsamer werden; (when driving / walking) langsamer fahren / gehen; **slowly** adv langsam; **slow motion** n in ~ in Zeitlupe

**slug** n ZOOL Nacktschnecke f

**slum** n Slum m

**slump 1.** n Rückgang m (in an + dat) **2.** vi (onto chair etc) sich fallen lassen; (prices) stürzen

**slung** pt, pp → **sling**

**slur** n (insult) Verleumdung f; **slurred** adj undeutlich

**slush** n (snow) Schneematsch m; **slushy** adj matschig; fig schmalzig

**slut** n pej Schlampe f

**smack 1.** n Klaps m **2.** vt ~ **sb** jdm einen Klaps geben

**small** adj klein; **small ads** npl (Brit) Kleinanzeigen pl; **small change** n Kleingeld nt; **small letters** npl **in ~** in Kleinbuchstaben; **smallpox** n Pocken pl; **small print** n **the ~** das Kleingedruckte; **small-scale** adj (map) in kleinem Maßstab; **small talk** n Konversation f, Smalltalk m

**smart** adj (elegant) schick; (clever) clever; **smartarse** f, **smartass** (US) n Klugscheißer(in) m(f); **smart card** n Chipkarte f; **smartly** adv (dressed) schick

**smash 1.** n (car crash) Zusammenstoß m, Schmetterball

m **2.** vt (break) zerschlagen; fig (record) brechen, deutlich übertreffen **3.** vi (break) zerbrechen; ~ **into** (car) krachen gegen

**smear 1.** n (mark) Fleck m; MED Abstrich m; fig Verleumdung f **2.** vt (spread) schmieren; (make dirty) beschmieren; fig verleumden

**smell 1.** vt riechen **2.** vi riechen (of nach); (unpleasantly) stinken **3.** n Geruch m; (unpleasant) Gestank m; **smelly** adj übel riechend; **smelt** pt, pp → **smell**

**smile 1.** n Lächeln nt **2.** vi lächeln; ~ **at sb** jdn anlächeln

**smog** n Smog m

**smoke 1.** n Rauch m **2.** vt rauchen; (food) räuchern **3.** vi rauchen; **smoke alarm** n Rauchmelder m; **smoked** adj (food) geräuchert; **smoke-free** adj (zone, building) rauchfrei; **smoker** n Raucher(in) m(f); **smoking** n Rauchen nt; **'no ~'** „Rauchen verboten"

**smooth 1.** adj glatt; (flight, crossing) ruhig; (movement) geschmeidig; (without problems) reibungslos; pej (person) aalglatt **2.** vt (hair, dress) glatt streichen; (surface) glätten; **smoothly** adv, reibungslos; **run ~** (engine) ruhig laufen

**smudge** vt (writing, lipstick) verschmieren

**smug** adj selbstgefällig

**smuggle** vt schmuggeln; ~ **in / out** herein- / herausschmuggeln

**smutty** adj (obscene) schmutzig

**snack** n Imbiss m; **have a ~** eine Kleinigkeit essen

**snail** n Schnecke f; **snail mail** n fam Schneckenpost f

**snake** n Schlange f

**snap** 1. n (photo) Schnappschuss m 2. adj (decision) spontan 3. vt (break) zerbrechen; (rope) zerreißen 4. vi (break) brechen; (rope) reißen; (bite) schnappen (at nach); **snap fastener** n (US) Druckknopf m; **snapshot** n Schnappschuss m

**snatch** vt (grab) schnappen

**sneak** vi (move) schleichen; **sneakers** npl (US) Turnschuhe pl

**sneeze** vi niesen

**sniff** 1. vi schniefen; (smell) schnüffeln (at an + dat) 2. vt schnuppern an + dat; (glue) schnüffeln

**snob** n Snob m; **snobbish** adj versnobt

**snog** vi, vt knutschen

**snooker** n Snooker nt

**snoop** vi ~ (**around**) (herum)schnüffeln

**snooze** n, vi (**have a**) ~ ein Nickerchen machen

**snore** vi schnarchen

**snorkel** n Schnorchel m; **snorkelling** n Schnorcheln

nt

**snout** n Schnauze f

**snow** 1. n Schnee m 2. vi schneien; **snowball** n Schneeball m; **snowboard** n Snowboard nt; **snowboarding** n Snowboarding nt; **snowdrift** n Schneewehe f; **snowflake** n Schneeflocke f; **snowman** n Schneemann m; **snowplough**, **snowplow** (US) n Schneepflug m; **snowstorm** n Schneesturm m; **snowy** adj (region) schneereich; (landscape) verschneit

**snug** adj (person, place) gemütlich

**snuggle up** vi ~ **to sb** sich an jdn ankuscheln

**so** 1. adv so; ~ **many / much** so viele / viel; ~ **do I** ich auch; **I hope** ~ hoffentlich; **30 or** ~ etwa 30; ~ **what?** na und?; **and** ~ on und so weiter 2. conj (therefore) also, deshalb

**soak** vt durchnässen; (leave in liquid) einweichen; **I'm ~ed** ich bin klatschnass; **soaking** adj ~ (**wet**) klatschnass

**soap** n Seife f; **soap** (**opera**) n Seifenoper f

**sob** vi schluchzen

**sober** adj nüchtern; **sober up** vi nüchtern werden

**so-called** adj sogenannt

**soccer** n Fußball m

**sociable** adj gesellig

**social** adj sozial; (sociable)

gesellig; **socialist 1.** *adj* sozialistisch **2.** *n* Sozialist(in) *m(f)*; **socialize** *vi* unter die Leute gehen; **social security** *n (Brit)* Sozialhilfe *f*; *(US)* Sozialversicherung *f*

**society** *n* Gesellschaft *f*; *(club)* Verein *m*

**sock** *n* Socke *f*

**socket** *n* ELEC Steckdose *f*

**soda** *n (soda water)* Soda *f*; *(US, pop)* Limo *f*

**sofa** *n* Sofa *nt*; **sofa bed** *n* Schlafcouch *f*

**soft** *adj* weich; *(quiet)* leise; *(lighting)* gedämpft; *(kind)* gutmütig; *(weak)* nachgiebig; ~ **drink** alkoholfreies Getränk; **softly** *adv* sanft; *(quietly)* leise; **software** *n* IT Software *f*

**soil** *n* Erde *f*; *(ground)* Boden *m*

**solar** *adj* Sonnen-, Solar-; **solarium** *n* Solarium *nt*

**sold** *pt, pp* → **sell**

**soldier** *n* Soldat(in) *m(f)*

**sole 1.** *n* Sohle *f*; *(fish)* Seezunge *f* **2.** *vt* besohlen **3.** *adj* einzig, *(owner, responsibility)* alleinig; **solely** *adv* nur

**solemn** *adj* feierlich; *(person)* ernst

**solicitor** *n (Brit)* Rechtsanwalt *m*, Rechtsanwältin *f*

**solid** *adj (hard)* fest; *(gold, oak etc)* massiv; *(solidly built)* solide; *(meal)* kräftig; *three hours* ~ drei volle

Stunden

**solitary** *adj* einsam; *(single)* einzeln; **solitude** *n* Einsamkeit *f*

**soluble** *adj* löslich; **solution** *n* Lösung *f (to + gen)*; **solve** *vt* lösen

**somber** *(US)*, **sombre** *adj* düster

**some 1.** *adj* etwas; *(with plural nouns)* einige; ~ **woman (or other)** irgendeine Frau; *would you like* ~ **more (wine)?** möchten Sie noch etwas (Wein)? **2.** *pron* etwas; *(plural)* einige (aus) der Mannschaft **3.** *adv* ~ **50 people (or so)** etwa 50 Leute

**somebody** *pron* jemand; ~ **(or other)** irgendjemand; ~ **else** jemand anders; **someday** *adv* irgendwann; **somehow** *adv* irgendwie; **someone** *pron* → **somebody**; **someplace** *adv (US)* → **somewhere**; **something 1.** *pron* etwas; ~ **else** etwas anderes; ~ **nice** etwas Nettes; *would you like* ~ **to drink?** möchtest du / möchten Sie etwas trinken? **2.** *adv* ~ **like 20** ungefähr 20; **sometime** *adv* irgendwann; **sometimes** *adv* manchmal; **somewhat** *adv* ein wenig; **somewhere** *adv* irgendwo; *(to a place)* irgendwohin; ~ **else** irgendwo anders; *(to* *another place)* irgendwo anders hin

**son** *n* Sohn *m*

**song** *n* Lied *nt*; Song *m*

**son-in-law** *n* Schwiegersohn *m*

**soon** *adv* bald; *(early)* früh; **too ~** *as* **as I ...** so bald ich ...; *as* **~** *as possible* so bald wie möglich; **sooner** *adv* *(time)* früher; *(for preference)* lieber

**soot** *n* Ruß *m*

**soothe** *vt* beruhigen; *(pain)* lindern

**sophisticated** *adj (person)* kultiviert; *(machine)* hoch entwickelt; *(plan)* ausgeklügelt

**soppy** *adj fam* rührselig

**soprano** *n* Sopran *m*

**sore 1.** *adj be ~* wehtun; *have a ~ throat* Halsschmerzen haben **2.** *n* wunde Stelle

**sorrow** *n* Kummer *m*

**sorry** *adj (sight, figure)* traurig; *(I'm) ~ (excusing)* Entschuldigung!; *I'm ~ (regretful)* es tut mir leid; *~?* wie bitte?; *I feel ~ for him* er tut mir leid

**sort 1.** *n* Art *f*; *what ~ of film is it?* was für ein Film ist das?; *a ~ of* eine Art + *gen*; *all ~s of things* alles Mögliche **2.** *adv ~ of fam* irgendwie **3.** *vt* sortieren; *everything's ~ed* alles ist geregelt; *(dealt with)* alles ist geregelt; **sort out** *vt (classify etc)* sortieren; *(problems)* lösen

**sought** *pt, pp* → **seek**

**soul** *n* Seele *f*; MUS Soul *m*

**sound 1.** *adj (healthy)* gesund; *(safe)* sicher; *(sensible)* vernünftig; *(theory)* stichhaltig; *(thrashing)* tüchtig **2.** *n (noise)* Geräusch *nt*; MUS Klang *m*; TV Ton *m* **3.** *vt ~ one's horn* hupen **4.** *vi (seem)* klingen *(like* wie); **soundcard** *n* IT Soundkarte *f*; **soundproof** *adj* schalldicht

**soup** *n* Suppe *f*

**sour** *adj* sauer; *fig* mürrisch

**source** *n* Quelle *f*; *fig* Ursprung *m*

**sour cream** *n* saure Sahne *f*

**south 1.** *n* Süden *m*; *to the ~ of* südlich von **2.** *adv (go, face)* nach Süden **3.** *adj* Süd-; **South Africa** *n* Südafrika *nt*; **South African 1.** *adj* südafrikanisch **2.** *n* Südafrikaner(in) *m(f)*; **South America** *n* Südamerika *nt*; **South American 1.** *adj* südamerikanisch **2.** *n* Südamerikaner(in) *m(f)*; **southbound** *adj (in)* Richtung Süden; **southern** *adj* Süd-, südlich; **southwards** *adv* nach Süden

**souvenir** *n* Andenken *nt* *(of* an + *acc)*

**sow 1.** *vt* säen; *(field)* besäen **2.** *n (pig)* Sau *f*

**soya bean** *n* Sojabohne *f*

**soy sauce** *n* Sojasoße *f*

**spa** *n (place)* Kurort *m*

**space** n (room) Platz m, Raum m; (outer space) Weltraum m; (gap) Zwischenraum m; (for parking) Lücke f; **space bar** n Leertaste f; **spacecraft** n Raumschiff nt; **space shuttle** n Raumfähre f

**spacing** n (in text) Zeilenabstand m; **double ~** zweizeiliger Abstand

**spacious** adj geräumig

**spade** n Spaten m; **~s**, Pik f

**spaghetti** nsing Spaghetti pl

**Spain** n Spanien nt

**spam** n IT Spam m

**Spaniard** n Spanier(in) m(f);

**Spanish 1.** adj spanisch **2.** n (language) Spanisch nt

**spanner** n (Brit) Schraubenschlüssel m

**spare 1.** adj (as replacement) Ersatz-; **~ part** Ersatzteil nt; **~ room** Gästezimmer nt; **~ time** Freizeit f; **~ tyre** Ersatzreifen m **2.** n (spare part) Ersatzteil m **3.** vt (lives, feelings) verschonen; **can you ~ (me) a moment?** hättest du / hätten Sie einen Moment Zeit?

**spark** n Funke m; **sparkle** vi funkeln; **sparkling wine** n Schaumwein m, Sekt m; **spark plug** n Zündkerze f

**sparrow** n Spatz m

**sparse** adj spärlich; **sparsely** adv **~ populated** dünn besiedelt

**spasm** n MED Krampf m

**spat** pt, pp → **spit**

**speak 1.** vt sprechen; **can you ~ French?** sprechen Sie Französisch?; **~ one's mind** seine Meinung sagen **2.** vi sprechen (to mit, zu); (make speech) reden; **~ing** TEL am Apparat; **so to ~** sozusagen; **speak up** vi (louder) lauter sprechen; **speaker** n Sprecher(in) m(f); (public speaker) Redner(in) m(f); (loudspeaker) Lautsprecher m, Box f

**special 1.** adj besondere(r, s), speziell **2.** n (on menu) Tagesgericht nt; TV, RADIO Sondersendung f; **special delivery** n Eilzustellung f; **specialist** n Spezialist(in) m(f); TECH Fachmann m, Fachfrau f; MED Facharzt m, Fachärztin f; **speciality** n Spezialität f; **specialize** vi sich spezialisieren (in auf + acc); **specially** adv besonders; (specifically) extra; **special offer** n Sonderangebot nt; **specialty** n (US) → **speciality**

**species** nsing Art f

**specific** adj spezifisch; (precise) genau; **specify** vt genau angeben

**specimen** n (sample) Probe f; (example) Exemplar m

**spectacle** n Schauspiel nt

**spectacles** npl Brille f

**spectacular** adj spektakulär

**spectator** n Zuschauer(in) m(f)

**sped** pt, pp → **speed**

**speech** n (address) Rede f; (faculty) Sprache f; **make a ~** eine Rede halten; **speechless** adj sprachlos (with vor + dat)

**speed 1.** vi rasen; **exceed ~ limit** zu schnell fahren **2.** n Geschwindigkeit f; (of film) Lichtempfindlichkeit f; **speed up 1.** vt beschleunigen **2.** vi schneller werden / fahren; **speedboat** n Rennboot nt; **speed bump** n Bodenschwelle f; **speed limit** n Geschwindigkeitsbegrenzung f; **speedometer** n Tachometer m; **speed trap** n Radarfalle f; **speedy** adj schnell

**spell 1.** vt buchstabieren; **how do you ~ ...?** wie schreibt man ...? **2.** n (period) Weile f; **a cold / hot ~** (weather) ein Kälteeinbruch / eine Hitzewelle; (enchantment) Zauber m; **spellchecker** n IT Rechtschreibprüfung f; **spelling** n Rechtschreibung f; **~mistake** Schreibfehler m

**spelt** pt, pp → **spell**

**spend** vt (money) ausgeben (on für); (time) verbringen

**spent** pt, pp → **spend**

**sperm** n Sperma nt

**sphere** n (globe) Kugel f; fig Sphäre f

**spice 1.** n Gewürz nt; fig Würze f **2.** vt würzen; **spicy** adj würzig

**spider** n Spinne f

**spike** n (on railing etc) Spitze f; (on shoe, tyre) Spike m

**spill** vt verschütten

**spin 1.** vi (turn) sich drehen; (washing) schleudern; **my head is ~ning** mir dreht sich alles **2.** vt (turn) drehen; (coin) hochwerfen **3.** n (turn) Drehung f

**spinach** n Spinat m

**spin doctor** n Spindoktor m (Verantwortlicher für die schönrednerische Öffentlichkeitsarbeit besonders von Politikern)

**spin-drier** n Wäscheschleuder f

**spine** n Rückgrat nt; (of animal, plant) Stachel m; (of book) Rücken m

**spiral 1.** n Spirale f **2.** adj spiralförmig; **spiral staircase** n Wendeltreppe f

**spire** n Turmspitze f

**spirit** n (essence, soul) Geist m; (humour, mood) Stimmung f; (courage) Mut m; (verve) Elan m; **~s pl** (drinks) Spirituosen pl

**spiritual** adj geistig, REL geistlich

**spit 1.** vi spucken **2.** n (for roasting) (Brat)spieß m; (saliva) Spucke f; **spit out** vt ausspucken

**spite** n Boshaftigkeit f; **in ~ of** trotz + gen; **spiteful** adj boshaft

**spitting image** n **he's the ~ of**

**you** er ist dir / Ihnen wie aus dem Gesicht geschnitten

**splash 1.** vt (*person, object*) bespritzen **2.** vi (*liquid*) spritzen; (*play in water*) planschen

**splendid** adj herrlich

**splinter** n Splitter m

**split 1.** vt (*stone, wood*) spalten; (*share*) teilen **2.** vi (*stone, wood*) sich spalten **3.** n (*in stone, wood*) Spalt m; (*in clothing*) Riss m; fig Spaltung f; **split up 1.** vi (*couple*) sich trennen **2.** vt (*divide up*) aufteilen; **split ends** npl (Haar)spliss m; **splitting** adj (*headache*) rasend

**spoil 1.** vt verderben; (*child*) verwöhnen **2.** vi (*food*) verderben

**spoilt** pt, pp → **spoil**

**spoke 1.** pt → **speak 2.** n Speiche f

**spoken** pp → **speak**

**spokesperson** n Sprecher(in) m(f)

**sponge** n (*for washing*) Schwamm m; **sponge cake** n Biskuitkuchen m

**sponsor 1.** n (*of event, programme*) Sponsor(in) m(f) **2.** vt unterstützen; (*event, programme*) sponsern

**spontaneous, spontaneously** adj, adv spontan

**spool** n Spule f

**spoon** n Löffel m

**sport** n Sport m; **sports car** n Sportwagen m; **sports centre** n Sportzentrum nt; **sportsman** n Sportler m; **sportswear** n Sportkleidung f; **sportswoman** n Sportlerin f; **sporty** adj sportlich

**spot 1.** n (*dot*) Punkt m; (*of paint, blood etc*) Fleck m; (*place*) Stelle f; (*pimple*) Pickel m; **on the ~** on Ort; (*at once*) auf der Stelle **2.** vt (*notice*) entdecken; (*difference*) erkennen; **spotless** adj (*clean*) blitzsauber; **spotlight** n (*lamp*) Scheinwerfer m; **spotty** adj (*pimply*) pickelig

**spouse** n Gatte m, Gattin f

**spout** n Schnabel m

**sprain** vt ~ **one's ankle** sich den Knöchel verstauchen

**sprang** pt → **spring**

**spray 1.** n (*liquid in can*) Spray nt or m; (*spray (can)*) Spraydose f **2.** vt (*plant, insects*) besprühen; (*car*) spritzen

**spread 1.** vt (*open out*) ausbreiten; (*news, disease*) verbreiten; (*butter, jam*) streichen **2.** vi (*news, disease, fire*) sich verbreiten **3.** n (*of disease, religion etc*) Verbreitung f; (*for bread*) Aufstrich m; **spreadsheet** n π Tabellenkalkulation f

**spring 1.** vi (*leap*) springen **2.** n (*season*) Frühling m; (*coil*) Feder f; (*water*) Quelle f; **springboard** n Sprungbrett *nt;* **spring onion** *n* (*Brit*) Frühlingszwiebel *f;* **spring roll** *n* (*Brit*) Frühlingsrolle *f*

**sprinkle** *vt* streuen; (*liquid*) beträufeln; **~ sth with sth** etw mit etw bestreuen / beträufeln; **sprinkler** *n* (*for lawn*) Rasensprenger *m;* (*for fire*) Sprinkler *m*

**sprint** *vi* rennen; SPORT sprinten

**sprout 1.** *n* (*of plant*) Trieb *m;* (*from seed*) Keim *m;* (**Brussels**)**~s** *pl* Rosenkohl *m* **2.** *vi* sprießen

**sprung** *pp* → **spring**

**spun** *pt, pp* → **spin**

**spy 1.** *n* Spion(in) *m(f)* **2.** *vi* spionieren; **~ on sb** jdm nachspionieren

**squad** *n* SPORT Kader *m*

**square 1.** *n* (*shape*) Quadrat *nt;* (*open space*) Platz *m;* (*on chessboard etc*) Feld *nt* **2.** *adj* (*in shape*) quadratisch; **2 ~ metres** 2 Quadratmeter; **2 metres ~** 2 Meter im Quadrat **3.** *vt* **3 ~d 3** hoch 2

**squash 1.** *n* (*drink*) Fruchtsaftgetränk *nt;* SPORT Squash *nt;* (*US, vegetable*) Kürbis *m* **2.** *vt* zerquetschen

**squeak** *vi* (*door, shoes etc*) quietschen; (*animal*) quieken

**squeal** *vi* (*person*) kreischen (*with* vor + *dat*)

**squeeze 1.** *vt* drücken; (*orange*) auspressen **2.** *vi* **~ into the car** sich in den Wagen hi-

neinzwängen

**squid** *n* Tintenfisch *m*

**squirrel** *n* Eichhörnchen *nt*

**St 1.** *abbr* → **saint** St. **2.** *abbr* → **street** Str.

**stab** *vt* (*person*) einstechen auf + *acc;* (*to death*) erstechen; **stabbing** *adj* (*pain*) stechend

**stabilize 1.** *vt* stabilisieren **2.** *vi* sich stabilisieren

**stable 1.** *n* Stall *m* **2.** *adj* stabil

**stack 1.** *n* (*pile*) Stapel *m* **2.** *vt* **~ (up)** (auf)stapeln

**stadium** *n* Stadion *nt*

**staff** *n* (*personnel*) Personal *nt,* Lehrkräfte *pl*

**stag** *n* Hirsch *m*

**stage 1.** *n* THEAT Bühne *f;* (*of project, life etc*) Stadium *nt;* (*of journey*) Etappe *f;* **at this ~** zu diesem Zeitpunkt **2.** *vt* THEAT aufführen, inszenieren; (*demonstration*) veranstalten

**stagger 1.** *vi* wanken **2.** *vt* (*amaze*) verblüffen; **staggering** *adj* (*amazing*) umwerfend; (*amount, price*) schwindelerregend

**stagnate** *vi* stagnieren

**stag night** *n* (*Brit*) Junggesellenabschied *m*

**stain** *n* Fleck *m;* **stained-glass window** *n* Buntglasfenster *nt;* **stainless steel** *n* rostfreier Stahl; **stain remover** *n* Fleck(en)entferner *m*

**stair** *n* (Treppen)stufe *f;* **~s** *pl*

Treppe *f*; **staircase** *n* Treppe
*f*

**stake** *n* (*post*) Pfahl *m*; (*in betting*) Einsatz *m*; FIN Anteil *m* (*in* an + *dat*); **be at** ~ auf dem Spiel stehen

**stale** *adj* (*bread*) alt; (*beer*) schal

**stalk** 1. *n* Stiel *m* 2. *vt* (*wild animal*) sich anpirschen an + *acc*; (*person*) nachstellen + *dat*

**stall** 1. *n* (*in market*) (Verkaufs)stand *m*; (*in stable*) Box *f*; ~**s** *pl* THEAT Parkett *nt* 2. *vt* (*engine*) abwürgen 3. *vi* (*driver*) den Motor abwürgen; (*car*) stehen bleiben

**stamina** *n* Durchhaltevermögen *nt*

**stammer** *vi, vt* stottern

**stamp** 1. *n* (*postage stamp*) Briefmarke *f*; (*for document*) Stempel *m* 2. *vt* (*passport etc*) stempeln; (*mail*) frankieren

**stand** 1. *vi* stehen; (*as candidate*) kandidieren 2. *vt* (*place*) stellen; (*endure*) aushalten; **I can't** ~ **her** ich kann sie nicht ausstehen 3. *n* (*stall*) Stand *m*; (*seats in stadium*) Tribüne *f*; (*for coats, bicycles*) Ständer *m*; (*for small objects*) Gestell *nt*; **stand around** *vi* herumstehen; **stand by 1.** *vi* (*be ready*) bereithalten; (*be inactive*) danebenstehen 2. *vt* (*person*) halten zu; (*deci-*

*sion, promise*) stehen zu; **stand for** *vt* (*represent*) stehen für; (*tolerate*) hinnehmen; **stand in for** *vt* einspringen für; **stand out** *vi* (*be noticeable*) auffallen; **stand up 1.** *vi* (*get up*) aufstehen 2. *vt* (*girlfriend, boyfriend*) versetzen; **stand up for** *vt* sich einsetzen für

**standard 1.** *n* (*norm*) Norm *f*; ~ **of living** Lebensstandard *m* 2. *adj* Standard-

**standardize** *vt* vereinheitlichen

**stand-by 1.** *n* (*thing in reserve*) Reserve *f*; **on** ~ in Bereitschaft 2. *adj* (*flight, ticket*) Stand-by-; **standing order** *n* (*at bank*) Dauerauftrag *m*; **standpoint** *n* Standpunkt *m*; **standstill** *n* Stillstand *m*; **come to a** ~ stehen bleiben; *fig* zum Erliegen kommen

**stank** *pt* → **stink**

**staple 1.** *n* (*for paper*) Heftklammer *f* 2. *vt* heften (*to* an + *acc*); **stapler** *n* Hefter *m*

**star 1.** *n* Stern *m*; (*person*) Star *m* 2. *vt* **the film** ~**s Hugh Grant** der Film zeigt Hugh Grant in der Hauptrolle 3. *vi* die Hauptrolle spielen

**starch** *n* Stärke *f*

**stare** *vi* starren; ~ **at** anstarren

**starfish** *n* Seestern *m*

**star sign** *n* Sternzeichen *nt*

**start 1.** *n* (*beginning*) Anfang *m*, Beginn *m*; SPORT Start *m*;

(*lead*) Vorsprung *m*; *from the* ~ von Anfang an **2.** *vt* anfangen; (*car, engine*) starten; (*business, family*) gründen; ~ *to do sth*, ~ *doing sth* anfangen, etw zu tun **3.** *vi* (*begin*) anfangen; (*car*) anspringen; (*on journey*) aufbrechen; SPORT starten; (*jump*) zusammenfahren; ~*ing from Monday* ab Montag; **start off 1.** *vt* (*discussion, process etc*) anfangen, beginnen **2.** *vi* (*begin*) anfangen, beginnen; (*on journey*) aufbrechen; **start up 1.** *vi* (*in business*) anfangen **2.** *vt* (*car, engine*) starten; (*business*) gründen; **starter** *n* (*Brit, first course*) Vorspeise *f*; AUTO Anlasser *m*; **starting point** *n* Ausgangspunkt *m*

**startle** *vt* erschrecken; **startling** *adj* überraschend

**starve** *vi* hungern; (*to death*) verhungern; *I'm starving* ich habe einen Riesenhunger

**state 1.** *n* (*condition*) Zustand *m*; POL Staat *m*; *the (United) States* die (Vereinigten) Staaten **2.** *adj* Staats-; (*control, education*) staatlich **3.** *vt* erklären; (*facts, name etc*) angeben; **stated** *adj* (*fixed*) festgesetzt; **statement** *n* (*official declaration*) Erklärung *f*; (*to police*) Aussage *f*; (*from bank*) Kontoauszug *m*; **state-of-the-art**

*adj* hochmodern, auf dem neuesten Stand der Technik

**static** *adj* (*unchanging*) konstant

**station 1.** *n* (*for trains, buses*) Bahnhof *m*; (*underground station*) Station *f*; (*police station, fire station*) Wache *f*; TV, RADIO Sender *m* **2.** *vt* MIL stationieren

**stationer's** *n* ~ (*shop*) Schreibwarengeschäft *nt*; **stationery** *n* Schreibwaren *pl*

**station wagon** *n* (*US*) Kombiwagen *m*

**statistics** *nsing* (*science*) Statistik *f*; (*figures*) Statistiken *pl*

**statue** *n* Statue *f*

**status** *n* Status *m*; (*prestige*) Ansehen *nt*

**stay 1.** *n* Aufenthalt *m* **2.** *vi* bleiben; (*with friends, in hotel*) wohnen (*with* bei); ~ *the night* übernachten; **stay away** *vi* wegbleiben; ~ *from sb* sich von jdm fernhalten; **stay behind** *vi* zurückbleiben; (*at work*) länger bleiben; **stay in** *vi* (*at home*) zu Hause bleiben; **stay out** *vi* (*not come home*) wegbleiben; **stay up** *vi* (*at night*) aufbleiben

**steady 1.** *adj* (*speed*) gleichmäßig; (*progress, increase*) stetig; (*job, income, girlfriend*) fest; (*worker*) zuverlässig; (*hand*) ruhig; *they've*

**sting**

***been going ~ for two years***
sie sind seit zwei Jahren fest
zusammen **2.** *vt (nerves)* beruhigen

**steak** *n* Steak *nt; (of fish)* Filet
*nt*

**steal** *vt* stehlen

**steam 1.** *n* Dampf *m* **2.** *vt*
GASTR dämpfen; **steam up**
*vi (window)* beschlagen;
**steamer** *n* GASTR Dampfkochtopf *m; (ship)* Dampfer
*m*

**steel 1.** *n* Stahl *m* **2.** *adj* Stahl-
**steep** *adj* steil

**steeple** *n* Kirchturm *m*

**steer** *vt, vi* steuern; *(car, bike
etc)* lenken; **steering** *n* AUTO
Lenkung *f*; **steering wheel** *n*
Steuer *nt*, Lenkrad *nt*

**stem** *n (of plant, glass)* Stiel *m*

**step 1.** *n* Schritt *m; (stair)* Stufe *f; (measure)* Maßnahme *f*;
**~ by** Schritt für Schritt **2.** *vi*
treten; **~ this way, please**
hier entlang, bitte; **step
down** *vi (resign)* zurücktreten

**stepbrother** *n* Stiefbruder *m*;
**stepchild** *n* Stiefkind *nt*;
**stepfather** *n* Stiefvater *m*;
**stepmother** *n* Stiefmutter
*f*; **stepsister** *n* Stiefschwester *f*

**stereo** *n* ~ **(system)** Stereoanlage *f*

**sterile** *adj* steril; **sterilize** *vt*
sterilisieren

**sterling** *n* FIN das Pfund Sterling

**stew** *n* Eintopf *m*

**steward** *n (on plane, ship)*
Steward *m*; **stewardess** *n*
Stewardess *f*

**stick 1.** *vt (with glue etc)* kleben; *(pin etc)* stecken; *fam
(put)* tun **2.** *vi (get jammed)*
klemmen; *(hold fast)* haften
**3.** *n* Stock *m; (hockey stick)*
Schläger *m; (of chalk)* Stück
*nt; (of celery, rhubarb)* Stange *f*; **stick out 1.** *vt* **stick
one's tongue out (at sb)**
(jdm) die Zunge herausstre-
cken **2.** *vi (protrude)* vorste-
hen; *(ears)* abstehen; *(be noticeable)* auffallen; **stick to**
*vt (rules, plan etc)* sich halten
an + *acc*; **sticker** *n* Aufkleber *m*; **sticky** *adj* klebrig;
*(weather)* schwül; ~ **label**
Aufkleber *m*; ~ **tape** Klebeband *nt*

**stiff** *adj* steif

**stifle** *vt (yawn etc, opposition)*
unterdrücken; **stifling** *adj*
drückend

**still 1.** *adj (drink)* ohne
Kohlensäure **2.** *adv (yet,
even now)* (immer) noch;
*(all the same)* immerhin;
*(sit, stand)* still; **he ~ doesn't
believe me** er glaubt mir immer noch nicht; **keep ~** halt
still!; **bigger / better ~** noch
größer / besser

**stimulate** *vt* anregen, stimu-
lieren; **stimulating** *adj* anre-
gend

**sting 1.** *vt (wound with sting)*

stechen 2. *vi (eyes, ointment etc)* brennen 3. *n (insect wound)* Stich *m*

**stingy** *adj fam* geizig

**stink 1.** *vi* stinken *(of nach)* 2. *n* Gestank *m*

**stir** *vt (mix)* (um)rühren; **stir up** *vt (mob)* aufhetzen; *(memories)* wachrufen; ~ **trouble** Unruhe stiften; **stir-fry** *vt (unter Rühren)* kurz anbraten

**stitch 1.** *n (in sewing)* Stich *m*; *(in knitting)* Masche *f*; **have a ~** *(pain)* Seitenstechen haben; **he had to have ~es** er musste genäht werden; **she had her ~es out** ihr wurden die Fäden gezogen; **be in ~es** *fam* sich kaputtlachen 2. *vt* nähen; **stitch up** *vt (hole, wound)* nähen

**stock 1.** *n (supply)* Vorrat *m (of an + dat)*; *(of shop)* Bestand *m*; *(for soup etc)* Brühe *f*; **~s and shares** *pl* Aktien und Wertpapiere *pl*; **be in / out of ~** vorrätig / nicht vorrätig sein; **take ~** Inventur machen; *fig* Bilanz ziehen 2. *vt (keep in shop)* führen; **stock up** *vi* sich eindecken *(on, with* mit)

**stockbroker** *n* Börsenmakler(in) *m(f)*

**stock cube** *n* Brühwürfel *m*

**stock exchange** *n* Börse *f*

**stocking** *n* Strumpf *m*

**stock market** *n* Börse *f*

**stole** *pt* → **steal**; **stolen** *pp* →

**steal**

**stomach** *n* Magen *m*; *(belly)* Bauch *m*; **on an empty ~** auf leeren Magen; **stomach-ache** *n* Magenschmerzen *pl*; **stomach upset** *n* Magenverstimmung *f*

**stone 1.** *n* Stein *m*; *(seed)* Kern *m*, Stein *m*; *(weight)* britische Gewichtseinheit *(6,35 kg)* 2. *adj* Stein-, aus Stein

**stony** *adj (ground)* steinig

**stood** *pt, pp* → **stand**

**stool** *n* Hocker *m*

**stop 1.** *n* Halt *m*; *(for bus, tram, train)* Haltestelle *f*; **come to a ~** anhalten 2. *vt (vehicle, passer-by)* anhalten; *(put an end to)* ein Ende machen + *dat*; *(cease)* aufhören mit; *(prevent from happening)* verhindern; *(bleeding)* stillen; *(engine, machine)* abstellen; *(payments)* einstellen; *(cheque)* sperren; **~ doing sth** aufhören, etw zu tun; **~ sb (from) doing sth** jdn daran hindern, etw zu tun; **~ it!** hör / hören Sie auf (damit)! 3. *vi (vehicle)* anhalten; *(during journey)* Halt machen; *(pedestrian, clock, heart)* stehen bleiben; *(rain, noise)* aufhören; *(stay)* bleiben; **stop by** *vi* vorbeischauen; **stop over** *vi* Halt machen; *(overnight)* übernachten; **stopgap** *n* Provisorium *nt*; Zwischenlösung *f*; **stop-**

**over** n (on journey) Zwischenstation f; **stopper** n Stöpsel m; **stop sign** n Stoppschild nt; **stopwatch** n Stoppuhr f

**storage** n Lagerung f. **store 1.** n (supply) Vorrat m (of an + dat); (place for storage) Lager nt; (large shop) Kaufhaus nt; (US, shop) Geschäft nt **2.** vt lagern; (in memory) speichern; **storeroom** n Lagerraum m

**storey** n (Brit) Stock m, Stockwerk nt

**storm 1.** n Sturm m; (thunderstorm) Gewitter nt **2.** vt, vi (with movement) stürmen; **stormy** adj stürmisch

**story** n Geschichte f; (plot) Handlung f; (US, of building) Stock m, Stockwerk nt

**stout** adj (fat) korpulent

**stove** n Herd m; (for heating) Ofen m

**stow** vt verstauen; **stowaway** n blinder Passagier

**straight 1.** adj (not curved) gerade; (hair) glatt; (honest) ehrlich (with zu); fam (heterosexual) hetero **2.** adv (directly) direkt; (immediately) sofort; (drink) pur; (think) klar; ~ **ahead** geradeaus; **go ~ on** geradeaus weitergehen / weiterfahren; **straightaway** adv sofort; **straightforward** adj einfach; (person) aufrichtig, unkompliziert

**strain 1.** n Belastung f **2.**

**vt** (eyes) überanstrengen; (rope, relationship) belasten; (vegetables) abgießen; ~ **a muscle** sich einen Muskel zerren; **strained** adj (relations) gespannt; ~ **muscle** Muskelzerrung f; **strainer** n Sieb nt

**strand 1.** n (of wool) Faden m; (of hair) Strähne f **2.** vt be (left) ~ed (person) festsitzen

**strange** adj seltsam; (unfamiliar) fremd; **strangely** adv seltsam; ~ **enough** seltsamerweise; **stranger** n Fremde(r) mf

**strangle** vt (kill) erdrosseln

**strap 1.** n Riemen m; (on dress etc) Träger m; (on watch) Band nt **2.** vt (fasten) festschnallen (to an + dat); **strapless** adj trägerlos

**strategy** n Strategie f

**straw** n Stroh nt; (drinking straw) Strohhalm m

**strawberry** n Erdbeere f

**stray 1.** n streunendes Tier **2.** adj (cat, dog) streunend **3.** vi streunen

**streak** n (of colour, dirt) Streifen m; (in hair) Strähne f; (in character) Zug m

**stream 1.** n (flow of liquid) Strom m; (brook) Bach m **2.** vi strömen

**street** n Straße f; **streetcar** n (US) Straßenbahn f; **street lamp, street light** n Straßenlaterne f; **street map** n Stadtplan m

**strength** n Kraft f, Stärke f;
**strengthen** vt verstärken;
fig stärken
**strenuous** adj anstrengend
**stress 1.** n Stress m; (on word)
Betonung f **2.** vt betonen;
(put under stress) stressen;
**stressed** adj ~ (out) ge-
stresst
**stretch 1.** n (of land) Stück nt;
(of road) Strecke f **2.** vt (material, shoes) dehnen; (rope,
canvas) spannen; (person in
job etc) fordern; ~ one's legs
(walk) sich die Beine vertreten **3.** vi (person) sich strecken; (area) sich erstrecken
(to bis zu); **stretch out 1.** vt
ausstrecken **2.** vi (reach) sich
strecken; (lie down) sich ausstrecken; **stretcher** n Trag-
bahre f
**strict, strictly** adj, adv (se-
vere(ly)) streng; (exact(ly))
genau; **strictly speaking** ge-
nauer gesagt
**strike 1.** vt (match) anzünden;
(hit) schlagen; (find) finden;
**it struck me as strange** es
kam mir seltsam vor **2.** vi
(stop work) streiken; (attack)
zuschlagen; (clock) schlagen
**3.** n (by workers) Streik m;
**be on** ~ streiken; **strike up**
vt (conversation) anfangen;
(friendship) schließen; **striking** adj auffallend
**string** n (for tying) Schnur f;
MUS Saite f; **the ~s** pl (section
of orchestra) die Streicher pl

**strip 1.** n Streifen m; (Brit, of
soccer player) Trikot nt **2.** vi
(undress) sich ausziehen,
strippen
**stripe** n Streifen m; **striped**
adj gestreift
**stripper** n Stripper(in) m(f);
(paint stripper) Farbentfer-
ner m
**stroke 1.** n MED, SPORT etc
Schlag m; (of pen, brush)
Strich m **2.** vt streicheln
**stroll 1.** n Spaziergang m **2.** vi
spazieren; **stroller** n (US, for
baby) Buggy m
**strong** adj stark; (healthy) robust; (wall, table) stabil;
(shoes) fest; (influence,
chance) groß; **strongly** adv
stark; (believe) fest; (con-
structed) stabil
**struck** pt, pp → **strike**
**structural, structurally** adj
strukturell; **structure** n
Struktur f; (building, bridge)
Konstruktion f, Bau m
**struggle 1.** n Kampf m (for
um) **2.** vi (fight) kämpfen
(for um); (do sth with difficulty) sich abmühen; ~ to
**do sth** sich abmühen, etw
zu tun
**stub 1.** n (of cigarette) Kippe f;
(of ticket, cheque) Abschnitt
m
**stubble** n Stoppelbart m;
(field) Stoppeln pl
**stubborn** adj (person) stur
**stuck 1.** pt, pp → **stick 2.** adj
**be** ~ (jammed) klemmen;

(at a loss) nicht mehr weiterwissen; **get ~** (car in snow etc) stecken bleiben

**student** n Student(in) m(f), Schüler(in) m(f)

**studio** n Studio nt

**study 1.** n (investigation) Untersuchung f; (room) Arbeitszimmer nt **2.** vt, vi studieren

**stuff 1.** n Zeug nt, Sachen pl **2.** vt (push) stopfen; GASTR füllen; **~ oneself** fam sich vollstopfen; **stuffing** n GASTR Füllung f

**stuffy** adj (room) stickig; (person) spießig

**stumble** vi stolpern; (when speaking) stocken

**stun** vt (shock) fassungslos machen; **I was ~ned** ich war fassungslos (or völlig überrascht)

**stung** pt, pp → **sting**

**stunk** pp → **stink**

**stunning** adj (marvellous) fantastisch; (beautiful) atemberaubend; (very surprising, shocking) überwältigend; unfassbar

**stupid** adj dumm; **stupidity** n Dummheit f

**sturdy** adj robust; (building, car) stabil

**stutter** vi, vt stottern

**stye** n MED Gerstenkorn nt

**style 1.** n Stil m **2.** vt (hair) stylen; **styling mousse** n Schaumfestiger m; **stylish** adj elegant, schick

**subconscious 1.** adj unterbewusst **2.** n **the ~** das Unterbewusstsein

**subject 1.** n (topic) Thema nt; (in school) Fach nt; (citizen) Staatsangehörige(r) mf; (of kingdom) Untertan(in) m(f); LING Subjekt nt; **change the ~** das Thema wechseln **2.** adj **be ~ to** (dependent on) abhängig von; (under control of) unterworfen sein + dat

**subjective** adj subjektiv

**sublet** irr vt untervermieten (to an + acc)

**submarine** n U-Boot nt

**submerge 1.** vt (put in water) eintauchen **2.** vi tauchen

**submit 1.** vt (application, claim) einreichen **2.** vi (surrender) sich ergeben

**subordinate 1.** adj untergeordnet (to + dat) **2.** n Untergebene(r) mf

**subscribe** vi **~ to** (magazine etc) abonnieren; **subscription** n (to magazine etc) Abonnement nt; (to club etc) (Mitglieds)beitrag m

**subsequent** adj nach(-folgend); **subsequently** adv später, anschließend

**subside** vi (floods) zurückgehen; (storm) sich legen; (building) sich senken

**substance** n Substanz f

**substantial** adj (improvement) wesentlich; (meal) reichhaltig

**substitute 1.** *n* Ersatz *m*; SPORT Ersatzspieler(in) *m(f)* **2.** *vt* ~ **A for B** B durch A ersetzen

**subtitle** *n* Untertitel *m*

**subtle** *adj* (*difference, taste*) fein; (*plan*) raffiniert

**subtract** *vt* abziehen (*from* von)

**suburb** *n* Vorort *m*; **suburban** *adj* vorstädtisch, Vorstadt-

**subway** *n* (*Brit*) Unterführung *f*; (*US*) RAIL U-Bahn *f*

**succeed 1.** *vi* erfolgreich sein; **he ~ed (in doing it)** es gelang ihm(, es zu tun) **2.** *vt* nachfolgen + *dat*; **succeeding** *adj* nachfolgend; **success** *n* Erfolg *m*; **successful, successfully** *adj, adv* erfolgreich

**successive** *adj* aufeinanderfolgend; **successor** *n* Nachfolger(in) *m(f)*

**such 1.** *adj* solche(r, s); ~ **a book** so ein Buch, ein solches Buch; **it was ~ a success that ...** es war solch ein Erfolg, dass ...; **~ as** wie ein solches Buch; **it was ~ a success that ...** es war solch ein Erfolg, dass ...; **~ as** wie **2.** *adv* so; ~ **a hot day** so ein heißer Tag **3.** *pron* **as** ~ als solche(r, s)

**suck** *vt* (*toffee etc*) lutschen; (*liquid*) saugen; **it ~s** *fam* das ist beschissen

**Sudan** *n* (**the**) ~ der Sudan

**sudden** *adj* plötzlich; **all of a** ~ ganz plötzlich; **suddenly** *adv* plötzlich

**sue** *vt* verklagen

**suede** *n* Wildleder *nt*

**suffer 1.** *vt* erleiden **2.** *vi* leiden; ~ **from** MED leiden an + *dat*

**sufficient, sufficiently** *adj, adv* ausreichend

**suffocate** *vi, vi* ersticken

**sugar 1.** *n* Zucker *m* **2.** *vt* zuckern; **sugary** *adj* (*sweet*) süß

**suggest** *vt* vorschlagen; (*imply*) andeuten; **I ~ saying nothing** ich schlage vor, nichts zu sagen; **suggestion** *n* (*proposal*) Vorschlag *m*; **suggestive** *adj* vielsagend; (*sexually*) anzüglich

**suicide** *n* (*act*) Selbstmord *m*; **suicide bomber** *n* Selbstmordattentäter(in) *m(f)*; **suicide bombing** *n* Selbstmordattentat *nt*

**suit 1.** *n* (*man's clothes*) Anzug *m*; (*lady's clothes*) Kostüm *nt*; (*cards*) Farbe *f* **2.** *vt* (*be convenient for*) passen + *dat*; (*clothes, colour*) stehen + *dat*; (*climate, food*) bekommen + *dat*; **suitable** *adj* geeignet (*for* für)

**suitcase** *n* Koffer *m*

**suite** *n* (*of rooms*) Suite *f*; (*sofa and chairs*) Sitzgarnitur *f*

**sulk** *vi* schmollen; **sulky** *adj* eingeschnappt

**sultana** *n* (*raisin*) Sultanine *f*

**sum** *n* Summe *f*; (*money a.*) Betrag *m*; (*calculation*) Rechenaufgabe *f*

**summarize** vt, vi zusammenfassen; **summary** n Zusammenfassung f

**summer** n Sommer m; **summer camp** n (US) Ferienlager m; **summertime** n **in (the)** ~ im Sommer

**summit** n a. POL Gipfel m

**summon** vt (doctor, fire brigade etc) rufen; (to one's office) zitieren; **summon up** vt (courage, strength) zusammennehmen

**summons** nsing LAW Vorladung f

**sumptuous** adj luxuriös; (meal) üppig

**sun 1.** n Sonne f 2. vt ~ **oneself** sich sonnen

**Sun** abbr → **Sunday** So.

**sunbathe** vi sich sonnen; **sunbed** n Sonnenbank f; **sunblock** n Sunblocker m; **sunburn** n Sonnenbrand m; **sunburnt** adj **be / get** ~ einen Sonnenbrand haben / bekommen

**sundae** n Eisbecher m

**Sunday** n Sonntag m; → **Tuesday**

**sung** pp → **sing**

**sunglasses** npl Sonnenbrille f; **sunhat** n Sonnenhut m

**sunk** pp → **sink**

**sunlamp** n Höhensonne f; **sunlight** n Sonnenlicht m; **sunny** adj sonnig; **sun protection factor** n Lichtschutzfaktor m; **sunrise** n Sonnenaufgang m; **sunroof** n

**sunscreen** n Sonnenschutzmittel nt; **sunset** n Sonnenuntergang m; **sunshade** n Sonnenschirm m; **sunshine** n Sonnenschein m; **sunstroke** n Sonnenstich m; **suntan** n (Sonnen)bräune f; ~ **lotion** (or **oil**) Sonnenöl nt

**super** adj fam toll

**superb, superbly** adj, adv ausgezeichnet

**superficial, superficially** adj, adv oberflächlich

**superfluous** adj überflüssig

**superior 1.** adj (better) besser (to als); (higher in rank) höhergestellt (to als), höher 2. n (in rank) Vorgesetzte(r) mf

**supermarket** n Supermarkt m

**supersonic** adj Überschall-; **superstition** n Aberglaube m; **superstitious** adj abergläubisch

**supervise** vt beaufsichtigen; **supervisor** n Aufsicht f; (at university) Doktorvater m

**supper** n Abendessen nt; (late-night snack) Imbiss m

**supplement 1.** n (extra payment) Zuschlag m; (of newspaper) Beilage f 2. vt ergänzen; **supplementary** adj zusätzlich

**supplier** n Lieferant(in) m(f);

**supply 1.** vt (deliver) liefern; (drinks, music etc) sorgen für; ~ **sb with sth** (provide) jdn mit etw versorgen **2.** n *(stock)* Vorrat *m (of* an + *dat)*

**support 1.** *n* Unterstützung *f*; TECH Stütze *f* **2.** *vt (hold up)* tragen, stützen; *(provide for)* ernähren, unterhalten; *(speak in favour of)* unterstützen; **he ~s Manchester United** er ist Manchester-United-Fan

**suppose** *vt (assume)* annehmen; *I~ so* ich denke schon; *I~ not* wahrscheinlich nicht; **you're not ~d to smoke here** du darfst / Sie dürfen hier nicht rauchen; **supposedly** *adv* angeblich

**suppress** *vt* unterdrücken

**surcharge** *n* Zuschlag *m*

**sure 1.** *adj* sicher; *I'm (not) ~* ich bin mir (nicht) sicher; **make ~ you lock up** vergiss / vergessen Sie nicht abzuschließen **2.** *adv ~I* klar!; **surely** *adv ~ you don't mean it?* das ist nicht dein / Ihr Ernst, oder?

**surf 1.** *n* Brandung *f* **2.** *vi* SPORT surfen **3.** *vt ~ the Net* im Internet surfen

**surface 1.** *n* Oberfläche *f* **2.** *vi* auftauchen

**surfboard** *n* Surfbrett *nt*; **surfer** *n* Surfer(in) *m(f)*; **surfing** *n* Surfen *nt*

**surgeon** *n* Chirurg(in) *m(f)*; **surgery** *n (operation)* Operation *f*; *(room)* Praxis *f*, Sprechzimmer *nt*; *(consulting time)* Sprechstunde *f*; **have ~** operiert werden

**surname** *n* Nachname *m*

**surpass** *vt* übertreffen

**surprise 1.** *n* Überraschung *f* **2.** *vt* überraschen; **surprising** *adj* überraschend; **surprisingly** *adv* überraschenderweise, erstaunlicherweise

**surrender 1.** *vi* sich ergeben *(to* + *dat)* **2.** *vt (weapon, passport)* abgeben

**surround** *vt* umgeben; *(stand all round)* umringen; **surrounding 1.** *adj (countryside)* umliegend **2.** *n ~s pl* Umgebung *f*

**survey 1.** *n (opinion poll)* Umfrage *f*; *(of literature etc)* Überblick *m (of* über + *acc)*; *(of land)* Vermessung *f* **2.** *vt (look out over)* überblicken; *(land)* vermessen

**survive** *vt, vi* überleben

**sushi** *n* Sushi *nt*

**suspect 1.** *n* Verdächtige(r) *mf* **2.** *adj* verdächtig **3.** *vt* verdächtigen *(of* + *gen)*; *(think likely)* vermuten

**suspend** *vt (from work)* suspendieren; *(payment)* vorübergehend einstellen; *(player)* sperren; *(hang up)* aufhängen; **suspender** *n (Brit)* Strumpfhalter *m*; **~s pl** *(US, for trousers)* Hosenträger *pl*

**suspense** *n* Spannung *f*

**suspicious** *adj* misstrauisch *(of sb / sth)* jdm / etw gegenüber); *(causing suspicion)* verdächtig

**swallow 1.** n (bird) Schwalbe f **2.** vt, vi schlucken

**swam** pt → **swim**

**swamp** n Sumpf m

**swan** n Schwan m

**swap** vt, vi tauschen; **~ sth for sth** etw gegen etw eintauschen

**sway** vi schwanken

**swear** vi (promise) schwören; (curse) fluchen; **~ at sb** jdn beschimpfen; **swear by** vt (have faith in) schwören auf + acc

**sweat 1.** n Schweiß m **2.** vi schwitzen; **sweater** n Pullover m; **sweaty** adj verschwitzt

**swede** n Steckrübe f

**Swede** n Schwede m, Schwedin f; **Sweden** n Schweden nt; **Swedish 1.** adj schwedisch **2.** n (language) Schwedisch nt

**sweep** vt, vi (with brush) kehren, fegen

**sweet 1.** n (Brit, candy) Bonbon nt; (dessert) Nachtisch m **2.** adj süß; (kind) lieb; **sweet-and-sour** adj süßsauer; **sweetcorn** n Mais m; **sweeten** vt (tea etc) süßen; **sweetener** n (substance) Süßstoff m; **sweet potato** n Süßkartoffel f

**swell 1.** vi **~ (up)** (an)schwellen **2.** adj (US) fam toll; **swelling** n MED Schwellung f

**sweltering** adj (heat) drückend

**swept** pt, pp → **sweep**

**swift, swiftly** adj, adv schnell

**swim 1.** vi schwimmen **2.** n **go for a ~** schwimmen gehen; **swimmer** n Schwimmer(in) m(f); **swimming** n Schwimmen nt; **go~** schwimmen gehen; **swimming cap** n (Brit) Badekappe f; **swimming costume** n (Brit) Badeanzug m; **swimming pool** n Schwimmbad nt; (private, in hotel) Swimmingpool m; **swimming trunks** npl (Brit) Badehose f; **swimsuit** n Badeanzug m

**swindle** vt betrügen (out of um)

**swine** n Schwein nt

**swing 1.** vt, vi (object) schwingen **2.** n (for child) Schaukel f

**swipe** vt (credit card etc) durchziehen; fam (steal) klauen; **swipe card** n Magnetkarte f

**Swiss 1.** adj schweizerisch **2.** n Schweizer(in) m(f)

**switch 1.** n ELEC Schalter m **2.** vi (change) wechseln (to zu); **switch off** vt abschalten, ausschalten; **switch on** vt anschalten, einschalten; **switchboard** n TEL Vermittlung f

**Switzerland** n die Schweiz

**swivel** vi sich drehen **2.** vt drehen

**swollen 1.** pp → **swell 2.** adj MED geschwollen; (stomach)

aufgebläht
swop → *swap*
sword *n* Schwert *nt*
swore *pt* → *swear*
sworn *pp* → *swear*
swum *pp* → *swim*
swung *pt*, *pp* → *swing*
syllable *n* Silbe *f*
symbol *n* Symbol *nt*; symbolic *adj* symbolisch; symbolize *vt* symbolisieren
symmetrical *adj* symmetrisch
sympathetic *adj* mitfühlend; (*understanding*) verständ-

nisvoll; sympathize *vi* mitfühlen (*with sb* mit jdm); sympathy *n* Mitleid *nt*; (*after death*) Beileid *nt*; (*understanding*) Verständnis *nt*
symphony *n* Sinfonie *f*
symptom *n* Symptom *nt*
synagogue *n* Synagoge *f*
synthetic *adj* (*material*) synthetisch
Syria *n* Syrien *nt*
syringe *n* Spritze *f*
system *n* System *nt*; systematic *adj* systematisch

# T

tab *n* (*for hanging up coat etc*) Aufhänger *m*; IT Tabulator *m*; **pick up the ~** *fam* die Rechnung übernehmen
table *n* Tisch *m*; (*list*) Tabelle *f*; **~ of contents** Inhaltsverzeichnis *nt*; tablecloth *n* Tischdecke *f*; tablespoon *n* Servierlöffel *m*; (*in recipes*) Esslöffel *m*
tablet *n* Tablette *f*
table tennis *n* Tischtennis *nt*; table wine *n* Tafelwein *m*
tabloid *n* Boulevardzeitung *f*
taboo **1.** *n* Tabu *nt* **2.** *adj* tabu
tack *n* (*small nail*) Stift *m*; (*US, thumbtack*) Reißzwecke *f*
tackle **1.** *n* SPORT Angriff *m*; (*equipment*) Ausrüstung *f* **2.** *vt* (*deal with*) in Angriff

nehmen; SPORT angreifen; (*verbally*) zur Rede stellen (*about* wegen)
tacky *adj* trashig, heruntergekommen
tact *n* Takt *m*; tactful, tactfully *adj*, *adv* taktvoll; tactic(s) *n*(*pl*) Taktik *f*; tactless, tactlessly *adj*, *adv* taktlos
tag *n* (*label*) Schild *nt*; (*with maker's name*) Etikett *nt*
tail *n* Schwanz *m*; **heads or ~s?** Kopf oder Zahl?; tailback *n* (*Brit*) Rückstau *m*; taillight *n* AUTO Rücklicht *nt*
tailor *n* Schneider(in) *m*(*f*)
tailpipe *n* (*US*) AUTO Auspuffrohr *nt*
Taiwan *n* Taiwan *nt*
take *vt* nehmen; (*take along with one*) mitnehmen; (*take*

*to a place*) bringen; (*subtract*) abziehen (*from* von); (*capture: person*) fassen; (*gain, obtain*) bekommen; FIN, COMM einnehmen; (*train, taxi*) nehmen, fahren mit; (*trip, walk, holiday, exam, course, photo*) machen; (*bath*) nehmen; (*phone call*) entgegennehmen; (*decision, precautions*) treffen; (*risk*) eingehen; (*advice, job*) annehmen; (*tablets*) nehmen; (*heat, pain*) ertragen; (*react to*) aufnehmen; (*have room for*) Platz haben für; **I'll ~ it** (*item in shop*) ich nehme es; **how long does it ~?** wie lange dauert es?; **it ~s 4 hours** man braucht 4 Stunden; **I ~ it that ...** ich nehme an, dass ...; **~ place** stattfinden; **~ part in** teilnehmen an; **take after** vt nachschlagen + dat; **take along** vt mitnehmen; **take apart** vt auseinandernehmen; **take away** vt (*remove*) wegnehmen (*from sb* jdm); (*subtract*) abziehen (*from* von); **take back** vt (*return*) zurückbringen; (*retract*) zurücknehmen; **take down** vt (*picture, curtains*) abnehmen; (*write down*) aufschreiben; **take in** vt (*understand*) begreifen; (*give accommodation to*) aufnehmen; (*deceive*) hereinlegen; (*include*) einschließen; (*show, film etc*) mitnehmen;

**take off 1.** vi (*plane*) starten **2.** vt (*clothing*) ausziehen; (*hat, lid*) abnehmen; (*deduct*) abziehen; **take a day off** sich einen Tag freinehmen; **take on** vt (*undertake*) übernehmen; (*employ*) einstellen; SPORT antreten gegen; **take out** vt (*wallet etc*) herausnehmen; (*person, dog*) ausführen; (*insurance*) abschließen; (*money from bank*) abheben; (*book from library*) ausleihen; **take over 1.** vt übernehmen **2.** vi he **took over** (*from me*) er hat mich abgelöst; **take to her I** *vt* ich mag sie / es; **~ doing sth** (*begin*) anfangen, etw zu tun; **take up** vt (*carpet*) hochnehmen; (*space*) einnehmen; (*time*) in Anspruch nehmen; (*hobby*) anfangen mit; (*new job*) antreten; (*offer*) annehmen

**taken 1.** pp → **take 2.** adj (*seat*) besetzt; **be ~ with** angetan sein von

**takeoff** n AVIAT Start m; **takeout** (*US*) → **takeaway**; **takeover** n Übernahme f

**tale** n Geschichte f

**talent** n Talent nt; **talented** adj begabt

**talk 1.** n (*conversation*) Gespräch nt; (*rumour*) Gerede nt; (*to audience*) Vortrag m **2.** vi sprechen, reden; (*have conversation*) sich unterhalten; ~ **to** (or with) sb (about sth) mit jdm (über etw acc) sprechen **3.** vt (language) sprechen; (nonsense) reden; (politics, business) reden über + acc; ~ **sb into doing/out of doing sth** jdn überreden/jdm ausreden, etw zu tun; **talk over** vt besprechen

**talkative** adj gesprächig

**tall** adj groß; (building, tree) hoch

**tame 1.** adj zahm **2.** vt (animal) zähmen

**tampon** n Tampon m

**tan 1.** n (on skin) (Sonnen)-bräune f; **get/have a** ~ braun werden/sein **2.** vi braun werden

**tangerine** n Mandarine f

**tango** n Tango m

**tank** n (for water) Hahn m **2.** vt, vi (strike) klopfen; ~ **sb on the shoulder** jdm auf die Schulter klopfen; **tap-dance** vi steppen

**tape 1.** n (adhesive tape) Klebeband nt; (for tape recorder) Tonband nt; (cassette) Kassette f; (video) Video nt **2.** vt (record) aufnehmen; **tape up** vt (parcel) zukleben; **tape measure** n Maß-

band nt; **tape recorder** n Tonbandgerät nt

**tapestry** n Wandteppich m

**tap water** n Leitungswasser nt

**target** n Ziel nt; (board) Zielscheibe f; **target group** n Zielgruppe f

**tariff** n (price list) Preisliste f; (tax) Zoll m

**tart** n (fruit tart) (Obst)kuchen m; (small) (Obst)törtchen nt; fam, pej (prostitute) Nutte f, Schlampe f

**tartan** n Schottenkaro nt

**tartar(e) sauce** n Remouladensoße f

**task** n Aufgabe f; (duty) Pflicht f

**Tasmania** n Tasmanien nt

**taste 1.** n Geschmack m; (sense of taste) Geschmackssinn m; (small quantity) Kostprobe f; **it has a strange** ~ es schmeckt komisch **2.** vt schmecken; (try) probieren **3.** vi (food) schmecken (of nach); **tasteful, tastefully** adj, adv geschmackvoll; **tasteless, tastelessly** adj, adv geschmacklos; **tasty** adj lecker

**taught** pt, pp → **teach**

**Taurus** n ASTR Stier m

**tax 1.** n Steuer f (on auf + acc) **2.** vt besteuern; **taxation** n Besteuerung f; **tax bracket** n Steuerklasse f; **tax-free** adj steuerfrei

**taxi 1.** n Taxi nt **2.** vi (plane) rollen; **taxi rank** (Brit), **taxi**

**stand** n Taxistand m

**tax return** n Steuererklärung f

**tea** n Tee m; (*afternoon tea*) ≈ Kaffee und Kuchen; (*meal*) frühes Abendessen; **teabag** n Teebeutel m; **tea break** n (Tee)pause f

**teach** 1. vt (*person, subject*) unterrichten; **~ sb (how) to dance** jdm das Tanzen beibringen 2. vi unterrichten; **teacher** n Lehrer(in) m(f)

**team** n SPORT Mannschaft f, Team nt; **teamwork** n Teamarbeit f

**teapot** n Teekanne f

**tear** n (*in eye*) Träne f

**tear** 1. vt zerreißen; **~ a muscle** sich einen Muskel zerren 2. vi (*in material etc*) Riss m; **tear down** vt (*building*) abreißen; **tear up** vt (*paper*) zerreißen

**tearoom** n Café, in dem in erster Linie Tee serviert wird

**tease** vt (*person*) necken (*about* wegen)

**teaspoon** n Teelöffel m; **tea towel** n Geschirrtuch nt

**technical** adj technisch; (*knowledge, term, dictionary*) Fach-; **technically** adv technisch; **technique** n Technik f

**techno** n Techno m

**technology** n Technologie f; Technik f

**tedious** adj langweilig

**teen(age)** adj (*fashions etc*) Teenager-; **teenager** n Teen-

ager m; **teens** npl **in one's ~** im Teenageralter

**teeth** pl → **tooth**

**teetotal** adj abstinent

**telephone 1.** n Telefon nt **2.** vi telefonieren **3.** vt anrufen; **telephone book** n Telefonbuch nt; **telephone booth, telephone box** (*Brit*) n Telefonzelle f; **telephone call** n Telefonanruf m; **telephone directory** n Telefonbuch nt; **telephone number** n Telefonnummer f

**telephoto lens** n Teleobjektiv nt

**telescope** n Teleskop nt

**television** n Fernsehen nt; **television (set)** n Fernseher m

**tell 1.** vt (*say, inform*) sagen (*sb sth* jdm etw); (*story*) erzählen; (*truth*) sagen; (*difference*) erkennen; (*reveal secret*) verraten; **~ sb about sth** jdm von etw erzählen; **~ sth from sth** etw von etw unterscheiden **2.** vi (*be sure*) wissen; **tell apart** vt unterscheiden; **tell off** vt schimpfen

**telling** adj aufschlussreich

**telly** n (*Brit*) fam Glotze f; **on (the) ~** in der Glotze

**temp 1.** n Aushilfskraft f **2.** vi als Aushilfskraft arbeiten

**temper** n (*anger*) Wut f; (*mood*) Laune f; **lose one's ~** die Beherrschung verlieren; **temperamental** adj (*moody*) launisch

**temperature** n Temperatur f; MED (*high temperature*) Fieber nt; **have a ~** Fieber haben

**temple** n Tempel m; ANAT Schläfe f

**temporarily** adv vorübergehend; **temporary** adj vorübergehend; (*road, building*) provisorisch

**tempt** vt in Versuchung führen; **temptation** n Versuchung f; **tempting** adj verlockend

**ten 1.** num zehn **2.** n Zehn f; → **eight**

**tenant** n Mieter(in) m(f); (*of land*) Pächter(in) m(f)

**tend** vi **~ to do sth** (*person*) dazu neigen, etw zu tun; **~ towards** neigen zu; **tendency** n Tendenz f

**tender** adj (*loving*) zärtlich; (*sore*) empfindlich; (*meat*) zart

**tendon** n Sehne f

**Tenerife** n Teneriffa f

**tenner** n (*Brit*) fam (*note*) Zehnpfundschein m

**tennis** n Tennis nt; **tennis court** n Tennisplatz m; **tennis racket** n Tennisschläger m

**tenor** n Tenor m

**tense** adj angespannt; (*stretched tight*) gespannt; **tension** n Spannung f; (*strain*) Anspannung f

**tent** n Zelt nt

**tenth 1.** adj zehnte(r, s) **2.** n (*fraction*) Zehntel nt; → **eighth**

**tent peg** n Hering m; **tent pole** n Zeltstange f

**term** n (*in school, at university*) Trimester nt; (*expression*) Ausdruck m; **~s** pl (*conditions*) Bedingungen pl; **be on good ~s with sb** mit jdm gut auskommen; **come to ~s with sth** sich mit etw abfinden; **in the long/short ~** langfristig/kurzfristig; **in ~s of ...** was ... betrifft

**terminal 1.** n (*bus terminal etc*) Endstation f; AVIAT Terminal m; IT Terminal m; ELEC Pol m **2.** adj MED unheilbar; **terminally** adv (*ill*) unheilbar

**terminate 1.** vt (*contract*) lösen; (*pregnancy*) abbrechen **2.** vi (*train, bus*) enden

**terrace** n (*of houses*) Häuserreihe f; (*in garden etc*) Terrasse f; **terraced** adj (*garden*) terrassenförmig angelegt; **terraced house** n (*Brit*) Reihenhaus nt

**terrible** adj schrecklich

**terrific** adj (*very good*) fantastisch

**terrify** vt erschrecken; **be terrified** schreckliche Angst haben (*of* vor + *dat*)

**territory** n Gebiet nt

**terror** n Schrecken m; POL Terror m; **terrorism** n Terrorismus m; **terrorist** n Terrorist(in) *m(f)*

**test 1.** *n* Test *m*, Klassenarbeit *f*; *(driving test)* Prüfung *f*; **put to the ~** auf die Probe stellen **2.** *vt* testen, prüfen

**Testament** *n* **the Old / New ~** das Alte / Neue Testament

**test-drive** *vt* Probe fahren

**testicle** *n* Hoden *m*

**testify** *vi* LAW aussagen

**test tube** *n* Reagenzglas *nt*

**tetanus** *n* Tetanus *m*

**text** *n* Text *m*; *(of document)* Wortlaut *m*; *(sent by mobile phone)* SMS *f* **2.** *vt (message)* simsen, SMSen; **~ sb** jdm simsen, jdm eine SMS schicken; **I'll ~ it to you** ich schicke es dir per SMS

**textbook** *n* Lehrbuch *nt*

**texting** *n* SMS-Messaging *nt*; **text message** *n* SMS *f*

**texture** *n* Beschaffenheit *f*

**Thailand** *n* Thailand *nt*

**Thames** *n* Themse *f*

**than** *prep, conj* als; *bigger / faster ~ me* größer / schneller als ich

**thank** *vt* danken + *dat*; **~ you** danke; *very much/~ you* vielen Dank; **thankful** *adj* dankbar; **thankfully** *adv (luckily)* zum Glück; **thankless** *adj* undankbar; **thanks** *npl* Dank *m*; **~** danke!; **~ to** dank + *gen*

**that 1.** *adj* der / die / das; *(opposed to this)* jene(r, s); *who's ~ woman?* wer ist die Frau?; *I like ~ one* ich

mag das **2.** *pron* das; *(in relative clauses)* der / die / das, die *pl*; **~ is very good** das ist sehr gut; *the wine ~ I drank* der Wein, den ich getrunken habe; **~ is** *(to say)* das heißt **3.** *conj* dass; *I think ~ ...* ich denke, dass ... **4.** *adv* so; **~ good** so gut

that's *contr* = that is; that has

**thaw 1.** *vi* tauen; *(frozen food)* auftauen **2.** *vt* auftauen lassen

the *art* der / die / das, die *pl*; *by ~ hour* pro Stunde; **~ ... ~ better** je ..., desto besser

**theater** *(US)*, **theatre** *n* Theater *nt*; *(for lectures etc)* Saal *m*

**theft** *n* Diebstahl *m*

**their** *adj* ihr; *they cleaned ~ teeth* sie putzten sich die Zähne; *someone has left ~ umbrella here* jemand hat seinen Schirm hier vergessen; **theirs** *pron* ihre(r, s); *it's ~* es gehört ihnen; *a friend of ~* ein Freund von ihnen; *someone has left ~ here* jemand hat seins hier liegen lassen

**them** *pron (direct object)* sie; *(indirect object)* ihnen; *do you know ~?* kennst du / kennen Sie sie?; *can you help ~?* kannst du / können Sie ihnen helfen?; *it's ~* sie sind's; *if anyone has a problem you should help ~* wenn jemand ein Problem hat,

solltest du / sollten Sie ihm
helfen
**theme** n Thema nt; MUS Motiv
nt; **~ song** Titelmusik f
**themselves** pron sich; **they
hurt ~** sie haben sich verletzt; **they ~ were not there**
sie selbst waren nicht da;
**they did it ~** sie haben es
selbst gemacht; **(all) by ~** allein
**then 1.** adv (at that time) damals; (next) dann; (therefore) also; (furthermore) ferner; **from ~ on** von da an; **by
~** bis dahin **2.** adj damalig
**theoretical, theoretically**
adj, adv theoretisch
**theory** n Theorie f; **in ~** theoretisch
**therapy** n Therapie f
**there** adv dort; (to a place)
dorthin; **~ is / are** (exists /
exist) es gibt; **it's over ~** es
ist da drüben; **~ you are**
(when giving) bitte schön;
**thereabouts** adv (approximately) so ungefähr; **therefore** adv daher, deshalb
**thermometer** n Thermometer nt
**Thermos® n ~ (flask)** Ther-
mosflasche® f
**these** pron, adj diese; **~ are
not my books** das sind nicht
meine Bücher
**thesis** n (for PhD) Doktorarbeit f
**they** pron pl sie; (people in
general) man; (unidentified

person) er / sie; **~ are rich**
sie sind reich; **~ say that ...**
man sagt, dass ...; **if anyone
looks at this, ~ will see that
...** wenn sich jemand dies an-
sieht, wird er erkennen, dass
...
**they'd** contr = **they had; they
would**
**they'll** contr = **they will; they
shall**
**they've** contr = **they have**
**thick** adj dick; (fog) dicht;
(liquid) dickflüssig; fam
(stupid) dumm; **thicken** vi
(fog) dichter werden; (sauce)
dick werden
**thief** n Dieb(in) m(f)
**thigh** n Oberschenkel m
**thimble** n Fingerhut m
**thin** adj dünn
**thing** n Ding nt; (affair) Sache
f; **how are ~s?** wie geht's?; **I
can't see a ~** ich kann nichts
sehen
**think** vt, vi denken; (believe)
meinen; **I ~ so** ich denke
schon; **I don't ~** ich glaube
nicht; **think about** vt denken
an + acc; (reflect on) nachdenken über + acc; (have
opinion of) halten von;
**think of** vt denken an
+ acc; (devise) sich ausdenken; (have opinion of) halten von; (remember) sich erinnern an + acc; **think over**
vt überdenken; **think up** vt
sich ausdenken
**third 1.** adj dritte(r, s) **2.** n

*(fraction)* Drittel *nt*; **in ~ (gear)** im dritten Gang; ~ **eighth**; thirdly *adv* drittens; **third-party insurance** *n* Haftpflichtversicherung *f*

**thirst** *n* Durst *m* *(for* nach); **thirsty** *adj* **be ~** Durst haben

**thirteen 1.** *num* dreizehn **2.** *n* Dreizehn *f*; ~ **eight; thirteenth** *adj* dreizehnte(r, s); → **eighth**; **thirtieth** *adj* dreißigste(r, s); → **eighth; thirty 1.** *num* dreißig; **~-one** einunddreißig **2.** *n* Dreißig *f*; **be in one's thirties** in den Dreißigern sein; → **eight**

**this 1.** *adj* diese(r, s); ~ **morning** heute Morgen **2.** *pron* das, dies; ~ **is Mark** *(on the phone)* hier spricht Mark

**thistle** *n* Distel *f*

**thong** *n* String *m*

**thorn** *n* Dorn *m*, Stachel *m*

**thorough** *adj* gründlich; **thoroughly** *adv* gründlich; *(agree etc)* völlig

**those 1.** *pron* die da, jene; ~ **who** diejenigen, die **2.** *adj* die, jene

**though 1.** *conj* obwohl; **as ~** als ob **2.** *adv* aber

**thought 1.** *pt, pp* → **think 2.** *n* Gedanke *m*; *(thinking)* Überlegung *f*; **thoughtful** *adj* *(kind)* rücksichtsvoll; *(attentive)* aufmerksam; *(in Gedanken versunken)* nachdenklich; **thoughtless** *adj* *(unkind)* rücksichtslos, gedankenlos

**thousand** *num* **(one)** ~, **a ~** tausend; **five ~, a ~** fünftausend; **~s of** Tausende von

**thrash** *vt* *(hit)* verprügeln; *(defeat)* vernichtend schlagen

**thread 1.** *n* Faden *m* **2.** *vt* *(needle)* einfädeln; *(beads)* auffädeln

**threat** *n* Drohung *f*; *(danger)* Bedrohung *f (to* für); **threaten** *vt* bedrohen; **threatening** *adj* bedrohlich

**three 1.** *num* drei **2.** *n* Drei *f*; → **eight; three-dimensional** *adj* dreidimensional; **three--quarters** *npl* drei Viertel *pl*

**threshold** *n* Schwelle *f*

**threw** *pt* → **throw**

**thrifty** *adj* sparsam

**thrilled** *adj* **be ~ (with sth)** sich *(über etw acc)* riesig freuen; **thrilling** *adj* aufregend

**thrive** *vi* gedeihen *(on* bei); *(business)* fig florieren

**throat** *n* Hals *m*, Kehle *f*

**throbbing** *adj* *(pain, headache)* pochend

**thrombosis** *n* Thrombose *f*

**throne** *n* Thron *m*

**through 1.** *prep* durch; *(time)* während + *gen*; *(because of)* aus, durch; *(US, up to and including)* bis **2.** *adv* durch; **put sb ~** TEL jdn verbinden *(to* mit) **3.** *adj* *(ticket, train)* durchgehend; ~ **flight** Direktflug *m*; **be ~ with sb / sth** mit jdm / etw fertig sein; **throughout 1.** *prep* *(place)* überall in + dat; (time) während + gen; **~ the night** die ganze Nacht hindurch **2.** adv überall; (time) die ganze Zeit

**throw 1.** vt werfen; (rider) abwerfen; (party) geben **2.** n Wurf m; **throw away** vt wegwerfen; **throw in** vt (include) dazugeben; **throw out** vt (unwanted object) wegwerfen; (person) hinauswerfen (of aus); **throw up** vt, vi fam (vomit) sich übergeben

**thrown** pp → **throw**

**thru** (US) → **through**

**thrush** n Drossel f

**thrust** vt, vi (push) stoßen

**thruway** n (US) Schnellstraße f

**thumb 1.** n Daumen m **2.** vt **~ a lift** per Anhalter fahren; **thumbtack** n (US) Reißzwecke f

**thunder 1.** n Donner m **2.** vi donnern; **thunderstorm** n Gewitter nt

**Thur(s)** abbr → **Thursday** Do.

**Thursday** n Donnerstag m; → **Tuesday**

**thus** adv (in this way) so; (therefore) somit, also

**thyme** n Thymian m

**Tibet** n Tibet nt

**tick 1.** n (Brit, mark) Häkchen nt **2.** vt (name) abhaken; (box, answer) ankreuzen **3.** vi (clock) ticken

**ticket** n (for train, bus) (Fahr)-karte f; (plane ticket) Flug-

schein m, Ticket nt; (for theatre, match, museum etc) (Eintritts)karte f; (price ticket) (Preis)schild nt; (raffle ticket) Los nt; (for car park) Parkschein m; (for traffic offence) Strafzettel m; **ticket collector**, **ticket inspector** (Brit) n Fahrkartenkontrolleur(in) m(f); **ticket machine** n (for public transport) Fahrscheinautomat m; (in car park) Parkscheinautomat m; **ticket office** n RAIL Fahrkartenschalter m; THEAT Kasse f

**tickle** vt kitzeln; **ticklish** adj kitzlig

**tide** n Gezeiten pl; **the ~ is in / out** es ist Flut / Ebbe

**tidy 1.** adj ordentlich **2.** vt aufräumen; **tidy up** vt, vi aufräumen

**tie 1.** n (necktie) Krawatte f; SPORT Unentschieden nt; (bond) Bindung f **2.** vt (attach, do up) binden (to an + acc); (tie together) zusammenbinden; (knot) machen; **tie down** vt festbinden (to an + dat); fig binden; **tie up** vt (dog) anbinden; (parcel) verschnüren; (shoelace) binden; (boat) festmachen

**tiger** n Tiger m

**tight 1.** adj (clothes) eng; (knot) fest; (screw, lid) fest sitzend; (control, security measures) streng; (timewise) knapp; (schedule) eng **2.** adv (*shut*) fest; (*pull*) stramm; **hold ~** festhalten!; **tighten** *vt* (*knot, rope, screw*) anziehen; (*belt*) enger machen; (*restrictions, control*) verschärfen; **tights** *npl* (*Brit*) Strumpfhose *f*

**tile** *n* (*on roof*) Dachziegel *m*; (*on wall, floor*) Fliese *f*

**till 1.** *n* Kasse *f* **2.** *prep, conj* → *until*

**tilt 1.** *vt* kippen; (*head*) neigen **2.** *vi* sich neigen

**time 1.** *n* Zeit *f*; (*occasion*) Mal *nt*; MUS Takt *m*; **local ~** Ortszeit; **what ~ is it?, what's the ~?** wie spät ist es?, wie viel Uhr ist es?; **take one's ~** (*over sth*) sich (*bei etw*) Zeit lassen; **have a good ~** Spaß haben; **in two weeks' ~** in zwei Wochen; **at ~s** manchmal; **at the same ~** gleichzeitig; **all the ~** die ganze Zeit; **by the ~ he ...** bis er ...; (*in past*) als er ...; **for the ~ being** vorläufig; **in ~** (*not late*) rechtzeitig; (*on time*) pünktlich; **the first ~** das erste Mal; **this ~** diesmal; **five ~s** fünfmal; **five ~s six** fünf mal sechs; **four ~s a year** viermal im Jahr; **three at a ~** drei auf einmal **2.** *vt* (*with stopwatch*) stoppen; **you ~d that well** das hast du / haben Sie gut getimt; **time difference** *n* Zeitunterschied *m*; **timer** *n* Timer *m*; (*switch*) Schaltuhr *f*; **time-saving** *adj* zeitspa-

rend; **time switch** *n* Schaltuhr *f*; **timetable** *n* (*for public transport*) Fahrplan *m*; (*school*) Stundenplan *m*; **time zone** *n* Zeitzone *f*

**timid** *adj* ängstlich

**timing** *n* (*coordination*) Timing *nt*

**tin 1.** *n* (*metal*) Blech *nt*; (*Brit, can*) Dose *f*; **tinfoil** *n* Alufolie *f*; **tinned** *adj* (*Brit*) aus der Dose; **tin opener** *n* (*Brit*) Dosenöffner *m*

**tinsel** *n* ≈ Lametta *nt*

**tint** *n* (*Farb*)ton *m*; (*in hair*) Tönung *f*; **tinted** *adj* getönt

**tiny** *adj* winzig

**tip 1.** *n* (*money*) Trinkgeld *nt*; (*hint*) Tipp *m*; (*end*) Spitze *f*; (*of cigarette*) Filter *m*; (*Brit, rubbish tip*) Müllkippe *f* **2.** *vt* (*waiter*) Trinkgeld geben + *dat*; **tip over** *vt, vi* (*overturn*) umkippen

**tipsy** *adj* beschwipst

**tiptoe** *n* **on ~** auf Zehenspitzen

**tire 1.** *n* (*US*) → *tyre* **2.** *vt* müde machen **3.** *vi* müde werden; **tired** *adj* müde; **be ~ of doing sth** es satthaben, etw zu tun; **tireless, tirelessly** *adv* unermüdlich; **tiresome** *adj* lästig; **tiring** *adj* ermüdend

**tissue** *n* ANAT Gewebe *nt*; (*paper handkerchief*) Papier(taschen)tuch *nt*; **tissue paper** *n* Seidenpapier *nt*

**tit** *n* (*bird*) Meise *f*; fam

(*breast*) Titte *f*

**title** *n* Titel *m*

**titter** *vi* kichern

**to** *prep* (*towards*) zu; (*with countries, towns*) nach; (*as far as*) bis; (*with infinitive of verb*) zu; ~ **Rome / Switzerland** nach Rom / in die Schweiz; **I've been** ~ **London** ich war schon mal in London; **go** ~ **town/** ~ **the theatre** in die Stadt / ins Theater gehen; **from Monday** ~ **Thursday** von Montag bis Donnerstag; **he came** ~ **say sorry** er kam, um sich zu entschuldigen; **20 minutes** ~ **4** 20 Minuten vor 4; **they won by 4 goals** ~ **3** sie haben mit 4 zu 3 Toren gewonnen

**toad** *n* Kröte *f*; **toadstool** *n* Giftpilz *m*

**toast** **1.** *n* (*bread, drink*) Toast *m*; **a piece** (*or* **slice**) **of** ~ eine Scheibe Toast; **propose a** ~ **to sb** einen Toast auf jdn ausbringen **2.** *vt* (*bread*) toasten; (*person*) trinken auf + *acc*; **toaster** *n* Toaster *m*

**tobacco** *n* Tabak *m*; **tobacconist's** *n* ~ (**-shop**) Tabakladen *m*

**toboggan** *n* Schlitten *m*

**today** *adv* heute; **a week** ~ heute in einer Woche; ~**'s newspaper** die Zeitung von heute

**toddler** *n* Kleinkind *nt*

**toe** *n* Zehe *f*, Zeh *m*; **toenail** *n*

Zehennagel *m*

**toffee** *n* (*sweet*) Karamellbonbon *m*; **toffee-nosed** *adj* hochnäsig

**tofu** *n* Tofu *m*

**together** *adv* zusammen; **I tied them** ~ ich habe sie zusammengebunden

**toilet** *n* Toilette *f*; **go to the** ~ auf die Toilette gehen; **toilet bag** *n* Kulturbeutel *m*; **toilet paper** *n* Toilettenpapier *nt*; **toiletries** *npl* Toilettenartikel *pl*; **toilet roll** *n* Rolle *f* Toilettenpapier

**token** *n* Marke *f*; (*in casino*) Spielmarke *f*; (*voucher, gift token*) Gutschein *m*; (*sign*) Zeichen *nt*

**Tokyo** *n* Tokio *nt*

**told** *pt*, *pp* → **tell**

**tolerant** *adj* tolerant (*of* gegenüber); **tolerate** *vt* tolerieren; (*noise, pain, heat*) ertragen

**toll** *n* (*charge*) Gebühr *f*; **toll-free** *adj*, *adv* (*US*) TEL gebührenfrei; **toll road** *n* gebührenpflichtige Straße

**tomato** *n* Tomate *f*; **tomato juice** *n* Tomatensaft *m*; **tomato sauce** *n* Tomatensoße *f*; (*Brit, ketchup*) Tomatenketchup *m or nt*

**tomb** *n* Grabmal *nt*; **tombstone** *n* Grabstein *m*

**tomorrow** *adv* morgen; ~ **morning** morgen früh; ~ **evening** morgen Abend; **the day after** ~ übermorgen

**toss**

*a week* (from) ~/~ *week* morgen in einer Woche

**ton** n (Brit) Tonne f (1016 kg); (US) Tonne f (907 kg); **~s of books** fam eine Menge Bücher

**tone** n Ton m; **toner** n (for printer) Toner m; **toner cartridge** n Tonerpatrone f

**tongs** npl Zange f; (curling tongs) Lockenstab m

**tongue** n Zunge f

**tonic** n MED Stärkungsmittel nt; ~ (water) Tonic nt

**tonight** adv heute Abend; (during night) heute Nacht

**tonsillitis** n Mandelentzündung f; **tonsils** n Mandeln pl

**too** adv zu; (also) auch; ~ **fast** zu schnell; ~ **much / many** zu viel / viele; **me** ~ ich auch; **she liked it** ~ ihr gefiel es auch

**took** pt → **take**

**tool** n Werkzeug nt; **toolbar** n IT Symbolleiste f; **toolbox** n Werkzeugkasten m

**tooth** n Zahn m; **toothache** n Zahnschmerzen pl; **toothbrush** n Zahnbürste f; **toothpaste** n Zahnpasta f; **toothpick** n Zahnstocher m

**top** 1. n (of tower, class, company etc) Spitze f; (of mountain) Gipfel m; (of tree) Krone f; (of street) oberes Ende; (of tube, pen) Kappe f; (of box) Deckel m; (of bikini) Oberteil nt; (sleeveless) Top nt; **at the ~ of the page** oben auf der Seite; **at the ~ of the league** an der Spitze der Liga; **on ~** oben; **on ~ of** auf + dat; (in addition to) zusätzlich zu; **over the ~** übertrieben 2. adj (floor, shelf) oberste(r, s); (price, note) höchste(r, s); (best) Spitzen-; (pupil, school) beste(r, s) 3. vt (exceed) übersteigen; (be better than) übertreffen; (league) an erster Stelle liegen in + dat; **~ped with cream** mit Sahne obendrauf; **top up** vt auffüllen; **can I top you up?** darf ich dir nachschenken?

**topic** n Thema nt; **topical** adj aktuell

**topless** adj, adv oben ohne

**topping** n (on top of pizza, ice-cream etc) Belag m, Garnierung f

**torch** n (Brit) Taschenlampe f

**tore** pt → **tear**

**torment** vt quälen

**torn** pp → **tear**

**tornado** n Tornado m

**torrential** adj (rain) sintflutartig

**tortoise** n Schildkröte f

**torture** 1. n Folter f; fig Qual f 2. vt foltern

**Tory** (Brit) n Tory m, Konservative(r) mf

**toss** 1. vt (throw) werfen; (salad) anmachen; ~ **a coin** eine Münze werfen 2. n **I don't give a** ~ fam es ist mir scheißegal

**total 1.** n (of figures, money) Gesamtsumme f; **a ~ of 30** insgesamt 30; **in ~** insgesamt **2.** adj total; (sum etc) Gesamt- **3.** vt (amount to) sich belaufen auf + acc; **totally** adv total

**touch 1.** n (act of touching) Berührung f; (sense of touch) Tastsinn m; (trace) Spur f; **be / keep in ~ with sb** mit jdm in Verbindung stehen / bleiben; **get in ~ with sb** sich mit jdm in Verbindung setzen **2.** vt (feel) berühren; (emotionally) bewegen; **touch on** vt (topic) berühren; **touchdown** n AVIAT Landung f; (touching) adj (moving) rührend; **touch screen** n Touchscreen m; **touchy** adj empfindlich, zickig

**tough** adj hart; (material) robust; (meat) zäh

**tour 1.** n Tour f (of durch); (of town, building) Rundgang m (of durch); (of pop group etc) Tournee f **2.** vt eine Tour / einen Rundgang / eine Tournee machen durch **3.** vi (on holiday) umherreisen; **tour guide** n Reiseleiter(in) m(f)

**tourism** n Tourismus m, Fremdenverkehr m; **tourist** n Tourist(in) m(f); **tourist guide** n (book) Reiseführer m; (person) Fremdenführer(in) m(f); **tourist office** n Fremdenverkehrsamt nt

**tournament** n Turnier nt

**tour operator** n Reiseveranstalter m

**towards** prep **~ me** mir entgegen, auf mich zu; **we walked ~ the station** wir gingen in Richtung Bahnhof; **my feelings ~ him** meine Gefühle ihm gegenüber

**towel** n Handtuch nt

**tower** n Turm m; **tower block** n (Brit) Hochhaus nt

**town** n Stadt f; **town center** (US), **town centre** n Stadtmitte f, Stadtzentrum nt; **town hall** n Rathaus nt

**towrope** n Abschleppseil nt; **tow truck** n (US) Abschleppwagen m

**toxic** adj giftig, Gift-

**toy** n Spielzeug nt; **toy with** vt spielen mit; **toyshop** n Spielwarengeschäft nt

**trace 1.** n Spur f; **without ~** spurlos **2.** vt (find) ausfindig machen; **tracing paper** n Pauspapier nt

**track** n (mark) Spur f; (path) Weg m; RAIL Gleis nt; (on CD, record) Stück nt; **keep / lose ~ of sb / sth** jdn / etw im Auge behalten / aus den Augen verlieren; **track down** vt ausfindig machen; **tracksuit** n Trainingsanzug m

**tractor** n Traktor m

**trade 1.** n (commerce) Handel

m; *(business)* Geschäft nt; *(skilled job)* Handwerk nt **2.** vi handeln *(in* mit) **3.** vt *(exchange)* tauschen *(for* gegen); **trademark** n Warenzeichen nt; **tradesman** n *(shopkeeper)* Geschäftsmann m; *(workman)* Handwerker m; **trade(s) union** n *(Brit)* Gewerkschaft f

**tradition** n Tradition f; **traditional, traditionally** adj, adv traditionell

**traffic** n Verkehr m; pej *(trading)* Handel m *(in* mit); **traffic circle** n *(US)* Kreisverkehr m; **traffic jam** n Stau m; **traffic lights** npl Verkehrsampel f; **traffic warden** n *(Brit)* ≈ Politesse f

**tragedy** n Tragödie f; **tragic** adj tragisch

**trail 1.** n Spur f; *(path)* Weg m **2.** vt *(follow)* verfolgen; *(drag)* schleppen; *(drag behind)* hinter sich herziehen; SPORT zurückliegen hinter + dat **3.** vi *(hang loosely)* schleifen; SPORT weit zurückliegen; **trailer** n Anhänger m; *(US, caravan)* Wohnwagen m; FILM Trailer m

**train 1.** n RAIL Zug m **2.** vt *(teach)* ausbilden; SPORT trainieren **3.** vi SPORT trainieren; **~ as** *(or* **to be)** **a teacher** eine Ausbildung als Lehrer machen; **trained** adj *(person, voice)* ausgebildet; **trainee** n Auszubildende(r) mf;

*(academic, practical)* Praktikant(in) m(f); **traineeship** n Praktikum nt; **trainer** n SPORT Trainer(in) m(f); **~s** *(Brit, shoes)* Turnschuhe pl; **training** n Ausbildung f; SPORT Training nt; **train station** n Bahnhof m

**tram** n *(Brit)* Straßenbahn f

**tramp** n Landstreicher(in) m(f)

**tranquillizer** n Beruhigungsmittel nt

**transaction** n *(piece of business)* Geschäft nt

**transatlantic** adj transatlantisch; **~ flight** Transatlantikflug m

**transfer 1.** n *(of money)* Überweisung f; *(ticket)* Umsteigekarte f **2.** vt *(money)* überweisen *(to sb* an jdn); *(patient)* verlegen; *(employee)* versetzen; SPORT transferieren **3.** vi *(on journey)* umsteigen; **transferable** adj übertragbar

**transform** vt umwandeln; **transformation** n Umwandlung f

**transfusion** n Transfusion f

**transistor** n Transistor m

**transition** n Übergang m *(from ... to* von ... zu)

**translate** vt, vi übersetzen; **translation** n Übersetzung f; **translator** n Übersetzer(in) m(f)

**transmission** n AUTO Getriebe nt

**transparent** *adj* durchsichtig

**transplant** MED **1.** *vt* transplantieren **2.** *n* (*operation*) Transplantation *f*

**transport 1.** *n* (*of goods, people*) Beförderung *f*; **public ~** öffentliche Verkehrsmittel *pl* **2.** *vt* befördern, transportieren; **transportation** *n* → **transport**

**trap 1.** *n* Falle *f* **2.** *vt* **be ~ped** (*in snow, job etc*) festsitzen

**trash** *n* (*book, film etc*) Schund *m*; (*US, refuse*) Abfall *m*; **trash can** *n* (*US*) Abfalleimer *m*; **trashy** *adj* (*novel*) Schund-

**traumatic** *adj* traumatisch

**travel 1.** *n* Reisen *nt* **2.** *vi* (*journey*) reisen **3.** *vt* (*distance*) zurücklegen; (*country*) bereisen; **travel agency**, **travel agent** *n* (*company*) Reisebüro *nt*; **traveler** (*US*) → **traveller**; **traveler's check** (*US*) → **traveller's cheque**; **traveller** *n* Reisende(r) *mf*; **traveller's cheque** *n* (*Brit*) Reisescheck *m*

**tray** *n* (*for meal etc*) Tablett *nt*; (*for mail etc*) Ablage *f*; (*of printer, photocopier*) Fach *nt*

**tread 1.** *n* (*on tyre*) Profil *nt*; **tread on** *vt* treten auf + *acc*

**treasure 1.** *n* Schatz *m* **2.** *vt* schätzen

**treat 1.** *n* besondere Freude; **it's my ~** das geht auf meine Kosten **2.** *vt* behandeln; **~ sb** (**to sth**) jdn (zu etw) einladen; **~ oneself to sth** sich etw leisten; **treatment** *n* Behandlung *f*

**treaty** *n* Vertrag *m*

**tree** *n* Baum *m*

**tremble** *vi* zittern

**tremendous** *adj* gewaltig; *fam* (*very good*) toll

**trench** *n* Graben *m*

**trend** *n* Tendenz *f*; (*fashion*) Mode *f*, Trend *m*; **trendy** *adj* trendy

**trespass** *n* '**no ~ing**' „Betreten verboten"

**trial** *n* LAW Prozess *m*; (*test*) Versuch *m*; **trial period** *n* (*for employee*) Probezeit *f*

**triangle** *n* Dreieck *nt*; MUS Triangel *m*; **triangular** *adj* dreieckig

**tribe** *n* Stamm *m*

**trick 1.** *n* Trick *m*; (*mischief*) Streich *m* **2.** *vt* hereinlegen

**tricky** *adj* (*difficult*) schwierig, heikel; (*situation*) verzwickt

**trifle** *n* Kleinigkeit *f*; (*Brit*) GASTR Trifle *nt* (*Nachspeise aus Biskuit, Wackelpudding, Obst, Vanillesoße und Sahne*)

**trigger 1.** *n* (*of gun*) Abzug *m* **2.** *vt* **~ (off)** auslösen

**trim 1.** *vt* (*hair, beard*) nachschneiden; (*nails*) schneiden; (*hedge*) stutzen **2.** *n* **just a ~, please** nur etwas nachschneiden, bitte; **trimmings** *npl* (*decorations*) Verzierungen *pl*; (*extras*) Zubehör *nt*; GASTR Beilagen *pl*

**trip 1.** n Reise f; (outing) Ausflug m **2.** vi stolpern (over über + acc)

**triple 1.** adj dreifach **2.** adv ~ **the price** dreimal so teuer **3.** vi sich verdreifachen; **triplet** n Drilling m

**tripod** n Stativ nt

**trite** adj banal

**triumph** n Triumph m

**trivial** adj trivial

**trod** pt → **tread**

**trodden** pp → **tread**

**trolley** n (Brit, in shop) Einkaufswagen m; (for luggage) Kofferkuli m; (serving trolley) Teewagen m

**trombone** n Posaune f

**troops** npl MIL Truppen pl

**trophy** n Trophäe f

**tropical** adj tropisch

**trouble 1.** n (problems) Schwierigkeiten pl; (worry) Sorgen pl; (effort) Mühe f; (unrest) Unruhen pl; MED Beschwerden pl; **be in ~** in Schwierigkeiten sein; **get into ~** (with authority) Ärger bekommen; **make ~** Schwierigkeiten machen **2.** vt (worry) beunruhigen; (disturb) stören; **sorry to ~ you** ich muss dich / Sie leider kurz stören; **troubled** adj (worried) beunruhigt; **trouble-free** adj problemlos; **troublemaker** n Unruhestifter(in) m(f); **troublesome** adj lästig

**trousers** npl Hose f; **trouser suit** n (Brit) Hosenanzug m

**trout** n Forelle f

**truck** n Lastwagen m; (Brit) RAIL Güterwagen m; **trucker** n (US, driver) Lastwagenfahrer(in) m(f)

**true** adj (factually correct) wahr; (genuine) echt; **come ~** wahr werden

**truly** adv wirklich; **Yours ~** (in letter) mit freundlichen Grüßen

**trumpet** n Trompete f

**trunk** n (of tree) Stamm m; ANAT Rumpf m; (of elephant) Rüssel m; (piece of luggage) Überseekoffer m; (US) AUTO Kofferraum m; **trunks** npl (swimming) ~ Badehose f

**trust 1.** n (confidence) Vertrauen nt (in zu) **2.** vt vertrauen + dat; **trusting** adj vertrauensvoll; **trustworthy** adj vertrauenswürdig

**truth** n Wahrheit f; **truthful** adj ehrlich; (statement) wahrheitsgemäß

**try 1.** n Versuch m **2.** vt (attempt) versuchen; (try out) ausprobieren; (sample) probieren; LAW (person) vor Gericht stellen; (courage, patience) auf die Probe stellen **3.** vi versuchen; (make effort) sich bemühen; **try on** vt (clothes) anprobieren; **try out** vt ausprobieren

**T-shirt** n T-Shirt nt

**tub** n (for ice-cream, margarine) Becher m

**tube** n (pipe) Rohr nt; (of rubber, plastic) Schlauch m; (for toothpaste, glue etc) Tube f; **the Tube** (in London) die U-Bahn; **tube station** n U-Bahn-Station f

**tuck** vt (put) stecken; **tuck in 1.** vt (shirt) in die Hose stecken; (person) zudecken **2.** vi (eat) zulangen

**Tue(s)** abbr → **Tuesday** Di.

**Tuesday** n Dienstag m; **on ~** (am) Dienstag; **on ~s** dienstags; **this / last / next ~** diesen / letzten / nächsten Dienstag; **(on) ~ morning / afternoon / evening** (am) Dienstagmorgen / -nachmittag / -abend; **every ~** jeden Dienstag; **a week on ~ / ~ week** Dienstag in einer Woche

**tug 1.** vt ziehen **2.** vi ziehen (at an + dat)

**tuition** n Unterricht m; (US, fees) Studiengebühren pl; **~ fees** pl Studiengebühren pl

**tulip** n Tulpe f

**tumble** vi (person, prices) fallen; **tumble dryer** n Wäschetrockner m

**tummy** n fam Bauch m

**tumor** (US), **tumour** n Tumor m

**tuna** n Thunfisch m

**tune 1.** n Melodie f; **be in / out of ~** (instrument) gestimmt / verstimmt sein; (singer) richtig / falsch singen **2.** vt (instrument) stim-

men; (radio) einstellen (to auf + acc)

**Tunisia** n Tunesien nt

**tunnel** n Tunnel m; (under road, railway) Unterführung f

**turbulence** n AVIAT Turbulenzen pl; **turbulent** adj stürmisch

**Turk** n Türke m, Türkin f

**turkey** n Truthahn m

**Turkey** n die Türkei; **Turkish 1.** adj türkisch **2.** n (language) Türkisch nt

**turmoil** n Aufruhr m

**turn 1.** n (rotation) Drehung f; (performance) Nummer f; **make a left ~** nach links abbiegen; **at the ~ of the century** um die Jahrhundertwende; **it's your ~** du bist / Sie sind dran; **in ~, by ~s** abwechselnd; **take ~s** sich abwechseln **2.** vt (wheel, key, screw) umdrehen; (to face other way) umdrehen; (corner) biegen um; (page) umblättern; (transform) verwandeln (into in + acc) **3.** vi (rotate) sich drehen; (to face other way) sich umdrehen; (change direction: driver, car) abbiegen; (become) werden; (weather) umschlagen; **~ into sth** (become) sich in etw acc verwandeln; **~ cold / green** kalt / grün werden; **~ left / right** links / rechts abbiegen; **turn away** vt (person) abweisen; **turn**

**back 1.** vt (person) zurückweisen **2.** vi (go back) umkehren; **turn down** vt (refuse) ablehnen; (radio, TV) leiser stellen; (heating) kleiner stellen; **turn off 1.** vi abbiegen **2.** vt (switch off) ausschalten; (tap) zudrehen; (engine, electricity) abstellen; **turn on** vt (switch on) einschalten; (tap) aufdrehen; (engine, electricity) anstellen; fam (person) anmachen, antörnen; **turn out 1.** vt (light) ausmachen; (pockets) leeren **2.** vi (develop) sich entwickeln; **as it turned out** wie sich herausstellte; **turn over 1.** vt umdrehen; (page) umblättern **2.** vi (person) sich umdrehen; (car) sich überschlagen; TV umschalten (to auf + acc); **turn round 1.** vt (to face other way) umdrehen **2.** vi (person) sich umdrehen; (go back) umkehren; **turn to** vi sich zuwenden + dat; **turn up 1.** vi (person, lost object) auftauchen **2.** vt (radio, TV) lauter stellen; (heating) höher stellen; **turning** n (in road) Abzweigung f; **turning point** n Wendepunkt m

**turnip** n Rübe f

**turnover** n FIN Umsatz m

**turnpike** n (US) gebührenpflichtige Autobahn

**turquoise** adj türkis

**turtle** n (Brit) Wasserschild-

kröte f; (US) Schildkröte f

**tutor** n (private) Privatlehrer(in) m(f); (Brit, at university) Tutor(in) m(f)

**tux, tuxedo** n (US) Smoking m

**TV 1.** n Fernsehen nt; (TV set) Fernseher m; **watch ~** fernsehen; **on ~** im Fernsehen **2.** adj Fernseh-; **~ programme** Fernsehsendung f

**tweed** n Tweed m

**tweezers** npl Pinzette f

**twelfth** adj zwölfte(r, s); → **eighth; twelve 1.** num zwölf **2.** n Zwölf f; → **eight**

**twentieth** adj zwanzigste(r, s); → **eighth; twenty 1.** num zwanzig; **~-one** einundzwanzig **2.** n Zwanzig f; **be in one's twenties** in den Zwanzigern sein; → **eight**

**twice** adv zweimal; **~ as much / many** doppelt so viel / viele

**twig** n Zweig m

**twilight** n (in evening) Dämmerung f

**twin 1.** n Zwilling m **2.** adj (brother etc) Zwillings-; **~ beds** zwei Einzelbetten **3.** vt **York is ~ned with Münster** York ist eine Partnerstadt von Münster

**twinkle** vi funkeln

**twin room** n Zweibettzimmer nt; **twin town** n Partnerstadt f

**twist** vt (turn) drehen, winden; (distort) verdrehen;

*I've ~ed my ankle* ich bin mit dem Fuß umgeknickt

**two 1.** *num* zwei; *break sth in ~* etw in zwei Teile brechen **2.** *n* Zwei *f*; *the ~ of them* die beiden; → **eight**; **two-dimensional** *adj* zweidimensional; *fig* oberflächlich; **two-piece** *adj* zweiteilig; **two-way** *adj* ~ *traffic* Gegenverkehr

**type** *n* (*sort*) Art *f*; (*typeface*)

Schrift(art) *f*; *he's not my ~* er ist nicht mein Typ; **typeface** *n* Schrift(art) *f*; **typewriter** *n* Schreibmaschine *f*
**typhoid** *n* Typhus *m*
**typhoon** *n* Taifun *m*
**typical** *adj* typisch (*of* für)
**typing error** *n* Tippfehler *m*
**tyre** *n* (*Brit*) Reifen *m*; **tyre pressure** *n* Reifendruck *m*
**Tyrol** *n* *the ~* Tirol *nt*

# U

**UFO** *acr* = **unidentified flying object**; Ufo *nt*
**Uganda** *n* Uganda *nt*
**ugly** *adj* hässlich
**UHT** *adj* *abbr* = **ultra-heat treated**; ~ *milk* H-Milch *f*
**UK** *abbr* = **United Kingdom** Vereinigtes Königreich *nt*
**Ukraine** *n* *the ~* die Ukraine
**ulcer** *n* Geschwür *nt*
**ultimate** *adj* (*final*) letzte(r, s); (*authority*) höchste(r, s); **ultimately** *adv* letzten Endes; (*eventually*) schließlich; **ultimatum** *n* Ultimatum *nt*
**ultra-** *pref* ultra-
**ultrasound** *n* MED Ultraschall *m*
**umbrella** *n* Schirm *m*
**umpire** *n* Schiedsrichter(in) *m(f)*
**umpteen** *num fam* zig; ~ *times* zigmal
**un-** *pref* un-

**UN** *nsing abbr* = **United Nations** VN, Vereinte Nationen *pl*
**unable** *adj* *be ~ to do sth* etw nicht tun können
**unacceptable** *adj* unannehmbar
**unaccustomed** *adj* *be ~ to sth* etw nicht gewohnt sein
**unanimous, unanimously** *adj, adv* einmütig
**unattached** *adj* (*without partner*) ungebunden
**unattended** *adj* (*luggage, car*) unbeaufsichtigt
**unauthorized** *adj* unbefugt
**unavailable** *adj* nicht erhältlich; (*person*) nicht erreichbar
**unavoidable** *adj* unvermeidlich
**unaware** *adj* *be ~ of sth* sich einer Sache *gen* nicht bewusst sein; *I was ~ that ...*

ich wusste nicht, dass …

**unbalanced** adj unausgewogen

**unbearable** adj unerträglich

**unbeatable** adj unschlagbar

**unbelievable** adj unglaublich

**uncertain** adj unsicher

**uncle** n Onkel m

**uncomfortable** adj unbequem

**unconditional** adj bedingungslos

**unconscious** adj MED bewusstlos; **be ~ of sth** sich einer Sache gen nicht bewusst sein; **unconsciously** adv unbewusst

**uncover** vt aufdecken

**undecided** adj unschlüssig

**undeniable** adj unbestreitbar

**under 1.** prep (beneath) unter + dat; (with motion) unter + acc; **~ an hour** weniger als eine Stunde **2.** adv (beneath) unten; (with motion) darunter; **children aged eight and ~** Kinder bis zu acht Jahren; **under-age** adj minderjährig

**undercarriage** n Fahrgestell nt

**underdog** n (outsider) Außenseiter(in) m(f)

**underdone** adj GASTR nicht gar, durch

**underestimate** vt unterschätzen

**underexposed** adj PHOT unterbelichtet

**undergo** irr vt (experience) durchmachen; (operation, test) sich unterziehen + dat

**undergraduate** n Student(in) m(f)

**underground 1.** adj unterirdisch **2.** n (Brit) U-Bahn f; **underground station** n U-Bahn-Station f

**underlie** irr vt zugrunde liegen + dat

**underline** vt unterstreichen

**underlying** adj zugrunde liegend

**underneath 1.** prep unter + dat; (with motion) unter + acc **2.** adv darunter

**underpants** npl Unterhose f; **undershirt** n (US) Unterhemd nt; **undershorts** npl (US) Unterhose f

**understand** irr vt, vi verstehen; **I ~ that …** (been told) ich habe gehört, dass …; (sympathize) ich habe Verständnis dafür, dass …; **make oneself understood** sich verständlich machen; **understanding** adj verständnisvoll

**undertake** irr vt (task) übernehmen; **~ to do sth** sich verpflichten, etw zu tun; **undertaker** n Leichenbestatter(in) m(f); **~'s** (firm) Bestattungsinstitut nt

**underwater 1.** adv unter Wasser **2.** adj Unterwasser-

**underwear** n Unterwäsche f

**undo** irr vt (unfasten) aufmachen; (work) zunichtemachen; **п** rückgängig machen

**undoubtedly** *adv* zweifellos

**undress 1.** *vt* ausziehen **2.** *vi* sich ausziehen

**unearth** *vt* (*dig up*) ausgraben; (*find*) aufstöbern

**unease** *n* Unbehagen *nt*; **uneasy** *adj* (*person*) unbehaglich; **I'm ~ about it** mir ist nicht wohl dabei

**unemployed 1.** *adj* arbeitslos **2.** *npl* **the ~** die Arbeitslosen *pl*; **unemployment** *n* Arbeitslosigkeit *f*; **unemployment benefit** *n* Arbeitslosengeld *nt*

**unequal** *adj* ungleich

**uneven** *adj* (*surface, road*) uneben; (*contest*) ungleich

**unexpected** *adj* unerwartet

**unfamiliar** *adj* **be ~ with sb / sth** jdn / etw nicht kennen

**unfasten** *vt* aufmachen

**unfit** *adj* ungeeignet (*for* für); (*in bad health*) nicht fit

**unforeseen** *adj* unvorhergesehen

**unforgettable** *adj* unvergesslich

**unforgivable** *adj* unverzeihlich

**unfortunate** *adj* (*unlucky*) unglücklich; **it is ~ that ...** es ist bedauerlich, dass ...; **unfortunately** *adv* leider

**unfounded** *adj* unbegründet

**unhappy** *adj* (*sad*) unglücklich, unzufrieden

**unhealthy** *adj* ungesund

**unheard-of** *adj* (*unknown*)

gänzlich unbekannt; (*outrageous*) unerhört

**unhitch** *vt* (*caravan, trailer*) abkoppeln

**unhurt** *adj* unverletzt

**uniform 1.** *n* Uniform *f* **2.** *adj* einheitlich

**unify** *vt* vereinigen

**unimportant** *adj* unwichtig

**uninhabited** *adj* unbewohnt

**uninstall** *vt* **п** deinstallieren

**unintentional** *adj* unabsichtlich

**union** *n* (*uniting*) Vereinigung *f*; (*alliance*) Union *f*

**unique** *adj* einzigartig

**unit** *n* Einheit *f*; (*of system, machine*) Teil *nt*; (*in school*) Lektion *f*

**unite 1.** *vt* vereinigen; **the United Kingdom** das Vereinigte Königreich; **the United Nations** *pl* die Vereinten Nationen *pl*; **the United States (of America)** *pl* die Vereinigten Staaten (von Amerika) *pl* **2.** *vi* sich vereinigen

**universe** *n* Universum *nt*

**university** *n* Universität *f*

**unkind** *adj* unfreundlich (*to* zu)

**unknown** *adj* unbekannt (*to* + *dat*)

**unleaded** *adj* bleifrei

**unless** *conj* es sei denn, wenn ... nicht; **don't do it ~ I tell you to** mach das nicht, es sei denn, ich sage es dir; **~ I'm mistaken ...** wenn ich mich nicht irre …

**unlicensed** adj (*to sell alcohol*) ohne Lizenz

**unlike** prep (*in contrast to*) im Gegensatz zu; *it's ~ her to be late* es sieht ihr gar nicht ähnlich, zu spät zu kommen;

**unlikely** adj unwahrscheinlich

**unload** vt ausladen

**unlock** vt aufschließen

**unlucky** adj unglücklich; *be ~* Pech haben

**unmistakable** adj unverkennbar

**unnecessary** adj unnötig

**unoccupied** adj (*seat*) frei; (*building, room*) leer stehend

**unpack** vt, vi auspacken

**unpleasant** adj unangenehm

**unplug ~ sth** den Stecker von etw herausziehen

**unprecedented** adj beispiellos

**unpredictable** adj (*person, weather*) unberechenbar

**unreasonable** adj unvernünftig; (*demand*) übertrieben

**unreliable** adj unzuverlässig

**unsafe** adj nicht sicher; (*dangerous*) gefährlich

**unscrew** vt abschrauben

**unskilled** adj (*worker*) ungelernt

**unsuccessful** adj erfolglos

**unsuitable** adj ungeeignet (*for* für)

**until 1.** prep bis; *not ~* erst;

*from Monday ~ Friday* von Montag bis Freitag; *he didn't come home ~ midnight* er kam erst um Mitternacht nach Hause; *~ then* bis dahin **2.** conj bis; *she won't come ~ you invite her* sie kommt erst, wenn du sie einlädst / Sie sie einladen

**unusual, unusually** adj, adv ungewöhnlich

**unwanted** adj unerwünscht, ungewollt

**unwell** adj krank; *feel ~* sich nicht wohlfühlen

**unwilling** adj *be ~ to do sth* nicht bereit sein, etw zu tun

**unwind** irr **1.** vt abwickeln **2.** vi (*relax*) sich entspannen

**unwrap** vt auspacken

**unzip** vt den Reißverschluss aufmachen an + *dat*; IT entzippen

**up 1.** prep *climb ~ a tree* einen Baum hinaufklettern; *go ~ the street / the stairs* die Straße entlanggehen / die Treppe hinaufgehen; *further ~ the hill* weiter oben auf dem Berg **2.** adv (*in higher position*) oben; (*to higher position*) nach oben; (*out of bed*) auf; *~ there* dort oben; *~ and down* (*walk, jump*) auf und ab; *what's ~?* fam was ist los?; *~ to £100* bis zu 100 Pfund; *what's she ~ to?* was macht sie da?; (*planning*) was hat sie vor?; *it's ~ to you* das liegt bei dir / Ihnen; *I don't feel ~ to it* ich fühle mich dem nicht gewachsen

**upbringing** n Erziehung f

**update 1.** n (*list etc*) Aktualisierung f; (*software*) Update nt **2.** vt (*list etc, person*) aktualisieren

**upgrade** vt (*computer*) aufrüsten; *we were ~d* das Hotel hat uns ein besseres Zimmer gegeben

**upheaval** n Aufruhr m; POL Umbruch m

**uphill** adv bergauf

**upon** prep → **on**

**upper** adj obere(r, s); (*arm, deck*) Ober-

**upright** adj, adv aufrecht

**uprising** n Aufstand m

**uproar** n Aufruhr m

**upset 1.** irr vt (*overturn*) umkippen; (*disturb*) aufregen; (*sadden*) bestürzen; (*offend*) kränken; (*plans*) durcheinanderbringen **2.** adj (*disturbed*) aufgeregt; (*sad*) bestürzt; (*offended*) gekränkt; *~ stomach* Magenverstimmung f

**upside down** adv verkehrt herum; *fig* drunter und drüber; *turn sth ~* (*box etc*) etw umdrehen / durchwühlen

**upstairs** adv oben; (*go, take*) nach oben

**up-to-date** adj modern; (*fashion, information*) aktuell; *keep sb ~* jdn auf dem Laufenden halten

**upwards** adv nach oben

**urban** adj städtisch, Stadt-

**urge 1.** n Drang m **2.** vt *~ sb to do sth* jdn drängen, etw zu tun; **urgent, urgently** adj, adv dringend

**urine** n Urin m

**us** pron uns; *can he help ~?* kann er uns helfen?; *it's ~* wir sind's; *both of ~* wir beide

**US, USA** nsing abbr = **United States (of America)** USA pl

**use 1.** n (*using*) Gebrauch m; (*for specific purpose*) Benutzung f; *in / out of ~* in / außer Gebrauch; *it's no ~ (do-ing that)* es hat keinen Zweck(, das zu tun); *it's (of) no ~ to me* das kann ich nicht brauchen **2.** vt benutzen, gebrauchen; (*for specific purpose*) verwenden; (*method*) anwenden; **use up** vt aufbrauchen

**used 1.** adj (*secondhand*) gebraucht **2.** *vaux be ~ to sb / sth* an jdn / etw gewöhnt sein; *get ~ to sb / sth* sich an jdn / etw gewöhnen; *she ~ to live here* sie hat früher mal hier gewohnt; **useful** adj nützlich; **useless** adj nutzlos; (*unusable*) unbrauchbar; (*pointless*) zwecklos; **user** n Benutzer(in) m(f); **user-friendly** adj benutzerfreundlich

**usual** adj üblich, gewöhnlich; *as ~* wie üblich; **usually** adv

normalerweise
**utensil** n Gerät nt
**uterus** n Gebärmutter f
**utilize** vt verwenden
**utmost** adj äußerst

**utter 1.** adj völlig **2.** vt von sich
geben; **utterly** adv völlig
**U-turn** n AUTO Wende f; *do a ~*
wenden

# V

**vacancy** n (job) offene Stelle;
(room) freies Zimmer; **va-**
**cant** adj (room, toilet) frei;
(post) offen; (building) leer
stehend; **vacate** vt (room,
building) räumen; (seat) frei
machen
**vacation** n (US) Ferien pl,
Urlaub m; (at university) (Semester)ferien pl; *go on ~* in
Urlaub fahren
**vaccinate** vt impfen; **vacci-**
**nation** n Impfung f; *~ card*
Impfpass m
**vacuum 1.** n Vakuum nt **2.** vt,
vi (staub)saugen; **vacuum**
(**cleaner**) n Staubsauger m
**vagina** n Scheide f
**vague** adj (imprecise) vage;
(resemblance) entfernt;
**vaguely** adv in etwa, irgendwie
**vain** adj (attempt) vergeblich;
(conceited) eitel; *in ~* vergeblich, umsonst
**valid** adj (ticket, passport etc)
gültig; (argument) stichhaltig
**valley** n Tal nt
**valuable** adj wertvoll; (time)
kostbar; **valuables** npl

Wertsachen pl
**value 1.** n Wert m **2.** vt (appreciate) schätzen; **value added**
**tax** n Mehrwertsteuer f
**valve** n Ventil nt
**van** n AUTO Lieferwagen m
**vanilla** n Vanille f
**vanish** vi verschwinden
**vanity** n Eitelkeit f; **vanity**
**case** n Schminkkoffer m
**vapor** (US), **vapour** n (mist)
Dunst m; (steam) Dampf m
**variable** adj (weather, mood)
unbeständig; (quality) unterschiedlich; (speed, height)
regulierbar; **varied** adj (interests, selection) vielseitig;
(career) bewegt; (work, diet)
abwechslungsreich; **variety**
n (diversity) Abwechslung
f; (assortment) Vielfalt f (of
an + dat); (type) Art f; **vari-**
**ous** adj verschieden
**varnish 1.** n Lack m **2.** vt lackieren
**vary 1.** vt (alter) verändern **2.**
vi (be different) unterschiedlich sein; (fluctuate) sich verändern; (prices) schwanken
**vase** (US) n Vase f
**vast** adj riesig; (area) weit

**VAT**

VAT *abbr* → **value added tax**
Mehrwertsteuer *f*, MwSt.

**Vatican** *n* **the ~** der Vatikan

**VCR** *abbr* = **video cassette recorder** Videorekorder *m*

**VD** *abbr* → **venereal disease** Geschlechtskrankheit *f*

**veal** *n* Kalbfleisch *nt*

**vegan** *n* Veganer(in) *m(f)*

**vegetable** *n* Gemüse *nt*

**vegetarian 1.** *n* Vegetarier(in) *m(f)* **2.** *adj* vegetarisch

**veggie** *fam* **1.** *n* Vegetarier(in) *m(f)*; Gemüse *nt* **2.** *adj* vegetarisch; **veggieburger** *fam n* Veggieburger *m*, Gemüseburger *m*

**vehicle** *n* Fahrzeug *nt*

**veil** *n* Schleier *m*

**vein** *n* Ader *f*

**Velcro®** *n* Klettband *nt*

**velvet** *n* Samt *m*

**vending machine** *n* Automat *m*

**venetian blind** *n* Jalousie *f*

**Venezuela** *n* Venezuela *nt*

**Venice** *n* Venedig *nt*

**venison** *n* Rehfleisch *nt*

**vent** *n* Öffnung *f*

**ventilate** *vt* lüften; **ventilation** *n* Belüftung *f*; **ventilator** *n* (*in room*) Ventilator *m*; **be on a ~** MED künstlich beatmet werden

**venture 1.** *n* (*project*) Unternehmung *f*; COMM Unternehmen *nt* **2.** *vi* (*go*) (sich) wagen

**venue** *n* (*for concert etc*) Veranstaltungsort *m*

**verb** *n* Verb *nt*

**verdict** *n* Urteil *nt*

**verge 1.** *n* (*of road*) (Straßen)rand *m*; **be on the ~ of doing sth** im Begriff sein, etw zu tun **2.** *vi* **~ on** grenzen an + *acc*

**verification** *n* (*confirmation*) Bestätigung *f*; (*check*) Überprüfung *f*; **verify** *vt* (*confirm*) bestätigen; (*check*) überprüfen

**vermin** *npl* Schädlinge *pl*; (*insects*) Ungeziefer *nt*

**verruca** *n* Warze *f*

**versatile** *adj* vielseitig

**verse** *n* (*poetry*) Poesie *f*; (*stanza*) Strophe *f*

**version** *n* Version *f*

**versus** *prep* gegen

**vertical** *adj* senkrecht, vertikal

**very 1.** *adv* sehr; **~ much** sehr **2.** *adj* **the ~ book I need** genau das Buch, das ich brauche; **at that ~ moment** gerade in dem Augenblick; **at the ~ top** ganz oben; **the ~ best** der / die / das Allerbeste

**vest** *n* (*Brit*) Unterhemd *nt*; (*US, waistcoat*) Weste *f*

**vet** *n* Tierarzt *m*, Tierärztin *f*

**veto 1.** *n* Veto *nt* **2.** *vt* sein Veto einlegen gegen

**via** *prep* über + *acc*

**vibrate** *vi* vibrieren; **vibration** *n* Vibration *f*

**vicar** *n* Pfarrer(in) *m(f)*

**vice 1.** *n* (*evil*) Laster *nt* **2.** *pref* Vize-; **~chairman** stellvertretender Vorsitzender;

**~-president** Vizepräsident(in) m(f)

**vice versa** adv umgekehrt

**vicinity** n **in the ~** in der Nähe (of + gen)

**vicious** adj (violent) brutal; (malicious) gemein; **vicious circle** n Teufelskreis m

**victim** n Opfer nt

**victory** n Sieg m

**video 1.** adj Video- **2.** n Video nt; (recorder) Videorekorder m **3.** vt (auf Video) aufnehmen; **video camera** n Videokamera f; **video cassette** n Videokassette f; **video clip** n Videoclip m; **video recorder** n Videorekorder m; **videotape 1.** n Videoband nt **2.** vt (auf Video) aufnehmen

**Vienna** n Wien nt

**Vietnam** n Vietnam nt

**view 1.** n (sight) Blick m (of auf + acc); (vista) Aussicht f; (opinion) Meinung f; **in ~ of** angesichts + gen **2.** vt (situation, event) betrachten; (house) besichtigen; **viewer** n (for slides) Diabetrachter m; TV Zuschauer(in) m(f); **viewpoint** n fig Standpunkt m

**village** n Dorf nt

**villain** n Schurke m; (in film, story) Bösewicht m

**vinegar** n Essig m

**vineyard** n Weinberg m

**vintage** n (of wine) Jahrgang m

**violate** vt (treaty) brechen; (rights, rule) verletzen

**violence** n (brutality) Gewalt f; (of person) Gewalttätigkeit f; **violent** adj (brutal) brutal; (death) gewaltsam

**violet** n Veilchen nt; (colour) Violett nt

**violin** n Geige f, Violine f

**virgin** n Jungfrau f

**Virgo** n ASTR Jungfrau f

**virtual** adj IT virtuell; **virtually** adv praktisch; **virtual reality** n IT virtuelle Realität f

**virtue** n Tugend f; **by ~ of** aufgrund + gen; **virtuous** adj tugendhaft

**virus** n MED, IT Virus nt

**visa** n Visum nt

**visibility** n METEO Sichtweite f; **good / poor ~** gute / schlechte Sicht; **visible** adj sichtbar; (evident) sichtlich; **visibly** adv sichtlich

**vision** n (power of sight) Sehvermögen nt; (foresight) Weitblick m; (dream, image) Vision f

**visit 1.** n Besuch m; (stay) Aufenthalt m **2.** vt besuchen; **visiting hours** npl Besuchszeiten pl; **visitor** n Besucher(in) m(f); **~s' book** Gästebuch m

**visual** adj Seh-; (image, joke) visuell; **visualize** vt sich vorstelle; **visually** adv visuell; **~ impaired** sehbehindert

**vital** adj (essential) unerlässlich, wesentlich; (argument, *moment)* entscheidend; **vitality** *n* Vitalität *f*; **vitally** *adv* äußerst

**vitamin** *n* Vitamin *nt*

**vivid** *adj (description)* anschaulich; *(memory)* lebhaft

**V-neck** *n* V-Ausschnitt *m*

**vocabulary** *n* Wortschatz *m*, Vokabular *nt*

**vocal** *adj (of the voice)* Stimm-; *(group)* Gesangs-; *(protest, person)* lautstark

**vocation** *n* Berufung *f*; **vocational** *adj* Berufs-

**vodka** *n* Wodka *m*

**voice 1.** *n* Stimme *f* **2.** *vt* äußern; **voice mail** *n* Voicemail *f*

**void 1.** *n* Leere *f* **2.** *adj* LAW ungültig

**volcano** *n* Vulkan *m*

**volleyball** *n* Volleyball *m*

**volt** *n* Volt *nt*; **voltage** *n* Spannung *f*

**volume** *n (of sound)* Lautstärke *f*; *(space occupied by sth)* Volumen *nt*; *(size, amount)* Umfang *m*; *(book)* Band *m*; **volume control** *n* Lautstärkeregler *m*

**voluntary, voluntarily** *adj, adv* freiwillig; *(unpaid)* ehrenamtlich; **volunteer 1.** *n* Freiwillige(r) *mf* **2.** *vi* sich freiwillig melden

**voluptuous** *adj* sinnlich

**vomit** *vi* sich übergeben

**vote 1.** *n* Stimme *f*; *(ballot)* Wahl *f*; *(result)* Abstimmungsergebnis *nt*; *(right to vote)* Wahlrecht *nt* **2.** *vt (elect)* wählen; **they ~d him chairman** sie wählten ihn zum Vorsitzenden **3.** *vi* wählen; **~ for / against sth** für / gegen etw stimmen; **voter** *n* Wähler(in) *m(f)*

**voucher** *n* Gutschein *m*

**vow** *n* Gelöbnis *nt*

**vowel** *n* Vokal *m*

**voyage** *n* Reise *f*

**vulgar** *adj* vulgär, ordinär

**vulnerable** *adj* verwundbar; *(sensitive)* verletzlich

**vulture** *n* Geier *m*

# W

**wade** *vi (in water)* waten

**wafer** *n* Waffel *f*; REL Hostie *f*; **wafer-thin** *adj* hauchdünn

**waffle** *n* Waffel *f*; *(Brit) fam (empty talk)* Geschwafel *nt*

**wag** *vt (tail)* wedeln mit

**wage** *n* Lohn *m*

**waggon** *(Brit)*, **wagon** *n*

*(horse-drawn)* Fuhrwerk *nt*; *(Brit)* RAIL Waggon *m*; *(US)* AUTO Wagen *m*

**waist** *n* Taille *f*; **waistcoat** *n* *(Brit)* Weste *f*; **waistline** *n* Taille *f*

**wait 1.** *n* Wartezeit *f* **2.** *vi* warten *(for* auf + *acc)*; **~ and see**

abwarten; **~ a minute** Moment mal!; **wait up** vi aufbleiben

**waiter** n Kellner m

**waiting** n *'no ~'* „Halteverbot"; **waiting list** n Warteliste f; **waiting room** n MED Wartezimmer nt; RAIL Wartesaal m

**waitress** n Kellnerin f

**wake 1.** vt wecken **2.** vi aufwachen; **wake up 1.** vt aufwecken **2.** vi aufwachen; **wake-up call** n TEL Weckruf m

**Wales** n Wales nt

**walk 1.** n Spaziergang m; (*ramble*) Wanderung f; (*route*) Weg m; **go for a ~** spazieren gehen; **it's only a five-minute ~** es sind nur fünf Minuten zu Fuß **2.** vi gehen; (*stroll*) spazieren gehen; (*ramble*) wandern **3.** vt (*dog*) ausführen; **walking** n **go ~** wandern; **walking shoes** npl Wanderschuhe pl

**wall** n (*inside*) Wand f; (*outside*) Mauer f

**wallet** n Brieftasche f

**wallpaper 1.** n Tapete f; IT Bildschirmhintergrund m **2.** vt tapezieren

**walnut** n (*nut*) Walnuss f

**waltz** n Walzer m

**wander** vi (*person*) herumwandern

**want 1.** n (*lack*) Mangel m (of an + dat); (*need*) Bedürfnis nt; **for ~ of** aus Mangel an

+ dat **2.** vt (*desire*) wollen; (*need*) brauchen; **he doesn't ~ to** er will nicht

**WAP phone** n WAP-Handy nt

**war** n Krieg m

**ward** n (*in hospital*) Station f; (*child*) Mündel nt

**warden** n Aufseher(in) m(f); (*in youth hostel*) Herbergsvater m, Herbergsmutter f

**wardrobe** n Kleiderschrank m

**warehouse** n Lagerhaus nt

**warfare** n Krieg m; (*techniques*) Kriegsführung f

**warm 1.** adj warm; (*welcome*) herzlich; **I'm ~** mir ist warm **2.** vt wärmen; (*food*) aufwärmen; **warm over** vt (US, *food*) aufwärmen; **warm up 1.** vt (*food*) aufwärmen; (*room*) erwärmen **2.** vi (*food, room*) warm werden; SPORT sich aufwärmen; **warmly** adv warm; (*welcome*) herzlich; **warmth** n Wärme f; (*of welcome*) Herzlichkeit f

**warn** vt warnen (*of, against* vor + dat); **~ sb not to do sth** jdn davor warnen, etw zu tun; **warning** n Warnung f; **warning light** n Warnlicht nt; **warning triangle** n AUTO Warndreieck nt

**warranty** n Garantie f

**wart** n Warze f

**wary** adj vorsichtig; (*suspicious*) misstrauisch

**was** pt → **be**

**wash** 1. n have a ~ sich waschen; **it's in the** ~ es ist in der Wäsche 2. vt waschen; (plates, glasses etc) abwaschen; ~ **the dishes** (das Geschirr) abwaschen 3. vi (clean oneself) sich waschen; **wash off** vt abwaschen; **wash up** vi (Brit, wash dishes) abwaschen; (US, clean oneself) sich waschen; **washable** adj waschbar; **washbag** n (US) Kulturbeutel m; **washbasin** n Waschbecken nt; **washcloth** n (US) Waschlappen m; **washer** n TECH Dichtungsring m; (washing machine) Waschmaschine f; **washing** n (laundry) Wäsche f; **washing machine** n Waschmaschine f; **washing powder** n Waschpulver nt; **washing-up** n (Brit) Abwasch m; **do the** ~ abwaschen; **washing-up liquid** n (Brit) Spülmittel nt; **washroom** n (US) Toilette f

**wasn't** contr = **was not**

**wasp** n Wespe f

**waste** 1. n (materials) Abfall m; (wasting) Verschwendung f; **it's a** ~ **of time** das ist Zeitverschwendung 2. adj (superfluous) überschüssig 3. vt verschwenden (on an + acc); (opportunity) vertun; **waste bin** n Abfalleimer m; **wastepaper basket** n Papierkorb m

**watch** 1. n (timepiece) (Armband)uhr f 2. vt (observe) beobachten; (guard) aufpassen auf + acc; (film, play, programme) sich dat ansehen; ~ **TV** fernsehen 3. vi zusehen; (guard) Wache halten; ~ **for sb / sth** nach jdm / etw Ausschau halten; ~ **out** pass auf!; **watchdog** n Wachhund m; **watchful** adj wachsam

**water** 1. n Wasser nt 2. vt (plant) gießen 3. vi (eye) tränen; **my mouth is** ~**ing** mir läuft das Wasser im Mund zusammen; **water down** vt verdünnen; **watercolor** (US), **watercolour** n (painting) Aquarell nt; (paint) Wasserfarbe f; **watercress** n (Brunnen)kresse f; **waterfall** n Wasserfall m; **watering can** n Gießkanne f; **water level** n Wasserstand m; **watermelon** n Wassermelone f; **waterproof** adj wasserdicht; **water-skiing** n Wasserskilaufen nt; **water sports** npl Wassersport m; **watertight** adj wasserdicht; **water wings** npl Schwimmflügel pl; **watery** adj wässerig

**wave** 1. n Welle f 2. vt (move to and fro) schwenken; (hand, flag) winken mit 3. vi (person) winken; (flag) wehen; **wavelength** n Wellenlänge f; **wavy** adj wellig

**wax** n Wachs nt; (in ear) Ohrenschmalz nt

**way** n Weg m; (direction) Richtung f; (manner) Art f; **can you tell me the ~ to ... ?** wie komme ich (am besten) zu ... ?; **we went the ~ wrong** wir sind in die falsche Richtung gefahren / gegangen; **lose one's ~** sich verirren; **make ~ for sb / sth** jdm / etw Platz machen; **get one's own ~** seinen Willen durchsetzen; **'give ~'** AUTO „Vorfahrt achten"; **the other~ round** andersherum; **one ~ or another** irgendwie; **in a ~** in gewisser Weise; **in the ~** im Weg; **by the ~** übrigens; **'~ in'** „Eingang"; **'~ out'** „Ausgang"; **no~** fam kommt nicht infrage!

**we** pron wir

**weak** adj schwach; **weaken 1.** vt schwächen **2.** vi schwächer werden

**wealth** n Reichtum m; **wealthy** adj reich

**weapon** n Waffe f

**wear 1.** vt (have on) tragen **2.** vi (become worn) sich abnutzen **3.** n ~ (and tear) Abnutzung f; **wear off** vi (diminish) nachlassen; **wear out 1.** vt abnutzen; (person) erschöpfen **2.** vi sich abnutzen

**weather** n Wetter nt; **weather forecast** n Wettervorhersage f

**weave** vt (cloth) weben; (basket etc) flechten

**web** n a. fig Netz nt; **the Web** das Web, das Internet; **webcam** n Webcam f; **web page** n Webseite f; **website** n Website f

**we'd** contr = **we had; we would**

**Wed** abbr → **Wednesday** Mi.

**wedding** n Hochzeit f; **wedding anniversary** n Hochzeitstag m; **wedding dress** n Hochzeitskleid nt; **wedding ring** n Ehering m; **wedding shower** n (US) Party für die zukünftige Braut

**wedge** n (under door etc) Keil m; (of cheese etc) Stück nt, Ecke f

**Wednesday** n Mittwoch m; → **Tuesday**

**wee 1.** adj klein **2.** vi fam pinkeln, Pipi machen

**weed 1.** n Unkraut nt **2.** vt jäten

**week** n Woche f; **twice a ~** zweimal in der Woche; **a ~ on Friday / Friday ~** Freitag in einer Woche; **in two ~s' time, in two ~s** in zwei Wochen; **weekday** n Wochentag m; **weekend** n Wochenende nt; **weekend break** n Wochenendurlaub m; **weekly** adj, adv wöchentlich; (magazine) Wochen-

**weep** vi weinen

**weigh** vt, vi wiegen; **weigh up** vt abwägen; (person) ein-

schätzen; **weight** n Gewicht
nt; **lose / put on ~** abnehmen / zunehmen; **weight-
lifting** n Gewichtheben nt;
**weight training** n Krafttrai-
ning nt

**weird** adj seltsam; **weirdo** n
Spinner(in) m(f)

**welcome 1.** n Empfang m **2.**
adj willkommen; (news) angenehm; **~ to London** willkommen in London! **3.** vt begrüßen; **welcoming** adj
freundlich

**welfare** n Wohl nt; (US, social
security) Sozialhilfe f; **welfare state** n Wohlfahrtsstaat
m

**well 1.** n Brunnen m **2.** adj (in
good health) gesund; **are
you ~?** geht es dir / Ihnen
gut?; **feel ~** sich wohlfühlen
**3.** interj nun; **~, I don't know**
nun, ich weiß nicht **4.** adv
gut; **~ done** gut gemacht!;
**it may ~ be** das kann wohl
sein; **as ~** (in addition) auch;
**~ over 60** weit über 60

**we'll** contr = **we will; we shall**

**well-behaved** adj brav; **well-
-done** adj (steak) durchgebraten

**wellingtons** npl Gummistiefel pl

**well-known** adj bekannt;
**well-off** adj (wealthy) wohlhabend; **well-paid** adj gut
bezahlt

**Welsh 1.** adj walisisch **2.** n
(language) Walisisch nt; **the**
**~ pl** die Waliser pl; **Welshman** n Waliser m; **Welshwoman** n Waliserin f

**went** pt → **go**

**wept** pt, pp → **weep**

**were** pt → **be**

**we're** contr = **we are**

**weren't** contr = **were not**

**west 1.** n Westen m **2.** adv (go,
face) nach Westen **3.** adj
West-; **westbound** adj (in)
Richtung Westen; **western**
**1.** adj West-, westlich; **Western Europe** Westeuropa nt
**2.** n FILM Western m; **West
Germany** n Westdeutsch-
land nt; **westwards** adv nach
Westen

**wet 1.** vt **~ oneself** in die Hose
machen **2.** adj nass, feucht;
**'~ paint'** „frisch gestrichen";
**wet suit** n Taucheranzug m

**we've** contr = **we have**

**whale** n Wal m

**wharf** n Kai m

**what 1.** pron, interj was; **~'s
your name?** wie heißt du /
heißen Sie?; **~ is the letter
about?** worum geht es in
dem Brief?; **~ are they talking about?** worüber reden
sie?; **~ for?** wozu? **2.** adj wel-
che(r, s); **~ colour is it?** welche Farbe hat es?; **whatever**
pron **I'll do ~ you want** ich
tue alles, was du willst / Sie
wollen; **~ he says** egal, was
er sagt

**what's** contr = **what is; what
has**

**wheat** n Weizen m

**wheel 1.** n Rad nt; (steering wheel) Lenkrad nt **2.** vt (bicycle, trolley) schieben; **wheelchair** n Rollstuhl m; **wheel clamp** n Parkkralle f

**when 1.** adv (in questions) wann; **on the day ~** an dem Tag, als **2.** conj wenn; (in past) als; **~ I was younger** als ich jünger war; **whenever** adv (every time) immer wenn; **come ~ you like** komm wann immer du willst / kommen Sie wann Sie wollen

**where 1.** adv wo; **~ are you going?** wohin gehst du / gehen Sie?; **~ are you from?** woher kommst du / kommen Sie? **2.** conj wo; **that's ~ I used to live** da habe ich früher gewohnt; **whereabouts 1.** adv wo **2.** npl Aufenthaltsort m; **whereas** conj während, wohingegen; **wherever** conj wo immer; **~ that may be** wo immer das sein mag

**whether** conj ob

**which 1.** adj welche(r, s); **~ car is yours?** welches Auto gehört dir / Ihnen?; **~ one?** welche(r, s)? **2.** pron (in questions) welche(r, s); (in relative clauses) der / die/das, die pl; **it rained, ~ upset his plans** es regnete, was seine Pläne durcheinanderbrachte; **whichever** adj, pron welche(r, s) auch im-

mer

**while 1.** n a **~** eine Weile; **for a ~** eine Zeit lang; **a short ~ ago** vor Kurzem **2.** conj während; (although) obwohl

**whine** v (person) jammern

**whip 1.** n Peitsche f **2.** vt (beat) peitschen; **~ped cream** Schlagsahne f

**whirl** vt, vi herumwirbeln; **whirlpool** n (in river, sea) Strudel m; (pool) Whirlpool m

**whisk 1.** n Schneebesen m **2.** vt (cream etc) schlagen

**whisker** n (of animal) Schnurrhaar nt; **~s** pl (of man) Backenbart m

**whisk(e)y** n Whisky m

**whisper** vi, vt flüstern

**whistle 1.** n Pfiff m, Pfeife f **2.** vt, vi pfeifen

**white 1.** n (of egg) Eiweiß nt; (of eye) Weiße nt **2.** adj weiß; (with fear) blass; (coffee) mit Milch / Sahne

**white lie** n Notlüge f; **white meat** n helles Fleisch; **white water rafting** n Rafting nt; **white wine** n Weißwein m

**Whitsun** n Pfingsten nt

**who** pron (in questions) wer; (in relative clauses) der / die/das, die pl; **~ did you see?** wen hast du / haben Sie gesehen?; **~ does that belong to?** wem gehört das?; **the people ~ live next door** die Leute, die nebenan wohnen; **whoever** pron wer auch immer; **~ you choose** wen auch immer du wählst / Sie wählen

**whole 1.** *adj* ganz **2.** *n* Ganze(s) *nt*; **the ~ of my family** meine ganze Familie; **on the ~** im Großen und Ganzen; **wholefood** *n* (*Brit*) Vollwertkost *f*; **~ store, ~ shop** Bioladen *m*; **wholeheartedly** *adv* voll und ganz; **wholemeal** *adj* (*Brit*) Vollkorn-; **wholesale** *adv* (*buy*, *sell*) im Großhandel; **wholesome** *adj* gesund; **whole wheat** *adj* Vollkorn-; **wholly** *adv* völlig

**whom** *pron* (*in questions*) wen; (*in relative clauses*) den / die/das, die *pl*; **with ~ did you speak?** mit wem hast du / haben Sie gesprochen?

**whooping cough** *n* Keuchhusten *m*

**whose 1.** *adj* (*in questions*) wessen; (*in relative clauses*) dessen / deren / deren, deren *pl* **2.** *pron* (*in questions*) wessen; **~ is this?** wem gehört das?

**why** *adv*, *conj* warum; **that's ~** deshalb

**wicked** *adj* böse; *fam* (*great*) geil

**wide 1.** *adj* breit; (*skirt*, *trousers*) weit; (*selection*) groß **2.** *adv* weit; **wide-angle lens** *n* Weitwinkelobjektiv *nt*; **wide-awake** *adj* hellwach;

**widely** *adv* weit; **~ known** allgemein bekannt; **widen** *vt* verbreitern; *fig* erweitern; **wide-open** *adj* weit offen; **widescreen TV** *n* Breitbildfernseher *m*; **widespread** *adj* weit verbreitet

**widow** *n* Witwe *f*; **widowed** *adj* verwitwet; **widower** *n* Witwer *m*

**width** *n* Breite *f*

**wife** *n* (Ehe)frau *f*

**wig** *n* Perücke *f*

**wild 1.** *adj* wild; (*violent*) heftig; (*plan*, *idea*) verrückt **2.** *n* **in the ~** in freier Wildbahn; **wildlife** *n* Tier- und Pflanzenwelt *f*; **wildly** *adv* wild; (*enthusiastic*, *exaggerated*) maßlos

**will 1.** *vaux* **he / they ~ come** er wird / sie werden kommen; **I won't be back until late** ich komme erst spät zurück; **the car won't start** das Auto will nicht anspringen; **~ you have some coffee?** möchtest du / möchten Sie eine Tasse Kaffee? **2.** *n* Wille *m*; (*wish*) Wunsch *m*; (*document*) Testament *nt*; **willing** *adj* bereitwillig; **be ~ to do sth** bereit sein, etw zu tun; **willingly** *adv* gern(e)

**willow** *n* Weide *f*

**wimp** *n* Weichei *nt*

**win 1.** *vt*, *vi* gewinnen **2.** *n* Sieg *m*; **win over**, **win round** *vt* für sich gewinnen

**wind** *vt* (*rope*, *bandage*) wickeln; **wind down** vt (car window) herunterkurbeln; **wind up** vt (clock) aufziehen; (car window) hochkurbeln; (meeting, speech) abschließen; (person) aufziehen, ärgern

**wind** n Wind m; MED Blähungen pl

**wind instrument** n Blasinstrument nt; **windmill** n Windmühle f

**window** n Fenster nt; (counter) Schalter m; **~ of opportunity** Chance f, Gelegenheit f; **windowpane** n Fensterscheibe f; **window-shopping** n **go ~** einen Schaufensterbummel machen; **windowsill** n Fensterbrett nt

**windpipe** n Luftröhre f; **windscreen** n (Brit) Windschutzscheibe f; **windscreen wiper** n (Brit) Scheibenwischer m; **windshield** n (US) Windschutzscheibe f; **windshield wiper** n (US) Scheibenwischer m; **windsurfer** n Windsurfer(in) m(f); (board) Surfbrett nt; **windsurfing** n Windsurfen nt

**windy** adj windig

**wine** n Wein m; **wine list** n Weinkarte f; **wine tasting** n (event) Weinprobe f

**wing** n Flügel m; (Brit) AUTO Kotflügel m

**wink** vi zwinkern; **~ at sb** jdm zuzwinkern

**winner** n Gewinner(in) m(f), Sieger(in) m(f); **winning** 1. adj (team, horse etc) siegreich 2. n **~s** pl Gewinn m

**winter** n Winter m; **winter sports** npl Wintersport m; **wint(e)ry** adj winterlich

**wipe** vt abwischen; **~ one's nose** sich dat die Nase putzen; **wipe off** vt abwischen; **wipe out** vt (destroy) vernichten; (data, debt) löschen

**wire** 1. n Draht m; ELEC Leitung f; (US, telegram) Telegramm nt 2. vt (plug in) anschließen; (US) TEL telegrafieren (sb sth jdm etw); **wireless** adj drahtlos

**wisdom** n Weisheit f; **wisdom tooth** n Weisheitszahn m

**wise, wisely** adj, adv weise

**wish** 1. n Wunsch m (for nach); **with best ~es** (in letter) herzliche Grüße 2. vt wünschen, wollen; **~ sb good luck / Merry Christmas** jdm viel Glück / frohe Weihnachten wünschen; **I ~ I'd never seen him** ich wünschte, ich hätte ihn nie gesehen

**witch** n Hexe f

**with** prep mit; (cause) vor + dat; **I'm pleased ~ it** ich bin damit zufrieden **he lives ~ his aunt** er wohnt bei seiner Tante

**withdraw** irr 1. vt zurückziehen; (money) abheben;

(*comment*) zurücknehmen
**2.** *vi* sich zurückziehen

**wither** *vi* (*plant*) verwelken

**withhold** *irr vt* vorenthalten
(*from sb* jdm)

**within** *prep* innerhalb + *gen*; ~
**walking distance** zu Fuß erreichbar

**without** *prep* ohne; ~ **asking**
ohne zu fragen

**withstand** *irr vt* standhalten
+ *dat*

**witness 1.** *n* Zeuge *m*, Zeugin
*f* **2.** *vt* Zeuge sein

**witty** *adj* geistreich

**wives** *pl* → **wife**

**WMD** *abbr* = **weapons of
mass destruction** Massenvernichtungswaffen *pl*

**wobble** *vi* wackeln; **wobbly**
*adj* wackelig

**wok** *n* Wok *m*

**woke** *pt* → **wake**

**woken** *pp* → **wake**

**wolf** *n* Wolf *m*

**woman** *n* Frau *f*

**womb** *n* Gebärmutter *f*

**women** *pl* → **woman**

**won** *pt, pp* → **win**

**wonder 1.** *n* (*marvel*) Wunder
*nt*; (*surprise*) Staunen *nt* **2.** *vt,
vi* (*speculate*) sich fragen; **I ~
what / if ...** ich frage mich,
was / ob ...; **wonderful,
wonderfully** *adj, adv* wunderbar

**won't** *contr* = **will not**

**wood** *n* Holz *nt*; **~s** Wald *m*;
**wooden** *adj* Holz-; *fig* hölzern; **woodpecker** *n* Specht

*m*

**wool** *n* Wolle *f*; **woollen,
woolen** (*US*) *adj* Woll-

**word 1.** *n* Wort *nt*; (*promise*)
Ehrenwort *nt*; **~s** *pl* (*of song*)
Text *m*; **have a ~ with sb** mit
jdm sprechen; **in other ~s**
mit anderen Worten **2.** *vt* formulieren; **word processor** *n*
(*program*) Textverarbeitungsprogramm *nt*

**wore** *pt* → **wear**

**work 1.** *n* Arbeit *f*; (*of art, literature*) Werk *nt*; **~ of art**
Kunstwerk *nt*; **he's at ~** er
ist in / auf der Arbeit; **out
of ~** arbeitslos **2.** *vi* arbeiten
(*at, on* an + *dat*); (*machine,
plan*) funktionieren; (*medicine*) wirken; (*succeed*) klappen **3.** *vt* (*machine*) bedienen; **work out 1.** *vi* (*plan*)
klappen; (*sum*) aufgehen; (*person*) trainieren **2.** *vt*
(*price, speed etc*) ausrechnen; (*plan*) ausarbeiten;
**work up** *vt* **get worked up**
sich aufregen; **workaholic**
*n* Arbeitstier *nt*; **worker** *n*
Arbeiter(in) *m(f)*; **work experience** *n* Praktikum *nt*;
**workman** *n* Handwerker
*m*; **workout** *n* SPORT Fitnesstraining *nt*, Konditionstraining *nt*; **work permit** *n* Arbeitserlaubnis *f*; **workplace**
*n* Arbeitsplatz *m*; **workshop**
*n* Werkstatt *f*; (*meeting*)
Workshop *m*

**world** *n* Welt *f*; **world cham-**

595

## wring out

**pionship** n Weltmeisterschaft f; **World War** n ~ I/II, **the First / Second** ~ der Erste / Zweite Weltkrieg; **world-wide** adj, adv weltweit; **World Wide Web** n World Wide Web nt

**worm** n Wurm m

**worn 1.** pp → **wear 2.** adj (clothes) abgetragen; (tyre) abgefahren; **worn-out** adj abgenutzt; (person) erschöpft

**worried** adj besorgt; **worry 1.** n Sorge f **2.** vt Sorgen machen + dat **3.** vi sich Sorgen machen (about um); **don't** ~ keine Sorge!; **worrying** adj beunruhigend

**worse 1.** adj comparative → **bad**; schlechter; (pain, mistake etc) schlimmer **2.** adv comparative → **badly**; schlechter; **worsen 1.** vt verschlechtern **2.** vi sich verschlechtern

**worship** vt anbeten, anhimmeln

**worst 1.** adj superlative → **bad**; schlechteste(r, s); (pain, mistake etc) schlimmste(r, s) **2.** adv superlative → **badly**; am schlechtesten **3.** n **the** ~ **is over** das Schlimmste ist vorbei; **at (the)** ~ schlimmstenfalls

**worth 1.** n Wert m **2.** adj **it is** ~ **£50** es ist 50 Pfund wert; ~ **seeing** sehenswert; **it's** ~ **it** (rewarding) es lohnt sich;

**worthless** adj wertlos; **worthwhile** adj lohnend, lohnenswert; **worthy** adj (deserving respect) würdig; **be** ~ **of sth** etw verdienen

**would** vaux **if you asked he / come** wenn du ihn fragtest / Sie ihn fragten, würde er kommen; **I** ~ **have told you, but** ... ich hätte es dir / Ihnen gesagt, aber ...; ~ **you like a drink?** möchtest du / möchten Sie etwas trinken?; **he** ~**n't help me** er wollte mir nicht helfen

**wouldn't** contr = **would not**

**would've** contr = **would have**

**wound 1.** n Wunde f **2.** vt verwunden, verletzen **3.** pt, pp → **wind**

**wove** pt → **weave**

**woven** pp → **weave**

**wrap** vt (parcel, present) einwickeln; **wrap up 1.** vt (parcel, present) einwickeln **2.** vi (dress warmly) sich warm anziehen; **wrapping paper** n Packpapier nt; (giftwrap) Geschenkpapier nt

**wreath** n Kranz m

**wreck 1.** n (ship, plane, car) Wrack nt; **a nervous** ~ ein Nervenbündel m (car) zu Schrott fahren; fig zerstören; **wreckage** n Trümmer pl

**wrench** n (tool) Schraubenschlüssel m

**wrestling** n Ringen nt

**wring out** vt auswringen

# wrinkle

**wrinkle** n Falte f

**wrist** n Handgelenk nt; **wristwatch** n Armbanduhr f

**write 1.** vt schreiben; (cheque) ausstellen **2.** vi schreiben; ~ **to sb** jdm schreiben; **write down** vt aufschreiben; **write off** vt (debt, person) abschreiben; (car) zu Schrott fahren; **write out** vt (name etc) ausschreiben; (cheque) ausstellen; **write-protected** adj ɪᴛ schreibgeschützt; **writer** n Verfasser(in) m(f); (author) Schriftsteller(in) m(f); **writing** n Schrift f; (profession) Schreiben nt; **in** ~ schriftlich; **writing paper** n

Schreibpapier nt

**written** pp → **write**

**wrong** adj (incorrect) falsch; (morally) unrecht; **you're** ~ du hast / Sie haben unrecht; **what's** ~ **with your leg?** was ist mit deinem / Ihrem Bein los?; **I dialled the** ~ **number** ich habe mich verwählt; **don't get me** ~ versteh / verstehen Sie mich nicht falsch; **go** ~ (plan) schiefgehen; **wrongly** adv falsch; (unjustly) zu Unrecht

**wrote** pt → **write**

**WWW** abbr → **World Wide Web** WWW

# X

**xenophobia** n Ausländerfeindlichkeit f

**XL** abbr = **extra large** XL, übergroß

**Xmas** n Weihnachten nt

**X-ray 1.** n (picture) Röntgenaufnahme f **2.** vt röntgen

**xylophone** n Xylophon nt

# Y

**yacht** n Jacht f; **yachting** n Segeln nt

**yam** n (US) Süßkartoffel f

**yard** n Hof m; (US, garden) Garten m; (measure) Yard nt (0,91 m)

**yawn** vi gähnen

**yd** abbr = **yard(s)**

**year** n Jahr nt; ~**s ago** vor Jahren; **a five-year-old** ein(e)

Fünfjährige(r); **yearly** adj, adv jährlich

**yearn** vi sich sehnen (for nach + dat)

**yeast** n Hefe f

**yell** vi, vt schreien; ~ **at sb** jdn anschreien

**yellow** adj gelb; ~ **fever** Gelbfieber nt; **the Yellow Pages®** pl die Gelben Seiten pl

**yes 1.** adv ja; (answering negative question) doch; **say~ to sth** ja zu etw sagen **2.** n Ja nt

**yesterday** adv gestern; **the day before ~** vorgestern; **~'s newspaper** die Zeitung von gestern

**yet 1.** adv (still) noch; (up to now) bis jetzt; (in a question: already) schon; **he hasn't arrived** ~ er ist noch nicht gekommen; **have you finished ~?** bist du / sind Sie schon fertig?; **~ again** schon wieder; **as ~** bis jetzt **2.** conj doch

**yield 1.** n Ertrag m **2.** vt (result, crop) hervorbringen; (profit, interest) bringen **3.** vi nachgeben (to + dat); MIL sich ergeben (to + dat); **'~'** (US) AUTO „Vorfahrt beachten"

**yoga** n Yoga nt

**yog(h)urt** n Jog(h)urt m

**yolk** n Eigelb nt

**Yorkshire pudding** n gebackener Eierteig, der meist zum Roastbeef gegessen wird

**you** pron (as subject) du / Sie/ihr; man; (as direct object) dich / Sie/euch; einen; (as indirect object) dir / Ihnen / ihnen; einem; **~ never can tell** man weiß nie

**you'd** contr = **you had; you would**; **~ better leave** du

solltest / Sie sollten gehen

**you'll** contr = **you will; you shall**

**young** adj jung; **youngster** n Jugendliche(r) mf

**your** adj dein; (polite form) Ihr; (pl) euer; (polite form) Ihr; **have you hurt ~ leg?** hast du dir / haben Sie sich das Bein verletzt?

**you're** contr = **you are**

**yours** pron (sg) deine(r, s); (polite form) Ihre(r, s); (pl) eure(r, s); (polite form) Ihre(r, s); **is this ~?** gehört das dir / Ihnen?; **a friend of ~** ein Freund von dir / Ihnen; (in letter) **~ ...** dein / deine ..., Ihr / Ihre ...

**yourself** pron sg dich; (polite form) sich; **have you hurt ~?** hast du dich / haben Sie sich verletzt?; **did you do it ~?** hast du / haben Sie es selbst gemacht?; **(all) by ~** allein; **yourselves** pron pl euch; (polite form) sich; **have you hurt ~?** habt ihr euch / haben Sie sich verletzt?

**you've** contr = **you have**

**yucky** adj fam eklig

**yummy** adj lecker

# Z

**zap 1.** *vt* IT löschen; *(in computer game)* abknallen **2.** *vi* TV zappen; **zapper** *n* TV Fernbedienung *f*

**zebra** *(US) n* Zebra *nt*; **zebra crossing** *n* *(Brit)* Zebrastreifen *m*

**zero** *n* Null *f*

**zest** *n* *(enthusiasm)* Begeisterung *f*

**zigzag 1.** *n* Zickzack *m* **2.** *vi* *(person, vehicle)* im Zickzack gehen / fahren

**zinc** *n* Zink *nt*

**zip 1.** *n* *(Brit)* Reißverschluss *m* **2.** *vt ~ (up)* den Reißverschluss zumachen; IT zippen;

**zip code** *n* *(US)* Postleitzahl *f*; **Zip disk** *n* IT ZIP-Diskette® *f*; **Zip drive** *n* IT ZIP-Laufwerk® *nt*; **Zip file** *n* IT ZIP-Datei® *f*; **zipper** *n* *(US)* Reißverschluss *m*

**zodiac** *n* Tierkreis *m*; *sign of the ~* Tierkreiszeichen *nt*

**zone** *n* Zone *f*; *(area)* Gebiet *nt*; *(in town)* Bezirk *m*

**zoo** *n* Zoo *m*

**zoom 1.** *vi* *(move fast)* brausen, sausen **2.** *n ~ (lens)* Zoomobjektiv *nt*; **zoom in** *vi* PHOT heranzoomen *(on* an + *acc)*

**zucchini** *n* *(US)* Zucchini *f*

# Appendices

## German irregular verbs

| | | | |
|---|---|---|---|
| **backen**–backt/bäckt | backte | hat gebacken |
| **befehlen**–befiehlt | befahl | hat befohlen |
| **beginnen**–beginnt | begann | hat begonnen |
| **beißen**–beißt | biss | hat gebissen |
| **bergen**–birgt | barg | hat geborgen |
| **betrügen**–betrügt | betrog | hat betrogen |
| **biegen**–biegt | bog | hat/ist gebogen |
| **bieten**–bietet | bot | hat geboten |
| **binden**–bindet | band | hat gebunden |
| **bitten**–bittet | bat | hat gebeten |
| **blasen**–bläst | blies | hat geblasen |
| **bleiben**–bleibt | blieb | ist geblieben |
| **braten**–brät | briet | hat gebraten |
| **brechen**–bricht | brach | hat/ist gebrochen |
| **brennen**–brennt | brannte | hat gebrannt |
| **bringen**–bringt | brachte | hat gebracht |
| **denken**–denkt | dachte | hat gedacht |
| **dringen**–dringt | drang | ist gedrungen |
| **dürfen**–darf | durfte | hat gedurft |
| **empfangen**–empfängt | empfing | hat empfangen |
| **empfehlen**–empfiehlt | empfahl | hat empfohlen |
| **empfinden**–empfindet | empfand | hat empfunden |
| **erschrecken**–erschrickt | erschrak | ist erschrocken |
| **essen**–isst | aß | hat gegessen |
| **fahren**–fährt | fuhr | hat/ist gefahren |
| **fallen**–fällt | fiel | ist gefallen |
| **fangen**–fängt | fing | hat gefangen |
| **finden**–findet | fand | hat gefunden |
| **flechten**–flicht | flocht | hat geflochten |
| **fliegen**–fliegt | flog | hat/ist geflogen |
| **fließen**–fließt | floss | ist geflossen |
| **fressen**–frisst | fraß | hat gefressen |
| **frieren**–friert | fror | hat gefroren |
| **geben**–gibt | gab | hat gegeben |
| **gehen**–geht | ging | ist gegangen |

| | | | |
|---|---|---|---|
| **gelingen**–gelingt | gelang | ist gelungen |
| **gelten**–gilt | galt | hat gegolten |
| **genießen**–genießt | genoss | hat genossen |
| **geschehen**–geschieht | geschah | ist geschehen |
| **gewinnen**–gewinnt | gewann | hat gewonnen |
| **gießen**–gießt | goss | hat gegossen |
| **gleichen**–gleicht | glich | hat geglichen |
| **gleiten**–gleitet | glitt | ist geglitten |
| **graben**–gräbt | grub | hat gegraben |
| **greifen**–greift | griff | hat gegriffen |
| **haben**–hat | hatte | hat gehabt |
| **halten**–hält | hielt | hat gehalten |
| **hängen**–hängt | hing | hat gehangen |
| **hauen**–haut | haute | hat gehauen |
| **heißen**–heißt | hieß | hat geheißen |
| **helfen**–hilft | half | hat geholfen |
| **kennen**–kennt | kannte | hat gekannt |
| **klingen**–klingt | klang | hat geklungen |
| **kneifen**–kneift | kniff | hat gekniffen |
| **kommen**–kommt | kam | ist gekommen |
| **können**–kann | konnte | hat gekonnt |
| **kriechen**–kriecht | kroch | ist gekrochen |
| **laden**–lädt | lud | hat geladen |
| **lassen**–lässt | ließ | hat gelassen |
| **laufen**–läuft | lief | ist gelaufen |
| **leiden**–leidet | litt | hat gelitten |
| **leihen**–leiht | lieh | hat geliehen |
| **lesen**–liest | las | hat gelesen |
| **liegen**–liegt | lag | hat gelegen |
| **lügen**–lügt | log | hat gelogen |
| **mahlen**–mahlt | mahlte | hat gemahlen |
| **meiden**–meidet | mied | hat gemieden |
| **messen**–misst | maß | hat gemessen |
| **misslingen**–misslingt | misslang | ist misslungen |
| **mögen**–mag | mochte | hat gemocht |
| **müssen**–muss | musste | hat gemusst |
| **nehmen**–nimmt | nahm | hat genommen |
| **nennen**–nennt | nannte | hat genannt |
| **pfeifen**–pfeift | pfiff | hat gepfiffen |
| **raten**–rät | riet | hat geraten |

| | | | |
|---|---|---|---|
| **reiben**–reibt | rieb | | hat gerieben |
| **reißen**–reißt | riss | | hat/ist gerissen |
| **reiten**–reitet | ritt | | hat/ist geritten |
| **rennen**–rennt | rannte | | ist gerannt |
| **riechen**–riecht | roch | | hat gerochen |
| **ringen**–ringt | rang | | hat gerungen |
| **rufen**–ruft | rief | | hat gerufen |
| **salzen**–salzt | salzte | | hat gesalzen |
| **saufen**–säuft | soff | | hat gesoffen |
| **saugen**–saugt | sog/saugte | | hat gesogen/gesaugt |
| **schaffen**–schafft | schuf | | hat geschaffen |
| **scheiden**–scheidet | schied | | hat/ist geschieden |
| **scheinen**–scheint | schien | | hat geschienen |
| **scheißen**–scheißt | schiss | | hat geschissen |
| **schieben**–schiebt | schob | | hat geschoben |
| **schießen**–schießt | schoss | | hat/ist geschossen |
| **schlafen**–schläft | schlief | | hat geschlafen |
| **schlagen**–schlägt | schlug | | hat geschlagen |
| **schleichen**–schleicht | schlich | | ist geschlichen |
| **schleifen**–schleift | schliff | | hat geschliffen |
| **schließen**–schließt | schloss | | hat geschlossen |
| **schmeißen**–schmeißt | schmiss | | hat geschmissen |
| **schmelzen**–schmilzt | schmolz | | ist geschmolzen |
| **schneiden**–schneidet | schnitt | | hat geschnitten |
| **schreiben**–schreibt | schrieb | | hat geschrieben |
| **schreien**–schreit | schrie | | hat geschrie(e)n |
| **schweigen**–schweigt | schwieg | | hat geschwiegen |
| **schwimmen**–schwimmt | schwamm | | hat/ist geschwommen |
| **schwören**–schwört | schwor | | hat geschworen |
| **sehen**–sieht | sah | | hat gesehen |
| **sein**–ist | war | | ist gewesen |
| **senden**–sendet | sandte | | hat gesandt |
| **singen**–singt | sang | | hat gesungen |
| **sinken**–sinkt | sank | | ist gesunken |
| **sitzen**–sitzt | saß | | hat gesessen |
| **spinnen**–spinnt | spann | | hat gesponnen |
| **sprechen**–spricht | sprach | | hat gesprochen |
| **springen**–springt | sprang | | ist gesprungen |
| **stechen**–sticht | stach | | hat gestochen |

| | | |
|---|---|---|
| **stehen**–steht | stand | hat gestanden |
| **stehlen**–stiehlt | stahl | hat gestohlen |
| **steigen**–steigt | stieg | ist gestiegen |
| **sterben**–stirbt | starb | ist gestorben |
| **stinken**–stinkt | stank | hat gestunken |
| **stoßen**–stößt | stieß | hat/ist gestoßen |
| **streichen**–streicht | strich | hat gestrichen |
| **streiten**–streitet | stritt | hat gestritten |
| **tragen**–trägt | trug | hat getragen |
| **treffen**–trifft | traf | hat getroffen |
| **treiben**–treibt | trieb | hat getrieben |
| **treten**–tritt | trat | hat/ist getreten |
| **trinken**–trinkt | trank | hat getrunken |
| **tun**–tut | tat | hat getan |
| **überwinden**–überwindet | überwand | hat überwunden |
| **verderben**–verdirbt | verdarb | hat/ist verdorben |
| **vergessen**–vergisst | vergaß | hat vergessen |
| **verlieren**–verliert | verlor | hat verloren |
| **verschwinden**– verschwindet | verschwand | ist verschwunden |
| **verzeihen**–verzeiht | verzieh | hat verziehen |
| **wachsen**–wächst | wuchs | ist gewachsen |
| **waschen**–wäscht | wusch | hat gewaschen |
| **weisen**–weist | wies | hat gewiesen |
| **wenden**–wendet | wendete/wandte | hat gewandt/gewendet |
| **werben**–wirbt | warb | hat geworben |
| **werden**–wird | wurde | ist geworden |
| **werfen**–wirft | warf | hat geworfen |
| **wiegen**–wiegt | wog | hat gewogen |
| **wissen**–weiß | wusste | hat gewusst |
| **ziehen**–zieht | zog | hat/ist gezogen |
| **zwingen**–zwingt | zwang | hat gezwungen |

# Numbers

## Cardinal numbers

| | | | |
|---|---|---|---|
| 0 | null *zero, nought* | 30 | dreißig *thirty* |
| 1 | eins *one* | 40 | vierzig *forty* |
| 2 | zwei *two* | 50 | fünfzig *fifty* |
| 3 | drei *three* | 60 | sechzig *sixty* |
| 4 | vier *four* | 70 | siebzig *seventy* |
| 5 | fünf *five* | 80 | achtzig *eighty* |
| 6 | sechs *six* | 90 | neunzig *ninety* |
| 7 | sieben *seven* | 100 | (ein)hundert |
| 8 | acht *eight* | | *a/one hundred* |
| 9 | neun *nine* | 101 | hundert(und)eins |
| 10 | zehn *ten* | | *a hundred and one* |
| 11 | elf *eleven* | 200 | zweihundert |
| 12 | zwölf *twelve* | | *two hundred* |
| 13 | dreizehn *thirteen* | 572 | fünfhundert(und)zwei- |
| 14 | vierzehn *fourteen* | | undsiebzig *five hundred* |
| 15 | fünfzehn *fifteen* | | *and seventy-two* |
| 16 | sechzehn *sixteen* | 1000 | (ein)tausend |
| 17 | siebzehn *seventeen* | | *a/one thousand* |
| 18 | achtzehn *eighteen* | 1998 | as year: |
| 19 | neunzehn *nineteen* | | neunzehnhundertacht- |
| 20 | zwanzig *twenty* | | undneunzig |
| 21 | einundzwanzig | | *nineteen (hundred and)* |
| | *twenty-one* | | *ninety-eight* |
| 22 | zweiundzwanzig | 2000 | zweitausend |
| | *twenty-two* | | *two thousand* |
| 23 | dreiundzwanzig | 2010 | as year: zweitausendzehn |
| | *twenty-three* | | *two thousand (and) ten* |
| 24 | vierundzwanzig | 61 48 25 | *as phone number:* |
| | *twenty-four* | | einundsechzig acht- |
| 25 | fünfundzwanzig | | undvierzig fünfund- |
| | *twenty-five* | | zwanzig |
| 26 | sechsundzwanzig | | *six one four eight* |
| | *twenty-six* | | *two five* |
| 27 | siebenundzwanzig | 1,000,000 | eine Million |
| | *twenty-seven* | | *a/one million* |
| 28 | achtundzwanzig | 2,000,000 | zwei Millionen |
| | *twenty-eight* | | *two million* |
| 29 | neunundzwanzig | 1,000,000,000 | eine Milliarde |
| | *twenty-nine* | | *a/one billion* |

## Ordinal numbers

1. erste *first*
2. zweite *second*
3. dritte *third*
4. vierte *fourth*
5. fünfte *fifth*
6. sechste *sixth*
7. siebte *seventh*
8. achte *eighth*
9. neunte *ninth*
10. zehnte *tenth*
11. elfte *eleventh*
12. zwölfte *twelfth*
13. dreizehnte *thirteenth*
14. vierzehnte *fourteenth*
15. fünfzehnte *fifteenth*
16. sechzehnte *sixteenth*
17. siebzehnte *seventeenth*
18. achtzehnte *eighteenth*
19. neunzehnte *nineteenth*
20. zwanzigste *twentieth*
21. einundzwanzigste
    *twenty-first*
22. zweiundzwanzigste
    *twenty-second*
23. dreiundzwanzigste
    *twenty-third*
24. vierundzwanzigste
    *twenty-fourth*
25. fünfundzwanzigste
    *twenty-fifth*
26. sechsundzwanzigste
    *twenty-sixth*
27. siebenundzwanzigste
    *twenty-seventh*
28. achtundzwanzigste
    *twenty-eighth*

29. neunundzwanzigste
    *twenty-ninth*
30. dreißigste *thirtieth*
40. vierzigste *fortieth*
50. fünfzigste *fiftieth*
60. sechzigste *sixtieth*
70. siebzigste *seventieth*
80. achtzigste *eightieth*
90. neunzigste *ninetieth*
100. (ein)hundertste *(one)
    hundredth*
101. hundert(und)erste
    *(one) hundred and first*
200. zweihundertste
    *two hundredth*
572. fünfhundert(und)zwei-
    undsiebzigste
    *five hundred and
    seventy-second*
1000. tausendste
    *(one) thousandth*
1998. neunzehnhundert(und)-
    achtundneunzigste
    *nineteen hundred and
    ninety-ninth*
2000. zweitausendste
    *two thousandth*
500 000. fünfhunderttausends-
    te *five hundred thou-
    sandth*
1 000 000. millionste
    *(one) millionth*
2 000 000. zweimillionste
    *two millionth*

## Fractions, decimals and mathematical calculation methods

| | |
|---|---|
| ¹/₂ | ein halb *one/a half* |
| ¹/₂ m | eine halbe Meile *half a mile* |
| 1 ¹/₂ | anderthalb/eineinhalb *one and a half* |
| 2 ¹/₂ | zweieinhalb *two and a half* |
| ¹/₃ | ein Drittel *one/a third* |
| ²/₃ | zwei Drittel *two thirds* |
| ¹/₄ | ein Viertel *one fourth, one/a quarter* |
| ³/₄ | drei Viertel *three fourths, three quarters* |
| ¹/₅ | ein Fünftel *one/a fifth* |
| 3 ⁴/₅ | drei vier Fünftel *three and four fifths* |
| 0,4 | null Komma vier *point four (.4)* |
| 2,5 | zwei Komma fünf *two point five (2.5)* |
| 1x | ein mal *once* |
| 2x | zwei mal *twice* |
| 3x | drei mal *three times* |
| 4x | vier mal *four times* |
| 7 + 8 = 15 | sieben plus acht ist fünfzehn *seven plus eight is fifteen* |
| 10 – 3 = 7 | zehn minus drei ist sieben *ten minus three is seven* |
| 2 x 3 = 6 | zwei mal drei ist sechs/zwei multpliziert mit drei ist sechs *two times three is six/two multiplied by three is six* |
| 20 : 5 = 4 | zwanzig (dividiert) durch fünf ist vier *twenty divided by five is four* |

# European currency

## Germany and Austria

1 euro (€) = 100 cent (ct)

| coins | banknotes |
|---|---|
| 1 ct | €   5 |
| 2 ct | €  10 |
| 5 ct | €  20 |
| 10 ct | €  50 |
| 20 ct | € 100 |
| 50 ct | € 200 |
| € 1 | € 500 |
| € 2 | |

## Switzerland

1 Swiss franc (Sfr) = 100 Rappen (Rp) / centimes (c)

| coins | banknotes |
| --- | --- |
| 1 Rp | 10 Sfr |
| 5 Rp | 20 Sfr |
| 10 Rp | 50 Sfr |
| 20 Rp | 100 Sfr |
| ½ Sfr (50 Rp) | 200 Sfr |
| 1 Sfr | 1,000 Sfr |
| 2 Sfr | |
| 5 Sfr | |

## Temperatures

| | °F (Fahrenheit) | °C (Celsius) |
| --- | --- | --- |
| | 400° | 204° |
| | 350° | 177° |
| | 300° | 149° |
| boiling point | 212° | 100° |
| | 100° | 38° |
| | 80° | 27° |
| | 60° | 16° |
| | 40° | 4° |
| freezing point | 32° | 0° |
| | 20° | – 7° |
| | 0° | –18° |

### How to convert Celsius into Fahrenheit and vice versa

To convert Celsius into Fahrenheit

multiply by 9, divide by 5 and add 32.

To convert Fahrenheit into Celsius

subtract 32, multiply by 5 and divide by 9.

# Weights and measures

## Length

| | | |
|---|---|---|
| 1 mm | *(Millimeter* millimeter/millimetre) | |
| | = 0.039 inches | |
| 1 cm | *(Zentimeter* centimeter/centimetre) | |
| | = 10 mm | = 0.39 inches |
| 1 m | *(Meter* meter/metre) | |
| | =100 cm | = 1.094 yards |
| | = 3.28 feet | = 39.37 inches |
| 1 km | *(Kilometer* kilometer/kilometre) | |
| | = 1000 m | 1094 yards = 0.62 miles |

| | | |
|---|---|---|
| 1 in (inch) | = 2.54 cm | |
| 1 ft (foot) | = 12 inches | = 30.48 cm |
| 1 yd (yard) | = 3 feet | = 91.4 cm |
| 1 m (mile) | = 1760 yards | = 1.61 km |

## Volume capacity

| | |
|---|---|
| 1 l *(Liter* liter/litre) | = 2.11 pints *(US)* |
| | = 1.06 quarts *(US)* |
| | = 0.26 gallons *(US)* |
| | = 1.76 pints *(Brit)* |
| | = 0.88 quarts *(Brit)* |
| | = 0.22 gallons *(Brit)* |
| 1 pint *(US)* | = 0.472 l |
| 1 pint *(Brit)* | = 0.567 l |
| 1 quart *(US)* | = 0.945 l |
| 1 quart *(Brit)* | = 1.136 l |
| 1 gallon *(US)* | = 3.785 l |
| 1 gallon *(Brit)* | = 4.54 l |

## Weight

| | |
|---|---|
| 1 g (*Gramm* gram/gramme) | = 15.432 grains |
| 1 Pfd (*Pfund* (German) pound) | = 500 g |
| | = 1.102 pounds avoirdupois |
| | = 1.34 pounds troy |
| 1 kg (*Kilogramm, Kilo* kilogram/kilogramme) | = 1000 g |
| | = 2.204 pounds avoirdupois |
| 1 Ztr (*Zentner* centner) | = 100 Pfd |
| | = 50 kg |
| | = 110.23 pounds avoirdupois |
| | = 1.102 US hundredweights |
| | = 0.98 British hundredweights |
| 1 t (*Tonne* ton) | = 1000 kg |
| | = 1.102 US tons |
| | = 0.984 British tons |
| 1 ton (of 2240 pounds) | = 1.01605 metric tonnes |
| | = 1016.05 kilograms/kilogrammes |
| 1 pound | = 0.4536 kilograms/kilogrammes |
| | = 453.6 grams/grammes |
| 1 ounce avoirdupois | = 28.3495 grams/grammes |
| 1 ounce troy | = 31.1035 grams/grammes |
| 1 grain | = 0.0648 grams/grammes |